Koren Talmud Bavli

THE NOÉ EDITION

SHABBAT • PART TWO

Steinsaltz Center

KOREN

תלמוד בבלי

KOREN TALMUD BAVLI

THE NOÉ EDITION

שבת

SHABBAT

Daf 20b through Daf 47b

COMMENTARY BY

Rabbi Adin Even-Israel Steinsaltz

EDITOR-IN-CHIEF

Rabbi Dr Tzvi Hersh Weinreb

SENIOR CONTENT EDITOR

Rabbi Dr Shalom Z Berger

EXECUTIVE EDITOR

Rabbi Joshua Schreier

•

STEINSALTZ CENTER

KOREN PUBLISHERS JERUSALEM

MATANEL
FOUNDATION
GRANTED TO GIVE

Supported by the Matanel Foundation

Koren Talmud Bavli, The Noe Edition
Vol. 2.2: Tractate Shabbat, Daf 20b through Daf 47b
Paperback, ISBN, 978-965-7765-27-2

First Hebrew/English paperback edition, 2019

Koren Publishers Jerusalem Ltd.
PO Box 4044, Jerusalem 91040, ISRAEL
PO Box 8531, New Milford, CT 06776, USA
www.korenpub.com

Steinsaltz Center

Steinsaltz Center is the parent organization of institutions established by Rabbi Adin Even-Israel Steinsaltz

PO Box 45187, Jerusalem 91450 ISRAEL
Telephone: +972 2 646 0900, Fax +972 2 624 9454
www.steinsaltz-center.org

Hardcover design by Ben Gasner

This book was published in cooperation with the Israel Institute for Talmudic Publications.

הִנֵּה יָמִים בָּאִים, נְאֻם אֲדֹנָי יֱהוִה, וְהִשְׁלַחְתִּי רָעָב בָּאָרֶץ,
לֹא־רָעָב לַלֶּחֶם וְלֹא־צָמָא לַמַּיִם, כִּי אִם־לִשְׁמֹעַ אֵת דִּבְרֵי יהוה.

Behold, days are coming – says the Lord God – I will send a hunger to the land, not a hunger for bread nor a thirst for water, but to hear the words of the Lord. (AMOS 8:11)

The Noé edition of the Koren Talmud Bavli
with the commentary of Rabbi Adin Even-Israel Steinsaltz
is dedicated to all those who open its covers
to quench their thirst for Jewish Knowledge,
in our generation of Torah renaissance.

This beautiful edition is for the young, the aged,
the novice and the savant alike,
as it unites the depth of Torah knowledge
with the best of academic scholarship.

Within its exquisite and vibrant pages,
words become worlds.

It will claim its place in the library of classics,
in the bookcases of the Beit Midrash,
the classrooms of our schools,
and in the offices of professionals and business people
who carve out precious time to grapple with its timeless wisdom.

For the Student and the Scholar

DEDICATED BY LEO AND SUE NOÉ

Steinsaltz Center

Executive Director, Steinsaltz Center

Rabbi Meni Even-Israel

Managing Editor

Rabbi Jason Rappoport

Senior Content Editor

Rabbi Dr. Shalom Z. Berger

Translators

Amy Fay Kaplan Benoff
Betzalel Philip Edwards
Rabbi Elli Fischer
Gila Hoch
Stephen Lauber
Elie Leshem
Rabbi Eli Ozarowski
Gavriel Reiss
Yosef Rosen
Jay Shapiro
Rabbi Ami Silver
Eliana Kinderlehrer Silver
Avi Steinhart
Amiel Vick
Rabbi Abe Y. Weschler

Editors

Mali Brofsky
Rabbi David Jay Derovan
Rabbi Dov Karoll
Rabbi Yaakov Komisar
Rabbi Adin Krohn
Rabbi Jason Leib
Sally Mayer
Rabbi Jonathan Mishkin
Rabbi Noam Shapiro
Rabbi Michael Siev
Rabbi David Strauss

Copy Editors

Aliza Israel, *Coordinator*
Bracha Hermon
Shira Finson
Ita Olesker
Nechama Unterman

Language Consultants

Dr. Stephanie E. Binder, *Greek & Latin*
Rabbi Yaakov Hoffman, *Arabic*
Dr. Shai Secunda, *Persian*
Shira Shmidman, *Aramaic*

KOREN

Design & Typesetting

Raphaël Freeman, *Design & Typesetting*
Dena Landowne Bailey, *Typesetting*
Tani Bayer, *Jacket Design*

Images

Eliahu Misgav, *Illustration*
Yehudit Cohen, *Image Acquisition*

Digital Edition

Raphaël Freeman, *Team Leader*
Eliyahu Skoczylas, *Senior Architect*
Tani Bayer, *User Interface Design*
Dena Landowne Bailey, *Concept*
Rabbi Hanan Benayahu, *Concept*
Laura Messinger, *Commercial Liaison*

Introduction by the Publisher

The Talmud has sustained and inspired Jews for thousands of years. Throughout Jewish history, an elite cadre of scholars has absorbed its learning and passed it on to succeeding generations. The Talmud has been the fundamental text of our people.

Beginning in the 1960s, Rabbi Adin Even-Israel Steinsaltz שליט״א created a revolution in the history of Talmud study. His translation of the Talmud, first into modern Hebrew and then into other languages, as well the practical learning aids he added to the text, have enabled millions of people around the world to access and master the complexity and context of the world of Talmud.

It is thus a privilege to present the *Koren Talmud Bavli*, an English translation of the talmudic text with the brilliant elucidation of Rabbi Steinsaltz. The depth and breadth of his knowledge are unique in our time. His rootedness in the tradition and his reach into the world beyond it are inspirational.

Working with Rabbi Steinsaltz on this remarkable project has been not only an honor, but a great pleasure. Never shy to express an opinion, with wisdom and humor, Rabbi Steinsaltz sparkles in conversation, demonstrating his knowledge (both sacred and worldly), sharing his wide-ranging interests, and, above all, radiating his passion. I am grateful for the unique opportunity to work closely with him, and I wish him many more years of writing and teaching.

Our intentions in publishing this new edition of the Talmud are threefold. First, we seek to fully clarify the talmudic page to the reader – textually, intellectually, and graphically. Second, we seek to utilize today's most sophisticated technologies, both in print and electronic formats, to provide the reader with a comprehensive set of study tools. And third, we seek to help readers advance in their process of Talmud study.

To achieve these goals, the *Koren Talmud Bavli* is unique in a number of ways:

- The classic *tzurat hadaf* of Vilna, used by scholars since the 1800s, has been reset for great clarity, and opens from the Hebrew "front" of the book. Full *nikkud* has been added to both the talmudic text and Rashi's commentary, allowing for a more fluent reading with the correct pronunciation; the commentaries of *Tosafot* have been punctuated. Upon the advice of many English-speaking teachers of Talmud, we have separated these core pages from the translation, thereby enabling the advanced student to approach the text without the distraction of the translation. This also reduces the number of volumes in the set. At bottom of each *daf*, there is a reference to the corresponding English pages. In addition, the Vilna edition was read against other manuscripts and older print editions, so that texts which had been removed by non-Jewish censors have been restored to their rightful place.
- The English translation, which starts on the English "front" of the book, reproduces the *menukad* Talmud text alongside the English translation (in bold) and commentary and explanation (in a lighter font). The Hebrew and Aramaic text is presented in logical paragraphs. This allows for a fluent reading of the text for the non-Hebrew or non-Aramaic reader. It also allows for the Hebrew reader to refer easily to the text alongside. Where the original text features dialogue or poetry, the English text is laid out in a manner appropriate to the genre. Each page refers to the relevant *daf*.

- Critical contextual tools surround the text and translation: personality notes, providing short biographies of the Sages; language notes, explaining foreign terms borrowed from Greek, Latin, Persian, or Arabic; and background notes, giving information essential to the understanding of the text, including history, geography, botany, archaeology, zoology, astronomy, and aspects of daily life in the talmudic era.
- Halakhic summaries provide references to the authoritative legal decisions made over the centuries by the rabbis. They explain the reasons behind each halakhic decision as well as the ruling's close connection to the Talmud and its various interpreters.
- Photographs, drawings, and other illustrations have been added throughout the text – in full color in the Standard and Electronic editions, and in black and white in the Daf Yomi edition – to visually elucidate the text.

This is not an exhaustive list of features of this edition, it merely presents an overview for the English-speaking reader who may not be familiar with the "total approach" to Talmud pioneered by Rabbi Steinsaltz.

Several professionals have helped bring this vast collaborative project to fruition. My many colleagues are noted on the Acknowledgements page, and the leadership of this project has been exceptional.

RABBI MENACHEM EVEN-ISRAEL, DIRECTOR OF THE STEINSALTZ CENTER, was the driving force behind this enterprise. With enthusiasm and energy, he formed the happy alliance with Koren and established close relationships among all involved in the work.

RABBI DR. TZVI HERSH WEINREB שליט״א, EDITOR-IN-CHIEF, brought to this project his profound knowledge of Torah, intellectual literacy of Talmud, and erudition of Western literature. It is to him that the text owes its very high standard, both in form and content, and the logical manner in which the beauty of the Talmud is presented.

RABBI JOSHUA SCHREIER, EXECUTIVE EDITOR, assembled an outstanding group of scholars, translators, editors, and proofreaders, whose standards and discipline enabled this project to proceed in a timely and highly professional manner.

RABBI MEIR HANEGBI, EDITOR OF THE HEBREW EDITION OF THE STEINSALTZ TALMUD, lent his invaluable assistance throughout the work process, supervising the reproduction of the Vilna pages.

RAPHAËL FREEMAN, EDITOR OF KOREN, created this Talmud's unique typographic design which, true to the Koren approach, is both elegant and user friendly.

It has been an enriching experience for all of us at Koren Publishers Jerusalem to work with the Steinsaltz Center to develop and produce the Koren Talmud Bavli. We pray that this publication will be a source of great learning and, ultimately, greater *avodat Hashem* for all Jews.

Matthew Miller, Publisher
Koren Publishers Jerusalem
Jerusalem 5772

Contents

For the vocalized Vilna Shas layout, please open as a Hebrew book.

Introduction to **Perek II**

You shall not kindle a fire throughout your settlements on the Shabbat day.

(Exodus 35:3)

You shall call the Shabbat a delight, the holy of the Lord honorable.

(Isaiah 58:13)

Delighting in Shabbat is not a mitzva by Torah law, but is first mentioned in the book of Isaiah. However, many of the *halakhot* and customs of Shabbat are based upon this mitzva.

Kindling the Shabbat lights in deference to Shabbat is based on the mitzva of delighting in Shabbat, as there can be no delight or enjoyment, even in a festive meal, in a house that is dark and bereft of illumination. With the lighting of the Shabbat lights, there is thus an element of delight, as well as deference to Shabbat day. However, since there is a strict prohibition against kindling fire or extinguishing it on the Shabbat day, special care must be taken to ensure that the kindling of the lights on Shabbat eve will not lead to kindling or extinguishing fire once Shabbat begins. Therefore, the Sages instituted safeguards and precautions with regard to the various substances that may be used in kindling the Shabbat lights as well as with regard to the manner in which their light may be utilized on Shabbat eve and on Shabbat day.

The primary focus of this chapter is the elucidation of the parameters of the prohibited labors of kindling and extinguishing, along with a discussion of precautionary measures enacted to enable use of the light of an oil lamp on Shabbat.

Other related topics, including the mitzva of the Hanukkah lights, are discussed in this chapter.

This mishna cites a list of fuels and wicks that one may not use in kindling the Shabbat lights, either because their use might induce one to perform a prohibited labor on Shabbat or because they are not in keeping with the deference due Shabbat. The mishna begins by listing the materials that one may not use as wicks. That is followed by a list of the substances that one may not use as fuel.

מתני׳ בַּמֶּה מַדְלִיקִין וּבַמָּה אֵין מַדְלִיקִין? אֵין מַדְלִיקִין לֹא בְּלֶכֶשׁ, וְלֹא בְּחוֹסֶן, וְלֹא בְּכָלָךְ, וְלֹא בִּפְתִילַת הָאִידָן, וְלֹא בִּפְתִילַת הַמִּדְבָּר, וְלֹא בִּירוֹקָה שֶׁעַל פְּנֵי הַמַּיִם. וְלֹא בְּזֶפֶת, וְלֹא בְּשַׁעֲוָה, וְלֹא בְּשֶׁמֶן קִיק, וְלֹא בְּשֶׁמֶן שְׂרֵיפָה, וְלֹא בְּאַלְיָה, וְלֹא בְּחֵלֶב. נַחוּם הַמָּדִי אוֹמֵר: מַדְלִיקִין בְּחֵלֶב מְבוּשָּׁל, וַחֲכָמִים אוֹמְרִים: אֶחָד מְבוּשָּׁל וְאֶחָד שֶׁאֵינוֹ מְבוּשָּׁל – אֵין מַדְלִיקִין בּוֹ.

MISHNA **With what may one light** the Shabbat lamp, **and with what may one not light**[N] it? With regard to types of prohibited wicks,[H] one may light **neither with cedar bast [*lekhesh*], nor with uncombed flax [*ḥosen*], nor with raw silk [*kalakh*],**[LB] **nor with willow bast [*petilat ha'idan*], nor with desert weed [*petilat hamidbar*], nor with green** moss **that is on the surface of the water.** With regard to types of prohibited oils,[H] one may light **neither with pitch [*zefet*], nor with wax [*sha'ava*], nor with castor oil [*shemen kik*], nor with burnt oil [*shemen sereifa*], nor with** fat from **a sheep's tail [*alya*], nor with tallow [*ḥelev*]. Naḥum the Mede says: One may light with boiled tallow. And the Rabbis say: Both** tallow that was **boiled and** tallow that was **not boiled, one may not light with them.**

גמ׳ ״לֶכֶשׁ״ – שׁוּכָא דְּאַרְזָא. שׁוּכָא דְּאַרְזָא עֵץ בְּעָלְמָא הוּא! בְּעַמְרָנִיתָא דְּאִית בֵּיהּ.

GEMARA Most of the terms used in the mishna were not understood in Babylonia. Therefore, the Gemara translated and clarified them. We learned in the mishna that one may not light with *lekhesh*. The Gemara explains that ***lekhesh*** is the **branch of the cedar** tree. The Gemara asks: Isn't the **cedar mere wood?** How would one fashion a wick out of wood? The Gemara answers: The mishna is referring to **the woolly** substance **that** is beneath its bark.

״וְלֹא בְּחוֹסֶן״. אָמַר רַב יוֹסֵף: נְעוֹרֶת שֶׁל פִּשְׁתָּן. אָמַר לֵיהּ אַבָּיֵי: וְהָכְתִיב: ״וְהָיָה הֶחָסֹן לִנְעֹרֶת״ מִכְּלָל דְּחוֹסֶן לָאו נְעוֹרֶת הוּא! אֶלָּא אָמַר אַבָּיֵי: כִּיתָּנָא דְּדַיֵּיק וְלָא נְפִיץ.

The mishna taught further that **one may not** light **with *ḥosen*. Rav Yosef said:** *Ḥosen* **is tow,** thin chaff that falls off the stalk **of** combed **flax.**[N] **Abaye said to him: Isn't it written: "And the *ḥason* shall be as tow"** (Isaiah 1:31)? **By inference, *ḥosen* is not tow. Rather, Abaye said:** *Ḥosen* **is flax** whose stalk **was crushed** but **not** yet **combed.** The threads in the stalk are still covered by a shell and therefore do not burn well.

״וְלֹא בְּכָלָךְ״. אָמַר שְׁמוּאֵל: שְׁאֶלְתִּינְהוּ לְכׇל נָחוֹתֵי יַמָּא, וְאָמְרִי (לָהּ): כּוּלְכָּא שְׁמֵיהּ. רַב יִצְחָק בַּר זְעִירָא אָמַר: גּוּשְׁקְרָא.

And we also learned in the mishna that **one may not** light **with *kalakh*. Shmuel said: I asked all seafarers, and they said to me** that the present-day **name** of *kalakh* mentioned in the mishna **is *kulka*. Rav Yitzḥak bar Ze'ira said:** *Kalakh* is **the cocoon of the silkworm [*gushkera*].**[L]

רָבִין וְאַבָּיֵי הֲווּ יָתְבִי קַמֵּיהּ דְּרַבָּנָא נְחֶמְיָה אֲחוּהּ דְּרֵישׁ גָּלוּתָא, חַזְיֵיהּ דַּהֲוָה לָבֵישׁ מְטַכְּסָא. אָמַר לֵיהּ רָבִין לְאַבָּיֵי: הַיְינוּ כָּלָךְ דִּתְנַן. אֲמַר לֵיהּ: אֲנַן שִׁירָא פְּרַנְדָּא קָרֵינַן לֵיהּ.

The Gemara relates that **Ravin and Abaye were sitting before Rabbana Neḥemya, brother of the Exilarch. Ravin saw that** Rabbana Neḥemya **was wearing *metaksa*,**[L] a type of silk. **Ravin said to Abaye: This is** the ***kalakh* that we learned** in our mishna. Abaye **said to him: We call it *shira*[L] *peranda*.**[L]

מֵיתִיבִי: הַשִּׁירָאִים וְהַכָּלָךְ וְהַסִּירִיקִין חַיָּיבִין בְּצִיצִית! תְּיוּבְתָּא דְּרָבִין תְּיוּבְתָּא. אִיבָּעֵית אֵימָא: שִׁירָא לְחוּד וְשִׁירָא פְּרַנְדָּא לְחוּד.

The Gemara **raises an objection** from that which we learned: **The *shira'im*, the *kalakh*, and the *sirikin*,**[L] different types of silk, all **require ritual fringes.** Apparently, *shira'im* and *kalakh* are different types of silk. This is **a conclusive refutation** of the statement of **Ravin** who identified *kalakh* with *shira peranda*. The Gemara responds: Indeed, it is **a conclusive refutation. If you wish, say** instead that ***shira*** is a **distinct** entity, **and *shira peranda*** is a **distinct** entity. *Shira peranda* is *kalakh*.

NOTES

With what may one light and with what may one not light, etc. – בַּמֶּה מַדְלִיקִין וּבַמָּה אֵין מַדְלִיקִין וכו׳: Lighting the Shabbat lamp with inferior wicks and oils, where the wick does not draw the oil properly, is prohibited because the purpose of this mitzva is to utilize the light. If the light emitted by inferior wicks and oils is weak and dim, the concern is that the person will abandon the Shabbat lights, defeating their purpose, which is to enjoy their light (see Rambam).

Tow of combed flax – נְעוֹרֶת שֶׁל פִּשְׁתָּן: According to the Gemara, the verse from Isaiah: "And the strong [*ḥason*] shall be as tow [*ne'oret*]," refers to processing the flax. In the course of that process, the raw flax is combed to break down the fibrous core and remove impurities. This is a metaphor for the wicked, who will undergo the same process and will ultimately be broken and crushed (Jerusalem Talmud).

HALAKHA

Disqualifications of wicks – פְּסוּלֵי פְּתִילוֹת: One may not make wicks for Shabbat lamps from material that will cause the flames to jump and flicker, as explained in the mishna and Gemara, regardless of where in the house they are lit. Even if the alternative is not fulfilling the mitzva at all, one may not light with the wicks listed in the mishna (*Peri Megadim*; Rambam *Sefer Zemanim*, *Hilkhot Shabbat* 5:5; *Shulḥan Arukh*, *Oraḥ Ḥayyim* 264:1).

Disqualification of oils – פְּסוּל שְׁמָנִים: It is only permitted to light Shabbat lamps using oil that is drawn easily by the wick, as per the list in the mishna. Even if the alternative is not fulfilling the mitzva at all, one may not light with the oils listed in the mishna (*Peri Megadim*; Rambam *Sefer Zemanim*, *Hilkhot Shabbat* 5:8; *Shulḥan Arukh*, *Oraḥ Ḥayyim* 264:3).

LANGUAGE

Raw silk [*kalakh*] – כָּלָךְ: Perhaps this word is related to the Persian kurg, which means a delicate, soft wool.

The cocoon of the silkworm [*gushkera*] – גּוּשְׁקְרָא: The source of this word appears to be from the Persian khuskar, which means coarse flour that is full of bran. This term was also used to connote a low-quality, coarse silk fabric.

Metaksa – מְטַכְּסָא: This is a Greek word μέταξα, *metaxa*, meaning silk, especially raw silk.

Shira – שִׁירָא: The words *shira'in* and *shira* are Aramaic. Apparently, their source is Chinese by way of the Greek σιρικόν, *sirikon*.

Peranda – פְּרַנְדָּא: From the Middle Persian parand, which means silk.

Sirikin – סִירִיקִין: From the Greek σιρικόν, *sirikon*, meaning a silk garment or silk.

BACKGROUND

Raw silk – כָּלָךְ:

Persian silk fabric

"וְלֹא בִּפְתִילַת הָאִידָן" אַחֲוִינָא. רָבִין וְאַבָּיֵי הֲווּ קָאָזְלוּ בְּפַקְתָּא דְּטַמְרוּרִיתָא, חֲזִינְהוּ לְהָנְהוּ אַרְבָתָא. אֲמַר לֵיהּ רָבִין לְאַבָּיֵי: הַיְינוּ אִידָן דִּתְנַן. אֲמַר לֵיהּ: הָהִיא עֵץ בְּעָלְמָא הוּא! קְלַף וְאַחְוֵי לֵיהּ עַמְרָנִיתָא דְּבֵינֵי בֵּינֵי. "וְלֹא בִּפְתִילַת הַמִּדְבָּר" שַׁבְרָא.

And we learned in the mishna that **one may not** light **with** ***petilat ha'idan***. The Gemara explains that *petilat ha'idan* is **willow,** which does not burn well. The Gemara relates that **Ravin and Abaye were walking in the valley of Tamrurita. They saw these willow** trees. **Ravin said to Abaye: This is** the ***idan*** **that we learned** in the mishna. Abaye **said to him:** But **this is mere wood.** How would one fashion a wick from it? Ravin **peeled** the bark **and showed him the wool**-like substance **between** the bark and the tree. We also learned in the mishna: **Nor with desert silk** [***petilat hamidbar***]. That is **the mullein** plant, which does not burn well.

"וְלֹא בִּירוֹקָה שֶׁעַל כו'". מַאי הִיא? אִילֵימָא אוּכָּמְתָּא דַּחֲרִיצֵי – אִיפְּרוּכֵי מִפָּרְכָן! אֶלָּא אָמַר רַב פָּפָּא: אוּכָּמְתָּא דְּאַרְבָּא.

And we learned in the mishna that **one may not** use the **green** moss **that is on** the surface of the water to fashion a wick for lighting the Shabbat lamp. The Gemara asks: **What is this** green moss? **If you say** that it is the **moss found on standing water,** isn't that moss **brittle** and therefore unfit material from which to fashion a wick? **Rather, Rav Pappa said:** It is referring to **the moss** that accumulates **on ships,** which is more pliable and when dried can be fashioned into a wick.

תָּנָא: הוֹסִיפוּ עֲלֵיהֶן שֶׁל צֶמֶר וְשֶׁל שֵׂעָר. וְתַנָּא דִּידַן: צֶמֶר מִכְוַוץ כָּוֵיץ, שֵׂעָר – אִיחְרוּכֵי מִיחֲרַךְ.

It was taught in a *baraita*: The Sages **added to** the list of prohibited wicks in the mishna those made **of wool and hair**[H] as well. The Gemara remarks: **And our** ***tanna*** did not consider it necessary to enumerate these because it is virtually impossible to fashion wicks from these materials, as, when they burn, **wool shrinks** and **hair is scorched.** Consequently, they are unsuitable for use as wicks.

"וְלֹא בְּזֶפֶת". זֶפֶת – זִיפְתָּא, שַׁעֲוָה – קִירוּתָא. תָּנָא: עַד כָּאן – פְּסוּל פְּתִילוֹת, מִכָּאן וְאֵילָךְ – פְּסוּל שְׁמָנִים. פְּשִׁיטָא! שַׁעֲוָה אִיצְטְרִיכָא לֵיהּ, מַהוּ דְּתֵימָא: לִפְתִילוֹת נָמֵי לָא חַזְיָא, קָא מַשְׁמַע לַן.

And we learned in the mishna that one may **not** use *zefet* or *sha'ava* as fuel in lighting the Shabbat lamp. The Gemara explains that *zefet* is **pitch,** and *sha'ava* is **wax. It was taught** in a *baraita*: **Until this point,** the word *zefet*, the mishna is dealing with **disqualification** of materials unfit for use as **wicks,** and **from this point on** it is dealing with **disqualification** of substances unfit for use as **oils.** The Gemara asks: **Obviously,** a wick cannot be made from pitch and similar materials. The Gemara answers: **It was necessary** for the mishna to mention **wax, lest you say** that it is **also unfit for use** as a coating **for wicks,**[H] in the manner that wicks are usually made. **Therefore, it teaches us** that even though wax is unfit for use as oil, it is fit for use as coating for wicks.

אָמַר רָמִי בַּר אָבִין: עִטְרָנָא – פְּסוֹלְתָּא דְּזִיפְתָּא, שַׁעֲוָה – פְּסוֹלְתָּא דְּדוּבְשָׁא.

Rami bar Avin said: Tar [*itran*] is the **by-product of pitch.**[B] When wood is burned to extract pitch, a clearer liquid oozes out after the pitch, and that is tar. Similarly, **wax** is the **by-product of honey.**

HALAKHA

The Sages added to the list wicks of wool and hair – הוֹסִיפוּ עֲלֵיהֶן שֶׁל צֶמֶר וְשֶׁל שֵׂעָר: One may not fashion wicks from wool or hair for use on Shabbat, as per the *baraita* (Rambam *Sefer Zemanim, Hilkhot Shabbat* 5:5; *Shulḥan Arukh, Oraḥ Ḥayyim* 264:1).

Lest you say it is also unfit for use for wicks – מַהוּ דְּתֵימָא לִפְתִילוֹת נָמֵי לָא חַזְיָא: It is permitted to light a wax candle or one made of pitch or fat on Shabbat, if the wick is made of a permitted material (*Mishna Berura*). These materials were disqualified for use only in their liquid state (Rambam *Sefer Zemanim, Hilkhot Shabbat* 5:8; *Shulḥan Arukh, Oraḥ Ḥayyim* 264:7).

BACKGROUND

Pitch and tar – זֶפֶת וְעִטְרָן: Until approximately one hundred years ago, most pitch and tar were extracted from trees. The manufacture of wood coal employed a method of dry, destructive distillation of trees, the derivatives of which were pitch and tar. These substances were used primarily for waterproofing utensils.

Perek **II**
Daf **21** Amud **a**

לְמַאי נָפְקָא מִינַּהּ? לְמִקַּח וּמִמְכָּר.

The Gemara asks: **What** is the **practical difference** that emerges from that which Rami bar Avin taught? The Gemara explains: Its significance is with regard **to buying and selling.** One who buys tar can insist upon receiving the by-product of pitch and no other material. The same is true with regard to wax and honey.

תָּנוּ רַבָּנַן: כׇּל אֵלּוּ שֶׁאָמְרוּ "אֵין מַדְלִיקִין בָּהֶן בְּשַׁבָּת" אֲבָל עוֹשִׂין מֵהֶן מְדוּרָה, בֵּין לְהִתְחַמֵּם כְּנֶגְדָּהּ בֵּין לְהִשְׁתַּמֵּשׁ לְאוֹרָהּ, בֵּין עַל גַּבֵּי קַרְקַע בֵּין עַל גַּבֵּי כִּירָה, וְלֹא אָסְרוּ אֶלָּא לַעֲשׂוֹת מֵהֶן פְּתִילָה לְנֵר בִּלְבַד.

The Sages taught in the *Tosefta*: With regard to **all of those** materials about **which they said** that **one may not light** the lamp **with them on Shabbat; however, one may** use **them** *ab initio* **to make a bonfire.**[H] One may do so **both to warm himself opposite it and to utilize its light,** and he may ignite it **both on the ground and on a stove. They prohibited** using **them only to make a wick for an oil lamp.**

HALAKHA

However, one may use them to make a bonfire – אֲבָל עוֹשִׂין מֵהֶן מְדוּרָה: It is permitted to light a bonfire for Shabbat using all the materials that may not be used for making wicks for a Shabbat lamp (Rambam *Sefer Zemanim, Hilkhot Shabbat* 3:19; *Shulḥan Arukh, Oraḥ Ḥayyim* 255:1).

״וְלֹא בְּשֶׁמֶן קִיק וכו׳״. מַאי שֶׁמֶן קִיק? אֲמַר שְׁמוּאֵל: שְׁאֵילְתִּינְהוּ לְכָל נְחוּתֵי יַמָּא וַאֲמַרוּ לִי: עוֹף אֶחָד יֵשׁ בִּכְרַכֵּי הַיָּם וְקִיק שְׁמוֹ. רַב יִצְחָק בְּרֵיהּ דְּרַב יְהוּדָה אָמַר: מִשְׁחָא דְּקָאזָא. רֵישׁ לָקִישׁ אָמַר: קִיקָיוֹן דְּיוֹנָה. אֲמַר רַבָּה בַּר בַּר חָנָה: לְדִידִי חֲזֵי לִי קִיקָיוֹן דְּיוֹנָה, וְלִצְלוֹלִיבָא דָּמֵי, וּמִדַּפְשְׁקֵי רָבֵי, וְעַל פּוּם חָנוּתָא מַדְלָן יָתֵיהּ, וּמִפַּרְצִידוֹהִי עָבְדִי מִשְׁחָא, וּבְעַנְפּוֹהִי נַיְיחָן כָּל בְּרִיחֵי דְּמַעַרְבָא.

And we learned in the mishna that **one may not** light the Shabbat lamp **with** ***kik*** **oil.** The Gemara asks: **What is** ***kik*** **oil? Shmuel said: I asked all the seafarers, and they said to me** that **there is a bird in the cities on the sea** coast, **and** ***kik*** **is its name.** *Kik* oil is produced from that bird. **Rav Yitzḥak, son of Rav Yehuda, said:** This is referring to **cotton oil. Reish Lakish said:** It is the oil made from the seed of a plant like the **castor plant** [*kikayon*][B] **of Jonah. Rabba bar bar Ḥana said: I have seen** the species of the **castor plant of Jonah, and it is similar to the ricinus tree and it grows in swamps, and they place it at the entrance of shops** for shade, **and they produce oil from its seeds, and all the sick people of the West,** Eretz Yisrael, **rest** beneath **its branches.**

אָמַר רַבָּה: פְּתִילוֹת שֶׁאָמְרוּ חֲכָמִים ״אֵין מַדְלִיקִין בָּהֶן בַּשַּׁבָּת״ – מִפְּנֵי שֶׁהָאוּר מְסַכְסֶכֶת בָּהֶן, שְׁמָנִים שֶׁאָמְרוּ חֲכָמִים ״אֵין מַדְלִיקִין בָּהֶן״ – מִפְּנֵי שֶׁאֵין נִמְשָׁכִין אַחַר הַפְּתִילָה.

Rabba said: Those **wicks** about **which the Sages said one may not light with them on Shabbat,** the reason is: **Because the fire flickers on them.** It sputters on the wick and does not burn well. Those **oils with which the Sages said** that **one may not light** on Shabbat, the reason is: **Because they are not drawn** effectively **by the wick.**

בְּעָא מִינֵּיהּ אַבַּיֵי מֵרַבָּה: שְׁמָנִים שֶׁאָמְרוּ חֲכָמִים אֵין מַדְלִיקִין בָּהֶן בַּשַּׁבָּת, מַהוּ שֶׁיִּתֵּן לְתוֹכָן שֶׁמֶן כָּל שֶׁהוּא וְיַדְלִיק? מִי גָּזְרִינַן דִּילְמָא אָתֵי לְאַדְלוֹקֵי בְּעֵינַיְיהוּ, אוֹ לֹא? אָמַר לֵיהּ: אֵין מַדְלִיקִין. מַאי טַעְמָא: לְפִי שֶׁאֵין מַדְלִיקִין.

Abaye raised a dilemma before Rabba: Those **oils with which the Sages said one may not light on Shabbat, what** is the ruling? May one, *ab initio*, **add to them any amount of oil**[H] with which it is permissible to light **and light** with that mixture? The sides of the dilemma are: **Do we issue a decree lest one come to light** these oils **in their natural form,** without mixing them with permissible oils? **Or no,** that possibility is **not** a source of concern? Rabba **said to him: One may not light** that mixture. **What is the reason** for this? The reason is **because** the *halakha* is that **one may not light** (*Arukh*).[N]

אֵיתִיבֵיהּ: כָּרַךְ דָּבָר שֶׁמַּדְלִיקִין בּוֹ עַל גַּבֵּי דָּבָר שֶׁאֵין מַדְלִיקִין בּוֹ – אֵין מַדְלִיקִין בּוֹ. (אָמַר) רַבָּן שִׁמְעוֹן בֶּן גַּמְלִיאֵל: שֶׁל בֵּית אַבָּא הָיוּ כּוֹרְכִין פְּתִילָה עַל גַּבֵּי אֱגוֹז וּמַדְלִיקִין. קָתָנֵי מִיהַת ״מַדְלִיקִין״!

Abaye raised an **objection** to Rabba's opinion from that which was taught in the *Tosefta*: **One who wrapped a material with which one may light around a material with which one may not light, may not light with** the bound wick. **Rabban Shimon ben Gamliel said: In the** ancestral **house of** my **father, they would wrap a wick** with which one is permitted to light **around a nut, and** that was how they would **light. In any case, it is teaching** that, according to Rabban Shimon ben Gamliel, **one may light.** Apparently, one is permitted to light with a combination of permitted and prohibited wicks.

אָמַר לֵיהּ: אַדְּמוֹתְבַתְּ לִי מִדְּרַבָּן שִׁמְעוֹן בֶּן גַּמְלִיאֵל – סַיְּיעִינְהוּ מִדְּתַנָּא קַמָּא! הָא לָא קַשְׁיָא, מַעֲשֶׂה רַב. מִכָּל מָקוֹם קַשְׁיָא! מַאי לָאו – לְהַדְלִיק? לֹא, לְהַקְפּוֹת. אִי לְהַקְפּוֹת – מַאי טַעְמָא דְּתַנָּא קַמָּא? כּוּלָּהּ רַבָּן שִׁמְעוֹן בֶּן גַּמְלִיאֵל הִיא, וְחַסּוּרֵי מִיחַסְּרָא וְהָכִי קָתָנֵי: כָּרַךְ דָּבָר שֶׁמַּדְלִיקִין בּוֹ עַל גַּבֵּי דָּבָר שֶׁאֵין מַדְלִיקִין בּוֹ – אֵין מַדְלִיקִין בּוֹ. בַּמֶּה דְּבָרִים אֲמוּרִים – לְהַדְלִיק, אֲבָל לְהַקְפּוֹת – מוּתָּר, שֶׁרַבָּן שִׁמְעוֹן בֶּן גַּמְלִיאֵל אוֹמֵר: שֶׁל בֵּית אַבָּא הָיוּ כּוֹרְכִין פְּתִילָה עַל גַּבֵּי אֱגוֹז.

Rabba **said to him: Before you raise an objection to my** opinion **from** the statement of **Rabban Shimon ben Gamliel, support it from** the statement of the **first** ***tanna*****,** who said that it is prohibited to light in that case. The Gemara answers: This is **not difficult,** as it is preferable to challenge from the statement of Rabban Gamliel with regard to the custom in his father's house. There is a principle that proof cited from **an action is great,** i.e., a practical precedent is more substantial than a theoretical *halakha*. **Nevertheless, the difficulty** from the statement of Rabban Shimon ben Gamliel remains: **Is he not** speaking of a case where he combined the wick and the nut **to light** them together? If so, one is permitted to combine the prohibited and the permitted. The Gemara answers: **No,** it is speaking in a case where he combined them **to float**[N] the wick on the oil with the help of the nut. The Gemara asks: **If** it is speaking only with regard to a case of **floating** the wick, **what is the reason** that the **first** ***tanna*** prohibits doing so? The Gemara answers: The **entire** *baraita* is the opinion of **Rabban Shimon ben Gamliel, and it is incomplete,**[N] **and it teaches the following: One who wrapped a material with which one may light around a material with which one may not light, may not light with it. In what** case is **this statement said?** When he combines the materials **to light** them together. **However,** if he utilizes that with which one may not light merely in order **to float** the wick, **it is permitted,**[H] as we learned **that Rabban Shimon ben Gamliel says: In the** ancestral **house of** my **father, they would wrap a wick** with which one is permitted to light **around a nut.** That was how they would light.

BACKGROUND

Castor plant – קִיקָיוֹן: The castor plant, *Ricinus communis* L., is a plant of diverse shapes. It can be an annual plant, bush or tree. Its height ranges from 1–4 m. Its stalks are erect and branch out at the top, with large leaves that are divided into finger-like lobes. Castor oil, used for medicinal purposes, is produced from the seeds of the plant, which is cultivated for that purpose. The castor plant grew in many countries, including Babylonia and Eretz Yisrael. In Aramaic, it is called *tzeloliva*.

Castor plant

HALAKHA

May one add to them any amount of oil – מַהוּ שֶׁיִּתֵּן לְתוֹכָן שֶׁמֶן כָּל שֶׁהוּא: One may not light prohibited oils even if he adds a small amount of permitted oil to them (Rambam *Sefer Zemanim, Hilkhot Shabbat* 5:9; *Shulḥan Arukh, Oraḥ Ḥayyim* 264:4).

However, to float it is permitted – אֲבָל לְהַקְפּוֹת מוּתָּר: One may wrap a wick made of permitted material around material that is prohibited for use as a wick on Shabbat in order to harden the wick or cause it to float on the oil. If the purpose was to thicken the wick and thereby produce light, it is prohibited (Rambam *Sefer Zemanim, Hilkhot Shabbat,* 5:6; *Shulḥan Arukh, Oraḥ Ḥayyim* 264:2).

NOTES

Because one may not light – לְפִי שֶׁאֵין מַדְלִיקִין: Many explanations were given for this cryptic answer. Some commentaries had a variant reading: Because they do not light. Rabba said that these oils do not ignite even in a mixture with other oils (Rambam; see *Me'iri*). Others explain that the answer is based on a decree. Since one may not use them in their pure form, the Sages prohibited using them even when they are mixed with other oils (Rashi; Rosh). Yet others said that the disqualified oil is not drawn by the wick in a mixture. The high quality oils would be drawn first, while the prohibited oil would not burn at all (Rabbeinu Ḥananel; *ge'onim*).

To float – לְהַקְפּוֹת: Some explain the term to mean thickening of the tip of the wick to produce more light (Rabbeinu Ḥananel; Rif).

And it is incomplete – וְחַסּוּרֵי מִיחַסְּרָא: The following expression: It is incomplete, is essentially an exegetical tool, i.e., adding words to clarify the statements of a mishna or a *baraita*. It should be read as if the added words appear in parentheses. No matter how the mishna is explained, in its present form it remains problematic due both to the difficulty in understanding the rationale of the first *tanna's* opinion and due to the incident that contradicts the *halakha* cited in the mishna. As a rule, a mishna does not cite a story that contradicts the statement that preceded it. These difficulties are resolved by means of the tool: It is incomplete.

אֵינִי? וְהָאָמַר רַב בְּרוּנָא אָמַר רַב: חֵלֶב מְהוּתָּךְ וְקִרְבֵי דָגִים שֶׁנִּמּוֹחוּ, אָדָם נוֹתֵן לְתוֹכוֹ שֶׁמֶן כׇּל שֶׁהוּא וּמַדְלִיק! הָנֵי מִימְשְׁכִי בְּעֵינַיְיהוּ, וְהָנֵי – לָא מִימְשְׁכִי בְּעֵינַיְיהוּ וּגְזַרוּ רַבָּנַן עַל חֵלֶב מְהוּתָּךְ מִשּׁוּם חֵלֶב שֶׁאֵינוֹ מְהוּתָּךְ, וְעַל קִרְבֵי דָגִים שֶׁנִּמּוֹחוּ מִשּׁוּם קִרְבֵי דָגִים שֶׁלֹּא נִמּוֹחוּ. וְלִיגְזוֹר נַמִי חֵלֶב מְהוּתָּךְ וְקִרְבֵי דָגִים שֶׁנִּמּוֹחוּ שֶׁנָּתַן לְתוֹכָן שֶׁמֶן, מִשּׁוּם חֵלֶב מְהוּתָּךְ וְקִרְבֵי דָגִים שֶׁנִּמּוֹחוּ שֶׁלֹּא נָתַן לְתוֹכָן שֶׁמֶן! הִיא גּוּפָהּ גְּזֵירָה, וַאֲנַן נֵיקוּם וְנִיגְזוֹר גְּזֵירָה לִגְזֵירָה?

In any case, to this point the conclusion is that one may not light with a mixture of permitted and prohibited oils. The Gemara asks: **Is that so? Didn't Rav Beruna say** that **Rav said:** With regard to **molten fat**[N] or **fish innards that dissolved**[H] and became like oil, **a person may place any amount of oil** fit for lighting **into it and light.** Apparently, one may light with a mixture of permitted and prohibited oils. Rabba answers: **These,** the fat and the fish innards, **are drawn by the wick** even **in their natural state, and those,** the prohibited oils, **are not drawn in their natural state.** Originally, **the Sages issued a decree** to prohibit **molten fat due to unmolten fat and** to prohibit **dissolved fish innards due to undissolved fish innards;** however, the Sages did not issue a decree in a case where one added to them any amount of oil suitable for lighting, and permitted lighting with it. The Gemara asks: **Let them also issue a decree** to prohibit **molten fat and** dissolved **fish innards to which he added oil due to molten fat and dissolved fish innards to which he did not add** permitted **oil.** The Gemara rejects this: **That** prohibition with regard to molten fat and dissolved fish innards **itself is** based on **a decree. And** will **we arise and issue** one **decree** to prevent violation **of** another **decree?** The Sages do not issue decrees under those circumstances. Therefore, there is no reason to prohibit their use.

תָּנֵי רָמִי בַּר חָמָא: פְּתִילוֹת וּשְׁמָנִים שֶׁאָמְרוּ חֲכָמִים אֵין מַדְלִיקִין בָּהֶן בַּשַּׁבָּת – אֵין מַדְלִיקִין בָּהֶן בַּמִּקְדָּשׁ, מִשּׁוּם שֶׁנֶּאֱמַר: ״לְהַעֲלוֹת נֵר תָּמִיד״. הוּא תָּנֵי לַהּ: וְהוּא אָמַר לַהּ: כְּדֵי שֶׁתְּהֵא שַׁלְהֶבֶת עוֹלָה מֵאֵילֶיהָ, וְלֹא שֶׁתְּהֵא עוֹלָה עַל יְדֵי דָּבָר אַחֵר.

Rami bar Ḥama taught a *baraita*: Those **wicks and oils, which the Sages said one may not light with them on Shabbat, one may not light** with them **in the Temple**[H] either **because it is stated** with regard to the Temple candelabrum: "And you shall command the children of Israel, that they bring unto you pure olive oil beaten for the light, **to cause a lamp to burn continually**" (Exodus 27:20). Rami bar Ḥama **taught that** *baraita* **and he** also **said its** explanation: What is the proof from the verse? One may interpret the verse homiletically: The requirement is to light the candelabrum **so that the flame ascends of itself** when it is kindled, **and not that it ascends by means of something else,** i.e., adjusting the wick after it was lit.

תְּנַן: מִבְּלָאֵי מִכְנְסֵי כֹהֲנִים וּמֵהֶמְיָינֵיהֶם הָיוּ מַפְקִיעִין, וּמֵהֶן מַדְלִיקִין! שִׂמְחַת בֵּית הַשּׁוֹאֵבָה שָׁאנֵי.

We learned in a mishna: **They would unravel the** threads of the **tattered trousers** of the **priests and their belts** in order to make wicks from them, **and from** those same wicks they would **light** at the Celebration of Drawing Water.[N] There was wool in the belts of the priests. It is said that their belts were made from, among other things, *tekhelet*, which in the Bible refers to dyed wool. Apparently, one may light with a mixture that includes a wick unsuitable for lighting. The Gemara answers: **The Celebration of Drawing Water is different,** as in that celebration, they did not light the Temple candelabrum. They lit special lanterns made specifically for that purpose and were not stringent with regard to the wicks placed in them.

תָּא שְׁמַע, דְּתָנֵי רַבָּה בַּר מַתָּנָה: בִּגְדֵי כְהוּנָּה שֶׁבָּלוּ מַפְקִיעִין אוֹתָן, וּמֵהֶן הָיוּ עוֹשִׂין פְּתִילוֹת לַמִּקְדָּשׁ. מַאי לָאו דִּכְלָאַיִם? לָא, דְּבוּץ.

Come and **hear** a related question from that which **Rabba bar Mattana taught: Priestly garments**[B] **that were tattered, they would unravel them** into threads **from which they would make wicks**[H] **for the Temple. Is this not** also referring to garments made of **diverse kinds,** like the sashes of the priests that were made of a mixture of wool and linen? The Gemara answers: **No,** these wicks were made from **linen** garments alone.

אָמַר רַב הוּנָא: פְּתִילוֹת וּשְׁמָנִים שֶׁאָמְרוּ חֲכָמִים אֵין מַדְלִיקִין בָּהֶן בַּשַּׁבָּת – אֵין מַדְלִיקִין בָּהֶן בַּחֲנוּכָּה, בֵּין בַּשַּׁבָּת בֵּין בַּחוֹל. אָמַר רָבָא: מַאי טַעְמָא דְּרַב הוּנָא – קָסָבַר: כָּבְתָה זָקוּק לָהּ, וּמוּתָּר לְהִשְׁתַּמֵּשׁ לְאוֹרָהּ. וְרַב חִסְדָּא אָמַר: מַדְלִיקִין בָּהֶן בַּחוֹל, אֲבָל לֹא בַּשַּׁבָּת, קָסָבַר: כָּבְתָה

Rav Huna said: Those **wicks and oils with which the Sages said** that **one may not light** the lamp **on Shabbat, one may not light** the lamp **with them on Hanukkah** either; **both** when it falls **on Shabbat and** when it falls **during the week. Rava said: What is the reason** for **Rav Huna's** statement? **He holds** that if the Hanukkah light **becomes extinguished,** even though one lit it properly, **one is bound** to attend to it and relight it so that it will burn properly. Therefore, one must ensure that the wick burns properly from the outset. **And utilizing the light** of the Hanukkah lamp **is permitted** during the week. Consequently, in order to prevent him from inadvertently sinning on Shabbat, he must ensure from the outset that the wick burns well, lest he come to adjust the flame on Shabbat. Those wicks and oils do not burn well at all. **And Rav Ḥisda said:** Those same oils and wicks with which the Sages prohibited to light on Shabbat, **one may light with them** on Hanukkah **during the week, but not on Shabbat. He holds** that if the Hanukkah light is extinguished

NOTES

Molten fat – חֵלֶב מְהוּתָּךְ: The molten fat mentioned here is fat that is actually in a liquid form, not fat that was merely previously cooked. This appears to be the understanding in the Jerusalem Talmud as well (Rashba).

The Celebration of Drawing Water – שִׂמְחַת בֵּית הַשּׁוֹאֵבָה: According to Rashi, the Sages were not as strict with regard to the Celebration of Drawing Water because it is not a Torah law. Others explain that they lit so many wicks that the fire was like a bonfire, and the quality of the wicks is of no concern in a bonfire (Rabbi Yehuda Bakhrakh).

HALAKHA

Molten fat or fish innards that dissolved – חֵלֶב מְהוּתָּךְ וְקִרְבֵי דָגִים: One may not light a Shabbat lamp with fuel made of molten fat or fish innards. However, if they are mixed together with permitted oil, one may light with them, as per the opinion of Rav Beruna (Rambam *Sefer Zemanim, Hilkhot Shabbat* 3:9; *Shulḥan Arukh, Oraḥ Ḥayyim* 255:5).

Wicks…one may not light in the Temple – פְּתִילוֹת...אֵין מַדְלִיקִין בָּהֶן בַּמִּקְדָּשׁ: All of the wicks that may not be utilized on Shabbat were also prohibited for use in the Temple candelabrum (Rambam *Sefer Avoda, Hilkhot Temidin UMusafin* 3:15).

Priestly garments that were tattered, they would unravel them into threads from which they would make wicks – בִּגְדֵי כְהוּנָּה שֶׁבָּלוּ מַפְקִיעִין אוֹתָן, וּמֵהֶן הָיוּ עוֹשִׂין פְּתִילוֹת: Wicks for the lights of the Celebration of Drawing Water were made from the tattered trousers and sashes of the priests. Wicks for the Temple candelabrum were not fashioned from those garments, since they contained wool. Rather, those wicks were made from the tattered tunics of the priests because they were made exclusively from linen (Rambam *Sefer Avoda, Hilkhot Temidin UMusafin* 8:6).

BACKGROUND

Priestly garments – בִּגְדֵי כְהוּנָּה: As described in the Torah, the priestly garments were made from different materials. The sashes and trousers were made from interwoven threads of multicolored linen and wool (Exodus 39:29), while the rest of their clothing was made exclusively from linen. Since it is prohibited to use priestly garments for mundane purposes and it is prohibited for priests to wear dirty clothing, the garments were not laundered. The tattered and dirty garments were used to fashion wicks for the Celebration of Drawing Water and for the Temple candelabrum.

אֵין זָקוּק לָהּ, וּמוּתָּר לְהִשְׁתַּמֵּשׁ לְאוֹרָהּ. אָמַר רַבִּי זֵירָא אָמַר רַב מַתְּנָה, וְאָמְרִי לַהּ אָמַר רַבִּי זֵירָא אָמַר רַב: פְּתִילוֹת וּשְׁמָנִים שֶׁאָמְרוּ חֲכָמִים אֵין מַדְלִיקִין בָּהֶן בַּשַּׁבָּת – מַדְלִיקִין בָּהֶן בַּחֲנוּכָּה, בֵּין בְּחוֹל בֵּין בַּשַּׁבָּת. אָמַר רַבִּי יִרְמְיָה: מַאי טַעְמָא דְּרַב – קָסָבַר: כָּבְתָה אֵין זָקוּק לָהּ, וְאָסוּר לְהִשְׁתַּמֵּשׁ לְאוֹרָהּ.

one is not bound to attend **to it.** Therefore, there is no reason to make certain from the outset to light it with materials that burn well, as even if it is extinguished, he is not required to relight it. However, he also holds that **it is permitted to use its light.** As a result, he must ensure that the wick burns well on Shabbat; if not, he is liable to come to adjust the flame in order to use its light. The third opinion is that which **Rabbi Zeira said** that **Rav Mattana said, and others say** that **Rabbi Zeira said** that **Rav said: The wicks and oils with which the Sages said one may not light on Shabbat, one may,** nevertheless, **light with them on Hanukkah,**[H] **both during the week and on Shabbat. Rabbi Yirmeya said: What is Rav's reason? He holds** that **if it is extinguished, one is not bound** to attend **to it**[H] and relight it, **and it is prohibited to use its light.**[NH] Therefore, even on Shabbat, there is no concern lest he come to adjust the wick, as it is prohibited to utilize its light.

אָמְרוּהָ רַבָּנַן קַמֵּיהּ דְּאַבָּיֵי מִשְּׁמֵיהּ דְּרַבִּי יִרְמְיָה – וְלָא קִיבְּלַהּ. כִּי אֲתָא רָבִין, אָמְרוּהָ רַבָּנַן קַמֵּיהּ דְּאַבָּיֵי מִשְּׁמֵיהּ דְּרַבִּי יוֹחָנָן – וְקִיבְּלַהּ. אָמַר: אִי זְכַאי גְּמִירְתֵּיהּ לִשְׁמַעְתֵּיהּ מֵעִיקָּרָא. וְהָא גְּמַרַהּ! נָפְקָא מִינַּהּ לְגִירְסָא דְּיַנְקוּתָא.

The Gemara relates that **the Sages said this** *halakha* **before Abaye in the name of Rabbi Yirmeya and he did not accept it,** as he did not hold Rabbi Yirmeya in high regard. However, subsequently, **when Ravin came** from Eretz Yisrael to Babylonia, **the Sages said** this *halakha* **before Abaye in the name of Rabbi Yoḥanan, and he accepted it.** Then Abaye **said** regretfully: **Had I merited, I would have learned this** *halakha* **from the outset.** The Gemara wonders: **Didn't he** ultimately **learn it** and accept it? What difference does it make from whom and at what point he learned it? The Gemara answers: **The practical difference** is with regard to **knowledge** acquired in one's **youth,** which is better remembered.

וְכָבְתָה אֵין זָקוּק לָהּ? וּרְמִינְהוּ: מִצְוָתָהּ מִשֶּׁתִּשְׁקַע הַחַמָּה עַד שֶׁתִּכְלֶה רֶגֶל מִן הַשּׁוּק. מַאי לָאו, דְּאִי כָּבְתָה הֲדַר מַדְלִיק לַהּ! לָא, דְּאִי לָא אַדְלִיק – מַדְלִיק. וְאִי נָמֵי: לְשִׁיעוּרָהּ.

With regard to the opinion that one need not rekindle the Hanukkah light if it is extinguished, the Gemara asks: **And is it** true that if the Hanukkah light **is extinguished one is not bound** to attend **to it?** The Gemara **raises a contradiction** from that which was taught in a *baraita*: **The mitzva** of kindling the Hanukkah lights **is from sunset**[H] **until traffic in the marketplace ceases. Does that not** mean **that if** the light **is extinguished, he must rekindle it** so that it will remain lit for the duration of that period? The Gemara answers: **No,** the *baraita* can be understood otherwise: **That if one did not** yet **light** at sunset, **he** may still **light**[H] the Hanukkah lights until traffic ceases. **Alternatively,** one could say that this is referring to the matter of **its measure.**[NH] One must prepare a wick and oil sufficient to burn for the period lasting from sunset until traffic ceases. If he did so, even if the light is extinguished beforehand, he need not relight it.

"עַד שֶׁתִּכְלֶה רֶגֶל מִן הַשּׁוּק", וְעַד כַּמָּה? אָמַר רַבָּה בַּר בַּר חָנָה אָמַר רַבִּי יוֹחָנָן: עַד דְּכָלְיָא רִיגְלָא דְּתַרְמוֹדָאֵי.

The expression **until traffic in the marketplace ceases** is mentioned here, and the Gemara asks: **Until when** exactly is this time? **Rabba bar bar Ḥana said** that **Rabbi Yoḥanan said: Until** the **traffic of** the people of **Tadmor** [*tarmoda'ei*][L] **ceases.** They sold kindling wood and remained in the marketplace later than everyone else. People who discovered at sunset that they had exhausted their wood supply could purchase wood from them.

NOTES

And it is prohibited to use its light – וְאָסוּר לְהִשְׁתַּמֵּשׁ לְאוֹרָהּ: The commentaries disagree about the rationale for this prohibition. Some say that the reason is because one is required to treat the mitzva with deference. Using the light for one's own needs is a display of contempt for the mitzva (Rashba, and others). According to Rashi, the prohibition ensures a differentiation between lights kindled to fulfill a mitzva and other lights. Others explain that since the Hanukkah lights commemorate the Temple candelabrum, deriving benefit from their light is prohibited just as benefiting from the light of the Temple candelabrum was prohibited for the priests (Ran; Rashba).

Its measure – לְשִׁיעוּרָהּ: The Rif rules that after the Hanukkah lights have burned for half an hour, it is permitted to use the oil or the light for other purposes.

LANGUAGE

People of Tadmor [*tarmoda'ei*] – תַּרְמוֹדָאֵי: One explanation of the word *tarmoda'ei* is related to *tadmari*, thin trees that grow wild. Workers who lacked the money to buy firewood would gather branches from these trees on their way home from work. They were called after these trees, with the letters *reish* and *dalet* reversed (*ge'onim*).

HALAKHA

Wicks and oils…one may light with them on Hanukkah – פְּתִילוֹת וּשְׁמָנִים...מַדְלִיקִין בָּהֶן בַּחֲנוּכָּה: Wicks and oils that are prohibited for use in lighting the Shabbat lamp are permitted for use in kindling the Hanukkah lights, even on Shabbat during Hanukkah, in accordance with the statement of Rabbi Zeira in the name of Rav, as Rabbi Yoḥanan and Abaye agreed with that opinion (Rambam *Sefer Zemanim, Hilkhot Megilla VaḤanukka* 4:6; *Shulḥan Arukh, Oraḥ Ḥayyim* 673:1).

If it is extinguished, he is not bound to attend to it – כָּבְתָה אֵין זָקוּק לָהּ: If the Hanukkah lights were extinguished, there is no requirement to relight them. If one seeks to be stringent, he may rekindle the lights without reciting a blessing, as per the statement of Rabbi Zeira in the name of Rav, as Rabbi Yoḥanan and Abaye agreed with that opinion (Rema; Rambam *Sefer Zemanim, Hilkhot Megilla VaḤanukka* 4:5; *Shulḥan Arukh, Oraḥ Ḥayyim* 673:2).

And it is prohibited to use its light – וְאָסוּר לְהִשְׁתַּמֵּשׁ לְאוֹרָהּ: One may not use the light of the Hanukkah lights for any purpose, not even an inconsequential one, e.g., counting money. In addition, the lights may not be utilized in the performance of a mitzva or for studying Torah. Other authorities permit using the light for sacred purposes (Rambam *Sefer Zemanim, Hilkhot Megilla VaḤanukka* 4:6; *Shulḥan Arukh, Oraḥ Ḥayyim* 673:1).

The mitzva is from sunset, etc. – מִצְוָתָהּ מִשֶּׁתִּשְׁקַע הַחַמָּה וכו׳: The proper time to perform the mitzva of lighting the Hanukkah lights is at sunset, which means the end of the sunset period, when the stars emerge (*Magen Avraham*). *Ab initio*, one may neither light later nor earlier than that time. If one forgot to light, or even if he intentionally chose not to light at that time, he may light the Hanukkah lights until the last people leave the marketplace, as per the *baraita* (Rambam *Sefer Zemanim, Hilkhot Megilla VaḤanukka* 4:5; *Shulḥan Arukh, Oraḥ Ḥayyim* 672:1).

That if one did not yet light – דְּאִי לָא אַדְלִיק: If the marketplace has emptied and one has yet to light the Hanukkah lights, he may light them and recite the blessings at any time during the night until the morning star appears, provided that members of his household are awake and witness the lighting. However, if the members of his household are asleep, he lights without reciting a blessing (*Hagahot Maimoniyot*; *Magen Avraham*; Rambam *Sefer Zemanim, Hilkhot Megilla VaḤanukka* 4:5; *Shulḥan Arukh, Oraḥ Ḥayyim* 672:2).

Its measure – לְשִׁיעוּרָהּ: The Hanukkah lamp must contain sufficient oil to burn from sunset until the marketplace empties completely, i.e., half an hour (Rambam *Sefer Zemanim, Hilkhot Megilla VaḤanukka* 4:5; *Shulḥan Arukh, Oraḥ Ḥayyim* 672:2).

תָּנוּ רַבָּנַן: מִצְוַת חֲנוּכָּה נֵר אִישׁ וּבֵיתוֹ. וְהַמְהַדְּרִין – נֵר לְכָל אֶחָד וְאֶחָד. וְהַמְהַדְּרִין מִן הַמְהַדְּרִין, בֵּית שַׁמַּאי אוֹמְרִים: יוֹם רִאשׁוֹן מַדְלִיק שְׁמֹנָה, מִכָּאן וְאֵילָךְ פּוֹחֵת וְהוֹלֵךְ; וּבֵית הִלֵּל אוֹמְרִים: יוֹם רִאשׁוֹן מַדְלִיק אַחַת, מִכָּאן וְאֵילָךְ מוֹסִיף וְהוֹלֵךְ.

The Sages taught in a *baraita*: **The** basic **mitzva of Hanukkah** is each day to have **a light** kindled by **a person,** the head of the household, for himself **and his household.**[N] **And the** ***mehadrin*****,**[L] i.e., those who are meticulous in the performance of mitzvot, kindle **a light for each and every one** in the household. **And the** ***mehadrin min hamehadrin*****,** who are even more meticulous, adjust the number of lights daily. Beit Shammai and Beit Hillel disagree as to the nature of that adjustment. **Beit Shammai say:** On **the first day one kindles eight** lights and, from **there on, gradually decreases** the number of lights until, on the last day of Hanukkah, he kindles one light. **And Beit Hillel say:** On **the first day one kindles one**[H] light, and from **there on, gradually increases** the number of lights until, on the last day, he kindles eight lights.

אָמַר עוּלָּא: פְּלִיגִי בָּהּ תְּרֵי אֲמוֹרָאֵי בְּמַעְרְבָא, רַבִּי יוֹסֵי בַּר אָבִין וְרַבִּי יוֹסֵי בַּר זְבִידָא, חַד אָמַר: טַעְמָא דְּבֵית שַׁמַּאי – כְּנֶגֶד יָמִים הַנִּכְנָסִין, וְטַעְמָא דְּבֵית הִלֵּל – כְּנֶגֶד יָמִים הַיּוֹצְאִין. וְחַד אָמַר: טַעְמָא דְּבֵית שַׁמַּאי – כְּנֶגֶד פָּרֵי הֶחָג, וְטַעְמָא דְּבֵית הִלֵּל – דְּמַעֲלִין בַּקֹּדֶשׁ וְאֵין מוֹרִידִין.

Ulla said: There were **two** ***amora'im*** **in the West,** Eretz Yisrael, who **disagreed** with regard to **this** dispute, **Rabbi Yosei bar Avin and Rabbi Yosei bar Zevida. One said** that **the reason** for **Beit Shammai's** opinion is that the number of lights **corresponds to the incoming days,** i.e., the future. On the first day, eight days remain in Hanukkah, one kindles eight lights, and on the second day seven days remain, one kindles seven, etc. **The reason** for **Beit Hillel's** opinion is that the number of lights **corresponds to the outgoing days.** Each day, the number of lights corresponds to the number of the days of Hanukkah that were already observed. **And one said** that **the reason** for **Beit Shammai's** opinion is that the number of lights **corresponds to the bulls of the festival** of *Sukkot*: Thirteen were sacrificed on the first day and each succeeding day one fewer was sacrificed (Numbers 29:12–31). **The reason** for **Beit Hillel's** opinion is that the number of lights is based on the principle: **One elevates** to a higher level **in** matters of **sanctity and one does not downgrade.** Therefore, if the objective is to have the number of lights correspond to the number of days, there is no alternative to increasing their number with the passing of each day.

אָמַר רַבָּה בַּר בַּר חָנָה אָמַר רַבִּי יוֹחָנָן: שְׁנֵי זְקֵנִים הָיוּ בְּצִידָן, אֶחָד עָשָׂה כְּבֵית שַׁמַּאי וְאֶחָד עָשָׂה כְּדִבְרֵי בֵית הִלֵּל, זֶה נוֹתֵן טַעַם לִדְבָרָיו – כְּנֶגֶד פָּרֵי הֶחָג, וְזֶה נוֹתֵן טַעַם לִדְבָרָיו – דְּמַעֲלִין בַּקֹּדֶשׁ וְאֵין מוֹרִידִין.

Rabba bar bar Ḥana said that **Rabbi Yoḥanan said: There were two Elders in Sidon,** and **one** of them **acted** in accordance with the opinion of **Beit Shammai, and one** of them **acted in accordance with** the opinion of **Beit Hillel.** Each provided a reason for his actions: **One gave a reason for his actions:** The number of lights **corresponds to the bulls of the Festival. And one gave a reason for his actions:** The number of lights is based on the principle: **One elevates** to a higher level **in** matters of **sanctity and one does not downgrade.**

תָּנוּ רַבָּנַן: נֵר חֲנוּכָּה מִצְוָה לְהַנִּיחָהּ עַל פֶּתַח בֵּיתוֹ מִבַּחוּץ. אִם הָיָה דָּר בַּעֲלִיָּיה – מַנִּיחָהּ בַּחַלּוֹן הַסְּמוּכָה לִרְשׁוּת הָרַבִּים. וּבִשְׁעַת הַסַּכָּנָה – מַנִּיחָהּ עַל שֻׁלְחָנוֹ, וְדַיּוֹ.

The Sages taught in a *baraita*: **It is a mitzva to place the Hanukkah lamp at the entrance to one's house**[H] **on the outside,** so that all can see it. **If he lived upstairs, he places it at the window adjacent to the public domain. And in a time of danger,**[B] when the gentiles issued decrees to prohibit kindling lights, **he places it on the table and that is sufficient** to fulfill **his** obligation.

אָמַר רָבָא: צָרִיךְ נֵר אַחֶרֶת לְהִשְׁתַּמֵּשׁ לְאוֹרָהּ. וְאִי אִיכָּא מְדוּרָה – לָא צְרִיךְ, וְאִי אָדָם חָשׁוּב הוּא, אַף עַל גַּב דְּאִיכָּא מְדוּרָה – צָרִיךְ נֵר אַחֶרֶת.

Rava said: One **must** kindle **another light** in addition to the Hanukkah lights **in order to use its light,**[H] as it is prohibited to use the light of the Hanukkah lights. **And if there is a bonfire, he need not** light an additional light, as he can use the light of the bonfire. However, **if he is an important person,** who is unaccustomed to using the light of a bonfire, **even though there is a bonfire, he must** kindle **another light.**

NOTES

A light, a person, and his household – נֵר אִישׁ וּבֵיתוֹ: Since the primary purpose of kindling the Hanukkah lights is to publicize the miracle, which is accomplished by passersby seeing the light, it is sufficient for one member of the household to light (*Penei Yehoshua*).

LANGUAGE

Mehadrin – מְהַדְּרִין: Two different roots combine to form this word. The Aramaic root, *hadar*, which means courted, as in one who courts a mitzva to ensure it is performed properly, and the Hebrew root *hadar* meaning beauty. Accordingly, *mehader* refers to one who takes steps to perform the mitzva in as beautiful a manner as possible. This is in accordance with the homiletic interpretation of the verse: "This is my God and I will exalt Him [*ve'anvehu*]," beautify yourself [*hitna'e*] before Him in mitzvot (see Rabbeinu Ḥananel).

HALAKHA

On the first day one kindles one – יוֹם רִאשׁוֹן מַדְלִיק אַחַת: Today, all Jews adopt the *mehadrin min hamehadrin* custom when kindling the Hanukkah lights, i.e., they light one light on the first night and add one light for each additional night of Hanukkah. Consequently, eight lights are lit on the eighth day, as per the opinion of Beit Hillel. In another commonly accepted custom among Ashkenazic communities, based on a variation of the opinion of the Rambam, each person in the house lights a Hanukkah lamp and adds one light corresponding to each day of Hanukkah because *mehadrin min hamehadrin* is understood to include the *mehadrin* custom, which calls for lighting a light for each family member (Rema; *Taz*; Rambam *Sefer Zemanim, Hilkhot Megilla VaḤanukka* 4:1; *Shulḥan Arukh, Oraḥ Ḥayyim* 671:2).

It is a mitzva to place the Hanukkah lamp at the entrance to one's house, etc. – נֵר חֲנוּכָּה מִצְוָה לְהַנִּיחָהּ עַל פֶּתַח בֵּיתוֹ וכו׳: *Ab initio*, one places the Hanukkah lamp outside the entrance of his home, facing the public domain. In dangerous times, one may place the lamp anywhere inside the house (Rambam *Sefer Zemanim, Hilkhot Megilla VaḤanukka* 4:7–8; *Shulḥan Arukh, Oraḥ Ḥayyim* 671:5).

One must kindle another light in order to use its light – צָרִיךְ נֵר אַחֶרֶת לְהִשְׁתַּמֵּשׁ לְאוֹרָהּ: In addition to the number of lights kindled each night to fulfill the mitzva, an additional light is added to provide light. If there are other lights burning nearby, described by the Gemara as a bonfire, the additional light is unnecessary. However, an important person is still required to light the additional light even then. The additional light must be distinct from the Hanukkah lights to emphasize that its kindling is not part of the mitzva (Rambam *Sefer Zemanim, Hilkhot Megilla VaḤanukka* 4:8; *Shulḥan Arukh, Oraḥ Ḥayyim* 671:5).

BACKGROUND

In a time of danger – בִּשְׁעַת הַסַּכָּנָה: Dangerous times are defined as periods of religious persecution, when it is decreed that the Jewish people may not observe the mitzvot. However, some commentaries explain that the dangerous times in this context are the occasions when the Zoroastrian priests of the Persian fire religion, the *ḥabarim*, passed the fire from their temples to the homes of their worshippers. At those times, they prohibited lighting fires anywhere outside the temples (*Tosafot*). Since the *ḥabarim* had significant influence on the authorities and the violators whom they reported were severely punished, the Jews dared not kindle lights that could be seen from the street.

מַאי חֲנוּכָּה? דְּתָנוּ רַבָּנַן: בְּכ״ה בְּכִסְלֵיו יוֹמֵי דַּחֲנוּכָּה תְּמָנְיָא אִינּוּן, דְּלָא לְמִסְפַּד בְּהוֹן וּדְלָא לְהִתְעַנּוֹת בְּהוֹן. שֶׁכְּשֶׁנִּכְנְסוּ יְוָנִים לַהֵיכָל טִמְּאוּ כׇּל הַשְּׁמָנִים שֶׁבַּהֵיכָל, וּכְשֶׁגָּבְרָה מַלְכוּת בֵּית חַשְׁמוֹנַאי וְנִצְּחוּם, בָּדְקוּ וְלֹא מָצְאוּ אֶלָּא פַּךְ אֶחָד שֶׁל שֶׁמֶן שֶׁהָיָה מוּנָּח בְּחוֹתָמוֹ שֶׁל כֹּהֵן גָּדוֹל, וְלֹא הָיָה בּוֹ אֶלָּא לְהַדְלִיק יוֹם אֶחָד, נַעֲשָׂה בּוֹ נֵס וְהִדְלִיקוּ מִמֶּנּוּ שְׁמוֹנָה יָמִים. לְשָׁנָה אַחֶרֶת קְבָעוּם וַעֲשָׂאוּם יָמִים טוֹבִים בְּהַלֵּל וְהוֹדָאָה.

The Gemara asks: **What is Hanukkah,** and why are lights kindled on Hanukkah?[N] The Gemara answers: **The Sages taught** in *Megillat Ta'anit*: **On the twenty-fifth of Kislev, the days of Hanukkah are eight. One may not eulogize on them**[H] **and one may not fast on them.** What is the reason? **When the Greeks entered the Sanctuary they defiled all the oils that were in the Sanctuary** by touching them. **And when the Hasmonean monarchy overcame them and emerged victorious over them, they searched and found only one cruse**[N] **of oil that was placed with the seal of the High Priest,** undisturbed by the Greeks. **And there was** sufficient oil **there to light** the candelabrum for **only one day. A miracle occurred and they lit** the candelabrum **from it eight days.**[N] **The next year** the Sages **instituted** those days **and made them holidays**[N] **with** recitation of ***hallel*** **and** special **thanksgiving** in prayer and blessings.

תְּנַן הָתָם: גֵּץ הַיּוֹצֵא מִתַּחַת הַפַּטִּישׁ וְיָצָא וְהִזִּיק – חַיָּב. גָּמָל שֶׁטָּעוּן פִּשְׁתָּן, וְהוּא עוֹבֵר בִּרְשׁוּת הָרַבִּים, וְנִכְנְסָה פִּשְׁתָּנוֹ לְתוֹךְ הַחֲנוּת וְדָלְקָה בְּנֵרוֹ שֶׁל חֶנְוָנִי, וְהִדְלִיק אֶת הַבִּירָה – בַּעַל הַגָּמָל חַיָּב. הִנִּיחַ חֶנְוָנִי אֶת נֵרוֹ מִבַּחוּץ – חֶנְוָנִי חַיָּב.

We learned there in a mishna with regard to damages: In the case of **a spark that emerges from under a hammer, and went out** of the artisan's workshop, **and caused damage,** the one who struck the hammer is **liable.** Similarly, in the case of **a camel that is laden with flax**[H] **and it passed** through **the public domain, and its flax entered into a store, and caught fire from the storekeeper's lamp, and set fire to the building, the camel owner is liable.** Since his flax entered into another's domain, which he had no permission to enter, all the damages were caused due to his negligence. However, if the **storekeeper placed his lamp outside** the store and it set fire to the flax, **the storekeeper is liable,** as he placed the lamp outside his domain where he had no right to place it.

רַבִּי יְהוּדָה אוֹמֵר: בְּנֵר חֲנוּכָּה פָּטוּר. אָמַר רָבִינָא (מִשּׁוּם דְּרַבָּה), זֹאת אוֹמֶרֶת: נֵר חֲנוּכָּה מִצְוָה לְהַנִּיחָהּ בְּתוֹךְ עֲשָׂרָה. דְּאִי סָלְקָא דַּעְתָּךְ לְמַעְלָה מֵעֲשָׂרָה – לֵימָא לֵיהּ: הָיָה לְךָ לְהַנִּיחַ לְמַעְלָה מִגָּמָל וְרוֹכְבוֹ! וְדִילְמָא: אִי מִיטְרְחָא לֵיהּ טוּבָא אָתֵי לְאִימְנוֹעֵי מִמִּצְוָה.

Rabbi Yehuda says: If the flax was set on fire **by the** storekeeper's **Hanukkah lamp** that he placed outside the entrance to his store, **he is not liable,** as in that case, it is permitted for the storekeeper to place his lamp outside. **Ravina said in the name of Rabba: That is to say** that it is a **mitzva to place** the **Hanukkah lamp within ten**[H] handbreadths of the ground. **As if it should enter your mind** to say that he may place it **above ten handbreadths,** why is the storekeeper exempt? **Let** the camel owner **say to** the storekeeper: **You should have placed** the lamp **above** the height **of a camel and its rider,** and then no damage would have been caused. By failing to do so, the storekeeper caused the damage, and the camel owner should not be liable. The Gemara rejects this: **And perhaps** one is also permitted to place the Hanukkah lamp above ten handbreadths, and the reason Rabbi Yehuda exempted the storekeeper was due to concern for the observance of the mitzva of kindling Hanukkah lights. He held that **if you burden** one **excessively, he will come to refrain from** performing the **mitzva** of kindling Hanukkah lights. Since the storekeeper placed the Hanukkah lamp outside at the behest of the Sages, the storekeeper should not be required to take extra precautions.

אָמַר רַב כָּהֲנָא, דָּרַשׁ רַב נָתָן בַּר מַנְיוּמִי מִשְּׁמֵיהּ דְּרַבִּי תַּנְחוּם:

With regard to the essence of the matter **Rav Kahana said** that **Rav Natan bar Manyumi taught in the name of Rabbi Tanhum:**

NOTES

Why is the miracle commemorated with lights – מַדּוּעַ מוּזְכָּר הַנֵּס בְּנֵרוֹת: The holiday of Hanukkah was instituted primarily to commemorate the rededication of the altar in the Temple. Nevertheless, the Sages instituted kindling lights as the mitzva of Hanukkah to underscore that the Maccabees went to war to preserve the sanctity of the nation and the sanctity of the Temple, not to defend their lives (*Bah*).

And found only one cruse – וְלֹא מָצְאוּ אֶלָּא פַּךְ אֶחָד: According to the fundamental *halakha*, kindling the Temple candelabrum with impure oil is permitted. Indeed, if the majority of the Jews are impure, Temple service may be performed in a state of ritual impurity. Furthermore, impure oil may be used in the offering of the daily sacrifices. Therefore, the miracle, which made it unnecessary to use impure oil, demonstrates the great love that God has for His people, Israel (*Penei Yehoshua*).

Eight days – שְׁמוֹנָה יָמִים: Some commentaries ask: Why couldn't a supply of pure oil have been procured sooner? They answer that the pure oil came from Tekoa, in the tribal territory of Asher, in the upper Galilee, and the round trip from Jerusalem took eight days (*ge'onim*). Others say that all the Jews were ritually impure from contact with corpses, and therefore they were required to wait seven days to complete the purification process (Rabbi Eliyahu Mizrahi).

The next year the Sages instituted it and made those days holidays – לְשָׁנָה אַחֶרֶת קְבָעוּם וַעֲשָׂאוּם יָמִים טוֹבִים: Since there was sufficient oil to burn for one day, the miracle lasted only seven days. Why, then, is Hanukkah celebrated for eight days? Many answers have been suggested. Rabbi Yosef Karo maintained that only one-eighth of the oil burned on the first day, so it was immediately clear that a miracle had been performed (*Beit Yosef*). Others explained that, from the outset, the priests placed only one-eighth of the oil from the cruse in the candelabrum, and it miraculously burned all day (*Me'iri*). Yet others suggested that Hanukkah commemorates two miracles; first, the discovery of the cruse of pure oil on the first day, and second, the fact that it lasted seven additional days (*She'erit Kenesset HaGedola*). There is also an opinion that the eight days commemorate the reinstitution of the mitzva of circumcision, banned by the Greeks, which is performed on the eighth day after birth (*Sefer Haltim*).

HALAKHA

The days of Hanukkah…one may not eulogize on them, etc. – יוֹמֵי דַּחֲנוּכָּה...דְּלָא לְמִסְפַּד בְּהוֹן וכו׳: Hanukkah is a time of joy and celebration, as well as a time for offering praise and thanks to God. Therefore, it is prohibited to eulogize the deceased and to fast on Hanukkah (*Megillat Ta'anit*). However, performing labors that are prohibited on Shabbat is permitted on Hanukkah (Rambam *Sefer Zemanim, Hilkhot Megilla VaHanukka* 3:3; *Shulhan Arukh, Orah Hayyim* 670:1).

Camel laden with flax – גָּמָל שֶׁטָּעוּן פִּשְׁתָּן: If a camel walks down a street with a load of flax that is so wide that it protrudes into a store and catches fire from the storekeeper's lamp and causes damage, the owner of the camel is liable. If the lamp is in the street in front of the store, then the storekeeper is liable for the damage, including the damage to the flax on the camel's back. This ruling also applies to a Hanukkah lamp adjacent to the entrance of the store, as the *halakha* is not in accordance with the opinion of Rabbi Yehuda, who said that the storekeeper is exempt in the case of a Hanukkah lamp (Rambam *Sefer Nezikin, Hilkhot Nizkei Mamon* 14:13; *Shulhan Arukh, Hoshen Mishpat* 418:12).

It is a mitzva to place the Hanukkah lamp within ten – נֵר חֲנוּכָּה מִצְוָה לְהַנִּיחָהּ בְּתוֹךְ עֲשָׂרָה: It is a mitzva to place the Hanukkah lamp within ten handbreadths of the ground, in accordance with the opinion of Rava. Although no support was cited for his statement, his opinion is reasonable. If one placed the lamp above ten handbreadths, he fulfilled the mitzva, as long as he did not place it above twenty cubits. One who lives on the second floor may place the Hanukkah lamp in a window *ab initio*, even though it is above ten handbreadths (*Magen Avraham*; *Shulhan Arukh, Orah Hayyim* 671:6).

נֵר שֶׁל חֲנוּכָּה שֶׁהִנִּיחָהּ לְמַעְלָה מֵעֶשְׂרִים אַמָּה – פְּסוּלָה, כְּסוּכָּה וּכְמָבוֹי. וְאָמַר רַב כָּהֲנָא, דָּרַשׁ רַב נָתָן בַּר מַנְיוּמִי מִשְּׁמֵיהּ דְּרַב תַּנְחוּם, מַאי דִּכְתִיב: ״וְהַבּוֹר רֵק אֵין בּוֹ מָיִם״. מִמַּשְׁמַע שֶׁנֶּאֱמַר: ״וְהַבּוֹר רֵק״ אֵינִי יוֹדֵעַ שֶׁאֵין בּוֹ מַיִם? אֶלָּא מָה תַּלְמוּד לוֹמַר: ״אֵין בּוֹ מָיִם״ – מַיִם אֵין בּוֹ, אֲבָל נְחָשִׁים וְעַקְרַבִּים יֵשׁ בּוֹ.

A Hanukkah lamp that one placed above twenty cubits[H] **is invalid, just as a** *sukka* whose roofing is more than twenty cubits high, **and just as an alleyway** whose beam, its symbolic fourth partition in order to place an *eiruv*, is more than twenty cubits high, are invalid. The reason is the same in all three cases: People do not usually raise their heads and see objects at a height above twenty cubits. As there is a requirement to see all of these, they are deemed invalid when placed above that height. **And** the Gemara cites another statement that **Rav Kahana said** that **Rav Natan bar Manyumi taught in the name of Rav Tanḥum: What** is the meaning of the verse **that is written** with regard to Joseph: "And they took him, and cast him into the pit; **and the pit was empty, there was no water in it"** (Genesis 37:24)? **By inference from that which is stated: And the pit was empty, don't I know that there was no water in it? Rather, why does the verse say: There was no water in it?** The verse comes to emphasize and teach that **there was no water in it, but there were snakes and scorpions in it.**

אָמַר רַבָּה: נֵר חֲנוּכָּה מִצְוָה לְהַנִּיחָהּ בְּטֶפַח הַסְּמוּכָה לַפֶּתַח. וְהֵיכָא מַנַּח לֵיהּ? רַב אַחָא בְּרֵיהּ דְּרָבָא אָמַר: מִיָּמִין, רַב שְׁמוּאֵל מִדִּפְתִּי אָמַר: מִשְּׂמֹאל. וְהִילְכְתָא – מִשְּׂמֹאל, כְּדֵי שֶׁתְּהֵא נֵר חֲנוּכָּה מִשְּׂמֹאל וּמְזוּזָה מִיָּמִין.

Rabba said: It is a mitzva to place the Hanukkah lamp within the handbreadth adjacent to the entrance. The Gemara asks: **And where,** on which side, **does he place it?** There is a difference of opinion: **Rav Aḥa, son of Rava, said: On the right** side of the entrance. **Rav Shmuel from Difti said: On the left.**[H] **And the** ***halakha*** **is** to place it **on the left so that the Hanukkah lamp will be on the left**[N] **and the** ***mezuza*** **on the right.** One who enters the house will be surrounded by mitzvot (*ge'onim*).

אָמַר רַב יְהוּדָה אָמַר רַב אַסִּי אָמַר רַב: אָסוּר לְהַרְצוֹת מָעוֹת כְּנֶגֶד נֵר חֲנוּכָּה. כִּי אָמְרִיתַהּ קַמֵּיהּ דִּשְׁמוּאֵל, אֲמַר לִי: וְכִי נֵר קְדוּשָּׁה יֵשׁ בָּהּ! מַתְקִיף לָהּ רַב יוֹסֵף: וְכִי דָּם קְדוּשָּׁה יֵשׁ בּוֹ? דְּתַנְיָא: ״וְשָׁפַךְ וְכִסָּה״ – בַּמֶּה שֶׁשָּׁפַךְ יְכַסֶּה, שֶׁלֹּא יְכַסֶּנּוּ בְּרֶגֶל, שֶׁלֹּא יְהוּ מִצְוֹת בְּזוּיוֹת עָלָיו. הָכָא נַמִי – שֶׁלֹּא יְהוּ מִצְוֹת בְּזוּיוֹת עָלָיו.

Rav Yehuda said that **Rav Asi said** that **Rav said: It is prohibited to count money**[N] **opposite a Hanukkah light.**[H] Rav Yehuda relates: **When I said this** ***halakha*** **before Shmuel, he said to me: Does the Hanukkah light have sanctity**[N] that would prohibit one from using its light? **Rav Yosef strongly objected to this** question: What kind of question is that; **does the blood** of a slaughtered undomesticated animal or fowl **have sanctity? As it was taught** in a *baraita* that the Sages interpreted the verse: **"He shall spill** its blood **and cover** it with dust" (Leviticus 17:13): **With that which he spilled, he shall cover.** Just as a person spills the blood of a slaughtered animal with his hand, so too, he is obligated to cover the blood with this hand and **not cover it with his foot.** The reason is so **that mitzvot will not be contemptible to him. Here too,** one should treat the Hanukkah lights as if they were sacred and refrain from utilizing them for other purposes, so that **mitzvot will not be contemptible to him.**

HALAKHA

Hanukkah lamp that one placed above twenty cubits – נֵר שֶׁל חֲנוּכָּה שֶׁהִנִּיחָהּ לְמַעְלָה מֵעֶשְׂרִים אַמָּה: One who places the Hanukkah lamp more than twenty cubits, 9–12 m, off the ground does not fulfill the mitzva (Rambam *Sefer Zemanim, Hilkhot Megilla VaḤanukka* 4:7; *Shulḥan Arukh, Oraḥ Ḥayyim* 671:6).

It is a mitzva to place the Hanukkah lamp in the handbreadth adjacent to the entrance…on the left – נֵר חֲנוּכָּה מִצְוָה לְהַנִּיחָהּ בְּטֶפַח הַסְּמוּכָה לַפֶּתַח...מִשְּׂמֹאל: When lighting the Hanukkah lamp outside the house, it is a mitzva to place it within one handbreadth adjacent to the left side of the door. In the synagogue, the Hanukkah lamp is placed along the southern wall or on a table adjacent to that wall (Rambam *Sefer Zemanim, Hilkhot Megilla VaḤanukka* 4:7; *Shulḥan Arukh, Oraḥ Ḥayyim* 671:7).

It is prohibited to count money opposite a Hanukkah light – אָסוּר לְהַרְצוֹת מָעוֹת כְּנֶגֶד נֵר חֲנוּכָּה: One may not use the light emanating from the Hanukkah lights for any purpose, even for an inconsequential one like counting money (Rambam *Sefer Zemanim, Hilkhot Megilla VaḤanukka* 4:6; *Shulḥan Arukh, Oraḥ Ḥayyim* 673:1).

NOTES

The Hanukkah lamp will be on the left – נֵר חֲנוּכָּה מִשְּׂמֹאל: Since the Temple candelabrum was on the left side of the Sanctuary, the Hanukkah lamp is placed on the left side as well (Rabbi Elazar Moshe Horowitz).

To count money – לְהַרְצוֹת מָעוֹת: The Gemara cites this example because it is a negligible use of the Hanukkah lights that does not diminish their sanctity. Nevertheless, it is prohibited (Ran).

Does the Hanukkah light have sanctity – וְכִי נֵר קְדוּשָּׁה יֵשׁ בָּהּ: In principle, the sanctity of the vessels used in the Temple, i.e., a Torah scroll, phylacteries, and the like, have inherent sanctity, unlike items used to perform a mitzva. The principle is as follows: Sanctified items no longer in use maintain their sanctity and must be buried. However, items used to perform a mitzva may be discarded. On that basis, Shmuel expressed surprise when the Gemara insists that Hanukkah lights be treated with the level of respect usually reserved for sacred items. Rav Yosef answered that while a mitzva is still being fulfilled, one must treat the items used for the mitzva with added deference, despite the fact that they do not retain their sanctity after the fulfillment of the mitzva (Ramban).

בָּעוּ מִינֵּיהּ מֵרַבִּי יְהוֹשֻׁעַ בֶּן לֵוִי: מַהוּ לְהִסְתַּפֵּק מִנּוֹיֵי סוּכָּה כׇּל שִׁבְעָה? אֲמַר לֵיהּ: הֲרֵי אָמְרוּ, אָסוּר לְהַרְצוֹת מָעוֹת כְּנֶגֶד נֵר חֲנוּכָּה. אֲמַר רַב יוֹסֵף: מָרֵיהּ דְּאַבְרָהָם! תָּלֵי תַּנְיָא בְּדְלָא תַּנְיָא. סוּכָּה – תַּנְיָא, חֲנוּכָּה – לָא תַּנְיָא. דְּתַנְיָא: סִכְּכָהּ כְּהִלְכָתָהּ, וְעִיטְּרָהּ בְּקְרָמִים וּבְסְדִינִין הַמְצוּיָּירִין, וְתָלָה בָּהּ אֱגוֹזִים אֲפַרְסְקִין שְׁקֵדִים וְרִמּוֹנִים וּפַרְכִּילֵי עֲנָבִים, וַעֲטָרוֹת שֶׁל שִׁבֳּלִים, יֵינוֹת (שֶׁל) שְׁמָנִים וּסְלָתוֹת – אָסוּר לְהִסְתַּפֵּק מֵהֶן עַד מוֹצָאֵי יוֹם טוֹב הָאַחֲרוֹן שֶׁל חָג, וְאִם הִתְנָה עֲלֵיהֶן – הַכֹּל לְפִי תְּנָאוֹ. אֶלָּא אֲמַר רַב יוֹסֵף: אֲבוּהוֹן דְּכוּלְּהוּ דָּם.

The Gemara relates that **they raised a dilemma before Rabbi Yehoshua ben Levi: What is the** *halakha* with regard to **using decorations of a** ***sukka*** **all seven** days of the festival of *Sukkot*? **He said to them: They** already **said** in a similar vein that **it is prohibited to count money opposite the Hanukkah light,** which proves that one may not use the object of a mitzva for another purpose. **Rav Yosef** replied in surprise: **Master of Abraham!**[N] **He makes** that **which was taught dependent upon** that which **was not taught. As,** with regard to ***sukka,*** the prohibition to enjoy use of its decorations **was taught** in a *baraita,* and the prohibition to enjoy use of the **Hanukkah** lights **was not taught** in a *baraita* at all. **As it was taught** in a *Tosefta* in tractate *Sukka:* With regard to **one who roofed** the *sukka* **in accordance with its halakhic** requirements, **and decorated it with colorful curtains**[H] **and sheets, and hung in it** ornamental **nuts, peaches, almonds, and pomegranates, and grape branches** [*parkilei*],[L] **and wreaths of stalks** of grain, **wines, oils, and** vessels full of **flour, it is prohibited to use them until the conclusion of the last day of the Festival. And, if** before he hung the decorations **he stipulated with regard to them** that he will be permitted to use them even during the Festival, **everything is according to his stipulation,** and he is permitted to use them. In any case, since the prohibition to benefit from the Hanukkah light is not explicitly taught, a proof should not be cited from there to resolve the dilemma with regard to *sukka* decorations. **Rather, Rav Yosef said:** There is no need to bring a proof for the *halakhot* of *sukka* from the Hanukkah light. Rather, **the paradigm of them all is blood.** The verse with regard to the covering of the blood of slaughter is the original source from which the prohibition to treat mitzvot with contempt is derived.

אִיתְּמַר, רַב אָמַר: אֵין מַדְלִיקִין מִנֵּר לְנֵר, וּשְׁמוּאֵל אָמַר: מַדְלִיקִין. רַב אָמַר: אֵין מַתִּירִין צִיצִית מִבֶּגֶד לְבֶגֶד, וּשְׁמוּאֵל אָמַר: מַתִּירִין מִבֶּגֶד לְבֶגֶד. רַב אָמַר: אֵין הֲלָכָה כְּרַבִּי שִׁמְעוֹן בִּגְרִירָה, וּשְׁמוּאֵל אָמַר: הֲלָכָה כְּרַבִּי שִׁמְעוֹן בִּגְרִירָה.

It was stated in a dispute between *amora'im* that **Rav said: One may not light from** one Hanukkah **lamp to** another **lamp. And Shmuel said: One may light** in that manner. The Gemara cites additional disputes between Rav and Shmuel. **Rav said: One may not untie ritual fringes from** one **garment** in order to affix them to another **garment. And Shmuel said: One may untie** them **from one garment** and affix them **to** another **garment.** And **Rav said: The** ***halakha*** **is not in accordance** with the opinion of **Rabbi Shimon in** the case of **dragging,** as Rabbi Shimon permitted dragging objects on Shabbat, even if, as a result, a furrow would be dug in the ground, as it was not the person's intent to dig that hole. **Shmuel said** that **the** ***halakha*** **is in accordance with** the opinion of **Rabbi Shimon in** the case of **dragging.**

אָמַר אַבָּיֵי: כׇּל מִילֵּי דְּמָר עָבֵיד כְּרַב, לְבַר מֵהָנֵי תְּלָת דְּעָבֵיד כִּשְׁמוּאֵל: מַדְלִיקִין מִנֵּר לְנֵר, וּמַתִּירִין מִבֶּגֶד לְבֶגֶד, וַהֲלָכָה כְּרַבִּי שִׁמְעוֹן בִּגְרִירָה. דְּתַנְיָא: רַבִּי שִׁמְעוֹן אוֹמֵר: גּוֹרֵר אָדָם מִטָּה כִּסֵּא וְסַפְסָל, וּבִלְבַד שֶׁלֹּא יִתְכַּוֵּין לַעֲשׂוֹת חָרִיץ.

Abaye said: In **all** halakhic **matters of the Master,** Rabba, **he conducted himself in accordance with** the opinion of **Rav, except these three where he conducted himself in accordance with** the opinion of **Shmuel.** He ruled: **One may light from** one Hanukkah **lamp to** another **lamp,**[H] **and one may untie** ritual fringes **from garment to garment,**[H] **and the** ***halakha*** **is in accordance with** the opinion of **Rabbi Shimon in** the case of **dragging.**[H] **As it was taught** in a *baraita,* **Rabbi Shimon says: A person may drag a bed, chair, and bench** on the ground, **as long as he does not intend to make a furrow** in the ground. Even if a furrow is formed inadvertently, one need not be concerned.

יָתֵיב הַהוּא מֵרַבָּנַן קַמֵּיהּ דְּרַב אַדָּא בַּר אַהֲבָה, וְיָתֵיב וְקָאָמַר: טַעְמָא דְּרַב – מִשּׁוּם בִּיזּוּי מִצְוָה. אֲמַר לְהוּ: לָא תַּצִיתוּ לֵיהּ, טַעְמֵיהּ דְּרַב – מִשּׁוּם דְּקָא מַכְחִישׁ מִצְוָה. מַאי בֵּינַיְיהוּ? אִיכָּא בֵּינַיְיהוּ: דְּקָא מַדְלִיק מִשְּׁרָגָא לִשְׁרָגָא. מַאן דְּאָמַר מִשּׁוּם בִּיזּוּי מִצְוָה – מִשְּׁרָגָא לִשְׁרָגָא מַדְלִיק, מַאן דְּאָמַר מִשּׁוּם אַכְחוֹשֵׁי מִצְוָה – מִשְּׁרָגָא לִשְׁרָגָא נַמִי אָסוּר.

One of the Sages sat before Rav Adda bar Ahava, and he sat and said: The reason for the opinion **of Rav,** who prohibited lighting from one Hanukkah lamp to another, is **due to contempt for the mitzva.** Using the light for a purpose other than illumination demeans the mitzva of Hanukkah lights. Rav Adda bar Ahava **said to** his students: **Do not listen to him,** as **the reason** for **Rav's** opinion is **due to** the fact **that he** thereby **weakens the mitzva.** By lighting from lamp to lamp he slightly diminishes the oil and wick designated for the purpose of the mitzva. The Gemara asks: **What is the** practical difference **between them?** The Gemara answers: The practical difference **between them** is in a case **where he lights** directly **from lamp to lamp,** without using a wood chip or another lamp to light the second lamp. According to the **one who said** that Rav's reason **is due to contempt for the mitzva,** directly **from lamp to lamp he may** even **light** *ab initio,* as, by lighting another Hanukkah lamp, he does not thereby demean the sanctity of the mitzva because the second lamp is also a mitzva. According to the **one who said** that Rav's reason **is because he weakens the mitzva,** lighting directly **from lamp to lamp is also prohibited,** as ultimately he utilizes the mitzva lamp for a task that he could have accomplished with a non-sacred lamp.

מֵתִיב רַב אַוְיָא: סֶלַע שֶׁל

Rav Avya raised an objection from that which was taught in a *Tosefta:* **A** ***sela*** **of**

NOTES

Master of Abraham – מָרֵיהּ דְּאַבְרָהָם: This expression of astonishment was commonly used by Rav Yosef. It is explained elsewhere that after Rav Yosef fell ill, he forgot his Torah knowledge. Therefore, he was uncertain whether or not he remembered Rabbi Yehoshua ben Levi's *halakha* accurately because the way he remembered it did not make sense (Rashi).

HALAKHA

One who roofed the ***sukka*** **in accordance with its halakhic requirements and decorated it with colorful curtains** – סִכְּכָהּ כְּהִלְכָתָהּ, וְעִיטְּרָהּ בִּקְרָמִים: No *sukka* decorations may be used for any other purpose during the festival of *Sukkot*. If one explicitly stipulated prior to the beginning of the Festival that he will use the decorations for a different purpose during the Festival (Rema), that use is permitted. Later commentaries wrote that the custom today is to refrain from making such stipulations (*Magen Avraham*). In general, the custom is to refrain from using the decorations hanging from the roofing of the *sukka*; however, ornaments hanging on the *sukka* walls may be used without prior stipulation. Nevertheless, it is preferable to stipulate with regard to those decorations as well (Rema), as per the *baraita* (Rambam *Sefer Zemanim, Hilkhot Sukka* 6:16; *Shulḥan Arukh, Oraḥ Ḥayyim* 638:2).

One may light from lamp to lamp – מַדְלִיקִין מִנֵּר לְנֵר: Lighting one Hanukkah lamp directly from another is permitted. However, one may not kindle one Hanukkah lamp from another by means of a non-Hanukkah lamp, as Shmuel agrees that when there is an action that displays contempt for the mitzva, it is prohibited. Others hold that Shmuel would permit lighting from one lamp to another even under those circumstances, as he rejected both explanations of Rav's opinion (*Taz*). Currently, the custom is to be stringent with Hanukkah lights and to refrain from lighting one lamp from another because the basic mitzva is to light just one light, while the rest of the lights serve merely to enhance the mitzva. Therefore, lighting one lamp from another involves contempt for the mitzva (Rema; Rambam *Sefer Zemanim, Hilkhot Megilla VaḤanukka* 4:9; *Shulḥan Arukh, Oraḥ Ḥayyim* 674:1).

One may untie from garment to garment – מַתִּירִין מִבֶּגֶד לְבֶגֶד: It is permitted to remove ritual fringes from one garment only in order to attach them to a different garment (*Magen Avraham*), as per Shmuel's statement and Rabba's custom (Rambam *Sefer Ahava Hilkhot Tzitzit* 1:13; *Shulḥan Arukh, Oraḥ Ḥayyim* 15:1).

The ***halakha*** **is in accordance with Rabbi Shimon in the case of dragging** – הֲלָכָה כְּרַבִּי שִׁמְעוֹן בִּגְרִירָה: It is permitted to drag even large objects, e.g., a bed or a bench, across the ground on Shabbat so long as he does not intend thereby to create a furrow in the ground. If creation of a furrow is an inevitable consequence [*pesik reishei*] of his action, it is prohibited to drag that object (*Magen Avraham*; Rambam *Sefer Zemanim, Hilkhot Shabbat* 1:5; *Shulḥan Arukh, Oraḥ Ḥayyim* 337:1).

LANGUAGE

Branches [*parkilei*] – פַּרְכִּילֵי: The origin of this word appears to be from the Greek φραγέλλιον, *phragellion*, from the Latin flagellum, meaning young, soft branches

מַעֲשֵׂר שֵׁנִי אֵין שׁוֹקְלִין כְּנֶגְדוֹ דִּינְרֵי זָהָב, וַאֲפִילּוּ לְחַלֵּל עָלָיו מַעֲשֵׂר שֵׁנִי אַחֵר. אִי אָמְרַתְּ בִּשְׁלָמָא כִּי פְּלִיגִי רַב וּשְׁמוּאֵל מִנֵּר לְנֵר, אֲבָל בְּקִינְסָא אָסַר שְׁמוּאֵל – הָא לָא תֶּיהֱוֵי תְּיוּבְתָּא. אֶלָּא אִי אָמְרַתְּ בְּקִינְסָא נַמִּי שָׁרֵי, הָא תֶּיהֱוֵי תְּיוּבְתָּא! אָמַר רַבָּה: גְּזֵירָה שֶׁמָּא לֹא יְכַוֵּין מִשְׁקְלוֹתָיו, וְקָא מַפֵּיק לְהוּ לְחוּלִּין.

the second tithe, one may not weigh gold dinars with it[H] in order to determine their precise weight. **And** doing so is prohibited **even** if he is weighing the coin in order **to redeem other second-tithe** produce **with it,**[N] as one may not derive benefit from tithe money. The Gemara discusses this matter: **Granted, if you say** that **when Rav and Shmuel disagree** it is with regard to a case when one lights **from lamp to lamp, but with a wood chip, Shmuel prohibits** lighting, **this will not be a conclusive refutation** of Shmuel's opinion. **But if you say** that he **permits** lighting from lamp to lamp **with a wood chip as well, this would be a conclusive refutation** of his opinion, as the Sages did not permit use of and benefit from a sacred object even for the purpose of a similar sacred need. **Rabba said:** This is not difficult, as in the case of weighing tithe money the Sages prohibited doing so as a **decree lest the weights not be precisely equal.**[N] One will discover that the weight of the gold dinars is not equal to the weight of the *sela* that he used to weigh them, **and he will reconsider and render them unsanctified,** i.e., they will maintain their original, non-sacred status. In that case, he will have used the tithe money for an unsanctified purpose. However, when one lights even a wood chip for the purpose of Hanukkah lights, it is clear that it is for the purpose of performing a mitzva, and there is no reason to issue a decree.

מְתִיב רַב שֵׁשֶׁת: ״מִחוּץ לְפָרוֹכֶת הָעֵדוּת יַעֲרוֹךְ״ וְכִי לְאוֹרָה הוּא צָרִיךְ? וַהֲלֹא כׇּל אַרְבָּעִים שָׁנָה שֶׁהָלְכוּ בְּנֵי יִשְׂרָאֵל בַּמִּדְבָּר לֹא הָלְכוּ אֶלָּא לְאוֹרוֹ; אֶלָּא עֵדוּת הִיא לְבָאֵי עוֹלָם שֶׁהַשְּׁכִינָה שׁוֹרָה בְּיִשְׂרָאֵל. מַאי עֵדוּת? אָמַר רַב: זוֹ נֵר מַעֲרָבִי, שֶׁנּוֹתֵן בָּהּ שֶׁמֶן כְּמִדַּת חַבְרוֹתֶיהָ, וּמִמֶּנָּה הָיָה מַדְלִיק וּבָהּ הָיָה מְסַיֵּים. וְהָא הָכָא, כֵּיוָן דִּקְבִיעִי נֵרוֹת לָא סַגְיָא דְּלָא מִשְׁקֵיל וְאַדְלוֹקֵי, קַשְׁיָא בֵּין לְמַאן דְּאָמַר מִשּׁוּם בִּזּוּי מִצְוָה, וּבֵין לְמַאן דְּאָמַר מִשּׁוּם אַכְחוּשֵׁי מִצְוָה!

Rav Sheshet raised an objection from that which was taught in a *baraita*. With regard to the Temple candelabrum,[B] it is stated: **"Outside the veil of the testimony,** in the Tent of Meeting, **shall** Aaron **order** it from evening to morning before the Lord continually; it shall be a statute forever throughout your generations" (Leviticus 24:3). It must be understood: **And does** God **require its light**[N] for illumination at night? **Didn't the children of Israel, all forty years that they walked in the wilderness, walk exclusively by His light,** the pillar of fire? **Rather,** the lighting of the candelabrum **is testimony to mankind that the Divine Presence rests among Israel.** The Gemara asks: **What is** this **testimony? Rav said: That is the westernmost lamp** in the candelabrum **in which the measure of oil placed was the same measure** of oil as was placed in **the other** lamps, **and** nevertheless **he would light the** others **from it** each day **and with it he would conclude,** i.e., the westernmost lamp would continue burning throughout the day after all the others were extinguished. The rest of the lamps burned only at night, and each night he would relight the rest of the lamps from the westernmost lamp. **But isn't it true that here,** in the Temple, **since the lamps were fixed** in the candelabrum, it was impossible to light directly from lamp to lamp? **There was no alternative to taking** a wood chip **and lighting** the rest of the lamps from the westernmost lamp. Consequently, **it is difficult both according to the one who said** that one may not light from lamp to lamp **due to contempt for the mitzva and according to the one who said** that one may not light from lamp to lamp **due to weakening** the **mitzva.**

תַּרְגְּמָא רַב פָּפָּא בִּפְתִילוֹת אֲרוּכּוֹת. סוֹף סוֹף, לְמַאן דְּאָמַר מִשּׁוּם אַכְחוּשֵׁי מִצְוָה קַשְׁיָא! קַשְׁיָא.

Rav Pappa explained that it need not necessarily be understood that way. Rather, there were **long wicks** in the candelabrum, which made it possible to reach and light directly from one lamp to another.[H] However, **ultimately, according to the one who said** that one may not light from lamp to lamp **due to weakening** the **mitzva, it is difficult.** The Gemara concludes: Indeed, the question remains **difficult.**

NOTES

To redeem other second-tithe produce with it – לְחַלֵּל עָלָיו מַעֲשֵׂר שֵׁנִי אַחֵר: As opposed to the fruits of the first tithe that are given to the Levites, the fruits of the second tithe must be brought to Jerusalem and eaten there. However, the distance to Jerusalem from certain places in Eretz Yisrael was great and transporting a large amount of fruit was a burden. In addition, there was the possibility that the fruit would spoil. The Torah allowed the redemption of the fruit of the second tithe with money, which would then be used to purchase food in Jerusalem (see Deuteronomy 14:22–27).

Decree lest the weights not be precisely equal – גְּזֵירָה שֶׁמָּא לֹא יְכַוֵּין מִשְׁקְלוֹתָיו: The *ge'onim* and the Rambam wrote that there is room for concern lest the weights not be precise, and one consequently undervalue the weight of the tithe. A variant text reads: Lest the weights be precisely equal. That reading suggests that one might discover that the weight of the coins used to redeem the tithe or even the fruits themselves corresponds to common weights. The concern is that he will use them to weigh non-sacred items (*Me'iri*).

And does God require its light – וְכִי לְאוֹרָה הוּא צָרִיךְ: Some commentaries explain the assumption that the phrase: Outside the veil of testimony, which seems extraneous, teaches that the purpose of the candelabrum was to provide light for the priests inside the Sanctuary, as they never ventured beyond the veil of testimony. Therefore, Rav Sheshet said that the candelabrum's light was not necessary for that purpose either, as the pillar of cloud provided light for the priests (see *Tosafot*).

BACKGROUND

The lamps of the Temple candelabrum – נֵרוֹת מְנוֹרַת הַמִּקְדָּשׁ: In this depiction of the Temple candelabrum, all of the wicks and flames face the middle branch. According to this opinion, the branches of the candelabrum are aligned along a north–south axis and the central light, which is the westernmost lamp of the candelabrum,. provides perpetual light.

Temple candelabrum

HALAKHA

The second tithe, one may not weigh gold dinars with it – מַעֲשֵׂר שֵׁנִי אֵין שׁוֹקְלִין כְּנֶגְדּוֹ דִּינְרֵי זָהָב: The coins used to redeem the second tithe may not be utilized as weights to ascertain the weight of other coins, even if one plans to use those coins to redeem other second-tithe produce (Rambam *Sefer Zera'im, Hilkhot Ma'aser Sheni VeNeta Revai* 3:19).

Lighting the Temple candelabrum – הַדְלָקָה בִּמְנוֹרַת הַמִּקְדָּשׁ: The priests kindle the lamps in the Temple candelabrum from the westernmost lamp by pulling the wick of the unlit lamp to the burning westernmost lamp, kindling it, and restoring the wick to its place (Rambam *Sefer Avoda, Hilkhot Temidin UMusafin* 3:14).

מַאי הָוֵי עֲלַהּ? אָמַר רַב הוּנָא בְּרֵיהּ דְּרַב יְהוֹשֻׁעַ: חָזֵינָא אִי הַדְלָקָה עוֹשָׂה מִצְוָה – מַדְלִיקִין מִנֵּר לְנֵר, וְאִי הַנָּחָה עוֹשָׂה מִצְוָה – אֵין מַדְלִיקִין מִנֵּר לְנֵר.

In summary, the Gemara asks: **What is** the halakhic conclusion reached[N] **about** this matter in terms of lighting from lamp to lamp? **Rav Huna, son of Rabbi Yehoshua, said: We see; if** the *halakha* is in accordance with the opinion of the one who said that **kindling** the Hanukkah light **accomplishes** the **mitzva** and the rest is secondary, **one may light from lamp**[B] **to lamp.** The lighting itself is the essence of the mitzva of Hanukkah lights. **And if** the *halakha* is in accordance with the opinion of the one who said that **placing** the lit lamp in a suitable place **accomplishes** the **mitzva,** then **one may not light from lamp to lamp.** According to that opinion, lighting is simply an auxiliary action that facilitates the fulfillment of the essence of the mitzva, which is placing the lamp in a place where its light can be seen by the public. Since lighting is merely a preparatory action, one may not demean the mitzva by lighting from lamp to lamp.

דְּאִיבַּעְיָא לְהוּ: הַדְלָקָה עוֹשָׂה מִצְוָה אוֹ הַנָּחָה עוֹשָׂה מִצְוָה?

After the issue of whether lighting accomplishes the mitzva or placing accomplishes the mitzva was raised in the context of the previous discussion, the Gemara cites the discussion in its entirety. **As a dilemma was raised before** the Sages: In the case of the Hanukkah light, does **lighting accomplish** the **mitzva,** and placing the lit lamp is simply a continuation of that action, **or** does **placing** the kindled lamp **accomplish** the **mitzva,** and lighting is simply a practical necessity that facilitates placing the lamp?

תָּא שְׁמַע. דְּאָמַר רָבָא: הָיָה תָּפוּשׂ נֵר חֲנוּכָּה וְעוֹמֵד – לֹא עָשָׂה וְלֹא כְּלוּם. שְׁמַע מִינָּהּ: הַנָּחָה עוֹשָׂה מִצְוָה. הָתָם: הָרוֹאֶה אוֹמֵר "לְצוֹרְכּוֹ הוּא דְּנָקֵיט לֵהּ".

The Gemara suggests: **Come** and **hear** a solution to this dilemma from that which **Rava said:** One who **was holding a burning Hanukkah lamp** in his hand **and standing,**[H] **he did nothing** in terms of fulfilling the mitzva. **Conclude from this that placing accomplishes** the **mitzva.** Until he sets the lamp down in its appropriate place, he did not fulfill the mitzva. The Gemara rejects this: **There,** they said that he did not fulfill his obligation for a different reason. One **who sees** it will **say** that he is not holding the lamp in order to fulfill the mitzva, but **he is holding it for his own needs.** Since holding the lamp can mislead onlookers, he does not fulfill the mitzva in that manner.

תָּא שְׁמַע. דְּאָמַר רָבָא: הִדְלִיקָהּ בִּפְנִים וְהוֹצִיאָהּ – לֹא עָשָׂה כְּלוּם. אִי אָמְרַתְּ בִּשְׁלָמָא הַדְלָקָה עוֹשָׂה מִצְוָה – הַדְלָקָה בִּמְקוֹמוֹ בָּעֵינַן, מִשּׁוּם הָכִי לֹא עָשָׂה כְּלוּם. אֶלָּא אִי אָמְרַתְּ "הַנָּחָה עוֹשָׂה מִצְוָה" אַמַּאי לֹא עָשָׂה וְלֹא כְּלוּם? הָתָם נַמִי; הָרוֹאֶה הוּא אוֹמֵר "לְצוֹרְכּוֹ הוּא דְּאַדְלְקָהּ".

Come and **hear** another resolution for this dilemma from that which **Rava said:** One who **lights** the Hanukkah lamp **inside** the house **and** then **takes it out** and places it at the entrance to his house **did nothing** in terms of fulfilling the mitzva. **Granted, if you say** that **lighting accomplishes the mitzva** it is understandable, as **lighting in its place is required. That is why** Rava ruled that **he did nothing** in terms of fulfilling the mitzva. **However, if you say** that **placing accomplishes the mitzva, why** did Rava rule that **he did nothing?** Didn't he set it down in its appropriate place? The Gemara answers: **There too,** even though he subsequently brought it outside, **one who sees** him lighting inside will **say** to himself that **he is lighting** the lamp **for his own needs** and not in fulfillment of the mitzva.

תָּא שְׁמַע, דְּאָמַר רַבִּי יְהוֹשֻׁעַ בֶּן לֵוִי:

Come and **hear** another resolution from that which **Rabbi Yehoshua ben Levi said:**

Perek **II**
Daf **23** Amud **a**

עֲשָׁשִׁית שֶׁהָיְתָה דּוֹלֶקֶת וְהוֹלֶכֶת כָּל הַיּוֹם כּוּלּוֹ, לְמוֹצָאֵי שַׁבָּת מְכַבָּהּ וּמַדְלִיקָהּ. אִי אָמְרַתְּ בִּשְׁלָמָא הַדְלָקָה עוֹשָׂה מִצְוָה – שַׁפִּיר. אֶלָּא אִי אָמְרַתְּ הַנָּחָה עוֹשָׂה מִצְוָה, הַאי "מְכַבָּהּ וּמַדְלִיקָהּ"? "מְכַבָּהּ וּמַגְבִּיהָהּ וּמַנִּיחָהּ וּמַדְלִיקָהּ" מִיבָּעֵי לֵיהּ! וְעוֹד, מִדְּקָא מְבָרְכִינַן "אֲשֶׁר קִדְּשָׁנוּ בְּמִצְוֹתָיו וְצִוָּנוּ לְהַדְלִיק נֵר שֶׁל חֲנוּכָּה" שְׁמַע מִינָּהּ: הַדְלָקָה עוֹשָׂה מִצְוָה, שְׁמַע מִינָּהּ.

A lantern that continued to burn[H] **the entire day** of Shabbat, **at the conclusion of Shabbat one extinguishes it and lights it** again as a Hanukkah light. **Granted, if you say** that **lighting accomplishes** the **mitzva,** the requirement to extinguish the lantern and relight it in order to fulfill the mitzva of kindling the Hanukkah light **works out well. However, if you say** that **placing accomplishes** the **mitzva, this** statement, which stated that one **extinguishes it and lights it,** is imprecise. According to this opinion, **it needed** to say: **One extinguishes it and lifts it** from its place **and sets it down and lights it,** as only by placing the lamp in an appropriate place could one fulfill the mitzva of the Hanukkah light. **Furthermore,** there is additional proof that lighting accomplishes the mitzva. **From** the fact **that we recite** the following blessing over the mitzva of kindling the Hanukkah light: **Who has made us holy through His commandments and has commanded us to light the Hanukkah light,** the Gemara suggests: **Conclude from this** that **lighting accomplishes** the **mitzva,** as it is over lighting that one recites the blessing. The Gemara concludes: Indeed, **conclude from this.**

NOTES

What is the conclusion about this matter – מַאי הָוֵי עֲלַהּ: This question is standard at the end of a discussion in which proofs are cited for both opinions, although neither is conclusive.

In this context, the question is twofold. The first question is whether or not the assumption that remained difficult, but was not conclusively refuted, was ultimately rejected by *halakha*. The second question is whether the *halakha* is in accordance with the opinion of Rav or in accordance with the opinion of Shmuel. Although Rabba's custom was in accordance with the opinion of Shmuel, the principle in ritual, as opposed to civil, cases is that the *halakha* is in accordance with the opinion of Rav (Rosh).

BACKGROUND

Lamp – נֵר:

Earthenware lamp from the talmudic period

HALAKHA

One who was holding a burning Hanukkah lamp in his hand and was standing – הָיָה תָּפוּשׂ נֵר חֲנוּכָּה וְעוֹמֵד: One who holds a Hanukkah lamp in his hand, lights it, and then remains standing with it did not fulfill the mitzva. Similarly, one who kindled a Hanukkah lamp inside his house and then placed it outside did not fulfill the mitzva (Rambam *Sefer Zemanim, Hilkhot Megilla VaḤanukka* 4:9; *Shulḥan Arukh, Oraḥ Ḥayyim* 675:1).

HALAKHA

Lantern that continued to burn, etc. – עֲשָׁשִׁית שֶׁהָיְתָה דּוֹלֶקֶת וְהוֹלֶכֶת וכו׳: One who wants to fulfill his obligation with a lantern or lamp that was burning during the day must first extinguish it and then relight it as a Hanukkah light. The ruling in the dispute in the Gemara is: The mitzva is accomplished by lighting the lights, as per the opinion of Rabbi Yehoshua ben Levi (Rambam *Sefer Zemanim, Hilkhot Megilla VaḤanukka* 4:9; *Shulḥan Arukh, Oraḥ Ḥayyim* 675:1).

וְהַשְׁתָּא דְּאָמְרִינַן הַדְלָקָה עוֹשָׂה מִצְוָה, הִדְלִיקָהּ חֵרֵשׁ שׁוֹטֶה וְקָטָן – לֹא עָשָׂה וְלֹא כְּלוּם. אִשָּׁה וַדַּאי מַדְלִיקָה, דְּאָמַר רַבִּי יְהוֹשֻׁעַ בֶּן לֵוִי: נָשִׁים חַיָּיבוֹת בְּנֵר חֲנוּכָּה, שֶׁאַף הֵן הָיוּ בְּאוֹתוֹ הַנֵּס.

And, the Gemara remarks, **now that we say** that **lighting accomplishes** the **mitzva,** there are practical ramifications. If **a deaf-mute,**[N] **an imbecile,** or **a minor,** all of whom are of limited intellectual capacity and not obligated in mitzvot, **kindled** the Hanukkah light, **he did nothing** in terms of fulfilling the mitzva, even if an adult obligated in mitzvot subsequently set it down in its appropriate place. That is because placing a lit lamp does not constitute fulfillment of the mitzva. The lighting must be performed by a person with full intellectual capacity, obligated in mitzvot. However, **a woman**[H] **certainly may light, as Rabbi Yehoshua ben Levi said: Women are obligated in** lighting **the Hanukkah light, as they too were included in that miracle**[N] of being saved from the decree of persecution.

אָמַר רַב שֵׁשֶׁת: אַכְסְנַאי חַיָּיב בְּנֵר חֲנוּכָּה. אָמַר רַבִּי זֵירָא: מֵרֵישׁ כִּי הֲוֵינָא בֵּי רַב מִשְׁתַּתַּפְנָא בִּפְרִיטֵי בַּהֲדֵי אוּשְׁפִּיזָא. בָּתַר דִּנְסִיבִי אִיתְּתָא אָמִינָא: הַשְׁתָּא וַדַּאי לָא צְרִיכְנָא, דְּקָא מַדְלִיקִי עֲלַי בְּגוֹ בֵּיתַאי.

Rav Sheshet said: A guest is obligated in lighting **the Hanukkah light**[H] in the place where he is being hosted. The Gemara relates that **Rabbi Zeira said: At first, when I was** studying **in the yeshiva, I would participate with *perutot*,** copper coins, **together with the host [*ushpiza*],**[L] so that I would be a partner in the light that he kindled. **After I married** my **wife, I said: Now I certainly need not** do so because **they light on my behalf in my house.**

אָמַר רַבִּי יְהוֹשֻׁעַ בֶּן לֵוִי: כָּל הַשְּׁמָנִים כּוּלָּן יָפִין לַנֵּר, וְשֶׁמֶן זַיִת מִן הַמּוּבְחָר. אָמַר אַבַּיֵי: מֵרֵישׁ הֲוָה מְהַדַּר מָר אַמִּשְׁחָא דְּשׁוּמְשְׁמֵי, אֲמַר: הַאי מָשַׁךְ נְהוֹרֵי טְפֵי. כֵּיוָן דִּשְׁמַע לָהּ לְהָא דְּרַבִּי יְהוֹשֻׁעַ בֶּן לֵוִי מְהַדַּר אַמִּשְׁחָא דְּזֵיתָא, אֲמַר: הַאי צְלִיל נְהוֹרֵיהּ טְפֵי.

Rabbi Yehoshua ben Levi said: All the oils are suitable for the Hanukkah **lamp, and olive oil is the most select**[H] of the oils. **Abaye said: At first, my Master,** Rabba, **would seek sesame oil,** as he said: **The light of** sesame oil **lasts longer** and does not burn as quickly as olive oil. **Once he heard that** statement **of Rabbi Yehoshua ben Levi, he sought olive oil** because **he said: Its light is clearer.**

וְאָמַר רַבִּי יְהוֹשֻׁעַ בֶּן לֵוִי: כָּל הַשְּׁמָנִים יָפִין לִדְיוֹ, וְשֶׁמֶן זַיִת מִן הַמּוּבְחָר. אִיבַּעְיָא לְהוּ: לְגַבֵּל אוֹ לְעַשֵּׁן? תָּא שְׁמַע, דְּתָנֵי רַב שְׁמוּאֵל בַּר זוּטְרֵי: כָּל הַשְּׁמָנִים יָפִין לִדְיוֹ וְשֶׁמֶן זַיִת מִן הַמּוּבְחָר. בֵּין לְגַבֵּל בֵּין לְעַשֵּׁן, רַב שְׁמוּאֵל בַּר זוּטְרָא מַתְנֵי הָכִי: כָּל הָעֲשָׁנִים יָפִין לִדְיוֹ וְשֶׁמֶן זַיִת מִן הַמּוּבְחָר. אָמַר רַב הוּנָא: כָּל הַשְּׂרָפִין יָפִין לִדְיוֹ, וּשְׂרָף קְטָף יָפֶה מִכּוּלָּם.

On a similar note, **Rabbi Yehoshua ben Levi said: All the oils are suitable for** making **ink,**[HB] **and olive oil is the most select. A dilemma was raised before** the Sages: What was Rabbi Yehoshua ben Levi's intention: Did he mean that olive oil is the most select in terms of being the best for use **to** mix and **knead** with the soot produced from a fire in manufacturing ink; **or** did he mean for use **to smoke,** i.e., burning olive oil to produce smoke is the most select method of producing the soot used in manufacturing ink? **Come** and **hear** a resolution to this from that which **Rav Shmuel bar Zutrei taught: All oils are suitable for ink, and olive oil is the most select, both to knead and to smoke. Rav Shmuel bar Zutra taught it this way: All types of smoke are good for ink, and olive oil is the most select.** Similarly, **Rav Huna said: All saps are good for** strengthening the **ink** compound, **and balsam sap is the best of all.**

אָמַר רַב חִיָּיא בַּר אַשִׁי אָמַר רַב: הַמַּדְלִיק נֵר שֶׁל חֲנוּכָּה צָרִיךְ לְבָרֵךְ. וְרַב יִרְמְיָה אָמַר: הָרוֹאֶה נֵר שֶׁל חֲנוּכָּה צָרִיךְ לְבָרֵךְ. אָמַר רַב יְהוּדָה: יוֹם רִאשׁוֹן – הָרוֹאֶה מְבָרֵךְ שְׁתַּיִם, וּמַדְלִיק מְבָרֵךְ שָׁלֹשׁ מִכָּאן וְאֵילָךְ – מַדְלִיק מְבָרֵךְ שְׁתַּיִם, וְרוֹאֶה מְבָרֵךְ אַחַת. מַאי מְמַעֵט? מְמַעֵט זְמַן. וְנִימְעוֹט נֵס! נֵס כָּל יוֹמֵי אִיתֵיהּ.

Rav Ḥiyya bar Ashi said that **Rav said: One who lights a Hanukkah light must recite a blessing. And Rabbi Yirmeya said: One who sees a burning Hanukkah light must recite a blessing** because the mitzva is not only to kindle the light but to see the light as well. Therefore, there is room to recite a blessing even when seeing them. **Rav Yehuda said:** On **the first day** of Hanukkah, the **one who sees** burning lights **recites two** blessings, **and the** one **who lights recites three** blessings.[H] **From there on,** from the second day of Hanukkah, **the one who lights recites two** blessings, **and the** one **who sees recites one** blessing. The Gemara asks: **What** blessing does he **omit** on the other days? The Gemara answers: He **omits** the blessing of **time:** Who has given us life, sustained us, and brought us to this time. The Gemara asks: **And let us omit** the blessing of the **miracle:** Who has performed miracles. The Gemara answers: The **miracle is** relevant on **all** of the **days,** whereas the blessing: Who has given us life, is only pertinent to the first time he performs the mitzva each year.

NOTES

A deaf-mute – חֵרֵשׁ: When the Sages employ the unmodified term *ḥeresh* the reference is to one who can neither hear nor speak. In the talmudic era, one with those disabilities did not, as a rule, have full mental capacity and was consequently exempt from all mitzvot in the Torah. However, if he has full mental capacity, he is considered like anyone else and is obligated (see *Tosefot Rabbeinu Yehuda HaḤasid*).

As they too were included in that miracle – שֶׁאַף הֵן הָיוּ בְּאוֹתוֹ הַנֵּס: The Torah principle is that women are exempt from time-bound positive mitzvot. There are exceptions, and lighting the Hanukkah lights is among them.

The phrase: They too were included in that miracle, can be understood in another way. The miracle was caused due to the merit of women (*Tosafot*). Various commentaries connect the episode of Judith and Holofernes, as well as the story of Hannah and her seven sons, to the miracle of Hanukkah. It is thanks to these righteous women that the miracle of Hanukkah transpired.

Reading the *Megilla* on Purim and drinking the four cups of wine at the Passover seder are other exceptions to the exemption from time-bound positive mitzvot. Esther was the catalyst for the miracle of Purim. Similarly, the Sages said: Due to the merit of righteous women, Israel was redeemed from Egypt (*Yalkut Shimoni* Psalms 68).

HALAKHA

If a deaf-mute, an imbecile, or a minor kindles it…a woman – הִדְלִיקָהּ חֵרֵשׁ שׁוֹטֶה וְקָטָן...אִשָּׁה: A woman's obligation to kindle the Hanukkah lights is the same as a man's. Indeed, a woman may recite the blessings on his behalf (*Magen Avraham*). A deaf-mute, an imbecile, or a minor who kindled the Hanukkah lights accomplished nothing. Some rule that a minor who reached the age of training is permitted to kindle Hanukkah lights. However, according to our custom, where each family member lights Hanukkah lights, a minor who has reached the age of training is obligated to light (Rema; Rambam *Sefer Zemanim, Hilkhot Megilla VaḤanukka* 4:9; *Shulḥan Arukh, Oraḥ Ḥayyim* 675:3).

A guest is obligated in lighting the Hanukkah light – אַכְסְנַאי חַיָּיב בְּנֵר חֲנוּכָּה: A guest whose family is not lighting for him at home is obligated to kindle Hanukkah lights where he is sleeping, assuming he has a lamp and a separate entrance where he could light (*Mishna Berura*). Alternatively, he could contribute a *peruta* to defray the cost of the light and have the host include him in his lighting (Rambam *Sefer Zemanim, Hilkhot Megilla VaḤanukka* 4:11; *Shulḥan Arukh, Oraḥ Ḥayyim* 677:1).

And olive oil is the most select – וְשֶׁמֶן זַיִת מִן הַמּוּבְחָר: Olive oil is the preferred oil for kindling lights, especially Hanukkah lights (Rambam *Sefer Zemanim, Hilkhot Shabbat* 5:11; *Shulḥan Arukh, Oraḥ Ḥayyim* 264:6, 673:1).

All the oils are suitable for making ink – כָּל הַשְּׁמָנִים יָפִין לִדְיוֹ: *Ab initio*, sacred texts are written with ink made from either the soot from the smoke of burnt wood or from oils soaked in gallnut juice (Rambam *Sefer Ahava, Hilkhot Tefillin UMezuza VeSefer Torah* 1:4; *Shulḥan Arukh, Oraḥ Ḥayyim* 32:3).

The blessings over the Hanukkah light – בִּרְכוֹת הַנֵּר: On the first evening of Hanukkah, three blessings are recited: To light the Hanukkah light, and: Who performed miracles, and: Who has given us life. On the second night, one recites the first two blessings. If one did not light, does not plan to light, and on whose behalf no one is lighting in his home sees a burning Hanukkah light, he recites: Who performed miracles, and: Who has given us life, on the first night. On all succeeding nights, he recites: Who performed miracles (Rambam *Sefer Zemanim, Hilkhot Megilla VaḤanukka* 3:4; *Shulḥan Arukh, Oraḥ Ḥayyim* 676:1–3).

LANGUAGE

Host [*ushpiza*] – אוּשְׁפִּיזָא: From the Middle Persian aspinj, meaning hotel or hospitality.

BACKGROUND

Making ink – עֲשִׂיַּית דְּיוֹ: In talmudic times, various writing utensils and colored inks were used for writing on parchment and paper. Black was the most common color of ink. This ink was similar to India ink, a thick ink made from the soot of the smoke of burnt wood or oil. The soot was collected and mixed with the appropriate quantity of oil. Sometimes sap was also added to the ink so that it would better adhere to the writing surface.

מַאי מְבָרֵךְ? מְבָרֵךְ ״אֲשֶׁר קִדְּשָׁנוּ בְּמִצְוֹתָיו וְצִוָּנוּ לְהַדְלִיק נֵר שֶׁל חֲנוּכָּה״. וְהֵיכָן צִוָּנוּ? רַב אָוְיָא אָמַר: מִ״לֹּא תָסוּר״. רַב נְחֶמְיָה אָמַר: ״שְׁאַל אָבִיךָ וְיַגֵּדְךָ זְקֵנֶיךָ וְיֹאמְרוּ לָךְ״.

And **what blessing** does one **recite? He recites: Who has made us holy through His commandments and has commanded us to light the Hanukkah light.** The Gemara asks: **And where did He command us?**[HN] The mitzva of Hanukkah is not mentioned in the Torah, so how is it possible to say that it was commanded to us by God? The Gemara answers that **Rav Avya said:** The obligation to recite this blessing is derived **from** the verse: **"You shall not turn aside** from the sentence which they shall declare unto you, to the right, nor to the left" (Deuteronomy 17:11). From this verse, the mitzva incumbent upon all of Israel to heed the statements and decrees of the Sages is derived. Therefore, one who fulfills their directives fulfills a divine commandment. **Rav Neḥemya said** that the mitzva to heed the voice of the Elders of Israel is derived from the verse: **"Ask your father, and he will declare unto you, your Elders, and they will tell you"** (Deuteronomy 32:7).

מְתִיב רַב עַמְרָם: הַדְּמַאי מְעָרְבִין בּוֹ וּמִשְׁתַּתְּפִין בּוֹ וּמְבָרְכִין עָלָיו וּמְזַמְּנִין עָלָיו, וּמַפְרִישִׁין אוֹתוֹ עָרוֹם וּבֵין הַשְּׁמָשׁוֹת. וְאִי אָמְרַתְּ: כֹּל מִדְּרַבָּנַן בָּעֵי בְּרָכָה, הָכָא כִּי קָאֵי עָרוֹם, הֵיכִי מְבָרֵךְ? וְהָא בָּעֵינַן ״וְהָיָה מַחֲנֶיךָ קָדוֹשׁ״ וְלֵיכָּא! אֲמַר אַבַּיֵי: וַדַּאי דְּדִבְרֵיהֶם – בָּעֵי בְּרָכָה, סְפֵק דְּדִבְרֵיהֶם – לָא בָּעֵי בְּרָכָה.

Rav Amram raised an objection from that which we learned in a mishna: With regard to **doubtfully tithed produce** [*demai*], i.e., grain that was acquired from an *am ha'aretz* about which there is uncertainty whether or not he tithed it; **one may** use it **to establish an** ***eiruv***, i.e., joining of courtyards and joining of borders, **and to establish the merging of alleys, and one recites a blessing** before and after eating **it, and one invites a quorum** for recitation of Grace after Meals after eating **it.** Although the Sages said that one is required to separate tithes from *demai*, they allowed it to be used for specific purposes and in exigent circumstances. **And** they said that **one may separate** the tithe from *demai* when he is **naked and at dusk** Shabbat eve, a time when separating tithes from actual untithed produce [*tevel*] is prohibited. **And if you say** that **every** action instituted by **rabbinic ordinance requires a blessing,** as fulfillment of rabbinic ordinances is based on the mitzva: You shall not turn aside, **here, when** he **stands naked, how** can he **recite a blessing? Don't we require** fulfillment of the mitzva: **"Therefore shall your camp be holy;** that He see no unseemly thing in you, and turn away from you" (Deuteronomy 23:15)? **And** the camp **is not** holy when one recites a blessing in a state of nakedness. **Abaye said:** There is room to distinguish between the cases: In **a case** where there is a **definite** mitzva **by rabbinic law, a blessing is required.** In a case where there is a **rabbinic** ordinance instituted due to **uncertainty**[N] with regard to the circumstances, as in the case of *demai*, which may or may not have been tithed already, **a blessing is not required.**[H]

וְהָא יוֹם טוֹב שֵׁנִי, דִּסְפֵק דִּבְרֵיהֶם הוּא, וּבָעֵי בְּרָכָה! הָתָם כִּי הֵיכִי דְּלָא לְזַלְזוּלֵי בָּהּ. רָבָא אָמַר: רוֹב עַמֵּי הָאָרֶץ מְעַשְּׂרִין הֵן.

The Gemara asks: **Isn't the second day of a Festival** in the Diaspora a **rabbinic** ordinance instituted due to **uncertainty** whether the first day or the second is the actual Festival, **and** nevertheless **a blessing is required?** On the second day of the Festival one recites the same blessings as he does on the first. The Gemara answers: **There,** in the case of the second day of the Festival, the reason that blessings are required is **so that people will not treat it with contempt.** If Festival blessings were not required on the second day of the Festival, people would take its sanctity lightly. **Rava said** another reason: *Demai* is not considered to be an ordinance instituted by the Sages due to uncertainty. In fact, in **most** cases, an ***am ha'aretz*** **tithes.** The concern lest they do not tithe is not a full-fledged case of uncertainty. It is merely a case of suspicion for which the Sages did not institute a blessing. That is not the case with regard to the second day of a Festival. Even though it was instituted due to uncertainty, one must recite the Festival blessings. Since it was instituted by the Sages, one is obligated to recite a blessing just as he recites blessings for other rabbinic ordinances.

HALAKHA

And where did He command us – וְהֵיכָן צִוָּנוּ: Performance of all rabbinic ordinances is preceded by a blessing with the formula: Who has made us holy through His mitzvot and has commanded us. In all those cases, the question arises: Where did He command us? He commanded us in the Torah: "Which they tell you, you shall do" (Deuteronomy 17:11). The meaning of the blessing is: God, Who sanctified us by means of His mitzvot, commanded us to obey those who commanded us to light Shabbat lights and Hanukkah lights and to read the *Megilla* (Rambam *Sefer Ahava, Hilkhot Berakhot* 11:3).

Definite mitzva by rabbinic law, a blessing is required…rabbinic ordinance instituted due to uncertainty, a blessing is not required – וַדַּאי דְּדִבְרֵיהֶם בָּעֵי בְּרָכָה, סְפֵק דְּדִבְרֵיהֶם לָא בָּעֵי בְּרָכָה: One does not recite a blessing before fulfilling an ordinance instituted by the Sages due to uncertainty, e.g., *demai*. The blessings recited on the second day of a Festival in the Diaspora are the exception. Blessings are recited then so that the day will not be treated with contempt. Blessings are recited over all other rabbinic ordinances that were not instituted due to uncertainty. In this matter, the *halakha* is in accordance with the opinion of Abaye because Rava did not dispute the actual *halakha* (*Maggid Mishne*). According to the Ra'avad, the *halakha* is in accordance with the opinion of Rava. Blessings are recited over all rabbinic ordinances, even those instituted due to uncertainty, with the exception of *demai*, which is not really a case of uncertainty. Most halakhic authorities (*ge'onim*; Ramban) ruled in accordance with the ruling of the Rambam in this case. Everyone agrees that blessings are not recited in a case where there is uncertainty with regard to a rabbinic ordinance (Rambam *Sefer Zemanim, Hilkhot Megilla VaḤanukka* 3:5).

NOTES

And where did He command us – וְהֵיכָן צִוָּנוּ: This question is often asked with regard to blessings recited over mitzvot of rabbinic origin. Here, the Gemara cites two sources. The first, "You shall not turn aside," which is both simple and accepted *halakha*, was sufficient. The Gemara preferred a source from a positive rather than a negative mitzva and therefore cited the verse: "Ask your father" (Rabbi Elazar Moshe Horowitz).

Rabbinic ordinance instituted due to uncertainty – סְפֵק דְּדִבְרֵיהֶם: *Demai* refers to crops or fruit that were acquired from an *am ha'aretz*. Even though the separation of tithes is a mitzva by Torah law, blessings are only by rabbinic law. Therefore, the question whether or not to recite a blessing when tithing *demai*, produce acquired from a *am ha'aretz*, is a case involving uncertainty with regard to rabbinic law (Ritva). Others say that since by Torah law the buyer is exempt from tithing, *demai* is always a case of a rabbinic ordinance instituted due to uncertainty (*Penei Yehoshua*).

אָמַר רַב הוּנָא: חָצֵר שֶׁיֵּשׁ לָהּ שְׁנֵי פְּתָחִים – צְרִיכָה שְׁתֵּי נֵרוֹת. (וְאָמַר) רָבָא: לָא אֲמַרַן אֶלָּא מִשְּׁתֵּי רוּחוֹת, אֲבָל מֵרוּחַ אַחַת – לָא צְרִיךְ. מַאי טַעְמָא? אִילֵימָא מִשּׁוּם חֲשָׁדָא, חֲשָׁדָא דְּמַאן? אִילֵימָא חֲשָׁדָא דְּעָלְמָא – אֲפִילּוּ בְּרוּחַ אַחַת נַמִי לִיבָּעֵי, אִי חֲשָׁדָא דִּבְנֵי מָתָא – אֲפִילּוּ מִשְּׁנֵי רוּחוֹת נַמִי לָא לִיבָּעֵי! לְעוֹלָם מִשּׁוּם חֲשָׁדָא דִּבְנֵי מָתָא, וְזִימְנִין דְּמִחַלְּפִי בְּהַאי וְלָא חָלְפִי בְּהַאי, וְאָמְרִי: כִּי הֵיכִי דִּבְהַאי פִּיתְחָא לָא אַדְלִיק, בְּהַךְ פִּיתְחָא נַמִי לָא אַדְלִיק.

Rav Huna said: A courtyard that has two entrances[H] **requires two lamps,** one lamp at each entrance, so that it will be obvious that the residents of this courtyard light properly. **And Rava said: We only said this** in a case where the two entrances face **two** different **directions.**[N] **However,** if they both face in **the same direction one need not** light at more than one entrance. The Gemara clarifies Rava's statement: **What is the reason** for this? **If you say** that it is **because** those who see the entrance without a lamp burning will harbor **suspicion** lest he does not kindle the Hanukkah light, **whose suspicion** concerns us? **If you say** that the concern is with regard to **the suspicion** of **people** who do not live in the city and are unfamiliar with the courtyard's tenants, **even** when both entrances face **the same direction let them be required** to light at both entrances because visitors are unaware that there are two entrances to that courtyard. **And if** the concern is with regard to the **suspicion of the residents of** that **city, even** when the two entrances face **two** different **directions let them not be required** to light at both entrances. The local residents know that only one person lives in the courtyard and will assume that if he did not light at one entrance he surely lit at the other. The Gemara answers: **Actually,** say that it is **because of the suspicion of the residents of** that **city, and sometimes** they **pass this** entrance **and do not pass that** one, **and they say: Just as he did not light in this entrance, in that** second **entrance he also did not light.** In order to avoid suspicion, it is preferable to light at both entrances.

וּמְנָא תֵּימְרָא דְּחָיְישִׁינַן לַחֲשָׁד – דְּתַנְיָא, אָמַר רַבִּי שִׁמְעוֹן: בִּשְׁבִיל אַרְבָּעָה דְּבָרִים אָמְרָה תּוֹרָה לְהַנִּיחַ פֵּיאָה בְּסוֹף שָׂדֵהוּ: מִפְּנֵי גֶּזֶל עֲנִיִּים, וּמִפְּנֵי בִּיטּוּל עֲנִיִּים, וּמִפְּנֵי הַחֲשָׁד, וּמִשּׁוּם "בַּל תְּכַלֶּה". מִפְּנֵי גֶּזֶל עֲנִיִּים – שֶׁלֹּא יִרְאֶה בַּעַל הַבַּיִת שָׁעָה פְּנוּיָה, וְיֹאמַר לִקְרוֹבוֹ עָנִי: הֲרֵי זוֹ פֵּאָה.

And from where do you say that we are concerned about suspicion? As it was taught in a *Tosefta* that **Rabbi Shimon said: On account of four things the Torah said** that one should **leave** ***pe'a***,[N] crops for the poor in the corner of his field, specifically **at the end of his field.**[H] Only after one has cut virtually the entire field should he leave an uncut corner for the poor. He should not designate an area for *pe'a* in the middle of the field in the course of cutting the field. The reasons for this ruling are: **Due to robbing the poor, and due to causing the poor to be idle, and due to suspicion, and due to** the verse: **"You shall not wholly reap** the corner of your field" (Leviticus 23:22). The Gemara explains: **Due to robbing the poor;** so **that the owner of the house will not see a time** when the field is **unoccupied** and there are no poor people in the area. If he could designate *pe'a* as he wished, there is room to suspect that **he** might **say to his poor relative: This is** ***pe'a***, in the place and at the time that he chooses. He would thereby conceal the fact that there is *pe'a* in his field from other poor people. The result would be that, for all intents and purposes, he robbed *pe'a* from those with whom he did not share the information.

HALAKHA

Courtyard that has two entrances, etc. – חָצֵר שֶׁיֵּשׁ לָהּ שְׁנֵי פְּתָחִים וכו׳: One whose house or courtyard has two entrances facing in different directions is obligated to light Hanukkah lamps at both entrances, so that he will not be suspected of failing to fulfill the mitzva. Some say that one who owns two houses, even if they face a single direction, is obligated to light in both houses (Rema in the name of *Kolbo*). In any case, one who lights in two entrances recites the blessings only once (Rambam *Sefer Zemanim, Hilkhot Megilla VaḤanukka* 4:10; *Shulḥan Arukh, Oraḥ Ḥayyim* 671:8).

The Torah said to leave *pe'a* at the end of his field – אָמְרָה תּוֹרָה לְהַנִּיחַ פֵּיאָה בְּסוֹף שָׂדֵהוּ: The *pe'a* is separated only at the end of a field because of the reasons cited by Rabbi Shimon. If one separates *pe'a* in the middle of his field, the produce that he separated goes to the poor, and he is nevertheless required to separate the requisite amount of *pe'a* at the end of the field. The calculation is based on what remained in the field after he separated the first *pe'a* from the middle. The manner of fulfilling the *halakha ab initio* was established in accordance with the opinion of Rabbi Shimon, and, apparently, there is no dispute with regard to that aspect of the *halakha* (*Kesef Mishne*; Rambam *Sefer Zera'im, Hilkhot Mattenot Aniyyim* 2:12).

NOTES

And Rava said: We only said this in a case where the two entrances face two different directions, etc. – וְאָמַר רָבָא: לָא אֲמַרַן אֶלָּא מִשְּׁתֵּי רוּחוֹת וכו׳: Most commentaries explain that Rava disagrees with Abaye and does not accept the distinction between cases of certainty and uncertainty with regard to rabbinic law. However, others say that Rava is merely offering a simpler explanation for not reciting a blessing on *demai*, and he does not disagree with Abaye with regard to the second day of a Festival and other cases (Ramban; Rashba). Apparently, the Rambam leans toward that explanation as well.

The mitzva of *pe'a* – מִצְוַות פֵּאָה: "And when you reap the harvest of your land, you shall not wholly reap the corner of your field, neither shall you gather the gleaning of your harvest. And you shall not glean your vineyard, neither shall you gather the fallen fruit of your vineyard; you shall leave them for the poor and for the stranger: I am the Lord your God" (Leviticus 19:9–10). Based on their understanding of these verses, the Sages established the *halakhot* of the mitzva of *pe'a* collected in tractate *Pe'a*. They even determined the percentage of the field that must be left as *pe'a*. Legally, *pe'a* is the property of all poor people, and the owner of the property is not allowed to give the *pe'a* to specific poor people whom he seeks to aid.

ומפני ביטול עניים – שלא יהו עניים יושבין ומשמרין: "עכשיו מניח בעל הבית פאה". ומפני חשד – שלא יהיו עוברין ושבין אומרים: תבא מארה לאדם שלא הניח פאה בשדהו. ומשום "בל תכלה". אטו כולהו לאו משום "בל תכלה" נינהו? אמר רבא: מפני הרמאין.

And due to causing the poor to be idle; so that the **poor,** who have no way of knowing when he is going to cut the grain and where in the field he is going to leave the *pe'a*, **will not be sitting and observing** until he designates the *pe'a* and constantly saying to themselves: **Now the owner** of the field **is placing *pe'a*.** Now that he leaves the *pe'a* in a defined area at the end of his field, and the poor people know exactly where they can receive their portion, they need not waste their time in anticipation. **And due to suspicion;** if one leaves the *pe'a* in the middle of the field, the poor will come and take their portion immediately when he designates the area of *pe'a*. When the owner then continues to cut and harvest the rest of the grain in the field, the *pe'a* will not be noticeable. Insisting that he leave *pe'a* at the end of the field ensures **that passersby will not say: A person who did not leave *pe'a* in his field should be cursed.** We learned that the fourth reason is **due to** the verse: **You shall not wholly reap.** The Gemara wonders: **Aren't all of** these reasons **due to: You shall not wholly reap?** All of the reasons explain that one may not reap his entire field and must leave *pe'a* at the end of his field. **Rava said:** The meaning of the last reason is that *pe'a* is separated that way **due to cheaters.** There is concern that a person would not leave *pe'a* at all. He would claim that he already separated it in the middle of his field and that the poor already came and took it. In order to bolster the mitzva of *pe'a*, the Sages instituted that it must be separated specifically at the end of one's field. In terms of the discussion in the Gemara, apparently, the desire to avoid arousing suspicion is a factor taken into consideration in determining *halakha*.

אמר רב יצחק בר רדיפה אמר רב הונא: נר שיש לה שני פיות – עולה לשני בני אדם. אמר רבא: מילא קערה שמן והקיפה פתילות, כפה עליה כלי – עולה לכמה בני אדם, לא כפה עליה כלי – עשאה כמין מדורה, ואפילו לאחד נמי אינה עולה.

Rav Yitzḥak bar Redifa said that **Rav Huna said: Lighting an oil lamp that has two spouts,**[HB] with one wick placed in each of the spouts, **is considered** to have fulfilled the obligation of kindling the Hanukkah light **for two people.** Similarly, **Rava said: One who filled a bowl with oil and placed wicks all around it,**[H] **if he overturned a vessel on top of it, it is considered** to have fulfilled the obligation of lighting the Hanukkah light **for several people,** corresponding to the number of wicks. By overturning a vessel atop the bowl, each wick appears to be burning independently. If **one did not overturn a vessel on top of it, he** thereby **made it** appear **like a type of bonfire.** From afar, the light from all of the flames appear to be a single flame. **And it is not even considered** to have fulfilled the obligation of lighting the Hanukkah light **for one** person because the mitzva is specifically to light a flame and not a bonfire.

אמר רבא, פשיטא לי: נר ביתו ונר חנוכה – נר ביתו עדיף, משום שלום ביתו. נר ביתו וקידוש היום – נר ביתו עדיף, משום שלום ביתו. בעי רבא: נר חנוכה וקידוש היום מהו? קידוש היום עדיף – דתדיר, או דילמא: נר חנוכה עדיף, משום פרסומי ניסא? בתר דאבעיא הדר פשטה: נר חנוכה עדיף, משום פרסומי ניסא.

Rava said: It is obvious to me that there is a fixed list of priorities. When a person is poor and must choose between purchasing oil to light a Shabbat **lamp for his home** or purchasing oil to light a **Hanukkah lamp,**[H] the Shabbat **lamp for his home takes precedence.** That is **due to peace in his home;** without the light of that lamp, his family would be sitting and eating their meal in the dark. Similarly, if there is a conflict between acquiring oil to light **a lamp for his home** and wine for **the sanctification** [***kiddush***] **of** Shabbat **day, the lamp for his home takes precedence due to peace in his home.** However, **Rava raised a dilemma:** When the conflict is between oil for **a Hanukkah lamp** or wine for ***kiddush*** **of** Shabbat **day,**[H] **what is** the ruling in that case? Does ***kiddush*** **of** Shabbat **day take priority** because it is **frequent,** i.e., it is performed every week, and there is a principle: When there is a conflict between a frequent practice and an infrequent practice, the frequent practice takes precedence? **Or, perhaps the Hanukkah lamp takes precedence due to publicity of the miracle? After he raised the dilemma, he then resolved it** on his own and he ruled that, in that case, the **Hanukkah lamp takes precedence due to publicity of the miracle.**

HALAKHA

Oil lamp that has two spouts – נר שיש לה שני פיות: A pottery lamp with two spouts may be used on Hanukkah by two people, according to the *mehadrin* custom that calls for each person to light one light each night. However, according to the *mehadrin min hamehadrin* custom that calls for each person to add a light for each night, two people may not use the same two-spouted pottery lamp (*Magen Avraham*; Rambam *Sefer Zemanim, Hilkhot Megilla VaḤanukka* 4:4; *Shulḥan Arukh, Oraḥ Ḥayyim* 671:3).

One who filled a bowl with oil and placed wicks all around it – מילא קערה שמן והקיפה פתילות: One who overturned a vessel onto a bowl of oil with wicks around its circumference before kindling the Hanukkah lights, each wick is considered an independent light. If he did not cover the bowl, it has the legal status of a bonfire and may not be used to fulfill the mitzva (Rambam *Sefer Zemanim, Hilkhot Megilla VaḤanukka* 4:4; *Shulḥan Arukh, Oraḥ Ḥayyim* 671:4).

Lamp for his home or a Hanukkah lamp – נר ביתו ונר חנוכה: One who lacks the means to purchase oil to kindle both the Shabbat and the Hanukkah lights should purchase and kindle the Shabbat lights (Rambam *Sefer Zemanim, Hilkhot Megilla VaḤanukka* 4:14; *Shulḥan Arukh, Oraḥ Ḥayyim* 263:3; 678:1).

Hanukkah lamp and *kiddush* of Shabbat day – נר חנוכה וקידוש היום: One who lacks the means to purchase both oil for the Hanukkah lights and wine for *kiddush* should purchase oil for Hanukkah, due to the obligation to publicize the miracle, as per the opinion of Rava. The same is true when the choice is between oil for Hanukkah and wine for *havdala* (Rambam *Sefer Zemanim, Hilkhot Megilla VaḤanukka* 4:13; *Shulḥan Arukh, Oraḥ Ḥayyim* 296:5; 678:1).

BACKGROUND

Oil lamp that has two spouts – נר שיש לה שני פיות:

Pottery lamp

HALAKHA

As long as he neither lights too early nor too late – שֶׁלֹּא יַקְדִּים וְשֶׁלֹּא יְאַחֵר: One may not kindle the Shabbat lights too early or too late. It is prohibited to kindle the Shabbat lights if one does not accept all of the prohibitions of Shabbat at that time. However, it is permitted for one to kindle the Shabbat lights less than one-and-a-quarter hours before sunset [*pelag haminḥa*] and accept all of the Shabbat prohibitions immediately (*Shulḥan Arukh, Oraḥ Ḥayyim* 263:4).

אָמַר רַב הוּנָא: הָרָגִיל בְּנֵר – הָוְיִין לֵיהּ בָּנִים תַּלְמִידֵי חֲכָמִים, הַזָּהִיר בִּמְזוּזָה – זוֹכֶה לְדִירָה נָאָה, הַזָּהִיר בְּצִיצִית – זוֹכֶה לְטַלִּית נָאָה, הַזָּהִיר בְּקִידּוּשׁ הַיּוֹם – זוֹכֶה וּמְמַלֵּא גַּרְבֵי יַיִן. רַב הוּנָא הֲוָה רָגִיל דַּהֲוָה חָלֵיף וְתָנֵי אַפִּתְחָא דְּרַבִּי אָבִין נַגָּרָא, חֲזָא דַּהֲוָה רָגִיל בִּשְׁרָגֵי טוּבָא, אֲמַר: תְּרֵי גַּבְרֵי רַבְרְבֵי נָפְקִי מֵהָכָא. נָפְקִי מִינַּיְיהוּ רַב אִידִי בַּר אָבִין וְרַב חִיָּיא בַּר אָבִין. רַב חִסְדָּא הֲוָה רָגִיל דַּהֲוָה חָלֵיף וְתָנֵי אַפִּיתְחָא דְּבֵי נָשָׁא דְּרַב שֵׁיזְבִי, חֲזָא דַּהֲוָה רָגִיל בִּשְׁרָגֵי טוּבָא, אָמַר: גַּבְרָא רַבָּא נָפֵק מֵהָכָא. נְפַק מִינַּיְיהוּ רַב שֵׁיזְבִי.

Rav Huna said: One who is accustomed to kindle **lights**[N] on Shabbat and Hanukkah will be rewarded and **have children who are Torah scholars,** who will disseminate the light of Torah. **One who is meticulous in** performing the mitzva of *mezuza* **merits a beautiful house** on which to affix his *mezuza*. **One who is meticulous in** performing the mitzva of ritual fringes **merits a beautiful garment. One who is meticulous in** performing the mitzva *of kiddush* **of the day merits and fills jugs of wine.** The Gemara relates: **Rav Huna was accustomed to pass by and teach at the entrance** of the house of **Rabbi Avin the carpenter. He saw that** Rabbi Avin **was accustomed to** kindle **many lights** in honor of Shabbat. Rav Huna **said: Two great men** will **emerge from here.** Indeed, **Rav Idi bar Avin and Rav Ḥiyya bar Avin,** his two oldest sons, **emerged from their** family. On a similar note, the Gemara relates: **Rav Ḥisda was accustomed to pass by and teach at the entrance of Rav Sheizvi's** father's family home. **He saw that** Rav Sheizvi's father **was accustomed** to kindle **many lights** in honor of Shabbat. Rav **Ḥisda said: A great person** will **emerge from here.** Indeed, **Rav Sheizvi emerged from them.**[N]

דְּבֵיתְהוּ דְּרַב יוֹסֵף הֲוַת מְאַחֲרָה וּמַדְלְקָת לָהּ, אָמַר לָהּ רַב יוֹסֵף, תַּנְיָא: ״לֹא יָמִישׁ עַמּוּד הֶעָנָן יוֹמָם וְעַמּוּד הָאֵשׁ לָיְלָה״ מְלַמֵּד שֶׁעַמּוּד עָנָן מַשְׁלִים לְעַמּוּד הָאֵשׁ, וְעַמּוּד הָאֵשׁ מַשְׁלִים לְעַמּוּד הֶעָנָן. סְבָרָה לְאַקְדּוֹמָהּ, אֲמַר לָהּ הַהוּא סָבָא: תָּנֵינָא, וּבִלְבַד שֶׁלֹּא יַקְדִּים וְשֶׁלֹּא יְאַחֵר.

The Gemara relates that **Rav Yosef's wife would kindle the** Shabbat lights **late. Rav Yosef said to her: Wasn't it taught** in a *baraita* with regard to the verse: **"The pillar of cloud by day, and the pillar of fire by night, departed not** from before the people" (Exodus 13:22), this **teaches that the pillar of cloud would overlap** with **the pillar of fire?** The pillar of fire would appear slightly before nightfall. **And the pillar of fire** would **overlap** with **the pillar of cloud,** as well. The pillar of cloud would appear slightly before daybreak. Therefore, in lighting the Shabbat lights it is also appropriate to light earlier, beginning Shabbat slightly before dark on Shabbat eve. **She thought to** kindle the lights much **earlier,** on Shabbat eve, long before nightfall. **An Elder said to her, we learned: As long as he neither** lights too **early nor** too **late.**[H]

אֲמַר רָבָא: דְּרָחֵים רַבָּנַן – הָווּ לֵיהּ בְּנִין רַבָּנַן, דְּמוֹקִיר רַבָּנַן – הָווּ לֵיהּ חֲתָנְוָותָא רַבָּנַן, דְּדָחֵיל מֵרַבָּנַן – הוּא גּוּפֵיהּ הָוֵי צוּרְבָא מֵרַבָּנַן, וְאִי לָאו בַּר הָכִי הוּא – מִשְׁתַּמְעָן מִילֵּיהּ כְּצוּרְבָא מֵרַבָּנַן.

Similar to the reward due one who kindles the Shabbat lights, **Rava said: One who loves Sages will have children who are Sages. One who honors Sages will have sons-in-law who are Sages. One who stands in awe of the Sages**[N] **will himself become a Torah scholar. And if he is not capable** and lacks the talent to become a Torah scholar, **his statements will be received like** the statements of **a Torah scholar.**

״וְלֹא בְּשֶׁמֶן שְׂרֵיפָה״ וכו׳. מַאי שֶׁמֶן שְׂרֵיפָה? אָמַר רַבָּה: שֶׁמֶן שֶׁל תְּרוּמָה שֶׁנִּטְמְאָה. וְאַמַּאי קָרוּ לָהּ שֶׁמֶן שְׂרֵיפָה – הוֹאִיל וְלִשְׂרֵיפָה עוֹמֵד. וּבְשַׁבָּת מַאי טַעְמָא לָא – מִתּוֹךְ שֶׁמִּצְוָה עָלָיו לְבַעֲרוֹ, גְּזֵירָה שֶׁמָּא יַטֶּה. אָמַר לֵיהּ אַבַּיֵי: אֶלָּא מֵעַתָּה, בְּיוֹם טוֹב לִישְׁתְּרֵי! אַלְמָה תְּנַן: אֵין מַדְלִיקִין בְּשֶׁמֶן שְׂרֵיפָה בְּיוֹם טוֹב! גְּזֵירָה יוֹם טוֹב אַטּוּ שַׁבָּת.

We learned in the mishna that **one may not** light **with burnt oil** on Shabbat. The Gemara asks: **What is burnt oil? Rabba said:** It is **oil of *teruma* that became ritually impure. And why did they call it burnt oil? Because its burning is imminent,** as it is prohibited to eat this oil and one is obligated to burn it. The Gemara asks: **And what is the reason** that one may **not** light with it **on Shabbat?** The Gemara explains: **Because it is a mitzva to burn it,** the Sages issued **a decree lest,** in doing so, **he** come to **adjust** the wick in order to hasten its burning. **Abaye said to him: But if** what you say **is so,** that the reason for the prohibition is a concern lest he adjust it, then, **on a Festival,** when adjusting a wick is permitted, **it should be permitted** to light with burnt oil. **Why** then **did we learn** in the mishna: **One may not light with burnt oil** even **on a Festival?** The Gemara answers: It is **a decree** issued by the Sages prohibiting burning it even on **a Festival, due to** the prohibition to burn it on **Shabbat.**

NOTES

One who is accustomed to kindle lights – הָרָגִיל בְּנֵר: Some commentaries explain that this statement refers to the Hanukkah lights that were discussed previously, while others hold that it refers to the Shabbat lights. Rashi indicates that it refers to both. Some interpret the phrase as referring to one who regularly lights lamps at home at night and uses the light for himself and his family to study Torah (*Panim Masbirot, Iyyun Ya'akov*).

Lights and their reward – הַנֵּרוֹת וּשְׂכָרָם: Various commentaries attempt to explain what led Rav Huna to say two great people would emerge from that home, while Rav Ḥisda spoke of only one great person. According to the variant reading of the Gemara in the Rif and *Tosafot*, the first story uses the plural: Were accustomed, meaning that both the husband and wife were accustomed to kindling lights. The second story uses the singular: Was accustomed, meaning that only one of them would kindle the lights. Other authorities point out that Rav Avin, the carpenter, was accustomed and careful to light both Hanukkah and Shabbat lights. In Rav Sheizvi's family, they were only accustomed to light one of them (*Me'iri*).

One who loves the Sages…one who honors the Sages…one who stands in awe of the Sages – דְּרָחֵים רַבָּנַן...דְּמוֹקִיר רַבָּנַן...דְּדָחֵיל מֵרַבָּנַן: Each reward mentioned here is measure for measure. One who loves the Sages will merit having children who will be loved both as children and as scholars. One who honors the Sages will have sons-in-law who will honor their in-laws and be honored by them. One who stands in awe of the Sages will merit the honor and awe of others, either as a Torah scholar or in other ways.

Some commentaries wonder: Ostensibly, love is more significant than awe. Why then is the reward here greater for awe than for love? The Vilna Gaon emended the text accordingly. Others explained that there is no mitzva to love the Sages beyond the mitzva to love all Jews. However, there is a mitzva to stand in awe of the Sages. Therefore, one who fulfills that mitzva merits a greater reward (Rabbi Ya'akov of Korvil).

רַב חִסְדָּא אֲמַר: לְ״שֶׁמָּא יַטֶּה״ – לָא חָיְישִׁינַן. אֶלָּא, הָכָא בְּיוֹם טוֹב שֶׁחָל לִהְיוֹת עֶרֶב שַׁבָּת עָסְקִינַן, לְפִי שֶׁאֵין שׂוֹרְפִין קָדָשִׁים בְּיוֹם טוֹב, וְהָא מִדְּקָתָנֵי סֵיפָא: ״אֵין מַדְלִיקִין בְּשֶׁמֶן שְׂרֵיפָה בְּיוֹם טוֹב״ מִכְּלָל דְּרֵישָׁא לָאו בְּיוֹם טוֹב עָסְקִינַן! אָמַר רַב חֲנִינָא מִסּוּרָא: ״מַה טַּעַם״ קָאָמַר: מַה טַּעַם אֵין מַדְלִיקִין בְּשֶׁמֶן שְׂרֵיפָה בְּיוֹם טוֹב – לְפִי שֶׁאֵין שׂוֹרְפִין קָדָשִׁים בְּיוֹם טוֹב.

Rav Ḥisda said: The reason for the prohibition against lighting a Shabbat lamp with burnt oil is different, as **we are not concerned lest one** come to **adjust** the wick. **Rather, here,** in our mishna, **we are dealing with a Festival that fell on Shabbat eve,** in which case he must kindle Shabbat lights on the Festival. One may not light a Shabbat lamp with burnt oil on a Festival **because one may not burn consecrated items on a Festival,**[N] a prohibition that applies to *teruma* as well. The Gemara asks: **But from the fact that we learned in the latter clause,** i.e., the next mishna, that **one may not light with burnt oil on a Festival, by inference,** in **the first clause** of the mishna **we are not dealing with a Festival** but rather with a standard Shabbat. **Rabbi Ḥanina from Sura said:** This mishna must be understood in the following manner: These are not two distinct *halakhot*; rather, this mishna was stated employing the didactic style of **what is the reason. What is the reason** that **one may not light with burnt oil on a Festival** or on a Festival that falls on Shabbat eve? It is **because one may not burn consecrated items on a Festival** at all.

NOTES

Because one may not burn consecrated items on a Festival – שֶׁאֵין שׂוֹרְפִין קָדָשִׁים בְּיוֹם טוֹב: According to some commentaries, Rabba ruled that the prohibition applies only to burning consecrated items. *Teruma* is not included in this prohibition (Rashba). Others state that Rabba did not dispute the *halakha* that one may not burn *teruma*. Rather, he held that since one may burn *teruma* for personal enjoyment, it would have been permitted on a Festival if not for the decree. Another opinion suggests that it is prohibited only when burned in a bonfire kindled for no purpose other than burning *teruma* (*Me'iri*).

Perek **II**
Daf **24** Amud **a**

תַּנְיָא כְּוָותֵיהּ דְּרַב חִסְדָּא: כָּל אֵלּוּ שֶׁאָמְרוּ אֵין מַדְלִיקִין בָּהֶן בַּשַּׁבָּת – מַדְלִיקִין בָּהֶן בְּיוֹם טוֹב, חוּץ מִשֶּׁמֶן שְׂרֵיפָה, לְפִי שֶׁאֵין שׂוֹרְפִין קָדָשִׁים בְּיוֹם טוֹב.

It was taught in a *baraita* **in accordance with** the opinion of **Rav Ḥisda. All of these** oils with which the Sages **said** that **one may not light on Shabbat, one may light with them on a Festival, with the exception of burnt oil, because one may not burn consecrated items on a Festival.**

אִיבַּעְיָא לְהוּ: מַהוּ לְהַזְכִּיר שֶׁל חֲנוּכָּה בְּבִרְכַּת הַמָּזוֹן? כֵּיוָן דִּמְדְּרַבָּנַן הוּא – לָא מַדְכְּרִינַן, אוֹ דִּילְמָא: מִשּׁוּם פַּרְסוּמֵי נִיסָּא מַדְכְּרִינַן? אָמַר רָבָא אָמַר רַב סְחוֹרָה אָמַר רַב הוּנָא: אֵינוֹ מַזְכִּיר, וְאִם בָּא לְהַזְכִּיר – מַזְכִּיר בְּהוֹדָאָה. רַב הוּנָא בַּר יְהוּדָה אִיקְּלַע לְבֵי רָבָא, סְבַר לְאַדְכּוּרֵי בְּ״בוֹנֵה יְרוּשָׁלַיִם״. אֲמַר לְהוּ רַב שֵׁשֶׁת: כִּתְפִלָּה, מַה תְּפִלָּה – בְּהוֹדָאָה, אַף בִּרְכַּת הַמָּזוֹן – בְּהוֹדָאָה.

A dilemma was raised before the Sages: **What is** the ruling **with regard to** the obligation **to mention Hanukkah**[N] **in Grace after Meals?**[N] The dilemma is: **Since it is merely an obligation by rabbinic law, do we not mention it? Or, perhaps due to publicity of the miracle, we mention it. Rava said** that **Rav Seḥora said** that **Rav Huna said: One does not mention** it. **And if,** nevertheless, **he comes to mention** it, **he mentions it in** the blessing of **thanksgiving.** The Gemara relates that **Rav Huna bar Yehuda happened by Rava's house** on Hanukkah. When, after eating, he came to recite Grace after Meals, **he thought to mention** Hanukkah **in** the blessing: **Who builds Jerusalem. Rav Sheshet said to** the yeshiva students: One mentions Hanukkah in Grace after Meals **just as** he does **in** the *Amida* **prayer. Just as** in the *Amida* **prayer** one mentions Hanukkah **in** the blessing of **thanksgiving, so too, in Grace after Meals** one mentions Hanukkah **in** the blessing of **thanksgiving.**[H]

NOTES

The topic of Hanukkah – עִנְיַן חֲנוּכָּה: *Tosafot* wondered why the *halakhot* of Hanukkah were not discussed consecutively and are instead interrupted by unrelated matters. Some commentaries explain that based on Rabba's reasoning, the Sages were especially concerned that one might come to adjust the flame when using burnt oil. Since the same prohibition applies to Hanukkah lights kindled just before Shabbat, it is a Hanukkah related issue as well (Ritva).

What is the ruling with regard to the obligation to mention Hanukkah in Grace after Meals – מַהוּ לְהַזְכִּיר שֶׁל חֲנוּכָּה בְּבִרְכַּת הַמָּזוֹן: Since the essence of the holiday is publicizing the miracle, all authorities agree that Hanukkah should be mentioned during the prayers that are conducted in public. However, the Sages were uncertain as to whether or not Hanukkah must be mentioned in Grace after Meals, which is an individual matter (Ritva).

HALAKHA

Just as in prayer one mentions Hanukkah in the blessing of thanksgiving, so too, in Grace after Meals one mentions Hanukkah in the blessing of thanksgiving – מַה תְּפִלָּה בְּהוֹדָאָה, אַף בִּרְכַּת הַמָּזוֹן בְּהוֹדָאָה: Throughout the eight days of Hanukkah, the paragraph: For the miracles, is added to the *Amida* prayer in the blessing of thanksgiving. The same paragraph is added to Grace after Meals in the blessing of the land. One who forgot to recite it and concluded the *Amida* prayer or Grace after Meals need not repeat either of them because the additional paragraph was not instituted as a full-fledged obligation. One who reached the end of the blessing into which: For the miracles, was inserted and did not yet recite the words: Blessed are You, Lord, repeats the blessing and includes the addition for Hanukkah. Once one recited the words: Blesssed are You, even if he did not yet recite the word Lord, he does not repeat the blessing (Rambam *Sefer Ahava, Hilkhot Tefilla* 2:13, *Hilkhot Berakhot* 2:6; *Shulḥan Arukh, Oraḥ Ḥayyim* 682:1).

אִיבַּעְיָא לְהוּ: מַהוּ לְהַזְכִּיר רֹאשׁ חוֹדֶשׁ בְּבִרְכַּת הַמָּזוֹן? אִם תִּימְצֵי לוֹמַר בַּחֲנוּכָּה דְּרַבָּנַן לָא צְרִיךְ, רֹאשׁ חוֹדֶשׁ דְּאוֹרַיְיתָא – צְרִיךְ, אוֹ דִּילְמָא: כֵּיוָן דְּלָא אָסוּר בַּעֲשִׂיַּית מְלָאכָה – לָא מַזְכְּרִינַן? רַב אָמַר: מַזְכִּיר, רַבִּי חֲנִינָא אָמַר: אֵינוֹ מַזְכִּיר. אֲמַר רַב זְרִיקָא: נְקוֹט דְּרַב בִּידָךְ, דְּקָאֵי רַבִּי אוֹשַׁעְיָא כְּוָותֵיהּ. דְּתָנֵי רַבִּי אוֹשַׁעְיָא: יָמִים שֶׁיֵּשׁ בָּהֶן קָרְבַּן מוּסָף, כְּגוֹן רֹאשׁ חוֹדֶשׁ וְחוּלּוֹ שֶׁל מוֹעֵד – עַרְבִית וְשַׁחֲרִית וּמִנְחָה מִתְפַּלֵּל שְׁמוֹנֶה עֶשְׂרֵה, וְאוֹמֵר מֵעֵין הַמְאוֹרָע בַּעֲבוֹדָה, וְאִם לֹא אָמַר – מַחֲזִירִין אוֹתוֹ, וְאֵין בָּהֶן קְדוּשָּׁה עַל הַכּוֹס, וְיֵשׁ בָּהֶן הַזְכָּרָה בְּבִרְכַּת הַמָּזוֹן. יָמִים שֶׁאֵין בָּהֶן קָרְבַּן מוּסָף, כְּגוֹן שֵׁנִי וַחֲמִישִׁי (וְשֵׁנִי), וְתַעֲנִיּוֹת וּמַעֲמָדוֹת.

Based on the previous dilemma, an additional **dilemma was raised before** the Sages: **What is** the ruling with regard to the obligation **to mention the New Moon in Grace after Meals?**[H] The dilemma is: **If you say that on Hanukkah,** since it is only **by rabbinic law, one need not** mention it in Grace after Meals; perhaps **the New Moon,** which is **by Torah law, one is required** to mention it. **Or, perhaps since it is not** a day on which it is **prohibited to perform labor, one need not mention it.** The Sages disputed this matter: **Rav said: One mentions** the New Moon in Grace after Meals. **Rabbi Ḥanina said: One does not mention** it. **Rav Zerika said: Take** the *halakha* **of Rav in your hand** as authoritative, since **Rabbi Oshaya holds in accordance with his** opinion. **As Rabbi Oshaya taught** in a *Tosefta*: **Days on which there is an additional offering sacrificed** in the Temple, i.e., **the New Moon and the intermediate days of a Festival;** in **the evening, morning, and afternoon prayers, one recites** the **eighteen** blessings of the *Amida* prayer **and says** a passage **pertaining to the event**[H] of the day **during** the blessing of **Temple service. And if he did not recite** it, **we require him to return** to the beginning of the prayer and repeat it. **And** on those days, **there is no *kiddush* recited over the cup** of wine at the start of the day, **but there is mention** of the day recited **in Grace after Meals,** in accordance with Rav's opinion. **Days on which there is no additional offering, i.e., Monday, and Thursday, and fast days, and** non-priestly **watches** [*ma'amadot*],[B] have a different legal status as detailed below.

שֵׁנִי וַחֲמִישִׁי מַאי עֲבִידְתַּיְיהוּ? אֶלָּא: שֵׁנִי וַחֲמִישִׁי וְשֵׁנִי שֶׁל תַּעֲנִיּוֹת וּמַעֲמָדוֹת. עַרְבִית וְשַׁחֲרִית וּמִנְחָה מִתְפַּלֵּל שְׁמוֹנֶה עֶשְׂרֵה, וְאוֹמֵר מֵעֵין הַמְאוֹרָע בְּ״שׁוֹמֵעַ תְּפִלָּה״, וְאִם לֹא אָמַר – אֵין מַחֲזִירִין אוֹתוֹ. (וְאֵין בָּהֶן קְדוּשָּׁה עַל הַכּוֹס) וְאֵין בָּהֶן הַזְכָּרָה בְּבִרְכַּת הַמָּזוֹן.

Before drawing a conclusion, the Gemara seeks to clarify: **Monday and Thursday, what is their purpose** in this discussion, i.e., why are Monday and Thursday mentioned here if no special prayers are recited on those days? The Gemara explains: **Rather,** certainly the reference is to **Monday and Thursday and Monday** that are **fast days**[H] for rain **and of *ma'amadot*.** On those days, in the **evening, morning, and afternoon prayers, one recites eighteen** blessings **and recites** a passage **pertaining to the event** of the day, i.e., the fast, **in** the blessing: **Who listens to prayer. However, if one did not mention** it, **we do not require him to return** to the beginning of the prayer and repeat it.[H] **And,** on those days, **there is no *kiddush* recited over a cup** of wine, **and there is no mention** of the day recited **in Grace after Meals.**

אִיבַּעְיָא לְהוּ: מַהוּ לְהַזְכִּיר שֶׁל חֲנוּכָּה בְּמוּסָפִין? כֵּיוָן דְּלֵית בֵּיהּ מוּסָף בְּדִידֵיהּ – לָא מַדְכְּרִינַן, אוֹ דִּילְמָא: יוֹם הוּא שֶׁחַיָּיב בְּאַרְבַּע תְּפִלּוֹת? רַב הוּנָא וְרַב יְהוּדָה דְּאָמְרִי תַּרְוַיְיהוּ: אֵינוֹ מַזְכִּיר, רַב נַחְמָן וְרַבִּי יוֹחָנָן דְּאָמְרִי תַּרְוַיְיהוּ: מַזְכִּיר.

An additional **dilemma was raised before** the Sages: **What is** the ruling with regard to the obligation **to mention Hanukkah in** the **additional prayer**[H] on Shabbat during Hanukkah or on the New Moon of Tevet, which falls during Hanukkah? The sides of the dilemma are: Do we say that **since** Hanukkah **has no** additional prayer **of its own,** and the additional prayer has no connection to Hanukkah, **we do not mention** it? **Or, perhaps it is** the essence of **the day that is obligated** in the mention of Hanukkah, in which case there is no distinction between the various prayers, and it should be mentioned **in all four prayers,** including the additional prayer on Shabbat and the New Moon. There is a dispute: **Rav Huna and Rav Yehuda both said: One does not mention** it. **Rav Naḥman and Rabbi Yoḥanan both said: One mentions** it.

HALAKHA

What is the ruling with regard to the obligation to mention the New Moon in Grace after Meals – מַהוּ לְהַזְכִּיר רֹאשׁ חוֹדֶשׁ בְּבִרְכַּת הַמָּזוֹן: One mentions the New Moon in the added paragraph: May there rise and come, in Grace after Meals. One who forgot to recite that paragraph need not repeat the blessing because there is no obligation to eat bread on the New Moon. However, if one did not begin the fourth blessing: Who is good and does good, he recites: Blessed…Who gave the New Moon to His people Israel for commemoration (Rambam *Sefer Ahava, Hilkhot Berakhot* 2:5; *Shulḥan Arukh, Oraḥ Ḥayyim* 424:1).

The New Moon and the intermediate days of the Festival…one recites a…passage pertaining to the event – רֹאשׁ חוֹדֶשׁ וְחוּלּוֹ שֶׁל מוֹעֵד...וְאוֹמֵר מֵעֵין הַמְאוֹרָע: On the New Moon or during the intermediate days of a Festival, the paragraph: May there rise and come, which includes mention of the New Moon or the Festival, is added to the *Amida* prayer. One who omitted that paragraph must recite the *Amida* prayer again. The only exception is the evening prayer on the New Moon.

If one remembered: May there rise and come, before starting the blessing of thanksgiving, the paragraph may be recited there. If one started to recite the blessing of thanksgiving and only then realized that he omitted the paragraph, he must repeat the *Amida* prayer from the beginning of the blessing of Temple service and include the paragraph that he omitted.

If one remembered after he finished the *Amida* prayer, while he is reciting the entreaties that he customarily recites after the *Amida* but before he moved his feet, he must repeat the *Amida* prayer from the beginning of the blessing of Temple service and include the paragraph that he omitted.

If one completed the *Amida* prayer and is uncertain whether or not he recited: May there rise and come, he need not repeat the *Amida* (Rema). The *Mishna Berura* writes that many authorities disagree with the Rema on this point and conclude that he must repeat the *Amida* prayer. Later commentaries add that if he had in mind to recite: May there rise and come, but some time after completing the *Amida* prayer he is uncertain whether or not he in fact recited it, he need not repeat the *Amida*. If the uncertainty arose immediately after he concluded the *Amida* prayer, he is required to repeat it (*Tosefta*; Rambam *Sefer Ahava, Hilkhot Tefilla* 2:10; *Shulḥan Arukh, Oraḥ Ḥayyim* 422:1; 490:2).

Mention on fast days – הַזְכָּרָה בְּתַעֲנִיּוֹת: On fast days, one adds the paragraph: Answer us, to each of the *Amida* prayers. The custom, based on the opinion of the *ge'onim*, is that an individual adds that paragraph to the afternoon prayer. There is concern that if one were to recite the paragraph in the morning prayer and then fail to complete the fast, he would end up contradicting the prayer that he recited in the added paragraph. During a communal fast, even an individual recites: Answer us, in the morning prayer. The Rema disagrees (Rambam *Sefer Ahava, Hilkhot Tefilla* 2:14; *Shulḥan Arukh, Oraḥ Ḥayyim* 565:1, 3).

If one did not mention it, we do not require him to return to the beginning of the prayer and repeat it – וְאִם לֹא אָמַר אֵין מַחֲזִירִין אוֹתוֹ: One who failed to recite: Answer us, on a communal fast need not repeat the *Amida* prayer. If he remembered prior to moving his feet at the end of the *Amida*, before he recited the verse: May the words of my mouth, he recites: Answer us, at that point without the concluding blessing (*Shulḥan Arukh, Oraḥ Ḥayyim* 565:2).

What is the ruling with regard to the obligation to mention Hanukkah in the additional prayer – מַהוּ לְהַזְכִּיר שֶׁל חֲנוּכָּה בְּמוּסָפִין: One mentions Hanukkah in the additional prayer on Shabbat and on the New Moon of Tevet, as per the opinions of Rav Naḥman and Rabbi Yoḥanan and the subsequent explicit ruling of the Gemara (Rambam *Sefer Ahava, Hilkhot Tefilla* 2:13; *Shulḥan Arukh, Oraḥ Ḥayyim* 682:2).

BACKGROUND

Non-priestly watches [*ma'amadot*] – מַעֲמָדוֹת: In the Temple era, priests and Levites were divided into twenty-four watches. Each watch served in the Temple for one week, twice or three times a year. The entire nation was also divided into twenty-four watches, with each watch attached to a specific group of priests. During the week when the priestly watch was on duty in the Temple, some members of the corresponding non-priestly watch were dispatched to Jerusalem to serve in the Temple, and others would assemble in various cities throughout the land. The representatives of the non-priestly watch would perform certain rituals, such as reading special portions of the Torah and fasting several days that week. Vestiges of the customs of the non-priestly watch are found in various prayer books.

אָמַר אַבַּיֵי לְרַב יוֹסֵף: הָא דְּרַב הוּנָא וְרַב יְהוּדָה – דְּרַב הוּא, דְּאָמַר רַב גִּידֵּל אָמַר רַב: רֹאשׁ חֹדֶשׁ שֶׁחָל לִהְיוֹת בְּשַׁבָּת – הַמַּפְטִיר בְּנָבִיא בְּשַׁבָּת אֵינוֹ צָרִיךְ לְהַזְכִּיר שֶׁל רֹאשׁ חֹדֶשׁ, שֶׁאִילְמָלֵא שַׁבָּת – אֵין נָבִיא בְּרֹאשׁ חֹדֶשׁ.

Abaye said to Rav Yosef: This opinion of **Rav Huna and Rav Yehuda is Rav's** opinion, **as Rav Giddel said** that **Rav said:** In the case of **the New Moon that occurs on Shabbat, the one who recites the portion from the Prophets** [*haftara*] **on Shabbat need not mention the New Moon** in the blessing, as, **if it were not Shabbat, there would be no** reading from **the Prophets on the New Moon.** The *haftara* is unrelated to the New Moon, and therefore the New Moon is not mentioned in the blessing. The same should be true with regard to mention of Hanukkah in the additional service on the New Moon, as, if it were not the New Moon, he would not be reciting the additional service on Hanukkah. Therefore, when he recites the additional prayer, he need not mention Hanukkah.

מִי דָּמֵי?! הָתָם – נָבִיא בְּרֹאשׁ חֹדֶשׁ לֵיכָּא כְּלָל, הָכָא – אִיתֵיהּ בְּעַרְבִית וְשַׁחֲרִית וּמִנְחָה! אֶלָּא, לְהָא דָּמְיָא: דְּאָמַר רַב אַחְדְּבוֹי אָמַר רַב מַתְּנָה אָמַר רַב: יוֹם טוֹב שֶׁחָל לִהְיוֹת בְּשַׁבָּת – הַמַּפְטִיר בַּנָּבִיא בְּמִנְחָה בְּשַׁבָּת אֵינוֹ צָרִיךְ לְהַזְכִּיר שֶׁל יוֹם טוֹב, שֶׁאִילְמָלֵא שַׁבָּת – אֵין נָבִיא בְּמִנְחָה בְּיוֹם טוֹב.

The Gemara rejects this comparison. **Is this comparable? There,** reading from the **Prophets** is **not at all part of** the service **on the New Moon. Here, there is** mention of Hanukkah **in the evening, morning, and afternoon prayers. Rather,** it is **comparable to this:** As **Rav Aḥadvoi said** that **Rav Mattana said** that **Rav said:** On **a Festival that occurs on Shabbat, one who recites the portion from the Prophets during the afternoon service**[B] **on Shabbat need not mention the Festival,** as, **if** it were **not Shabbat, there would be no** reading from the **Prophets during the afternoon service on a Festival.** If so, even though there is a *haftara* during the morning service on a Festival, since they do not read from the Prophets in the afternoon, the reading is considered totally unrelated to the Festival and one does not mention the Festival. The same is true with regard to Hanukkah. One does not mention Hanukkah in the additional prayer.

BACKGROUND

Portion from the Prophets [*haftara*] during the afternoon service – הַפְטָרָה בְּמִנְחָה: The mishna states explicitly that the Torah is read during the afternoon service on Shabbat, but no portion from the Prophets [*haftara*] is read then. However, apparently, that statement reflected the specific local custom, while in other locales, throughout many generations, there was a custom to read a portion from the Prophets after the Torah reading during the Shabbat afternoon service. These readings were always from the chapters of consolation in the book of Isaiah and were ten verses long. Persecution of the Jews by the Persian kings brought this custom to a halt in Babylonia and in other Jewish centers. Nevertheless, in certain communities in Persia and in Media, this custom was preserved through the period of the *ge'onim*.

Perek **II**
Daf **24** Amud **b**

וְלֵית הִילְכְתָא כְּכׇל הָנֵי שְׁמַעְתָּתָא, אֶלָּא כִּי הָא דְּאָמַר רַבִּי יְהוֹשֻׁעַ בֶּן לֵוִי: יוֹם הַכִּפּוּרִים שֶׁחָל לִהְיוֹת בְּשַׁבָּת הַמִּתְפַּלֵּל נְעִילָה צָרִיךְ לְהַזְכִּיר שֶׁל שַׁבָּת, יוֹם הוּא שֶׁנִּתְחַיֵּיב בְּאַרְבַּע תְּפִלּוֹת.

The Gemara concludes: **And the *halakha* is not in accordance with any of these *halakhot*;**[H] **rather,** it is **in accordance with that which Rabbi Yehoshua ben Levi said:** On **Yom Kippur that falls on Shabbat, one who recites** the day's **closing prayer** [***ne'ila***][H] **must mention Shabbat** even in that prayer, although *ne'ila* is not recited every Shabbat. The reason for this is that on Yom Kippur, the **day** itself **is obligated in four prayers,** i.e., morning, additional, afternoon, and closing. When it occurs on Shabbat, one must mention Shabbat in each of the prayers. Apparently, on a day that has a unique character, that character is manifest in all sacred aspects of the day; those engendered by the day itself as well as those engendered by other factors.

קַשְׁיָא הִילְכְתָא אַהִילְכְתָא! אָמְרַתְּ: הִילְכְתָא כְּרַבִּי יְהוֹשֻׁעַ בֶּן לֵוִי, וְקַיְימָא לַן: הִילְכְתָא כְּרָבָא. דְּאָמַר רָבָא: יוֹם טוֹב שֶׁחָל לִהְיוֹת בְּשַׁבָּת, שְׁלִיחַ צִיבּוּר הַיּוֹרֵד לִפְנֵי הַתֵּיבָה עַרְבִית אֵינוֹ צָרִיךְ לְהַזְכִּיר שֶׁל יוֹם טוֹב, שֶׁאִילְמָלֵא שַׁבָּת אֵין שְׁלִיחַ צִבּוּר יוֹרֵד עַרְבִית בְּיוֹם טוֹב.

The Gemara challenges this: It is **difficult,** as there is a contradiction between one ***halakha*** and another ***halakha.*** On the one hand, **you said** that **the *halakha*** is **in accordance with** the opinion of **Rabbi Yehoshua ben Levi. And,** on the other hand, **we hold** that **the *halakha* is in accordance with** the opinion of **Rava,** which contradicts the first *halakha*, **as Rava said:** On **a Festival that occurs on Shabbat,**[H] **the prayer leader who descends before the ark** to recite the prayer abridged from the seven blessings of the Shabbat **evening** *Amida* **prayer need not mention** the Festival, **as, if it were not** also **Shabbat, the prayer leader would not descend before the ark** to recite this prayer during **the evening prayer on a Festival.** The Gemara reverts to the previous assumption that an element that does not arise from the essential *halakhot* of the day is considered foreign to it and is not mentioned.

HALAKHA

And the *halakha* is not in accordance with any of these *halakhot* – וְלֵית הִילְכְתָא כְּכׇל הָנֵי שְׁמַעְתָּתָא: It is not clear to which of the aforementioned *halakhot* this statement is referring. Certainly, those *halakhot* with regard to prayers are rejected. However, some authorities rule that mention of the New Moon in the blessings recited after the portion read from the Prophets on Shabbat is not required because Rav Giddel's statement was not categorically rejected. Other commentaries explain that although one need not mention the New Moon at the conclusion of the blessing, the phrase: This day of rest and this day of the New Moon, is mentioned in the body of the blessing. The *halakha* is in accordance with the first opinion (Rambam *Sefer Ahava, Hilkhot Tefilla* 12:15; *Shulḥan Arukh, Oraḥ Ḥayyim* 284:2).

On Yom Kippur that falls on Shabbat, one who recites the closing prayer [*ne'ila*], etc. – יוֹם הַכִּפּוּרִים שֶׁחָל לִהְיוֹת בְּשַׁבָּת הַמִּתְפַּלֵּל נְעִילָה וכו׳: When Yom Kippur occurs on Shabbat, Shabbat is mentioned even in the closing prayer. If either an individual or the prayer leader neglected to mention Shabbat, the closing prayer must be repeated. In the confession that follows the *Amida* prayer, the prayer leader, not the individual, mentions Shabbat. If the prayer leader forgot to mention Shabbat during the confession, he need not repeat the prayer (Rambam *Sefer Ahava, Hilkhot Tefilla* 2:7; *Shulḥan Arukh, Oraḥ Ḥayyim* 623:3).

Festival that occurs on Shabbat – יוֹם טוֹב שֶׁחָל לִהְיוֹת בְּשַׁבָּת: In the blessing abridged from the seven blessings of the Shabbat *Amida* prayer, recited by the prayer leader after the silent evening prayer, there is neither mention of a Festival nor of Yom Kippur (Rambam *Sefer Ahava, Hilkhot Tefilla* 9:12; *Shulḥan Arukh, Oraḥ Ḥayyim* 268:9, 619:3).

הָכִי הָשְׁתָּא! הָתָם – בְּדִין הוּא דַּאֲפִילּוּ בְּשַׁבָּת נַמִי לָא צְרִיךְ, וְרַבָּנַן הוּא דְּתַקּוּנֵי מִשּׁוּם סַכָּנָה, אֲבָל הָכָא – יוֹם הוּא שֶׁנִּתְחַיֵּיב בְּאַרְבַּע תְּפִלּוֹת.

This challenge is rejected: **How can you compare? There, actually, even on Shabbat,** the prayer leader **need not** repeat the prayer, just as the prayer is not repeated any other evening. **It was the Sages who instituted** repetition of the prayer **due to** concern for potential **danger.** The Sages sought to slightly delay those leaving the synagogue to enable people who came late to leave together with the rest of the worshippers. This was necessary because synagogues were often located beyond the city limits, and it was dangerous to walk alone at night. This repetition of the prayer does not stem from the obligation of the day but was instituted for another purpose. **However, here,** on Yom Kippur, **it is the day that is obligated in four prayers,** and therefore on each day that there are added prayers, one must mention the events that occurred on that day in those prayers just as he does in all the standard prayers.

״וְלֹא בְּאַלְיָה כו׳״. חֲכָמִים הַיְינוּ תַּנָּא קַמָּא! אִיכָּא בֵּינַיְיהוּ דְּרַב בְּרוּנָא אָמַר רַב, וְלָא מְסַיְּימִי.

And we learned in the mishna that **one may not** light **with the sheep's tail**[B] or with fat. Naḥum the Mede says that one may light using cooked fat. And the Rabbis say that one may not light with it whether or not it is cooked. The Gemara asks: Isn't the opinion of the **Rabbis identical** to the unattributed opinion of the **first** ***tanna*** in the mishna? The Gemara answers: The practical difference **between them is** with regard to what **Rav Beruna said** that **Rav** said that one may light with cooked fat to which oil was added. One of the *tanna'im* accepts this opinion as *halakha* and permits lighting with it, and the other prohibits it, **and** the opinions **are not defined.**[B] Although it seems from the formulation of the mishna that they differ on this point, it is unclear what the opinion of each *tanna* is.

מתני׳ אֵין מַדְלִיקִין בְּשֶׁמֶן שְׂרֵיפָה בְּיוֹם טוֹב. רַבִּי יִשְׁמָעֵאל אוֹמֵר: אֵין מַדְלִיקִין בְּעִטְרָן, מִפְּנֵי כְבוֹד הַשַּׁבָּת. וַחֲכָמִים מַתִּירִין בְּכָל הַשְּׁמָנִים; בְּשֶׁמֶן שׁוּמְשְׁמִין, בְּשֶׁמֶן אֱגוֹזִים, בְּשֶׁמֶן צְנוֹנוֹת, בְּשֶׁמֶן דָּגִים, בְּשֶׁמֶן פַּקּוּעוֹת, בְּעִטְרָן וּבְנֵפְטְ. רַבִּי טַרְפוֹן אוֹמֵר: אֵין מַדְלִיקִין אֶלָּא בְּשֶׁמֶן זַיִת בִּלְבַד.

MISHNA In continuation of the previous mishna, this mishna adds that **one may not light with burnt oil on a Festival,** as the Gemara will explain below. With regard to lighting Shabbat lamps, there were Sages who prohibited the use of specific oils. **Rabbi Yishmael says** that **one may not light with tar** [*itran*][H] **in deference to Shabbat** because tar smells bad and disturbs those in the house. **And the Rabbis permit** lighting **with all oils**[H] for lamps as long as they burn properly; **with sesame oil, with nut oil, with turnip oil, with fish oil, with gourd oil, with tar, and even with naphtha** [*neft*].[B] **Rabbi Tarfon says: One may light only with olive oil** in deference to Shabbat, as it is the choicest and most pleasant of the oils.

גמ׳ מַאי טַעְמָא? לְפִי שֶׁאֵין שׂוֹרְפִין קָדָשִׁים בְּיוֹם טוֹב. מְנָהָנֵי מִילֵּי? אָמַר חִזְקִיָּה, וְכֵן תָּנָא דְּבֵי חִזְקִיָּה, אָמַר קְרָא: ״וְלֹא תוֹתִירוּ מִמֶּנּוּ עַד בֹּקֶר וְהַנּוֹתָר מִמֶּנּוּ עַד בֹּקֶר״, שֶׁאֵין תַּלְמוּד לוֹמַר ׳עַד בֹּקֶר׳ מַה תַּלְמוּד לוֹמַר ׳עַד בֹּקֶר׳ – בָּא הַכָּתוּב לִיתֵּן לוֹ בֹּקֶר שֵׁנִי לִשְׂרֵיפָתוֹ.

GEMARA With regard to the statement of the mishna that one may not light with burnt oil on a Festival, the Gemara asks: **What is the reason** for this? The Gemara answers: **Because,** in general, **one may not burn consecrated items on a Festival.**[H] With regard to the fundamental principle that one may not burn consecrated items on a Festival, the Gemara asks: **From where are these matters** derived?[N] **Ḥizkiya said, and** one of the Sages **from the school of Ḥizkiya taught the same,** that which **the verse said: "And you shall let nothing of it remain until morning; but that which remains of it until morning** you shall burn with fire" (Exodus 12:10), requires explanation. **As the Torah did not need to state until morning** the second time. It would have been sufficient to state: But that which remains of it you shall burn with fire. Rather, **why does the Torah state until morning? The verse comes to provide him** with **the second morning for burning.** Leftover meat of the Paschal lamb is not burned on the following morning, which is a Festival, but rather on the following day, the first of the intermediate days of the Festival. From there it is derived that burning consecrated items on a Festival is prohibited.

אַבַּיֵי אָמַר, אָמַר קְרָא: ״עֹלַת שַׁבַּת בְּשַׁבַּתּוֹ״ – וְלֹא עוֹלַת חוֹל בְּשַׁבָּת, וְלֹא עוֹלַת חוֹל בְּיוֹם טוֹב.

Abaye said: This is derived from another verse, as **the verse said: "This is the burnt-offering of each Shabbat on its Shabbat"** (Numbers 28:10). Only the burnt-offering of Shabbat is sacrificed on Shabbat, **and not a weekday burnt-offering on Shabbat, and not a weekday burnt-offering on a Festival.** Apparently, performing this mitzva is prohibited even on a Festival, since it was not explicitly enumerated among the actions permitted on a Festival.

BACKGROUND

Sheep's tail [*alya*] – אַלְיָה: The *alya* is the long, thick, fatty tail of the genus of sheep that was common in Eretz Yisrael and the surrounding areas during the Temple era. The tail covered the entire back of the sheep to the extent that it was difficult to ascertain the gender of the sheep, particularly in younger animals. The Torah commands that when a sheep is brought as a peace-offering, the tail is one of the parts of the animal burned on the altar. This applied only to sheep, as other animals that were sacrificed, e.g., goats, did not have this kind of tail.

Sheep

And the opinions are not defined – וְלָא מְסַיְּימִי: This expression describes a situation where two opinions are discussed and it is unclear which Sage holds which opinion, although there is clearly a dispute. At times, the Gemara seeks to determine which of the Sages stated which opinion.

Naphtha [*neft*] – נֵפְטְ: Naphtha, crude oil extracted from the ground, was a common fuel in several countries in the ancient world. During the Middle Ages it was not used and it was virtually unknown in Europe (see Rashi here). It is apparent from the description in the Gemara that not only did they use crude oil that burst from the ground, like the people of Cappadocia that have nothing but naphtha, as described below on 26a, p. 122, they even successfully refined it. The Gemara is apparently the first historical source that describes the production of white naphtha, which is one of the products of refining crude oil. Since white naphtha was refined, it would vaporize and burn more quickly, as the Gemara said: White naphtha is volatile. The techniques of refining crude oil first appear in other sources approximately five hundred years after the talmudic era.

HALAKHA

One may not light with tar [*itran*] – אֵין מַדְלִיקִין בְּעִטְרָן: One may not use tar as fuel for lighting the Shabbat lamp because it has a foul odor. Consequently, there is concern that one might light the lamp and leave without fulfilling the obligation to eat by the light of the Shabbat lights (*Tosafot*), as per the explanation of Rava (Rambam *Sefer Ahava, Hilkhot Tefilla* 5:10; *Shulḥan Arukh, Oraḥ Ḥayyim* 264:3).

With all oils – בְּכָל הַשְּׁמָנִים: One is permitted to light the Shabbat lamp with any oil. However, everyone agrees that olive oil is preferred (Rambam *Sefer Ahava, Hilkhot Tefilla* 5:11; *Shulḥan Arukh, Oraḥ Ḥayyim* 264:6).

Burning consecrated items on a Festival – שְׂרֵיפַת קָדָשִׁים בְּיוֹם טוֹב: On a Festival, one may not burn ritually impure consecrated items (Rambam *Sefer Zemanim, Hilkhot Yom Tov* 3:8).

NOTES

From where are these matters derived – מְנָהָנֵי מִילֵּי: It would have been appropriate to ask, why is burning consecrated items and specifically burning *teruma* prohibited on a Festival? First of all, there is a positive mitzva to burn consecrated items, which should override the negative mitzva of the Festival. Second, since lighting a fire is permitted on Festivals, burning consecrated items should have been permitted as well (Rashba).

רָבָא אָמַר, אָמַר קְרָא: ״הוּא לְבַדּוֹ יֵעָשֶׂה לָכֶם״, ׳הוּא׳ – וְלֹא מַכְשִׁירִין, ׳לְבַדּוֹ׳ – וְלֹא מִילָה שֶׁלֹּא בִּזְמַנָּהּ, דְּאָתְיָא בְּקַל וָחוֹמֶר.

Rava said: This is derived from a different verse, as **the verse said** with regard to the laws of a Festival: "No manner of work shall be done in them, save that which every man must eat, **that alone may be done by you**" (Exodus 12:16). From the word **that,** it is derived that for sustenance, one is permitted to perform prohibited labor on a Festival, **but not** for **facilitators** of sustenance. Although cooking is permitted, actions that involve prohibited labors for the purpose of facilitating cooking are prohibited. From the word **alone,** it is derived: **And not circumcision** performed **not at its** appointed **time,** i.e., a circumcision may be performed on a Festival only if it is on the eighth day. A circumcision that was postponed may not be performed on a Festival. It is possible **that** license to perform the postponed circumcision on a Festival could have been **derived by means of an *a fortiori* inference.**[N] Therefore, the verse explicitly prohibited doing so. The same is true with regard to burning consecrated items. Although the Torah commands burning consecrated items, it was not permitted on a Festival since there is no obligation to do so specifically on that day.

רַב אַשִׁי אָמַר: (׳שַׁבָּת׳) ׳שַׁבָּתוֹן׳ –

Rav Ashi said: It is derived from a different source. In the verses that speak of the Festivals, as opposed to the term **Shabbat,** the term ***shabbaton*** (Leviticus 23:24) appears.

NOTES

Derived by means of an *a fortiori* inference – דְּאָתְיָא בְּקַל וָחוֹמֶר: Many commentaries discussed the essence of this *a fortiori* inference (see *Tosafot*). Contrary to the majority of the commentaries, who explained that the Gemara means that, if not for the verse, circumcision would have been derived by means of an *a fortiori* inference, there is another explanation. The prohibition of burning consecrated items on a Festival is derived by means of an *a fortiori* inference from circumcision. The mitzva of circumcision is so significant a mitzva that it overrides Shabbat. Nevertheless, when its appropriate time has passed, it no longer overrides the prohibition of Shabbat or even that of a Festival. All the more so the obligation to burn consecrated items, which, unlike circumcision, lacks a definite time, and the thirteen covenants of circumcision do not apply to it, is prohibited on a Festival (Rav Hai Gaon).

Perek **II**
Daf **25** Amud **a**

עֲשֵׂה, וַהֲוָה לֵיהּ יוֹם טוֹב עֲשֵׂה וְלֹא תַעֲשֶׂה, וְאֵין עֲשֵׂה דּוֹחֶה אֶת לֹא תַעֲשֶׂה וַעֲשֵׂה.

The latter term is a positive **mitzva** to rest. **And,** if so, observance of **a Festival is** a mitzva that was commanded with both **a positive mitzva** to rest **and a prohibition:**[N] "You shall do no manner of servile work" (Leviticus 23:8). **And** there is a principle that **a positive mitzva,** e.g., burning consecrated items whose time has expired, **does not override** a mitzva that was commanded with both **a prohibition and a positive mitzva,** e.g., observance of the Festival.

בְּיוֹם טוֹב הוּא דְּאָסִיר, הָא בְּחוֹל – שַׁפִּיר דָּמֵי, מַאי טַעְמָא? אָמַר רַב: כְּשֵׁם שֶׁמִּצְוָה לִשְׂרוֹף הַקֳּדָשִׁים שֶׁנִּטְמְאוּ, כָּךְ מִצְוָה לִשְׂרוֹף אֶת הַתְּרוּמָה שֶׁנִּטְמֵאת. וְאָמְרָה תּוֹרָה: בִּשְׁעַת בִּיעוּרָהּ תֵּיהָנֵי מִמֶּנָּה. הֵיכָן אָמְרָה תּוֹרָה? מִדְּרַב נַחְמָן. דְּאָמַר רַב נַחְמָן אָמַר רַבָּה בַּר אֲבוּהּ: אָמַר קְרָא ״וַאֲנִי הִנֵּה נָתַתִּי לְךָ אֶת מִשְׁמֶרֶת תְּרוּמֹתָי״ בִּשְׁתֵּי תְרוּמוֹת הַכָּתוּב מְדַבֵּר, אַחַת תְּרוּמָה טְהוֹרָה וְאַחַת תְּרוּמָה טְמֵאָה. וְאָמַר רַחֲמָנָא ׳לְךָ׳ – שֶׁלְּךָ תְּהֵא, לְהַסִּיקָהּ תַּחַת תַּבְשִׁילְךָ.

By inference, the conclusion is that, specifically **on a Festival,** lighting with burnt oil **is prohibited.** During the week one may **well** do so. The Gemara asks: **What is the reason** for this distinction? It would be reasonable to say that it is prohibited to derive any benefit from *teruma* that became ritually impure. **Rav said: Just as there is a mitzva to burn consecrated items that became ritually impure, so too, there is a mitzva to burn *teruma* that became ritually impure, and the Torah said: While it is being destroyed, derive benefit from it.** The Gemara asks: **Where did the Torah say** this? Where is there an allusion to this in the Bible? The Gemara answers: It can be derived **from** the statement of **Rav Naḥman,** as **Rav Naḥman said** that **Rabba bar Avuh said: The verse said: "And I, behold, I have given you the charge of My *terumot*"** (Numbers 18:8). From the amplification of the plural: My *terumot*, it is derived that **the verse is speaking of two *terumot*, one *teruma* that is ritually pure and one *teruma* that is ritually impure. And God said:** "I have given **you,"** i.e., **it shall be yours,** and you may derive benefit from it.[H] Since there is a stringent prohibition against eating it, the benefit permitted is **to burn it beneath your cooked dish.** Similar forms of benefit may also be derived from burning *teruma*.

NOTES

Positive mitzva and a prohibition – עֲשֵׂה וְלֹא תַעֲשֶׂה: The Gemara in tractate *Yevamot* arrives at a conclusion accepted throughout the Talmud that a positive mitzva overrides a negative mitzva in a case where both are in effect simultaneously. However, as a rule, a positive mitzva does not override another positive mitzva, unless explicitly stated otherwise in the Torah. All the more so, a positive mitzva does not override both a positive mitzva and a prohibition. Therefore, it was important in this context to emphasize that on a Festival there is the positive mitzva to rest and refrain from performing labor in addition to the prohibition against performing labor.

HALAKHA

Benefiting from *teruma* that is ritually impure – הֲנָאָה בִּתְרוּמָה טְמֵאָה: Although eating ritually impure *teruma* is prohibited, a priest is permitted to benefit from burning it. It is prohibited for all other Jews to derive benefit from burning *teruma*. However, if a priest is benefitting from burning *teruma*, a non-priest may benefit along with him. Therefore, in the Jerusalem Talmud, the Sages permitted burning ritually impure *teruma* for certain communal purposes with the permission of the priests (Rambam *Sefer Zera'im, Hilkhot Terumot* 2:14; *Shulḥan Arukh, Yoreh De'a* 331:19, and in the comment of the Rema).

BACKGROUND

And what did you see – וּמָה רָאִיתָ: This expression has a standard meaning. It is used when an apparently arbitrary distinction is suggested between different matters. In that case, the question: What did you see that led you to that conclusion, forces the Gemara to provide a rationale for distinguishing between those matters in that manner.

Mnemonic – סִימָן: Acronyms are used throughout the Talmud as mnemonic devices. In general, the acronyms assist the Sages in remembering discussions in which numerous opinions are cited consecutively, potentially leading to confusion between the names of the speakers or their opinions. Acronyms were also composed as summaries of *halakhot*, as in the case of *yod, ayin, lamed, kuf, gimmel* and *mem* that represent the disputes between Abaye and Rava where, anomalously, the *halakha* is in accordance with the opinion of Abaye.

Not all mnemonics are identical. Most are acronyms, although they do not always consist of the first letter of each word. The mnemonic on 25b, p. 120, *mem, tet, kuf, samekh*, is a mnemonic of the Sages who addressed the issue at hand: *Meir, Tarfon, Akiva*, and *Yosei*. There are also mnemonics in the form of a sentence composed of several key words, and sometimes folk expressions served as mnemonics for a series of *halakhot* (see below, 63a, p. 305).

וְאִיבָּעֵית אֵימָא – מִדְּרַבִּי אַבָּהוּ, דְּאָמַר רַבִּי אַבָּהוּ אָמַר רַבִּי יוֹחָנָן: ״וְלֹא בִעַרְתִּי מִמֶּנּוּ בְּטָמֵא״ – מִמֶּנּוּ אִי אַתָּה מְבַעֵר, אֲבָל אַתָּה מְבַעֵר שֶׁמֶן שֶׁל תְּרוּמָה שֶׁנִּטְמֵאת. וְאֵימָא: מִמֶּנּוּ אִי אַתָּה מְבַעֵר, אֲבָל אַתָּה מְבַעֵר שֶׁמֶן שֶׁל קֹדֶשׁ שֶׁנִּטְמָא!

And if you wish, say instead an alternative manner to derive this *halakha*, from the statement of **Rabbi Abbahu, as Rabbi Abbahu said** that **Rabbi Yoḥanan said:** It is written in the confession of the tithes: "I have not eaten thereof in my mourning, **neither have I destroyed from it while impure**" (Deuteronomy 26:14). By inference: **From it**[N] **you may not destroy, but you may destroy the oil of *teruma* that has become ritually impure.** The Gemara asks: **And say** differently: **From it you may not destroy, but you may destroy** and derive benefit from burning **consecrated oil that became ritually impure.**

לָאו קַל וָחוֹמֶר הוּא? מַה מַּעֲשֵׂר הַקַּל אָמְרָה תּוֹרָה ״לֹא בִעַרְתִּי מִמֶּנּוּ בְּטָמֵא״, קֹדֶשׁ חָמוּר לֹא כׇּל שֶׁכֵּן?

The Gemara responds: That possibility is unacceptable. Is it **not an *a fortiori* inference? If** with regard to **the tithe which is lenient, the Torah said: Neither have I destroyed from it, while impure, items consecrated** to the Temple, **which are** more **stringent, all the more so** that it is prohibited to burn it while ritually impure.

אִי הָכִי, תְּרוּמָה נַמִי, לֵימָא: קַל וָחוֹמֶר הוּא! הָא כְּתִיב ׳מִמֶּנּוּ׳.

The Gemara rejects this: **If so,** that this matter is derived through an *a fortiori* inference, then, with regard to ***teruma* as well, let us say** that **it is an *a fortiori* inference,** as *teruma* is more stringent than tithes. If it is prohibited to benefit from tithes while they are burning, all the more so would one be prohibited to benefit from the *teruma* while it is burning. The Gemara answers: **Doesn't it say: From it?** From there it is derived that there is an item excluded from the prohibition of burning in ritual impurity.

וּמָה רָאִיתָ? מִסְתַּבְּרָא, קֹדֶשׁ לָא מְמַעֵיטְנָא שֶׁכֵּן סִימָן פנ״ק עכ״ס: פִּיגּוּל, נוֹתָר, קָרְבַּן מְעִילָה, וְכָרֵת, אָסוּר לְאוֹנֵן.

The Gemara asks: **And what did you see**[B] that led you to conclude that "from it" comes to exclude *teruma*? Perhaps "from it" comes to exclude consecrated items. The Gemara replies: **It is reasonable** that **I do not exclude consecrated items** from the prohibition against benefiting from its burning, as with regard to consecrated items there are many stringent elements. **Their** Hebrew acronym is ***peh, nun, kuf, ayin, kaf, samekh,*** which is a **mnemonic**[BN] for **the following terms. *Piggul*:** With regard to an offering, if, during one of the services involved in its sacrifice, i.e., slaughter, receiving the blood, bringing it to the altar, sprinkling it on the altar, the priest or the one bringing the offering entertains the thought of eating the sacrifice at a time that is unfit for eating, it is thereby invalidated. *Notar*: Meat of a sacrifice that **remained** beyond its allotted time may not be eaten and must be burned. ***Korban me'ila*:** One who unwittingly derives benefit from consecrated items is required to bring a guilt-**offering for misuse of consecrated items. *Karet*:** The punishment of one who eats consecrated items while ritually impure is *karet*. ***Asur le'onen*:** **An acute mourner,** i.e., one whose relative died that same day and has not yet been buried, **is prohibited** to eat consecrated items. None of these *halakhot* applies to *teruma*. Therefore, consecrated items are more stringent than *teruma*, and therefore it is consecrated items that are not excluded from the prohibition against deriving benefit while ritually impure.

NOTES

The Talmud's approach to the matter of "from it" – שִׁיטַת הַתַּלְמוּד בְּעִנְיַן ״מִמֶּנּוּ״: The fundamental difficulty in this derivation is to find a middle ground between two conclusions derived from a single verse. From the verse in the confession of the tithes, one could derive that use of ritually impure second-tithe produce for any purpose is prohibited and that one may not even derive benefit from burning it. At the same time, the verse does not establish a general *halakha*. On the contrary, the prohibition is apparently restricted to second-tithe as derived from the emphasis on the word "from" in the expression: "Neither did I destroy from it", as opposed to: And I did not destroy, or: I did not destroy it.

On the other hand, it is well-known that Torah law can be derived by means of an *a fortiori* inference. The second tithe is the most lenient of all types of consecrated items and *teruma* because it lacks intrinsic sanctity and is not prohibited to non-priests. Its only restriction is that it must be eaten in Jerusalem. More stringent consecrated items, such as *teruma* and sacrifices, may be derived from it *a fortiori*. Therefore, with regard to burning ritually impure consecrated items, there is, on the one hand, a tendency to prohibit doing so by means of an *a fortiori* inference from second tithe. On the other hand, one could permit doing so because of the exclusionary phrase, "from it," which restricts the prohibition to a case of second tithe. Since there is room both to expand and restrict the prohibition, one must consider what elements are included and what elements are not included within that prohibition.

Mnemonic – סִימָן: There are different methods used to create these mnemonics: Here the acronym *peh, nun, kuf, ayin, kaf,* and *samekh* is formed from the first or other significant letters of the words *piggul, notar, korban, me'ila, karet,* and *asur*. The other mnemonic, *mem, ḥet, peh,* and *zayin,* is an acronym for *mita, ḥomesh, pidyon,* and *zarim*.

אַדְּרַבָּה, תְּרוּמָה לָא מְמַעֵיטְנָא, שֶׁכֵּן מחפ״ז סִימָן: מִיתָה, חוֹמֶשׁ,

The Gemara rejects this: **On the contrary, it is *teruma* that I would not exclude** from the prohibition, **as,** with regard to *teruma*, there are many stringent elements represented by the acronym ***mem, ḥet, peh, zayin,*** which is a **mnemonic** for the following: ***Mita*:** One for whom *teruma* is prohibited who ate it intentionally is punishable by **death** at the hand of Heaven. ***Ḥomesh*:** A non-priest, for whom *teruma* is prohibited, who unwittingly ate *teruma* is obligated to pay its value to the priest plus **one-fifth** of the sum.

Perek **II**
Daf **25** Amud **b**

וְאֵין לָהּ פִּדְיוֹן, וַאֲסוּרָה לְזָרִים. הָנָךְ נְפִישָׁן.

And, *teruma* **does not have** the possibility of ***pidyon*: redemption,** as, once it is sanctified, it may not be redeemed and rendered non-sacred. And it is **prohibited to *zarim*: non-priests** may not eat it. These stringencies do not apply to consecrated items. The Gemara answers: Nevertheless, **those** stringencies that apply to consecrated items **are more** numerous than those that apply to *teruma*. Therefore, it is appropriate to be more stringent with consecrated items and exclude impure *teruma* from the prohibition against deriving benefit when burning it.

וְאִיבָּעֵית אֵימָא: קֹדֶשׁ חָמוּר, שֶׁכֵּן עָנוּשׁ כָּרֵת. רַב נַחְמָן בַּר יִצְחָק אָמַר: אָמַר קְרָא ״תִּתֶּן לוֹ״, ״לוֹ״ וְלֹא לְאוּרוֹ, מִכְּלָל דְּבַת אוּרוֹ הוּא.

And if you wish, say instead a different reason, without counting the number of stringencies: **Consecrated items are** more **stringent because** one who eats them while ritually impure is **punishable by *karet*,** while in the case of *teruma* the punishment is death at the hand of Heaven.[N] In this regard, the Torah is more stringent vis-à-vis consecrated items than it is vis-à-vis *teruma*. **Rav Naḥman bar Yitzḥak said** that there is a different proof that one is permitted to benefit from *teruma* while it is burning. As **the verse said:** "The first fruits of your grain, of your wine, and of your oil, and the first of the fleece of your sheep **shall you give him**" (Deuteronomy 18:4). The Sages derived from this verse: Give the priest *teruma* that is ritually pure, that is fit for **him** to consume, **and do not** give the priest *teruma* that is suitable only **for his fire,** to be burned. **By inference,** ritually impure *teruma* **is suitable for his fire,** i.e., a priest may derive benefit from it.

״רַבִּי יִשְׁמָעֵאל אוֹמֵר כו׳״. מַאי טַעְמָא? אָמַר רָבָא: מִתּוֹךְ שֶׁרֵיחוֹ רַע, גְּזֵרָה שֶׁמָּא יַנִּיחֶנָּה וְיֵצֵא. אֲמַר לֵיהּ אַבָּיֵי: וְיֵצֵא! אָמַר לֵיהּ, שֶׁאֲנִי אוֹמֵר: הַדְלָקַת נֵר בְּשַׁבָּת – חוֹבָה, דְּאָמַר רַב נַחְמָן בַּר רַב זַבְדָּא, וְאָמְרִי לַהּ אָמַר רַב נַחְמָן בַּר רָבָא אָמַר רַב: הַדְלָקַת נֵר בְּשַׁבָּת – חוֹבָה, רְחִיצַת יָדַיִם וְרַגְלַיִם בְּחַמִּין עַרְבִית – רְשׁוּת, וַאֲנִי אוֹמֵר: מִצְוָה.

We learned in the mishna that **Rabbi Yishmael says** that kindling a lamp on Shabbat[H] with tar is prohibited. The Gemara asks: **What is the reason** for this? **Rava said: Because its odor is bad** the Sages issued a **decree** prohibiting the use of tar, **lest one forsake** the light **and leave. Abaye said to him: And let him leave.** What obligation is there to sit next to the light? Rava **said to him: Because I say** that **kindling Shabbat lights** is **an obligation,** and one is required to eat specifically by that light in deference to Shabbat. As **Rav Naḥman bar Rav Zavda said, and others say** that it was **Rav Naḥman bar Rava** who **said** that **Rav said: Kindling the Shabbat lamps** is **an obligation,** whereas **washing** one's **hands and feet with hot water**[H] **in the evening** prior to Shabbat is merely **optional. And I say:** Washing is not merely optional; it is a **mitzva** even though it is not an obligation.

NOTES

***Karet* and death at the hand of Heaven – כָּרֵת וּמִיתָה בִּידֵי שָׁמַיִם:** There are significantly diverse definitions for *karet* and death at the hand of Heaven (see *Tosafot* on 25a, s.v. *karet*). Nevertheless, it is clear from the Torah that *karet* is the more severe punishment, and consequently a transgression punishable by *karet* is egregious.

HALAKHA

Kindling a lamp on Shabbat – הַדְלָקַת נֵר בְּשַׁבָּת: Kindling the lights is one of the obligations of Shabbat and it takes precedence even over wine for *kiddush*. One who only has the means to purchase either wine for *kiddush* or oil for the lamp should purchase oil. However, if the choice is between bread for the Shabbat meal and oil for the lamp, one should purchase bread (*Mishna Berura*). Other foods do not take precedence over the Shabbat lights because light is one of the essential components of the mitzva to enjoy Shabbat (Rambam *Sefer Zemanim, Hilkhot Shabbat* 5:1; *Shulḥan Arukh, Oraḥ Ḥayyim* 263:2).

Washing one's hands and feet with hot water – רְחִיצַת יָדַיִם וְרַגְלַיִם בְּחַמִּין: It is a mitzva to wash one's entire body with hot water before Shabbat as preparation for fulfillment of the mitzva to enjoy Shabbat. If one does not have the opportunity to wash his entire body, he should at least wash his face, hands, and feet in that order (*Sha'arei Teshuva* in the name of the Rabbi Yitzḥak Luria; Rambam *Sefer Zemanim, Hilkhot Shabbat* 30:2; *Shulḥan Arukh, Oraḥ Ḥayyim* 260:1 and in the comment of the Rema).

מַאי מִצְוָה? דְּאָמַר רַב יְהוּדָה אָמַר רַב: כָּךְ הָיָה מִנְהָגוֹ שֶׁל רַבִּי יְהוּדָה בַּר אֶלְעַאי, עֶרֶב שַׁבָּת מְבִיאִים לוֹ עֲרֵיבָה מְלֵאָה חַמִּין, וְרוֹחֵץ פָּנָיו יָדָיו וְרַגְלָיו, וּמִתְעַטֵּף וְיוֹשֵׁב בִּסְדִינִין הַמְצוּיָּיצִין, וְדוֹמֶה לְמַלְאַךְ ה׳ צְבָאוֹת, וְהָיוּ תַּלְמִידָיו מְחַבִּין מִמֶּנּוּ כַּנְפֵי כְסוּתָן, אָמַר לָהֶן: בָּנַי, לֹא כָּךְ שָׁנִיתִי לָכֶם, סָדִין בְּצִיצִית, בֵּית שַׁמַּאי פּוֹטְרִין וּבֵית הִלֵּל מְחַיְּיבִין. וַהֲלָכָה כְּדִבְרֵי בֵית הִלֵּל! וְאִינְהוּ סָבְרִי – גְּזֵירָה מִשּׁוּם כְּסוּת לַיְלָה.

The Gemara asks: **What mitzva** is there? The Gemara explains that **Rav Yehuda said** that **Rav said: This was the custom of Rabbi Yehuda bar Elai: On Shabbat eve,** they **would bring him a bowl full of hot water and** he would use it to **wash his face, hands, and feet, and he would wrap himself, and sit in** linen **cloaks with ritual fringes,**[N] **and** he was **like an angel of the Lord**[N] **of hosts.** He did all this in deference to Shabbat. **And** the Gemara relates that **his students,** who also sat wrapped in linen cloaks, **would conceal the corners of their garments from him** so that he would not see that they did not have ritual fringes on their garments. **He said to them: My sons, did I not teach you** with regard to the obligation to attach ritual fringes to **a** linen **cloak: Beit Shammai exempt** the linen sheet because at least part of the ritual fringes is always made from wool, and there is a Torah prohibition against a mixture of wool and linen that applies even to ritual fringes? **And Beit Hillel obligate** linen sheets in the mitzva of ritual fringes, as they hold that the positive mitzva of ritual fringes overrides the prohibition of mixing wool and linen. **The *halakha* is in accordance with** the opinion of **Beit Hillel,** and therefore the sheets require ritual fringes. **And** the students **held:** Although it is permitted by Torah law to attach ritual fringes to a linen garment, the Sages issued a **decree** that one may not do so **due to garments** worn at **night.**[H] The Sages were concerned lest a person wear this cloak at night. Since one is not obligated in the mitzva of ritual fringes at night, he would be wearing the prohibited mixture of wool and linen at a time when he is not fulfilling the mitzva of ritual fringes. Therefore, attaching ritual fringes made of wool to a linen garment is prohibited, even to a garment worn during the day.

״וַתִּזְנַח מִשָּׁלוֹם נַפְשִׁי נָשִׁיתִי טוֹבָה״. מַאי ״וַתִּזְנַח מִשָּׁלוֹם נַפְשִׁי״? אָמַר רַבִּי אַבָּהוּ: זוֹ הַדְלָקַת נֵר בַּשַּׁבָּת. ״נָשִׁיתִי טוֹבָה״ – אָמַר רַבִּי יִרְמְיָה: זוֹ בֵּית הַמֶּרְחָץ. (אָמַר רַבִּי יוֹחָנָן): זוֹ רְחִיצַת יָדַיִם וְרַגְלַיִם בְּחַמִּין. רַבִּי יִצְחָק נַפָּחָא אָמַר: זוֹ מִטָּה נָאָה וְכֵלִים נָאִים שֶׁעָלֶיהָ. רַבִּי אַבָּא אָמַר: זוֹ מִטָּה מוּצַּעַת וְאִשָּׁה מְקוּשֶּׁטֶת לְתַלְמִידֵי חֲכָמִים.

Since bathing as preparation for enjoyment of Shabbat was discussed, the Gemara cites the homiletic interpretation of the verse describing those heading into exile: **"And my soul is removed far off from peace, I forgot prosperity"** (Lamentations 3:17). **What is: And my soul is removed far off from peace? Rabbi Abbahu said: That is** the lack of opportunity to engage in **kindling the Shabbat lights,** which a refugee is unable to do. **I forgot prosperity, Rabbi Yirmeya said: That is** the lack of opportunity to bathe in **the bathhouse. Rabbi Yoḥanan said: That is** the lack of opportunity to engage in **washing one's hands and feet in hot water. Rabbi Yitzḥak Nappaḥa said:** Prosperity **is a pleasant bed and** the **pleasant bedclothes that are on it,** which are not available in exile. **Rabbi Abba said: That is a made bed, and a wife adorned,** i.e., worthy of and suitable (Rashba) **for Torah scholars.**

תָּנוּ רַבָּנַן: אֵיזֶהוּ עָשִׁיר? כֹּל שֶׁיֵּשׁ לוֹ נַחַת רוּחַ בְּעָשְׁרוֹ, דִּבְרֵי רַבִּי מֵאִיר. סִימָן מ״ט ק״ס. רַבִּי טַרְפוֹן אוֹמֵר: כֹּל שֶׁיֵּשׁ לוֹ מֵאָה כְּרָמִים וּמֵאָה שָׂדוֹת, וּמֵאָה עֲבָדִים שֶׁעוֹבְדִין בָּהֶן. רַבִּי עֲקִיבָא אוֹמֵר: כָּל שֶׁיֵּשׁ לוֹ אִשָּׁה נָאָה בְּמַעֲשִׂים. רַבִּי יוֹסֵי אוֹמֵר: כֹּל שֶׁיֵּשׁ לוֹ בֵּית הַכִּסֵּא סָמוּךְ לְשׁוּלְחָנוֹ.

Incidental to the discussion of prosperity, the Gemara mentions that on a similar topic, **the Sages taught: Who is wealthy?**[N] **Anyone who gets pleasure from his wealth,** that is **the statement of Rabbi Meir. The letters *mem*** (Meir), ***tet*** (Tarfon), ***kuf*** (Akiva), ***samekh*** (Yosei) are a **mnemonic** for the *tannaim* who expressed opinions on this matter. **Rabbi Tarfon says:** A wealthy person is **anyone who has one hundred vineyards, and one hundred fields, and one hundred slaves working in them. Rabbi Akiva says: Anyone who has a wife whose actions are pleasant. Rabbi Yosei says: Anyone who has a bathroom close to his table.**

תַּנְיָא, רַבִּי שִׁמְעוֹן בֶּן אֶלְעָזָר אוֹמֵר: אֵין מַדְלִיקִין בָּצֳרִי. מַאי טַעְמָא? אֲמַר רַבָּה: מִתּוֹךְ שֶׁרֵיחוֹ נוֹדֵף, גְּזֵירָה שֶׁמָּא יִסְתַּפֵּק מִמֶּנּוּ. אֲמַר לֵיהּ אַבָּיֵי:

It was taught in a *baraita* that **Rabbi Shimon ben Elazar says: One may not light** on Shabbat **with sap from balsam trees** [*tzori*].[HB] The Gemara asks: **What is the reason** for this? **Rabba said: Since its pleasant smell diffuses,** the Sages were concerned **lest** one forget and come to **take** some sap **from it** on Shabbat. That is tantamount to extinguishing the lamp, as removing oil from a burning lamp curtails the amount of time that it will burn. **Abaye said to him:**

NOTES

In linen cloaks with ritual fringes – בִּסְדִינִין הַמְצוּיָּיצִין: The commentaries differed significantly with regard to the obligation to place ritual fringes on a linen garment and the material from which those fringes are made. One opinion is that the students of Rabbi Yehuda had ritual fringes on their garments but they were not dyed sky blue [*tekhelet*]. The fringes themselves may be made of linen; however, everyone agrees that the strand dyed sky blue must be fashioned from wool. The combination of a strand of wool with the linen garment constitutes a forbidden mixture of wool and linen. Rabbi Yehuda's students concealed the corners of their garments so their teacher would not see that the blue dye was missing from their ritual fringes (Ran).

And he was similar to an angel of the Lord – וְדוֹמֶה לְמַלְאַךְ ה׳: The simple understanding is that since Rabbi Yehuda was wrapped in a white sheet with ritual fringes, he resembled an angel, described as: "The man clothed in linen" (Ezekiel 9:11; see Rashi).

Who is wealthy – אֵיזֶהוּ עָשִׁיר: Each Sage based his statement on his own personal experience. For Rabbi Meir, to be wealthy is to be satisfied with one's portion. Rabbi Tarfon who was, in fact, very wealthy, quantified that wealth. Rabbi Akiva, whose wife Raḥel was responsible for his greatness, praised wives. Rabbi Yosei, who suffered from intestinal disease, said that from his perspective to be wealthy is to be comfortable in that regard (*Panim Masbirot*).

BACKGROUND

Balsam – אֲפַרְסְמוֹן: According to many scholars, the *tzori* that is mentioned in the Torah and here in the Gemara is identified with balsam, which is apparently the *Commiphora opobalsamum*, a bush or short tree, 3–5 m in height. The tree has extremely thin branches, complex leaves, and small white flowers.

The highest quality balsamic perfume is sap which drips in small amounts from the ends of the stems. However, the perfume is generally extracted by boiling the branches. After a certain period of time, the balsam sap evaporates, leaving a sticky residue. Even though it is also quite fragrant, it was used for medicinal purposes, in addition to its use as incense and as fragrant oil.

During the second Temple period, the finest balsam grew in the Jordan Valley. It was so highly valued that it was literally worth its weight in gold.

Balsam branch

HALAKHA

The Sages issued a decree due to garments worn at night – סָבְרִי גְּזֵירָה מִשּׁוּם כְּסוּת לַיְלָה: With regard to ritual fringes, the authorities disputed the definition of daytime versus nighttime garments. According to the Rambam, any garment that one wears during the day, even if its primary designation is for nighttime use, is considered a daytime garment and requires ritual fringes. Conversely, a garment that is worn at night is exempt from the obligation of ritual fringes even if its primary designation is for daytime use.

However, according to the Rosh, any garment whose primary designation is for nighttime use is considered to be a nighttime garment even if it is worn during the day, and a garment whose primary designation is for daytime use is considered to be a daytime garment even if it is worn at night.

Because of their dispute in this matter, one recites a blessing only over a garment that is both designated for daytime use and one wears during the day, as one does not recite the blessing in a case of uncertainty (Rema in the name of *Hagahot Maimoniyot*). Nevertheless, one must attach ritual fringes to a nighttime garment worn during the day (*Mishna Berura*; Rambam *Sefer Ahava, Hilkhot Tzitzit* 3:7; *Shulḥan Arukh, Oraḥ Ḥayyim* 18:1).

One may not light with sap from balsam trees [*tzori*] – אֵין מַדְלִיקִין בָּצֳרִי: One may not light with balsam oil on Shabbat because its pleasant fragrance may lead one to unwittingly use some of it. Furthermore, balsam oil is also dangerous because it is volatile and sticks to the walls of the house when it burns. Therefore, there is concern that a person who is anxious to protect his property might come to extinguish the flame on Shabbat (*Mishna Berura*; Rambam *Sefer Zemanim, Hilkhot Shabbat* 5:10; *Shulḥan Arukh, Oraḥ Ḥayyim* 264:3).

לֵימָא מָר: ״מִפְּנֵי שֶׁהוּא עָף״! חֲדָא וְעוֹד קָאָמַר, חֲדָא – מִפְּנֵי שֶׁהוּא עָף, וְעוֹד: גְּזֵירָה שֶׁמָּא יִסְתַּפֵּק מִמֶּנּוּ.

Let the Master say a different reason: **Because** tar **is volatile,** i.e., it is liable to evaporate quickly and cause a fire. The Gemara answers: **He stated one** reason **and another: One, because it is volatile** and potentially dangerous; **and, furthermore,** due to **a decree lest one take** sap **from it.**

הַהִיא חֲמָתָא דַּהֲוַת סְנִיאָה לַהּ לְכַלָּתַהּ, אֲמַרָה לַהּ: זִיל אִיקַּשִּׁיט בְּמִשְׁחָא דַּאֲפַרְסְמָא. אֲזַלָא אִיקַּשִּׁיט. כִּי אֲתַת, אֲמַרָה לַהּ: זִיל אִיתְלִי שְׁרָגָא! אֲזַלָא אַתְלָא שְׁרָגָא, אִינְפַּח בָּהּ נוּרָא וַאֲכַלְתַּהּ.

The Gemara relates: **A mother-in-law who hated her daughter-in-law said to her: Go adorn yourself with balsam oil. She went** and **adorned herself. When she came,** her mother-in-law **said to her: Go light the lamp. She went** and **lit the lamp. She caught fire and was burned.**

״וּמִדַּלַּת הָאָרֶץ הִשְׁאִיר נְבוּזַרְאֲדָן רַב טַבָּחִים לְכוֹרְמִים וּלְיוֹגְבִים״. ׳כּוֹרְמִים׳ תָּנֵי רַב יוֹסֵף: אֵלּוּ מְלַקְּטֵי אֲפַרְסְמוֹן מֵעֵין גֶּדִי וְעַד רָמָתָא. ׳יוֹגְבִים׳ – אֵלּוּ צַיָּידֵי חִלָּזוֹן, מִסּוּלָּמוֹת שֶׁל צוֹר וְעַד חֵיפָה.

Since balsam oil was discussed, the Gemara cites the verse: **"But Nebuzaradan the captain of the guard left of the poorest of the land to be vinedressers and husbandmen"** (Jeremiah 52:16). The Gemara explains the verse: With regard to **vinedressers, Rav Yosef taught: These** poorest of the land were **the balsam collectors** in the south of Eretz Yisrael, in the expanse **from Ein Gedi to Ramata. And** the **husbandmen; these are the trappers of the snail** [*ḥilazon*], from which the sky blue dye is produced in the north of the country, in the area **between the Promontory of Tyre and Ḥaifa.** Only a small number of poor people could barely eke out a living from these tasks, which involved mere gathering.

תָּנוּ רַבָּנַן: אֵין מַדְלִיקִין בְּטֶבֶל טָמֵא בַּחוֹל, וְאֵין צָרִיךְ לוֹמַר בַּשַּׁבָּת. כַּיּוֹצֵא בּוֹ: אֵין מַדְלִיקִין בְּנֵפְט לָבָן בַּחוֹל, וְאֵין צָרִיךְ לוֹמַר בַּשַּׁבָּת. בִּשְׁלָמָא נֵפְט לָבָן – מִפְּנֵי שֶׁהוּא עָף, אֲבָל טֶבֶל טָמֵא, מַאי טַעְמָא?

The Sages taught: One may not light with ritually impure untithed produce [*tevel*][NH] **during the week, and needless to say** one may not light with it **on Shabbat. On a similar note, one may not light with white naphtha**[H] **during the week, and needless to say** one may not light with it **on Shabbat. Granted,** with regard to **white naphtha,** its prohibition is understandable **because it is volatile** and potentially dangerous. **However,** with regard to **ritually impure *tevel*, what is the reason** that the Sages prohibited lighting with it?

אָמַר קְרָא: ״וַאֲנִי הִנֵּה נָתַתִּי לְךָ אֶת מִשְׁמֶרֶת תְּרוּמֹתָי״ בִּשְׁתֵּי תְרוּמוֹת הַכָּתוּב מְדַבֵּר, אַחַת תְּרוּמָה טְהוֹרָה וְאַחַת תְּרוּמָה טְמֵאָה. מַה תְּרוּמָה טְהוֹרָה – אֵין לְךָ בָּהּ אֶלָּא מִשְּׁעַת הֲרָמָה וְאֵילָךְ, אַף תְּרוּמָה טְמֵאָה – אֵין לְךָ בָּהּ אֶלָּא מִשְּׁעַת הֲרָמָה וְאֵילָךְ.

The Gemara answers that **the verse said: "And I, behold, I have given you the charge of My *terumot*"** (Numbers 18:8). From the fact that *terumot* is plural, the Sages derived that **the verse is speaking of two *terumot*: Both *teruma* that is ritually pure and *teruma* that is ritually impure. Just as** with regard to ***teruma* that is ritually pure, you,** the priest, **have** permission to benefit **from it only from the time *teruma* was separated and onward, so too,** with regard to ***teruma* that is ritually impure, you have** permission to benefit from **it only from the time *teruma* was separated and onward.** Since a portion of the untithed produce is *teruma* that has not yet been separated, it is prohibited even for a priest to use it.

גּוּפָא, רַבִּי שִׁמְעוֹן בֶּן אֶלְעָזָר אוֹמֵר: אֵין מַדְלִיקִין בַּצֳּרִי. וְכֵן הָיָה רַבִּי שִׁמְעוֹן בֶּן אֶלְעָזָר אוֹמֵר: צֳרִי אֵינוֹ אֶלָּא שְׂרָף מֵעֲצֵי הַקְּטָף. רַבִּי יִשְׁמָעֵאל אוֹמֵר: כֹּל הַיּוֹצֵא מִן הָעֵץ אֵין מַדְלִיקִין בּוֹ. רַבִּי יִשְׁמָעֵאל בֶּן בְּרוֹקָה אוֹמֵר: אֵין מַדְלִיקִין אֶלָּא בַּיּוֹצֵא מִן הַפְּרִי. רַבִּי טַרְפוֹן אוֹמֵר: אֵין מַדְלִיקִין אֶלָּא בְּשֶׁמֶן זַיִת בִּלְבַד.

The Gemara proceeds to discuss **the matter** of the *Tosefta* **itself,** the case of lighting with sap from balsam trees on Shabbat. **Rabbi Shimon ben Elazar says: One may not light with *tzori*** on Shabbat. **And Rabbi Shimon ben Elazar would also say: *Tzori*,** which is one of the component spices of the incense in the Temple, **is merely the sap** that emerges **from balsam trees,**[N] and is not part of the balsam tree itself. **Rabbi Yishmael says: Anything that originates from the tree, one may not light with it;** only materials that do not come from trees may be used. **Rabbi Yishmael ben Beroka says: One may only light with** a substance **that emerges from the fruit. Rabbi Tarfon says: One may only light with olive oil alone.**

NOTES

Using untithed produce – שִׁימּוּשׁ בְּטֶבֶל: It is prohibited to eat produce from which the *teruma* and tithes have not been separated. There is an opinion among early commentaries that *tevel* is not a distinct halakhic status that applies to untithed produce. It is rather a mixture of *teruma* and unconsecrated produce. Separating *teruma* retroactively designates which part of the *tevel* was *teruma*. Therefore, while there is a prohibition to eat *tevel*, even for priests, the legal status of the produce before tithing is based on the *teruma* it contains.

Sap that emerges from balsam trees – שְׂרָף מֵעֲצֵי הַקְּטָף: In the Jerusalem Talmud and according to Rashi's first explanation, Rabbi Shimon ben Elazar provides another reason why one may not light with sap of balsam trees. Like all other sap, sap of a balsam tree is not drawn easily by the wick (Rashba). However, there is an alternative explanation. Rabbi Shimon ben Elazar is referring to the nature of the sap from balsam trees as an aside and not specifically with regard to Shabbat (*Tosafot*).

HALAKHA

One may not light with untithed produce – אֵין מַדְלִיקִין בְּטֶבֶל: This applies to lighting a lamp with ritually impure untithed produce and all the more so if it is ritually pure (*Shakh*). It is prohibited during the week, and all the more so on Shabbat (*Shakh*; Rambam *Sefer Zera'im, Hilkhot Ma'aser* 6:2; *Shulḥan Arukh Yoreh De'a* 331:116).

One may not light with white naphtha – אֵין מַדְלִיקִין בְּנֵפְט לָבָן: One may neither light with white naphtha on Shabbat nor may he do so during the week because it is dangerous (Rambam *Sefer Zemanim, Hilkhot Shabbat* 5:10).

עָמַד רַבִּי יוֹחָנָן בֶּן נוּרִי עַל רַגְלָיו וְאָמַר: מַה יַּעֲשׂוּ אַנְשֵׁי בָבֶל שֶׁאֵין לָהֶם אֶלָּא שֶׁמֶן שׁוּמְשְׁמִין, וּמַה יַּעֲשׂוּ אַנְשֵׁי מָדַי שֶׁאֵין לָהֶם אֶלָּא שֶׁמֶן אֱגוֹזִים, וּמַה יַּעֲשׂוּ אַנְשֵׁי אֲלֶכְּסַנְדְּרִיָּא שֶׁאֵין לָהֶם אֶלָּא שֶׁמֶן צְנוֹנוֹת, וּמַה יַּעֲשׂוּ אַנְשֵׁי קַפּוֹטְקִיָּא שֶׁאֵין לָהֶם לֹא כָּךְ וְלֹא כָּךְ אֶלָּא נֵפְטְ? אֶלָּא: אֵין לְךָ אֶלָּא מַה שֶּׁאָמְרוּ חֲכָמִים אֵין מַדְלִיקִין.

The Gemara relates: **Rabbi Yoḥanan ben Nuri stood on his feet**[N] **and,** contrary to this statement, **said: And what shall the people of Babylonia, who have only sesame oil, do? And what shall the people of Medea, who have only nut oil, do? And what shall the people of Alexandria, who have only radish oil,**[B] **do? And what shall the people of Cappadocia, who have neither this nor that but only naphtha, do? Rather, you have** a prohibition **only** with regard to those substances with regard to **which the Sages said:**[H] **One may not light with them.** All other oils are permitted.

וּמַדְלִיקִין בְּשֶׁמֶן דָּגִים וּבְעִטְרָן, רַבִּי שִׁמְעוֹן שְׁזוּרִי אוֹמֵר: מַדְלִיקִין בְּשֶׁמֶן פַּקּוּעוֹת וּבְנֵפְטְ, סוּמָכוֹס אוֹמֵר: כֹּל הַיּוֹצֵא מִן הַבָּשָׂר אֵין מַדְלִיקִין בּוֹ, אֶלָּא בְּשֶׁמֶן דָּגִים. סוּמָכוֹס הַיְינוּ תַּנָּא קַמָּא! אִיכָּא בֵּינַיְיהוּ דְּרַב בְּרוּנָא אָמַר רַב, וְלָא מְסַיְּימִי.

And one may light with fish oil and tar. Rabbi Shimon Shezuri says: One may light with gourd oil[B] **and naphtha. Sumakhos says: Among the** substances **that emerge from the flesh** of living beings, **one may light only with fish oil.** The Gemara asks: The opinion of **Sumakhos** is identical to the opinion of the **first *tanna*,** who also permits lighting with fish oil. The Gemara answers: **There is** a practical difference **between them** with regard to what **Rav Beruna said** that **Rav said:** One is permitted to use molten fat to which oil was added for lighting. They disagree with regard to this *halakha*; however, their opinions **are not defined** and it is unclear which of them permits using it and which prohibits using it.

תַּנְיָא, רַבִּי שִׁמְעוֹן בֶּן אֶלְעָזָר אוֹמֵר: כֹּל הַיּוֹצֵא מִן הָעֵץ – אֵין בּוֹ מִשּׁוּם שָׁלֹשׁ עַל שָׁלֹשׁ, וּמְסַכְּכִין בּוֹ, חוּץ מִפִּשְׁתָּן. אָמַר אַבָּיֵי:

It was taught in a *baraita* that **Rabbi Shimon ben Elazar says: Anything that emerges from the tree** does **not have** the legal status of an area of **three by three** fingerbreadths.[H] Even if it is three by three fingerbreadths, it is not considered sufficiently large to become ritually impure. **And,** therefore, **one may roof** his *sukka*[H] **with it,** as the roofing of his *sukka* may not be made from any material that can become ritually impure. This is the case for everything that originates from a tree **with the exception of linen,** which has a unique legal status. **Abaye said:**

HALAKHA

You have only those which the Sages said – אֵין לְךָ אֶלָּא מַה שֶּׁאָמְרוּ חֲכָמִים: The *halakha* is in accordance with the Sages and with Rabbi Yoḥanan ben Nuri, who stated with regard to the laws of wicks and oils on Shabbat that the *halakha* is no more stringent than the guidelines established by the Sages. This is according to the unattributed mishna and the discussion in the Gemara (Rambam *Sefer Zemanim, Hilkhot Shabbat* 5:11; *Shulḥan Arukh, Oraḥ Ḥayyim* 264:6).

Anything that emerges from the tree with regard to ritual impurity – הַיּוֹצֵא מִן הָעֵץ לְעִנְיַן טוּמְאָה: Anything that comes from a tree, with the exception of flax, cannot become ritually impure unless it measures a minimum of three by three handbreadths. This rule also applies to torn garments. However, if one weaves a complete garment, regardless of its size, the garment can become ritually impure with all forms of ritual impurity, except for the ritual impurity imparted by treading. The Gemara elaborates in a later discussion (Rambam *Sefer Tahara, Hilkhot Kelim* 22:1).

Anything that emerges from the tree with regard to roofing for the *sukka* – הַיּוֹצֵא מִן הָעֵץ לְסִיכּוּךְ: Anything that comes from a tree may be used as roofing for the *sukka* unless it has been crafted into a vessel, as per the

NOTES

Rabbi Yoḥanan ben Nuri stood on his feet – עָמַד רַבִּי יוֹחָנָן בֶּן נוּרִי עַל רַגְלָיו: All of the Sages sat in the study hall and voiced their opinions on different topics while seated. Since certain Sages wanted to rule stringently with regard to enhancement of the mitzva, Rabbi Yoḥanan ben Nuri stood to emphasize his objection to these stringencies. He asserted that the restrictions would eventually become too burdensome and would ultimately prevent people from fulfilling the mitzva of kindling the Shabbat lights.

BACKGROUND

Radish oil – שֶׁמֶן צְנוֹנוֹת: This oil is produced from radish seeds, probably from the radish species *Raphunus sativus*, whose seeds contain a high concentration of oil. Ancient writers indicate that radish oil was prevalent in Egypt during the talmudic period.

Gourd oil – שֶׁמֶן פַּקּוּעוֹת: The gourds mentioned in the Bible and the Mishna have been identified with the plant known as the bitter apple, the *Citrullus colocynthis* L. of the gourd family.

This plant is similar to a watermelon and is found along the coastal plain and the other sandy regions of Israel. The plant has finger-like leaves that are somewhat similar to grape leaves and round fruits that are approximately 10 cm in diameter with a thick rind. The fruit is spongy, filled with seeds, and has a bitter taste.

It is possible to extract oil from the seeds, generally as much as 15 percent of the weight of the seeds. The oil can be used for food or light.

Bitter apple

רַבִּי שִׁמְעוֹן בֶּן אֶלְעָזָר וְתַנָּא דְּבֵי רַבִּי יִשְׁמָעֵאל אָמְרוּ דָּבָר אֶחָד. רַבִּי שִׁמְעוֹן בֶּן אֶלְעָזָר – הָא דַּאֲמַרַן, תַּנָּא דְּבֵי רַבִּי יִשְׁמָעֵאל מַאי הִיא – דְּתָנֵי דְּבֵי רַבִּי יִשְׁמָעֵאל: הוֹאִיל וְנֶאֶמְרוּ בְּגָדִים בַּתּוֹרָה סְתָם, וּפָרַט לְךָ הַכָּתוּב בְּאֶחָד מֵהֶן "צֶמֶר וּפִשְׁתִּים", מַה לְּהַלָּן – צֶמֶר וּפִשְׁתִּים, אַף כֹּל – צֶמֶר וּפִשְׁתִּים.

Rabbi Shimon ben Elazar and the ***tanna* of the school of Rabbi Yishmael** essentially **said the same thing,** even though they said it in different ways. The Gemara elaborates: The statement of **Rabbi Shimon ben Elazar** is **that which we said:** The only fabrics woven from plant materials that are considered bona fide fabrics are those made of linen. **What is** the statement of the ***tanna* from the school of** Rabbi Yishmael? **As it was taught in the school of Rabbi Yishmael: Since** the word **garments is stated in the Torah unmodified,** without stating from what materials those garments were made, **and the verse specified in one of** its references to garments, in the *halakhot* of ritual impurity of leprosy, **wool and linen:** "And the garment in which there will be the plague of leprosy, whether it be a woolen garment, or a linen garment" (Leviticus 13:47), the conclusion can be drawn: **Just as below,** when it mentions a garment in the case of leprosy,[B] the Torah is referring to one made of **wool** or **linen, so too, all** garments mentioned in the Torah are those made from **wool** or **linen.** Other fabrics are not classified as garments.

רָבָא אָמַר: שְׁלֹשָׁה עַל שְׁלֹשָׁה בִּשְׁאָר בְּגָדִים אִיכָּא בֵּינַיְיהוּ, דְּרַבִּי שִׁמְעוֹן בֶּן אֶלְעָזָר אִית לֵיהּ, לְתַנָּא דְּבֵי רַבִּי יִשְׁמָעֵאל – לֵית לֵיהּ.

In contrast to Abaye, who viewed the opinions expressed by Rabbi Shimon ben Elazar and the *tanna* of the school of Rabbi Yishmael as expressing the same idea, **Rava said** that the two opinions are not identical. **There is** a difference **between them** when the cloth is **three by three**[B] handbreadths, **with regard to other garments** that are neither wool nor linen. **As Rabbi Shimon ben Elazar** says explicitly: If it is less than three by three fingerbreadths, indicating that he **is of** the opinion that a cloth that is three by three handbreadths that is suitable for use even by wealthy people can become ritually impure. In his opinion, the uniqueness of linen fabric is not that it can become ritually impure, but rather that a linen rag, even if it is very small, can become ritually impure. The *tanna* **of the school of Rabbi Yishmael is not of** the opinion that other garments can become ritually impure.

דְּכוּלֵּי עָלְמָא מִיהַת שָׁלֹשׁ עַל שָׁלֹשׁ בְּצֶמֶר וּפִשְׁתִּים מִיטַּמֵּא בִּנְגָעִים, מְנָלַן? דְּתַנְיָא: 'בֶּגֶד' אֵין לִי אֶלָּא בֶּגֶד, שָׁלֹשׁ עַל שָׁלֹשׁ מִנַּיִן? תַּלְמוּד לוֹמַר: 'וְהַבֶּגֶד'. וְאֵימָא לְרַבּוֹת שְׁלֹשָׁה עַל שְׁלֹשָׁה! לָאו קַל וָחוֹמֶר הוּא? הָשְׁתָּא שְׁתִי וָעֵרֶב מִיטַּמֵּא, שְׁלֹשָׁה עַל שְׁלֹשָׁה מִיבַּעְיָא!

In any case, based on the above, **everyone agrees** that, clearly, **three by three** fingerbreadths **in a wool** or **linen** garment can **become ritually impure with** the impurity of **leprosy.**[H] The Gemara asks: **From where do we** derive this? The Gemara responds that it is derived **as it was taught** in a *baraita* with regard to this matter. When the Torah states: **Garment,** unmodified, **I have** derived that **nothing other** than a whole **garment** can become ritually impure. However, with regard to a cloth that is **three by three** fingerbreadths, **from where** do I derive that it is also included in this *halakha*? **The verse states: "And the garment**[N] in which there will be the plague of leprosy" (Leviticus 13:47).[H] From the addition of the word: And the garment [*vehabeged*], it is derived that all woven swatches are subsumed within the category of garment in this matter. The Gemara asks: **And** perhaps **say** that it comes **to include** a woven garment that is **three by three**[N] handbreadths? The Gemara answers: That is inconceivable. **Is that not** derived through **an *a fortiori* inference?** As, **now,** even the threads of the **warp** or the threads of the **woof** can **become ritually impure, is it necessary** to mention that a cloth **three by three**[N] handbreadths can become ritually impure as well? A garment that is three by three handbreadths is comprised of several warp and woof threads that can themselves become ritually impure.

BACKGROUND

Leprosy of clothing – נִגְעֵי בְּגָדִים: By Torah law, if bright red or green spots appear on clothing, the clothing must be brought to a priest to determine whether or not the spots indicate leprosy of clothing (Leviticus 13:47–59). The affected garment is then put aside for a week, after which it is reexamined by the priest. If the spots spread, the clothing is immediately declared ritually impure by the priest and burned. If, however, the spots did not spread, the clothing is laundered and then put aside for another week, after which the priest reexamines it. If the spots have disappeared or become darker, the garment is laundered and immersed in a ritual bath, after which it is considered ritually pure. Otherwise, the affected part, and sometimes the entire garment, must be burned. A leprous garment may not be used, and it renders people and items that come in contact with it ritually impure, in the same way a leprous person does. The laws of leprosy of clothing apply only to leather, wool, and linen garments that are not dyed.

Three feminine and masculine – שָׁלֹשׁ וּשְׁלֹשָׁה: When referring to garments, measures mentioned by the Sages using feminine numbers are fingerbreadths. Measurements mentioned by the Sages using masculine numbers are handbreadths. In the discussion of other topics, feminine numbers connote cubits.

The thumb is the basic measure of a fingerbreadth and is measured at its widest part. The handbreadth is the size of a clenched fist, which equals four fingerbreadths. Three by three fingerbreadths is equal to 6 × 6 cm or, according to another opinion, 7.5 × 7.5 cm. Three by three handbreadths equal 24 × 24 cm or 30 × 30 cm, according to the alternate opinion.

HALAKHA

The measure of a garment with regard to ritual impurity from leprosy – שִׁיעוּר הַבֶּגֶד לְעִנְיַן טוּמְאַת נְגָעִים: The minimal size of a garment that can become ritually impure from leprosy is three by three fingerbreadths, as per the *baraita* (Rambam *Sefer Tahara, Hilkhot Tumat Tzara'at* 12:10 and *Hilkhot Kelim* 22:12).

Types of garments with regard to ritual impurity from leprosy – סוּגֵי בֶּגֶד בְּטוּמְאַת נְגָעִים: Leprosy can only transmit ritual impurity to woolen or linen garments and not to clothing fashioned from other materials, as per the *baraita* (Rambam *Sefer Tahara, Hilkhot Tumat Tzara'at* 13:1).

NOTES

The verse states: "And the garment" – תַּלְמוּד לוֹמַר וְהַבֶּגֶד: Although, in the study hall of Rabbi Yishmael the general practice was not to derive *halakhot* from unclear amplifications in the Torah text, e.g., an extra letter *vav*, the Gemara already stated that the students of Rabbi Yishmael would derive *halakhot* from the addition of *vav* and *heh*, meaning: And the (*Yevamot* 72b). In this case, the text could have simply read: Garment. Therefore, the prefix meaning: And the, is an uncommon linguistic form whose purpose is to teach that garment should be understood in its broadest sense.

Three by three – שְׁלֹשָׁה עַל שְׁלֹשָׁה: It is apparent from the discussion in the Gemara that the fact that a cloth that is three by three handbreadths is considered a garment requires no derivation. Since it is fit for use by both wealthy and poor people, a garment of three by three handbreadths is indeed an article of clothing. There is no reason to enlarge the minimum measure of a garment beyond a reasonable size (Ramban; Rashba).

Now that the warp and the woof can become ritually impure… a cloth that is three by three – הָשְׁתָּא שְׁתִי וָעֵרֶב מִיטַּמֵּא...שְׁלֹשָׁה עַל שְׁלֹשָׁה: Some commentaries say that it is not self-evident that the criterion for becoming ritually impure in the case of the warp and woof is the same with regard to a garment. From the additional language in the verse, apparently, each case is derived independently (*Tziyyun LeNefesh Ḥayya*).

אִי הָכִי, שָׁלֹשׁ עַל שָׁלֹשׁ נַמִּי לֵיתֵי בְּקַל וָחוֹמֶר! אֶלָּא: שְׁלֹשָׁה עַל שְׁלֹשָׁה דַּחֲזוּ בֵּין לַעֲשִׁירִים בֵּין לַעֲנִיִּים – אָתֵי בְּקַל וָחוֹמֶר, שָׁלֹשׁ עַל שָׁלֹשׁ – לַעֲנִיִּים הוּא דַּחֲזְיָין, לַעֲשִׁירִים לָא חַזְיָין, לָא אָתֵי בְּקַל וָחוֹמֶר. טַעְמָא דִּכְתַבֵיהּ קְרָא, הָא לָא כְּתַבֵיהּ קְרָא – לָא גָּמְרִינַן בְּקַל וָחוֹמֶר,

The Gemara rejects this: **If so,** then **let us also derive** a cloth that is **three by three** fingerbreadths through the same *a fortiori* **inference** from the warp and woof threads. **Rather,** it must be that this *a fortiori* inference is flawed. Threads woven into fabric do not maintain their previous status as they are no longer suitable to be used as warp and woof threads. **Rather,** cloths that are **three by three** handbreadths, **which are suitable** for use **by both the wealthy and the poor** as they are multipurpose cloths, can **be derived through an** ***a fortiori*** **inference,** as they are certainly more significant than the warp and woof threads and they become ritually impure. However, cloths that are **three by three** fingerbreadths, which **are suitable for** use by **the poor** but **are unsuitable for** use by **the wealthy, are not derived through an** ***a fortiori*** **inference.** Therefore, **the reason** that they can become ritually impure is specifically **because it was written in the Torah. Had it not been written in the Torah, we would not derive** it **through an** ***a fortiori*** **inference.**

וְאֵימָא: לְרַבּוֹת שְׁלֹשָׁה עַל שְׁלֹשָׁה בִּשְׁאָר בְּגָדִים! אֲמַר קְרָא: ״בֶּגֶד צֶמֶר וּפִשְׁתִּים״, בֶּגֶד צֶמֶר וּפִשְׁתִּים – אִין, מִידֵּי אַחֲרִינֵי – לָא. וְאֵימָא: כִּי אִימְעוּט – מִשָּׁלֹשׁ עַל שָׁלֹשׁ, אֲבָל שְׁלֹשָׁה עַל שְׁלֹשָׁה – מִיטַּמֵּא! תְּרֵי מִיעוּטֵי כְּתִיבִי: ״בֶּגֶד צֶמֶר אוֹ [בְּבֶגֶד] פִּשְׁתִּים״, חַד – לְמַעוּטֵי מִשָּׁלֹשׁ עַל שָׁלֹשׁ, וְחַד – לְמַעוּטֵי מִשְּׁלֹשָׁה עַל שְׁלֹשָׁה,

The Gemara also asks: Indeed, there is amplification in the Torah, derived from the term: And the garment, which is a generalization that comes to expand upon the details that follow. **And say** that it comes **to include** the ruling that cloth that is **three by three** handbreadths **in garments** made of materials **other** than wool or linen can become ritually impure. The Gemara answers: That is inconceivable. **The verse said: A garment of wool** or **linen,** indicating that a garment made of **wool** or **linen, yes,** it becomes ritually impure; a garment made of **other materials, no,** it does not become ritually impure. The Gemara asks: **And say** that **when** the verse **excluded,** it excluded specifically a garment that is **three by three** fingerbreadths; **however,** a garment that is **three by three** handbreadths **can become ritually impure.** The Gemara replies: **Two exclusions are written;** once it is stated: "A garment of wool or linen" (Leviticus 13:59), and it is also stated: **"Whether it be a woolen garment, or a linen garment"** (Leviticus 13:47). **One** verse comes **to exclude** cloth of **three by three** fingerbreadths, **and one** verse comes **to exclude** cloth of **three by three** handbreadths, to emphasize that a garment made of a material that is neither wool nor linen cannot become ritually impure at all. This corresponds to Abaye's opinion that garments not made of wool or linen cannot become ritually impure.

וּלְרָבָא, דְּאָמַר: שְׁלֹשָׁה עַל שְׁלֹשָׁה בִּשְׁאָר בְּגָדִים אִיכָּא בֵּינַיְיהוּ, לְרַבִּי שִׁמְעוֹן בֶּן אֶלְעָזָר – אִית לֵיהּ, לְתַנָּא דְּבֵי רַבִּי יִשְׁמָעֵאל – לֵית לֵיהּ, שְׁלֹשָׁה עַל שְׁלֹשָׁה בִּשְׁאָר בְּגָדִים

The Gemara asks: **And according to** the opinion of **Rava, who said** that the practical difference **between** the two opinions is with regard to cloth **three by three** handbreadths **in other garments, that Rabbi Shimon ben Elazar is of** the opinion that they can become ritually impure, whereas the ***tanna*** **of the school of Rabbi Yishmael is not of** the opinion that they can become ritually impure, in the case of a cloth that is **three by three** handbreadths **in other garments,**

מְנָא לֵיהּ? נָפְקָא מֵ׳אוֹ בֶגֶד׳, דְּתַנְיָא: ׳בֶגֶד׳ – אֵין לִי אֶלָּא בֶּגֶד, שְׁלֹשָׁה עַל שְׁלֹשָׁה בִּשְׁאָר בְּגָדִים מִנַּיִין? תַּלְמוּד לוֹמַר: ׳אוֹ בֶגֶד׳.

from where does Rabbi Shimon ben Elazar derive that it can become ritually impure? The Gemara answers: In his opinion, it **is derived from** the verse that speaks of the ritual impurity of creeping animals: **"Or a garment,** or skin, or sack" (Leviticus 11:32). The additional "or" comes to include items that are not generally included in the definition of garment. **As it was taught** in a *baraita*: From the fact that it says **garment, I have** derived **nothing other** than **a** whole **garment;** however, a swatch that is **three by three** handbreadths **in other garments, from where** is it derived that it can become ritually impure? **The verse states: Or a garment.**

וְאַבַּיֵי, הַאי 'אוֹ בֶגֶד' מַאי עָבֵיד לֵיהּ? מִיבְּעֵי לֵיהּ לְרַבּוֹת שָׁלֹשׁ עַל שָׁלֹשׁ בְּצֶמֶר וּפִשְׁתִּים דְּמִטַּמֵּא בִּשְׁרָצִים.

The Gemara asks: **And Abaye,** who says that everyone agrees that other garments do not become ritually impure at all, **this** phrase: **Or a garment, what does he do with it** and what does it come to add? The Gemara answers: **He needs it to include** a small swatch of fabric that is **three by three** fingerbreadths made **of wool or linen.** Despite its size, **it can become ritually impure**[H] **from** contact with **creeping animals.**

וְרָבָא: גַּלֵּי רַחֲמָנָא גַּבֵּי נְגָעִים, וְהוּא הַדִּין לִשְׁרָצִים.

And Rava holds that there is no need for the verse to discuss that matter explicitly, as **the Torah revealed in the case of leprosy** that it is considered to be a garment, **and the same is true with regard to** the ritual impurity of **creeping animals.**

וְאַבַּיֵי: אִיכָּא לְמִיפְרַךְ; מָה לִנְגָעִים – שֶׁכֵּן שְׁתִי וָעֵרֶב מִטַּמֵּא בָּהֶם.

And Abaye holds that one cannot derive the *halakhot* of creeping animals from the *halakhot* of leprosy, as **there is room to refute** that comparison in the following manner: **What** comparison is there to **leprosy,** which has more stringent *halakhot* of ritual impurity, **as** even the **warp and woof** threads alone **can become ritually impure from it,** which is not the case with regard to ritual impurity from creeping animals? Therefore, even small scraps can become ritually impure from leprosy.

וְאִידָךְ: אִי סָלְקָא דַּעְתָּךְ נְגָעִים חֲמִירִי, לִכְתּוֹב רַחֲמָנָא גַּבֵּי שְׁרָצִים – וְלֵיתוּ נְגָעִים מִינַּיְיהוּ.

The other *amora*, Rava, **says: If it should enter your mind** to say that **leprosy is more stringent,** then **the Torah should have written** the *halakha* **with regard to creeping animals, and let leprosy be derived from them.** Ultimately, the two *halakhot* are paralleled to one another in the Torah. It would have been simpler to explicitly write the laws of creeping animals and to derive leprosy from them. Since that is not the case, it is proof that the *halakhot* of creeping animals can be derived from leprosy.

וְאִידָךְ: נְגָעִים מִשְּׁרָצִים לָא אָתוּ, דְּאִיכָּא לְמִיפְרַךְ: מָה לִשְׁרָצִים שֶׁכֵּן מְטַמֵּא בְּכַעֲדָשָׁה.

The other *amora*, Abaye, said that this contention is fundamentally unsound, as **leprosy could not be derived from creeping animals because there is room to refute** this idea and challenge: **What** is the comparison **to** the ritual impurity of **creeping animals,** which is more stringent than the ritual impurity of leprosy, **as** the creeping animal **makes one ritually impure even in** a case where it is **a lentil-bulk,**[N] which is not true of other types of ritual impurity? Therefore, verses were necessary to teach about the ritual impurity of both creeping animals and leprosy.

אָמַר אַבַּיֵי: הַאי תַּנָּא דְּבֵי רַבִּי יִשְׁמָעֵאל מַפִּיק מֵאִידָךְ תַּנָּא דְּבֵי רַבִּי יִשְׁמָעֵאל. דְּתָנֵי דְּבֵי רַבִּי יִשְׁמָעֵאל: 'בֶּגֶד' אֵין לִי אֶלָּא בֶּגֶד צֶמֶר וּפִשְׁתִּים, מִנַּיִין לְרַבּוֹת צֶמֶר גְּמַלִּים וְצֶמֶר אַרְנָבִים נוֹצָה שֶׁל עִזִּים וְהַשִּׁירָיִין וְהַכָּלָךְ וְהַסְּרִיקִין – תַּלְמוּד לוֹמַר "אוֹ בֶגֶד".

Abaye said: This statement of the *tanna* **of the school of Rabbi Yishmael diverges from another** statement of the *tanna* **of the school of Rabbi Yishmael,** as the *tanna* **of the school of Rabbi Yishmael taught:** From the fact that the verse says **garment, I have** derived **nothing other than** the *halakha* that **a garment of wool or linen** can become ritually impure. However, **from where** is it derived to **include** garments made of **camels' hair**[H] **and rabbits' wool, goats' hair**[B] **or** the types of silk, **the** *shirayin*, **the** *kalakh*, **and the** *serikin* among the fabrics that can become ritually impure? **The verse states: Or a garment.** The word "or" serves as an amplification to include all types of fabric.

רָבָא אָמַר: כִּי לֵית לֵיהּ לְהַךְ תַּנָּא דְּבֵי רַבִּי יִשְׁמָעֵאל בִּשְׁאָר בְּגָדִים – שָׁלֹשׁ עַל שָׁלֹשׁ, שְׁלֹשָׁה עַל שְׁלֹשָׁה – אִית לֵיהּ.

Whereas **Rava said:** There is no need to say that there is a dispute in this case between two *tanna'im* from a single school. Rather, **when this** *tanna* **from the school** of Rabbi Yishmael, quoted above, **is not of** the opinion that there is ritual impurity **in other garments,** it is only with regard to a swatch that is **three by three** fingerbreadths; however, with regard to a cloth that is **three by three** handbreadths **he is** of the opinion that it becomes ritually impure. His previous statement came to exclude a small garment from becoming ritually impure. This statement is referring to a larger garment that is three by three handbreadths.

וְהָא רָבָא הוּא דַּאֲמַר שְׁלֹשָׁה עַל שְׁלֹשָׁה בִּשְׁאָר בְּגָדִים לְרַבִּי שִׁמְעוֹן בֶּן אֶלְעָזָר – אִית לֵיהּ, לְתַנָּא דְּבֵי רַבִּי יִשְׁמָעֵאל – לֵית לֵיהּ! הֲדַר בֵּיהּ רָבָא מֵהַהִיא. וְאִי בָּעֵית אֵימָא: הָא – רַב פַּפָּא אֲמָרָהּ.

The Gemara asks: **Isn't Rava** the one who **said** above that, in the case of **three by three** handbreadths **in other garments, Rabbi Shimon ben Elazar is** of the opinion that they can become ritually impure, whereas **the** *tanna* **of the school of Rabbi Yishmael is not** of the opinion that they become ritually impure? The Gemara answers: **Rava retracted that opinion** in order to reconcile the opinions of the *tanna'im* of the school of Rabbi Yishmael. **And if you wish, say** instead a different answer: **Rav Pappa said this**[N] statement and not Rava. Since Rav Pappa was the primary disciple of Rava, the Gemara attributed his statement to Rava.

HALAKHA

The size for a garment to become ritually impure – שִׁיעוּר טוּמְאַת בְּגָדִים: All garments, other than those made of wool and linen, can become ritually impure only if they are at least three by three handbreadths, as per the *baraita* cited in the Gemara. Apparently, Abaye's rejection of the proof was only according to the opinion of Rabbi Shimon ben Elazar (Rambam *Sefer Tahara, Hilkhot Kelim* 22:1 and 23:2).

From where is it derived to include garments made of camels' hair, etc. – מִנַּיִין לְרַבּוֹת צֶמֶר גְּמַלִּים וכו׳: Garments woven from anything that grows on land, i.e., from both plants and animals, are considered garments in terms of ritual impurity, as per the *tanna* of the school of Rabbi Yishmael (Rambam *Sefer Tahara, Hilkhot Kelim* 1:11).

NOTES

Makes one ritually impure even in a case where it is a lentil-bulk – מְטַמֵּא בְּכַעֲדָשָׁה: With regard to creeping animals, the size of a lentil is the smallest measure of any item that can make another item ritually impure. In all other types of ritual impurity, e.g., a corpse, or an animal carcass, the minimum size capable of making another item ritually impure is larger. The rationale for this rule is that the smallest creeping animal capable of making another item ritually impure is a lentil-bulk at birth.

Rav Pappa said this – רַב פַּפָּא אֲמָרָהּ: This phrase appears several times in the Gemara. Rav Pappa was the preeminent student of Rava and, after his death, he even succeeded him as the head of the yeshiva. When Rav Pappa cited a statement without attribution, the students attributed it to Rava (see Rashi).

BACKGROUND

Goats' hair – נוֹצָה שֶׁל עִזִּים: The Torah and the Sages do not refer to the material sheared from goats as wool. Rather, it is called either hair or feathers. Goats' hair is also called feathers because it is not soft like other types of wool. Rather, it is stiff like bird feathers (Rashi).

רַב פַּפָּא אָמַר: אַף כֹּל – לְאַתּוֹיֵי כִּלְאַיִם. כִּלְאַיִם, בְּהֶדְיָא כְּתִיבִי בֵּיהּ ״לֹא תִלְבַּשׁ שַׁעַטְנֵז צֶמֶר וּפִשְׁתִּים יַחְדָּיו״! סָלְקָא דַּעְתָּךְ אָמִינָא: הָנֵי מִילֵּי – דֶּרֶךְ לְבִישָׁה, אֲבָל בְּהַעֲלָאָה – כָּל תְּרֵי מִינֵי אָסוּר.

Rav Pappa himself understood the first statement of the *tanna* of the school of Rabbi Yishmael and **stated** it in a completely different manner. In his opinion, the derivation from the *halakhot* of leprosy, which concluded that **even all** nonspecific mentions of garments in the Torah refer to wool or linen, came **to include** the *halakhot* of **diverse kinds,**[H] the Torah prohibition to wear clothing made from a mixture of wool and linen threads. He sought to prove that the *halakhot* of prohibited mixtures of threads apply only to wool and linen. The Gemara asks: Why does he require this derivation with regard to the prohibition of **diverse kinds?** The fact that the prohibition is limited to wool and linen is **explicitly written,** as it is stated: **"You shall not wear diverse kinds, wool and linen together"** (Deuteronomy 22:11). The Gemara answers: Nevertheless, an additional derivation was necessary, as **it would have entered your mind to say** that **this,** the restriction of the prohibition of diverse kinds to wool and linen, **applies** specifically to a case when one uses them together **in the manner of wearing** them; **however, in** merely **placing** the garments upon oneself, **any two kinds are prohibited.** Therefore, it was necessary to derive that the garment mentioned is restricted to wool and linen.

וְלָאו קַל וָחוֹמֶר הוּא? וּמַה לְבִישָׁה, דְּקָא מִיתְהַנֵּי כּוּלֵּי גּוּפֵיהּ מִכִּלְאַיִם, אָמַרְתְּ: צֶמֶר וּפִשְׁתִּים – אִין, מִידֵּי אַחֲרִינָא – לָא, הַעֲלָאָה לֹא כָּל שֶׁכֵּן! אֶלָּא, דְּרַב פַּפָּא בְּדוּתָא הִיא.

This claim is rejected: **And is it not an *a fortiori* inference? Just as** in the case of **wearing** the garment, **where one's entire body derives benefit from** the **diverse kinds, you said** that **wool and linen, yes,** are included in the prohibition, **other materials, no,** are not included; in the case of merely **placing** the garment upon himself, **all the more so** that the *halakha* should not be more stringent. **Rather,** certainly the *halakha* that was attributed to **Rav Pappa is a mistake,**[N] and he did not say it.

רַב נַחְמָן בַּר יִצְחָק אָמַר: אַף כֹּל –

Rav Naḥman bar Yitzḥak also **said** that those statements of the *tanna* of the school of Rabbi Yishmael do not refer to the *halakhot* of ritual impurity. They refer to another topic. In his opinion, the *tanna* of the school of Rabbi Yishmael came to say that just as the *halakhot* of leprosy are limited to garments made from wool or linen, **so too, all**

HALAKHA

To include diverse kinds – לְאַתּוֹיֵי כִּלְאַיִם: The prohibition of a mixture of diverse kinds applies only to sheep's wool and linen and not to any other materials (Rambam *Sefer Zera'im, Hilkhot Kil'ayim* 10:1; *Shulḥan Arukh, Yoreh De'a* 298:1).

NOTES

Is a mistake – בְּדוּתָא הִיא: There is a variant reading in several sources: It is external [*berota hi*]. According to this reading, when the Sages wanted to suggest that a certain opinion was without basis, they would do so in a respectful manner, saying: It is external, indicating that it is an outside opinion and should not be introduced into the study hall (*Arukh*).

Perek **II**
Daf **27** Amud **b**

לְאַתּוֹיֵי צִיצִית. צִיצִית, בְּהֶדְיָא כְּתִיב: ״לֹא תִלְבַּשׁ שַׁעַטְנֵז צֶמֶר וּפִשְׁתִּים״ וּכְתִיב: ״גְּדִילִים תַּעֲשֶׂה לָּךְ״! סָלְקָא דַּעְתָּךְ אָמִינָא כִּדְרָבָא, דְּרָבָא רָמֵי: כְּתִיב ׳הַכָּנָף׳ – מִין כָּנָף, וּכְתִיב ״צֶמֶר וּפִשְׁתִּים יַחְדָּיו״ הָא כֵּיצַד? צֶמֶר וּפִשְׁתִּים פּוֹטְרִין בֵּין בְּמִינָן בֵּין שֶׁלֹּא בְּמִינָן; שְׁאָר מִינִין, בְּמִינָן – פּוֹטְרִין, שֶׁלֹּא בְּמִינָן – אֵין פּוֹטְרִין. סָלְקָא דַּעְתָּךְ כִּדְרָבָא – קָא מַשְׁמַע לָן.

garments mentioned in the Torah are made from wool and linen. This comes **to include** the law of **ritual fringes;**[H] the obligation of ritual fringes applies only to those materials. The Gemara asks: Why is that derivation necessary? With regard to **ritual fringes it is written explicitly: "You shall not wear diverse kinds, wool and linen** together" (Deuteronomy 22:11); **and** juxtaposed to it, **it is written: "You shall make for you twisted fringes** upon the four corners of your covering, with which you cover yourself" (Deuteronomy 22:12). From the juxtaposition of these two verses it is derived that the mitzva of ritual fringes applies only to garments to which the laws of diverse kinds apply. Rav Naḥman bar Yitzḥak responded that the matter is not so clear, as **it could have entered your mind to say in accordance with** the statement of **Rava. As Rava raised a contradiction:** On the one hand, **it is written:** "And that they put with the fringe of each **corner** a thread of sky blue" (Numbers 15:39); apparently, the threads of the ritual fringes must be of the same **type** of fabric as the **corner** of the garment. **However,** in Deuteronomy, in the laws of ritual fringes, **it is written** in juxtaposition to the laws of diverse kinds: **Wool and linen together.** The ritual fringes may only be made of those materials. **How** can **that** contradiction be resolved? Rather, Rava says: Ritual fringes made of **wool and linen exempt** the garment and fulfill the obligation of ritual fringes **whether** the garment is **of their own type,** wool or linen, **whether it is not**[H] **of their own type.** Whereas with regard to **other types,** a garment of **their** own **type, they exempt;**[H] a garment **not of their** own **type, they do not exempt. It would have entered your mind** to explain this **in accordance with** the approach of **Rava.** Therefore, the *tanna* **taught us** that the obligation of ritual fringes applies only to wool and linen and not to other materials.

HALAKHA

To include ritual fringes – לְאַתּוֹיֵי צִיצִית: Dating back to the *ge'onim*, there is a halakhic dispute whether or not one is obligated by Torah law to place ritual fringes on garments made from materials other than wool or linen. Some authorities ruled in accordance with the opinion of Rav Naḥman bar Yitzḥak that the mitzva by Torah law applies only to garments made of wool or linen. This is the ruling of the *Shulḥan Arukh*. The Rema rules in accordance with the opinion of Rava, who says that one is obligated by Torah law to place ritual fringes on all garments. However, they require ritual fringes made either of wool or linen or of the same material as the garment (Rambam *Sefer Ahava, Hilkhot Tzitzit* 3:1; *Shulḥan Arukh, Oraḥ Ḥayyim* 9:1).

Wool and linen exempt whether it is of their own type, whether it is not of their own type – צֶמֶר וּפִשְׁתִּים פּוֹטְרִין בֵּין בְּמִינָן בֵּין שֶׁלֹּא בְּמִינָן: Ritual fringes made from wool or linen may be placed on all garments. The exceptions are wool fringes on a linen garment or linen fringes on a wool garment. Since there is no universally accepted sky blue dye today, these combinations violate the prohibition of diverse kinds. Others say that one may never attach linen fringes to any garment, even one made of linen, because of the appearance of wrongdoing (Rema; *Magen Avraham*; Rambam *Sefer Ahava, Hilkhot Tzitzit* 3:3, 5–6; *Shulḥan Arukh, Oraḥ Ḥayyim* 9:2).

Other types, a garment of their own type, they exempt – שְׁאָר מִינִין, בְּמִינָן פּוֹטְרִין: All authorities agree that ritual fringes made from materials other than wool or linen may be attached only to garments made from the same material as the ritual fringes and not to garments made from other materials, as per the opinion of Rava (Rambam *Sefer Ahava, Hilkhot Tzitzit* 3:5; *Shulḥan Arukh, Oraḥ Ḥayyim* 9:3).

אָמַר רַב אַחָא בְּרֵיהּ דְּרָבָא לְרַב אַשִׁי: לְתַנָּא דְּבֵי רַבִּי יִשְׁמָעֵאל מַאי שְׁנָא לְעִנְיַן טוּמְאָה דִּמְרַבֵּי שְׁאָר בְּגָדִים – דִּכְתִיב 'אוֹ בֶגֶד' הָכָא נַמִי לֵימָא: לְרַבּוֹת שְׁאָר בְּגָדִים מֵ"אֲשֶׁר תְּכַסֶּה בָּהּ" – הַהוּא לְאַתּוֹיֵי כְּסוּת סוּמָא הוּא דַּאֲתָא, דְּתַנְיָא: "וּרְאִיתֶם אוֹתוֹ" – פְּרָט לִכְסוּת לַיְלָה. אַתָּה אוֹמֵר פְּרָט לִכְסוּת לַיְלָה, אוֹ אֵינוֹ אֶלָּא פְּרָט לִכְסוּת סוּמָא? כְּשֶׁהוּא אוֹמֵר: "אֲשֶׁר תְּכַסֶּה בָּהּ" – הֲרֵי כְּסוּת סוּמָא אָמוּר, הָא מָה אֲנִי מְקַיֵּים "וּרְאִיתֶם אוֹתוֹ" – פְּרָט לִכְסוּת לַיְלָה.

Rav Aḥa, son of Rava, said to Rav Ashi: According to the *tanna* of the school of Rabbi Yishmael, what is different about ritual impurity that he includes other garments not made of wool and linen because it is written: Or a garment, which is a term of amplification? Here too, in the matter of ritual fringes, say that it comes to include other garments from the phrase: Of your covering, with which you cover yourself. Rav Ashi answered: That amplification is necessary to include the garment of a blind person[H] in the obligation of ritual fringes. As it was taught in a *baraita*, with regard to ritual fringes it is stated: "And it shall be unto you for a fringe, that you may look upon it and remember all the mitzvot of the Lord" (Numbers 15:39). The phrase: That you may look, comes to exclude a night garment, which cannot be seen and is therefore exempt from the mitzva of ritual fringes. The *tanna* continues: Do you say[B] that the verse comes to exclude a night garment? Or is it only to exclude the garment of a blind person who is also unable to fulfill the verse: That you may look upon it? The *tanna* explains: When it says in Deuteronomy: Of your covering, with which you cover yourself, the garment of a blind person is mentioned, as he too covers himself with a covering. If so, then how do I fulfill the exclusion: That you may look upon it? It comes to exclude a night garment.

וּמָה רָאִיתָ לְרַבּוֹת סוּמָא וּלְהוֹצִיא כְּסוּת לַיְלָה? מְרַבֶּה אֲנִי כְּסוּת סוּמָא – שֶׁיֶּשְׁנָהּ בִּרְאִיָּיה אֵצֶל אֲחֵרִים, וּמוֹצִיא אֲנִי כְּסוּת לַיְלָה – שֶׁאֵינָהּ בִּרְאִיָּיה אֵצֶל אֲחֵרִים.

The Gemara asks: Since there is one verse that includes and another verse that excludes, what did you see that led you to include a blind person and to exclude a night garment in the obligation of ritual fringes? The Gemara answers: I include the garment of a blind person because it is, at least, visible to others, and I exclude a night garment because it is not even visible to others.

וְאֵימָא לְרַבּוֹת שְׁאָר בְּגָדִים! מִסְתַּבְּרָא: קָאֵי בְּצֶמֶר וּפִשְׁתִּים – מְרַבֶּה צֶמֶר וּפִשְׁתִּים, קָאֵי בְּצֶמֶר וּפִשְׁתִּים – מְרַבֶּה שְׁאָר בְּגָדִים?!

The Gemara asks: And say that this amplification does not come to include a blind person's garments, but rather, as Rava said, to include other garments not made from wool or linen in the obligation of ritual fringes. The Gemara answers: It is logical to say that since the Torah is standing and discussing a garment made of wool or linen, it is certainly including another garment made of wool or linen. Therefore, an amplification with regard to the garment of a blind person made of wool or linen is derived. However, when the Torah is standing and discussing a garment made from wool or linen, is it reasonable to say that it is including other garments with them? Rather, other garments are certainly not derived from there.

אָמַר אַבַּיֵי: רַבִּי שִׁמְעוֹן בֶּן אֶלְעָזָר וְסוּמָכוֹס אָמְרוּ דָּבָר אֶחָד. רַבִּי שִׁמְעוֹן בֶּן אֶלְעָזָר – הָא דַּאֲמַרַן, סוּמָכוֹס, דְּתַנְיָא, סוּמָכוֹס אוֹמֵר: סִיכְּכָהּ בִּטְווּי – פְּסוּלָה, מִפְּנֵי שֶׁמִּטַּמְּאָה בִּנְגָעִים.

The Gemara returns to discuss the opinion of Rabbi Shimon ben Elazar, who disqualified even small cloths from being used as roofing in the *sukka* because they can become ritually impure. Abaye said: Rabbi Shimon ben Elazar and Sumakhos said the same thing.[B] The Gemara specifies: Rabbi Shimon ben Elazar; that which we stated above. Sumakhos; as it was taught in a *baraita*: Sumakhos says: A *sukka* that he roofed with roofing made from spun thread[H] is disqualified because spun thread can become ritually impure from leprosy.

כְּמַאן – כִּי הַאי תַּנָּא, דִּתְנַן: שְׁתִי וָעֵרֶב מִטַּמֵּא בִּנְגָעִים מִיָּד, דִּבְרֵי רַבִּי מֵאִיר. וְרַבִּי יְהוּדָה אוֹמֵר: הַשְּׁתִי מִשֶּׁיִּשָּׁלֶה, וְהָעֵרֶב מִיָּד, וְהָאוּנִין שֶׁל פִּשְׁתָּן מִשֶּׁיִּתְלַבְּנוּ.

In accordance with whose opinion is Sumakhos' statement? It is in accordance with the opinion of this *tanna*, as we learned in a mishna: Warp and woof can become ritually impure from leprosy[H] immediately after they are spun; this is the statement of Rabbi Meir. Rabbi Yehuda says: The warp can become ritually impure only after it is removed from the cauldron in which it is boiled, and it is only the woof that can become ritually impure immediately. However, the bundles of unprocessed flax can become ritually impure after they are bleached in the oven and their processing is at least half-completed. Sumakhos, the student of Rabbi Meir, adheres to his position.

HALAKHA

The garment of a blind person – כְּסוּת סוּמָא: A blind man is obligated by Torah law in the mitzva of ritual fringes. This ruling is based on the *baraita*, which was apparently accepted throughout the Talmud (Rambam *Sefer Ahava, Hilkhot Tzitzit* 3:7; *Shulḥan Arukh, Oraḥ Ḥayyim* 17:1).

***Sukka* that he roofed with spun thread – סִיכְּכָהּ בִּטְווּי:** Spun flax may not be used for the roofing of a *sukka* because it can become ritually impure. The same is true with regard to half-processed flax because it no longer looks like something that grows in the ground (Rambam) and is suitable for stuffing for a pillow. Therefore, it can become ritually impure (Ra'avad) and is disqualified for use in the roofing of a *sukka* (Rambam *Sefer Zemanim, Hilkhot Sukka* 5:4; *Shulḥan Arukh, Oraḥ Ḥayyim* 629:4).

Warp and woof can become ritually impure from leprosy – שְׁתִי וָעֵרֶב מִטַּמֵּא בִּנְגָעִים: Immediately after being spun, the warp and woof threads from either wool or linen can become ritually impure from leprosy, as per the unattributed mishna. How large must a skein of spun thread be for it to become impure with the ritual impurity of leprosy? There must be enough thread in the skein to weave a swatch of cloth that is at least three by three fingerbreadths in size, as per the opinions of several *tanna'im* (Rambam *Sefer Tahara, Hilkhot Tumat Tzara'at* 13:8).

BACKGROUND

Do you say, etc. – אַתָּה אוֹמֵר וכו׳: This didactic method of clarifying issues is commonly found in the halakhic midrash. It involves one of the Sages challenging his own statements and answering his own questions. In this way, the issues under discussion as well as the connection between the verses and the *halakha* are effectively clarified.

They said the same thing – אָמְרוּ דָּבָר אֶחָד: This phrase refers to the consolidation of several opinions into a single view, which the Talmud calls a *shita*, a halakhic position. There is an ancient, controversial, and not universally accepted tradition that asserts: The *halakha* is not established in accordance with a *shita*. According to that tradition, when several opinions are consolidated into a *shita*, the purpose is to highlight those Sages whose statements were not accepted. As mentioned above, the validity of that principle is not universally accepted and many commentaries partially or completely dispute it.

BACKGROUND

Flax – **פִּשְׁתָּן**: Cultivated flax, *Linum usitatissimum*, is an annual plant that grows erect to a height of 40–120 cm. Its flowers are blue or white. Its stiff stalks contain flax fibers, and oil is extracted from its seeds.

After the plant is cut, the stalks are soaked in water, called *mei mishra* in the language of the Sages, for several days. Various bacteria cause the materials that attach the fibers to the stalks to decompose. Afterward the shell is beaten and opened and the fibers are extracted to be used in weaving linen, *bad* or *shesh* in the language of the Torah.

The flax plant has been cultivated since ancient times, especially in ancient Egypt.

Flower of the flax plant

HALAKHA

And of all substances that emerge from the tree, the only substance that becomes ritually impure with impurity transmitted by tents over a corpse, etc. – **כָּל הַיּוֹצֵא מִן הָעֵץ אֵינוֹ מְטַמֵּא טוּמְאַת אֹהָלִים וכו׳**: The only material made from plant fibers that is suspended over a dead body that becomes ritually impure is linen. Some commentaries say that this law applies specifically to a permanent tent (*Tosafot*; Ra'avad; Rambam *Sefer Tahara, Hilkhot Tumat Met* 5:12).

מתני׳ כָּל הַיּוֹצֵא מִן הָעֵץ – אֵין מַדְלִיקִין בּוֹ, אֶלָּא פִּשְׁתָּן. וְכָל הַיּוֹצֵא מִן הָעֵץ אֵינוֹ מְטַמֵּא טוּמְאַת אֹהָלִים אֶלָּא פִּשְׁתָּן.

MISHNA Of **all** substances **that emerge from the tree, one may light only with flax**[B] on Shabbat (*Tosafot*) because the other substances do not burn well. **And** of **all** substances **that emerge from the tree, the only** substance **that becomes ritually impure** with impurity transmitted by **tents** over a corpse **is flax.**[H] If there is a dead body inside a house or a tent that is made from any materials that originate from a tree, everything in the house becomes ritually impure. However, only in the case of flax does the tent itself become impure.

גמ׳ מְנָלַן דְּפִשְׁתָּן אִיקְרִי עֵץ? אָמַר מָר זוּטְרָא, דְּאָמַר קְרָא: ״וְהִיא הֶעֱלָתַם הַגָּגָה וַתִּטְמְנֵם בְּפִשְׁתֵּי הָעֵץ״.

GEMARA The mishna mentioned flax as a material that comes from a tree. The Gemara asks: **From where do we** derive that **flax is called a tree?** Based on appearance, it does not resemble a tree at all. **Mar Zutra said:** It is derived from that which the **verse said: "And she had taken them up to the roof and hidden them under the trees of flax"** (Joshua 2:6).

״וְהַיּוֹצֵא מִן הָעֵץ אֵינוֹ מְטַמֵּא טוּמְאַת אֹהָלִים אֶלָּא פִּשְׁתָּן״. מְנָלַן? אָמַר רַבִּי אֶלְעָזָר: גָּמַר ׳אֹהֶל׳ ׳אֹהֶל׳

And we also learned in the mishna that with regard to **any** substance **that emerges from the tree, the only** substance **that becomes ritually impure** with impurity transmitted by **tents** over a corpse **is flax.** The Gemara asks: **From where do we** derive this? **Rabbi Elazar said:** The *tanna* **learned** a verbal analogy [*gezera shava*] between the word **tent,** written in the context of ritual impurity, and the word **tent,**

Perek **II**
Daf **28** Amud **a**

HALAKHA

What is considered a tent – **מַהוּ הַקָּרוּי אֹהֶל**: With regard to the *halakhot* of ritual impurity imparted by a corpse, a tent is limited to a roof fashioned out of a garment, a sack, a wooden vessel, or leather, either from a kosher or non-kosher animal. Roofing made of bone or metal does not constitute a tent and does not become ritually impure when it extends over a corpse (Rambam *Sefer Tahara, Hilkhot Tumat Met* 5:12).

NOTES

Twisted and the threads were folded – **שְׁזוּרִין וְחוּטָן כָּפוּל**: The key discussion of this issue appears elsewhere in the Talmud. There, the Sages derive that everywhere the term *shesh* is employed in the Torah, it is referring to a linen cloth fashioned from a special thread composed of six threads spun into one. This is based on various derivations, including a verbal analogy and the juxtaposition of verses.

מִמִּשְׁכָּן; כְּתִיב הָכָא: ״זֹאת הַתּוֹרָה אָדָם כִּי יָמוּת בְּאֹהֶל״ וּכְתִיב הָתָם: ״וַיִּפְרוֹשׂ אֶת הָאֹהֶל עַל הַמִּשְׁכָּן״. מָה לְהַלָּן – שֶׁל פִּשְׁתָּן קָרוּי אֹהֶל, אַף כָּאן – שֶׁל פִּשְׁתָּן קָרוּי אֹהֶל. אִי מָה לְהַלָּן – שְׁזוּרִין וְחוּטָן כָּפוּל שִׁשָּׁה, אַף כָּאן שְׁזוּרִין וְחוּטָן כָּפוּל שִׁשָּׁה? תַּלְמוּד לוֹמַר: ׳אֹהֶל׳, ׳אֹהֶל׳ רִיבָּה. אִי אֹהֶל אֹהֶל רִיבָּה, אֲפִילּוּ כׇּל מִילֵּי נָמֵי! אִם כֵּן, גְּזֵירָה שָׁוָה מַאי אַהֲנִי לֵיהּ?

written in the context of the **Tabernacle. It is written here,** in the discussion of the laws of ritual impurity: **"This is the law: When a man dies in a tent,** every one that comes into the tent, and everything that is in the tent, shall be impure seven days" (Numbers 19:14), **and it is written there: "And he spread the tent over the Tabernacle,** and put the covering of the tent above upon it; as the Lord commanded Moses" (Exodus 40:19). **Just as below,** with regard to the Tabernacle, the tent was made **of linen** and **is considered a tent, so too, here,** with regard to the *halakhot* of ritual impurity imparted by a corpse, only a tent made **of linen is considered a tent.**[H] The Gemara asks: **If** so, derive the following from that same verbal analogy: **Just as below** the linen threads in the Tabernacle were specifically threads that were **twisted** and **the threads were folded**[N] **six times, so too, here,** in all of the *halakhot* pertaining to a tent over a corpse, the threads must be **twisted and their threads folded six times. The verse states** the word **tent, tent** several times to **amplify** and include even a tent made of linen not identical to the Tabernacle. The Gemara asks: **If** the repetition of the word **tent, tent** several times **amplifies, even all things** should be included among those items that can receive ritual impurity as a tent. The Gemara answers: This amplification cannot be that far-reaching, as, **if so,** the **verbal analogy** of tent, tent, that teaches us to derive the tent over a corpse from the Tabernacle, **what purpose does it serve** if everything is included? Rather, certainly the amplification is not absolute. Through the combination of the verbal analogy and the amplification, it is derived that this *halakha* applies specifically to linen.

וְאֵימָא: מַה לְּהַלָּן קְרָשִׁים, אַף כָּאן קְרָשִׁים! אָמַר קְרָא: "וְעָשִׂיתָ קְרָשִׁים לַמִּשְׁכָּן", מִשְׁכָּן – קָרוּי מִשְׁכָּן, וְאֵין קְרָשִׁים קְרוּיִין מִשְׁכָּן. אֶלָּא מֵעַתָּה "וְעָשִׂיתָ מִכְסֶה לָאֹהֶל" הָכִי נַמִי, מִכְסֶה לָא אִיקְּרִי אֹהֶל! אֶלָּא הָא דְּבָעֵי רַבִּי אֶלְעָזָר: עוֹר בְּהֵמָה טְמֵאָה מַהוּ שֶׁיִּטַּמֵּא בְּאֹהֶל הַמֵּת? הַשְׁתָּא עוֹר בְּהֵמָה טְהוֹרָה לָא מִטַּמֵּא, עוֹר בְּהֵמָה טְמֵאָה מִיבַּעְיָא?! שָׁאנֵי הָתָם דַּהֲדַר אַהַדְרֵיהּ קְרָא, דִּכְתִיב: "וְנָשְׂאוּ אֶת יְרִיעֹת הַמִּשְׁכָּן וְאֶת אֹהֶל מוֹעֵד מִכְסֵהוּ וּמִכְסֵה הַתַּחַשׁ אֲשֶׁר עָלָיו" מַקִּישׁ עֶלְיוֹן לַתַּחְתּוֹן, מַה תַּחְתּוֹן קָרוּי אֹהֶל – אַף עֶלְיוֹן קָרוּי אֹהֶל.

And perhaps say: **Just as below,** in the Tabernacle, there were **beams** supporting the tent, **so too, here,** in the laws of ritual impurity, a tent made of **beams** should also be considered a tent. The Gemara responds that **the verse said: "And you shall make the beams for the Tabernacle** of acacia wood, standing up" (Exodus 26:15). From the language of the verse, it is derived that the **Tabernacle,** i.e., the curtains alone, is **called Tabernacle, and the beams are not called Tabernacle,** because they merely facilitate the Tabernacle. The Gemara rejects this: **But if that is so,** based on an analysis of the language of the verse, it says there: **"And you shall make a covering for the tent** of rams' skins dyed red and a covering of *teḥashim*[N] above" (Exodus 26:14), then in **that** case, **too,** say that **the covering is not considered a tent.** If so, **however,** what of **the dilemma raised by Rabbi Elazar:** With regard to **the hide of a non-kosher animal** over a corpse, **what** is the ruling? **Can it become ritually impure as a tent over a corpse?** If the covering of the Tabernacle is not considered a tent, **now, the hide of a kosher animal** that covered the Tabernacle **cannot become ritually impure.** If that is so, **is it necessary to mention that the hide of a non-kosher animal** cannot become ritually impure? The Gemara answers: The cases are not comparable because **it is different there,** in the case of the covering of animal hides, **because the verse subsequently restored** its status as a tent by uniting the tent and its covering, **as it is written: "They shall bear the curtains of the Tabernacle, and the Tent of Meeting, its covering, and the covering of *taḥash* that is upon it"** (Numbers 4:25). The verse **juxtaposes the upper to the lower** covering; **just as the lower** covering **is considered a tent, so too,** the **upper** covering **is considered a tent.**

גּוּפָא, בָּעֵי רַבִּי אֶלְעָזָר: עוֹר בְּהֵמָה טְמֵאָה, מַהוּ שֶׁיִּטַּמֵּא טוּמְאַת אֹהָלִין? מַאי קָמִיבַּעְיָא לֵיהּ? – אָמַר רַב אַדָּא בַּר אַהֲבָה: תַּחַשׁ שֶׁהָיָה בִּימֵי מֹשֶׁה קָמִיבַּעְיָא לֵיהּ, טָמֵא הָיָה אוֹ טָהוֹר הָיָה? אָמַר רַב יוֹסֵף: מַאי תִּיבְּעֵי לֵיהּ? תְּנֵינָא: לֹא הוּכְשְׁרוּ לִמְלֶאכֶת שָׁמַיִם אֶלָּא עוֹר בְּהֵמָה טְהוֹרָה בִּלְבַד!

Rabbi Elazar's dilemma was mentioned above, and now the Gemara discusses **the matter itself. Rabbi Elazar raised a dilemma:** With regard to **the hide of a non-kosher animal** over a corpse, **what** is the ruling? **Can it become ritually impure as a tent** over a corpse? The Gemara clarifies: **What is** the essence of **his dilemma? Rav Adda bar Ahava said: The *taḥash* that existed in the time of Moses is** at the crux of Rabbi Elazar's **dilemma. Was it non-kosher or was it kosher? Rav Yosef said: What is his dilemma?** Didn't **we learn** explicitly: **Only the hide of a kosher animal was deemed suitable for heavenly service?** Certainly, the *taḥash* was a kosher species.

מְתִיב רַבִּי אַבָּא, רַבִּי יְהוּדָה אוֹמֵר: שְׁנֵי מִכְסָאוֹת הָיוּ, אֶחָד שֶׁל עוֹרוֹת אֵילִים מְאָדָּמִים וְאֶחָד שֶׁל עוֹרוֹת תְּחָשִׁים. רַבִּי נְחֶמְיָה אוֹמֵר: מִכְסֶה אֶחָד הָיָה, וְדוֹמֶה כְּמִין תְּלָא אִילָן. וְהָא תְּלָא אִילָן טָמֵא הוּא! הָכִי קָאָמַר: כְּמִין תְּלָא אִילָן הוּא, שֶׁיֵּשׁ בּוֹ גְּוָונִין הַרְבֵּה, וְלֹא תְּלָא אִילָן, דְּאִילּוּ הָתָם – טָמֵא, וְהָכָא – טָהוֹר. אָמַר רַב יוֹסֵף: אִי הָכִי הַיְינוּ דְּמִתַּרְגְּמִינַן "סַסְגּוֹנָא" – שֶׁשָּׂשׂ בִּגְוָונִין הַרְבֵּה.

Rabbi Abba raised an objection. Rabbi Yehuda says: There were two coverings for the Tabernacle, **one** made **of the reddened hides of rams and one of the hides of *teḥashim*. Rabbi Neḥemya says: There was** only **one covering** for the Tabernacle, half of which was made of rams' hides and half from the hides of *teḥashim*. **And** *teḥashim* **were similar to the** species of undomesticated animals called ***tela ilan***.[B] The Gemara asks: **But isn't** a ***tela ilan*** a non-**kosher** creature? The Gemara emends this statement: **This is what** Rabbi Neḥemya intended **to say:** It was **like a *tela ilan* in that it was multicolored;** however, it was **not** an actual ***tela ilan*. There,** the *tela ilan* is **non-kosher, and here,** the covering of the tent was made from **kosher** animals. **Rav Yosef said: If so, that is** the reason **that we translate** the word *taḥash* as ***sasgona***,[L] which means **that it rejoices** [*sas*] in many **colors** [*gevanim*].

רָבָא אָמַר: עוֹר בְּהֵמָה טְמֵאָה דְּמִטַּמֵּא בְּאֹהֶל הַמֵּת מֵהָכָא, דְּתַנְיָא: 'עוֹר' 'אוֹ בְעוֹר' – רִיבָּה עוֹר בְּהֵמָה טְמֵאָה, וְשֶׁלְּקָה בְּיַד כֹּהֵן. קָצַץ מִכּוּלָּן וְעָשָׂה אַחַת מֵהֶן מִנַּיִן? תַּלְמוּד לוֹמַר: 'אוֹ בְּכָל מְלֶאכֶת עוֹר'. וְאִיכָּא לְמִיפְרַךְ: מַה לִּנְגָעִים – שֶׁכֵּן שְׁתִי וָעֵרֶב טָמֵא בָּהֶן!

Rava said that the proof that **the hide of a non-kosher animal becomes ritually impure in a tent over a corpse** is derived **from here, as it was taught** in a *baraita* that it is stated in the *halakhot* of ritual impurity of leprosy that the leprosy could be: "Either in the warp, or in the woof, whether they be of linen, or of wool; or in a hide, or in any thing made of hide" (Leviticus 13:48). The verse could have simply stated: **Or hide,** and it said instead: **Or in a hide.** The Sages said: These words, or in a hide, **amplify** to include **the hide of a non-kosher animal** as well as hide **that was afflicted in the hands of a priest,**[H] i.e., before the owner showed it to the priest there was no leprosy but it became leprous while in the hands of the priest, that they too become ritually impure. **If one cut** pieces from each of these types **and made of them a single** cloth,[H] **from where** is it derived that it can become ritually impure? **The verse states** from the broader amplification: **Or in anything made of hide.** The Gemara remarks: **There is** room **to refute** this parallel, rendering it impossible to derive the laws of ritual impurity imparted by a corpse from the laws of leprosy. **What** is the comparison **to leprosy** with regard to which the Torah is stringent, as even **the warp and woof** that have not been woven into a garment **can become ritually impure from it,** which is not the case in impurity imparted by a corpse?

NOTES

The hides of *teḥashim* – עוֹרוֹת תְּחָשִׁים: In the Jerusalem Talmud, the Sages disputed whether or not the *taḥash* was a kosher or a non-kosher animal. The resolution to Rabbi Elazar's dilemma here depends on the resolution of that tannaitic dispute.

BACKGROUND

***Tela ilan* – תְּלָא אִילָן:** There are divergent opinions as to the identity of this creature. According to the *ge'onim*, the *tela ilan* belongs to the *Genetta* species, and it is possibly the *Genetta terrasanctae*, unique to Eretz Yisrael. The *tela* is approximately the size of a cat, with yellow or light-orange skin and black stripes. This creature is a quick predator that also climbs trees. The ancient Egyptians domesticated them and used them to hunt mice.

Spotted genet

LANGUAGE

***Sasgona* – סַסְגּוֹנָא:** It is assumed that the origin of this word, which is the Aramaic translation of the biblical *taḥash*, is from the Persian word gōn, meaning color. The word *sasgona* is conceivably a form of the word shast-gon, meaning possessing sixty colors, or in other words, multicolored.

HALAKHA

That was afflicted in the hands of a priest – וְשֶׁלְּקָה בְּיַד כֹּהֵן: The Torah teaches that a garment with a leprous-like growth is brought before a priest. Upon inspection, the priest could quarantine it. However, if clear signs of ritual impurity appear on the garment before he quarantines it, he confirms the leprosy immediately. The garment need not have been leprous before it was brought to the priest (Rambam *Sefer Tahara, Hilkhot Tumat Tzara'at* 6:7).

One cut and made of them a single cloth – קָצַץ מִכּוּלָּן וְעָשָׂה אַחַת מֵהֶן: If one takes swatches of various materials, none of which is three by three fingerbreadths, and sews them together, the resulting fabric can become ritually impure because a sewn garment has the same legal status as a woven garment (Rambam *Sefer Tahara, Hilkhot Tumat Tzara'at* 12:12).

אֶלָּא: גָּמַר מִשְּׁרָצִים, דְּתַנְיָא: 'עוֹר' אֵין לִי אֶלָּא עוֹר בְּהֵמָה טְהוֹרָה, עוֹר בְּהֵמָה טְמֵאָה מִנַּיִן – תַּלְמוּד לוֹמַר: 'אוֹ עוֹר'. וְאִיכָּא לְמִיפְרַךְ: מָה לִשְׁרָצִים – שֶׁכֵּן מְטַמְּאִין בְּכַעֲדָשָׁה – נְגָעִים יוֹכִיחוּ. וְחָזַר הַדִּין, לֹא רְאִי זֶה כִּרְאִי זֶה, וְלֹא רְאִי זֶה כִּרְאִי זֶה, הַצַּד הַשָּׁוֶה שֶׁבָּהֶן – שֶׁעוֹר טָמֵא בָּהֶן, וְעָשָׂה עוֹר בְּהֵמָה טְמֵאָה כְּעוֹר בְּהֵמָה טְהוֹרָה, אַף אֲנִי אָבִיא אֹהֶל הַמֵּת, שֶׁעוֹר טָמֵא בּוֹ, וְנַעֲשָׂה בּוֹ עוֹר בְּהֵמָה טְמֵאָה כְּעוֹר בְּהֵמָה טְהוֹרָה.

Rather, one could say that **he derived** it **from** the laws of the ritual impurity of **creeping animals,** as it is stated with regard to them: "And upon whatsoever any of them, when they are dead, does fall, it shall be impure; whether it be any vessel of wood, or garment, or hide, or sack, whatsoever vessel it be, with which any work is done" (Leviticus 11:32). **As it was taught** in a *baraita*: From the use of the word **hide, I have** derived **nothing other** than the fact that **the hide of a kosher animal** becomes ritually impure from contact with a creeping animal; however, **from where** is it derived that **the hide of a non-kosher animal** can become ritually impure? This is derived from the amplification, as **the verse states: Or hide.** Since, with regard to the ritual impurity of creeping animals the laws of the hides of kosher and non-kosher animals are identical, it is derived that this is also true with regard to the *halakhot* of ritual impurity imparted by a corpse. Once again, the Gemara says: **There is** room **to refute** this derivation and say: **What** is the comparison **to creeping animals,** as their legal status is stringent **because** they **become ritually impure** even if they are as small **as a lentil-bulk,** which is not true in the case of a corpse? In order for a corpse to transmit ritual impurity, it must be larger, an olive-bulk. Therefore, the Gemara says: If so, the case of **leprosy can prove** that the fact that creeping animals that are a lentil-bulk transmit impurity is not a factor in whether or not a non-kosher animal hide can become ritually impure. Leprosy that is a lentil-bulk does not transmit impurity and, nevertheless, the hide of a non-kosher animal becomes ritually impure from it. **And the derivation has reverted** to its starting point. **The aspect of this** case **is not like the aspect of that** case **and the aspect of that** case **is not like the aspect of this** case, as each case has its own unique stringencies. However, **their common denominator is that hide,** in general, **is ritually impure in** both cases, **and** the Torah **rendered the hide of a non-kosher animal equal** to **the hide of a kosher animal** in that it becomes ritually impure. **I will also bring** the additional *halakha* of a **tent over a corpse** made of the **hide of a non-kosher animal, and in** that case as well, **the hide of a non-kosher animal will be rendered equal to the hide of a kosher animal.**

אֲמַר לֵיהּ רָבָא מִבַּרְנִישׁ לְרַב אַשִׁי: אִיכָּא לְמִיפְרַךְ, מָה לְהַצַּד הַשָּׁוֶה שֶׁבָּהֶן – שֶׁכֵּן טְמֵאִין בִּפְחוֹת מִכַּזַּיִת, תֹּאמַר בְּמֵת שֶׁאֵינוֹ מְטַמֵּא אֶלָּא בְּכַזַּיִת!

Rava from Barnish said to Rav Ashi: There is still room **to refute** this statement and say: **What** is the comparison to leprosy and creeping animals? Their **common denominator is that they** both **transmit ritual impurity when smaller than an olive-bulk.** Can **you say** the same **in the case of a corpse, which only transmits ritual impurity when** it is at least **an olive-bulk?** Therefore, despite the differences between them, these two *halakhot* are both more stringent than the laws of ritual impurity imparted by a corpse, and the status of a non-kosher animal hide cannot be derived from them.

אֶלָּא אָמַר רָבָא מִבַּרְנִישׁ:

Rather, Rava from Barnish said it can be derived in the following manner:

Perek **II**
Daf **28** Amud **b**

אָתְיָא בְּקַל וָחוֹמֶר מִנּוֹצָה שֶׁל עִזִּים שֶׁאֵין מִטַּמֵּא בִּנְגָעִים – מִטַּמֵּא בְּאֹהֶל הַמֵּת, עוֹר בְּהֵמָה טְמֵאָה שֶׁמִּטַּמְּאָה בִּנְגָעִים – אֵינוֹ דִּין שֶׁמִּטַּמְּאָה בְּאֹהֶל הַמֵּת.

It is derived through an *a fortiori* inference from goats' hair. Although goats' hair **does not become ritually impure from leprosy,** it does **become ritually impure as a tent over a corpse;** with regard to **the hide of a non-kosher animal that becomes ritually impure from leprosy, is it not the case that it becomes ritually impure as a tent over a corpse?**

וְאֶלָּא הָא דְּתָנֵי רַב יוֹסֵף: לֹא הוּכְשְׁרוּ בִּמְלֶאכֶת שָׁמַיִם אֶלָּא עוֹר בְּהֵמָה טְהוֹרָה בִּלְבַד, לְמַאי הִלְכְתָא? לִתְפִילִּין. תְּפִילִּין?! בְּהֶדְיָא כְּתִיב בְּהוּ: ״לְמַעַן תִּהְיֶה תּוֹרַת ה׳ בְּפִיךָ״ – מִן הַמּוּתָּר בְּפִיךָ.

Since the conclusion was that the hide of even a non-kosher animal can become ritually impure as a tent over a corpse, it is not necessary to assume that the covering of the Tabernacle was made specifically from the hide of a kosher animal. **And,** if so, **that which Rav Yosef taught: Only the hide of a kosher animal was suitable for heavenly service, for what *halakha*** is that relevant,[N] as it is clearly not relevant to the Tabernacle? The Gemara replies: This *halakha* was stated with regard **to phylacteries,**[BH] which may be prepared only from the hide of a kosher animal. The Gemara asks: **Phylacteries?** Why did Rav Yosef need to state that *halakha*? It is **written explicitly**[N] **with regard to them:** "And it shall be for a sign unto you upon your hand, and for a memorial between your eyes, **that the law of the Lord may be in your mouth**" (Exodus 13:9). The Sages derived from there that the phylacteries must be prepared **from that which is permitted** to be eaten **in your mouth.**

אֶלָּא לְעוֹרָן. וְהָאָמַר אַבָּיֵי: שִׁי״ן שֶׁל תְּפִילִּין הֲלָכָה לְמֹשֶׁה מִסִּינַי!

Rather, the Gemara explains that this *halakha* of Rav Yosef was said only with regard **to the leather**[H] of the boxes that house the phylacteries, which must be crafted from the hide of a kosher animal. It was not referring to the parchment on which the portions of the Torah inserted into the phylacteries are written. The Gemara asks: **Didn't Abaye say:** The obligation to make a letter ***shin*** protruding **on the phylacteries**[H] of one's head is a ***halakha*** transmitted **to Moses from Sinai?** Since Torah law addresses the boxes of the phylacteries, presumably their legal status is parallel to that of the parchment and the prohibition against preparing them from the hide of a non-kosher animal is by Torah law as well.

אֶלָּא לְכוֹרְכָן בִּשְׂעָרָן וּלְתוֹפְרָן בְּגִידָן. הָא נַמִי הֲלָכָה לְמֹשֶׁה מִסִּינַי הוּא, דְּתַנְיָא: תְּפִילִּין מְרוּבָּעוֹת הֲלָכָה לְמֹשֶׁה מִסִּינַי, נִכְרָכוֹת בִּשְׂעָרָן וְנִתְפָּרוֹת בְּגִידָן.

Rather, the Gemara explains that Rav Yosef's *halakha* comes to teach that one must **tie** the parchments upon which the portions of the Torah are written in the phylacteries **with** a kosher animal's **hair, as well as sew** the phylacteries **with** a kosher animal's **sinews.** The Gemara asks: The source of **these** *halakhot* is **also** a ***halakha*** transmitted **to Moses from Sinai, as it was taught** in a *baraita*: The requirement that **phylacteries** must be **square**[H] is a *halakha* transmitted **to Moses from Sinai,** as is the requirement that they must be **tied with their hair**[H] **and sewn with their sinews.**[H]

אֶלָּא לִרְצוּעוֹת. וְהָאָמַר רַבִּי יִצְחָק: רְצוּעוֹת שְׁחוֹרוֹת הֲלָכָה לְמֹשֶׁה מִסִּינַי. נְהִי דִּגְמִירִי שְׁחוֹרוֹת – טְהוֹרוֹת מִי גְּמִירִי?

Rather, the Gemara says that Rav Yosef came to teach with regard **to** the *halakha* of **the straps** of the phylacteries. The Gemara asks: **Didn't Rabbi Yitzḥak say:** The **straps** of the phylacteries must be **black**[H] is a *halakha* transmitted **to Moses from Sinai?** The Gemara responds: **Although we learned** this *halakha*, which states that the straps must be **black, did we** also **learn** that they must be from **kosher** animals? Rav Yosef was certainly referring to straps when he said that all heavenly service must be performed with the hides of kosher animals.

NOTES

For what *halakha* is that relevant – לְמַאי הִלְכְתָא: Some commentaries explain this question as follows: Since Rava of Barnish states that the hide of a non-kosher animal becomes ritually impure as a tent over a corpse, it is then possible to draw an analogy between the case of a tent over a corpse and the laws of the Tabernacle, which was covered with the hide of a non-kosher animal, i.e., the *taḥash*. Consequently, it is possible to ask: For what *halakha* is Rav Yosef's statement relevant? (Rav Hai Gaon).

Phylacteries is written explicitly – תְּפִילִּין בְּהֶדְיָא כְּתִיב: The *Tosafot* asked: What is so surprising about this? Rav Yosef is certainly permitted to repeat a principle that was derived in the *baraita* with regard to phylacteries. Some explain that Rav Yosef meant to say that the laws of the *taḥash* are the source from which the fact that only kosher animals were permitted was derived. On that basis, the Gemara asked with regard to phylacteries: Wasn't this *halakha* derived directly from an explicit verse in the Torah and not from the Tabernacle?

BACKGROUND

Phylacteries – תְּפִילִּין: The boxes housing the phylacteries are sewn using the sinews of animals. The parchments with the Torah portions that are rolled up and inserted into the phylacteries of both the head and the arm are tied using the hair of a kosher animal.

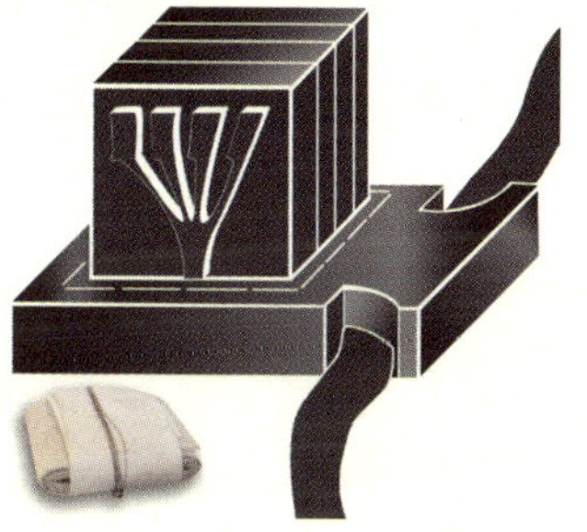

Phylacteries for the head and parchment on which a Torah portion is written, from inside the phylacteries

HALAKHA

With regard to phylacteries – לִתְפִילִּין: The Torah portions of the phylacteries, a Torah scroll, and other sacred writings that contain the names of God may be written only on parchment made from the hides of kosher animals. However, one is permitted to use the hides of kosher animals that were not slaughtered properly or the hides of animals with a life expectancy of less than a year, as per the Gemara (Rambam *Sefer Ahava, Hilkhot Tefillin UMezuza VeSefer Torah* 1:10, 10:1; *Shulḥan Arukh, Oraḥ Ḥayyim* 32:12 and *Yoreh De'a* 271:1).

With regard to their leather – לְעוֹרָן: The leather of the boxes of the phylacteries may be made only from the hides of kosher animals. However, here too, one is permitted to use the hides of kosher animals that were not slaughtered properly or the hides of animals with a life expectancy of less than a year (Rambam *Sefer Ahava, Hilkhot Tefillin UMezuza VeSefer Torah* 3:15; *Shulḥan Arukh, Oraḥ Ḥayyim* 32:37).

The *shin* on the phylacteries – שִׁי״ן שֶׁל תְּפִילִּין: It is a *halakha* transmitted to Moses from Sinai that the box of the phylacteries of the head must have an embossed letter *shin* on either side. The *shin* on the right side of the box has three heads, like the standard letter *shin*, while the one on the left side has four heads (Rambam *Sefer Ahava, Hilkhot Tefillin UMezuza VeSefer Torah* 3:1; *Shulḥan Arukh, Oraḥ Ḥayyim* 32:42).

Phylacteries must be square – תְּפִילִּין מְרוּבָּעוֹת: The boxes of the phylacteries must be a perfect square, whose sides are of equal length and width and form a right angle. The base of the phylacteries must also be square. Some say that the height of the box need not be equal to the length and width of the box (*Beit Yosef*; Rema). However, others insist that the height of the box must also equal its length and its width (Rambam *Sefer Ahava, Hilkhot Tefillin UMezuza VeSefer Torah* 3:1–4; *Shulḥan Arukh, Oraḥ Ḥayyim* 32:39).

Tied with their hair – נִכְרָכוֹת בִּשְׂעָרָן: Each Torah portion placed in the phylacteries is rolled in a small piece of parchment and tied with the hair of a kosher animal. It is customary to tie the Torah portion itself and then roll it in a piece of parchment and tie it again. It is also customary to use the hair of a calf. If one does not have calf's hair, one may tie it with the hair of a cow or an ox. The hair must first be washed. The ends of the hair must be visible outside the box, customarily, in a specific place (*Be'er Hetev*; Rambam *Sefer Ahava, Hilkhot Tefillin UMezuza VeSefer Torah* 3:1; *Shulḥan Arukh, Oraḥ Ḥayyim* 32:44).

Sewn with their sinews – וְנִתְפָּרוֹת בְּגִידָן: The boxes of the phylacteries are sewn shut using the sinews of a kosher domesticated or non-domesticated animal, even those of kosher animals that were not slaughtered properly or with a life expectancy of less than a year. *Ab initio* it is preferable to use the sinews of an ox (Rambam *Sefer Ahava, Hilkhot Tefillin UMezuza VeSefer Torah* 3:9; *Shulḥan Arukh, Oraḥ Ḥayyim* 32:49).

Straps of the phylacteries must be black – רְצוּעוֹת שְׁחוֹרוֹת: The leather straps of the phylacteries are made from the hides of kosher animals, as per the statement of Rav Yosef. It is a *halakha* transmitted to Moses from Sinai that the straps must be colored black on the outside (Rambam *Sefer Ahava, Hilkhot Tefillin UMezuza VeSefer Torah* 3:14–15; *Shulḥan Arukh, Oraḥ Ḥayyim* 33:3).

מַאי הֲוֵי עֲלָהּ דְּתַחַשׁ שֶׁהָיָה בִּימֵי מֹשֶׁה? אָמַר רַבִּי אִלְעָא אָמַר רַבִּי שִׁמְעוֹן בֶּן לָקִישׁ, אוֹמֵר הָיָה רַבִּי מֵאִיר: תַּחַשׁ שֶׁהָיָה בִּימֵי מֹשֶׁה בְּרִיָּה בִּפְנֵי עַצְמָהּ הָיָה, וְלֹא הִכְרִיעוּ בָּהּ חֲכָמִים אִם מִין חַיָּה הוּא אִם מִין בְּהֵמָה הוּא, וְקֶרֶן אַחַת הָיְתָה לוֹ בְּמִצְחוֹ, וּלְפִי שָׁעָה נִזְדַּמֵּן לוֹ לְמֹשֶׁה, וְעָשָׂה מִמֶּנּוּ מִשְׁכָּן וְנִגְנַז.

The Gemara asks: **What is** the halakhic conclusion reached **about** this matter of the ***taḥash***[B] **that existed in the days of Moses? Rabbi Ela said** that **Rabbi Shimon ben Lakish said** that **Rabbi Meir used to say:** The ***taḥash*** **that existed in the days of Moses was a creature unto itself, and the Sages did not determine whether it was a type of undomesticated animal or a type of domesticated animal. And it had a single horn on its forehead, and** this *taḥash* **happened** to come **to Moses for the moment** while the Tabernacle was being built, **and he made** the covering for **the Tabernacle from it. And** from then on the *taḥash* **was suppressed** and is no longer found.

מִדְּקָאָמַר קֶרֶן אַחַת הָיְתָה לוֹ בְּמִצְחוֹ – שְׁמַע מִינַּהּ טָהוֹר הָיָה, דְּאָמַר רַב יְהוּדָה: שׁוֹר שֶׁהִקְרִיב אָדָם הָרִאשׁוֹן קֶרֶן אַחַת הָיְתָה לוֹ בְּמִצְחוֹ, שֶׁנֶּאֱמַר: ״וְתִיטַב לַה׳ מִשּׁוֹר פָּר מַקְרִן מַפְרִיס״. ׳מַקְרִן׳ תַּרְתֵּי מַשְׁמַע! אָמַר רַב נַחְמָן בַּר יִצְחָק: ׳מִקֶּרֶן׳ כְּתִיב. וְלִיפְשׁוֹט מִינֵּיהּ דְּמִין בְּהֵמָה הוּא! כֵּיוָן דְּאִיכָּא קֶרֶשׁ דְּמִין חַיָּה הוּא, וְלֵית לֵיהּ אֶלָּא חֲדָא קֶרֶן – אִיכָּא לְמֵימַר מִין חַיָּה הוּא.

The Gemara comments: **From** the fact **that it is said** that the *taḥash* **had a single horn on its forehead, conclude from this** that it was kosher, **as Rav Yehuda said** in a similar vein: The **ox that Adam, the first** man,[N] **sacrificed** as a thanks-offering for his life being spared, **had a single horn on its forehead, as it is stated: "And it shall please the Lord better than a horned** [***makrin***] **and hooved ox"** (Psalms 69:32). The word *makrin* means one with a horn. The Gemara asks: On the contrary, ***makrin*** **indicates** that it has **two** horns. **Rav Naḥman bar Yitzḥak said:** Despite the fact that it is vocalized in the plural, **it is written *mikeren*** without the letter *yod* to indicate that it had only a single horn. The Gemara asks: If so, **let us resolve from** the same *baraita* that just as it was derived from the ox of Adam, the first man, that an animal with one horn is kosher, derive that an animal with one horn **is a type of domesticated animal.** The Gemara answers: **Since there is** the ***keresh***[BH] **which is a type of undomesticated animal, and it has only a single horn, it** is also possible **to say** that the *taḥash* **is a type of undomesticated animal.** This dilemma was not resolved.

מתני׳ פְּתִילַת הַבֶּגֶד שֶׁקִּיפְּלָהּ וְלֹא הִבְהֲבָהּ, רַבִּי אֱלִיעֶזֶר אוֹמֵר: טְמֵאָה הִיא וְאֵין מַדְלִיקִין בָּהּ, רַבִּי עֲקִיבָא אוֹמֵר: טְהוֹרָה הִיא וּמַדְלִיקִין בָּהּ.

MISHNA

The wick of a garment, i.e., cloth made into a wick for a lamp, **that one folded it** into a size and shape suitable for a wick, **but did not** yet **singe it**[H] slightly in order to facilitate its lighting, **Rabbi Eliezer says:** This wick is **ritually impure.** With regard to the laws of ritual impurity, it can, like other garments, still become ritually impure **and one may not light with it** on Shabbat. **Rabbi Akiva says: It is ritually pure and one may** even **light with it** on Shabbat.

גמ׳ בִּשְׁלָמָא לְעִנְיַן טוּמְאָה – בְּהָא פְּלִיגִי, דְּרַבִּי אֱלִיעֶזֶר סָבַר: קִיפּוּל אֵינוֹ מוֹעִיל, וּבְמִילְּתֵיהּ קַמַּיְיתָא קָיְימָא. וְרַבִּי עֲקִיבָא סָבַר: קִיפּוּל מוֹעִיל וּבְטוּלֵי בָּטֵיל.

GEMARA

The Gemara asks: **Granted, with regard to ritual impurity,** the reasons for their disagreement are clear and **this is** their **dispute: Rabbi Eliezer holds** that **folding** alone **is ineffective** in altering the identity of the garment **and it retains its original status.** It can become ritually impure like any other garment. **Rabbi Akiva holds** that **folding is effective, and it negates** its garment status, and therefore, it can no longer become ritually impure.

BACKGROUND

***Taḥash* – תַּחַשׁ**: The identity of the *taḥash* is a matter of great controversy and was never resolved. Some authorities explain that the *taḥash* is a monodon or narwhal, a species of whale. Narwhals travel in small groups, especially in northern ocean waters. It can grow to 6 m in length. Its primary color is light yellow and it is spotted with numerous dark spots, the only cetacean with spots. A twisted tooth, up to 3 m long, grows out of one side of its mouth, to the extent that for many years it was thought to be the horn of the unicorn. It is possible that a group of these creatures approached the Red Sea and were thrown onto the shore or trapped there.

The narwhal's appearance closely parallels the descriptions here: It is spotted like the *tela ilan*; compare it to the depiction in the Gemara (28a, p. 129). It has a single horn on its forehead and the Sages were unable to determine its precise nature: domesticated or non-domesticated; kosher or non-kosher.

Narwhal

Prof. Yehuda Feliks, one of the foremost scholars in the field of nature in the Bible, suggests that the *taḥash* may have been a giraffe, which has many of the characteristics mentioned by Rabbi Meir: A multicolored hide, a horn-like protrusion on its forehead, and some of the signs that determine that an animal is kosher.

Giraffe

***Keresh* – קֶרֶשׁ**: Apparently, from the Greek word **κέρας**, *keras*, which means horn. Similarly, the Greek word **μονόκερως**, *monokeros*, refers to a one-horned animal. It may also be a reference to a wild ox, especially in the Septuagint. The identity of the *keresh* is unclear. Some say that the *keresh* is an imaginary animal, a unicorn, and some think that it refers to a single-horned rhinoceros.

HALAKHA

Since there is the *keresh* – דְּאִיכָּא קֶרֶשׁ: Although the *keresh* only has a single horn, it is considered a non-domesticated animal (Rambam *Sefer Kedusha, Hilkhot Ma'akhalot Asurot* 1:12; *Shulḥan Arukh, Yoreh De'a* 80:4).

The wick of a garment, that one folded it, but did not yet singe it – פְּתִילַת הַבֶּגֶד שֶׁקִּיפְּלָהּ וְלֹא הִבְהֲבָהּ: One is not required to singe the wick before lighting it. However, it is customary to light the wick and extinguish it immediately to splay it so that it will hold the flame well. The mishna is interpreted in accordance with the opinion of Rava, who explained that the dispute is whether or not one is required to singe the wick. The *halakha* is in accordance with the opinion of Rabbi Akiva, who says that one need not singe the wick (*Shulḥan Arukh, Oraḥ Ḥayyim* 264:9 and in the comment of Rema).

NOTES

The ox of Adam, the first man – שׁוֹרוֹ שֶׁל אָדָם הָרִאשׁוֹן: The ox that Adam sacrificed is explained metaphorically. The horn is a general symbol of strength and basic faith. This statement teaches that after his banishment from the Garden of Eden, Adam reestablished his world on the basis of one fundamental principle, symbolized by the single horn, namely, the belief in God (Rashba).

אֶלָּא לְעִנְיַן הַדְלָקָה בְּמַאי פְּלִיגִי? אָמַר רַבִּי אֶלְעָזָר אָמַר רַב אוֹשַׁעְיָא, וְכֵן אָמַר רַב אַדָּא בַּר אַהֲבָה: הָכָא בְּשָׁלֹשׁ עַל שָׁלֹשׁ מְצוּמְצָמוֹת עָסְקִינַן, וּבְיוֹם טוֹב שֶׁחָל לִהְיוֹת עֶרֶב שַׁבָּת עָסְקִינַן, דְּכוּלֵּי עָלְמָא אִית לְהוּ דְּרַבִּי יְהוּדָה, דְּאָמַר: מַסִּיקִין בְּכֵלִים וְאֵין מַסִּיקִין בְּשִׁבְרֵי כֵלִים, וּדְכוּלֵּי עָלְמָא אִית לְהוּ דְּעוּלָּא, דְּאָמַר עוּלָּא: הַמַּדְלִיק צָרִיךְ שֶׁיַּדְלִיק בְּרוֹב הַיּוֹצֵא. רַבִּי אֱלִיעֶזֶר סָבַר: קִיפּוּל אֵינוֹ מוֹעִיל, וְכֵיוָן דְּאַדְלִיק בֵּיהּ פּוּרְתָּא – הָוְיָא לֵיהּ שֶׁבֶר כְּלִי, וְכִי קָא מַדְלִיק – בְּשֶׁבֶר כְּלִי קָמַדְלִיק. וְרַבִּי עֲקִיבָא סָבַר: קִיפּוּל מוֹעִיל, וְאֵין תּוֹרַת כְּלִי עָלָיו, וְכִי קָמַדְלִיק – בְּעֵץ בְּעָלְמָא קָמַדְלִיק.

However, with regard to lighting on Shabbat **what is** at the crux of their **dispute? Rabbi Elazar said** that **Rav Oshaya said, and Rav Adda bar Ahava said likewise: Here we are dealing with** a cloth that is **precisely three by three fingerbreadths and we are dealing with a Festival that occurred on Shabbat eve. And everyone is of** the opinion that the *halakha* is in accordance with the opinion of **Rabbi Yehuda, who said that on a Festival one may** only **kindle** a fire **with** whole **vessels,** as it is permitted to carry them and they do not have set-aside [*muktze*] status; **however, one may not kindle** a fire **using broken vessels,** i.e., vessels that broke on the Festival. Since they broke on the Festival itself, they are classified as an entity that came into being [*nolad*][B] on the Festival, and the *halakha* prohibits moving them. **And,** similarly, **everyone is of** the opinion that the *halakha* is **in accordance with** the opinion of **Ulla,** as **Ulla said: One who lights** a lamp **must light most** of the wick **that protrudes**[H] from the lamp. Based on these assumptions, the dispute in the mishna can be understood as follows: **Rabbi Eliezer holds** that **folding** alone **is ineffective** in negating the wick's vessel status, **and once** one **lights** only **a small part of it,** it thereby **becomes a broken vessel,** as part of it burns and the remainder is less than three by three fingerbreadths. A smaller cloth is no longer considered significant. Since he is required to light most of the protruding wick and, as mentioned above, it is prohibited to light broken vessels, he may not light the folded garment. **And Rabbi Akiva held** that **folding is effective and,** immediately when he folded it, the garment **no longer has the status of a vessel.** It was not considered a vessel even before he lit it, **and when he lights** it, it is as if **he were lighting plain wood,** not a vessel that broke on the Festival.

אָמַר רַב יוֹסֵף, הַיְינוּ דְּתָנֵינָא: ״שָׁלֹשׁ עַל שָׁלֹשׁ מְצוּמְצָמוֹת״ וְלָא יָדַעְנָא לְמַאי הִלְכְתָא.

Rav Yosef said, that is what I learned: Three by three exactly. And I did not know to what *halakha* this was relevant. Rav Yosef received from his teachers that the *baraita* is referring to a case of three by three exactly, and he did not know why it was significant to establish the *baraita* in a case of exactly three by three and no more.

וּמִדְּקָא מְתָרֵץ רַב אַדָּא בַּר אַהֲבָה אַלִּיבָּא דְּרַבִּי יְהוּדָה – שְׁמַע מִינַּהּ כְּרַבִּי יְהוּדָה סְבִירָא לֵיהּ; וּמִי אָמַר רַב אַדָּא בַּר אַהֲבָה הָכִי? וְהָאָמַר רַב אַדָּא בַּר אַהֲבָה:

The Gemara adds incidentally: **And from the fact** that **Rav Adda bar Ahava interpreted**[N] this mishna **in accordance** with the opinion of **Rabbi Yehuda, conclude from this** that **he holds in accordance with** the opinion of **Rabbi Yehuda. Did Rav Adda bar Ahava** actually **say this? Didn't Rav Adda bar Ahava** himself **say:**

Perek **II**
Daf **29** Amud **a**

גּוֹי שֶׁחָקַק קַב בִּבְקַעַת, יִשְׂרָאֵל מַסִּיקָהּ בְּיוֹם טוֹב. וְאַמַּאי? נוֹלָד הוּא! לְדִבְרֵיהֶם דְּרַבִּי אֱלִיעֶזֶר וְרַבִּי עֲקִיבָא קָאָמַר לֵיהּ, וְלֵיהּ לָא סְבִירָא לֵיהּ.

When a gentile carved out a vessel the size of a *kav* from a **piece of wood** on a Festival and thereby rendered it a new vessel, **a Jew may burn** the vessel **on a Festival** *ab initio*. **And why** may he do so? This new vessel that was made from the wood **is** an object that **came into being [*nolad*]** on a Festival, and is set-aside [*muktze*]. Since Rav Adda bar Ahava permitted doing so, apparently he holds that the laws of set-aside do not apply on a Festival, contrary to the opinion of Rabbi Yehuda. The Gemara answers: Rav Adda bar Ahava **said this** statement **in** explanation of **the statements** of **Rabbi Eliezer and Rabbi Akiva** in the mishna; **however, he** himself **does not hold that way.** Although he explained the opinions in the mishna in accordance with the opinion of Rabbi Yehuda, he himself does not hold that that is the *halakha*.

HALAKHA

One who lights must light most of the wick that protrudes – הַמַּדְלִיק צָרִיךְ שֶׁיַּדְלִיק בְּרוֹב הַיּוֹצֵא: One must light most of the wick that protrudes from the oil lamp before Shabbat, while it is still day, as per the opinion of Ulla (Rambam *Sefer Zemanim, Hilkhot Shabbat* 5:5; *Shulḥan Arukh, Oraḥ Ḥayyim* 264: 8).

NOTES

From the fact that Rav Adda bar Ahava interpreted, etc. – וּמִדְּקָא מְתָרֵץ רַב אַדָּא וכו׳: The fact that a given mishna is interpreted in accordance with the opinion of one of the Sages does not always prove that the one who interpreted the mishna personally agrees with that opinion. A Sage often explains the statements of a mishna in a certain way, although he does not accept that opinion as *halakha*. However, in this case, since it was not a single opinion that was explained in this way, but the fundamental basis of the entire mishna, i.e., everyone is of the opinion that the *halakha* is in accordance with the opinion of Rabbi Yehuda, apparently that is Rav Adda's opinion as well.

BACKGROUND

Came into being [*nolad*] – נוֹלָד: In the context of the *halakhot* of Shabbat and Festivals, this describes an object that came into being or assumed its present form on Shabbat or a Festival, e.g., an egg that was laid or a utensil that was broken on Shabbat or a Festival. These objects are set aside from use and may not be moved or handled on Shabbat and Festivals.

רָבָא אָמַר: הַיְינוּ טַעְמָא דְּרַבִּי אֱלִיעֶזֶר – לְפִי שֶׁאֵין מַדְלִיקִין בִּפְתִילָה שֶׁאֵינָהּ מְחוּרֶכֶת, וְלֹא בִּסְמַרְטוּטִין שֶׁאֵינָן מְחוּרָכִין. אֶלָּא הָא דְּתָנֵי רַב יוֹסֵף: ״שָׁלֹשׁ עַל שָׁלֹשׁ מְצוּמְצָמוֹת״ לְמַאי הִלְכְתָא? לְעִנְיַן טוּמְאָה, דִּתְנַן: שָׁלֹשׁ עַל שָׁלֹשׁ שֶׁאָמְרוּ – חוּץ מִן הַמְּלָל, דִּבְרֵי רַבִּי שִׁמְעוֹן. וַחֲכָמִים אוֹמְרִים: שָׁלֹשׁ עַל שָׁלֹשׁ מְכוּוָּנוֹת.

Rava said, this is the reasoning behind **Rabbi Eliezer's** opinion with regard to lighting the wick: **Because** he holds **that one may neither light** on Shabbat **using a wick that is not** slightly **singed** and prepared for lighting **nor light with rags that were not singed** before Shabbat. If a person singes the wick slightly before lighting it, it will burn well. A wick that has not been singed does not burn well and will not show the appropriate deference to Shabbat. The Gemara asks: If so, **that which Rav Yosef taught: Three by three exactly,**[H] **to what *halakha*** is it relevant? According to Rava's explanation, the precise size of the garment used in making the wick is irrelevant. The Gemara responds: Rav Yosef's statement was **with regard to** another **matter,** the *halakhot* of **ritual impurity. As we learned** in a mishna in tractate *Kelim*: **Three by three** fingerbreadths **that they stated** as the smallest sized garment that can become ritually impure, **excludes the** portion used for the **hem,**[BN] i.e., those threads that emerge at the edge of the garment and are sewn into a hem; this is **the statement of Rabbi Shimon. And the Rabbis say: Three by three exactly,** even including the hem. That is the context of Rav Yosef's statement: Three by three exactly.

אָמַר רַב יְהוּדָה אָמַר רַב: מַסִּיקִין בְּכֵלִים וְאֵין מַסִּיקִין בְּשִׁבְרֵי כֵלִים, דִּבְרֵי רַבִּי יְהוּדָה, וְרַבִּי שִׁמְעוֹן מַתִּיר. מַסִּיקִין בִּתְמָרִין, אֲכָלָן – אֵין מַסִּיקִין בְּגַרְעִינֵיהֶן, דִּבְרֵי רַבִּי יְהוּדָה, וְרַבִּי שִׁמְעוֹן מַתִּיר. מַסִּיקִין בֶּאֱגוֹזִים, אֲכָלָן – אֵין מַסִּיקִין בִּקְלִיפּוֹתֵיהֶן, דִּבְרֵי רַבִּי יְהוּדָה, וְרַבִּי שִׁמְעוֹן מַתִּיר.

With regard to the statement cited above, **Rav Yehuda said** that **Rav said** that there is a dispute between the *tanna'im* on this issue: **One may** only **kindle** a fire **with** whole **vessels and one may not kindle** a fire **with broken vessels;**[H] this is **the statement of Rabbi Yehuda. And Rabbi Shimon permits** kindling a fire even with broken vessels. An additional *halakha*: **One may kindle** a fire **with** whole **dates**[H] on a Festival, and if **he ate them, he may not kindle** a fire **with their pits** as they are set-aside; this is **the statement of Rabbi Yehuda. And Rabbi Shimon permits** kindling a fire with the pits. Furthermore, **one may kindle** a fire **with** whole **nuts** on a Festival, and if **he ate them, he may not kindle** a fire **with their shells;** this is **the statement of Rabbi Yehuda. And Rabbi Shimon permits** doing so.

וּצְרִיכָא, דְּאִי אַשְׁמְעִינַן קַמַּיְיתָא – בְּהַהִיא קָאָמַר רַבִּי יְהוּדָה – מִשּׁוּם דְּמֵעִיקָּרָא כְּלִי וְהָשְׁתָּא שֶׁבֶר כְּלִי, וַהֲוָה לֵיהּ נוֹלָד – וְאָסוּר. אֲבָל תְּמָרִים, דְּמֵעִיקָּרָא גַּרְעִינִין וְהָשְׁתָּא גַּרְעִינִין – אֵימָא שַׁפִּיר דָּמֵי. וְאִי אַשְׁמְעִינַן גַּרְעִינִין – הֲוָה אָמִינָא: דְּמֵעִיקָּרָא מְכַסְּיָין, וְהָשְׁתָּא מִיגַלְּיָין. אֲבָל קְלִיפֵּי אֱגוֹזִין, דְּמֵעִיקָּרָא מִיגְלוּ וְהָשְׁתָּא מִיגְלוּ – אֵימָא שַׁפִּיר דָּמֵי, צְרִיכָא.

The Gemara comments: **And it was necessary** to cite all three of these cases because each teaches a novel idea. **As,** had Rav **taught us** only **the first** *halakha*, we would have thought that it is specifically **in that** case, with regard to burning broken vessels, that **Rabbi Yehuda said** that it is prohibited, **as initially** it was **a vessel and now** it is **a broken vessel, and therefore it is** considered an object that **came into being** [*nolad*] **and prohibited; however, dates, initially** there were **pits** in the dates **and now** they remain **pits, say** that one may **well** do so. **And had** Rav **taught us** only with regard to date **pits I would have said** that they are prohibited because **initially** they were **concealed** within the fruit **and now** they are **exposed,** it is a case of an object that came into being and prohibited. **However, nutshells, which initially** were **exposed and now** are **exposed,** as they were before, **say** that one may **well** do so. Therefore, it was necessary to teach all of these cases.

וְהָא דְּרַב – לָאו בְּפֵירוּשׁ אִיתְּמַר, אֶלָּא מִכְּלָלָא אִיתְּמַר. דְּרַב אֲכַל תַּמְרֵי וּשְׁדָא קַשְׁיָיתָא לְבוּכְיָא, אֲמַר לֵיהּ רַבִּי חִיָּיא: בַּר פַּחֲתֵי, כְּנֶגְדּוֹ בְּיוֹם טוֹב – אָסוּר. קִיבְּלָהּ מִינֵּיהּ אוֹ לֹא קִיבְּלָהּ מִינֵּיהּ?

And the Gemara adds: **This** *halakha* of **Rav was not stated explicitly; rather, it was stated by inference** based on conclusions drawn from Rav's actions and not from his explicit statements. There was an instance where **Rav ate dates** on a weekday and **threw** the **pits into the oven. Rabbi Ḥiyya said to him: Son of noblemen,** the **corresponding** action, throwing pits into an oven, **is prohibited on a Festival.** The Gemara asks: **Did** Rav **accept** this *halakha* **from him**[N] **or did he not accept** it **from him?**

HALAKHA

Three by three exactly – שָׁלֹשׁ עַל שָׁלֹשׁ מְכוּוָּנוֹת: According to the laws of ritual impurity, a garment can become ritually impure if it is a minimum of three by three fingerbreadths. This applies to both linen and wool and includes the hem, as per the opinion of the Rabbis (Rambam *Sefer Tahara, Hilkhot Kelim* 22:1).

One may only kindle a fire with whole vessels and one may not kindle a fire using broken vessels – מַסִּיקִין בְּכֵלִים וְאֵין מַסִּיקִין בְּשִׁבְרֵי כֵלִים: A vessel that broke on a Festival may not be used to feed a fire because it is considered to be something that came into being on a Festival; it is set-aside, and one may not move it. However, one may feed a fire with whole vessels or vessels that broke before the Festival, as per the opinion of Rabbi Yehuda (Rambam *Sefer Zemanim, Hilkhot Yom Tov* 2:12; *Shulḥan Arukh, Oraḥ Ḥayyim* 501:6).

One may kindle a fire with dates – מַסִּיקִין בִּתְמָרִין: One may burn the shells of almonds and walnuts and the pits of dates that he ate before a Festival (*Mishna Berura*). If he ate them on the Festival itself, he may not use their shells and pits to feed a fire. Similarly, because nuts are primarily for eating, not burning, one may only burn the nuts themselves on a Festival when still in their shells, if there is no other material to burn. Otherwise, doing so would be in violation of the prohibition against wanton destruction. This is in accordance with the opinion of Rabbi Yehuda (Rambam *Sefer Zemanim, Hilkhot Yom Tov* 2:12; *Shulḥan Arukh, Oraḥ Ḥayyim* 501:7).

BACKGROUND

The hem – הַמְּלָל: When the edge of the fabric, where the threads stick out, is hemmed, as shown here, the size of the garment decreases. The folded and hemmed portion of the fabric is not calculated in the area of a sewn garment. However, the Rabbis argue that the hem is calculated in the area of the fabric before it is sewn.

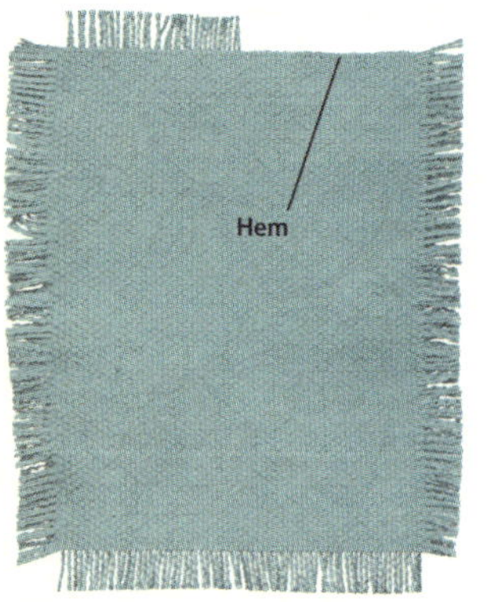

Piece of fabric and its hem

NOTES

Excludes the hem – חוּץ מִן הַמְּלָל: According to Rabbi Shimon, one must assess each object in terms of its practical use. Since this piece of cloth has a hem that will be folded when the garment is worn, the hem cannot be considered part of the garment. The Rabbis disagree. Since at present, the garment is the requisite, minimum size, that is sufficient to render it capable of becoming ritually impure.

Did he accept it from him – קִיבְּלָהּ מִינֵּיהּ: Since the fundamental assertion was that Rav did not explicitly prohibit the use of date pits on a Festival due to set-aside, the Gemara cites as proof, the action of Rav and that which his uncle and teacher, Rabbi Ḥiyya, said to him. Had that been the extent of it, together with the added information that Rav generally rules in accordance with the opinion of Rabbi Yehuda (see *Tosafot*), it would have been sufficient to determine Rav's position. However, Rav's opinion was only stated by inference, resulting in the dilemma: Did Rav accept Rabbi Ḥiyya's opinion or did he not? This question is compounded by a different incident involving Rav on a Festival, which seems contradictory. Although based on the explanation of the Gemara there is no contradiction, the conclusion is that neither is there any proof (see *Penei Yehoshua*).

תא שמע, דכי אתא רב לבבל אכל תמרי ושדא קשייתא לחיותא. מאי לאו בפרסייאתא ולא קיבלה! לא, בארמיאתא – הואיל וחזי אגב אימייהו.

Come and hear: **When Rav came** from Eretz Yisrael **to Babylonia, he ate dates** on a Festival **and threw their pits to the animals** so that they may eat them. **Wasn't it** a case involving **Persian** dates, which are quality dates whose fruit comes completely off the pits, leaving the pits with no trace of fruit? Ostensibly, they are completely set-aside as they are of no use at all to people. **And** the fact that Rav threw the pits to the animals indicates that **he did not accept** this *halakha* from Rabbi Ḥiyya, and he holds that there is no prohibition in that case. The Gemara replies: **No,** this is a case involving **Aramean** dates whose fruit does not come off completely, and remnants of the date remain attached to the pit. These pits, **since they are** still **fit** for use **due to their mother,** i.e., the fruit itself, one is permitted to carry them.[N]

אמר ליה רב שמואל בר בר חנה לרב יוסף: לרבי יהודה דאמר "מסיקין בכלים ואין מסיקין בשברי כלים" כיון דאדליק בהו פורתא – הוה ליה שברי כלים, וכי קא מהפך – באיסורא קא מהפך! דעבד כדרב מתנה, דאמר רב מתנה אמר רב: עצים שנשרו מן הדקל לתנור ביום טוב מרבה עצים מוכנין, ומסיקן.

Rav Shmuel bar bar Ḥana said to Rav Yosef: According to the opinion **of Rabbi Yehuda,** who said that **one may kindle** a fire **with** whole **vessels, and one may not kindle** a fire **with broken vessels,** how it is possible to use whole vessels? **Once they are ignited a bit, they become broken vessels, and when one turns** the wood **over** to accelerate their ignition, **he turns** them **over in a prohibited** manner,[H] as it is prohibited to light with broken vessels. The Gemara answers: This is a case **where he acted in accordance with** the statement of **Rav Mattana.** As **Rav Mattana said** that **Rav said: Branches that fell from a palm tree into an oven on a Festival,**[H] since these branches were attached to the tree at the onset of the Festival, they are set-aside and it is prohibited to move them. Nevertheless, he can remedy the situation if he **adds wood** that was **prepared** for burning prior to the Festival, until the majority of the wood in the oven is not set-aside, **and then kindles them.** Since the majority of the wood is permitted, he need not concern himself with the minority. One may do the same when burning vessels by adding wood that is not set-aside.

רב המנונא אמר: הכא בפחות משלשה על שלשה עסקינן, מקולי מטלניות שנו כאן.

Rav Hamnuna said a different explanation of the dispute in the mishna. In his opinion, **here we are dealing with** a garment that is **smaller than three by three** handbreadths, **and they taught here** *halakhot* established by the Sages **with regard to insignificant small cloths.**

ואזדא רבי אליעזר לטעמיה ורבי עקיבא לטעמיה, דתנן: פחות משלשה על שלשה שהתקינו לפקק בו את המרחץ, ולנער בו את הקדירה, ולקנח בו את הרחיים – בין מן המוכן ובין שאין מן המוכן – טמא, דברי רבי אליעזר. ורבי יהושע אומר: בין מן המוכן ובין שלא מן המוכן – טהור. רבי עקיבא אומר: מן המוכן – טמא ושלא מן המוכן – טהור. ואמר עולא, ואיתימא רבה בר בר חנה אמר רבי יוחנן, הכל מודים: זרקו באשפה – דברי הכל טהור,

And Rabbi Eliezer followed his line of **reasoning** expressed elsewhere, **and Rabbi Akiva** followed **his** line of **reasoning** expressed elsewhere. **As we learned** in a mishna in tractate *Kelim*: A cloth **smaller than three by three** handbreadths **that was utilized to plug the bath, and to pour** from a boiling **pot, and to wipe the millstone,**[N] **whether** this cloth was expressly **prepared** for that purpose or **whether it was not prepared,** it can become **ritually impure;** this is **the statement of Rabbi Eliezer. And Rabbi Yehoshua says: Whether** it was **prepared or whether** it was **not prepared,** it is **ritually pure,** i.e., it cannot become ritually impure. **Rabbi** Akiva distinguishes between the cases and **says:** If it was **prepared** it is **ritually impure,** and if it was **not prepared** it is **ritually pure. And Ulla said, and some say** that **Rabba bar bar Ḥana said** that **Rabbi Yoḥanan said: Everyone agrees** that a cloth this size, if **one threw it into the garbage dump, it is ritually pure.** His discarding of the cloth indicates that he no longer considers this cloth a garment and no longer considers it significant.

NOTES

Date – **תמר**: The date palm *Phoenix dactylifera* is cultivated for its edible sweet fruit. It is a medium-sized tree, 15–25 m tall, growing singly or forming a clump with several stems from a single root system. The leaves are 3–5 m long, and the full span of the crown ranges from 6–10 m. Dates were eaten fresh or dried, and were boiled into a thick, durable syrup called date honey and used as a sweetener. The honey in the biblical reference of "a land flowing with milk and honey" (Exodus 3:8, for example), is date honey.

Remnants of dates and pits found in Qumran

Millstone – **רחיים**: Millstones are stones used for grinding wheat and other grains.

Millstone

HALAKHA

Once they are ignited a bit…he turns them over in a prohibited manner – **כיון דאדליק בהו פורתא...באיסורא קא מהפך**: One who placed whole vessels into a fire on a Festival may not stoke the fire after they catch fire, unless he adds wood already designated to be burnt (*Shulḥan Arukh, Oraḥ Ḥayyim* 501:6 and the comment of the Rema).

Branches that fell from a palm tree into an oven on a Festival – **עצים שנשרו מן הדקל לתנור ביום טוב**: When palm branches fall from a tree into an oven on a Festival, one may add branches that were designated for burning prior to the Festival so that they obscure the palm branches (Rema). The palm branches are thereby nullified and he may burn the wood. That is permitted as long as he does not move the prohibited palm branches while adding the other branches (Rambam *Sefer Zemanim, Hilkhot Yom Tov* 2:11; *Shulḥan Arukh, Oraḥ Ḥayyim* 507:2).

הניחו בקופסא – דברי הכל טמא, לא נחלקו אלא שתלאו במגוד או שהניחו לאחורי הדלת. רבי אליעזר סבר: מדלא זרקו באשפה – דעתיה עילויה, ומאי קרי ליה ׳שלא מן המוכן׳ – דלגבי קופסא לאו מוכן הוא. ורבי יהושע סבר: מדלא הניחו בקופסא – בטולי בטליה, ומאי קרי ליה ׳מוכן׳ – דלגבי אשפה מוכן הוא. ורבי עקיבא, בתלאו במגוד – סבר כרבי אליעזר, בהניחו אחורי הדלת – סבר לה כרבי יהושע.

If one placed it in a box, everyone agrees that it can become ritually impure because his placing the cloth in a box indicates that he considers the cloth significant and is keeping it in order to use it. **They only disagreed** in a case **where one hung** the garment **on a dryer,**[H] i.e., a stake in the wall, **or where he placed it behind a door. Rabbi Eliezer held: From** the fact that **he did not throw it in the garbage** dump, **it is** certainly **on his mind** and he is planning to use it. **And what** is the reason that **he called it not prepared?** It is because, **relative to** a cloth placed in **a box, it is not** considered **prepared** for use. **And Rabbi Yehoshua held** that **since he did not place it in a box,** certainly **he has negated its** garment status. **And what** is the reason that **he called it prepared?** Because **relative** to one thrown in **the garbage,** this garment **is prepared** for use, although, in fact, the cloth has already been negated. **And Rabbi Akiva,** in the case **where he hung it on a dryer, held in accordance with** the opinion of **Rabbi Eliezer** that one has not yet negated it from use and it can therefore become ritually impure. In the case **where he placed it behind a door, Rabbi Akiva held in accordance with** the opinion of **Rabbi Yehoshua** that, in doing so, he negated its garment status, and it can no longer become ritually impure.

והדר ביה רבי עקיבא לגביה דרבי יהושע. ממאי? אמר רבא: מדקתני ׳פתילת הבגד׳, מאי איריא דתני ׳פתילת הבגד׳, ליתני ״פתילה של בגד״! מאי ׳פתילת הבגד׳ – דעדיין בגד הוא.

The Gemara comments: **And Rabbi Akiva retracted his** opinion in favor of the opinion of **Rabbi Yehoshua** and held in accordance with his opinion. And **from where** do we know this? **Rava said: From** the term that **we learned** in our mishna: **The wick** of a **garment** [*petilat habeged*]. **Why did it** specifically **teach: The wick** of a **garment? Teach** that *halakha* using the phrase: **A wick** made **from a garment. What is** the reason that the mishna taught: **A wick** of a **garment?** It is because **it remains a garment.** Nevertheless, Rabbi Akiva deemed it ritually pure, in accordance with the opinion of Rabbi Yehoshua.

מתני׳ לא יקוב אדם שפופרת של ביצה וימלאנה שמן ויתננה על פי הנר בשביל שתהא מנטפת, ואפילו היא של חרס, ורבי יהודה מתיר. אבל אם חברה היוצר מתחלה – מותר, מפני שהוא כלי אחד. לא ימלא אדם קערה של שמן ויתננה בצד הנר ויתן ראש הפתילה בתוכה בשביל שתהא שואבת, ורבי יהודה מתיר.

MISHNA The fundamental dispute in this mishna is with regard to the determination whether or not indirect acts of kindling and extinguishing fall within the parameters of the prohibition on Shabbat. The Rabbis said: **A person may not pierce** a hole in **an eggshell**[HN] **and fill it with oil, and place it over** the mouth of **a lamp**[B] **so that** the egg **will drip** additional oil into the lamp and thereby extend the time that it burns. **And** this is the ruling **even if it is** not an actual egg but an **earthenware** vessel. **And Rabbi Yehuda permits** doing so. **However, if the craftsman,** who crafts ceramic vessels, **attached** the egg to the lamp **from the outset, one is permitted** to fill it with oil **because it** constitutes **a single,** large **vessel.** The Rabbis decreed that **a person may not fill a bowl**[H] **with oil, and place it beside the lamp, and place the** unlit **head of the wick into** the bowl **so that it draws** additional oil from the bowl and thereby extend the time that the lamp burns. **And Rabbi Yehuda permits** doing so.

HALAKHA

One hung it on a dryer – שתלאו במגוד: The Rambam ruled that a cloth smaller than three by three handbreadths that was hung on a dryer or placed in a basket can still become ritually impure. Only if one throws it in the garbage can it no longer become ritually impure, as per the opinion of Rabbi Eliezer. The early commentaries on the Rambam were surprised that he did not rule in accordance with the opinion of Rabbi Yehoshua, since Rabbi Akiva agrees with his opinion (*Kesef Mishne*; Rambam *Sefer Tahara, Hilkhot Kelim* 22:22).

A person may not pierce an eggshell, etc. – לא יקוב אדם שפופרת של ביצה וכו׳: One may not place a pierced eggshell or any other vessel filled with oil above a lamp that is burning on Shabbat so that the oil will drip into the lamp. The reason is that one might take oil from it and thereby extinguish the light. If one attaches the additional vessel to the lamp with plaster or clay before Shabbat, it is permitted, as per the unattributed mishna (Rambam *Sefer Zemanim, Hilkhot Shabbat* 5:12; *Shulḥan Arukh, Oraḥ Ḥayyim* 265:1).

A person may not fill a bowl – לא ימלא אדם קערה: It is prohibited to fill a bowl with oil and place it next to a lamp so that the wick of the lamp will draw oil from the bowl (Rambam *Sefer Zemanim, Hilkhot Shabbat* 5:12; *Shulḥan Arukh, Oraḥ Ḥayyim* 265:2).

BACKGROUND

Lamp and a tube – נר ושפופרת:

Oil lamp with a receptacle attached to supply it with additional oil

NOTES

A person may not pierce an eggshell, etc. – לא יקוב אדם שפופרת של ביצה וכו׳: In the Babylonian Talmud, the rationale for this *halakha* is the concern lest one come to use the additional oil. However, in the Jerusalem Talmud, the Sages questioned this reason and offer a different one in its place. Only in the case of an oil lamp with a wick can one claim that the burning of each and every drop of oil began before Shabbat and is merely continuing on Shabbat. However, oil added from an eggshell or from an additional vessel will only reach the wick on Shabbat itself. It will only begin burning then, which is tantamount to having been lit on Shabbat.

גמ׳ וּצְרִיכָא, דְּאִי אַשְׁמְעִינַן שְׁפוֹפֶרֶת שֶׁל בֵּיצָה – בְּהָא קָאָמְרִי רַבָּנַן דְּכֵיוָן דְּלָא מְאִיסָא – אָתֵי לְאִסְתַּפּוֹקֵי מִינָּהּ, אֲבָל שֶׁל חֶרֶס דִּמְאִיסָא – אֵימָא מוֹדוּ לֵיהּ לְרַבִּי יְהוּדָה, וְאִי אַשְׁמְעִינַן שֶׁל חֶרֶס – בְּהָא קָאָמַר רַבִּי יְהוּדָה, אֲבָל בְּהַהִיא – אֵימָא מוֹדֵי לְהוּ לְרַבָּנַן, וְאִי אַשְׁמְעִינַן הָנָךְ תַּרְתֵּי – בְּהָנֵי קָאָמַר רַבִּי יְהוּדָה מִשּׁוּם דְּלָא מִיפְסַק. אֲבָל קְעָרָה דְּמִיפְסְקָא – אֵימָא מוֹדֵי לְהוּ לְרַבָּנַן, וְאִי אַשְׁמְעִינַן בְּהַהִיא – בְּהַהִיא קָאָמְרִי רַבָּנַן, אֲבָל בְּהָנֵי תַּרְתֵּי – אֵימָא מוֹדוּ לְרַבִּי יְהוּדָה, צְרִיכָא.

GEMARA The Gemara comments on the fact that the mishna cited three cases that all share the same rationale: **And** it was **necessary** to cite all of the aforementioned cases because it is impossible to derive one from the other. **As, had** the Gemara only **taught us** the prohibition of **an eggshell,** I would have said that, specifically **in that** case, **the Rabbis said** that it is prohibited to do so. **Since** the egg **is not** dirty and **disgusting,** there is room for concern that one might **come to take** oil **from it,** which would be tantamount to taking oil from a burning lamp on Shabbat, because it causes the flame to be extinguished faster. **However,** an **earthenware** tube **that is disgusting, say** that the Rabbis **agree with Rabbi Yehuda** that there is no room for concern, and even according to their opinion it would be permitted. **And,** conversely, **had** the Gemara only **taught us** the prohibition of an **earthenware** tube, I would have said that, specifically **in that** case, **Rabbi Yehuda says** that one is permitted to do so because it is disgusting, as explained above; **however, in that** case of the eggshell that is not disgusting, **say** that **he agrees with the Rabbis** that it is prohibited. **And had** the Gemara **taught us** only **those two** cases of the eggshell and the earthenware tube, I would have said that, specifically **in those** cases, **Rabbi Yehuda said** that it is permitted **because there is no separation** between the lamp and the second receptacle. **However, in the case of a bowl, which is separate, say** that **he agrees with the Rabbis** that it is prohibited. **And,** conversely, **had** the Gemara **only taught us in that** case of the added bowl, I would have said that only **in that** case did **the Rabbis say** it is prohibited because it is separate. **However, in these two** cases of the eggshell and the ceramic tube, **I would say** that the Rabbis **agree with Rabbi Yehuda** and permit doing so. Therefore, **it was necessary** for the mishna to specifically state the *halakha* in each of the cases cited.

״וְאִם חִבְּרָהּ הַיּוֹצֵר מִתְּחִלָּה מוּתָּר וכו׳״. תָּנָא: אִם חִבְּרָהּ בְּסִיד וּבְחַרְסִית – מוּתָּר, וְהָאֲנַן ׳יוֹצֵר׳ תְּנַן! מַאי יוֹצֵר – כְּעֵין יוֹצֵר.

And we also learned in our mishna that **if the craftsman attached** the tube to the lamp **from the outset, it is permitted** to fill it with oil and use it. **It was taught** in a *baraita* that even **if** a homeowner **attached it** to the vessel before Shabbat **by means of plaster or with** dry **potter's clay, it is permitted.** The Gemara asks: **Didn't we** specifically **learn** in the mishna: If the **craftsman** attached it from the outset, not a layman? The Gemara answers: **What** is the meaning of **craftsman** in the mishna? It refers to any attachment **similar to** the attachment of the **craftsman.**

תַּנְיָא, אָמַר רַבִּי יְהוּדָה: פַּעַם אַחַת שָׁבַתְנוּ בַּעֲלִיַּית בֵּית נִתְזָה בְּלוֹד וְהֵבִיאוּ לָנוּ שְׁפוֹפֶרֶת שֶׁל בֵּיצָה וּמִלֵּאנוּהָ שֶׁמֶן וּנְקַבְנוּהָ וְהִנַּחְנוּהָ עַל פִּי הַנֵּר וְהָיָה שָׁם רַבִּי טַרְפוֹן וּזְקֵנִים וְלֹא אָמְרוּ לָנוּ דָּבָר. אָמְרוּ לוֹ: מִשָּׁם רְאָיָה?! שָׁאנֵי בֵּית נִתְזָה דִּזְרִיזִין הֵן.

With regard to the dispute between Rabbi Yehuda and the Rabbis, **it was taught** in a *baraita* that **Rabbi Yehuda said** to the Rabbis: **One time** we spent **our Shabbat in the upper story of the house of Nit'za in** the city of **Lod. And they brought us an eggshell, and we filled it with oil, and pierced it, and left it over the lamp** in order to extend its burning. **And Rabbi Tarfon and** other **Elders were there and they did not say anything to us.** Apparently, there is no prohibition. The Rabbis **said to him:** Do you bring **proof from there?**[B] The legal status of the Elders who were sitting in the house of **Nit'za is different. They are vigilant.** There is no room for concern lest they use the oil in the eggshell and accelerate the extinguishing of the lamp. However, in every other circumstance, doing so is prohibited.

אָבִין צִיפּוֹרָאָה גְּרַר סַפְסָלָא בְּעִילִּיתָא דְּשֵׁישָׁא לְעֵילָּא מֵרַבִּי יִצְחָק בֶּן אֶלְעָזָר, אָמַר לֵיהּ: אִי שְׁתוֹקִי לָךְ כִּדְשַׁתִּיקוּ לֵיהּ חַבְרַיָּא לְרַבִּי יְהוּדָה נָפֵיק מִינֵּיהּ חוּרְבָּא: גְּזֵירָה עִלִּיתָא דְּשֵׁישָׁא אַטּוּ עִלִּיתָא דְּעָלְמָא.

The Gemara relates: **Avin from** the city of **Tzippori dragged a bench in an upper story,** whose floor was made of **marble, before Rabbi Yitzḥak ben Elazar.** Rabbi Yitzḥak ben Elazar **said to him: If I remain silent** and say nothing **to you, as** Rabbi Tarfon and **the members of the group** of Elders **were silent** and said nothing **to Rabbi Yehuda, damage will result,** as it will lead to unfounded leniency in the future. Had they told Rabbi Yehuda at that time that it is prohibited to puncture the eggshell, he would not have disagreed with the Rabbis. He would not have mistakenly derived a general leniency. So too, here the Sages issued a **decree** on a **marble**-floored **upper story due to a standard upper story** with an earth floor. One who drags a bench on an earth floor will create a furrow.

רֵישׁ כְּנִישְׁתָּא דְּבָצְרָה גְּרַר סַפְסָלָא לְעֵילָּא מֵרַבִּי יִרְמְיָה רַבָּה, אָמַר לֵיהּ: כְּמַאן – כְּרַבִּי שִׁמְעוֹן? אֵימַר דַּאֲמַר רַבִּי שִׁמְעוֹן בִּגְדוֹלִים, דְּלָא אֶפְשָׁר, בִּקְטַנִּים מִי אֲמַר?! וּפְלִיגָא דְּעוּלָּא, דְּאָמַר עוּלָּא: מַחֲלוֹקֶת – בִּקְטַנִּים, אֲבָל בִּגְדוֹלִים – דִּבְרֵי הַכֹּל מוּתָּר.

On the topic of dragging, the Gemara relates that **the Head of the** ***Kenesset***[B] **of Batzra dragged a bench before Rabbi Yirmeya the Great** on Shabbat. Rabbi Yirmeya **said to him: In accordance with whose** opinion do you permit yourself to drag a bench on Shabbat? Is it **in accordance with** the opinion of **Rabbi Shimon? Say** that **Rabbi Shimon said** his statement specifically **with** regard to **large** benches **that** are **impossible** to move from place to place in any other way, **but in** the case of **small** benches **did he say** that one is permitted to drag them? **And** this **disagrees with** the opinion **of Ulla, as Ulla said:** The **dispute** with regard to dragging is **in** the case of **small** benches; **however, in** the case of **large** benches, **everyone agrees that one is permitted** to drag them, as there is no other way to move them.

BACKGROUND

Do you bring proof from there – מִשָּׁם רְאָיָה: This common phrase is employed when one seeks to reject a proof from a certain source. It indicates that there is a significant difference between the case under discussion and the source cited as proof.

The Head of the *Kenesset* – רֵישׁ כְּנִישְׁתָּא: The Head of the *Kenesset* was the title given to a significant leader in the Jewish community. The Head of the *Kenesset* was in charge of all synagogue matters, honors, and appointments. In Jewish communities in the Diaspora, the Head of the *Kenesset* was apparently the head of the local Jewish community. There was a Head of the *Kenesset* in the Temple, who was subject to the authority of the Deputy High Priest.

HALAKHA

Clothing merchants, etc. – מוכרי כסות וכו׳: Merchants who sell clothing made from the prohibited mixture of wool and linen are permitted to don those garments that are for sale in the usual manner, as long as they do not intend to derive benefit from them (Rambam *Sefer Zera'im, Hilkhot Kilayim* 10:16; *Shulḥan Arukh Yoreh De'a* 301: 6).

When one does not intend, Rabbi Shimon permits – לא מתכוין שרי רבי שמעון: It is permitted *ab initio* to perform an action on Shabbat from which a prohibited labor may ensue as long as one does not intend to perform the labor, in accordance with the opinion of Rabbi Shimon. This does not apply when the prohibited consequence is inevitable (Rambam *Sefer Zemanim, Hilkhot Shabbat* 1:5; *Shulḥan Arukh, Oraḥ Ḥayyim* 337:1).

One who extinguishes the lamp, etc. – המכבה את הנר וכו׳: One is permitted *ab initio* to extinguish a lamp on Shabbat to enable a critically ill person to sleep, or due to danger posed by gentiles or thieves, as per the mishna and the explanation of the Gemara. That is only the case where the possibility of moving the sick person, covering the light source, or moving the lamp to another room does not exist. Despite the fact that the lamp is set-aside, it is preferable to move it rather than violate the Torah prohibition of extinguishing a flame on Shabbat (Rambam *Sefer Zemanim, Hilkhot Shabbat* 2:2; *Shulḥan Arukh, Oraḥ Ḥayyim* 278:1).

מתיב רב יוסף, רבי שמעון אומר: גורר אדם מטה כסא וספסל ובלבד שלא יתכוין לעשות חריץ. קתני גדולים וקתני קטנים, קשיא לתרווייהו!

Rav Yosef raised an objection from what was taught in a *baraita*, **Rabbi Shimon says: One may drag a bed, a chair, and a bench** across the floor on Shabbat even though it creates a furrow, **as long as he does not intend to create a furrow.** This *baraita* **teaches** about **large** objects, like a bed, **and teaches** about small objects, like a chair. If so, **this is difficult for both** Rabbi Yirmeya the Great and for Ulla. Rabbi Yirmeya holds that Rabbi Shimon prohibits dragging even small furniture. Ulla holds that even Rabbi Yehuda permits dragging large pieces of furniture. According to his opinion, there is no need for Rabbi Shimon to state that it is permitted.

עולא מתרץ לטעמיה, ורבי ירמיה רבה מתרץ לטעמיה. עולא מתרץ לטעמיה: מטה דומיא דכסא. ורבי ירמיה רבה מתרץ לטעמיה: כסא דומיא דמטה.

The Gemara answers that **Ulla reconciles** the objection **in accordance with his reasoning and Rabbi Yirmeya the Great reconciles** the objection **in accordance with his reasoning.** The Gemara explains: **Ulla reconciles** the objection **in accordance with his reasoning: A bed, similar** to **a chair;** the *baraita* is referring here to a small bed that can be carried like a chair, with regard to which there is a dispute between Rabbi Shimon and Rabbi Yehuda. **And Rabbi Yirmeya the Great reconciles** the objection **in accordance with his reasoning: A chair, similar** to **a bed;** the *baraita* is referring to dragging a heavy chair that cannot be moved in any other way.

מתיב רבה: מוכרי כסות מוכרין כדרכן, ובלבד שלא יתכוין בחמה מפני החמה ובגשמים מפני הגשמים, והצנועין מפשילין במקל לאחוריהן. והא הכא, דאפשר למיעבד כצנועין, דכי קטנים דמי, וכי לא מתכוין – שרי רבי שמעון לכתחלה! תיובתא דרבי ירמיה רבה! תיובתא.

Rabba raised an objection to Rabbi Yirmeya's statement from that which we learned in a mishna: **Clothing merchants**[H] who sell garments made of diverse kinds, a prohibited mixture of wool and linen, **may sell them as they normally would**[N] to gentiles, and they may place the garments that they are selling on their shoulders and need not be concerned about the prohibition against wearing diverse kinds, **as long as** the merchant **does not intend**[N] to benefit from the garments **in the sun** as protection **from the sun, or in the rain** as protection **from the rain. However, the modest** people, those who are particularly fastidious in performing mitzvot, would **suspend** the wool and linen garments **on a stick behind them. And here,** in the case of dragging benches, **where it is possible to act like** the **modest** people, **as** the clothes are **similar to small** benches, **and** nevertheless, **when** one **does not intend** to perform the prohibited action, **Rabbi Shimon permits**[H] dragging even ***ab initio***. Rabbi Shimon holds that one who does not intend to violate a prohibition need not take an alternative course of action due to concern that resulting from his action, the prohibited act might come to be performed. Based on that principle, it is clear that Rabbi Shimon would permit dragging small benches since one does not intend to create a furrow in dragging them. This is a **conclusive refutation** of the statement of **Rabbi Yirmeya the Great,** who held that dragging small objects is prohibited according to Rabbi Shimon. The Gemara concludes: Indeed, it is a **conclusive refutation.**

מתני׳ המכבה את הנר מפני שהוא מתירא מפני גוים ומפני ליסטים, מפני רוח רעה, מפני החולה שיישן – פטור. כחס על הנר, כחס על השמן, כחס על הפתילה – חייב. רבי יוסי פוטר בכולן, חוץ מן הפתילה, מפני שהוא עושה פחם.

MISHNA One who extinguishes the lamp[H] on Shabbat **because he is afraid due to gentiles,** from whom he is hiding in his home, **and due to thieves,** or if one is afraid **due to an evil spirit,** i.e., he is depressed and prefers sitting in the dark, or if he extinguished the flame **due to the sick person** so that he **will sleep,** he is **exempt.** However, in a case where he extinguishes the flame in order to **spare the lamp, spare the oil, or spare the wick,** he is **liable. Rabbi Yosei exempts** him **in all of** those cases, as in his opinion no labor prohibited by Torah law is being performed by extinguishing the flame, **except for** the case where he seeks to spare **the wick.** Only in that case is extinguishing a creative action **because he makes** the wick into **charcoal** by extinguishing the flame.

NOTES

Clothing merchants may sell them as they normally would, etc. – מוכרי כסות מוכרין כדרכן וכו׳: Some question Rabbi Shimon's opinion: Doesn't the one wearing a garment fashioned from a prohibited mixture of the diverse kinds of wool and linen benefit from wearing it? This is, then, an inevitable consequence [*pesik reishei*] and Rabbi Shimon holds that one is liable in that case. The Gemara was sensitive to that problem and that is why it limited Rabbi Shimon's ruling to a case where the merchant was wearing other clothing to protect himself from the elements. In that case, he derives no benefit from the additional, prohibited garment (Rashba).

As long as he does not intend, etc. – ובלבד שלא יתכוין וכו׳: In general, a person's intent plays a significant role in the *halakhot* of Shabbat. Indeed, a prohibited labor performed without intent is not considered a labor by Torah law. Rabbi Shimon's opinion, with regard to all cases of Torah law, is that one's intention is the decisive factor in determining whether or not the action is prohibited. In his opinion, one who does not intend to perform an action, and it ensued unintended, is not responsible for that action and he is even permitted to perform the action *ab initio*. However, there is one caveat to this approach: The prohibited consequence of his action must be only one of several possible results and not an inevitable consequence. If it were inevitable, he would not be able to claim that it was not his intention to perform the action.

גמ׳ מִדְּקָתָנֵי סֵיפָא ׳חַיָּיב׳ – שְׁמַע מִינָּהּ רַבִּי יְהוּדָה הִיא. רֵישָׁא בְּמַאי עָסְקִינַן? אִי בְּחוֹלֶה שֶׁיֵּשׁ בּוֹ סַכָּנָה – ׳מוּתָּר׳ מִיבָּעֵי לֵיהּ! וְאִי בְּחוֹלֶה שֶׁאֵין בּוֹ סַכָּנָה – ׳חַיָּיב חַטָּאת׳ מִיבָּעֵי לֵיהּ!

GEMARA From the fact that **it was taught in the latter clause** of the mishna that one who extinguishes a flame on Shabbat is **liable, conclude from it** that this mishna **is** in accordance with the opinion of **Rabbi Yehuda,** who holds that one who performs a prohibited labor on Shabbat is liable to bring a sin-offering even it is a labor that is not necessary for its own sake [*melakha she'eina tzerikha legufa*]. In the mishna, one does not extinguish the flame to achieve the product produced by extinguishing it. He does so to prevent the light from shining. If so, **with what is the first clause** of the mishna **dealing? If** it is referring to one who extinguished the flame due **to a critically ill person,** the term exempt is imprecise. **It should have** said **permitted,** as it is permitted even *ab initio* to perform a prohibited labor on Shabbat in a case of danger. **And if** it is speaking **about a non-critically ill person,** why is one who extinguished the flame exempt? **It should have** said that one is **liable** to bring a **sin-offering.**

לְעוֹלָם בְּחוֹלֶה שֶׁיֵּשׁ בּוֹ סַכָּנָה, וּבְדִין הוּא דְּלִיתְנֵי ׳מוּתָּר׳, וְאַיְּידֵי דְּבָעֵי לְמִתְנֵי סֵיפָא ׳חַיָּיב׳ – תְּנָא נַמִי רֵישָׁא ׳פָּטוּר׳. וְהָדְתָנֵי רַבִּי אוֹשַׁעְיָא: ״אִם בִּשְׁבִיל הַחוֹלֶה שֶׁיִּישַׁן – לֹא יְכַבֶּה, וְאִם כִּבָּה – פָּטוּר אֲבָל אָסוּר״ – הַהִיא בְּחוֹלֶה שֶׁאֵין בּוֹ סַכָּנָה, וְרַבִּי שִׁמְעוֹן הִיא.

The Gemara replies: **Actually,** the first clause was referring **to a critically ill person, and it should have taught** that it is **permitted. And since the latter clause** of the mishna **had to teach** that one is **liable, in the first clause too, it taught** employing the opposite term, **exempt,** so that the mishna would maintain stylistic uniformity. The *halakha* is, indeed, that not only is one exempt if he extinguished a light for a critically ill person, it is even permitted to do so *ab initio*. The Gemara asks: **What of that which Rabbi Oshaya taught: If** one wants to extinguish a flame on Shabbat **for a sick person** so he **can sleep, he may not extinguish** it, **and if he extinguished** it, **he is not liable** after the fact, **but** *ab initio* he is **prohibited** to do so? The Gemara answers: This is not similar, as **that** *baraita* is referring **to a non-critically ill person and it** is in accordance with the opinion of **Rabbi Shimon,** who said that one who performs a prohibited labor not necessary for its own sake is exempt. Our mishna is referring to a critically ill person.

שַׁאוּל שְׁאֵילָה זוֹ לְעֵילָּא מֵרַבִּי תַּנְחוּם דְּמִן נְוֵי: מַהוּ לְכַבּוֹת בּוּצִינָא דְּנוּרָא מִקַּמֵּי בְּאִישָׁא בְּשַׁבְּתָא? פְּתַח וַאֲמַר: אַנְתְּ שְׁלֹמֹה, אָן חָכְמָתָךְ אָן סוּכְלְתָנוּתָךְ! לֹא דַּיֶּיךָ שֶׁדְּבָרֶיךָ סוֹתְרִין דִּבְרֵי דָּוִד אָבִיךָ אֶלָּא שֶׁדְּבָרֶיךָ סוֹתְרִין זֶה אֶת זֶה! דָּוִד אָבִיךָ אָמַר: ״לֹא הַמֵּתִים יְהַלְלוּ יָהּ״ וְאַתְּ אָמַרְתְּ: ״וְשַׁבֵּחַ אֲנִי אֶת הַמֵּתִים שֶׁכְּבָר מֵתוּ״, וְחָזַרְתְּ וְאָמַרְתְּ: ״כִּי לְכֶלֶב חַי הוּא טוֹב מִן הָאַרְיֵה הַמֵּת״!

The Gemara relates: **This question was asked before Rabbi Tanḥum**[N] from the village of **Nevi: What is the ruling with regard to extinguishing a burning lamp before a sick person on Shabbat?** The Gemara relates that Rabbi Tanḥum delivered an entire homily[B] touching upon both aggadic and halakhic materials surrounding this question. **He began and said: You,** King **Solomon, where is your wisdom, where is your understanding? Not only do your statements contradict** the **statements of your father David, but your statements** even **contradict each other. Your father David said: "The dead praise not the Lord,** neither any that go down into silence" (Psalms 115:17); **and you said: "And I praised the dead that are already dead** more than the living that are yet alive" (Ecclesiastes 4:2). **And then again you said: "For a living dog is better than a dead lion"** (Ecclesiastes 9:4). These are different assessments of life and death.

לָא קַשְׁיָא, הָא דְּקָאָמַר דָּוִד: ״לֹא הַמֵּתִים יְהַלְלוּ יָהּ״ הָכִי קָאָמַר: לְעוֹלָם יַעֲסוֹק אָדָם בְּתוֹרָה וּבְמִצְוֹת קוֹדֶם שֶׁיָּמוּת, שֶׁכֵּיוָן שֶׁמֵּת – בָּטֵל מִן הַתּוֹרָה וּמִן הַמִּצְוֹת, וְאֵין לְהַקָּדוֹשׁ בָּרוּךְ הוּא שֶׁבַח בּוֹ, וְהַיְינוּ דְּאָמַר רַבִּי יוֹחָנָן, מַאי דִּכְתִיב: ״בַּמֵּתִים חָפְשִׁי״ – כֵּיוָן שֶׁמֵּת אָדָם נַעֲשָׂה חָפְשִׁי מִן הַתּוֹרָה וּמִן הַמִּצְוֹת.

He resolved the contradictions in the following manner: This is **not difficult. That which David said: "The dead praise not the Lord," this is what he is saying: A person should always engage in Torah and mitzvot before he dies, as once** he is **dead he is idle from Torah and mitzvot and there is no praise for the Holy One, Blessed be He,** from **him. And that is what Rabbi Yoḥanan said: What** is the meaning **of that which is written: "Set free among the dead,** like the slain that lie in the grave, whom You remember no more" (Psalms 88:6)? **When a person dies** he then **becomes free of Torah and mitzvot.**

NOTES

Before Rabbi Tanḥum – לְעֵילָּא מֵרַבִּי תַּנְחוּם: This is a common phrase in the Talmud, which literally means above Rabbi Tanḥum. Some understand it as a figure of speech meaning that the student was standing before Rabbi Tanḥum (see Rashi). Elsewhere, Rashi explains that this expression was based on the prevailing circumstances. The Sage would sit and teach and the one posing a question would stand. Consequently, the student actually asked his question while standing above Rabbi Tanḥum, corresponding to the literal meaning of the phrase.

BACKGROUND

The teaching of Rabbi Tanḥum – דְּרָשַׁת רַבִּי תַּנְחוּם: This style of teaching, which opens with a halakhic question and proceeds to deal extensively with *aggada* and ethical teachings, only to conclude with a *halakha*, is typical of the teachings of the Sages beginning with the generation of Rabbi Tanḥum. Here, the Gemara presents a complete homiletic interpretation of a Sage with all the external trappings, including the surprising question to King Solomon: Where is your wisdom, where is your understanding? This style was especially common in Eretz Yisrael and in the aggadic midrash *Yelamdenu*, as well as *Midrash Tanḥuma*, which is attributed to Rabbi Tanḥum. In those two anthologies of midrash, the halakhic question opens with the words: Teach us, our Rabbi [*yelamdenu rabbeinu*], switches to an aggadic discussion, and ultimately returns to a halakhic conclusion. The *She'iltot* of Rav Aḥai Gaon was also influenced by this style of presentation. This tradition was also preserved in the teachings of the Sages in many Jewish communities.

וּדְקָאָמַר שְׁלֹמֹה "וְשַׁבֵּחַ אֲנִי אֶת הַמֵּתִים שֶׁכְּבָר מֵתוּ" – שֶׁכְּשֶׁחָטְאוּ יִשְׂרָאֵל בַּמִּדְבָּר עָמַד מֹשֶׁה לִפְנֵי הַקָּדוֹשׁ בָּרוּךְ הוּא, וְאָמַר כַּמָּה תְּפִלּוֹת וְתַחֲנוּנִים לְפָנָיו וְלֹא נַעֲנָה, וּכְשֶׁאָמַר "זְכוֹר לְאַבְרָהָם לְיִצְחָק וּלְיִשְׂרָאֵל עֲבָדֶיךָ" – מִיָּד נַעֲנָה, וְלֹא יָפֶה אָמַר שְׁלֹמֹה "וְשַׁבֵּחַ אֲנִי אֶת הַמֵּתִים שֶׁכְּבָר מֵתוּ"? דָּבָר אַחֵר: מִנְהָגוֹ שֶׁל עוֹלָם, שַׂר בָּשָׂר וָדָם גּוֹזֵר גְּזֵרָה סָפֵק מְקַיְּימִין אוֹתָהּ סָפֵק אֵין מְקַיְּימִין אוֹתָהּ, וְאִם תִּמְצֵי לוֹמַר מְקַיְּימִין אוֹתָהּ – בְּחַיָּיו מְקַיְּימִין אוֹתָהּ, בְּמוֹתוֹ – אֵין מְקַיְּימִין אוֹתָהּ. וְאִילּוּ מֹשֶׁה רַבֵּינוּ, גָּזַר כַּמָּה גְּזֵירוֹת וְתִיקֵּן כַּמָּה תַּקָּנוֹת, וְקַיָּימוֹת הֵם לְעוֹלָם וּלְעוֹלְמֵי עוֹלָמִים. וְלֹא יָפֶה אָמַר שְׁלֹמֹה "וְשַׁבֵּחַ אֲנִי אֶת הַמֵּתִים וגו'"?

And that which Solomon said: "And I praised the dead that are already dead"; he was not speaking of all dead people, but rather in praise of certain dead people. **As when Israel sinned in the desert, Moses stood before the Holy One, Blessed be He, and he said several prayers and supplications before Him, and his prayers were not answered. And when he said: "Remember Abraham, Isaac, and Israel, Your servants"** (Exodus 32:13), his prayers **were answered immediately.** Consequently, **did Solomon not speak appropriately** when **he said: "Wherefore I praised the dead that are already dead"?** Certainly the merit of the deceased forefathers is greater than that of the righteous people who are alive. **Alternatively, the way of the world** is such that when **a flesh-and-blood prince issues a decree** on the public it is **uncertain whether they fulfill it** and **uncertain whether they do not fulfill it. And** even **if you want to say** that **they fulfill it,** it is only **during his lifetime** that **they fulfill it; after he dies they do not fulfill it. But Moses our teacher issued several decrees and instituted several ordinances,**[N] **and they are in effect forever and ever. And,** if so, **is it not appropriate** that which **Solomon said: "Wherefore I praised the dead that are already dead"?**

דָּבָר אַחֵר: "וְשַׁבֵּחַ אֲנִי וגו'" – כִּדְרַב יְהוּדָה אָמַר רַב, דְּאָמַר רַב יְהוּדָה אָמַר רַב: מַאי דִּכְתִיב "עֲשֵׂה עִמִּי אוֹת לְטוֹבָה וְיִרְאוּ שׂוֹנְאַי וְיֵבוֹשׁוּ" – אָמַר דָּוִד לִפְנֵי הַקָּדוֹשׁ בָּרוּךְ הוּא: רִבּוֹנוֹ שֶׁל עוֹלָם, מְחוֹל לִי עַל אוֹתוֹ עָוֹן! אָמַר לוֹ: מָחוּל לָךְ. אָמַר לוֹ: עֲשֵׂה עִמִּי אוֹת בְּחַיַּי! אָמַר לוֹ: בְּחַיֶּיךָ אֵינִי מוֹדִיעַ, בְּחַיֵּי שְׁלֹמֹה בִּנְךָ אֲנִי מוֹדִיעַ.

Alternatively, another explanation is given for the verse: **"And I praised** the dead that are already dead," **is in accordance with** that which **Rav Yehuda said** that **Rav said. As Rav Yehuda said** that **Rav said: What** is the meaning of the verse **that was written: "Work on my behalf a sign for good; that they that hate me may see it, and be put to shame"** (Psalms 86:17)? **David said before the Holy One, Blessed be He: Master of the Universe, forgive me for that sin** in the matter of Bathsheba. **He said to him: It is forgiven you.** David **said to Him: Show me a sign in my lifetime** so that all will know that You have forgiven me. God **said to him: In your lifetime I will not make it known** that you were forgiven; however, **in the lifetime of your son Solomon I will make it known.**

כְּשֶׁבָּנָה שְׁלֹמֹה אֶת בֵּית הַמִּקְדָּשׁ בִּיקֵּשׁ לְהַכְנִיס אָרוֹן לְבֵית קָדְשֵׁי הַקֳּדָשִׁים, דָּבְקוּ שְׁעָרִים זֶה בָּזֶה. אָמַר שְׁלֹמֹה עֶשְׂרִים וְאַרְבָּעָה רְנָנוֹת וְלֹא נַעֲנָה. פָּתַח וְאָמַר: "שְׂאוּ שְׁעָרִים רָאשֵׁיכֶם וְהִנָּשְׂאוּ פִּתְחֵי עוֹלָם וְיָבֹא מֶלֶךְ הַכָּבוֹד" רְהַטוּ בַּתְרֵיהּ לְמִיבְלְעֵיהּ, אָמְרוּ: "מִי הוּא זֶה מֶלֶךְ הַכָּבוֹד?" אָמַר לְהוּ: "ה' עִזּוּז וְגִבּוֹר". חָזַר וְאָמַר: "שְׂאוּ שְׁעָרִים רָאשֵׁיכֶם וּשְׂאוּ פִּתְחֵי עוֹלָם וְיָבֹא מֶלֶךְ הַכָּבוֹד. מִי הוּא זֶה מֶלֶךְ הַכָּבוֹד ה' צְבָאוֹת הוּא מֶלֶךְ הַכָּבוֹד סֶלָה" וְלֹא נַעֲנָה. כֵּיוָן שֶׁאָמַר: "ה' אֱלֹהִים אַל תָּשֵׁב פְּנֵי מְשִׁיחֶךָ זָכְרָה לְחַסְדֵי דָּוִד עַבְדֶּךָ" – מִיָּד נַעֲנָה. בְּאוֹתָהּ שָׁעָה נֶהֶפְכוּ פְּנֵי כׇּל שׂוֹנְאֵי דָוִד כְּשׁוּלֵי קְדֵירָה, וְיָדְעוּ כׇּל הָעָם וְכׇל יִשְׂרָאֵל שֶׁמָּחַל לוֹ הַקָּדוֹשׁ בָּרוּךְ הוּא עַל אוֹתוֹ עָוֹן. וְלֹא יָפֶה אָמַר שְׁלֹמֹה: "וְשַׁבֵּחַ אֲנִי אֶת הַמֵּתִים שֶׁכְּבָר מֵתוּ"?!

When Solomon built the Temple and **sought to bring the Ark into the Holy of Holies,** the **gates**[N] **clung together** and could not be opened. **Solomon uttered twenty-four songs** of praise,[N] as in his prayer there are twenty-four expressions of prayer, song, etc. (I Kings 8), **and** his prayer **was not answered. He began and said: "Lift up your heads, O you gates, and be you lifted up, you everlasting doors; that the King of glory may come in"** (Psalms 24:7). Immediately, the gates **ran after him to swallow him,** as they thought that in the words: "King of glory" he was referring to himself, **and they said** to him: **"Who is the King of glory?"** (Psalms 24:8). **He said to them: "The Lord strong and mighty,** the Lord mighty in battle" (Psalms 24:8). And **he said** again: **"Lift up your heads, O you gates, yea, lift them up, you everlasting doors; that the King of glory may come in. Who then is the King of glory? The Lord of hosts; He is the King of glory. Selah"** (Psalms 24:9–10), **and he was not answered. When he said: "O Lord God, turn not away the face of Your anointed; remember the good deeds of David Your servant"** (II Chronicles 6:42), **he was immediately answered,** and a fire descended from Heaven (II Chronicles 7:1). **At that moment, the faces of all of David's enemies turned** dark **like the** charred **bottom of a pot. And all of Israel knew that the Holy One, Blessed be He, forgave him for that sin. And** if so, is it **not appropriate** what **Solomon said: "And I praised the dead that are already dead,"** David, more than the living, Solomon, to whose request to open the gates of the Temple God did not respond?

וְהַיְינוּ דִּכְתִיב: "בַּיּוֹם הַשְּׁמִינִי שִׁלַּח אֶת הָעָם וַיְבָרְכוּ אֶת הַמֶּלֶךְ וַיֵּלְכוּ לְאׇהֳלֵיהֶם שְׂמֵחִים וְטוֹבֵי לֵב עַל כׇּל הַטּוֹבָה אֲשֶׁר עָשָׂה ה' לְדָוִד עַבְדּוֹ וּלְיִשְׂרָאֵל עַמּוֹ": 'וַיֵּלְכוּ לְאׇהֳלֵיהֶם' – שֶׁמָּצְאוּ נְשׁוֹתֵיהֶן בְּטׇהֳרָה. 'שְׂמֵחִים' – שֶׁנֶּהֱנוּ מִזִּיו הַשְּׁכִינָה. 'וְטוֹבֵי לֵב' – שֶׁנִּתְעַבְּרוּ נְשׁוֹתֵיהֶן שֶׁל כׇּל אֶחָד וְאֶחָד וְיָלְדָה זָכָר. "עַל כׇּל הַטּוֹבָה אֲשֶׁר עָשָׂה ה' לְדָוִד עַבְדּוֹ (וּלְיִשְׂרָאֵל עַמּוֹ", 'לְדָוִד עַבְדּוֹ') – שֶׁמָּחַל לוֹ עַל אוֹתוֹ עָוֹן, 'וּלְיִשְׂרָאֵל עַמּוֹ' – דְּאַחֵיל לְהוּ עֲוֹן דְּיוֹם הַכִּפּוּרִים.

And that is what is written: "On the eighth day he sent the people away, and they blessed the king, and went unto their tents joyful and glad of heart for all the goodness that the Lord had shown unto David His servant and to Israel His people" (I Kings 8:66). The Gemara explains: **And went unto their tents,** in accordance with the common expression: One's house is his wife. It is explained **that** when they returned home **they found their wives ritually pure** from the ritual impurity of menstruation. **Joyful** means **that they enjoyed the aura of the Divine Presence** at the dedication of the Temple. **And glad of heart** means **that the wife of each and every one of them was impregnated and gave birth to a male.** The verse continues: **For all the goodness that the Lord had shown unto David His servant and to Israel His people. Unto David His servant** means that at that opportunity they all saw **that** God **forgave him for that sin. And to Israel His people** means **that He forgave them** for the **sin** of **Yom Kippur,** as they did not fast that year (see I Kings 8:65).

NOTES

Moses our teacher issued several decrees and instituted several ordinances – מֹשֶׁה רַבֵּינוּ גָּזַר כַּמָּה גְּזֵירוֹת וְתִיקֵּן כַּמָּה תַּקָּנוֹת: This is not referring to the contents of the Torah itself, which are not attributable to Moses. Rather, it is referring to ordinances that he instituted on his own, e.g., public Torah reading, blessings, the order of the priestly watches, etc. (see Rashi and Rav Nissim Gaon).

Gates – שְׁעָרִים: *Midrash Tanḥuma* explains that the width of the entrance to the Holy of Holies was identical to the width of the Holy Ark and the cherubs. This situation is described metaphorically as: The gates clung together. Since the Holy Ark could not enter by natural means, Solomon prayed, a miracle occurred, and the Holy Ark entered the Holy of Holies.

Twenty-four songs of praise – עֶשְׂרִים וְאַרְבָּעָה רְנָנוֹת: It is explained in *Midrash Rabba* that the twenty-four songs correspond to the twenty-four verses of praise that precede this verse in Solomon's prayer.

וּדְקָאָמַר שְׁלֹמֹה: ״כִּי לְכֶלֶב חַי הוּא טוֹב מִן הָאַרְיֵה הַמֵּת״ – כִּדְרַב יְהוּדָה אָמַר רַב, דְּאָמַר רַב יְהוּדָה אָמַר רַב: מַאי דִּכְתִיב: ״הוֹדִיעֵנִי ה׳ קִצִּי וּמִדַּת יָמַי מַה הִיא אֵדְעָה מֶה חָדֵל אָנִי״, אָמַר דָּוִד לִפְנֵי הַקָּדוֹשׁ בָּרוּךְ הוּא: רִבּוֹנוֹ שֶׁל עוֹלָם, ״הוֹדִיעֵנִי ה׳ קִצִּי״! אָמַר לוֹ: גְּזֵירָה הִיא מִלְּפָנַי שֶׁאֵין מוֹדִיעִין קִצּוֹ שֶׁל בָּשָׂר וָדָם. ״וּמִדַּת יָמַי מַה הִיא״? גְּזֵירָה הִיא מִלְּפָנַי שֶׁאֵין מוֹדִיעִין מִדַּת יָמָיו שֶׁל אָדָם. ״וְאֵדְעָה מֶה חָדֵל אָנִי״, אָמַר לוֹ: בְּשַׁבָּת תָּמוּת. אָמוּת בְּאֶחָד בְּשַׁבָּת! אָמַר לוֹ: כְּבָר הִגִּיעַ מַלְכוּת שְׁלֹמֹה בִּנְךָ, וְאֵין מַלְכוּת נוֹגַעַת בַּחֲבֶרְתָּהּ אֲפִילּוּ כִּמְלֹא נִימָא. אָמוּת בְּעֶרֶב שַׁבָּת! אָמַר לוֹ: ״כִּי טוֹב יוֹם בַּחֲצֵרֶיךָ מֵאָלֶף״ טוֹב לִי יוֹם אֶחָד שֶׁאַתָּה יוֹשֵׁב וְעוֹסֵק בַּתּוֹרָה מֵאֶלֶף עוֹלוֹת שֶׁעָתִיד שְׁלֹמֹה בִּנְךָ לְהַקְרִיב לְפָנַי עַל גַּבֵּי הַמִּזְבֵּחַ.

The Gemara continues: **And that which Solomon said: "For a living dog is better than a dead lion"** (Ecclesiastes 9:4), **is in accordance with** that which **Rav Yehuda** said that **Rav said. As Rav Yehuda said** that **Rav said: What** is the meaning of that verse which David said: **"Lord, make me to know my end, and the measure of my days, what it is; let me know how short-lived I am"** (Psalms 39:5)? It means that **David said before the Holy One, Blessed be He: Master of the Universe, Lord, make me to know my end;** in how long will I die? God **said to him: It is decreed before Me that** I do **not reveal the end of** the life of **flesh and blood.** He asked further: **And the measure of my days;** on **what** day of the year will I die? He said to him: **It is decreed before Me not to reveal the measure of a person's days.** Again he requested: **Let me know how short-lived I am;** on what day of the week will I die? **He said to him: You will die on Shabbat.** David requested of God: **Let me die on the first** day **of the week** so that the honor of Shabbat will not be tarnished by the pain of death. **He said to him:** On that day **the** time of **the kingdom of your son Solomon has already arrived, and one kingdom does not overlap with another** and subtract from the time allotted to another **even a hairbreadth.** He said to him: **I will** cede a day of my life and **die on Shabbat eve.** God **said to him: "For a day in your courts is better than a thousand"** (Psalms 84:11); **a single day in which you sit and engage in Torah is preferable to Me than the thousand burnt-offerings that your son Solomon will offer before Me on the altar** (see 1 Kings 3:4).

Perek **II**
Daf **30** Amud **b**

כָּל יוֹמָא דְּשַׁבְּתָא הֲוָה יָתֵיב וְגָרֵיס כּוּלֵּי יוֹמָא, הַהוּא יוֹמָא דִּבְעֵי לְמֵינַח נַפְשֵׁיהּ קָם מַלְאַךְ הַמָּוֶת קַמֵּיהּ וְלָא יָכֵיל לֵיהּ, דְּלָא הֲוָה פָּסֵק פּוּמֵיהּ מִגִּירְסָא. אֲמַר: מַאי אַעֲבֵיד לֵיהּ? הֲוָה לֵיהּ בּוּסְתָּנָא אֲחוֹרֵי בֵּיתֵיהּ, אֲתָא מַלְאַךְ הַמָּוֶת סָלֵיק וּבָחֵישׁ בְּאִילָנֵי, נְפַק לְמֶיחֱזֵי. הֲוָה סָלֵיק בְּדַרְגָּא. אִיפְּחִית דַּרְגָּא מִתּוּתֵיהּ, אִישְׁתִּיק וְנָח נַפְשֵׁיהּ.

What did David do? **Every Shabbat he would sit and learn all day** long to protect himself from the Angel of Death. On **that day on which** the Angel of Death **was supposed to put his soul to rest,** the day on which David was supposed to die, **the Angel of Death stood before him and was unable** to overcome him because **his mouth did not pause from study.** The Angel of Death **said: What shall I do to him? David had a garden** [*bustana*][L] **behind his house; the Angel of Death came, climbed, and shook the trees.** David **went out to see. As he climbed the stair, the stair broke beneath him.** He was startled and **was silent,** interrupted his studies for a moment, **and died.**

שָׁלַח שְׁלֹמֹה לְבֵי מִדְרְשָׁא: אַבָּא מֵת וּמוּטָל בַּחַמָּה, וּכְלָבִים שֶׁל בֵּית אַבָּא רְעֵבִים, מָה אֶעֱשֶׂה? שָׁלְחוּ לֵיהּ: חֲתוֹךְ נְבֵלָה וְהַנַּח לִפְנֵי הַכְּלָבִים, וְאָבִיךָ – הַנַּח עָלָיו כִּכָּר אוֹ תִּינוֹק וְטַלְטְלוֹ. וְלֹא יָפֶה אָמַר שְׁלֹמֹה: ״כִּי לְכֶלֶב חַי הוּא טוֹב מִן הָאַרְיֵה הַמֵּת״? וּלְעִנְיַן שְׁאֵילָה דְּשָׁאִילְנָא קֳדָמֵיכוֹן: נֵר קְרוּיָה נֵר, וְנִשְׁמָתוֹ שֶׁל אָדָם קְרוּיָה נֵר, מוּטָב תִּכְבֶּה נֵר שֶׁל בָּשָׂר וָדָם מִפְּנֵי נֵרוֹ שֶׁל הַקָּדוֹשׁ בָּרוּךְ הוּא.

Since David died in the garden, **Solomon sent** the following question **to the study hall: Father died and is lying in the sun, and the dogs of father's house are hungry.** There is room for concern lest the dogs come and harm his body. What shall I do? **They sent** an answer **to him: Cut up an** animal **carcass and place it before the dogs.**[H] Since the dogs are hungry, handling the animal carcass to feed them is permitted. **And** with regard to **your father,** it is prohibited to move his body directly. **Place a loaf** of bread **or an infant on top of him, and** you can **move him**[H] into the shade due to the bread or the infant. **And is it not appropriate** what **Solomon said: "For a living dog is better than a dead lion."** The ultimate conclusion of this discussion is that life is preferable to death. **And** now, **with regard to the question that I asked before you;** Rav Tanḥum spoke modestly, as, actually, they had asked him the question. **A lamp is called** ***ner*** **and a person's soul is** also **called** ***ner*****,**[N] as it is written: "The spirit of man is the lamp [*ner*] of the Lord" (Proverbs 20:27). **It is preferable** that **the lamp of** a being of **flesh and blood,** an actual lamp, **will be extinguished in favor of the lamp of the Holy One, Blessed be He,** a person's soul. Therefore, one is permitted to extinguish a flame for the sake of a sick person.

LANGUAGE

Garden [*bustana*] – בּוּסְתָּנָא: From the Iranian *bōstān*, meaning a fragrant place, i.e., a garden or orchard.

NOTES

A lamp is called *ner* and a person's soul is also called *ner* – נֵר קְרוּיָה נֵר וְנִשְׁמָתוֹ שֶׁל אָדָם: According to the Gemara in tractate *Yoma* (85b), the *halakha* that requires one to perform prohibited labors on Shabbat in order to save human life is not based on this homily. The actual source is the verse that states that the mitzvot of the Torah were given so that one should "live by them" (Leviticus 18:4–5), from which it is inferred that, as a rule, one is not commanded to give his life in order to fulfill a positive mitzva or to avoid violating a prohibition. Since this teaching was presented before an unlearned crowd, it was expounded in a manner that would appeal to a wide audience (Rashi).

HALAKHA

Cut up a carcass and place it before the dogs – חֲתוֹךְ נְבֵלָה וְהַנַּח לִפְנֵי הַכְּלָבִים: On Shabbat, it is permitted to cut up an animal carcass that is difficult for dogs to eat whole, even if the animal died on Shabbat. However, it is prohibited to do so if the dogs are able to eat the carcass uncut (Rambam *Sefer Zemanim*, *Hilkhot Shabbat* 21:18; *Shulḥan Arukh*, *Oraḥ Ḥayyim* 324:7).

And with regard to your father, place a loaf of bread or an infant on top of him and move him – וְאָבִיךָ הַנַּח עָלָיו כִּכָּר אוֹ תִּינוֹק וְטַלְטְלוֹ: On Shabbat, it is permitted to move a corpse that is lying in a place where it might be disgraced by placing upon it a loaf of bread, or an infant, or any other object that may be moved on Shabbat (*Mishna Berura*). If there is neither bread nor an infant available, but one has two beds available, he may move the corpse by continuously rolling it from one bed to the other until he moves it to a more suitable place. If neither of those options is available, he may simply move the corpse.

All of the above applies to moving the corpse within a single domain. However, moving a corpse from one domain to another is not permitted under any circumstances (*Shulḥan Arukh*). According to many of the later commentaries, one is permitted to move a corpse into a *karmelit* or even into another domain to prevent dishonoring the dead. Some commentaries add that it is preferable to move the corpse without bread or an infant to minimize that which is being carried from one domain to another on Shabbat (Rambam *Sefer Zemanim*, *Hilkhot Shabbat* 26:21; *Shulḥan Arukh*, *Oraḥ Ḥayyim* 311:1).

אָמַר רַב יְהוּדָה בְּרֵיהּ דְּרַב שְׁמוּאֵל בַּר שֵׁילַת מִשְּׁמֵיהּ דְּרַב: בִּקְשׁוּ חֲכָמִים לִגְנוֹז סֵפֶר קֹהֶלֶת מִפְּנֵי שֶׁדְּבָרָיו סוֹתְרִין זֶה אֶת זֶה, וּמִפְּנֵי מָה לֹא גְּנָזוּהוּ – מִפְּנֵי שֶׁתְּחִילָּתוֹ דִּבְרֵי תוֹרָה וְסוֹפוֹ דִּבְרֵי תוֹרָה, תְּחִילָּתוֹ דִּבְרֵי תוֹרָה – דִּכְתִיב: "מַה יִּתְרוֹן לָאָדָם בְּכָל עֲמָלוֹ שֶׁיַּעֲמוֹל תַּחַת הַשָּׁמֶשׁ" וְאָמְרִי דְּבֵי רַבִּי יַנַּאי: תַּחַת הַשָּׁמֶשׁ הוּא דְּאֵין לוֹ, קוֹדֶם שֶׁמֶשׁ – יֵשׁ לוֹ. סוֹפוֹ דִּבְרֵי תוֹרָה – דִּכְתִיב: "סוֹף דָּבָר הַכֹּל נִשְׁמָע אֶת הָאֱלֹהִים יְרָא וְאֶת מִצְוֹתָיו שְׁמוֹר כִּי זֶה כׇּל הָאָדָם". מַאי "כִּי זֶה כׇּל הָאָדָם"? אָמַר רַבִּי (אֱלִיעֶזֶר): כׇּל הָעוֹלָם כּוּלּוֹ לֹא נִבְרָא אֶלָּא בִּשְׁבִיל זֶה. רַבִּי אַבָּא בַּר כָּהֲנָא אָמַר: שָׁקוּל זֶה כְּנֶגֶד כׇּל הָעוֹלָם כּוּלּוֹ. שִׁמְעוֹן בֶּן עַזַּאי אוֹמֵר, וְאָמְרִי לַהּ שִׁמְעוֹן בֶּן זוֹמָא אוֹמֵר: לֹא נִבְרָא כׇּל הָעוֹלָם כּוּלּוֹ אֶלָּא לְצַוּוֹת לָזֶה.

Since contradictions in Ecclesiastes were mentioned, the Gemara cites additional relevant sources. **Rav Yehuda, son of Rav Shmuel bar Sheilat, said in the name of Rav: The Sages sought to suppress the book of Ecclesiastes**[N] and declare it apocryphal **because its statements contradict each other** and it is liable to confuse its readers. **And why did they not suppress it? Because its beginning** consists of **matters of Torah and its end** consists of **matters of Torah.** The ostensibly contradictory details are secondary to the essence of the book, which is Torah. The Gemara elaborates: **Its beginning** consists of **matters of Torah, as it is written: "What profit has man of all his labor which he labors under the sun?"** (Ecclesiastes 1:3), **and** the Sages of **the school of** Rabbi **Yannai said:** By inference: **Under the sun is where** man **has no** profit from his labor; however, **before the sun,** i.e., when engaged in the study of Torah, which preceded the sun, **he does have** profit. **Its ending** consists of **matters of Torah, as it is written: "The end of the matter, all having been heard: Fear God, and keep His mitzvot; for this is the whole man"** (Ecclesiastes 12:13). With regard to this verse, the Gemara asks: **What is** the meaning of the phrase: **For this is the whole man? Rabbi Eliezer said: The entire world was only created for this** person. **Rabbi Abba bar Kahana said: This** person **is equivalent to the entire world. Shimon ben Azzai says and some say** that **Shimon ben Zoma says: The entire world was only created as companion to this** man, so that he will not be alone.

וּמַאי דְּבָרָיו סוֹתְרִין זֶה אֶת זֶה? כְּתִיב: "טוֹב כַּעַס מִשְּׂחוֹק" וּכְתִיב: "לִשְׂחוֹק אָמַרְתִּי מְהוֹלָל". כְּתִיב: "וְשִׁבַּחְתִּי אֲנִי אֶת הַשִּׂמְחָה" וּכְתִיב: "וּלְשִׂמְחָה מַה זֹּה עוֹשָׂה". לָא קַשְׁיָא, "טוֹב כַּעַס מִשְּׂחוֹק" – טוֹב כַּעַס שֶׁכּוֹעֵס הַקָּדוֹשׁ בָּרוּךְ הוּא עַל הַצַּדִּיקִים בָּעוֹלָם הַזֶּה, מִשְּׂחוֹק שֶׁמְּשַׂחֵק הַקָּדוֹשׁ בָּרוּךְ הוּא עַל הָרְשָׁעִים בָּעוֹלָם הַזֶּה. "וְלִשְׂחוֹק אָמַרְתִּי מְהוֹלָל" – זֶה שְׂחוֹק שֶׁמְּשַׂחֵק הַקָּדוֹשׁ בָּרוּךְ הוּא עִם הַצַּדִּיקִים בָּעוֹלָם הַבָּא.

And to the essence of the matter, the Gemara asks: **What is** the meaning of: **Its statements** that **contradict each other? It is written: "Vexation is better than laughter"** (Ecclesiastes 7:3), **and it is written: "I said of laughter: It is praiseworthy"** (Ecclesiastes 2:2), which is understood to mean that laughter is commendable. Likewise in one verse **it is written: "So I commended mirth"** (Ecclesiastes 8:15), **and** in another verse **it is written: "And of mirth: What does it accomplish?"** (Ecclesiastes 2:2). The Gemara answers: This is **not difficult,** as the contradiction can be resolved. **Vexation is better than laughter** means: The **vexation of the Holy One, Blessed be He, toward the righteous in this world is preferable to the laughter which the Holy One, Blessed be He, laughs with the wicked in this world** by showering them with goodness. **I said of laughter: It is praiseworthy,** that is the **laughter which the Holy One, Blessed be He, laughs with the righteous in the World-to-Come.**

"וְשִׁבַּחְתִּי אֲנִי אֶת הַשִּׂמְחָה" שִׂמְחָה שֶׁל מִצְוָה, "וּלְשִׂמְחָה מַה זֹּה עוֹשָׂה" – זוֹ שִׂמְחָה שֶׁאֵינָהּ שֶׁל מִצְוָה. לְלַמֶּדְךָ שֶׁאֵין שְׁכִינָה שׁוֹרָה לֹא מִתּוֹךְ עַצְבוּת וְלֹא מִתּוֹךְ עַצְלוּת וְלֹא מִתּוֹךְ שְׂחוֹק וְלֹא מִתּוֹךְ קַלּוּת רֹאשׁ וְלֹא מִתּוֹךְ שִׂיחָה וְלֹא מִתּוֹךְ דְּבָרִים בְּטֵלִים, אֶלָּא מִתּוֹךְ דְּבַר שִׂמְחָה שֶׁל מִצְוָה, שֶׁנֶּאֱמַר: "וְעַתָּה קְחוּ לִי מְנַגֵּן וְהָיָה כְּנַגֵּן הַמְנַגֵּן וַתְּהִי עָלָיו יַד ה'". אָמַר רַב יְהוּדָה: וְכֵן לִדְבַר הֲלָכָה. אָמַר רָבָא: וְכֵן לַחֲלוֹם טוֹב.

Similarly, **"So I commended mirth,"** that is **the joy of a mitzva.**[H] **"And of mirth: What does it accomplish?"** that is **joy that is not** the joy **of a mitzva.** The praise of joy mentioned here is **to teach you that the Divine Presence rests** upon an individual **neither from** an atmosphere of **sadness, nor from** an atmosphere of **laziness, nor from** an atmosphere of **laughter, nor from** an atmosphere of **frivolity, nor from** an atmosphere of **idle conversation, nor from** an atmosphere of **idle chatter, but rather from** an atmosphere imbued with **the joy of a mitzva.**[H] **As it was stated** with regard to Elisha that after he became angry at the king of Israel, his prophetic spirit left him until he requested: **"But now bring me a minstrel; and it came to pass, when the minstrel played, that the hand of the Lord came upon him"** (II Kings 3:15). **Rav Yehuda said: And, so** too, one should be joyful before stating **a matter of** ***halakha.*** **Rava said: And, so** too, one should be joyful before going to sleep in order **to** have a **good dream.**

אִינִי?! וְהָאָמַר רַב גִּידֵּל אָמַר רַב: כׇּל תַּלְמִיד חָכָם שֶׁיּוֹשֵׁב לִפְנֵי רַבּוֹ וְאֵין שִׂפְתוֹתָיו נוֹטְפוֹת מֹר – תִּכָּוֶינָה, שֶׁנֶּאֱמַר: "שִׂפְתוֹתָיו שׁוֹשַׁנִּים נוֹטְפוֹת מוֹר עוֹבֵר", אַל תִּקְרֵי 'מוֹר עוֹבֵר', אֶלָּא 'מַר עוֹבֵר', אַל תִּקְרֵי 'שׁוֹשַׁנִּים' אֶלָּא 'שֶׁשּׁוֹנִים'! לָא קַשְׁיָא, הָא – בְּרַבָּה וְהָא – בְּתַלְמִיד. וְאִיבָּעֵית אֵימָא: הָא וְהָא בְּרַבָּה, וְלָא קַשְׁיָא, הָא – מִקַּמֵּי דְּלִפְתַּח, הָא – לְבָתַר דִּפְתַח. כִּי הָא דְּרַבָּה, מִקַּמֵּי דְּפָתַח לְהוּ לְרַבָּנַן אֲמַר מִילְּתָא דִּבְדִיחוּתָא, וּבָדְחִי רַבָּנַן. לְסוֹף יָתֵיב בְּאֵימְתָא וּפָתַח בִּשְׁמַעְתָּא.

The Gemara asks: Is **that so,** that one should introduce matters of *halakha* joyfully? **Didn't Rav Giddel say** that **Rav said: Any Torah scholar who sits before his teacher and his lips are not dripping with myrrh** due to fear of his teacher, those lips **shall be burnt,** as **it is stated: "His lips are as lilies, dripping with flowing myrrh [*shoshanim notefot mor over*]"** (Song of Songs 5:13)? He interpreted homiletically: **Do not read** ***mor over,*** **flowing myrrh; rather,** read ***mar over,*** **flowing bitterness.** Likewise, **do not read** ***shoshanim,*** **lilies; rather,** read ***sheshonim,*** **that are studying,** meaning that lips that are studying Torah must be full of bitterness. The Gemara explains: This is **not difficult,** there is no contradiction here, as **this,** where it was taught that one should introduce matters of *halakha* joyfully, is referring **to a rabbi, and that,** where it was taught that one must be filled with bitterness, is referring **to a student,** who must listen to his teacher with trepidation. **And if you wish,** say instead that **this and that** are referring **to a rabbi,** and it is **not difficult. This,** where it was taught that he must be joyful, is **before** he **begins** teaching, whereas **that,** where it was taught that he must be filled with bitterness and trepidation, is **after** he already **began** teaching *halakha.* That explanation is **like that which Rabba** did. **Before he began** teaching *halakha* **to the Sages, he would say something humorous and the Sages would be cheered. Ultimately, he sat in trepidation and began** teaching the *halakha.*

NOTES

The Sages sought to suppress the book of Ecclesiastes – בִּקְשׁוּ חֲכָמִים לִגְנוֹז סֵפֶר קֹהֶלֶת: The proposed suppression of Ecclesiastes was not an attempt to repudiate its contents. Rather, the Sages feared that its apparent contradictions would confuse those who study it. Nevertheless, since they found significant Torah content in Ecclesiastes, they made the effort to resolve the contradictions.

HALAKHA

The joy of a mitzva – שִׂמְחָה שֶׁל מִצְוָה: The Rambam wrote: The joy of performing mitzvot…is a great service…and there is no greatness and honor other than being joyful before God, as it is stated: "King David leaping and dancing before God" (II Samuel 6:16; see Rambam *Sefer Zemanim, Hilkhot Shofar VeSukka VeLulav* 8:15).

The Divine Presence does rests upon an individual neither from an atmosphere of sadness…but rather from an atmosphere imbued with the joy of a mitzva – שֶׁאֵין שְׁכִינָה שׁוֹרָה לֹא מִתּוֹךְ עַצְבוּת...אֶלָּא מִתּוֹךְ דְּבַר מִצְוָה לְשִׂמְחָה שֶׁ: None of the prophets could prophesy at will. Rather, they would meditate in solitude, focus their thoughts, and fill their hearts with joy. By the same token, the prophetic spirit does not rest upon one who is sad or lazy but only upon one filled with joy. Therefore, the novice prophets would play the drums, lyres, flutes, and harps while the prophets sought to prophesy (Rambam *Sefer HaMadda, Hilkhot Yesodei HaTorah* 7:4).

ואף ספר משלי בקשו לגנוז, שהיו דבריו סותרין זה את זה. ומפני מה לא גנזוהו – אמרי: ספר קהלת לאו עיינינן ואשכחינן טעמא? הכא נמי ליעיינן. ומאי דבריו סותרים זה את זה – כתיב: "אל תען כסיל כאולתו" וכתיב: "ענה כסיל כאולתו" לא קשיא, הא – בדברי תורה, הא במילי דעלמא.

And, the Gemara continues, the Sages **sought to suppress the book of Proverbs as well** because **its statements contradict each other. And why did they not suppress it? They said:** In the case of **the book of Ecclesiastes, didn't we analyze it and find an explanation** that its statements were not contradictory? **Here too, let us analyze it. And what** is the meaning of: **Its statements contradict each other?** On the one hand, **it is written: "Answer not a fool according to his folly,** lest you also be like him" (Proverbs 26:4), **and** on the other hand, **it is written: "Answer a fool according to his folly,** lest he be wise in his own eyes" (Proverbs 26:5). The Gemara resolves this apparent contradiction: This is **not difficult,** as **this,** where one should answer a fool, is referring to a case where the fool is making claims **about Torah matters;** whereas **that,** where one should not answer him, is referring to a case where the fool is making claims **about mundane matters.**

כי הא דההוא דאתא לקמיה דרבי, אמר ליה: אשתך אשתי ובניך בני. אמר ליה: רצונך שתשתה כוס של יין? שתה ופקע. ההוא דאתא לקמיה דרבי חייא, אמר ליה: אמך אשתי ואתה בני. אמר ליה: רצונך שתשתה כוס של יין? שתה ופקע. אמר רבי חייא: אהניא ליה צלותיה לרבי דלא לשווייה בני ממזירי. דרבי כי הוה מצלי, אמר: "יהי רצון מלפניך ה׳ אלהינו שתצילני היום מעזי פנים ומעזות פנים".

The Gemara relates how Sages conducted themselves in both of those circumstances. **As in the case of that man who came before Rabbi** Yehuda HaNasi and **said to him: Your wife is my wife**[N] **and your children are my children,** Rabbi Yehuda HaNasi **said to him:** Would **you like to drink a cup of wine? He drank and burst** and died. Similarly, the Gemara relates: **There was that man who came before Rabbi Ḥiyya and said to him: Your mother is my wife, and you are my son. He said to him:** Would **you like to drink a cup of** wine? **He drank and burst** and died. **Rabbi Ḥiyya said** with regard to the incident involving Rabbi Yehuda HaNasi: **Rabbi** Yehuda HaNasi's **prayer** that **his children will not be rendered** *mamzerim*, children of illicit relations, **was effective for him. As when Rabbi** Yehuda HaNasi **would pray, he said** after his prayer: **May it be Your will, O Lord, my God, that You will deliver me today from impudent people and from insolence.**[N] Insolence, in this case, refers to *mamzerut*. It was due to his prayer that that man burst and was unsuccessful in disparaging Rabbi Yehuda HaNasi's children.

בדברי תורה מאי היא? כי הא דיתיב רבן גמליאל וקא דריש: עתידה אשה שתלד בכל יום, שנאמר: "הרה ויולדת יחדיו". ליגלג עליו אותו תלמיד, אמר: "אין כל חדש תחת השמש"! אמר ליה: בא ואראך דוגמתן בעולם הזה, נפק אחוי ליה תרנגולת.

In matters of Torah, what is the case with regard to which the verse said that one should respond to a fool's folly? **As in the case where Rabban Gamliel was sitting and he interpreted** a verse **homiletically: In the future,** in the World-to-Come, **a woman will give birth every day, as it says: "The woman with child and her that gives birth together"** (Jeremiah 31:7), explaining that birth will occur on the same day as conception. **A certain student**[N] **scoffed at him** and **said:** That cannot be, as it has already been stated: **"There is nothing new under the sun"** (Ecclesiastes 1:9). Rabban Gamliel **said to him: Come and I will show you an example** of this **in this world. He took him outside and showed him a chicken** that lays eggs every day.

ותו יתיב רבן גמליאל וקא דריש: עתידים אילנות שמוציאין פירות בכל יום, שנאמר: "ונשא ענף ועשה פרי", מה ענף בכל יום – אף פרי בכל יום. ליגלג עליו אותו תלמיד, אמר: והכתיב "אין כל חדש תחת השמש"! אמר ליה: בא ואראך דוגמתם בעולם הזה, נפק אחוי ליה צלף.

And furthermore: Rabban Gamliel sat and interpreted a verse **homiletically: In the future,** in the World-to-Come, **trees will produce fruits every day, as it is stated: "And it shall bring forth branches and bear fruit"** (Ezekiel 17:23); **just as a branch** grows every day, **so too, fruit** will be produced **every day. A certain student scoffed at him and said: Isn't it written: There is nothing new under the sun? He said to him: Come and I will show you an example** of this **in this world. He went outside and showed him a caper bush,**[B] part of which is edible during each season of the year.

ותו יתיב רבן גמליאל וקא דריש: עתידה ארץ ישראל שתוציא גלוסקאות וכלי מילת, שנאמר "יהי פסת בר בארץ". ליגלג עליו אותו תלמיד, ואמר: "אין כל חדש תחת השמש"! אמר ליה: בא ואראך דוגמתן בעולם הזה, נפק אחוי ליה כמיהין ופטריות, ואכלי מילת – נברא בר קורא.

And furthermore: Rabban Gamliel sat and interpreted a verse **homiletically: In the future,** the World-to-Come, **Eretz Yisrael will produce cakes and fine wool garments** that will grow in the ground, **as it is stated: "Let abundant grain be in the land." A certain student scoffed at him and said: There is nothing new under the sun. He said to him: Come and I will show you an example in this world. He went outside** and **showed him truffles and mushrooms,** which emerge from the earth over the course of a single night and are shaped like a loaf of bread. **And with regard to wool garments,** he showed him **the covering of a heart of palm,** a young palm branch, which is wrapped in a thin net-like covering.

NOTES

Your wife is my wife – אשתך אשתי: The man who came to Rabbi Yehuda Hanasi claimed in the course of a confession that Rabbi Yehuda Hanasi's wife had been unfaithful, and that Rabbi Yehuda Hanasi was not the father of her children. The man who came before Rabbi Ḥiyya made a similar claim. Although these are very serious charges, the Sages did not consider it proper to argue with those who brought them. Therefore, they found a way to discreetly be rid of these people.

From impudent people and from insolence – מעזי פנים ומעזות פנים: In tractate *Kiddushin* (70b), the Sages state that impudence is an indication of tarnished lineage, as one of distinguished lineage is shy and modest. Therefore, impudence became known as a characteristic of a *mamzer*.

Rabban Gamliel and the student – רבן גמליאל והתלמיד: Rabban Gamliel spoke metaphorically when he explained that in messianic times there will be plenty in the world and life will be much easier and more comfortable. However, the student did not understand his metaphors and thought they were to be taken literally. This led the student to challenge Rabban Gamliel with a verse from the Bible. Therefore, the Sages said that Rabban Gamliel acted in accordance with the maxim: Answer a fool according to his folly. Since that student was a fool and asked questions that indicated his lack of understanding, the response was in kind (Rambam's Commentary on the Mishna).

BACKGROUND

Caper bush – צלף: The most common species of caper bush in Israel is the thorny caper bush, *Capparis spinosa*, a thorny, deciduous bush that grows to a height of 1.5 m. Its rounded leaves range in color from purple to green and alongside each leaf there is a pair of thorns. The caper has large white flowers, approximately 6 cm in diameter, with purple stamens.

The buds of the caper bush, the *kaprisin*, from the Greek κάππαρις, *kapparis*, meaning caper bush or fruit of the caper bush, are the buds of flowers that have not yet bloomed. Nowadays, in Provence, Greece, and other Mediterranean countries, the caper-bush is grown primarily for its buds, which are pickled and eaten.

If not harvested, these buds open into new flowers on a daily basis and are then pollinated and wither on that same day. The *evyona*, the ripe berry of the caper bush, is similar in shape to a date or small squash and grows to 6 cm.

The young fronds are apparently the caper bush's young, purple-green branches and their leaves, which in ancient times were pickled and eaten. They are called *shuta* in Aramaic.

Botanically, the fruit of the caper bush is the berry, which even today is generally eaten pickled.

Flower of the caper bush

HALAKHA

A person should always be patient like Hillel, etc. – **לְעוֹלָם יְהֵא אָדָם עַנְוְותָן כְּהִלֵּל וכו׳**: To the best of one's ability, one should adopt the trait of patience and humility, distancing himself from arrogance and anger, as per the Gemara's depiction of Hillel (Rambam *Sefer HaMadda*, *Hilkhot Deot* 2:3).

תָּנוּ רַבָּנַן: לְעוֹלָם יְהֵא אָדָם עַנְוְותָן כְּהִלֵּל וְאַל יְהֵא קַפְּדָן כְּשַׁמַּאי. מַעֲשֶׂה בִּשְׁנֵי בְּנֵי אָדָם

Since the Gemara discussed the forbearance of Sages, who remain silent in the face of nonsensical comments, it cites additional relevant examples. **The Sages taught** in a *baraita*: **A person should always be patient like Hillel**[H] **and not impatient like Shammai.** The Gemara related: There was **an incident** involving **two people**

Perek **II**
Daf **31** Amud **a**

שֶׁהִמְרוּ זֶה אֶת זֶה, אָמְרוּ: כָּל מִי שֶׁיֵּלֵךְ וְיַקְנִיט אֶת הִלֵּל – יִטּוֹל אַרְבַּע מֵאוֹת זוּז. אָמַר אֶחָד מֵהֶם: אֲנִי אַקְנִיטֶנּוּ. אוֹתוֹ הַיּוֹם עֶרֶב שַׁבָּת הָיָה, וְהִלֵּל חָפַף אֶת רֹאשׁוֹ. הָלַךְ וְעָבַר עַל פֶּתַח בֵּיתוֹ, אָמַר: מִי כָּאן הִלֵּל? מִי כָּאן הִלֵּל? נִתְעַטֵּף וְיָצָא לִקְרָאתוֹ. אָמַר לוֹ: בְּנִי, מָה אַתָּה מְבַקֵּשׁ? אָמַר לוֹ: שְׁאֵלָה יֵשׁ לִי לִשְׁאוֹל. אָמַר לוֹ: שְׁאַל בְּנִי, שְׁאַל! מִפְּנֵי מָה רָאשֵׁיהֶן שֶׁל בַּבְלִיִּים סְגַלְגַּלּוֹת? אָמַר לוֹ: בְּנִי, שְׁאֵלָה גְּדוֹלָה שָׁאַלְתָּ – מִפְּנֵי שֶׁאֵין לָהֶם חַיּוֹת פִּקְחוֹת.

who wagered with each other and **said: Anyone who will go and aggravate Hillel** to the point that he reprimands him, **will take**[N] **four-hundred** *zuz*. **One of them said: I will aggravate him. That day** that he chose to bother Hillel **was Shabbat eve, and Hillel was washing** the hair on **his head. He went and passed the entrance to** Hillel's **house** and in a demeaning manner **said: Who here is Hillel, who here is Hillel?** Hillel **wrapped himself** in a dignified garment **and went out to greet him. He said to him: My son, what do you seek? He said to him: I have a question to ask.** Hillel **said to him: Ask, my son, ask.** The man asked him: **Why are the heads of Babylonians oval?** He was alluding to and attempting to insult Hillel, who was Babylonian. **He said to him: My son, you have asked a significant question.**[N] The reason is **because they do not have clever midwives.** They do not know how to shape the child's head at birth.

הָלַךְ וְהִמְתִּין שָׁעָה אַחַת, חָזַר וְאָמַר: מִי כָּאן הִלֵּל? מִי כָּאן הִלֵּל? נִתְעַטֵּף וְיָצָא לִקְרָאתוֹ. אָמַר לוֹ: בְּנִי, מָה אַתָּה מְבַקֵּשׁ? אָמַר לוֹ: שְׁאֵלָה יֵשׁ לִי לִשְׁאוֹל. אָמַר לוֹ: שְׁאַל בְּנִי, שְׁאַל! מִפְּנֵי מָה עֵינֵיהֶן שֶׁל תַּרְמוֹדִיִּין תְּרוּטוֹת? אָמַר לוֹ: בְּנִי, שְׁאֵלָה גְּדוֹלָה שָׁאַלְתָּ – מִפְּנֵי שֶׁדָּרִין בֵּין הַחוֹלוֹת.

That man **went and waited one hour**, a short while, **returned** to look for Hillel, **and said: Who here is Hillel, who here is Hillel?** Again, Hillel **wrapped himself and went out to greet him.** Hillel **said to him: My son, what do you seek?** The man **said to him: I have a question to ask. He said to him: Ask, my son, ask.** The man asked: **Why are the eyes of the residents of Tadmor bleary** [*terutot*]?[L] Hillel **said to him: My son, you have asked a significant question.** The reason is **because they live among the sands** and the sand gets into their eyes.

הָלַךְ וְהִמְתִּין שָׁעָה אַחַת, חָזַר וְאָמַר: מִי כָּאן הִלֵּל? מִי כָּאן הִלֵּל? נִתְעַטֵּף וְיָצָא לִקְרָאתוֹ. אָמַר לוֹ: בְּנִי, מָה אַתָּה מְבַקֵּשׁ? אָמַר לוֹ: שְׁאֵלָה יֵשׁ לִי לִשְׁאוֹל. אָמַר לוֹ: שְׁאַל בְּנִי, שְׁאַל! מִפְּנֵי מָה רַגְלֵיהֶם שֶׁל אַפְרִקִיִּים רְחָבוֹת? אָמַר לוֹ: בְּנִי, שְׁאֵלָה גְּדוֹלָה שָׁאַלְתָּ – מִפְּנֵי שֶׁדָּרִין בֵּין בִּצְעֵי הַמַּיִם.

Once again the man **went, waited one hour, returned, and said: Who here is Hillel, who here is Hillel?** Again, he, Hillel, **wrapped himself and went out to greet him. He said to him: My son, what do you seek? He said to him: I have a question to ask. He said to him: Ask, my son, ask.** The man asked: **Why do Africans**[B] **have wide feet?** Hillel **said to him: You have asked a significant question.** The reason is **because they live in marshlands** and their feet widened to enable them to walk through those swampy areas.

אָמַר לוֹ: שְׁאֵלוֹת הַרְבֵּה יֵשׁ לִי לִשְׁאוֹל, וּמִתְיָרֵא אֲנִי שֶׁמָּא תִּכְעוֹס. נִתְעַטֵּף וְיָשַׁב לְפָנָיו, אָמַר לוֹ: כָּל שְׁאֵלוֹת שֶׁיֵּשׁ לְךָ לִשְׁאוֹל – שְׁאַל. אָמַר לוֹ: אַתָּה הוּא הִלֵּל שֶׁקּוֹרִין אוֹתְךָ נְשִׂיא יִשְׂרָאֵל? אָמַר לוֹ: הֵן. אָמַר לוֹ: אִם אַתָּה הוּא – לֹא יִרְבּוּ כְּמוֹתְךָ בְּיִשְׂרָאֵל. אָמַר לוֹ: בְּנִי, מִפְּנֵי מָה? אָמַר לוֹ: מִפְּנֵי שֶׁאִבַּדְתִּי עַל יָדְךָ אַרְבַּע מֵאוֹת זוּז. אָמַר לוֹ: הֱוֵי זָהִיר בְּרוּחֲךָ, כְּדַי הוּא הִלֵּל שֶׁתְּאַבֵּד עַל יָדוֹ אַרְבַּע מֵאוֹת זוּז וְאַרְבַּע מֵאוֹת זוּז – וְהִלֵּל לֹא יַקְפִּיד.

That man **said to him: I have many** more **questions to ask, but I am afraid lest you get angry.** Hillel **wrapped himself and sat before him,** and **he said to him: All of the questions that you have to ask, ask** them. The man got angry and **said to him: Are you Hillel whom they call** the *Nasi* **of Israel? He said to him: Yes. He said to him: If it is you,** then **may there not be many like you in Israel.** Hillel **said to him: My son, for what** reason do you say this? The man **said to him: Because I lost four hundred** *zuz*[B] **because of you.** Hillel **said to him: Be vigilant of your spirit** and avoid situations of this sort. **Hillel is worthy of having you lose four hundred** *zuz* **and** another **four hundred** *zuz* **on his account, and Hillel will not get upset.**

NOTES

They said that anyone who will go and aggravate Hillel will take, etc. – **אָמְרוּ כָּל מִי שֶׁיֵּלֵךְ וְיַקְנִיט אֶת הִלֵּל יִטּוֹל וכו׳**: The attempt to provoke Hillel combined several factors, each of which was aggravating. The first was the choice of the day and time. Shabbat eve is a busy time, in general, and the person chose to disturb Hillel while he was washing his hair. Hillel was forced to interrupt his shampoo in order to respond. The second factor was the contemptuous manner in which he addressed Hillel, as if he did not know who Hillel was. Finally, the series of ridiculous questions with inflammatory implications was particularly irritating (Maharsha).

You have asked a significant question – **שְׁאֵלָה גְּדוֹלָה שָׁאַלְתָּ**: Hillel's approach was to respond seriously and deliberately to anyone who asked him a question. If the questioner was turned away and embarrassed when asking a frivolous question, he would not return to ask significant questions that required meaningful answers (*Iyyun Ya'akov*).

LANGUAGE

Bleary [*terutot*] – **תְּרוּטוֹת**: There are several opinions as to the origin of this word and its meaning. One possibility is that it is a derivative of the Greek verb δρύπτειν, to tear. Another possibility is the Latin teres, genitive teretis, meaning round.

BACKGROUND

Tadmorians and Africans – **תַּרְמוֹדִיִּים וְאַפְרִקִיִּים**: The Tadmorians are the residents of Tadmor, Palmyra, a city located in the heart of the Syrian desert and visited by sandstorms from time to time.

The Africans mentioned here are apparently the inhabitants of the southern Nile Valley, the swampy regions adjacent to southern Sudan.

Four hundred *zuz* – **אַרְבַּע מֵאוֹת זוּז**: The easiest way to appreciate the value of this sum is by quantifying its buying power. Four hundred *zuz* was approximately four months' salary.

תָּנוּ רַבָּנַן: מַעֲשֶׂה בְּגוֹי אֶחָד שֶׁבָּא לִפְנֵי שַׁמַּאי, אָמַר לוֹ: כַּמָּה תוֹרוֹת יֵשׁ לָכֶם? אָמַר לוֹ: שְׁתַּיִם, תּוֹרָה שֶׁבִּכְתָב וְתוֹרָה שֶׁבְּעַל פֶּה. אָמַר לוֹ: שֶׁבִּכְתָב – אֲנִי מַאֲמִינְךָ, וְשֶׁבְּעַל פֶּה – אֵינִי מַאֲמִינְךָ. גַּיְּירֵנִי עַל מְנָת שֶׁתְּלַמְּדֵנִי תּוֹרָה שֶׁבִּכְתָב. גָּעַר בּוֹ וְהוֹצִיאוֹ בִּנְזִיפָה. בָּא לִפְנֵי הִלֵּל – גַּיְירֵיהּ, יוֹמָא קַמָּא אֲמַר לֵיהּ: א״ב ג״ד, לְמָחָר אַפֵּיךְ לֵיהּ. אֲמַר לֵיהּ: וְהָא אֶתְמוֹל לָא אֲמַרְתְּ לִי הָכִי?! אֲמַר לֵיהּ: לָאו עֲלַי דִּידִי קָא סָמְכַתְּ? דְּעַל פֶּה נַמִּי סְמוֹךְ עֲלַי.

The Sages taught: There was **an incident involving one gentile who came before Shammai.** The gentile **said to** Shammai: **How many Torahs do you have? He said to him: Two, the Written Torah and the Oral Torah.** The gentile **said to him:** With regard to **the Written** Torah, **I believe you, but** with regard to **the Oral** Torah, **I do not believe you. Convert me on condition that you will teach me** only the **Written Torah.** Shammai **scolded him and cast him out with reprimand.** The same gentile **came before Hillel,** who **converted him** and began teaching him Torah. **On the first day, he** showed him the letters of the alphabet and **said to him:** ***Alef, bet, gimmel, dalet.*** **The next day he reversed** the order of the letters and told him that an *alef* is a *tav* and so on. The convert **said to him: But yesterday you did not tell me that.** Hillel **said to him:** You see that it is impossible to learn what is written without relying on an oral tradition. **Didn't you rely on me?** Therefore, you should **also rely on me** with regard to the matter **of the Oral** Torah, and accept the interpretations that it contains.

שׁוּב מַעֲשֶׂה בְּגוֹי אֶחָד שֶׁבָּא לִפְנֵי שַׁמַּאי, אָמַר לוֹ: גַּיְּירֵנִי עַל מְנָת שֶׁתְּלַמְּדֵנִי כָּל הַתּוֹרָה כּוּלָּהּ כְּשֶׁאֲנִי עוֹמֵד עַל רֶגֶל אַחַת. דְּחָפוֹ בְּאַמַּת הַבִּנְיָן שֶׁבְּיָדוֹ. בָּא לִפְנֵי הִלֵּל, גַּיְירֵיהּ. אָמַר לוֹ: דַּעֲלָךְ סְנֵי לְחַבְרָךְ לָא תַּעֲבֵיד – זוֹ הִיא כָּל הַתּוֹרָה כּוּלָּהּ, וְאִידָּךְ – פֵּירוּשָׁהּ הוּא, זִיל גְּמוֹר.

There was **another incident involving one gentile who came before Shammai** and said to Shammai: **Convert me on condition that you teach me the entire Torah while I am standing on one foot.**[N] Shammai **pushed him** away **with the builder's cubit in his hand.** This was a common measuring stick and Shammai was a builder by trade. The same gentile **came before Hillel. He converted him and said to him:** That **which is hateful to you do not do to another;**[N] **that is the entire Torah, and the rest is its interpretation. Go study.**

שׁוּב מַעֲשֶׂה בְּגוֹי אֶחָד שֶׁהָיָה עוֹבֵר אֲחוֹרֵי בֵּית הַמִּדְרָשׁ, וְשָׁמַע קוֹל סוֹפֵר שֶׁהָיָה אוֹמֵר: ״וְאֵלֶּה הַבְּגָדִים אֲשֶׁר יַעֲשׂוּ חֹשֶׁן וְאֵפוֹד״. אָמַר: הַלָּלוּ לְמִי? אָמְרוּ לוֹ: לְכֹהֵן גָּדוֹל, אָמַר אוֹתוֹ גּוֹי בְּעַצְמוֹ: אֵלֵךְ וְאֶתְגַּיֵּיר, בִּשְׁבִיל שֶׁיְּשִׂימוּנִי כֹּהֵן גָּדוֹל. בָּא לִפְנֵי שַׁמַּאי, אָמַר לֵיהּ: גַּיְּירֵנִי עַל מְנָת שֶׁתְּשִׂימֵנִי כֹּהֵן גָּדוֹל. דְּחָפוֹ בְּאַמַּת הַבִּנְיָן שֶׁבְּיָדוֹ. בָּא לִפְנֵי הִלֵּל – גַּיְירֵיהּ.

There was **another incident involving one gentile who was passing behind the study hall and heard the voice of a teacher who** was teaching Torah to his students and **saying** the verse: **"And these are the garments**[B] **which they shall make: A breastplate, and an** ***efod***, and a robe, and a tunic of checkered work, a mitre, and a girdle" (Exodus 28:4). **The gentile said: These** garments, **for whom are they** designated? The students **said to him: For the High Priest. The gentile said to himself: I will go and convert so that they will install me as High Priest. He came before Shammai and said to him: Convert me on condition that you install me** as High Priest. Shammai **pushed him with the builder's cubit in his hand. He came before Hillel; he converted him.**

אָמַר לוֹ: כְּלוּם מַעֲמִידִין מֶלֶךְ אֶלָּא מִי שֶׁיּוֹדֵעַ טַכְסִיסֵי מַלְכוּת? לֵךְ לְמוֹד טַכְסִיסֵי מַלְכוּת. הָלַךְ וְקָרָא, כֵּיוָן שֶׁהִגִּיעַ ״וְהַזָּר הַקָּרֵב יוּמָת״ אָמַר לֵיהּ: מִקְרָא זֶה עַל מִי נֶאֱמַר? אָמַר לוֹ: אֲפִילּוּ עַל דָּוִד מֶלֶךְ יִשְׂרָאֵל. נָשָׂא אוֹתוֹ גֵּר קַל וָחוֹמֶר בְּעַצְמוֹ: וּמַה יִּשְׂרָאֵל שֶׁנִּקְרְאוּ בָּנִים לַמָּקוֹם, וּמִתּוֹךְ אַהֲבָה שֶׁאֲהֵבָם קָרָא לָהֶם: ״בְּנִי בְכֹרִי יִשְׂרָאֵל״ – כְּתִיב עֲלֵיהֶם: ״וְהַזָּר הַקָּרֵב יוּמָת״, גֵּר הַקַּל שֶׁבָּא בְּמַקְלוֹ וּבְתַרְמִילוֹ – עַל אַחַת כַּמָּה וְכַמָּה!

Hillel **said to him,** to the convert: **Is it not** the way of the world that **only one who knows the protocols** [*takhsisei*][L] **of royalty is appointed king? Go and learn the royal protocols** by engaging in Torah study. **He went and read** the Bible. **When he reached** the verse which says: **"And the common man that draws near shall be put to death"** (Numbers 1:51), the convert **said to** Hillel: **With regard to whom is the verse speaking?** Hillel **said to him: Even with regard to David, king of Israel. The convert reasoned an** ***a fortiori*** **inference himself: If the Jewish people are called God's children, and due to the love that God loved them he called them: "Israel is My son, My firstborn"** (Exodus 4:22), and nevertheless **it is written about them: And the common man that draws near shall be put to death; a mere convert who came** without merit, **with** nothing more than **his staff and traveling bag, all the more so** that this applies to him, as well.

בָּא לִפְנֵי שַׁמַּאי, אָמַר לוֹ: כְּלוּם רָאוּי אֲנִי לִהְיוֹת כֹּהֵן גָּדוֹל? וַהֲלֹא כְּתִיב בַּתּוֹרָה: ״וְהַזָּר הַקָּרֵב יוּמָת״! בָּא לִפְנֵי הִלֵּל, אָמַר לוֹ: עַנְוְותָן הִלֵּל, יָנוּחוּ לְךָ בְּרָכוֹת עַל רֹאשְׁךָ שֶׁהִקְרַבְתַּנִי תַּחַת כַּנְפֵי הַשְּׁכִינָה. לְיָמִים נִזְדַּוְּוגוּ שְׁלָשְׁתָּן לְמָקוֹם אֶחָד, אָמְרוּ: קַפְּדָנוּתוֹ שֶׁל שַׁמַּאי בִּקְּשָׁה לְטוֹרְדֵנוּ מִן הָעוֹלָם, עַנְוְותָנוּתוֹ שֶׁל הִלֵּל קֵרְבָנוּ תַּחַת כַּנְפֵי הַשְּׁכִינָה.

The convert **came before Shammai** and **told him** that he retracts his demand to appoint him High Priest, saying: **Am I at all worthy to be High Priest? Is it not written in the Torah: And the common man that draws near shall be put to death? He came before Hillel and said to him: Hillel the patient, may blessings rest upon your head as you brought me under the wings of the Divine Presence.** The Gemara relates: **Eventually, the three** converts **gathered together in one place, and they said: Shammai's impatience sought to drive us from the world; Hillel's patience brought us beneath the wings of the Divine Presence.**[N]

NOTES

On one foot – עַל רֶגֶל אַחַת: Apparently, his intention was to ask the Sage for a single fundamental principle, one foot, upon which all of Judaism is based. Indeed, just as Hillel based the Torah upon this single principle, so too Rabbi Akiva and ben Azzai later attempted to formulate the same concept in different, broader terms (Maharsha).

That which is hateful to you do not do to another – דַּעֲלָךְ סְנֵי לְחַבְרָךְ לָא תַּעֲבֵיד: This phrase appears in the Aramaic translation, *Targum Yonatan*, of the Torah verse: "And you shall love your neighbor as yourself" (Leviticus 19:18). It is not a precise translation; rather, it is a limited interpretation. It does not express the positive mitzva to love another, but the prohibition, proscribing actions harmful to others. Apparently, Hillel sought to express through this principle that at the basis of the Torah are those mitzvot, which are fundamental principles that may be universally applied (Maharsha).

Accepting converts – קַבָּלַת גֵּרִים: In practice, people like the ones Hillel converted are not accepted as converts because the *halakha* insists that a convert accept upon himself the entire Torah without intention to accrue personal benefit. However, Hillel apparently relied on the fact that these converts could eventually accept Judaism in its entirety at a later time.

BACKGROUND

And these are the garments, etc. – וְאֵלֶּה הַבְּגָדִים וכו׳: These are the priestly garments worn by the High Priest, also referred to as the golden garments (Exodus 28). Four of them, the breastplate, the *efod*, the robe, and the frontplate, were unique to the High Priest. Four other garments, the trousers, the tunic, the sash, and the miter, resembled those worn by common priests. There was a debate among the Sages whether the sash worn by the High Priest was identical to that worn by the common priests. It appears that the miters differed, at least in the way they were worn.

Priestly garments

LANGUAGE

Protocols [*takhsisei*] – טַכְסִיסֵי: From the Greek τάξις, *taxis*, which means, among other things, order, protocol, and observances.

אָמַר רֵישׁ לָקִישׁ, מַאי דִּכְתִיב: ״וְהָיָה אֱמוּנַת עִתֶּיךָ חוֹסֶן יְשׁוּעוֹת חָכְמַת וָדָעַת וגו׳״ – ׳אֱמוּנַת׳ זֶה סֵדֶר זְרָעִים, ׳עִתֶּיךָ׳ – זֶה סֵדֶר מוֹעֵד, ׳חוֹסֶן׳ – זֶה סֵדֶר נָשִׁים, ׳יְשׁוּעוֹת׳ – זֶה סֵדֶר נְזִיקִין, ׳חָכְמַת׳ – זֶה סֵדֶר קָדָשִׁים, ׳וָדָעַת׳ – זֶה סֵדֶר טְהָרוֹת. וַאֲפִילּוּ הָכִי ״יִרְאַת ה׳ הִיא אוֹצָרוֹ״.

The Gemara continues discussing the conduct of the Sages, citing that **Reish Lakish said: What** is the meaning of **that which is written: "And the faith of your times shall be a strength of salvation, wisdom, and knowledge,** the fear of the Lord is his treasure" (Isaiah 33:6)? **Faith; that is the order of *Zera'im*, Seeds,** in the Mishna, because a person has faith in God and plants his seeds (Jerusalem Talmud). **Your times; that is the order of *Moed*, Festival,** which deals with the various occasions and Festivals that occur throughout the year. **Strength; that is the order of *Nashim*,**[N] **Women. Salvations; that is the order of *Nezikin*, Damages,** as one who is being pursued is rescued from the hands of his pursuer. **Wisdom; that is the order of *Kodashim*, Consecrated Items. And knowledge; that is the order of *Teharot*, Purity,** which is particularly difficult to master. **And even** if a person studies and masters all of these, **"the fear of the Lord is his treasure,"** it is preeminent.

אָמַר רָבָא: בְּשָׁעָה שֶׁמַּכְנִיסִין אָדָם לַדִּין אוֹמְרִים לוֹ: נָשָׂאתָ וְנָתַתָּ בֶּאֱמוּנָה, קָבַעְתָּ עִתִּים לַתּוֹרָה, עָסַקְתָּ בִּפְרִיָּה וּרְבִיָּה, צִפִּיתָ לִישׁוּעָה, פִּלְפַּלְתָּ בְּחָכְמָה, הֵבַנְתָּ דָּבָר מִתּוֹךְ דָּבָר? וַאֲפִילּוּ הָכִי: אִי יִרְאַת ה׳ הִיא אוֹצָרוֹ – אִין, אִי לָא – לָא. מָשָׁל לְאָדָם שֶׁאָמַר לִשְׁלוּחוֹ: הַעֲלֵה לִי כּוֹר חִטִּין לַעֲלִיָּיה. הָלַךְ וְהֶעֱלָה לוֹ. אָמַר לוֹ: עֵירַבְתָּ לִי בָּהֶן קַב חוֹמְטוֹן? אָמַר לוֹ: לָאו. אָמַר לוֹ: מוּטָב אִם לֹא הֶעֱלִיתָה.

With regard to the same verse, **Rava said:** After departing from this world, **when a person is brought to judgment** for the life he lived in this world, **they say to him** in the order of that verse: Did **you conduct business faithfully?**[H] Did **you designate times for Torah study?**[H] Did **you engage in procreation? Did you await salvation? Did you engage** in the dialectics of **wisdom** or understand **one matter from another? And, nevertheless,** beyond all these, **if the fear of the Lord is his treasure, yes,** he is worthy, and **if not, no,** none of these accomplishments have any value. There is **a parable** that illustrates this. **A person who said to his emissary: Bring a *kor* of wheat up to the attic for me** to store there. The messenger **went and brought it up for him. He said to the emissary:** Did **you mix a *kav* of *ḥomton*,**[L] a preservative to keep away worms, **into it for me? He said to him: No. He said to him:** If so, it would have been **preferable had you not brought it up.** Of what use is worm-infested wheat? Likewise, Torah and mitzvot without the fear of God are of no value.

תָּנָא דְּבֵי רַבִּי יִשְׁמָעֵאל: מְעָרֵב אָדָם קַב חוֹמְטוֹן בְּכוֹר שֶׁל תְּבוּאָה, וְאֵינוֹ חוֹשֵׁשׁ.

On a related note, the Gemara cites a *halakha* that was **taught** in **the school** of **Rabbi Yishmael: A person** who sells wheat **may,** *ab initio*, **mix a *kav* of *ḥomton* into a *kor***[B] **of grain and need not be concerned** that by selling it all at the price of grain he will be guilty of theft, as the *kav* of *ḥomton* is essential for the preservation of the wheat.

אָמַר רַבָּה בַּר רַב הוּנָא: כָּל אָדָם שֶׁיֵּשׁ בּוֹ תּוֹרָה וְאֵין בּוֹ

Rabba bar Rav Huna said: Any person who has Torah in him but does not have

NOTES

Strength, that is the order of *Nashim* – ׳חוֹסֶן׳ זֶה סֵדֶר נָשִׁים: The order of *Nashim* in the Mishna, which deals with the *halakhot* pertaining to women and marriage, is called strength because a man who lives without a wife, lives without a protective wall (*Yevamot* 62b).

HALAKHA

Did you conduct business faithfully – נָשָׂאתָ וְנָתַתָּ בֶּאֱמוּנָה: From the outset, a person engaging in business should conduct himself honestly and faithfully. There should be no theft or deceit in one's business affairs. Indeed, that is one of the questions that a person is asked when standing before the heavenly court: Did you conduct your business honestly and faithfully? (*Mishna Berura*; *Shulḥan Arukh*, *Oraḥ Ḥayyim* 156).

Did you designate times for Torah study – קָבַעְתָּ עִתִּים לַתּוֹרָה: Every person must designate specific times for Torah study on a regular basis. Optimally, one should study Torah after prayer. If one does not have the skills to study classic texts, he should nevertheless study material that he does understand. For example, focusing one's attention and assessing his actions to ascertain whether or not he sinned, and then resolving to change his conduct falls under the rubric of Torah study.

To ensure that no day will pass without Torah study, the Sages introduced several paragraphs of Torah study at the conclusion of the prayer service, following the *Amida* prayer (*Be'er Heitev*). This too is one of the questions that a person is asked when standing before the heavenly court: Did you designate times for Torah? (*Mishna Berura*; Rambam *Sefer HaMadda*, *Hilkhot Talmud Torah* 1:8; *Shulḥan Arukh*, *Oraḥ Ḥayyim* 155:1).

LANGUAGE

***Ḥomton* – חוֹמְטוֹן:** Some commentaries state that the proper reading should be *ḥomoton*, from the Greek word ἄμαθος, *amathos*, meaning sand or sandy earth. It also refers to the sand and salts near the sea.

BACKGROUND

A *kav* into a *kor* – קַב בְּכוֹר: There are 180 *kav* in a *kor*. Therefore, one is only permitted to mix a small percentage, a little more than one half of one percent, of *ḥomton* into a *kor* of wheat.

Perek **II**
Daf **31** Amud **b**

יִרְאַת שָׁמַיִם, דּוֹמֶה לְגִזְבָּר שֶׁמָּסְרוּ לוֹ מַפְתְּחוֹת הַפְּנִימִיּוֹת וּמַפְתְּחוֹת הַחִיצוֹנוֹת לֹא מָסְרוּ לוֹ. בְּהֵי עָיֵיל? מַכְרִיז רַבִּי יַנַּאי: חֲבָל עַל דְּלֵית לֵיהּ דַּרְתָּא, וְתַרְעָא לְדַרְתָּא עָבֵיד. אָמַר רַב יְהוּדָה: לֹא בָּרָא הַקָּדוֹשׁ בָּרוּךְ הוּא אֶת עוֹלָמוֹ אֶלָּא כְּדֵי שֶׁיִּירְאוּ מִלְּפָנָיו, שֶׁנֶּאֱמַר: ״וְהָאֱלֹהִים עָשָׂה שֶׁיִּירְאוּ מִלְּפָנָיו״.

fear of Heaven is like a treasurer [*gizbar*][L] **to whom they gave keys to the inner doors** of the treasury **but they did not give keys** to the **outer** door. **With what** key **will he enter?** Although the Torah is the inner key, without fear of Heaven one cannot gain access to the genuine Torah. Similarly, **Rabbi Yannai** would **proclaim: Woe unto** one **who does not have a courtyard, and who makes a fence for the courtyard,** i.e., a person who lacks fear of Heaven and is nevertheless involved in Torah study. **Rav Yehuda said: The Holy One, Blessed be He, only created His world so that people would fear before Him, as it is stated: "And God has so made it that men should fear before Him"** (Ecclesiastes 3:14).

LANGUAGE

Treasurer [*gizbar*] – גִּזְבָּר: This word, which appears in the Bible (Ezra 1:8), was apparently borrowed from the Old Persian word ganzabara, referring to the one in charge of the treasury. Ganz means treasury and bara means carrier.

רַבִּי סִימוֹן וְרַבִּי אֶלְעָזָר הֲווּ יָתְבִי, חֲלֵיף וַאֲזֵיל רַבִּי יַעֲקֹב בַּר אַחָא. אֲמַר לֵיהּ חַד לְחַבְרֵיהּ: נֵיקוּ מִקַּמֵּיהּ, דִּגְבַר דָּחֵיל חֲטָאִין הוּא, אֲמַר אִידָּךְ: נֵיקוּ מִקַּמֵּיהּ; דִּגְבַר בַּר אוֹרְיָין הוּא. אֲמַר: אֲמִינָא לָךְ אֲנָא דִּגְבַר דָּחֵיל חֲטָאִין הוּא – וְאָמְרַתְּ לִי אַתְּ "בַּר אוֹרְיָין הוּא"?!

The Gemara also related that **Rabbi Simon and Rabbi Elazar were sitting. Rabbi Ya'akov bar Aḥa passed and went** adjacent to them. **One said to the other: Let us stand before him as he is a man who fears sin. The other said to him** in response: **Let us stand before him, as he is a man of Torah study. He said** to him: **I said to you that he is a man who fears sin, and you said me that he is a man of Torah study?**[N] The former is much greater praise than the latter.

תִּסְתַּיֵּים דְּרַבִּי אֶלְעָזָר הוּא דַּאֲמַר "דִּגְבַר דָּחֵיל חֲטָאִין הוּא", דְּאָמַר רַבִּי יוֹחָנָן מִשּׁוּם רַבִּי אֶלְעָזָר: אֵין לוֹ לְהַקָּדוֹשׁ בָּרוּךְ הוּא בְּעוֹלָמוֹ אֶלָּא יִרְאַת שָׁמַיִם בִּלְבַד, שֶׁנֶּאֱמַר: "וְעַתָּה יִשְׂרָאֵל מָה ה׳ אֱלֹהֶיךָ שׁוֹאֵל מֵעִמָּךְ כִּי אִם לְיִרְאָה וגו׳" וּכְתִיב: "וַיֹּאמֶר לָאָדָם הֵן יִרְאַת ה׳ הִיא חָכְמָה וגו׳", שֶׁכֵּן בִּלְשׁוֹן יְוָנִי קוֹרִין לְאַחַת הֵן. תִּסְתַּיֵּים.

The Gemara remarks: **Conclude that Rabbi Elazar is** the **one who said** that he is praiseworthy **because he is a man who fears sin,** as elsewhere he also spoke in praise of fear. **As Rabbi Yoḥanan said in the name of Rabbi Elazar: The Holy One, Blessed be He, has in His world only fear of Heaven alone, as it is stated: "And now, Israel, what does the Lord your God ask of you, but to fear** the Lord your God" (Deuteronomy 10:12). **And it is written: "And unto man He said: Behold [*hen*], the fear of the Lord, that is wisdom;** and to depart from evil is understanding" (Job 28:28), **as in the Greek language they call one *hen*.**[L] Apparently, fear of God is of primary importance. The Gemara concludes: Indeed, **conclude** that Rabbi Elazar is the one who said so.

דָּרַשׁ רַב עוּלָּא, מַאי דִּכְתִיב: "אַל תִּרְשַׁע הַרְבֵּה וגו׳", הַרְבֵּה הוּא דְּלָא לִירְשַׁע, הָא מְעַט לִירְשַׁע? אֶלָּא: מִי שֶׁאָכַל שׁוּם וְרֵיחוֹ נוֹדֵף, יַחֲזוֹר וְיֹאכַל שׁוּם אַחֵר וִיהֵא רֵיחוֹ נוֹדֵף?!

Rav Ulla taught: What is the meaning of **that which is written: "Be not overmuch wicked"**[N] (Ecclesiastes 7:17)? This appears difficult, as, is that to say that only **overmuch** one should not be wicked; **a little, one should be wicked? Rather,** this can be understood based on the following adage: **One who ate** a clove of **garlic and its odor spreads,** should **he again eat** another clove of **garlic so that its odor will spread** further? If you were somewhat wicked, do not think that it is legitimate to continue and be very wicked.

דָּרַשׁ רָבָא בַּר רַב עוּלָּא, מַאי דִּכְתִיב: "כִּי אֵין חַרְצֻבּוֹת לְמוֹתָם וּבָרִיא אוּלָם" – אָמַר הַקָּדוֹשׁ בָּרוּךְ הוּא: לֹא דַּיָּין לָרְשָׁעִים שֶׁאֵינָן חֲרֵדִין וַעֲצֵבִין מִיּוֹם הַמִּיתָה, אֶלָּא שֶׁלִּבָּם בָּרִיא לָהֶן כְּאוּלָם. וְהַיְינוּ דְּאָמַר רַבָּה, מַאי דִּכְתִיב: "זֶה דַּרְכָּם כֶּסֶל לָמוֹ" – יוֹדְעִין רְשָׁעִים שֶׁדַּרְכָּם לְמִיתָה, וְיֵשׁ לָהֶם חֵלֶב עַל כִּסְלָם. שֶׁמָּא תֹּאמַר: שִׁכְחָה הִיא מֵהֶן – תַּלְמוּד לוֹמַר: "וְאַחֲרֵיהֶם בְּפִיהֶם יִרְצוּ סֶלָה".

Rava bar Rav Ulla taught: What is the meaning of **that which is written: "For there are no pangs [*ḥartzubot*] at their death and their body is sound"** (Psalms 73:4)? **The Holy One, Blessed be He, said: Is it not enough for wicked people that they are not anxious [*ḥared*] or sad [*atzuv*],** *ḥartzubot* is an acronym of *ḥared* and *atzuv*, in anticipation **of the day** of their **death, but** also, **their heart is as unyielding for them** as the entrance to a **hall** is wide, and they devote no thought to it. **And that is** what **Rabba said: What is** the meaning of **that which is written: "This is the way of them that are foolish** and of those who after them speak approvingly, Selah" (Psalms 49:14)? It means that the **wicked know that their path** leads **to** eternal **death, but they have fat on their kidneys** that prevents that realization from entering their hearts. **Lest you say that it is** simply **forgotten from them;** therefore, **the verse states: "And of those who after them speak approvingly, Selah"** (Psalms 49:14). They are aware of their fate and speak of it, but it does not affect them.

"כְּחָס עַל הַנֵּר כו׳". רַבִּי יוֹסֵי כְּמַאן סְבִירָא לֵיהּ? אִי כְּרַבִּי יְהוּדָה סְבִירָא לֵיהּ – אֲפִילּוּ בְּהָנָךְ נַמִי לִיחַיֵּיב, וְאִי כְּרַבִּי שִׁמְעוֹן סְבִירָא לֵיהּ – פְּתִילָה נַמִי לִיפְטַר! אָמַר עוּלָּא: לְעוֹלָם כְּרַבִּי יְהוּדָה סְבִירָא לֵיהּ. וְקָסָבַר רַבִּי יוֹסֵי: סוֹתֵר עַל מְנָת לִבְנוֹת בִּמְקוֹמוֹ – הָוֵי סוֹתֵר, עַל מְנָת לִבְנוֹת שֶׁלֹּא בִּמְקוֹמוֹ – לָא הָוֵי סוֹתֵר.

We learned in the mishna that if one extinguished a flame on Shabbat because he sought to **spare the lamp,** the oil, or the wick, he is liable, but Rabbi Yosei exempts in all cases except in a case in which he extinguished the flame to spare the wick. The Gemara asks with regard to **Rabbi Yosei: In accordance with whose** opinion **does he hold** with regard to prohibited labor performed on Shabbat not for its own sake?[N] **If he holds in accordance with** the opinion of **Rabbi Yehuda,** who holds that one is liable for a prohibited labor performed on Shabbat not for its own sake, then **even in** all **those** cases **he should also deem** him **liable. And if he holds in accordance with** the opinion of **Rabbi Shimon,** who holds that one is exempt for a prohibited labor performed on Shabbat not for its own sake, then even in the case of **a wick he should also deem** him **exempt. Ulla said: Actually,** Rabbi Yosei **holds in accordance with** the opinion of **Rabbi Yehuda. However, Rabbi Yosei holds** that with regard to every destructive action, if **he dismantles in order to rebuild**[H] **in the same place,** then **it is considered** to be **dismantling,** and he is liable for having performed a prohibited labor on Shabbat. However, one who demolishes **in order to build elsewhere it is not considered** performance of the prohibited labor of **dismantling.** He merely performed a destructive act and is not liable. When one extinguishes the flame to spare the lamp or the oil, he does not do so in order to relight them. When he does so to spare the wick, he indicates that he intends to relight the wick.

NOTES

Fear and wisdom – הַיִּרְאָה וְהַחָכְמָה: There is a distinction between the statements of Rabba bar Rav Huna and Rabbi Yannai. Rabbi Yannai praises fear more because, in his opinion, fear is more sublime and more intrinsic than wisdom. Torah is nothing more than the gateway to fear. Others explained that there are various levels of fear. There is fear that serves as a prelude to acquiring the wisdom of the Torah, and Torah serves as a prelude to a higher level of fear (*Shenei Luḥot HaBerit*; Maharsha).

Be not overmuch wicked – אַל תִּרְשַׁע הַרְבֵּה: The commentaries explain that this quotation was introduced at this point because the Gemara had previously discussed Ecclesiastes and its internal contradictions. Therefore, the Gemara cited another verse that seems self-contradictory, since it warns against both righteousness and wickedness. The Gemara answers that there are indeed wicked people who gradually exacerbate their wickedness (Maharsha; *Iyyun Ya'akov*).

Prohibited labor performed on Shabbat not for its own sake – מְלָאכָה שֶׁאֵינָהּ צְרִיכָה לְגוּפָהּ: The parameters of a prohibited labor by Torah law incorporate myriad details, including the intention to perform a complete action. As a result, there are differing opinions with regard to a prohibited labor performed not for its own sake, i.e., the labor was indeed performed, but the one performing the labor has no interest in its performance. If one needs dirt and digs a hole for that purpose, creating a pit is not part of his objective. The labor of extinguishing a flame is rarely performed for its own sake; rather, it is usually extinguished to prevent light or danger. In essence, the one extinguishing the flame is indifferent to whether or not the flame itself continues to burn.

LANGUAGE

One [*hen*] – הֵן: The reference is to the Greek word ἕν, *hen*, which means one.

HALAKHA

He dismantles in order to rebuild – סוֹתֵר עַל מְנָת לִבְנוֹת: One who dismantles or ruins a structure with the intent to repair it or to rebuild it, even if the intent is to rebuild it elsewhere, is liable. If his purpose in dismantling is destructive, he is exempt (Rambam *Sefer Zemanim*, *Hilkhot Shabbat* 10:15).

NOTES

And in lighting the Shabbat lamp – וּבְהַדְלָקַת הַנֵּר: Some commentaries explain that women are not punished for failure to kindle the Shabbat lights. Rather, lack of caution results in their lighting after Shabbat has begun, and they are then punished for violating the Shabbat (Rashash).

HALAKHA

And in lighting the Shabbat lamp – וּבְהַדְלָקַת הַנֵּר: Although both men and women are commanded to kindle the Shabbat lights, this mitzva has nevertheless become the purview of women, and it is their responsibility because they are generally in charge of the home. Furthermore, it comes as compensation for the fact that the first woman, Eve, extinguished the light of the world, as per the mishna and Gemara (Rambam *Sefer Zemanim, Hilkhot Shabbat* 5:3; *Shulḥan Arukh, Oraḥ Ḥayyim* 263:3).

BACKGROUND

A quarter of a *log* of blood – רְבִיעִית דָּם: A quarter of a *log* of blood, approximately 80–150 ml according to the varying opinions of the authorities, is halakhically considered to be the minimum amount of blood required to sustain a person. Apparently, the Sages arrived at this measurement by checking the amount of blood in an embryo at a certain stage of its development. As a result, it is possible to call a quarter of a *log* of blood the blood of the soul because it is the amount required to sustain a person at the beginning of his life.

אָמַר לֵיהּ רַבָּה: מִכְּדִי, כָּל מְלָאכוֹת יַלְפִינַן לְהוּ מִמִּשְׁכָּן וְהָתָם סוֹתֵר עַל מְנָת לִבְנוֹת שֶׁלֹּא בִּמְקוֹמוֹ הוּא! אָמַר לֵיהּ: שָׁאנֵי הָתָם, כֵּיוָן דִּכְתִיב: ״עַל פִּי ה׳ יַחֲנוּ״ – כְּסוֹתֵר עַל מְנָת לִבְנוֹת בִּמְקוֹמוֹ דָּמֵי,

Rabba said to him: That reasoning is implausible. **After all, all labors** prohibited on Shabbat, **we derive them from** the labors performed in the Tabernacle, **and there it was** a case of **dismantling in order to build elsewhere.** They would dismantle the Tabernacle and reconstruct it at the next encampment. Ulla **said to** Rabba: That is not a proof, as **there,** in the case of the Tabernacle, **it is different. Since it is written: "At the commandment of the Lord they encamped"** (Numbers 9:23). The time and place of their travels and their encampments were not determined by them but rather by the word of God. Consequently, when they took down the Tabernacle **it was tantamount to demolishing in order to build in the same place.** Since the demolition and the construction were both accomplished at the command of God, there was never a case of destruction without a constructive purpose.

וְרַבִּי יוֹחָנָן אָמַר: לְעוֹלָם כְּרַבִּי שִׁמְעוֹן סְבִירָא לֵיהּ, וּמַאי שְׁנָא פְּתִילָה – כִּדְאָמַר רַב הַמְנוּנָא וְאִיתֵימָא רַב אַדָּא בַּר אַהֲבָה: הָכָא בִּפְתִילָה שֶׁצָּרִיךְ לְהַבְהֲבָהּ עָסְקִינַן, דִּבְהַהִיא אֲפִילּוּ רַבִּי שִׁמְעוֹן מוֹדֵי דְּקָא מְתַקֵּן מָנָא. אָמַר רָבָא: דַּיְקָא נַמִי דְּקָתָנֵי ״שֶׁהוּא עוֹשֶׂה פֶּחָם״ וְלָא קָתָנֵי ״מִפְּנֵי שֶׁנַּעֲשֵׂית פֶּחָם״ – שְׁמַע מִינָּהּ.

And Rabbi Yoḥanan said: Actually, Rabbi Yosei **holds in accordance with** the opinion of **Rabbi Shimon. And** as far as the question, **what is different** about **a wick,** that can be answered **as Rav Hamnuna said, and some say, Rav Adda bar Ahava** said: **Here, we are dealing with a wick that one must singe** before lighting it in order to facilitate its burning, **as, in that** case, **even Rabbi Shimon agrees** that extinguishing the flame is prohibited, **as,** by doing so, **he prepares a vessel** for use. **Rava said:** That interpretation is **also precise** in the language of the mishna, **as it was taught** in the mishna that one who extinguished a wick is liable **because he makes** the wick into **charcoal** intentionally, **and it was not taught because charcoal was made** on its own. The Gemara concludes: **Conclude from it** that the mishna is to be understood in that manner.

מתני׳ עַל שָׁלֹשׁ עֲבֵירוֹת נָשִׁים מֵתוֹת בִּשְׁעַת לֵידָתָן: עַל שֶׁאֵינָן זְהִירוֹת בְּנִדָּה, בְּחַלָּה, וּבְהַדְלָקַת הַנֵּר.

MISHNA This mishna concludes the aggadic treatment of the topic of kindling the Shabbat lights. **For three transgressions women** are punished and **die during childbirth: For** the fact **that they are not careful in** observing the laws of **a menstruating woman,** and **in** separating ***ḥalla*** from the dough, **and in lighting** the Shabbat **lamp.**[NH]

גמ׳ נִדָּה מַאי טַעְמָא? אָמַר רַבִּי יִצְחָק: הִיא קִלְקְלָה בְּחַדְרֵי בִטְנָהּ – לְפִיכָךְ תִּלְקֶה בְּחַדְרֵי בִטְנָהּ. תֵּינַח נִדָּה, חַלָּה וְהַדְלָקַת הַנֵּר מַאי אִיכָּא לְמֵימַר? כִּדְדָרַשׁ הַהוּא גָּלִילָאָה עֲלֵיהּ דְּרַב חִסְדָּא, אָמַר הַקָּדוֹשׁ בָּרוּךְ הוּא: רְבִיעִית דָּם נָתַתִּי בָּכֶם – עַל עִסְקֵי דָם הִזְהַרְתִּי אֶתְכֶם,

GEMARA The Gemara asks: A woman who was not careful in observing the laws of **menstruation, what is the reason** that she is punished during childbirth? **Rabbi Yitzḥak said: She sinned with** regard to **the chambers of her womb; therefore, she is afflicted in the chambers of her womb.** The Gemara asks: **Granted,** with regard to **menstruation;** but with regard to a woman who was not careful in separating ***ḥalla* and in kindling the Shabbat lights, what is there to say?** Rather, it must be explained **in accordance with that which that Galilean taught before Rav Ḥisda. The Holy One, Blessed be He, said: I placed a quarter** [*revi'it*] of a *log* **of blood**[B] **in you** when you were formed, and **about matters of** the **blood** of menstruation **I warned you.**

Perek **II**
Daf **32** Amud **a**

רֵאשִׁית קְרָאתִי אֶתְכֶם – עַל עִסְקֵי רֵאשִׁית הִזְהַרְתִּי אֶתְכֶם, נְשָׁמָה שֶׁנָּתַתִּי בָּכֶם קְרוּיָה נֵר – עַל עִסְקֵי נֵר הִזְהַרְתִּי אֶתְכֶם. אִם אַתֶּם מְקַיְּימִים אוֹתָם – מוּטָב, וְאִם לָאו – הֲרֵינִי נוֹטֵל נִשְׁמַתְכֶם.

I called you first, as it is stated: "Israel is the Lord's hallowed portion, His first fruits of the increase" (Jeremiah 2:3) **and I warned you about matters of the first:** "Of the first of your dough you shall set apart *ḥalla* for a gift" (Numbers 15:20). **The soul that I have placed in you is called *ner*:** "The spirit of man is the lamp [*ner*] of the Lord" (Proverbs 20:27), and **I warned you about matters of the** Shabbat **lamp. If you fulfill these** mitzvot, **fine, and if not, then I will take your soul.**

ומאי שנא בשעת לידתן? אמר רבא: נפל תורא – חדד לסכינא. אביי אמר: תפיש תירוס אמתא – בחד מחטרא ליהוי. רב חסדא אמר: שבקיה לרויא, דמנפשיה נפיל. מר עוקבא אמר: רעיא חגרא ועיזי ריהטן, אבב חוטרא – מילי, ואבי דרי – חושבנא. רב פפא אמר: אבב חנואתא נפישי אחי ומרחמי, אבב בזיוני – לא אחי ולא מרחמי.

And, if so, **what is different during childbirth?**[N] Why does the divine attribute of judgment punish them for dereliction in fulfillment of these mitzvot specifically then? The Gemara cites several folk sayings expressing the concept that when a person is in danger, he is punished for his sins. **Rava said: If the ox fell, sharpen the knife** to slaughter it. **Abaye said: If the maidservant's insolence abounds, she will be struck by a single blow** as punishment for all her sins. So too, when a woman is giving birth and her suffering is great due to Eve's sin of eating from the Tree of Knowledge, all the punishments for her own sins are added to that suffering. **Rav Ḥisda said: Leave the drunk, as he falls on his own.** Similarly, the time of birth is a time of danger, and if the Holy One, Blessed be He, does not come to her assistance at that time, that is sufficient to cause her death. **Mar Ukva said: The shepherd is crippled, and the goats are running,** and he cannot catch them. However, **next to the gate,** he speaks harsh **words, and inside the pen** he settles the **account.** Similarly, as long as a woman is in a healthy state, her sins are in abeyance, and she is not held accountable for them. However, when she is giving birth, which is a time of danger, she is held accountable for her sins and a calculation is made whether or not she is worthy of a miracle. **Rav Pappa said: At the entrance to the stores,** during a time of prosperity, **brothers and loved ones abound.** When a person is prospering financially, everyone acts like his brother or friend. However, **at the gate of disgrace,** during a time of loss and poverty, he has **no brothers and no loved ones;** everyone abandons him.

וגברי היכא מיבדקי? אמר ריש לקיש: בשעה שעוברים על הגשר. גשר ותו לא?! אימא: כעין גשר. רב לא עבר במברא דיתיב ביה גוי, אמר: דילמא מיפקיד ליה דינא עליה, ומתפיסנא בהדיה. שמואל לא עבר אלא במברא דאית ביה גוי, אמר: שטנא בתרי אומי לא שליט.

And the Gemara asks: **And where are men examined?** When are men vulnerable to judgment and held accountable for their actions? **Reish Lakish said: When they are crossing a bridge.** The Gemara wonders: Only when they are crossing **a bridge and at no other** time? Rather, **say:** Anything **like a bridge,** any place where danger is commonplace. On a similar note, the Gemara relates: **Rav would not cross** a river **in a ferry in which a gentile sat. He said** to himself: **Perhaps a judgment will be reckoned with him, and I will be caught together with him** when he is punished. Whereas, **Shmuel would only cross in a ferry if there was a gentile in it. He said: Satan does not have dominion over two nations.** He settles his accounts with people from each nationality separately.

רבי ינאי בדיק ועבר. רבי ינאי לטעמיה, דאמר: לעולם אל יעמוד אדם במקום סכנה לומר שעושין לו נס – שמא אין עושין לו נס. ואם עושין לו נס – מנכין לו מזכיותיו. אמר רבי חנין: מאי קראה – "קטנתי מכל החסדים ומכל האמת". רבי זירא ביומא דשותא לא נפיק לביני דיקלא.

Rabbi Yannai would examine the ferry **and cross.** The Gemara comments that **Rabbi Yannai** acted **in accordance with his reasoning** stated elsewhere, as **he said: A person should never stand in a place of danger**[H] **saying that they** on High **will perform a miracle for him, lest** in the end **they do not perform a miracle for him. And,** moreover, even **if they do perform a miracle for him, they will deduct it from his merits. Rabbi Ḥanin said: What is the verse** that alludes to this? When Jacob said: **"I am not worthy of all the mercies, and of all the truth,** which You have shown unto Your servant" (Genesis 32:11), and he explains: Since You have bestowed upon me so much kindness and truth, my merits have been diminished. Similarly, the Gemara relates that **Rabbi Zeira would not go out** and walk **among the palm trees on a day when there was a southern wind**[B] blowing due to the fear that the trees might fall on him.

אמר רב יצחק בריה דרב יהודה: לעולם יבקש אדם רחמים שלא יחלה, שאם יחלה – אומרים לו: הבא זכות והפטר. אמר מר עוקבא: מאי קראה – "כי יפול הנופל ממנו" ממנו להביא ראיה. תנא דבי רבי ישמעאל: "כי יפול הנופל ממנו" (ממנו) ראוי זה ליפול מששת ימי בראשית, שהרי לא נפל, והכתוב קראו נופל. אלא שמגלגלין זכות על ידי זכאי וחובה על ידי חייב.

In a similar vein, **Rav Yitzḥak, son of Rav Yehuda, said: A person should always pray that he will not become ill, as if he becomes ill they say to him: Bring** proof of your **virtue and exempt yourself.** It is preferable for a person not to be forced to prove that he merits staying alive, as he might not be able to prove it. **Mar Ukva said: What is the verse** that alludes to this? As it says: "When you build a new house, then you shall make a parapet for your roof, that you bring not blood upon your house, **if the fallen falls *mimenu*"** (Deuteronomy 22:8). He explains: ***Mimenu*, from him proof must be brought.** When one falls from his previous situation, it is his own responsibility to prove his innocence and emerge unharmed. **The school of Rabbi Yishmael taught:** What is the meaning of the phrase: **If the fallen falls from it?** This person **was destined to fall** from that roof **from the six days of Creation,** it was ingrained into nature. **As,** although **he did not yet fall, the verse calls him fallen. Nevertheless,** the owner of the house is indicted for this, as **merit is engendered by means of** the **innocent and guilt by means of** the **guilty.**

NOTES

During childbirth – שעת לידתן: The fundamental concept underlying all of these statements is that only rarely do divine punishments come with no material foreshadowing. Nevertheless, the time for retribution is when one is in a dangerous situation engendered by external factors. The folk expressions cited here seek, in different ways and to varying degrees, to express the same concept: In times of distress, all of one's outstanding debts with God are settled.

HALAKHA

A person should never stand in a place of danger – לעולם אל יעמוד אדם במקום סכנה: One is required to distance himself from elements or places that are potentially dangerous and refrain from relying on miracles. The Sages even said: One must treat danger with greater stringency than he treats prohibition. Therefore, one must be more vigilant in avoiding potential danger than in avoiding potential prohibition (Rambam *Sefer Nezikin, Hilkhot Rotze'aḥ UShemirat HaNefesh* 12:6; *Shulḥan Arukh, Yoreh De'a* 116:5 and in the comment of the Rema).

BACKGROUND

Southern wind – שותא: The *Arukh* explains that this refers to a strong easterly wind that is apparently very hot and dry, causes food to spoil, and causes discomfort and fatigue among the people.

תָּנוּ רַבָּנַן: מִי שֶׁחָלָה וְנָטָה לָמוּת, אוֹמְרִים לוֹ: הִתְוַדֵּה, שֶׁכֵּן כׇּל הַמּוּמָתִין מִתְוַדִּין. אָדָם יוֹצֵא לַשּׁוּק – יְהִי דּוֹמֶה בְּעֵינָיו כְּמִי שֶׁנִּמְסַר לְסַרְדְּיוֹט, חָשׁ בְּרֹאשׁוֹ – יְהִי דּוֹמֶה בְּעֵינָיו כְּמִי שֶׁנְּתָנוּהוּ בְּקוֹלָר, עָלָה לַמִּטָּה וְנָפַל – יְהִי דּוֹמֶה בְּעֵינָיו כְּמוֹ שֶׁהֶעֱלוּהוּ לַגַּרְדּוֹם לִידּוֹן; שֶׁכׇּל הָעוֹלֶה לַגַּרְדּוֹם לִידּוֹן אִם יֵשׁ לוֹ פְּרַקְלִיטִין גְּדוֹלִים – נִיצּוֹל, וְאִם לָאו – אֵינוֹ נִיצּוֹל.

The Sages taught: One who became ill and tended toward death, they say to him: Confess,[H] **as all those executed** by the courts **confess.** Even if he is dying of natural causes, it is worthwhile for him to consider his death atonement for his sins. The Sages said: When **a person goes out to the marketplace** where there are fights and disputes, **he should consider himself as someone who has been handed over to a soldier** [*seradiyot*].[L] **If his head hurt, he should consider it as if they placed him in a chain** [*kolar*][L] around his neck. If **he climbed into bed and fell ill, he should consider himself as if they took him up to the gallows to be judged,** as with regard to **anyone who goes up to the gallows to be judged, if he has great advocates** [*peraklitin*],[L] **he is spared, and if not, he is not spared.**

וְאֵלּוּ הֵן פְּרַקְלִיטִין שֶׁל אָדָם – תְּשׁוּבָה וּמַעֲשִׂים טוֹבִים. וַאֲפִילּוּ תְּשַׁע מֵאוֹת וְתִשְׁעִים וְתִשְׁעָה מְלַמְּדִים עָלָיו חוֹבָה, וְאֶחָד מְלַמֵּד עָלָיו זְכוּת – נִיצּוֹל, שֶׁנֶּאֱמַר: ״אִם יֵשׁ עָלָיו מַלְאָךְ מֵלִיץ אֶחָד מִנִּי אָלֶף לְהַגִּיד לְאָדָם יׇשְׁרוֹ וַיְחֻנֶּנּוּ וַיֹּאמֶר פְּדָעֵהוּ מֵרֶדֶת שַׁחַת וגו׳״. רַבִּי אֱלִיעֶזֶר בְּנוֹ שֶׁל רַבִּי יוֹסֵי הַגְּלִילִי אוֹמֵר: אֲפִילּוּ תְּשַׁע מֵאוֹת וְתִשְׁעִים וְתִשְׁעָה בְּאוֹתוֹ מַלְאָךְ לְחוֹבָה וְאֶחָד לִזְכוּת – נִיצּוֹל, שֶׁנֶּאֱמַר: ״מֵלִיץ אֶחָד מִנִּי אָלֶף״.

And with regard to divine judgment, **these are a person's advocates: Repentance and good deeds.** The Gemara comments: **And even** if there are **nine hundred ninety-nine asserting his guilt and** only **one** asserting his **innocence, he is spared,** as **it is stated: "If there be for him an angel, an advocate, one among a thousand, to vouch for a man's uprightness; then He is gracious unto him, and says: Deliver him from going down to the pit,** I have found a ransom" (Job 33:23–24). **Rabbi Eliezer, son of Rabbi Yosei HaGelili, says: Even** if there are **nine hundred ninety-nine** portions **within that same angel**[N] accusing him, **and one** portion asserting **his innocence, he is spared, as it stated: "An advocate, one among a thousand."** Even when the advocate who asserts his innocence finds only one-tenth of one percent of innocence in this man, even then, he is gracious unto him, and says: Deliver him from going down to the pit, I have found a ransom.

תָּנוּ רַבָּנַן: עַל שָׁלֹשׁ עֲבֵירוֹת נָשִׁים מֵתוֹת יוֹלְדוֹת, רַבִּי אֶלְעָזָר אוֹמֵר: נָשִׁים מֵתוֹת יְלָדוֹת. רַבִּי אַחָא אוֹמֵר: בַּעֲוֹן שֶׁמְּכַבְּסוֹת צוֹאַת בְּנֵיהֶם בְּשַׁבָּת, וְיֵשׁ אוֹמְרִים: עַל שֶׁקּוֹרִין לַאֲרוֹן הַקֹּדֶשׁ ״אַרְנָא״.

The Sages taught in a *baraita*: **For three transgressions women die in childbirth** [*yoledot*]. **Rabbi Elazar** has a different version and **says** that **women die** when they are **young** [*yeladot*]. These transgressions are those enumerated in the mishna: The *halakhot* of a menstruating woman, *ḥalla*, and Shabbat lights. **Rabbi Aḥa says** they are punished **for the sin of laundering their children's feces** from clothing **on Shabbat. And some say: Because they call the Holy Ark** simply **ark.**[B]

תַּנְיָא, רַבִּי יִשְׁמָעֵאל בֶּן אֶלְעָזָר אוֹמֵר: בַּעֲוֹן שְׁנֵי דְבָרִים עַמֵּי הָאָרֶץ מֵתִים – עַל שֶׁקּוֹרִין לַאֲרוֹן הַקֹּדֶשׁ ״אַרְנָא״, וְעַל שֶׁקּוֹרִין לְבֵית הַכְּנֶסֶת ״בֵּית עַם״. תַּנְיָא, רַבִּי יוֹסֵי אוֹמֵר: שְׁלֹשָׁה בִּדְקֵי מִיתָה נִבְרְאוּ בָּאִשָּׁה, וְאָמְרִי לַהּ: שְׁלֹשָׁה דִּבְקֵי מִיתָה, נִדָּה וְחַלָּה וְהַדְלָקַת הַנֵּר. חֲדָא כְּרַבִּי אֶלְעָזָר, וַחֲדָא כְּרַבָּנַן.

Similarly, **we learned** in a *baraita* that **Rabbi Yishmael ben Elazar says: On account of two sins, ignoramuses** [*amei ha'aretz*] **die** young (Rav Ya'akov Emden): **Because they call the Holy Ark** simply **ark, and because they call the synagogue the house of the people. It was taught** in a *baraita* that **Rabbi Yosei says: Three crucibles** potentially leading to **death were created in the woman, and some say: Three accelerants of death.** They are: **Menstruation, *ḥalla*, and lighting the Shabbat lights.** The Gemara explains that **one** version, accelerants of death, is **in accordance with** the opinion of **Rabbi Elazar,** who said that women die young. **And** the other **one,** crucibles of death, is **in accordance with** the opinion of **the Rabbis,** who said that women die in childbirth.

תַּנְיָא, רַבָּן שִׁמְעוֹן בֶּן גַּמְלִיאֵל אוֹמֵר: הִלְכוֹת הֶקְדֵּשׁ תְּרוּמוֹת וּמַעַשְׂרוֹת הֵן הֵן גּוּפֵי תוֹרָה,

Similarly, **it was taught** in a *baraita* that **Rabbi Shimon ben Gamliel says: The *halakhot* of consecrated items, *terumot*, and tithes are themselves** the **essence of Torah** and are extremely severe,

Perek **II**
Daf **32** Amud **b**

וְנִמְסְרוּ לְעַמֵּי הָאָרֶץ.

and they were given, among others, **to ignoramuses**[N] to fulfill. When they are negligent in the performance of these mitzvot, they are punished for it.

HALAKHA

One who became ill and tended toward death, they say to him: Confess – מִי שֶׁחָלָה וְנָטָה לָמוּת, אוֹמְרִים לוֹ הִתְוַדֵּה: They also say to him: Many people have confessed and survived, and many have not confessed and died. As a reward for confessing, you live, and anyone who confesses has a portion in the World-to-Come. If one is unable to verbalize his confession, he may confess in his heart. If he does not know how to confess, he is told to say: My death shall be atonement for my sins (Rambam *Sefer HaMadda, Hilkhot Teshuva* 1:1; *Shulḥan Arukh Yoreh De'a* 338:1).

LANGUAGE

Soldier [*seradiyot*] – סַרְדְּיוֹט: From the Greek στρατιώτης, *stratiotes*, meaning soldier. Beginning in mishnaic times, it meant specifically a professional soldier or mercenary.

Chain [*kolar*] – קוֹלָר: From the Latin collare, meaning a chain around the neck of an animal or a prisoner.

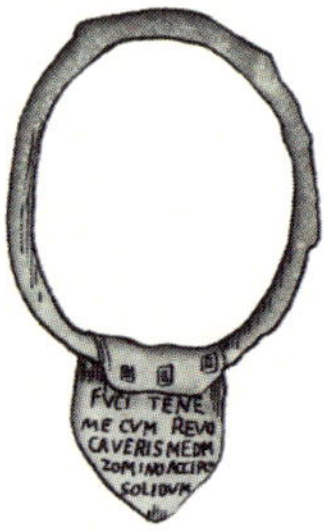

Kolar

Advocates [*peraklitin*] – פְּרַקְלִיטִין: from the Greek παράκλητος, *parakletos*, meaning one who pleads on another's behalf or a lawyer.

NOTES

Nine hundred…within that same angel – תְּשַׁע מֵאוֹת...בְּאוֹתוֹ מַלְאָךְ: Clearly, repentance and good deeds are identified with the advocate angel, since a good deed is itself an angel that advocates on one's behalf. Rabbi Eliezer, son of Rabbi Yosei HaGelili, added that even if the good deed contains other aspects that are not completely good, if there is just a kernel of good in the action, that is sufficient.

BACKGROUND

They call it ark – שֶׁקּוֹרִין אַרְנָא: Medieval and modern talmudic commentaries (see *Tosafot*) ask: What is the sin in referring to the Holy Ark as simply ark [*arna*]? The Sages refer to it the same way [*aron*]. Perhaps the distinction is that the proper Aramaic term for ark is *arona*, while *arna* also means wild goat. Therefore, the use of that term is inappropriate when referring to the Holy Ark.

NOTES

And they were given to ignoramuses – וְנִמְסְרוּ לְעַמֵּי הָאָרֶץ: For all intents and purposes, observance of these mitzvot is in the purview of all, including ignoramuses. These mitzvot were underscored in particular because once an item achieves consecrated or *teruma* status, that is its status, not only for the one who consecrated it but for everyone. Therefore, ignoramuses also determine the sanctity of items, even in these stringent areas of *halakha*.

תַּנְיָא, רַבִּי נָתָן אוֹמֵר: בַּעֲוֹן נְדָרִים מֵתָה אִשְׁתּוֹ שֶׁל אָדָם, שֶׁנֶּאֱמַר: ״אִם אֵין לְךָ לְשַׁלֵּם לָמָּה יִקַּח מִשְׁכָּבְךָ מִתַּחְתֶּיךָ״. רַבִּי אוֹמֵר: בַּעֲוֹן נְדָרִים בָּנִים מֵתִים כְּשֶׁהֵן קְטַנִּים, שֶׁנֶּאֱמַר: ״אַל תִּתֵּן אֶת פִּיךָ לַחֲטִיא אֶת בְּשָׂרֶךָ וְאַל תֹּאמַר לִפְנֵי הַמַּלְאָךְ כִּי שְׁגָגָה הִיא לָמָּה יִקְצֹף הָאֱלֹהִים עַל קוֹלֶךָ וְחִבֵּל אֶת מַעֲשֵׂה יָדֶיךָ״. אֵיזֶה הֵן מַעֲשֵׂה יָדָיו שֶׁל אָדָם – הֱוֵי אוֹמֵר: בָּנָיו וּבְנוֹתָיו שֶׁל אָדָם.

It was taught in a *baraita* that **Rabbi Natan says: Due to the sin of vows** unfulfilled **a person's wife dies.** The allusion is **as it is stated: "If you have not the wherewithal to pay, why should He take away your bed from under you?"** (Proverbs 22:27). **Rabbi Yehuda HaNasi says: Due to the sin of vows** unfulfilled, **children die when they are young, as it is stated:** "Better is it that you should not vow, than that you should vow and not pay. **Suffer not your mouth to bring your flesh into guilt, neither say you before the messenger that it was an error; wherefore should God be angry at your voice and destroy the work of your hands?"** (Ecclesiastes 5:4–5). **What is the work of a person's hands? You must say** that it is **a person's sons and daughters.**

תָּנוּ רַבָּנַן, בַּעֲוֹן נְדָרִים בָּנִים מֵתִים – דִּבְרֵי רַבִּי אֶלְעָזָר בְּרַבִּי שִׁמְעוֹן, רַבִּי יְהוּדָה הַנָּשִׂיא אוֹמֵר: בַּעֲוֹן בִּיטּוּל תּוֹרָה. בִּשְׁלָמָא לְמַאן דְּאָמַר בַּעֲוֹן נְדָרִים – כִּדְאֲמַרַן, אֶלָּא לְמַאן דְּאָמַר בַּעֲוֹן בִּיטּוּל תּוֹרָה – מַאי קְרָאָה? דִּכְתִיב: ״לַשָּׁוְא הִכֵּיתִי אֶת בְּנֵיכֶם מוּסָר לֹא לָקָחוּ״. רַב נַחְמָן בַּר יִצְחָק אָמַר: לְמַאן דְּאָמַר בַּעֲוֹן נְדָרִים נַמִי מֵהָכָא – ״לַשָּׁוְא הִכֵּיתִי אֶת בְּנֵיכֶם״ – עַל עִסְקֵי שָׁוְא. מִכְּדִי, רַבִּי יְהוּדָה הַנָּשִׂיא הַיְינוּ רַבִּי, וְרַבִּי בַּעֲוֹן נְדָרִים קָאָמַר! בָּתַר דִּשְׁמַעָהּ מֵרַבִּי אֶלְעָזָר בְּרַבִּי שִׁמְעוֹן.

In order to clarify which sins cause one's young children to die, the Gemara cites what **the Sages taught** in a *baraita*: **For the sin of vows, one's children die,** this is **the statement of Rabbi Elazar, son of Rabbi Shimon. Rabbi Yehuda HaNasi says: For the sin of dereliction in** the study of **Torah.**[N] The Gemara asks: **Granted, according to** the opinion of **the one who said** that one's children die **due to the sin of vows, as we stated** above. **However, according to the** opinion of **the one who said** that one's children die **due to sin of dereliction in** the study of **Torah, what is the verse** that supports this? The Gemara replies: **As it is written: "In vain have I smitten your children; they received no morality"** (Jeremiah 2:30). Children die because their fathers did not accept the morality, the Torah. **Rav Naḥman bar Yitzḥak said: According to the one who said** that one's children die **because of the sin of vows, it can also** be derived **from here: In vain have I smitten your children; on matters of vanity,** i.e., when one vows in vain and does not fulfill it. The Gemara asks: **After all, Rabbi Yehuda HaNasi is Rabbi, and** it was taught in a *Tosefta* that **Rabbi said** that one's children die **because of the sin of vows.** How then could it be that Rabbi Yehuda HaNasi said that it is due to the sin of dereliction in the study of Torah? The Gemara answers: **After he heard it from Rabbi Elazar, son of Rabbi Shimon,** he reconsidered and taught in accordance with Rabbi Elazar's opinion.

NOTES

For the sin of dereliction in the study of Torah – בַּעֲוֹן בִּיטּוּל תּוֹרָה: In tractate *Kalla* a similar concept is expressed, but a different proof is cited: "You have forgotten the Torah of your God; I too will forget your children" (Hosea 4:6).

פְּלִיגִי בָּהּ רַבִּי חִיָּיא בַּר אַבָּא וְרַבִּי יוֹסֵי, חַד אָמַר: בַּעֲוֹן מְזוּזָה, וְחַד אָמַר: בַּעֲוֹן בִּיטּוּל תּוֹרָה. לְמַאן דְּאָמַר ״בַּעֲוֹן מְזוּזָה״ – מִקְרָא נִדְרָשׁ לְפָנָיו וְלֹא לִפְנֵי פָנָיו. וּלְמַאן דְּאָמַר ״בַּעֲוֹן בִּיטּוּל תּוֹרָה״ מִקְרָא נִדְרָשׁ לְפָנָיו וְלִפְנֵי פָנָיו.

On the same topic, **Rabbi Ḥiyya bar Abba and Rabbi Yosei disagree. One said** that children die **due to the sin of** not affixing a *mezuza* to one's doorpost. **And one said** children die **due to the sin of dereliction in** the study of **Torah. According to the one who said** that children die **because of the sin of** not affixing a *mezuza*, his opinion there is based on an exegetical principle, which states that **a verse is interpreted homiletically** based on juxtaposition to the verse immediately **preceding it and not** on juxtaposition to the verse **before the one preceding it.** In this case, it says: "That your days may be multiplied, and the days of your children" (Deuteronomy 11:21), and the preceding verse says: "And you shall write them upon the doorposts of your house, and upon your gates" (Deuteronomy 11:20). **And according to the one who said** that children die due to **the sin of dereliction in** the study of **Torah,** that is because in his opinion the exegetical principle is that **a verse is interpreted homiletically** based on juxtaposition to the verse immediately **preceding it, as well as** to the verse **before the one preceding it.** In his opinion, the blessing of long life also relates to the verse before the one immediately preceding it: "And you shall teach them your children, talking of them" (Deuteronomy 11:19).

פְּלִיגִי בָּהּ רַבִּי מֵאִיר וְרַבִּי יְהוּדָה; חַד אָמַר: בַּעֲוֹן מְזוּזָה, וְחַד אָמַר: בַּעֲוֹן צִיצִית. בִּשְׁלָמָא לְמַאן דְּאָמַר בַּעֲוֹן מְזוּזָה – דִּכְתִיב: ״וּכְתַבְתָּם עַל מְזוּזוֹת בֵּיתֶךָ״ וּכְתִיב בַּתְרֵיהּ: ״לְמַעַן יִרְבּוּ יְמֵיכֶם וִימֵי בְנֵיכֶם״. אֶלָּא לְמַאן דְּאָמַר בַּעֲוֹן צִיצִית, מַאי טַעְמָא? אָמַר רַב כָּהֲנָא וְאִיתֵימָא שֵׁילָא מָרִי, דִּכְתִיב: ״גַּם בִּכְנָפַיִךְ נִמְצְאוּ דַּם נַפְשׁוֹת אֶבְיוֹנִים נְקִיִּים״. רַב נַחְמָן בַּר יִצְחָק אָמַר: לְמַאן דְּאָמַר בַּעֲוֹן מְזוּזָה נַמִי מֵהָכָא, דִּכְתִיב: ״לֹא בַמַּחְתֶּרֶת מְצָאתִים״ – שֶׁעָשׂוּ פְּתָחִים כְּמַחְתֶּרֶת.

The *tanna'im* **Rabbi Meir and Rabbi Yehuda** also **disagreed about this. One said:** Children die **due to the sin of** *mezuza*, **and one said** children die **due to the sin of** not affixing **ritual fringes.** The Gemara asks: **Granted,** according **to** the opinion of **the one who said** that children die **due to the sin of** *mezuza*, it is based on the juxtaposition of the verses, **as it is written: "And you shall write them upon the doorposts of your house,** and upon your gates," **and it says thereafter: "That your days may be multiplied, and the days of your children." However, according to the one who said** that children die **because of the sin of ritual fringes, what is the reason?** What is the connection between these matters? **Rav Kahana said, and some say** that it was **Sheila Mari:** It is homiletically interpreted **as is written: "Also in your corners is found the blood of the souls of the innocent poor"** (Jeremiah 2:34). Due to one's failure to affix ritual fringes to the corners of his garments, the innocent poor, young children, who have not had opportunity to sin, die. **Rav Naḥman bar Yitzḥak said:** According **to the one who said** that children die **because of the sin of** *mezuza*, **it is also** derived **from here, as it is written** in the continuation of that verse: **"You did not find them breaking in;** yet for all these things." We see that this punishment comes **because they made entrances like** a thief's **breach** in the wall. They did not place *mezuzot* in their entrances.

HALAKHA

Anyone who is vigilant in performing the mitzva of ritual fringes, etc. – כׇּל הַזָּהִיר בְּצִיצִית וכו׳: The mitzva of ritual fringes is a significant one, as the Torah equated it to all the mitzvot, as it is stated: "That you may look upon it, and remember all the commandments of the Lord" (Numbers 19:39). Therefore, one must be vigilant with regard to this mitzva and perform it in a beautiful manner (Rambam *Sefer Ahava, Hilkhot Tzitzit* 3:12; *Tur Oraḥ Ḥayyim* 24).

NOTES

Mnemonic – סִימָן: This mnemonic includes all the cases subsequently discussed, although the Gemara cited them with slight emendations. It is a mnemonic for hate, for gratuitous hatred; *ḥalla*; *teruma*; theft; judgment, for distortion and perversion of justice; oath, for a vain oath; pouring, for murder; uncovering, for prohibited sexual relations; and vulgarity, for vulgar speech.

Consume the snow waters – יִגְזְלוּ מֵימֵי שֶׁלֶג: Apparently, the word consume applies to both the beginning and the end of the verse. It should be interpreted as follows: As drought and heat will consume, i.e., if people steal the gifts that they are meant to give to others in the summer, then ultimately, that will cause the snow waters to be consumed. The verse itself can also mean that when drought and heat consume the snow waters, it is a sign that: "So does the netherworld [consume] those that have sinned" (Rashi).

BACKGROUND

Meḥoza – מְחוֹזָא: Meḥoza was a large city on the banks of the Tigris River, not far from the Malka River that connects the Tigris with the Euphrates River. Its location in the center of Babylonia led to its development as a wealthy commercial city. The people of Meḥoza were known for their great wealth, to the extent that even the male residents would wear special, ornamented clothing. A large portion of the city's population was Jewish, and included many converts. Rava was the head of the yeshiva in Meḥoza, which later merged with the yeshiva of Neharde'a-Pumbedita. He regularly rebuked the people of the city for their self-indulgence, dishonesty, and lack of fear of God.

אָמַר רֵישׁ לָקִישׁ: כׇּל הַזָּהִיר בְּצִיצִית זוֹכֶה וּמְשַׁמְּשִׁין לוֹ שְׁנֵי אֲלָפִים וּשְׁמוֹנֶה מֵאוֹת עֲבָדִים, שֶׁנֶּאֱמַר: ״כֹּה אָמַר ה׳ [צְבָאוֹת] בַּיָּמִים הָהֵמָּה אֲשֶׁר יַחֲזִיקוּ עֲשָׂרָה אֲנָשִׁים מִכֹּל לְשׁוֹנוֹת הַגּוֹיִם [וְהֶחֱזִיקוּ] בִּכְנַף אִישׁ יְהוּדִי לֵאמֹר נֵלְכָה עִמָּכֶם וגו׳״.

Since the Gemara discussed the importance of the mitzva of ritual fringes, it cites that which **Reish Lakish said: Anyone who is vigilant in** performing the mitzva of **ritual fringes**[H] **merits** that **two thousand eight hundred servants will serve him** in the World-to-Come. **As it is stated: "Thus says the Lord of hosts: In those days it shall come to pass, that ten men shall take hold, out of all the languages of the nations, shall even take hold of the corner of the garment of him that is a Jew, saying: We will go with you,** for we have heard that God is with you" (Zechariah 8:23). On each corner of a Jewish person's garment with ritual fringes, ten people from each of the seventy nations will take hold. That totals seven hundred people on each corner; 2,800 people altogether.

סִימָן: שָׂנֵא חַלָּה תְּרוּמָה נְגֶזֶלֶת דִּינָא שְׁבוּעָה שִׁיפּוּכְתָא גִּילּוּיָא וְנַבְלוּתָא. תַּנְיָא, רַבִּי נְחֶמְיָה אוֹמֵר: בַּעֲוֹן שִׂנְאַת חִנָּם – מְרִיבָה רַבָּה בְּתוֹךְ בֵּיתוֹ שֶׁל אָדָם, וְאִשְׁתּוֹ מַפֶּלֶת נְפָלִים, וּבָנָיו וּבְנוֹתָיו שֶׁל אָדָם מֵתִים כְּשֶׁהֵן קְטַנִּים. רַבִּי אֶלְעָזָר בְּרַבִּי יְהוּדָה אוֹמֵר: בַּעֲוֹן חַלָּה אֵין בְּרָכָה בַּמְּכוּנָּס, וּמְאֵרָה מִשְׁתַּלַּחַת בַּשְּׁעָרִים, וְזוֹרְעִין זְרָעִים וַאֲחֵרִים אוֹכְלִין, שֶׁנֶּאֱמַר: ״אַף אֲנִי אֶעֱשֶׂה זֹּאת לָכֶם וְהִפְקַדְתִּי עֲלֵיכֶם בֶּהָלָה אֶת הַשַּׁחֶפֶת וְאֶת הַקַּדַּחַת מְכַלּוֹת עֵינַיִם וּמְדִיבוֹת נָפֶשׁ וּזְרַעְתֶּם לָרִיק זַרְעֲכֶם וַאֲכָלֻהוּ אֹיְבֵיכֶם״, אַל תִּקְרֵי ״בֶּהָלָה״ אֶלָּא ״בְּחַלָּה״. וְאִם נוֹתְנִין – מִתְבָּרְכִין, שֶׁנֶּאֱמַר: ״[וְ]רֵאשִׁית עֲרִיסוֹתֵיכֶם תִּתְּנוּ לַכֹּהֵן לְהָנִיחַ בְּרָכָה אֶל בֵּיתֶךָ״.

Together with these statements, the Gemara cites **a mnemonic**[N] for additional rabbinic adages with regard to punishments for various sins: **Hate, *ḥalla*, *teruma*, stolen, judgment, oath, pouring, uncovering, and vulgarity. It was taught** in a *baraita*, **Rabbi Neḥemya says: Due to the sin of gratuitous hatred** that one has for another, the punishment is **great discord within a person's home, and his wife miscarries, and his sons and daughters die when they are young. Rabbi Elazar, son of Rabbi Yehuda, said: Due to the sin** of failure to separate ***ḥalla*** from the dough, **no blessing takes effect on the** grain **gathered** in the storehouse **and a curse spreads to the prices** of crops, which increase, **and they plant seeds and others eat** their yield, **as it is stated: "I also will do this unto you: I will appoint terror [*behala*] over you, even consumption and fever, that shall make the eyes to fail and the soul to languish; and you shall sow your seed in vain, for your enemies shall eat it"** (Leviticus 26:16). **Do not read** it ***behala*;** **rather,** read it as ***beḥalla*.** Due to negligence in the separation of *ḥalla* from the dough, these punishments come. **And if they give** *ḥalla*, **they are blessed, as it is stated: "And the first of your dough you shall give unto the priest to cause a blessing to rest on your house"** (Ezekiel 44:30).

בַּעֲוֹן בִּיטּוּל תְּרוּמוֹת וּמַעַשְׂרוֹת שָׁמַיִם נֶעֱצָרִין מִלְּהוֹרִיד טַל וּמָטָר, וְהַיּוֹקֶר הוֹוֶה, וְהַשָּׂכָר אָבֵד, וּבְנֵי אָדָם רָצִין אַחַר פַּרְנָסָתָן וְאֵין מַגִּיעִין, שֶׁנֶּאֱמַר: ״צִיָּה גַם חוֹם יִגְזְלוּ מֵימֵי שֶׁלֶג שְׁאוֹל חָטָאוּ״. מַאי מַשְׁמַע? תָּנָא דְּבֵי רַבִּי יִשְׁמָעֵאל: בִּשְׁבִיל דְּבָרִים שֶׁצִּוִּיתִי אֶתְכֶם בִּימוֹת הַחַמָּה וְלֹא עֲשִׂיתֶם – יִגְזְלוּ מִכֶּם מֵימֵי שֶׁלֶג בִּימוֹת הַגְּשָׁמִים. וְאִם נוֹתְנִין – מִתְבָּרְכִין, שֶׁנֶּאֱמַר: ״הָבִיאוּ אֶת כׇּל הַמַּעֲשֵׂר אֶל בֵּית הָאוֹצָר וִיהִי טֶרֶף בְּבֵיתִי וּבְחָנוּנִי נָא בָּזֹאת אָמַר ה׳ צְבָאוֹת אִם לֹא אֶפְתַּח לָכֶם אֵת אֲרֻבּוֹת הַשָּׁמַיִם וַהֲרִיקוֹתִי לָכֶם בְּרָכָה עַד בְּלִי דָי״, מַאי ״עַד בְּלִי דַי״? אָמַר רָמִי בַּר (רַב) אָמַר רַב: עַד שֶׁיִּבְלוּ שִׂפְתוֹתֵיכֶם מִלּוֹמַר דַּי.

They also said: **Due to the sin of abrogation of *terumot* and tithes, the heavens are prevented from pouring down dew and rain, and expense prevails, and profit is lost, and people pursue their livelihood but do not attain it, as it is stated: "Drought and heat consume the snow waters;**[N] **so does the netherworld those that have sinned"** (Job 24:19). The Gemara asks: **What is the inference?** How is that concept derived from this verse? **The school of Rabbi Yishmael taught** that it should be explained as follows: **Due to the things that I commanded you during the summer,** separating *terumot* and tithes from the summer crops, **and you did not do them, the snow waters will be robbed from you during the rainy season. And if** people **give** *terumot* and tithes, **they are blessed, as it is stated: "Bring you the whole tithe into the storehouse, that there may be food in My house, and try Me now with this, says the Lord of Hosts, if I will not open you the windows of heaven, and pour you out a blessing, that there shall be more than sufficiency [*ad bli dai*]"** (Malachi 3:10). The Gemara asks: **What** is the meaning of: **More than sufficiency [*ad bli dai*]? Rami bar Rav said** that **Rav said:** It means that the abundance will be so great **that your lips will be worn out [*yivlu*],** similar to the word *beli*, **from saying enough [*dai*].**

בַּעֲוֹן גָּזֵל הַגּוֹבַאי עוֹלֶה, וְהָרָעָב הוֹוֶה, וּבְנֵי אָדָם אוֹכְלִים בְּשַׂר בְּנֵיהֶן וּבְנוֹתֵיהֶן, שֶׁנֶּאֱמַר: ״שִׁמְעוּ הַדָּבָר הַזֶּה פָּרוֹת הַבָּשָׁן אֲשֶׁר בְּהַר שׁוֹמְרוֹן הָעוֹשְׁקוֹת דַּלִּים הָרוֹצְצוֹת אֶבְיוֹנִים״ אָמַר רָבָא: כְּגוֹן הָנֵי נְשֵׁי דִּמְחוֹזָא,

Due to the sin of robbery, locusts emerge, and famine prevails, and people eat the flesh of their sons and daughters, as it is **stated: "Hear this word, you cows of Bashan, that are in the mountain of Samaria, that oppress the poor, that crush the needy,** that say unto their lords: Bring, that we may feast" (Amos 4:1). Afterward it says: "And I also have given you cleanness of teeth in all your cities, and want of bread in all your places" (Amos 4:6), which refers to famine. **Rava said:** The cows of Bashan; **like those women of** the city of **Meḥoza,**[B]

דְּאָכְלָן וְלָא עָבְדָן. וּכְתִיב: ״הִכֵּיתִי אֶתְכֶם בַּשִּׁדָּפוֹן וּבַיֵּרָקוֹן הַרְבּוֹת גַּנּוֹתֵיכֶם וְכַרְמֵיכֶם וּתְאֵנֵיכֶם וְזֵיתֵיכֶם יֹאכַל הַגָּזָם״. וּכְתִיב: ״יֶתֶר הַגָּזָם אָכַל הָאַרְבֶּה וְיֶתֶר הָאַרְבֶּה אָכַל הַיָּלֶק וְיֶתֶר הַיֶּלֶק אָכַל הֶחָסִיל״. וּכְתִיב: ״וַיִּגְזוֹר עַל יָמִין וְרָעֵב וַיֹּאכַל עַל שְׂמֹאל וְלֹא שָׂבֵעוּ אִישׁ בְּשַׂר זְרוֹעוֹ יֹאכֵלוּ״, אַל תִּקְרֵי ׳בְּשַׂר זְרוֹעוֹ׳ אֶלָּא ׳בְּשַׂר זַרְעוֹ׳.

who eat and do nothing to support themselves, and cause their husbands to commit the sin of theft. **And it is written: “I have smitten you with blight and mildew; the multitude of your gardens and your vineyards and your fig trees and your olive trees has the palmerworm devoured”** (Amos 4:9). **And it is written: “That which the palmerworm has left the locust has eaten; and that which the locust has left the cankerworm has eaten; and that which the cankerworm has left the caterpillar has eaten”** (Joel 1:4). **And it is written: “And one snatches on the right hand, and is hungry; and he eats on the left hand, and is not satisfied; they eat every man the flesh of his own arm** [*besar zero’o*]**”** (Isaiah 9:19). **Do not read** it: **The flesh of his own arm** [*besar zero’o*]; **rather, the flesh of his own offspring** [*besar zaro*]. All the punishments for theft listed above were explicitly mentioned in the verses.

בַּעֲוֹן עִינּוּי הַדִּין וְעִיוּוּת הַדִּין וְקִלְקוּל הַדִּין וּבִיטּוּל תּוֹרָה חֶרֶב וּבִיזָּה רַבָּה, וְדֶבֶר וּבַצּוֹרֶת בָּא, וּבְנֵי אָדָם אוֹכְלִין וְאֵינָן שְׂבֵעִין, וְאוֹכְלִין לַחְמָם בְּמִשְׁקָל, דִּכְתִיב: ״וְהֵבֵאתִי עֲלֵיכֶם חֶרֶב נוֹקֶמֶת נְקַם בְּרִית וגו׳״. וְאֵין בְּרִית אֶלָּא תּוֹרָה, שֶׁנֶּאֱמַר: ״אִם לֹא בְרִיתִי יוֹמָם וָלָיְלָה וגו׳״. וּכְתִיב: ״בְּשִׁבְרִי לָכֶם מַטֵּה לֶחֶם וְאָפוּ עֶשֶׂר נָשִׁים וגו׳״. וּכְתִיב: ״יַעַן וּבְיַעַן בְּמִשְׁפָּטַי מָאָסוּ״.

Furthermore, the Sages said that **due to the sin of delay of justice,** i.e., judges delay issuing their rulings due to personal considerations, **and for distortion of justice,** i.e., judges intentionally distort their verdicts, **and for miscarriage of justice**[N] that results from negligence, **and for dereliction in** the study of **Torah, violence and looting abound** in the world, **and pestilence and famine come, and people eat and are not sated, and they eat their bread** measured **by weight. As it is written: “And I will bring a sword upon you, that shall execute the vengeance of the covenant;** and you shall be gathered together within your cities; and I will send the pestilence among you; and you shall be delivered into the hand of the enemy” (Leviticus 26:25). **And covenant means nothing other than Torah, as it is stated: “If My covenant be not with day and night,** if I have not appointed the ordinances of heaven and earth” (Jeremiah 33:25). The study of Torah is the mitzva practiced both day and night. **And it is written** with regard to this punishment: **“When I break your staff of bread, ten women shall bake** your bread in one oven, and they shall deliver your bread again by weight; and ye shall eat, and not be satisfied” (Leviticus 26:26). **And it is written: “Even because they rejected My ordinances,** and their soul abhorred My statutes” (Leviticus 26:43). All of these punishments result from breaching the covenant of the Torah and the perversion of justice.

בַּעֲוֹן שְׁבוּעַת שָׁוְא וּשְׁבוּעַת שֶׁקֶר וְחִילּוּל הַשֵּׁם וְחִילּוּל שַׁבָּת – חַיָּה רָעָה רַבָּה, וּבְהֵמָה כָּלָה, וּבְנֵי אָדָם מִתְמַעֲטִין, וְהַדְּרָכִים מִשְׁתּוֹמְמִין, שֶׁנֶּאֱמַר: ״וְאִם בְּאֵלֶּה לֹא תִוָּסְרוּ לִי״ אַל תִּקְרֵי בְּאֵלֶּה אֶלָּא בְּאָלָה, וּכְתִיב: ״וְהִשְׁלַחְתִּי בָכֶם אֶת חַיַּת הַשָּׂדֶה וגו׳״. וּכְתִיב בִּשְׁבוּעַת שֶׁקֶר: ״וְלֹא תִשָּׁבְעוּ בִשְׁמִי לַשָּׁקֶר וְחִלַּלְתָּ אֶת שֵׁם אֱלֹהֶיךָ״ וּבְחִילּוּל הַשֵּׁם כְּתִיב: ״וְלֹא תְחַלְּלוּ אֶת שֵׁם קָדְשִׁי״ וּבְחִילּוּל שַׁבָּת כְּתִיב: ״מְחַלְלֶיהָ מוֹת יוּמָת״, וְיָלֵיף חִילּוּל חִילּוּל מִשְּׁבוּעַת שֶׁקֶר.

Due to the sin of an oath taken **in vain**[B] **and a false oath, and desecration of** God’s **name, and desecration of Shabbat, wild beasts abound** in the world, and domesticated **animals cease** to exist, **and human beings decrease** in number, **and the roads become desolate, as it is stated: “And if in spite of these** [*be’eleh*] **things you will not be corrected unto Me,** but will walk contrary unto Me casually” (Leviticus 26:23). **Do not read of these** [*be’eleh*]; **rather,** due to a vain **oath** [*be’ala*]. **And it is written** that the punishment for this is: **“And I will send the beast of the field among you,** which shall rob you of your children, and destroy your cattle, and make you few in number; and your ways shall become desolate” (Leviticus 26:22). **And it is written with regard to a false oath: “And you shall not swear by My name falsely, so that you desecrate** [*veḥillalta*] **the name of your God:** I am the Lord” (Leviticus 19:12). **And it is written with regard to desecrating the name of God: “And you shall not desecrate** [*teḥallelu*] **My Holy Name”** (Leviticus 22:32). **And it is written with regard to desecrating Shabbat: “Every one that desecrates it** [*meḥaleleha*] **shall surely be put to death”** (Exodus 31:14). **And derive** by means of a verbal analogy [*gezera shava*] **desecration** [*ḥillul*] **of Shabbat from desecration** [*ḥillul*] **of a false oath.** Just as punishment for a false oath is desolation and wild beasts, one receives the same punishment for desecrating Shabbat and the name of God.

NOTES

And distortion of justice and miscarriage of justice – וְעִיוּוּת הַדִּין וְקִלְקוּל הַדִּין: Apparently, distortion of justice, does not refer to the judge himself, but to his attendants and aides who do not see to it that his rulings are implemented appropriately (Maharsha).

BACKGROUND

An oath taken in vain – שְׁבוּעַת שָׁוְא: There is no halakhic difference between an oath taken in vain and a false oath. Whenever someone swears to an untruth, it falls into this category. However, a vain oath refers specifically to an oath that is patently untrue, i.e., one who takes two contradictory oaths and one of the two is a vain oath. If a person intentionally takes a vain oath, he is punishable by lashes. If he does so unwittingly, there is no punishment unless the oath also violates another prohibition, e.g., taking the name of God in vain. In addition, if one takes an oath that a known object is precisely what everyone perceives it to be, e.g., if one swears that a particular man is indeed a man, that oath falls under the rubric of an oath taken in vain.

בַּעֲוֹן שְׁפִיכוּת דָּמִים בֵּית הַמִּקְדָּשׁ חָרֵב, וּשְׁכִינָה מִסְתַּלֶּקֶת מִיִּשְׂרָאֵל, שֶׁנֶּאֱמַר: ״וְלֹא תַחֲנִיפוּ וגו׳ וְלֹא תְטַמֵּא אֶת הָאָרֶץ אֲשֶׁר אַתֶּם יוֹשְׁבִים בָּהּ אֲשֶׁר אֲנִי שׁוֹכֵן בְּתוֹכָהּ״, הָא אַתֶּם מְטַמְּאִים אוֹתָהּ – אֵינְכֶם יוֹשְׁבִים בָּהּ, וְאֵינִי שׁוֹכֵן בְּתוֹכָהּ.

Due to the sin of bloodshed, the Holy Temple is destroyed, and the Divine Presence leaves Israel, as it says: "So you shall not pollute the land wherein you are; for blood, it pollutes the land; and no expiation can be made for the land for the blood that is shed therein, but by the blood of him that shed it. **And you shall not defile the land which you inhabit, in the midst of which I dwell;** for I the Lord dwell in the midst of the children of Israel" (Numbers 35:33–34). However, if **you defile** the land, **you will not inhabit it, and I will not dwell in it.**

בַּעֲוֹן גִּלּוּי עֲרָיוֹת וַעֲבוֹדָה זָרָה וְהַשְׁמָטַת שְׁמִיטִּין וְיוֹבְלוֹת – גָּלוּת בָּא לָעוֹלָם, וּמַגְלִין אוֹתָן, וּבָאִין אֲחֵרִים וְיוֹשְׁבִין בִּמְקוֹמָן, שֶׁנֶּאֱמַר: ״כִּי אֶת כָּל הַתּוֹעֵבוֹת הָאֵל עָשׂוּ אַנְשֵׁי הָאָרֶץ וגו׳״ וּכְתִיב: ״וַתִּטְמָא הָאָרֶץ וָאֶפְקוֹד עֲוֹנָהּ עָלֶיהָ וגו׳״ וּכְתִיב: ״וְלֹא תָקִיא הָאָרֶץ אֶתְכֶם בְּטַמַּאֲכֶם אוֹתָהּ״

Due to the sin of prohibited sexual relations, and idol worship, and failure to let the land **lie fallow** during **the Sabbatical and Jubilee Years, exile comes to the world and they exile** the Jewish people from their land, **and others come and settle in their place. As it is stated** with regard to illicit sexual relations: **"For all these abominations have the men of the land done,** that were before you, and the land is defiled; that the land expel not you also, when you defile it, as it expelled the nation that was before you" (Leviticus 18:27–28). **And it is written: "And the land was defiled, therefore I did visit the iniquity thereof upon it,** and the land expelled her inhabitants" (Leviticus 18:25). **And it is written: "That the land expel not you also, when you defile it,** as it expelled the nation that was before you."

וּבַעֲבוֹדָה זָרָה כְּתִיב: ״וְנָתַתִּי אֶת פִּגְרֵיכֶם וגו׳״ וּכְתִיב: ״וַהֲשִׁמּוֹתִי אֶת מִקְדְּשֵׁיכֶם וגו׳ וְאֶתְכֶם אֱזָרֶה בַגּוֹיִם״.

And with regard to idol worship it is written: "And I will cast your carcasses upon the carcasses of your idols" (Leviticus 26:30). **And it is written: "And I will bring your sanctuaries unto desolation,** and I will not smell the savor of your sweet odors" (Leviticus 26:31). **"And you will I scatter among the nations,** and I will draw out the sword after you; and your land shall be a desolation, and your cities shall be a waste" (Leviticus 26:33).

בִּשְׁמִיטִּין וּבַיּוֹבְלוֹת כְּתִיב: ״אָז תִּרְצֶה הָאָרֶץ אֶת שַׁבְּתוֹתֶיהָ כֹּל יְמֵי הָשַּׁמָּה וְאַתֶּם בְּאֶרֶץ אוֹיְבֵיכֶם וגו׳״ וּכְתִיב: ״כָּל יְמֵי הָשַּׁמָּה תִּשְׁבּוֹת״.

With regard to the sin of failure to observe **the Sabbatical and Jubilee Years it is written: "Then shall the land be paid her Sabbaths, as long as it lies desolate, and you are in your enemies' land;** even then shall the land rest, and repay her Sabbaths" (Leviticus 26:34). **And it is written: "As long as it lies desolate it shall have rest;** even the rest which it had not in your Sabbaths, when you dwelt upon it" (Leviticus 26: 35).

בַּעֲוֹן נַבְלוּת פֶּה צָרוֹת רַבּוֹת, וּגְזֵירוֹת קָשׁוֹת מִתְחַדְּשׁוֹת, וּבַחוּרֵי שׂוֹנְאֵי יִשְׂרָאֵל מֵתִים, יְתוֹמִים וְאַלְמָנוֹת צוֹעֲקִין וְאֵינָן נַעֲנִין, שֶׁנֶּאֱמַר: ״עַל כֵּן עַל בַּחוּרָיו לֹא יִשְׂמַח ה׳ וְאֶת יְתוֹמָיו [וְאֶת] (וְ)אַלְמְנוֹתָיו לֹא יְרַחֵם כִּי כֻלּוֹ חָנֵף וּמֵרַע וְכָל פֶּה דּוֹבֵר נְבָלָה בְּכָל זֹאת לֹא שָׁב אַפּוֹ וְעוֹד יָדוֹ נְטוּיָה״.

Due to the sin of vulgar speech, troubles abound, and harsh decrees are renewed, and the youth among the enemies of Israel, a euphemistic reference to Israel, **die,** and **orphans and widows cry out** for help **and are not answered, as it is stated: "Therefore the Lord shall have no joy in their young men, neither shall He have compassion on their fatherless and widows; for everyone is ungodly and an evildoer, and every mouth speaks wantonness. For all this His anger is not turned away, but His hand is stretched out still"** (Isaiah 9:16).[N]

מַאי וְעוֹד יָדוֹ נְטוּיָה? אָמַר רַבִּי חָנָן בַּר רָבָא: הַכֹּל יוֹדְעִין כַּלָּה לָמָּה נִכְנְסָה לַחוּפָּה, אֶלָּא כׇּל הַמְנַבֵּל פִּיו אֲפִילּוּ חוֹתְמִין עָלָיו גְּזַר דִּין שֶׁל שִׁבְעִים שָׁנָה לְטוֹבָה – הוֹפְכִין עָלָיו לְרָעָה. אָמַר רַבָּה בַּר שֵׁילָא אָמַר רַב חִסְדָּא: כׇּל הַמְנַבֵּל אֶת פִּיו – מַעֲמִיקִין לוֹ גֵּיהִנָּם, שֶׁנֶּאֱמַר: ״שׁוּחָה עֲמוּקָּה פִּי זָרוֹת״. רַב נַחְמָן בַּר יִצְחָק אָמַר: אַף שׁוֹמֵעַ וְשׁוֹתֵק, שֶׁנֶּאֱמַר: ״זְעוּם ה׳ יִפּוֹל שָׁם״.

The Gemara explains: **What** is the meaning of the phrase: **But His hand is stretched out still? Rabbi Ḥanan bar Rava said: Everybody knows why the bride enters the wedding canopy.** There is no secret revealed. **Nevertheless, anyone who speaks vulgarly** about it, **even if they,** on High, **sealed for him a decree of seventy years of good** fortune, **they will reverse it to bad** fortune because of this sin. **And Rabba bar Sheila said** that **Rav Ḥisda said: Anyone who speaks vulgarly, they deepen Gehenna for him, as it is stated: "The mouth that speaks perversity is a deep pit:** he that is abhorred of the Lord shall fall therein" (Proverbs 22:14), i.e., Gehenna is deepened for one who speaks vulgarly. **Rav Naḥman bar Yitzḥak said: Even** one who **hears** vulgar speech **and is silent** is punished, **as it is stated: "He that is abhorred of the Lord shall fall therein,"**[N] even if he himself does not speak at all.

NOTES

But His hand is stretched out still [*ve'od*] – וְעוֹד יָדוֹ נְטוּיָה: In this context, *ve'od* is understood as *va'ed*, forever. In human terms, this refers to the life expectancy of seventy years. When one commits this sin, the evil decree is forever (Rashi).

Shall fall therein – יִפּוֹל שָׁם: Some commentaries explain that the phrase: Shall fall therein, can be understood in two ways. The first is that one shall fall therein, in Gehenna. The second is: He shall fall therein, in the sense of the verse: "Over against all his brethren he did fall" (Genesis 25:18). One who is present and remains silent is sentenced to the same punishment (Maharsha).

אָמַר רַב אוֹשַׁעְיָא: כׇּל הַמְמָרֵק עַצְמוֹ לַעֲבֵירָה – חַבּוּרוֹת וּפְצָעִין יוֹצְאִין בּוֹ, שֶׁנֶּאֱמַר: ״חַבּוּרוֹת פֶּצַע תַּמְרוּק בְּרָע״ וְלֹא עוֹד אֶלָּא שֶׁנִּדּוֹן בְּהִדְרוֹקָן, שֶׁנֶּאֱמַר: ״וּמַכּוֹת חַדְרֵי בָטֶן״. אָמַר רַב נַחְמָן בַּר יִצְחָק: סִימָן לַעֲבֵירָה הִדְרוֹקָן.

And in a similar vein, **Rav Oshaya said: Anyone who** prepares **himself to commit a sin, wounds and bruises emerge on him, as it is stated: "Sharp wounds for one devoted to evil;** so do stripes that reach the inward parts" (Proverbs 20:30). **And not only that, but he is sentenced to** suffer from the disease of **edema** [*hidrokan*],[LB] **as it is stated: So do stripes that reach the inward parts. Rav Naḥman bar Yitzḥak said: A sign** indicating one who **committed** a sin is the disease *hidrokan,* which afflicts the inner parts.

תָּנוּ רַבָּנַן, שְׁלֹשָׁה מִינֵי הִדְרוֹקָן הֵן: שֶׁל עֲבֵירָה – עָבֶה, וְשֶׁל רָעָב – תָּפוּחַ, וְשֶׁל כְּשָׁפִים – דַּק.

The Sages taught in a *baraita*: **There are three types of** *hidrokan*: The one that comes as punishment **for sin is thick; and** that which is the result **of hunger is swollen,** but not as thick; **and** the one caused **by witchcraft is thin,** and the flesh of the sick person becomes thin in other places.

שְׁמוּאֵל הַקָּטָן חָשׁ בֵּיהּ אָמַר: רִבּוֹנוֹ שֶׁל עוֹלָם, מִי מֵפִיס? אִיתַּסִּי. אַבָּיֵי חָשׁ בֵּיהּ, אָמַר רָבָא: יָדַעְנָא בֵּיהּ בְּנַחְמָנִי דְּמַכְפֵּין נַפְשֵׁיהּ. רָבָא חָשׁ בֵּיהּ. וְהָא רָבָא הוּא דְּאָמַר: נְפִישִׁי קְטִילֵי קְדָר מִנְּפִיחֵי כָפָן! שָׁאנֵי רָבָא, דְּאָנְסִי לֵיהּ רַבָּנַן בְּעִידָּנֵיהּ בְּעַל כּוֹרְחֵיהּ.

The Gemara relates: **Shmuel HaKatan fell ill with** *hidrokan*. **He said: Master of the Universe, who will draw lots,** meaning, who will be able to determine that this *hidrokan* is not the consequence of sin? **He was cured. Abaye** also **fell ill with** *hidrokan*. **Rava** testified and **said** about him: **I know about Naḥmani,** Abaye, **that** he **starves himself** and that his *hidrokan* is the result of hunger. The Gemara relates that **Rava fell ill with** *hidrokan,* and they asked: **But Rava** did not starve himself, and there is no reason to suspect him of sin, and we cannot say that he contracted *hidrokan* because he did not relieve himself on time. Rava knew to relieve himself, as it is **he** who **said: More have been killed** due to the **chamber pot,** because they were not careful about relieving themselves in a timely manner, **than those swollen** due to **starvation.** The Gemara answers: **Rava is different because the Sages compel him** to remain in place **against his will while he** lectures. Since he could not relieve himself, he became sick with *hidrokan.*

תָּנוּ רַבָּנַן, אַרְבָּעָה סִימָנִין הֵן: סִימָן לַעֲבֵירָה הִדְרוֹקָן, סִימָן לְשִׂנְאַת חִנָּם יֵרָקוֹן, סִימָן לְגַסּוּת הָרוּחַ עֲנִיּוּת, סִימָן לְלָשׁוֹן הָרָע אַסְכָּרָה.

On a related note, **the Sages taught** in a *baraita* that **there are four signs: A sign of sin is** *hidrokan*, **a sign of gratuitous hatred is jaundice, a sign of arrogance is poverty,**[N] **and a sign of slander is** *askara.*

תָּנוּ רַבָּנַן: אַסְכָּרָה בָּאָה לָעוֹלָם

The Sages taught: *Askara* **comes to the world** as punishment

Perek **II**
Daf **33** Amud **b**

עַל הַמַּעֲשֵׂר, רַבִּי אֶלְעָזָר בְּרַבִּי יוֹסֵי אוֹמֵר: עַל לָשׁוֹן הָרָע. אָמַר רָבָא, וְאִיתֵּימָא רַבִּי יְהוֹשֻׁעַ בֶּן לֵוִי: מַאי קְרָאָה – ״וְהַמֶּלֶךְ יִשְׂמַח בֵּאלֹהִים יִתְהַלֵּל כׇּל הַנִּשְׁבָּע בּוֹ כִּי יִסָּכֵר פִּי דוֹבְרֵי שָׁקֶר״.

for neglecting to separate **tithes. Rabbi Elazar, son of Rabbi Yosei, says:** *Askara*[B] comes as punishment for **slander. Rava said, and some say** that it was **Rabbi Yehoshua ben Levi** who said it: **What is the verse** that alludes to this? **"But the king shall rejoice in God; every one that swears by Him shall glory; for the mouth of them that speak lies shall be stopped"** (Psalms 63:12). The punishment for lying is that the mouth will be stopped. *Askara* affects the mouth along with other parts of the body.

LANGUAGE

Edema [*hidrokan*] – הִדְרוֹקָן: From the Greek ὑδρωπικός *hydropikos*, which means one who is ill with edema.

BACKGROUND

Edema [*hidrokan*] – הִדְרוֹקָן: Edema is a symptom characterized by swelling, which is the result of fluid that collects in body tissue. It is caused either by disruption in the blood circulation or by cirrhosis of the liver. All types of edema are called *hidrokan*. One type, known as *anasarca* or *hidropsia sicca* is a condition where the entire body is swollen. Another, known as *ascites*, is a condition in which the whole body is thin, yet the stomach is swollen, similar to the symptoms associated with cirrhosis of the liver. Similar swelling, hunger edema, occurs as a result of prolonged starvation. Constipation does not cause edema, although it can cause a one's stomach to swell.

NOTES

A sign of arrogance is poverty – סִימָן לְגַסּוּת הָרוּחַ עֲנִיּוּת: In tractate *Kiddushin*, the Sages explain that poverty in this context is not defined in terms of wealth; rather, it refers to poverty in terms of Torah. In this sense, poverty results from a person failing to take the opportunity to travel to a place of Torah scholars to study with them. Due to his arrogance, he is not even aware of his own ignorance (Rashi).

BACKGROUND

***Askara* – אַסְכָּרָה:** *Askara* is diphtheria, an infectious disease of the throat that causes the mucous membrane in the throat to swell, causing a choking sensation. Diphtheria is very common among children, and until the discovery of innovative medical treatments it was extremely deadly. Those who contracted the illness would die of asphyxiation. During the Second Temple period, members of the non-priestly watch would fast once a week so that *askara* would not befall young children.

Apparently, the description of the illness as beginning in the intestines comes from the symptoms that children display when contracting infectious diseases like this one, which include vomiting and stomachaches.

BACKGROUND

The vineyard in Yavne – **כֶּרֶם בְּיַבְנֶה**: Apparently, the seat of the Sanhedrin in Yavne was called the vineyard in Yavne. According to an ancient tradition, the Sanhedrin was called a vineyard because when it was in session, the Sages themselves, along with their students, would sit in rows, like the rows of a vineyard (Jerusalem Talmud). The seat of the Sanhedrin may also have been located near vineyards, lending the name a double meaning. Since most of the prominent Sages of that generation assembled there and their decisions were especially significant for the future existence of the Jewish people, the vineyard in Yavne was held in high regard. The *halakhot* studied there, known as the *baraitot* of the vineyard, are extremely authoritative.

אִיבַּעְיָא לְהוּ: רַבִּי אֶלְעָזָר בְּרַבִּי יוֹסֵי "עַל לְשׁוֹן הָרַע קָאָמַר" אוֹ דִּילְמָא "אַף עַל לְשׁוֹן הָרַע" נַמִּי קָאָמַר? תָּא שְׁמַע, כְּשֶׁנִּכְנְסוּ רַבּוֹתֵינוּ לַכֶּרֶם בְּיַבְנֶה הָיָה שָׁם רַבִּי יְהוּדָה וְרַבִּי אֶלְעָזָר בְּרַבִּי יוֹסֵי וְרַבִּי שִׁמְעוֹן. נִשְׁאֲלָה שְׁאֵלָה זוֹ בִּפְנֵיהֶם: מַכָּה זוֹ מִפְּנֵי מָה מַתְחֶלֶת בִּבְנֵי מֵעַיִים וְגוֹמֶרֶת בַּפֶּה? נַעֲנָה רַבִּי יְהוּדָה בְּרַבִּי אִלְעָאִי רֹאשׁ הַמְדַבְּרִים בְּכָל מָקוֹם וְאָמַר: אַף עַל פִּי שֶׁכְּלָיוֹת יוֹעֲצוֹת, וְלֵב מֵבִין, וְלָשׁוֹן מְחַתֵּךְ – פֶּה גּוֹמֵר. נַעֲנָה רַבִּי אֶלְעָזָר בְּרַבִּי יוֹסֵי וְאָמַר: מִפְּנֵי שֶׁאוֹכְלִין בָּהּ דְּבָרִים טְמֵאִין. דְּבָרִים טְמֵאִים סָלְקָא דַּעְתָּךְ? אֶלָּא: שֶׁאוֹכְלִין בָּהּ דְּבָרִים שֶׁאֵינָן מְתוּקָּנִים. נַעֲנָה רַבִּי שִׁמְעוֹן וְאָמַר: בַּעֲוֹן בִּיטּוּל תּוֹרָה.

A dilemma was raised before those who were sitting in the study hall: Did **Rabbi Elazar, son of Rabbi Yosei, say** that *askara* comes as punishment only **for slander, or perhaps he said** it was **also for slander? Come** and **hear** a resolution to this dilemma from that which was taught in a *baraita*: **When our Sages entered the vineyard in Yavne,**[B] **Rabbi Yehuda, and Rabbi Elazar, son of Rabbi Yosei, and Rabbi Shimon were there, and a question was asked before them** with regard to **this plague** of *askara*: **Why does it begin in the intestines and end in the mouth? Rabbi Yehuda, son of Rabbi Ila'i,** who was **the head of the speakers in every place, responded and said: Even though the kidneys advise, and the heart understands, and the tongue shapes** the voice that emerges from the mouth, still, **the mouth completes** the formation of the voice. Therefore, the disease begins in the same place that slander begins and it ends in the mouth. **Rabbi Elazar, son of Rabbi Yosei, responded and said:** This disease ends in the mouth **because one eats with it non-kosher things.** They immediately wondered about this: **Does it enter your mind** to say that *askara* is caused by eating **non-kosher food?** Are those who eat non-kosher food so numerous? **Rather,** it comes as a punishment **for eating** foods **that were not** ritually **prepared,** i.e., were not tithed. **Rabbi Shimon responded and said:** This disease comes as a punishment **for the sin of dereliction in** the study of **Torah.**

אָמְרוּ לוֹ: נָשִׁים יוֹכִיחוּ! שֶׁמְּבַטְּלוֹת אֶת בַּעֲלֵיהֶן. גּוֹיִם יוֹכִיחוּ! שֶׁמְּבַטְּלִין אֶת יִשְׂרָאֵל. תִּינוֹקוֹת יוֹכִיחוּ! שֶׁמְּבַטְּלִין אֶת אֲבִיהֶן. תִּינוֹקוֹת שֶׁל בֵּית רַבָּן יוֹכִיחוּ!

They said to him: Women will prove that dereliction in the study of Torah is not the cause, as they are not obligated to study Torah and, nevertheless, they contract *askara*. He answered them: They are punished because **they cause their husbands to be idle** from the study of Torah. They said to him: **Gentiles will prove** that this is not the cause, as they also contract *askara* even though they are not obligated to study Torah. He answered them: They are also punished because **they cause Israel to be idle** from the study of Torah. They said to him: **Children will prove** that this is not the cause, for they are not at all obligated to study Torah and they also suffer from *askara*. He answered them: They are punished because **they cause their fathers to be idle** from the study of Torah. They said to him: **School children will prove** that this is not the cause, as they study Torah and, nevertheless, they suffer from *askara*.

הָתָם כִּדְרַבִּי גּוּרְיוֹן, דְּאָמַר רַבִּי גּוּרְיוֹן, וְאִיתֵימָא רַב יוֹסֵף בְּרַבִּי שְׁמַעְיָה: בִּזְמַן שֶׁהַצַּדִּיקִים בַּדּוֹר – צַדִּיקִים נִתְפָּסִים עַל הַדּוֹר, אֵין צַדִּיקִים בַּדּוֹר – תִּינוֹקוֹת שֶׁל בֵּית רַבָּן נִתְפָּסִים עַל הַדּוֹר. אָמַר רַבִּי יִצְחָק בַּר זְעִירִי וְאָמְרִי לָהּ אָמַר רַבִּי שִׁמְעוֹן בֶּן נְזִירָא: מַאי קְרָאָה – "אִם לֹא תֵדְעִי לָךְ הַיָּפָה בַּנָּשִׁים צְאִי לָךְ בְּעִקְבֵי הַצֹּאן וגו'" וְאָמְרִינַן: גְּדָיִים הַמְּמוּשְׁכָּנִין עַל הָרוֹעִים. שְׁמַע מִינָּהּ: אַף עַל לְשׁוֹן הָרַע נַמִּי קָאָמַר, שְׁמַע מִינָּהּ.

The Gemara answers: **There,** it must be understood **in accordance with** the statement of **Rabbi Guryon,** as **Rabbi Guryon said, and some say** that it was **Rav Yosef, son of Rabbi Shemaya,** who said it: **At a time when** there are **righteous people in the generation,** the **righteous are seized,** i.e., they die or suffer, **for** the sins of **the generation.**[N] **If there are no righteous people in the generation, school children,** who are also without sin, **are seized for** the sins **of the generation. Rabbi Yitzḥak bar Ze'iri said, and some say** that **Rabbi Shimon ben Nezira said: What is the verse** that alludes to this? **"If you know not, you fairest among women, go your way forth by the footsteps of the flock** and feed your kids, beside the shepherds' tents [*mishkenot*]" (Song of Songs 1:8). **And we say** in explanation of this verse: They are the **lambs that are taken as collateral** [***hamemushkanin***], which is etymologically similar to the word *mishkenot*, **in place of the shepherds.** If the shepherds and leaders of the generation corrupt the multitudes, young children die because of their sins. With regard to the dilemma, **conclude from it** that Rabbi Elazar, son of Rabbi Yosei, **said** that the illness of *askara* **also** results from **slander,** as the *baraita* provides an additional cause of the illness. The Gemara comments: Indeed, **conclude from it.**

NOTES

The righteous are seized for the sins of the generation – **צַדִּיקִים נִתְפָּסִים עַל הַדּוֹר**: Due to the general principle that all members of the Jewish people are mutually responsible for each other, clearly, leaders and the righteous suffer for the sins of the multitudes. Furthermore, the wicked are punished by means of a plague that afflicts everyone, while the punishment meted out to the righteous is by God's hand and they alone are punished (*Sha'arei Ora*).

וְאַמַּאי קָרוּ לֵיהּ ״רֹאשׁ הַמְדַבְּרִים בְּכׇל מָקוֹם״? דְּיָתְבִי רַבִּי יְהוּדָה וְרַבִּי יוֹסֵי וְרַבִּי שִׁמְעוֹן, וְיָתֵיב יְהוּדָה בֶּן גֵּרִים גַּבַּיְיהוּ. פָּתַח רַבִּי יְהוּדָה וְאָמַר: כַּמָּה נָאִים מַעֲשֵׂיהֶן שֶׁל אוּמָּה זוֹ: תִּקְּנוּ שְׁוָוקִים, תִּקְּנוּ גְּשָׁרִים, תִּקְּנוּ מֶרְחֲצָאוֹת. רַבִּי יוֹסֵי שָׁתַק. נַעֲנָה רַבִּי שִׁמְעוֹן בֶּן יוֹחַאי וְאָמַר: כׇּל מַה שֶּׁתִּקְּנוּ – לֹא תִּקְּנוּ אֶלָּא לְצוֹרֶךְ עַצְמָן, תִּקְּנוּ שְׁוָוקִין – לְהוֹשִׁיב בָּהֶן זוֹנוֹת, מֶרְחֲצָאוֹת – לְעַדֵּן בָּהֶן עַצְמָן, גְּשָׁרִים – לִיטּוֹל מֵהֶן מֶכֶס. הָלַךְ יְהוּדָה בֶּן גֵּרִים וְסִיפֵּר דִּבְרֵיהֶם, וְנִשְׁמְעוּ לַמַּלְכוּת. אָמְרוּ: יְהוּדָה שֶׁעִילָּה – יִתְעַלֶּה, יוֹסֵי שֶׁשָּׁתַק – יִגְלֶה לְצִיפּוֹרִי, שִׁמְעוֹן שֶׁגִּינָּה – יֵהָרֵג.

In this *baraita* Rabbi Yehuda is described as head of the speakers in every place. The Gemara asks: **And why did they call him head of the speakers in every place?** The Gemara relates that this resulted due to an incident that took place **when Rabbi Yehuda and Rabbi Yosei and Rabbi Shimon were sitting, and Yehuda, son of converts, sat beside them. Rabbi Yehuda opened and said: How pleasant are the actions of this nation,** the Romans,[B] as **they established marketplaces, established bridges,** and **established bathhouses. Rabbi Yosei was silent. Rabbi Shimon ben Yoḥai responded and said: Everything that they established, they established only for their own purposes. They established marketplaces, to place prostitutes in them; bathhouses, to pamper themselves;** and **bridges, to collect taxes from** all who pass over **them. Yehuda, son of converts, went and related their statements**[H] to his household, **and** those statements continued to spread until **they were heard by the monarchy. They** ruled and **said: Yehuda, who elevated** the Roman regime, **shall be elevated** and appointed as head of the Sages, the head of the speakers in every place. **Yosei, who remained silent, shall be exiled** from his home in Judea as punishment, and sent **to** the city of **Tzippori** in the Galilee. **And Shimon, who denounced** the government, **shall be killed.**

אֲזַל הוּא וּבְרֵיהּ טְשׁוֹ בֵּי מִדְרְשָׁא. כׇּל יוֹמָא הֲוָה מַיְיתִי לְהוּ דְּבֵיתְהוּ רִיפְתָּא וְכוּזָא דְּמַיָּא וְכָרְכִי. כִּי תְּקִיף גְּזֵירְתָא, אֲמַר לֵיהּ לִבְרֵיהּ: נָשִׁים דַּעְתָּן קַלָּה עֲלֵיהֶן, דִּילְמָא מְצַעֲרִי לַהּ וּמְגַלְּיָא לַן. אֲזַלוּ טְשׁוֹ בִּמְעָרְתָּא. אִיתְרְחִישׁ נִיסָּא, אִיבְּרִי לְהוּ חָרוּבָא וְעֵינָא דְמַיָּא. וַהֲווֹ מְשַׁלְּחִי מָנַיְיהוּ, וַהֲווֹ יָתְבִי עַד צַוְּארַיְיהוּ בְּחָלָא, כּוּלֵּי יוֹמָא גָּרְסִי, בְּעִידָּן צַלּוֹיֵי לָבְשׁוּ מִיכַּסּוּ וּמְצַלּוּ, וַהֲדַר מְשַׁלְּחִי מָנַיְיהוּ כִּי הֵיכִי דְּלָא לִיבְלוּ. אִיתִּיבוּ תְּרֵיסַר שְׁנֵי בִּמְעָרְתָּא. אֲתָא אֵלִיָּהוּ וְקָם אַפִּיתְחָא דִּמְעָרְתָּא, אֲמַר: מַאן לוֹדְעֵיהּ לְבַר יוֹחַי דְּמִית קֵיסָר וּבְטִיל גְּזֵירְתֵיהּ?

Rabbi Shimon bar Yoḥai **and his son,** Rabbi Elazar, **went and hid in the study hall. Every day** Rabbi Shimon's **wife would bring them bread and a jug of water and they would eat. When the decree intensified,** Rabbi Shimon **said to his son: Women are easily impressionable**[N] and, therefore, there is room for concern **lest** the authorities **torture her and she reveal our** whereabouts. **They went and they hid in a cave. A miracle occurred** and **a carob** tree **was created for them** as well as **a spring of water. They would remove their clothes and sit** covered **in sand up to their necks. They would study** Torah **all day** in that manner. **At the time of prayer, they would dress, cover themselves, and pray,**[N] **and they would again remove their clothes afterward so that they would not become tattered. They sat in the cave for twelve years. Elijah** the Prophet **came**[N] **and stood at the entrance to the cave** and **said: Who will inform bar Yoḥai that** the **emperor died and his decree has been abrogated?**

נְפַקוּ. חֲזוֹ אִינָשֵׁי דְּקָא כָּרְבִי וְזָרְעִי, אָמַר: מַנִּיחִין חַיֵּי עוֹלָם וְעוֹסְקִין בְּחַיֵּי שָׁעָה! כׇּל מָקוֹם שֶׁנּוֹתְנִין עֵינֵיהֶן – מִיָּד נִשְׂרָף. יָצְתָה בַּת קוֹל וְאָמְרָה לָהֶם: לְהַחְרִיב עוֹלָמִי יְצָאתֶם? חִיזְרוּ לִמְעָרַתְכֶם! הֲדוּר אֲזוּל אִיתִּיבוּ תְּרֵיסַר יַרְחֵי שַׁתָּא. אָמְרִי: מִשְׁפַּט רְשָׁעִים בְּגֵיהִנָּם – שְׁנֵים עָשָׂר חֹדֶשׁ. יָצְתָה בַּת קוֹל וְאָמְרָה: צְאוּ מִמְּעָרַתְכֶם! נְפַקוּ, כׇּל הֵיכָא דַּהֲוָה מָחֵי רַבִּי אֶלְעָזָר – הֲוָה מָסֵי רַבִּי שִׁמְעוֹן. אָמַר לוֹ: בְּנִי, דַּי לָעוֹלָם אֲנִי וְאַתָּה.

They emerged from the cave, and **saw people who were plowing and sowing.** Rabbi Shimon bar Yoḥai **said:** These people **abandon eternal life** of Torah study **and engage in temporal life** for their own sustenance. The Gemara relates that **every place that** Rabbi Shimon and his son Rabbi Elazar **directed their eyes was immediately burned.**[N] **A Divine Voice emerged and said to them:** Did you **emerge** from the cave in order **to destroy My world? Return to your cave. They again went** and sat there **for twelve months. They said: The judgment of the wicked in Gehenna lasts** for **twelve months.** Surely their sin was atoned in that time. **A Divine Voice emerged and said** to them: **Emerge from your cave. They emerged. Everywhere that Rabbi Elazar would strike, Rabbi Shimon would heal.** Rabbi Shimon **said to** Rabbi Elazar: **My son, you and I suffice for the** entire **world,** as the two of us are engaged in the proper study of Torah.

בַּהֲדֵי פַּנְיָא דְּמַעֲלֵי שַׁבְּתָא חֲזוֹ הָהוּא סָבָא דַּהֲוָה נָקֵיט תְּרֵי מְדָאנֵי אָסָא, וְרָהֵיט בֵּין הַשְּׁמָשׁוֹת. אָמְרוּ לֵיהּ: הָנֵי לְמָה לָךְ? אָמַר לְהוּ: לִכְבוֹד שַׁבָּת. וְתִיסְגֵּי לָךְ בְּחַד? חַד כְּנֶגֶד ״זָכוֹר״, וְחַד כְּנֶגֶד ״שָׁמוֹר״. אָמַר לֵיהּ לִבְרֵיהּ: חֲזִי כַּמָּה חֲבִיבִין מִצְוֹת עַל יִשְׂרָאֵל! יָתֵיב דַּעְתַּיְיהוּ.

As the sun was setting on Shabbat eve, they saw an elderly man who was holding two bundles of myrtle branches and running at twilight. They said to him: Why do you have these? He said to them: In honor of Shabbat. They said to him: **And let one suffice.** He answered them: **One** is **corresponding to: "Remember** the Shabbat day, to keep it holy" (Exodus 20:8), **and** one is **corresponding to: "Observe** the Shabbat day, to keep it holy" (Deuteronomy 5:12). Rabbi Shimon **said to his son: See how beloved the mitzvot are to Israel. Their minds were** put at ease and they were no longer as upset that people were not engaged in Torah study.

BACKGROUND

The actions of the Romans – מַעֲשֵׂי הָרוֹמָאִים: As opposed to the Greeks, the Romans did not directly impose cultural or spiritual changes on the peoples they conquered. Instead, the Romans excelled in effective organization and comprehensive building projects. In all of the lands they conquered, they expertly paved roads, many of which are intact to this day in Eretz Yisrael and in other countries. They erected bridges over rivers and streams and constructed well-planned cities and public establishments, such as bathhouses and theaters. All of these developments resulted in the improvement of the quality of life in the countries they conquered within a short period of time. Rabbi Yehuda's praise for them is understandable. Rabbi Shimon saw all of the Roman accomplishments merely as measures to facilitate domination and exploitation of the people they ruled.

HALAKHA

Yehuda, son of converts, went and related their statements – הָלַךְ יְהוּדָה בֶּן גֵּרִים וְסִיפֵּר דִּבְרֵיהֶם: One who accepts information that could potentially cause pain or harm to an individual if it became public, even if that was not the intention of the source of the information, violates the prohibition against evil speech. That was the case of Yehuda, son of converts (Rambam *Sefer HaMadda, Hilkhot Deot* 7:5).

NOTES

Women are easily impressionable – נָשִׁים דַּעְתָּן קַלָּה עֲלֵיהֶן: In other words, women are more easily appeased and persuaded and are not always sensitive to the danger inherent in a given situation (Rashi).

They would dress, cover themselves, and pray – לָבְשׁוּ מִיכַּסּוּ וּמְצַלּוּ: Although they were covered in sand, they still donned their clothing during prayer because of the verse: "Prepare to meet your God" (Amos 4:12; see Maharsha).

Elijah the Prophet came – אֲתָא אֵלִיָּהוּ: Some commentaries explain that any bearer of good news is referred to as Elijah. In this case, a person passed by and recounted what had happened in an incidental, unconsidered remark (*Beit Ya'akov*).

Every place they directed their eyes was immediately burned – כׇּל מָקוֹם שֶׁנּוֹתְנִין עֵינֵיהֶן מִיָּד נִשְׂרָף: Some commentaries explain this incident homiletically. Rabbi Shimon and his son convinced people to abandon their business and engage in Torah study for its own sake (*Beit Ya'akov*).

שָׁמַע רַבִּי פִּנְחָס בֶּן יָאִיר חֲתָנֵיהּ וּנְפַק לְאַפֵּיהּ, עַיְילֵיהּ לְבֵי בָנְיָה הֲוָה קָא אָרֵיךְ לֵיהּ לְבִישְׂרֵיהּ, חֲזֵי דַּהֲוָה בֵּיהּ פִּילֵי בְּגוּפֵיהּ, הֲוָה קָא בָּכֵי, וְקָא נָתְרוּ דִּמְעַת עֵינֵיהּ וְקָמְצַוְּחָא לֵיהּ. אָמַר לוֹ: אוֹי לִי שֶׁרְאִיתִיךָ בְּכָךְ! אָמַר לוֹ: אַשְׁרֶיךָ שֶׁרְאִיתַנִי בְּכָךְ, שֶׁאִילְמָלֵא לֹא רְאִיתַנִי בְּכָךְ – לֹא מָצָאתָ בִּי כָּךְ. דִּמֵּעִיקָּרָא כִּי הֲוָה מַקְשֵׁי רַבִּי שִׁמְעוֹן בֶּן יוֹחַי קוּשְׁיָא – הֲוָה מְפָרֵק לֵיהּ רַבִּי פִּנְחָס בֶּן יָאִיר תְּרֵיסַר פֵּירוּקֵי, לַסּוֹף כִּי הֲוָה מַקְשֵׁי רַבִּי פִּנְחָס בֶּן יָאִיר קוּשְׁיָא – הֲוָה מְפָרֵק לֵיהּ רַבִּי שִׁמְעוֹן בֶּן יוֹחַי עֶשְׂרִין וְאַרְבָּעָה פֵּירוּקֵי.

Rabbi Pineḥas ben Ya'ir,[P] Rabbi Shimon's **son-in-law, heard and went out to** greet **him. He brought him into the bathhouse and** began **tending to his flesh. He saw that** Rabbi Shimon **had cracks in** the skin on **his body. He was crying, and the tears fell from his eyes and caused** Rabbi Shimon **pain.** Rabbi Pineḥas **said to** Rabbi Shimon, his father-in-law: **Woe is me, that I have seen you like this.** Rabbi Shimon **said to him: Happy are you that you have seen me like this, as had you not seen me like this, you would not have found in me this** prominence in Torah, as the Gemara relates: **At first, when Rabbi Shimon ben Yoḥai would raise a difficulty, Rabbi Pineḥas ben Ya'ir would respond** to his question **with twelve answers. Ultimately, when Rabbi Pineḥas ben Ya'ir would raise a difficulty, Rabbi Shimon ben Yoḥai would respond** with **twenty-four answers.**

אָמַר: הוֹאִיל וְאִיתְרְחִישׁ נִיסָּא – אֵיזִיל אַתְקִין מִילְּתָא, דִּכְתִיב: "וַיָּבֹא יַעֲקֹב שָׁלֵם" וְאָמַר רַב: שָׁלֵם בְּגוּפוֹ, שָׁלֵם בְּמָמוֹנוֹ, שָׁלֵם בְּתוֹרָתוֹ. "וַיִּחַן אֶת פְּנֵי הָעִיר" אָמַר רַב: מַטְבֵּעַ תִּיקֵּן לָהֶם, וּשְׁמוּאֵל אָמַר: שְׁוָוקִים תִּיקֵּן לָהֶם, וְרַבִּי יוֹחָנָן אָמַר: מֶרְחֲצָאוֹת תִּיקֵּן לָהֶם. אָמַר: אִיכָּא מִילְּתָא דְּבָעֵי לְתַקּוּנֵי? אֲמַרוּ לֵיהּ: אִיכָּא דּוּכְתָּא דְּאִית בֵּיהּ סְפֵק טוּמְאָה,

Rabbi Shimon **said: Since a miracle transpired** for me, **I will go** and **repair something** for the sake of others in gratitude for God's kindness, **as it is written: "And Jacob came whole to the city of Shechem,** which is in the land of Canaan, when he came from Paddan-aram; and he graced the countenance of the city" (Genesis 33:18). **Rav said,** the meaning of: And Jacob came whole, is: **Whole in his body, whole in his money, whole in his Torah.** And what did he do? **And he graced the countenance of the city;** he performed gracious acts to benefit the city. **Rav said:** Jacob **established a currency for them. And Shmuel said: He established marketplaces for them. And Rabbi Yoḥanan said: He established bathhouses for them.** In any event, clearly one for whom a miracle transpires should perform an act of kindness for his neighbors as a sign of gratitude. **He said: Is there something that needs repair? They said to him: There is a place where there is uncertainty with regard to ritual impurity**

PERSONALITIES

Rabbi Pineḥas ben Ya'ir – רַבִּי פִּנְחָס בֶּן יָאִיר: Rabbi Pineḥas ben Ya'ir was one of the Sages of the Mishna and among the outstanding righteous individuals of talmudic times. He also had a reputation for being a miracle worker.

Rabbi Pineḥas ben Ya'ir was a contemporary of Rabbi Shimon bar Yoḥai. According to the text here, Rabbi Shimon was his father-in-law, but in other sources he is described as Rabbi Shimon's father-in-law. Even during his lifetime, he was revered by all of the Sages. There are so many miraculous stories told about him that in the Talmud it was said about him: How much greater was this man than Moses our teacher.

Even Rabbi Pineḥas ben Ya'ir's donkey was righteous: He would not eat produce that was not tithed. Indeed, the Talmud relates several stories about the donkey of Rabbi Pineḥas ben Ya'ir.

Only a few of his Torah statements are recorded. His most famous statement is his enumeration of the succession of character traits that ultimately lead one to prophecy and the advent of the Messiah.

Perek **II**
Daf **34** Amud **a**

וְאִית לְהוּ צַעֲרָא לְכֹהֲנִים לְאַקּוּפֵי. אָמַר: אִיכָּא אִינִישׁ דְּיָדַע דְּאִיתַּחְזַק הָכָא טָהֳרָה? אָמַר לֵיהּ הַהוּא סָבָא: כָּאן קִיצֵּץ בֶּן זַכַּאי תּוּרְמְסֵי תְרוּמָה. עֲבַד אִיהוּ נַמִי הָכִי, כָּל הֵיכָא דַּהֲוָה קָשֵׁי – טַהֲרֵיהּ, וְכָל הֵיכָא דַּהֲוָה רָפֵי – צַיְּינֵיהּ.

and the priests are troubled by being forced **to circumvent it,** as it is prohibited for them to become ritually impure from contact with a corpse. There was suspicion, but no certainty, that a corpse was buried there. Therefore, they were unable to definitively determine its status. Rabbi Shimon **said: Is there a person who knows that there was a presumption of ritual purity here?** Is there anyone who remembers a time when this place was not considered ritually impure, or that at least part of it was considered to be ritually pure? **An Elder said to him: Here ben Zakkai** planted and **cut the *teruma* of lupines.** In this marketplace Rabbi Yoḥanan ben Zakkai, who himself was a priest, once planted lupines that were given to him as *teruma*. On that basis, the conclusion can be drawn that it was definitely ritually pure. Rabbi Shimon, like Jacob, **also did so** and took steps to improve the city and examined the ground (*Tosafot*). **Everywhere that** the ground **was hard, he pronounced it ritually pure** as there was certainly no corpse there, **and every place that** the ground **was soft, he marked it** indicating that perhaps a corpse was buried there. In that way, he purified the marketplace so that even priests could walk through it.

אֲמַר הַהוּא סָבָא: טִיהֵר בֶּן יוֹחַי בֵּית הַקְּבָרוֹת! אָמַר לֵיהּ: אִילְמָלֵי (לֹא) הָיִיתָ עִמָּנוּ, וַאֲפִילּוּ הָיִיתָ עִמָּנוּ וְלֹא נִמְנֵיתָ עִמָּנוּ – יָפֶה אַתָּה אוֹמֵר. עַכְשָׁיו שֶׁהָיִיתָ עִמָּנוּ וְנִמְנֵיתָ עִמָּנוּ, יֹאמְרוּ: זוֹנוֹת מְפַרְכְּסוֹת זוֹ אֶת זוֹ, תַּלְמִידֵי חֲכָמִים לֹא כָּל שֶׁכֵּן? יְהַב בֵּיהּ עֵינֵיהּ, וְנָח נַפְשֵׁיהּ. נְפַק לְשׁוּקָא, חַזְיֵיהּ לִיהוּדָה בֶּן גֵּרִים, אֲמַר: עֲדַיִין יֵשׁ לָזֶה בָּעוֹלָם? נָתַן בּוֹ עֵינָיו, וַעֲשָׂהוּ גַּל שֶׁל עֲצָמוֹת.

A certain Elder said in ridicule and surprise: **Ben Yoḥai purified the cemetery.**[N] Rabbi Shimon got angry and **said to him: Had you not been with us, and even had you been with us and were not counted with us** in rendering this ruling, what **you say is fine.** You could have said that you were unaware of my intention or that you did not agree or participate in this decision. **Now that you were with us and were counted with us** in rendering this ruling, you will cause people to say that Sages are unwilling to cooperate with one another. **They will say:** If competing **prostitutes** still **apply makeup to each other** to help one another look beautiful, **all the more so** that **Torah scholars** should cooperate with each other. **He directed his eyes toward him and** the Elder **died.** Rabbi Shimon **went out to the marketplace** and **he saw Yehuda, son of converts,**[P] who was the cause of this entire incident. Rabbi Shimon, **said: This one still has a place in the world? He directed his eyes toward him and turned him into a pile of bones.**[N]

NOTES

Ben Yoḥai purified the cemetery – טִיהֵר בֶּן יוֹחַי בֵּית הַקְּבָרוֹת: It is explained in the Jerusalem Talmud (*Shevi'it* 9:1) that Rabbi Shimon bar Yoḥai accomplished this miraculously. Everywhere that a corpse was buried, it would rise up from the earth. Although the Samaritans attempted to sabotage his effort, they were unsuccessful. Here, it is explained that Rabbi Shimon bar Yoḥai purified the ground by examining the texture of the soil to see whether or not the soil had been overturned at some point in the past.

A pile of bones – גַּל שֶׁל עֲצָמוֹת: The implication is that he died, since with the passage of time a corpse turns into a mere pile of bones (Rashi).

PERSONALITIES

Yehuda, son of converts – יְהוּדָה בֶּן גֵּרִים: He was called son of converts because his parents were indeed converts. He is counted among the students of Rabbi Shimon bar Yoḥai, who referred to him as a man of stature and treated him with respect. The fact that he sat in the company of the most prominent Sages indicates his significance and proves that they considered him loyal. However, Rabbi Shimon became angry with him because he violated a basic principle: Matters discussed in the study hall, whether statements about politics or topics that warrant discretion, should not to be discussed outside the study hall (see *Tosafot*).

מתני׳ שְׁלֹשָׁה דְּבָרִים צָרִיךְ אָדָם לוֹמַר בְּתוֹךְ בֵּיתוֹ עֶרֶב שַׁבָּת עִם חֲשֵׁכָה: עִשַּׂרְתֶּם, עֵרַבְתֶּם? הַדְלִיקוּ אֶת הַנֵּר. סָפֵק חֲשֵׁכָה סָפֵק אֵינוֹ חֲשֵׁכָה – אֵין מְעַשְּׂרִין אֶת הַוַּדַּאי, וְאֵין מַטְבִּילִין אֶת הַכֵּלִים, וְאֵין מַדְלִיקִין אֶת הַנֵּרוֹת. אֲבָל מְעַשְּׂרִין אֶת הַדְּמַאי, וּמְעָרְבִין וְטוֹמְנִין אֶת הַחַמִּין.

MISHNA There are **three things a person must say**[H] **in his home on Shabbat eve at nightfall** and not before. The mishna elaborates: He should ask the members of his household, **have you tithed** the crop that required tithing? **Have you placed the *eiruv*** for joining the courtyards and joining the Shabbat borders? If you have done so, **light the lamp** in honor of Shabbat. The Sages stated a principle: If the time arrives on Friday when there is **uncertainty** whether it is **nightfall** and **uncertainty** whether it is **not** yet **nightfall,**[NH] **one may not tithe** the crop that has **definitely** not been tithed, **and one may not immerse** ritually impure **vessels** in a ritual bath to render them ritually pure, **and one may not light the** Shabbat **lights. However, one may tithe *demai*,** doubtfully tithed produce, which must be tithed due to mere suspicion. **And one may place an *eiruv* and insulate the hot water** to be used on Shabbat.

גמ׳ מְנָא הָנֵי מִילֵּי? אָמַר רַבִּי יְהוֹשֻׁעַ בֶּן לֵוִי, אָמַר קְרָא: ״וְיָדַעְתָּ כִּי שָׁלוֹם אָהֳלֶךָ וּפָקַדְתָּ נָוְךָ וְלֹא תֶחֱטָא״. אָמַר רַבָּה בַּר רַב הוּנָא: אַף עַל גַּב דְּאָמוּר רַבָּנַן שְׁלֹשָׁה דְּבָרִים צָרִיךְ אָדָם לוֹמַר וכו׳, צָרִיךְ לְמֵימְרִינְהוּ בִּנְיחוּתָא, כִּי הֵיכִי דְּלִיקַבְּלִינְהוּ מִינֵּיהּ. אָמַר רַב אַשִׁי: אֲנָא לָא שְׁמִיעַ לִי הָא דְּרַבָּה בַּר רַב הוּנָא, וְקַיֵּימְתִּיהָ מִסְּבָרָא.

GEMARA The Gemara attempts to clarify: **From where are these matters,** that one must ask these questions in his home at nightfall of Shabbat, derived? **Rabbi Yehoshua ben Levi said:** As **the verse said: "And you shall know that your tent is in peace;**[N] **and you shall visit your habitation, and shall not sin"** (Job 5:24). From here it is derived that one should visit his habitation, i.e., ask in his home, so that he will not come to sin. **Rabba bar Rav Huna said: Although the Sages said** that there are **three things a person should,** indeed he is required to, **say** in his home on Shabbat eve at nightfall, **one must say them calmly so that** the members of his household **will accept them from him.** If he says them harshly, his family members may mislead him and cause him to sin. **Rav Ashi said: I did not hear this** *halakha* **of Rabba bar Rav Huna, but I fulfilled** it **based on** my own **reasoning.**

הָא גּוּפָא קַשְׁיָא; אָמְרַתְּ שְׁלֹשָׁה דְּבָרִים צָרִיךְ אָדָם לוֹמַר בְּתוֹךְ בֵּיתוֹ עֶרֶב שַׁבָּת עִם חֲשֵׁכָה, עִם חֲשֵׁכָה – אִין, סָפֵק חֲשֵׁכָה סָפֵק אֵינוֹ חֲשֵׁכָה – לָא. וַהֲדַר תָּנֵי: סָפֵק חֲשֵׁכָה סָפֵק אֵינוֹ חֲשֵׁכָה מְעָרֵב!

The Gemara asks: **This** mishna **itself is difficult,** as it contains an internal contradiction. On the one hand, **you stated** initially that there are **three things a person must say in his home before Shabbat at nightfall,** and this means: **At nightfall,** i.e., before nightfall, **yes,** he should say those things; when there is **uncertainty** whether it is **nightfall** and **uncertainty** whether it is **not** yet **nightfall, no,** he should not say them. Even if one were to ask then, it is no longer permitted to correct these matters. **And then it taught:** When there is **uncertainty** whether it is **nightfall** and **uncertainty** whether it is **not** yet **nightfall, one may place an *eiruv*.** One may correct the situation even then. Why did the mishna restrict asking these questions to an earlier time?

סִימָן: בְּגוּפַיְא זִימְרָא צִיפְּרָא בְּחַבְלָא דְּמִילְתָא.

Incidentally, prior to answering this question, the Gemara lists all of the other *halakhot* in tractate *Shabbat* stated by the Sage who answers the question, with the **mnemonic: Self,**[N] **pruning, bird, cord, silk.**

אָמַר רַבִּי אַבָּא אָמַר רַב חִיָּיא בַּר אַשִׁי אָמַר רַב: לָא קַשְׁיָא, כָּאן – בְּעֵירוּבֵי תְחוּמִין, כָּאן – בְּעֵירוּבֵי חֲצֵרוֹת.

Rabbi Abba said that **Rabbi Ḥiyya bar Ashi said** that **Rav said:** This is **not difficult** and there is no contradiction here. **Here,** at the beginning of the mishna, where it indicates that the *eiruv* can only be placed while it is still day, it is referring **to the joining of Shabbat boundaries,**[N] which is based on a Torah law. Therefore, one must place this *eiruv* while it is definitely day. And **here,** where the mishna said that it is permitted even when it is uncertain whether or not it is already nighttime, it is referring **to the joining of courtyards,** which is more lenient and based merely on a stringency.

HALAKHA

Three things a person must say – שְׁלֹשָׁה דְּבָרִים צָרִיךְ אָדָם לוֹמַר: A person should calmly ask the members of his household three questions before Shabbat begins, just before twilight (*Mishna Berura*): Have you tithed the produce? Have you placed the *eiruv*? Have you separated *ḥalla*? After doing so, he says to them: Light the lamp, as per the statement of Rabba bar Rav Huna. Nowadays, when the joining of courtyards is placed for an entire year, or in a location where there is no mitzva to tithe, one need not ask those questions (Rema; *Be'er Heitev*; Rambam *Sefer Zemanim*, *Hilkhot Shabbat* 5:3; *Shulḥan Arukh*, *Oraḥ Ḥayyim* 260:2).

Uncertainty whether it is nightfall and uncertainty whether it is not yet nightfall – סָפֵק חֲשֵׁכָה סָפֵק אֵינוֹ חֲשֵׁכָה: When there is uncertainty whether or not night has fallen on Friday evening, one may not tithe the produce that definitely has not been tithed, including fruit, for which tithing is required by rabbinic law (*Mishna Berura*). One may not immerse vessels in a ritual bath, one may not light the lamp, and one may not place a joining of the Shabbat boundaries. However, one may tithe *demai*, insulate hot water in a manner that does not add heat (*Mishna Berura*), and place a joining of the courtyards (Rambam *Sefer Zemanim*, *Hilkhot Shabbat* 4:4; *Shulḥan Arukh*, *Oraḥ Ḥayyim* 261:1).

NOTES

Uncertainty whether it is nightfall and uncertainty whether it is not yet nightfall – סָפֵק חֲשֵׁכָה סָפֵק אֵינוֹ חֲשֵׁכָה: Some commentaries explain that this period is not definitely twilight. It is uncertain twilight (*Penei Yehoshua*). Others explain that the phrase: Uncertainty whether it is nightfall, refers to the onset of Shabbat. Uncertainty whether it is not yet nightfall, refers to the conclusion of Shabbat (*Melo HaRo'im*).

That your tent is in peace – כִּי שָׁלוֹם אָהֳלֶךָ: The verse alludes to the three actions mentioned in the mishna. "And you shall know that your tent is in peace" refers to the Shabbat light, as mentioned above: "And my soul is removed far off from peace," that is kindling the Shabbat light. "And you shall visit your habitation" refers to the *eiruv*, which is a stage in preparing the house for Shabbat. "And you shall not sin" refers to the tithe, as it is written with regard to eating untithed produce: "And you shall bear no sin by reason of it" (Numbers 18:32; see the Ran).

The mnemonic: Self, etc. – סִימָן: בְּגוּפַיְא וכו׳: This is a mnemonic of the *halakhot* that Rabbi Abba said in the name of Rabbi Ḥiyya bar Ashi in the name of Rav throughout tractate *Shabbat*. Self refers to the solution to the question: This itself is difficult. Pruning refers to his statement: One who prunes is liable for the labor of planting (73b, p. 356). Bird refers to the *halakha* of a bird that flies under one's clothing (107a). Cord refers to the *halakha* that one may bring a rope from his house and tie it (113a). Silk refers to the issue of silk brooms (124b; see Maharsha).

Here, it is referring to the joining of Shabbat boundaries – כָּאן בְּעֵירוּבֵי תְחוּמִין: The stringency of the joining of Shabbat boundaries [*eiruv teḥumin*] stems from the dispute whether or not the prohibition to travel beyond city limits on Shabbat is by Torah law. Some *tanna'im* are of the opinion that the *halakha* of Shabbat boundaries is by Torah law, as it is stated: "Abide you every man in his place, let no man go out of his place" (Exodus 16:29). Even those who hold that the two-thousand-cubit Shabbat boundary is by rabbinic law understand that the essential Shabbat boundary, twelve *mil* beyond city limits, is by Torah law (Rambam).

NOTES

One to whom two people said: Go and place an *eiruv* for us – אָמְרוּ לוֹ שְׁנַיִם צֵא וְעָרֵב עָלֵינוּ: The Gemara cited a case where two people asked a third to place an *eiruv* for them, rather than the simple case of two people who each placed his own *eiruv*, to underscore the *halakha* that even if the third person, the messenger, was to ask about the status of each *eiruv*, the Sages deemed them both valid (*Penei Yehoshua*). Although the essential basis of this issue is not fully developed here, the Gemara raises this basic problem in a similar case in which there are two paths, one ritually impure and one ritually pure, and one person took one path and one took the other, and they do not know which person took which path. Clearly, one of them must have been exposed to ritual impurity. The ruling is dependent on a dispute between the *tanna'im* with regard to the extent to which each case is treated independently. If the uncertainty is with regard to one person, it is prohibited, despite the fact that it is an uncertainty involving rabbinic law (*Melo HaRo'im*).

HALAKHA

One to whom two people said: Go and place an *eiruv* for us – אָמְרוּ לוֹ שְׁנַיִם צֵא וְעָרֵב עָלֵינוּ: If two people deputized a third person to place an *eiruv* for them, and he placed the *eiruv* for one while it was still day and the *eiruv* food was eaten during twilight, and he placed the *eiruv* for the second one during twilight, then the *halakha* is that each *eiruv* is valid. For the one whose *eiruv* was eaten, twilight is considered nighttime, and it is as if the *eiruv* were eaten after Shabbat begun. For the one whose *eiruv* was placed during twilight, it is considered to be daytime, and it is as if the *eiruv* were placed during the day. Joining of courtyards is a rabbinic edict, and there is a principle that rulings in cases of uncertainty with regard to rabbinic ordinances are lenient. If the *eiruv* was both placed during twilight and eaten during twilight, it is invalid (Rambam *Sefer Zemanim, Hilkhot Eiruvin* 6:13; *Shulḥan Arukh, Oraḥ Ḥayyim* 393:3).

One may not insulate in something that does not add heat from nightfall – אֵין טוֹמְנִין בְּדָבָר שֶׁאֵינוֹ מוֹסִיף הֶבֶל מִשֶּׁחֲשֵׁכָה: One may not insulate food at night on Friday even in a substance that does not add heat. The decree is based on the fear that he might come to cook food on Shabbat. Therefore, this *halakha* applies only in a case where there is concern that the Torah prohibition against cooking might be violated (Rambam *Sefer Zemanim, Hilkhot Shabbat* 4:3; *Shulḥan Arukh, Oraḥ Ḥayyim* 257:1, 318:4).

וְאָמַר רָבָא: אָמְרוּ לוֹ שְׁנַיִם ״צֵא וְעָרֵב עָלֵינוּ״. לְאֶחָד עֵירֵב עָלָיו מִבְּעוֹד יוֹם, וּלְאֶחָד עֵירֵב עָלָיו בֵּין הַשְּׁמָשׁוֹת. זֶה שֶׁעֵירֵב עָלָיו מִבְּעוֹד יוֹם – נֶאֱכַל עֵירוּבוֹ בֵּין הַשְּׁמָשׁוֹת, וְזֶה שֶׁעֵירֵב עָלָיו בֵּין הַשְּׁמָשׁוֹת – נֶאֱכַל עֵירוּבוֹ מִשֶּׁחֲשֵׁכָה, שְׁנֵיהֶם קָנָה עֵירוּב.

In connection to this, the Gemara cites the *halakha* that **Rava said** in order to emphasize the rabbinic aspect of the *halakhot* of *eiruv*: One **to whom two people said: Go and place an *eiruv*,** a joining of courtyards (Rabbeinu Ḥananel), **for us.**[NH] **For one** of them **he placed an *eiruv* while it was still day, and for one he placed an *eiruv* at twilight,** when it is uncertain whether it is day or night. **The one for whom he placed an *eiruv* while it was still day had his *eiruv* eaten during twilight, and the one for whom he placed an *eiruv* during twilight had his *eiruv* eaten after nightfall.** The principle is as follows: Whether or not an *eiruv* takes effect is determined at the moment that Shabbat begins. If one placed the *eiruv* beforehand, and it remains intact at the moment Shabbat begins, the *eiruv* is in effect. However, if the *eiruv* that was placed at the appropriate time was eaten during twilight, it is problematic. Twilight is a period of uncertainty. There is uncertainty whether it is day, and consequently the *eiruv* was not in place at the moment that Shabbat began, or whether it is night, and it was in place. In the latter case, there is still uncertainty as to whether or not the *eiruv* was in place prior to Shabbat, so that it could take effect at all. In that case, Rava ruled that **both of them acquired** the ***eiruv*.**

מַה נַּפְשָׁךְ, אִי בֵּין הַשְּׁמָשׁוֹת יְמָמָא הוּא – בַּתְרָא לִיקְנֵי, קַמָּא לָא לִיקְנֵי! וְאִי בֵּין הַשְּׁמָשׁוֹת לֵילְיָא הוּא, קַמָּא לִיקְנֵי, בַּתְרָא לָא לִיקְנֵי! בֵּין הַשְּׁמָשׁוֹת סְפֵקָא הוּא, וּסְפֵקָא דְּרַבָּנַן לְקוּלָּא.

The Gemara is surprised by this: **Whichever** way **you** look at it, this ruling is difficult. **If** the **twilight** period **is** considered **day,** let **the latter** one **acquire** his *eiruv*, but let **the first one not acquire** his because his *eiruv* was eaten while it was still day. **And if** the **twilight** period **is night, let the first one acquire** his *eiruv*, but **let the latter one not acquire** his *eiruv* because his was not placed before Shabbat. In any event, it is impossible for the *eiruv* in both of these cases to be valid. The Gemara answers this according to Rava's position: The status of **twilight is uncertain,** as it is unknown whether it is day, or night, or both, **and uncertainty** in the case of a **rabbinic** ordinance is ruled **leniently.** Therefore, in both cases the *eiruv* is acquired.

(וְאָמַר) רָבָא: מִפְּנֵי מָה אָמְרוּ: אֵין טוֹמְנִין בְּדָבָר שֶׁאֵינוֹ מוֹסִיף הֶבֶל מִשֶּׁחֲשֵׁכָה – גְּזֵרָה שֶׁמָּא יַרְתִּיחַ. אֲמַר לֵיהּ אַבָּיֵי: אִי הָכִי, בֵּין הַשְּׁמָשׁוֹת נָמֵי נִיגְזַר! אֲמַר לֵיהּ: סְתָם קְדֵירוֹת רוֹתְחוֹת הֵן.

And Rava said: Why did they say that **one may not insulate** hot water even **in something that does not add heat,** but only retains the pre-existing heat, **from nightfall**[H] on Friday? It is **a decree lest one** come to **boil** the pot on Shabbat. **Abaye said to him: If so,** if it is due to concern that one may boil it, then **during twilight we should also issue a decree** and prohibit insulating in something that does not add heat. Rava **said to him:** During twilight, there is no reason to be concerned because at that time **most pots are boiling,** as they have just been taken off of the fire. Later at night the pots cool down and it is conceivable that one may come to boil them in order to restore the heat.

וְאָמַר רָבָא:

And Rava said:

Perek **II**
Daf **34** Amud **b**

HALAKHA

One may not insulate in something that adds heat – אֵין טוֹמְנִין בְּדָבָר הַמּוֹסִיף הֶבֶל: One may not insulate food in a substance that adds heat, even while it is still day. If one did so, even unintentionally (*Magen Avraham*), it is prohibited to eat the food (Rambam *Sefer Zemanim, Hilkhot Shabbat* 4:2; *Shulḥan Arukh, Oraḥ Ḥayyim* 257:1).

מִפְּנֵי מָה אָמְרוּ אֵין טוֹמְנִין בְּדָבָר הַמּוֹסִיף הֶבֶל וַאֲפִילּוּ מִבְּעוֹד יוֹם – גְּזֵירָה שֶׁמָּא יַטְמִין בְּרֶמֶץ שֶׁיֵּשׁ בָּהּ גַּחֶלֶת. אֲמַר לֵיהּ אַבָּיֵי: וְיַטְמִין! גְּזֵירָה שֶׁמָּא יַחְתֶּה בַּגֶּחָלִים.

Why did the Sages **say** that **one may not insulate** hot water for Shabbat **in something that adds heat,**[H] **even while it is still day?** It is **a decree lest one come to cover it in hot ashes that contain** a glowing **ember.** People may not differentiate between addition of heat by means of hot ashes and other additions of heat. **Abaye said to him: Let him insulate** it with hot ashes, what is the problem? Rava answered him: It is **a decree lest one come to stoke the coals** in order to make them burn on Shabbat and thereby violate a Torah prohibition.

תָּנוּ רַבָּנַן: בֵּין הַשְּׁמָשׁוֹת סָפֵק מִן הַיּוֹם וּמִן הַלַּיְלָה, סָפֵק כּוּלּוֹ מִן הַיּוֹם, סָפֵק כּוּלּוֹ מִן הַלַּיְלָה – מַטִּילִין אוֹתוֹ לְחוֹמֶר שְׁנֵי יָמִים.

The Sages taught a *baraita* which discusses the range of problems that arise with regard to the twilight period. **Twilight** is a period of **uncertainty.** It is uncertain whether it consists of both **day and night,** it is **uncertain** whether **it is completely day,** and it is **uncertain** whether it is **completely night.** Therefore, the Sages **impose the stringencies of both days upon it.** If there is a stringency that applies on either of the days, one is obligated to adhere to it during the twilight period.

וְאֵיזֶהוּ בֵּין הַשְּׁמָשׁוֹת – מִשֶּׁתִּשְׁקַע הַחַמָּה כׇּל זְמַן שֶׁפְּנֵי מִזְרָח מַאֲדִימִין, הִכְסִיף הַתַּחְתּוֹן וְלֹא הִכְסִיף הָעֶלְיוֹן – בֵּין הַשְּׁמָשׁוֹת, הִכְסִיף הָעֶלְיוֹן וְהִשְׁוָה לַתַּחְתּוֹן – זֶהוּ לַיְלָה, דִּבְרֵי רַבִּי יְהוּדָה. רַבִּי נְחֶמְיָה אוֹמֵר: כְּדֵי שֶׁיְּהַלֵּךְ אָדָם מִשֶּׁתִּשְׁקַע הַחַמָּה חֲצִי מִיל. רַבִּי יוֹסֵי אוֹמֵר: בֵּין הַשְּׁמָשׁוֹת כְּהֶרֶף עַיִן, זֶה נִכְנָס וְזֶה יוֹצֵא, וְאִי אֶפְשָׁר לַעֲמוֹד עָלָיו.

Nevertheless, the definition of twilight is uncertain. **And what is twilight? From when the sun sets, as long as the eastern face** of the sky **is reddened** by the light of the sun. If **the lower** segment of the sky has **lost its color, and the upper** segment **has not** yet **lost** its **color,** that is the **twilight** period. If **the upper** segment **has lost its color, and** its color **equals** that of **the lower one, it is night;** this is **the statement of Rabbi Yehuda. Rabbi Neḥemya says:** The duration of the twilight period is **the time** it takes **for a person to walk half a *mil* after the sun sets. Rabbi Yosei says: Twilight** does not last for a quantifiable period of time; rather, it is **like the blink of an eye: This,** night, **enters and that,** day, **leaves, and it is impossible to calculate it** due to its brevity.

אָמַר מָר: ״מַטִּילִין אוֹתוֹ לְחוֹמֶר שְׁנֵי יָמִים״, לְמַאי הִלְכְתָא? אָמַר רַב הוּנָא בְּרֵיהּ דְּרַב יְהוֹשֻׁעַ: לְעִנְיַן טוּמְאָה, כְּדִתְנַן: רָאָה שְׁנֵי יָמִים בֵּין הַשְּׁמָשׁוֹת – סָפֵק לְטוּמְאָה וּלְקׇרְבָּן, רָאָה יוֹם אֶחָד בֵּין הַשְּׁמָשׁוֹת סָפֵק לְטוּמְאָה.

It was taught in the *baraita* that **the Master said:** The Sages **impose the stringencies of both days upon** twilight. The Gemara asks: **With regard to what *halakha*** was this stated? **Rav Huna, son of Rav Yehoshua, said:** With regard to the **matter of ritual impurity, as we learned** in a mishna: With regard to a *zav* who **saw** an emission for **two** consecutive **days during twilight,**[H] it is unclear whether it should be considered as if he only saw the emission for a single day, as perhaps twilight of the first day was part of the following day, and twilight of the second day was part of the previous day; or, whether it should be considered as two days, attributing each twilight to either the previous or the following day; or, whether it should be considered three days, as it is possible to view the twilight period as two days. By Torah law, a *zav* who saw two emissions is ritually impure, and all of the stringencies of a *zav* apply to him. If he sees a third emission, he is liable to bring an offering as part of his purification ritual. Therefore, this *zav*, with regard to whom there is uncertainty whether he saw emissions for one day, two days, or three days, has **uncertain** status **with regard to both ritual impurity and to sacrifice.** If **he saw** an emission **one day during twilight,** he has **uncertain** status **with regard to ritual impurity** because it may be considered two days.

הָא גּוּפָהּ קַשְׁיָא; אָמְרַתְּ: אֵיזֶהוּ בֵּין הַשְּׁמָשׁוֹת – מִשֶּׁתִּשְׁקַע הַחַמָּה, כׇּל זְמַן שֶׁפְּנֵי מִזְרָח מַאֲדִימִין. הָא הִכְסִיף הַתַּחְתּוֹן וְלֹא הִכְסִיף הָעֶלְיוֹן – לַיְלָה הוּא. וַהֲדַר תְּנָא: הִכְסִיף הַתַּחְתּוֹן וְלֹא הִכְסִיף הָעֶלְיוֹן – בֵּין הַשְּׁמָשׁוֹת! אָמַר רַבָּה אָמַר רַב יְהוּדָה אָמַר שְׁמוּאֵל: כְּרוֹךְ וּתְנִי, אֵיזֶהוּ בֵּין הַשְּׁמָשׁוֹת – מִשֶּׁתִּשְׁקַע הַחַמָּה כׇּל זְמַן שֶׁפְּנֵי מִזְרָח מַאֲדִימִין, וְהִכְסִיף הַתַּחְתּוֹן וְלֹא הִכְסִיף הָעֶלְיוֹן – נַמִי בֵּין הַשְּׁמָשׁוֹת, הִכְסִיף הָעֶלְיוֹן וְהִשְׁוָה לַתַּחְתּוֹן – לַיְלָה. וְרַב יוֹסֵף אָמַר רַב יְהוּדָה אָמַר שְׁמוּאֵל: הָכִי קָתָנֵי: מִשֶּׁתִּשְׁקַע הַחַמָּה כׇּל זְמַן שֶׁפְּנֵי מִזְרָח מַאֲדִימִין – יוֹם, הִכְסִיף הַתַּחְתּוֹן וְלֹא הִכְסִיף הָעֶלְיוֹן – בֵּין הַשְּׁמָשׁוֹת, הִכְסִיף הָעֶלְיוֹן וְהִשְׁוָה לַתַּחְתּוֹן – לַיְלָה.

The Gemara comments on the *baraita* cited by the Gemara. **This** *baraita* **is itself difficult,** self-contradictory. Initially **you said, what is twilight?**[H] **From when the sun sets, as long as the eastern face** of the sky **is reddened** by the light of the sun. By inference, **if the bottom** segment **lost** its **color, and the upper one has not lost** its **color, it is night. And then** the *baraita* **taught:** If **the lower** segment of the sky has **lost** its **color, and the upper** segment **has not** yet **lost** its **color,** that is the **twilight** period. There is an apparent internal contradiction in the *baraita*. **Rabba said** that **Rav Yehuda said** that **Shmuel said:** In order to resolve the contradiction, **unify** the two statements **and teach** it as follows: **What is twilight? From when the sun sets, as long as the eastern face** of the sky **is reddened** by the light of the sun. If **the lower** segment of the sky has **lost** its **color and the upper** segment **has not** yet **lost** its **color,** that is **also** the **twilight** period. Only if **the upper** segment **lost** its **color, and** it **equals** that of **the lower** one, is it **night. And Rav Yosef** said that **Rav Yehuda said** that **Shmuel said** otherwise: **From when the sun sets, as long as the eastern face** of the sky **is reddened** by the light of the sun, it is **day.** If **the lower** segment of the sky has **lost** its **color, and the upper** segment **has not** yet **lost** its **color,** that is the **twilight** period. If **the upper** segment **lost** its **color and** it **equals** that **of the lower** one, it is **night.**

וְאַזְדוּ לְטַעְמַיְיהוּ, דְּאִיתְּמַר: שִׁיעוּר בֵּין הַשְּׁמָשׁוֹת בְּכַמָּה? אָמַר רַבָּה אָמַר רַב יְהוּדָה אָמַר שְׁמוּאֵל: שְׁלֹשָׁה חֶלְקֵי מִיל. מַאי שְׁלֹשָׁה חֶלְקֵי מִיל? אִילֵימָא תְּלָתָא פַּלְגֵי מִילָא – נֵימָא מִיל וּמֶחֱצָה! אֶלָּא תְּלָתָא תִּילְתֵּי מִילָא – נֵימָא מִיל! אֶלָּא: תְּלָתָא רִיבְעֵי מִילָא. וְרַב יוֹסֵף אָמַר רַב יְהוּדָה אָמַר שְׁמוּאֵל: שְׁנֵי חֶלְקֵי מִיל. מַאי שְׁנֵי חֶלְקֵי מִיל? אִילֵימָא תְּרֵי פַּלְגֵי מִילָא – לֵימָא מִיל! וְאֶלָּא תְּרֵי רִבְעֵי מִילָא – לֵימָא חֲצִי מִיל! אֶלָּא:

And the Gemara remarks: In this dispute over the precise definition of twilight both Rabba and Rav Yosef **follow their** line of **reasoning** stated elsewhere. **As it was stated: What is the measure** of the duration **of twilight? Rabba said** that **Rav Yehuda said** that **Shmuel said:** The time it takes to walk **three parts of a *mil*.**[N] The Gemara asks: **What is** the meaning of **three parts of a *mil*? If you say** that it refers to **three halves of a *mil*, let him say a *mil* and a half. Rather,** if you say that it means **three-thirds of a *mil*, let him** simply **say** one ***mil*. Rather,** it means **three-quarters of a *mil*. And Rav Yosef said** that **Rav Yehuda said** that **Shmuel said:** The duration of twilight is **two parts of a *mil*.** Again the Gemara asks: **What is** the meaning of **two parts of a *mil*? If you say** that it means **two halves of a *mil*, let him** simply **say** one ***mil*. Rather,** if you say that it means **two-quarters of a *mil*, let him say** instead: **Half of a *mil*. Rather,**

HALAKHA

Saw two days during twilight – רָאָה שְׁנֵי יָמִים בֵּין הַשְּׁמָשׁוֹת: A *zav* who saw an emission during twilight is considered ritually impure based on an uncertainty. If a *zav* saw an emission on two consecutive days during twilight, his status is uncertain with regard to both ritual impurity and the sacrifice. Consequently, the sacrifice may not be eaten, as per the mishna (Rambam *Sefer Korbanot, Hilkhot Meḥusrei Kappara* 2:12–14).

What is twilight – אֵיזֶהוּ בֵּין הַשְּׁמָשׁוֹת: The duration of twilight lasts as long as it takes to walk three-quarters of a *mil* before nightfall. The *halakha* was decided in accordance with the opinion of Rabbi Yehuda, the ruling of Rabbi Yoḥanan, below, and the opinion of Rabba, in accordance with whose opinion the *halakha* is established in disputes with Rav Yosef (Rambam *Sefer Zemanim, Hilkhot Shabbat* 5:4; *Shulḥan Arukh, Oraḥ Ḥayyim* 261:2).

NOTES

Three parts of a *mil* – שְׁלֹשָׁה חֶלְקֵי מִיל: The assumption in establishing the duration of twilight is that as simple a number as possible was chosen to quantify it. The possibility that Shmuel was referring to three-fifths or three-sevenths of a *mil* was not considered (Rashash).

תְּרֵי תִּילְתֵּי מִיל. מַאי בֵּינַיְיהוּ? אִיכָּא בֵּינַיְיהוּ פַּלְגָא דְּדַנְקָא.

it means **two-thirds of a *mil*.** The Gemara explains: **What is** the practical difference **between them? The** practical difference **between them is half of one-sixth** [*danka*],[L] i.e., one-twelfth of a *mil*. Their disputes are consistent, as the duration of twilight according to Rav Yosef is shorter than its duration according to Rabba.

וְחִילּוּפָהּ בְּחַלְתָּא, דַּאֲמַר רַבָּה: חַלְתָּא בַּת תְּרֵי כּוֹרֵי שָׁרֵי לְטַלְטוּלָהּ, וּבַת תְּלָתָא כּוֹרֵי אָסוּר לְטַלְטוּלָהּ. וְרַב יוֹסֵף אֲמַר: בַּת תְּלָתָא כּוֹרֵי נַמִי שָׁרֵי, בַּת אַרְבָּעָה כּוֹרֵי אָסוּר.

The Gemara comments: **And** with regard to the legal status of a **wicker vessel** their dispute **is the opposite.** In that case, the size of the vessel permitted by Rav Yosef is larger than the size of the vessel permitted by Rabba. **As Rabba said** with regard to **a wicker vessel with a capacity of two *kor*, one is permitted to move it** on Shabbat. **And one with a capacity of three *kor*,**[N] **one is prohibited to move it** on Shabbat.[H] It is much larger than the dimensions of a vessel and one is only permitted to move vessels on Shabbat. **And Rav Yosef said:** A vessel **with a capacity of three *kor*, one is also permitted** to move it, and only **one with a capacity of four *kor*,** it **is prohibited** to move.

אָמַר אַבַּיֵי: בְּעֵי מִינֵּיהּ דְּמָר בִּשְׁעַת מַעֲשֶׂה, וַאֲפִילּוּ בַּת תְּרֵי כּוֹרֵי לָא שְׁרָא לִי, כְּמַאן – כְּהַאי תַּנָּא, דִּתְנַן: כַּוֶּורֶת הַקַּשׁ וְכַוֶּורֶת הַקָּנִים וּבוֹר סְפִינָה אֲלֶכְּסַנְדְּרִית, אַף עַל פִּי שֶׁיֵּשׁ לָהֶם שׁוּלַיִם וְהֵן מַחֲזִיקוֹת אַרְבָּעִים סְאָה בְּלַח שֶׁהֵן כּוֹרַיִים בְּיָבֵשׁ – טְהוֹרִים. אָמַר אַבַּיֵי: שְׁמַע מִינָּהּ – הַאי גּוּדְשָׁא תִּילְתָּא הָוֵי.

Abaye said: I raised the dilemma before my Master, Rabba, **when it was practical,** when I actually needed to know what to do, **and he did not permit me** to move **even** a vessel **with a capacity of two *kor*.** The Gemara explains: **In accordance with whose** opinion did Rabba issue his practical halakhic ruling? **In accordance with** the opinion of **this *tanna*** that **we learned** in the mishna discussing the laws of ritual purity: **A round straw barrel, and a round barrel** made **of reeds,**[N] **and the cistern of an Alexandrian ship,**[B] which is a large vessel placed on a boat and filled with potable water, **although** these vessels **have bottoms,** i.e., they are receptacles, since they **have a capacity of forty *se'a*** of liquid, **which is the** equivalent of **two *kor*** of **dry** goods, they are **ritually pure.** Even if they come into contact with a source of ritual impurity, they do not become impure. Beyond a certain size, containers are no longer considered vessels and, consequently, cannot become ritually impure.[H] Rabba held: Since with regard to the *halakhot* of ritual impurity a vessel of two *kor* is not considered a vessel, it may not be moved on Shabbat. With regard to this mishna, **Abaye said: Learn from it** that **the surplus** of dry goods in a vessel relative to liquids **is one-third** of the contents of the vessel. It says in the mishna that a vessel that can hold forty *se'a* of liquid holds two *kor* of dry produce, which is the equivalent of sixty *se'a*.

אַבַּיֵי חַזְיֵיהּ לְרָבָא דְּקָא דָּאוֵי לְמַעֲרָב, אֲמַר לֵיהּ: וְהָתַנְיָא כָּל זְמַן שֶׁפְּנֵי מִזְרָח מַאֲדִימִין! אֲמַר לֵיהּ: מִי סָבְרַתְּ פְּנֵי מִזְרָח מַמָּשׁ? לֹא, פָּנִים הַמַּאֲדִימִין אֶת הַמִּזְרָח. אִיכָּא דְּאָמְרִי, רָבָא חַזְיֵיהּ לְאַבַּיֵי דְּקָא דָּאוֵי לְמִזְרָח, אֲמַר לֵיהּ: מִי סָבְרַתְּ פְּנֵי מִזְרָח מַמָּשׁ? פָּנִים הַמַּאֲדִימִין אֶת הַמִּזְרָח! וְסִימָנֵיךְ כַּוְּותָא.

The Gemara relates: **Abaye saw** that **Rava was gazing westward** on Shabbat eve to determine whether or not the sky was red and whether or not it was twilight. Abaye **said to** Rava: **Wasn't it taught** in a *baraita* that twilight **is from when the sun sets, as long as the eastern face** of the sky **is reddened** by the light of the sun? Why, then, are you looking westward? Rava **said to him: Do you hold** that the reference is actually to **the eastern face** of the sky? **No,** it is referring to **the face** of the sky **that causes the east** to **redden,** i.e., the west. **Some say** a different version of that incident. **Rava saw** that **Abaye was gazing eastward. He said to him, do you hold** that the reference is to **the actual eastern face** of the sky? The reference is to **the face** of the sky **that causes the east to redden,** i.e., the west. **And your mnemonic is a window,** as it is on the wall opposite the window that one can see how much sunlight is shining through.

רַבִּי נְחֶמְיָה אוֹמֵר: כְּדֵי שֶׁיְּהַלֵּךְ אָדָם מִשֶּׁתִּשְׁקַע הַחַמָּה חֲצִי מִיל – אָמַר רַבִּי חֲנִינָא: הָרוֹצֶה לֵידַע שִׁיעוּרוֹ שֶׁל רַבִּי נְחֶמְיָה יַנִּיחַ חַמָּה בְּרֹאשׁ הַכַּרְמֶל, וְיֵרֵד וְיִטְבּוֹל בַּיָּם וְיַעֲלֶה, וְזֶהוּ שִׁיעוּרוֹ שֶׁל רַבִּי נְחֶמְיָה.

With regard to that which was taught in the *baraita* that **Rabbi Neḥemya says:** The duration of twilight is **the time** it takes **for a person to walk half a *mil* after the sun sets. Rabbi Ḥanina said: One who wants to know** the precise measure of **Rabbi Neḥemya's** twilight should do the following: **Leave the sun at the top of** Mount **Carmel,** as when one is standing on the seashore he can still see the top of Mount Carmel in sunlight, **and descend and immerse himself in the sea, and emerge,**[N] **and that is Rabbi Neḥemya's measure** of the duration of twilight.

LANGUAGE

One-sixth [*danka*] – דַּנְקָא: *Danka* is the name of a Persian coin. In Middle Persian, the word dāng means a tiny particle. *Ma'a* is the Aramaic equivalent of *danka*. Since the *ma'a* is one-sixth of a *dinar*, the Sages used the word *danka* to refer to one-sixth in many contexts.

NOTES

A wicker vessel with a capacity of two *kor*…three *kor*, etc. – חַלְתָּא בַּת תְּרֵי כּוֹרֵי...תְּלָתָא כּוֹרֵי וכו׳: In tractate *Eiruvin*, where this statement of Abaye is mentioned, a biblical allusion is cited. In the Bible, two contradictory measures were cited for the Sea of Solomon. One verse states: "It held two thousand baths" (I Kings 7:26), and another states: "It received and held three thousand baths" (II Chronicles 4:5). Abaye explains that the larger size is a dry measure and the smaller size is a liquid measure.

Round straw barrel or a round barrel made of reeds, etc. – כַּוֶּורֶת הַקַּשׁ וְכַוֶּורֶת הַקָּנִים וכו׳: The halakhic principle is as follows: In order for a vessel to be able to become ritually impure, it must be similar to a sack that can be carried full or empty. Therefore, any vessel that is so large that it cannot be carried when it is full is not considered a vessel and cannot become ritually impure.

And descend and immerse himself in the sea and emerge – וְיֵרֵד וְיִטְבּוֹל בַּיָּם וְיַעֲלֶה: Some commentaries explain that the reference is to a person standing at the peak of Mount Carmel who descends and immerses himself in the sea and then emerges and climbs back to the peak of the mountain (Rashba).

HALAKHA

Moving a large vessel on Shabbat – טִלְטוּל כְּלִי גָּדוֹל בְּשַׁבָּת: Any vessel, even a very large one, does not lose its status as a vessel and one is permitted to move it on Shabbat. This ruling is in contrast to the statement of Rabba and Rav Yosef, and in accordance with the conclusion reached in tractate *Eiruvin* (*Shulḥan Arukh, Oraḥ Ḥayyim* 308:2).

Large vessel in matters of ritual impurity – כְּלִי גָּדוֹל לְעִנְיַן טוּמְאָה: A vessel that is made to permanently remain in a single place and not to be moved cannot become ritually impure if it holds forty *se'a* (Rambam *Sefer Tahara, Hilkhot Kelim* 3:2).

BACKGROUND

The cistern of an Alexandrian ship – בּוֹר סְפִינָה אֲלֶכְּסַנְדְּרִית: Given the need for large quantities of potable water on long sea journeys, a very large receptacle fashioned from animal hides was placed on the deck of the ship and filled with water. From time to time, they would even allow it to be filled with the rain that fell at sea. The Alexandrian ship mentioned here refers to a large ship that not only sails in rivers or along the shore but also travels longer distances, e.g., from Alexandria to Rome.

אָמַר רַבִּי חִיָּיא: הָרוֹצֶה לִרְאוֹת בְּאֵרָהּ שֶׁל מִרְיָם, יַעֲלֶה לְרֹאשׁ הַכַּרְמֶל וְיִצְפֶּה וְיִרְאֶה כְּמִין כְּבָרָה בַּיָּם, וְזוֹ הִיא בְּאֵרָהּ שֶׁל מִרְיָם. אָמַר רַב: מַעְיָן הַמִּיטַּלְטֵל – טָהוֹר, וְזֶהוּ בְּאֵרָהּ שֶׁל מִרְיָם.

Because of its similarity to Rabbi Ḥanina's statement, the Gemara cites that which **Rabbi Ḥiyya said: One who wants to see Miriam's well,**[N] which accompanied the Jewish people throughout their sojourn in the desert, should do the following: **He should climb to the top of** Mount **Carmel and look out, and** he will **see** a rock that looks **like a sieve in the sea, and that is Miriam's well. Rav said: A spring that is portable,** i.e., that moves from place to place, **is ritually pure** and is regarded as an actual spring and not as drawn water. **And** what is a movable spring? **It is Miriam's well.**

אָמַר רַב יְהוּדָה אָמַר שְׁמוּאֵל: בֵּין הַשְּׁמָשׁוֹת דְּרַבִּי יְהוּדָה כֹּהֲנִים טוֹבְלִין בּוֹ. לְמַאן? אִילֵימָא לְרַבִּי יְהוּדָה – סְפֵקָא הוּא! אֶלָּא בֵּין הַשְּׁמָשׁוֹת דְּרַבִּי יְהוּדָה לְרַבִּי יוֹסֵי כֹּהֲנִים טוֹבְלִין בּוֹ.

Rav Yehuda said that **Shmuel said:** During **Rabbi Yehuda's twilight,** ritually impure **priests** who want to immerse themselves during the day to become ritually pure, so that sunset will follow immersion and they will be permitted to eat *teruma*, **can** still **immerse** themselves **during** that period. According to this opinion, twilight is still considered to be day. The Gemara asks: **In accordance with whose** opinion is that true? **If you say** that it is **in accordance with Rabbi Yehuda**'s own opinion, his opinion cited above is that twilight is a period of **uncertainty.** Therefore, one who immerses at that time may not eat *teruma* until after the sunset of the following day. **Rather,** the reference is to **twilight** of **Rabbi Yehuda,** in accordance with the opinion of **Rabbi Yosei. Priests** can **immerse then,** as Rabbi Yosei considers that time to still be day, and sunset will follow.

פְּשִׁיטָא! מַהוּ דְּתֵימָא: בֵּין הַשְּׁמָשׁוֹת דְּרַבִּי יוֹסֵי – מֵישַׁךְ שָׁיֵיךְ בִּדְרַבִּי יְהוּדָה, קָא מַשְׁמַע לָן: דְּשָׁלֵים בֵּין הַשְּׁמָשׁוֹת דְּרַבִּי יְהוּדָה, וַהֲדַר מַתְחִיל בֵּין הַשְּׁמָשׁוֹת דְּרַבִּי יוֹסֵי.

The Gemara asks: It is **obvious** that according to Rabbi Yosei they are immersing themselves during the day. The Gemara answers: **Lest you say** that the **twilight of Rabbi Yosei is subsumed within**[N] and takes place at the end of the twilight **of Rabbi Yehuda.** When the twilight of Rabbi Yehuda ends, Rabbi Yosei's twilight is also over. It is already night, sunset of that day has already passed, and there is no sunset to enable them to eat *teruma*. Therefore, **he teaches us** that **Rabbi Yehuda's twilight ends, and** only **thereafter** does **Rabbi Yosei's twilight begin.**

אָמַר רַבָּה בַּר בַּר חָנָה אָמַר רַבִּי יוֹחָנָן: הֲלָכָה כְּרַבִּי יְהוּדָה לְעִנְיַן שַׁבָּת, וַהֲלָכָה כְּרַבִּי יוֹסֵי לְעִנְיַן תְּרוּמָה. בִּשְׁלָמָא הֲלָכָה כְּרַבִּי יְהוּדָה לְעִנְיַן שַׁבָּת – לְחוּמְרָא, אֲבָל לְעִנְיַן תְּרוּמָה מַאי הִיא? אִילֵימָא לִטְבִילָה – סְפֵקָא הִיא!

Rabba bar bar Ḥana said that **Rabbi Yoḥanan said: The *halakha* is in accordance with** the opinion of **Rabbi Yehuda with regard to the matter of Shabbat, and the *halakha* is in accordance with** the opinion of **Rabbi Yosei with regard to the matter of *teruma*.** The Gemara asks: **Granted,** concerning the statement that **the *halakha* is in accordance with** the opinion of **Rabbi Yehuda with regard to the matter of Shabbat,** as like all other cases of uncertainty, the ruling is **stringent** with regard to Torah prohibitions. **However, with regard to *teruma*, what is** the case under discussion? **If you say** that it is referring **to** the matter of **immersion,** immersion is also a case of **uncertainty** with regard to a Torah law. Why would the ruling be more lenient in that case than in the case of Shabbat?

NOTES

Miriam's well – בְּאֵרָהּ שֶׁל מִרְיָם: Miriam's well was the source of water for the Jews in the desert. It was attributed to Miriam because the verse relating her death (Numbers 20:1) is followed immediately by the verse: "And there was no water for the congregation" (Numbers 20:2). According to rabbinic tradition, the well was a rock that rolled and accompanied Israel wherever they went in the desert. Other sources state that Miriam's well is now located in the center of the Sea of Galilee.

Lest you say that the twilight of Rabbi Yosei is subsumed within, etc. – מַהוּ דְּתֵימָא בֵּין הַשְּׁמָשׁוֹת דְּרַבִּי יוֹסֵי מֵישַׁךְ שָׁיֵיךְ וכו׳: There were those who explained that even the *amora'im* did not know clearly whether twilight as defined by Rabbi Yosei was proximate to twilight as determined by Rabbi Yehuda, or whether it was considerably later than that. Consequently, it was necessary for Rabbi Yoḥanan to rule that the *halakha* is in accordance with Rabbi Yosei in certain cases (Rosh).

Perek **II**
Daf **35** Amud **b**

אֶלָּא לַאֲכִילַת תְּרוּמָה, דְּלָא אָכְלִי כֹּהֲנִים תְּרוּמָה עַד דְּשָׁלֵים בֵּין הַשְּׁמָשׁוֹת דְּרַבִּי יוֹסֵי.

Rather, it must be that the reference is with regard **to eating *teruma*. Priests may not eat *teruma* until twilight is completed, which according to Rabbi Yosei's** opinion is slightly later than it is according to Rabbi Yehuda's opinion.

אָמַר רַב יְהוּדָה אָמַר שְׁמוּאֵל: כּוֹכָב אֶחָד – יוֹם, שְׁנַיִם – בֵּין הַשְּׁמָשׁוֹת, שְׁלֹשָׁה – לַיְלָה. תַּנְיָא נַמִי הָכִי: כּוֹכָב אֶחָד – יוֹם, שְׁנַיִם – בֵּין הַשְּׁמָשׁוֹת, שְׁלֹשָׁה – לַיְלָה. אָמַר רַבִּי יוֹסֵי: לֹא כּוֹכָבִים גְּדוֹלִים הַנִּרְאִין בַּיּוֹם, וְלֹא כּוֹכָבִים קְטַנִּים שֶׁאֵין נִרְאִין אֶלָּא בַּלַּיְלָה, אֶלָּא בֵּינוֹנִים.

With regard to the period of twilight, **Rav Yehuda said** that **Shmuel said:** When one can see **one star** in the evening sky, it is still **day;**[N] **two stars, twilight; three**[H] **stars, night. That was also taught** in a *baraita*: When one can see **one star** in the evening sky, it is still **day; two stars, twilight; three stars, night. Rabbi Yosei said:** This is **neither** referring to **large stars that are visible** even **during the day, nor to small stars that are visible only** late **at night. Rather,** it is referring to **medium**-sized stars.

HALAKHA

One star…three, etc. – כּוֹכָב אֶחָד...שְׁלֹשָׁה וכו׳: In practice, night begins when three small stars are visible, even if they are dispersed in the sky (*Mishna Berura*) because we are not considered experts in the parameters of medium-sized stars (*Taz*; *Magen Avraham*). On a fast day, medium-sized stars are sufficient to constitute the end of the fast, so as not to impose on the public (Rambam *Sefer Zemanim*, *Hilkhot Shabbat* 5:4; *Sefer Zera'im*, *Hilkhot Terumot* 7:2; *Shulḥan Arukh*, *Oraḥ Ḥayyim* 235:1).

NOTES

One star it is still day, etc. – כּוֹכָב אֶחָד יוֹם וכו׳: The determinations with regard to the stars rely on the basic Torah principle: Night begins with the emergence of the stars. Indeed, there is an opinion, cited in tractate *Berakhot* in the Jerusalem Talmud, that when one sees two stars it is already night because the word stars, in the plural, denotes a minimum of two. When there are two stars in the sky, the stars have emerged. As far as the practical *halakha* is concerned, there are numerous opinions. In the Jerusalem Talmud there is a comment that certain stars, such as Venus, are visible even during the day. They are not taken into consideration in the tally of stars that determine night.

אָמַר רַבִּי יוֹסֵי בְּרַבִּי זְבִידָא: הָעוֹשֶׂה מְלָאכָה בִּשְׁנֵי בֵּין הַשְּׁמָשׁוֹת – חַיָּיב חַטָּאת מִמָּה נַפְשָׁךְ. אֲמַר לֵיהּ רָבָא לְשַׁמָּעֵיהּ: אַתּוּן דְּלָא קִים לְכוּ בְּשִׁיעוּרָא דְרַבָּנַן, אַדְּשִׁמְשָׁא אַרֵישׁ דִּיקְלֵי – אַתְלוּ שְׁרָגָא. בְּיוֹם הַמְעוּנָּן מַאי? בְּמָתָא חֲזִי תַּרְנְגוֹלָא, בְּדַבְרָא – עוֹרְבֵי, אִי נַמִּי אַדָּאנֵי.

Rabbi Yosei, son of Rabbi Zevida, said: One who performs a prohibited labor during two twilights,[H] one between Friday and Shabbat and one between Shabbat and the conclusion of Shabbat on Saturday night, **is liable** to bring a **sin-offering** for performing a prohibited labor on Shabbat **whichever** way **you** look at it. Whether we say that twilight is day or night, certainly one of those labors was performed on Shabbat. **Rava said to his servant: You, who are not expert in the measures of the Sages,**[H] **when the sun is at the top of the palm trees, light the** Shabbat **lights.** His servant asked him: **What** should we do **on a cloudy day,** when the sun is not visible at the top of the trees? Rava said to him: **In the city, watch the roosters** because as evening approaches they sit on their beams. **In a field,** watch **the ravens** because they return to their nests as evening approaches. **Alternatively,** you can watch **the plants** [*adanei*][B] that turn westward in the evening. When they begin to turn westward evening is approaching.

תָּנוּ רַבָּנַן, שֵׁשׁ תְּקִיעוֹת תּוֹקְעִין עֶרֶב שַׁבָּת: רִאשׁוֹנָה לְהַבְטִיל אֶת הָעָם מִמְּלָאכָה שֶׁבַּשָּׂדוֹת, שְׁנִיָּה – לְהַבְטִיל עִיר וַחֲנוּיוֹת, שְׁלִישִׁית – לְהַדְלִיק אֶת הַנֵּר, דִּבְרֵי רַבִּי נָתָן. רַבִּי יְהוּדָה הַנָּשִׂיא אוֹמֵר: שְׁלִישִׁית לַחֲלוֹץ תְּפִילִּין. וְשׁוֹהֶה כְּדֵי צְלִיַּית דָּג קָטָן, אוֹ כְּדֵי לְהַדְבִּיק פַּת בַּתַּנּוּר, וְתוֹקֵעַ וּמֵרִיעַ וְתוֹקֵעַ וְשׁוֹבֵת.

The Sages taught in a *baraita*: **They sound six blasts on Shabbat eve**[H] to announce that Shabbat is approaching. The Gemara details what each blast signifies. The **first blast** is in order **to stop the people from work in the fields.** The **second** blast **is to stop** those who are working in **the city, and** to inform the proprietors to close the **stores.** The **third** is to inform them **to light the** Shabbat **light;** that is **the statement of Rabbi Natan. Rabbi Yehuda HaNasi says:** The **third** blast is to inform those who don phylacteries throughout the day **to remove** their **phylacteries,**[N] as one does not don phylacteries on Shabbat. **And he pauses** after the third blast for the length of **time** it takes to **fry a small fish or to stick bread to the** sides of the **oven.** One who forgot to do so and needs those foods for Shabbat may do so then. **And he sounds a *tekia*, and sounds a *terua*, and sounds a *tekia*, and he accepts Shabbat.**[N] It is then that Shabbat begins in every sense.

אָמַר רַבָּן שִׁמְעוֹן בֶּן גַּמְלִיאֵל: מַה נַּעֲשֶׂה לָהֶם לַבַּבְלִיִּים, שֶׁתּוֹקְעִין וּמְרִיעִין וְשׁוֹבְתִין – מִתּוֹךְ מְרִיעִין. ״תּוֹקְעִין וּמְרִיעִין״?! הָווּ לְהוּ חֲמִשָּׁה! אֶלָּא: שֶׁתּוֹקְעִין, וְחוֹזְרִין וְתוֹקְעִין, וּמְרִיעִין וְשׁוֹבְתִין מִתּוֹךְ מְרִיעִין – מִנְהַג אֲבוֹתֵיהֶן בִּידֵיהֶן.

Rabban Shimon ben Gamliel said: What shall we do to the Babylonian Jews? They stray from the custom, **as they sound a *tekia* and a *terua*,** and **they accept Shabbat during the *terua*,** i.e., upon hearing the blast of the *terua*. The Gemara asks about this: Do the Babylonians really **sound** only **a *tekia* and a *terua*** and no more blasts? If so, **there are** only **five** blasts and not six, as it was taught in the *baraita*. **Rather,** the correct version is: **They sound a *tekia*, and they again sound a *tekia*, and** then they **sound a *terua*, and they accept Shabbat during the *terua*.** They do so because they continue **the custom of their fathers that was handed** down **to them.**

מַתְנֵי לֵיהּ רַב יְהוּדָה לְרַב יִצְחָק בְּרֵיהּ: שְׁנִיָּה – לְהַדְלִיק אֶת הַנֵּר. כְּמַאן? לָא כְּרַבִּי נָתָן וְלָא כְּרַבִּי יְהוּדָה הַנָּשִׂיא! אֶלָּא: שְׁלִישִׁית לְהַדְלִיק אֶת הַנֵּר, כְּמַאן? כְּרַבִּי נָתָן.

Rav Yehuda taught to Rav Yitzḥak, his son: The **second** blast that is sounded before Shabbat is to inform people **to light the light.** The Gemara asks: **In accordance with whose** opinion did he say this? It is **neither in accordance with** the opinion of **Rabbi Natan nor in accordance with** the opinion of **Rabbi Yehuda HaNasi. Rather,** certainly he told him that the **third** blast is in order to inform people **to light the light, and in accordance with whose** opinion did he say this? It is in accordance **with** the opinion of **Rabbi Natan.**

HALAKHA

One who performs a prohibited labor during two twilights – הָעוֹשֶׂה מְלָאכָה בִּשְׁנֵי בֵּין הַשְּׁמָשׁוֹת: One who performs labor during twilight (*Kesef Mishne*) on Shabbat eve and at twilight at the conclusion of Shabbat is liable to bring a sin-offering (Rambam *Sefer Zemanim, Hilkhot Shabbat* 5:4).

You, who are not expert in the measures of the Sages – אַתּוּן דְּלָא קִים לְכוּ בְּשִׁיעוּרָא דְרַבָּנַן: One who is not an expert in the duration of twilight should light the Shabbat lights while the sun is still visible at the treetops. On a cloudy day, when it is difficult to see this, one should watch the roosters. When the roosters sit on their roosts, one should light the Shabbat lights, since the roosters sit at twilight. In a field, one should watch for when the crows return to their roosts and then light, as per the statement of Rava (*Shulḥan Arukh, Oraḥ Ḥayyim* 261:3).

They sound six blasts on Shabbat eve – שֵׁשׁ תְּקִיעוֹת תּוֹקְעִין עֶרֶב שַׁבָּת: When the Jewish people lived in their land, they would sound six *shofar* blasts before Shabbat to inform the people to stop working. It was customary in the sacred communities that a special messenger would inform the people a half an hour or an hour before Shabbat that Shabbat was approaching, so that they would complete their Shabbat preparations. This practice replaced the blasts of the *shofar*, and it is appropriate to inform the people that Shabbat is approaching (Rambam *Sefer Zemanim, Hilkhot Shabbat* 5:18–19; *Shulḥan Arukh, Oraḥ Ḥayyim* 256:1).

BACKGROUND

The plants [*adanei*] – אַדָּאנֵי: According to Rashi and other commentaries, the *adanei* mentioned here are one of the mallow species. The mallow, *Malva nicaeensis All.*, is a leafy annual plant, one variety of which is indigenous to Israel. The mallow plant is common on roadsides and in fields throughout the Middle East. The round leaf of the mallow is slightly split, like the palm of a hand. The leaf adjusts its position during daylight hours and, as a rule, its wider surface faces in the direction of the sun. Apparently, this phenomenon can also be observed on cloudy days.

Common mallow whose leaves follow the direction of the sun

NOTES

The third is to remove phylacteries – שְׁלִישִׁית לַחֲלוֹץ תְּפִילִּין: To a certain extent, the emphasis on phylacteries is connected to the dispute between Rabbi Eliezer ben Hyrcanus and his son with regard to the significance of removing phylacteries with the advent of Shabbat. The opinion of Rabbi Eliezer, and apparently that of Rabbi Natan, is that there is no urgency to remove the phylacteries, and one may begin Shabbat while still donning phylacteries. According to this opinion, which is the accepted *halakha*, even though one does not don phylacteries on Shabbat, there is no serious prohibition against wearing them on Shabbat (Rav Nissim Gaon, based on the Jerusalem Talmud).

And he accepts Shabbat – וְשׁוֹבֵת: In other words, from that point on, Shabbat has begun for all (Ran).

תָּנָא דְּבֵי רַבִּי יִשְׁמָעֵאל, שֵׁשׁ תְּקִיעוֹת תּוֹקְעִין עֶרֶב שַׁבָּת: הִתְחִיל לִתְקוֹעַ תְּקִיעָה רִאשׁוֹנָה – נִמְנְעוּ הָעוֹמְדִים בַּשָּׂדֶה מִלַּעֲדוֹר וּמִלַּחֲרוֹשׁ וּמִלַּעֲשׂוֹת כׇּל מְלָאכָה שֶׁבַּשָּׂדוֹת, וְאֵין הַקְּרוֹבִין רַשָּׁאִין לִיכָּנֵס עַד שֶׁיָּבוֹאוּ רְחוֹקִין וְיִכָּנְסוּ כּוּלָּם כְּאֶחָד. וַעֲדַיִין חֲנוּיוֹת פְּתוּחוֹת וּתְרִיסִין מוּנָּחִין, הִתְחִיל לִתְקוֹעַ תְּקִיעָה שְׁנִיָּה – נִסְתַּלְּקוּ הַתְּרִיסִין וְנִנְעֲלוּ הַחֲנוּיוֹת, וַעֲדַיִין חַמִּין מוּנָּחִין עַל גַּבֵּי כִּירָה. וּקְדֵירוֹת מוּנָּחוֹת עַל גַּבֵּי כִּירָה הִתְחִיל לִתְקוֹעַ תְּקִיעָה שְׁלִישִׁית – סִילֵּק הַמְסַלֵּק, וְהִטְמִין הַמַּטְמִין, וְהִדְלִיק הַמַּדְלִיק. וְשׁוֹהֶה כְּדֵי צְלִיַּית דָּג קָטָן, אוֹ כְּדֵי לְהַדְבִּיק פַּת בַּתַּנּוּר, וְתוֹקֵעַ וּמֵרִיעַ וְתוֹקֵעַ וְשׁוֹבֵת.

On a similar note, **the school of Rabbi Yishmael taught** in greater detail: **Six blasts are sounded on Shabbat eve.**[N] When **one begins sounding the first** ***tekia*****, the people standing** and working **in the fields refrained from hoeing, and from plowing and from performing all labor in the fields. And** those **workers** who work **close** to the city **are not permitted to enter** the city **until** those who work **farther** away **come, so that they will all enter together.** Otherwise, people would suspect that the workers who came later continued to work after the blast. **And still,** at this time, the **stores** in the city **are open and** the **shutters** of the stores, upon which the storekeepers would arrange their merchandise in front of the stores, remain **in place.** When **he began sounding the second blast, the shutters were removed** from where they were placed **and the stores were locked and** in the homes, however, **hot water was still** cooking **on the stove and pots** remained **in place on the stove.** When **he began sounding the third blast,** the **one** charged with **removing** food from the stove **removed** it, **and the one** charged with **insulating** hot water for Shabbat so that it would not cool off **insulated** it, **and** the **one** charged with **kindling** the Shabbat lights **lit. And** the one sounding the *shofar* **pauses for** the amount of time it takes to **fry a small fish or to stick bread to the** sides of the **oven, and he sounds a** ***tekia*****, and sounds a** ***terua*****, and sounds a** ***tekia*****, and accepts Shabbat.**

אָמַר רַבִּי יוֹסֵי (בַּר) חֲנִינָא: שָׁמַעְתִּי שֶׁאִם בָּא לְהַדְלִיק אַחַר שֵׁשׁ תְּקִיעוֹת – מַדְלִיק, שֶׁהֲרֵי נָתְנוּ חֲכָמִים שִׁיעוּר לְחַזַּן הַכְּנֶסֶת לְהוֹלִיךְ שׁוֹפָרוֹ לְבֵיתוֹ. אָמַר לוֹ: אִם כֵּן, נָתַתָּ דְּבָרֶיךָ לְשִׁיעוּרִין! אֶלָּא: מָקוֹם צָנוּעַ יֵשׁ לוֹ לְחַזַּן הַכְּנֶסֶת בְּרֹאשׁ גַּגּוֹ, שֶׁשָּׁם מַנִּיחַ שׁוֹפָרוֹ, לְפִי שֶׁאֵין מְטַלְטְלִין לֹא אֶת הַשּׁוֹפָר וְלֹא אֶת הַחֲצוֹצְרוֹת.

Rabbi Yosei bar Ḥanina, said: I heard that a person who was pressed for time and **comes to light** Shabbat lights **after six blasts may light** without concern, as even the moment of the sixth blast is not yet Shabbat. Proof for this is **that the Sages provided the sexton of the synagogue a period** of time **to take his** ***shofar*****,** which he used to sound the blasts on a tall roof in the middle of the city, **to his house.** Clearly, during that interval it is not yet Shabbat. He **said to him: If so,** then **you have rendered your statement** subject **to circumstances,**[B] and it would not apply uniformly to all. Shabbat would start at a different time in each place based on the distance between the site where the *shofar* is sounded and the home of the sexton. **Rather,** Shabbat began immediately after the final blast with no pause in between. **The sexton had a concealed place on top of his roof,** where he would sound the *shofar*, **in which he would place his** ***shofar*** **because** the consensus is **that one may move neither the** ***shofar*** **nor the trumpets** on Shabbat.

וְהָתַנְיָא: שׁוֹפָר מִיטַּלְטֵל וַחֲצוֹצְרוֹת אֵינָם מִיטַּלְטְלִין! אָמַר רַב (יוֹסֵי): לָא קַשְׁיָא, כָּאן – בְּיָחִיד, כָּאן – בְּצִבּוּר. אָמַר לֵיהּ אַבַּיֵי: וּבְיָחִיד לְמַאי חֲזֵי – הוֹאִיל וְרָאוּי לְגַמַּע בּוֹ מַיִם

The Gemara asks with regard to this last *halakha*: **Wasn't it taught** in a *baraita* that **the** ***shofar*** **may be moved** on Shabbat, **and the trumpets may not be moved? Rav Yosei said:** This is **not difficult,** as one could say that **here,** where moving a *shofar* was permitted, it is referring **to a** *shofar* belonging to **an individual.** Because it has a use even on Shabbat, it may be moved. **There,** where moving a *shofar* was prohibited, it is referring **to a** *shofar* that belongs to **a community.** Because it has no use on Shabbat, it is, therefore, considered set-aside [*muktze*]. **Abaye said to him: And** in the case of **an individual, for what** permitted action is a *shofar* **fit** to be used on Shabbat? It is fit for use **since it is suitable to give water with it**

NOTES

Blasts are sounded on Shabbat eve – תְּקִיעוֹת תּוֹקְעִין עֶרֶב שַׁבָּת: The *shofar* blasts advising the people of the imminent onset of Shabbat had to be heard throughout the city of Jerusalem and beyond, especially by those working in the fields. The Gemara, though, does not identify the location from where the *shofar* blasts were sounded. Josephus refers to the spot as being on one of the towers of the Temple (*Judean Wars* 4:9:12).

During the archaeological excavations conducted adjacent to the Western Wall in the wake of the Six-Day War, a large stone was discovered at the southwest corner of the walls surrounding the Temple Mount, with the inscription: To the trumpeting to… Apparently, it fell from a tower atop the wall and shattered during the destruction of the Temple by the Romans in 70 CE.

Blowing the *shofar* on top of the tower

BACKGROUND

You have rendered your statement subject to circumstances – נָתַתָּ דְּבָרֶיךָ לְשִׁיעוּרִין: This expression appears throughout the Talmud as a rationale for rejecting a *halakha* that does not include fixed parameters. Although in certain cases it is possible that, due to the rationale for a specific *halakha*, there is room for leniency or stringency, the concern remains that if the standards are subject to change, the authority of the halakhic determination will be undermined. Therefore, *halakhot* are established with fixed parameters without reference to specific circumstances.

HALAKHA

Moving a *shofar* and a trumpet – טִלְטוּל שׁוֹפָר וַחֲצוֹצְרָה: Sounding a *shofar* or a trumpet is prohibited on Shabbat. However, since the ruling with regard to set-aside is in accordance with Rabbi Shimon's opinion, one may move them to utilize them for a permitted use or to utilize their place (Rambam *Sefer Zemanim*, *Hilkhot Shabbat* 25:3; *Shulḥan Arukh*, *Oraḥ Ḥayyim* 308:3).

לְתִינוֹק, בְּצִיבּוּר נַמִּי חֲזֵי – לְגַמֵּעַ לְתִינוֹק עָנִי! וְתוּ, הָא דְּתַנְיָא: כְּשֵׁם שֶׁמְּטַלְטְלִין אֶת הַשּׁוֹפָר – כָּךְ מְטַלְטְלִין אֶת חֲצוֹצְרוֹת, מַנִּי? אֶלָּא, לָא קַשְׁיָא, הָא – רַבִּי יְהוּדָה, הָא – רַבִּי שִׁמְעוֹן, הָא – רַבִּי נְחֶמְיָה.

to a child. Because the mouth of a *shofar* is bent, one can pour a little water at a time. If so, a *shofar* belonging **to the community is also suitable to feed** water **to a poor infant** whose sustenance is provided by the community. **And furthermore, that** *halakha* **which was taught** in a *baraita*: **Just as one may move the *shofar*, so too one may move** the **trumpets,**[H] is contrary to that which was taught previously that there is a difference between moving the *shofar* and moving the trumpet. In accordance with **whose** opinion is that *baraita*? **Rather,** this is **not difficult,** as it can be explained that these three *baraitot* correspond to the three opinions with regard to these *halakhot*. **This** *baraita*, which permits moving the *shofar* but not the trumpet, is in accordance with the opinion of **Rabbi Yehuda,** who holds that the laws of set-aside apply to these items on Shabbat and one may not move a utensil whose only function is prohibited. Since a trumpet has no permitted use on Shabbat, it may not be moved. On the other hand, one is permitted to move a *shofar*, which can be used to feed a child. And **that** *baraita*, which permits moving both a *shofar* and a trumpet, is in accordance with the opinion of **Rabbi Shimon,** who holds that the *halakhot* of set-aside do not apply to utensils of this kind on Shabbat. Whereas **this** other *baraita*, which prohibits moving both a *shofar* and a trumpet, is in accordance with the opinion of **Rabbi Neḥemya,**[N] who holds that one may not use a utensil whose primary function is prohibited on Shabbat, even for a permissible purpose.

וּמַאי שׁוֹפָר – נַמִּי חֲצוֹצְרוֹת, כִּדְרַב חִסְדָּא. דְּאָמַר רַב חִסְדָּא: הָנֵי תְּלָת מִילֵּי אִישְׁתַּנִּי שְׁמַיְיהוּ מִכִּי חֲרַב בֵּית הַמִּקְדָּשׁ: חֲצוֹצַרְתָּא שׁוֹפָרָא, שׁוֹפָרָא חֲצוֹצַרְתָּא. לְמַאי נָפְקָא מִינַּהּ – לְשׁוֹפָר שֶׁל רֹאשׁ הַשָּׁנָה.

However, this explanation raises a slight difficulty with regard to the statement that one may move neither a *shofar* nor a trumpet. There was no need to mention the trumpet. If one may not move a *shofar*, certainly he may not move a trumpet. However, it can be explained as follows: **What is** the ***shofar*** mentioned in this *baraita*? It refers to **trumpets, in accordance with** the statement of **Rav Ḥisda, as Rav Ḥisda said: These three objects, their names changed since the Holy Temple was destroyed.** That which was called **trumpet** was called ***shofar*** in later generations, and that which was called ***shofar*** was called **trumpet** in later generations. The *baraita* that was cited employed the style that switches trumpet and *shofar*, and they were mentioned in that order. Incidentally, the Gemara asks: **What is the** practical halakhic **difference** whether a *shofar* is called *shofar* or trumpet? The Gemara answers: It is significant with regard **to the** *halakhot* of ***shofar* of Rosh HaShana.** On Rosh HaShana one fulfills his obligation only by sounding a *shofar*. If one comes today and asks what instrument he should use to sound the requisite blasts, he should be told to use a trumpet.

BACKGROUND

Willow and *tzaftzafa* – עֲרָבָה וְצַפְצָפָה: Even though the Talmud provides several distinguishing characteristics of both a willow and a *tzaftzafa*, scholars disagree with regard to their identity. Apparently, both belong to the species of willow called *Salix*, and they are both short trees that grow quickly. Both come in many variations, and there are even trees that are a hybrid of the two.

Willow branch with pointed leaves, *Salix acmophylla* Boiss

The *tzaftzafa* has differently shaped leaves. Branches from the willow are used with the palm branch on the festival of *Sukkot*. Apparently, one of the trees is the modern-day white willow, *Salix alba* L.

Tzaftzafa

עֲרָבָה צַפְצָפָה, צַפְצָפָה עֲרָבָה. לְמַאי נָפְקָא מִינָּהּ – לְלוּלָב.

The second object whose name was changed: That which was called **willow** [*arava*] was called in later generations ***tzaftzafa***,[B] and that which was called ***tzaftzafa* was** called **willow.** Here too the Gemara asks: **What is the** practical halakhic **difference** that emerges from the name change? The Gemara answers: With regard **to** the mitzva of the four species, referred to by the name of one of the species, as taking the **palm branch,** as one of the four species is a willow branch, not a *tzaftzafa*.

NOTES

This is Rabbi Neḥemya – הָא רַבִּי נְחֶמְיָה: Rabbi Neḥemya's opinion, which is the most stringent with regard to the *halakhot* of set-aside, is very different from the mainstream understanding of this concept. Generally speaking, the category of set-aside applies to an object whose use is prohibited on Shabbat. Due to that prohibition, one removes that object from his consciousness and it is set aside from use on Shabbat. Apparently, Rabbi Neḥemya's position is based on an alternative understanding of set-aside. In his opinion, objects are set aside to reinforce the restriction against carrying out on Shabbat, so that one will not come to carry objects from one domain to another (Rambam).

פְּתוֹרָה פְּתוֹרְתָא, פְּתוֹרְתָא פְּתוֹרָה, לְמַאי נָפְקָא מִינַּהּ – לְמִקָּח וּמִמְכָּר.

The third item whose name was changed: A large table that was originally called *petora* was called in later generations by the name previously used for a small table, ***petorata*.** And a ***petorata*** was called ***petora*.** And the Gemara asks: **What is the** practical halakhic **difference** that emerges from the change of name? The Gemara answers: With regard **to** the laws of **buying and selling.**[N] A person who orders a *petora* should know that he ordered a small table and not a large one.

אָמַר אַבַּיֵי: אַף אָנוּ נֹאמַר, הוּבְלִילָא בֵּי כָּסֵי, בֵּי כָּסֵי הוּבְלִילָא. לְמַאי נָפְקָא מִינַּהּ – לְמַחַט שֶׁנִּמְצֵאת בְּעוֹבִי בֵּית הַכּוֹסוֹת, דְּמִצַּד אֶחָד כְּשֵׁירָה וּמִשְּׁנֵי צְדָדִים טְרֵיפָה.

Abaye said: We too shall speak and comment on changes in the meaning of terms in our generation. What was called ***huvlila*,** the first stomach of animals that chew their cud, is, in recent generations, called ***bei kasei*,** the name of the animal's second stomach.[N] Similarly, what was once called in the past ***bei kasei*** is called ***huvlila*** in recent generations. **What is the** practical halakhic **difference** that emerges from this change of names? **With regard to a needle that is found in the thick** wall **of the second stomach.** In the *halakhot* of *tereifot*, one is prohibited to eat animals with a life expectancy of less than a year. It was established that if a needle punctured the wall of the second stomach **from** only **one side,** the animal is **kosher.** If the needle penetrated through the wall in a manner visible **from both sides,** the animal assumes the halakhic status of a ***tereifa*.** In the first stomach, even if the needle penetrated only one side of the wall, the animal assumes the halakhic status of a *tereifa*. Therefore, it is crucial to distinguish between the first and the second stomachs.

אָמַר רַב אַשִׁי: אַף אָנוּ נֹאמַר, בָּבֶל בּוּרְסִיף, בּוּרְסִיף בָּבֶל.

Rav Ashi said: We too shall speak of matters whose name changed over the generations. The city that, in biblical times, was called **Babylon** was called **Bursif** in later generations, and **Bursif** was called **Babylon** in later generations.

NOTES

To the laws of buying and selling – לְמִקָּח וּמִמְכָּר: In the *halakhot* governing business transactions, there are a significant number of restrictions on the type of proof that is valid in these cases. For example: Money is not proof (*Bava Metzia* 40b). The fact that one paid a larger sum of money cannot be cited as proof that he actually bought a larger table. As a result, it is crucial to know the term used for a given item in determining commercial transactions.

The first stomach and the second stomach – בֵּית הַכּוֹסוֹת וְהַהֶמְסֵס: A mortally wounded animal is a *tereifa* and may not be eaten. Generally, in talmudic times, those who slaughtered animals were not professionals. Consequently, they would often pose questions to the Sages. Therefore, the Gemara emphasized the importance of familiarity with the colloquial terms for the parts of an animal's body.

Perek **II**
Daf **36** Amud **b**

לְמַאי נָפְקָא מִינַּהּ – לְגִיטֵּי נָשִׁים.

What is the practical halakhic **difference** that emerges from this change of names? It is in the area **of women's bills of divorce.**[N] With regard to bills of divorce, special care is devoted to ensuring that the name of the place where the bill is written is not altered. Therefore, it is important to be aware that Babylon underwent a name change in later generations.

הדרן עלך במה מדליקין

NOTES

Of women's bills of divorce – לְגִיטֵּי נָשִׁים: When writing a bill of divorce [*get*], the *halakha* requires that the names of the people, their nicknames, and the name of the place where the divorce takes place be written as accurately as possible. This is to prevent any reason for invalidating the document. Therefore, it is vitally important to determine the precise name of that particular place. Consequently, many commentaries understand that the discussion here is about the relationship of Bursif to Babylon. Babylon was a center of Torah study, and the Babylonian communities adopted the custom of Eretz Yisrael and did not require a messenger who delivered a bill of divorce from Babylonia to Eretz Yisrael to testify that he was present when the bill of divorce was properly drafted. Below is a picture of the archaeological remains of the city of Babylon, which, at its height, extended over both banks of the Euphrates River. Over the course of generations, the city center moved from the right side of the river to Bursif on its left side.

Bursif and Babylon

Summary of **Perek II**

The nature of the mitzva of kindling the Shabbat lights is the fundamental problem that was addressed in this chapter. It was clearly resolved in one direction. The conclusion was that the Shabbat lights essentially have a functional purpose: To introduce light into the experience of delighting in Shabbat, to enhance the atmosphere, and to make partaking in the festive Shabbat meal more comfortable. Therefore, it was concluded that the oil suitable for kindling the Shabbat lights must provide a clear, consistent glow. Although there were Sages who sought to restrict the use of certain oils in an attempt to further enhance the stature of the mitzva, their opinions were not incorporated into the ultimate halakhic ruling. Certain oils and wicks were ultimately prohibited either because they do not provide effective illumination or because their use is liable to result in the desecration of Shabbat.

The comprehensive discussion of the Hanukkah lights found in this chapter, which, in effect, included all the *halakhot* of Hanukkah, underscored the role of the Shabbat lights. The conclusion was that, in virtually every matter, there is a contrast between Hanukkah lights and Shabbat lights. The objective of the mitzva to kindle the Shabbat lights is to illuminate. The mitzva of kindling the Hanukkah lights has no such practical objective; the mitzva is the act of kindling itself. The Shabbat lights are kindled so that the entire family can derive benefit from them. It is prohibited to derive benefit from the Hanukkah candles at all. Consequently, the Shabbat lamp must be equipped with materials that burn clearly and consistently. There is no such requirement for the Hanukkah candles. Their sole purpose is to publicize the miracle of Hanukkah.

Although the *halakha* has determined that the essence of the Shabbat lights lies in their practical function, the Sages, in a series of aggadic statements, enhanced the stature of the mitzva and its symbolic essence, transforming it into a manifestation of the very sanctity of Shabbat.

Introduction to **Perek III**

And he [Moses] said to them: This is what the Lord meant: Tomorrow is a day of rest, a holy Shabbat of the Lord. Bake what you would bake and boil what you would boil, and all that is left put aside to be kept until morning.

(Exodus 16:23)

Cooking on Shabbat is explicitly prohibited in the Torah, and this prohibited labor is listed among the thirty-nine primary categories of labor prohibited on Shabbat. Since cooking is generally completed as Shabbat begins, the discussion of the labor of cooking precedes the discussion of the other prohibited labors in the sequence of this tractate.

This chapter occupies itself primarily with the clarification and precise definition of the prohibited labor of cooking. That undertaking carries with it numerous problems. Unlike other categories of labor, there is an interval between the action and the desired result. It is a process, and therefore the question arises: At what stage in the process can it be said that an act of cooking has been performed? Shall we say that one who undertakes any action in the course of the entire process is considered to have engaged in that prohibited labor? Or perhaps, that is the case only with regard to one who initiates the process? Moreover, since the cooking process, once initiated, continues without the need for any additional action by the one cooking, the question can be raised: Is the mere act of placing an item on the fire defined as labor, or is it considered an incomplete segment of that labor?

There is a question as to whether the essence of the labor of cooking is transforming inedible into edible, unusable into usable, or whether it is the act of cooking that is prohibited, independent of the result. In practical terms, is it prohibited to further cook a cooked item?

The fundamental definition of cooking requires clarification and precision. In a very general sense, one could posit that cooking or baking are activities that render substances fit for use by means of heat. However, that leaves open the question of whether any activity that renders a substance usable is considered cooking, or perhaps, the essence of cooking is merely the softening or hardening of that substance?

It is also important to clarify whether the prohibited labor of cooking applies to all substances, or perhaps only to food, or perhaps only to specific types of food. Another related question is whether the halakhic definition of cooking depends upon some specific level of heat, e.g., the boiling point, or the intensity of the heat, or perhaps its effect is of no significance. Additionally, it must be ascertained whether the definition of cooking is restricted to the use of fire or whether it extends to other sources of heat. Similarly, is there a distinction between natural sources of heat and artificial ones in this context?

Most of these problems are resolved in various manners in this chapter. Some are discussed in Chapter Four and some in Chapter Seven, which discusses the primary categories of prohibited labor.

מתני׳ כִּירָה שֶׁהִסִּיקוּהָ בְּקַשׁ וּבִגְבָבָא – נוֹתְנִים עָלֶיהָ תַּבְשִׁיל. בְּגֶפֶת וּבְעֵצִים – לֹא יִתֵּן עַד שֶׁיִּגְרוֹף, אוֹ עַד שֶׁיִּתֵּן אֶת הָאֵפֶר. בֵּית שַׁמַּאי אוֹמְרִים, חַמִּין אֲבָל לֹא תַּבְשִׁיל וּבֵית הִלֵּל אוֹמְרִים, חַמִּין וְתַבְשִׁיל. בֵּית שַׁמַּאי אוֹמְרִים, נוֹטְלִין אֲבָל לֹא מַחֲזִירִין וּבֵית הִלֵּל אוֹמְרִים, אַף מַחֲזִירִין.

MISHNA With regard to **a stove that was lit**[N] on Shabbat eve **with straw** or **with rakings**, scraps collected from the field, one may **place** a pot of **cooked food atop it** on Shabbat. The fire in this stove was certainly extinguished while it was still day, as both straw and rakings are materials that burn quickly. However, if the stove was lit **with pomace**, pulp that remains from sesame seeds, olives, and the like after the oil is squeezed from them, **and** if it was lit **with wood,**[H] one may **not place** a pot atop it on Shabbat **until he sweeps**[N] the coals from the stove while it is still day **or until he places ashes** on the coals, so that the fire will not ignite on Shabbat. **Beit Shammai say:** Even after one has swept away the coals, it is only permitted to place **hot water** on it, as it is sufficiently hot and does not require additional cooking, **but not cooked food.** Since, in general, one prefers that food will cook more, there is concern lest he come to ignite the fire by stoking the coals. **And Beit Hillel say:** Both **hot water and cooked food** may be placed. **Beit Shammai say: One may remove** a pot from the stove on Shabbat **but** may **not return** it. **And Beit Hillel say:** One may **even return it.**

גמ׳ אִיבַּעְיָא לְהוּ: הַאי ׳לֹא יִתֵּן׳ – לֹא יַחֲזִיר הוּא, אֲבָל לַשְׁהוֹת – מַשְׁהִין אַף עַל פִּי שֶׁאֵינוֹ גָּרוּף וְאֵינוֹ קָטוּם, וּמַנִּי – חֲנַנְיָה הִיא. דְּתַנְיָא, חֲנַנְיָה אוֹמֵר: כׇּל שֶׁהוּא כְּמַאֲכַל בֶּן דְּרוֹסַאי – מוּתָּר לַשְׁהוֹתוֹ עַל גַּבֵּי כִּירָה, אַף עַל פִּי שֶׁאֵינוֹ גָּרוּף וְאֵינוֹ קָטוּם; אוֹ דִילְמָא: לַשְׁהוֹת תְּנַן, וְאִי גָּרוּף וְקָטוּם – אִין, אִי לָא – לָא, וְכׇל שֶׁכֵּן לְהַחֲזִיר.

GEMARA The students **raised a dilemma** with regard to the explanation of the mishna. **That** which we learned in the mishna: One may **not place, does it** mean that **one may not return**[N] a pot that he took off the fire and wishes to return on Shabbat; **however, to leave** the pot from Shabbat eve into Shabbat, **one may leave** it **even though** this stove **is not swept** of its coals **and** its coals **are not covered with ashes? And,** according to this, **whose** opinion **is it** in this mishna? **It** is the opinion of **Ḥananya. As it was taught** in a *baraita*, **Ḥananya says: Any** food **that** has already been cooked to the extent **of the food of ben Drosai,** who would only cook his food the minimum amount necessary, **one is permitted to leave it atop a stove** on Shabbat **even though** the stove **is not swept and not covered with ashes. Or perhaps,** that which **we learned** in the mishna: One may not place, means one may not **leave** it on the fire from Shabbat eve. **And if** the coals in the stove were **swept** or **covered with ashes, yes,** one may leave the pot on the stove. **And if not, no,** one may not leave it, **and all the more so** one may not **return** it to the stove on Shabbat under any circumstances.

תָּא שְׁמַע, מִדְּקָתָנֵי תְּרֵי בָּבֵי בְּמַתְנִיתִין: בֵּית שַׁמַּאי אוֹמְרִים: חַמִּין אֲבָל לֹא תַּבְשִׁיל, וּבֵית הִלֵּל אוֹמְרִים: חַמִּין וְתַבְשִׁיל. בֵּית שַׁמַּאי אוֹמְרִים: נוֹטְלִין אֲבָל לֹא מַחֲזִירִין, וּבֵית הִלֵּל אוֹמְרִים: אַף מַחֲזִירִין. אִי אָמְרַתְּ בִּשְׁלָמָא לַשְׁהוֹת תְּנַן – הָכִי קָתָנֵי: כִּירָה שֶׁהִסִּיקוּהָ בְּקַשׁ וּבִגְבָבָא – מַשְׁהִין עָלֶיהָ תַּבְשִׁיל, בְּגֶפֶת וּבְעֵצִים – לֹא יַשְׁהֶא עַד שֶׁיִּגְרוֹף אוֹ עַד שֶׁיִּתֵּן אֵפֶר, וּמָה הֵן מַשְׁהִין? בֵּית שַׁמַּאי אוֹמְרִים: חַמִּין אֲבָל לֹא תַּבְשִׁיל, וּבֵית הִלֵּל אוֹמְרִים: חַמִּין וְתַבְשִׁיל. וְכִי הֵיכִי דִּפְלִיגִי בְּלַשְׁהוֹת – פְּלִיגִי נַמִי בְּלְהַחֲזִיר, שֶׁבֵּית שַׁמַּאי אוֹמְרִים: נוֹטְלִין אֲבָל לֹא מַחֲזִירִין, וּבֵית הִלֵּל אוֹמְרִים: אַף מַחֲזִירִין.

In order to resolve this dilemma, the Gemara suggests: **Come** and **hear** a resolution to this **from the fact that two sections were taught in our mishna.** In the first, **Beit Shammai say: Hot water but not cooked food. And Beit Hillel say:** Both **hot water and cooked food.** And in the second, **Beit Shammai say: One may remove** it **but may not return** it. **And Beit Hillel say: One may even return** it. **Granted, if you say** that when **we learned** in the mishna that one may not place it means that it is prohibited **to leave** it; in that case, the mishna **is teaching as follows:** With regard to **a stove that was lit with straw** or **with rakings, one may leave cooked food on it.** If it was lit **with pomace** or **with wood, one may not leave** the cooked food on it **until he sweeps** the coals **out** while it is still day **or until he places ashes on it. And what may they leave? Beit Shammai say: Hot water but not cooked food. And Beit Hillel say:** One may leave both **hot water and cooked food** on it. **And just as** they **disagree with regard to leaving** a pot on the stove, **so too,** they **disagree with regard to** whether or not it is permitted **to return** it to the stove. **As Beit Shammai say: One may take** the pot from the stove on Shabbat **but may not return** it to the stove at all. **And Beit Hillel say: One may even return** it.

NOTES

A stove that was lit – כִּירָה שֶׁהִסִּיקוּהָ: The early commentaries explained this issue in different ways. Many of the *ge'onim* and those who adopted their approach state that this mishna and those that follow are not discussing the question of inserting the pot into the stove. Rather, they are discussing a case where the pot is suspended over the stove. Consequently, there is no concern lest one come to stoke the coals. Sweeping the coals or covering them with ashes is merely an indication that he has diverted his attention from the coals (Rav Hai Gaon; Ran).

Until he sweeps – עַד שֶׁיִּגְרוֹף: Some commentaries explain that sweeping does not mean that one must sweep all of the coals out of the stove. It is sufficient if he sweeps them all to one side within the stove itself (Rabbeinu Zeraḥia HaLevi).

That which we learned in the mishna: One may not place, does it mean that one may not return – הַאי לֹא יִתֵּן לֹא יַחֲזִיר הוּא: Some explain that the essence of the question is not an attempt to draw a halakhic conclusion from the mishna; rather, the goal is to define terms in a manner that will enable the Gemara to establish the mishna in accordance with the opinion of Ḥananya (see *Tosafot*). The Gemara seeks to clarify whether a simple reading of the mishna corresponds to his opinion or whether, in order to align the mishna with Ḥananya's approach, it is necessary to emend the mishna and add passages to it (*Derush VeḤiddush*).

HALAKHA

Stove that was lit…with pomace and with wood – כִּירָה שֶׁהִסִּיקוּהָ...בְּגֶפֶת וּבְעֵצִים: Before Shabbat, it is prohibited to place a pot with food that would benefit from additional cooking on a stove that was lit with wood, pomace, sesame seed pulp, or olive-pit pulp. One may do so if the coals were swept or if the coals were covered with ashes. This is according to Beit Hillel and Ḥananya. Some commentaries explain that it is permitted to place a pot on any stove, even if it were lit with pomace or wood and even if the coals were neither swept nor covered with ashes before Shabbat, as long as the food was cooked to the extent of the food of ben Drosai, which is half-cooked or, according to some, one-third cooked (see *Mishna Berura*). That is the accepted custom (Rema; Rambam *Sefer Zemanim, Hilkhot Shabbat* 3:4–5; *Shulḥan Arukh, Oraḥ Ḥayyim* 253:1).

אֶלָּא אִי אָמְרַתְּ לְהַחֲזִיר תְּנַן, הָכִי קָתָנֵי: כִּירָה שֶׁהִסִּיקוּהָ בְּקַשׁ וּבִגְבָבָא – מַחֲזִירִין עָלֶיהָ תַּבְשִׁיל, בְּגֶפֶת וּבְעֵצִים – לֹא יַחֲזִיר עַד שֶׁיִּגְרוֹף אוֹ עַד שֶׁיִּתֵּן אֵפֶר. וּמָה הֵן מַחֲזִירִין? בֵּית שַׁמַּאי אוֹמְרִים: חַמִּין אֲבָל לֹא תַּבְשִׁיל, וּבֵית הִלֵּל אוֹמְרִים: חַמִּין וְתַבְשִׁיל. בֵּית שַׁמַּאי אוֹמְרִים: נוֹטְלִין אֲבָל לֹא מַחֲזִירִין, וּבֵית הִלֵּל אוֹמְרִים: אַף מַחֲזִירִין. הָא תּוּ לָמָּה לִי?!

However, **if you say** that when **we learned** in the mishna that one may not place, it means that it is prohibited **to return** it, then the mishna **is teaching as follows: A stove that was lit with straw** or **with rakings, one may return cooked food onto it.** If it was lit **with pomace** or **with wood, one may not return** cooked food to it **until one sweeps** the coals **out** while it is still day **or until one places ashes** on them. **And what may they return? Beit Shammai say: Hot water but not cooked food. And Beit Hillel say:** Both **hot water and cooked food. Beit Shammai say: One may remove but may not return. And Beit Hillel say: One may even return.** If in the first section the question of what may be returned was already addressed, **why do I need this additional** dispute in the second section? The gist of Beit Shammai's statement that cooked food may not be returned to the stove is that one may remove but may not return. Apparently, the mishna can only be understood in accordance with the first explanation. The first clause discusses leaving and the latter clause discusses returning.

Perek **III**
Daf **37** Amud **a**

NOTES

To return – לְהַחֲזִיר: Contrary to Rashi's approach, some commentaries emphasize that there is no concern lest one bury the pot in the coals. However, the concern is that the inside of the stove will add heat even if the coals are swept or covered. In that case, placing a pot inside the oven on Shabbat would be considered cooking on Shabbat. This would not be the case if one places the pot atop the stove (Ramban).

לְעוֹלָם אֵימָא לָךְ לְהַחֲזִיר תְּנַן, וְחַסּוֹרֵי מִיחַסְּרָא וְהָכִי קָתָנֵי: כִּירָה שֶׁהִסִּיקוּהָ בְּקַשׁ וּבִגְבָבָא – מַחֲזִירִין עָלֶיהָ תַּבְשִׁיל, בְּגֶפֶת וּבְעֵצִים – לֹא יַחֲזִיר עַד שֶׁיִּגְרוֹף אוֹ עַד שֶׁיִּתֵּן אֶת הָאֵפֶר. אֲבָל לִשְׁהוֹת – מַשְׁהִין, אַף עַל פִּי שֶׁאֵינוֹ גָּרוּף וְאֵינוֹ קָטוּם. וּמָה הֵן מַשְׁהִין? בֵּית שַׁמַּאי אוֹמְרִים: חַמִּין אֲבָל לֹא תַּבְשִׁיל, וּבֵית הִלֵּל אוֹמְרִים: חַמִּין וְתַבְשִׁיל. וְהָךְ חֲזָרָה דְּאָמְרִי לָךְ – לָאו דִּבְרֵי הַכֹּל הִיא אֶלָּא מַחְלוֹקֶת בֵּית שַׁמַּאי וּבֵית הִלֵּל; שֶׁבֵּית שַׁמַּאי אוֹמְרִים: נוֹטְלִין וְלֹא מַחֲזִירִין, וּבֵית הִלֵּל אוֹמְרִים: אַף מַחֲזִירִין.

The Gemara rejects this proof. **Actually, you can say** that in the first clause of the mishna **we learned to return**[N] **and the mishna is incomplete.** A clause must be added to the mishna, **and it teaches the following:** With regard to **a stove that was lit with straw** or **rakings, one may return** a pot of **cooked food to it.** If it was lit **with pomace** or **with wood, one may not return** a pot to it **until one sweeps** the coals out while it is still day **or until one covers** the coals **with ashes. However, to leave** the pot on the flame on Shabbat, **one may leave it, even though it is not swept and not covered with ashes.** Through this addition, the continuation of the dispute can be understood as follows: **And what may they leave? Beit Shammai say: Hot water but not cooked food. And Beit Hillel say:** Both **hot water and cooked food.** Furthermore: **And that return that I said to you** at the start of the mishna **is not according to everyone. Rather,** it too is subject to **a dispute** between **Beit Shammai and Beit Hillel, as Beit Shammai say: One may remove but not return. And Beit Hillel say: One may even return.** The dilemma with regard to the interpretation of the mishna has not been resolved.

תָּא שְׁמַע, דְּאָמַר רַבִּי חֶלְבּוֹ אָמַר רַב חָמָא בַּר גּוּרְיָא אָמַר רַב: לֹא שָׁנוּ אֶלָּא עַל גַּבָּהּ, אֲבָל לְתוֹכָהּ – אָסוּר. אִי אָמְרַתְּ בִּשְׁלָמָא לְהַחֲזִיר תְּנַן – הַיְינוּ דְּשָׁנֵי בֵּין תּוֹכָהּ לְעַל גַּבָּהּ, אֶלָּא אִי אָמְרַתְּ לִשְׁהוֹת תְּנַן – מָה לִי תּוֹכָהּ מָה לִי עַל גַּבָּהּ! מִי סָבְרַתְּ רַבִּי חֶלְבּוֹ אַרֵישָׁא קָאֵי? אַסֵּיפָא קָאֵי: ״וּבֵית הִלֵּל אוֹמְרִים אַף מַחֲזִירִין״. וְאָמַר רַבִּי חֶלְבּוֹ אָמַר רַב חָמָא בַּר גּוּרְיָא אָמַר רַב: לֹא שָׁנוּ אֶלָּא עַל גַּבָּהּ, אֲבָל תּוֹכָהּ – אָסוּר.

Come and hear another resolution to this dilemma from that which **Rabbi Ḥelbo said** that **Rav Ḥama bar Gurya said** that **Rav said: They only taught** that placing is permitted with regard to a stove as far as placing a pot **atop it** is concerned. **However,** placing a pot **inside it** is **prohibited. Granted, if you say** that **we learned returning** in the mishna, **that is why there is a** halakhic **difference between** placing a pot **inside it and** placing a pot **atop it.** If one returns it on Shabbat, placing it inside a stove that might have burning coals, there is concern that Shabbat would be desecrated. Therefore, it was only permitted to place cooked food atop the stove. **However, if you say** that **we learned leaving** in the mishna, **what is** the difference **to me** whether it is **inside** the stove and **what is** the difference **to me** whether it is **atop it?** Ultimately, he does nothing on Shabbat with the hot ashes in the stove. The Gemara rejects this proof: **Do you think that Rabbi Ḥelbo is referring to the first clause** of the mishna? No, he **is referring to the latter clause** of the mishna, which states: **And Beit Hillel say that one may even return. And** with regard to this **Rabbi Ḥelbo said** that **Rav Ḥama bar Gurya said** that **Rav said: They only taught** that one may return the cooked food **atop** the stove; **however, inside it** is **prohibited.** If so, there is still no resolution to the dilemma.

תָּא שְׁמַע: ״שְׁתֵּי כִּירוֹת הַמַּתְאִימוֹת, אַחַת גְּרוּפָה וּקְטוּמָה וְאַחַת שֶׁאֵינָהּ גְּרוּפָה וְאֵינָהּ קְטוּמָה – מַשְׁהִין עַל גַּבֵּי גְּרוּפָה וּקְטוּמָה, וְאֵין מַשְׁהִין עַל שֶׁאֵינָהּ גְּרוּפָה וְאֵינָהּ קְטוּמָה. וּמָה הֵן מַשְׁהִין? בֵּית שַׁמַּאי אוֹמְרִים: וְלֹא כְלוּם, וּבֵית הִלֵּל אוֹמְרִים: חַמִּין אֲבָל לֹא תַּבְשִׁיל. עָקַר – דִּבְרֵי הַכֹּל לֹא יַחֲזִיר, דִּבְרֵי רַבִּי מֵאִיר. רַבִּי יְהוּדָה אוֹמֵר, בֵּית שַׁמַּאי אוֹמְרִים: חַמִּין אֲבָל לֹא תַּבְשִׁיל, וּבֵית הִלֵּל אוֹמְרִים: חַמִּין וְתַבְשִׁיל. בֵּית שַׁמַּאי אוֹמְרִים: נוֹטְלִין אֲבָל לֹא מַחֲזִירִין, וּבֵית הִלֵּל אוֹמְרִים: אַף מַחֲזִירִין״.

Come and hear a resolution to this dilemma from that which was taught in the *Tosefta*: In the case of **two adjoining stoves**[HB] that share a common wall, in **one** of them, the coals were **swept** or **covered with ashes, and in one** the coals **were not swept and not covered with ashes;** the ruling with regard to leaving a pot atop them on Shabbat is as follows: **One may leave** food **atop** the one that was **swept** or **covered with ashes, and one may not leave** food **atop the** one **that was not swept and not covered with ashes. And** to the crux of the matter, **what may one leave? Beit Shammai say: Nothing at all.** They dispute the *halakha* cited above. **And Beit Hillel say:** One may leave **hot water but not cooked food.** However, if one **removed** the cooked dish from atop the stove, **everyone,** Beit Shammai and Beit Hillel, **agrees** that **one may not return** it atop the stove; this is **the statement of Rabbi Meir.** According to the tradition that he received, that is the issue disputed between Beit Shammai and Beit Hillel. **Rabbi Yehuda says** that the dispute is different. **Beit Shammai say:** One may leave **hot water** on it **but not cooked food. And Beit Hillel say:** One may leave both **hot water and cooked food.** Furthermore, **Beit Shammai say: One may remove** a pot from the stove on Shabbat **but may not return** it. **And Beit Hillel say: One may even return** it.[H]

אִי אָמְרַתְּ בִּשְׁלָמָא לְשַׁהוֹת תְּנַן; מַתְנִיתִין מַנִּי – רַבִּי יְהוּדָה הִיא, אֶלָּא אִי אָמְרַתְּ לְהַחֲזִיר תְּנַן, מַתְנִיתִין מַנִּי? לָא רַבִּי יְהוּדָה וְלָא רַבִּי מֵאִיר. אִי רַבִּי מֵאִיר – קַשְׁיָא לְבֵית שַׁמַּאי בַּחֲדָא, וּלְבֵית הִלֵּל בִּתַרְתֵּי. אִי רַבִּי יְהוּדָה – קַשְׁיָא גְּרוּפָה וּקְטוּמָה!

Granted, if you say that the case **we learned** in our mishna was with regard to **leaving** the pot on the stove, in accordance with **whose** opinion is **our mishna? It is** in accordance with the opinion of **Rabbi Yehuda. However, if you say** that the case **we learned** in our mishna was with regard to **returning** the pot to the stove, in accordance with **whose** opinion is **our mishna?** It is **neither** in accordance with the opinion of **Rabbi Yehuda nor** with the opinion of **Rabbi Meir. If** you say that the mishna is in accordance with the opinion of **Rabbi Meir,** it is **difficult for Beit Shammai in one** respect. In our mishna, Beit Shammai permit some use of a stove on Shabbat; while according to Rabbi Meir in the *baraita,* Beit Shammai prohibit any use. **And for Beit Hillel** it is difficult **in two** respects. According to our understanding of the mishna, Beit Hillel permit both hot water and cooked food, contrary to Rabbi Meir's version of their opinion as stated in the *baraita.* Similarly, in our mishna, Beit Hillel permit returning the pot to the stove, contrary to Rabbi Meir's version of their opinion. **If** you explain that our mishna is in accordance with the opinion of **Rabbi Yehuda** in the *baraita,* it is **difficult** with regard to the issue of **sweeping** the coals **and covering** them **with ashes.** In the mishna, both Beit Hillel and Beit Shammai allow leaving it on a stove whose coals were not swept or covered with ashes. According to Rabbi Yehuda in the *baraita,* apparently a stove whose coals are neither swept nor covered with ashes may not be used at all. Since this interpretation leads to contradictions, it is preferable to explain the mishna in accordance with the other approach, so that the mishna will at least correspond to one opinion.

לְעוֹלָם אֵימָא לָךְ: לְהַחֲזִיר תְּנַן, וְתַנָּא דִּידַן סָבַר לָהּ כְּרַבִּי יְהוּדָה בַּחֲדָא, וּפְלִיג עֲלֵיהּ בַּחֲדָא. סָבַר לָהּ כְּרַבִּי יְהוּדָה בַּחֲדָא – בְּחַמִּין וְתַבְשִׁיל, וְנוֹטְלִין וּמַחֲזִירִין. וּפְלִיג עֲלֵיהּ בַּחֲדָא – דְּאִילּוּ תַּנָּא דִּידַן סָבַר: לְשַׁהוֹת, וְאַף עַל פִּי שֶׁאֵינוֹ גָּרוּף וְקָטוּם, וְרַבִּי יְהוּדָה סָבַר: בִּלְשַׁהוֹת נַמִי, גָּרוּף וְקָטוּם – אִין, אִי לָא – לָא.

This claim is rejected: **Actually, you can say** that the case **we learned** in our mishna was with regard to **returning** the pot to the stove, **and our** ***tanna*** in the mishna **holds in accordance with Rabbi Yehuda in one** matter,[N] **and disagrees with him in one** matter. **He holds in accordance with Rabbi Yehuda in one** matter, with regard to the matter of **hot water and cooked food, and** what may be **taken** from the stove **and** what may even be **returned. And** he **disagrees with him in one** matter: **While our** ***tanna*** in the mishna **held** that **to leave** a pot on a stove is permitted **even though it is not swept or covered with ashes, Rabbi Yehuda held: With regard to** permitting one **to leave** a pot on the stove **as well,** if the stove was **swept or covered with ashes, yes,** it is permitted; **if** it was **not** swept or covered with ashes, **no,** it is prohibited.

אִיבַּעְיָא לְהוּ: מַהוּ לִסְמוֹךְ בָּהּ? תּוֹכָהּ וְגַבָּהּ – אָסוּר, אֲבָל לִסְמוֹךְ בָּהּ שַׁפִּיר דָּמֵי, אוֹ דִּילְמָא לָא שְׁנָא?

A dilemma was raised before the Sages: With regard to a stove that was neither swept nor covered with ashes, **what is** the *halakha* with regard to permitting one **to lean** a cooked dish **against it,**[N] so that it may be heated from the sides of the stove? The dilemma is: Was it only placing a pot **inside it and atop it** that **is prohibited,** but **to lean** the pot **against it** he may **well** do so? **Or, perhaps,** leaning **is no different** and it is prohibited in every case.

HALAKHA

Two adjoining stoves – שְׁתֵּי כִּירוֹת הַמַּתְאִימוֹת: If there are two adjoining stoves that share a common wall and in one of them the coals are swept or covered with ashes and in the other the coals are not swept or covered with ashes, it is permitted to leave a pot atop the stove in which the coals are swept or covered with ashes, as per the *baraita* (*Shulḥan Arukh, Oraḥ Ḥayyim* 353:1, and in the comment of the Rema).

Taking and returning – נוֹטְלִין וּמַחֲזִירִין: On Shabbat, if one removed a pot of cooked food from a stove in which the coals were swept or covered with ashes or a stove that was lit with straw and rakings, he is permitted to return the pot to the stove on Shabbat, as long as the pot has not cooled off completely (*Magen Avraham*). This *halakha* is in accordance with Beit Hillel and Ḥananya (Rambam *Sefer Zemanim, Hilkhot Shabbat* 3:10; *Shulḥan Arukh, Oraḥ Ḥayyim* 353:2).

BACKGROUND

Two adjoining stoves – שְׁתֵּי כִּירוֹת הַמַּתְאִימוֹת:

Sketch of two adjoining stoves found on Masada, from the period of the destruction of the Temple. On each one of the stoves there is room for two pots.

NOTES

He holds in accordance with Rabbi Yehuda in one matter – סָבַר לָהּ כְּרַבִּי יְהוּדָה בַּחֲדָא: Even though this phrasing appears often in the Talmud, it is not considered an optimal solution. It is only used when the Gemara has no alternative. This solution does not answer the question: In accordance with whose opinion is the mishna? The difficulty is that, without any basis, the Gemara assumes the existence of a new opinion.

There is another issue. The Gemara is certainly aware of a *tanna* who apparently shares this opinion, namely, Ḥananya (see above 20a, p. 89, and 36b, p. 173). Why in order to answer the question does the Gemara seek other opinions? The rationale of the Gemara is that Ḥananya's opinion does not relate to the entire case in the mishna but only to part of it. Therefore, the Gemara prefers the solution offered here (Rashba).

What is the ***halakha*** **with regard to the allowance to lean a cooked dish against it – מַהוּ לִסְמוֹךְ בָּהּ:** Apparently, this question was asked according to all opinions. The question is relevant to each and every opinion based on what each permits on Shabbat (Rashba).

תָּא שְׁמַע: שְׁתֵּי כִּירוֹת הַמַּתְאִימוֹת, אַחַת גְּרוּפָה וּקְטוּמָה וְאַחַת שֶׁאֵינָהּ גְּרוּפָה וּקְטוּמָה – מַשְׁהִין עַל גַּבֵּי גְּרוּפָה וּקְטוּמָה, וְאַף עַל גַּב דְּקָא סָלֵיק לֵיהּ הַבְלָא מֵאִידָךְ. דִּילְמָא שָׁאנֵי הָתָם – דְּכֵיוָן דְּמִידַּלְיָא שָׁלֵיט בָּהּ אֲוִירָא.

Come and **hear** a resolution to this dilemma from that which was taught in a *baraita*: If there are **two adjoining stoves, one** that was **swept** or **covered with ashes and one that was not swept and covered with ashes, one may leave** cooked food **atop** the stove that is **swept and covered with ashes** on Shabbat. Apparently, it is permitted to lean a pot on a stove that was not swept, **even though heat rises to it from the other** stove. The Gemara rejects this: **Perhaps that** case of two adjoining stoves **is different. Since** the pot **is elevated, the air affects it** and cools it. Therefore, it is not comparable to actually leaning it against the stove.

תָּא שְׁמַע, דְּאָמַר רַב סָפְרָא אָמַר רַב חִיָּיא: קְטָמָהּ וְנִתְלַבְּתָה – סוֹמְכִין לָהּ, וּמְקַיְּימִין עָלֶיהָ, וְנוֹטְלִין מִמֶּנָּה, וּמַחֲזִירִין לָהּ. שְׁמַע מִינָּהּ: לִסְמוֹךְ נַמִי, קְטָמָהּ – אִין, לֹא קְטָמָהּ – לָא. וּלְטַעֲמִיךְ ׳נוֹטְלִין מִמֶּנָּה׳ דְּקָתָנֵי, קְטָמָהּ – אִין, לֹא קְטָמָהּ – לָא?! אֶלָּא: תְּנָא, ׳נוֹטְלִין׳ מִשּׁוּם ׳מַחֲזִירִין׳ הָכָא נַמִי: תְּנָא סוֹמְכִין מִשּׁוּם מְקַיְּימִין.

Come and **hear** another resolution to this dilemma from that which **Rav Safra said** that **Rav Ḥiyya said:** If there is a stove whose coals **one covered** with ashes on Shabbat eve **and it** subsequently **reignited** on Shabbat, **one may lean** a pot **against it, and leave** cooked food **on it, and remove** food **from it, and** even **return** food **to it. Conclude from this** the following with regard to **leaning, as well:** If **he covered** them **with ashes, yes,** if **he did not cover** them **with ashes, no,** as the Gemara is speaking about a stove whose ashes were covered properly during the day. The Gemara rejects this proof too. **And according to your opinion, that which was taught: One may remove** the food **from it,** would you say there too that if **he covered them, yes,** and if **he did not cover them, no?** Everyone agrees that it is permitted to take the pot off of the stove even if it is not swept or covered with ashes. **Rather,** it must be understood that **he taught** permission **to remove** the pot **due to** the fact that it taught permission **to return** it. **Here too, it taught** permission **to lean** the pot **due to** the fact that it taught permission **to leave** the pot on the stove. Consequently, a conclusion cannot be drawn that leaning a pot on an unswept stove is prohibited.

הָכִי הָשְׁתָּא! הָתָם – נוֹטְלִין וּמַחֲזִירִין בְּחַד מָקוֹם הוּא, תְּנָא נוֹטְלִין מִשּׁוּם מַחֲזִירִין. אֶלָּא הָכָא, סוֹמְכִין – בְּחַד מָקוֹם הוּא, וּמְקַיְּימִין – בְּחַד מָקוֹם הוּא.

The Gemara is astonished by this comparison. **How can you compare** them? **There, one removes** the pot from **and returns it** to **one** and the same **place.** Therefore, **it taught removing due to returning,** as one cannot return a pot before he removes it. **However, here,** where **one leans** the pot **is in one place and** where **one leaves** the pot **is in one,** another, **place,** there is no connection between the two. If the *tanna* did not intend to teach that leaning is permitted only on a swept stove, there would be no reason to mention permission to lean in conjunction with permission to leave. In any event, this is not an absolute proof, and the dilemma has not been resolved.

מַאי הָוֵי עֲלָהּ? תָּא שְׁמַע: כִּירָה שֶׁהִסִּיקוּהָ בְּגֶפֶת וּבְעֵצִים – סוֹמְכִין לָהּ, וְאֵין מְקַיְּימִין אֶלָּא אִם כֵּן גְּרוּפָה וּקְטוּמָה. גֶּחָלִים שֶׁעָמְמוּ, אוֹ שֶׁנָּתַן עָלֶיהָ נְעוֹרֶת שֶׁל פִּשְׁתָּן דַּקָּה – הֲרֵי הִיא כִּקְטוּמָה.

The Gemara asks: **What conclusion was reached** with regard to this dilemma? **Come** and **hear** a resolution to this from that which was taught in the *Tosefta*: With regard to **a stove that was lit with pomace** or **with wood, one may lean** a pot of cooked food **against it;**[H] **however, one may not leave** a pot inside it **unless** the stove is **swept out** or **covered with ashes. Coals that dimmed or on which a strip of** thinly **beaten flax was placed**[H] and the fire did not ignite, **it is as** if it were **covered with ashes,** and one need not add more ashes to it. In any case, the conclusion is drawn from here that one is permitted to lean a dish of cooked food against a stove, even though it is not covered with ashes or swept out.

אָמַר רַבִּי יִצְחָק בַּר נַחְמָנִי אָמַר רַב אוֹשַׁעְיָא: קְטָמָהּ וְהוּבְעֲרָה מַשְׁהִין עָלֶיהָ חַמִּין שֶׁהוּחַמּוּ כָּל צוֹרְכָּן, וְתַבְשִׁיל שֶׁבִּישֵּׁל כָּל צוֹרְכּוֹ.

Rabbi Yitzḥak bar Naḥmani said that **Rav Oshaya said:** With regard to a stove that **he covered with ashes and** that **reignited** on Shabbat, **one may leave hot water that was** already **completely heated and cooked food that was** already **completely cooked upon it.** In that case, there is no need for additional cooking, and therefore there is no concern that one might come to stoke the coals and ignite the fire.

HALAKHA

Stove that was lit with pomace or with wood, one may lean a pot of cooked food against it, etc. – **כִּירָה שֶׁהִסִּיקוּהָ בְּגֶפֶת וּבְעֵצִים סוֹמְכִין לָהּ וכו׳**: It is permitted to place a pot of cooked food against the side of a stove that was lit with pomace and wood, even if the coals were not swept or covered with ashes. It is permitted to do so even on Shabbat itself (Rema). The Rambam and the Ramban prohibit doing so. In *Shulḥan Arukh HaRav* the ruling is that it is appropriate to adopt the stringency of the second opinion. If the coals were swept or covered with ashes, everyone agrees that it is permitted (Rambam *Sefer Zemanim, Hilkhot Shabbat* 3:7; *Shulḥan Arukh, Oraḥ Ḥayyim* 353:1).

Coals that dimmed or on which a strip of thinly beaten flax was placed – **גֶּחָלִים שֶׁעָמְמוּ, אוֹ שֶׁנָּתַן עָלֶיהָ נְעוֹרֶת שֶׁל פִּשְׁתָּן**: It is permitted to leave a pot on a stove whose coals have dimmed or were covered by a strip of thinly beaten flax. This is the equivalent of being covered with ashes (Rambam *Sefer Zemanim, Hilkhot Shabbat* 3:4).

שמע מינה: מצטמק ויפה לו מותר – שאני הכא, דקטמה. אי הכי, מאי למימרא? הובערה איצטריכא ליה, מהו דתימא: כיון דהובערה – הדרא לה למילתא קמייתא, קמשמע לן.

Conclude from this *halakha* that even when it is food that **shrivels and improves**[H] by remaining on the fire, it is nevertheless **permitted** to leave it. The food is already completely cooked and there is no concern lest one come to stoke the coals and ignite the fire. Rabbi Oshaya did not distinguish between different types of foods in permitting this. The Gemara rejects this conclusion: **Here,** it **is different** because **he covered** the coals in the stove **with ashes,** and that is the reason that he is **permitted** to leave food on the stove. The Gemara asks: **If so, what** purpose was there **to say** this *halakha*? Is it to teach that if the coals are covered with ashes, there is no room for concern? That is obvious. The Gemara answers: The case where he covered it with ashes and it **reignited** on Shabbat **was necessary** and required additional articulation. **Lest you say** that **since it reignited, it returns to its original status** and is prohibited, therefore **it taught us** that this is not the case.

אמר רבה בר בר חנה אמר רבי יוחנן: קטמה והובערה – משהין עליה חמין שהוחמו כל צורכן ותבשיל שבישל כל צורכו, ואפילו גחלים של רותם. שמע מינה: מצטמק ויפה לו מותר. שאני הכא דקטמה. אי הכי, מאי למימרא? הובערה איצטריכא ליה. היינו הך! גחלים של רותם איצטריכא ליה.

Rabba bar bar Ḥana said that **Rabbi Yoḥanan said:** With regard to a stove that **he** swept out or **covered with ashes** before Shabbat **and** subsequently **reignited** on Shabbat, **one may leave hot water that** was already **completely heated and cooked food that** was already **completely cooked upon it, even if** the **coals** were **from** the wood of **a broom** tree,[B] which are very hot and long-burning. If so, **conclude from this** that even if food **shrivels and improves** while on the stove, it is permitted. The Gemara rejects this: **Here,** in this case, **it is different** because **he covered it with ashes.** Therefore, it is permitted to leave it on the stove. The Gemara asks: **If so, what** was the purpose **of saying** this *halakha*? The Gemara answers: Mention of the case where he covered it with ashes and it **reignited** on Shabbat **was necessary.** The Gemara challenges that explanation: **This case is identical to the** previous **one.**[N] Why did Rabbi Yoḥanan find it necessary to repeat what was already said? The Gemara responds that there is a novel element in his statement. It **was necessary** to teach the case of **coals** from the wood of **a broom** tree. Even in a case of especially hot coals it is permitted.

אמר רב ששת אמר רבי יוחנן: כירה שהסיקוה בגפת ובעצים משהין עליה חמין שלא הוחמו כל צורכן ותבשיל שלא בישל כל צורכו, עקר – לא יחזיר עד שיגרוף או עד שיתן אפר. קסבר: מתניתין להחזיר תנן, אבל לשהות משהין אף על פי שאינו גרוף ואינו קטום.

Rav Sheshet said that **Rabbi Yoḥanan said:** With regard to **a stove that was lit with pomace** or **with wood, one may leave**[H] **hot water on it even if** the water **has not** yet **been completely heated, and** the same is true for **cooked food** even **if it was not** yet **completely cooked.** However, if **one removed** the food from the stove, **one may** only **return** it **if he sweeps** the coals out of the stove while it is still day, **or if he places ashes** on the coals. The reason for mentioning this *halakha* is because **he holds** that in **our mishna we learned** with regard to **returning** the cooked food to the stove; **however,** with regard to **leaving** a pot on top of the stove, if it was placed there while it was still day, **one may leave it** on the stove **even if it is not swept and not covered with ashes.**

אמר רבא: תרווייהו תננהי, לשהות תנינא: אין נותנין את הפת בתוך התנור עם חשיכה, ולא חררה על גבי גחלים, אלא כדי שיקרמו פניה. הא קרמו פניה – שרי. להחזיר נמי תנינא: בית הלל אומרים: אף מחזירין. ועד כאן לא קשרו בית הלל אלא בגרופה וקטומה, אבל בשאינה גרופה וקטומה לא. ורב ששת נמי – דיוקא דמתניתין קמשמע לן.

Rava said: We already **learned**[N] **both** aspects of Rav Sheshet's *halakha* and there is no need to teach us something that was already stated explicitly in the mishna. **We** already **learned** that it is permitted **to leave** a pot on the stove. **One may not put bread into the oven at nightfall and** may **not** place **cake on top of coals unless** there is enough time before Shabbat **that its surface will form a crust.** However, if **its surface already formed a crust** before Shabbat, **it is permitted** to leave it even in an oven that was not swept and not covered with coals. Likewise, **we also** already **learned** in our mishna the second aspect of Rav Sheshet's *halakha* that it is permitted **to return** the pot to the fire, as **Beit Hillel say: One may even return. And** it is clear that **Beit Hillel only went so far as permitting** the return of the pot **in** a stove that is **swept** or **covered with ashes; however, in one that is not swept** or **covered with ashes,** they did **not** permit doing so. If so, Rav Sheshet's statement is superfluous. The Gemara answers: **Rav Sheshet also** only came to **teach us the inference from the mishna** and not to introduce new *halakhot*.

HALAKHA

Food that shrivels and improves – מצטמק ויפה לו: In a case where food shrivels and improves when left on the fire, i.e., on a stove where the coals are neither swept nor covered with ashes, it is prohibited to leave it on the stove, even if it was placed on the stove during the day, on Friday. It is permitted to do so only when leaving it on the fire causes the food to shrivel and the taste to deteriorate (Rambam *Sefer Zemanim, Hilkhot Shabbat* 3:4; *Shulḥan Arukh, Oraḥ Ḥayyim* 353:1).

A stove that was lit with pomace or with wood, one may leave, etc. – כירה שהסיקוה בגפת ובעצים משהין וכו׳: One may place a pot of cooked food on Shabbat eve on a stove that was lit with pomace or wood, even if the coals were not swept or covered with ashes, as long as the food does not shrivel and taste does not improve (Rambam *Sefer Zemanim, Hilkhot Shabbat* 3:4; *Shulḥan Arukh, Oraḥ Ḥayyim* 353:1).

BACKGROUND

Broom tree – רותם: The broom tree, known as the desert broom, *Retama raetam*, is a tall bush with branches that sometimes reach the height of a tree. It grows primarily in sand and in dry riverbeds. The branches of the broom are greenish-gray, and during most of the year they do not grow leaves. The broom blooms at the end of winter with an abundance of white flowers. It was common to make coals from the roots and trunk of the broom. In the Bible (Psalms 120:4) and in several places in the Talmud, it is emphasized that the coals made from the broom burn and retain their heat longer than other types of coals.

Broom branches in bloom

NOTES

This case is identical to the previous one – היינו הך: This statement is problematic. It is one thing to inquire about a Sage who repeats himself, but where is the difficulty when one Sage says the exact same thing as another? Perhaps the Gemara's question is based on the fact that Rabba bar bar Ḥana failed to note in his statement that Rabbi Yoḥanan followed the approach of Rabbi Oshaya in this matter.

We already learned – תננהי: This term challenges an *amora* when he says something that apparently already appears in the mishna. It would have been more appropriate for him to cite the mishna verbatim, thereby establishing the *halakha* in accordance with the mishna. In general, the Gemara answers by delineating the novel element in the *amora's* statement. Or, as in this instance, Rav Sheshet used deduction and logic to teach something that was not apparent from the mishna.

BACKGROUND

Fried fish [*kasa deharsena*]– כסא דהרסנא: Fried fish was a popular dish in Babylonia and was commonly eaten by the poor. This dish is made primarily from small, flour-coated salted fish, fried in oil with vinegar. The origin of the word *harsana* is not clear. It is probably connected to the Syrian word *harsana*, which is a type of fish that lives among the rocks in the water.

LANGUAGE

Dishes made of figs [*lafda*] – לפדא: This is the Greek word λοπάς, λοπάδος, *lopas*, genitive *lopados*, a prepared dish. Others think the origin is λέπιδι, *lapidi*, which means a dish made of figs.

אמר רב שמואל בר יהודה אמר רבי יוחנן: כירה שהסיקוה בגפת ובעצים משהין עליה תבשיל שבישל כל צורכו וחמין שהוחמו כל צורכן ואפילו מצטמק ויפה לו. אמר ליה ההוא מדרבנן לרב שמואל בר יהודה: הא רב ושמואל דאמרי תרווייהו: מצטמק ויפה לו אסור!

Rav Shmuel bar Yehuda said that **Rabbi Yoḥanan said:** With regard to **a stove that was lit with pomace** or **with wood,** on Shabbat eve **one may leave a cooked dish that was** already **completely cooked,** as well as **hot water that was** already **completely heated, upon it and even if** it is the type of food that when left for a prolonged period of time on the fire it **shrivels and improves.** There is no concern lest one come to stoke the coals. The Gemara relates that **one of the Sages said to Rav Shmuel bar Yehuda: Isn't it Rav and Shmuel who both say,** contrary to your opinion, that if food **shrivels and improves** when placed on the stove, leaving it on there on Shabbat is **prohibited?**

אמר ליה: אטו לית אנא ידע דאמר רב יוסף אמר רב יהודה אמר שמואל: מצטמק ויפה לו אסור! כי קאמינא לך – לרבי יוחנן קאמינא. אמר ליה רב עוקבא ממישן לרב אשי: אתון דמקרביתו לרב ושמואל – עבידו כרב ושמואל, אנן – נעביד כרבי יוחנן.

Rav Shmuel bar Yehuda **said to him: Is that to say** that **I do not know** that **Rav Yosef said** that **Rav Yehuda said** that **Shmuel said: If** food **shrivels and improves** when left on the fire for an extended period, it is **prohibited** to leave it there? **When I said to you** that it is permitted to leave it, **I said** it **in accordance with** the opinion of **Rabbi Yoḥanan. Rav Ukva from Meishan said to Rav Ashi: You, who are close**[N] to the place where **Rav and Shmuel** lived, **act in accordance with** the ruling of **Rav and Shmuel; we will act in accordance with** the ruling of **Rabbi Yoḥanan.**

אמר ליה אביי לרב יוסף: מהו לשהות? אמר ליה: הא רב יהודה משהו ליה ואכיל. אמר ליה: בר מיניה דרב יהודה, דכיון דמסוכן הוא – אפילו בשבת נמי שרי למעבד ליה, לי ולך מאי? אמר ליה: בסורא משהו, דהא רב נחמן בר יצחק מרי דעובדא הוה ומשהו ליה ואכיל. אמר רב אשי: קאימנא קמיה דרב הונא ושהין ליה כסא דהרסנא ואכל ולא ידענא אי משום דקסבר מצטמק ויפה לו מותר, אי משום דכיון דאית ביה מיחא מצטמק ורע לו הוא.

Abaye said to Rav Yosef: What is the ruling with regard **to leaving** food on the stove from Shabbat eve? Rav Yosef **said to him: Didn't they leave** food **for Rav Yehuda and** he **ate** it? Apparently, it is permitted to do so. Abaye **said to him: No proof can be brought from Rav Yehuda. Since he is in danger,** as he is sick and needs hot food, **even on Shabbat as well, it is permitted to** heat up food **for him.** However, **for me and you** as well as for all other people **what** is the ruling? Rav Yosef **said to** Abaye: **In Sura, they leave** food on the stove from Shabbat eve, **as Rav Naḥman bar Yitzḥak** from Sura **was a master of** good **deeds** who was meticulous in his performance of mitzvot, **and they would leave** food **for him and he would eat it. Rav Ashi said: I stood before Rav Huna and** saw that **they left fish fried in oil** [*kasa deharsena*][B] for him atop the stove on Shabbat, **and he ate** the fish on Shabbat. **And I do not know if** his reason for doing so is **because he holds** that **it is permitted** to leave food that **shrivels and improves** when left on the stove for a long time. Or, **if** it is **because this** dish **has flour** in it, and therefore it **shrivels and deteriorates.** Everyone agrees that it is permitted to leave food atop the stove that shrivels and deteriorates.

אמר רב נחמן: מצטמק ויפה לו – אסור, מצטמק ורע לו – מותר. כללא דמלתא: כל דאית ביה מיחא – מצטמק ורע לו, לבר מתבשיל דליפתא, דאף על גב דאית ביה מיחא מצטמק ויפה לו הוא. והני מילי – דאית ביה בשרא, אבל לית ביה בשרא – מצטמק ורע לו הוא. וכי אית ביה בשרא נמי לא אמרן אלא דלא קבעי לה לאורחין, אבל קבעי לה לאורחין – מצטמק ורע לו. לפדא דייסא ותמרי – מצטמק ורע להן.

Rav Naḥman said: Food that **shrivels and improves** when left on the stove, **it is prohibited** to leave it on the stove; if it **shrivels and deteriorates, it is permitted. The principle in this matter** is as follows: Any food **that has flour in it shrivels and deteriorates, except for a cooked turnip** dish, **which, even though it has flour, shrivels and improves. And this applies only** when **there is meat in it, but** when **there is no meat in it, it shrivels and deteriorates. And when there is meat in it, too, we only said** that it shrivels and improves **when** one **does not need it for guests, but** when one **needs it for guests,** it **shrivels and deteriorates** because it is not polite to serve guests overcooked food, which is not aesthetic. Furthermore: Leaving dishes made **of figs** [*lafda*],[L] **porridge,** or **dates** on the stove causes them to **shrivel and deteriorate.**

בעו מיניה מרבי חייא בר אבא:

They raised a dilemma before Rabbi Ḥiyya bar Abba:

NOTES

You who are close – אתון דמקרביתו: Rav Ukva is saying that, in fact, this is permitted in accordance with the opinion of Rabbi Yoḥanan. Indeed, the Sages rule in accordance with the opinion of Rabbi Yoḥanan, even in disputes with Rav and Shmuel, especially when other Sages agree with him. Nevertheless, for those who lived near the towns of Rav and Shmuel, it was appropriate that they follow their custom for two reasons: First, because Rav and Shmuel's opinion is stricter; and second, because it was the local custom (Rabbeinu Ḥananel).

שָׁכַח קְדֵירָה עַל גַּבֵּי כִּירָה וּבִשְּׁלָה בַּשַּׁבָּת, מַהוּ? אִישְׁתֵּיק וְלָא אָמַר לֵיהּ וְלָא מִידֵּי. לְמָחָר נְפַק דְּרַשׁ לְהוּ: הַמְבַשֵּׁל בַּשַּׁבָּת, בְּשׁוֹגֵג – יֹאכַל, בְּמֵזִיד – לֹא יֹאכַל, וְלָא שְׁנָא.

If **one forgot a pot**[N] on Shabbat eve **atop a stove and it cooked on Shabbat, what is** the ruling in that case? Is one permitted to eat that food, or not? **He was silent and did not say a thing to him. The next day, he emerged** and publicly **taught them** the following *halakha*: With regard to **one who cooks on Shabbat,**[H] if he did so **unwittingly, he may eat** it, and if he cooked **intentionally, he may not eat** it; and the *halakha* **is no different.**

מַאי 'וְלָא שְׁנָא'? רַבָּה וְרַב יוֹסֵף דְּאָמְרִי תַּרְוַיְיהוּ לְהֶיתֵּירָא: מְבַשֵּׁל הוּא דְּקָא עָבֵיד מַעֲשֶׂה, בְּמֵזִיד – לֹא יֹאכַל, אֲבָל הַאי דְּלָא קָא עָבֵיד מַעֲשֶׂה – בְּמֵזִיד נַמִי יֹאכַל. רַב נַחְמָן בַּר יִצְחָק אָמַר לְאִיסּוּרָא: מְבַשֵּׁל הוּא דְּלָא אָתֵי לְאִיעֲרוּמֵי – בְּשׁוֹגֵג יֹאכַל, אֲבָל הַאי דְּאָתֵי לְאִיעֲרוּמֵי – בְּשׁוֹגֵג נַמִי לֹא יֹאכַל.

The last part of Rabbi Ḥiyya bar Abba's statement is unclear. The Gemara asks: **What is** the practical halakhic meaning of the phrase: **And it is no different? Rabba and Rav Yosef both said** to interpret the phrase **permissively**[N] in the following manner: **One who cooks is one who performs an action.** If he did so **intentionally, he may not eat** what he cooked. **However, this** one who forgot the pot on the stove, **who does not perform an action,** even if he **intentionally** left the pot on Shabbat eve, he **may also eat** the food. However, **Rav Naḥman bar Yitzḥak said** that the phrase: And it is no different, should be interpreted **restrictively** in the following manner: It is **one who cooks** who **will not come to deceive,** as there is no room for suspicion that a person will intentionally cook on Shabbat. Therefore, if one cooks **unwittingly, he may eat** it. **However, one who would come to deceive,** intentionally leaving the pot on the stove and saying: I forgot it, the Sages penalize him and decree that if he did so **unwittingly as well, he may not eat** it.

מֵיתִיבֵי: שָׁכַח קְדֵירָה עַל גַּבֵּי כִּירָה וּבִישְּׁלָה בַּשַּׁבָּת, בְּשׁוֹגֵג – יֹאכַל, בְּמֵזִיד – לֹא יֹאכַל. בַּמֶּה דְּבָרִים אֲמוּרִים – בְּחַמִּין שֶׁלֹּא הוּחַמּוּ כׇּל צוֹרְכָּן, וְתַבְשִׁיל שֶׁלֹּא בִּישֵּׁל כׇּל צוֹרְכּוֹ. אֲבָל חַמִּין שֶׁהוּחַמּוּ כׇּל צוֹרְכָּן וְתַבְשִׁיל שֶׁבִּישֵּׁל כׇּל צוֹרְכּוֹ, בֵּין בְּשׁוֹגֵג בֵּין בְּמֵזִיד – יֹאכַל, דִּבְרֵי רַבִּי מֵאִיר.

The Gemara raises an objection to this statement from that which was taught in a *baraita*: **One who forgot a pot**[H] **atop a stove and it cooked on Shabbat, if** he did so **unwittingly, he may eat** it; if he did so **intentionally, he may not eat** it. **In what case is this statement said?** It is in a case **where** the pot contains **hot water that** was **not** yet **completely heated,** and the same applies to **cooked food that** was **not** yet **completely cooked. However,** if it contains **hot water that** was already **completely heated and cooked food that** was already **completely cooked, whether** the pot was left there **unwittingly, or whether** the pot was left there **intentionally, one may eat** it; this is **the statement of Rabbi Meir.**

רַבִּי יְהוּדָה אוֹמֵר: חַמִּין שֶׁהוּחַמּוּ כׇּל צוֹרְכָּן – מוּתָּרִין, מִפְּנֵי שֶׁמִּצְטַמֵּק וְרַע לוֹ. וְתַבְשִׁיל שֶׁבִּישֵּׁל כׇּל צוֹרְכּוֹ – אָסוּר, מִפְּנֵי שֶׁמִּצְטַמֵּק וְיָפֶה לוֹ, וְכׇל הַמִּצְטַמֵּק וְיָפֶה לוֹ, כְּגוֹן כְּרוּב וּפוֹלִים וּבָשָׂר טָרוּף – אָסוּר, וְכׇל הַמִּצְטַמֵּק וְרַע לוֹ – מוּתָּר.

Rabbi Yehuda says that there is a distinction: **Hot water that** was already **completely heated is permitted because,** in that case, the longer it remains on the fire, the more it **shrivels,** i.e., evaporates, **and deteriorates.** In that case, one would certainly not come to increase the heat because he would not want to lose more water through evaporation. **However, cooked food that was completely cooked,** it **is prohibited** to leave it on the fire **because** it **shrivels and improves.** There is room for concern that he will stoke the coals to increase the heat under the food. **And** there is a general principle: **Anything that shrivels and improves, e.g., cabbage, and beans, and meat cut** into small pieces[B] **is prohibited; and anything that shrivels and deteriorates is permitted.**

קָתָנֵי מִיהָא: תַּבְשִׁיל שֶׁלֹּא בִּישֵּׁל כׇּל צוֹרְכּוֹ, בִּשְׁלָמָא לְרַב נַחְמָן בַּר יִצְחָק לָא קַשְׁיָא: כָּאן – קוֹדֶם גְּזֵירָה, כָּאן – לְאַחַר גְּזֵירָה. אֶלָּא רַבָּה וְרַב יוֹסֵף דְּאָמְרִי לְהֶיתֵּירָא, אִי קוֹדֶם גְּזֵירָה – קַשְׁיָא מֵזִיד, אִי לְאַחַר גְּזֵירָה – קַשְׁיָא נַמִי שׁוֹגֵג! קַשְׁיָא.

In any event, it was taught in that *baraita* that in the case of **cooked food that was not completely cooked,** if it was cooked unwittingly, it is permitted. **Granted,** according **to** the opinion of **Rav Naḥman bar Yitzḥak,** this is **not difficult.** Although there is an apparent contradiction, as he prohibits eating from a pot that was unwittingly forgotten on the stove, and the *baraita* prohibits it only when it was left intentionally, he could explain the following: **Here,** the *baraita,* which permits eating it, was taught **prior to** the **decree** that was issued lest a person act deceitfully, whereas **there,** the *halakha* of Rav Naḥman bar Yitzḥak, was taught **after** the **decree,** which prohibited eating food even if it was forgotten unwittingly. **However,** according to the opinion of **Rabba and Rav Yosef, who said** to interpret the phrase **permissively,** whether he left it on the stove unwittingly or he did so intentionally, it is difficult. **If** this *baraita* was taught **prior to** the **decree,**[N] the ruling with regard to when he did so **intentionally is difficult,** as Rabba and Rav Yosef permit eating the food even in that case. **If** this *baraita* was taught **after** the **decree,** the ruling with regard to when he did so **unwittingly is also difficult,** as Rabba and Rav Yosef permit eating the food in every case. No answer was found to this objection and the Gemara concludes: It is indeed **difficult.**

NOTES

One forgot a pot – **שָׁכַח קְדֵירָה**: This is a case where a person placed a pot on top of a stove with the intention of removing it before nightfall but forgot to do so. When the Gemara speaks of doing so intentionally, it is a case where one remembered before nightfall and nevertheless failed to remove the pot from the stove. In either case, one did not even perform an act prohibited by rabbinic law (Rashi).

Permissively – **לְהֶיתֵּירָא**: Permissively means: Had Rabbi Ḥiyya bar Abba sought to prohibit eating food on which a prohibited labor was performed, he would have expressed himself unambiguously. Therefore, apparently he intended to permit it (*Adderet Eliyahu*).

If this was prior to the decree – **אִי קוֹדֶם גְּזֵירָה**: This phrasing is imprecise. Although there is no dispute that the *baraita* preceded the decree, there is a possibility that perhaps this Sage held that no such decree was issued (Ramban).

HALAKHA

One who cooks on Shabbat – **הַמְבַשֵּׁל בַּשַּׁבָּת**: If one unwittingly cooks on Shabbat for himself or for others, it is prohibited to eat the food on Shabbat itself but it may be eaten immediately after Shabbat. If one cooks the food intentionally, others may eat it after Shabbat. However, it is prohibited forever for the one who cooked the food. The *halakha* was decided on the basis of explicit cases from other sources (Rambam *Sefer Zemanim, Hilkhot Shabbat* 3:4, 6:23; *Shulḥan Arukh, Oraḥ Ḥayyim* 318:1).

One who forgot a pot – **שָׁכַח קְדֵירָה**: If one intentionally left a pot of food on a stove on Shabbat, it is prohibited for him to eat the food until after Shabbat (*Magen Avraham*). Others rule that before eating the food, he must wait after Shabbat the amount of time it takes to cook that food (Rema). If one placed food that was not completely cooked on a stove on Friday and he forgot and left the pot on the stove, the food may not be eaten until after Shabbat. If the food was completely cooked before Shabbat, one may eat it on Shabbat, as per the opinion of Rav Naḥman bar Yitzḥak as supported by the *baraita* (Rambam *Sefer Zemanim, Hilkhot Shabbat* 3:9; *Shulḥan Arukh, Oraḥ Ḥayyim* 253:1).

BACKGROUND

Meat cut into small pieces – **בָּשָׂר טָרוּף**: Some explain that the meat was chopped finely to be mixed into a soup or a stew. Therefore, the more the meat is cooked, the better it mixes into the dish (*Arukh*).

NOTES

One who transgressed and left – **עָבַר וְשִׁהָה**: According to this version of the text, the question itself is the crux of the dispute between Rabbi Meir and Rabbi Yehuda. Since the *halakha* had not been determined, the Sages raised the issue as a practical question (Ramban).

Like crab apples – **כְּעוּזָרְדִין**: The *ge'onim* explained that the eggs turned red like crab apples from being cooked so long. However, in the Jerusalem Talmud, there is an explanation that they shrunk to the size of crab apples. Rav Ḥama said there that the flavor of those eggs is especially tasty.

BACKGROUND

Crab apples – **עוּזָרְדִין**: A crab apple comes from the *Crataegus azarolus*, the thorny crab apple plant from the Rosaceae family. The plant reaches 2–4 m in height, and at times reaches the height of tall trees, up to 8 m. It grows wild in mountainous areas. In the spring the crab apple plant blossoms with bunches of white flowers. The orange- or red-colored fruit of the crab apple tree resembles a small apple, with a diameter of 1–1.5 cm. There are two or three pits in each. Its taste is also slightly sour like an apple. In Mediterranean countries, like Greece and Italy, crab apples are cultivated.

Crab apples

מַאי גְּזֵירְתָּא? דְּאָמַר רַב יְהוּדָה בַּר שְׁמוּאֵל אָמַר רַבִּי אַבָּא אָמַר רַב כָּהֲנָא אָמַר רַב: בַּתְּחִילָּה הָיוּ אוֹמְרִים הַמְבַשֵּׁל בַּשַּׁבָּת, בְּשׁוֹגֵג – יֹאכַל, בְּמֵזִיד – לֹא יֹאכַל, וְהוּא הַדִּין לְשׁוֹכֵחַ. מִשֶּׁרַבּוּ מַשְׁהִין בְּמֵזִיד וְאוֹמְרִים ׳שְׁכֵחִים אָנוּ׳ – חָזְרוּ וְקָנְסוּ עַל הַשּׁוֹכֵחַ.

With regard to the matter itself, the Gemara asks: **What is the decree** that was discussed above in terms of the distinction between before the decree and after the decree? The Gemara says: This is the decree that **Rav Yehuda bar Shmuel said** that **Rabbi Abba said** that **Rav Kahana said** that **Rav said: Initially, they would say:** With regard to **one who cooks on Shabbat,** if it was **unwitting, one may eat** it; if it was **intentional, one may not eat** it. **And the same is true with regard to one who forgets** the pot atop the stove before Shabbat and it cooks on Shabbat. **When** the number of those who **leave** their pots **intentionally and say we forgot** to justify their actions, **increased,** the Sages **then penalized those who forgot.** Even one who forgets unwittingly may not eat it.

קַשְׁיָא דְּרַבִּי מֵאִיר אַדְּרַבִּי מֵאִיר, קַשְׁיָא דְּרַבִּי יְהוּדָה אַדְּרַבִּי יְהוּדָה! דְּרַבִּי מֵאִיר אַדְּרַבִּי מֵאִיר לָא קַשְׁיָא; הָא – לְכַתְּחִילָּה, הָא – דִּיעֲבַד. דְּרַבִּי יְהוּדָה אַדְּרַבִּי יְהוּדָה נַמִי לָא קַשְׁיָא: כָּאן – בִּגְרוּפָה וּקְטוּמָה, כָּאן – בְּשֶׁאֵינָהּ גְּרוּפָה וּקְטוּמָה.

In the *Tosefta* cited earlier, which deals with one who forgot a pot atop the stove and the food cooked on Shabbat, Rabbi Meir ruled leniently and permitted both hot water that was completely heated and cooked food that was completely cooked, even when it was left on the stove intentionally. Rabbi Yehuda ruled stringently and distinguished between different cases. However, in the *Tosefta* cited at the beginning of the chapter, it was taught that Rabbi Meir and Rabbi Yehuda disagree with regard to the opinions of Beit Hillel and Beit Shammai as far as leaving food on the stove on Shabbat is concerned. Rabbi Meir says that it is completely prohibited to leave cooked food on the stove *ab initio*, even according to Beit Hillel who rule leniently. Rabbi Yehuda said that Beit Hillel ruled leniently and permitted doing so. There is a **contradiction** between one statement **of Rabbi Meir** and the other statement **of Rabbi Meir,** and there is a **contradiction** between one statement **of Rabbi Yehuda** and the other statement **of Rabbi Yehuda.** The Gemara responds: Between one statement **of Rabbi Meir** and the other statement **of Rabbi Meir** there is **no contradiction. That** which we learned: Rabbi Meir prohibits leaving cooked food under any circumstances, is speaking ***ab initio***; whereas **this,** where he permits eating the food even if it was left on the stove intentionally, is speaking **after the fact.** Between one statement **of Rabbi Yehuda** and the other statement **of Rabbi Yehuda** there **is also no contradiction. There,** where he permitted leaving the food on the stove, it is referring to the case **of** a stove that was **swept and covered with ashes,** whereas **here,** where he prohibited doing so, is referring to the case **of** a stove **that is not swept and covered with ashes.**

אִיבַּעְיָא לְהוּ: עָבַר וְשִׁהָה מַאי, מִי קְנַסוּהוּ רַבָּנַן אוֹ לָא? תָּא שְׁמַע, דְּאָמַר שְׁמוּאֵל בַּר נָתָן אָמַר רַבִּי חֲנִינָא: כְּשֶׁהָלַךְ רַבִּי יוֹסֵי לְצִיפּוֹרִי מָצָא חַמִּין שֶׁנִּשְׁתַּהוּ עַל גַּבֵּי כִּירָה – וְלֹא אָסַר לָהֶן, בֵּיצִים מְצוּמָּקוֹת שֶׁנִּשְׁתַּהוּ עַל גַּבֵּי כִּירָה – וְאָסַר לָהֶן. מַאי לָאו – לְאוֹתוֹ שַׁבָּת? לֹא, לְשַׁבָּת הַבָּאָה.

A dilemma was raised before the Sages: **One** who **transgressed and left**[N] his pot on the fire on Shabbat, **what** is his legal status? **Did the Sages penalize him** and prohibit him from eating the food, **or did they not** penalize him? **Come** and **hear** a resolution to this dilemma from that which **Shmuel bar Natan said** that **Rabbi Ḥanina said: When Rabbi Yosei went to** the city of **Tzippori, he found hot water that was left on the stove, and he did not prohibit them** from drinking **it.** He found **eggs shriveled** from overcooking **that were left on the stove** on Shabbat **and he prohibited them** from eating **them. Is** this **not** referring to permitting and prohibiting their consumption **for that same Shabbat?** If so, apparently he prohibits eating cooked food that was intentionally left on the stove on Shabbat. The Gemara immediately rejects this assumption: **No.** Rather, he prohibited them from doing so *ab initio* **the following Shabbat,** but he did not prohibit them from eating the eggs on that same Shabbat.

מִכְּלָל דְּבֵיצִים מְצוּמָּקוֹת מִצְטַמְּקוֹת וְיָפֶה לָהֶן נִינְהוּ?! אִין, דְּאָמַר רַב חָמָא בַּר חֲנִינָא: פַּעַם אַחַת נִתְאָרַחְתִּי אֲנִי וְרַבִּי לְמָקוֹם אֶחָד, וְהֵבִיאוּ לְפָנֵינוּ בֵּיצִים מְצוּמָּקוֹת כְּעוּזָרְדִין, וְאָכַלְנוּ מֵהֶן הַרְבֵּה.

The Gemara is surprised: **From this** statement it can be **inferred** that **eggs shriveled** from overcooking **shrivel and improve** when left on the fire for a long time, and that is the reason that Rabbi Yosei made a distinction between hot water, which he permitted leaving on the stove, and eggs, which he prohibited leaving on the stove. The Gemara replies: **Yes,** overcooking improves the eggs. **As Rav Ḥama bar Ḥanina said: One time Rabbi** Yehuda HaNasi **and I were guests in the same place, and they brought before us overcooked eggs** that shriveled to the size **of crab apples** [***uzradin***][NB] **and we ate many of them.** Apparently, extended cooking improves eggs. Therefore, when they are left on the fire on Shabbat there is room for concern lest one stoke the coals in order to shrivel them more.

״בֵּית הִלֵּל אוֹמְרִים: אַף מַחֲזִירִין״. אָמַר רַב שֵׁשֶׁת: לְדִבְרֵי הָאוֹמֵר

We learned in the mishna: **Beit Hillel say** that **one may even return** a pot taken off the stove to the stove on Shabbat. **Rav Sheshet said: According to the one who says**

מחזירין – אפילו בשבת. ואף רבי אושעיא סבר: אף מחזירין – אפילו בשבת; דאמר רבי אושעיא: פעם אחת היינו עומדים לעילא מרבי חייא רבה, והעלנו לו קומקמוס של חמין מדיוטא התחתונה לדיוטא העליונה, ומזגנו לו את הכוס והחזרנוהו למקומו, ולא אמר לנו דבר.

that one may even **return** it, doing so is permitted **even on Shabbat**[NH] and not only on Shabbat eve. **And Rav Oshaya also holds:** One may **even return** it **even on Shabbat. As Rav Oshaya said: Once we were standing** on Shabbat **before Rabbi Ḥiyya the Great and we passed up to him a kettle** [*kumkemos*][L] **of hot** water **from the bottom floor** [*deyota*][L] **to the top floor, and we poured him** a **cup and returned** the kettle **to its place** on top of the stove, **and he did not say anything to us.** Apparently, he is of the opinion that even on Shabbat it is permitted to return a pot to the stove.

אמר רבי זריקא אמר רבי אבא אמר רבי תדאי: לא שנו אלא שעודן בידו, אבל הניחן על גבי קרקע – אסור. אמר רבי אמי: רבי תדאי דעבד – לגרמיה הוא דעבד, אלא הכי אמר רבי חייא אמר רבי יוחנן: אפילו הניחה על גבי קרקע – מותר.

Rabbi Zerika said that **Rabbi Abba said** that **Rabbi Tadai said: They only taught** that it is permitted to return vessels with the food inside them when **they are still in his hand;**[H] **however,** if he already **placed them on the ground,** he obviously regretted placing them on the fire and **it is prohibited** to replace them on the stove. **Rabbi Ami said:** That which **Rabbi Tadai did** and said, **he did on his own,**[N] and not in accordance with the accepted *halakha*. **Rather, Rabbi Ḥiyya said** that **Rabbi Yoḥanan said as follows: Even if** one **placed** the pot **on the ground,** it **is permitted** to return it to the stove.

פליגי בה רב דימי ורב שמואל בר יהודה, ותרוייהו משמיה דרבי אלעזר אמרי. חד אמר: עודן בידו – מותר, על גבי קרקע – אסור. וחד אמר: הניחן על גבי קרקע – נמי מותר. אמר חזקיה משמיה דאביי: הא דאמרת עודן בידו מותר – לא אמרן אלא שדעתו להחזיר, אבל אין דעתו להחזיר – אסור. מכלל דעל גבי קרקע, אף על פי שדעתו להחזיר – אסור.

The Gemara remarks that **Rav Dimi and Rav Shmuel bar Yehuda disagreed about this** matter, **and both stated** their opinion **in the name of Rabbi Elazar. One said** that when **they are still in his hand, it is permitted** to return them to the stove; when they were already **placed on the ground, it is prohibited** to do so. **And one said** that even if **one placed them on the ground, it is also permitted** to return it to the stove. **Ḥizkiya said in the name of** Abaye: **That** which **you said,** that when **it is still in his hand, it is permitted** to return it to the stove; **we only said** that *halakha* **when his** original **intention** was **to return** it to the stove. **However,** when **it was not his** original **intention to return** it, and he reconsidered and decided to return it, **it is prohibited** to return it. This proves **by inference** that if one placed it **on the ground, even if his intention** was **to return** it, **it is prohibited.**

איכא דאמרי, אמר חזקיה משמיה דאביי: הא דאמרת על גבי קרקע אסור – לא אמרן אלא שאין דעתו להחזיר, אבל דעתו להחזיר – מותר. מכלל שבעודן בידו, אף על פי שאין דעתו להחזיר – מותר. בעי רבי ירמיה: תלאן במקל מהו? הניחן על גבי מטה מהו? בעי רב אשי: פינן ממיחם למיחם מהו? תיקו.

Some say a different version of what **Ḥizkiya said in the name** of **Abaye: That** which **you said,** if one placed it **on the ground it is prohibited; we only said** that *halakha* **when it was not his** original **intention to return it. However,** if **his** original **intention was to return** it, **it is permitted.** With regard to this matter, **Rabbi Yirmeya raised a dilemma:** In a case where he neither placed them on the floor nor held them in his hand, but he **hung them on a stick, what is the ruling?** In a case where he **placed it on top of a bed, what is** the ruling? Similarly, **Rav Ashi raised a dilemma:** If **one transferred them from** one **urn to** another **urn what is** the ruling? The Gemara said: These dilemmas **stand** unresolved.

NOTES

One may return it even on Shabbat – מחזירין אפילו בשבת: According to the conclusion in the Jerusalem Talmud, it is permitted for one who removed a pot from a stove on Shabbat to replace it. The discussion here is limited to the question whether or not one who removed a pot before Shabbat is considered to have initiated an act of cooking on Shabbat if he returns it after nightfall? (See the Ran.) Based on this and similar cases, some commentaries explain that when Rav Sheshet said: Even on Shabbat, he meant even after nightfall and not only on Friday before Shabbat (*Tosafot*; Ramban; Rosh).

He did on his own – לגרמיה הוא דעבד: The Gemara chose to employ this phrase even though the person did not perform an action to which this phrase would apply. Nonetheless, it is used as a colloquial expression to imply that Rabbi Tadai's statement is not meant to teach practical *halakha*. He merely cited a stringent custom (Rashash).

LANGUAGE

Kettle [*kumkemos*] – קומקמוס: *Kumkemos* comes from the Latin cucuma or cucumis, and it is reasonable to assume that it was adopted from the Greek word **κουκκούμιον**, *koukkoumion*, which means a kettle or a vessel for water.

Floor [*deyota*] – דיוטא: From the Greek word **δίαιτα**, *diaita*, which means a room, or a dwelling.

HALAKHA

One may return it even on Shabbat – מחזירין אפילו בשבת: In a situation where it is permitted to replace a pot to a stove on Friday night, e.g., a stove in which the coals are swept or covered or a *kupah* that was lit with straw or rakings, it is permitted to replace the pot even on Shabbat day, as per the opinion of Rav Sheshet (*Shulḥan Arukh, Oraḥ Ḥayyim* 253:2).

They are still in his hand – עודן בידו: If one placed a pot that was on the fire onto the floor, it is prohibited to replace it on the stove. According to the Rema, who is of the opinion that unresolved dilemmas are resolved stringently, in accordance with the Rosh, it is prohibited to return the pot in each of the following cases: If one put it down onto a bed; if one transferred the water from one kettle to another; or if one did not intend to return it from the outset. In the *Beit Yosef*, where, according to the Rambam, the ruling in cases of unresolved dilemmas is lenient, it is permitted to replace the pot on the stove in all of those cases (Rambam *Sefer Zemanim, Hilkhot Shabbat* 3:10; *Shulḥan Arukh, Oraḥ Ḥayyim* 253:2; see the Vilna Gaon).

מַתְנִי׳ תַּנּוּר שֶׁהִסִּיקוּהוּ בְּקַשׁ וּבִגְבָבָא לֹא יִתֵּן בֵּין מִתּוֹכוֹ בֵּין מֵעַל גַּבָּיו. כּוּפָּח שֶׁהִסִּיקוּהוּ בְּקַשׁ וּבִגְבָבָא – הֲרֵי זֶה כִּכִירַיִם, בְּגֶפֶת וּבָעֵצִים – הֲרֵי הוּא כְּתַנּוּר.

MISHNA The *halakhot* that were stated with regard to a stove were specific to a stove's unique structure and the manner in which it retains heat. However, with regard to other baking apparatuses, i.e., an oven or a *kupaḥ*, there are different rules. The mishna delineates: **An oven**[H] **that they lit** even **with straw** or **rakings, one may neither place** a pot **inside it nor atop it** on Shabbat. Whereas a ***kupaḥ***[HB] **that was lit with straw** or **rakings, its** legal status is **like** that of **a stove,** and one is permitted to place a pot atop it on Shabbat. If it were lit **with pomace** or **with wood, its** legal status is **like** that of **an oven** and it is prohibited to place a pot atop it on Shabbat.

גְּמָ׳ ׳תַּנּוּר שֶׁהִסִּיקוּהוּ׳ סָבַר רַב יוֹסֵף לְמֵימַר: ׳תּוֹכוֹ׳ – תּוֹכוֹ מַמָּשׁ, ׳עַל גַּבָּיו׳ – עַל גַּבָּיו מַמָּשׁ, אֲבָל לִסְמוֹךְ – שַׁפִּיר דָּמֵי. אֵיתִיבֵיהּ אַבָּיֵי: כּוּפָּח שֶׁהִסִּיקוּהוּ בְּקַשׁ וּבִגְבָבָא – הֲרֵי הוּא כִּכִירַיִם, בְּגֶפֶת וּבָעֵצִים – הֲרֵי הוּא כְּתַנּוּר, וְאָסוּר. הָא כְּכִירָה שָׁרֵי! בְּמַאי עָסְקִינַן? אִילֵּימָא עַל גַּבָּיו, וּבְמַאי? אִילֵּימָא כְּשֶׁאֵינוֹ גָּרוּף וְקָטוּם, אֶלָּא כִּירָה כִּי אֵינָהּ גְּרוּפָה וּקְטוּמָה עַל גַּבָּיו מִי שָׁרֵי?! אֶלָּא לָאו – לִסְמוֹךְ, וְקָתָנֵי: הֲרֵי הוּא כְּתַנּוּר, וַאֲסִיר?

GEMARA With regard to that which we learned in the mishna that **an oven that they lit** even with straw or rakings, one may neither place a pot atop it nor inside it, **Rav Yosef thought to say** that when the mishna says **inside it,** it means **actually inside it;** and when it says **atop it,** it means **actually atop it. However, to lean** a pot against an oven, it may **well** be done. **Abaye raised an objection** to Rav Yosef from that which we learned in our mishna: **A *kupaḥ* that was lit with straw** or **rakings, its** legal status is **like** that of **a stove.** If it were lit **with pomace** or **with wood, its** legal status is **like** that of **an oven, and it is prohibited.** By inference: If it were **like a stove,** it would be **permitted. With what** circumstances **are we dealing? If you say** that he placed the pot **atop** the *kupaḥ*, **and in what** case? **If you say** it is referring to a case where **it is not swept and covered with ashes; a stove** that **is not swept and covered with ashes, is it permitted** even to place a pot **atop it** on Shabbat? **Rather, isn't** it referring to a case where one seeks **to lean** a pot against a *kupaḥ*, and **it taught: It is like an oven, and prohibited?**

אָמַר רַב אַדָּא בַּר אַהֲבָה: הָכָא בְּכוּפָּח גָּרוּף וְקָטוּם, וְתַנּוּר גְּרוּפָה וּקְטוּמָה עָסְקִינַן. הֲרֵי הוּא כְּתַנּוּר – דְּאַף עַל גַּב דְּגָרוּף וְקָטוּם, עַל גַּבָּיו אָסוּר. דְּאִי כְּכִירָה – כִּי גְּרוּפָה וּקְטוּמָה, שַׁפִּיר דָּמֵי. תַּנְיָא כְּוָותֵיהּ דְּאַבָּיֵי: תַּנּוּר שֶׁהִסִּיקוּהוּ בְּקַשׁ וּבִגְבָבָא – אֵין סוֹמְכִין לוֹ, וְאֵין צָרִיךְ לוֹמַר עַל גַּבָּיו, וְאֵין צָרִיךְ לוֹמַר לְתוֹכוֹ, וְאֵין צָרִיךְ לוֹמַר בְּגֶפֶת וּבָעֵצִים. כּוּפָּח שֶׁהִסִּיקוּהוּ בְּקַשׁ וּבִגְבָבָא – סוֹמְכִין לוֹ, וְאֵין נוֹתְנִין עַל גַּבָּיו. בְּגֶפֶת וּבָעֵצִים – אֵין סוֹמְכִין לוֹ.

Rav Adda bar Ahava said: **Here we are dealing with** the cases of **a *kupaḥ* that is swept and covered with ashes and an oven that is swept and covered with ashes,** and the mishna is to be understood as follows: **It is like an oven in** the sense **that, although** it is **swept and covered with ashes, it is prohibited to place** a pot **atop it;** as, **if** its legal status were **like** that of **a stove, when** it is **swept and covered** it may **well** be done. The Gemara comments that there is a *baraita* that **taught in accordance with** the opinion of **Abaye: An oven that one lit with straw and with rakings, one may not lean** a pot against **it, and needless to say** one may not place a pot **atop it, and needless to say** one may not place a pot **inside it, and, needless to say** if it was lit **with pomace** or **with wood** it is prohibited. While with regard to a ***kupaḥ* that was lit with straw** or **with rakings, one may lean** a pot **against it, but he may not place** a pot **atop it.** If it was lit **with pomace** or **with wood, one may not lean** a pot against **it.**

אֲמַר לֵיהּ רַב אַחָא בְּרֵיהּ דְּרָבָא לְרַב אַשִׁי: הַאי כּוּפָּח הֵיכִי דָּמֵי? אִי כְּכִירָה דָּמֵי – אֲפִילּוּ בְּגֶפֶת וּבָעֵצִים נַמִי, אִי כְּתַנּוּר דָּמֵי – אֲפִילּוּ בְּקַשׁ וּבִגְבָבָא נַמִי לָא! אֲמַר לֵיהּ: נָפֵישׁ הַבְלֵיהּ מִדְּכִירָה, וְזוּטָר הַבְלֵיהּ מִדְּתַנּוּר.

Rav Aḥa, son of Rava, said to Rav Ashi: This *kupaḥ*, what are its circumstances? If it is **considered like a stove, even** if it was lit **with pomace** or **with wood,** it should **also** be permitted. **And if** it is **considered like an oven, even with straw** or **with rakings,** it should **also not** be permitted. Rav Ashi **said to him:** From a halakhic perspective, a *kupaḥ* has intermediate status. **Its heat is greater than** that of **a stove;** however **its heat is less than** that of **an oven.**

הֵיכִי דָּמֵי כּוּפָּח, הֵיכִי דָּמֵי כִּירָה? אָמַר רַבִּי יוֹסֵי בַּר חֲנִינָא: כּוּפָּח – מְקוֹם שְׁפִיתַת קְדֵרָה אַחַת, כִּירָה מְקוֹם שְׁפִיתַת שְׁתֵּי קְדֵרוֹת. אָמַר אַבָּיֵי, וְאִיתֵּימָא רַבִּי יִרְמְיָה: אַף אֲנַן נַמִי תְּנֵינָא: כִּירָה שֶׁנֶּחְלְקָה – לְאוֹרְכָּהּ טְהוֹרָה, לְרׇחְבָּהּ – טְמֵאָה. כּוּפָּח בֵּין לְאוֹרְכּוֹ בֵּין לְרׇחְבּוֹ – טָהוֹר.

The Gemara asks: **What are the circumstances of a *kupaḥ*? What are the circumstances of a stove** in terms of the configuration of the vessels? **Rabbi Yosei bar Ḥanina said: A *kupaḥ*** is a small vessel that is similar to a stove; however, it only has one hole with enough **space to place a single pot. A stove** is like a double *kupaḥ* with enough **space to place two pots. Abaye said, and some say** that **Rabbi Yirmeya** said: **We also learned** this matter in a mishna dealing with the laws of ritual purity and impurity: **An** impure **stove that was divided lengthwise is pure** because it can no longer be considered a vessel. It is a broken vessel, and a broken vessel cannot become ritually impure. However, if the stove was divided **widthwise,** between the spaces for the pots, then it remains **impure** because it became two small stoves. However, a ***kupaḥ*, whether** it was divided **lengthwise** or **whether** it was divided **widthwise, is pure** because it can no longer be used as there is no way to put even a single pot on it. That is the difference between a *kupaḥ* and a stove.[H]

HALAKHA

Oven – תַּנּוּר: It is prohibited to leave food atop an oven when the oven is very hot, even if it was lit with straw and rakings. Nowadays, ovens are large and spacious. Therefore, it is permitted to leave a pot on an oven (Rema). However, placing a pot of food up against a hot oven is prohibited because the *halakha* is in accordance with the opinion of Abaye. This *halakha* applies specifically to an oven that is so hot that one's hand spontaneously recoils from it. When it is not that hot, it is permitted (Rambam *Sefer Zemanim, Hilkhot Shabbat* 3:5; *Shulḥan Arukh, Oraḥ Ḥayyim* 253:2).

***Kupaḥ* – כּוּפָּח:** It is permitted to leave a pot of food on or inside a *kupaḥ* that was lit with straw or with rakings on Shabbat, and the same goes for placing a pot against it. If it was lit with wood, it is prohibited, as per our mishna (Rambam *Sefer Zemanim, Hilkhot Shabbat* 3:7; *Shulḥan Arukh, Oraḥ Ḥayyim* 253:2).

Stove and a *kupaḥ* that were divided – כִּירָה וְכוּפָּח שֶׁנֶּחְלְקוּ: A ritually impure stove that was separated lengthwise becomes ritually pure. If it was separated widthwise, it remains ritually impure. A *kupaḥ* that was split either way becomes pure, as per the mishna in tractate *Kelim* (Rambam *Sefer Tahara, Hilkhot Kelim* 16:13).

BACKGROUND

***Kupaḥ* – כּוּפָּח:** A *kupaḥ* was a half stove. It was a ceramic vessel in which one would light a fire; on top of it there was space for a single pot.

Kupaḥ

מתני׳ אֵין נוֹתְנִין בֵּיצָה בְּצַד הַמֵּיחַם בִּשְׁבִיל שֶׁתִּתְגַּלְגֵּל וְלֹא יַפְקִיעֶנָּה בַּסּוּדָרִין, וְרַבִּי יוֹסֵי מַתִּיר. וְלֹא יַטְמִינֶנָּה בַּחוֹל וּבַאֲבַק דְּרָכִים בִּשְׁבִיל שֶׁתִּצָּלֶה.

MISHNA In addition to the *halakhot* that deal with cooking on the fire on Shabbat, several related *halakhot* are discussed. The mishna says: **One may not place a** raw **egg next to an urn**[H] full of hot water **so that it will roast slightly. And one may not** even **wrap it in cloths,** i.e., one may not heat the egg inside cloths that were heated in the sun. **And Rabbi Yosei permits** doing so in that case. **And,** similarly, **one may not insulate it in sand** or **in road dust** that was heated in the sun **so that it will roast.**[H] Although there is no actual cooking with fire here, it is similar to cooking and the Sages issued a decree to prohibit doing so.

מַעֲשֶׂה שֶׁעָשׂוּ אַנְשֵׁי טְבֶרְיָא וְהֵבִיאוּ סִילוֹן שֶׁל צוֹנֵן לְתוֹךְ אַמָּה שֶׁל חַמִּין, אָמְרוּ לָהֶם חֲכָמִים: אִם בַּשַּׁבָּת - כְּחַמִּין שֶׁהוּחַמּוּ בַּשַּׁבָּת, וַאֲסוּרִין בִּרְחִיצָה וּבִשְׁתִיָּה. אִם בְּיוֹם טוֹב - כְּחַמִּין שֶׁהוּחַמּוּ בְּיוֹם טוֹב, וַאֲסוּרִין בִּרְחִיצָה וּמוּתָּרִין בִּשְׁתִיָּה.

The mishna relates **a story about the people of** the city of **Tiberias,**[B] **and they ran a cold-water pipe** [*silon*][HL] **through a canal of hot** water from the Tiberias hot springs. They thought that by doing so, they could heat the cold potable water on Shabbat. **The Rabbis said to them: If** the water passed through **on Shabbat,**[N] its legal status is **like** that of **hot water that was heated on Shabbat, and** the water is **prohibited** both **for bathing and for drinking. And if** the water passed through **on a Festival, then it is prohibited** for **bathing but permitted for drinking.** On Festivals, one is even permitted to boil water on actual fire for the purposes of eating and drinking.

גמ׳ אִיבַּעְיָא לְהוּ: גִּלְגֵּל מַאי? אֲמַר רַב יוֹסֵף: גִּלְגֵּל - חַיָּיב חַטָּאת. אֲמַר מָר בְּרֵיהּ דְּרָבִינָא: אַף אֲנַן נַמִי תְּנֵינָא:

GEMARA A dilemma was raised before the Sages: One who violated the *halakha* in the mishna and **slightly roasted** an egg next to an urn, **what is the ruling?**[N] **Rav Yosef said: One who slightly cooked** an egg **is liable to bring a sin-offering,** as he performed the act of cooking on Shabbat, which is prohibited by Torah law. **Mar, son of Ravina, said: We also learned** something similar in the mishna:

HALAKHA

Cooking with derivatives of fire – בִּישּׁוּל בְּתוֹלְדוֹת הָאֵשׁ: Just as it is prohibited to cook with fire on Shabbat, so too, it is prohibited to cook with an object heated by fire. Therefore, one may not place an egg next to a kettle that was heated by fire, and one may not wrap an egg in a cloth that was heated by fire. One who did so unwittingly is liable to bring a sin-offering (Rambam *Sefer Zemanim, Hilkhot Shabbat* 9:2; *Shulḥan Arukh, Oraḥ Ḥayyim* 318:3).

Derivatives of the sun – תּוֹלְדוֹת חַמָּה: The Sages issued a decree prohibiting cooking even with an item that was heated by the sun. For example, cooking food in sand or road dust that was heated by the sun or in the hot springs of Tiberias is prohibited lest one come to cook with derivatives of fire (Rambam *Sefer Zemanim, Hilkhot Shabbat* 9:3, *Shulḥan Arukh, Oraḥ Ḥayyim* 318:3).

And they ran a cold-water pipe, etc. – וְהֵבִיאוּ סִילוֹן שֶׁל צוֹנֵן וכו׳: It is prohibited to run a cold water pipe through hot water, even on Friday before Shabbat, in order to heat the water on Shabbat. If one did so, the water is prohibited for both drinking and washing. On a Festival, one may not wash with it, but he may drink it (Rambam *Sefer Zemanim, Hilkhot Shabbat* 22:3; *Shulḥan Arukh, Oraḥ Ḥayyim* 326:3).

BACKGROUND

The pipe of the people of Tiberias – סִילוֹן אַנְשֵׁי טְבֶרְיָא: For many years, the people of Tiberias drew their water from springs adjacent to their city and not from the Sea of Galilee. However, the water from the Tiberias hot springs is not potable. Therefore, the people of Tiberias tried to use the hot springs to heat potable water, transported by means of aqueducts, by running a pipe through the hot springs.

LANGUAGE

Pipe [*silon*] – סִילוֹן: From the Greek σωλήν, *solen*, which means a pipe or channel.

NOTES

If on Shabbat – אִם בַּשַּׁבָּת: That is to say, if the heated water passed through on Shabbat (Rashi).

One who slightly roasted an egg, what is the ruling – גִּלְגֵּל מַאי: Rav Yosef's dilemma is: Is it a Torah prohibition or is it merely prohibited by rabbinic decree to cook with an item heated by fire but not with fire itself (Ritva)? Apparently, this dilemma can be resolved by that which is stated in the mishna. Since the Sages issued a decree prohibiting derivatives of the sun due to derivatives of fire, apparently derivatives of fire must be prohibited by Torah law as well. However, it is possible that the derivatives of the sun were prohibited due to their similarity to actual fire, and the *halakhot* of the derivatives of fire are no more stringent than the *halakhot* of the derivatives of the sun (*Tziyyun LeNefesh Ḥayyah*).

Perek **III**
Daf **39** Amud **a**

כָּל שֶׁבָּא בְּחַמִּין מִלִּפְנֵי הַשַּׁבָּת - שׁוֹרִין אוֹתוֹ בְּחַמִּין בַּשַּׁבָּת, וְכָל שֶׁלֹּא בָּא בְּחַמִּין מִלִּפְנֵי הַשַּׁבָּת - מְדִיחִין אוֹתוֹ בְּחַמִּין בַּשַּׁבָּת, חוּץ מִן הַמָּלִיחַ יָשָׁן וְקוֹלְיַיס הָאִיסְפָּנִין שֶׁהֲדָחָתָן זוֹ הִיא גְּמַר מְלַאכְתָּן. שְׁמַע מִינָּהּ.

Any salted food item **that was already placed in hot water,**[H] i.e., cooked, **before Shabbat one may soak it in hot water** even **on Shabbat. And anything that was not placed in hot water before Shabbat, one may rinse it in hot water on Shabbat,** but may not soak it, **with the exception of old salted** fish or the **colias of the Spaniards** [*kolyas ha'ispanin*][L] fish, **for which rinsing** with hot water **itself is completion of the prohibited labor** of cooking. Once it is rinsed in hot water, it does not require any additional cooking. The same is true with regard to an egg that was slightly cooked. Since it thereby becomes edible, one who brought it to that state has violated the prohibition of cooking. The Gemara sums up: Indeed, **conclude from it** that this is its meaning.

HALAKHA

Any salted food item that was already placed in hot water – כָּל שֶׁבָּא בְּחַמִּין: With regard to soaking dry food that was completely cooked before Shabbat, it is permitted to soak it in hot water on Shabbat. It is permitted to pour hot water from a secondary vessel onto food that was not cooked before Shabbat. However, it is prohibited to pour hot water from a primary vessel that was actually on the fire at one point (*Magen Avraham*). Rinsing old salted fish, known as *kolyas* of the Spaniards, and the like (Rema) in hot water completes its preparation because it cannot be eaten without being rinsed. Therefore, it is prohibited to do so on Shabbat. It is permitted to do so in cold water (Taz; Rambam *Sefer Zemanim, Hilkhot Shabbat* 9:2; *Shulḥan Arukh, Oraḥ Ḥayyim* 318:4).

LANGUAGE

Colias of the Spaniards [*kolyas ha'ispanin*] – קוֹלְיַיס הָאִיסְפָּנִין: The name of this fish is from the Greek κολίας, *kolias*, meaning coly-mackerel, *Scomber colias*. The Gemara is discussing a fish imported from Spain (*Espania*).

״וְלֹא יַפְקִיעֶנָּה בַּסּוּדָרִין״ וְהָא דִּתְנַן: ״נוֹתְנִין תַּבְשִׁיל לְתוֹךְ הַבּוֹר בִּשְׁבִיל שֶׁיְּהֵא שָׁמוּר, וְאֶת הַמַּיִם הַיָּפִים בָּרָעִים בִּשְׁבִיל שֶׁיִּצַּנּוּ, וְאֶת הַצּוֹנֵן בַּחַמָּה בִּשְׁבִיל שֶׁיֵּחַמּוּ״ לֵימָא רַבִּי יוֹסֵי הִיא וְלָא רַבָּנַן!

We also learned in the mishna according to the first *tanna*: **And one may not wrap** an egg **in cloths** that were heated by the sun in order to heat up the egg, and Rabbi Yosei permits doing so. **And** with regard to **that which we learned** in a mishna that **one may place cooked food into a pit** on Shabbat **to protect it** from the heat; **and** one may place **good**, potable **water into bad**, non-potable water **so that it will cool; and** one may put **cold water** out **in the sun to heat it**, the Gemara asks: **Let us say** that this mishna **is in accordance with** the opinion of **Rabbi Yosei**[N] in our mishna **and not** the opinion of **the Rabbis** as represented by the first *tanna* in the mishna. The Rabbis prohibited heating food with the heat of the sun.

אָמַר רַב נַחְמָן: בַּחַמָּה – דְּכוּלֵּי עָלְמָא לָא פְּלִיגִי דְּשָׁרֵי, בְּתוֹלְדוֹת הָאוּר – כּוּלֵּי עָלְמָא לָא פְּלִיגִי דַּאֲסִיר, כִּי פְּלִיגִי – בְּתוֹלְדוֹת הַחַמָּה; מָר סָבַר: גָּזְרִינַן תּוֹלְדוֹת הַחַמָּה אַטּוּ תּוֹלְדוֹת הָאוּר, וּמָר סָבַר: לָא גָּזְרִינַן.

Rav Naḥman said: With regard to heating food **in the sun** itself, **everyone agrees that one is permitted**[H] to place food in the sun to heat it, as it is certainly neither fire nor a typical form of cooking. Likewise, **with derivatives of fire,** i.e., objects that were heated by fire, **everyone agrees that it is prohibited** to heat food with them, as heating with them is tantamount to heating with fire itself. **Where they argue** is with regard to heating **with derivatives of the sun,**[N] i.e., objects heated with the heat of the sun. **This Sage,** who represents the opinion of the Rabbis, **holds** that **we issue a decree** prohibiting a person to heat with **derivatives of the sun due to derivatives of fire,** which are prohibited. People have no way of knowing how the cooking vessel was heated. If the Sages permit the use of objects heated in the sun, people will come to permit use of objects heated by fire as well. **And this Sage**, Rabbi Yosei, **holds** that **we do not issue a decree.** Even though it is prohibited to heat with derivatives of fire, heating with derivatives of the sun is permitted.

״וְלֹא יַטְמִינֶנָּה בַּחוֹל״. וְלִיפְלוֹג נַמִי רַבִּי יוֹסֵי בְּהָא! רַבָּה אָמַר: גְּזֵרָה שֶׁמָּא יַטְמִין בָּרֶמֶץ. רַב יוֹסֵף אָמַר: מִפְּנֵי שֶׁמֵּזִיז עָפָר מִמְּקוֹמוֹ. מַאי בֵּינַיְיהוּ? אִיכָּא בֵּינַיְיהוּ: עָפָר תִּיחוּחַ.

We learned in the mishna: **And one may not insulate it in sand** or **in road dust** that was heated in the sun. The Gemara asks: **And let Rabbi Yosei disagree with this** *halakha* **as well.** If he holds that one is permitted to cook on Shabbat using objects heated by the sun, the same should apply with regard to sand. The Gemara cites two answers. **Rabba said:** Rabbi Yosei agrees with the opinion of the Rabbis in this case. The Sages issued a **decree** in this case due to concern **lest** one come **to insulate** it **in hot ashes,** which is certainly prohibited, if he is permitted to insulate food in sand or road dust. Insulating in sand and insulating in hot ashes appear to be very similar. **Rav Yosef said:** Rabbi Yosei prohibits it in this case **because** when insulating it in the sand, **he displaces dirt.** It is as if he dug a hole in the sand, which is prohibited. The Gemara asks: **What is** the practical difference **between** the answers proposed by Rabba and Rav Yosef? Apparently, the two answers lead to the same practical conclusion. The Gemara answers: **There is** a practical difference **between them** in the case of **loose earth.**[N] Loose earth does not require digging a hole. According to Rav Yosef's explanation, there is no reason to prohibit insulating food in loose earth, as displacing loose earth involves no prohibition. However if the decree was issued lest one insulate an egg in hot ashes, then it applies even in the case of loose earth.

מֵיתִיבֵי, רַבָּן שִׁמְעוֹן בֶּן גַּמְלִיאֵל אוֹמֵר: מְגַלְגְּלִין בֵּיצָה עַל גַּבֵּי גַּג רוֹתֵחַ, וְאֵין מְגַלְגְּלִין בֵּיצָה עַל גַּבֵּי סִיד רוֹתֵחַ. בִּשְׁלָמָא לְמַאן דְּאָמַר ״גְּזֵירָה שֶׁמָּא יַטְמִין בָּרֶמֶץ״ – לֵיכָּא לְמִיגְזַר. אֶלָּא לְמַאן דְּאָמַר ״מִפְּנֵי שֶׁמֵּזִיז עָפָר מִמְּקוֹמוֹ״ – לִיגְזַר! סְתָם גַּג לֵית בֵּיהּ עָפָר.

The Gemara **raises an objection** from that which was taught in a *baraita*: **Rabban Shimon ben Gamliel says: One may slightly roast an egg on a hot rooftop** heated by the sun; **however, one may not slightly roast an egg on top of boiling limestone. Granted,** this works out well **according to** the opinion of **the one who said** that insulating an egg in sand is prohibited due to a **decree lest he come insulate** it **in hot ashes. There is no** reason **to issue a decree** on a hot rooftop, as it is not at all similar to hot ashes. **However, according to the** opinion of the one **who said** that the reason is **because he is displacing dirt, let him issue a decree** and prohibit warming an egg on the rooftop as well because there is sometimes dirt on the roof. The Gemara answers: This is not difficult because, **in general, a rooftop does not have dirt,** and there is no reason to issue a decree in uncommon cases.

NOTES

Let us say that this is in accordance with the opinion of Rabbi Yosei – לֵימָא רַבִּי יוֹסֵי הִיא: According to the explanation in the Jerusalem Talmud, Rabbi Yosei, holds that only those matters that are unequivocal cases of cooking are prohibited. Since utilizing items heated by the sun in order to cook food is not a clear case of cooking, Rabbi Yosei does not prohibit doing so.

Derivatives of the sun – תּוֹלְדוֹת הַחַמָּה: The Sages of Eretz Yisrael in the Jerusalem Talmud hold that the derivatives of the sun are permitted on Shabbat, and the mishna's prohibition against burying food in sand and in dirt is for other reasons, like those cited by Rabba and Rav Yosef.

Loose earth – עָפָר תִּיחוּחַ: Some commentaries explain this statement in a manner that completely changes its meaning. They say that the Sage who prohibits burying an egg in sand because a person will come to bury it in ashes permits burying an egg in loose earth because it is not similar to ashes. However, the one who prohibits burying it in sand because he thereby displaces dirt prohibits doing so in loose earth because in the process of burying the egg loose earth is also displaced (Rav Hai Gaon).

HALAKHA

Cooking in the sun and its derivatives – בִּישּׁוּל בַּחַמָּה וּבְתוֹלְדוֹתֶיהָ: Cooking and heating food in the heat of the sun itself are permitted on Shabbat. However, cooking and heating food in a derivative of the sun, e.g., a cloth, sand, or road dust heated in the sun is prohibited. Even leaving food in a derivative of the sun before Shabbat to be heated during Shabbat is prohibited by rabbinic decree, as per the opinion of the Rabbis (Rambam *Sefer Zemanim*, *Hilkhot Shabbat* 9:3; *Shulḥan Arukh*, *Oraḥ Ḥayyim* 318:3).

תא שמע: מעשה שעשו אנשי טבריא והביאו סילון של צונן לתוך אמה של חמין וכו׳. בשלמא למאן דאמר ״גזרה שמא יטמין ברמץ״ – היינו דדמיא להטמנה, אלא למאן דאמר ״מפני שמזיז עפר ממקומו״ – מאי איכא למימר?

Come and **hear** a different objection to the opinion of the *amora* from our mishna: The Sages prohibited **the people of** the city of **Tiberias, who ran a cold-water pipe through a canal of hot** water from the Tiberias hot springs, from using the water. **Granted, according to** the opinion of **the one who said** that the prohibition is due to a **decree lest one insulate** food **in hot ashes, that** is the reason that this was prohibited, as **it is similar** to insulating. The cold-water pipe was placed inside the hot water and was surrounded by it. **However, according to** the opinion of **the one who said** that the reason is **because one displaces dirt, what is there to say** to explain the prohibition?

מי סברת מעשה טבריא אסיפא קאי? ארישא קאי: לא יפקיענה בסודרין, ורבי יוסי מתיר. והכי קאמרי ליה רבנן לרבי יוסי: הא מעשה דאנשי טבריא דתולדות חמה הוא, ואסרי להו רבנן! אמר להו: ההוא – תולדות אור הוא, דחלפי אפיתחא דגיהנם.

The Gemara answers: **Do you think** that **the story about Tiberias refers to the latter clause** of the mishna? No, it **refers to the first clause** of the mishna, and it should be understood as follows: The Rabbis and Rabbi Yosei disagree with regard to wrapping an egg in cloths. The Rabbis say: **One may not wrap it in cloths and Rabbi Yosei permits doing so. And the Rabbis said the following to Rabbi Yosei: Wasn't the incident involving the people of Tiberias with derivatives of the sun,** as the hot springs of Tiberias are not heated by fire, and nevertheless **the Sages prohibited them** from using the water? Rabbi Yosei **said to them:** That is not so. **That** incident involved **derivatives of fire,** as the hot springs of Tiberias are hot because **they pass over the entrance to Gehenna.**[N] They are heated by hellfire, which is a bona fide underground fire. That is not the case with derivatives of the sun, which are not heated by fire at all.

אמר רב חסדא

On the same topic, **Rav Hisda said:**

NOTES

They pass over the entrance to Gehenna – דחלפי אפיתחא דגיהנם: The Sages who say that the hot springs of Tiberias are heated by the sun mean that the water is not heated by fire. Any source of heat other than fire is comparable to the sun in the sense that cooking with it is significantly different from cooking with fire and should be permitted. Rabbi Yosei, on the other hand, believes that the hot springs are heated by the fire that arises from beneath the ground, called here hellfire. The legal status of the hot springs is analogous to water heated by fire although their fire was not lit by human hand.

ממעשה שעשו אנשי טבריא ואסרי להו רבנן – בטלה הטמנה בדבר המוסיף הבל, ואפילו מבעוד יום. אמר עולא: הלכה כאנשי טבריא. אמר ליה רב נחמן: כבר תברינהו אנשי טבריא לסילונייהו.

From this **action performed by the people of Tiberias and the** fact that the **Sages prohibited them** from using the water, the conclusion is that the practice of **insulating** a pot **in something that increases the heat** over the course of Shabbat **was abolished**[N] on Shabbat. **And** not only is it prohibited to do so on Shabbat itself, but it is also prohibited **while it is still day** before Shabbat. Running pipes of cold water through hot water is similar to insulating water in something that adds heat. **Ulla said: The *halakha* is in accordance with the people of Tiberias.**[N] **Rav Naḥman said to him: The people of Tiberias have already broken their pipes.** Even they reconsidered their position.

״מעשה שעשו אנשי טבריא״. מאי רחיצה? אילימא רחיצת כל גופו, אלא חמין שהוחמו בשבת – הוא דאסורין, הא חמין שהוחמו מערב שבת – מותרין?! והתניא: חמין שהוחמו מערב שבת, למחר רוחץ בהן פניו ידיו ורגליו, אבל לא כל גופו?! אלא – פניו ידיו ורגליו.

We learned in the mishna with regard to the **incident,** which related **what the people of Tiberias did,** that the legal status of water that was heated in the Tiberias hot springs is like that of water heated on Shabbat, and it is prohibited for use in bathing. The Gemara clarifies this matter: **What** type of **bathing** is this? **If you say** that it is referring to **bathing one's entire body,**[N] that is difficult. That would indicate that only **water heated on Shabbat is prohibited** for use in bathing one's entire body; however, bathing one's entire body in **hot water heated before Shabbat is permitted.** That cannot be. **Wasn't it taught** in a *baraita*: With regard to **hot water that was heated on Shabbat eve, one may** use **it the next day** to **wash his face, his hands, and his feet** incrementally; **however, not** to wash **his entire body? Rather,** it must be that the bathing prohibited in the mishna with water heated on Shabbat is, in fact, washing **his face, his hands, and his feet.**

NOTES

Insulating a pot in something that increases the heat over the course of Shabbat was abolished – בטלה הטמנה בדבר המוסיף הבל: The early commentaries asked (see *Tosafot*): Why did the Gemara need to derive this *halakha* from a source from which it it is derived tangentially? Isn't there an explicit mishna that states that one may not insulate food in something that increases the heat? Some commentaries answer that the source for the *halakha* that one may not insulate a pot of food in a substance that adds heat is indeed the story of the people of Tiberias, and the general *halakha* is derived from the ruling in that case (Rashba).

The *halakha* is in accordance with the people of Tiberias – הלכה כאנשי טבריא: Some commentaries believe that Ulla disagreed with the opinion of Rav Ḥisda, who held that the people of Tiberias buried their pipe in the hot springs of Tiberias. Therefore, the Gemara discussed the insulation of a pot. In fact, Ulla held that the issue was raised because insulation is comparable to cooking. In this regard, the *halakha* is in accordance with the opinion of Rabbi Yosei (*Penei Yehoshua*).

If you say bathing one's entire body – רחיצת כל גופו: It was not necessary for the Gemara to mention the prohibition to bathe one's entire body. Obviously, since washing even part of the body is prohibited, all the more so washing one's entire body would be prohibited. The reason that the Gemara mentioned this was to prevent drawing the following inference: If bathing one's entire body was prohibited due to the prohibition of washing in water that was heated on Shabbat, the implication would be that had it been heated on Shabbat eve, it would have been permitted. That is not the case, as bathing one's entire body is prohibited even in water heated prior to Shabbat (Ramban).

אֵימָא סֵיפָא: בְּיוֹם טוֹב – כְּחַמִּין שֶׁהוּחַמּוּ בְּיוֹם טוֹב, וַאֲסוּרִין בִּרְחִיצָה וּמוּתָּרִין בִּשְׁתִיָּה. לֵימָא תְּנַן סְתָמָא כְּבֵית שַׁמַּאי; דִּתְנַן, בֵּית שַׁמַּאי אוֹמְרִים: לֹא יָחֵם אָדָם חַמִּין לְרַגְלָיו אֶלָּא אִם כֵּן רְאוּיִין לִשְׁתִיָּה, וּבֵית הִלֵּל מַתִּירִין!

However, if so, say the **latter clause** of the mishna: **On a Festival,** the legal status of the water is **like** that of **water that was heated** by fire **on a Festival,**[H] **and it is prohibited for bathing and permitted for drinking.** Even on a Festival, washing one's face, hands, and feet is prohibited with this hot water. If so, **let us say** that **we learned the unattributed mishna in accordance with** the opinion of **Beit Shammai. As we learned** in a mishna, **Beit Shammai say: A person may not heat water for his feet** on a Festival **unless it is** also **fit for drinking, and Beit Hillel permit** doing so. According to Beit Hillel, it is permitted to heat water on a Festival for the purpose of washing one's feet. According to the proposed interpretation of the term bathing in the mishna, as referring to washing one's face, hands, and feet, our mishna is in accordance with the opinion of Beit Shammai. This is problematic, as the halakhic opinion of Beit Shammai is rejected and only rarely cited in an unattributed mishna.

אָמַר רַב אִיקָא בַּר חֲנַנְיָא: לְהִשְׁתַּטֵּף בָּהֶן כָּל גּוּפוֹ עָסְקִינַן; וְהַאי תַּנָּא הוּא, דְּתַנְיָא: לֹא יִשְׁתַּטֵּף אָדָם כָּל גּוּפוֹ, בֵּין בְּחַמִּין וּבֵין בְּצוֹנֵן – דִּבְרֵי רַבִּי מֵאִיר, רַבִּי שִׁמְעוֹן מַתִּיר, רַבִּי יְהוּדָה אוֹמֵר: בְּחַמִּין – אָסוּר, בְּצוֹנֵן – מוּתָּר.

Rav Ika bar Ḥananya said: In our mishna, **we are dealing with** water that was heated in order **to rinse one's entire body**[H] **with it.** Rinsing does not have the same legal status as bathing. **And** that which we learned in the mishna: Water that was heated on Shabbat is prohibited for bathing, from which it can be inferred that water heated before Shabbat is permitted for bathing on Shabbat, **is** in accordance with the opinion of **this** ***tanna***, the opinion of Rabbi Shimon in the *Tosefta*. **As it was taught** in a *Tosefta*: **One may neither rinse**[N] **his entire body with hot water,** even if it was heated before Shabbat, **nor with cold water;** this is **the statement of Rabbi Meir. Rabbi Shimon permits doing so** even with hot water because it was heated before Shabbat. **Rabbi Yehuda says: With hot water,** it is **prohibited; with cold water,** it is **permitted.** According to Rabbi Shimon, it is completely prohibited to rinse with water that was heated on Shabbat itself. Consequently, our mishna, which does not differentiate between hot and cold water, is in accordance with the opinion of Rabbi Shimon.

אָמַר רַב חִסְדָּא: מַחֲלוֹקֶת בִּכְלִי, אֲבָל בְּקַרְקַע – דִּבְרֵי הַכֹּל מוּתָּר. וְהָא מַעֲשֶׂה דְּאַנְשֵׁי טְבֶרְיָא בְּקַרְקַע הֲוָה, וְאָסְרִי לְהוּ רַבָּנַן! אֶלָּא, אִי אִיתְּמַר הָכִי אִיתְּמַר: מַחֲלוֹקֶת – בְּקַרְקַע, אֲבָל בִּכְלִי – דִּבְרֵי הַכֹּל אָסוּר.

Rav Ḥisda said: This **dispute** over washing with water heated before Shabbat is specifically with regard to water **in a vessel,**[N] as one might mistakenly think that it was heated on Shabbat, and there is then concern lest one permit the use of water heated with fire on Shabbat. **However,** when the water was collected **in the ground, everyone agrees that it is permitted.** The Gemara challenges this: **Wasn't the incident** involving **the people of Tiberias** with regard to water **in the ground, and** nevertheless **the Sages prohibited it? Rather, if this was stated, this is what was stated,** i.e., this is the correct version of Rav Ḥisda's statement: This **dispute** is specifically when the water is collected **in the ground. However,** when it is **in a vessel, everyone agrees that it is prohibited.**[H]

אָמַר רַבָּה בַּר בַּר חָנָה אָמַר רַבִּי יוֹחָנָן: הֲלָכָה כְּרַבִּי יְהוּדָה. אָמַר לֵיהּ רַב יוֹסֵף: בְּפֵירוּשׁ שְׁמִיעַ לָךְ, אוֹ מִכְּלָלָא שְׁמִיעַ לָךְ? מַאי כְּלָלָא? דְּאָמַר רַב תַּנְחוּם אָמַר רַבִּי יוֹחָנָן אָמַר רַבִּי יַנַּאי אָמַר (רַב): כָּל מָקוֹם שֶׁאַתָּה מוֹצֵא שְׁנַיִם חֲלוּקִין וְאֶחָד מַכְרִיעַ – הֲלָכָה כְּדִבְרֵי הַמַּכְרִיעַ, חוּץ מִקּוּלֵּי מַטְלָנִיּוֹת, שֶׁאַף עַל פִּי שֶׁרַבִּי אֱלִיעֶזֶר מַחְמִיר וְרַבִּי יְהוֹשֻׁעַ מֵיקֵל, וְרַבִּי עֲקִיבָא מַכְרִיעַ – אֵין הֲלָכָה כְּדִבְרֵי הַמַּכְרִיעַ. חֲדָא: דְּרַבִּי עֲקִיבָא תַּלְמִיד הוּא, וְעוֹד: הָא

Rabba bar bar Ḥana said that **Rabbi Yoḥanan said: The** ***halakha*** in this dispute is **in accordance with** the opinion of **Rabbi Yehuda. Rav Yosef said to him:** Did **you learn** this from Rabbi Yoḥanan **explicitly, or** did **you learn** it **by inference** from something else that he said? The Gemara remarks: **What** was the statement of Rabbi Yoḥanan from which this conclusion could be **inferred? As Rav Tanḥum said** that **Rabbi Yoḥanan said** that **Rabbi Yannai said** that **Rav said: Every place that you find two** who **disagree** and each one of them establishes his opinion in a series of cases, **and one** of the Sages, a third one, adopts a **compromise** opinion and says that in some cases the *halakha* is in accordance with one, and in some cases the *halakha* is in accordance with the other, the ***halakha*** **is in accordance with** the opinion of **the compromiser.**[N] This principle holds true **except for** the case of the ritual impurity of **insignificant strips** of material. In that case, **even though Rabbi Eliezer is stringent, and Rabbi Yehoshua is lenient, and Rabbi Akiva compromises, the** ***halakha*** **is not in accordance with the statement of the compromiser: First,** because **Rabbi Akiva is a student** of Rabbi Eliezer and Rabbi Yehoshua and lacks the authority to decide between the opinions of his rabbis. **And furthermore, didn't**

HALAKHA

Like water that was heated on a Festival – כְּחַמִּין שֶׁהוּחַמּוּ בְּיוֹם טוֹב: Heating water on a Festival for use in washing one's face, hands, and feet is permitted (see *Mishna Berura*). Heating water to wash one's entire body is prohibited, as per the opinion of Beit Hillel (Rambam *Sefer Zemanim, Hilkhot Yom Tov* 1:16; *Shulḥan Arukh, Oraḥ Ḥayyim* 511:2).

To rinse one's entire body on Shabbat – לְהִשְׁתַּטֵּף בָּהֶן כָּל גּוּפוֹ: Rinsing one's entire body with hot water on Shabbat is prohibited whether the water was heated on Shabbat or before Shabbat. However, doing so in cold water is permitted, as per the opinion of Rabbi Yehuda and the ruling of Rabbi Yoḥanan (Rambam *Sefer Zemanim, Hilkhot Shabbat* 22:3; *Shulḥan Arukh, Oraḥ Ḥayyim* 326:1).

Bathing on Shabbat – רְחִיצָה בְּשַׁבָּת: It is prohibited to bathe in hot water on Shabbat, even if the water was heated on Friday. It is permitted to bathe in the hot springs of Tiberias in water collected in the ground but not in water collected in a vessel (*Shulḥan Arukh, Oraḥ Ḥayyim* 326:1).

NOTES

One may neither rinse – לֹא יִשְׁתַּטֵּף: In this context, rinsing means pouring water on one's entire body. Since this was not the usual method of bathing, it could conceivably have been permitted (Rashi).

In a vessel – בִּכְלִי: The implication here is that one is pouring water from a vessel onto himself in the manner that one typically washes. Consequently, there is greater reason to prohibit this, especially due to the potential of the appearance of transgression (*ge'onim*; Ritva).

The ***halakha*** **is in accordance with the opinion of the compromiser – הֲלָכָה כְּדִבְרֵי הַמַּכְרִיעַ:** The basic assumption is that the *halakha* is established in accordance with the majority opinion. Therefore, when two Sages argue and a third Sage tends toward a certain aspect of the opinion of one of the Sages, a majority of two is formed. The compromise opinion of a student in a dispute involving his teacher does not determine the *halakha* because the student lacks the authority to determine the *halakha* in accordance with or contrary to the opinion of his mentor.

הֲדַר בֵּיהּ רַבִּי עֲקִיבָא לְגַבֵּיהּ דְּרַבִּי יְהוֹשֻׁעַ. וְאִי מִכְּלָלָא מַאי? דִּילְמָא, הָנֵי מִילֵּי – בְּמַתְנִיתִין, אֲבָל בְּבָרַיְיתָא – לָא. אֲמַר לֵיהּ: אֲנָא בְּפֵירוּשׁ שְׁמִיעַ לִי.

Rabbi Akiva reconsider and adopt **Rabbi Yehoshua's** opinion? In the dispute over the laws of bathing as well, the ruling should have been in accordance with the opinion of Rabbi Yehuda because his is the compromise opinion. Therefore, Rav Yosef asked whether the ruling was based on that principle alone. The Gemara asks: **And if** the *halakha* was derived **by inference, what of it?** It is legitimate to draw conclusions by inference. The Gemara responds: **Perhaps this** principle, that the *halakha* is established in accordance with the compromise opinion, **applies only in a mishna; but in a** ***baraita*****, no,**[N] it does not apply. Perhaps the *baraita* is not a sufficiently reliable source to establish the *halakha* in accordance with the compromise opinion based on its formulation. Rabba bar bar Ḥana **said to** Rav Yosef: **I heard it explicitly.**

אִתְּמַר: חַמִּין שֶׁהוּחַמּוּ מֵעֶרֶב שַׁבָּת; רַב אָמַר: לְמָחָר רוֹחֵץ בָּהֶן כָּל גּוּפוֹ אֵבֶר אֵבֶר, וּשְׁמוּאֵל אָמַר: לֹא הִתִּירוּ לִרְחוֹץ אֶלָּא פָּנָיו יָדָיו וְרַגְלָיו. מֵיתִיבֵי: חַמִּין שֶׁהוּחַמּוּ מֵעֶרֶב שַׁבָּת – לְמָחָר רוֹחֵץ בָּהֶן פָּנָיו יָדָיו וְרַגְלָיו, אֲבָל לֹא כָּל גּוּפוֹ, תְּיוּבְתָּא דְּרַב! אָמַר לָךְ רַב: לֹא כָּל גּוּפוֹ – בְּבַת אַחַת, אֶלָּא אֵבֶר אֵבֶר. וְהָא ״פָּנָיו יָדָיו וְרַגְלָיו״ קָתָנֵי! כְּעֵין פָּנָיו יָדָיו וְרַגְלָיו.

An amoraic dispute **was stated:** With regard to **hot water that was heated on Shabbat eve**[H] before Shabbat, **Rav said: The next day,** on Shabbat, **one may wash his entire body with it;** however, not all at once. Rather, he washes **one limb** at a time, in a departure from the standard practice, to remind him that it is Shabbat. **And Shmuel said: They only permitted washing one's face, his hands, and his feet** with hot water, even if it was heated on Shabbat eve; however, they did not permit washing his entire body, even in increments. The Gemara **raises an objection** from what was taught in a *baraita*: **Hot water that was heated on Shabbat eve, the next day one may wash his face, his hands, and his feet with it but not his entire body.** This is **a conclusive refutation** of **Rav's** opinion. **Rav** could have **said to you:** When the *baraita* says: **Not one's entire body,** it means not his entire body **at once, but one limb** and then another **limb** until he washes his entire body is permitted. The Gemara asks: **Doesn't it say one's face, his hands, and his feet,** and no more? Rav answers: It means that one washes his body in a manner **similar to** the manner that one washes **his face, his hands, and his feet,** i.e., each limb separately, and they were cited as examples of washing one limb at a time.

תָּא שְׁמַע: לֹא הִתִּירוּ לִרְחוֹץ בְּחַמִּין שֶׁהוּחַמּוּ מֵעֶרֶב שַׁבָּת, אֶלָּא פָּנָיו יָדָיו וְרַגְלָיו! הָכָא נַמִי: כְּעֵין פָּנָיו יָדָיו וְרַגְלָיו.

The Gemara cites an additional proof. **Come** and **hear** from what was taught in a *baraita*: **They only permitted to wash one's face, his hands, and his feet with hot water that was heated before Shabbat.** This poses a difficulty to Rav. Rav answers: **Here too,** this refers to washing one limb at a time, in a manner **similar to** the way one washes **his face, his hands, and his feet.**

תַּנְיָא כְּוָותֵיהּ דִּשְׁמוּאֵל: חַמִּין שֶׁהוּחַמּוּ מֵעֶרֶב שַׁבָּת, לְמָחָר רוֹחֵץ בָּהֶן פָּנָיו יָדָיו וְרַגְלָיו, אֲבָל לֹא כָּל גּוּפוֹ אֵבֶר אֵבֶר, וְאֵין צָרִיךְ לוֹמַר חַמִּין שֶׁהוּחַמּוּ בְּיוֹם טוֹב. רַבָּה מַתְנֵי לָהּ לְהָא שְׁמַעְתָּא דְּרַב בְּהַאי לִישָּׁנָא: חַמִּין שֶׁהוּחַמּוּ מֵעֶרֶב שַׁבָּת, לְמָחָר, אָמַר רַב: רוֹחֵץ בָּהֶן כָּל גּוּפוֹ, וּמְשַׁיֵּיר אֵבֶר אֶחָד. אֵיתִיבֵיהּ כָּל הָנֵי תְּיוּבְתָּא – תְּיוּבְתָּא.

The Gemara remarks: A *baraita* **was taught in accordance with** the opinion of **Shmuel: Hot water that was heated on Shabbat eve, the next day one may wash his face, his hands, and his feet with it but not his entire body,** even **one limb** at a time. **And, needless to say,** this is the *halakha* with regard to **hot water that was heated on a Festival. Rabba would teach this** ***halakha*** **of Rav in this language: Hot water that was heated on Shabbat eve, the next day, Rav said: One may bathe his entire body in it and exclude one limb** to remind himself that today is Shabbat. **They raised all of these conclusive refutations,** with which they objected to the previous version of Rav's statement, against him and the Gemara concludes: Indeed, it is **a conclusive refutation.**

אָמַר לֵיהּ רַב יוֹסֵף לְאַבַּיֵי: רַבָּה מִי קָא עָבֵיד כִּשְׁמַעְתֵּיהּ דְּרַב? אָמַר לֵיהּ: לָא יָדַעְנָא. מַאי תִּיבְּעֵי לֵיהּ: פְּשִׁיטָא דְּלָא עָבֵיד, דְּהָא אִיתּוֹתַב! (דִּילְמָא) לָא שְׁמִיעָא לֵיהּ.

Rav Yosef said to Abaye: Does Rabba act in accordance with this ***halakha*** **of Rav? He said to him: I do not know.** The Gemara asks: **What is his dilemma? It is obvious** that Rabba **did not** act in accordance with Rav's statement, **as** Rav's statement **was conclusively refuted.** The Gemara answers: **Perhaps he did not hear,**[N] i.e., he did not know of the challenges or he did not consider them substantial. Perhaps, in his opinion, it is still reasonable to act in accordance with Rav's statement.

NOTES

Applies only in a mishna but in a ***baraita*** **no** – **בְּמַתְנִיתִין אֲבָל בְּבָרַיְיתָא לָא:** Many of the principles used in determining the *halakha* in the Mishna are not applied to *baraitot*. The major reason is that the text of a *baraita* is generally not as concisely crafted as the text of a mishna, and any conclusions based on the precise style of the text cannot be reached from the text of a *baraita*. It was already established (*Tosafot*) that the *halakha* is in accordance with the compromise opinion only when the Sages disagree about precisely the same topic. There is no way to ascertain whether or not that degree of precision exists in a particular *baraita*.

He did not hear – **לָא שְׁמִיעָא לֵיהּ:** In most instances, the talmudic phrase: He did not hear, is not to be taken literally. Rather, it means that one of the Sages did not accept a specific idea. In this case, apparently Rabba accepted the principle: Rav has the status of a *tanna* and has the authority to disagree with *tanna'im*. Therefore, there is no proof from the challenge brought from the *baraita* (*Melo HaRo'im*).

HALAKHA

Hot water that was heated on Shabbat eve – **חַמִּין שֶׁהוּחַמּוּ מֵעֶרֶב שַׁבָּת:** Hot water that was heated before the beginning of Shabbat or a Festival may be used for washing one's face, hands, and feet but may not be used to wash all or most of one's body (*Magen Avraham*), even if he washes one limb at a time (Rambam *Sefer Zemanim, Hilkhot Shabbat* 22:2; *Shulḥan Arukh, Oraḥ Ḥayyim* 326:1).

וְאִי לָא שְׁמִיעָא לֵיהּ – וַדַּאי עָבֵיד, דַּאֲמַר אַבָּיֵי: כׇּל מִילֵּי דְּמָר עָבֵיד כְּרַב, בַּר מֵהָנֵי תְּלָת דְּעָבֵיד כִּשְׁמוּאֵל: מַתִּירִין מִבֶּגֶד לְבֶגֶד, וּמַדְלִיקִין מִנֵּר לְנֵר, וַהֲלָכָה כְּרַבִּי שִׁמְעוֹן בִּגְרִירָה. כְּחוּמְרֵי דְּרַב – עָבֵיד, כְּקוּלֵּי דְּרַב – לָא עָבֵיד.

The Gemara says: If so, there is still no room for the dilemma. **And if** Rabba **did not hear** this refutation, **certainly he acted** in accordance with Rav's opinion, **as Abaye said:** In **all** halakhic **matters of the Master,** Rabba, **he conducted himself in accordance with** the opinion of **Rav, except these three where he conducted himself in accordance with** the opinion of **Shmuel.** He ruled: **One may not light from** one Hanukkah **lamp to** another **lamp, and one may untie** ritual fringes **from garment to garment, and the *halakha* is in accordance with** the opinion of **Rabbi Shimon in** the case of **dragging.** According to Rabbi Shimon, it is permitted to drag heavy objects, and there is no concern that, as a result, a ditch might be dug in the ground. In any case, it is certainly reasonable to say that he acted in accordance with the opinion of Rav in the case of bathing on Shabbat as well. The Gemara answers: His is not an absolute proof. Perhaps Rabba's custom was that **he acted in accordance with the stringencies of Rav** and **he did not act in accordance with the leniencies of Rav.** Washing with hot water on Shabbat is one of Rav's leniencies. Therefore, it is not clear how Rabba acted in practice.

תָּנוּ רַבָּנַן: מֶרְחָץ שֶׁפָּקְקוּ נְקָבָיו מֵעֶרֶב שַׁבָּת, לְמוֹצָאֵי שַׁבָּת – רוֹחֵץ בּוֹ מִיָּד. פָּקְקוּ נְקָבָיו מִיּוֹם טוֹב – לְמָחָר נִכְנָס וּמֵזִיעַ, וְיוֹצֵא וּמִשְׁתַּטֵּף בַּבַּיִת הַחִיצוֹן.

The Sages taught in a *Tosefta*: **A bathhouse whose openings were sealed on Shabbat eve**[H] so that the heat would not diminish, **after Shabbat one may bathe in it immediately.** If **its openings were sealed on the eve of a Festival,**[H] **the next day,** on the Festival itself, **one may enter and sweat** in the heat produced by the hot water **and emerge and rinse** with cold water **in the outer room** of the bathhouse.

אָמַר רַב יְהוּדָה: מַעֲשֶׂה בְּמֶרְחָץ שֶׁל בְּנֵי בְרַק שֶׁפָּקְקוּ נְקָבָיו מֵעֶרֶב יוֹם טוֹב, לְמָחָר נִכְנַס רַבִּי אֶלְעָזָר בֶּן עֲזַרְיָה וְרַבִּי עֲקִיבָא, וְהֵזִיעוּ בּוֹ וְיָצְאוּ וְנִשְׁתַּטְּפוּ בַּבַּיִת הַחִיצוֹן. אֶלָּא שֶׁחַמִּין שֶׁלּוֹ מְחוּפִּין בִּנְסָרִים. כְּשֶׁבָּא הַדָּבָר לִפְנֵי חֲכָמִים, אָמְרוּ: אַף עַל פִּי שֶׁאֵין חַמִּין שֶׁלּוֹ מְחוּפִּין בִּנְסָרִין. וּמִשֶּׁרַבּוּ עוֹבְרֵי עֲבֵירָה הִתְחִילוּ לֶאֱסוֹר. אַמְבַּטְיָאוֹת שֶׁל כְּרַכִּין – מְטַיֵּיל בָּהֶן וְאֵינוֹ חוֹשֵׁשׁ.

Rabbi Yehuda said: There was **an incident in the bathhouse of Benei Berak, whose openings were sealed on the eve of a Festival. The next day,** on the Festival itself, **Rabbi Elazar ben Azarya and Rabbi Akiva entered and sweated there, and emerged and rinsed themselves in the outer room. However,** this bathhouse was unique **because** the **hot water** was **covered by** wooden **boards** and there was no concern lest a person bathe in the hot water. **When this matter came before the Sages, they said: Even if its hot water is not covered by boards,** it is permitted to sweat from the heat in the bathhouse. **When the** number of **transgressors increased,** the Sages **began to prohibit** this. However, the **large bathhouses** [*ambatyaot*][L] **in cities,**[B] **one may stroll through them** as usual **and need not be concerned** about the prohibitions of Shabbat, even if he sweats while doing so.

מַאי ״עוֹבְרֵי עֲבֵירָה״? דְּאָמַר רַבִּי שִׁמְעוֹן בֶּן פָּזִי אָמַר יְהוֹשֻׁעַ בֶּן לֵוִי מִשּׁוּם בַּר קַפָּרָא: בַּתְּחִילָּה הָיוּ רוֹחֲצִין בְּחַמִּין שֶׁהוּחַמּוּ מֵעֶרֶב שַׁבָּת, הִתְחִילוּ הַבַּלָּנִים לְהָחֵם בְּשַׁבָּת וְאוֹמְרִים: מֵעֶרֶב שַׁבָּת הוּחַמּוּ, אָסְרוּ אֶת הַחַמִּין וְהִתִּירוּ אֶת הַזֵּיעָה. וַעֲדַיִין הָיוּ רוֹחֲצִין בְּחַמִּין, וְאוֹמְרִים ״מְזִיעִין אֲנַחְנוּ״ – אָסְרוּ לָהֶן אֶת הַזֵּיעָה, וְהִתִּירוּ חַמֵּי טְבֶרְיָה. וַעֲדַיִין הָיוּ רוֹחֲצִין בְּחַמֵּי הָאוּר, וְאוֹמְרִים ״בְּחַמֵּי טְבֶרְיָה רָחַצְנוּ״ – אָסְרוּ לָהֶן חַמֵּי טְבֶרְיָה וְהִתִּירוּ לָהֶן אֶת הַצּוֹנֵן. רָאוּ שֶׁאֵין הַדָּבָר עוֹמֵד לָהֶן – הִתִּירוּ לָהֶן חַמֵּי טְבֶרְיָה, וְזֵיעָה בִּמְקוֹמָהּ עוֹמֶדֶת.

And the Gemara asks: **What are these transgressors?** The Gemara answers: **Rabbi Shimon ben Pazi said** that **Rabbi Yehoshua ben Levi said in the name of bar Kappara: Initially, people would bathe** even on Shabbat **in hot water that was heated before Shabbat. The** bathhouse **attendants began to heat** water **on Shabbat**[N] **and say** that **it was heated before Shabbat.** Therefore, the Sages **prohibited** bathing in **hot water and permitted sweating. And they would still bathe in hot water and say: We are sweating,** and that is why we entered the bathhouse. Therefore, the Sages **prohibited sweating and permitted** bathing in **the hot springs of Tiberias.**[H] **And people would still bathe in hot water heated by fire and say: We bathed in the hot springs of Tiberias.** Therefore, **they prohibited** even **the hot springs of Tiberias and permitted them** to bathe in **cold water.** When the Sages **saw that their** decrees **were not upheld**[N] by the people because of their stringency, **they permitted them** to bathe in **the hot springs of Tiberias,** and the decree prohibiting **sweating remained in place.**[H]

HALAKHA

A bathhouse whose openings were sealed on Shabbat eve – מֶרְחָץ שֶׁפָּקְקוּ נְקָבָיו מֵעֶרֶב שַׁבָּת: Immediately after Shabbat, it is permitted to bathe in a bathhouse whose openings were sealed before Shabbat to prevent it from cooling. If the openings were not sealed, one must wait sufficient time after Shabbat for the water to be heated (*Shulḥan Arukh, Oraḥ Ḥayyim* 326:11).

If its openings were sealed on the eve of a Festival – פָּקְקוּ נְקָבָיו מֵעֶרֶב יוֹם טוֹב: One is permitted to sweat in a bathhouse whose openings were sealed on the eve of a Festival so that it would not cool off. Some authorities rule that one is even permitted to bathe his entire body in water that was heated before a Festival. However, he may only use that water to wash himself outside the bathhouse. Using it even in the outer room is prohibited (*Magen Avraham*). Other authorities prohibit washing even outside the bathhouse (*Tur*), and that is the accepted *halakha* (Rema; Rambam *Sefer Zemanim, Hilkhot Yom Tov* 1:16; *Shulḥan Arukh, Oraḥ Ḥayyim* 511:2).

They permitted bathing in the hot springs of Tiberias – הִתִּירוּ לָהֶן חַמֵּי טְבֶרְיָה: It is permitted to bathe in the water that is in the ground of the hot springs of Tiberias on Shabbat. When the water is in a vessel, bathing is prohibited (Rambam *Sefer Zemanim, Hilkhot Shabbat* 22:2; *Shulḥan Arukh, Oraḥ Ḥayyim* 326:1).

And the decree prohibiting sweating remained in place – וְזֵיעָה בִּמְקוֹמָהּ עוֹמֶדֶת: Entering a bathhouse on Shabbat in order to sweat there is prohibited. Some authorities hold that even passing through a bathhouse in a manner that will inevitably cause one to sweat, e.g., a small bathhouse where there is considerable heat, is prohibited (*Mishna Berura*; Rambam *Sefer Zemanim, Hilkhot Shabbat* 22:2; *Shulḥan Arukh, Oraḥ Ḥayyim* 326:12).

LANGUAGE

Bathhouses [*ambatyaot*] – אַמְבַּטְיָאוֹת: The word *ambati* or *ambatiya* is from the Greek word ἐμβατή, *embate*, which means, among other things, a bath.

BACKGROUND

Large bathhouses in cities – אַמְבַּטְיָאוֹת שֶׁל כְּרַכִּין: The bathhouses in the big cities consisted of several large rooms. It was customary to walk through them for purposes other than bathing. The heating in most of these bathhouses was under the floor, so simply walking through the bathhouse would cause one to sweat.

Hall of a Roman bathhouse in Pompeii, from the talmudic period

NOTES

The attendants began to heat water on Shabbat – הִתְחִילוּ הַבַּלָּנִים לְהָחֵם בְּשַׁבָּת: This does not mean that the attendants actually heated the water on Shabbat by lighting a fire and boiling it. Indeed, the general principle is that Jews are never suspected of willfully desecrating the Shabbat. Rather, the statement must be understood to mean that the attendants added wood to the fire just before Shabbat and sealed the openings of the bathhouse. This act was prohibited lest the attendants come to stir the coals. This explanation is found in the Jerusalem Talmud (Ran).

The Sages saw that their decrees were not upheld – רָאוּ שֶׁאֵין הַדָּבָר עוֹמֵד לָהֶן: It is stated in the Jerusalem Talmud that since the Sages saw that people began to restrain themselves and no longer violated the decrees of the Sages, they reconsidered and permitted certain activities that they had previously prohibited.

אָמַר רָבָא: הַאי מַאן דְּעָבַר אַדְּרַבָּנַן – שָׁרֵי לְמִיקְרֵי לֵיהּ עֲבַרְיָינָא, כְּמַאן –

In this context, **Rava said: One who violates** a decree **of the Sages, it is permitted to call him a transgressor.**[N] Transgressor is not a term limited to one who violates a severe Torah prohibition. The Gemara asks: **In accordance with whose opinion** did Rabba make this statement?

NOTES

To call him a transgressor – **לְמִיקְרֵי לֵיהּ עֲבַרְיָינָא:** Although calling people names is generally prohibited, publicizing and denouncing one who violates a prohibition to warn the public about his actions is wholly appropriate. Here, the Gemara emphasized that this applies even to one who violates rabbinic decrees (*Me'iri*).

Perek **III**
Daf **40** Amud **b**

כִּי הַאי תַּנָּא.

Rabba's statement is **according to this *tanna*** in the *baraita*, who referred to those who violated a rabbinic decree as transgressors.

״אַמְבַּטְיָאוֹת שֶׁל כְּרַכִּים מְטַיֵּיל בָּהֶן וְאֵינוֹ חוֹשֵׁשׁ״. אָמַר רָבָא: דַּוְקָא כְּרַכִּין, אֲבָל דִּכְפָרִים – לָא. מַאי טַעְמָא? כֵּיוָן דְּזוּטְרִין, נְפִישׁ הַבְלַיְיהוּ.

It was taught in a *Tosefta*: In **bathhouses in cities, one may stroll through them and,** even if he sweats while doing so, **need not be concerned. Rava said:** This applies **specifically** to bathhouses in **cities; but in villages, no,** it does not apply. **What is the reason** for this distinction? **Since** the bathhouses in the villages **are small, their heat is great,** and even merely walking through them will certainly cause one to sweat.

תָּנוּ רַבָּנַן: מִתְחַמֵּם אָדָם כְּנֶגֶד הַמְּדוּרָה וְיוֹצֵא וּמִשְׁתַּטֵּף בְּצוֹנֵן, וּבִלְבַד שֶׁלֹּא יִשְׁתַּטֵּף בְּצוֹנֵן וְיִתְחַמֵּם כְּנֶגֶד הַמְּדוּרָה, מִפְּנֵי שֶׁמַּפְשִׁיר מַיִם שֶׁעָלָיו. תָּנוּ רַבָּנַן: מֵיחַם אָדָם אֲלוּנְטִית וּמַנִּיחָהּ עַל בְּנֵי מֵעַיִם בְּשַׁבָּת, וּבִלְבַד שֶׁלֹּא יָבִיא קוּמְקוּמוֹס שֶׁל מַיִם חַמִּין וְיַנִּיחֶנּוּ עַל בְּנֵי מֵעַיִם בְּשַׁבָּת, וְדָבָר זֶה אֲפִילּוּ בַּחוֹל אָסוּר מִפְּנֵי הַסַּכָּנָה.

The Sages taught: One may warm himself opposite a bonfire on Shabbat **and emerge and rinse in cold** water **as long as he does not** first **rinse in cold** water **and** then **warm himself**[H] **opposite the bonfire.**[N] This is prohibited **because he** thereby **warms** the **water on his** body and renders it lukewarm. **The Sages** also **taught: A person** whose intestines are painful **may heat up a towel** [*aluntit*][L] **and place it on** his **intestines even on Shabbat.** This is permitted **as long as one does not bring a kettle**[H] **of water and place it on his intestines on Shabbat,** lest the water spill and he come to wring it out (*Tosafot*), which is a prohibited labor on Shabbat. **And** placing a kettle directly on his intestines **is prohibited even on a weekday due to the danger** involved. If the water is extremely hot it could spill and scald him.

תָּנוּ רַבָּנַן: מֵבִיא אָדָם קִיתוֹן מַיִם וּמַנִּיחוֹ כְּנֶגֶד הַמְּדוּרָה, לֹא בִּשְׁבִיל שֶׁיֵּחַמּוּ, אֶלָּא בִּשְׁבִיל שֶׁתָּפִיג צִינָּתָן. רַבִּי יְהוּדָה אוֹמֵר: מְבִיאָה אִשָּׁה פַּךְ שֶׁל שֶׁמֶן וּמַנִּיחַתּוֹ כְּנֶגֶד הַמְּדוּרָה, לֹא בִּשְׁבִיל שֶׁיְּבַשֵּׁל אֶלָּא בִּשְׁבִיל שֶׁיּפְשֵׁר. רַבָּן שִׁמְעוֹן בֶּן גַּמְלִיאֵל אוֹמֵר: אִשָּׁה סָכָה יָדָהּ שֶׁמֶן וּמְחַמַּמְתָּהּ כְּנֶגֶד הַמְּדוּרָה, וְסָכָה לִבְנָהּ קָטָן, וְאֵינָהּ חוֹשֶׁשֶׁת.

Similarly, **the Sages taught: One may bring a jug** [*kiton*][L] full of cold **water and place it opposite the bonfire** on Shabbat; **not so that** the water **will heat up,**[N] as it is prohibited to cook on Shabbat, **rather to temper the cold,** as one is permitted to render water less cold on Shabbat. **Rabbi Yehuda says: A woman may take a cruse of oil and place it opposite the bonfire;**[H] **not so** the oil **will cook, rather, so it will warm** until it is lukewarm. **Rabban Shimon ben Gamliel says: A woman may smear** her **hand with oil, and heat it opposite the fire, and** afterward **smear her young son** with the heated oil, **and she need not be concerned** about cooking on Shabbat.

NOTES

As long as he does not rinse in cold water and warm himself opposite the bonfire – **וּבִלְבַד שֶׁלֹּא יִשְׁתַּטֵּף בְּצוֹנֵן וְיִתְחַמֵּם כְּנֶגֶד הַמְּדוּרָה:** The reason provided in the Gemara, that the water is warmed, is difficult since it is not prohibited to make water lukewarm on Shabbat. Nevertheless, the Sages prohibited one who rinsed in cold water to warm himself next to a bonfire, as that could create the impression that he had been in a bathhouse, potentially leading people to conclude that bathing in a bathhouse is permitted (Ramban).

Not so that the water will heat up – **לֹא בִּשְׁבִיל שֶׁיֵּחַמּוּ:** Some commentaries explain that one must be careful when tempering cold water. If the water is close enough to the fire that it could become hotter than lukewarm, it is prohibited. This is also the conclusion in the Jerusalem Talmud (Rosh and others).

LANGUAGE

Towel [*aluntit*] – **אֲלוּנְטִית:** From the Latin linteum, a towel or napkin made of linen, probably by way of the Greek.

Jug [*kiton*] – **קִיתוֹן:** From the Greek **κύαθος**, *kyathos*, meaning a cup for drawing wine from a mixing bowl.

HALAKHA

Rinsing and warming – **לְהִשְׁתַּטֵּף וּלְהִתְחַמֵּם:** It is prohibited to rinse oneself with cold water and then warm oneself by standing next to the fire, as that is tantamount to heating water on Shabbat. However, heating oneself next to a fire and then rinsing with cold water is permitted (Rambam *Sefer Zemanim, Hilkhot Shabbat* 22:3; *Shulḥan Arukh, Oraḥ Ḥayyim* 326:4).

As long as one does not bring a kettle, etc. – **וּבִלְבַד שֶׁלֹּא יָבִיא קוּמְקוּמוֹס וכו׳:** Placing a vessel containing hot water on one's stomach on Shabbat is prohibited, as per the *baraita*. Even on a weekday it is prohibited because of the danger involved. However, placing a hot garment on one's stomach on Shabbat is permitted (Rambam *Sefer Zemanim, Hilkhot Shabbat* 22:4; *Shulḥan Arukh, Oraḥ Ḥayyim* 326:6).

Liquids opposite the bonfire – **מַשְׁקִין כְּנֶגֶד הַמְּדוּרָה:** Placing water, oil, and other liquids near a fire is permitted as long as they will not reach a temperature at which one's hand spontaneously recoils from them. This applies equally to water and oil, as per the opinion of Shmuel (*Shulḥan Arukh, Oraḥ Ḥayyim* 318:14).

איבעיא להו: שמן מה הוא לתנא קמא? רבה ורב יוסף דאמרי תרווייהו להתירא, רב נחמן בר יצחק אמר לאיסורא. רבה ורב יוסף דאמרי תרווייהו להתירא: שמן אף על פי שהיד סולדת בו – מותר, קסבר תנא קמא: שמן אין בו משום בשול. ואתא רבי יהודה למימר: שמן יש בו משום בשול, והפשרו לא זה הוא בשולו. ואתא רבן שמעון בן גמליאל למימר: שמן – יש בו משום בשול, והפשרו זהו בשולו.

A dilemma was raised before the Sages: With regard to heating **oil** in this manner on Shabbat, **what is its** legal status **according to the first *tanna*,** who permits doing so with water? Does he permit oil as well? **Rabba and Rav Yosef both said** that the opinion of the first *tanna* is **to permit** doing so in the case of oil. **Rav Naḥman bar Yitzḥak said** that the opinion of the first *tanna* is **to prohibit** doing so. **Rabba and Rav Yosef both said** that the opinion of the first *tanna* is **to permit** doing so. The Gemara explains the dispute in the mishna: **Oil, even though** it is heated to the point at which **the hand** spontaneously **recoils** [*soledet*][L] **from its** heat, **is permitted** to be heated in this manner. The reason is because the **first *tanna* holds** that **oil is not subject to** the prohibition of **cooking.** Cooking oil to its boiling point requires a very high temperature; merely heating it is not considered cooking. **And Rabbi Yehuda came to say** that **oil is subject to** the prohibition of **cooking; however, warming it** to a lukewarm temperature **is not** tantamount to **cooking it.** Therefore, it is permitted to place a jar of oil near the fire in order to raise its temperature, though it is prohibited to heat it to the point of cooking. **And Rabban Shimon ben Gamliel came to say** that **oil is subject to** the prohibition of **cooking, and warming it is** tantamount to **cooking it.** He permitted it only in the specific case of a woman who smeared her hand with oil, heated it, and smeared her son with it.

רב נחמן בר יצחק אמר לאיסורא: שמן אף על פי שאין היד סולדת בו – אסור, קסבר: שמן יש בו משום בשול, והפשרו זהו בשולו. ואתא רבי יהודה למימר: הפשרו לא זהו בשולו. ואתא רבן שמעון בן גמליאל למימר: שמן יש בו משום בשול, והפשרו זהו בשולו. רבן שמעון בן גמליאל היינו תנא קמא! איכא בינייהו כלאחר יד.

Rav Naḥman bar Yitzḥak said: The opinion of the first *tanna* is **to prohibit** doing so. He explains the dispute in the following manner: According to the first *tanna*, with regard to **oil, even if** the heat is **not** so great that **the hand** spontaneously **recoils from it, it is prohibited** to heat it. **He holds** that **oil is subject to** the prohibition of **cooking, and warming it is** tantamount to **cooking it. And Rabbi Yehuda came to say,** leniently, that **warming it is not** tantamount to **cooking it. And Rabban Shimon ben Gamliel came** to disagree with Rabbi Yehuda and **to say** that **oil is subject to** the prohibition of **cooking, and warming it is** tantamount to **cooking it.** The Gemara questions: According to this explanation, the opinion of **Rabban Shimon ben Gamliel is** identical to the opinion of **the first *tanna*.** What is the difference between them? The Gemara answers: **There is** a practical difference **between them** in a case where this is done **in a backhanded** manner, i.e., not as it is typically done. According to the first *tanna,* it is totally prohibited to heat the oil, whereas according to Rabban Shimon ben Gamliel, it is permitted to heat the oil in a backhanded manner.

אמר רבי יהודה אמר שמואל: אחד שמן ואחד מים, יד סולדת בו – אסור, אין יד סולדת בו – מותר. והיכי דמי יד סולדת בו? אמר רחבא: כל שכריסו של תינוק נכוית.

Rav Yehuda said that **Shmuel said** that the *halakha* is: With regard to **both oil and water,** heating either one to the point where the **hand** spontaneously **recoils from it is prohibited.** Heating either one to the point where the **hand does not** spontaneously **recoil from it is permitted.** The Gemara asks: **And what are the circumstances** in which **a hand** spontaneously **recoils from it?** Not all hands are equal in their sensitivity to heat. The Sage, **Raḥava, said: Any** water that could cause **a baby's stomach** to be **scalded** is considered water from which the hand spontaneously recoils.

אמר רבי יצחק בר אבדימי: פעם אחת נכנסתי אחר רבי לבית המרחץ ובקשתי להניח לו פך של שמן באמבטי, ואמר לי: טול בכלי שני ותן. שמע מינה תלת, שמע מינה: שמן יש בו משום בשול, ושמע מינה: כלי שני אינו מבשל, ושמע מינה: הפשרו זהו בשולו.

Rav Yitzḥak bar Avdimi said: One time I followed Rabbi Yehuda HaNasi **into the bathhouse** on Shabbat to assist him, **and I sought to place a jar of oil in the bathtub for him,** to heat the oil somewhat before rubbing it on him. **And he said to me: Take** water from the bath **in a secondary vessel**[H] **and place** the oil into it. The Gemara remarks: **Learn from this** comment of Rabbi Yehuda HaNasi **three *halakhot*: Learn from it** that **oil is subject to** the prohibition of **cooking.** This explains why he prohibited placing it in the bathtub. **And learn from it** that a **secondary vessel** is not hot and **does not cook.**[N] **And learn from it** with regard to oil that **warming it is** tantamount to **cooking it.**

LANGUAGE

Spontaneously recoils [*soledet*] – **סולדת:** According to Rashi, who bases his opinion on an ambiguous verse in Job (6:10), the word means to recoil. Radak bases his explanation of the verse in Job on the usage of the word in the Gemara. He states that it means heated or boiling. However, Rabbeinu Ḥananel compares the use of this expression here with the expression in the Jerusalem Talmud: The hand can control [*sholetet*] it. In this context, as long as the hand is capable of holding it, it is permitted.

HALAKHA

Secondary vessel – **כלי שני:** Placing a jug of cold water into a secondary vessel is permitted; placing it into a primary vessel is prohibited. A primary vessel is defined as a vessel that was heated on the fire, while a secondary vessel is one into which water or food was poured from a primary vessel. The Sages established a principle that a secondary vessel is not hot enough to cook what is inside it (*Shulḥan Arukh, Oraḥ Ḥayyim* 318:13).

NOTES

Secondary vessel does not cook – **כלי שני אינו מבשל:** The reason seems to be as follows: A primary vessel, which was actually on the fire, is often heated to a degree that it will cook whatever is inside it. The Sages extended their decree to include even a primary vessel that is not that hot. However, it is inconceivable that water in a secondary vessel, which is not as hot, could boil. Therefore, the Sages allowed certain leniencies with regard to secondary vessels.

הֵיכִי עָבֵיד הָכִי? וְהָאָמַר רַבָּה בַּר בַּר חָנָה אָמַר רַבִּי יוֹחָנָן: בְּכָל מָקוֹם מוּתָּר לְהַרְהֵר – חוּץ מִבֵּית הַמֶּרְחָץ וּבֵית הַכִּסֵּא! וְכִי תֵּימָא בִּלְשׁוֹן חוֹל אָמַר לֵיהּ, וְהָאָמַר אַבָּיֵי: דְּבָרִים שֶׁל חוֹל – מוּתָּר לְאוֹמְרָן בִּלְשׁוֹן קוֹדֶשׁ, שֶׁל קוֹדֶשׁ – אָסוּר לְאוֹמְרָן בִּלְשׁוֹן חוֹל! אַפְרוּשֵׁי מֵאִיסּוּרָא שָׁאנֵי.

The Gemara is astonished by this story: **How did** Rabbi Yehuda HaNasi **do this?**[N] How did he teach his student *halakha* in the bathhouse? **Didn't Rabba bar bar Ḥana say that Rabbi Yoḥanan said: In all places, it is permitted to contemplate** Torah matters **except for the bathhouse and the bathroom?**[H] **And if you say that he spoke to him in a secular language, didn't Abaye say: Secular matters are permitted to be spoken in the sacred language,** Hebrew, even in the bathhouse, and **sacred matters may not be spoken** in the bathhouse even **in a secular language?** The Gemara answers: It was permitted for Rabbi Yehuda HaNasi to conduct himself in that manner because he was **preventing** an individual **from** violating **a prohibition,**[N] which **is different.**

תֵּדַע, דְּאָמַר רַב יְהוּדָה אָמַר שְׁמוּאֵל: מַעֲשֶׂה בְּתַלְמִידוֹ שֶׁל רַבִּי מֵאִיר שֶׁנִּכְנַס אַחֲרָיו לְבֵית הַמֶּרְחָץ, וּבִקֵּשׁ לְהָדִיחַ קַרְקַע. וְאָמַר לוֹ: אֵין מְדִיחִין. לָסוּךְ לוֹ קַרְקַע, אָמַר לוֹ: אֵין סָכִין. אַלְמָא: אַפְרוּשֵׁי מֵאִיסּוּרָא – שָׁאנֵי, הָכָא נַמִי: לְאַפְרוּשֵׁי מֵאִיסּוּרָא שָׁאנֵי.

Know that this is so, as **Rav Yehuda said** that **Shmuel said:** There was **an incident where a student of Rabbi Meir followed him into the bathhouse** on Shabbat **and sought to rinse the floor** in order to clean it. **And** Rabbi Meir **said to him: One may not rinse** the floor on Shabbat. The student asked if it was permitted **to smear the floor** with oil.[H] **He said to him: One may not smear** the floor with oil. **Apparently, preventing** one **from** violating **a prohibition is different. Here too,** in the incident involving Rabbi Yehuda HaNasi, **preventing** one **from** violating **a prohibition is different** and permitted.

אָמַר רָבִינָא: שְׁמַע מִינָּהּ, הַמְבַשֵּׁל בְּחַמֵּי טְבֶרְיָא בְּשַׁבָּת – חַיָּיב. דְּהָא מַעֲשֶׂה דְּרַבִּי לְאַחַר גְּזֵירָה הֲוָה, וַאֲמַר לֵיהּ: טוֹל בִּכְלִי שֵׁנִי וְתֵן. אִינִי?! וְהָאָמַר רַב חִסְדָּא: הַמְבַשֵּׁל בְּחַמֵּי טְבֶרְיָא בְּשַׁבָּת – פָּטוּר! מַאי 'חַיָּיב' נַמִי דְּקָאָמַר – מַכַּת מַרְדּוּת.

Ravina said: Learn from it that **one who cooks in the hot springs of Tiberias**[H] **on Shabbat is liable, as the incident** with **Rabbi** Yehuda HaNasi **was after the decree, and he said to** his student: **Take** hot water **in a secondary vessel and place** the oil into it. Had he cooked the oil in the hot water itself, he would have violated a Torah prohibition. Since the incident with Rabbi Yehuda HaNasi took place after the Sages issued a decree to prohibit bathing in hot water on Shabbat, it must have taken place in a bath in the hot springs of Tiberias. The Gemara challenges this: **Is that so? Didn't Rav Ḥisda say that one who cooks in the Tiberias hot springs on Shabbat is not liable?** The Gemara answers: There is no contradiction. **What, too, is** the meaning of the term **liable that** Ravina **said?** It does not mean that one who cooked in the hot springs of Tiberias is liable to be stoned or to bring a sin-offering like one who violates a Torah prohibition. Rather, it means liable to receive **lashes for rebelliousness,**[N] which one receives for intentionally violating rabbinic decrees.

אָמַר רַבִּי זֵירָא: אֲנָא חֲזִיתֵיהּ לְרַבִּי אַבָּהוּ דְּשָׁט בְּאַמְבַּטֵי, וְלָא יָדַעְנָא אִי עֲקַר אִי לָא עֲקַר. פְּשִׁיטָא דְּלָא עֲקַר. דְּתַנְיָא: לֹא יָשׁוּט אָדָם בִּבְרֵיכָה מְלֵאָה מַיִם, וַאֲפִילּוּ עוֹמֶדֶת בֶּחָצֵר! לָא קַשְׁיָא, הָא

Rabbi Zeira said: I saw Rabbi Abbahu floating in a bath on Shabbat, **and I do not know if he lifted** his feet and was actually swimming in the water, or **if he did not lift**[N] his feet. The Gemara questions Rabbi Zeira's uncertainty. **It is obvious that he did not lift** his feet, **as it was taught** in a *baraita*: **A person may not float in a pool full of water**[H] on Shabbat, **and even** if the pool **was in a courtyard,** where there is no room for concern lest he violate a prohibition. This is **not difficult; this** *baraita* is referring to a place

HALAKHA

In all places, it is permitted to contemplate Torah matters except for the bathhouse and the bathroom – מָקוֹם מוּתָּר לְהַרְהֵר חוּץ מִבֵּית הַמֶּרְחָץ וּבֵית הַכִּסֵּא: It is prohibited to speak or even think of matters of Torah in a bathroom or even within four cubits, 1.92–2.3 m, of a bathroom (*Mishna Berura*). The same applies to a bathhouse. This is a corollary of the prohibition against speaking sacred matters in a bathroom or a bathhouse, even in a language other than Hebrew. However, in the course of preventing oneself or someone else from violating a more severe prohibition, it is permitted to speak of Torah matters in a bathroom or bathhouse, as per the conclusion of the Gemara (Rambam *Sefer Ahava, Hilkhot Keriat Shema* 3:4–5; *Shulḥan Arukh, Oraḥ Ḥayyim* 85:2).

And sought to rinse the floor…to smear the floor with oil – וּבִקֵּשׁ לְהָדִיחַ קַרְקַע...לָסוּךְ לוֹ קַרְקַע: One may not oil or wash the floor of a bathhouse on Shabbat, even if the floor is made of stone tiles. Since there is no great need to do so on Shabbat, the Sages were stringent in this regard (*Magen Avraham*; Rambam *Sefer Zemanim, Hilkhot Shabbat* 21:3; *Shulḥan Arukh, Oraḥ Ḥayyim* 337:3).

Cooking in the hot springs of Tiberias – בִּישּׁוּל בְּחַמֵּי טְבֶרְיָא: One who cooks in the hot springs of Tiberias is not liable by Torah law; however, he violates a rabbinic decree. Even though the water of the hot springs is not heated by fire and it is unlike standard cases of cooking, nevertheless the Sages issued a decree. Cooking in hot springs is punishable by lashes for rebelliousness (*Maggid Mishne*; Rambam *Sefer Zemanim, Hilkhot Shabbat* 9:3).

A person may not float in a pool full of water, etc. – לֹא יָשׁוּט אָדָם בִּבְרֵיכָה מְלֵאָה מַיִם וכו׳: It is prohibited to swim on Shabbat, even in a pool in a courtyard. It is permitted, though, to swim in a pool with an edge around it that prevents the water from splashing outside the pool, as per the conclusion of the Gemara (Rambam *Sefer Zemanim, Hilkhot Shabbat* 23:5; *Shulḥan Arukh, Oraḥ Ḥayyim* 339:2).

NOTES

How did Rabbi Yehuda HaNasi do this – הֵיכִי עָבֵיד הָכִי: Why did the Gemara challenge the custom of Rabbi Yehuda HaNasi from the statement of Rabbi Yoḥanan, who was his student? Rather, Rabbi Yoḥanan's statement was based on a long-standing tradition; Rabbi Yoḥanan merely publicized it. Once it is widely accepted, it can be used to challenge even Rabbi Yehuda HaNasi (Rabbeinu Ḥananel).

Preventing an individual from violating a prohibition – אַפְרוּשֵׁי מֵאִיסּוּרָא: Many actions that involve disdain for an individual's honor, e.g., treating one's rabbi without the requisite deference, were permitted in order to prevent one from violating a prohibition. In that context, it is permitted to speak of Torah matters in a place where doing so is generally prohibited. Although those Sages could have told the person to refrain from his actions without citing the Torah source prohibiting those actions, they cited the prohibition in order to distance him from transgression in the future as well (Rashba).

Lashes for rebelliousness – מַכַּת מַרְדּוּת: The violation of a Torah prohibition is generally punishable by thirty-nine lashes. The lashes were administered by a court based on the testimony of witnesses only if the defendant was forewarned, as explained in tractate *Makkot*. However, there were also lashes for rebelliousness that were administered to anyone who defiantly and intentionally violated a rabbinic ordinance or decree, even if it was a relatively minor infraction. The lashes of rebelliousness have neither an upper nor a lower limit. Rather, the number depends solely on the assessment of the judges. According to Rav Sa'adia Gaon, lashes for rebelliousness were thirteen in number, one-third the number of lashes instituted by the Torah.

And I do not know if he lifted his feet or if he did not lift – וְלָא יָדַעְנָא אִי עֲקַר אִי לָא עֲקַר: Some commentaries explained the verb lifted in this context to mean splashed water outside the pool. The fundamental prohibition of swimming is based on the concern that one will splash water from the private domain to the public domain. This is contrary to Rashi's opinion, which maintains that swimming is prohibited because one might tie wood or other objects to oneself as a flotation device to facilitate his swimming (Rabbeinu Zeraḥya HaLevi; Ran).

דְּלֵית לֵיהּ גִּידוּדֵי, הָא – דְּאִית לֵיהּ גִּידוּדֵי.

that does not have embankments surrounding it. Since there are no partitions, it appears like an ocean or a river. **That** incident involving Rabbi Abbahu occurred in a place **that has embankments** and looks like a vessel. Therefore, the Sages did not prohibit it.

וְאָמַר רַבִּי זֵירָא: אֲנָא חֲזֵיתֵיהּ לְרַבִּי אַבָּהוּ שֶׁהִנִּיחַ יָדָיו כְּנֶגֶד פָּנָיו שֶׁל מַטָּה, וְלָא יָדַעְנָא אִי נָגַע אִי לָא נָגַע. פְּשִׁיטָא דְּלָא נָגַע! דְּתַנְיָא, רַבִּי אֱלִיעֶזֶר אוֹמֵר: כׇּל הָאוֹחֵז בְּאַמָּה וּמַשְׁתִּין כְּאִילּוּ מֵבִיא מַבּוּל לָעוֹלָם!

After citing what Rabbi Zeira related with regard to Rabbi Abbahu, the Gemara cites that **Rabbi Zeira said: I saw that Rabbi Abbahu,** while he was bathing, **placed his hands over his genitals** for the sake of modesty, **and I do not know whether he touched** them **or did not touch** them. The Gemara questions Rabbi Zeira's uncertainty. **It is obvious** that **he did not touch** his genitals, **as it was taught** in a *baraita*: **Rabbi Eliezer says: One who holds his penis and urinates**[H] it is **as if he were bringing a flood to the world.**[N] He is liable to become aroused by that contact and that is an extremely severe transgression, comparable to the transgressions violated in the generation of the flood.

אָמַר אַבָּיֵי: עֲשָׂאוּהָ כְּבוֹלֶשֶׁת. דִּתְנַן: בּוֹלֶשֶׁת שֶׁנִּכְנְסָה לָעִיר, בִּשְׁעַת שָׁלוֹם, חָבִיּוֹת פְּתוּחוֹת – אֲסוּרוֹת, סְתוּמוֹת – מוּתָּרוֹת. בִּשְׁעַת מִלְחָמָה – אֵלּוּ וָאֵלּוּ מוּתָּרוֹת, לְפִי שֶׁאֵין פְּנַאי לְנַסֵּךְ. אַלְמָא: כֵּיוָן דְּבָעִיתִי – לָא מְנַסְּכִי, הָכָא נָמֵי כֵּיוָן דְּבָעִית – לָא אָתֵי לְהַרְהוּרֵי. הָכָא מַאי בִּיעֲתוּתָא? בִּיעֲתוּתָא דְּנַהֲרָא.

Abaye said: Nevertheless, no proof can be cited from that *baraita*. Perhaps the Sages **rendered** the legal status of this situation **like** that of **a military unit, as we learned** in a mishna: **A military unit that entered a city,**[N] if it entered **during peacetime,** after the soldiers leave, the **open barrels** of wine are **prohibited** and the wine in them may not be drunk due to suspicion that the gentile soldiers may have poured this wine as a libation for idolatry. The **sealed** barrels **are permitted.** However, if the unit entered **in wartime, both are permitted because** in wartime **there is no respite to pour** wine for idolatry, and one can be certain that the soldiers did not do so. **Apparently, since** they **are afraid, they do not pour libations. Here too,** in the case of bathing, **since he is afraid, he will not come to** have impure **thoughts.** The Gemara asks: **And what fear** is there **here** that would prevent one bathing from having impure thoughts? The Gemara answers: **Fear of the river.** Since he needs to be careful that the water does not wash him away, he is too distracted to think of other matters.

אִינִי?! וְהָאָמַר רַבִּי אַבָּא אָמַר רַב הוּנָא אָמַר רַב: כׇּל הַמַּנִּיחַ יָדָיו כְּנֶגֶד פָּנָיו שֶׁל מַטָּה כְּאִילּוּ כּוֹפֵר בִּבְרִיתוֹ שֶׁל אַבְרָהָם אָבִינוּ! לָא קַשְׁיָא, הָא – כִּי נָחֵית, הָא – כִּי סָלֵיק. כִּי הָא דְּרָבָא שָׁחֵי, רַבִּי זֵירָא זָקֵיף. רַבָּנַן דְּבֵי רַב אָשֵׁי, כִּי קָא נָחְתִי – זָקְפִי, כִּי קָא סָלְקִי – שָׁחִי.

The Gemara questions the story itself: **And is that so?** Is it permitted under any circumstances to cover one's genitals while bathing? **Didn't Rabbi Abba say** that **Rav Huna said** that **Rav said: Anyone who places his hands over his genitals** is **as if he denies the covenant of our father Abraham?** It appears as if he is covering himself to obscure the fact that he is circumcised. The Gemara answers: This is **not difficult,** as there is room to distinguish and say that **this,** the case where it is prohibited to cover oneself, **is when he is descending** into the river and there are no people facing him and he need not be concerned with modesty. In that case covering oneself is prohibited as he appears to be renouncing the covenant of Abraham. **That,** the case where, in certain circumstances, this prohibition does not apply, is **when he is emerging** from the river. When he emerges, he is facing the people on the riverbank and it is then permitted to cover himself in the interest of modesty, **as that** which **Rava** would do. He would **bend over**[N] when he was naked. **Rabbi Zeira would stand upright,** in accordance with Rav's statement that it is prohibited to appear to be renouncing the covenant of Abraham. **When the Sages of the school of Rav Ashi descended** into the river **they stood upright. When they emerged** from the river **they bent over.**

רַבִּי זֵירָא הֲוָה קָא מִשְׁתַּמֵּיט מִדְּרַב יְהוּדָה, דְּבָעֵי לְמִיסַּק לְאַרְעָא דְיִשְׂרָאֵל. דְּאָמַר רַב יְהוּדָה: כׇּל הָעוֹלֶה מִבָּבֶל לְאֶרֶץ יִשְׂרָאֵל עוֹבֵר בַּעֲשֵׂה, שֶׁנֶּאֱמַר: ״בָּבֶלָה יוּבָאוּ וְשָׁמָּה יִהְיוּ״. אָמַר: אֵיזִיל וְאֶשְׁמַע מִינֵּיהּ מִילְּתָא, וְאֵיתֵי וְאֵיסַּק. אֲזַל אַשְׁכְּחֵיהּ דְּקָאֵי בֵּי בָּאנֵי, וְקָאָמַר לֵיהּ לְשַׁמָּעֵיהּ: הָבִיאוּ לִי נֶתֶר, הָבִיאוּ לִי מַסְרֵק, פִּתְחוּ פּוּמַיְיכוּ וְאַפִּיקוּ הַבְלָא וְאִשְׁתּוּ מִמַּיָּא דְּבֵי בָּאנֵי. אָמַר: אִילְמָלֵא (לֹא) בָּאתִי אֶלָּא לִשְׁמוֹעַ דָּבָר זֶה – דַּיִּי.

Speaking of bathing and its *halakhot*, the Gemara relates: **Rabbi Zeira was avoiding** being seen **by** his teacher, **Rav Yehuda,** as Rabbi Zeira **sought to ascend to Eretz Yisrael**[N] and his teacher disapproved. **As Rav Yehuda said: Anyone who ascends from Babylonia to Eretz Yisrael transgresses a positive commandment,**[H] **as it is stated: "They shall be taken to Babylonia and there they shall remain** until the day that I recall them, said the Lord" (Jeremiah 27:22). Based on that verse, Rav Yehuda held that since the Babylonian exile was by divine decree, permission to leave Babylonia for Eretz Yisrael could only be granted by God. Rabbi Zeira did not want to discuss his desire to emigrate with Rav Yehuda, so that he would not be forced to explicitly disobey him. Nevertheless, **he said: I will go and hear something from him and then I will leave. He went and found** Rav Yehuda **standing in the bathhouse and telling his servant: Bring me natron** [*neter*] with which to wash, **bring me a comb, open your mouths and let out air, and drink from the water of the bathhouse.** Rabbi Zeira **said: If I had come only to hear this matter** from Rav Yehuda, **it would suffice for me.**

HALAKHA

One who holds his penis and urinates – כׇּל הָאוֹחֵז בְּאַמָּה וּמַשְׁתִּין: An unmarried man may only hold his penis while urinating in a way that will not cause arousal, i.e., he must not touch the glans, the tip of the penis. If he is married, it is permitted, but he should refrain from doing so as an act of piety (Rambam *Sefer Kedusha, Hilkhot Issurei Bia* 21:23; *Shulḥan Arukh, Oraḥ Ḥayyim* 3:14 and *Even HaEzer* 23:4).

Anyone who ascends from Babylonia to Eretz Yisrael transgresses a positive commandment – כׇּל הָעוֹלֶה מִבָּבֶל לְאֶרֶץ יִשְׂרָאֵל עוֹבֵר בַּעֲשֵׂה: Some authorities ruled that leaving Babylonia to live in other countries is prohibited. Some include Eretz Yisrael in this prohibition (*Kessef Mishne*). However, according to this opinion, for the same reasons that one is permitted to leave Eretz Yisrael, Torah, marriage and business, one may leave Babylonia as well (Rambam *Sefer Shoftim, Hilkhot Melakhim* 5:12).

NOTES

It is as if he were bringing a flood to the world – כְּאִילּוּ מֵבִיא מַבּוּל לָעוֹלָם: The Talmud explains that one of the reasons for the Flood was masturbation, as it says: "For all flesh had corrupted their way" (Genesis 6:12). Therefore, one who arouses himself sexually it is as if he is bringing a flood to the world.

A military unit that entered a city, etc. – בּוֹלֶשֶׁת שֶׁנִּכְנְסָה לָעִיר וכו׳: There was an idolatrous custom in talmudic times for a gentile to pour out a small portion of the wine from a cup as an offering to the gods. As a result, any wine touched by gentiles had the legal status of a prohibited idolatrous offering from which it is prohibited to derive any benefit. Therefore, when gentiles entered a city without supervision, there was an assumption that they poured wine for idolatrous purposes from all of the open barrels and thereby rendered the wine prohibited.

As that which Rava would do. He would bend over – כִּי הָא דְּרָבָא שָׁחֵי: Since Rava did not accept the opinion of Abaye in tractate *Nidda*, which permits one to hold his genitals if he is afraid, Rava was careful to obscure his genitals by bending over rather than concealing them with his hand (Rav Avraham Moshe Horowitz).

Rabbi Zeira was avoiding…as he sought to ascend to Eretz Yisrael – הֲוָה קָא מִשְׁתַּמֵּיט...דְּבָעֵי לְמִיסַּק לְאַרְעָא דְיִשְׂרָאֵל: Rav Yehuda, whose opinion is cited in detail in tractate *Ketubot*, states that the Jews in Babylonia who did not ascend to Eretz Yisrael during the immigrations of the Second Temple period were obligated to remain in Babylonia. In addition, Rav Yehuda claimed that living in Babylonia is of comparable value to living in Eretz Yisrael. Rabbi Zeira explained the verse: "They shall be taken to Babylonia and there they shall remain," does not refer to the Jewish people, but to the Temple vessels. Consequently, no prohibition may be derived from it. On the other hand, Rabbi Zeira was concerned that Rav Yehuda would explicitly prohibit him from leaving Babylonia and he did not want to defy him (Rashi).

בִּשְׁלָמָא הָבִיאוּ נֶתֶר הָבִיאוּ מַסְרֵק, קָמַשְׁמַע לָן: דְּבָרִים שֶׁל חוֹל מוּתָּר לְאוֹמְרָם בִּלְשׁוֹן קֹדֶשׁ. פִּתְחוּ פּוּמַיְיכוּ וְאַפִּיקוּ הַבְלָא – נַמִּי כְּדִשְׁמוּאֵל, דַּאֲמַר שְׁמוּאֵל: הַבְלָא מַפֵּיק הַבְלָא, אֶלָּא, אִשְׁתּוּ מַיָּא דְּבֵי בָּאנֵי, מַאי מַעַלְיוּתָא? דְּתַנְיָא: אָכַל וְלֹא שָׁתָה – אֲכִילָתוֹ דָּם וְזֶהוּ תְּחִילַּת חוֹלִי מֵעַיִם. אָכַל וְלֹא הָלַךְ אַרְבַּע אַמּוֹת – אֲכִילָתוֹ מַרְקֶבֶת, וְזֶהוּ תְּחִילַּת רֵיחַ רַע. הַנִּצְרָךְ לִנְקָבָיו וְאָכַל – דּוֹמֶה לְתַנּוּר שֶׁהִסִּיקוּהוּ עַל גַּבֵּי אֶפְרוֹ, וְזֶהוּ תְּחִילַּת רֵיחַ זוּהֲמָא. רָחַץ בְּחַמִּין וְלֹא שָׁתָה מֵהֶן – דּוֹמֶה לְתַנּוּר שֶׁהִסִּיקוּהוּ מִבַּחוּץ וְלֹא הִסִּיקוּהוּ מִבִּפְנִים, רָחַץ בְּחַמִּין וְלֹא נִשְׁתַּטֵּף בְּצוֹנֵן – דּוֹמֶה לְבַרְזֶל שֶׁהִכְנִיסוּהוּ לָאוּר וְלֹא הִכְנִיסוּהוּ לַצּוֹנֵן. רָחַץ וְלֹא סָךְ – דּוֹמֶה לַמַּיִם עַל גַּבֵּי חָבִית.

The Gemara analyzes the lessons learned from this story. **Granted,** when Rav Yehuda said: **Bring me natron, bring me a comb, he was teaching us** that **mundane matters are permitted to be spoken** in the bathhouse, even **in the sacred language.** When he said: **Open your mouths and let out air,** that too **is in accordance with** that which **Shmuel** said, **as Shmuel said: Heat produces heat.** The hot air that one inhales causes him to sweat more quickly. **However, drink the water of the bathhouse, what benefit** is there in doing that? The Gemara answers: **As it was taught** in a *baraita*: One who **ate and did not drink** at all, **what he ate** becomes **blood and** that causes **the onset of intestinal disease. One who ate and did not walk four cubits** after eating, **what he ate rots and that** causes **the onset of bad breath. One who needs to defecate and ate is similar to an oven that was lit on top of its ashes.**[H] When ashes from a previous fire are not swept out, and new logs are placed on top of the old ones, it inhibits the burning and dirties the oven, and **that** causes **the onset of odor of** the **filth** of perspiration in a person. As far as our matter is concerned, the *baraita* teaches: **One who bathed in hot water and did not drink from it is like an oven that was lit from the outside and not lit from the inside.** The lighting is ineffective and the oven does not heat properly. Rav Yehuda told his servants to drink the hot water while bathing so that they would be heated from the inside and the outside. The *baraita* continues: **One who bathed in hot water and did not rinse** afterward **with cold water is like iron that was placed in the fire and not placed** afterward **in cold water,** which leaves the iron soft. And one who **bathed and did not smear** himself with oil afterward **is like water** that was poured **on top of a barrel,** and not into it. The water spills outside the barrel.

מתני׳ מוּלְיָאר הַגָּרוּף שׁוֹתִין הֵימֶנּוּ בְּשַׁבָּת. אַנְטִיכִי, אַף עַל פִּי שֶׁגְּרוּפָה – אֵין שׁוֹתִין הֵימֶנָּה.

MISHNA

In this mishna, the Sages discuss two vessels used for heating water. With regard to **a** ***mulyar***,[LB] a bronze vessel into which coals are placed in an outer compartment and water is placed into an adjacent inner compartment, whose coals were **swept, one may drink from it on Shabbat.** With regard to **an** ***antikhi***,[LBN] which is a vessel with a different configuration, **even if** its coals were **swept, one may not drink from it** on Shabbat.

גמ׳ הֵיכִי דָּמֵי מוּלְיָאר הַגָּרוּף? תָּנָא: מַיִם מִבִּפְנִים וְגֶחָלִים מִבַּחוּץ. אַנְטִיכִי, רַבָּה אָמַר: בֵּי כִּירֵי. רַב נַחְמָן בַּר יִצְחָק אָמַר: בֵּי דוּדֵי. מַאן דְּאָמַר בֵּי דוּדֵי – כׇּל שֶׁכֵּן בֵּי כִּירֵי. וּמַאן דְּאָמַר בֵּי כִּירֵי, אֲבָל בֵּי דוּדֵי – לָא. תַּנְיָא כְּוָותֵיהּ דְּרַב נַחְמָן: אַנְטִיכִי אַף עַל פִּי שֶׁגְּרוּפָה וּקְטוּמָה – אֵין שׁוֹתִין הֵימֶנָּה, מִפְּנֵי שֶׁנְּחוֹשְׁתָּהּ מְחַמַּמְתָּהּ.

GEMARA

The Gemara asks: **What are the circumstances of a swept** ***mulyar***? The Gemara answers: A *mulyar* is the vessel, explained in the *Tosefta* on our mishna, that has **water on the inside and coals on the outside.** With regard to the identity of an ***antikhi*** there are different opinions. **Rabba said** that it refers to a **stove.** A space is created in the wall of a stove and filled with water. Since the stove is very hot, it is prohibited to use this water. **Rav Naḥman bar Yitzhak said:** An *antikhi* is **a cauldron,** i.e., a vessel made from two cauldrons stacked one on top of the other with coals in the bottom one and water in the upper one. These two different opinions have halakhic implications. **The one who says** that it is prohibited to use a vessel composed of two **cauldrons, all the more so** it is prohibited to use the space inside of a **stove. And the one who says** that it is prohibited to use the space inside a **stove,** a vessel composed of **two cauldrons, no,** it is not prohibited. **It was taught** in a *baraita* **in accordance with** the opinion of **Rav Naḥman: An** ***antikhi*****, even if it was swept and covered with ashes, one may not drink from it** on Shabbat **because its copper heats it.** The heating in an *antikhi* is by means of the coals beneath the water.

מתני׳ הַמֵּיחַם שֶׁפִּינָּהוּ – לֹא יִתֵּן לְתוֹכוֹ צוֹנֵן בִּשְׁבִיל שֶׁיֵּחַמּוּ, אֲבָל נוֹתֵן הוּא לְתוֹכוֹ, אוֹ לְתוֹךְ הַכּוֹס כְּדֵי לְהַפְשִׁירָן.

MISHNA

The Sages added to the laws of leaving food on a source of heat and cooking food on Shabbat: **An urn that was emptied** of its hot water on Shabbat, **one may not place cold water into it so that** the cold water **will be heated. However, one may place** cold water **into** an urn **or into a cup** that were emptied of their hot water **in order to warm it** but not in order to heat it.

גמ׳ מַאי קָאָמַר? אָמַר רַב אַדָּא בַּר מַתְנָא, הָכִי קָאָמַר: הַמֵּיחַם שֶׁפִּינָּה מִמֶּנּוּ מַיִם חַמִּין – לֹא יִתֵּן לְתוֹכָן מַיִם מוּעָטִים כְּדֵי שֶׁיֵּחַמּוּ, אֲבָל נוֹתֵן לְתוֹכוֹ מַיִם מְרוּבִּים – כְּדֵי לְהַפְשִׁירָן.

GEMARA

The mishna seems to contradict itself. The first statement completely prohibits placing water into an urn, and later it was partially permitted. The Gemara asks: **What is** the mishna **saying?**[N] **Rav Adda bar Mattana said that it said the following: An urn that was emptied of its hot water,**[H] **one may not put a small amount of water into it so that it will become** very **hot. However, one may put a large quantity of water into it in order to warm it.** A large quantity of cold water will not be heated in those circumstances.

HALAKHA

Modes of eating, etc. – **דַּרְכֵי אֲכִילָה וכו׳**: A person is obligated to preserve his own physical health and accustom himself to eat, drink, conduct himself in a manner deemed beneficial by medical experts, and follow the advice of the Gemara (Rambam *Sefer HaMadda, Hilkhot Deot* 4:2).

Urn that was emptied of its hot water, etc. – **הַמֵּיחַם שֶׁפִּינָּה מִמֶּנּוּ מַיִם וכו׳**: It is permitted to pour a large quantity of cold water into an urn from which hot water was emptied. One need not be concerned about the prohibition of hardening the metal of the urn, since he does not intend to perform that labor (Rambam *Sefer Zemanim, Hilkhot Shabbat* 12:1, 22:6, *Shulḥan Arukh, Oraḥ Ḥayyim* 318:12).

LANGUAGE

Mulyar – **מוּלְיָאר**: From the Latin miliarium, or the Greek **μιλιάριον**, *miliarion,* derived from the Latin. It is a tall, copper vessel with a narrow top, furnished with winding tubes.

Antikhi – **אַנְטִיכִי**: Apparently, this word comes from the Greek **ἀγγοθήκη**, *angotheke*. It means, among other things, a vessel heated by coals.

BACKGROUND

Mulyar – **מוּלְיָאר**: The water is poured into the elevated cylindrical section, while the coals are placed in the section of the vessel attached to it.

Depiction of a *mulyar* from Pompeii, from the period of the Mishna

Antikhi – **אַנְטִיכִי**: The vessel has double walls where the coals are placed, with the water inside the vessel. The water is poured through a faucet on the left.

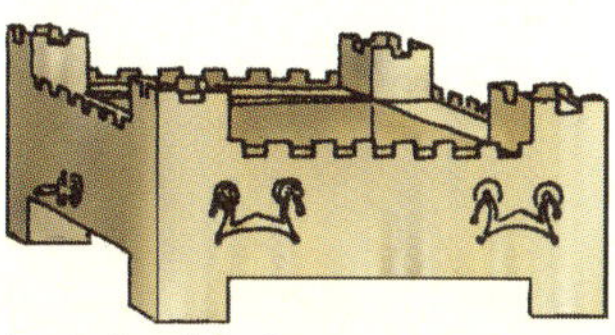

Depiction of an *antikhi* from Pompeii

NOTES

Mulyar…antikhi – **מוּלְיָאר...אַנְטִיכִי**: There are various explanations with regard to what is permitted and what is prohibited in this matter. Some explained that the reason for permitting a *mulyar* is because the water is not above the coals. Therefore, it is not considered a primary vessel. However, an *antikhi* is considered to be a primary vessel because the water is above the coals (Ran).

What is the mishna saying – **מַאי קָאָמַר**: The Ritva explained that this question means: What is the precise meaning of the word *shepinahu* in the mishna? Does it mean that the urn itself was removed from its place on the fire, or does it mean that the water was removed from the urn, as subsequently interpreted in the Gemara?

וְהָלֹא מְצָרֵף! רַבִּי שִׁמְעוֹן הִיא, דְּאָמַר: דָּבָר שֶׁאֵין מִתְכַּוֵּין – מוּתָּר. מַתְקִיף לָהּ אַבָּיֵי: מִידֵּי ״מֵיחַם שֶׁפִּינָּה מִמֶּנּוּ מַיִם״ קָתָנֵי? ״מֵיחַם שֶׁפִּינָּהוּ״ קָתָנֵי!

The Gemara questions this leniency: By putting cold water into the urn, **doesn't it harden** the vessel?[N] Cold water poured into a heated metal vessel reinforces the vessel. It is one of the stages in the labor of a blacksmith. How is it permitted to do something similar on Shabbat? The Gemara answers: This mishna **is** in accordance with the opinion of **Rabbi Shimon,** who **stated** a principle with regard to the laws of Shabbat: **An unintentional act,**[N] i.e., a permitted action from which a prohibited labor inadvertently ensues, **is permitted.** Here too, his intention was to warm the water, not to reinforce the vessel. **Abaye strongly objects to this** explanation: **Does it say** in the mishna: **An urn from which water was emptied?** That would indicate that he sought to fill the vessel with other water and warm up that water. Rather, **an urn that was removed**[N] **was taught** in the mishna, meaning that the urn was removed from the fire, not that the water was emptied from it.

אֶלָּא אָמַר אַבָּיֵי, הָכִי קָאָמַר: הַמֵּיחַם שֶׁפִּינָּהוּ וְיֵשׁ בּוֹ מַיִם חַמִּין – לֹא יִתֵּן לְתוֹכוֹ מַיִם מוּעָטִין בִּשְׁבִיל שֶׁיָּחוֹמּוּ, אֲבָל נוֹתֵן לְתוֹכוֹ מַיִם מְרוּבִּים כְּדֵי לְהַפְשִׁירָן. וּמֵיחַם שֶׁפִּינָּה מִמֶּנּוּ מַיִם – לֹא יִתֵּן לְתוֹכוֹ מַיִם כׇּל עִיקָּר, מִפְּנֵי שֶׁמְּצָרֵף. וְרַבִּי יְהוּדָה הִיא, דְּאָמַר: דָּבָר שֶׁאֵין מִתְכַּוֵּין – אָסוּר.

Rather, Abaye said this is what the mishna **is saying: An urn that was removed** from the fire **and contains hot water, one may not place a small quantity of water in it so that** the water will **become hot; rather, one may place a large quantity of water in it so that** the water will **become warm. And** with regard to **an urn from which water was removed; one may not place any water into it because he hardens** the vessel by placing cold water into a hot vessel. **And,** according to this explanation, our mishna is in accordance with the opinion of **Rabbi Yehuda,** who **said** that **an unintentional act** from which a prohibited labor inadvertently ensues **is prohibited** on Shabbat.

אָמַר רַב: לֹא שָׁנוּ אֶלָּא לְהַפְשִׁיר, אֲבָל לְצָרֵף – אָסוּר. וּשְׁמוּאֵל אָמַר: אֲפִילּוּ לְצָרֵף נָמֵי מוּתָּר. לְצָרֵף לְכַתְּחִילָּה מִי שָׁרֵי? אֶלָּא, אִי אִיתְּמַר הָכִי אִיתְּמַר, אָמַר רַב: לֹא שָׁנוּ אֶלָּא שִׁיעוּר לְהַפְשִׁיר, אֲבָל שִׁיעוּר לְצָרֵף – אָסוּר. וּשְׁמוּאֵל אָמַר: אֲפִילּוּ שִׁיעוּר לְצָרֵף

With regard to the matter itself, **Rav said: They taught** that one is permitted to place cold water into an urn with hot water after it was removed from the fire, when his intention is **only to warm**[N] the cold water. **However,** if he did this in order **to harden** the vessel, **it is prohibited. And Shmuel said: Even** if he does so in order **to harden** the vessel, it **is also permitted.** The Gemara wonders: **Is hardening permitted** ***ab initio*****?** Isn't it a full-fledged prohibited labor on Shabbat? Rather, **if** the dispute between Rav and Shmuel **was stated, it was stated as follows. Rav said: They taught** that it is permitted to add water **only** in **a measure** that is sufficient **to warm** the water, i.e., to only partially fill the vessel. **However,** filling it completely with **a measure** sufficient **to harden** the vessel **is prohibited. And Shmuel said: Even a measure** sufficient **to harden** the vessel

NOTES

Doesn't it harden the vessel – וְהָלֹא מְצָרֵף: The process of hardening a vessel falls in the general category of the prohibited labor of "striking with a hammer," which includes any act that completes the crafting of a vessel. Any action that serves to complete the crafting of a vessel or its repair is prohibited. In this context, since the vessel is strengthened by the cold water, that constitutes the final step in making the vessel.

Unintentional act – דָּבָר שֶׁאֵין מִתְכַּוֵּין: One might have thought that hardening, even though it unintended, is a case of: If you cut off its head will it not die, i.e., an inevitable consequence, in which case, even Rabbi Shimon agrees that the action is prohibited. Therefore, the Gemara explains that Rabbi Shimon does not consider this a case of hardening but only a case where the potential of hardening exists (Ra'avad).

Urn that was removed – מֵיחַם שֶׁפִּינָּהוּ: Although in the Bible, the word *pina* means to empty a vessel of its contents, rabbinic Hebrew is not always consistent with biblical Hebrew. Since the word *pina* has two different meanings in talmudic literature, it is imperative to understand the word correctly in this context because the *halakha* depends on an unambiguous understanding of the language (Rashba; *Tosafot*).

They taught only to warm – לֹא שָׁנוּ אֶלָּא...לְהַפְשִׁיר: The statements of Rav and Shmuel can be interpreted according to the opinions of both Rav Adda bar Ahava and Abaye. However, each interprets the matter according to the specific case with which he is dealing (Ritva).

מוּתָּר.

is permitted, since one did not intend to perform that prohibited labor.

לְמֵימְרָא דִּשְׁמוּאֵל כְּרַבִּי שִׁמְעוֹן סְבִירָא לֵיהּ? וְהָאָמַר שְׁמוּאֵל: מְכַבִּין גַּחֶלֶת שֶׁל מַתֶּכֶת בִּרְשׁוּת הָרַבִּים בִּשְׁבִיל שֶׁלֹּא יִזּוֹקוּ בָּהּ רַבִּים, אֲבָל לֹא גַּחֶלֶת שֶׁל עֵץ. וְאִי סָלְקָא דַּעְתָּךְ סָבַר לָהּ כְּרַבִּי שִׁמְעוֹן – אֲפִילּוּ שֶׁל עֵץ נַמִי!

The Gemara asks: **Is that to say that Shmuel,** who permits adding water even in an amount sufficient to harden a vessel, **holds in accordance with** the opinion of **Rabbi Shimon,** who says that one may perform an action that inadvertently results in a prohibited labor? **Didn't Shmuel say: One may extinguish a piece of white-hot metal**[H] **in a public area** on Shabbat **so that the masses will not be injured?** That is because the piece of white-hot metal is not actual fire and extinguishing it is prohibited by rabbinic decree, not Torah law. The Sages did not issue decrees in situations where there is concern for public safety. **However,** one may **not** extinguish a red-hot **wood coal**[N] because extinguishing it is prohibited by Torah law. **And if it would enter your mind** that Shmuel **holds in accordance with** the opinion of **Rabbi Shimon,** it should **even** be permitted to extinguish **wood as well.** When one extinguishes the coal, he intends neither to perform a prohibited labor nor to derive any benefit. He merely intends to prevent the coal from causing injury. Extinguishing the coal is a labor not necessary for its own sake. Rabbi Shimon says that one who performs a labor not necessary for its own sake is exempt.

בְּדָבָר שֶׁאֵין מִתְכַּוֵּין – סָבַר לָהּ כְּרַבִּי שִׁמְעוֹן, בִּמְלָאכָה שֶׁאֵינָהּ צְרִיכָה לְגוּפָהּ – סָבַר לָהּ כְּרַבִּי יְהוּדָה. אָמַר רָבִינָא: הִלְכָּךְ קוֹץ בִּרְשׁוּת הָרַבִּים – מוֹלִיכוֹ פָּחוֹת פָּחוֹת מֵאַרְבַּע אַמּוֹת, וּבְכַרְמְלִית אֲפִילּוּ טוּבָא.

The Gemara responds: **In the case of an unintentional act,** Shmuel **holds in accordance with** the opinion of **Rabbi Shimon.** In the case of **labor not necessary for its own sake,**[N] **he holds** that he is liable, **in accordance with** the opinion of **Rabbi Yehuda. Ravina said: Therefore, a thorn in the public domain**[H] that is liable to cause injury, **one may move it** from there in increments, **each less than four cubits,** on Shabbat. Although the Torah prohibits carrying an object four cubits in the public domain on Shabbat, carrying less than four cubits is prohibited only by rabbinic law. From Shmuel's statement, it is clear that the Sages did not issue a decree in any case where there is a threat to the masses. **And,** therefore, if the thorn was **in a *karmelit*,** where the prohibition to carry is by rabbinic law, one is permitted to carry it **even more** than four cubits.

"אֲבָל נוֹתֵן כו׳". תָּנוּ רַבָּנַן: נוֹתֵן אָדָם חַמִּין לְתוֹךְ הַצּוֹנֵן, וְלֹא הַצּוֹנֵן לְתוֹךְ הַחַמִּין, דִּבְרֵי בֵּית שַׁמַּאי. וּבֵית הִלֵּל אוֹמְרִים: בֵּין חַמִּין לְתוֹךְ הַצּוֹנֵן, וּבֵין צוֹנֵן לְתוֹךְ הַחַמִּין מוּתָּר. בַּמֶּה דְּבָרִים אֲמוּרִים – בְּכוֹס, אֲבָל בְּאַמְבַּטֵי – חַמִּין לְתוֹךְ הַצּוֹנֵן, וְלֹא צוֹנֵן לְתוֹךְ הַחַמִּין. וְרַבִּי שִׁמְעוֹן בֶּן מְנַסְיָא אוֹסֵר. אָמַר רַב נַחְמָן: הֲלָכָה כְּרַבִּי שִׁמְעוֹן בֶּן מְנַסְיָא.

We learned in the mishna: **However, one may place** water into an urn in order to warm it. **The Sages taught** in a *baraita*: **A person may place hot** water **into cold**[H] water, **but not cold into hot;**[HN] this is **the statement of Beit Shammai.** In their opinion the cold water becomes heated by the hot water beneath it. **And Beit Hillel say: Both hot into cold and cold into hot** are **permitted.** However, Beit Hillel did not permit this in all cases. **In what case is this said?** It is in the case of **a cup. However, in a bath** with a lot of water, it is permitted to pour **hot into cold but not cold into hot. And Rabbi Shimon ben Menasya prohibits** even putting hot into cold. **Rav Naḥman said: The *halakha* is in accordance with** the opinion of **Rabbi Shimon ben Menasya** in this matter.

HALAKHA

One may extinguish a piece of white-hot metal, etc. – מְכַבִּין גַּחֶלֶת שֶׁל מַתֶּכֶת וכו׳: It is permitted to extinguish on Shabbat a lump of white-hot metal located in a place where it could cause injury, as per the ruling of Shmuel. As for wood coal, the Rambam prohibits extinguishing it, while other authorities permit doing so because most halakhic authorities ruled in accordance with the opinion of Rabbi Shimon with regard to an action that is not necessary for its own sake. That is the *halakha* (*Mishna Berura* in the name of *Eliyahu Rabba*; Rambam *Sefer Zemanim, Hilkhot Shabbat* 1:7; *Shulḥan Arukh, Oraḥ Ḥayyim* 334:27).

Thorn in the public domain – קוֹץ בִּרְשׁוּת הָרַבִּים: On Shabbat, one may move a thorn or other obstacles in the public domain to the sides of the public domain in increments of less than four cubits at a time so that people will not be injured by them. In a *karmelit*, one may move the obstacle even more than four cubits at a time, as per the opinion of Ravina (Rambam *Sefer Zemanim, Hilkhot Shabbat* 1:7; *Shulḥan Arukh, Oraḥ Ḥayyim* 308:18).

Hot water into cold – חַמִּין לְתוֹךְ הַצּוֹנֵן: Pouring a large quantity of cold water into an urn that was emptied of hot water in order to warm the cold water is permitted. In addition, there is no reason for concern that one will thereby harden the metal of the urn, since he did not intend to perform that action, as per the statement of Beit Hillel and Abaye's explanation of Rabbi Shimon ben Menasya's statement (Rambam *Sefer Zemanim, Hilkhot Shabbat* 22:6; *Shulḥan Arukh, Oraḥ Ḥayyim* 318:12).

Cold into hot – צוֹנֵן לְתוֹךְ הַחַמִּין: Adding cold water to hot water in a primary vessel on Shabbat is prohibited. If there is so much cold water that it will not become exceedingly hot, it is permitted, as long as the vessel is not on the fire (Rema). If the hot water is in a secondary vessel, it is permitted. There are authorities who prohibit this in a large tub, even if it is a secondary vessel (*Shulḥan Arukh HaRav* according to the *Tur*; Rambam *Sefer Zemanim, Hilkhot Shabbat* 22:6; *Shulḥan Arukh, Oraḥ Ḥayyim* 318:12).

NOTES

One may extinguish a piece of white-hot metal…however, not a red-hot wood coal – מְכַבִּין גַּחֶלֶת שֶׁל מַתֶּכֶת...אֲבָל לֹא גַּחֶלֶת שֶׁל עֵץ: Some of the early commentaries explain that the difference between extinguishing burning wood and metal is not in the severity of the prohibition but in the danger posed by each case. When a wooden coal is hot, it is red, which prompts people to avoid it. Metal can be hot enough to cause damage even when it is not red. That is dangerous, as people tend to be less careful to avoid it (*Ba'al Halakhot Gedolot*; Rabbeinu Ḥananel; Rav Hai Gaon).

An unintentional act…labor not necessary for its own sake – בְּדָבָר שֶׁאֵין מִתְכַּוֵּין...בִּמְלָאכָה שֶׁאֵינָהּ צְרִיכָה לְגוּפָהּ: The Gemara is based on the assumption that an unintentional action and a labor that is not necessary for its own sake are interdependent. Indeed, there is a certain relationship between the two: If an action is not necessary for its own sake, then, at the very least, the person did not intend to perform that aspect of the action. Conversely, one who performs an unintentional action clearly did not perform the prohibited labor for its own sake. Therefore, despite the resolution in the Gemara, apparently the Sages agree that those who exempt a person from labor that is not necessary for its own sake would certainly exempt a person from an unintentional act. However, according to the answer that rejects the close connection between these two actions, a distinction must be made between an unintentional act, where one had no intention at all of performing the action or the prohibition, even if it ensued as an unintended but not inevitable consequence of a different action, and an action that is not necessary for its own sake where the person intentionally performs the action but did not perform it in order to achieve the standard objective of that action.

Hot water into cold, but not cold into hot – חַמִּין לְתוֹךְ הַצּוֹנֵן וְלֹא הַצּוֹנֵן לְתוֹךְ הַחַמִּין: According to Rashi, the difference in the *halakha* is based on the concept that the water below prevails, as hot air or water is lighter and rises upward. Therefore, cold water poured into hot water is heated, while hot water poured into cold water is cooled. Other commentaries explain that the reason for the prohibition was a decree based on the prohibition against cooking. Since cooking, including placing food in a primary vessel, is prohibited, pouring cold water into a vessel in which there is hot water, even if it is a secondary vessel, is tantamount to cooking the water and is prohibited (Rashba).

סָבַר רַב יוֹסֵף לְמֵימַר: סֵפֶל הֲרֵי הוּא כְּאַמְבַּטִי. אֲמַר לֵיהּ אַבָּיֵי: תָּנֵי רַבִּי חִיָּיא: סֵפֶל אֵינוֹ כְּאַמְבַּטִי. וּלְמַאי דִּסְלֵיק אַדַּעְתָּא מֵעִיקָּרָא דְּסֵפֶל הֲרֵי הוּא כְּאַמְבַּטִי, וְאָמַר רַב נַחְמָן: הֲלָכָה כְּרַבִּי שִׁמְעוֹן בֶּן מְנַסְיָא, אֶלָּא בְּשַׁבָּת רְחִיצָה בְּחַמִּין לֵיכָּא?!

Rav Yosef thought to say that the legal status of **a basin** [*sefel*],[L] which is a vessel used for washing, **is like** that of **a bath,** and it is prohibited to pour water into it. **Abaye said to him** that **Rabbi Ḥiyya taught** a *baraita*: **A basin is not like a bath** in terms of pouring water into it. The Gemara asks: **And according to what entered** Rav Yosef's **mind initially,** that **a basin is like a bath** with regard to this *halakha*, **and Rav Naḥman said** that **the *halakha* is in accordance with** the opinion of **Rabbi Shimon ben Menasya** in this matter, does that mean that **on Shabbat there is no** possibility of **washing with hot** water? No all-encompassing prohibition of washing with hot water on Shabbat was ever taught.

מִי סָבְרַתְּ רַבִּי שִׁמְעוֹן אַסֵּיפָא קָאֵי? אַרֵישָׁא קָאֵי: וּבֵית הִלֵּל מַתִּירִין בֵּין חַמִּין לְתוֹךְ צוֹנֵן, וּבֵין צוֹנֵן לְתוֹךְ הַחַמִּין, וְרַבִּי שִׁמְעוֹן בֶּן מְנַסְיָא אוֹסֵר צוֹנֵן לְתוֹךְ חַמִּין. לֵימָא רַבִּי שִׁמְעוֹן בֶּן מְנַסְיָא דְּאָמַר כְּבֵית שַׁמַּאי! הָכִי קָאָמַר: לֹא נֶחְלְקוּ בֵּית שַׁמַּאי וּבֵית הִלֵּל בְּדָבָר זֶה.

The Gemara replies: **Do you think** that **Rabbi Shimon** ben Menasya **is referring to the latter clause of the mishna?** No, **he is referring to the first clause of the mishna,** where we learned that **Beit Hillel permit both hot** water **into cold and cold** water **into hot, and Rabbi Shimon ben Menasya prohibits** placing **cold** water **into hot.** The Gemara asks: If so, **say** that **Rabbi Shimon ben Menasya stated** his opinion **in accordance with** the opinion of **Beit Shammai.** Isn't the *halakha* generally established according to Beit Hillel? The Gemara explains: **He said the following: Beit Shammai and Beit Hillel did not dispute this matter.**[N] Rabbi Shimon ben Menasya had a different tradition with regard to the opinions of Beit Shammai and Beit Hillel.

אָמַר רַב הוּנָא בְּרֵיהּ דְּרַב יְהוֹשֻׁעַ: חֲזֵינָא לֵיהּ לְרָבָא דְּלָא קָפֵיד אַמָּנָא, מִדְּתָנֵי רַבִּי חִיָּיא: נוֹתֵן אָדָם קִיתוֹן שֶׁל מַיִם לְתוֹךְ סֵפֶל שֶׁל מַיִם, בֵּין חַמִּין לְתוֹךְ צוֹנֵן וּבֵין צוֹנֵן לְתוֹךְ חַמִּין. אֲמַר לֵיהּ רַב הוּנָא לְרַב אָשֵׁי: דִּילְמָא שָׁאנֵי הָתָם דְּמִיפְסַק כְּלִי? אֲמַר לֵיהּ ׳מְעָרֶה׳ אִיתְּמַר, מְעָרֶה אָדָם קִיתוֹן שֶׁל מַיִם לְתוֹךְ סֵפֶל שֶׁל מַיִם, בֵּין חַמִּין לְתוֹךְ צוֹנֵן, בֵּין צוֹנֵן לְתוֹךְ חַמִּין.

Rav Huna, son of Rav Yehoshua, said: I saw that Rava was not strict in the case **of a vessel** and made no distinction between cold and hot. From where did he derive this leniency? **From** a *baraita* **that Rabbi Ḥiyya taught: A person may place a jug of water into a basin of water, both hot into cold and cold into hot. Rav Huna said to Rav Ashi:** There is a weakness in this proof, as **perhaps there it is different because the vessel forms a partition** between the hot and cold water. He is not pouring cold water into the basin itself but is placing a jug whose sides form a partition into the basin. **He said to him:** The term **pour was stated** in that *baraita*. This is the correct version: **A person may pour a jug of water into a basin of water, both hot into cold or cold into hot.** Therefore, there is no room to distinguish between the two cases.

מתני׳ הָאִילְפָּס וְהַקְּדֵרָה שֶׁהֶעֱבִירָן מְרוּתָּחִין – לֹא יִתֵּן לְתוֹכָן תְּבָלִין,

MISHNA In continuation of the discussion of vessels where the prohibition of cooking applies even though the vessels are not actually on the fire itself, the mishna establishes: **A stew pot** [*ilpas*][L] **and a pot that were removed** from the fire while they were still **boiling,** even if they were removed before Shabbat, **one may not place spices into them**[H] on Shabbat itself. Even though the pot is not actually standing on the fire, the spices are still cooked in it because the pot is a primary vessel, i.e., a vessel whose contents were cooked on the fire.

LANGUAGE

Basin [*sefel*] – סֵפֶל: From the usage of this word here and in many other sources it seems clear that this is a large vessel into which significant quantities of liquid are poured either for the purpose of drinking or for washing one's feet. In popular usage today, it refers to a small vessel used for drinking but that is not reflected in the sources.

Stew pot [*ilpas*] – אִילְפָּס: From the Greek word λοπάς, *lopas*, genitive λοπάδος, *lopados*, which means a flat dish, or a vessel used for frying or deep frying.

NOTES

Beit Shammai and Beit Hillel did not dispute this matter – לֹא נֶחְלְקוּ בֵּית שַׁמַּאי וּבֵית הִלֵּל בְּדָבָר זֶה: It is difficult to assume that a *tanna* from a later generation would rule in accordance with the opinion of Beit Shammai. In instances where a Sage apparently rules in accordance with the opinion of Beit Shammai, it must be explained that the ruling is not contrary to the opinion of Beit Hillel. It must be that the Sage has a different tradition with regard to the opinions of Beit Shammai and Beit Hillel, and his opinion corresponds to the opinion of Beit Hillel as well.

HALAKHA

One may not place spices into them – לֹא יִתֵּן לְתוֹכָן תְּבָלִין: It is prohibited to place spices into a primary vessel even after it was removed from the fire as long as one's hand spontaneously recoils from it due to its heat, as per the mishna. Other authorities are more stringent, stating that it is prohibited to do so even when the primary vessel is not so hot that one's hand spontaneously recoils from it (*Magen Avraham* based on the Jerusalem Talmud; *Shulḥan Arukh HaRav*). Adding spices to a secondary vessel is permitted, even if it is so hot that one's hand spontaneously recoils from it (*Mishna Berura*; Rambam *Sefer Zemanim, Hilkhot Shabbat* 22:6; *Shulḥan Arukh, Oraḥ Ḥayyim* 318:9).

Perek **III**
Daf **42** Amud **b**

אֲבָל נוֹתֵן הוּא לְתוֹךְ הַקְּעָרָה אוֹ לְתוֹךְ הַתַּמְחוּי. רַבִּי יְהוּדָה אוֹמֵר: לַכֹּל הוּא נוֹתֵן, חוּץ מִדָּבָר שֶׁיֵּשׁ בּוֹ חוֹמֶץ וְצִיר.

However, one may place the spices **into a bowl or into a tureen** [*tamḥui*],[B] which is a large bowl into which people pour the contents a stew pot or a pot. Bowls and tureens are both secondary vessels and food placed into them does not get cooked. **Rabbi Yehuda says: One may place** spices **into anything** on Shabbat **except for** a vessel that has in it **something containing vinegar** or **brine** of salted fish.

גמ׳ אִיבַּעְיָא לְהוּ: רַבִּי יְהוּדָה אַרֵישָׁא קָאֵי, וּלְקוּלָּא, אוֹ דִּילְמָא, אַסֵּיפָא קָאֵי וּלְחוּמְרָא?

GEMARA **A dilemma was raised before** the Sages: Is **Rabbi Yehuda referring to the first clause** of the mishna **and** being **lenient?** According to that possibility, the mishna prohibits placing spices into any boiling pot and Rabbi Yehuda holds that this only applies if there is fish brine or vinegar inside the pot. **Or perhaps he is referring to the latter clause of** the mishna **and** is being **stringent?** The Rabbis said that one is permitted to place spices into a bowl or a tureen, and Rabbi Yehuda came to add a stringency and say that if the bowl or tureen contains vinegar or brine, it is prohibited to place spices into it.

BACKGROUND

Tureen [*tamḥui*] – תַּמְחוּי: A *tamḥui* is a large, flat vessel used to hold food after it was removed from a pot before it was distributed into bowls. In every city, the charity collectors would collect money to be distributed to the poor for their needs, such as clothing, shelter, and the like. The money was also used to purchase food for the *tamḥui*, which was a large tureen full of food that was apportioned to the poor in need of a meal. Consequently, the place where charity was distributed was named for this vessel, a house of *tamḥui*.

תָּא שְׁמַע: דְּתַנְיָא, רַבִּי יְהוּדָה אוֹמֵר: לְכָל אִילְפָּסִין הוּא נוֹתֵן, לְכָל הַקְּדֵירוֹת רוֹתְחוֹת הוּא נוֹתֵן, חוּץ מִדָּבָר שֶׁיֵּשׁ בּוֹ חוֹמֶץ וְצִיר.

Come and hear a resolution to this dilemma from that which was taught explicitly in a *baraita* that Rabbi Yehuda says: Into all stew pots one may place spices on Shabbat; into all pots, even those that are boiling, one may place spices, except for one that contains vinegar or brine. The *baraita* clearly indicates that Rabbi Yehuda disputes the first clause of the mishna and is being lenient.

סָבַר רַב יוֹסֵף לְמֵימַר: מֶלַח הֲרֵי הוּא כִּתְבָלִין, דִּבִכְלִי רִאשׁוֹן – בָּשְׁלָה, וּבִכְלִי שֵׁנִי לֹא בָּשְׁלָה. אֲמַר לֵיהּ אַבָּיֵי, תָּנֵי רַבִּי חִיָּיא: מֶלַח אֵינָהּ כִּתְבָלִין, דְּבִכְלִי שֵׁנִי נַמִּי בָּשְׁלָה. וּפְלִיגָא דְּרַב נַחְמָן, דְּאָמַר רַב נַחְמָן: צְרִיכָא מִילְחָא בִּישּׁוּלָא כְּבִשְׂרָא דְּתוֹרָא.

Rav Yosef thought to say that salt is like a spice whose legal status is: In a primary vessel that was on the fire, salt gets cooked and therefore it is prohibited to place salt into it on Shabbat. And in a secondary vessel, into which the contents of a primary vessel were poured, salt does not get cooked. Abaye said to him: Didn't Rabbi Ḥiyya already teach that salt is not like a spice?[H] Certainly he meant that in a secondary vessel it also gets cooked. And the Gemara remarks that this conclusion disputes the statement of Rav Naḥman, as Rav Naḥman said: Salt requires cooking[B] for as long as the meat of an ox does, i.e., it requires extensive cooking.

וְאִיכָּא דְּאָמְרִי, סָבַר רַב יוֹסֵף לְמֵימַר: מֶלַח הֲרֵי הוּא כִּתְבָלִין, דִּבִכְלִי רִאשׁוֹן – בָּשְׁלָה, בִּכְלִי שֵׁנִי לֹא בָּשְׁלָה. אֲמַר לֵיהּ אַבָּיֵי, תָּנֵי רַבִּי חִיָּיא: מֶלַח אֵינָהּ כִּתְבָלִין, דְּבִכְלִי רִאשׁוֹן נַמִּי לֹא בָּשְׁלָה. וְהַיְינוּ דַּאֲמַר רַב נַחְמָן: צְרִיכָא מִילְחָא בִּישּׁוּלָא כְּבִישְׂרָא דְּתוֹרָא.

And some say a very different version of this: Rav Yosef thought to say that salt is like a spice, i.e., in a primary vessel it gets cooked, whereas in a secondary vessel it does not get cooked.[N] Abaye said to him: Didn't Rabbi Ḥiyya already teach that salt is not like a spice, meaning that in a primary vessel, it also does not get cooked? And that is precisely what Rav Naḥman said: Salt requires cooking for as long as the meat of an ox does.

מתני׳ אֵין נוֹתְנִין כְּלִי תַּחַת הַנֵּר לְקַבֵּל בּוֹ אֶת הַשֶּׁמֶן, וְאִם נְתָנוּהָ מִבְּעוֹד יוֹם – מוּתָּר. וְאֵין נֵיאוֹתִין מִמֶּנּוּ, לְפִי שֶׁאֵינוֹ מִן הַמּוּכָן.

MISHNA From a discussion of the *halakhot* of insulation and preparation for Shabbat followed by a brief tangent dealing with the prohibited labor of cooking on Shabbat, the mishna proceeds to briefly discuss prohibitions relating to set-aside [*muktze*] items in terms of Shabbat lamps. One may not place a vessel beneath the oil lamp,[H] the vessel containing the oil and the wick, on Shabbat in order to receive the oil that drips from the wick. And if one placed the vessel on Friday while it was still day, it is permitted.[N] However, in any case, one may not make use of the oil on Shabbat because it is not from the oil prepared from Shabbat eve for use on Shabbat. The oil in the lamp was already set aside and designated solely for the purpose of lighting the lamp.

גמ׳ אָמַר רַב חִסְדָּא: אַף עַל פִּי שֶׁאָמְרוּ אֵין נוֹתְנִין כְּלִי תַּחַת תַּרְנְגוֹלֶת לְקַבֵּל בֵּיצָתָהּ – אֲבָל כּוֹפֶה עָלֶיהָ כְּלִי שֶׁלֹּא תִּשָּׁבֵר. אָמַר רַבָּה: מַאי טַעְמָא דְּרַב חִסְדָּא – קָסָבַר: תַּרְנְגוֹלֶת עֲשׂוּיָה לְהַטִּיל בֵּיצָתָהּ בְּאַשְׁפָּה, וְאֵינָהּ עֲשׂוּיָה לְהַטִּיל בֵּיצָתָהּ בִּמְקוֹם מִדְרוֹן, וְהַצָּלָה מְצוּיָה – הִתִּירוּ, וְהַצָּלָה שֶׁאֵינָהּ מְצוּיָה – לֹא הִתִּירוּ.

GEMARA Rav Ḥisda said: Although the Sages said that one may not place a vessel beneath a hen preparing to lay an egg on Shabbat on an inclined surface, in order to receive its egg and prevent it from breaking when it falls; however, they permitted overturning a vessel onto an egg[H] on Shabbat so that it will not be trampled and break. Rabba said: What is Rav Ḥisda's reason? He holds that a hen is likely to lay its egg in a garbage dump and people or animals will oftentimes step on it, but it is not likely to lay its egg on an inclined surface where the egg could roll down and break. And in a common case of preservation, the Sages permitted overturning a vessel onto the egg that is located in the garbage dump to protect it from being broken. And in an uncommon case of preservation, i.e., placing a vessel beneath a hen to receive its egg so that it would not roll down an inclined surface, they did not permit[N] doing so.

HALAKHA

Salt is not like a spice – מֶלַח אֵינָהּ כִּתְבָלִין: Sprinkling salt into a primary vessel after it was taken off the fire is permitted, as per the second version in the Gemara, because *halakha* tends to be established according to the second version. Moreover, in that version Rav Naḥman and Abaye are in agreement. Other authorities state that putting salt even into a secondary vessel is prohibited (Rema). According to that approach, the first statement in the Gemara is accepted (*Taz*). It is proper to be stringent in this matter (Rema; Rambam *Sefer Zemanim, Hilkhot Shabbat* 22: 6; *Shulḥan Arukh, Oraḥ Ḥayyim* 318:9).

Vessel beneath the oil lamp – כלי תחת הנר: One may not place a vessel beneath an oil lamp on Shabbat to receive the oil. Placing a vessel beneath the oil lamp before Shabbat begins is permitted; however, the oil may not be used on Shabbat, as per the mishna (Rambam *Sefer Zemanim, Hilkhot Shabbat* 25:23; *Shulḥan Arukh, Oraḥ Ḥayyim* 265:3).

Overturning a vessel onto an egg – כְּפִיַּית כְּלִי עַל בֵּיצָה: Overturning a vessel onto an egg that was laid on Shabbat is permitted. This *halakha* applies to protecting other set-aside objects from damage, both on Shabbat and on Festivals, as per the opinion of Rav Ḥisda (Rambam *Sefer Zemanim, Hilkhot Shabbat* 25:23; *Shulḥan Arukh, Oraḥ Ḥayyim* 310:6, 322:1, 513:4).

BACKGROUND

Cooking salt – בִּישּׁוּל מֶלַח: It is difficult to articulate a precise and unequivocal definition of cooking salt, because the concept of cooking, in general, is not clear in the Talmud. In any case, water with even a very small quantity of salt requires a significantly higher temperature to reach boiling. Since salt boils only at a very high temperature or after cooking for a long time, its cooking is said to be like cooking the meat of an ox.

NOTES

In a primary vessel it gets cooked, whereas in a secondary vessel it does not get cooked – דִּבִכְלִי רִאשׁוֹן בָּשְׁלָה, וּבִכְלִי שֵׁנִי לֹא בָּשְׁלָה: In the Jerusalem Talmud, the Sages discussed whether the rationale for prohibiting placing food in a primary vessel is because in most instances it is so hot that a hand will spontaneously recoil from it or because a primary vessel is, at times, so hot that one could actually cook with it, which is not the case with a secondary vessel.

If one placed it while it was still day, it is permitted – נְתָנוּהָ מִבְּעוֹד יוֹם מוּתָּר: This language is problematic, as apparently permission is only granted after the fact. It should have said: However, one may place it while it is still day (*Tosafot*). Some commentaries explain that the language is precise: Even on Friday it is prohibited *ab initio* to place a vessel under a candle to receive the dripping oil, as people might assume that the bowl was placed there after Shabbat began (*Tziyyun LeNefesh Ḥayya*).

And in an uncommon case of preservation, they did not permit – וְהַצָּלָה שֶׁאֵינָהּ מְצוּיָה לֹא הִתִּירוּ: Some commentaries explain that the Sages did not permit an uncommon method of preservation, even for food suitable to be eaten on Shabbat (*Tosafot*, but not according to Rashi). The rationale is that permitting an uncommon method of preservation might lead a person in desperation to perform an action that is actually prohibited. That is the same reason that rescuing objects from a fire is prohibited. Nevertheless, the Sages permitted common methods of preservation because in standard situations, the necessary preparations will be in place before Shabbat and one will not come to desecrate the Shabbat (Rambam).

LANGUAGE

Barrels [*gulfei*] – **גּוּלְפֵי**: Some authorities believe that the origin of this word is from the Greek κάλαθος, *kalathos*, which means a basket, jug, or water vessel.

אֵיתִיבֵיהּ אַבַּיֵי: וְהַצָּלָה שֶׁאֵינָהּ מְצוּיָה – לֹא הִתִּירוּ?! וְהָתַנְיָא: נִשְׁבְּרָה לוֹ חָבִית שֶׁל טֶבֶל בְּרֹאשׁ גַּגּוֹ – מֵבִיא כְּלִי וּמַנִּיחַ תַּחְתֶּיהָ! בְּגוּלְפֵי חַדְתֵּי, דִּשְׁכִיחִי דְּפָקְעִי.

Abaye raised an objection to Rabba's opinion from a *baraita*: **And is it** so that **in an uncommon** case of **preservation they did not permit** taking steps to protect the object on Shabbat? **Wasn't it taught** in a *baraita*: One whose **barrel of untithed produce** [*tevel*], which may not be eaten until it is tithed, **broke on top of his roof** on Shabbat, **may bring a vessel and place it beneath** the barrel so that the untithed produce is not lost. Even though eating untithed produce is prohibited on Shabbat, they permitted carrying a vessel to preserve it even in the uncommon case of a barrel that breaks. Apparently, even in an uncommon case of preservation the Sages permit taking the necessary steps. Rabba answered: This too, is a common case of preservation because it is an instance of **new barrels** [*gulfei*],[L] **which commonly break.**

אֵיתִיבֵיהּ: נוֹתְנִין כְּלִי תַּחַת הַנֵּר לְקַבֵּל נִיצוֹצוֹת! נִיצוֹצוֹת נַמִי שְׁכִיחִי.

Abaye **raised** another **objection** to Rabba's opinion from the last mishna in this chapter: **One may place a vessel beneath the** oil **lamp** in order **to receive** burning **sparks** of oil that drip from the burning wick even though this is not common. Rabba answered: **Sparks are also common** and therefore, it is a common case of preservation.

Perek **III**
Daf **43** Amud **a**

HALAKHA

He negates a vessel's preparedness – **דְּקָא מְבַטֵּל כְּלִי מֵהֵיכָנוֹ**: It is prohibited to place a vessel that one is permitted to move, beneath an object whose use is prohibited on Shabbat. By doing so a person negates the vessel's availability, as per the opinion of Rav Yosef (Rambam *Sefer Zemanim, Hilkhot Shabbat* 25:23; *Shulḥan Arukh, Oraḥ Ḥayyim* 310:6).

Barrel of untithed wine – **חָבִית שֶׁל טֶבֶל**: It is permitted to place a vessel beneath a barrel of untithed produce that broke on Shabbat in order to preserve its contents because although tithing untithed produce on Shabbat is prohibited *ab initio*, it is effective after the fact (Rambam *Sefer Zemanim, Hilkhot Shabbat* 25:25).

NOTES

Barrel of untithed wine – **חָבִית שֶׁל טֶבֶל**: There is no Torah prohibition against separating tithes on Shabbat because it entails no prohibited labor. However, the Sages prohibited tithing because by doing so, one renders the untithed produce edible, which is somewhat comparable to repairing or completing a vessel, an act prohibited on Shabbat.

The permission to move untithed produce when necessary is not based upon the assumption that without that permission a person will violate the law and separate the tithes. If that were the case, that assumption would apply to all set-aside objects, and would undermine the very basis of the prohibition of set-aside (*Tosafot*). Rather, since by Torah law, separating *teruma* and tithes from untithed produce on Shabbat is permitted, the prohibition of set-aside is not applied as stringently (Rashba).

אֵיתִיבֵיהּ: כּוֹפִין קְעָרָה עַל הַנֵּר שֶׁלֹּא יֹאחַז בַּקּוֹרָה! בְּבָתֵּי גְּחִינֵי, דִּשְׁכִיחַ בְּהוּ דְּלֵיקָה.

Abaye **raised** another **objection to** Rabba's opinion from a *baraita*: **One may overturn a bowl on the** oil **lamp** so that the flame **will not set** fire **to the beam.** Apparently, the Sages permitted moving a vessel, even though this is not a common case of preservation. Rabba answered him: This is a case **of low-ceilinged houses in which fires are common.**

וְכֵן קוֹרָה שֶׁנִּשְׁבְּרָה סוֹמְכִין אוֹתָהּ בְּסַפְסָל וּבַאֲרוּכוֹת הַמִּטָּה! בִּכְשׁוּרֵי חַדְתֵּי, דַּעֲבִידִי דְּפָקְעִי.

And it is **likewise** difficult from a mishna: **The beam** of a roof **that broke, one may support it with a bench and with the lengths of a bed** frame so that it will not fall. Even though this is an uncommon case of preservation, it is permitted. Rabba answered: This is a case **of new beams, which commonly break.** This too is a common case of preservation.

נוֹתְנִין כְּלִי תַּחַת הַדֶּלֶף בַּשַּׁבָּת! בְּבָתֵּי חַדְתֵּי דִּשְׁכִיחִי דְּדָלְפִי.

And Abaye raised another objection from a mishna: **One may place a vessel beneath a leak** in the ceiling **on Shabbat.** Apparently, even an uncommon case of preservation is permitted. Rabba answered: This is a case of **new houses, which frequently leak.**

רַב יוֹסֵף אָמַר: הַיְינוּ טַעְמָא דְּרַב חִסְדָּא – מִשּׁוּם דְּקָא מְבַטֵּל כְּלִי מֵהֵיכָנוֹ.

Rav Yosef said: This is the reasoning of Rav Ḥisda, who allowed covering a hen's egg, but not placing a vessel underneath the hen, in order to receive the egg when it is laid: **Because** by receiving the egg in the vessel, **he negates a vessel's preparedness.**[H] Initially, the vessel was available for any use. Since it now contains an egg that may neither be used nor moved, the vessel too may no longer be carried. It is tantamount to breaking the vessel.

אֵיתִיבֵיהּ אַבַּיֵי: חָבִית שֶׁל טֶבֶל שֶׁנִּשְׁבְּרָה מֵבִיא כְּלִי אַחֵר וּמַנִּיחַ תַּחְתֶּיהָ! אָמַר לֵיהּ: טֶבֶל מוּכָן הוּא אֵצֶל שַׁבָּת, שֶׁאִם עָבַר וְתִקְּנוֹ – מְתוּקָּן.

Abaye raised an objection to Rav Ḥisda's opinion, just as he had to Rabba's opinion, from the *Tosefta*: One whose **barrel of untithed produce,**[HN] which may not be eaten until it is tithed, **broke** on Shabbat, **may bring another vessel and place it beneath** the barrel so that the untithed produce is not lost. Even though eating untithed produce is prohibited on Shabbat, they permitted carrying a vessel to preserve it even in the uncommon case of a barrel that breaks. Apparently, one is permitted to negate the vessel's preparedness. Rav Yosef **said to him:** This is not difficult. Fundamentally, **untithed produce is available for** use on **Shabbat. As, if one sins and prepares it** for use by tithing it on Shabbat, it is **prepared** and may be eaten and carried.

נוֹתְנִין כְּלִי תַּחַת הַנֵּר לְקַבֵּל נִיצוֹצוֹת! אָמַר רַב הוּנָא בְּרֵיהּ דְּרַב יְהוֹשֻׁעַ: נִיצוֹצוֹת אֵין בָּהֶן מַמָּשׁ.

Abaye raised another objection from a mishna: **One may place a vessel underneath the** oil **lamp** in order **to receive** the burning **sparks** of oil that drip from the wick. Once the vessel is filled with the drops of oil, it will no longer be available. **Rav Huna, son of Rav Yehoshua, said: Sparks have no substance.** They burn and dissolve as they fall into the bowl and do not accumulate. Therefore, the vessel may still be used.

וְכֵן קוֹרָה שֶׁנִּשְׁבְּרָה סוֹמְכִין אוֹתָהּ בְּסַפְסָל אוֹ בַּאֲרוּכּוֹת הַמִּטָּה! דְּרָפֵי, דְּאִי בָּעֵי – שָׁקֵיל לֵיהּ.

And he **also** raised another objection from a mishna: **A beam that broke,**[H] **one may support it with a bench and with the lengths of a bed** frame so that it will not fall. By doing so, he negates the preparedness of the bench or bed frame. He answered: This is a case **in which** the bench **is loosely** supporting the beam and not supporting its entire weight. **If one wants** to do so, **he can take** the bench. Therefore, the preparedness of the bench is not negated.

נוֹתְנִין כְּלִי תַּחַת הַדֶּלֶף בַּשַּׁבָּת! בְּדֶלֶף הָרָאוּי.

And he also raised another objection from a mishna: **One may place a vessel beneath a leak**[H] that is dripping from the ceiling **on Shabbat.** The dripping water has no use and is set-aside; therefore, the water negates the vessel's preparedness. He answered him: This is a case **of a leak that is suitable** for drinking. Since it has a use, one is permitted to carry the water that is in the vessel. Consequently, he does not negate the vessel's preparedness by placing it beneath the leak.

כּוֹפִין אֶת הַסַּל לִפְנֵי הָאֶפְרוֹחִין שֶׁיַּעֲלוּ וְיֵרְדוּ! קָסָבַר: מוּתָּר לְטַלְטְלוֹ. וְהָתַנְיָא: אָסוּר לְטַלְטְלוֹ! בְּעוֹדָן עָלָיו. וְהָתַנְיָא: אַף עַל פִּי שֶׁאֵין עוֹדָן עָלָיו אָסוּר! אָמַר רַבִּי אַבָּהוּ: בְּעוֹדָן עָלָיו כׇּל בֵּין הַשְּׁמָשׁוֹת, מִיגּוֹ דְּאִיתְּקַצַּאי לְבֵין הַשְּׁמָשׁוֹת – אִיתְּקַצַּאי לְכוּלֵּי יוֹמָא.

And he also raised another objection from a *Tosefta*: **One may overturn a basket in front of chicks**[H] so that **they can climb on and climb off** of it. By doing so, he negates the vessel's preparedness due to the chicks, as moving them is prohibited on Shabbat. The Gemara answers: Rav Yosef **holds** that it **is permitted to move** the basket on Shabbat. The Gemara asks: **Wasn't it taught** in a *baraita* that **it is prohibited to move** the basket? The Gemara replies: This prohibition was stated **when they are still on it;** however, once the chicks climbed off the basket, it may be carried immediately. The Gemara asks: **Wasn't it taught** in a *baraita* that **even though they are no longer on it, it is prohibited** to move the basket? Consequently, the vessel's preparedness is negated. **Rabbi Abbahu said:** That *baraita* is referring to the unique case **where** the chicks **remained on top of** the basket **for the entire twilight** period on Shabbat eve. This is in accordance with the principle: **Since it was set aside** from use during **twilight** of Shabbat eve, **it was set aside for the entire day** of Shabbat. The status of every vessel, i.e., whether or not it may be used on Shabbat, is determined at twilight.

אָמַר רַבִּי יִצְחָק: כְּשֵׁם שֶׁאֵין נוֹתְנִין כְּלִי תַּחַת תַּרְנְגוֹלֶת לְקַבֵּל בֵּיצָתָהּ – כָּךְ אֵין כּוֹפִין עָלֶיהָ כְּלִי בִּשְׁבִיל שֶׁלֹּא תִּשָּׁבֵר. קָסָבַר: אֵין כְּלִי נִיטָּל אֶלָּא לְדָבָר הַנִּיטָּל בַּשַּׁבָּת. מֵיתִיבֵי כׇּל הָנֵי תְּיוּבְתָּא, וְשָׁנֵי: בְּצָרִיךְ לִמְקוֹמוֹ.

With regard to the basic *halakha* of a hen that lays an egg on Shabbat, **Rabbi Yitzhak said:**[N] **Just as one may not place a vessel beneath a hen** on Shabbat in order **to receive its egg, so too, one may not overturn a vessel onto** the egg **so that it will not break.** The Gemara explains that **he holds: A vessel may only be carried** on Shabbat **for the sake of an object that may be carried on Shabbat.** Since the egg may not be carried on Shabbat, it is prohibited to carry a vessel for its sake. The Gemara **raises all of these objections** that were raised to Rav Hisda's opinion, which permitted doing so. **And he answered:** All of those *halakhot* are referring to cases **where** one needs to move the vessel that he is using for the set-aside item, because he **requires its location.** This is in accordance with the principle that once it is permitted, for whatever reason, to move any vessel, one may place it anywhere he chooses.

תָּא שְׁמַע: אַחַת בֵּיצָה שֶׁנּוֹלְדָה בַּשַּׁבָּת, וְאַחַת בֵּיצָה שֶׁנּוֹלְדָה בְּיוֹם טוֹב – אֵין מְטַלְטְלִין לֹא לְכַסּוֹת בָּהּ אֶת הַכְּלִי, וְלִסְמוֹךְ בָּהּ כַּרְעֵי הַמִּטָּה, אֲבָל כּוֹפֶה עָלֶיהָ כְּלִי בִּשְׁבִיל שֶׁלֹּא תִּשָּׁבֵר! הָכָא נַמִי – בְּצָרִיךְ לִמְקוֹמוֹ.

To clarify whether or not the opinion of Rabbi Yitzhak is valid, **come** and **hear** what was taught in a *baraita*: With regard to **both an egg that was laid on Shabbat and an egg that was laid on a Festival, one may neither move it to cover**[N] **a vessel with it, nor to support the legs of a bed**[B] **with it. However, one may cover it with a vessel so that it does not break.** This is contrary to Rabbi Yitzhak's opinion. **Here too,** it is referring **to** a vessel that one seeks to move because he **requires its location.** Since he was permitted to move it from its place, he is also permitted to cover an egg with it.

תָּא שְׁמַע: פּוֹרְסִין מַחְצָלוֹת עַל גַּבֵּי אֲבָנִים בַּשַּׁבָּת! בַּאֲבָנִים מְקוּרְזָלוֹת, דַּחֲזַיִין לְבֵית הַכִּסֵּא.

Come and **hear** an additional proof from that which we learned: **One may spread mats on top of stones on Shabbat.** Apparently, it is permissible to move a vessel for the sake of something that may not be moved on Shabbat. The Gemara responds: This is a case **of rounded rocks that are suitable to** be used in **the bathroom.** Therefore, it is permitted to carry them on Shabbat.

HALAKHA

A beam that broke – קוֹרָה שֶׁנִּשְׁבְּרָה: It is permitted to support a ceiling beam that broke on Shabbat with the long side of a bed frame, provided that it is loosely supported and that the beam is not thereby raised, but is merely prevented from falling any further. This does not negate the bed frame's preparedness. Raising the beam, is prohibited as it constitutes the prohibited labor of building (Rambam *Sefer Zemanim, Hilkhot Shabbat* 25:25; *Shulḥan Arukh, Oraḥ Ḥayyim* 313:7).

A vessel underneath a leak – כְּלִי תַּחַת הַדֶּלֶף: It is permitted to place a vessel beneath a leak on Shabbat, specifically when the water is at least minimally suitable for use, for example, for bathing. If it is unsuitable for use, it is prohibited (Rambam *Sefer Zemanim, Hilkhot Shabbat* 25:24; *Shulḥan Arukh, Oraḥ Ḥayyim* 338:8, 521:3).

One may overturn a basket in front of chicks – כּוֹפִין אֶת הַסַּל לִפְנֵי הָאֶפְרוֹחִין: One may overturn a basket in front on chicks so that they may climb into it. Moving the basket while they are inside it is prohibited. If the chicks were atop the basket during twilight when Shabbat began, it is prohibited to move it, because an object that is set aside at twilight remains set aside for the entire Shabbat (*Magen Avraham*; Rambam *Sefer Zemanim, Hilkhot Shabbat* 25:25; *Shulḥan Arukh, Oraḥ Ḥayyim* 308:39).

NOTES

Rabbi Yitzḥak said – אָמַר רַבִּי יִצְחָק: Many commentaries agree that Rabbi Yitzḥak also holds that negating a vessel's preparedness is prohibited. However, he adds an additional prohibition: A person may not move a vessel for the sake of some other object that may not be moved on Shabbat (Rabbeinu Yona; Rashba; Ritva).

Both an egg…one may neither move it to cover, etc. – אַחַת בֵּיצָה...אֵין מְטַלְטְלִין לֹא לְכַסּוֹת וכו׳: Why does the Gemara cite the *halakha* of the egg to challenge Rabbi Yitzḥak's opinion? He already rebuffed similar challenges by saying that it is referring to a case where the person requires the object's location; there is no point in raising it again. Based on the style of the *baraita* concerning the egg, one may overturn a vessel onto an egg for the sake of the egg, which emphasizes the challenge to Rabbi Yitzḥak (Rashba).

Other commentaries explain that the case here is completely different. It is referring to a case where the person seeks to sit in the place where the egg is located. Since one cannot sit on the egg itself, he brings a vessel to protect the egg and sits upon the vessel (Rabbeinu Ḥananel).

BACKGROUND

An egg and the legs of a bed – בֵּיצָה וְכַרְעֵי הַמִּטָּה: How is it possible to support the leg of a bed with an egg? A variety of answers were suggested. According to Rashi, one places the egg underneath the leg of the bed when the egg is standing vertically. An egg or any similarly shaped object is very strong and difficult to break in that position. Other commentaries explain that in talmudic times the legs of the beds were positioned atop small, overturned, cup-like vessels. The egg was placed inside the overturned cup. In that way, it was positioned beneath the legs of the bed. However, the *Me'iri* explains that *mitta* in this context refers to a bowl-like vessel, placed on the table, that could be supported by an egg.

Other authorities explain that it is indeed referring to an actual bed. The egg was not used to support the bed. Rather, the egg was placed alongside the leg of the bed as a talisman for fertility.

HALAKHA

One may spread a mat over a beehive – פּוֹרְסִין מַחֲצֶלֶת עַל גַּבֵּי כַּוֶּורֶת דְּבוֹרִים: Covering a beehive with a mat to protect it from the sun or rain is permitted, provided that one does not intend to trap the bees inside the hive. In addition, one is required to leave a small opening so that the bees will not be trapped inside with no means of escape. In that case, trapping the bees would be an inevitable consequence of his action and placing the mat would be prohibited (Rambam *Sefer Zemanim, Hilkhot Shabbat* 25:25; *Shulḥan Arukh, Oraḥ Ḥayyim* 316:4).

תָּא שְׁמַע: פּוֹרְסִין מַחְצָלוֹת עַל גַּבֵּי לְבֵנִים בְּשַׁבָּת! דְּאִישְׁתַּיּוּר מִבִּנְיָנָא, דַּחֲזְיָין לְמִיזְגָּא עֲלַיְיהוּ.

Come and **hear** another proof from that which we learned: **One may spread mats on top of bricks on Shabbat.** Bricks may not be used on Shabbat. Nevertheless, one is permitted to carry mats for the sake of bricks that are prohibited for use on Shabbat. The Gemara replies: This is referring to a case of bricks that are not set aside for construction, but **are left over from a** completed **building and are suitable** for people **to lean on them.** Consequently, they are like other household vessels, and moving them and moving mats to protect them is permitted.

תָּא שְׁמַע: פּוֹרְסִין מַחֲצֶלֶת עַל גַּבֵּי כַּוֶּורֶת דְּבוֹרִים בְּשַׁבָּת, בַּחַמָּה מִפְּנֵי הַחַמָּה, וּבַגְּשָׁמִים מִפְּנֵי הַגְּשָׁמִים, וּבִלְבַד שֶׁלֹּא יִתְכַּוֵּין לָצוּד! הָכָא בְּמַאי עָסְקִינַן – דְּאִיכָּא דְּבַשׁ. אָמַר לֵיהּ רַב עוּקְבָא מִמֵּישָׁן לְרַב אַשִׁי: תֵּינַח בִּימוֹת הַחַמָּה –

Come and **hear** another proof for this from that which we learned: **One may spread a mat over a beehive**[H] **on Shabbat in the sun due to** the need to protect it **from the sun, and in the rain due to** the need to protect it **from the rain, as long as he does not intend to trap** the bees by covering them. In any event, apparently it is permitted to move a mat for the sake of the beehive even though the beehive itself may not be moved on Shabbat. The Gemara rejects this: **With what are we dealing here?** With a case **where there is honey** in the beehive. He is permitted to cover it for the sake of the honey. **Rav Ukva from Meishan said to Rav Ashi: Granted,** you could say this **in the summer,**

Perek **III**
Daf **43** Amud **b**

BACKGROUND

Honeycombs in a beehive – חַלּוֹת בַּכַּוֶּורֶת: In general, bees do not leave their hives during the rainy season, due to the rain and the lack of blossoming plants. Consequently, honeycombs are removed before the rainy season, at the end of the month of Tishrei. However, the bees require a few honeycombs to sustain themselves through the winter. The number of honeycombs necessary varies depending on the size of the beehive. During the talmudic period, beehives were very small and typically, two honeycombs were sufficient to feed the bees during the rainy season. In springtime, during the month of Nisan, the bees emerge to collect pollen from flowers and then there is honey in the beehives again.

NOTES

Let him distinguish and teach with regard to that same *halakha* itself – לִפְלוֹג וְלִתְנֵי בְּדִידַהּ: The mishna and even the *baraita* are assumed to be as succinct and precise as possible in their formulation. Therefore, whenever the possibility of making a more subtle distinction between cases that are more similar arises, the question is, why did the mishna or *baraita* prefer a more obvious distinction between clearly disparate cases, when the more subtle distinction could have taught a novel lesson of greater value?

דְּאִיכָּא דְּבַשׁ, בִּימוֹת הַגְּשָׁמִים דְּלֵיכָּא דְּבַשׁ – מַאי אִיכָּא לְמֵימַר? לֹא נִצְרְכָא אֶלָּא לְאוֹתָן שְׁתֵּי חַלּוֹת. וְהָא מוּקְצוֹת נִינְהוּ! דְּחָשֵׁיב עֲלַיְיהוּ. הָא לָא חָשֵׁיב עֲלַיְיהוּ מַאי – אָסוּר?

as there is honey in the beehive during the summer. However, **during the rainy season in which there is not honey** in the beehive, **what can be said** according to Rabbi Yitzḥak to explain why it is permitted to cover the beehive at that time? The Gemara answers: This *halakha* **is only applicable** in order to permit covering the beehive for **those two honeycombs**[B] that remain in the hive even during the rainy season so that the bees can feed off of them. The Gemara asks: **Aren't** these honeycombs **set aside** for the bees alone? The Gemara responds: This is a case **where one thought of them** before Shabbat and, in his mind, prepared them to be eaten. The Gemara asks: By inference, if **one did not think about them, what** would be the ruling? It would be **prohibited** to cover the beehive.

אִי הָכִי, הָא דְּתָנֵי: ״וּבִלְבַד שֶׁלֹּא יִתְכַּוֵּין לָצוּד״ לִפְלוֹג וְלִתְנֵי בְּדִידַהּ, בַּמֶּה דְּבָרִים אֲמוּרִים – כְּשֶׁחִישֵּׁב עֲלֵיהֶן, אֲבָל לֹא חִישֵּׁב עֲלֵיהֶן – אָסוּר! הָא קָמַשְׁמַע לַן: אַף עַל פִּי שֶׁחִישֵּׁב עֲלֵיהֶן – וּבִלְבַד שֶׁלֹּא יִתְכַּוֵּין לָצוּד.

If so, this *tanna* **who taught** in that same *baraita*: **As long as he does not intend to trap** the bees, **let him distinguish and teach with regard to** that same *halakha* **itself:**[N] **In what case are these matters stated,** that one is permitted to cover the hive? It is in a case **where he thought of them** before Shabbat. **However, if he did not think of them,** it is **prohibited.** The Gemara answers: **This teaches us** a novel understanding. **Even though he thought of them** before Shabbat, it is only permitted **as long as he did not intend to trap** them.

מַנִּי? אִי רַבִּי שִׁמְעוֹן – לֵית לֵיהּ מוּקְצֶה, אִי רַבִּי יְהוּדָה – כִּי לֹא מִתְכַּוֵּין מַאי הָוֵי? הָא דָּבָר שֶׁאֵין מִתְכַּוֵּין אָסוּר! לְעוֹלָם רַבִּי יְהוּדָה, מַאי ״וּבִלְבַד שֶׁלֹּא יִתְכַּוֵּין לָצוּד״ – שֶׁלֹּא יַעֲשֶׂנָּה כִּמְצוּדָה, דְּלִישְׁבּוֹק לְהוּ רַוְוחָא כִּי הֵיכִי דְּלָא לִיתְצְדוּ מִמֵּילָא.

With regard to the matter itself, the Gemara asks: In accordance with **whose** opinion **is this** *baraita*? **If** it is in accordance with the opinion of **Rabbi Shimon, he does not hold** that there is a prohibition of **set-aside.** Consequently, there is no distinction between the different beehives. **If** it is in accordance with the opinion of **Rabbi Yehuda, when** he **does not have intention** to trap the bees, **what** of it? **Doesn't** Rabbi Yehuda hold that even an **unintentional act is prohibited?** The Gemara replies: **Actually,** this *baraita* is in accordance with the opinion of **Rabbi Yehuda. What** does: **And as long as one does not intend to trap** the bees, mean? It means **that one should not make** the mat **like a trap.** He must **leave space so that** the bees **will not get trapped on their own.**

רַב אַשִׁי אָמַר: מִי קָתָנֵי ׳בִּימוֹת הַחַמָּה׳ וּ׳בִימוֹת הַגְּשָׁמִים׳? ׳בַּחַמָּה מִפְּנֵי הַחַמָּה וּבַגְּשָׁמִים מִפְּנֵי הַגְּשָׁמִים׳ קָתָנֵי – בְּיוֹמֵי נִיסָן וּבְיוֹמֵי תִשְׁרֵי, דְּאִיכָּא חַמָּה (וְאִיכָּא צִינָּה) וְאִיכָּא גְּשָׁמִים, וְאִיכָּא דְּבַשׁ.

Rav Ashi said that it can be resolved differently: **Did** the *baraita* **teach: In the summer and in the rainy season?** Actually, **it taught: In the sun due to the sun and in the rain due to the rain.** That can be interpreted as follows: **In the days of Nisan and in the days of Tishrei,** as then **there is sun** shining **and there is** also **cold** weather; **and there is rain and there is honey** in the beehives.

אָמַר לְהוּ רַב שֵׁשֶׁת: פּוּקוּ וְאִמְרוּ לֵיהּ לְרַבִּי יִצְחָק: כְּבָר תַּרְגְּמָא רַב הוּנָא לִשְׁמַעְתֵּיךְ בְּבָבֶל. דְּאָמַר רַב הוּנָא: עוֹשִׂין מְחִיצָה לַמֵּת בִּשְׁבִיל חַי, וְאֵין עוֹשִׂין מְחִיצָה לַמֵּת בִּשְׁבִיל מֵת.

Rav Sheshet said to the Sages: **Go out and tell Rabbi Yitzḥak** in Eretz Yisrael: **Rav Huna already explained your *halakha*[N] in Babylonia.** There is nothing novel in the principle that you established that a vessel may only be moved for the sake of something that may be moved, **as Rav Huna said: One may make a partition for the dead** for the benefit of **a living person, and one may not make a partition for the dead for** the benefit of the **dead person.** It is prohibited to move objects for the sake of a corpse because it is prohibited to move the corpse itself on Shabbat.

מַאי הִיא? דְּאָמַר רַב שְׁמוּאֵל בַּר יְהוּדָה, וְכֵן תָּנָא שֵׁילָא מָרִי: מֵת הַמּוּטָּל בַּחַמָּה בָּאִים שְׁנֵי בְּנֵי אָדָם וְיוֹשְׁבִין בְּצִדּוֹ, חַם לָהֶם מִלְּמַטָּה – זֶה מֵבִיא מִטָּה וְיוֹשֵׁב עָלֶיהָ, וְזֶה מֵבִיא מִטָּה וְיוֹשֵׁב עָלֶיהָ. חַם לָהֶם מִלְּמַעְלָה – מְבִיאִים מַחֲצֶלֶת וּפוֹרְסִין עֲלֵיהֶן. זֶה זוֹקֵף מִטָּתוֹ וְנִשְׁמָט וְהוֹלֵךְ לוֹ, וְזֶה זוֹקֵף מִטָּתוֹ וְנִשְׁמָט וְהוֹלֵךְ לוֹ, וְנִמְצֵאת מְחִיצָה עֲשׂוּיָה מֵאֵלֶיהָ.

The Gemara asks: **What is** the practical application of this *halakha*? As **Rav Shmuel bar Yehuda said, and likewise** the Sage, **Sheila Mari taught** in a *baraita*: **A corpse that is laid out in the sun**[H] and there is concern that it will putrefy and smell, what can be done? **Two people come and sit beside it.** After a while, when **they** feel **hot from beneath** them, **this** one **brings a bed and sits on it and that** one **brings a bed and sits on it** on either side of the corpse, as they are permitted to carry the beds for their own use. When **they** feel **hot from above** them, **they bring a mat and spread it over their** heads. Then, **this** one **stands his bed up** so the mat will remain resting atop it **and slips away and leaves, and that** one **stands his bed up and slips away and leaves, and a partition is then created** over the corpse as if **on its own** without erecting it directly for the sake of the corpse. Apparently, the Sages did not permit carrying a mat to cover a corpse for the sake of the corpse. They only permitted doing so in an indirect manner for the benefit of the living.

אִיתְּמַר, מֵת הַמּוּטָּל בַּחַמָּה, רַב יְהוּדָה אָמַר שְׁמוּאֵל: הוֹפְכוֹ מִמִּטָּה לְמִטָּה. רַב חֲנִינָא בַּר שְׁלַמְיָא מִשְּׁמֵיהּ דְּרַב אָמַר: מַנִּיחַ עָלָיו כִּכָּר אוֹ תִּינוֹק וּמְטַלְטְלוֹ. הֵיכָא דְּאִיכָּא כִּכָּר אוֹ תִּינוֹק – כּוּלֵּי עָלְמָא לָא פְּלִיגִי דְּשָׁרֵי, כִּי פְּלִיגִי – דְּלֵית לֵיהּ. מָר סָבַר: טִלְטוּל מִן הַצַּד – שְׁמֵיהּ טִלְטוּל, וּמָר סָבַר: לָא שְׁמֵיהּ טִלְטוּל.

Incidental to the mention of *halakhot* related to a corpse on Shabbat, the Gemara cites an amoraic dispute in which **it was stated: A corpse that was laid out in the sun, Rav Yehuda said** that **Shmuel said: One turns it over from bed to bed** until it reaches the shade. **Rav Hanina bar Shelamiyya said in the name of** Rav: **One places a loaf** of bread **or an infant on** the corpse **and moves it.** The corpse becomes a base for an object that one is permitted to move on Shabbat and, consequently, one may move the corpse due to the permitted object. The Gemara adds: In a case **where there is a loaf or an infant, everyone agrees that it is permitted** to use that method to move the corpse. **Where they argue** is in a case **where he does not have** a loaf or an infant. **One Sage,** Rav, **holds:** Moving an object **in an atypical manner**[N] **is considered** a bona fide act of **moving.** Therefore, one may not move the corpse by passing it from bed to bed. **And the other Sage,** Shmuel, **holds** that moving an object in an atypical manner **is not considered moving.** Therefore, it is permitted to move a corpse by passing it from bed to bed.

לֵימָא כְּתַנָּאֵי: אֵין מַצִּילִין אֶת הַמֵּת מִפְּנֵי הַדְּלֵיקָה. אָמַר רַבִּי יְהוּדָה בֶּן לָקִישׁ: שָׁמַעְתִּי שֶׁמַּצִּילִין אֶת הַמֵּת מִפְּנֵי הַדְּלֵיקָה. הֵיכִי דָמֵי? אִי דְּאִיכָּא כִּכָּר אוֹ תִּינוֹק – מַאי טַעְמָא דְּתַנָּא קַמָּא? אִי דְּלֵיכָּא – מַאי טַעְמָא דְּרַבִּי יְהוּדָה בֶּן לָקִישׁ? אֶלָּא לָאו בְּטִלְטוּל מִן הַצַּד פְּלִיגִי: דְּמָר סָבַר: טִלְטוּל מִן הַצַּד – שְׁמֵיהּ טִלְטוּל. וּמָר סָבַר לָא שְׁמֵיהּ טִלְטוּל. לָא, דְּכוּלֵּי עָלְמָא – טִלְטוּל מִן הַצַּד שְׁמֵיהּ טִלְטוּל, וְהַיְינוּ טַעְמָא דְּרַבִּי יְהוּדָה בֶּן לָקִישׁ: דְּמִתּוֹךְ שֶׁאָדָם בָּהוּל עַל מֵתוֹ,

With regard to this dispute between Rav and Shmuel, the Gemara remarks: **Let us say** that this dispute is **parallel** to a dispute between *tanna'im* in the *Tosefta*. The Rabbis said: **One may not rescue a corpse from a fire** on Shabbat.[H] **Rabbi Yehuda ben Lakish said: I heard that one may rescue a corpse from a fire.** The Gemara seeks to clarify the matter: **What are the circumstances? If there is a loaf or an infant** available, **what is the rationale** for the opinion **of the first *tanna*,** who prohibited rescuing the corpse from the fire? **If there is not** a loaf or an infant, **what is the reason** of **Rabbi Yehuda ben Lakish** who permits rescuing the corpse from the fire? **Rather, is it not that they disagree over moving** an object **in an atypical manner? As this Sage,** the first *tanna*, **holds** that **moving** an object **in an atypical manner is considered moving.** Therefore, it is prohibited to rescue the corpse in that manner. **And this Sage,** Rabbi Yehuda ben Lakish, **holds** that **moving** an object **in an atypical manner is not considered moving.** Therefore, it is permitted to rescue the corpse in this manner. The amoraic dispute deals with an issue already disputed by the *tanna'im*. The Gemara rejects this: **No, everyone,** both *tanna'im*, **agrees that moving** an object **in an atypical manner is considered moving. Rather, this is the rationale** for the opinion **of Rabbi Yehuda ben Lakish: Since a person is agitated about his deceased** relative and is concerned about maintaining the dignity of the dead,

NOTES

Rav Huna already explained your *halakha* – תַּרְגְּמָא רַב הוּנָא לִשְׁמַעְתֵּיךְ: For reasons related to a possible contradiction between Rav Huna's statement here and his statements elsewhere, some commentaries explain that Rav Sheshet meant to say that Rav Huna agrees with only part of Rav Yitzḥak's ruling. Other commentaries explain that the phrase: Go out and tell Rav Yitzḥak, means that although there was a Sage in Babylonia who agreed, the *halakha* is still not in accordance with his ruling (*Me'iri*).

Moving an object in an atypical manner – טִלְטוּל מִן הַצַּד: From the discussion here it appears that moving an object in an atypical manner means moving it in any manner that deviates from the norm, not necessarily limited to moving it by means of another object, e.g., a bed (Ritva).

HALAKHA

A corpse that is laid out in the sun – מֵת הַמּוּטָּל בַּחַמָּה: If a corpse was out in the sun on Shabbat and there was no place to move it or, for some reason, they did not want to move it, two people should sit on either side of the corpse. When the ground feels hot, each brings a bed upon which to sit. When the sun is hot, each spreads a mat over the bed to shield him from the sun. Then, each stands the bed on its side and leaves. The two beds and the two mats together form an impromptu structure to protect the corpse from the sun (Rambam *Sefer Zemanim, Hilkhot Shabbat* 25:6, 26:23; *Shulḥan Arukh, Oraḥ Ḥayyim* 311:6).

A corpse in a fire – מֵת בִּמְקוֹם דְּלֵיקָה: When there is a corpse in a place that caught fire on Shabbat, one places a loaf of bread or an infant on top of the dead body or beside it on the bed and moves it out of the house. If there is no loaf of bread or infant available, but there are two beds, then one moves the corpse from one bed to the other until it is outside the house. If those options are unavailable, one may lift the corpse and carry it outside (Rambam *Sefer Zemanim, Hilkhot Shabbat* 26:21; *Shulḥan Arukh, Oraḥ Ḥayyim* 311:1).

אי לא שרית ליה – אתי לכבויי. אמר רבי יהודה בן שילא אמר רב אסי אמר רבי יוחנן: הלכה כרבי יהודה בן לקיש במת.

if you do not permit him to move the corpse in an atypical manner, **he will come to extinguish**[N] the fire. The Sages permitted performing an act prohibited by rabbinic law so that one will not come to transgress a Torah prohibition. **Rabbi Yehuda ben Sheila said** that **Rav Asi said** that **Rabbi Yoḥanan said: The** ***halakha*** **is in accordance with** the opinion of **Rabbi Yehuda ben Lakish with regard to** the issue of rescuing **a corpse** from a fire.

״אין ניאותין הימנו לפי שאינו מן המוכן״. תנו רבנן: מותר השמן שבנר ושבקערה – אסור, ורבי שמעון מתיר.

We learned in the mishna that **one may not make use of** the oil that drips from the candle on Shabbat **because it is not among** the oil **prepared** from Shabbat eve for use on Shabbat. With regard to this same issue, **the Sages taught** in a *baraita*: **The remaining oil that is in the lamp**[H] **or in a bowl** in which a wick was burning **is prohibited** for use on Shabbat. However, **Rabbi Shimon permits** using the remaining oil as, according to his opinion, there is virtually nothing prohibited due to the prohibition of set-aside.

מתני׳ מטלטלין נר חדש אבל לא ישן. רבי שמעון אומר: כל הנרות מטלטלין, חוץ מן הנר הדולק בשבת.

MISHNA The dispute in this mishna seems to be a local one; however, it is the key to several *halakhot* in the area of the prohibition of set-aside [*muktze*]. **One may move a new** oil **lamp** on Shabbat **but not** an **old** one that was already used. A lamp that was used is covered with soot and unsuitable for use. It is therefore considered set aside from use due to its disgusting nature. **Rabbi Shimon says: All** oil **lamps may be moved** on Shabbat **except for an** oil **lamp** that is **burning on Shabbat,** due to the concern that it might be extinguished.

גמ׳ תנו רבנן: מטלטלין נר חדש אבל לא ישן, דברי רבי יהודה. רבי מאיר אומר: כל הנרות מטלטלין, חוץ מן הנר שהדליקו בו בשבת. רבי שמעון אומר: חוץ מן הנר הדולק בשבת. כבתה – מותר לטלטלה, אבל כוס וקערה ועששית לא יזיזם ממקומם. ורבי אליעזר ברבי שמעון אומר: מסתפק מן הנר הכבה, ומן השמן המטפטף, ואפילו בשעה שהנר דולק.

GEMARA **The Sages taught** the dispute in the mishna in greater detail in a *Tosefta*: **One may move a new** oil **lamp** on Shabbat **but not an old one;** this is **the statement of Rabbi Yehuda. Rabbi Meir says: All** oil **lamps may be moved** on Shabbat **except for an** oil **lamp that they kindled on** that **Shabbat.**[H] Rabbi Meir does not hold that one must distance himself from objects that are disgusting. However, since the lamp was burning on Shabbat, it may not be moved, as it is an object set aside due to prohibition for the entire Shabbat. **Rabbi Shimon says:** All lamps may be moved **except for an** oil **lamp** that is **burning on Shabbat.** If the flame **was extinguished, one is permitted to move it. However, a cup and a bowl and a lantern** that are full of oil with a wick lit in them, **one may not move them from their place** even after the flame is extinguished. **And Rabbi Eliezer, son of Rabbi Shimon, says:**[N] **One may supply** himself with oil **from an extinguished candle and from the oil that drips** from the lamp, **and even while the lamp is burning.**

אמר אביי: רבי אליעזר ברבי שמעון סבר לה כאבוה בחדא, ופליג עליה בחדא. סבר לה כאבוה בחדא – דלית ליה מוקצה, ופליג עליה בחדא, דאילו אבוה סבר: כבה – אין, לא כבה – לא, ואיהו סבר: אף על גב דלא כבה.

Abaye said: Rabbi Eliezer, son of Rabbi Shimon, holds in accordance with the opinion of **his father in one** matter **and disagrees with him in one** matter. **He holds in accordance with** the opinion of **his father in one** matter, **as he is not** of the opinion that moving **set-aside** objects is prohibited. **And he disagrees with him in one** matter; **as his father holds** that **if** the flame **was extinguished, yes,** he may move it, if **it was not extinguished, no,** he may not move it. **And** Rabbi Eliezer **holds: Even though** the flame **was not extinguished,** it is permitted to carry the lamp and to use the oil that drips from it. In his opinion, doing so in no way extinguishes the flame and it is in no way comparable to extinguishing the flame.

NOTES

He will come to extinguish – אתי לכבויי: This reasoning is only stated with regard to rescuing a corpse from a fire and not with regard to salvaging other items from a fire. On the contrary, in the case of a fire where there is no corpse, several otherwise permitted acts were prohibited because a person in panic over his belongings might extinguish the fire. However, when a corpse is present, it is paramount in the mourner's mind. Furthermore, there is the issue of human dignity in terms of both the living and the dead. The assumption is that a person will transgress rabbinic prohibitions to preserve human dignity. In general, the Sages did not apply their decrees to situations which conflict with human dignity.

The opinion of Rabbi Eliezer, son of Rabbi Shimon – שיטת רבי אליעזר ברבי שמעון: In several places in the Talmud, apparently, Rabbi Shimon himself agrees to a significant number of the *halakhot* of set-aside with regard to objects whose use is prohibited on Shabbat. On the other hand, his son, Rabbi Eliezer, adopts his father's fundamental ruling without exception both in terms of rejecting the halakhic category of set-aside altogether, as well as in terms of the need for intent in violating the prohibited labor of extinguishing. The connection between these ideas is: Since Rabbi Eliezer, son of Rabbi Shimon, permits making use of oil from an oil lamp, all the more so does he permit moving the oil lamp, even while it is burning (*Penei Yehoshua*).

HALAKHA

The remaining oil that is in the lamp – מותר השמן שבנר: It is prohibited to use the oil remaining in an oil lamp on Shabbat because it was set aside from use when Shabbat began (*Magen Avraham* according to the Ran; Rambam *Sefer Zemanim*, *Hilkhot Shabbat* 5:12, 26:14; *Shulḥan Arukh*, *Oraḥ Ḥayyim* 279:1, 265:3).

All oil lamps may be moved on Shabbat except for an oil lamp that they lit on that Shabbat – כל הנרות מטלטלין, חוץ מן הנר שהדליקו בו בשבת: It is prohibited to move an oil lamp that was burning on Shabbat, even after it is no longer burning and no oil remains, because it was set aside while burning at twilight (Rambam *Sefer Zemanim*, *Hilkhot Shabbat* 25:10; *Shulḥan Arukh*, *Oraḥ Ḥayyim* 279:1).

"אֲבָל כּוֹס וּקְעָרָה וַעֲשָׁשִׁית לֹא יְזִיזֵם מִמְּקוֹמָם" מַאי שְׁנָא הָנֵי? אָמַר עוּלָּא: סֵיפָא אֲתָאן לְרַבִּי יְהוּדָה.

Following Rabbi Shimon's statement, it was taught in the *Tosefta*: **However, a cup, and a bowl, and a lantern, one may not move them from their place.** The Gemara asks: **What is different about these,** that even Rabbi Shimon prohibits moving them? **Ulla said:** In **the latter clause** of this *Tosefta*, **we came** back **to**[B] explain the opinion of **Rabbi Yehuda,** who prohibits moving items that are set-aside.

מַתְקִיף לַהּ מָר זוּטְרָא: אִי הָכִי מַאי 'אֲבָל'? אֶלָּא אָמַר מָר זוּטְרָא: לְעוֹלָם רַבִּי שִׁמְעוֹן, וְכִי קָשָׁרֵי רַבִּי שִׁמְעוֹן - בְּנֵר זוּטָא דְּדַעְתֵּיהּ עִלָּוֵיהּ, אֲבָל הָנֵי דִּנְפִישִׁי - לָא.

Mar Zutra strongly objects to Ulla's explanation: **If so, what** is the meaning of the word **however** in the phrase: **However,** a cup and a bowl, etc.? Rabbi Yehuda prohibited moving an oil lamp as well. In what way could the legal status of a bowl be any different? **Rather, Mar Zutra said: Actually,** this must be explained differently. That phrase was stated by **Rabbi Shimon. And when Rabbi Shimon permitted** moving a lamp, that was **in** the case of **a small lamp, which he has in mind,** i.e., he is certain that the flame will be extinguished on Shabbat and that he will have the opportunity to use the remaining oil that day. **However, these,** the bowl and the lantern, **which have much** oil, **no,** he does not expect them to be extinguished and he sets them aside from use for the entire Shabbat.

וְהָתַנְיָא: מוֹתַר הַשֶּׁמֶן שֶׁבַּנֵּר וְשֶׁבַּקְּעָרָה - אָסוּר, וְרַבִּי שִׁמְעוֹן מַתִּיר. הָתָם - קְעָרָה דּוּמְיָא דְּנֵר, הָכָא - קְעָרָה דּוּמְיָא דְּכוֹס.

The Gemara asks: **Wasn't it taught** in a *baraita*: Using **the remaining oil that is in an oil lamp or in a bowl is prohibited** on Shabbat, **and Rabbi Shimon permits** using it. Apparently, Rabbi Shimon does not distinguish between a candle and a bowl. The Gemara answers: **There,** where Rabbi Shimon permitted **a bowl,** was specifically in a case where it is **similar to a lamp,** i.e., a small bowl in which the flame will quickly extinguish. **Here,** where Rabbi Shimon prohibited using the oil remaining in a bowl, it is referring to **a bowl that is similar to a cup,** which is large.

אָמַר רַבִּי זֵירָא: פָּמוֹט שֶׁהִדְלִיקוּ בּוֹ בְּשַׁבָּת, לְדִבְרֵי הַמַּתִּיר אָסוּר, לְדִבְרֵי הָאוֹסֵר - מוּתָּר. לְמֵימְרָא דְּרַבִּי יְהוּדָה מוּקְצֶה מֵחֲמַת מִיאוּס - אִית לֵיהּ, מוּקְצֶה מֵחֲמַת אִיסּוּר - לֵית לֵיהּ? וְהָתַנְיָא, רַבִּי יְהוּדָה אוֹמֵר: כׇּל הַנֵּרוֹת שֶׁל מַתֶּכֶת מְטַלְטְלִין, חוּץ מִן הַנֵּר שֶׁהִדְלִיקוּ בּוֹ בְּשַׁבָּת! אֶלָּא, אִי אִיתְּמַר - הָכִי אִיתְּמַר: אָמַר רַבִּי זֵירָא: פָּמוֹט שֶׁהִדְלִיקוּ עָלָיו בְּשַׁבָּת - דִּבְרֵי הַכֹּל אָסוּר, לֹא הִדְלִיקוּ עָלָיו - דִּבְרֵי הַכֹּל מוּתָּר.

Rabbi Zeira said: A metal **candlestick** [*pamot*][L] **that was kindled on Shabbat,**[N] **according to** Rabbi Shimon, **who permits** moving a lamp, **it is prohibited** because it is large. Whereas, **according to** Rabbi Yehuda, **who prohibits** moving a lamp, a metal candlestick **is permitted** because it does not become disgusting (Rabbeinu Ḥananel). The Gemara asks: **Is that to say** that **Rabbi Yehuda is of** the opinion that an object that is **set-aside** [*muktze*] **due to repugnance** may not be moved, and **he is not of** the opinion that an object that is **set-aside due to prohibition** may not be moved, and therefore permits moving the candlestick? **Wasn't it taught** in a *baraita* that **Rabbi Yehuda says: All metal candlesticks may be moved** on Shabbat **with the exception of a candlestick that was kindled on Shabbat** itself? Apparently, he prohibits moving the metal candlestick, not because it is disgusting but because it is set-aside due to prohibition. **Rather, if it was stated, it was stated as follows, Rabbi Zeira said:** A metal **candlestick that was kindled on Shabbat, everyone agrees** that **it is prohibited.** One that **was not kindled** on Shabbat, **everyone agrees** that **it is permitted** because it is neither set aside due to prohibition nor set aside due to repugnance.

אָמַר רַב יְהוּדָה אָמַר רַב: מִטָּה שֶׁיִּחֲדָהּ לְמָעוֹת - אָסוּר לְטַלְטְלָהּ. מֵיתִיבֵיהּ רַב נַחְמָן בַּר יִצְחָק: מְטַלְטְלִין נֵר חָדָשׁ, אֲבָל לֹא יָשָׁן.

Rav Yehuda said that **Rav said: A bed which one designated to** place **money** upon it **may not be moved** on Shabbat because it is set-aside. It is prohibited even though it no longer has money upon it. **Rav Naḥman bar Yitzḥak raised an objection to** Rav Yehuda from our mishna: **One may move a new** oil **lamp** on Shabbat **but not** an **old** one.

BACKGROUND

In the latter clause of this *Tosefta*, we came back to – סֵיפָא אֲתָאן: This expression is utilized to explain that the mishna or *baraita* contains more than one opinion. Consequently, the concluding section presents a different opinion that may or may not have been mentioned previously. In general, this explanation is only employed in situations where there is no alternative. It is far preferable to explain a mishna in its entirety in accordance with the opinion of a single Sage, even if the explanation leaves something to be desired.

LANGUAGE

Candlestick [*pamot*] – פָּמוֹט: The origin of this word is unclear. There are those who believe that it is a corruption of the Greek φωτισμός, *photismos*, meaning illumination or light. An alternative opinion is that the word is from the Latin pavimentum, which means base, since a *pamot* is indeed the base for a candle.

NOTES

A candlestick that was lit on Shabbat – פָּמוֹט שֶׁהִדְלִיקוּ בּוֹ בְּשַׁבָּת: The commentaries explain that since a candlestick is made of metal and more valuable than a standard earthenware oil lamp, one might assume that it has a fixed location and people are very careful with it. Nevertheless, even those who rule leniently with regard to the *halakhot* of set-aside, accept that a valuable object, which is set aside due to monetary loss, i.e., concern that the object may be ruined, is set aside from use. Therefore, it was necessary to emphasize the laws of a candlestick (Ran).

HALAKHA

Money on the bed – מָעוֹת עַל הַמִּטָּה: It is prohibited to move a bed that has money on it on Shabbat, or even one that no longer has money on it but had money on it when Shabbat began. The prohibition is applicable even if someone wants to use the bed or requires the area where the bed is located (Rema), as per Rav's opinion. However, if there is no money on the bed, and there was none when Shabbat began, even though it is designated and utilized for placing money on during the week, it is permitted to move the bed, which is like any other vessel whose use is prohibited on Shabbat, because Rabbi Shimon holds that the *halakha* of set-aside does not apply in this case (Rambam *Sefer Zemanim*, *Hilkhot Shabbat* 25:10; *Shulḥan Arukh*, *Oraḥ Ḥayyim* 310:7, and in the comment of the Rema).

LANGUAGE

Undercarriage [*mukheni*] – מוּכְנִי: The origin is from the Greek word **μηχανή**, *mekhane*, which means a machine or a hoist-like vessel used for lifting.

וּמַה נֵּר דִּלְהָכִי עֲבִידָא, כִּי לֹא הִדְלִיק בָּהּ – שָׁרֵי לְטַלְטוּלָהּ, מִטָּה דְּלָאו לְהָכִי עֲבִידָא – לֹא כׇּל שֶׁכֵּן! אֶלָּא, אִי אִיתְּמַר – הָכִי אִיתְּמַר: אָמַר רַב יְהוּדָה אָמַר רַב: מִטָּה שֶׁיִּחֲדָהּ לְמָעוֹת, הִנִּיחַ עָלֶיהָ מָעוֹת – אָסוּר לְטַלְטְלָהּ, לֹא הִנִּיחַ עָלֶיהָ מָעוֹת – מוּתָּר לְטַלְטְלָהּ. לֹא יִחֲדָהּ לְמָעוֹת, יֵשׁ עָלֶיהָ מָעוֹת – אָסוּר לְטַלְטְלָהּ, אֵין עָלֶיהָ מָעוֹת – מוּתָּר לְטַלְטְלָהּ, וְהוּא שֶׁלֹּא הָיוּ עָלֶיהָ בֵּין הַשְּׁמָשׁוֹת.

He explains his objection: **And just as a lamp, which** is **made for this** purpose, for lighting, **when he did not light it, he is permitted to move it, a bed, which is not made for that** purpose, for placing money on it, **all the more so** moving it would be permitted. **Rather, if it was stated, it was stated as follows: Rav Yehuda said** that **Rav said: A bed that one designated for money**[N] to be placed upon **it,** if **one left money upon it** one day, it becomes designated for that purpose and **it is prohibited to move it** on Shabbat. If **one did not leave money upon it, it is permitted to move it** on Shabbat. A bed, which **one did not designate for money** to be placed upon it, if **there is money upon it** on Shabbat itself, **it is prohibited to move it** on Shabbat. If **there is not money on it, it is permitted to move it. And that is** only **when there was not** money **on it during** the **twilight** period between Shabbat eve and Shabbat. If there was money on it at that time, the bed itself becomes set aside due to prohibition for the entire Shabbat, even if the money fell off the bed in the course of the day.[H]

אָמַר עוּלָּא, מְתִיב רַבִּי אֱלִיעֶזֶר: ״מוּכְנִי שֶׁלָּהּ, בִּזְמַן שֶׁהִיא נִשְׁמֶטֶת – אֵין חִבּוּר לָהּ, וְאֵין נִמְדֶּדֶת עִמָּהּ, וְאֵין מַצֶּלֶת עִמָּהּ בְּאֹהֶל הַמֵּת, וְאֵין גּוֹרְרִין אוֹתָהּ בְּשַׁבָּת בִּזְמַן שֶׁיֵּשׁ עָלֶיהָ מָעוֹת״.

Ulla said: Rabbi Eliezer raised an objection to Rav's statement from that which we learned in a mishna. This mishna deals primarily with the laws of ritual impurity and discusses the relationship between a wagon and its undercarriage [*mukheni*],[LB] the system of wheels and the frame at the base of the wagon. And the Sages said: The wagon's **undercarriage, when it is detachable** from the wagon, it is **not** considered **connected to it** and they are considered independent units as far as the *halakhot* of ritual impurity are concerned. **And it is not measured with it.** This refers to calculating the volume of forty *se'a*, as a vessel with a volume larger than forty *se'a* does not have the legal status of a vessel and cannot become ritually impure. **And** the undercarriage likewise **does not protect** together **with** the wagon **in a tent** over **the corpse.**[N] A large wagon is considered a tent in and of itself and the vessels inside the wagon do not become impure if the wagon is over a corpse. However, the undercarriage is not included with the wagon in this regard. If a hole in the wagon is sealed by the undercarriage, it is not considered sealed with regard to preventing ritual impurity. **And,** likewise, **one may not pull** the wagon **on Shabbat when there is money upon it.**

הָא אֵין עָלֶיהָ מָעוֹת – שַׁרְיָא, אַף עַל גַּב דַּהֲווּ עָלֶיהָ בֵּין הַשְּׁמָשׁוֹת! הַהִיא רַבִּי שִׁמְעוֹן הִיא, דְּלֵית לֵיהּ מוּקְצֶה, וְרַב כְּרַבִּי יְהוּדָה סְבִירָא לֵיהּ.

By inference: **If there is not money on it,** one is **permitted** to move the wagon **even though there was** money **on it at twilight.** In this mishna, the prohibition is contingent exclusively on whether or not there is money on the wagon at that time. The Gemara answers: **That** mishna **is** in accordance with the opinion of **Rabbi Shimon,**[N] **who is not of** the opinion that there is a prohibition of **set-aside. And Rav holds in accordance with** the opinion of **Rabbi Yehuda.** Since according to Rabbi Yehuda there is a prohibition of set-aside, the wagon became set aside from use during the twilight period and remains prohibited for the entire Shabbat.

BACKGROUND

A wagon and undercarriage – עֲגָלָה וּמוּכְנִי: The wagon is the compartment in which objects are kept, while the undercarriage is the wheel system, the axles and gears that support the wagon.

Wagon obtained from the Pompeii ruins

NOTES

A bed that one designated for money – מִטָּה שֶׁיִּחֲדָהּ לְמָעוֹת: There are several areas of *halakha* where significance is accorded to an act of designation for a specific purpose. By means of that designation, the object assumes the legal status as if it had always been utilized for that purpose. However, in other areas of *halakha*, there is a dispute whether or not designation alone is sufficient to accord that status to an object.

And the undercarriage likewise does not protect together with the wagon in a tent over the corpse – וְאֵין מַצֶּלֶת עִמָּהּ בְּאֹהֶל הַמֵּת: Preventing objects from becoming ritually impure in a tent over a corpse can be accomplished in any number of ways. In this context, the discussion is with regard to an object covering a corpse like a tent. The object itself remains ritually pure and the objects above that object also remain ritually pure. Objects beneath it become impure. With regard to a ceramic vessel in a tent over a corpse there is a similar *halakha*. If it is sealed, it protects its contents from ritual impurity (Numbers 19:15). According to *Tosafot*, a large wooden vessel, which cannot become ritually impure because it has a capacity of more than forty *se'a* and does not, therefore, have the legal status of a vessel, preserves the ritual purity of items inside it when it is closed on all sides. In the case at hand, if we understand the undercarriage to be the entire bottom part of the wagon and not just the wheels alone, as Rashi explains, then when there is an opening in the bottom of the wagon that is sealed by the undercarriage, the wagon is not considered sealed and does not protect its contents from ritual impurity in the case of a tent over a corpse.

That mishna is in accordance with the opinion of Rabbi Shimon – הַהִיא רַבִּי שִׁמְעוֹן הִיא: At first, the Gemara held that this mishna was in accordance with the opinion of Rabbi Yehuda because it mentions a *halakha* that has an element of set-aside, as Rabbi Yehuda holds the prohibition of set-aside. Only after analysis does the Gemara suggest that even Rabbi Shimon agrees that money, which is neither fit for any use on Shabbat nor is it a vessel, is completely prohibited because it is set-aside (*Penei Yehoshua*).

הכי נמי מיסתברא דרב כרבי יהודה סבירא ליה, דאמר רב: מניחין נר על גבי דקל בשבת, ואין מניחין נר על גבי דקל ביום טוב. אי אמרת בשלמא דרב כרבי יהודה סבירא ליה – היינו דשני בין שבת ליום טוב, אלא אי אמרת כרבי שמעון סבירא ליה – מה לי שבת ומה לי יום טוב!

The Gemara adds: **So too, it is reasonable** to say that **Rav holds in accordance with** the opinion **of Rabbi Yehuda,**[N] **as Rav said: One may place a lamp atop a palm tree**[H] on Shabbat eve to burn **on Shabbat,**[N] **and one may not place a lamp atop a palm tree on a Festival. Granted, if you say** that **Rav holds in accordance with** the opinion of **Rabbi Yehuda** in this matter; **that is** why there **is a distinction between Shabbat and a Festival.** Since the lamp is set-aside [*muktze*] on Shabbat one will not come to carry it. Since one is permitted to carry a lamp on a Festival, there is concern that one might climb the palm tree or make use of the tree on the Festival and thereby transgress the rabbinic prohibition against making use of something connected to the ground on a Festival. **However, if you say** that Rav **holds in accordance with** the opinion of **Rabbi Shimon,** who maintains that the lamp is not set-aside even on Shabbat, **what** difference **is** there **to me** between **Shabbat and a Festival?** Ostensibly, there should be no distinction between the two.

ורב כרבי יהודה סבירא ליה?! והא בעו מיניה דרב: מהו לטלטולי שרגא דחנוכתא מקמי חברי בשבתא? ואמר להו: שפיר דמי. שעת הדחק שאני. דהא אמרו להו רב כהנא ורב אשי לרב: הכי הלכתא? אמר להו: כדי הוא רבי שמעון לסמוך עליו בשעת הדחק.

The Gemara asks: **And does Rav** really **hold in accordance with** the opinion of **Rabbi Yehuda** that it is prohibited to move an object that is set-aside? **Didn't they raise a dilemma before Rav: What is** the ruling with regard to **moving a Hanukkah candle from before the *ḥabarei*,** Persian Zoroastrian fire priests, **on Shabbat?** Those priests prohibited lighting fires on certain days. In order to prevent them from discovering that he lit Hanukkah candles it was necessary to quickly move them. **And he said to them:** One may **well** do so. Apparently, Rav does not hold that there is a prohibition of set-aside. The Gemara answers: This is not a proof, as **exigent circumstances are different** and Rav permitted this due to the danger involved. **As Rav Kahana and Rav Ashi said to Rav** on this matter: Is **that the *halakha*?** He said to them: **Rabbi Shimon is worthy to rely upon in exigent circumstances** like this one.

בעא מיניה ריש לקיש מרבי יוחנן: חטים שזרען בקרקע, וביצים שתחת תרנגולת מהו? כי לית ליה לרבי שמעון מוקצה – היכא דלא דחייה בידים, היכא דדחייה בידים – אית ליה מוקצה, או דילמא לא שנא? אמר ליה: אין מוקצה לרבי שמעון אלא שמן שבנר בשעה שהוא דולק, הואיל והוקצה למצותו הוקצה לאיסורו.

On this same matter **Reish Lakish raised a dilemma before Rabbi Yoḥanan: Wheat** kernels **that he sowed in the ground** that have not yet taken root and he could still gather them, **and eggs that** were placed **beneath the hen** and the incubation process has begun, **what is** the *halakha* in these cases? Would Rabbi Shimon agree that in these cases it is prohibited for use on Shabbat? One side of the dilemma is: **When is Rabbi Shimon not** of the opinion that there is a prohibition of **set-aside?** In a case **where** one did **not reject** the object **with his own hands,**[N] i.e., he did not perform an action setting the object aside. However, in a case **where he rejected it with** his own **hands,**[H] **he is of** the opinion that there is a prohibition of **set-aside.** When he sowed the wheat, he rejected it with his own hands. The same is true with regard to the egg; by placing it under the hen to hatch, he actively rejected it. The other side of the dilemma is: **Or, perhaps there is no difference** between the cases and Rabbi Shimon holds that there is no prohibition of set-aside in either case. Rabbi Yoḥanan **said to him: There is only** a prohibition of **set-aside, according to Rabbi Shimon,** in the case of **oil that is in the lamp while it is burning. Since it was set aside for its mitzva,** the lighting of Shabbat candles, and it was also **set aside for its prohibition,**[N] it is prohibited due to the concern that one might inadvertently extinguish the flame if he moves it while it is burning.

ולית ליה הוקצה למצותו?! והתניא: סיככה כהלכתה, ועיטרה בקרמים ובסדינין המצויירין, ותלה בה אגוזין, אפרסקין, שקדים ורמונין, ואפרכלי של ענבים, ועטרות של שבולין, יינות, שמנים וסלתות – אסור להסתפק מהן עד מוצאי יום טוב האחרון, ואם התנה עליהן הכל לפי תנאו.

The Gemara asks: **And does he not hold** that the prohibition of set-aside applies to an object **set aside** only **for its mitzva** without any prohibition? **Wasn't it taught** in a *baraita*: **One who roofed** the *sukka* **in accordance with its halakhic** requirements **and decorated it** for aesthetic purposes **with colored hangings and tapestries, and hung** as decorations **nuts, peaches, almonds and pomegranates, and grape branches, and wreaths made of stalks, wine, oils, and fine flour, it is prohibited to supply** himself **from them until the conclusion of the last day of the Festival.** Since they were all set aside for the mitzva of *sukka*, all other uses are prohibited. **And if one stipulated** at the time that he hung them in the *sukka* that he is not designating them exclusively for this purpose, but he intends to use **them** for other purposes as well, their use **is entirely in accordance with his stipulation.** He is permitted to use them as he chooses.

NOTES

So too, it is reasonable to say that Rav holds in accordance with the opinion of Rabbi Yehuda – הכי נמי מיסתברא דרב כרבי יהודה סבירא ליה: This proof seems superfluous. Not only is it clear in other places that this is Rav's opinion, but the matter that opened the discussion, i.e., the case of moving a wagon with set-aside items on it, is in accordance with the opinion of Rabbi Yehuda. One proposed explanation is: Since the case of the wagon is not absolutely clear, as it can also be explained in accordance with the opinion of Rabbi Shimon, there is no proof that Rav agrees with Rabbi Yehuda (Rashba).

Using a tree on Shabbat – שימוש באילן בשבת: The Sages decreed that one may not climb a tree on Shabbat and on a Festival. Indeed, one may not even use a tree in any manner similar to climbing it. The rationale for this decree is the concern that one might unwittingly cut branches or pick fruit while climbing and thereby violate a Torah prohibition.

When is Rabbi Shimon not of the opinion that there is a prohibition of set-aside? In a case where one did not reject the object with his own hands – כי לית ליה לרבי שמעון מוקצה היכא דלא דחייה בידים: It is necessary to complete this statement: When the Sages said that Rabbi Shimon only holds the prohibition of set-aside in the case of the oil in an oil lamp, it was with regard to an object that is usable but was set aside from use on Shabbat. Indeed, in the case of figs and raisins that are drying, Rabbi Shimon certainly agrees.

Essentially, the rejection involved in planting wheat is much greater than that of placing oil into a bowl or an oil lamp. Rabbi Shimon distinguishes between the cases. The oil in the oil lamp is consciously rejected from use by the individual due to a Shabbat prohibition. As a result, Rabbi Shimon agrees that it is set-aside on Shabbat. However, in the case of wheat, the rejection is not tied to a Shabbat prohibition. Therefore, Rabbi Shimon holds that its rejection has no significance vis-à-vis the *halakhot* of Shabbat (*Tziyyun LeNefesh Ḥayya*).

Since it was set aside for its mitzva it was set aside for its prohibition – הואיל והוקצה למצותו הוקצה לאיסורו: There are commentaries who have a variant reading of the conclusion: It was set aside for its mitzva and it was set aside for its prohibition. However, they interpret the conjunction, and, to mean or. That is to say, an object that was set aside either for its mitzva or for its prohibited use is set aside from use according to Rabbi Shimon. Apparently, that is the correct interpretation, as Rabbi Shimon certainly agrees in the case of an item set aside due to a prohibition. The dispute is limited to Rabbi Shimon's opinion with regard to an item that was set aside due to its mitzva (*Me'iri*).

HALAKHA

Lamp atop a palm tree – נר על גבי דקל: Placing an oil lamp atop a palm tree on Shabbat eve with the intention of leaving it there over Shabbat is permitted. However, doing so before a Festival is prohibited, as per the opinion of Rav (Rambam *Sefer Zemanim, Hilkhot Shabbat* 5:17 and *Hilkhot Yom Tov* 4:5; *Shulḥan Arukh, Oraḥ Ḥayyim* 277:4, 514:6).

Where he rejected it with his own hands – דדחייה בידים: An object that was set aside from use by means of a specific action, e.g., wheat planted before Shabbat that has not yet taken root, is not set-aside and it is permitted to move it according to Rabbi Shimon (Rambam *Sefer Zemanim, Hilkhot Shabbat* 26:14; *Shulḥan Arukh, Oraḥ Ḥayyim* 310:2).

BACKGROUND

Dried figs – גרוגרות: After picking the fig from the tree, its stem and tip are cut to allow the liquid to drain. The figs are then spread on broad surfaces and left there until they are sun-dried.

וּמִמַּאי דְּרַבִּי שִׁמְעוֹן הִיא – דְּתָנֵי רַבִּי חִיָּיא בַּר יוֹסֵף קַמֵּיהּ דְּרַבִּי יוֹחָנָן: אֵין נוֹטְלִין עֵצִים מִן הַסּוּכָּה בְּיוֹם טוֹב אֶלָּא מִן הַסָּמוּךְ לָהּ, וְרַבִּי שִׁמְעוֹן מַתִּיר. וְשָׁוִין בְּסוּכַּת הֶחָג בֶּחָג שֶׁהִיא אֲסוּרָה. וְאִם הִתְנָה עָלֶיהָ – הַכֹּל לְפִי תְּנָאוֹ – כְּעֵין שֶׁמֶן שֶׁבַּנֵּר קָאָמְרִינַן, הוֹאִיל וְהוּקְצָה לְמִצְוָתוֹ הוּקְצָה לְאִיסּוּרוֹ. אִיתְּמַר נָמֵי, אָמַר רַבִּי חִיָּיא בַּר אַבָּא אָמַר רַבִּי יוֹחָנָן: אֵין מוּקְצֶה לְרַבִּי שִׁמְעוֹן אֶלָּא כְּעֵין שֶׁמֶן שֶׁבַּנֵּר בְּשָׁעָה שֶׁהוּא דּוֹלֵק, הוֹאִיל וְהוּקְצָה לְמִצְוָתוֹ – הוּקְצָה לְאִיסּוּרוֹ.

And from where do we know that this unattributed *baraita* **is** in accordance with the opinion of **Rabbi Shimon?** We ascertained this from a comparison to a *baraita* that was taught by Rabbi Ḥiyya bar Yosef. **As Rabbi Ḥiyya bar Yosef taught before Rabbi Yoḥanan: One may not take wood from the *sukka*** that was constructed for shade **on** any **Festival,** even if the wood fell from the *sukka* on the Festival. Because it is prohibited to destroy the *sukka* on the Festival, it was set aside before the Festival for the entire duration of the Festival. **Rather,** one may take wood only **from what is beside** the *sukka*, i.e., bundles of wood that are not being used for the *sukka*. When he placed them there, his intention was to use them during the Festival. **And Rabbi Shimon permits** taking wood even from the *sukka* itself, since he holds that there is no prohibition of set-aside. **And** Rabbi Yehuda and Rabbi Shimon **agree that** taking wood from **the *sukka*** constructed **for the *Sukkot* festival is prohibited during the Festival. And if one stipulated about** the wood that he will be able to use it during the Festival, **everything is in accordance with his stipulation.** Apparently, Rabbi Shimon prohibits using an object that was set aside due only to a mitzva, even though it was not set aside due to a prohibition. Therefore, the Gemara emends Rabbi Yoḥanan's statement: There is no *halakha* of set-aside according to Rabbi Shimon except in a case **similar to oil in the candle.** It is not necessary that there be both a prohibited labor and a prohibition due to the mitzva. Rather, **since it was set aside for the mitzva** alone, it is thereby **set aside for the prohibition.** It **was also stated: Rabbi Ḥiyya bar Abba said** that **Rabbi Yoḥanan said: There is only** a prohibition of **set-aside according to Rabbi Shimon in** a case **similar to oil in the candle while it is burning; since it was set aside for its mitzva, it was set aside for its prohibition.**

אָמַר רַב יְהוּדָה אָמַר שְׁמוּאֵל: אֵין מוּקְצֶה לְרַבִּי שִׁמְעוֹן אֶלָּא גְּרוֹגָרוֹת וְצִימּוּקִים בִּלְבַד. וּמִידֵּי אַחֲרִינָא לָא?! וְהָתַנְיָא: הָיָה אוֹכֵל בִּתְאֵנִים וְהוֹתִיר וְהֶעֱלָן לַגַּג לַעֲשׂוֹת מֵהֶן גְּרוֹגָרוֹת. בַּעֲנָבִים וְהוֹתִיר וְהֶעֱלָן לַגַּג לַעֲשׂוֹת מֵהֶן צִימּוּקִין – לֹא יֹאכַל עַד שֶׁיַּזְמִין. וְכֵן אַתָּה אוֹמֵר בָּאֲפַרְסְקִין וְחַבּוּשִׁין, וּבִשְׁאָר כׇּל מִינֵי פֵירוֹת.

Rav Yehuda said that **Shmuel said: There is only** a prohibition of **set-aside according to Rabbi Shimon** in the cases of **dried figs**[B] **and raisins alone.** The case of one who takes figs and raisins up to his roof in order to dry them in the sun is the only situation in which Rabbi Shimon holds that they are prohibited on Shabbat due to the prohibition of set-aside. Since in the initial stages of the process they emit a bad odor and are unfit for consumption, one consciously sets them aside. The Gemara challenges: **And other items** are **not** included in the prohibition of set-aside? **Wasn't it taught** in a *baraita*: One who **was eating figs and left** some over **and took them up to the roof to make them** into **dried figs,** and likewise one who was eating **grapes and left** some over **and took them up to the roof to make them** into **raisins, one may not eat** them on Shabbat **unless he designates** them to be eaten before Shabbat. Otherwise, they are prohibited as set-aside. **And you** would **say the same with regard to peaches, and quinces, and all other types of fruit** that one left out to dry. It is prohibited to eat them all on Shabbat due to set-aside.

מַנִּי? אִילֵימָא רַבִּי יְהוּדָה – וּמָה הֵיכָא דְּלָא דַּחְיֵיהּ בְּיָדַיִם – אִית לֵיהּ מוּקְצֶה, הֵיכָא דְּדַחְיֵיהּ בְּיָדַיִם לֹא כׇּל שֶׁכֵּן?

The Gemara seeks to clarify: **Whose** opinion **is** it in the *baraita*? **If you say** that it is the opinion of **Rabbi Yehuda,** this *baraita* is superfluous. **If** in a case **where one did not reject it with** his own **hands, he holds** that there is a prohibition of **set-aside,** in a case **where he rejected it by** his own **hand, all the more so** that it is prohibited. There is no need to articulate the *halakha* in this unique case.

אֶלָּא לָאו – רַבִּי שִׁמְעוֹן הִיא! לְעוֹלָם – רַבִּי יְהוּדָה, וְ״אוֹכֵל״ אִצְטְרִיכָא לֵיהּ, סָלְקָא דַּעְתָּךְ אָמֵינָא: כֵּיוָן דְּקָאָכֵיל וְאָזֵיל – לָא לִיבְּעֵי הַזְמָנָה, קָמַשְׁמַע לַן: כֵּיוָן דְּהֶעֱלָן לַגַּג – אַסּוּחֵי אַסְּחֵי לְדַעְתֵּיהּ מִינַּיְיהוּ.

Rather, isn't this *baraita* in accordance with the opinion of **Rabbi Shimon?** Apparently, he expands the *halakhot* of set-aside beyond dried figs and raisins. The Gemara rejects this: **Actually,** this *halakha* is in accordance with **Rabbi Yehuda** who holds that there is a prohibition of set-aside. **And** the case cited here, where he was **eating** figs, **is necessary** in order to teach us a novel *halakha*. **It may enter your mind to say** that **since one was in the course of eating, he does not require** prior **designation;** and if he changed his mind he may immediately retrieve the dried figs that he placed on the roof. Therefore, the *baraita* **teaches us** that **since he brought them up to the roof, he diverted his attention from them** and they are completely set-aside.

בְּעָא מִינֵּיהּ רַבִּי שִׁמְעוֹן בַּר רַבִּי מֵרַבִּי:

On the same topic: **Rabbi Shimon bar Rabbi** Yehuda HaNasi, **raised a dilemma before** his father, **Rabbi** Yehuda HaNasi:

פַּצְעִילֵי תְּמָרָה לְרַבִּי שִׁמְעוֹן מַהוּ? אָמַר לוֹ: אֵין מוּקְצֶה לְרַבִּי שִׁמְעוֹן אֶלָּא גְּרוֹגָרוֹת וְצִימּוּקִין בִּלְבַד.

Unripe dates[NB] that are placed in baskets to ripen and until they are ripe can only be eaten with difficulty, **according to** the opinion of **Rabbi Shimon, what is** their legal status as far as moving them on Shabbat is concerned? Are they considered set-aside? Rabbi Yehuda HaNasi **said to him: There is only** a prohibition of **set-aside according to Rabbi Shimon**[H] in the cases of **dried figs and raisins alone.**

וְרַבִּי לֵית לֵיהּ מוּקְצֶה?! וְהָתְנַן: אֵין מַשְׁקִין וְשׁוֹחֲטִין אֶת הַמִּדְבָּרִיּוֹת, אֲבָל מַשְׁקִין וְשׁוֹחֲטִין אֶת הַבַּיְיתוֹת. וְתַנְיָא: אֵלּוּ הֵן מִדְבָּרִיּוֹת – כׇּל שֶׁיּוֹצְאוֹת בְּפֶסַח וְנִכְנָסוֹת בָּרְבִיעָה. בַּיָּיתוֹת – כׇּל שֶׁיּוֹצְאוֹת וְרוֹעוֹת חוּץ לַתְּחוּם, וּבָאוֹת וְלָנוֹת בְּתוֹךְ הַתְּחוּם. רַבִּי אוֹמֵר: אֵלּוּ וָאֵלּוּ בַּיָּיתוֹת הֵן, וְאֵלּוּ הֵן מִדְבָּרִיּוֹת – כׇּל שֶׁרוֹעוֹת בָּאֲפָר וְאֵין נִכְנָסוֹת לַיִּשּׁוּב לֹא בִּימוֹת הַחַמָּה וְלֹא בִּימוֹת הַגְּשָׁמִים.

The Gemara challenges this: **And does Rabbi** Yehuda HaNasi **not hold** that there is a prohibition of **set-aside? Didn't we learn** in a mishna that on a Festival, before they are slaughtered, **one may neither give water to,** in order to ease removal of their hides, **nor slaughter** non-domesticated, **desert** animals,[H] animals that are always grazing in the fields? Since people do not generally tend to them, they are considered set-aside and may not be used. **However, one may give water to and slaughter**[N] **domesticated animals. And it was taught** in a *baraita* that **these are** non-domesticated, **desert** animals: Any animals **that leave** their sheds **on Passover and** only **enter** their sheds with the advent of the **rainy season. Domesticated** animals are **any** animals **that go out to graze beyond the** city **limits, and come and sleep within the** city **limits. Rabbi** Yehuda HaNasi **says: These and those are** both **domesticated. And these are** the non-domesticated, **desert** animals that are prohibited due to the prohibition of set-aside: **Any** animals **that graze in the grazing area and neither enter the town during the summer nor during the rainy season.** It is these animals that it is prohibited to give water to or slaughter on a Festival. Apparently, Rabbi Yehuda HaNasi holds that there is a prohibition of set-aside even in the case of animals.

אִיבָּעֵית אֵימָא: הָנֵי נַמִּי כִּגְרוֹגְרוֹת וְצִימּוּקִין דָּמְיָין. וְאִי בָּעֵית אֵימָא: לְדִבְרָיו דְּרַבִּי שִׁמְעוֹן קָאָמַר לֵיהּ, וְלֵיהּ לָא סְבִירָא לֵיהּ.

Several resolutions are proposed to this contradiction: **If you wish, say** that **these** non-domesticated animals that graze in the grazing areas throughout the year **are also** considered **like dried figs and raisins.** Even Rabbi Shimon would agree to this *halakha*. **And if you wish, say** instead: When Rabbi Yehuda HaNasi told his son that answer, **he was saying it to him in accordance with** the opinion of **Rabbi Shimon, and he** himself **does not hold** that way.

וְאִיבָּעֵית אֵימָא: לְדִבְרֵיהֶם דְּרַבָּנַן קָאָמַר לְהוּ: לְדִידִי – לֵית לִי מוּקְצֶה כְּלָל, לְדִידְכוּ – אוֹדוּ לִי מִיהַת, דְּהֵיכָא דְּיוֹצְאוֹת בְּפֶסַח וְנִכְנָסוֹת בָּרְבִיעָה, דְּבַיָּיתוֹת נִינְהוּ. וְרַבָּנַן אֲמַרוּ לֵיהּ: לָא, מִדְבָּרִיּוֹת נִינְהוּ.

And if you wish, say instead: In that *baraita*, **he spoke to them in accordance with the statement of the Rabbis,** and this is how his statement must be understood: **In my opinion I do not hold** that there is a prohibition of **set-aside at all.** However, **according to your** opinion, **at least agree with me that** animals that leave their sheds **on Passover and** only **enter** their sheds with the advent of the **rainy season are domesticated. And the Rabbis said to him: No,** those **are non-domesticated** animals.

אָמַר רַבָּה בַּר בַּר חָנָה אָמַר רַבִּי יוֹחָנָן: אָמְרוּ ״הֲלָכָה כְּרַבִּי שִׁמְעוֹן״. וּמִי אָמַר רַבִּי יוֹחָנָן הָכִי? וְהָא בְּעָא מִינֵּיהּ הַהוּא סָבָא קְרוּיָא, וְאָמְרִי לַהּ סְרוּיָא, מֵרַבִּי יוֹחָנָן: קִינָּה שֶׁל תַּרְנְגוֹלֶת מַהוּ לְטַלְטוּלֵי בְּשַׁבָּת? אֲמַר לֵיהּ: כְּלוּם עָשׂוּי אֶלָּא לְתַרְנְגוֹלִין? הָכָא בְּמַאי עָסְקִינַן – דְּאִית בֵּיהּ אֶפְרוֹחַ מֵת.

As to the essential dispute with regard to the laws of set-aside, **Rabba bar bar Ḥana said** that **Rabbi Yoḥanan said: They said that the *halakha* is in accordance with** the opinion of **Rabbi Shimon** who holds that there is no prohibition of set-aside. The Gemara asks: **Did Rabbi Yoḥanan** actually **say this? Didn't an Elder** from **Keruya, and some say** that he was from **Seruya, raise a dilemma before Rabbi Yoḥanan:** With regard to **a hen's roost,**[N] **what is** its legal status as far as **moving it on Shabbat** is concerned? Rabbi Yoḥanan **said to him: Isn't** the roost **made exclusively for hens** to be inside it? Since it is not designated for use by people, moving it is prohibited. Apparently, he holds in accordance with the opinion of Rabbi Yehuda with regard to set-aside. The Gemara answers: **With what are we dealing here?** With a special case, **when there is a dead chick in** the roost. Moving the roost is prohibited due to the dead chick, which is set-aside.

NOTES

Unripe dates – **פַּצְעִילֵי תְּמָרָה:** Some explain the difference between unripe dates, on the one hand, and dried figs and raisins, on the other. Figs and raisins are expressly set-aside, while unripe dates are not. They are simply not yet edible, but they will become so over time. Therefore, because one only set them aside temporarily, they are not prohibited (*Tosefot Yeshanim*).

One may give water to and slaughter – **מַשְׁקִין וְשׁוֹחֲטִין:** Although, apparently, this is referring to giving water to the animal before slaughtering it, it is also related to another *halakha*: An animal that may not be eaten on a Festival is set-aside. Providing it with food or water on a Festival is prohibited.

A hen's roost – **קִינָּה שֶׁל תַּרְנְגוֹלֶת:** When Rabbi Yoḥanan was initially asked about a roost, the assumption was that the reference was to a roost that has chickens in it during the week and is specifically designated for them, like a bed designated for money. Therefore, moving the hen's roost is prohibited (Ritva). In Rabbi Yoḥanan's rhetorical question: Isn't the roost made exclusively for hens, he essentially includes all of the answers in the Gemara, as a dead chick, an egg, or an egg with a chick inside it are commonly found in a roost (*Penei Yehoshua*).

BACKGROUND

Unripe dates – **פַּצְעִילֵי תְּמָרָה:** Many species of dates do not become fully ripe on the tree; they must be picked while they are still unripe and allowed to ripen afterward in baskets or in storage. There are several methods that accelerate the ripening process. As opposed to other species of dates, these dates generally do not spoil in the course of the artificial ripening process. Rather, their flavor continues to improve in the baskets.

HALAKHA

Set-aside according to Rabbi Shimon – **מוּקְצֶה לְרַבִּי שִׁמְעוֹן:** Rabbi Shimon only applies the *halakha* of set-aside to the specific case of dried figs and raisins. The rationale is twofold: They are set aside from use by means of a specific action, and they are not yet suitable for consumption (Rambam *Sefer Zemanim*, *Hilkhot Shabbat* 26:14; *Shulḥan Arukh*, *Oraḥ Ḥayyim* 310:2).

One may neither give water to nor slaughter non-domesticated, desert animals, etc. – **אֵין מַשְׁקִין וְשׁוֹחֲטִין אֶת הַמִּדְבָּרִיּוֹת וכו׳:** With regard to animals that graze beyond the city limits and come back to sleep inside the city, even if only on occasion (*Mishna Berura*), if they returned to the city on the Festival, they are considered prepared for use, since their owners have them in mind, and one is permitted to slaughter them on the Festival. However, if the animals graze and sleep beyond the city limits, they are not considered prepared for use and it is prohibited to slaughter them on a Festival because it never enters their owners' minds that these animals will return to sleep inside the city, as per the unattributed mishna (Rambam *Sefer Zemanim*, *Hilkhot Yom Tov* 2:2; *Shulḥan Arukh*, *Oraḥ Ḥayyim* 497:2, 498:3).

NOTES

And a candelabrum fell onto Rabbi Asi's cloak and he did not move it – וְנָפַל מְנַרְתָּא עַל גְּלִימֵיהּ דְּרַבִּי אַסִי וְלָא טִילְטְלָהּ: Although the candelabrum was not intentionally placed on Rabbi Asi's cloak and he could have shaken it off, apparently he did not do so because he was concerned that he might break the candelabrum. He did not want to move the candelabrum itself because of the prohibition of set-aside (*Ḥokhmat Mano'aḥ*).

Because Rabbi Asi was a student of Rabbi Yoḥanan – מִשּׁוּם דְּרַבִּי אַסִי תַּלְמִידֵיהּ דְּרַבִּי יוֹחָנָן הֲוָה: Although proof for the statement of one *amora* is not usually cited from the statement of another, occasionally the opinion of a Sage is derived from the statements or the customs of his preeminent disciple.

In the case of an oil lamp and according to the opinion of Rabbi Shimon – בְּנֵר כְּרַבִּי שִׁמְעוֹן: There is no proof from here that Rabbi Yoḥanan holds in accordance with the opinion of Rabbi Shimon that it is permitted to move an oil lamp. Rather, Rabbi Yoḥanan is stating that among all of the *tanna'im*, the only Sage who permits moving an oil lamp is Rabbi Shimon, and even he did not permit moving a candelabrum (Ritva).

הָנִיחָא לְמָר בַּר אַמֵימָר מִשְּׁמֵיהּ (דְּרַב) דְּאָמַר: מוֹדֶה הָיָה רַבִּי שִׁמְעוֹן בְּבַעֲלֵי חַיִּים שֶׁמֵּתוּ שֶׁאֲסוּרִין, אֶלָּא לְמָר בְּרֵיהּ דְּרַב יוֹסֵף מִשְּׁמֵיהּ דְּרָבָא דְּאָמַר: חָלוּק הָיָה רַבִּי שִׁמְעוֹן [אֲפִילּוּ] בְּבַעֲלֵי חַיִּים שֶׁמֵּתוּ, שֶׁהֵן מוּתָּרִין, מַאי אִיכָּא לְמֵימַר? הָכָא בְּמַאי עָסְקִינַן – בִּדְאִית בֵּיהּ בֵּיצָה.

The Gemara continues to ask: This **works out well according to** the opinion of **Mar bar Ameimar in the name of Rav, who said: Rabbi Shimon agreed in** the case of **animals that died** on Shabbat, **that they are prohibited** on Shabbat due to set-aside. **However, according to** the opinion of **Mar, son of Rav Yosef, in the name of Rava, who said: Rabbi Shimon was in disagreement even in** the case of **animals that died,** and said that **they are permitted** and are not prohibited as set-aside, **what can be said?** The Gemara responds: **With what are we dealing here?** With a case **where there is an egg** that was laid on Shabbat in the roost. Because it was laid on Shabbat it is considered set-aside, and using the egg is prohibited. The thought of using it never entered anyone's mind before Shabbat.

וְהָאָמַר רַב נַחְמָן: מַאן דְּאִית לֵיהּ מוּקְצֶה – אִית לֵיהּ נוֹלָד, דְּלֵית לֵיהּ מוּקְצֶה – לֵית לֵיהּ נוֹלָד! דְּאִית בֵּיהּ בֵּיצַת אֶפְרוֹחַ.

The Gemara asks: **Didn't Rav Naḥman say: One who is of** the opinion that there is a prohibition of **set-aside, is** also **of** the opinion that there is a prohibition of an object that **came into being** on Shabbat or on a Festival; and one **who is not of** the opinion that there is a prohibition of **set-aside, is** also **not of** the opinion that there is a prohibition of an object that **came into being.** This case is no different than other cases of set-aside. The Gemara responds: This is referring to a case **where** the roost **has an egg with a chick in it.** Even Rabbi Shimon would agree that moving an egg of that sort is prohibited since it is fit for neither human nor animal consumption.

כִּי אֲתָא רַב יִצְחָק בְּרַבִּי יוֹסֵף אָמַר רַבִּי יוֹחָנָן: הֲלָכָה כְּרַבִּי יְהוּדָה, וְרַבִּי יְהוֹשֻׁעַ בֶּן לֵוִי אָמַר: הֲלָכָה כְּרַבִּי שִׁמְעוֹן. אָמַר רַב יוֹסֵף: הַיְינוּ דְּאָמַר רַבָּה בַּר בַּר חָנָה אָמַר רַבִּי יוֹחָנָן: אָמְרוּ ״הֲלָכָה כְּרַבִּי שִׁמְעוֹן״. ׳אָמְרוּ׳ – וְלֵיהּ לָא סְבִירָא לֵיהּ.

This explanation was cited to explain that Rabbi Yoḥanan could hold in accordance with the opinion of Rabbi Shimon. However, **when Rav Yitzḥak, son of Rabbi Yosef, came** from Eretz Yisrael to Babylonia, **he said** that **Rabbi Yoḥanan said: The *halakha* is in accordance with** the opinion of **Rabbi Yehuda** that there is a prohibition of set-aside. **And Rabbi Yehoshua ben Levi said: The *halakha* is in accordance with** the opinion of **Rabbi Shimon,** that there is no prohibition of set-aside. **Rav Yosef said: That is** what **Rabba bar bar Ḥana said** that **Rabbi Yoḥanan said: They said that the *halakha* is in accordance with** the opinion of **Rabbi Shimon.** The inference is: **They said; however, he** himself **does not hold** that this is the *halakha.*

אָמַר לֵיהּ אַבַּיֵי לְרַב יוֹסֵף: וְאַתְּ לָא תִּסְבְּרָא דְּרַבִּי יוֹחָנָן כְּרַבִּי יְהוּדָה? הָא רַבִּי אַבָּא וְרַבִּי אַסִי אִיקְלְעוּ לְבֵי רַבִּי אַבָּא דְּמִן חֵיפָא, וְנָפַל מְנַרְתָּא עַל גְּלִימֵיהּ דְּרַבִּי אַסִי וְלָא טִילְטְלָהּ. מַאי טַעְמָא? לָאו מִשּׁוּם דְּרַבִּי אַסִי תַּלְמִידֵיהּ דְּרַבִּי יוֹחָנָן הֲוָה, וְרַבִּי יוֹחָנָן כְּרַבִּי יְהוּדָה סְבִירָא לֵיהּ דְּאִית לֵיהּ מוּקְצֶה?

Abaye said to Rav Yosef: And you yourself **did not hold that Rabbi Yoḥanan** rules **in accordance with** the opinion of **Rabbi Yehuda,** even before Rav Yitzḥak came and cited this statement in his name? **Didn't Rabbi Abba and Rabbi Asi happen** to come **to the house of Rabbi Abba who was from** the city **Haifa, and a candelabrum fell onto Rabbi Asi's cloak and he did not move it?**[N] **What is the reason** that he did not lift it? **Is it not because Rabbi Asi was a student of Rabbi Yoḥanan,**[N] and **Rabbi Yoḥanan holds in accordance with** the opinion of **Rabbi Yehuda, who holds** that there is a prohibition of **set-aside?** Apparently, Rabbi Yoḥanan holds in accordance with the opinion of Rabbi Yehuda.

אָמַר לֵיהּ: מְנַרְתָּא קָאָמְרַתְּ? מְנַרְתָּא שָׁאנֵי. דְּאָמַר רַבִּי אַחָא בַּר חֲנִינָא אָמַר רַבִּי אַסִי: הוֹרָה רֵישׁ לָקִישׁ בְּצִידָן: מְנוֹרָה הַנִּיטֶּלֶת בְּיָדוֹ אַחַת – מוּתָּר לְטַלְטְלָהּ, בִּשְׁתֵּי יָדָיו – אָסוּר לְטַלְטְלָהּ. וְרַבִּי יוֹחָנָן אָמַר: אָנוּ אֵין לָנוּ אֶלָּא בְּנֵר כְּרַבִּי שִׁמְעוֹן. אֲבָל מְנוֹרָה, בֵּין נִיטְּלָה בְּיָדוֹ אַחַת בֵּין נִיטְּלָה בִּשְׁתֵּי יָדָיו – אָסוּר לְטַלְטְלָהּ.

Rav Yosef **said to** Abaye: **Candelabrum you say;** are you citing a proof from the case of a candelabrum? **A candelabrum is different** because there is a unique *halakha* in that case. **As Rabbi Aḥa bar** Rabbi **Ḥanina said** that **Rabbi Asi said** that **Reish Lakish issued a ruling in** the city of **Sidon: A candelabrum that can be moved in one of his hands, one is permitted to move it** on Shabbat. However, if it is so heavy that one must move it **with his two hands, it is prohibited to move it. And Rabbi Yoḥanan said: We have** permission to carry **only in the case of an** oil **lamp, according to** the opinion of **Rabbi Shimon.**[N] However, with regard to a candelabrum, **both** one **that is carried in one hand** and one **that is carried in two hands, it is prohibited to move it.**

וְטַעְמָא מַאי? רַבָּה וְרַב יוֹסֵף דְּאָמְרִי תַּרְוַיְיהוּ: הוֹאִיל וְאָדָם קוֹבֵעַ לָהּ מָקוֹם. אָמַר לֵיהּ אַבַּיֵי לְרַב יוֹסֵף: וַהֲרֵי כִּילַּת חֲתָנִים, דְּאָדָם קוֹבֵעַ לוֹ מָקוֹם, וְאָמַר שְׁמוּאֵל מִשּׁוּם רַבִּי חִיָּיא: כִּילַּת חֲתָנִים

The Gemara asks: **And what is the reason** that there is a unique prohibition in the case of a candelabrum? **Rabba and Rav Yosef both said: Since a person** usually **designates** a fixed **place for it** due to its size and its use, it is considered a built-in part of the house, and moving the candelabrum is like dismantling the house. **Abaye said to Rav Yosef: A groom's canopy** is an object **for** which **a person designates a** set **place, and,** nevertheless, **Shmuel said in the name of Rabbi Ḥiyya:** With regard to a **groom's canopy,**

מותר לנטותה ומותר לפרקה בשבת! אלא אמר אביי: בשל חוליות. אי הכי, מאי טעמא דרבי שמעון בן לקיש דשרי?

it is permitted to assemble it and it is permitted to dismantle it on Shabbat. If a permanent object like that one may be assembled on Shabbat and there is no concern for the prohibition of building, all the more so it should not be considered building and dismantling in the case of a candelabrum. **Rather, Abaye said:** Here it is referring to a special candelabrum made **of joints,**[B] removable parts, and there is concern lest it fall and break into its component parts when it is moved, and one may come to reassemble it, which would be tantamount to crafting a vessel on Shabbat. The Gemara asks: **If so,** if it is referring to that type of candelabrum, **what is the reason** for the opinion of **Rabbi Shimon ben Lakish who permits** moving the candelabrum?

מאי "חוליות" – כעין חוליות, דאית בה חידקי. הלכך: חוליות – בין גדולה בין קטנה אסורה לטלטלה. גדולה נמי דאית בה חידקי – גזירה אטו גדולה דחוליות. כי פליגי – בקטנה דאית בה חידקי. מר סבר: גזרינן, ומר סבר: לא גזרינן.

The Gemara replies: It is not referring to a candelabrum that can actually be dismantled. Rather, **what** is the meaning of **joints? Similar to joints,**[N] i.e., **there are grooves in it** and it appears as if it is made of different components. **Therefore,** in summary: With regard to a candelabrum made of actual **joints, both** one that is **large** and one that is **small, it is prohibited to move it.**[H] **In addition,** a **large** candelabrum **that has grooves,** everyone agrees that it is prohibited to move it by rabbinic **decree,** which was issued **due to a large** candelabrum made of **joints.** Because it is common for a large candelabrum to be made of joints, if one saw someone carrying a large, grooved candelabrum, he would mistakenly assume that it had joints due to the similarity between them, and would mistakenly permit carrying a large candelabrum actually composed of joints. **Where** Rabbi Yoḥanan and Reish Lakish **disagree** is **in** the case of a **small** candelabrum **that has grooves. This Sage,** Rabbi Yoḥanan, **holds** that **we issue a decree** prohibiting moving even a small, grooved candelabrum due to a large one. **And this Sage,** Reish Lakish, **holds** that **we do not issue a decree.** Because a small candelabrum is not typically made of joints, everyone realizes that the grooves are strictly decorative.

ומי אמר רבי יוחנן הכי? והאמר רבי יוחנן: הלכה כסתם משנה, ותנן: "מוכני שלה בזמן שהיא נשמטת – אין חיבור לה, ואין נמדדת עמה, ואין מצלת עמה באהל המת, ואין גוררין אותה בשבת בזמן שיש עליה מעות".

The Gemara questions: **And did Rabbi Yoḥanan** actually **say that**[N] the *halakha* is in accordance with the opinion of Rabbi Yehuda? **Didn't Rabbi Yoḥanan state** the following principle: **The *halakha* is in accordance with an unattributed mishna? And we learned** in the mishna that discusses ritual impurity of a wagon with a detachable undercarriage: The wagon's **undercarriage, when it is detachable** from the wagon, it is **not** considered **connected to it** and they are considered independent units as far as the *halakhot* of ritual impurity are concerned. **And it is not measured with it.** This refers to calculating the volume of forty *se'a*, as a vessel with a volume larger than forty *se'a* does not have the legal status of a vessel and cannot become ritually impure. **And** the undercarriage likewise **does not protect** together **with** the wagon **in a tent** over **the corpse.** A large wagon is considered a tent in and of itself, and the vessels inside the wagon do not become impure if the wagon is over a dead body. However, the undercarriage is not included with the wagon in this regard. If a hole in the wagon is sealed by the undercarriage, it is not considered to be sealed with regard to preventing ritual impurity. **And,** likewise, **one may not pull** the wagon **on Shabbat when there is money upon it.**

BACKGROUND

A collapsible candelabrum – מנורה מתפרקת:

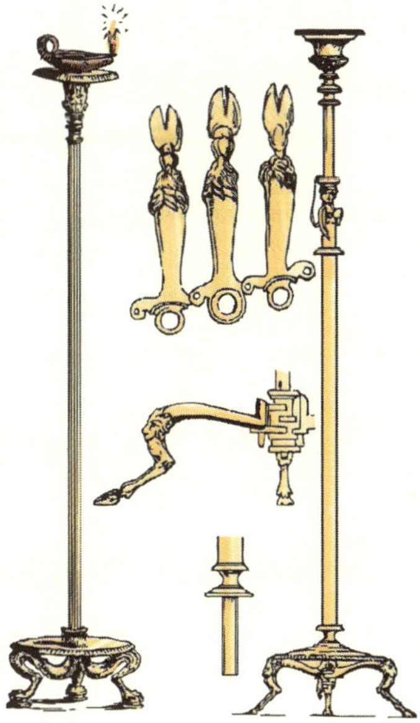

Depiction of a mishnaic-era, collapsible candelabrum and its component parts found in Pompeii

HALAKHA

With regard to a candelabrum made of actual joints, both one that is large and one that is small, it is prohibited to move it – חוליות בין גדולה בין קטנה אסורה לטלטלה: It is prohibited to carry a candelabrum made of joints, whether large or small, on Shabbat, even if it is new (*Mishna Berura*). It is also prohibited by rabbinic decree to carry a candelabrum on Shabbat that has grooves that create the impression that it is made of joints, as per the opinion of Rabbi Yoḥanan (Rambam *Sefer Zemanim, Hilkhot Shabbat* 26:11; *Shulḥan Arukh, Oraḥ Ḥayyim* 279:7).

NOTES

Similar to joints – כעין חוליות: Some commentaries explain that this type of candelabrum was initially made of separate components that were then attached with nails so that the candelabrum could no longer be dismantled (*Me'iri*).

Did Rabbi Yoḥanan actually say that – ומי אמר רבי יוחנן הכי: The commentaries questioned this based on several talmudic sources where the unattributed mishna is in accordance with the opinion of Rabbi Yehuda, and Rabbi Yoḥanan rules in accordance with the opinion of Rabbi Shimon. One explanation is that Rabbi Yoḥanan does, in fact, rule in accordance with Rabbi Shimon's opinion with regard to most *halakhot* of Shabbat. However, with regard to the prohibition of set-aside, which is the issue here, he rules in accordance with the opinion of Rabbi Yehuda (Rashba).

NOTES

Naphtha lamp – דנפטא: Rabbeinu Ḥananel has a variant reading here: A naphtha lamp may be used to cover a naphtha vessel. This is an appropriate reading in our Gemara, as, if the naphtha lamp is too disgusting to be held or used, why would he use it to cover a vessel? Rather, the Gemara is discussing a vessel used with naphtha and there is no concern with regard to its cleanliness. The same is true in the continuation, in the case of pebbles in the yard. They, too, can be used to cover a vessel with naphtha, since the cleanliness of its cover is not an issue.

הא אין עליה מעות – שריא, ואף על גב דהוו עליה בין השמשות! אמר רבי זירא: תהא משנתינו שלא היו עליה מעות כל בין השמשות, שלא לשבור דבריו של רבי יוחנן.

By inference: **If there is not money on it,** one is **permitted** to move the wagon **even though there was** money **on it at twilight.** An object that was set aside at twilight is set aside for the entire Shabbat. In this mishna, moving the wagon is permitted. Clearly, the unattributed mishna is in accordance with the opinion of Rabbi Shimon, who holds that there is no prohibition of set-aside. Why, then, did Rabbi Yoḥanan, who always rules in accordance with an unattributed mishna, not rule in accordance with the opinion of Rabbi Shimon? **Rabbi Zeira said: Let our mishna** apply only to a case **in which there was no money on** the wagon **throughout** the entire duration of **twilight.** This strained interpretation is accepted **so as not to contradict** and reject **Rabbi Yoḥanan's statement.**

אמר רבי יהושע בן לוי: פעם אחת הלך רבי לדיוספרא, והורה במנורה כרבי שמעון בנר. איבעיא להו: הורה במנורה כרבי שמעון בנר – להיתרא, או דילמא: הורה במנורה – לאיסורא וכרבי שמעון בנר – להיתרא? תיקו.

Rabbi Yehoshua ben Levi said: One time, Rabbi Yehuda HaNasi **went to** the town of **Deyosfera, and issued a ruling with regard to a candelabrum in accordance with** the ruling that **Rabbi Shimon** made **with regard to an oil lamp.** This description is insufficiently clear, therefore **a dilemma was raised before** the Sages: Does this mean that **he issued a ruling in** the case of a candelabrum, **like** the ruling that **Rabbi Shimon** made **in** the case of **an oil lamp, to permit** moving it? **Or, perhaps, he issued a ruling in** the case of **a candelabrum to prohibit** moving it, **and** in another case he ruled **in accordance with** the ruling that **Rabbi Shimon** made **in** the case of **an oil lamp, to permit** moving it. There was no resolution found to this dilemma and therefore it **stands** unresolved.

רב מלכיא איקלע לבי רבי שמלאי וטילטל שרגא ואיקפד רבי שמלאי. רבי יוסי גלילאה איקלע לאתריה דרבי יוסי ברבי חנינא, טילטל שרגא ואיקפד רבי יוסי ברבי חנינא. רבי אבהו, כי איקלע לאתריה דרבי יהושע בן לוי – הוה מטלטל שרגא, כי איקלע לאתריה דרבי יוחנן – לא הוה מטלטל שרגא. מה נפשך, אי כרבי יהודה סבירא ליה – ליעבד כרבי יהודה, אי כרבי שמעון סבירא ליה – ליעבד כרבי שמעון! לעולם כרבי שמעון סבירא ליה, ומשום כבודו דרבי יוחנן הוא דלא הוה עביד.

It is told that **Rav Malkiya happened** to come **to the house of Rabbi Simlai and moved an** extinguished oil **lamp, and Rabbi Simlai became angry,** as in his opinion it is prohibited to move an oil lamp because it is set-aside. Likewise, **Rabbi Yosei the Galilean happened** to come **to the place of Rabbi Yosei, son of Rabbi Ḥanina, and moved an** oil **lamp, and Rabbi Yosei, son of Rabbi Ḥanina, became angry.** The Gemara also relates that **Rabbi Abbahu, when he happened** to come **to the place of Rabbi Yehoshua ben Levi, he would move an** oil **lamp.** However, **when he happened** to come **to the place of Rabbi Yoḥanan, he would not move an** oil **lamp.** The Gemara wondered: **Whichever** way **you** look at it there is a difficulty. **If he holds in accordance with** the opinion of **Rabbi Yehuda, let him act in accordance with** the opinion of **Rabbi Yehuda** everywhere and refrain from moving the lamp. **And if he holds in accordance with** the opinion of **Rabbi Shimon, let him act in accordance with** the opinion of **Rabbi Shimon** everywhere and move the oil lamp. The Gemara answers: **Actually,** it can be explained that Rabbi Abbahu **holds in accordance with** the opinion of **Rabbi Shimon; however, in deference to Rabbi Yoḥanan he did not act** accordingly, so as not to act contrary to his ruling in the place where he was the authority.

אמר רב יהודה: שרגא דמשחא – שרי לטלטולה, דנפטא – אסור לטלטולה. רבה ורב יוסף דאמרי תרווייהו: דנפטא נמי שרי לטלטולה. (דהואיל וחזי לכסות ביה מנא).

With regard to the *halakhot* of moving lamps on Shabbat, **Rav Yehuda said:** With regard to **an** extinguished **oil lamp, it is permitted to move it,** whereas a **naphtha** lamp, **it is prohibited to move it.** Since the smell of naphtha is unpleasant, the lamp is used exclusively for lighting. Therefore, moving it is prohibited. **Rabba and Rav Yosef both said:** With regard to **a naphtha** lamp, **too, it is permitted to move it.**

רב אויא איקלע לבי רבא, הוה מאיסן בי כרעיה בטינא, אתיבי אפוריא קמיה דרבא. איקפד רבא, בעא לצעוריה. אמר ליה: מאי טעמא רבה ורב יוסף דאמרי תרווייהו שרגא דנפטא נמי שרי לטלטוליה? אמר ליה: הואיל וחזיא לכסויי בה מנא. אלא מעתה כל צרורות שבחצר מטלטלין, הואיל וחזיא לכסויי בהו מנא! אמר ליה: הא – איכא תורת כלי עליה, הני – ליכא תורת כלי עליה. מי לא תניא

The Gemara relates: **Rav Avya happened** to come **to Rava's house. His feet were dirty with clay and he put them on the bed before Rava. Rava became angry** at him for dirtying the bed and, therefore, **sought to torment him** with questions that he could not answer. Rava **said to him: What is the reason** that **Rabba and Rav Yosef both said** that with regard to **a naphtha lamp,**[N] **too, that it is permitted to move it?** Rav Avya **said to him: Since it is suitable to cover a vessel with it.** Rava **said to him: But if that is so, all pebbles** in the yard **may** also **be carried** *ab initio* on Shabbat, **since it is suitable to cover a vessel with them.** Rav Avya **said to him:** There is a distinction between these cases. **This,** the lamp, **the status of a vessel** applies **to it** and there are leniencies that apply to vessels with regard to the *halakhot* of set-aside. **These,** the pebbles, **the status of a vessel does not** apply **to it,** as they are a raw material. Carrying them is prohibited unless designated for a specific purpose before Shabbat. **Was it not taught** in a *baraita* that

הַשֵּׁירִים וְהַנְּזָמִים וְהַטַּבָּעוֹת הֲרֵי הֵן כְּכׇל הַכֵּלִים הַנִּטָּלִים בֶּחָצֵר, וְאָמַר עוּלָּא: מַה טַּעַם – הוֹאִיל וְאִיכָּא תּוֹרַת כְּלִי עֲלֵיהּ. הָכָא נַמִי – הוֹאִיל וְאִיכָּא תּוֹרַת כְּלִי עֲלֵיהּ. אָמַר רַב נַחְמָן בַּר יִצְחָק: בְּרִיךְ רַחֲמָנָא דְּלָא כְּסִיפֵיהּ רָבָא לְרַב אַוְיָא.

bracelets,[B] **nose-rings and rings,** although it is prohibited to go out into the public domain wearing them on Shabbat, **they are like all the vessels that may be moved in the courtyard;** in the private domain, one may move them and they are not set-aside. **And Ulla said: What is the reason** that it is permitted to move nose-rings in the yard? It is **because the status of a vessel** applies **to it.**[N] Apparently, vessel status is sufficient to permit moving it on Shabbat. **Rav Naḥman bar Yitzḥak said: Thank God** that **Rava did not embarrass Rav Avya** and Rav Avya managed to successfully answer Rava's questions.

רָמֵי לֵיהּ אַבַּיֵי לְרַבָּה: תַּנְיָא, מוֹתַר הַשֶּׁמֶן שֶׁבַּנֵּר וְשֶׁבַּקְּעָרָה – אָסוּר, וְרַבִּי שִׁמְעוֹן מַתִּיר. אַלְמָא: לְרַבִּי שִׁמְעוֹן לֵית לֵיהּ מוּקְצֶה. וּרְמִינְהוּ, רַבִּי שִׁמְעוֹן אוֹמֵר: כׇּל שֶׁאֵין מוּמוֹ נִיכָּר מֵעֶרֶב יוֹם טוֹב – אֵין זֶה מִן הַמּוּכָן!

Abaye raised a contradiction before Rabba citing two sources with regard to set-aside on Shabbat. **It was taught** in a *baraita*: With regard to **the remaining oil that is in an oil lamp and in a bowl** in which a wick was lit, it **is prohibited** to use it on Shabbat **and Rabbi Shimon permits** using it. **Apparently, Rabbi Shimon is not of** the opinion that there is a prohibition of **set-aside. And a contradiction is raised** from a parallel source, in which the Sages discussed the *halakha* of the firstborn of a kosher animal that developed a blemish on a Festival. The firstborn must be examined to determine whether or not that type of blemish disqualifies the animal from being sacrificed as an offering. If it is disqualified, it may be redeemed, slaughtered, and eaten as non-sacred meat on the Festival.[N] **Rabbi Shimon says: Any** firstborn animal **whose blemish is not perceptible before the Festival is not among** the animals **prepared** prior to the Festival for use on the Festival, and it is prohibited to slaughter it. Apparently, an item not prepared in advance has set-aside status according to Rabbi Shimon.

הָכִי הָשְׁתָּא! הָתָם – אָדָם יוֹשֵׁב וּמְצַפֶּה אֵימָתַי תִּכְבֶּה נֵרוֹ, הָכָא – אָדָם יוֹשֵׁב וּמְצַפֶּה מָתַי יִפּוֹל בּוֹ מוּם?! מֵימַר אָמַר: מִי יֵימַר דְּנָפֵיל בֵּיהּ מוּמָא, וְאִם תִּמְצֵי לוֹמַר דְּנָפֵיל בֵּיהּ מוּמָא – מִי יֵימַר דְּנָפֵיל בֵּיהּ מוּם קָבוּעַ, וְאִם תִּמְצֵי לוֹמַר דְּנָפֵל בֵּיהּ מוּם קָבוּעַ – מִי יֵימַר דְּמִזְדַּקֵּק לֵיהּ חָכָם?

Rabba said to him: **How can you compare** these cases? **There,** in the case of the lamp, **a person sits and anticipates when his candle will be extinguished.** It is clear to him that it will be extinguished, and he can safely assume that a certain amount of oil will remain in the lamp or the bowl. **Here,** does **a person sit and anticipate when a blemish will befall** his animal? The owner of the animal **says: Who says that a blemish will befall** his animal? **And** even **if you say that a blemish will befall it, who says that a permanent blemish** that would enable it to be slaughtered **will befall it? And** even **if you say that a permanent blemish will befall it, who says that a Sage will** agree to **engage** in examining the blemish? Since there are so many uncertainties involved, if the blemish is not perceptible before the Festival, the possibility of the firstborn animal becoming available does not enter a person's mind at all.

מְתִיב רָמִי בַּר חָמָא: מְפִירִין נְדָרִים בַּשַּׁבָּת, [וְנִשְׁאָלִין לִנְדָרִים שֶׁהֵן] לְצוֹרֶךְ הַשַּׁבָּת. וְאַמַּאי? לֵימָא: מִי יֵימַר דְּמִיזְדַּקֵּק לָהּ בַּעַל?

Rami bar Ḥama raised an objection to this last point from that which we learned in a mishna: **One may nullify vows**[N] **on Shabbat.** A woman who vowed that certain food is prohibited to her, her husband can nullify her vow on Shabbat. **And** likewise **one may request** that a Sage find an opening **to** dissolve his **vows,**[N] i.e., a factor that the one taking the vow failed to take into account or an element of regret, if that nullification or dissolution is **for the purpose of Shabbat.** The question arises: **And why,** after a man has nullified his wife's vow, should she be permitted to eat that food? When the woman vowed not to eat that food, she consciously set it aside. Even if some way to dissolve the vow is found, the food should remain set-aside. On the basis of the same uncertainty that was raised above, **say: Who says that** her husband **will** agree to **engage** in nullifying her oath? Perhaps he will refuse to nullify it.

BACKGROUND

Ankle bracelet – שֵׁיר לְרַגְלַיִם:

Ankle bracelet from the period of the Mishna

NOTES

Because the status of a vessel applies to it – הוֹאִיל וְאִיכָּא תּוֹרַת כְּלִי עֲלֵיהּ: The rationale for this distinction is that raw material is not a vessel and therefore is typically set aside from use on Shabbat for two reasons: It has no use in its present state, and fashioning a vessel from raw material is prohibited. That is not the case with a vessel, which is complete and ready for use. It is only due to Shabbat prohibitions or other external reasons that its use is prohibited for a certain period of time.

Permitting non-sacred slaughter of firstborn animals – הֶיתֵּר בְּכוֹרוֹת לִשְׁחִיטַת חוּלִּין: The Torah commands the giving of the firstborn male of all kosher animals to a priest (see Numbers 18). When the Temple was standing, the unblemished firstborn of a kosher animal was offered as a sacrifice, and the priest would eat the meat; a blemished firstborn animal was eaten by the priest without it being sacrificed. After the destruction of the Temple, the sanctity of the firstborn is still in effect; however, using the animal is prohibited. If it develops a permanent blemish that would invalidate it as a sacrifice, the animal is given to the priest and he may eat it. Great expertise is required to distinguish between the different blemishes, and the responsibility resting upon the shoulders of the one performing the examination is great, as it can result in the misuse of consecrated property. Consequently, only a Sage who received special authorization has license to examine firstborn animals.

One may nullify vows – מְפִירִין נְדָרִים: The *halakhot* of vows and their nullification are articulated in the Torah (Numbers 30), and the entire tractate of *Nedarim* is devoted to those *halakhot*. By Torah law, a husband may nullify his wife's vows on the day that he hears them. The Gemara explains that this applies only to those vows that affect her husband in some way. Since the verse itself states: "Every vow, and every binding oath to afflict the soul, her husband may let it stand, or her husband may make it void" (Numbers 30:14), the statement of Rav Pineḥas is readily understood. From the time she takes the vow, she is aware that it is contingent upon her husband's consent (see the Ran).

One may request to dissolve his vows – נִשְׁאָלִין לִנְדָרִים: In tractate *Nedarim*, it is explained at length that one may dissolve a vow that he made by consulting with a Sage. There are several reasons that a Sage would agree to dissolve a vow. The simplest reason is if the one who took the vow realizes afterward that it is difficult for him to fulfill it, and, therefore, he regrets taking the vow. Since regret is a valid reason to dissolve the vow, in exigent circumstances, even three common people who are not experts can comprise a court to dissolve a vow.

הָתָם כִּדְרַב פִּנְחָס מִשְּׁמֵיהּ דְּרָבָא, דְּאָמַר רַב פִּנְחָס מִשְּׁמֵיהּ דְּרָבָא: כׇּל הַנּוֹדֶרֶת – עַל דַּעַת בַּעְלָהּ הִיא נוֹדֶרֶת.

The Gemara answers: **There,** in the case of vows, it can be explained **in accordance with** that which **Rav Pineḥas** said **in the name** of **Rava,** who came to explain some of the fundamentals of the *halakhot* of vows, **as Rav Pineḥas said in the name** of Rava: **Every** woman **who takes a vow,** it is from the outset contingent **on her husband's consent that she takes the vow.** Since she knows that her husband has the ability to nullify it, her vows are not absolute and their final validation comes only through her husband's agreement. When a woman vows, she does not set aside the food absolutely from potential use.

תָּא שְׁמַע: נִשְׁאָלִין לִנְדָרִים שֶׁל צוֹרֶךְ הַשַּׁבָּת בְּשַׁבָּת. וְאַמַּאי? לֵימָא: מִי יֵימַר דְּמִזְדַּקֵּק לֵיהּ חָכָם? הָתָם אִי לָא מִיזְדַּקֵּק לֵיהּ חָכָם סַגְיָא לֵיהּ בִּשְׁלֹשָׁה הֶדְיוֹטוֹת, הָכָא – מִי יֵימַר דְּמִיזְדַּקֵּק לֵיהּ חָכָם.

Moreover, the Gemara cites proof for this from that which was taught: **Come** and **hear: One may request** that a Sage dissolve his **vows**[B] **for the purpose of Shabbat on Shabbat,** i.e., one who vowed on Shabbat that eating on that day is prohibited for him. **And why** is he permitted to eat something that was prohibited to him by his vow? **Say** again: **Who says that** the **Sage will** agree to **engage** in dissolution of **his** vow? Consequently, one has certainly diverted his attention from the food, set it aside, and it should be prohibited to eat it. The Gemara answers: Nevertheless, there is a difference, as **there,** in the *halakhot* of vows, even **if** the **Sage does not** agree to **engage** in dissolution of **his** vow, **he** can **suffice** with renouncing the vow **before three common people.** Even though it is preferable to have a Sage dissolve his vow, in exigent circumstances one may turn to a court of three common people to dissolve it. He will certainly find a way to dissolve his vow. However, **here,** in the case of the firstborn animal, **who says that** the **Sage will** agree to **engage** in examination of the blemish? In the *halakhot* of firstborn animals only an ordained Sage, who received special license to do so, is authorized to verify that it is a permanent blemish and permit redemption and slaughter of the animal as a non-sacred animal.

רָמֵי לֵיהּ אַבָּיֵי לְרַב יוֹסֵף: מִי אָמַר רַבִּי שִׁמְעוֹן "כָּבְתָה מוּתָּר לְטַלְטְלָהּ", כָּבְתָה – אִין, לֹא כָּבְתָה – לָא. מַאי טַעְמָא – דִּילְמָא בַּהֲדֵי דְּנָקֵיט לָהּ כָּבְתָה, הָא שָׁמְעִינַן לֵיהּ לְרַבִּי שִׁמְעוֹן דְּאָמַר: דָּבָר שֶׁאֵין מִתְכַּוֵּין מוּתָּר; דְּתַנְיָא, רַבִּי שִׁמְעוֹן אוֹמֵר: גּוֹרֵר אָדָם כִּסֵּא מִטָּה וְסַפְסָל, וּבִלְבַד שֶׁלֹּא יִתְכַּוֵּין לַעֲשׂוֹת חָרִיץ!

Abaye raised a contradiction before Rav Yosef: Did Rabbi Shimon actually **say** that when a lamp **is extinguished,** it **is permitted to move it** on Shabbat? By inference: After **it is extinguished, yes,** moving it is permitted; so long as it **is not extinguished, no,** moving it is prohibited. **What is the reason** that it is prohibited to move a burning candle? It is due to concern that **perhaps, as he moves** the lamp, the flame **will be extinguished.** However, is Rabbi Shimon really concerned that a flame will be extinguished under those circumstances? **Didn't we learn** that **Rabbi Shimon stated** a principle: **An unintentional act,** a permitted action from which an unintended prohibited labor ensues on Shabbat, since he did not intend to perform the prohibited action, **is permitted? As it was taught** in a *baraita*, **Rabbi Shimon says: A person may drag a bed, chair, and bench** on the ground, **as long as he does not intend** to **make a furrow** in the ground. Even if a furrow is formed inadvertently, one need not be concerned. Since that was not his intention, there is no prohibition according to Rabbi Shimon. Consequently, according to Rabbi Shimon there should be no prohibition in moving a burning candle, even though it may be extinguished. Since that is not the intention of the one moving it, no prohibition would be violated.

כׇּל הֵיכָא דְּכִי מִיכַּוֵּין אִיכָּא אִיסּוּרָא דְּאוֹרַיְיתָא – כִּי לָא מִיכַּוֵּין גְּזַר רַבִּי שִׁמְעוֹן מִדְּרַבָּנָן, כׇּל הֵיכָא דְּכִי מִיכַּוֵּין אִיכָּא אִיסּוּרָא דְּרַבָּנַן – כִּי לָא מִיכַּוֵּין שָׁרֵי רַבִּי שִׁמְעוֹן לְכַתְּחִילָּה.

The Gemara answers that there is a distinction between the cases: In **every** case **where if** he **intends** to perform the action, **there is a prohibition by Torah law,** e.g. extinguishing a candle; even **when he does not intend** to do so, **Rabbi Shimon issued a decree** prohibiting it **by rabbinic law.** However, in **every** case **where** even **if** he **intends** to perform the action, **there is** merely **a prohibition by rabbinic law,** e.g., digging a furrow which is not a full-fledged act of plowing that is prohibited by Torah law, but is prohibited only by rabbinic law, **when he does not intend** to perform the action, **Rabbi Shimon** even **permits** performing this action ***ab initio.***

BACKGROUND

Vows – **נְדָרִים**: This refers to a personal vow, i.e., a voluntary obligation to refrain from performing a certain action or from deriving benefit from someone. This is, in effect, a type of reverse consecration. The person pledges to regard the object or person as if it, or he, were consecrated to the Temple. Any object can be forsworn, and one who fails to fulfill his vow violates the commandment: "He shall not profane his word" (Numbers 30:3). It is also possible to prohibit one's own property to another by means of a vow; the other person must then treat that property as consecrated. However, one cannot prohibit another's property to anyone other than himself. The vows of a female minor, a young woman, or a wife may be annulled by her father or husband, respectively. Other individuals can be released from their vows by a Torah scholar or a rabbinical court, if they can show that their vows were not taken with full knowledge and intent. The Sages were very strongly opposed to the taking of vows and encouraged people who had taken vows to have them dissolved. If one makes a statement worded in the form of a vow, and it is evident that the intention was not to utter a vow but rather to make a point by means of exaggeration or hyperbole, that vow is not considered binding.

מְתִיב רָבָא: מוֹכְרֵי כְסוּת מוֹכְרִין כְּדַרְכָּן, וּבִלְבַד שֶׁלֹּא יִתְכַּוֵּין בַּחַמָּה מִפְּנֵי הַחַמָּה, וּבַגְּשָׁמִים מִפְּנֵי הַגְּשָׁמִים, וְהַצְּנוּעִין מַפְשִׁילִין בְּמַקֵּל לַאֲחוֹרֵיהֶן. וְהָא הָכָא, דְּכִי מִיכַּוֵּין – אִיסּוּרָא דְּאוֹרַיְיתָא אִיכָּא, כִּי לָא מִיכַּוֵּין – שָׁרֵי רַבִּי שִׁמְעוֹן לְכַתְּחִילָּה!

Rava raised an objection to this distinction from that which we learned in a mishna: **Clothing merchants** who sell garments made of diverse kinds, a prohibited mixture of wool and linen, **may sell them as they normally would** to gentiles. A merchant may place the garments he is selling on his shoulders and need not be concerned about the prohibition against wearing diverse kinds, **as long** as the merchant **does not intend** to benefit from the garments **in the sun** as protection **from the sun, or in the rain** as protection **from the rain. However, the modest** people, those who are particularly meticulous in their performance of mitzvot, would **suspend** the wool and linen garments **on a stick behind them. And here, isn't it** a case where **if** one **intends** to wear the clothing, **there is a prohibition by Torah law,** and even so **when** he **does not intend** to wear it, **Rabbi Shimon permits** it ***ab initio.*** Apparently, Rabbi Shimon does not distinguish between cases on that basis.

אֶלָּא אָמַר רָבָא:

Rather, Rava said a different explanation for Rabbi Shimon's prohibition in the case of an oil lamp:

Perek **III**
Daf **47** Amud **a**

הַנַּח לְנֵר שֶׁמֶן וּפְתִילָה – הוֹאִיל דְּנַעֲשָׂה בָּסִיס לְדָבָר הָאָסוּר.

Leave the candle, oil, and wick, since they **became a base for a prohibited object.**[N] Even Rabbi Shimon agrees that a flame burning on Shabbat is set-aside. Since it is prohibited to move the flame, moving the lamp, oil, and wick is also prohibited.

אָמַר רַבִּי זֵירָא אָמַר רַבִּי אַסִי אָמַר רַבִּי יוֹחָנָן אָמַר רַבִּי חֲנִינָא אָמַר רַבִּי רוֹמָנוּס: לִי הִתִּיר רַבִּי לְטַלְטֵל מַחְתָּה בְּאֶפְרָהּ. אָמַר לֵיהּ רַבִּי זֵירָא לְרַבִּי אַסִי: מִי אָמַר רַבִּי יוֹחָנָן הָכִי? וְהָתְנַן: נוֹטֵל אָדָם בְּנוֹ וְהָאֶבֶן בְּיָדוֹ, אוֹ כַּלְכָּלָה וְהָאֶבֶן בְּתוֹכָהּ. וְאָמַר רַבָּה בַּר בַּר חָנָה אָמַר רַבִּי יוֹחָנָן: בְּכַלְכָּלָה מְלֵאָה פֵּירוֹת עָסְקִינַן. טַעְמָא – דְּאִית בָּהּ פֵּירֵי, הָא לֵית בָּהּ פֵּירֵי – לָא!

Rabbi Zeira said that **Rabbi Asi said** that **Rabbi Yoḥanan said** that **Rabbi Ḥanina said** that **Rabbi Romanus said: Rabbi** Yehuda HaNasi **permitted me to carry a coal pan with its ashes. Rabbi Zeira said to Rabbi Asi: Did Rabbi Yoḥanan** actually **say that? Didn't we learn** in a mishna: **A person may carry his son** in his hands **and** even if the son has **a stone,** which is prohibited to carry, **in his hands; or,** one may carry **a basket with a stone inside it? And Rabba bar bar Ḥana said** that **Rabbi Yoḥanan said: We are dealing with a basket that is full of fruit.** Due to the fruit, carrying the stone is also permitted. **The reason** for the leniency is because **there is fruit inside** the basket; **however, if there is no fruit inside it, no,** one may not move it. With regard to the coal pan that is filled with ashes, how can moving it be permitted according to Rabbi Yoḥanan?

״אֶשְׁתּוֹמַם כְּשָׁעָה חֲדָא״ וַאֲמַר: הָכָא נַמִי – דְּאִית בָּהּ קְרָטִין. אֲמַר אַבַּיֵי: קְרָטִין בֵּי רַבִּי מִי חֲשִׁיבִי?

"He was astonished for a while" (Daniel 4:16) and could not find an answer. **And,** ultimately, Rabbi Asi **said: Here, too,** it is referring to a case where the coal pan **has bits** of frankincense that were not yet burned. Due to those bits, moving the pan is permitted. **Abaye said:** Are small **bits in the house of Rabbi** Yehuda HaNasi **significant?** Since they are not significant, they are nullified by the ashes and the mixture is entirely unsuitable for use.

וְכִי תֵּימָא – חֲזוּ לַעֲנִיִּים, וְהָתַנְיָא: בִּגְדֵי עֲנִיִּים – לַעֲנִיִּים, בִּגְדֵי עֲשִׁירִים – לַעֲשִׁירִים, אֲבָל דַּעֲנִיִּים לַעֲשִׁירִים – לֹא! אֶלָּא אָמַר אַבַּיֵי: מִידֵּי דַּהֲוָה אַגְּרָף שֶׁל רֵיעִי.

And if you say: The bits **are suitable** for the **poor.** We will explain that the value of an object is determined not by its context, but by its intrinsic value. **Wasn't it taught** in a *baraita* that there is a difference with regard to the *halakhot* of ritual impurity between garments belonging to poor people, which can become ritually impure even if they are very small, and garments belonging to the wealthy, which are not considered significant unless they contain a larger amount of fabric? Garments the size of **poor people's clothing** are **for the poor,** and garments the size of **rich people's clothing** are **for the rich;** **however,** clothes of **the poor for the rich**[N] **are not** significant. Apparently, the significance of an object is determined by its context and its owner. **Rather, Abaye said** an alternative explanation: The *halakha* here is **just as** it is **in** the case of **a chamber pot of feces.** Since it is disgusting, removing it from the house is permitted, even though clearly there is no use for it.

NOTES

Leave the candle, oil, and wick, since they became a base for a prohibited object – הַנַּח לְנֵר שֶׁמֶן וּפְתִילָה הוֹאִיל דְּנַעֲשָׂה בָּסִיס לְדָבָר הָאָסוּר: The question was raised: Why does the Gemara say that the wick is a base for a prohibited object? It is a prohibited object itself (*Tosafot*). Some commentaries explain that the discussion is with regard to a burning wick. Since it is serving its designated purpose, i.e., burning, it is not set-aside. It is only prohibited to move the wick because it is a base for the flame (*Derush VeḤiddush*).

Clothes of the poor for the rich – דַּעֲנִיִּים לַעֲשִׁירִים: Some commentaries explain that for poor people, thick, coarse clothes are measured as garments as far as ritual impurity is concerned. For rich people, who do not wear coarse garments, a larger measure is required, and they are measured as a sack (*Me'iri*).

אָמַר רָבָא: שְׁתֵּי תְּשׁוּבוֹת בַּדָּבָר: חֲדָא: גְּרָף שֶׁל רֵיעִי – מְאִיס, וְהַאי – לָא מְאִיס. וְעוֹד: גְּרָף שֶׁל רֵיעִי – מִיגַּלֵּי, וְהַאי מִיכְסֵי! אֶלָּא אָמַר רָבָא: כִּי הֲוֵינַן בֵּי רַב נַחְמָן הֲוָה מְטַלְטְלִינַן כָּנוּנָא אַגַּב קִיטְמָא וְאַף עַל גַּב דְּאִיכָּא עֲלֵיהּ שִׁבְרֵי עֵצִים. מֵיתִיבֵי: וְשָׁוִין שֶׁאִם יֵשׁ בָּהּ שִׁבְרֵי פְתִילָה – שֶׁאָסוּר לְטַלְטֵל! אָמַר אַבַּיֵי: בְּגָלִילָא שָׁנוּ.

Rava said: There are **two answers to** reject **this** analogy: **One, a chamber pot with feces is disgusting,** and the coal pan **is not disgusting. And furthermore: A chamber pot with feces is uncovered** and smells, **and** the coal pan **is covered. Rather, Rava said** an alternative explanation: **When we were at the house of Rav Naḥman we would move a coal pan** [*kanuna*][L] **on account of the ashes, and we did this even though there were broken pieces of wood on it.** Since the ashes can be used to cover filth, it is not set-aside and the coal pan may be moved due to the ashes. Even if there were also broken sticks on the pan that are useless, nevertheless they are nullified by the ashes. The Gemara **raises an objection** to this last remark from that which was cited previously: **And** Rabbi Yehuda and Rabbi Shimon **agree that if there were fragments of a wick in** the lamp, **that it is prohibited to move** it. Apparently, these fragments are not null and render the entire lamp set-aside. **Abaye said:** No proof can be cited from that *baraita* because **they taught** it **in the Galilee,**[NH] where oil is abundant and inexpensive. That is why broken wicks are not nullified relative to the oil (Rav Nissim Gaon).

לֵוִי בַּר שְׁמוּאֵל אַשְׁכְּחִינְהוּ לְרַבִּי אַבָּא וּלְרַב הוּנָא בַּר חִיָּיא דַּהֲווּ קָיְימִי אַפִּיתְחָא דְּבֵי רַב הוּנָא, אֲמַר לְהוּ: מַהוּ לְהַחֲזִיר מִטָּה שֶׁל טַרְסִיִּים בְּשַׁבָּת? אֲמַרוּ לֵיהּ: שַׁפִּיר דָּמֵי. אֲתָא לְקַמֵּיהּ דְּרַב יְהוּדָה, אֲמַר: הָא רַב וּשְׁמוּאֵל דְּאָמְרִי תַּרְוַיְיהוּ: הַמַּחֲזִיר מִטָּה שֶׁל טַרְסִיִּים בְּשַׁבָּת – חַיָּיב חַטָּאת.

The Gemara relates that **Levi bar Shmuel found Rabbi Abba and Rav Huna bar Ḥiyya, who were standing at the entrance of Rav Huna's house.** Levi bar Shmuel **said to them: What is** the *halakha* with regard to **reassembling a weaver's loom,**[NH] which was typically a collapsible frame, **on Shabbat? They said to him:** It may **well** be done. **He came before Rav Yehuda,** asking him the same question, and Rav Yehuda **said** to him that **Rav and Shmuel both said: One who reassembles a weaver's loom on Shabbat is liable to** bring **a sin-offering,** as he performed a labor prohibited by Torah law on Shabbat.

מֵיתִיבֵי: הַמַּחֲזִיר קְנֵה מְנוֹרָה בְּשַׁבָּת – חַיָּיב חַטָּאת, קְנֵה סַיָּידִין – לֹא יַחֲזִיר, וְאִם הֶחֱזִיר – פָּטוּר אֲבָל אָסוּר. רַבִּי סִימַאי אוֹמֵר: קֶרֶן עֲגוּלָּה – חַיָּיב, קֶרֶן פְּשׁוּטָה – פָּטוּר! אִינְהוּ דַּאֲמוּר כִּי הַאי תַּנָּא – דְּתַנְיָא: מַלְבְּנוֹת הַמִּטָּה, וְכַרְעוֹת הַמִּטָּה, וּלְוָוחִים שֶׁל סְקִיבָּס – לֹא יַחֲזִיר, וְאִם הֶחֱזִיר – פָּטוּר

The Gemara **raises an objection** to the statement of Levi bar Shmuel from the *Tosefta*: **One who reassembles the branch of a** disassembled **candelabrum on Shabbat is liable to** bring **a sin-offering.** With regard to **the plasterer's pole,** which has several component parts, **one may not reassemble it** *ab initio*, **and if he reassembled it, he is exempt** from bringing a sin-offering, **although it is prohibited. Rabbi Simai says:** With regard to **a rounded horn,** which is a trumpet that can be dismantled and whose assembly is complicated, one who reassembled it **is liable.** However, **a straight horn,**[B] which is easy to assemble, one who assembled it **is exempt.** Apparently, assembling an object that consists of several components on Shabbat is prohibited by Torah law, and one is liable to bring a sin-offering for doing so. The Gemara answers: **They said** that it is permitted **in accordance with** the opinion of **this** *tanna*, **as it was taught** in a *baraita*: **A bed frame,** which is a wooden frame through which the ropes of the bed were interlaced, **and the legs of the bed, and the archer's tablets** [*skibas*],[LB] which refers to the part of a bow upon which one pulls the arrow back, if they were detached from the bed or from the bow, **one may not reassemble** them, **and if he reassembled** them **he is exempt.**

LANGUAGE

Coal pan [*kanuna*] – כָּנוּנָא: This word is found in the same form in Syriac and in Arabic, and it means a vessel in which coals are placed, i.e., a pan.

NOTES

They taught it in the Galilee – בְּגָלִילָא שָׁנוּ: The commentaries explain that the legal status of the Galilee was different not due to poverty or wealth. Rather, the Galilee was not considered a place of Torah, and the Sages adopted a more stringent policy with regard to issuing decrees in places where there were few Torah scholars (Rav Nissim Gaon).

Weaver's loom – מִטָּה שֶׁל טַרְסִיִּים: This *halakha* is connected to the previous discussion with regard to moving a lamp. The conclusion was that a lamp that can be disassembled may not be reassembled, as in doing so one would perform the prohibited labor of building on Shabbat (*Penei Yehoshua*).

BACKGROUND

A rounded horn and a straight horn – קֶרֶן עֲגוּלָּה וְקֶרֶן פְּשׁוּטָה:

Round Roman horn

Straight Roman horn

Archer's tablet – סְקִיבָּס: According to Rashi, the *skibas* in this image is the kind of bow mentioned in the Talmud. The wooden components of the bow are the boards of the *skibas*.

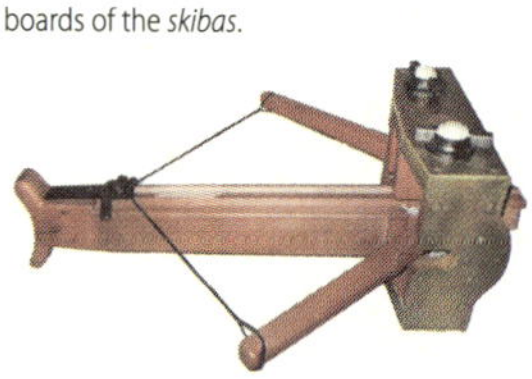

Bow installed on a rod

LANGUAGE

Archer's tablet [*skibas*] – סְקִיבָּס: This word is a distortion of the Greek word στιβάς, *stibas*, which means a bed of straw or leaves. According to the context of the Gemara, it appears to refer to a mattress, although most commentators understand it as relating to a kind of bow (see Background, left).

HALAKHA

We would move a coal pan on account of its ashes…They taught it in the Galilee – הֲוָה מְטַלְטְלִינַן כָּנוּנָא אַגַּב קִיטְמָא...בְּגָלִילָא שָׁנוּ: The case of carrying a coal pan, which was lit before Shabbat and contains ashes and sticks, serves as the basis for the principle that one is permitted to carry an object that serves as a base for both prohibited and permitted objects. The *Mishna Berura* rules that this principle applies only if the permitted object is more significant than the prohibited one. However, if the prohibited object is worth more, or the value of the two is equal, then carrying the base is prohibited. The value of an object is determined subjectively by each individual (*Magen Avraham*; Rambam *Sefer Zemanim, Hilkhot Shabbat* 26:13; *Shulḥan Arukh, Oraḥ Ḥayyim* 310:8).

Weaver's loom – מִטָּה שֶׁל טַרְסִיִּים: Assembling an object whose component parts are loosely connected is permitted on Shabbat. One may not attach the components tightly. If he does so, he is liable to bring a sin-offering, as per the opinion of Rabban Shimon ben Gamliel (Rambam *Sefer Zemanim, Hilkhot Shabbat* 22:26; *Shulḥan Arukh, Oraḥ Ḥayyim* 313:6).

אֲבָל אָסוּר. וְלֹא יִתְקַע, וְאִם תָּקַע – חַיָּיב חַטָּאת. רַבָּן שִׁמְעוֹן בֶּן גַּמְלִיאֵל אוֹמֵר: אִם הָיָה רָפוּי – מוּתָּר.

However, doing so is **prohibited. And one may not fasten** the pieces together forcefully, **and if he fastens** them, **he is liable to** bring **a sin-offering** for performing a labor prohibited by Torah law. **Rabban Shimon ben Gamliel says: If it was loose** and could be assembled with ease, **it is permitted.**[N] Rabbi Abba and Rav Huna bar Hiyya relied on this opinion.

בֵּי רַב חָמָא הֲוָה מִטָּה גְּלַלְנִיתָא, הֲוָה מְהַדְּרִי לָהּ בְּיוֹמָא טָבָא. אֲמַר לֵיהּ הַהוּא מִדְּרַבָּנַן לְרָבָא: מַאי דַּעְתִּיךְ, בִּנְיָן מִן הַצַּד הוּא, נְהִי דְּאִיסּוּרָא דְּאוֹרַיְיתָא – לֵיכָּא, אִיסּוּרָא דְּרַבָּנַן מִיהָא אִיכָּא! אֲמַר לֵיהּ: אֲנָא כְּרַבָּן שִׁמְעוֹן בֶּן גַּמְלִיאֵל סְבִירָא לִי, דְּאָמַר: אִם הָיָה רָפוּי – מוּתָּר.

The Gemara relates: **In the house of Rav Ḥama,** Rava's grandfather, **there was a collapsible bed,**[R] similar to a weaver's loom, **and they would reassemble it on a Festival. One of the Sages said to Rava: What is your opinion?** Do you hold that this **is allowed** because **it is building in an atypical manner?**[N] In other words, one is not performing the prohibited labor of building since it is was not performed in the standard manner? **Although there is no Torah prohibition, there is, in any case, a rabbinic prohibition.** Rava **said to him: I hold in accordance with** the opinion of **Rabban Shimon ben Gamliel** who said that **if it were loose, it is permitted** even *ab initio*.

מתני׳ נוֹתְנִין כְּלִי תַּחַת הַנֵּר לְקַבֵּל נִיצוֹצוֹת. וְלֹא יִתֵּן לְתוֹכוֹ מַיִם – מִפְּנֵי שֶׁהוּא מְכַבֶּה.

MISHNA **One may place a vessel beneath the** oil **lamp** in order **to receive burning sparks**[H] of oil that fall from the lamp so that they will not cause a fire. **And he may not place water into** the vessel **because he** thereby **extinguishes** the sparks.

גמ׳ וְהָא קָמְבַטֵּל כְּלִי מֵהֵיכָנוֹ! אָמַר רַב הוּנָא בְּרֵיהּ דְּרַב יְהוֹשֻׁעַ: נִיצוֹצוֹת אֵין בָּהֶן מַמָּשׁ.

GEMARA The Gemara asks: How is it permitted to position this vessel to receive the sparks, **doesn't he** thereby **negate** the **vessel's preparedness?** It is no longer prepared for any use on Shabbat as the sparks accord it set-aside status. The opinion that negating the preparedness of a vessel is prohibited has already been stated. **Rav Huna, son of Rav Yehoshua, said: Sparks have no substance.** They burn immediately and do not leave behind any trace of oil in the vessel. Therefore, the vessel remains suitable to be moved.

״וְלֹא יִתֵּן לְתוֹכוֹ מַיִם מִפְּנֵי שֶׁהוּא מְכַבֶּה״. לֵימָא תְּנַן סְתָמָא כְּרַבִּי יוֹסֵי, דְּאָמַר: גּוֹרֵם לְכִיבּוּי – אָסוּר!

And we also learned in the mishna that **one may not place water into** the vessel situated beneath the candle **because he** thereby **extinguishes** the sparks. The Gemara remarks: **Is that to say** that **we learned** an **unattributed** mishna **in accordance with** the opinion of **Rabbi Yosei,** who **said** that even an action that **causes extinguishing** indirectly **is prohibited?** The extinguishing in this case, where water was placed into a vessel, was not accomplished by means of a direct action. His action only caused it to extinguish indirectly.

וְתִסְבְּרָא?! אֵימוּר דְּאָמַר רַבִּי יוֹסֵי – בְּשַׁבָּת, בְּעֶרֶב שַׁבָּת מִי אֲמַר? וְכִי תֵּימָא הָכָא נַמִי בְּשַׁבָּת – וְהָתַנְיָא: נוֹתְנִין כְּלִי תַּחַת הַנֵּר לְקַבֵּל נִיצוֹצוֹת בְּשַׁבָּת – וְאֵין צָרִיךְ לוֹמַר בְּעֶרֶב שַׁבָּת, וְלֹא יִתֵּן לְתוֹכוֹ מַיִם מִפְּנֵי שֶׁהוּא מְכַבֶּה מֵעֶרֶב שַׁבָּת, וְאֵין צָרִיךְ לוֹמַר בְּשַׁבָּת! אֶלָּא אָמַר רַב אַשִׁי: אֲפִילּוּ תֵּימָא רַבָּנַן, שָׁאנֵי הָכָא – מִפְּנֵי שֶׁמְּקָרֵב אֶת כִּיבּוּיוֹ.

The Gemara rejects this question in astonishment: **And** how can **you understand** it in that manner? Say that **Rabbi Yosei said** that indirectly causing extinguishing is prohibited **on Shabbat; on Shabbat eve did he say** this? **And if you say** that **here, too,** it is referring to a case where he placed water in the vessel **on Shabbat, wasn't it taught** in a *baraita*: **One may place a vessel underneath an** oil **lamp to receive sparks** that fall from the lamp **on Shabbat, and, needless to say,** placing it there is permitted **on Shabbat eve? And one may not put water into** the vessel **because he will** thereby **extinguish** the spark, even if he placed it there **on Shabbat eve, and, needless to say,** doing so is prohibited **on Shabbat** itself. Apparently, the prohibition in the mishna is not at all connected to Rabbi Yosei's approach. **Rather, Rav Ashi said: Even if you say** that this mishna is in accordance with the opinion of **the Rabbis, it is different here because,** in this case, he is not only causing the spark to extinguish. He is **hastening its extinguishing,**[N] as the sparks are extinguished immediately when they fall into the water (Rabbeinu Ḥananel). In this matter even the Rabbis would prohibit doing so.

הדרן עלך כירה

NOTES

If it was loose it is permitted – רָפוּי מוּתָּר: Rabban Shimon ben Gamliel's rationale is that the prohibition only applies to an object that cannot be easily dismantled and reassembled. Assembling that object violates the prohibition of creating a vessel on Shabbat. However, when the object is loosely assembled and no expertise is required to assemble it, there is no prohibition involved.

In an atypical manner – מִן הַצַּד: In the context of Shabbat law, the Hebrew phrase, *min hatzad*, which literally means from the side, is translated as: In an atypical manner. This phrase indicates that the action is not performed in the manner that it is generally performed. One is not liable for performing a prohibited labor on Shabbat unless the action is performed in the appropriate manner. In general, this phrase refers to the consequences of the action. The objective of a full-fledged prohibited labor was not achieved. This is as opposed to the phrase: In a backhanded manner [*kilaḥar yad*], which refers to a difference in the manner in which the action was performed, e.g., using the left hand, and not to the consequences of the action.

Causes extinguishing…he is hastening its extinguishing – גּוֹרֵם לְכִיבּוּי...שֶׁמְּקָרֵב אֶת כִּיבּוּיוֹ: Indirect extinguishing of a flame is explained later in this tractate (*Shabbat* 120a) as positioning a ceramic vessel full of water so that it will burst when the fire reaches it and the water will extinguish the fire. The difference between indirect extinguishing and hastening extinguishing is extremely subtle. The conclusion in the Jerusalem Talmud is that our mishna is in accordance with the opinion of Rabbi Yosei, who prohibits indirectly causing a flame to extinguish. Nevertheless, there is a distinction between the two. Indirectly extinguishing a flame refers to a case where the fire has not yet reached a certain place and an obstacle is placed to prevent it from spreading further. That obstacle causes the flame to be extinguished. On the other hand, hastening extinguishing applies to a case where the fire is already there, as in the case of the sparks, but one takes action that will extinguish it faster (Ritva). Other commentaries explain that the rationale for the prohibition in the case of a vessel and sparks is that the vessel is empty, and there is room for concern lest one come to pour water on the sparks burning there on Shabbat (*Me'iri*).

BACKGROUND

Collapsible bed – מִטָּה גְּלַלְנִיתָא:

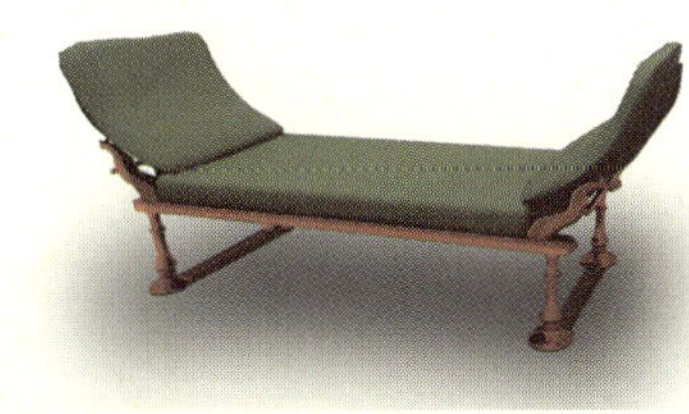

Collapsible bed in the style of the mishnaic era

HALAKHA

A vessel beneath the oil lamp to receive sparks – כְּלִי תַּחַת הַנֵּר לְקַבֵּל נִיצוֹצוֹת: It is permitted to position a vessel to receive sparks from a lamp even on Shabbat (*Mishna Berura*). However, according to all opinions, it is prohibited to place a vessel with water because it hastens the extinguishing of the sparks (Rambam *Sefer Zemanim*, *Hilkhot Shabbat* 5:13; *Shulḥan Arukh*, *Oraḥ Ḥayyim* 265:4).

Summary of **Perek III**

This chapter, whose primary focus was on the details of the labor of cooking on Shabbat, discussed the issue from a practical perspective. Matters relating to concluding the cooking process on Shabbat were underscored.

First, the Gemara clarified the permitted and prohibited manners in which one may leave cooked food on different types of stoves, so that the cooking process may be completed, and the food will remain hot for Shabbat day. The Gemara concluded that it is permitted to leave the item upon the stove if the item is sufficiently cooked at the onset of Shabbat, i.e., it could be eaten in exigent circumstances, and if there is no room for concern lest one come to stoke the coals, e.g., in a case where the possibility of stoking the coals on Shabbat is physically precluded.

The fundamental discussion of the *halakhot* of cooking concluded with the ruling that there is a distinction between cooking with fire, which is prohibited by Torah law, and cooking with other heat sources, e.g., the heat of the sun, which, if it is prohibited, the prohibition is only by rabbinic decree. It was also ruled that the prohibition of cooking applies to all types of foods, solids and liquids, in accordance with the level of heat that renders them cooked. There are also different substances that accelerate or impede the cooking process and influence the degree of heat required for cooking.

Matters relating to moving utensils used for cooking and illuminating accompanied the discussion of the laws of cooking. The questions were: To what extent are these utensils that are designated for prohibited labor or objects that are unsuited for use on Shabbat set aside from use on Shabbat? To what extent is moving them prohibited on Shabbat?

תלמוד בבלי

— מהדורת נאה —

שבת · חלק ב

Steinsaltz Center

KOREN

Please note that the number ranges that appear at the bottom of each daf of the Vilna pages indicate the corresponding pages of the Koren Talmud Bavli translation and commentary.

תלמוד בבלי

הוצאת קורן ירושלים

— מהדורת נאה —

מסכת שבת
דף כ: עד דף מז:

COMMENTARY BY
Rabbi Adin Even-Israel
Steinsaltz

EDITOR-IN-CHIEF
Rabbi Dr Tzvi Hersh Weinreb

SENIOR CONTENT EDITOR
Rabbi Dr Shalom Z Berger

EXECUTIVE EDITOR
Rabbi Joshua Schreier

•

STEINSALTZ CENTER
KOREN PUBLISHERS JERUSALEM

אָמַר רַב כָּהֲנָא: [א]קָנִים שֶׁאֲגָדָן[א] – צְרִיכִין רוֹב,[ב] לֹא אֲגָדָן אֵין צְרִיכִין רוֹב. גַּרְעִינִין – צְרִיכִין רוֹב, נְתָנָן בְּחוּתָלוֹת – אֵין צְרִיכִין רוֹב. תָּנֵי רַב יוֹסֵף, [ב]אַרְבַּע מְדוּרוֹת אֵין צְרִיכִין רוֹב: שֶׁל זֶפֶת, וְשֶׁל גָּפְרִית, וְשֶׁל[ג] גְּבִינָה, *וְשֶׁל רְבָב. בְּמַתְנִיתָא תָּנָא: [ג]אַף שֶׁל קַשׁ וְשֶׁל גְּבָבָא. א"ר יוֹחָנָן: עֵצִים שֶׁל בָּבֶל אֵין צְרִיכִין רוֹב. מַתְקִיף לָהּ רַב יוֹסֵף: מַאי הִיא? אִילֵימָא סִילְתֵי, הַשְׁתָּא פְּתִילָה אָמַר עוּלָּא: *הַמַּדְלִיק צָרִיךְ שֶׁיַּדְלִיק בְּרוֹב הַיּוֹצֵא, סִילְתֵי מִבַּעְיָא! אֶלָּא אָמַר רַב יוֹסֵף: שׁוּכָא דְּאַרְזָא. רָמֵי בַּר אַבָּא אָמַר: *זַאזָא.§

הדרן עלך יציאות השבת

*בַּמֶּה מַדְלִיקִין וּבַמָּה אֵין מַדְלִיקִין? [ד]אֵין מַדְלִיקִין לֹא *בְּלֶכֶשׁ, וְלֹא בְּחוֹסֶן, וְלֹא בְּכָלָךְ, וְלֹא בִּפְתִילַת הָאִידָן, וְלֹא בִּפְתִילַת הַמִּדְבָּר, וְלֹא בִּירוֹקָה שֶׁעַל פְּנֵי הַמַּיִם. *[ה]וְלֹא בְּזֶפֶת, וְלֹא בְּשַׁעֲוָה, וְלֹא בְּשֶׁמֶן קִיק, וְלֹא בְּשֶׁמֶן שְׂרֵיפָה, וְלֹא בְּאַלְיָה, וְלֹא בְּחֵלֶב. *נַחוּם הַמָּדִי אוֹמֵר: מַדְלִיקִין בְּחֵלֶב מְבוּשָּׁל, וחכ"א: אֶחָד מְבוּשָּׁל וְאֶחָד שֶׁאֵינוֹ מְבוּשָּׁל – אֵין מַדְלִיקִין בּוֹ.§

גמ' "לֶכֶשׁ" – שׁוּכָא דְּאַרְזָא. שׁוּכָא דְּאַרְזָא עֵץ בְּעָלְמָא הוּא! בְּעַמְרָנִיתָא דְּאִית בֵּיהּ.§ "וְלֹא בְּחוֹסֶן".§ אָמַר רַב יוֹסֵף: נְעוֹרֶת שֶׁל פִּשְׁתָּן. אֲמַר לֵיהּ אַבַּיֵי: וְהָכְתִיב: °"וְהָיָה *הֶחָסֹן לִנְעֹרֶת" (מִכְּלָל דְּחוֹסֶן לָאו נְעוֹרֶת הוּא!) אֶלָּא אָמַר אַבַּיֵי: כִּיתָּנָא דְּדַיֵיק וְלָא נְפִיץ.§ "וְלֹא בְּכָלָךְ".§ אָמַר שְׁמוּאֵל: שְׁאֶלְתִּינְהוּ לְכָל נָחוֹתֵי יַמָּא, וְאָמְרִי (*לָהּ): כּוּלְכָּא שְׁמֵיהּ. רַב יִצְחָק בַּר זְעֵירָא אָמַר: גּוּשְׁקְרָא. רָבִין וְאַבַּיֵי הֲווּ יָתְבִי קַמֵּיהּ דְּרַבָּנָא נְחֶמְיָה אֲחוּהּ דְּרֵישׁ גָּלוּתָא, חַזְיֵיהּ דַּהֲוָה לָבֵישׁ מְטַכְסָא. א"ל רָבִין לְאַבַּיֵי: הַיְינוּ כָּלָךְ דִּתְנַן. א"ל: אֲנַן שִׁירָא פַרְנְדָא קָרֵינַן לֵיהּ. °מֵיתִיבִי: *הַשִּׁירָאִים וְהַכָּלָךְ וְהַסִּירִיקִין חַיָּיבִין בְּצִיצִית! (תְּיוּבְתָּא דְּרָבִין) *תְּיוּבְתָּא. אִיבָּעֵית אֵימָא: שִׁירָא לְחוּד וְשִׁירָא פַרְנְדָא לְחוּד*).§ "וְלֹא בִּפְתִילַת הָאִידָן".§ אַחֲוָינָא.§ רָבִין וְאַבַּיֵי הֲווּ קָאָזְלוּ בְּפַקְתָּא דְּטַמְרוּרִיתָא, חֲזֵינְהוּ לְהָנְהוּ *אַרְבָּתָא. אֲמַר לֵיהּ רָבִין לְאַבַּיֵי: הַיְינוּ אִידָן דִּתְנַן. אֲמַר לֵיהּ: הַהִיא עֵץ בְּעָלְמָא הוּא! קְלַף וְאַחֲוֵי לֵיהּ עַמְרָנִיתָא דְּבֵינֵי בֵּינֵי.§ "וְלֹא בִּפְתִילַת הַמִּדְבָּר".§ שַׁבְרָא.§ "וְלֹא בִּירוֹקָה שֶׁעַל כו'".§ מַאי הִיא? אִילֵימָא אוּכָּמְתָּא דְּחַרִיצֵי – אִיפְּרוֹכֵי מִפָּרְכָן! אֶלָּא אָמַר רַב פָּפָּא: אוּכָּמְתָּא דְּאַרְבָּא. תָּנָא: [ו]הוֹסִיפוּ עֲלֵיהֶן שֶׁל צֶמֶר וְשֶׁל שֵׂעָר. וְתַנָּא דִּידַן: צֶמֶר מִכְוַוץ כַּוּוֹיֵץ, שֵׂעָר – אִיחֲרוּכֵי מִיחֲרַךְ.§ "וְלֹא בְּזֶפֶת".§ זֶפֶת – זִיפְתָּא, שַׁעֲוָה – קִירוּתָא. תָּנָא: עַד כָּאן – פְּסוּל פְּתִילוֹת, מִכָּאן וְאֵילָךְ – פְּסוּל שְׁמָנִים. פְּשִׁיטָא! [ז]שַׁעֲוָה אִיצְטְרִיכָא לֵיהּ, מַהוּ דְּתֵימָא: לִפְתִילוֹת נַמִי לָא חַזְיָא, קָא מַשְׁמַע לָן. אֲמַר רָמֵי בַּר אָבִין: עִטְרָנָא – פְּסוֹלְתָּא דְּזִיפְתָּא, שַׁעֲוָה – פְּסוֹלְתָּא דְּדוּבְשָׁא.

לְמַאי

*) רש"ל גורס ואב"א פירושא קא מפרש.

רש"י

רַב כָּהֲנָא אָמַר קָנִים שֶׁאֲגָדָן צְרִיכִין רוֹב. כְּרַב הוּנָא, דְּלָא עַיְילָא בְּהֶן נוּרָא. וּלְאַחְדּוּדֵי לָא קַיְישִׁינַן, דִּמְרוּבִּין הֵן וּכְבֵדִין: גַּרְעִינִין שֶׁנְּתָנָן בְּחוּתָלוֹת אֵין צְרִיכִין רוֹב. כְּרַב חִסְדָּא, שֶׁנּוֹחִין לִידָּלֵק. אֲבָל בְּלָא חוּתָלוֹת מִבַּדְרִי: מְדוּרָה. לְשׁוֹן הֶיסֵּק גָּדוֹל: רְבָב. שׁוּמָּן וְשַׁעֲוָה וְכָל דָּבָר הַנִּיתָּךְ: גְּבָבָא. שֶׁגּוֹבְבִין מִן הַשָּׂדֶה, בְּלַ"ע שטובל"א: קַשׁ. זַנְבוֹת שִׁבּוֹלִין, אשטרי"ם: סִילְתֵי. לְאַחַר שֶׁעֲשָׂאוּם עֵצִים דַּקִּים, וּבְבָבֶל נוֹהֲגִין כֵּן: הַשְׁתָּא פְּתִילָה. שֶׁל בֶּגֶד הַטְּבוּלָה בְּשֶׁמֶן, וְנוֹחַ לִידָּלֵק: אָמַר עוּלָּא הַמַּדְלִיק. נֵר שֶׁל שַׁבָּת – צָרִיךְ שֶׁיַּדְלִיק בְּרוֹב הַיּוֹצֵא מֵרֹאשׁ הַפְּתִילָה חוּץ לַנֵּר: שׁוּכָא דְּאַרְזָא. יָבֵשׁ הוּא וְדַק, וְיֵשׁ כְּמִין צֶמֶר בֵּין קְלִיפָּה לָעֵץ, וְהוּא מַבְעִירוֹ מִשֶּׁמַּחֲזֶה בּוֹ אוּר: זַאזָא. מולס"א בְּלַעַז:

הדרן עלך יציאות השבת

בַּמֶּה מַדְלִיקִין. לַעֲשׂוֹת פְּתִילָה. כָּל הָנֵי דְּמַתְנִי' מְפָרֵשׁ בַּגְּמָרָא: לֹא בְּזֶפֶת וְלֹא בְּשַׁעֲוָה. לָאו לְעִנְיַן פְּתִילָה, אֶלָּא לָתֵת בִּמְקוֹם שֶׁמֶן. וְכָל הָנֵי מִזֶּפֶת וְאֵילָךְ – פְּסוּלֵי שְׁמָנִים הֵן: **גמ'** עֵץ בְּעָלְמָא הוּא. וּפְשִׁיטָא דְּלָא חַזֵי לִפְתִילָה אֶלָּא לִמְדוּרָה: עַמְרָנִיתָא. כְּמִין צֶמֶר יֵשׁ בֵּין קְלִיפָּתוֹ לְעֵצוֹ: וְהָיָה הֶחָסֹן לִנְעֹרֶת. אַלְמָא: חָסוֹן לָאו נְעוֹרֶת הוּא: כִּיתָּנָא דְּדַיֵיק וְלָא נְפִיץ. דְּכֵיוָן דְּלָא נְפִיץ אֵין שֶׁמֶן נִמְשָׁךְ אַחֲרָיו: נְפִיץ. קרפר"י. וּנְעוֹרֶת מִן הַדַּק שֶׁבּוֹ, וְהָכִי קָאָמַר קְרָא: פִּשְׁתָּן הֶחָזָק יֵהָפֵךְ לִנְעוֹרֶת, כְּלוֹמַר: הַגִּבּוֹר יִהְיֶה חַלָּשׁ: גּוּשְׁקְרָא. פְּסוֹלֶת שֶׁל מֶשִׁי הֶעָשׂוּי כְּכוֹבָעִים, וְהוּא בֵּית הַתּוֹלַעַת, וְקוֹרִין לוֹ פולוי"ל. וְנוֹפְּצִים אוֹתוֹ, וְטוֹוִין וְעוֹשִׂין מִמֶּנּוּ בֶּגֶד. וְאָסוּר לַעֲשׂוֹת מִמֶּנּוּ פְּתִילָה כִּדְאָמַר בְּכָל פְּסוּלֵי פְּתִילוֹת דְּמַתְנִיתִין – שֶׁהָאוּר מְסַכְסֶכֶת בָּהֶן – קוֹפֶצֶת וְנִפְסֶקֶת, וְאֵין הַשַּׁלְהֶבֶת עוֹמֶדֶת בִּמְקוֹמָהּ: גּוּשְׁקְרָא. עַל שֵׁם פְּסוֹלֶת, וְגַם פַּת סוּבִּין כְּמוֹ כֵן נִקְרֵאת בְּמַסֶּכֶת גִּיטִּין (דף ע:): מְטַכְסָא. לְבוּשׁ הֶעָשׂוּי מֵאוֹתוֹ כָּלָךְ: שִׁירָאִים. מְעִיל הֶעָשׂוּי מֵעִיקַּר הַמֶּשִׁי: סִירִיקִין. עָשׂוּי מִן הַמֶּשִׁי הָרַךְ הַמִּתְפַּצֵּל, וּמָלוּי בַּמֶּשִׁי, וְקוֹרִין לוֹ בִּמְקוֹמֵנוּ יד"ש: חַיָּיבִין בְּצִיצִית. וּדְלָא כְּמַאן דְּאָמַר כָּל בִּגְדֵי צֶמֶר וּפִשְׁתִּים דַּוְקָא חַיָּיבִין בְּצִיצִית מִדְּאוֹרַיְיתָא. אִי נַמִי – מִדְּרַבָּנַן קָתָנֵי מִיהָא "הַשִּׁירָאִים וְהַכָּלָךְ", אַלְמָא: שִׁירָאִין לָאו הַיְינוּ כָּלָךְ! אַחֲוָינָא. עֲרָבָה, וְיֵשׁ כְּמִין צֶמֶר בֵּין קְלִיפָּה לָעֵץ: בְּפַקְתָּא. בִּקְעָה: עֵץ בְּעָלְמָא הוּא. וְהֵיכִי לֵיחֲזֵי לִפְתִילָה? שַׁבְרָא. מִין עֵשֶׂב אָרוֹךְ, וְקוֹרִין אוֹתוֹ אורטי"א: אוּכָּמְתָּא דְּחַרִיצֵי. מְקוֹם כִּנּוּס מַיִם גָּדֵל עֲלֵיהֶם כְּמִין יְרַקְרוֹקֶת: אִיפְּרוֹכֵי מִיפָּרְכָן. וְלָא מָצֵי לְמֶעְבַּד פְּתִילָה מִינָּהּ: אוּכָּמְתָּא דְּאַרְבָּא. סְפִינָה הַמִּתְעַכֶּבֶת בְּמָקוֹם אֶחָד בַּמַּיִם גָּדֵל יְרַקְרוֹקֶת סָבִיב שׁוּלֶיהָ מִבַּחוּץ: מְכַוֵּוץ כַּוּוֹיֵץ. מִפְּנֵי הָאוּר, וְאֵין דּוֹלֵק כְּלָל, וְאֵין שַׁלְהֶבֶת אוֹחֶזֶת בּוֹ, וְלָא צָרִיךְ לְמִתְנְיֵיהּ: עַד כָּאן. עַד יְרוֹקָה שֶׁעַל פְּנֵי הַמַּיִם – פְּסוּל פְּתִילוֹת: מִכָּאן וְאֵילָךְ פְּסוּל שְׁמָנִים. שֶׁלֹּא יִתֵּן חֲתִיכָה זֶפֶת אוֹ שַׁעֲוָה בַּנֵּר בִּמְקוֹם שֶׁמֶן: שַׁעֲוָה אִיצְטְרִיכָא לֵיהּ. לְפִי שֶׁרְגִילִין לַעֲשׂוֹת כְּמִין פְּתִילָה אֲרוּכָּה וְהַפְּתִילָה לְתוֹכָהּ, כְּמוֹ שֶׁאָנוּ עוֹשִׂין: מַהוּ דְּתֵימָא לִפְתִילָה נַמִי. קָמַשְׁמַע לָן: פְּסוֹלְתָּא דְּזִיפְתָּא. לְאַחַר שֶׁיּוֹצֵאת הַזֶּפֶת מִן הָעֵץ זָב מִמֶּנּוּ עַל יְדֵי הָאוּר פְּסוֹלֶת גָּלוּל כְּשֶׁמֶן, וְהוּא עִיטְרָן[א]:

לְמִקָּם

תוספות

במה מדליקין כו'. פעמים מפרש מאי דסליק מיניה, ופעמים במה שהתחיל*: **אחד** מבושל כו'. הכא מוזכר שאינו פשוט תחילה, וכן בכמה מקומות. ומה שקשה על גירסת רש"י דסוכה [דף ז.] מפורש במקום אחר*: **בעמרניתא** דאית ביה. וא"ת: הא מסיפא שמעינן ליה: "כל היוצא מן העץ אין מדליקין בו אלא פשתן". וכן קשה גבי אידן! ויש לומר: דאין למדין מן הכללות, אפילו במקום שנאמר בהן חוץ*: **אנן** שירא פרנדא קרינן ליה. פר"ת: דכלך דמתניתין קרינן שירא פרנדא, אבל מטכסא – לאו היינו שירא פרנדא, דלא הוה אחר חורבן, כדאמר בפ' בתרא דסוטה: (דף מח:): משחרב בית המקדש בטל שמיר וזכוכית לבנה ושירא פרנדא. ור"י מפרש: דקאי נמי אמטכסא. והא דקאמר התם "בטל" – לא לגמרי בטל, אלא שלא היה נמצא כ"כ. דהא זכוכי' לבנה היתה אחר חורבן, דאמרי' בפ' "אין עומדין" (ברכות דף לא.): "תבר קמייהו זכוכית חיורתא" בחופת בנו*: **ותנא** דידן צמר מכווץ כווץ ושער איחרוכי מחרך. ולא איצטריך תנא דמתני' למיתני. וא"ת: כיון דמתני' נמי סברה דצמר ושער פסולים להדלקה, א"כ מאי הוסיפו? וי"ל: דהוסיפו היינו טעמא מפני שאין מושכין השמן יפה. ותנא דמתניתין פסיל להו משום דצמר כווץ ושער מחרך, ולא איצטריך למתני: **עד** כאן פסול פתילות מכאן ואילך פסול שמנים. בני נרבונא אוסרין נר שעוה שלנו. ומפרשי הכי: מהו דתימא לפתילות נמי לא, שאם שם נר שעוה בנר שמן יהא אסור – קמ"ל: מכאן ואילך פסול שמנים, כיון שיש בו שמן כשר – מותר. אבל נר של שעוה בלא שמן – אסור להדליק. ולי נראה: דאם אסור להדליק בלא שמן – כי הניחה בשמן נמי אסור, כדאמרינן לקמן כרך דבר שמדליקין על גבי דבר שאין מדליקין דאסור, אלא ודאי, כי לא הניח בשמן – נמי שרי:

לְמַאי

עין משפט נר מצוה

[כך מסיק הש"ס נדרים ב: ובנזיר ב.]

[עי' תוס' פסחים פה. קת: ד"ה אחד ובסוכה כ. ד"ה אחת זבחים נב: ד"ה אי הכי מנחות סג: ד"ה ר"י ועי' תוספות קידושין יג. ד"ה כשם]

[כדאיתא עירובין כז.]

קסג א ב ג מיי' פ"ג מהל' שבת הלכה כא כב סמג לאוין סה טוש"ע או"ח סי' רנה ס"ג:

א ד מיי' פ"ה מהלכות שבת הלכה ה סמג שם טור או"ח סימן רסד:

ב ה מיי' שם הלכה ח סמג שם טור שו"ע שם סעיף ג:

ג ו מיי' שם הלכה ה טוש"ע שם סעיף א:

ד ז מיי' שם הלכה ח טוש"ע שם סעיף ז:

[ועי' תוס' ב"ת כט: ד"ה בזכוכית ותוספות חולין פד: ד"ה בזוגיתא]

[עי' רש"י לקמן כד: ד"ה ה"ג נחום וכו']

רבינו חננאל

האח לפניו מבוערת רב אמר אהואגה. פי' עצי (מערבה) [ערבות] תני רב יוסף ארבע מדורות אין צריכות רוב של זפת ס"א של נפט ושל גפרית ושל רבב ושל גבינה. פתילה אמר עולא צריך להדליק ברוב היוצא עצים של בבל שוכא דארזא פי' זאזא גוותא יבש דרומני:

פ"ב במה מדליקין כו' לכש עמרניתא וביני ביני דארזא. חוסן כיתנא דדייק ולא נפיץ. כלך רבין אמר מיטכס' השיראים והכלך והסיריקין חייבין בציצי' פתילת האידן ערמניתא דביני ביני ערבה. פתילת המדבר שיברא. **ירושלמי** אמר שמואל בר רב יצחק כתיב להעלות נר תמיד שערו לומר אין לך עושה שלהבת אלא פשתן: **לא** בזפת ולא בשעוה תנא ע"כ פסול פתילות

הגהות הגר"א

[א] גמ' קנים שאגדן. נ"ב אין. גירסת הרא"ש אבל הרי"ף והמג"ס גרסי כל הא' שמעתא בהיפך מגירסת הרא"ש: [ב] שם (לא אגדן א"ל רוב גרעינין צריכין רוב נתנן בחותלות א"צ רוב) מא"ת וכ"צ הרי"ף והרא"ש לא גרסי כל זה: [ג] שם גבינה. נ"ב גירסת הרי"ף קורה:

מסורת הש"ס

תורה אור השלם: שעיה ...

גי' הרי"ף גפרית ושל רבב ושל קורה

לקמן כח:

ערך של עץ [עי' ערוך]

[נדרים ב: נזיר ב.]

[גי' הערוך בלגש ע"ש]

[גי' רש"י וכן הרב מברטנורה לא בזפת וכן נכון כי זה התחלת בבא דפסול שמנים]

יש מפרשים דקרא משמע שהנעורת דולק ואין נראה דקש נמי דולק יפה ואין דומה לפתילה [ת"י]

מנחות לט:

[גיטין כח. זבחים פה.]

נ"ל ערבתא

הגהות הב"ח

(א) רש"י ד"ה פסולתא דזיפתא וכו' והוא עיטרן שקורין דוזיט בלשון כנען סס"ד:

גליון הש"ס

גמ' מיתיבי השיראים והכלך. ק"ל אמאי פריך מהברייתא ולא פריך ממתניתין פ"ט מ"ב דכלאים: תוס' ד"ה אנן שירא כו' שלא היה נמצא כל כך. עיין בר"ש פ"ט מ"ב דכלאים:

למאי נפקא מינה? למקח וממכר.§ *ת"ר: כל אלו שאמרו "אין מדליקין בהן בשבת" אאבל עושין מהן מדורה, בין להתחמם כנגדה בין להשתמש לאורה, בין ע"ג קרקע בין על גבי [א]*כירה, ולא אסרו אלא לעשות מהן פתילה לנר בלבד.§ "ולא בשמן קיק וכו'".§ מאי שמן קיק? אמר שמואל: שאילתינהו לכל נחותי ימא ואמרו לי: עוף אחד יש בכרכי הים וקיק שמו. רב יצחק בריה דרב יהודה אמר: משחא דקאזא. ריש לקיש אמר: קיקיון דיונה. אמר רבה בר בר חנה: לדידי חזי לי קיקיון דיונה, *ולצלוליבא דמי, ומדפשקי רבי, ועל פום חנותא מדלן יתיה, ומפרצידוהי עבדי משחא, ובענפוהי נייחן כל *בריחי דמערבא. אמר רבה: בפתילות שאמרו חכמים "אין מדליקין בהן בשבת" – מפני שהאור מסכסכת בהן, שמנים שאמרו חכמים "אין מדליקין בהן" – מפני שאין נמשכין אחר הפתילה. בעא מיניה אביי מרבה: שמנים שאמרו חכמים אין מדליקין בהן בשבת, מהו שיתן לתוכן שמן כל שהוא וידליק? מי גזרינן דילמא אתי לאדלוקי בעינייהו, או לא? א"ל: גאין מדליקין. מאי טעמא; *לפי *שאין מדליקין. איתיביה: *כורך דבר שמדליקין בו ע"ג דבר שאין מדליקין בו – אין מדליקין בו. (אמר) *רשב"ג: [נ"ל רשב"ג אומר] של בית אבא היו כורכין פתילה על גבי אגוז ומדליקין. קתני מיהת "מדליקין"! א"ל: אדמותבת לי מדרשב"ג – סייעינהו מדתנא קמא! הא לא קשיא, *מעשה רב. מ"מ קשיא! מאי לאו – להדליק? לא, להקפות. אי להקפות – מ"ט דת"ק? כולה רשב"ג היא, וחסורי מיחסרא והכי קתני: כורך דבר שמדליקין בו ע"ג דבר שאין מדליקין בו – אין מדליקין בו. דבד"א – להדליק, אבל להקפות – מותר, שרבן שמעון בן גמליאל אומר: של בית אבא היו כורכין פתילה ע"ג אגוז. איני? והאמר רב ברונא *אמר רב: החלב מהותך וקרבי דגים שנמוחו, אדם נותן לתוכו שמן כל שהוא ומדליק! הני מימשכי בעינייהו, והני – לא מימשכי בעינייהו וגזרו רבנן על חלב מהותך משום חלב שאינו מהותך, ועל קרבי דגים שנמוחו משום קרבי דגים שלא נמוחו. וליגזור נמי חלב מהותך וקרבי דגים שנמוחו שנתן לתוכן שמן, משום חלב מהותך וקרבי דגים שנמוחו שלא נתן לתוכן שמן! *)היא גופה גזירה, *ואנן ניקום וניגזור גזירה לגזירה?§ תני רמי בר חמא: פתילות ושמנים שאמרו חכמים אין מדליקין בהן בשבת – ואין מדליקין בהן במקדש, משום שנא': °"להעלות נר תמיד" (שמות כז). הוא תני לה: והוא אמר לה: כדי *שתהא שלהבת עולה מאיליה, ולא שתהא עולה על ידי דבר אחר. תנן: *מבלאי מכנסי כהנים ומהמייניהם היו מפקיעין, ומהן מדליקין! שמחת בית השואבה שאני. ת"ש, דתני רבה בר מתנה: ובגדי כהונה שבלו מפקיעין אותן, ומהן היו עושין פתילות למקדש. מאי לאו דכלאים? לא, חדבוץ.§ אמר רב הונא: פתילות ושמנים שאמרו חכמים אין מדליקין בהן בשבת – אין מדליקין בהן בחנוכה, בין בשבת בין בחול. אמר רבא: מאי טעמא דרב הונא – קסבר: כבתה זקוק לה, ומותר להשתמש לאורה. ורב חסדא אמר: מדליקין בהן בחול, אבל לא בשבת, קסבר: כבתה אין

תורה אור: שמות כז; לעיל כ.

רש"י

למקח וממכר. למאן דמתני למזבן שעוה – ליתיב ליה פסולתא דדובשא: אבל עושין מהן מדורה. היסק גדול, שאחד מבעיר חבירו: לנר. קרויז"ל: בשמן קיק. שמן של עוף אחד נותנין בנר, ודולק: משחא דקאזא. שמן שעושין מגרעיני צמר גפן, שקורין קוטו"ן: קיקיון. כעין אותה של יונה: לדידי חזי לי. מין קיקיון דיונה: ומדפשקי רבי. בגלעי המים הוא גדל: ועל פום חנוותא מדלן יתיה. על פוס החנויות מדלין אותו, לצל ולריח טוב: מפרצידוהי. מגרעיניו: נייחין. שוכבין: בריחי. אולין: מסכסכת. כמין סכין פגומה מסכסכת בבשר, אנמילי"ד בלע"ז. שאין אורו זקוף ונוח במקום אחד, אלא נדעך וקופץ. לישנא אחרינא: מסכסכת בהן – אינה נכנסת תוך הפתילה, אלא סביב מבחוץ, כמו "סיכסכה אבניו", ברואט"ש בלע"ז: שאין נמשכין. ואתי להטות: שמן כל שהוא. שמן הניתן בתוכו, ממשיכו לאחר הפתילה: לפי שאין מדליקין. בעינייהו, וגזרינן הא אטו הא: כורך דבר לעשות פתילה על גבי דבר שאין מדליקין בו. כגון פסול פתילות דמתני': קתני מיהא. בדר"ש מדליקין, ואע"ג דאגוז לא חזי לפתילה – על ידי תערובות שפיר דמי: מעשה רב. הואיל ומעיד שכך היו של בית אביו עושין – הלכה היא: מאי לאו להדליק. היו כורכים, שמדליק הפתילה עם האגוז: לא להקפות. לא היו מדליקין האגוז, אלא סומך עליה הפתילה להציפה שלא תטבע בשמן. "ויצף הברזל" מתרגמינן "וקפא פרזלא" (מלכים ב ו): חלב מהותך. פונד"ר בלע"ז: הני מימשכי בעינייהו. אחר הפתילה, ובלא תערובות שמן נמי חזו, אלא דגזור רבנן מהותך אטו אינו מהותך. הלכך בעינייהו גופה – גזירה, ואנן ניקום וניגזור ע"י תערובת אטו בעינייהו?! והוא אמר לה. מפרש מאי תלמודא, והיכי משמע מהאי קרא: ולא שתהא עולה כו'. ולא שתהא צריכה תיקון והטייה: מבלאי מכנסי הכהנים. ממכנסי הכהנים הבלואים: היו מפקיעין. קורעין ועושין פתילות בשמחת בית השואבה, שהיא בעזרת נשים: ומהמייניהם. של כלאים הם, דכתיב: "ואת האבנט שש משזר ותכלת וארגמן", וקי"ל: תכלת עמרא הוא. ותני לעיל לענין שבת: הוסיפו עליהן של צמר לפסול, וקתני: מדליקין בהן במקדש! שמחת בית השואבה שאני. דלא כתיב להעלות בה, ולאו דאורייתא היא: מאי לאו דכלאים. כגון אבנט: כבתה. נר חנוכה: זקוק לה. לתקנה. הלכך: צריך לכתחלה לעשות יפה, דילמא פשע ולא מתקן לה: ומותר להשתמש לאורה. הלכך בשבת אסור, שמא יטה לצורך תשמיש: אין

תוספות

למאי נ"מ למקח וממכר. פשיטא ליה להתלמוד שהיו מכירין השעוה והעיטרן, כדאמרינן: שעוה – קירותא. לכך קאמר: למאי נ"מ – למקח וממכר, שאם נדר לתת לחבירו שעוה – יתן לו פסולתא דדובשא, ואין יכול לכופו לתקן לו, וכן עיטרן. אבל לעיל דקאמר: "מאי לכש – שוכא דארזא" לא קאמר למאי נ"מ – לפי שלא היו מכירין בשם לכש, ומפרש שהוא שוכא דארזא:

מפני שאין נמשכין כו' – שמעתי ממהר"א ז"ל: שמשע באם שיש רק נר א' כשר בבית – ע"י זה יזכור ולא יטה שאר נרות שבחדר ושבמרתף. ור"ש מקולי אומר: דבר שיכול לעשות בלא נר כגון להוציא יין מן החבית – מותר להשתמש לאור כל נר [תוספות ישנים]:

חלב מהותך וקרבי דגים שנימוחו נותן לתוכן שמן כו'. קרבי דגים לאו היינו שמן דגים, דשמן דגים שרי ליה מתני' בעיניה (לקמן דף כד:):

שמחת בית השואבה שאני. תימה: היכי שרי להדליק? והא לאו צורך קרבן הוא?! ואמר בפ"ב דקידושין (דף נד. ושם): בגדי כהונה שבלו – מועלין בהן! ודוחק לומר: לב ב"ד מתנה עליהן, *דמה צורך יש להן להתנות בשביל זה? ונראה לר"י: דהואיל ולכבוד הקרבן היו עושין, דכתיב: "ושאבתם מים בששון" (ישעיה יב) – צורך קרבן חשוב ליה. והא דאמר (סוכה פ"ה דף נג.): בוררת אשה חטין לאור בית השואבה – לא שהיתה בוררת, אלא שהיתה יכולה לברור. ומיהו: בירושלמי דייק מהכא דקול ומראה וריח אין בהן משום מעילה. וקשה לר"י: מאי פריך *ממכנסי הכהנים, הלא היה בהן פשתן, דכתיב: "תכלת וארגמן ותולעת שני ושש משזר" (שמות כח) וטוב לפתילה, דהוי ככרך דבר שמדליקין בו ע"ג דבר שאין מדליקין בו, ובשבת הוא דאסור – שמא ידליק בעיניה, אבל במקדש לא שייכא הך גזירה! ונראה לר"י: דכיון שאין מן הפשתן אלא רביע – בטל בשאר מינים, והוי כאילו אין בו פשתן כלל:

ומותר להשתמש לאורה. וא"ת: מנא ליה לרבא דסבר רב הונא דמותר להשתמש לאורה? דילמא הא דאמר: "אין מדליקין בשבת" – משום דסבר: כבתה זקוק לה, ואין

עין משפט נר מצוה

ה א מיי' פ"ג מהלכות שבת הלכה יט סמג לאוין סה טור שו"ע או"ח סימן רנה סעיף א:

ו ב מיי' פ"ה מהל' שבת הלכה ה סמג שם טור שו"ע או"ח סימן רסד סעיף א ג:

ז ג מיי' שם הלכה ט טור שו"ע שם סעיף ד:

ח ד מיי' שם הלכה ו טוש"ע שם סעיף ב:

ט ה מיי' שם הלכה ט טוש"ע שם סעיף ה:

י ו מיי' פ"ג מהלכות תמידין ומוספין הלכה טו:

יא ז ה מיי' פ"ח מהלכות כלי המקדש הלכה ו:

מסורת הש"ס (הגהות בשוליים)

תוספתא פ"ב

ס"א מנורה

ערוך פי' אילן סרק

[נ"ל בריחי עי' ערוך ערך כרח ובמתורגמן]

מ"ט א"ל לפי שאין כצ"ל רש"ל [ועי' בערוך ערך לפי פי' שאין מדליקין כלומר קבלה היא כך שאין מדליקין]

[לקמן קכו: ב"ב פג. קל.] נדה סה:

[לקמן כד:]

ועוד דלא מצינו לב ב"ד בזה דכיון דכבר קדשו בגדי כהונה לא נפקי לחולין בלא פדיון [ת"י]

כ"א שאינן נדלקין

תוספתא פ"ב

[נ"ל מהמיני' דהיינו אבנט ועי' רש"א]

[illegible]

רבינו חננאל

מיכן ואילך פסול שמנים: ת"ר כל אלו שאמרו חכמים אין מדליקין בהם בשבת משום פסול פתילות אבל עושה בהם מדורה בין להתחמם כנגדה בין להשתמש לאורה בין ע"ג קרקע בין ע"ג מנורה לא אסרו אלא לעשותן פתילה לנר בלבד. בשמן קיק שמואל אמר (עץ) [עוף] ושמו קיק ר"ל אמר קיקיון דיונה. אמר רבה פתילות שאמרו חכמים אין מדליקין בהן מפני שהאור מסכסכת בהן שמנים שפסלו [חכמי'] מפני שאין נמשכין אחר הפתילה. בעא מיניה אביי מרבה שמנים שאסרו חכמים להדליק בהן בשבת מהו לתת לתוכן שמן ולהדליק א"ל אסור לפי שאין מדליקין כלומר כיון שאין מדליקין בפני עצמן כשישלים השמן שתתן בתוכו שוב אין מדליקין שכבר אמרו אין נמשכין אחר הפתילה ואותיב עלה ותרצה הכי כורך דבר שמדליקין בו על גבי דבר שאין מדליקין בו אין מדליקין בו בד"א להדליק אבל להקפות

פירוש להעבות ראש הפתילה להרבות אורה מותר שרשב"ג אומר של בית אבא היו כורכין כו' וקיי"ל (כרבא) [כרבה] איני והא אמר רב ברונא אמר רב חלב מהותך (מ"ש) [פי'] מלשון היתוך כדכתיב (יחזקאל כב) כהתוך כסף בתוך כור וכתיב (איוב ג) ויתכו כמים וקרבי דגים שנימוחו נותן לתוכן שמן כל שהוא ומדליק ושנינן הני ממשכי בעינייהו אבל הני לא ממשכי בעינייהו ואסיק' לקמן*) דשני הני משמן דגים לפיכך שמן דגים מזוקק הוא ודולק ונמשך אחר הפתילה ואין צריך תערובת. תני רמי בר חמא פתילות שאסרו חכמים להדליק בהן בשבת גם במקדש אין מדליקין בהם שנאמר להעלות נר תמיד והא דתנן מבלאי מכנסי כהנים ומהמייניהם מהן היו מפקיעין ובהן היו מדליקין והאבנט יש בו צמר הני לשמחת בית השואבה אבל למנורה אין מדליקין אלא בשל (בוץ) [פשתן] וכבר פירשנוהו היטב בראיות בפרק החליל.

*) לפנינו ליתא בגמ' הני משמן דגים ואולי דכוון למ"ש לקמן דף כ"ו ע"א איכא בינייהו דרב ברונא ומפרש כפי' ר"ת שם בתוס' ודו"ק היטב. ועי' תוס' כאן ד"ה חלב:

גליון הש"ס גמ' אין מדליקין מ"ט לפי שאין מדליקין. כעין זה עירובין דף לו ע"א מו"ק דף כו ע"ב גיטין דף ס ע"א נדה דף ס ע"א וכן בלשון התורה ויקרא כ"ב אשר יהיה בו מום לא יקרב כי כל איש אשר בו מום לא יקרב ועי' ריטב"א קידושין דף ו ע"ב ד"ה ה"ג: שם שמנים ופתילות כו' אין מדליקין בהם במקדש. ק"ל למאי נקט שמנים הא במקדש אין מדליקין רק בשמן זית זך: תוס' ד"ה חלב מהותך כו' קרבי דגים לאו היינו. ע"ל דף כו ע"א תוס' ד"ה איכא בינייהו דרב ברונא:

אין זקוק לה, ומותר להשתמש לאורה. א"ר זירא אמר רב מתנה, ואמרי לה א"ר זירא אמר רב: [א]פתילות ושמנים שאמרו חכמים אין מדליקין בהן בשבת – מדליקין בהן בחנוכה, בין בחול בין בשבת. א"ר ירמיה: מאי טעמא דרב – קסבר: [ב]כבתה אין זקוק לה, [ג]ואסור להשתמש לאורה. אמרוה רבנן קמיה דאביי משמיה דר' ירמיה – ולא קיבלה. כי אתא רבין, אמרוה רבנן קמיה דאביי משמיה דר' יוחנן – וקיבלה. אמר: אי זכאי גמירתיה לשמעתיה מעיקרא. והא גמרה! נפקא מינה לגירסא דינקותא. וכבתה אין זקוק לה? ורמינהו: [ד]מצותה *משתשקע החמה עד שתכלה רגל מן השוק. מאי לאו, דאי כבתה הדר מדליק לה! לא, [ה]דאי לא אדליק – מדליק. וא"נ: לשיעורה.§ "עד שתכלה רגל מן השוק", ועד כמה? אמר רבה בר בר חנה אמר ר' יוחנן: עד דכליא ריגלא דתרמודאי.§ ת"ר: [ו]מצות חנוכה נר איש וביתו. והמהדרין – נר לכל אחד ואחד. והמהדרין מן המהדרין, ב"ש אומרים: יום ראשון מדליק שמנה, מכאן ואילך פוחת והולך; וב"ה אומרים: [ז]יום ראשון מדליק אחת, מכאן ואילך מוסיף והולך. אמר עולא: פליגי בה תרי אמוראי במערבא, ר' יוסי בר אבין ור' יוסי בר זבידא, חד אמר: טעמא דב"ש – כנגד ימים הנכנסין, וטעמא דב"ה – כנגד ימים היוצאין. וחד אמר: טעמא דב"ש – כנגד פרי החג, וטעמא דבית הלל – *דמעלין בקדש ואין מורידין. אמר רבה בר בר חנה א"ר יוחנן: שני זקנים היו בצידן, אחד עשה כב"ש ואחד עשה כדברי ב"ה, זה נותן טעם לדבריו – כנגד פרי החג, וזה נותן טעם לדבריו – דמעלין בקדש ואין מורידין. ת"ר: *[ח]נר חנוכה מצוה להניחה על פתח ביתו מבחוץ. אם היה דר בעלייה – מניחה בחלון הסמוכה לרה"ר. ובשעת הסכנה – מניחה על שלחנו, ודיו. אמר רבא: [ט]צריך נר אחרת [א]להשתמש לאורה. ואי איכא מדורה – לא צריך, ואי אדם חשוב הוא, אע"ג דאיכא מדורה – צריך נר אחרת.§ מאי חנוכה? דתנו רבנן: [י]בכ"ה בכסליו יומי דחנוכה תמניא אינון, דלא למספד בהון [ב] ודלא להתענות בהון. שכשנכנסו יוונים להיכל טמאו °כל השמנים שבהיכל, וכשגברה מלכות בית חשמונאי ונצחום, בדקו ולא מצאו אלא פך אחד של שמן שהיה מונח בחותמו של כהן גדול, ולא היה בו אלא להדליק יום אחד, נעשה בו נס והדליקו ממנו שמונה ימים. לשנה אחרת קבעום ועשאום ימים טובים בהלל והודאה. *)תנן התם: גץ היוצא מתחת הפטיש ויצא והזיק – חייב. *[כ]גמל שטעון פשתן, והוא עובר ברשות הרבים, ונכנסה פשתנו לתוך החנות ודלקה בנרו של חנוני, והדליק את הבירה – בעל הגמל חייב. [ל]הניח חנוני את נרו מבחוץ – חנוני חייב. רבי יהודה אומר: בנר חנוכה פטור. *אמר רבינא *(משום דרבה), זאת אומרת: [מ]נר חנוכה מצוה להניחה בתוך עשרה. דאי ס"ד למעלה מעשרה – לימא ליה: היה לך להניח למעלה מגמל ורוכבו! ודילמא: אי מיטרחא ליה טובא אתי לאימנועי ממצוה.§ *אמר רב כהנא, דרש רב נתן בר מניומי משמיה דרבי תנחום: נר

*) ב"ק סב: ב"ב ט:

רש"י

אין זקוק לה. הלכך בחול שרי: ואסור להשתמש לאורה. שיהא ניכר שהוא נר מצוה, וליכא למיחש לכבייה: ולא קבלה. שלא חששו לסמוך על דבריו: אי זכאי. אילו הייתי זוכה ללומדה הייתי גורסה כששמעתיה ראשון: גירסא דינקותא. מתקיים יותר משל זקנה: לשיעורה. שיהא בה שמן כשיעור הזה, ומיהו, אם כבתה – אין זקוק לה: רגלא דתרמודאי. שם אומה, מלקטי עצים דקים, ומתעכבין בשוק עד שהולכים בני השוק לבתיהם משחשכה ומבעירים בבתיהם אור, וכשצריכין לעצים – יוצאים וקונין מהן: נר איש וביתו. נר אחד בכל לילה. ואיש ואנשי ביתו סגי להו בנר אחד: והמהדרין. אחר המצות – עושין נר אחד בכל לילה לכל אחד ואחד מבני הבית: כנגד ימים הנכנסים. העתידים לבא: ימים היוצאין. שיצאו כבר, וזה שהוא עומד בו נמנה עם היוצאין: פרי החג. מתמעטים והולכים, כקרבנות דפרשת פנחס: מעלין בקדש ואין מורידין. מקרא ילפינן לה, במנחות בפרק "שתי הלחם" (דף צט.): מבחוץ. משום פרסומי ניסא. ולא ברה"ר אלא בחצרו, שבתיהן היו פתוחין לחצר: ואם היה דר בעלייה. שאין לו מקום בחצרו להניחה שם: מניחה. מבפנים, כנגד חלון הסמוך לרה"ר: הסכנה. שהיה להם לפרסיים חוק ביום אידם שלא יבעירו נר אלא בבית ע"ז שלהם, כדאמרינן בגיטין (פ"ב דף יז:): נר אחרת. לעשות היכר לדבר: ואי איכא מדורה. אש, לא צריך נר אחרת, לפי שמשתמש לאור המדורה, ויש היכרא שהנר של מצוה היא: ואי אדם חשוב הוא. שאינו רגיל להשתמש לאור המדורה: צריך נר אחרת. דאי לא – לא הוי היכר: מאי חנוכה. על איזה נס קבעוה: בחותמו. בהצנע, וחתום בטבעתו, והכיר שלא נגעו בו: ה"ג: ועשאום ימים טובים בהלל והודאה. לא שאסורין במלאכה, שלא נקבעו אלא לקרות הלל ולומר "על הנסים" בהודאה: גץ. ניצוץ, אישטינצל"ש: פטיש. קורנס גדול של נפחים: בעל גמל חייב. שלא היה לו להגדיל בחבילתו שתכנס לחנות: בנר חנוכה פטור. חנוני, שברשות פירסום מצוה הניחה שם: זאת אומרת. הא דקתני "בנר חנוכה פטור": פסולה

תוספות

ואין יכול להדליק בשבת. וי"ל: דא"כ לא הוה צריך ליה למימר "בין בחול בין בשבת" – כיון דחד טעמא הוא, אלא ה"ל למימר: *"אין מדליקין" סתם. מדקאמר "בין בחול בין בשבת" – ש"מ שעוד יש טעם אחר בשבת שלא להדליק, לבד מטעם חול. והיינו – שמא יטה. וא"כ סבר: דמותר להשתמש לאורה. ומיהו, רב דקאמר: "מדליקין בין בחול בין בשבת", לא היה מצי למימר מדליק סתם – דה"א דוקא בחול, אבל בשבת – אין מדליקין, שמא יטה. דבסתמא לא הייתי אומר שמשום אדם יחמיר לאסור להשתמש לאורה. וכן הלכתא: דנר חנוכה אסור להשתמש לאורה כרב וכר' יוחנן, ואביי נמי קיבלה, ורב יוסף נמי משמע לקמן דס"ל הכי. וכבתה – אין זקוק לה, דכולהו סבירא להו הכי. ורב הונא – יחיד הוא, ולית הלכתא כוותיה:

דאי לא אדליק מדליק. אבל מכאן ואילך – עבר הזמן. אומר הר"י פורת: דיש ליזהר ולהדליק בלילה מיד, שלא יאחר יותר מדאי. ומ"מ: אם איחר – ידליק מספק. דהא משני שינויי אחרינא. ולר"י נראה: דעתה אין לחוש מתי ידליק, דאנו אין לנו היכרא אלא לבני הבית – שהרי מדליקין מבפנים:

והמהדרין מן המהדרין. נראה לר"י: דב"ש וב"ה לא קיימי אלא אנר איש וביתו, שכן יש יותר הידור – דאיכא היכרא כשמוסיף והולך או מחסר, שהוא כנגד ימים הנכנסים או היוצאים. אבל אם עושה נר לכל אחד, אפי' יוסיף מכאן ואילך – ליכא היכרא, שיסברו שכך יש בני אדם בבית:

מצוה להניחה על פתח ביתו מבחוץ. ומיירי דליכא חצר, אלא בית עומד סמוך לרה"ר. אבל אם יש חצר לפני הבית – מצוה להניח על פתח חצר, דאמר לקמן: *חצר שיש לה ב' פתחים – צריכה ב' נרות. ואמרי' נמי: נר שיש לה שני פיות – עולה לשני בני אדם. משמע: לשני בתים, ואם היו מניחים על פתחי בתיהם – היה לזה מימין ולזה משמאל! אבל אי מניחים על פתח החצר – אתי שפיר:

ובשעת הסכנה. נראה לר"י: דהיינו מכי אתו חברי לבבל, כדאמר בפ' "כירה" (לקמן דף מה. ושם): מהו לטלטל שרגא דחנוכתא מקמי חברי בשבתא. וא"ת: דעל השלחן נמי יקחו אותו, כדאמר בגיטין (דף יז.): רבה בר בר חנה חלש, אתא חברא שקל שרגא מקמייהו! וי"ל: דאין רגילות כ"כ לחפש בבתים*:

שהיה מונח בחותמו של כ"ג. אם כבר גזרו על הגוים להיות כזבים *(נדה פ"ד דף לד.) צ"ל שהיה מונח בקופסא בקרקע, שלא °הסיטו הכלי:

עין משפט נר מצוה

ובהא ליכא למימר דאי הוי אמר אין מדליקין סתם ה"א דהיינו בשבת ומשום דמותר להשתמש לאורה אבל בחול מדליקין דכבתה אין זקוק לה דא"כ לא ה"ל למימר אין מדליקין בחנוכה אלא בהדיא הל"ל נ"ח מותר להשתמש לאורה [תוספות ישנים]

יב א מיי' פ"ד מהלכות חנוכה הלכה ו סמג לאוין ס ועשין ה טוש"ע או"ח סימן תרעג סעיף א:

יג ב מיי' שם הלכה ה טוש"ע שם סעיף ב:

יד ג מיי' שם הלכה ו טוש"ע שם סעיף א:

טו ד מיי' שם הלכה ה סמג שם טוש"ע או"ח סימן תרעב סעיף א:

טז ה מיי' שם טור שו"ע שם סעיף ב:

יז ו ז מיי' שם הלכה א סמג שם טוש"ע או"ח סימן תרעא סעיף ב:

יח ח ט מיי' שם הלכה ז ח טור שו"ע שם סעיף ה:

יט י מיי' פ"ג מהלכות חנוכה הלכה א ב סמג שם טור שו"ע או"ח סימן תרע סעיף א:

כ כ ל מיי' פי"ד מהל' נזקי ממון הלכה יג טוש"ע חו"מ סימן תיח סעיף יב:

כא מ טוש"ע או"ח סי' תרעא סעיף ו:

רבינו חננאל

אמר רב פתילו' ושמנים שאמרו חכמים אין מדליקין בהן בשבת מדליקין בהם בחנוכה בין בחול בין בשבת מ"ט קסבר כבתה אין זקוק לה ואסו' להשתמש לאורה. מיתיבי מצותה משתשקע החמה ועד שתכלה רגל מן השוק מאי לאו דאי כבתה הדר מדליק לה ושנינן לא אי לא אדליק נר של חנוכה עדיין לא יאמר כבר עבר זמנה אלא מדליק עד דכלי ריגלא דתרמודאי אי נמי שיעורא דשמן דנר חנוכה כמה הוא כדי שיהא דולק משקיעת החמה עד שתכלה רגלא דתרמודאי: **ת"ר** מצות חנוכה נר איש וביתו והמהדרין נר לכל אחד ואחד והמהדרין מן המהדרין ב"ה אומרים יום ראשון מדליק אחד מיכן והילך מוסיף והולך. פי' המהדרין מהדרי מצות כדאמרינן (ב"ק ט ב) להדור מצוה עד שליש במצוה. ת"ר נר חנוכה מצוה להניחה על פתח ביתו מבחוץ ואם היה דר בעליה מניחה בחלון הסמוך לרה"ר ובשעת הסכנה מניחו על השולחן ודי אמר רבא וצריך נר (אחד) [אחר] לתשמישו [ואי איכא מדורה לא צריך] ואי אדם חשוב הוא אף על גב דאית ליה מדורה צריך נר (אחד) [אחר] לתשמישו ואסיק'

מסורת הש"ס

[מס' סופרים פ"כ הלכה ד ועי' תוספות זבחים ט. ד"ה מנין ותוספות מנחות כ: ד"ה נפסל]

[ברכות כח. יומא יב: עג. מגילה ט: כא: הוריות יב: מנחו' לט: לט.]

[מס' סופרים פ"כ הלכה ה]

ב"ק כב. סב:

[נ"ל משמיה דרבא]

[ב"ק סב:]

גליון הש"ס

גמ' כל השמנים שבהיכל. עי' ברמב"ם פ"ה מהלכות בית הבחירה הלכה ח ועיין בתשובת בתי כהונה ח"א בבית ועד סימן א': תוס' ד"ה שהיה מונח וכו' שלא הסיטו. עיין לקמן דף פד ע"ב תוספות ד"ה שטהורים בזב:

הגהות הגר"א

[א] גמרא (להשתמש לאורה) תא"מ: [ב] שם (ודלא להתענות בהון) תא"מ:

נֵר *[א]שֶׁל חֲנוּכָּה שֶׁהִנִּיחָהּ לְמַעְלָה מִכ' אַמָּה – פְּסוּלָה, כְּסוּכָּה וּכְמָבוֹי.§ וְאָמַר *רַב כָּהֲנָא, דָּרַשׁ רַב נָתָן בַּר מַנְיוֹמֵי מִשְּׁמֵיהּ דְּרַב תַּנְחוּם, מַאי דִּכְתִיב: °"וְהַבּוֹר רֵק אֵין בּוֹ מָיִם". מִמַּשְׁמַע שֶׁנֶּאֱ': "וְהַבּוֹר רֵק" אֵינִי יוֹדֵעַ שֶׁאֵין בּוֹ מַיִם? אֶלָּא מַה ת"ל: "אֵין בּוֹ מָיִם" – מַיִם אֵין בּוֹ, אֲבָל נְחָשִׁים וְעַקְרַבִּים יֵשׁ בּוֹ.§ אָמַר רַבָּה: [ב]נֵר חֲנוּכָּה מִצְוָה לְהַנִּיחָהּ בְּטֶפַח הַסְּמוּכָה לַפֶּתַח. וְהֵיכָא מַנַּח לֵיהּ? רַב אַחָא בְּרֵיהּ דְּרָבָא אָמַר: מִיָּמִין, רַב *שְׁמוּאֵל מִדִּפְתִּי אָמַר: מִשְּׂמֹאל. וְהִילְכְתָא – [ג]מִשְּׂמֹאל, כְּדֵי שֶׁתְּהֵא נֵר חֲנוּכָּה מִשְּׂמֹאל וּמְזוּזָה מִיָּמִין.§ אָמַר רַב יְהוּדָה אָמַר רַב אַסִּי (אָמַר *רַב): [ד]אָסוּר לְהַרְצוֹת מָעוֹת כְּנֶגֶד נֵר חֲנוּכָּה. כִּי אָמְרִיתָהּ קַמֵּיהּ דִּשְׁמוּאֵל, אֲמַר לִי: וְכִי נֵר קְדוּשָּׁה יֵשׁ בָּהּ! מַתְקִיף לַהּ רַב יוֹסֵף: וְכִי דָּם קְדוּשָּׁה יֵשׁ בּוֹ? *דְּתַנְיָא: °"וְשָׁפַךְ וְכִסָּה" – בְּמָה שֶׁשָּׁפַךְ יְכַסֶּה, שֶׁלֹּא יְכַסֶּנּוּ בָּרֶגֶל, שֶׁלֹּא יְהוּ מִצְוֹת בְּזוּיוֹת עָלָיו. ה"נ – שֶׁלֹּא יְהוּ מִצְוֹת בְּזוּיוֹת עָלָיו.§ בָּעוּ מִינֵּיהּ מֵרַבִּי יְהוֹשֻׁעַ בֶּן לֵוִי: מַהוּ לְהִסְתַּפֵּק מִנּוֹיֵי סוּכָּה כָּל שִׁבְעָה? א"ל: הֲרֵי אָמְרוּ, אָסוּר לְהַרְצוֹת מָעוֹת כְּנֶגֶד נֵר חֲנוּכָּה. אֲמַר רַב יוֹסֵף: *מָרֵיהּ דְּאַבְרָהָם! תָּלֵי תַּנְיָא בִּדְלָא תַּנְיָא. סוּכָּה – תַּנְיָא, חֲנוּכָּה – לָא תַּנְיָא. *דְּתַנְיָא: [ה]סִכְּכָהּ כְּהִלְכָתָהּ, וְעִיטְּרָהּ בְּקְרָמִים וּבִסְדִינִין הַמְצוּיָּירִין, וְתָלָה בָּהּ אֱגוֹזִים אֲפַרְסְקִין שְׁקֵדִים וְרִמּוֹנִים וּפַרְכִּילֵי עֲנָבִים, וַעֲטָרוֹת שֶׁל שִׁבֳּלִים, יֵינוֹת (שֶׁל) שְׁמָנִים וּסְלָתוֹת – אָסוּר לְהִסְתַּפֵּק מֵהֶן עַד מוֹצָאֵי יוֹם טוֹב הָאַחֲרוֹן שֶׁל חָג, וְאִם הִתְנָה עֲלֵיהֶן – הַכֹּל לְפִי תְּנָאוֹ. אֶלָּא אֲמַר רַב יוֹסֵף: [ו]אֲבוּהוֹן דְּכוּלְּהוּ דָּם.§ *אִיתְּמַר, רַב אָמַר: אֵין מַדְלִיקִין מִנֵּר לְנֵר, וּשְׁמוּאֵל אָמַר: [ז]מַדְלִיקִין. רַב אָמַר: אֵין מַתִּירִין צִיצִית מִבֶּגֶד לְבֶגֶד, וּשְׁמוּאֵל אָמַר: [ח]מַתִּירִין מִבֶּגֶד לְבֶגֶד. רַב אָמַר: אֵין הֲלָכָה כְּרַבִּי שִׁמְעוֹן בִּגְרִירָה, וּשְׁמוּאֵל אָמַר: [ט]הֲלָכָה כְּרַבִּי שִׁמְעוֹן בִּגְרִירָה. *אָמַר אַבַּיֵי: כָּל מִילֵּי דְּמָר עָבֵיד כְּרַב, לְבַר מֵהָנֵי תְּלָת דְּעָבֵיד כִּשְׁמוּאֵל: מַדְלִיקִין מִנֵּר לְנֵר, וּמַתִּירִין מִבֶּגֶד לְבֶגֶד, וַהֲלָכָה כְּרַבִּי שִׁמְעוֹן בִּגְרִירָה. *דְּתַנְיָא: רַבִּי שִׁמְעוֹן אוֹמֵר: גּוֹרֵר אָדָם מִטָּה כִּסֵּא וְסַפְסָל, וּבִלְבַד שֶׁלֹּא יִתְכַּוֵּין לַעֲשׂוֹת חָרִיץ. יָתֵיב הַהוּא מֵרַבָּנַן קַמֵּיהּ דְּרַב אַדָּא בַּר אַהֲבָה, וְיָתֵיב וְקָאָמַר: טַעְמָא דְּרַב – מִשּׁוּם בִּיזּוּי מִצְוָה. אֲמַר לְהוּ: לָא תַּצִּיתוּ לֵיהּ, טַעְמֵיהּ דְּרַב – מִשּׁוּם דְּקָא מַכְחִישׁ מִצְוָה. מַאי בֵּינַיְיהוּ? אִיכָּא בֵּינַיְיהוּ: דְּקָא מַדְלִיק מִשְּׁרָגָא לִשְׁרָגָא. מ"ד מִשּׁוּם בִּיזּוּי מִצְוָה – מִשְּׁרָגָא לִשְׁרָגָא מַדְלִיק, מ"ד מִשּׁוּם אַכְחוּשֵׁי מִצְוָה – מִשְּׁרָגָא לִשְׁרָגָא נַמִּי אָסוּר. מֵתִיב רַב אַוְיָא[א]: *סֶלַע שֶׁל מַעֲשֵׂר

רש"י

פְּסוּלָה. דְּלָא שָׁלְטָא בָּהּ עֵינָא לְמַעְלָה מִכ' אַמָּה, וְלֵיכָּא פִּרְסוּמֵי נִיסָּא: כְּסוּכָּה וּכְמָבוֹי. דִּתְנַן בְּהוּ בְּהֶדְיָא בְּעֵירוּבִין וּמַסֶּכֶת סוּכָּה דִּפְסִילִי: מִצְוָה לְהַנִּיחָהּ. בְּחָצֵר אוֹ בִּרה"ר בְּטֶפַח הַסָּמוּךְ לַפֶּתַח, שֶׁאִם יַרְחִיקֶנּוּ לְהַלָּן מִן הַפֶּתַח – אֵינוֹ נִיכָּר שֶׁבַּעַל הַבַּיִת הִנִּיחוֹ שָׁם: מִיָּמִין. בִּכְנִיסָתוֹ לְבֵיתוֹ לְיָמִין: מְזוּזָה. קי"ל דְּבְיָמִין, דִּכְתִיב: °"בֵּיתֶךָ" – דֶּרֶךְ בִּיאָתְךָ, וְכִי עָקַר אֱינָשׁ – כַּרְעֵיהּ דְּיָמִינָא עָקַר בְּרֵישָׁא*: לְהַרְצוֹת. לִמְנוֹת: בְּמָה שֶׁשָּׁפַךְ. בְּיָדוֹ שֶׁשָּׁפַךְ בָּהּ, וְלֹא בְּרַגְלוֹ: נוֹיֵי סוּכָּה. פֵּירוֹת שֶׁתּוֹלִין בָּהּ לְנוֹי: מָרֵיהּ דְּאַבְרָהָם. לְשׁוֹן תְּמִיָּה הוּא: תָּלֵי. סוּכָּה דְּתַנְיָא בְּבָרַיְיתָא בְּהֶדְיָא, כִּדְמְפָרֵשׁ וְאָזֵיל: בִּדְלָא תַּנְיָא. בְּנֵר חֲנוּכָּה, דְּמֵימְרָא דְּרַב אַסִּי הוּא, וְאֵינוֹ בָּרַיְיתָא: וְעִטְּרָהּ בִּקְרָמִים. פַּתָּרָהּ בִּירִיעוֹת שֶׁל צְבָעִים, שֶׁקּוֹרִין אוֹברי"ן: הִתְנָה עֲלֵיהֶן. בְּמַסֶּ' בֵּיצָה (דף ל:) אוֹקִימְנָא בְּאוֹמֵר: "אֵינִי בּוֹדֵל מֵהֶן כָּל בֵּין הַשְּׁמָשׁוֹת שֶׁל קִידּוּשׁ יו"ט רִאשׁוֹן" – דְּלָא חָל עֲלַיְיהוּ קְדוּשָּׁה כְּלָל. אֲבָל תְּנַאי אַחֵר – אֵינוֹ מוֹעִיל: אֲבוּהוֹן דְּכוּלְּהוּ. שֶׁיִּלָּמְדוּ כּוּלָּן מִמֶּנּוּ: דָּם. כִּיסּוּי הַדָּם. דְּנָפְקָא לָן מִקְּרָא: "וְשָׁפַךְ וְכִסָּה", וּמְפָרֵשׁ בָּהּ טַעְמָא: שֶׁלֹּא יִהְיוּ מִצְוֹת בְּזוּיוֹת עָלָיו: מִנֵּר לְנֵר. דַּחֲנוּכָּה, כִּדְמְפָרֵשׁ טַעְמָא לְקַמֵּיהּ: מַתִּירִין. לְהַטִּיל צִיצִית מִטַּלִּית יָשָׁן לְטַלִּית חָדָשׁ, וּבִמְנָחוֹת מְפָרֵשׁ טַעְמָא דְּמַאן דְּאָסַר: הֲלָכָ' כְּר"ש. דְּאָמַר: דָּבָר שֶׁאֵין מִתְכַּוֵּין – מוּתָּר, וְאַע"ג דְּקָעָבֵיד חָרִיץ, וַהֲוֵי תּוֹלָדָה דְּחוֹרֵשׁ אוֹ בּוֹנֶה. וּמִשּׁוּם דְּהִילְכְתָא *כְּרַב בְּאִיסּוּרֵי בְּכוּלֵּיהּ תַּלְמוּדָא בַּר מֵהָנֵי תְּלָת – נָקְטִינְהוּ גַּבֵּי הֲדָדֵי: כָּל מִילֵּי דְּמָר. רַבָּה בַּר נַחְמָנִי: לַעֲשׂוֹת חָרִיץ גָּרְסִינַן: טַעְמָא דְּרַב. מִנֵּר לְנֵר – מִשּׁוּם בִּיזּוּי מִצְוָה, שֶׁמַּדְלִיק קֵיסָם שֶׁאֵינָהּ מִן הַמִּצְוָה מִנֵּר שֶׁל מִצְוָה, וּמִמֶּנּוּ מַדְלִיק הָאַחֵר: אַכְחוּשֵׁי. דְּמֶיחֱזֵי כְּמַאן דְּשָׁקֵיל נְהוֹרָא, וְשׁוֹאֵב קְצָת מִלַּחְלוּחִית שַׁמְנוֹ: מִשְּׁרָגָא לִשְׁרָגָא. מַדְלִיק נֵר אֵצֶל נֵר, וּשְׁתֵּיהֶן שֶׁל מִצְוָה, וְלֹא בְּקֵיסָם:

תוספות

נר חנוכה שהניחה למעלה מכ' אמה פסולה כסוכה וכמבוי. וא"ת: הוה ליה למימר "ימעט" כמו גבי מבוי, דאמר התם: מבוי דרבנן – תני תקנתא. ואיכא למימר: דנקט פסולה – משום דבעי למימר כסוכה שהיא מן התורה. אי נמי: לא רצה להאריך "יכבנה וימעטנה ויחזור וידליקנ"", דלמעטה ולהניחה כמו שהיא דולקת – אי אפשר, כדמוכח לקמן*:

אסור להסתפק מהן עד מוצאי יו"ט האחרון. והא דשרי אתרוג ביו"ט האחרון טפי מסוכה – מפרש בפרק "לולב וערבה" (סוכה מו:) משום דסוכה בספק שביעי ספק שמיני – יתובי יתבינן, ואי מתרמי ליה סעודה בין השמשות – אכיל ליה התם, והואיל ואיתקצי בין השמשות – איתקצי כוליה יומא של ספק ח' וט'. אבל אתרוג – אינו ניטל בספק ז' וח', *ולא איתסר בספק שמיני(א) אלא משום דאיתקצי בין השמשות של ז'. ואע"פ דבין השמשות של ח' נמי אסור משום שהוא ספק יום – הואיל ולא אסור אלא משום ספק יום וספק לילה – לא איתקצי בכך כולי יומא – מידי דהוה אבילה שנולדה בזה דמותרת בזה, אע"פ דבין השמשות אסור משום ספק יום וספק לילה:

סוכה תניא. משמע דטעמא דנויי סוכה משום ביזוי מצוה. וקשה לר"י: בפרק "כירה" (לקמן דף מה. ושם) משמע דטעמא משום "מיגו דאיתקצי למצותה"! ותירץ: דצריכי לתרווייהו; דמשום דאיתקצי למצותה – לא הוה אסרינן בחולו של מועד, דלא שייך מוקצה אלא (בנפל) בשבת וביו"ט. ומשום ביזוי מצוה – לא הוה אסרינן להו היכא דנפלו. אבל השתא דאמרי' דאיתקצי, וביזוי מצוה – אסרינן אפילו נפלו, ואפי' בחוה"מ. *וקשה לר"י: כיון דנויי סוכה אסורין משום ביזוי, א"כ מאי פריך בביצה בפ' "המביא" (דף ל: ושם) מנויי סוכה אעצי סוכה – דקאמר: וסוכת החג לא מהני בה תנאה, והתני': סככה כהלכתה כו'. ומאי קושיא? דילמא עצי סוכה לא מהני ביה תנאה – דמקרא נפקא, כדדריש התם: מניין לעצי סוכה שאסורין כל שבעה ת"ל: "חג הסוכות ז' ימים וגו'". ודרשה גמורה היא, כדמוכח בפ"ק דסוכה (דף ט. ושם) דב"ש פסלי מהאי קרא סוכה ישנה, וב"ה מכשירין. דההוא מיבעי ליה לעצי סוכה שאסורין כל שבעה. אבל נויי סוכה דלא אסירי אלא משום ביזוי – מהני בהו תנאה. ועוד, בפרק "כירה" (לקמן דף מה.) משמע בהדיא *דעצי סוכה לא אסור אלא משום דאיתקלאי למצותה! *והשיב ר"ת: דבין נויי סוכה ובין עצי סוכה היתרים על הכשר סוכה – לא אסירי אלא משום ביזוי, או משום "הואיל והוקצה למצותו". ולא אסירי מקרא – אלא דווקא כדי הכשר סוכה. והמקשה דפריך בביצה (דף ל:) מנויי סוכה אעצי סוכה – לא ידע שיש חילוק בין יותר מכדי הכשר סוכה לכדי הכשר סוכה, ומשני: באומר "איני בודל מהם כל בה"ש", דלא חיילא קדושה על נויי סוכה, וכן על עצים היתרין על הכשר סוכה מהני בה תנאה. אבל עצי סוכה כדי הכשר – חיילא קדושה עלייהו על כרחו דבר תורה כל שבעה, ולא מהני תנאה. והא דקאמר התם: ואם התנה עליהן – הכל לפי תנאו, ופריך: למימרא דמהני בה תנאה כו', ומשני: סיפא אתאן לסוכה דעלמא. ובתר הכי פריך: וסוכת החג לא מהני בה תנאה? והתניא סככה כו' – לא בעי לשנויי "הכל לפי תנאו" על יתרות מכדי הכשר סוכה – "דהכל לפי תנאו" – משמע בכל הסוכה:

אבוהון דכולהו דם. הא דלא קאמר: אבוהון דכולהו עצי סוכה, דנפקי מקרא כדאמר בריש "המביא" בביצה (דף ל: ושם). אומר ר"י: דמשום דמעצי סוכה לא הוה ילפינן – דשאני סוכה, דבמסתפק מהן איכא ביטול מצוה. אבל בנויי סוכה והרצאת מעות לאור נר חנוכה – ליכא ביטול מצוה:

רב אמר אין מתירין מבגד לבגד. לא מבעיא אי חובת טלית הוא דאסור, אלא אפילו חובת גברא הוא – נמי אסור, כדאשכחן במזוזה דנענש אותו שנטלה, בבבא מליעא בסוף פרק "השואל" (דף קב.), אף על גב דחובת הדר היא. ושמואל אמר: מתירין. אע"ג דשמואל גופי' סבר *דחובת טלית היא – אפ"ה מתירין, כיון שעושהו לצורך בגד אחר. וגבי מזוזה שנענש – שמא לא היה בדעתו להניח בבית אחר. א"נ: מזוזה שאני, שעשויה להציל מן המזיקין. ואע"ג דלכ"ע אין מתירין שלא להניח בבגד אחר – אין קשה מה שנהגו להתיר ציצית מטליתות של מתים, דדווקא בטלית של חי שהוא בר חיובא אין מתירין:

כל מילי דמר עביד כרב. קושיא דפ"ק דכתובות (ד' ו) שם כתובה: וכי

מסורת הש"ס

[יומא יא:]

[בשאלתות פ' וישלח סי' כו איתא ירמי']

[בהרא"ש ליתא וכן משמע מלשון רש"י ד"ה תלי]

חולין פז.

[עירובין עה:] כתובות ג. ב"ב קלד:

לקמן מה. ביצה ל: סוכה י. [תוספתא סוכה פ"א]

מנחות מא:

שם לקמן מ. פסחים קא.

לקמן כט: מו. [פסחים קא.] ביצה כג: [מנחות מא:] [תוספתא ביצה פ"ב]

[תוספתא דמעשר שני רפ"א]

[ועי' תוס' עירובין ב. ד"ה סוכה ותוס' סוכה ב. ד"ה לאורייתא]

[מנחות מא.]

עין משפט נר מצוה

כב א מיי' פ"ד מהל' חנוכה הל' ז סמג עשין ה טוש"ע א"ח סי' תרעא סעיף ו:

כג ב ג מיי' שם טוש"ע שם סעיף ז:

כד ד מיי' שם הל' ו סמג שם טוש"ע א"ח סי' תרעג סעיף א:

כה ה מיי' פ"ו מהל' סוכה הל' טז סמג עשין מג טוש"ע א"ח סימן תרלח סעיף ב:

כו ו טוש"ע א"ח סימן תרעז סעיף ד:

כז ז מיי' פ"ד מהלכות חנוכה הל' ט סמג עשין ה טוש"ע א"ח סי' תרעד סעיף א:

כח ח מיי' פ"א מהל' ציצית הל' יג סמג עשין כו טוש"ע א"ח סי' טו סעיף א:

כט ט מיי' פ"א מהל' שבת הלכה ה סמג לאוין סה טוש"ע א"ח סי' שלז סעיף א:

ר"ל לא איתסר בה"ש של ח' וט' אלא משום דאתקלי בה"ש של ז' וח' ורש"ל גורס ולא איתסר בשמיני משום דאתקלי כו' דבה"ש של ז' נמי אסור:

אי נמי טעמא דהוקצה למצותו נ"מ לאסורי אפי' ביו"ט האחרון משום דאתקלי בה"ש דלטעמא דביזוי ליכא א"כ הכל אחד אתקלי למצותו משום ביזוי מצוה [ת"י]

*אולי צ"ל דנויי

פי' ר"ת נראה דחוק דלא ה"ל למימר באומר איני בודל ס' אלא בהדיא התם בהכשר סוכה ומיהו נראה דאצטריך לשנויי באומר איני בודל דהכא אחר לא מהני בהו משום ביזוי מצוה אבל בקשות אומר איני בודל לא חייל עלייהו קדושה כלל וליכא ביזוי [ת"י]

גליון הש"ס

גמרא אמר אביי כל מילי דמר. עיין לקמן דף מו ע"א תוספות ד"ה דנפשה ובעירובין דף לג ע"ב תוספות ד"ה לא תימא:

הגהות הב"ח

(א) תום' ד"ה אסור וכו' ולא איתסר בספק שביעי ושמיני אלא וכו' של ז' וח' ואע"ג דבין השמשות של ח' וט' נמי אסור:

הגהות הגר"א

[א] גמ' (סלע של) א"מ:

רבינו חננאל

נר חנוכה למעלה מעשרים אמה פסולה כמבוי וכסוכה ומצוה להניחה מבחוץ בתוך י' טפחים בטפח הסמוך לפתח בצד שמאל כדי שתהא מזוזה מימין ונר חנוכה משמאל דרך ביאתו לביתו. ואסור להרצות מעות כנגד נר של חנוכה שלא יהא מצות בזויות עליו כמו הדם דאמר רחמנא ושפך וכסה שלא יכסנו ברגל וכו' וכן סככה כהלכתה כו' אמר רב יוסף אבוהון דכולהו דם פי' כל המצות לומדות שלא יהא מצות בזויות עליו: **תניא** בב"ה בכסליו חנוכה תמניא יומי דלא למספד שכשנכנסו גוים להיכל טמאו כל שמן שבמקדש וכשגברו כו': **אתמר** רב אמר אין מתירין ציצית מבגד לבגד כלומר מזו הטלית ומטילין לטלית אחרת וכו'. אין מדליקין מנר של חנוכה נר אחר ואין הלכה כרבי שמעון בגרירה. רבה בר נחמני לעולם היה עושה כרב בר מהני תלתי דעביד כשמואל דהוה שרי להתיר ציצית מבגד לבגד ולהדליק מנר של חנוכה נר אחר של חנוכה והלכתא כר"ש דאמר גורר אדם

עין משפט נר מצוה

ל א ב מיי' פ"ג מהל' מעשר שני הלכ' יט:
לא ג מיי' פ"ג מהל' תמידין הלכה יד:
לב ד ה מיי' פ"ד מהל' חנוכה הל' ט סמג עשין ה טוש"ע א"ח סי' תרעה סעיף א:

מסורת הש"ס

^א^מַעֲשֵׂר שֵׁנִי אֵין שׁוֹקְלִין כְּנֶגְדּוֹ דִּינְרֵי זָהָב, וַאֲפִילּוּ לְחַלֵּל עָלָיו מַעֲשֵׂר שֵׁנִי אַחֵר. אִי אָמְרַתְּ בִּשְׁלָמָא כִּי פְּלִיגִי רַב וּשְׁמוּאֵל מִנֵּר לְנֵר, אֲבָל בְּקִינְסָא אָסַר שְׁמוּאֵל – הָא לָא תֶּהֱוֵי תְּיוּבְתָּא. אֶלָּא אִי אָמְרַתְּ בְּקִינְסָא נַמִי שָׁרֵי, הָא תֶּהֱוֵי תְּיוּבְתָּא! אָמַר רַבָּה: ^ב^גְּזֵירָה שֶׁמָּא לֹא יְכַוֵּין מִשְׁקְלוֹתָיו, וְקָא מַפֵּיק לְהוּ לְחוּלִּין. מְתִיב רַב שֵׁשֶׁת: °"מִחוּץ לְפָרוֹכֶת הָעֵדוּת יַעֲרוֹךְ" *וְכִי לְאוֹרָה הוּא צָרִיךְ? וַהֲלֹא כָּל אַרְבָּעִים שָׁנָה שֶׁהָלְכוּ בְּנֵי יִשְׂרָאֵל בַּמִּדְבָּר לֹא הָלְכוּ אֶלָּא לְאוֹרוֹ; אֶלָּא עֵדוּת הִיא לְבָאֵי עוֹלָם שֶׁהַשְּׁכִינָה שׁוֹרָה בְּיִשְׂרָאֵל. מַאי עֵדוּת? אָמַר *רַב: זוֹ נֵר מַעֲרָבִי, שֶׁנּוֹתֵן בָּהּ שֶׁמֶן כְּמִדַּת חַבְרוֹתֶיהָ, *וּמִמֶּנָּה הָיָה מַדְלִיק °וּבָהּ הָיָה מְסַיֵּים. וְהָא הָכָא, כֵּיוָן דִּקְבִיעִי נֵרוֹת לָא סַגְיָא דְּלָא מִשְׁקִיל וְאַדְלוּקֵי, קַשְׁיָא בֵּין לְמ"ד מִשּׁוּם בִּזּוּי מִצְוָה, וּבֵין לְמ"ד מִשּׁוּם אַכְחוּשֵׁי מִצְוָה! תַּרְגְּמָא ר"פ ^ג^בִּפְתִילוֹת אֲרוּכּוֹת. סוֹף סוֹף, לְמ"ד מִשּׁוּם אַכְחוּשֵׁי מִצְוָה קַשְׁיָא! קַשְׁיָא. מַאי הָוֵי עֲלַהּ? א"ר הוּנָא בְּרֵיהּ דְּרַב יְהוֹשֻׁעַ: חָזֵינָא אִי הַדְלָקָה עוֹשָׂה מִצְוָה – מַדְלִיקִין מִנֵּר לְנֵר, וְאִי הַנָּחָה עוֹשָׂה מִצְוָה – אֵין מַדְלִיקִין מִנֵּר לְנֵר. דְּאִיבַּעְיָא לְהוּ: הַדְלָקָה עוֹשָׂה מִצְוָה אוֹ הַנָּחָה עוֹשָׂה מִצְוָה – ת"ש. דְּאָמַר רָבָא: ^ד^הָיָה תָּפוּשׂ נֵר חֲנוּכָּה וְעוֹמֵד – לֹא עָשָׂה וְלֹא כְּלוּם. שְׁמַע מִינַּהּ: הַנָּחָה עוֹשָׂה מִצְוָה. הָתָם: הָרוֹאֶה אוֹמֵר "לְצוֹרְכּוֹ הוּא דְּנָקֵיט לַהּ". ת"ש. דְּאָמַר רָבָא: ^ה^הִדְלִיקָהּ בִּפְנִים וְהוֹצִיאָהּ – לֹא עָשָׂה כְּלוּם. אא"ב הַדְלָקָה עוֹשָׂה מִצְוָה – הַדְלָקָה בִּמְקוֹמוֹ בָּעֵינַן, מִשּׁוּם הָכִי לֹא עָשָׂה כְּלוּם. אֶלָּא אִי אָמְרַתְּ "הַנָּחָה עוֹשָׂה מִצְוָה" אַמַּאי לֹא עָשָׂה וְלֹא כְּלוּם? הָתָם נַמִי; הָרוֹאֶה הוּא אוֹמֵר "לְצוֹרְכּוֹ הוּא דְּאַדְלְקָהּ". תָּא שְׁמַע, דְּאָמַר רַבִּי יְהוֹשֻׁעַ בֶּן לֵוִי:
עֲשָׁשִׁית

תורה אור: ויקרא כד

מַעֲשֵׂר שֵׁנִי. דִּינָרִין שֶׁמְּחַלֵּל עֲלֵיהֶם מַעֲשֵׂר שֵׁנִי אֵין שׁוֹקְלִין כְּנֶגְדָּן דִּינָרִין שֶׁל חוּלִּין, לִרְאוֹת שֶׁיִּהְיוּ שְׁלֵימִים: אִי אָמְרַתְּ בִּשְׁלָמָא כִּי פְּלִיגִי רַב וּשְׁמוּאֵל מִנֵּר לְנֵר. מַמָּשׁ, וְלֹא בְּקֵיסָם. וּבְהָא הוּא דְּשָׁרֵי שְׁמוּאֵל – דְּלָא חָיֵישׁ לְאַכְחוּשֵׁי, אֲבָל בְּקִינְסָא דְּבִיזּוּי הוּא – מוֹדֶה, הָא לָאו הָוְיָא תְּיוּבְתֵּיהּ; דְּהָנָךְ דִּינָרִים דְּחוּלִּין לָא גּוּפַיְיהוּ מִצְוָה, וְאַע"ג דִּלְמִצְוָה קָבָעֵי לְהוּ – לְקִינְסָא דָּמְיָא. אֶלָּא אִי אָמְרַתְּ בְּקִינְסָא נַמִי שָׁרֵי שְׁמוּאֵל, הוֹאִיל וְצוֹרֶךְ מִצְוָה הוּא – הָא הָוְיָא תְּיוּבְתֵּיהּ, דְּאָסַר לִשְׁקוֹל וְאַע"ג דְּצוֹרֶךְ מִצְוָה! לֹא יְכַוֵּין מִשְׁקְלוֹתָיו. שֶׁמָּא לֹא יִמְצְאֵם טוֹבִים, אוֹ יִמְצָאֵם יְתֵירִים, וְיָחוּס עֲלֵיהֶן וְלֹא יְחַלֵּל הַמַּעֲשֵׂר עֲלֵיהֶן. וְנִמְצָא שֶׁבִּיזָּה הַמַּעֲשֵׂר שֶׁלֹּא לְצוֹרֶךְ: וּמַפֵּיק לְהוּ לְחוּלִּין. כְּלוֹמַר: יַנִּיחֵם בְּחוּלֵּיהֶן כְּמוֹ שֶׁהֵן: נֵר מַעֲרָבִי. לְמ"ד בִּמְנָחוֹת: *"מִזְרָח וּמַעֲרָב מוּנָּחִין" סֵדֶר הַקָּנִים – קָרֵי "מַעֲרָבִי" נֵר שֵׁנִי שֶׁבְּצַד הַחִיצוֹן, שֶׁהוּא בַּמִּזְרָח. וּלְמ"ד: "צָפוֹן וְדָרוֹם מוּנָּחִים" – אֶמְצָעִי קָרֵי "מַעֲרָבִי", עַל שֵׁם שֶׁהָיָה פִּיו כְּנֶגֶד מַעֲרָב, וְכָל שְׁאָר הַנֵּרוֹת כְּלַפֵּי הָאֶמְצָעִית, דִּכְתִיב: "אֶל מוּל פְּנֵי הַמְּנוֹרָה" דְּהַיְינוּ אֶמְצָעִי "יָאִירוּ" וגו'. שֶׁל צָפוֹן הָיוּ פּוֹנוֹת לְדָרוֹם, וְשֶׁבְּדָרוֹם פּוֹנוֹת לְצָפוֹן: נֵרוֹת. בזי"ך שֶׁל זָהָב, שֶׁנּוֹתְנִין לְתוֹכָן שֶׁמֶן וּפְתִילָה: כְּמִדַּת חַבְרוֹתֶיהָ. חֲצִי לוֹג שִׁיעֲרוּ בָּהּ לְלֵילֵי תְּקוּפַת טֵבֵת הַגְּדוֹלִים, וְאִם יִדְלַק בַּיּוֹם (וּבַלַּיְלָה) בַּלֵּילוֹת הַקְּצָרִים – יִדְלַק. אֲבָל פָּחוֹת – לֹא, שֶׁלֹּא יִכְבֶּה בְּטֵבֵת בַּלַּיְלָה, וְהַתּוֹרָה אָמְרָה: "מֵעֶרֶב עַד בֹּקֶר": וּמִמֶּנָּה הָיָה מַדְלִיק. הַנֵּרוֹת בֵּין הָעַרְבַּיִם: וּבָהּ הָיָה מְסַיֵּים. הֲטָבַת הַנֵּרוֹת שֶׁדָּלַק כָּל הַיּוֹם, וְאֵינוֹ מֵטִיבוֹ עַד הָעֶרֶב. וּמִשְׁנָה זוֹ בְּת"כ שְׁנוּיָה, וּסְבִירָא לֵיהּ דְּמִזְרָח וּמַעֲרָב מוּנָּחִין. וְהָכִי תַּנְיָא לְעֵיל מִינֵּיהּ: "לְהַעֲלוֹת נֵר תָּמִיד" – שֶׁתְּהֵא נֵר מַעֲרָבִי תָּמִיד, שֶׁמִּמֶּנּוּ יְהֵא מַתְחִיל וּבוֹ יְהֵא מְסַיֵּים. וּמִדְּלָא כְּתִיב "לְהַעֲלוֹת נֵרוֹת" – ש"מ: הוּקְבַּע נֵר אֶחָד לְהַתְחִיל בּוֹ בְּכָל יוֹם, וְזֶהוּ נֵר מַעֲרָבִי הַשֵּׁנִי שֶׁל מִזְרָח. וְהָכִי תְּנַן (תמיד לג.): נִכְנַס וּמָצָא נֵרוֹת מִזְרָחִים דּוֹלְקוֹת – מְדַשֵּׁן הַמִּזְרָחִי וּמַנִּיחַ אֶת הַמַּעֲרָבִי דּוֹלֵק, שֶׁמִּמֶּנּוּ מַדְלִיק אֶת הַמְּנוֹרָה בֵּין הָעַרְבַּיִם. מְצָאוֹ שֶׁכָּבָה, כְּגוֹן מִשֶּׁמֵּת שִׁמְעוֹן הַצַּדִּיק – מַדְלִיקוֹ מִמִּזְבַּח הָעוֹלָה. וְנִרְאֶה בְּעֵינַי דְּאָמוּר רַבָּנַן קְבִיעוּתָא בְּנֵר שֵׁנִי – מִשּׁוּם דְּאֵין מַעֲבִירִין עַל הַמִּצְוֹת, וְכִי עָיֵיל בַּהֵיכָל – בְּקַמָּא פָּגַע בְּרֵישָׁא, וּבֵיהּ לָא מָצֵי לְאַתְחוּלֵי, דִּכְתִיב: "יַעֲרוֹךְ אוֹתוֹ לִפְנֵי ה'" – צָרִיךְ שֶׁיְּהֵא אֶחָד חוּצָה לוֹ, דְּאִי לָא, לָא קָרֵינַן בֵּיהּ "לִפְנֵי ה'". וְהָכִי אָמְרִינַן בִּמְנָחוֹת (דף נח:), דִּכְתִיב בְּנֵר מַעֲרָבִי "לִפְנֵי ה'" – מִכְּלָל דְּכוּלְּהוּ לָאו לִפְנֵי ה' כו'. וּבָהּ הָיָה מְסַיֵּים הַהֲטָבָה – לְפִי שֶׁהַשְּׁאָר הָיָה מֵטִיב שַׁחֲרִית, וְזוֹ מֵטִיב בֵּין הָעַרְבַּיִם. וְאוֹחֵז הַיְשָׁנָה בְּיָדוֹ, אוֹ מַנִּיחָהּ בִּכְלִי עַד^(א)^ שֶׁנּוֹתֵן שֶׁמֶן וּפְתִילָה, וּמַדְלִיקָהּ וּמַדְלִיק מִמֶּנָּה אֶת הַשְּׁאָר. וְהָא דְּאָמְרִינַן בְּסֵדֶר יוֹמָא (דף לג.): הֲטָבַת ה' נֵרוֹת קוֹדֶם לַהֲטָבַת ב' נֵרוֹת, מַשְׁמַע: כּוּלְּהוּ הֲוָה מֵטִיב שַׁחֲרִית, וְיָלֵיף לָהּ מִקְּרָאֵי – הַיְינוּ בְּשֶׁלֹּא הָיָ' הַנֵּס מִתְקַיֵּים וְהָיָ' מוֹצְאוֹ שֶׁכָּבָה. דְּלָא סָמַךְ קְרָא אַנִּיסָּא, וְכָל זְמַן שֶׁהָיוּ יִשְׂרָאֵל חֲבִיבִין – הָיָה דּוֹלֵק כָּל הַיּוֹם, וְהַיְינוּ עֵדוּתָהּ: וְהָא הָכָא כֵּיוָן דִּקְבִיעִי נֵרוֹת. בַּמְּנוֹרָה, וְלֹא הָיָה יָכוֹל לְנַתֵּק נֵר מַעֲרָבִי מִן הַמְּנוֹרָה לְהַדְלִיק בּוֹ הָאֲחֵרִים – עַל כָּרְחֵיךְ הָא דְּקָתָנֵי "מִמֶּנָּה הָיָ' מַדְלִיק" – לָא סַגֵּי דְּלָאו מִשְׁקַל קִינְסָא: וְאַדְלוּקֵי. לְקִינְסָא מִנֵּר מַעֲרָבִי, וּבְהַהִיא קִינְסָא מַדְלִיק אֶת הַשְּׁאָר: בִּפְתִילוֹת אֲרוּכּוֹת. כָּל הַפְּתִילוֹת יוֹצְאוֹת חוּץ לְנֵרוֹתֵיהֶם עַד שֶׁמַּגִּיעוֹת זוֹ לָזוֹ, וּמַדְלִיק מִמֶּנָּה הַסְּמוּכָה לָהּ, וְהַשְּׁאָר זוֹ מִזּוֹ: סוֹף סוֹף לְמ"ד כו'. דְּהָא לְדִידֵיהּ מִשְׁרָגָא לִשְׁרָגָא אָסוּר: אִי הַדְלָקָה עוֹשָׂה מִצְוָה. אִי הַמִּצְוָה שֶׁל חֲנוּכָּה תְּלוּיָה בְּהַדְלָקָה – מַדְלִיקִין, כִּדְאַשְׁכְּחַן בַּמְּנוֹרָה: וְאִי הַנָּחָה עוֹשָׂה מִצְוָה. וְעִיקַּר מִצְוָתָהּ תַּלְיָא בְּהַנָּחָה: אֵין מַדְלִיקִין מִנֵּר לְנֵר. דְּהַדְלָקָה לָאו מִצְוָה הִיא כּוּלֵּי הַאי: דְּאִיבַּעְיָא לְהוּ גָּרְסִי'. כְּלוֹמַר: דְּהָא מִילְּתָא כְּבָר אִיבַּעְיָא לַן, וּמִפְּשָׁטָא דְּהַהִיא בָּעְיָא מִיפְשְׁטָא לַן הָךְ: הָיָה תָּפוּשׂ נֵר חֲנוּכָּה. בְּיָדוֹ מִשֶּׁהִדְלִיקָהּ עַד שֶׁכָּבְתָה: וְעוֹמֵד. לָאו דַּוְקָא, אֶלָּא כֵּן לְשׁוֹן הַתַּלְמוּד: לְצָרְכּוֹ. לְהִשְׁתַּמֵּשׁ, וְלֵיכָּא הֶיכֵּר נִיסָּא: בִּפְנִים. בַּבַּיִת: וְהוֹצִיאָהּ לַחוּץ. כְּדַאֲמַר לְעֵיל, דְּצָרִיךְ לְהַנִּיחָהּ עַל פֶּתַח בֵּיתוֹ מִבַּחוּץ: אִי אָמְרַתְּ בִּשְׁלָמָא הַדְלָקָה עוֹשָׂה מִצְוָה מִשּׁוּם הָכִי לֹא עָשָׂה וְלֹא כְּלוּם. דְּכֵיוָן דְּזוֹ הִיא מִצְוָתָהּ – צָרִיךְ שֶׁתֵּיעָשֶׂה בִּמְקוֹם חִיוּבָא:
עֲשָׁשִׁית

וכי לאורה הוא צריך והלא כל אותם מ' שנה כו'. תימה: אמאי נקט מ' שנה? לעולם כל העולם כולו לאורו של מקום הולכין! וי"מ: וכי אהרן כשהיה נכנס לפנים לאורה היה צריך? והלא מ' שנה היה מאיר להם עמוד ענן בכל המקומות, כדאמרינן בברייתא דמלאכת המשכן היה מסתכל בטפיח *(ורואה בו) ויודע מה בתוכו, בחבית ויודע מה בתוכה. וכן משמע בת"כ דאכהנים קאי, דגרס התם: וכי צריכים לנר? והלא כל אותן מ' שנה לא הוצרכו לנר, שנא': "כי ענן ה' על המשכן וגו'". ומיהו, בשלהי "כל קרבנות" (מנחות ד' פו: ושם) משמע דאשכינה קאי, דמייתי לה גבי הא דא"ר אליעזר: לא לאכילה אני צריך ולא לאורה אני צריך. וקאמר נמי התם: "לפרוכת העדות" – עדות היא לכל באי עולם שהשכינה שורה בישראל. וא"ת: לאורה אני צריך – והלא כל אותן ארבעים שנה: **ובה** היה מסיים. פירש בקונטרס: ובה היה מסיים ההטבה, שהשאר היה מטיב שחרית וזה היה מטיב בין הערבים, ואוחז הישנה בידו או מניחה בכלי עד שנותן לתוך מערבית שמן ופתילה ומדליקה, ומדליק השאר ממנה. וקשה לריב"א: שאם^(ב)^ אפשר להדליק מן הישנה – א"כ גם השאר ידליק ממנה ומאי פריך לרב! כיון דהוציא הפתילה הישנה מן הנר – תו ליכא לא משום בזיון מצוה ולא משום אכחושי מצוה. אלא ודאי א"א לעשות כן. וכשבא להטיב – היה מטיב כל מה שבנר, והפתילה היתה כבה מאליה. אלא בעוד שהפתילה ישנה בנר מערבי דולקת – היה מדליק ממנה השאר, והיה מטיבה ונותן בה שמן ופתילה חדשה ומדליקה מן השאר – "ובה היה מסיים" – היינו ההדלקה*: **והא** הכא כיון דקביעי נרות כו'. כמ"ד בפרק "ב' מדות" (מנחות ד' פח:) דנר של פרקים היה, דמשמע התם דמחובר הוה והיה של פרקים כדי שיוכל להטיבו יפה. ואיכא מ"ד התם דלא הוה קבוע, אלא היה מסלקו לגמרי בשעת הטבה ואחר כך מניחו: **מאי** הוי עלה. תימה: מאי קמיבעיא ליה? ומאי קאמר נמי "חזינן אי הדלקה כו'"? הא לכאורה משמע דהלכה כשמואל, דהא רבה עבד כוותיה – וא"כ קינסא נמי שרי, דהא ע"כ בקינסא פליגי, ובביזוי מצוה. דהא מאן דמפרש טעמא דרב משום אכחושי מצוה – איתותב! וצ"ל דאינו תופס דברי רבה עיקר, ומבעיא ליה: אי הנחה עושה מצוה – ואסור לרב מנר לנר משום ביזוי מצוה כמו בקינסא, או הדלקה עושה מצוה ושרי כמו במנורה – דלא חיישינן לאכחושי מצוה. ומסיק: דהדלקה עושה מצוה, ושרי. א"נ, מצאתי בשם ריב"ס: דמיבעיא ליה אליבא דשמואל דהילכתא כוותיה, אי שרי בקינסא אי לאו. ומיבעיא ליה: אי קי"ל כמו שאמר למעלה דלמ"ד משום בזויי מצוה – שרי להדליק מנר לנר לרב, ואם כן בקינסא פליגי – ושרי שמואל בקינסא. או דילמא: לא קי"ל הכי, ומנר לנר נמי איכא ביזוי מצוה, ואסר רב. (פי') דהנחה עושה מצוה, ולא דמי למנורה. ודוקא מנר לנר שרי שמואל, אבל בקינסא – אפילו שמואל מודה דאסור. ומסיק: חזינן דאיבעיא לן ואפשיט דהדלקה עושה מצוה, ומדליק לרב מנר לנר כמו במנורה. ולשמואל אפילו בקינסא שרי: **דאיבעיא** להו הדלקה עושה מצוה כו'. ונפקא מינה אם הדליקה חש"ו או הניחה:
מכבה

[בילקוט סוף פקודי לית']

[במנחות פו: אית' רבא וכ"א בילקוט פרשת תצוה רמז שעח]

[וע"ע תוס' מנחות פו: ד"ה ממנה וכו']

מנחות פו:

[דף נח:]

תמיד לג. פ"ו מ"א

רבינו חננאל

אדם מטה כסא וספסל ובלבד שלא יתכוון לעשות חריץ ואסיקנ' דטעמא דרב משום בזוי מצוה וכיון דנר של מצוה הוא [דמדליק מנר של] מצוה ליכא בזיון מצוה והדלקה היא המצוה ולא הנחת הנר בטפח הסמוך לפתח הלכך מותר להדליק נר של חנוכה מנר של חנוכה שנמצא מדליק מצוה ממצוה שהדלקת נר השני היא מצותו

הגהות הב"ח

(א) רש"י ד"ה ובה היה מסיים וכו' מניחה בכלי עד שנותן לתוך מערבית שמן ופתילה וכו': (ב) תוס' ד"ה ובה היה וכו' וקשה לריב"א שאם היה אפשר להדליק בישנה א"כ:

גליון הש"ס

גמרא ובה היה מסיים. עיין חגיגה ד' כו ע"ב תוס' ד"ה מנורה:

עֲשָׁשִׁית. כְּלִי גָּדוֹל שֶׁל זְכוּכִית, בְּלַעַ"ז לנטרנ"א: דּוֹלֶקֶת. שֶׁהִדְלִיקָהּ לְמִצְוַת חֲנוּכָּה בְּעֶ"שׁ: וּמַדְלִיקָהּ. לְמִצְוַת הַלַּיְלָה: הָיוּ בְּאוֹתוֹ הַנֵּס. שֶׁגָּזְרוּ יְוָונִים עַל כָּל בְּתוּלוֹת הַנְּשׂוּאוֹת לְהִיבָּעֵל לְטַפְסַר תְּחִלָּה, וְעַל יַד אִשָּׁה נַעֲשָׂה הַנֵּס: אַכְסְנַאי. אוֹרֵחַ: בָּתַר דְּנְסִיבִי. וּפְעָמִים שֶׁהָיִיתִי אַכְסְנַאי לִלְמוֹד תּוֹרָה: עֲלַי. בִּשְׁבִילִי: בְּגוֹ בֵּיתַאי. בְּבֵיתִי: מָשִׁיךְ נְהוֹרֵיהּ. אֵינוֹ מְמַהֵר לִכְלוֹת כְּשֶׁמֶן זַיִת: צְלִיל נְהוֹרֵיהּ. צָלוּל וּמֵאִיר: לְגַבֵּל. מָצָאתִי בִּתְשׁוּבַת הַגְּאוֹנִי': שֶׁמְּעַשְּׁנִין כְּלִי זְכוּכִית בְּעָשָׁן שֶׁמֶן זַיִת עַד שֶׁמַּשְׁחִיר, וְגוֹרֵר הַשַּׁחֲרוּרִי' וְנוֹתֵן בּוֹ שֶׁמֶן קִימְעָא, וּמְגַבֵּל בּוֹ וּמְיַיבְּשׁוֹ בַּחַמָּה, וּמְמַחֶה אוֹתוֹ לְתוֹךְ הַדְּיוֹ: לְעַשֵּׁן. נַמִי כְּדְפָרִישִׁית: שָׂרָף. גּוֹמָא: קֶטֶף. פרוייר"ל שֶׁל יַעַר, כְּמוֹ שֶׁאָנוּ עוֹשִׂים מִשֶּׁל שָׂרָף: הָרוֹאֶה. הָעוֹבֵר בַּשּׁוּק וְרוֹאֶה בְּאַחַד הַמִּגְדָּלוֹת דּוֹלֵק. וּמָצָאתִי בְּשֵׁם רַבֵּינוּ יִצְחָק בֶּן יְהוּדָה, שֶׁאָמַר מִשֵּׁם רַבֵּינוּ יַעֲקֹב, דְּלֹא הוּזְקְקָה בְּרָכָה זוֹ אֶלָּא לְמִי שֶׁלֹּא הִדְלִיק בְּבֵיתוֹ עֲדַיִין, אוֹ לְיוֹשֵׁב בִּסְפִינָה: הָרוֹאֶה מְבָרֵךְ שְׁתַּיִם. "שֶׁעָשָׂה נִסִּים" וְ"שֶׁהֶחֱיָינוּ". שֶׁאֵין עָלָיו לְבָרֵךְ "לְהַדְלִיק" – דְּהָא לָא אַדְלִיק אִיהוּ: מַאי מְמַעֵט. הַמַּדְלִיק בִּשְׁאָר יָמִים, אֵיזוֹ מִן הַשָּׁלֹשׁ מְמַעֵט: כָּל יוֹמֵי אִיתֵיהּ. שֶׁהֲרֵי כָּל שְׁמוֹנָה הִדְלִיקוּ מִן הַפַּךְ. אֲבָל זְמַן מִשֶּׁהִגִּיעָנוּ לְהַתְחָלַת זְמַן הִגִּיעָנוּ: הֵיכָן צִוָּנוּ. הָא לָאו דְּאוֹרַיְיתָא הִיא, אֶלָּא מִדִּבְרֵיהֶם: מִ"לֹּא תָסוּר. מִן הַדָּבָר אֲשֶׁר יַגִּידוּ לְךָ" וגו': מְעָרְבִין בּוֹ. עֵירוּבֵי חֲצֵרוֹת וּתְחוּמִין: מִשְׁתַּתְּפִין בּוֹ. בְּמָבוֹי, דְּאִי בָּעֵי מַפְקַר לְנִכְסֵיהּ וַהֲוָה עָנִי וַחֲזֵי לֵיהּ. כְּדִתְנַן: מַאֲכִילִין אֶת הָעֲנִיִּים דְּמַאי. הִלְכָּךְ חָשׁוּב דִּידֵיהּ: וּמְבָרְכִין עָלָיו. "הַמּוֹצִיא": וּמְזַמְּנִין עָלָיו. בִּרְכַּת הַזִּימּוּן: וּמַפְרִישׁ אוֹתוֹ. אָדָם שֶׁהוּא עָרוֹם. כְּלוֹמַר: דְּלָא צָרִיךְ לְבָרוֹכֵי עֲלֵיהּ בְּהַפְרָשָׁתוֹ: "וְהָיָה מַחֲנֶיךָ קָדוֹשׁ. וְלֹא יִרְאֶה בְךָ עֶרְוַת דָּבָר" – אֲפִילּוּ דִּבּוּר דְּהַזְכָּרַת הַשֵּׁם לֹא יִרְאֶה בְךָ עֶרְוַת דָּבָר: וַדַּאי דְּדִבְרֵיהֶם. כְּגוֹן נֵר חֲנוּכָּה: סָפֵק דְּדִבְרֵיהֶם. כְּגוֹן דְּמַאי, שֶׁהַפְרָשָׁתוֹ אֵינָהּ אֶלָּא מִסָּפֵק: וּבָעֵי בְּרָכָה. קִידּוּשׁ הַיּוֹם: רָבָא אָמַר. סָפֵק דְּדִבְרֵיהֶם בָּעֵי בְּרָכָה, וּדְמַאי – אֲפִילּוּ סָפֵק לָא הֲוֵי אֶלָּא חוּמְרָא בְּעָלְמָא, דְּרוֹב עַמֵּי הָאָרֶץ מְעַשְּׂרִין: חָצֵר שֶׁיֵּשׁ לָהּ ב' פְּתָחִים. שֶׁיֵּשׁ לַבַּיִת ב' פְּתָחִים פְּתוּחִים לֶחָצֵר – צְרִיכָ' שְׁתֵּי נֵרוֹת, נֵר לְכָל פֶּתַח. כִּדְמְפָ' טַעְמָא מִשּׁוּם חֲשָׁדָא: שֶׁהָרוֹאֶה יְהֵא סָבוּר שֶׁהַבַּיִת חָלוּק, וַהֲרֵי הוּא שֶׁל שְׁנֵי בְּנֵי אָדָם, וְיֹאמְרוּ: הָאֶחָד אֵינוֹ מְקַיֵּים מִצְוַת נֵר: מִב' רוּחוֹת. אֶחָד בַּצָּפוֹן וְאֶחָד בַּמִּזְרָח: חֲשָׁדָא דְעָלְמָא. בְּנֵי עִיר אַחֶרֶת הָעוֹבְרִין מִשָּׁם בַּשּׁוּק: אֲפִי' מֵרוּחַ אַחַת נַמִי. סְבוּרִין הֵן שֶׁהַבַּיִת חָלוּק מִתּוֹכוֹ: וְאִי חֲשָׁדָא דִבְנֵי מָתָא. שֶׁיּוֹדְעִים שֶׁאֵין חָלוּק: לְסוֹף שָׂדֵהוּ. בִּגְמַר קְצִירוֹ. כִּדְכְתִי': "לֹא תְכַלֶּה" מַשְׁמַע בִּשְׁעַת כִּילּוּי, וְלֹא שֶׁיַּקְצֶה אוֹתָהּ קוֹדֶם לָכֵן: מִפְּנֵי בִּטּוּל עֲנִיִּים. וְכוּלְּהוּ מְפָרֵשׁ לְהוּ: שָׁעָה פְּנוּיָה. שֶׁאֵין עֲנִיִּים אֶצְלוֹ, וְיֹאמַר לִקְרוֹבוֹ עָנִי: מַהֵר וְטוֹל כָּאן עַד שֶׁלֹּא יָבֹאוּ אֲחֵרִים. אֲבָל עַכְשָׁיו שֶׁמַּנִּיחָהּ בִּגְמַר קְצִיר הַשָּׂדֶ' – הָעֲנִיִּים רוֹאִין וּבָאִין:

תורה אור

עֲשָׁשִׁית שֶׁהָיְתָה דּוֹלֶקֶת וְהוֹלֶכֶת כָּל הַיּוֹם כּוּלּוֹ, לְמוֹצָ"שׁ מְכַבָּה וּמַדְלִיקָהּ. אִי אָמְרַתְּ בִּשְׁלָמָא הַדְלָקָה עוֹשָׂה מִצְוָה – שַׁפִּיר אֶלָּא אִי אָמְרַתְּ הַנָּחָה עוֹשָׂה מִצְוָה, הַאי "מְכַבָּה וּמַדְלִיקָהּ"? "מְכַבָּה וּמַגְבִּיהָהּ וּמַנִּיחָהּ וּמַדְלִיקָהּ" מִיבָּעֵי לֵיהּ! וְעוֹד, מִדְּקָא מְבָרְכִינַן "אֲשֶׁר קִדְּשָׁנוּ בְּמִצְוֹתָיו וְצִוָּנוּ לְהַדְלִיק נֵר שֶׁל חֲנוּכָּה" ש"מ: הַדְלָקָה עוֹשָׂה מִצְוָה, ש"מ. וְהָשְׁתָּא דְּאָמְרִינַן הַדְלָקָה עוֹשָׂה מִצְוָה, הִדְלִיקָהּ חֵרֵשׁ שׁוֹטֶה וְקָטָן – לֹא עָשָׂה וְלֹא כְּלוּם. אִשָּׁה וַדַּאי מַדְלִיקָה, דְּא"ר יְהוֹשֻׁעַ בֶּן לֵוִי: נָשִׁים חַיָּיבוֹת בְּנֵר חֲנוּכָּה, *שֶׁאַף הֵן הָיוּ בְּאוֹתוֹ הַנֵּס. אָמַר רַב שֵׁשֶׁת: אַכְסְנַאי חַיָּיב בְּנֵר חֲנוּכָּה. א"ר זֵירָא: מֵרֵישׁ כִּי הֲוֵינָא בֵּי רַב מִשְׁתַּתַּפְנָא בִּפְרִיטֵי בַּהֲדֵי אוּשְׁפִּיזָא. בָּתַר דִּנְסִיבִי אִיתְּתָא אָמִינָא: הָשְׁתָּא וַדַּאי לָא צְרִיכְנָא, דְּקָא מַדְלְקֵי עֲלַי בְּגוֹ בֵּיתַאי. א"ר יְהוֹשֻׁעַ בֶּן לֵוִי: כָּל הַשְּׁמָנִים כּוּלָּן יָפִין לַנֵּר, וְשֶׁמֶן זַיִת מִן הַמּוּבְחָר. אָמַר אַבַּיֵי: מֵרֵישׁ הֲוָה מְהַדַּר מָר אַמִּשְׁחָא דְּשׁוּמְשְׁמֵי, אָמַר: הַאי מָשֵׁךְ נְהוֹרֵי טְפֵי. כֵּיוָן דִּשְׁמַע לַהּ לְהָא דְּרַבִּי יְהוֹשֻׁעַ בֶּן לֵוִי מְהַדַּר אַמִּשְׁחָא דְּזֵיתָא, אָמַר: הַאי צְלִיל נְהוֹרֵיהּ טְפֵי. וְאריב"ל: כָּל הַשְּׁמָנִים יָפִין לַדְּיוֹ, וְשֶׁמֶן זַיִת מִן הַמּוּבְחָר. אִיבַּעְיָא לְהוּ: לְגַבֵּל אוֹ לְעַשֵּׁן? ת"ש, דְּתָנֵי רַב שְׁמוּאֵל בַּר זוּטְרָא: כָּל הַשְּׁמָנִים יָפִין לַדְּיוֹ וְשֶׁמֶן זַיִת מִן הַמּוּבְחָר. בֵּין לְגַבֵּל בֵּין לְעַשֵּׁן, רַב שְׁמוּאֵל בַּר זוּטְרָא מַתְנֵי הָכִי: כָּל הָעֲשָׁנִים יָפִין לַדְּיוֹ וְשֶׁמֶן זַיִת מִן הַמּוּבְחָר. אָמַר רַב הוּנָא: כָּל הַשְּׂרָפִין יָפִין לַדְּיוֹ, וּשְׂרָף קֶטֶף יָפֶה מִכּוּלָּם. *א"ר חִיָּיא בַּר אַשִׁי אָמַר רַב: הַמַּדְלִיק נֵר שֶׁל חֲנוּכָּה צָרִיךְ לְבָרֵךְ. וְרַב יִרְמְיָה אָמַר: הָרוֹאֶה נֵר שֶׁל חֲנוּכָּה צָרִיךְ לְבָרֵךְ. אָמַר רַב יְהוּדָה: *יוֹם רִאשׁוֹן – הָרוֹאֶה מְבָרֵךְ ב', וּמַדְלִיק מְבָרֵךְ ג'. מִכָּאן וְאֵילָךְ – מַדְלִיק מְבָרֵךְ שְׁתַּיִם, וְרוֹאֶה מְבָרֵךְ אַחַת. מַאי מְמַעֵט? מְמַעֵט זְמַן. וְנִימְעוֹט נֵס! נֵס כָּל יוֹמֵי אִיתֵיהּ. מַאי מְבָרֵךְ? מְבָרֵךְ "אֲשֶׁר קִדְּשָׁנוּ בְּמִצְוֹתָיו וְצִוָּנוּ לְהַדְלִיק נֵר שֶׁל חֲנוּכָּה".* וְהֵיכָן צִוָּנוּ? רַב אָוְיָא אָמַר: מִ"לֹּא תָסוּר". רַב *נְחֶמְיָה אָמַר: "שְׁאַל אָבִיךָ וְיַגֵּדְךָ זְקֵנֶיךָ וְיֹאמְרוּ לָךְ". מֵתִיב רַב עַמְרָם: *) הַדְּמַאי מְעָרְבִין בּוֹ וּמִשְׁתַּתְּפִין בּוֹ *וּמְבָרְכִין עָלָיו וּמְזַמְּנִין עָלָיו, וּמַפְרִישִׁין אוֹתוֹ עָרוֹם וּבֵין הַשְּׁמָשׁוֹת. וְאִי אָמְרַתְּ: כֹּל מִדְּרַבָּנַן בָּעֵי בְּרָכָה, הָכָא כִּי קָאֵי עָרוֹם, הֵיכִי מְבָרֵךְ? וְהָא בָּעֵינַן *"וְהָיָה מַחֲנֶיךָ קָדוֹשׁ" וְלֵיכָּא! אָמַר אַבַּיֵי: וַדַּאי דְּדִבְרֵיהֶם – בָּעֵי בְּרָכָה, סָפֵק דְּדִבְרֵיהֶם – לָא בָּעֵי בְּרָכָה. וְהָא יו"ט שֵׁנִי, דְּסָפֵק דִּבְרֵיהֶם הוּא, וּבָעֵי בְּרָכָה! הָתָם כִּי הֵיכִי דְּלָא לְזִילְזוּלֵי בָּהּ. *רָבָא אָמַר: רוֹב עַמֵּי הָאָרֶץ מְעַשְּׂרִין הֵן. אָמַר רַב הוּנָא: חָצֵר שֶׁיֵּשׁ לָהּ ב' פְּתָחִים – צְרִיכָה שְׁתֵּי נֵרוֹת. (*וְאָמַר) רָבָא: לָא אֲמַרַן אֶלָּא מִשְּׁתֵּי רוּחוֹת, אֲבָל מֵרוּחַ אַחַת – לָא צְרִיךְ. מ"ט? אִילֵימָא מִשּׁוּם חֲשָׁדָא, חֲשָׁדָא דְּמַאן? אִילֵימָא חֲשָׁדָא דְּעָלְמָא – אֲפִילּוּ בְּרוּחַ אַחַת נַמִי לִיבָּעֵי, אִי חֲשָׁדָא דִּבְנֵי מָתָא – אֲפִי' מִשְּׁנֵי רוּחוֹת נַמִי לָא לִיבָּעֵי! לְעוֹלָם מִשּׁוּם חֲשָׁדָא דִּבְנֵי מָתָא, וְזִימְנִין דְּמַחַלְפִי בְּהַאי וְלָא חָלְפִי בְּהַאי, וְאָמְרִי: כִּי הֵיכִי דִּבְהַאי פִּיתְחָא לָא אַדְלִיק, בְּהַךְ פִּיתְחָא נַמִי לָא אַדְלִיק. וּמְנָא תֵּימְרָא דְּחָיְישִׁינַן לַחֲשָׁד – *דְּתַנְיָא, אָמַר רַבִּי שִׁמְעוֹן: בִּשְׁבִיל אַרְבָּעָה דְּבָרִים אָמְרָה תּוֹרָה לְהַנִּיחַ פֵּאָה בְּסוֹף שָׂדֵהוּ: מִפְּנֵי גֶּזֶל עֲנִיִּים, וּמִפְּנֵי בִּיטּוּל עֲנִיִּים, וּמִפְּנֵי הַחֲשָׁד, וּמִשּׁוּם "בַּל תְּכַלֶּה". מִפְּנֵי גֶּזֶל עֲנִיִּים – שֶׁלֹּא יִרְאֶה בַּעַל הַבַּיִת שָׁעָה פְּנוּיָה, וְיֹאמַר לִקְרוֹבוֹ עָנִי: הֲרֵי זוֹ פֵּאָה. וּמִפְּנֵי

*) דמאי פ"א מ"ד

מכבה ומגביהה ומניחה וחוזר ומדליק מיבעי ליה. וא"ת: אמאי מכבה וחוזר ומדליק? בהגבהה סגי! כיון דהנחה עושה מצוה. דאטו מי גרע דלוקה ועומדת מהדליקה חש"ו? וי"ל: דמיירי שהדליקה מתחלתה לצורך שבת, ולכך גרע מהדליקה חש"ו. דהתם שמדליקה בעתה – ניכר הדבר שהוא מדליקה לשם חנוכה. ריב"א:

שמע מינה הדלקה עושה מצוה. וא"כ: מותר להדליק מנר לנר, ומכל מקום, כיון שנהגו העולם להחמיר – אין לשנות המנהג:

מריש הוה מהדר מר אמשחא דשומשמי. נראה דאנר חנוכה קאי, ומשום טעמא דמסיק – דנפיש נהוריה טפי. אבל לנר שבת – פשיטא דשמן זית מצוה מן המובחר, לפי שנמשך אחר הפתילה טפי מכולהו. כדמוכח במתניתין דכולהו מודו ביה דמדליקין:

כל השרפים יפים לדיו. פירש בקונטרס: שרף – גומא ואין נראה לר"ת, דהא דיו אין זה גומא. כדאמרינן בפ"ב דגיטין (דף יט. ושם): "בכל כותבין בדיו בסם ובסקרא ובקומוס" ומפרש בגמרא: קומוס – גומא. ודיו נמי אין זה מי עפצים שרגילין להניח בהן גומא, דהא בברייתא קתני התם: כתבו במי טריא ועפצא, דהיינו עפצים – כשר. משמע: דלאו היינו דיו דקתני במתניתין. ועוד ד"כשר" – משמע דיעבד, ובדיו היא עיקר הכתיבה. ועוד, דבפרק "כל היד" (נדה דף כ. ושם) אמרינן: פלי קורטא דדיותא ובדיק. דהיינו דיו שלנו שהוא קשה, ולא של עפצים. ואין דרך להניח גומא לתוך דיו שלנו. אלא שרף [דהכא] היינו לחלוחית של אילן, כמו שאנו עושין דיו שלנו, וכן יש בנדה בפ"ק (דף י:) גבי בתולה, זו שירפה מלוי, וזו אין שירפה מלוי. וכן בפ' "כל שעה" (פסחים לט. ושם): ירק מר יש לו שרף, ופניו מכסיפין. דע"כ – ההוא שרף היינו לחלוחית. ועל כן היה פוסל ר"ת ס"ת שאין כותבין בדיו שלנו, דשאר לא מיקרי דיו כדפי' ואמרי' בפ' "הבונה" (לקמן קג:): כתבו שלא בדיו – הרי אלו יגנזו. ומוקמי' לה ב"הקומץ רבה" (מנחות דף לד*) בס"ת:

הדר

לג א ב מיי' פ"ד מהל' חנוכה הל' ט סמג עשין ה טוש"ע א"ח סי' תרעה סעיף א:
לד ג ד מיי' שם טוש"ע שם סעיף ג:
לה ה ו ז מיי' פ"ד שם הל' יא סמג שם טוש"ע א"ח סימן רסג סעיף ז וסימן תרעז סעיף א:
לו ח מיי' פ"ה מהל' שבת הל' יא סמג לאוין סה טוש"ע א"ח סי' רסד סעיף ו וסימן תרעג סעיף א:
לז ט מיי' פ"א מהל' תפילין הל' ד סמג עשין כה טוש"ע א"ח סי' לב סעיף ג:
לח י מיי' פ"ג מהל' חנוכה הל' ד סמג עשין ה טוש"ע א"ח סי' תרעו סעי' א ב ג:
לט כ מיי' פי"א מהל' ברכות הל' ג סמג עשין כז:
מ ל מיי' פ"ג מהלכות חנוכה הל' ה וע"ש במ"מ:
מא מ נ מיי' פ"ד מהל' חנוכה הל' י סמג עשין ה טוש"ע א"ח סי' תרעא סעיף א:
מב ס מיי' פ"ב מהל' מתנות עניים הלכה יב:

[נ"ל בא"י אמ"ה שעשה נסים וכו' ושהחיינו וכו' וכ"א בהרי"ף והרא"ש]

[לפי פרש"י ד"ה והיה מחניך כו' סמיך הש"ס אסיפא דקרא כמ"ש תוס' כתובות כט. סד"ה אלו וכן כתבו בשאר דוכתא ועי' ב"מ קיד: מנין לערום שלא יתרום דכתי' ולא יראה בך ערות דבר ע"ש פרש"י]

[פסחים קח. מגילה ד. ערכין ג.]

גליון הש"ס
גמ' איבעיא להו לגבל. עי' לעיל דף יח ע"א תוס' ד"ה אבל דיו.

סוכה מו.

[מס' סופרים פ"כ הלכה ו]

[בשאלתות סי' כו איתא רב נחמן בר יצחק]
*ומברכין היינו ברהמ"ז בג' ומזמנין בי' דאילו ברכת המוציא פשיטא דמברכין דאסו' ליהנות מהעוה"ז בלא ברכה [ת"י]

לעיל יג. כתובות כד. כו: גיטין סא. [ביצה לה: מנחות לא.]

תוספת' דפאה פ"א ת"כ פ' קדושים

דברים יז | שם לב | שם כג | נ"ל אמר | ויקרא יט

רבינו חננאל

ובעי' (להדליק) [שדליק] מי שהי' חייב ובר מצות והנשים מדליקות עששיות שהיתה דולקת כל היום כולו לערב מכבה ומדליקה ואכסנאי חייב בנר חנוכה ואי משתתף בהדי אושפיזי או אם היה נסיב תו לא צריך. כל השמנים יפין לנר ושמן זית יפה מכולם המדליק ביום ראשון מברך להדליק ושעשה נסים וזמן. מיכן והילך מברך שתים ומניח זמן. היכן צונו דמברכין אשר קדשנו במצותיו וצונו להדליק רב נחמן בר יצחק אמר שאל אביך ויגדך כו' [רב] אויא אמר לא תסור מן הדבר אשר יגידו לך הנה צונו אלהינו לשמוע דברי חכמים ואקשינן וכי מצוה מדרבנן בעי ברכה והתנן הדמאי מערבין בו ומשתתפין בו ומברכין ומזמנין עליו ומפרישין אותו ערום בין השמשות ואי אמרת דכל מצוה מדרבנן בעי ברכה היכי מברך ערום הא בעינן והיה מחניך קדוש ולא יראה בך ערות דבר וליכא ושני אביי ודאי דדבריהם כגון חנוכה וכיוצא בו בעי ברכה אבל דמאי דאפי' לרבנן ספק הוא לא בעי ברכה איני והא יו"ט שני דספק מדרבנן הוא ומברכינן ומשנינן התם משום דלא ליזלזלו בה רבא אמר רוב עמי הארץ מעשרין הן לפיכך לא בעי ברכה בדמאי השתא מן רבנן דדייק ואמרי לענין נולד כשהוא מהול אע"ג דקיי"ל (כרבא) [כרבה] דאמר שמא ערלה כבושה הוא לפיכך צריך להטיף ממנו דם ברית בחול כיון שהוא ספק מדבריהם כד מהיל ליה בחול לא צריך ברכה כמו הדמאי. אמר רב הונא חצר שיש לה ב' פתחים בב' רוחות צריך ב' נרות דחיישינן לחשדא ומנלן דחיישינן דתני

וּמִפְּנֵי בִּיטּוּל עֲנִיִּים – שֶׁלֹּא יְהוּ עֲנִיִּים יוֹשְׁבִין וּמְשַׁמְּרִין: "עַכְשָׁיו מַנִּיחַ בעה"ב פֵּאָה". וּמִפְּנֵי חֲשָׁד – שֶׁלֹּא יְהוּ עוֹבְרִין וְשָׁבִין אוֹמְרִים: תָּבֹא מְאֵרָה לְאָדָם שֶׁלֹּא הִנִּיחַ פֵּאָה בְּשָׂדֵהוּ. וּמִשּׁוּם °"בַּל תְּכַלֶּה". אַטּוּ כּוּלְּהוּ לָאו מִשּׁוּם "בַּל תְּכַלֶּה" נִינְהוּ? אָמַר רָבָא: מִפְּנֵי הָרַמָּאִין.§ אָמַר רַב יִצְחָק בַּר רְדִיפָה א"ר הוּנָא: [א]נֵר שֶׁיֵּשׁ לָהּ שְׁנֵי פִּיּוֹת – עוֹלָה לְב' בְּנֵי אָדָם. אָמַר רָבָא: [ב]מִילֵּא קְעָרָה שֶׁמֶן וְהִקִּיפָהּ פְּתִילוֹת, כָּפָה עָלֶיהָ כְּלִי – עוֹלָה לְכַמָּה בְּנֵי אָדָם, לֹא כָּפָה עָלֶיהָ כְּלִי – עֲשָׂאָהּ כְּמִין מְדוּרָה, וַאֲפִילּוּ לְאֶחָד נַמִּי אֵינָהּ עוֹלָה.§ אֲמַר רָבָא, פְּשִׁיטָא לִי: [ג]נֵר בֵּיתוֹ וְנֵר חֲנוּכָּה – נֵר בֵּיתוֹ עָדִיף, מִשּׁוּם שְׁלוֹם בֵּיתוֹ. נֵר בֵּיתוֹ וְקִידּוּשׁ הַיּוֹם – נֵר בֵּיתוֹ עָדִיף, מִשּׁוּם שְׁלוֹם בֵּיתוֹ. בָּעֵי רָבָא: נֵר חֲנוּכָּה וְקִידּוּשׁ הַיּוֹם מַהוּ? קִידּוּשׁ הַיּוֹם עָדִיף – דִּתְדִיר, אוֹ דִילְמָא: נֵר חֲנוּכָּה עָדִיף, מִשּׁוּם *פִּרְסוּמֵי נִיסָּא? בָּתַר דְּאִבַּעְיָא הֲדַר פְּשָׁטָהּ: [ד]נֵר חֲנוּכָּה עָדִיף, מִשּׁוּם פִּרְסוּמֵי נִיסָּא.§ אָמַר רַב הוּנָא: [ה]הָרָגִיל בְּנֵר – הָוְיָין לֵיהּ בָּנִים תַּלְמִידֵי חֲכָמִים, הַזָּהִיר בִּמְזוּזָה – זוֹכֶה לְדִירָה נָאָה, הַזָּהִיר בְּצִיצִית – זוֹכֶה לְטַלִּית נָאָה, הַזָּהִיר בְּקִידּוּשׁ הַיּוֹם – זוֹכֶה וּמְמַלֵּא גַּרְבֵּי יַיִן. רַב הוּנָא הֲוָה רְגִיל דַּהֲוָה חָלֵיף וְתָנֵי אַפִּתְחָא דְּרַבִּי אָבִין נַגָּרָא, חֲזָא דַּהֲוָה רְגִיל בְּשְׁרָגֵי טוּבָא, אֲמַר: תְּרֵי גַּבְרֵי רַבְרְבֵי נָפְקִי מֵהָכָא. נָפְקִי מִינַּיְיהוּ רַב אִידִי בַּר אָבִין וְרַב חִיָּיא בַּר אָבִין. רַב חִסְדָּא הֲוָה רְגִיל דַּהֲוָה חָלֵיף וְתָנֵי אַפִּיתְחָא דְּבֵי נָשָׁא דְּרַב שֵׁיזְבִי, חֲזָא דַּהֲוָה רְגִיל בִּשְׁרָגֵי טוּבָא, אֲמַר: גַּבְרָא רַבָּא נָפֵק מֵהָכָא. נְפַק מִינַּיְיהוּ רַב שֵׁיזְבִי. דְּבֵיתְהוּ דְּרַב יוֹסֵף הֲוַת מְאַחֲרָה וּמַדְלְקָת לָהּ, אֲמַר לָהּ רַב יוֹסֵף, תַּנְיָא: *°"לֹא יָמִישׁ עַמּוּד הֶעָנָן יוֹמָם וְעַמּוּד הָאֵשׁ לָיְלָה" מְלַמֵּד שֶׁעַמּוּד עָנָן מַשְׁלִים לְעַמּוּד הָאֵשׁ, וְעַמּוּד הָאֵשׁ מַשְׁלִים לְעַמּוּד הֶעָנָן. סְבַרָה לְאַקְדּוֹמֵהּ, אֲמַר לָהּ הַהוּא סָבָא: תָּנֵינָא, [ו]וּבִלְבַד שֶׁלֹּא יַקְדִּים וְשֶׁלֹּא יְאַחֵר.§ אָמַר רָבָא: דְּרָחֵים רַבָּנַן – הָווּ לֵיהּ בְּנִין רַבָּנַן[א], דְּמוֹקִיר רַבָּנַן – הָווּ לֵיהּ חַתְנְוָותָא רַבָּנַן[ב], דְּדָחֵיל מֵרַבָּנַן – הוּא גּוּפֵיהּ הָוֵי צוּרְבָא מֵרַבָּנַן, וְאִי לָאו בַּר הָכִי הוּא – מִשְׁתַּמְעָן מִילֵּיהּ כְּצוּרְבָא מֵרַבָּנַן.§ "וְלֹא בְּשֶׁמֶן שְׂרֵיפָה" וכו'.§ מַאי שֶׁמֶן שְׂרֵיפָה? אָמַר רַבָּה: [ז]שֶׁמֶן שֶׁל תְּרוּמָה שֶׁנִּטְמְאָה. וְאַמַּאי קָרוּ לָהּ שֶׁמֶן שְׂרֵיפָה – הוֹאִיל וְלִשְׂרֵיפָה עוֹמֵד. וּבְשַׁבָּת מ"ט לָא – מִתּוֹךְ שֶׁמִּצְוָה עָלָיו לְבַעֲרוֹ, גְּזֵרָה שֶׁמָּא יַטֶּה. א"ל אַבַּיֵי: אֶלָּא מֵעַתָּה, בְּיוֹ"ט לִישְׁתְּרֵי! אַלְמָּה תְּנַן: *אֵין מַדְלִיקִין בְּשֶׁמֶן שְׂרֵיפָה בְּיוֹ"ט! גְּזֵרָה יוֹ"ט אַטּוּ שַׁבָּת. רַב חִסְדָּא אֲמַר: לְ"שֶׁמָּא יַטֶּה" – לָא חָיְישִׁינַן. אֶלָּא, הָכָא בְּיוֹ"ט שֶׁחָל לִהְיוֹת ע"ש עָסְקִינַן, לְפִי *שֶׁאֵין שׂוֹרְפִין קָדָשִׁים בְּיוֹ"ט, וְהָא מִדְּקָתָנֵי סֵיפָא: "אֵין מַדְלִיקִין בְּשֶׁמֶן שְׂרֵיפָה בְּיוֹ"ט" מִכְּלַל דְּרֵישָׁא לָאו בְּיוֹ"ט עָסְקִי'! א"ר חֲנִינָא מִסּוּרָא: "מַה טַּעַם" קָאָמַר: מַה טַּעַם אֵין מַדְלִיקִין בְּשֶׁמֶן שְׂרֵיפָה בְּיוֹ"ט – לְפִי שֶׁאֵין שׂוֹרְפִין קָדָשִׁים בְּיוֹ"ט. תַּנְיָא

ויקרא יט | שמות יג

רש"י

וּמִפְּנֵי בִּטּוּל עֲנִיִּים. שֶׁלֹּא הָיוּ יוֹדְעִים מָתַי יִקְצוֹר אוֹתָם: מִפְּנֵי הַחֲשָׁד. שֶׁהָעוֹבְרִין רוֹאִין בִּגְמַר קְצִירוֹ שֶׁהוּא מְכַלֶּה אֶת הַכֹּל, לֹא יֵדְעוּ שֶׁנִּתְּנָה כְּבָר: וּמִשּׁוּם לֹא תְכַלֶּה. דְּמַשְׁמַע שְׁעַת כִּלּוּי: אַטּוּ כּוּלְּהוּ. הָנֵי דַּאֲמַרַן, לֹא טַעְמָא דְ"לֹא תְכַלֶּה" קָא מְפָרְשִׁי, מַאי שְׁנָא שְׁעַת כִּלּוּי: אָמַר רָבָא מִפְּנֵי הָרַמָּאִין. הָעוֹבְרִין עַל "לֹא תְכַלֶּה" וְאוֹמְרִים: כְּבָר הִנַּחְתִּיהָ: שְׁתֵּי פִּיּוֹת. שֶׁהַנֵּרוֹת שֶׁלָּהֶם שֶׁל חֶרֶס הֵן, וּמְכוּסִּין, וְעוֹשִׂים לוֹ נֶקֶב בְּצִדֵּי כִּסּוּיוֹ לְהַכְנִיס לוֹ הַפְּתִילָה – וְהוּא הַפֶּה. וּלְמַעְלָה בְּכִסּוּיוֹ יֵשׁ נֶקֶב קָטָן, וְגַם חָלָל יֵשׁ לְמַעְלָה מִן הַכִּסּוּי וּמְמַלְּאוֹ שֶׁמֶן, וְהוּא נִכְנָס דֶּרֶךְ הַנֶּקֶב מְעַט מְעַט. אִם יֵשׁ בּוֹ שְׁנֵי נְקָבִים מִשְּׁנֵי צְדָדִין – עוֹלֶה לִשְׁנֵי בְּנֵי אָדָם, לַמְהַדְּרִין הָעוֹשִׂין נֵר לְכָל אֶחָד וְאֶחָד: עֲשָׂאָהּ כִּמְדוּרָה. שֶׁהָאֵשׁ מִתְחַבֶּרֶת לְאֶמְצָעִיתָהּ, וְאֵינוֹ דּוֹמֶה לְנֵר: נֵר בֵּיתוֹ וְנֵר חֲנוּכָּה. נֵר בֵּיתוֹ בְּשַׁבָּת, וְהוּא עָנִי וְאֵין לוֹ כְּדֵי לִקְנוֹת שֶׁמֶן לִשְׁתֵּי נֵרוֹת: שְׁלוֹם בֵּיתוֹ. וְהָכִי אָמְרִינַן לְקַמָּן (דף כה:): "וַתִּזְנַח מִשָּׁלוֹם נַפְשִׁי" – זוֹ הַדְלָקַת נֵר בְּשַׁבָּת, שֶׁבְּנֵי בֵיתוֹ מִצְטַעֲרִין לֵישֵׁב בַּחֹשֶׁךְ: בָּנִים תַּלְמִידֵי חֲכָמִים. דִּכְתִיב (משלי ו): "כִּי נֵר מִצְוָה וְתוֹרָה אוֹר", עַל יְדֵי נֵר מִצְוָה דְּשַׁבָּת וַחֲנוּכָּה – בָּא אוֹר דְּתוֹרָה: דְּרַבִּי אָבִין נַגָּרָא. חָרָשׁ עֵצִים: בִּשְׁרָגָא. דְּשַׁבָּת: חָלֵיף וְתָנֵי. עוֹבֵר וְשׁוֹנֶה כְּלוֹמַר: עוֹבֵר תָּמִיד: דְּבֵי נָשָׁא(א). אָבִיו, וְאִיכָּא דְּאָמְרִי חָמִיו: נְפַק מִינַּיְיהוּ. דַּחֲתָנוֹ כִּבְנוֹ: מְאַחֲרָה וּמַדְלֶקֶת. נֵר שֶׁל שַׁבָּת סָמוּךְ לַחֲשֵׁכָה: לֹא יָמִישׁ. קְרָא יְתֵירָא הוּא לְהָךְ דְּרָשָׁה. דְּהָא כְּתִיב: "וַה' הוֹלֵךְ לִפְנֵיהֶם יוֹמָם": עַמּוּד הֶעָנָן. שֶׁל יוֹם מַשְׁלִים אוֹרוֹ לְעַמּוּד הָאֵשׁ, שֶׁהָיָה עַמּוּד הָאֵשׁ בָּא קוֹדֶם שֶׁיִּשְׁקַע עַמּוּד הֶעָנָן. אַלְמָא: אוֹרַח אַרְעָא בְּהָכִי: לְאַקְדּוּמֵי. בְּעוֹד הַיּוֹם גָּדוֹל: תָּנֵינָא. שׁוֹנֶה אֲנִי: שֶׁלֹּא יַקְדִּים. דְּלָא מִינְכְּרָא שֶׁהִיא שֶׁל שַׁבָּת: דְּרָחֵים. אוֹהֵב: הָווּ לֵיהּ בְּנִין רַבָּנַן.(ב) וְאַהֲבָתוֹ עֲלֵיהֶם כְּתַב עַל בֵּן: וְאִי לָאו בַּר הָכִי(ג). שֶׁאֵינוֹ רָגִיל לַעֲסוֹק בַּתּוֹרָה: וְלִשְׂרֵיפָה עוֹמֵד. שֶׁאָסוּר בַּאֲכִילָה: שֶׁמִּצְוָה עָלָיו לְבַעֲרוֹ. דִּילְמָא אָתֵי בֵּיהּ לִידֵי תַּקָּלָה דַּאֲכִילָה: שֶׁמָּא יַטֶּה. כְּדֵי שֶׁיִּתְבַּעֵר מַהֵר: בְּיוֹם טוֹב. דְּלֵיכָּא לְמֵיחַשׁ לְהַטָּיָיה לִישְׁתְּרֵי: בְּעֶרֶב שַׁבָּת. וְהוּא צָרִיךְ לְהַדְלִיקָהּ מִבְּעוֹד יוֹם, וְנִמְצָא שׂוֹרֵף קֳדָשִׁים בְּיוֹ"ט. וּלְקַמָּן בְּפִרְקִין (דף כד:) יָלְפִינַן מִקְּרָאֵי דְּאֵין שׂוֹרְפִין: בְּבִרְכַּת

תוספות

הדר פשטה נר חנוכה עדיף משום פרסומי ניסא. ונראה לרשב"א: כשחל ר"ח טבת להיות בשבת – שיש להפטיר בנרות דזכריה משום פרסומי ניסא ולא ב"השמים כסאי" שהיא הפטרת ר"ח. ועוד: כיון שהמפטיר קורא בשל חנוכה – יש לו להפטיר מענין שקרא. ומה שמקדימים לקרות בשל ר"ח – משום דבקריאת התורה, כיון דמצי למיעבד תרוייהו, תדיר ופרסומי ניסא – עבדינן תרוייהו, ותדיר קודם. אבל היכא דלא אפשר למעבד תרוייהו – פרסומי ניסא עדיף. ועוד: דבקריאת התורה אין כל כך פרסומי ניסא, שאינו מזכיר בה נרות כמו בהפטרה. ועוד נראה לרשב"א: דעל כן הקדימו של ר"ח – כדי שהמפטיר יקרא בשל חנוכה, ויפטיר בנרות דזכריה:

ה"ג חזא דהוו רגילי בשרגא. פי': הבעל והאשה, לכך אמר: תרי גברי רברבי נפקי מהכא. ולקמן אמר, חזא דהוה רגילה האשה לבדה, לכך קאמר דנפיק חד גברא רבא בזכותה:

דבי נשא דרב שיזבי. אומר ר"ת: דכבר נפטר אביו, לכך קאמר בהאי לישנא. דאי מחיים הוה ליה למימר "דבי אבוה". ואומר ר"ת בשם רבינו שמואל: שכשכותבין כתובה, אם אבי הכלה מחיים – כותבין "דהנעלת ליה מבי אבוה", ואם כבר מת – כותבין "דהנעלת ליה מבי נשא". ולרשב"א נרא' דאפי' מחיים אשכחן דקאמר "בי נשא" בפרק "מי שהחשיך" (לקמן דף קנו.): לוי בריה דרב הונא בר חייא אשכחיה לגבלא דבי נשא דקגביל וספי לתוריה בטש ביה, אתא אבוה אשכחיה כו' ויכול לכתוב בכתובה כאשר ירצה*:

גזרה יו"ט אטו שבת. וא"ת: בכל שמנים שאין מדליקין בהן בשבת נגזור יו"ט אטו שבת. ובמתני' תנן: אין מדליקין בשמן שריפה ביו"ט. משמע דבשאר שמנים מדליקין! וי"ל דבשאר שמנים דכיון דאין נמשכין אחר הפתילה, כי שרי ביו"ט – לא אתי למישרי בשבת, דפשיטא הוא דאיכא למיגזר בהן שמא יטה. אבל שמן שריפה, אי שרי ביו"ט – איכא למטעי, ואתי למשרי בשבת כיון דנמשך אחר הפתילה. לפי שאינו פשוט לעולם דטעמא דמתוך שמצוה עליו לשורפו גזרה שמא יטה. הקשה ה"ר אליעזר: דהכא מפרש רבה דטעמא "גזרה יו"ט אטו שבת", ולקמן (דף כד:) מפיק מקרא ד"הוא לבדו". והשיב לו רבינו שמואל: דע"כ לקמן הוי רבא, שהוא אחר אביי, והכא רבה. שהרי משיב לו אביי תלמידו, וגם פליג עליה רב חסדא חבירו. אך קשה: מאי פריך הכא אביי "אלא מעתה ביו"ט לישתרי", והוא גופיה מפיק לקמן דאין מדליקין בשמן שריפה מ"עולת שבת בשבתו"! ונראה לפרש: דאביי ורבא לקמן לא קיימי אמאי דקאמר "מ"ט אין מדליקין לפי שאין שורפין קדשים ביו"ט", ולית להו האי גזרה [תרומה אטו קדשים]. אלא קיימי לפרושי מנ"ל שאין שורפין קדשים ביום טוב. ורשב"א מפרש הכי: אלא מעתה ביום טוב לישתרי, אי אמרת בשלמא דמיירי ביום טוב שחל בערב שבת – וטעמא לפי שאין שורפין קדשים ביום טוב, כדמוקי לה רב חסדא – שפיר. אלא כיון שאמרת טעמא דאין מדליקין בשבת – גזירה שמא יטה, השתא לא מצי לפרושי דביום טוב אין מדליקין לפי שאין שורפין קדשים ביו"ט, דהא מה שייך יו"ט למיתני הכא? כיון דביו"ט טעמא אחרינא הוא! אלא צריך לפרש – דביו"ט נמי שמא יטה, ומאי יטה שייך ביו"ט? ולפ"ז מתיישב לישנא "אלא מעתה", דמשמע שיש לפרש בענין אחר שלא יקשה ביו"ט לישתרי, ולא קשה דאביי אדאביי. ואם תאמר: דהכא גזר רבה יו"ט אטו שבת, ושבת גופיה – שמא יטה, א"כ סבר דגזרינן גזרה לגזרה. ובריש פירקין קאמר: היא גופה גזרה ואנן ניקום ונגזור גזרה לגזרה! ולא

רבינו חננאל

דתניא' ר' שמעון בשביל ד' דברים אמרה תורה הנח פאה בסוף שדה מפני החשד כו' אמר רב הונא [נר] שיש לו ב' פיות עולה לב' בני אדם אמר רב מילא קערה שמן והקיפה פתילות עולה מנין פתילות לבני אדם. אלו הן מן המהדרין שצריכין לנר לכל אחד ואחד ואם לא כפה עליה כלי נעשת כמדורה ואפילו לאחד אינו עולה. אמר רבה נר ביתו עדיף מנר חנוכה ומקדוש היום משום שלום ביתו שנאמר (איוב ה) וידעת כי שלום אהלך ונר חנוכה עדיף מקדוש היום כדי לפרסומי ניסא. אמר רב הונא הרגיל בנר חנוכה הויין לו בנים ת"ח הזהיר במזוזה כו'. דביתהו דרב יוסף הוית מאחרה ומדלקה סמוך לחשיכה בע"ש. אמר רב יוסף תנינא לא ימיש עמוד הענן יומם וגו' מלמד שעמוד הענן משלים לעמוד האש כלומר בא עמוד האש ועדיין עמוד הענן קיים. סברה לאקדומי טובא תנא ליה ההוא סבא ובלבד שלא יקדים ובלבד שלא יאחר אלא בעת שקיעת החמה קודם בכמעט תהיה הדלקה: **ולא** בשמן שרפה. אוקמה רב חסדא ביו"ם שחל להיות ע"ש עסקי' דבעי' אדלוקי נר של שבת מבעוד יום ונמצא מדליקין ביו"ט ואין מדליקין בשמן שרפה ביו"ט דקיי"ל שאין שורפין קדשים ביו"ט ותניא

עין משפט נר מצוה

מג א מיי' פ"ד מהל' חנוכה הל' ד סמג עשין ה טוש"ע א"ח סי' תרעג סעיף ג:

מד ב מיי' שם טוש"ע שם סעיף ד:

מה ג ד מיי' פ"ד מהל' חנוכה הל' יב טוש"ע א"ח סי' רסג סעי' ג וסי' רצו סעיף ה וסי' תרעח:

מו ה מיי' פ"ה מהל' שבת הל' א' סמג לאוין סה טוש"ע א"ח סי' רסג סעיף א ב:

מז ו מיי' פ"ד מהל' חנוכה הל' ה] טוש"ע א"ח שם סעיף ד:

מח ז מיי' פי"א מהל' תרומות הלכה ה:

מסורת הש"ס

[ברכות יז.]

[ועי' תוס' ב"ב יב: ד"ה ואמגרא]

[תוספתא' סוטה פ"ד]

[לקמן כד:]

[לקמן כד: מנחות מו:]

הגהות הב"ח

(א) רש"י ד"ה דבי נשא. נ"ב ע"ל בדף קנו ע"ב מבואר דבי נשא פי' אביו: (ב) ד"ה הוו ליה בנין רבנן הואיל ואהבתו: (ג) ד"ה ואי לאו בר הכי הוא שאינו:

הגהות הגר"א

[א] גמ' למוקיר רבנן. נ"ל לדחיל מרבנן: [ב] שם לדחיל מרבנן. נ"ל למוקיר רבנן:

גליון הש"ס

גמ' אמר רבא לרחים רבנן. עי' מסכת יו"ד ע"א:

רש"י

בְּבִרְכַּת הַמָּזוֹן. בִּתְפִלָּה פְּשִׁיטָא לָן, שֶׁהֲרֵי לְהַלֵּל וּלְהוֹדָאָה נִקְבְּעוּ, כִּדְאָמְרִינַן לְעֵיל*: [דף כא:] לָא מַזְכְּרִינַן. לֹא חִיְּיבוּ לְהַזְכִּיר: אֵינוֹ מַזְכִּיר. אֵינוֹ צָרִיךְ לְהַזְכִּיר: מַה תְּפִלָּה בְּבִרְכַּת הוֹדָאָה. דְּהָא כּוּלַּהּ מִילְּתָא דַּחֲנוּכָּה עִיקָּרָהּ לְהוֹדָאָה נִתְקְנָה: בְּהוֹדָאָה. בְּבִרְכַּת הָאָרֶץ: וְאוֹמֵר מֵעֵין הַמְּאוֹרָע בַּעֲבוֹדָה. לְבַקֵּשׁ רַחֲמִים עַל יִשְׂרָאֵל וְעַל יְרוּשָׁלַיִם לְהָשִׁיב עֲבוֹדָה לִמְקוֹמָהּ, לַעֲשׂוֹת קָרְבְּנוֹת הַיּוֹם: [תוספתא פ"ב] שֵׁנִי וַחֲמִישִׁי. מַשְׁמַע: שֶׁל כָּל שַׁבְּתוֹת הַשָּׁנָה, וּמַאי עֲבִידְתַּיְיהוּ לְזוֹכְרָם וּלְחַלְּקָם מִשְּׁאָר יְמוֹת הַשָּׁנָה? שֶׁל תַּעֲנִיּוֹת. שֶׁהָיוּ גּוֹזְרִים תַּעֲנִיּוֹת עַל הַגְּשָׁמִים שֵׁנִי וַחֲמִישִׁי [וְשֵׁנִי], בְּמַסֶּ' תַּעֲנִית (דף י.): וְשֶׁל מַעֲמָדוֹת. כְּלוֹמַר: לְיָמִים שֶׁל מַעֲמָדוֹת, שֶׁהָיוּ מִתְעַנִּין אַרְבָּעָה תַּעֲנִיּוֹת בְּשַׁבָּת: שֵׁנִי וּשְׁלִישִׁי וּרְבִיעִי וַחֲמִישִׁי, וּמֵעֵין הַמְּאוֹרָע דִּידְהוּ תְּפִלַּת תַּעֲנִית: עַרְבִית. לֵילֵי כְּנִיסָתָן. וְאַע"פ שֶׁאוֹכֵל וְשׁוֹתֶה כָּל הַלַּיְלָה, מִתְפַּלֵּל תְּפִלַּת תַּעֲנִית, מֵאַחַר שֶׁנִּכְנַס הַיּוֹם וְהָכִי נַמִי אָמַר רַב הוּנָא בְּמַסֶּכֶת תַּעֲנִית (דף יא:): יָחִיד שֶׁקִּבֵּל עָלָיו תַּעֲנִית, אַף עַל פִּי שֶׁאוֹכֵל וְשׁוֹתֶה כָּל הַלַּיְלָה – מִתְפַּלֵּל תְּפִלַּת תַּעֲנִית. וּבִתְשׁוּ' הַגְּאוֹנִים מָצָאתִי בְּרַיְיתָא, שָׁנוּ רַבּוֹתֵינוּ: פְּעָמִים שֶׁאָדָם שָׁרוּי בְּתַעֲנִית וְאֵינוֹ מִתְפַּלֵּל, וּפְעָמִים שֶׁאֵינוֹ שָׁרוּי בְּתַעֲנִית וּמִתְפַּלֵּל. הָא כֵּיצַד? כָּאן בִּכְנִיסָתָהּ, כָּאן בִּיצִיאָתָהּ. כְּלוֹמַר: עֶרֶב תַּעֲנִית, אַע"פ שֶׁעָתִיד לֶאֱכוֹל לְאַחַר תְּפִלָּה – מִתְפַּלֵּל תְּפִלַּת תַּעֲנִית. וְלֵיל מָחֳרָתוֹ, אַף עַל פִּי שֶׁעוֹדֵנּוּ בְּתַעֲנִית כְּשֶׁמִּתְפַּלֵּל תְּפִלַּת עַרְבִית – אֵינוֹ מִתְפַּלֵּל תְּפִלַּת תַּעֲנִית. [תוספתא ברכות פ"ג ע"ש וקנ"ע] וְסוֹף דִּבְרֵי הַגְּאוֹנִים כָּתְבוּ: אֲבָל אֵין אָנוּ רְגִילִים לוֹמַר עַרְבִית וַאֲפִילּוּ שַׁחֲרִית, שֶׁמָּא יֶאֱרַע לוֹ אוֹנֶס חוֹלִי אוֹ בּוּלְמוּס וְיִטְעוֹם כְּלוּם, וְנִמְצָא שַׁקְרָן בִּתְפִלָּתוֹ: אֵין מַחֲזִירִין אוֹתוֹ. דְּלָאו דְּאוֹרַיְיתָא נִינְהוּ: בְּבִרְכַּת הַמָּזוֹן. שֶׁל עַרְבִית בִּכְנִיסָתוֹ, וְכ"ש בִּיצִיאָתוֹ, שֶׁכְּבָר עָבַר הַיּוֹם: [ס"א ל"ג] שֶׁל חֲנוּכָּה בְּמוּסָפִין. בִּתְפִלַּת מוּסָפִין דְּשַׁבָּת וְר"ח שֶׁבְּתוֹךְ יְמֵי חֲנוּכָּה, מַהוּ לְהַזְכִּיר "עַל הַנִּסִּים" בְּהוֹדָאָה: בְּד' תְּפִלּוֹת. עַרְבִית וְשַׁחֲרִית וּמוּסָף וּמִנְחָה. וְכֵיוָן שֶׁחוֹבַת תְּפִלָּה זֶה הַיּוֹם, אֵינָהּ פְּחוּתָה מִשְּׁאָר תְּפִלּוֹת שֶׁל יוֹם: אֵין נָבִיא בְּר"ח. הָכָא נַמִי, הוֹאִיל אִלְמָלֵא ר"ח אֵין מוּסָפִין בַּחֲנוּכָּה – לָא בָּעֵי לְאַזְכּוּרֵי: הָכָא אִיתֵיהּ (*בְּשַׁחֲרִית וְעַרְבִית) [נ"ל בערבית ושחרית] וּמִנְחָה, וְכֵיוָן שֶׁהַיּוֹם מְחוּיָּב בְּאַרְבַּע תְּפִלּוֹת – כְּאוֹ כֵּן זוֹ: הַמַּפְטִיר בַּנָּבִיא בְּמִנְחָה בְּשַׁבָּת. מָצָאתִי בִּתְשׁוּבַת הַגְּאוֹנִים שֶׁהָיוּ רְגִילִים לִקְרוֹת בַּנָּבִיא בְּשַׁבָּתוֹת בְּמִנְחָה עֲשָׂרָה פְּסוּקִים, וּבִימֵי פַּרְסִיִּים גָּזְרוּ גְּזֵרָה שֶׁלֹּא לַעֲשׂוֹת, וְכֵיוָן שֶׁנִּסְתַּלְּקוּ – נִסְתַּלְּקוּ: אֵין נָבִיא בְּמִנְחָה בְּיוֹם טוֹב. וְאַף עַל גַּב דְּאִיתֵיהּ שַׁחֲרִית, הוֹאִיל וּמִנְחָה לָאו מִשּׁוּם יוֹם טוֹב אָתֵי – לָא מַזְכְּרִינַן: כְּלָל

גמרא

תַּנְיָא כְּווֹתֵיהּ דְּרַב חִסְדָּא: *כָּל אֵלּוּ שֶׁאָמְרוּ אֵין מַדְלִיקִין בָּהֶן בַּשַּׁבָּת – מַדְלִיקִין בָּהֶן בְּיוֹם טוֹב, חוּץ מִשֶּׁמֶן שְׂרֵיפָה, לְפִי שֶׁאֵין שׂוֹרְפִין קָדָשִׁים בְּיוֹם טוֹב.§ אִיבַּעְיָא לְהוּ: מַהוּ לְהַזְכִּיר שֶׁל חֲנוּכָּה בְּבִרְכַּת הַמָּזוֹן? כֵּיוָן דְּמִדְּרַבָּנַן הוּא – לָא מַדְכְּרִינַן, אוֹ דִילְמָא: מִשּׁוּם פִּרְסוּמֵי נִיסָּא מַדְכְּרִינַן? אָמַר רָבָא אָמַר רַב סְחוֹרָה אָמַר רַב הוּנָא: אֵינוֹ מַזְכִּיר, וְאִם בָּא לְהַזְכִּיר – מַזְכִּיר בְּהוֹדָאָה. רַב הוּנָא בַּר יְהוּדָה אִיקְלַע לְבֵי רָבָא, סָבַר לְאַדְכּוּרֵי בְּ"בוֹנֵה יְרוּשָׁלַיִם". אֲמַר לְהוּ רַב שֵׁשֶׁת: כִּתְפִלָּה, [א]מַה תְּפִלָּה – בְּהוֹדָאָה, אַף בִּרְכַּת הַמָּזוֹן – בְּהוֹדָאָה.§ אִיבַּעְיָא לְהוּ: מַהוּ לְהַזְכִּיר רֹאשׁ חוֹדֶשׁ בְּבִרְכַּת הַמָּזוֹן? אִם תִּימְצֵי לוֹמַר בַּחֲנוּכָּה דְּרַבָּנַן לָא צְרִיךְ, רֹאשׁ חוֹדֶשׁ דְּאוֹרַיְיתָא – צְרִיךְ, אוֹ דִילְמָא: כֵּיוָן דְּלָא אָסוּר בַּעֲשִׂיַּית מְלָאכָה – לָא מַזְכְּרִינַן? רַב אָמַר: [ב]מַזְכִּיר, רַבִּי חֲנִינָא אָמַר: אֵינוֹ מַזְכִּיר. אֲמַר רַב זְרִיקָא: נְקוֹט דְּרַב בִּידָךְ, דְּקָאֵי רַבִּי אוֹשַׁעְיָא כְּווֹתֵיהּ. דְּתָנֵי ר' אוֹשַׁעְיָא: *[ג]יָמִים שֶׁיֵּשׁ בָּהֶן קָרְבַּן מוּסָף, כְּגוֹן ר"ח וְחוש"מ – עַרְבִית וְשַׁחֲרִית וּמִנְחָה מִתְפַּלֵּל שְׁמוֹנֶה עֶשְׂרֵה, וְאוֹמֵר מֵעֵין הַמְּאוֹרָע בַּעֲבוֹדָה, וְאִם לֹא אָמַר – מַחֲזִירִין אוֹתוֹ, וְאֵין בָּהֶן קְדוּשָּׁה עַל הַכּוֹס, וְיֵשׁ בָּהֶן הַזְכָּרָה בְּבִרְכַּת הַמָּזוֹן. יָמִים שֶׁאֵין בָּהֶן קָרְבַּן מוּסָף, כְּגוֹן שֵׁנִי וַחֲמִישִׁי (וְשֵׁנִי), וְתַעֲנִיּוֹת וּמַעֲמָדוֹת. שֵׁנִי וַחֲמִישִׁי מַאי עֲבִידְתַּיְיהוּ? אֶלָּא: שֵׁנִי וְה' וּב' שֶׁל תַּעֲנִיּוֹת וּמַעֲמָדוֹת. [ד]עַרְבִית וְשַׁחֲרִית וּמִנְחָה מִתְפַּלֵּל שְׁמוֹנֶה עֶשְׂרֵה, וְאוֹמֵר מֵעֵין הַמְּאוֹרָע בְּ"שׁוֹמֵעַ תְּפִלָּה", [ה]וְאִם לֹא אָמַר – אֵין מַחֲזִירִין אוֹתוֹ. *(וְאֵין בָּהֶן קְדוּשָּׁה עַל הַכּוֹס) וְאֵין בָּהֶן הַזְכָּרָה בְּבִרְכַּת הַמָּזוֹן.§ אִיבַּעְיָא לְהוּ: מַהוּ לְהַזְכִּיר שֶׁל חֲנוּכָּה בְּמוּסָפִין? כֵּיוָן דְּלֵית בֵּיהּ מוּסָף בְּדִידֵיהּ – לָא מַדְכְּרִינַן, אוֹ דִילְמָא: יוֹם הוּא שֶׁחַיָּיב בְּאַרְבַּע תְּפִלּוֹת? רַב הוּנָא וְרַב יְהוּדָה דְּאָמְרִי תַּרְוַיְיהוּ: אֵינוֹ מַזְכִּיר, רַב נַחְמָן וְרַבִּי יוֹחָנָן דְּאָמְרִי תַּרְוַיְיהוּ: [ו]מַזְכִּיר. אֲמַר אַבָּיֵי לְרַב יוֹסֵף: הָא דְּרַב הוּנָא וְרַב יְהוּדָה – דְּרַב הוּא, דְּאָמַר רַב גִּידֵּל אָמַר רַב: רֹאשׁ חֹדֶשׁ שֶׁחָל לִהְיוֹת בְּשַׁבָּת – הַמַּפְטִיר בַּנָּבִיא בְּשַׁבָּת אֵינוֹ צָרִיךְ לְהַזְכִּיר שֶׁל רֹאשׁ חֹדֶשׁ, שֶׁאִילְמָלֵא שַׁבָּת – אֵין נָבִיא בְּרֹאשׁ חֹדֶשׁ. מִי דָּמֵי?! הָתָם – נָבִיא בְּדר"ח לֵיכָּא כְּלָל, הָכָא – אִיתֵיהּ בְּעַרְבִית וְשַׁחֲרִית וּמִנְחָה! אֶלָּא, לְהָא דָּמְיָא: דְּאָמַר רַב אַחְדְּבוֹי אָמַר רַב מַתָּנָה אָמַר רַב: יוֹם טוֹב שֶׁחָל לִהְיוֹת בְּשַׁבָּת – הַמַּפְטִיר בַּנָּבִיא בְּמִנְחָה בְּשַׁבָּת א"צ לְהַזְכִּיר שֶׁל יוֹם טוֹב, שֶׁאִילְמָלֵא שַׁבָּת – אֵין נָבִיא בְּמִנְחָה בְּיוֹם טוֹב.

וְלֵית

תוספות

ולא גזרי' נתן לתוך חלב מהותך שמן, אטו לא נתן. דבלא נתן נמי לא אסור אלא אטו שאין מהותך. אע"ג דבחלב מהותך גזרינן גזרה לגזרה, דגזרי' אטו שאינו מהותך, ושאינו מהותך אטו "שמא יטה" – הא לא חשיב גזרה לגזרה, דכשאינו מהותך – ודאי יטה, לפי שאינו נמשך אחר הפתילה. אבל הכא, משום שמלוה עליו – לית לן למימר ודאי יטה. ותירץ ר"י: דהכא לא חשיב גזירה לגזרה, דיו"ט ושבת כי הדדי נינהו. כדאמרינן בפרק "במה אשה" (לקמן דף ס. ושם) גבי סנדל המסומר. וקשה לרשב"א: דהכא גזרינן יו"ט אטו שבת, ובריש "כל הכלים" (לקמן דף קכד. ושם) מסקינן דלא גזרינן. ושמא אין להשוות גזרות של חכמים זו לזו, אותם שאינם במלאכה אחת: **גזירה** יו"ט אטו שבת. וקשה לרשב"א, הא דתנן בפ"ג דבילה (דף כז: ושם): מעשה ושאל ר' טרפון עליה ועל החלה שנטמאת, ואמרו לו: לא יזיזם ממקומם. והשתא, לרבה אמאי לא יזיזנה? והא חזיא להיסק תחת תבשילו דלא שייך בה למיגזר יו"ט אטו שבת כמו בשמן! ולפי טעמא דאין שורפין קדשים ביום טוב – ניחא. וצריך לדחוק: דגזרינן חלה בשבת אטו שמן*:

תניא כוותיה דרב חסדא. וא"ת: והא משמע חוץ משמן שריפה דאין מדליקין בשבת ולא ביו"ט, והיינו דלא כרב חסדא, דלדידי' מדליקין בשבת! וי"ל דה"ק: כל אלו שאמרו אין מדליקין בשבת – מדליקין ביום טוב, וכ"ש אותו שמדליקין בשבת מדליקין ביום טוב. חוץ משמן שריפה, שאף על פי שמדליקין בשבת – אין מדליקין ביום טוב וכו':

איבעיא להו מהו להזכיר של חנוכה בברכת המזון. תימה: דהך מילתא הוה ליה לאסוקי לעיל, גבי מילי דחנוכה:

מהו להזכיר של חנוכה בבהמ"ז. בתפלה פשיטא ליה דמזכיר, משום דתפלה בצבור הוא ואיכא פרסומי ניסא. אבל בבהמ"ז שבבית, ליכא פרסומי ניסא כולי האי:

מזכיר בהודאה. ד"על הנסים" הודאה היא, ולא תפלה:

בבונה ירושלים. כמו בר"ח שאומר "יעלה ויבא" בבונה ירושלים. ומשום דיעלה ויבא היא תפלה ותחנונים – תקנוה בבונה ירושלים דהיא נמי תפלה, ובי"ח תיקנוה בעבודה, שהיא תפלה להשב ישראל לירושלים: **או** דילמא כיון דלא אסור בעשיית מלאכה כו'. והא דאמר בפ"ג דמגילה (דף כב: ושם): כל שיש בו ביטול מלאכה לעם כגון תענית ציבור וט' באב – קורין שלשה, ושאין בו ביטול מלאכה לעם – כגון ראש חודש וחולו של מועד – קורין ד'. היינו מנהג בעלמא, שאין רגילין לעשות מלאכה*:

דתני ר' אושעיא (כוותיה) כו'. מהכא לא הוי בעי למיפשט לעיל דאינו מזכיר חנוכה בברכת המזון, דאיכא למידחי: דדוקא נקט תעניות ומעמדות, אבל חנוכה ופורים, אף על פי שאין בהן קרבן מוסף – צריך להזכיר, משום פרסומי ניסא. ואיפכא ליכא למיפשט, דדילמא נקיט תעניות ומעמדות משום תפלת מוסף, והוא הדין לחנוכה. ומיהו, אף בחנוכה ופורים, אם לא אמר בתפלה – אין מחזירין אותו, כדתניא בהדיא בתוספתא דברכות (פרק ת"ה): **תעניות** ומעמדות ערבית שחרית ומנחה כו'. מה שפי' הגאונים שאין אנו רגילין לאומרה ערבית ואפילו שחרית – שמא יארע לו אונס חולי או בולמוס, ונמצא שקרן בתפלתו. ומה שש"צ מתפלל שחרית – היינו לפי שא"א שלא יתענה אחד מהם. וקשה לר"י: אם כן, היאך לוה אדם תעניתו ופורע? הלא ימצא שקרן בתפלתו קודם תקנת הגאונים! ולעיל בפ"ק (דף יא.) דאמר "ליזוף מר וליפרע", הלא כבר התפלל תפלת תענית! **אלא** להא דמיא דאמר רב אחדבוי כו'. תימה: תרתי מילתא דרב למה לי לאשמועינן יום טוב שחל להיות בשבת, וכ"ש ראש חודש דליכא נביא כלל! ותירץ ר"י: דחדא מכלל חבירתה איתמר:

שאלמלא שבת אין נביא במנחה. וקשה לר"י: דתנן בפרק שלישי דמגילה (דף כא. ושם ע"ש): "בשני ובחמישי ובשבת במנחה קורין שלשה ואין מפטירין בנביא"! ותירץ ר"ת: דנביא דהכא היינו כתובים, שהיו מפטירין בכתובים בשבת במנחה. כדאמר בפרק "כל כתבי" (לקמן דף קטז:): בנהרדעא פסקי סידרא בכתובים במנחתא דשבתא ובמגילה איירי בנביא ממש:

ולית

עין משפט נר מצוה

מט א מיי' פ"ב (מהל' תפלה הל' יג ופ"ב) מהלכות ברכות הלכה ו סמג עשין כז טוש"ע א"ח סי' תרפב סעיף א:
נ ב מיי' פ"ב מהל' ברכות הלכה ה סמג שם טוש"ע א"ח סי' תכד:
נא ג מיי' פ"ב מהל' תפלה הלכה י סמג עשין יט טוש"ע א"ח סי' תכב סעי' א וסימן תל סעיף ב:
נב ד מיי' שם הל' יד טור וש"ע א"ח סי' תקסה סעיף א ג:
נג ה שם סעיף ב:
נד ו מיי' שם הל' יג סמג שם טוש"ע א"ח סי' תרפב סעיף ב:

עיין רש"א

[ועי' תוספות תענית יח. ד"ה ר"ח ותוס' ר"ה כב. ד"ה משום ותוס' מגילה כב: ד"ה ואין]

רבינו חננאל

ותניא כותיה כל השמנים שאמרו חכמים אין מדליקין בהן בשבת אבל מדליקין בהן ביו"ט חוץ משמן שריפה שאין שורפין קדשים [פסולין] ביו"ט: **אמר** רבא מזכיר של חנוכה בברכת המזון כתפלה מה תפלה בהודאה אף ברכת המזון בהודאה אמר רב מזכיר של ר"ח בברכת המזון דתני רב הושעיא ימים שיש בהן קרבן מוסף כגון ר"ח וחוש"מ ערבית שחרית ומנחה מתפלל י"ח ואומרין מעין המאורע בעבודה ואם לא אמר מחזירין אותו ואין בהם קדושה על הכוס ויש בהן הזכרה בבהמ"ז. ימים שאין בהם קרבן מוסף כגון שני וחמישי ושל תעניות ומעמדות ערבי' ושחרית ומנחה מתפלל י"ח ואומר מעין המאורע בשומע תפלה ואם לא אמר אין מחזירין אותו ואין בהם קידוש על הכוס ולא הזכרה

תורה אור

ולית הילכתא [א]ככל הני שמעתתא, אלא כי הא דא"ר יהושע בן לוי: [ב]יום הכפורים שחל להיות בשבת המתפלל נעילה צריך להזכיר של שבת, יום הוא שנתחייב בארבע תפלות. קשיא הילכתא אהילכתא! אמרת: הילכתא כריב"ל, וקיימא לן: הילכתא כרבא. דאמר רבא: [ג]יו"ט שחל להיות בשבת, שליח ציבור היורד לפני התיבה ערבית אינו צריך להזכיר של יום טוב, שאילמלא שבת אין שליח צבור יורד ערבית ביו"ט. הכי השתא! התם – בדין הוא דאפילו בשבת נמי לא צריך, ורבנן הוא דתקוני משום סכנה, אבל הכא – יום הוא שנתחייב בארבע תפלות. "ולא באליה כו'". חכמים היינו תנא קמא! איכא בינייהו *דרב ברונא אמר רב, ולא מסיימי.

מתני' *אין מדליקין בשמן שריפה ביו"ט. רבי ישמעאל אומר: [ד]אין מדליקין בעטרן, מפני כבוד השבת. וחכמים מתירין [ה]בכל השמנים; בשמן שומשמין, בשמן אגוזים, בשמן צנונות, בשמן דגים, בשמן פקועות, בעטרן ובנפט. ר' טרפון אומר: אין מדליקין אלא בשמן זית בלבד.

גמ' *מ"ט? [ו]לפי *שאין שורפין קדשים ביו"ט. מנהני מילי? אמר חזקיה, וכן *תנא דבי חזקיה, אמר קרא: (שמות יב) °"ולא תותירו ממנו עד בקר והנותר ממנו עד בקר*", שאין ת"ל 'עד בקר' מה ת"ל 'עד בקר' – בא הכתוב ליתן לו בקר שני לשריפתו. אביי אמר, *אמר קרא: (במדבר כח) °"עולת שבת בשבתו" – *ולא עולת חול בשבת, ולא עולת חול ביו"ט. רבא אמר, אמר קרא: (שמות יב) °"הוא לבדו יעשה לכם", 'הוא' – ולא מכשירין, 'לבדו' – ולא מילה שלא בזמנה, דאתיא בק"ו. רב אשי אמר: ('שבת') (ויקרא כג) °'שבתון' עשה

רש"י

בכל הני שמעתתא. רב הונא ורב יהודה ורב גידל ורב אחדבוי, אלא כתפלה אחת כך תברכה לכל דבר היום, ומזכיר: **צריך להזכיר של שבת.** לומר: "ותתן לנו את יום המנוח ואת יום הכפורים הזה", וחותם: "מקדש השבת ויה"כ", ואע"פ שאין תפלת נעילה בשבת: **יום הוא שנתחייב בד' תפלות.** לאו תפלת הלילה בכלל, אלא תפלות היום: שחרית מוסף מנחה ונעילה: **שליח ציבור היורד ערבית.** המתפלל ברכת מעין שבע: "קונה שמים וארץ מגן אבות בדברו": **משום סכנה.** מזיקין. שלא היו בתי כנסיות שלהן בישוב, וכל שאר לילי החול היו עסוקין במלאכתן, ובגמרן מלאכתן מתפללין ערבית בביתן, ולא היו באין בבית הכנסת. אבל לילי שבת באין לבית הכנסת, וחשו שיש שאין ממהרין לבא ושוהין לאחר תפלה, לכך האריכו תפלת הצבור: *הכי גרסינן: נחום(א) **אומר** מדליקין בחלב מבושל. והוא מהותך: **היינו ת"ק.** דקאמר: "ולא בחלב" – כל חלב במשמע: **דרב ברונא.** דשרי ע"י תערובת שמן כל שהוא: **ולא מסיימי.** אין ניכר מי אוסר ומי מתיר:

מתני' שמן שריפה. שמן של תרומה טמאה. ובגמ' מפרש טעמא: **רבי ישמעאל אומר כו'.** בשבת: **עטרן.** פסולתא דזיפתא: **מפני כבוד השבת.** שריחו רע: **שמן שומשמין כו'.** מסקנא דמילתא דחכמים היא: **צנונות.** לנון: **שמן דגים.** מקרבי דגים שנימוחו: **פקועות.** דלעת מדברי: **נפט.** מין שמן שריחו רע, כדאמרינן בסדר יומא (דף לט.): בא למדוד נפט, אומרים לו "מדוד לעצמך", שאין אדם רוצה לסייעו:

גמ' מנהני מילי. דאין שורפין. דאי לא ממעט לה קרא, אית לן למימר: ליתי עשה ד"באש תשרופו" וידחה את "לא תעשה כל מלאכה": **שאין ת"ל עד בקר.** זימנא אחריתי, אלא "והנותר ממנו באש תשרופו", דהא כתיב "עד בקר" ברישא: **בקר שני.** שהוא חולו של מועד, והכי משמע: והנותר ממנו לבקר ראשון – עד בקר שני המתינו ותשרפהו: **עולת חול.** כגון אברי תמיד של ערב יו"ט שלא הוקטרו מבעוד יום, אין מעלין אותן משחשכה. וכ"ש קדשים פסולים לא שרפינן: **הוא לבדו.** קראי יתירי נינהו, דמצי למכתב "אך אשר יאכל לכל נפש יעשה לכם": **מכשירין.** מכשירי האוכל, כגון לעשות שפוד וסכין ותנור וכירים: **לבדו.** למעוטי מילה שלא בזמנה, דלא דחיא שבת ויו"ט. דאי לא מעטיה קרא, אתיא בק"ו דתידחי בפ' "ר' אליעזר" (לקמן קלב:), דהכי תניא התם: ומה צרעת שדוחה את עבודה ועבודה דוחה את השבת, מילה שלא בזמנה דוחה אותה – דהכי תניא התם: מילה דוחה את הצרעת בין בזמנה בין שלא בזמנה, ויליף לה מקראי – שבת שנדחית מפני עבודה, אינו דין שתהא מילה שלא בזמנה דוחה אותה?! אתא "לבדו" לאפוקי מהאי ק"ו, דלא תדרוש ליה. ומתמילא שמעינן מינה דמלוה שאין זמנה קבוע ויכול לעשותה למחר – אינה דוחה יום טוב, וה"ה לשריפת קדשים טמאים:

עשה

תוספות

ולית הילכתא ככל הני שמעתתא. פי' בקונטרס: כרב הונא ורב יהודה ורב גידל ורב אחדבוי. ואומר ר"י: דלא היה לו למנות דרב גידל בהדייהו, דאפילו ריב"ל מודה דאין צריך להזכיר של ראש חדש בנעילה, כיון דנעילה בר"ח ליכא כלל. וכן אנו נוהגין שלא להזכיר*:

איכא בינייהו דרב ברונא אמר רב ולא מסיימי. הקשה ריב"א: אמאי לא מסיימי? והא אמר ב"המוכר פירות" (ב"ב דף צג.): דכל תנא בתרא לטפויי אתא! וי"ל: דהכא דאיכא ג' תנאים איכא למימר דלא אתא לטפויי אלא אנחום המדי, דאמר מדליקין בחלב מבושל בעיניה, ואתו חכמים למימר אפילו במבושל אין מדליקין בעיניה, אבל בנתינת שמן לתוכו – מותר. וטעמא דת"ק נמי איכא למימר דאסר בנתינת שמן דומיא דזפת ושעוה, ולא מסיימי משום דאיכא למימר תנא בתרא לטפויי אתא:

לפי שאין שורפין קדשים ביו"ט. וא"ת: היכי ילפינן תרומה מקדשים? דקדשים דין הוא שאין שריפתן דוחה יו"ט – לפי שאין יכול ליהנות בשעת שריפה, ולא אמרינן מתוך שהותרה הבערה לצורך, הותר' נמי שלא לצורך – אלא שלא לצורך אוכל נפש, אבל צריך שיהא קצת צורך – להתחמם או לשום הנאה, אבל הבערה לגמרי שלא לצורך – לא הותרה. אלא שריפת תרומה טמאה, שמותר ליהנו' בשעת שריפה למה יאסר? מאי שנא משמן חולין שמותר לשורפו ולהדליקו להנאתו. דאטו תרומה, לפי שיש מצוה בשריפתה מיגרע גרע? ואומר ריב"א: דודאי גרע. *דכיון שאסרה תורה כל הנאות רק הנאת שריפה, אם כן הבערה זו אינה לצורך הנאתו, אלא לשם מצות שריפה. אלא שהתורה לא הקפידה שיהנה ממנה בשעת ביעור', ולהכי לא דחיא יו"ט. מידי דהוה אנדרים ונדבות *דאין קרבים ביו"ט, למ"ד משלחן גבוה קא זכו. וכן שתי הלחם לדידיה אין אפייתן דוחה יו"ט, אע"פ שיש בהן אכילת אדם משום דעיקרן לצורך גבוה. ולמ"ד קריבין ביו"ט – היינו משום דקסבר דעיקר שחיטתן ואפייתן נמי לצורך אדם. אבל שריפת תרומה טמאה – ודאי לשם מצות ביעור, ולא לשם הנאה, הלכך אסור ביו"ט כשאר קדשים. ולר"י נראה: דלא שייך בשריפת תרומה לומר "משולחן גבוה קא זכו" ולא דמו לשתי הלחם שהאפייה היא לצורך גבוה, שהרי אחר אפייה צריך לעשות בהם תנופה. וכן אחר שחיטת נדרים ונדבות – עושין מהן לגבוה. אבל תרומה טמאה אין עושין ממנה לגבוה כלום, וליכא למימר בה "משולחן גבוה קא זכו". והכי מפרש ר"י: "לפי שאין שורפין קדשים ביו"ט", פי': גזרו תרומה אטו קדשים. *וא"ת: ומאי אירא אטו קדשים, משום דאין שורפין קדשים ביו"ט, נגזור משום תרומה שלא לצורך, דאפילו שורפין קדשים ביו"ט. דאתי עשה ודחי לא תעשה – תרומה שלא לצורך אין שורפין. דמשמע מתוך פרש"י בסמוך, דאין עשה בשריפתה אלא מדרבנן! וי"ל: דשריפת תרומה שלא לצורך לא שכיח, דשום אדם לא ישרפנה חנם, כיון שיוכל ליהנות בשריפתה. וכדמוכח בירושלמי כלשון הזה:

בקר שני לשריפתו. וא"ת: אי בקר שני דוקא ואינו יכול לשורפו בליל מוצאי יו"ט, היכי מוכח דאין שריפת קדשים דוחה יום טוב? הא ע"כ אינו מטעם דאין שריפת קדשים דוחה יום טוב, דהא בליל מוצאי יום טוב נמי אין שורפו, ואם כן גזרת הכתוב הוא לשרוף בבקר שני! וי"ל: הא דאין שורפין בלילה – היינו משום דהקפיד הכתוב שלא לשרוף הקדשים בלילה, כדאשכחן בשלמים דאין נאכלין לאור שלישי, ואפילו הכי אין נשרפין אלא ביום שלישי, כדדריש בריש פסחים (דף ג. ושם): "ביום השלישי באש ישרף", ביום אתה שורפו כו':

ולא עולת חול בשבת ולא עולת חול ביום טוב. תימה: כיון דקרא בשבת איירי, מנא ליה למדרש "ולא עולת חול ביום טוב"? דילמא דוקא ולא חול בשבת דחמיר מיום טוב, וי"ל: דאביי סבר כרבי עקיבא, דדריש בפרק "אלו קשרים" (לקמן דף קיד.): עולת שבת בשבת אחרת – לימד על חלבי שבת שקריבין ביום טוב. מדאיצטריך קרא למשרי עולת שבת ביום טוב – אם כן עולת חול ביום טוב אסור. דקסבר נדרים ונדבות אין קרבין ביום טוב, כדאמר התם. ורבי ישמעאל פליג התם, ודריש "עולת שבת בשבתו" – לימד על חלבי שבת שקריבין בי"ה אבל שקריבין ביום טוב לא איצטריך דקסבר נדרים ונדבות קריבין ביום טוב:

ולא מילה שלא בזמנה דאתיא בק"ו. פירש בקונטרס: מה צרעת שדוחה את העבודה, ועבודה דוחה את השבת – מילה דוחה אותה, שבת שנדחית כו'. וקשה, בפרק "ר"א דמילה" (לקמן דף קלג: ושם) לית ליה לרבא(א) האי קל וחומר. דקסבר: האי דצרעת דוחה את העבודה – לאו משום דחמירא, אלא משום דגברא הוא דלא חזי. והר"ר יוסף פורת לא גריס "דאתיא

(א) ור"ח עשה ק"ו מאוכל נפש שלא נכרתו עליו [י"ג בריתות] ואיכא למיפרך מה לאוכל נפש שכן מצוה עוברת [ת"י]:

בק"ו

עין משפט נר מצוה

[ועי' תוספות כתובות נד. ד"ה לית]

נה א מיי' פי"ב מהל' תפלה הל' טו טוש"ע א"ח סי' רפד ס"ב וסי' תכה סעיף ג:

נו ב מיי' פ"ב מהל' תפלה הל' ז טוש"ע א"ח סי' תרכג סעיף ג:

נז ג מיי' פ"ט מהלכות תפלה הל' יב סמג עשין יט טוש"ע א"ח סי' רסח ס"ב וסי' תריט סעיף ג:

נח ד מיי' פ"ה מהל' שבת הלכה י סמג לאוין סה טור וש"ע א"ח סי' רסד סעיף ג:

נט ה מיי' שם הל' יא טוש"ע שם סעיף ו:

ס ו מיי' פ"ג מהל' י"ט הל' ח:

תוספתא פ"ב

[ועי' מ"ש רש"י במשנה ביצה כז: ד"ה חלה שנטמאת וכו']

[ועי' תוס' לעיל כג: ד"ה גזרה]

[ביצה יט.]

בדפו"י ליתא

[ועי' תוס' פסחים מו. ד"ה לא תקרא ותוס' ביצה כז: ד"ה ועל]

מסורת הש"ס

[שייך לעיל במשנה כ:]

[לעיל כח.]

[לעיל כג:]

[לעיל כג: וש"נ]

לקמן קלג. פסחים פג: תמורה ל: ע"ש

[נ"ל באש תשרופו שאין כו']

[פסחים נט:]

הגהות הב"ח

(א) רש"י ד"ה ה"ג נחום המדי אומר:

גליון הש"ס

רש"י ד"ה עטרן פסולתא דזיפתא. עי' לעיל כ ע"ב: שם ד"ה שמן דגים מקרבי דגים שנמוחו. עי' לקמן טו ע"א תוס' ד"ה איכא בינייהו: שם ד"ה פקועות דלעת מדברי. עיין רד"ק (מ"ב ד לט): תוס' ד"ה איכא בינייהו דרב ברונא כו' וי"ל דהכא דאיכא שלשה תנאים. עיין בב"ק נט ע"א תוס' ד"ה איכא בינייהו כתב גופנא: שם ד"ה לפי כו' נגזור משום תרומה שלא לצורך. ק"ל הא גם בשלא לצורך הוי רק דרבנן דמדאורייתא שרי הואיל ואי מקלעי אורחים מש"ה לא גזרי בכך. ואולי דקושייתם אההיא דלעיל כג ע"ב ר"ח אמר כו' לפי שאין שורפין קדשים דאיהו לא ס"ל הואיל גבי האופה מיום טוב לחול:

רבינו חננאל

בבהמ"ז ואסיקנא נמי דמזכיר של חנוכה בתפלת המוסף של שבת ושל ר"ח טבת כרבי יהושע בן לוי דאמר יוה"כ שחל להיות בשבת המתפלל תפלת נעילה צריך להזכיר של שבת יום הוא שנתחייב בד' תפלות והלכתא כרבא דאמר ש"ץ היורד ערבית ביום טוב שחל להיות בשבת א"צ להזכיר של יו"ט שאלמלא שבת אין ש"ץ יורד ערבית ביום טוב ומשום סכנה הוא בשבת אין ביום טוב לא אבל הא דאמר רב ר"ח שחל להיות בשבת המפטיר בנביא א"צ להזכיר של ר"ח שאלמלא שבת אין נביא בר"ח וגם זה שאמר המפטיר בנביא במנחה ביו"ט שחל להיות בשבת א"צ להזכיר של יו"ט שאלמלא שבת אין נביא במנחה ביו"ט בהני (תלת) [תרתי] לית הלכתא כוותיה דרב: **ואקשינן** אהא דתנן וחכ"א אחד חלב מבושל ואחד שאינו מבושל אין מדליקין בו היינו ת"ק דתני לא באליה ולא בחלב ונחום פליג עלייהו ואמר מדליקין בחלב מבושל מכלל דת"ק אסר אפילו בחלב מבושל ושנינן יש לומר כן ת"ק סבר אין מדליקין בחלב מבושל בפני עצמו ואם נתן בהו שמן מותר כרב ברונא אמר רב נחום מתיר בחלב מבושל אע"פ שלא נתן בהו שמן ורבנן בתראי אסרי אפילו בשנתן בהו שמן: **ומנא** לן שאין שורפין קדשים ביו"ט חזקיה תני מלא תותירו אביי אמר עולת שבת בשבתו זו לבדה ולא עולת שבת בשבת ולא עולת חול בשבת ולא עולת יו"ט בשבת וכן לא עולת חול ביו"ט רבא אמר כתיב הוא

רב נסים גאון

פרק ב לבדו ולא מילה שלא בזמנה הבאה מק"ו. עיקרה בפ' ר' אליעזר אומר אם לא הביא כלי מערב שבת (דף קלג) דת"ר מילה דוחה את הצרעת בין בזמנה בין שלא בזמנה יו"ט אינה דוחה אלא בזמנה ואמרי' (שם דף קלג) מנא הני מילי אמר חזקיה וכן תנא דבי חזקיה (שמות יב) לא תותירו ממנו עד בוקר וכו' והכין כתב אדונינו האיי גאון בפירושיה מילה אינה דוחה יו"ט אלא בזמנה ומי שעבר שמיני שלו אינו נימול ביו"ט ותנן (שבת דף קלז) קטן נימול לח' לט' לי' לי"א לי"ב ותני בה יו"ט אחר שבת נימול לי"א ואפי' י"ט שני אינה דוחה דקתני ב' ימים טובים של ראש השנה נימול לי"ב מנהני מילי ושמעתא דעיקר דילה בגמ' דכיצד צולין (פסחים דף פג) דתנן העצמות והגידים והנותר כו' שאין דוחה לא את השבת ולא את יו"ט ואיתמרו בה הני ד' טעמי וקאמר רבה מילה הבאה שלא בזמנה לא דחיא יו"ט

– עֲשֵׂה, וַהֲוָה לֵיהּ *יוֹם טוֹב עֲשֵׂה וְלֹא תַעֲשֶׂה, וְאֵין עֲשֵׂה דּוֹחֶה אֶת לֹא תַעֲשֶׂה וַעֲשֵׂה. בְּיוֹם טוֹב הוּא דַּאֲסִיר, הָא בַּחוֹל – שַׁפִּיר דָּמֵי, מ"ט? אָמַר רַב: כְּשֵׁם שֶׁמִּצְוָה לִשְׂרוֹף הַקֳּדָשִׁים שֶׁנִּטְמְאוּ, *כָּךְ מִצְוָה לִשְׂרוֹף אֶת הַתְּרוּמָה שֶׁנִּטְמֵאת. וְאָמְרָה תּוֹרָה: א בִּשְׁעַת בִּיעוּרָהּ תֵּיהָנֵי מִמֶּנָּה. הֵיכָן אָמְרָה תּוֹרָה? מִדְּרַב נַחְמָן. *דְּאָמַר רַב נַחְמָן אָמַר רַבָּה בַּר אֲבוּהּ: אָמַר קְרָא °"וַאֲנִי הִנֵּה נָתַתִּי לְךָ אֶת מִשְׁמֶרֶת תְּרוּמוֹתָי" *ב בִּשְׁתֵּי תְּרוּמוֹת הַכָּתוּב מְדַבֵּר, אַחַת תְּרוּמָה טְהוֹרָה וְאַחַת תְּרוּמָה טְמֵאָה. וְאָמַר רַחֲמָנָא 'לְךָ' – שֶׁלְּךָ תְּהֵא, לְהַסִּיקָהּ תַּחַת תַּבְשִׁילְךָ. וְאִיבָּעֵית אֵימָא – מִדְּרַבִּי אַבָּהוּ, דְּאָמַר *רַבִּי אַבָּהוּ א"ר יוֹחָנָן: °"וְלֹא בִעַרְתִּי מִמֶּנּוּ בְּטָמֵא" – מִמֶּנּוּ אִי אַתָּה מְבָעֵיר, אֲבָל אַתָּה מְבָעֵיר שֶׁמֶן שֶׁל תְּרוּמָה שֶׁנִּטְמֵאת. וְאֵימָא: מִמֶּנּוּ אִי אַתָּה מְבָעֵיר, אֲבָל אַתָּה מְבָעֵיר שֶׁמֶן שֶׁל קֹדֶשׁ שֶׁנִּטְמָא! לָאו קַל וָחוֹמֶר הוּא? *מָה מַּעֲשֵׂר הַקַּל אָמְרָה תּוֹרָה "לֹא בִעַרְתִּי מִמֶּנּוּ בְּטָמֵא", קֹדֶשׁ חָמוּר לֹא כ"ש? א"ה, תְּרוּמָה נַמִי, לֵימָא: ק"ו הוּא! הָא כְּתִיב 'מִמֶּנּוּ'. וּמָה רָאִיתָ? מִסְתַּבְּרָא, קֹדֶשׁ לָא מְמַעֵיטְנָא שֶׁכֵּן סִימָן פנ"ק עכ"ם: פִּיגּוּל, נוֹתָר, קָרְבָּן מְעִילָה, וְכָרֵת, אָסוּר לְאוֹנֵן. אַדְּרַבָּה, תְּרוּמָה לָא מְמַעֵיטְנָא, שֶׁכֵּן מחפ"ז סִימָן: מִיתָה, חוֹמֶשׁ, וְאֵין

תורה אור: [נ"ל הכיתר] במדבר יח; דברים כו

רש"י

עֲשֵׂה הוּא. דְּמַשְׁמַע שְׁבוּת בּוֹ: וְאֵין עֲשֵׂה. דְּ"בָאֵשׁ תִּשְׂרוֹפוּ" דּוֹחֶה יו"ט, דְּהוּא לֹא תַעֲשֶׂה וַעֲשֵׂה. וְאע"ג דְּהַדְלָקַת נֵר בְּיו"ט מְלָאכָה הַמּוּתֶּרֶת הִיא, הוֹאִיל וְהַבְעָרַת שְׁאָר קֳדָשִׁים שֶׁאֵין נֶהֱנִין מֵהֶן נֶאֱסָרִין – גַּם זוֹ לֹא יָצְאָה מִן הַכְּלָל: הָא בַּחוֹל שַׁפִּיר דָּמֵי. לְאִיתְהַנּוּיֵי מִינָּהּ: מִצְוָה לִשְׂרוֹף אֶת הַתְּרוּמָה שֶׁנִּטְמֵאת. דְּדָמְיָא לְקֹדֶשׁ, וְעוֹד: מִשּׁוּם תַּקָּלָה: לֹא בִעַרְתִּי מִמֶּנּוּ. בְּמַעֲשֵׂר שֵׁנִי כְּתִיב: בְּטָמֵא. בֵּין שֶׁאֲנִי טָמֵא בֵּין שֶׁהוּא טָמֵא: קֹדֶשׁ לָא מְמַעֵיטְנָא. מֵהָךְ חוּמְרָא: שֶׁכֵּן. יֵשׁ בּוֹ חוּמְרֵי פנקעכ"ם, וְרָאוּי גַּם לָזוֹ. חַיָּיבִין עָלָיו מִשּׁוּם פִּיגּוּל – שָׁחַט עַל מְנָת לֶאֱכוֹל חוּץ לִזְמַנּוֹ וְאָכַל אֲפִילּוּ בִּזְמַנּוֹ. וּמִשּׁוּם נוֹתָר – חוּץ לִזְמַנּוֹ מַמָּשׁ, וְלֹא חָשַׁב מִתְּחִלָּה. וְקָרוּי קָרְבָּן – וְיֵשׁ בּוֹ מְעִילָה. וְאַף עַל גַּב שֶׁקֹּדֶשׁ *(הַנּוֹתָר) לַאֲכִילַת כֹּהֲנִים אֵין בָּהֶן מְעִילָה, מ"מ תּוֹרַת מְעִילָה שַׁיְּיכָא בֵּיהּ. אִם קָדְשֵׁי קָדָשִׁים הֵן – יֵשׁ בָּהֶן מְעִילָה לִפְנֵי זְרִיקָה לְכָל הַנֶּהֱנֶה מֵהֶן, וְאִם קָדָשִׁים קַלִּים הֵן – יֵשׁ מְעִילָה בְּאֵימוּרֵיהֶן לְאַחַר זְרִיקַת דָּמִים, לְאַפּוּקֵי תְּרוּמָה דְּלֵית בָּהּ כְּלָל: וְכָרֵת. לְאוֹכְלָהּ בְּטוּמְאַת הַגּוּף. וּתְרוּמָה בְּמִיתָה בִּידֵי שָׁמַיִם – יָמָיו נִקְצָרִים, אֲבָל אֵינוֹ הוֹלֵךְ עֲרִירִי: אָסוּר לְאוֹנֵן. ק"ו מִמַּעֲשֵׂר. אֲבָל תְּרוּמָה מוּתֶּרֶת לְאוֹנֵן, כִּיבָמוֹת בְּפֶרֶק "הֶעָרֵל" (דף ע:), "זָר" "זָר" ב' פְּעָמִים, זָרוּת אֲמַרְתִּי לְךָ וְלֹא אֲנִינוּת. אוֹנֵן כָּל זְמַן שֶׁלֹּא נִקְבַּר מֵתוֹ: מחפ"ז. מִיתָה בִּידֵי שָׁמַיִם לְזָר הָאוֹכְלָהּ, אוֹ כֹּהֵן טָמֵא, וְחוֹמֶשׁ לְזָר הָאוֹכְלָהּ בְּשׁוֹגֵג, דִּכְתִיב (ויקרא כב): "כִּי יֹאכַל קֹדֶשׁ בִּשְׁגָגָה, וְיָסַף חֲמִישִׁיתוֹ עָלָיו". אֲבָל קֹדֶשׁ, מִשָּׁעָה שֶׁיֵּשׁ הֶיתֵּר לְכֹהֲנִים כִּתְרוּמָה וְיָצָא מִידֵי מְעִילָה – שׁוּב אֵין חוֹמֶשׁ בְּשִׁגְגַת אֲכִילָתוֹ. וְיֵשׁ דְּמוֹקְמֵי לָהּ בְּחוֹמָשִׁין דְּחוּמְשָׁא; וְלָא נְהִירָא, דְּהָא רַבִּינַן בֵּיהּ חוֹמֶשׁ דְּחוֹמֶשׁ בְּהֶקְדֵּשׁ, בְּפֶרֶק "הַזָּהָב" (בבא מציעא דף נד:): וְאֵין

תוספות

בק"ו", דהא בלאו ק"ו נמי אתיא, דאתי עשה ודחי לא תעשה. ורב אשי הוא דמשני דיו"ט עשה ולא תעשה הוא, ואין עשה דוחה לא תעשה ועשה. וקשה לר"י: דבפ"ק דבילה (דף ח: ושם) משמע *דאית ליה לרבא דיו"ט עשה ולא תעשה הוא, גבי אפר כירה. דפריך: סוף סוף יו"ט עשה ולא תעשה הוא, ואין עשה דכיסוי דוחה לא תעשה ועשה. אלא אמר רבא כו'. ודוחק למימר דהתלמוד ניחא ליה למיפרך דיו"ט עשה ולא תעשה הוא, דקי"ל כרב אשי אבל רבא אע"ג דלית ליה ליו"ט עשה ולא תעשה – מ"מ אין כיסוי דוחה יו"ט מלבדו. ור"י מפרש: דאתיא בק"ו מנדרים ונדבות, דדחו יו"ט אף על גב שלא נכרתו עליהם י"ג בריתות – מילה לכ"ש. וקסבר רבא דקריבין ביו"ט. וליכא למיפרך: מה לנדרים ונדבות שהן לצורך גבוה, כדפריך בפ' "ר' אליעזר דמילה" (לקמן קלא:): מה לעומר ושתי הלחם – שהן לצורך גבוה. דהא לאו חובה נינהו, ואפילו חטאות ואשמות לא מיקרו צורך גבוה, כיון דאי לא חטא – לא בעי לאייתינהו. ואית ליה לרבא דיום טוב עשה ולא תעשה, כדמוכח בבילה. להכי איצטריך ק"ו, דאי לאו ק"ו – לא הוה צריך קרא למיסר. ורבא לא קאי אשריפת קדשים, אלא התלמוד מייתי, משום דמינה נמי שמעינן דאין שריפת קדשים דוחה יו"ט:

ה"ל יו"ט עשה כו'. וא"ת: הנך אמוראי דלעיל, דסברי דיו"ט לא תעשה גרידא – נילף מהכא דלא דחי עשה את ל"ת. וכי האי גוונא פריך בפ"ק דיבמות (דף ו.) ושמא מיכן לא נילף, לפי שיכול לעשות אחר יו"ט [ת"י]:

הא בחול שפיר דמי מ"ט כו'. תימה: מהיכא תיתי דתרומה טמאה אסורה בהנאה, דבעי מ"ט? אי ממעשר הקל כדמשמע בסמוך – איכא למיפרך: מה למעשר שכן הד"ס ט"ב כדפריך ב"הערל" (יבמות דף עד:). וליכא למימר דהוה אסרינן ליה משום דאיקרי "קדש" דכתיב (ויקרא כב): "ונתן לכהן את הקדש", או משום דהוקשה לקדשים כדאמר במעילה בפרק "הנהנה" (דף יט.) דקדש אקשי רחמנא לתרומה, וקדש גופיה אסור בהנאה כשניטמא אפילו אותו קדש שהיה מותר בהנאה קודם כמו שלמים, נפקא לן שפיר מק"ו דמעשר, או מהיקשא דמעשר, כדאמר בפרק "כל שעה" (פסחים דף כב.) דא"כ: מאי פריך "ומה ראית"? ואימא: "ממנו" אתא למעוטי קדש ולא תרומה, ואם נמעט קדש, מהיכא תיתי איסור תרומה? וי"ל: דהוה גמרינן תרומה מדאיתקש לבכורים, ובכורים למעשר, כדאמרינן ב"הערל" (יבמות דף עג:) ולקמן לא סמיך אק"ו אלא אהיקשא סמיך. ומיהו, קדש אתי שפיר בק"ו ממעשר, כדאמרי' בפ' "כל שעה" (פסחים דף כב.). וליכא למיפרך שכן הד"ס ט"ב – דכולהו איתנהו בקדש, בר מוידוי. ואר"ת: דמוידוי לא שייך למיפרך, דלא שייך וידוי גבי קדש. אבל בתרומה שייך, דהא אגב מעשר מתודה נמי אתרומה, כדאמר: *"וגם נתתיו ללוי" – זו תרומה, ואין לה וידוי בפני עצמה. וא"ת: אכתי היכי יליף בק"ו קדש ממעשר? מה למעשר שכן טעון כסף צורה, כדפריך בפרק בתרא דמכות (דף יז:)! ואור"י: דלא שייך האי פירכא אלא דוקא גבי חוץ לחומה, כדהתם, דבעי למילף דאוכל תודה או שלמים חוץ לחומה דלוקה ממעשר. ואם תאמר: הכא אסרינן הסקה והדלקה באיסורי הנאה וערלה דאסורה בהנאה ושרי ליהנות בשעת ביעור, כדאמר בפרק "כל שעה" (פסחים כו:) ולא משכח התם עצים לרבנן דאסורים אלא בשרשיפא! וצריך לדחות ולומר: דשמן ובשר ותבואה חשיבי בעין טפי בשעת היסק מעצים: **כך אתה מצווה לשרוף את התרומה.** פי' בקונטרס: משום דלא ליתי בה לידי תקלה. לפי טעם זה נראה דלאו דוקא שריפה, אלא ה"ה שאר ביעור. וכ"פ בהדיא ב"אלו עוברין". ול"נ, דבסוף תמורה (דף לג:) קתני תרומה טמאה בהדי הנשרפין, וקתני התם: הנשרפין לא יקברו. ע"כ נראה: דשריפה דוקא, משום דדמיא לקדש, ומדרבנן. א"נ: מדאורייתא, מדאיקרי "קדש". ואם תאמר: דאמר בספ"ק דפסחים (דף כ:) גבי תרומה טמאה שתעשה זילוף, הא תנן בתמורה: הראוי לקבורה – קבורה. פירוש: כגון משקין. ויש לומר: דלא קאי אלא אערלה וכלאי הכרם, ולא אתרומה דשריא בהנאה*: **אחת** תרומה טמאה ואחת תרומה טהורה. ואף על גב דדריש רבי אליעזר (בכורות דף לד. ושם): אחת תרומה טהורה ואחת תלויה, יניחנה במקום המוצנע ולא במקום התורפה דאסור לגרום לה טומאה, התם דריש "משמרת תרומותי" משמע: שתי תרומות לריכות שימור, דהיינו טהורה ותלויה. והכא דריש מ"לך": **שכן** פנקעכ"ם. תימה: דמאי לאחשובי נמי דחמירי קדשים מתרומה בהא: העריב שמשו – אוכל בתרומה, הביא כפרתו – אוכל בקדשים*: **פגול.** היינו חישב לאוכלו חוץ למקומו, ובכלל זה הוי אוכל חוץ לחומה דלוקה בקדשים. ונותר היינו חישב לאוכלו חוץ לזמנו, והוי נותר בכלל זה, והוי האי פיגול ונותר כי ההוא ד"אם עון פיגול הוא – הרי כבר נאמר לא יחשב, ואם עון נותר" כו' (פסחים דף טז:). ולא כמו פיגול שבכל התלמוד דקרי פיגול דחישב לאוכלו חוץ לזמנו – דהיינו נותר דהכא: **כרת.** שאינו מגיע לששים שנה, שהוא מיתת כל אדם, כדמשמע בשילהי מ"ק (דף כח. ושם), דאמר התם: רב יוסף כי הוה בר שיתין שנין עבד יומא טבא לרבנן, אמר: השתא נפקי לי מכרת. א"ל אביי: נהי דנפק מר מכרת דשני, מכרת דיומי מי נפק מר? פירוש, כדאמר התם: מת ביום א' – מיתה של זעם, שנים – מיתה של בהלה, שלשה – מיתה של כרת. ומיתה בידי שמים אין לה זמן קבוע, אלא שמת בשביל עון זה, אפי' אין בידו עון אחר. ואפי' למ"ד (לקמן דף נה.) "יש מיתה בלא חטא" – בשביל עון זה יקצרו ימיו. ומיהו בירושל'* קאמר: דכרת אינו מגיע לחמשים, ומפיק לה מ"אל תכריתו את שבט הקהתי וגו' וזאת עשו להם וחיו", פי': אמרה תורה עשו להם תקנה שלא ימותו בעבודתן קודם חמשים, וכתיב "אל תכריתו" משמע כרת, היינו שמת קודם חמישים. ומיתה האמורה בתורה דקאמר התם – היינו שמת עד ששים, דכתיב "במדבר הזה יתמו ושם ימותו" ולא נגזרה גזירה אלא על בני עשרים שימותו קודם ארבעים, וקרי לה מיתה. אבל זרעו, אומר ריב"א דאין בכרת אלא בהנהו דכתיב בהו ערירי. ואין נראה לר"ת, דהא בפרק "הבא על יבמתו" (יבמות דף נה.) קאמר: ערירי דכתב רחמנא גבי דודתו למה לי – לכדרבא כו'. ואי אין זרעו נכרת אלא דוקא בהנהו דכתיב ערירי, *מאי קבעי? והא דלא קאמר במועד קטן (דף כח. ושם): נהי דנפק מר מכרת דשני, מכרת דבני מי נפק מר – התם מיירי כשאין לו בנים קטנים. ודוקא קטנים נענשים בעון אביהם, ולא גדולים כדמשמע בפירקין (דף לג:). ומיהו, קשה: דבתורת כהנים ממעט אשת אח מן האם מכרת, מדכתיב: "אשת אחיו נדה היא" מה נדה יש לה היתר – אף אשת אח דיש לה היתר, דהיינו מן האב דשריא כשאין לה בנים. ובכולי התלמוד משמע דיש בה כרת כמו בשאר עריות, דהא מני לה גבי "חמש עשרה נשים פוטרות צרותיהן". ולפירוש ריב"א אתי שפיר, דמצינן למימר דממעט לה מערירי, ואין להאריך [וע"ע תוספות יבמות ג: ד"ה אשת]:

תתן

עין משפט נר מצוה

סא א ב מיי' פ"ב מהל' תרומות הי"ד ופ"א ה"א טוש"ע י"ד סימן שלא סי"ט בהג"ה:

*וע"כ אית ליה לרבא דיו"ט עשה ול"ת הוא דאי לא הוי אלא ל"ת גרידא אמאי מוקי קרא אמילתא דליכא ק"ו ולוקמא בנותר או בשאר דליכא ק"ו ומיהו אכולהו ק"ו איכא למיפרך שכן נוהגים בנשים כבאנשים תאמר במילה שאינה נוהגת כ"א באנשים ואיכא למימר עולת ראייה תוכיח לב"ה ביו"ט. וא"ת בפרק ר' אליעזר דמילה דבעי למילף מילה שלא בזמנה דלא דחי יו"ט לחזקיה מנותר ולאביי מעולת שבת והיכא בעי למילף הא במילה איכא ק"ו [ת"י]:

רבינו חננאל

לבדו יעשה לכם הוא ולא מכשירין לבדו ולא מילה שלא בזמנה דאתיא בק"ו ומה מילה שנכרתו עליה י"ג בריתות שלא בזמנה אין דוחה יום טוב קדשים שלא נכרתו עליהן ברית אינו דין שלא ידחו יו"ט שלא בזמנם כגון קדשים שעבר זמנן שנעשו נותר וטעונין שריפה: **תרומה** טמאה ביו"ט אסור לשורפה הא בחול מותר מנלן אמר רבא כשם שמצוה לשרוף קדשים הפסולים בחול כן מצוה לשרוף התרומה שנטמאת ואמרה תורה בשעת שרפתה תהנה ממנה שנאמר ואני נתתי לך את משמרת תרומותי בב' תרומות הכתוב מדבר אחת תרומה טהורה ואחת תרומה טמאה ואמר רחמנא בשתיהן נתתי לך שלך תהא להסקה תחת תבשילך להנות ממנה ור' יוחנן אמר מהכא לא בערתי ממנו בטמא (מן המעשר) ממנו אינו מבעיר בטמא אבל מבעיר בשמן תרומה שנטמאה: **ואקשינן** אמאי קא מרבית תרומה להנאה תרבה קודש שנטמא שמותר להנות ממנו ודחי' (קאי') ק"ו הוא ומה מעשר הקל (יום) [אם] נטמא אסור בהנא' קדש החמור לא כ"ש אי הכי תרומה נמי נימא ק"ו ותהיה אסורה בהנאה ודחי הא כתיב במעשר ממנו מכלל שיש אחד שמותר בהנאה כו' ומייתינן בק"ו הקדש שכן חומר מן התרומה כי הקדש יש בו חומרא שנעשה פיגול ונותר כי בשר הוא וקבוע לו זמן לאכילתו ואם עבר [הזמן] נעשה נותר והאוכל קודש וטומאתו עליו חייב כרת והנהנה מן הקדש מביא קרבן

רב נסים גאון

יו"ט מק"ו והיכי ראמי מה עצמות וגידים ונותר דפסח לא דחו ועולת חול לא דחיא יו"ט מילה שלא בזמנה לא כל שכן ושמעתי בה פירוש אחר בפנים אחרות והכין איתמר לבדו ולא מילה שלא בזמנה הבאה בק"ו הראה כי המילה שלא בזמנה ביו"ט הייתי סבור שהיא מותרת מק"ו והיה לי לומר (א"כ) [דמה] עשיית אוכל נפש שהוא רשות כגון שחיטה ובישול ואפיה פטריה רחמנא עשייתו ביו"ט מילה שלא בזמנה שהיא מצוה לא כל שכן שתעשה ביו"ט לפיכך הוצרך לבדו להודיענו כי אוכל נפש לבדו מותר לעשותו ביו"ט ולא מילה שלא בזמנה ונדחה מה שהייתי סבור מק"ו בזה המיעוט שמיעט

מסורת הש"ס / גליון הש"ס

[ביצה ח:]
תמורה לג:
בכורות לג. ע"ש יבמות עד. ע"ש
[יבמות שם. ולקמן סו.]
יבמות עג:
[פסחים כב.]

גליון הש"ס: תוס' ד"ה הא בחול וכו' וא"ת אכתי היכי יליף בק"ו. עיין זבחים קא ע"א תוס' ד"ה אמעשר: שם ד"ה כך אתה מצווה וכו' ומדרבנן אי נמי מדאורייתא מדאיקרי קדש. עיין פסחים פ"ב ע"ב תוס' ד"ה אבל נטמאת וצ"ע:

[במעשר שני פ"ה מ"י]
[ועי' תוספות פסחים כ: ד"ה ראוין]
[ביבמות וכו': ד"ה שכן וכו' כתבו בפסיקתות מחוסר כפורים לא חשיב משום דמהאי טעמא גופה נפקא לן וכו']
פ"ב דבכורים
אע"ג דהוקשו כל עריות זה לזה דילמא קרא אתא לאשוויינהו בי' כתובים הבאים כאחד. [ת"י]

עין משפט
נר מצוה

סב א מיי' פ"ה מהל' שבת הלכה א' סמג לאוין סה טוש"ע א"ח סי' רסג סעיף ב:
סג ב מיי' פ"ל מהל' שבת הלכה ב' סמג עשין ל טוש"ע א"ח סי' רס סעיף א:
סד ג מיי' פ"ג מהלכו' ציצית הלכה ז סמג עשין כו טוש"ע א"ח סי' יח סעיף ב:
סה ד מיי' פ"ה מהל' שבת הלכה י סמג לאוין סה טוש"ע א"ח סי' רסל סעיף ג:

ואין לה פדיון, ואסורה לזרים. הנך נפישן. ואיבעית אימא: קדש חמור, שכן ענוש כרת. *רב נחמן בר יצחק אמר: אמר קרא °"תתן לו", 'לו' ולא לאורו, מכלל דבת אורו הוא.§ "רבי ישמעאל אומר כו'".§ מאי טעמא? אמר (א)רבא: מתוך שריחו רע, גזרה שמא יניחנה ויצא. אמר ליה אביי: ויצא! אמר ליה, שאני אומר: אהדלקת נר בשבת – חובה, דאמר רב נחמן בר רב זבדא, ואמרי לה אמר רב נחמן בר רבא אמר רב: הדלקת נר בשבת – חובה, רחיצת ידים ורגלים בחמין ערבית – רשות, ואני אומר: במצוה. מאי מצוה? דאמר רב יהודה אמר רב: כך היה מנהגו של ר' יהודה בר אלעאי, ע"ש מביאים לו עריבה מלאה חמין, ורוחץ פניו ידיו ורגליו, ומתעטף ויושב בסדינין המצוייצין°, ודומה למלאך ה' צבאות, והיו תלמידיו מחבין ממנו כנפי כסותן, אמר להן: בני, לא כך שניתי לכם, *סדין בציצית, בית שמאי פוטרין וב"ה מחייבין. והלכה כדברי בית הלל! ואינהו גסברי – גזירה משום כסות לילה.§ °"ותזנח משלום נפשי נשיתי טובה". מאי "ותזנח משלום נפשי"? אמר ר' אבהו: זו הדלקת נר בשבת. "נשיתי טובה" – אמר רבי ירמיה: זו בית המרחץ(ב). (*אמר רבי יוחנן): זו רחיצת ידים ורגלים בחמין. ר' יצחק נפחא אמר: זו מטה נאה וכלים נאים שעליה. ר' אבא אמר: זו מטה מוצעת ואשה מקושטת לתלמידי חכמים.§ ת"ר: איזה עשיר? כל שיש לו נחת רוח בעשרו, דברי רבי מאיר.§ סימן מ"ט ק"ס.§ רבי טרפון אומר: כל שיש לו ק' כרמים ומאה שדות, וק' עבדים שעובדין בהן. רבי עקיבא אומר: כל שיש לו אשה נאה במעשים. רבי יוסי אומר: כל שיש לו בית הכסא סמוך לשולחנו. *תניא, רבי שמעון בן אלעזר אומר: דאין מדליקין בצרי. מאי טעמא? אמר רבה: מתוך שריחו נודף, גזרה שמא יסתפק ממנו. אמר ליה אביי: לימא

דברים יח | איכה ג | תורה אור

ואין לה פדיון. להוציאה לחולין. אבל קדש יש קדש שנפדה, כגון שהומם לפני שחיטה: ואסורה לזרים. לעולם. אבל קדש – יש קדש שמותר לזרים לאחר זריקה, כגון מעשר בהמה ותודה ושלמים: הנך נפישין. בשם: כרת. עדיפא, דאית בה תרי חומרי: ימיו נכרתין, והולך ערירי: ראשית דגנך תתן לו ולא לאורו. מכאן שאין תורמין מן הטמא על הטהור, דכתיב: "תתן לו", דבר הראוי לו לאכול, ולא לתת לאורו להסיק. ומדאיצטריך למעוטי – מכלל דבת אורו היא להסקה: ויצא. מאי איכפת לן? חובה. כבוד שבת הוא, שאין סעודה חשובה אלא במקום אור כעין יממא. בפרק בתרא דיומא (דף עה:): רחיצת ידים ורגלים. ערבית ליל שבת: בסדינין המצוייצין. סדינים של פשתן, ובהן ציצית של תכלת. כלאים, אלא שמותר מן התורה, דדרשינן סמוכין: "לא תלבש שעטנז" "גדילים תעשה לך" (מנחות פ"ד לט.): מחבין ממנו כנפי כסותן. שהיו להם סדינים שאינן מצוייצין: בית שמאי פוטרין. ואף על גב דציצית חובה הוא בכל טליתות שיש לו לאדם, ואפילו מונחים בקופסא – הני דפשתן פטורין, משום דכלאים לא שרא רחמנא. דלא דרשי סמוכין: וב"ה מחייבין. דדרשי סמוכין: ואינהו סברי. [תלמידיו] שהיו אוסרין, סבור: נהי דהלכה כב"ה וחייבין מדאורייתא, מיהו: [רבנן] גזור בהו משום כסות לילה. שמא יהא לו כסות שמיוחד ללילות, ויטיל בו ציצית, ונמצא לובש כלאים שלא במקום מצוה. דכסות לילה לא מיחייב בציצית, דכתיב: "וראיתם אותו". וביבמות *פרכינן: וכי ב"ד מתנין לעקור דבר מן התורה לפטור את החייב? ומשני: שב ואל תעשה שאני: הדלקת נר בשבת. שלא היה לו ממה להדליק. ובמקום שאין נר אין שלום, שהולך ונכשל(ג) והולך באפילה: איזהו עשיר. נפקא מיניה למטרח להדורי אמילתא: נחת רוח בעשרו. שמח בחלקו, אם מעט אם רב: שעובדין בהן. בשדות, עבודה הצריכה להם: שמא יסתפק ממנו. ותניא בתוספתא*: הנותן שמן לנר – חייב משום מבעיר, והמסתפק – חייב משום מכבה, במסכת ביצה בגמרא דיום טוב (דף כב.): שהוא

תתן לו ולא לאורו מכלל דבת אורו היא. ואם תאמר: מידי "ולא לאורו" כתיב? אימא: "תתן לו" – ולא דבר שאין ראוי לו כלל! וי"ל: דאם כן לא לכתוב אלא "תתן" – דאין נתינה פחות משוה פרוטה,° מדכתיב "לו" משמע: לו ולא לאורו:

הדלקת נר בשבת חובה. פי': במקום סעודה, דחובה היא שיסעוד במקום הנר משום עונג. אבל מהדלקת נר גופיה לא הוה פריך אביי, דפשיטא דחובה היא. דהתנן (לקמן דף לא:): על ג' עבירות נשים כו' על שאינן זהירות בהדלקת הנר: חובה. לגבי רחילת(ד) ידים בחמין קרי ליה חובה, דלא הוי כל כך מלוה. ומים אחרונים קרי ליה חובה – *משום סכנה דמלח סדומית, ושהרגו הנפש, ואמירי טפי מן הראשוני'. ויש שרולים לומר דאין לברך אהדלקת נר מדקרי ליה חובה, כדאמרינן (חולין קה.): מים אחרונים חובה, ואין טעונין ברכה. ואומר ר"ת: דשיבוש הוא, דלא דמי למים אחרונים – דלא הוי אלא להללה בעלמא, אבל הדלקת נר – היא חובה של מלות עונג שבת. וכמה חובו' הן דטעונין ברכה. ומה שאומר טעם אחר שלא לברך: משום שאם היתה מודלקת ועומדת לא היה לרי' לכבותה ולחזור ולהדליקה, ולא להדליק אחרת – אין נראה. דהא גבי כיסוי הדם (שם פז.), אם כסהו הרוח – פטור מלכסותו. אפ"ה: כשמכסה – לריך לברך. וכן נולד מהול, איכא למ"ד *דאין לריך להטיף ממנו דם ברית. וכשמל, תניא בשילהי פר' "ר' אליעזר דמילה" (לקמן דף קלז:): המל אומר כו'. ובסדר רב עמרם יש: המדליק נר בשבת מברך "אשר קדשנו כו'". ועוד נראה לר"ת: שאם היה הנר מודלק ועומד – שלריך לכבות ולחזור ולהדליק, כדאמר ליה ההוא סבא: ובלבד שלא יקדים ובלבד שלא יאחר (לעיל דף כג:):

מתוך שריחו רע. ואף על גב דנפט נמי ריחו רע, כדאמר בפ"ק (דף יב:): הא בדמשחא והא בדנפטא. ובפרק "אמר להם הממונה" (יומא דף לט.): בא למדוד נפט אומרים לו מדוד לעצמך – אין ריחו רע כמו עטרן:

סדין בציצית ב"ש פוטרין. פירש בקונטרס: ב"ש לא דרשי סמוכין. והא דלא קאמר "אוסרין" – משום דסברי בעלמא כלי קופסא חייבין בציצית, והכא פטירי – דלא שייך למיתני בהו אוסרין. ובסיפא דהך ברייתא קתני בפ' "התכלת" (מנחות דף מ.), א"ר אליעזר: כל המטיל תכלת בסדינו בירושלים אינו אלא מן המתמיהין. אמר ר': אם כן למה אסרוה. פי': *א"כ (כל אותן) שמתמיהין עליו, למה עושין כן? כיון דהלכה כב"ה. ומשני: גזרה שמא יקרע סדינו כו'. ועוד מתרץ: גזרה משום כסות לילה. ופירש"י בתשובה אחת: שלא גזרו אלא על התכלת, אבל במינו – חייב. והא דא"ל *מלאכא לרב קטינא: סדינא בקייטא, סרבלא בסיתוא – ציצית מה תהא עליה? היינו ציצית מן המובחר מה תהא עליה, אבל ציצית במינו היה עושה. ובשמעתין נמי – היה להם ציצית של מינו, והיו מתביישים מר' יהודה. לפי שהיה מחייב לעשות תכלת, והיה סבור שעושין כב"ש מדאורייתא, ואינהו סבור אפי' לב"ה אסור מדרבנן משום כסות לילה. וקשה לר"י: דבפרק "התכלת" (שם דף מא.) מהדר לאתויי דציצית חובת טלית הוא מחסידים הראשונים, משארגו בבגד ג' היו מטילין בו ציצית. ודחי לה, ואמאי לא מייתי מהכא דלא קתני אוסרין? ועוד, דבה"ג פוסק: דחובת גברא הוא, מדמברכינן "להתעטף בציצית". ועוד: דאמרינן בפ"ק דיבמות (ד' ד.) גבי כלאים בציצית, דאפילו מאן דלא דריש סמוכין בעלמא – במשנה תורה דריש, ואיך יתכן לומר דב"ש לא דרשי סמוכין? ועוד: דרב עמרם גאון פוסק כב"ש בששה דברים, וחשיב הך בהדייהו. ועוד: אמאי נקט סדין בציצית, הוה ליה למנקט כלאים בציצית! ונראה לר"ת: דכ"ע דרשי סמוכין. וב"ש פטרי מדרבנן משום כסות לילה, או משום שמא יקרע. ופטרי אפילו ממינו, מדקתני "סדין בציצית" ולא קתני סדין בתכלת. כדאמר ר' אליעזר בר' לדוק: "כל המטיל תכלת בסדינו" כו' וב"ה מחייבין – אפי' תכלת, דלית להו הנהו גזרות דב"ש. וכב"ש קי"ל, כדמוכח בסיפא דהך ברייתא. והשתא ניחא דרב קטינא שלא היה לו ציצית כלל, וכן תלמידיו של רבי יהודה לא היה להם כלל ציצית, דסברי כב"ש. ואומר ר"ת: דאין לעשות טליתות של פשתן ולעשות בו ציצית אפילו מינו, דכב"ש קיימא לן דפטרי, והמברך מברך ברכה לבטלה*: גזירה משום כסות לילה. מדנקט סתמא דתלמוד האי טעמא, ולא נקט טעמא שמא יקרע – משמע דקי"ל כרבי שמעון, דפוטר כסות לילה בפ' "התכלת" (מנחות ד' מג.). וכן משמע בפ"ב דברכות (דף יד:) דאמר: במערבא לא היו אומרים פרשת ציצית בלילה, אלא מתחילין "דבר אל בני ישראל". אמר אביי: כיון דאינהו מתחילין – אנן נמי מתחילין, וכיון דמתחילינן – מסיימינן. משמע דמודו כולהו דאין מלות ציצית בלילה, ולכך נשים פטורות מן הציצית. ורב יהודה ורב עמרם דהוו רמי תכלתא לפרזומא דאינשי ביתיה ב"התכלת" (ד' מג.) ובפרק קמא דסוכה (ד' יא. ושם) משום דסברי דהויא מלות עשה שלא הזמן גרמא – לא קיימא לן כוותייהו. דהא משמע שהם דווקא היו עושין, ולא האחרים. ובפרק קמא דקדושין (ד' לג:) תנו רבנן: מלות עשה שהזמן גרמא – שופר ולולב סוכה וציצית: ולימא

רבינו חננאל

מעילה והוא קרבן לפיכך אסור לאונן משא"כ בתרומה כי לא תמצא מאלו כולן בתרומ' אע"פ שהתרומה יש בה מיתה שנאמר ומתו בו כי יחללוהו והנהנה ממנה משלם אותה וחומשה ואין לה פדיון ואסורה לזרים מה שאין כן בקודש כי השלמים מותרין לישראל שאין זרים ואם נפסלו*) יש להן פדיון אפ"ה חומרות דקודש נפישי: אמרו משמיה דרב הדלקת נר בשבת (חנוכה) [חובה] וכן אמר רבא הדלקת נר בשבת (חנוכה) [חובה] **) ורב חנן אמר אפילו רחיצת ידים ורגלים בחמין חובה ממנהג של רבי אלעזר וי"א רחיצת ידים ורגלים בחמין מצוה: סדין בציצית ב"ש פוטרין וב"ה מחייבין והלכה כב"ה: ותזנח משלום נפשי זו הדלקת הנר נשיתי טובה זו בית המרחץ רבי יוחנן אמר רחיצת ידים ורגלים

*) ר"ל אם נפסלו ע"י מום קודם שחיטה וכ"ה בפירש"י.
**) נ"ל דכן צ"ל רב חנן משמיה דרב אמר רחילת ידים ורגלים בחמין ערבית רשות ואני אומר מלוה ממנהג של ר"י בר אלעאי.

רב נסים גאון

שמיעט בו הכתוב דהיינו לבדו ולולי הוא היה עולה על דעתנו כי מילה שלא בזמנה ביום טוב מותרת מקל וחומר: אינהו סבור גזירה משום כסות לילה. עיקר דילה במס' מנחות בפ' התכלת (דף מ) דתנו רבנן סדין בציצית בית שמאי פוטרין ובית הלל מחייבין והלכה כב"ה וכו' רב זירא אמר גזירה משום כסות לילה:

הגהות הב"ח

(א) גמ' אמר רבה מתוך שריחו: (ב) שם זו בית המרחץ רבי יוחנן זו רחיצה: (ג) רש"י ד"ה הדלקת וכו' ונכשל (והולך) תא"מ ונ"ב ס"א והולך: (ד) תו' ד"ה חובה לגבי רחיצת ידים ורגלים בחמין דלא הוי (אב) כל כך מצוה קרי ליה חובה ומים אחרונים:

א"כ כיון דהל' כב"ה למה עושין כן שמתמיהין עליו כל"ל מהרש"א וכת"ה א"י א"כ שמתמיהין עליו למה אסרן כיון דהלכה כב"ה:

מסורת הש"ס: פסחים לג. | [חולין קה:] | מנחות מ. עדיות פ"ד [מ"י] | [נ"ל ר' יוחנן אמר] | [לקמן קלו.] | [דף ל:] | [תוספתא פ"ב] | [פי"ב] | [שם מא.] | [ועי' תוספות יבמות ל: ד"ה כולהו ותוס' מנחות מ. ד"ה סדין]

גליון הש"ס גמרא ודומה למלאך ה' צבאות. עיין קדושין דף עב ע"א ברש"י ד"ה דומים למלאכי השרת: רש"י ד"ה כרת עדיפא דאית בה תרי וכו'. עיין בהרע"ב ספ"ט דסנהדרין: תוס' ד"ה תתן לו וכו' דאין נתינה פחות משוה פרוטה. עיין גיטין דף כ ע"א תוספות ד"ה דלמא:

לימא מר: "מפני שהוא עף"! חדא ועוד קאמר, חדא – מפני שהוא עף, ועוד: גזירה שמא יסתפק ממנו. ההיא חמתא דהות סניאה לה לכלתה, אמרה לה: זיל איקשיט במשחא דאפרסמא. אזלא איקשיט. כי אתת, אמרה לה: זיל איתלי שרגא! אזלא אתלא שרגא, אינפח בה נורא ואכלתה.§ °"ומדלת הארץ השאיר נבוזראדן רב טבחים לכורמים וליוגבים". 'כורמים' תני רב יוסף: אלו מלקטי אפרסמון מעין גדי ועד רמתא. 'יוגבים' – אלו צידי חלזון, מסולמות של צור ועד חיפה.§ ת"ר: [א]אין מדליקין בטבל טמא בחול, ואצ"ל בשבת. כיוצא בו: [ב]אין מדליקין בנפט לבן בחול, ואצ"ל בשבת. בשלמא נפט לבן – מפני שהוא עף, אבל טבל טמא, מאי טעמא? אמר קרא: °"ואני הנה נתתי לך את משמרת תרומתי" *בשתי תרומות הכתוב מדבר, אחת תרומה טהורה ואחת תרומה טמאה. מה תרומה טהורה – אין לך בה אלא משעת הרמה ואילך, אף תרומה טמאה – אין לך בה אלא משעת הרמה ואילך.§ גופא, ר"ש בן אלעזר אומר: אין מדליקין בצרי. וכן היה רבי שמעון בן אלעזר אומר: *צרי אינו אלא שרף מעצי הקטף. *ר' ישמעאל אומר: כל היוצא מן העץ אין מדליקין בו. ר' ישמעאל בן ברוקה אומר: אין מדליקין אלא ביוצא מן הפרי. ר' טרפון אומר: אין מדליקין אלא בשמן זית בלבד. עמד רבי יוחנן בן נורי על רגליו ואמר: מה יעשו אנשי בבל שאין להם אלא שמן שומשמין, ומה יעשו אנשי מדי שאין להם אלא שמן אגוזים, ומה יעשו אנשי אלכסנדריא שאין להם אלא שמן צנונות, ומה יעשו אנשי קפוטקיא שאין להם לא כך ולא כך אלא נפט? אלא: [ג]אין לך אלא מה שאמרו חכמים אין מדליקין. ומדליקין בשמן דגים ובעטרן, רבי שמעון שזורי אומר: מדליקין בשמן פקועות ובנפט, סומכוס אומר: כל היוצא מן הבשר אין מדליקין בו, אלא בשמן דגים. סומכוס היינו ת"ק! איכא ביניהו דרב ברונא אמר רב, ולא מסיימי. *תניא, רבי שמעון בן אלעזר אומר: [ד]כל היוצא מן העץ אין בו משום שלש על שלש, ומסככין בו, חוץ מפשתן. אמר אביי: ר'

רש"י

שהוא עף. ונדבק בכותלי הבית ומדליק את הבית: חמתא. חמותה: איתלי שרגא. הדלק את הנר: עד רמתא. שם מקום: לכורמים. לשון מקפים, כמו "כורמים עליו את הכלים" לקמן בפרק "רבי עקיבא" (דף פח:): וליוגבים. לשון יקבים, שעוצרין ופוצעין את החלזון להוציא דמו, כדאמרן בפרק "כלל גדול" לקמן (דף עה.). והכניס נבוזראדן ללבושי המלך: סולמא דצור. מעלה הר, וקורה המסילה וגבוהה, וקורין אותה פוייאי"ה: אין מדליקין בטבל טמא. וכ"ש בטהור, ולקמיה מפרש טעמא: מה תרומה טהורה. שהיא לאכילה אין לך בה אלא משעת הרמה ואילך, ומוקמי הכי אסירא, שהרי טבל במיתה לאוכלה. אף תרומה טמאה, אע"פ שאין אתה אוכלה אלא מסיקה – אסור להסיקו בטבלו: אין מדליקין בצרי. כדמפרש לעיל. ועוד, כדקתני ואזיל, דאינו בא מן הפרי אלא מן העץ שרף בעלמא, והוה ליה כזפת ואינו נמשך. לישנא אחרינא: וכן היה רבי שמעון בן אלעזר אומר כו', לאו טעמא למילתיה יהיב, אלא הכי קאמר: ועוד היה אומר דבר אחר בצרי: עצי הקטף. כך שמם: מן הפרי. לאפוקי שמן דגים ועטרן וצרי: אין לך אלא מה שאמרו חכמים אין מדליקין בהן. כגון פסולי שמנים דמתניתין: ומדליקין בשמן דגים. ואע"ג דדמי לחלב ואינו יוצא מפרי: ובעטרן. ואע"ג דמזופת קאתי: סומכוס היינו ת"ק. רבי יוחנן בן נורי דפסיל כל הנך דמתניתין, וחלב אימני בהדייהו דהוא יוצא מן הבשר, ואכשר בשמן דגים: איכא ביניהו דרב ברונא. דאמר: צריך לתת לתוכו שמן כל שהוא. אי נמי: דאכשר חלב מהותך בתערובת שמן כל שהוא. חד מהנך תנאי סבר לדרב ברונא דחלב ניתר בתערובת, אבל שמן דגים – אפילו בעיניה, וחד סבר שמן דגים על ידי תערובת, אבל חלב כלל וכלל לא: אין בו משום שלש על שלש. לקבל טומאה בג' אצבעות: יוצא מן העץ. כמו קנבוס וצמר גפן: ומסככים בו. סוכה, הואיל ואינו מקבל טומאה. דאין מסככין בדבר המקבל טומאה, כדילפינן במס' סוכה (דף יב:) "מגרנך ומיקבך": חוץ מפשתן. דילפינן לקמן דאיקרי עץ, ומקבל טומאת נגעים אפילו אוגין שבו, כדלקמן. הלכך אין מסככין באוגין: – ר'

תוספות

ולימא מר מפני שהוא עף. ויהא בהול על ממונו, ויבא לכבות. תימה: דה"ל למימר אפילו בחול נמי ליתסר. כדאמר לקמן דאין מדליקין בנפט לבן אפילו בחול, מפני שהוא עף:

חדא ועוד קאמר. וקשה לר"י, דתניא בסמוך: "הצרי אינו אלא שרף מעצי הקטף" משמע דהטעם לפי שאינו נמשך אחר הפתילה, ומה הוצרך לבדות הטעם מדעתו:

אין מדליקין בטבל טמא. פירש בקונטרס: וכ"ש בטבל טהור. ואין נראה, דלא הוי כ"ש. דמהיכא תיתי? אלא ה"ה בטבל טהור, דילפינן טבל טהור מטבל טמא: מה טבל טמא אין לך בו שום הנאה של כילוי אלא מהרמה ואילך, אף טבל טהור כן. אבל הנאה שאינה של כילוי – שרי, דלא מצינו בשום מקום שיהא טבל אסור בהנאה. ומהכא נמי ילפינן, כהן ששכר פרה מישראל לא יאכילנה כרשיני תרומה (יבמות פ"ז דף סו:), דהנאה של כילוי אסורה לזרים – אבל שאר הנאות שרי. דתנן בפרק "בכל מערבין" (עירובין דף כו:): דמערבין לישראל בתרומה*:

רבי ישמעאל אומר כל היוצא מן העץ אין מדליקין בו. הא דלא קתני אלא פשתן כדקתני במתני' – משום דמתניתין איירי בפסול פתילות, והכא איירי בפסול שמנים. קשה לרשב"א: דרבי ישמעאל דתני במתני' דאין מדליקין בעטרן מפני כבוד השבת – משמע שנמשך אחר הפתילה יפה, אלא דגזרינן שמא יניחנו וילא, כדמפרש לעיל. והכא משמע כל היוצא מן העץ אינו נמשך אחר הפתילה, ועטרן יוצא מן העץ הוא – דהוא פסולתא דזיפתא, כדאמר לעיל:

רבי שמעון שזורי אומר מדליקין בשמן פקועות ובנפט. *קשה לרשב"א: מה בא לומר רבי שמעון שזורי, דהא לרבי יוחנן בן נורי נמי מדליקין בהן, מדקאמר: אין לך אלא מה שאמרו חכמים "אין מדליקין" משמע דוקא הנהו, אבל שמן פקועות ונפט מכשיר. ועוד: דנפט מכשיר בהדיא רבי יוחנן. ואין לומר דרבי שמעון שזורי איירי בנפט לבן, דהא אפי' בחול אמר לעיל: אין מדליקין בו. ואי גרסינן "אין מדליקין" במילתיה דרבי שמעון שזורי – אתי שפיר:

איכא בינייהו דרב ברונא. פירש בקונטרס: דחד מינייהו סבר דחלב מהותך שרי בתערובות, אבל שמן דגים אפילו בעיניה. וחד סבר: שמן דגים בתערובות, אבל חלב כלל וכלל לא. והשתא תרווייהו לא סברי בכולה מילתא כרב ברונא. ולא משמע הכי, ובקונטרס דחק לפי שפירש במתניתין דשמן דגים היינו קרבי דגים שנימוחו. ונראה לר"ת: דשמן דגים היינו שמן שבא מעינו של דג, כדאמר ב"המוכר את הספינה" (ב"ב דף עג:): נגדו מגלגלתא דעינא תלת מאה גרבי מישחא. ובשמן דגים מודה רב ברונא דשרי בעיניה. והשתא, חד מינייהו סבר לגמרי כרב ברונא:

ולא מסיימי. ולא שייך הכא תנא בתרא לטפויי אתא. *דמוכח קצת דת"ק להחמיר, מדקאמר: אין לך אלא מה כו' ומדליקין בשמן דגים ובעטרן, משמע דווקא הנך מדנחת לפרושי, ולא פי' נמי דרב ברונא:

אין בו משום שלש על שלש ומסככין בו חוץ מפשתן. קשה לריב"א: דמשמע דפחות משלש על שלש – מסככין, אפי' בשל פשתן. ובפ"ק דסוכה (דף טז.) אמרינן: סיככה במטלניות שאין בהן שלש על שלש – פסולה! ותירץ דהתם איירי דבאות מבגד גדול, שכבר היו ראויות לקבל טומאה. אבל הכא מיירי בהנהו שלא היה בהם מעולם שלש על שלש. וקשה לרשב"א: דאפי' אם לא נארג בו מעולם שלש על שלש מקבל טומאה, כדאמר בפרק "במה אשה" (לקמן דף סג:): אריג כל שהוא – טמא, ואין מסככין בו. וי"ל: דהתם מיירי כשאין בדעתו לארוג בו יותר, והכא מיירי כשיש בדעתו לארוג בו יותר. הלכך – אם אין בו שלש על שלש – טהור:

עין משפט נר מצוה

סו א מיי׳ פ״ו מהלכות מעשר הל׳ ב טוש״ע י״ד סי׳ שלא סעיף קטז:

סז ב מיי׳ פ״ה מהל׳ שבת הלכה י:

סח ג ד מיי׳ שם הלכה יא ופכ״ב מהלכות כלים הלכ׳ א סמג לאוין סה טוש״ע א״ח סי׳ רסד סעיף ו:

מסורת הש"ס / תורה אור

ירמיהו נב | במדבר יח | [לעיל כה. וש״נ] | [כריתות ו.] | תוספתא פ״ב | תוספתא שם

[וע״ע תוס׳ מנחות סז: ד״ה כדי שתהא ותוספ׳ פסחי׳ לג. ד״ה מתחמין לו]

[לפני מ״ש תוס׳ בחולין עה: ד״ה אנא כי האי ס״ל כו׳ דר״ש שזורי דוקא קאמר ולא בא להוסיף אלא רק בהנך דקחשיב בלחוד מכשיר ע״ש אין מקום לקושית הרשב״א ודע עוד התם בחולין הביאו תוס׳ במלתא דר״ש שזורי בעטרן ובנפט]

[עי׳ תוס׳ לעיל כד: ד״ה איכא בינייהו וכו׳]

רב נסים גאון

איכא בינייהו דרב ברונא אמר רב ולא מסיימי. [והוא] שמעתתא דאיתמרא בפירקא (דף כג) חלב מהותך וקירבי דגים שנימוחו:

רבינו חננאל

בחמין: ת"ר אין מדליקין בטבל טמא בחול. ואין צ"ל בשבת מ"ט (בתרומה) [בב' תרומות הכתוב מדבר] מה תרומה טהורה אין לך בה אלא משעת הרמה ואילך אף תרומה טמאה אין לך בה אלא משעת הרמה. תניא אין מדליקין בעטרן מפני שריחו רע שמא יניח הנר ויצא. אין מדליקין בצרי מפני שריחו נודף שמא יסתפק ממנו. ועוד מפני שהוא עף. רבי [טרפון] אומר אין מדליקין אלא בשמן זית בלבד. א"ר יוחנן בן נורי מה יעשו אנשי בבל שאין להם אלא שמן שומשמין. מה יעשו אנשי מדי שאין להם אלא שמן אגוזים. ואנשי אלכסנדריא שאין להם אלא שמן צנונות. אין לך אלא השמנים שאמרו חכמים אין מדליקין בהן וכן הלכה. רבי שמעון בן אלעזר אומר כל היוצא מן העץ אין בו משום שלש על שלש. ומסככין בו חוץ מן הפשתן שבגד פשתן מקבל טומאה אפילו אין בו אלא שלש על שלש אצבעות ואין מסככין בו. ואתא אביי למימר כי רבי

עין משפט
נר מצוה

סט א מיי' פי"ב מהל' טומאת צרעת הל' י ופכ"ב מהל' כלים הל' יב:
ע ב מיי' פי"ג שם הל' א סמג עשין רלת:

מסורת הש"ס

ר' שמעון בן אלעזר ותנא דבי ר' ישמעאל אמרו דבר אחד. ר' שמעון בן אלעזר – הא דאמרן, תנא דבי ר' ישמעאל מאי היא – *דתני דבי ר' ישמעאל: הואיל ונאמרו בגדים בתורה סתם, ופרט לך הכתוב באחד מהן "צמר ופשתים", מה להלן – צמר ופשתים, אף כל – צמר ופשתים. רבא אמר: שלשה על שלשה בשאר בגדים איכא בינייהו, *דר' שמעון בן אלעזר אית ליה, לתנא דבי ר' ישמעאל – לית ליה. דכולי עלמא מיהת שלש על שלש בצמר ופשתים מיטמא בנגעים, מנלן? דתניא: 'בגד' אין לי אלא בגד, אשלש על שלש מנין? ת"ל: °'והבגד'. ואימא לרבות שלשה על שלשה! ויקרא יג
לאו ק"ו הוא? השתא שתי וערב מיטמא, שלשה על שלשה מיבעיא! אי הכי, שלש על שלש נמי ליתי בק"ו! אלא: שלשה על שלשה דחזו בין לעניים בין לעשירים – אתי בק"ו, שלש על שלש – לעניים הוא דחזיין, לעשירים לא חזיין, לא אתי בק"ו. טעמא דכתביה קרא, הא לא כתביה קרא – לא גמרינן בק"ו, ואימא: לרבות שלשה על שלשה בשאר בגדים! אמר קרא: °"בגד צמר ופשתים", שם
בבגד צמר ופשתים – אין, מידי אחריני – לא. ואימא: כי אימעוט – משלש על שלש, אבל שלשה על שלשה – מיטמא! (א) תרי מיעוטי כתיבי: °"בגד צמר או [בבגד] פשתים", חד – למעוטי משלש על שלש, וחד – למעוטי משלשה על שלשה, ולרבא, דאמר: שלשה על שלשה בשאר בגדים איכא בינייהו, לרשב"א – אית ליה, לתנא דבי רבי ישמעאל – לית ליה, שלשה על שלשה בשאר בגדים שם
מנא

תורה אור

ר' שמעון בן אלעזר ותנא דבי ר' ישמעאל אמרו דבר אחד. דמהיכא תיתי לר' שמעון למעוטי שאר בגדים מטומאה אי לאו דאית ליה הא דתנא דבי ר' ישמעאל. והלכך: יוצא מן העץ לאו דווקא נקט, דה"ה לנוצה של עזים, וכל מידי דלאו צמר ופשתים הוא. ואיידי דנקט יוצא מן העץ לענין סוכה, נקט לה נמי לענין טומאה: הואיל ונאמרו בגדים בתורה סתם. כגון בטומאת שרצים וטומאת מת, דכתיב בטומאת שרצים "או בגד או עור", ובמת "וכל בגד וכל כלי עור", וכן בשכבת זרע "וכל בגד וכל עור אשר יהיה עליו שכבת זרע" וגו', ובציצית "על כנפי בגדיהם": ופרט לך הכתוב באחד מהן. בטומאת נגעים, כלל תחלה ואח"כ פרט: "והבגד כי יהיה בו נגע צרעת" – כלל, "בבגד צמר" כו' – פרט. אף כל בגדים הסתומים ילפי' ב"מה מצינו", דהוא בנין אב, דאינו אלא צמר ופשתים: שלשה. טפחים: לר' שמעון אית ליה. דבהדיא תנא: אין בו משום שלש על שלש. אבל שלשה על שלשה דחזי אף לעשירים – מיטמא. ולקמן יליף מנליה בהו טומאה כלל, הואיל ומנגעים יליף. דאי לא יליף מנגעים – מהיכא תיתי ליה לחלק בין פשתן לשאר מינין? דכולי עלמא. בין לאביי בין לרבא, אליבא דהני תנאי: בגד אין לי כו'. כלומר: אי הוה כתיב בנגעים 'בגד', אין לי דמיטמא בנגעים אלא בגד שלם: לעשירים לא חזיין. אין מקפידין להצניע, ובטולי מבטלי להו – לא אתיין בק"ו: וטעמא דכתביה קרא כו'. מסקנא דפירושה דמילתא היא, ובניחותא, כלומר: הלכך טעמא דכתב קרא "והבגד" – לרבויינהו, הלכך מיטמו. הא לא רבינהו – לא מיטמו: ואימא לרבות שלשה על שלשה בשאר בגדים. ושלש על שלש בצמר ופשתים מיטמו מק"ו. והאי רבויא לשלשה על שלשה אתא, ולשאר בגדים: אמר קרא בבגד צמר. פרט אחר כלל, למימר דאפי' גדול דשאר מינין לא מיטמו בנגעים: ואימא כי אמעיט. שאר בגדים משלש על שלש, דבצמר ופשתים אתי בק"ו משתי וערב, אבל שלשה על שלשה – מיטמו מריבויא ד'והבגד': תרי מיעוטי כתיבי. תרי זימני כתיבי: "בגד צמר ופשתים", "זאת תורת נגע הצרעת, בגד הצמר או הפשתים": מנא ליה. לרבי שמעון שום טומאה בשאר בגדים, הואיל ושאר בגדים הסתומים למדין הן מן המפורש:
מאי

רבי שמעון בן אלעזר ותנא דבי ר' ישמעאל אמרו דבר אחד. וא"ת: כיון דבשאר בגדים אפי' שלשה על שלשה טהור לר' שמעון בן אלעזר, אמאי נקט שלש על שלש? ותירץ הרב פורת: דנקט שלש על שלש משום פשתן, דאפי' שלש על שלש טמא. ואע"ג דאמר לקמן (דף כט:): ר"ש בן אלעזר וסומכוס אמרו דבר אחד, דאמר סומכוס: סיככה בטווי – פסולה. משמע דהא דקאמר הכא חוץ מפשתן, היינו טווי ולא בגד! וי"ל: דעיקר מילתיה איירי בבגדי פשתן. ומ"מ דייק לקמן מדלא קאמר "חוץ מבגד פשתן" דבטווי נמי איירי. וא"ת: מאי דוחקיה דאביי לאוקמה דתנא שלש על שלש משום פשתן, ולימא דדוקא נקט, כמו שאמר רבא. ואי משום דלא ליפלוג ר"ש בן אלעזר אתנא דבי ר' ישמעאל – הא אביי גופיה קאמר לקמן דהאי תנא דבי ר' ישמעאל מפיק מאידך תנא דבי ר' ישמעאל! וי"ל: דסבירא ליה לאביי הא דמרבה לקמן תנא דבי ר' ישמעאל שאר בגדים – היינו אפי' שלש על שלש, וסבר דשאר בגדים או יהיה בהן טומאה כמו בצמר ופשתים, או יהיו טהורים לגמרי:

השתא שתי וערב מיטמא. תימה לר"י: דילמא הא דתנן בפי"א דנגעים (משנה ח): "כמה יהא בפקיע ויטמא – כדי לארוג בו שלש על שלש", היינו בתר דקיי"ל באריג דמיטמא בשלש על שלש – אבל כל כמה דלא ידעינן באריג – גם שתי וערב לא יטמא אלא כשיהיה כדי לארוג בו הרבה. וא"כ, היכי אתי שלשה על שלשה בק"ו דשתי וערב? ותירץ ר"י: דנראה לו להתלמוד סברא דאריג שלשה על שלשה עדיף משתי וערב, אפי' כדי לארוג בו אלף על אלף. ולרשב"א נראה: דודאי בבגד שייך לחלק בשיעורו, משום דכתב רחמנא "בגד" דמשמע בגד שלם. אבל שתי וערב – השיעור תלוי בסברא, והיינו שלש על שלש דחזי אפילו לעשירים, דהא חזי לאיצטרופי לבגד גדול: *אתי בק"ו. מפרש הרב פורת: דהאי ק"ו לא נקט אלא להרווחא דמילתא, ובלאו ק"ו נמי אין צריך ריבוי לשלשה על שלשה, דכיון דחזו לעניים ולעשירים בגד חשוב הוא. דמה לי שלשה על שלשה, ומה לי ד' או ה' אמות, כיון שגם זה ראוי כמו זה. וכן מוכח מדברי רבא דאמר: שלשה על שלשה בשאר בגדים מ"או בגד". ומנא ליה, דילמא איצטריך קרא לבגד שלם? אלמא משמע: דאין חילוק בין בגד שלם לשלשה על שלשה. וכן אביי דמוקי "או בגד" לשלש על שלש בצמר ופשתים דמיטמא בשרצים, ולא מוקי לשלשה על שלשה – משום דשלשה על שלשה הוי בכלל בגד, ולא צריך ריבוי. וכן משמע ממאי דפריך: ואימא כי אימעוט משלש על שלש, ושם אפרש. ויש ליישב: דאיצטריך ק"ו, דאי לאו ק"ו ה"א: "בגד" משמע בגד שלם, אבל השתא דאיכא ק"ו – גלי לן דבכל מקום דכתיב "בגד" הוי שלשה על שלשה:

ואימא לרבות שלשה על שלשה בשאר בגדים. פי' בקונטרס: אבל שלש על שלש בצמר ופשתים – אתי בק"ו. ולא נהירא, דהא אמרן: כיון דלא חזי לעניים ולעשירים לא אתי בק"ו. ונראה לפרש(ב) דהכי פריך: ואימא לרבות שלשה על שלשה. פי': שנרבה שלשה על שלשה בשאר בגדים, דהא ליכא מיעוטא למעוטינהו. וצמר ופשתים – אתי למעוטי שאר בגדים משלש על שלש. דאי לאו צמר ופשתים הוה מרבינן בכל בגדים מ"והבגד" שלש על שלש, כיון דקרא סתמא כתיב. ומשני: "צמר ופשתים" כתיב. והמתרץ לא הבין קושייתו, והיה סבור שהמקשה לא ידע דצמר ופשתים כתיב, ולהכי הדר פריך: אימא כי אימעוט משלש על שלש, היינו קושיא ראשונה אלא שמפרש היטב:

ואימא כי אימעוט משלש על שלש. מכאן נמי משמע כפי' הרב פורת, דשלשה על שלשה הוי בכלל בגד, וק"ו להרווחא דמילתא נקט. דאי שלשה על שלשה לא שמעי' מבגד אלא מק"ו – א"כ מאי פריך: כי אימעוט משלש על שלש. מה צריך מיעוט, מהיכא תיתי לרבות שלש על שלש בשאר בגדים? דריבויא ד"והבגד" – בצמר ופשתים מוקמית לה, אפי' בשלש על שלש. דשלשה על שלשה לא איצטריך בצמר ופשתים, דהא מק"ו דשתי וערב אתי. אבל בשאר בגדים דלא אתי בק"ו, דהא בשתי וערב בהדיא כתיב: "צמר ופשתים" – איצטריך ריבוי מ"והבגד" *לשלש על שלש. ומיהו, שמא המקשה סבר דיש לרבות בשאר בגדים שלש על שלש כמו בצמר ופשתים, כיון דקרא סתמא כתיב, וחד ריבוי לכולהו:

תרי מיעוטי כתיבי. ואם תאמר: לשתוק מריבויא ד"והבגד" וע"כ שלש על שלש טמא בצמר ופשתים, דאי לאו הכי – תרי מיעוטי למה לי? וי"ל: *דאי לאו ריבויא ד"והבגד" הוה מוקמינן תרי מיעוטי – לרבות שלשה על שלשה בשאר בגדים, דאין מיעוט אחר מיעוט אלא לרבות. (ולפי מהסס, דהיאך נאמר דאין מיעוט אחר מיעוט אלא לרבות שלשה על שלשה בשאר בגדים? ויותר נראה לומר: כיון דאיכא לאוקמי שפיר תרי מיעוטי, ליכא למימר דאתי לרבות) [ת"י]. ושלש על שלש בצמר ופשתים ה"א דטהור. אבל השתא דכתיב ריבוי ד"והבגד" ע"כ הנך תרי מיעוטי אתי למעוטי, ולאו לרבות. דאי לרבות מ"והבגד" וחד מיעוט הוה ידעינן שלשה על שלשה בשאר בגדים, כדפרישית לעיל. וא"ת: אכתי לשתוק מריבויא ד"והבגד" וחד מיעוטא, ולא ניכתב אלא חד "צמר ופשתים" ואנא ידענא דשאר בגדים דלא יטמאו בנגעים, דמהיכא תיתי? וידעינן נמי דצמר ופשתים מיטמו בשלש על שלש, דאי לאו הכי – אמאי כתב רחמנא טומאה כלל בבגד צמר ופשתים? דשלשה על שלשה שמעינן מק"ו דשתי וערב, אלא ודאי לשלש על שלש אתיא. וי"ל: דהשתא דגלי לן קרא דשייכי טומאה דנגעים בבגדים – ילפינן השיעור שפיר בק"ו דשתי וערב. אבל אי לאו איכתיב טומאת בגדים לא הוה ילפינן מק"ו דשייך טומאה בבגד, וה"א: דאין שייך נגע אלא בשתי וערב, אבל בבגד לא שייך נגע, דשמא לא יבא בו נגע כלל:
נפקא

רבינו חננאל

רבי שמעון בן אלעזר כתנא דבי ר' ישמעאל תני הא מתניתא דיליה ודחי רבא ואמר שלשה על שלשה טפחים בשאר בגדים זולתי בגדי פשתן איכא בינייהו. ר' שמעון בן אלעזר לא מיעט שאר בגדים אלא משלשה על שלשה. אבל ג' על ג' טפחים אפילו דשאר בגדים מקבלי טומאה ותנא דבי רבי ישמעאל סבר לא איקרי בגד אלא צמר ופשתים. ובגדים אחרים שעושין משאר עצים לאו בגדים נינהו ולא מיטמא ג' על ג' ולא שלשה על שלשה. ושקלינן וטרינן

יבמות ד: מנחות לט:

בנ"י לד

(א) תרי מיעוטי כתיבי בגד צמר ופשתים כו"ל ובת"י כתבו על זה גם זה משמע כפי' הר"פ פורת דאי שלשה על שלשה אינו בכלל בגד נוקי תרי מיעוטי חדא לשלש על שלש וחדא לשלשה על שלשה ואיכא בגד שלם בשאר בגדים דלא מטמא בנגעים מנא ליה אלא משמע כפי' ואין זה הוכחה דבמיעוט א' נמתעט גם משלשה על שלשה דשלש על שלש ושלשה על שלשה שניהם איתרבו לשאר בגדים מריבוי אחד מוהבגד אבל מ"מ קצת יש להוכיח מדלא קאמר כי אימעוט מג' על ג' ומשלשה על שלשה דמחד ריבוי נפקא תרוייהו אבל בגד שלם מטמא [ת"י]:

כ"ה גירסת הרש"ל שזהו דיבור בפ"ע וגרים לעיל דאריג שלש על שלש עדיף אבל בת"י גרים לעיל דאריג שלשה על שלשה כו' והך מפ' הרב פורת שייך לדיבור א' עם דלעיל וקאי אק"ו דשלשה על שלשה

(ב) אבל אין לפרש ואימא לרבות מוהבגד שלשה על שלשה בשאר בגדים ולא שלש על שלש בצמר ופשתים דהא מדאיצטריך ריבוי לשאר בגדים ידע דצמר ופשתים כתיב ועוד דבקושיא שניה ידע דצמר ופשתים כתיב ועוד דבקושיא שניה ידע דצמר ופשתים כתיב א"כ מה פריך כיון דצמר ופשתים כתיב טפי הוי לן לאוקמי ריבוי לג' על ג' בצמר ופשתים ממה שנרבה שלשה על שלשה בשאר בגדים כמו בצמר ופשתים דהא רבוי צמר ופשתים נכתב בחנם כדאמר לקמן קאי בצמר ופשתים מרבה שאר בגדים ועוד מה פריך אימא כי אימעוט מג' על ג' אבל שלשה על שלשה מטמא מנ"ל כיון דאיצטריך ריבוי לג' על ג' בצמר ופשתים וי"ל ואימא לרבות נמי שלשה על שלשה בשאר בגדים וזהו כפי' המפורש בפנים [ת"י]:

[נ"א לשלשה על שלשה]

מצאתי בשם ה"ר שלמה אשטרוביצ"ג ז"ל ק"ל א"כ יהיו שוין כל הבגדים ולמה כתב ד' תיבות הללו בגד צמר בגד פשתים אלא י"ל אי לא יתורא דוהבגד ה"א אין מיעוט אחר מיעוט אלא לרבות שלש על שלש בצמר ופשתים וממילא נרבה שלש על שלש בשאר בגדים דסברא הוא שיהא שוין אם אין מיעוט כדפיר' לעיל וכך מועיל יתור של שני מיעוטים כמו והבגד אבל השתא דכתיב ריבוי דוהבגד לרבות ג' על ג' בצמר ופשתים אם כן אתי תרי מיעוטי למעט ולמעוטי זה וזה משאר בגדים דאי לרבות ליסתוק מרבוי דוהבגד [ת"י]:

מנא ליה? נפקא °מ'או בגד', דתניא: 'בגד' – אין לי אלא בגד, אשלשה על שלשה בשאר בגדים מנין? ת"ל: 'או בגד' ואביי, האי 'או בגד' מאי עביד ליה? מיבעי ליה לרבות שלש על שלש בצמר ופשתים דמטמא בשרצים. ורבא: גלי רחמנא גבי נגעים, והוא הדין לשרצים. ואביי: איכא למיפרך; מה לנגעים – שכן שתי וערב מטמא בהם. ואידך: אי ס"ד נגעים חמירי, לכתוב רחמנא גבי שרצים – וליתו נגעים מינייהו. ואידך: נגעים משרצים לא אתו, דאיכא למיפרך: מה לשרצים שכן מטמא בכעדשה. *אמר אביי: האי תנא דבי רבי ישמעאל מפיק מאידך תנא דבי ר' ישמעאל. דתני דבי רבי ישמעאל: 'בגד' אין לי אלא בגד צמר ופשתים, במנין לרבות צמר גמלים וצמר ארנבים נוצה של עזים והשירין והכלך והסריקין – תלמוד לומר "או בגד". רבא אמר: כי לית ליה להך תנא דבי רבי ישמעאל בשאר בגדים - שלש על שלש, שלשה על שלשה – אית ליה. והא רבא הוא דאמר שלשה על שלשה בשאר בגדים לרשב"א – אית ליה, לתנא דבי רבי ישמעאל – לית ליה! הדר ביה רבא מההיא. ואב"א: *הא – *רב פפא אמרה. רב פפא אמר: אף כל – גלאתויי כלאים. כלאים, בהדיא כתיבי ביה °"לא תלבש שעטנז צמר ופשתים יחדיו"! ס"ד אמינא: ה"מ – דרך לבישה, אבל בהעלאה – כל תרי מיני אסור. ולאו ק"ו הוא? ומה לבישה, דקא מיתהני כולי גופיה מכלאים, אמרת: צמר ופשתים – אין, מידי אחרינא – לא, העלאה לא כ"ש! אלא, דרב פפא *בדותא היא. רב נחמן בר יצחק אמר: אף כל – לאתויי

רש"י

מאו בגד. דכתיב בשרצים. "או" – ריבויא הוא: דתניא ל"ג. דאי מתניתא היא – היכי פליג עלה אביי ואמר: מיבעיא ליה לשלש על שלש, הא תנא תני בהדיא "שלשה על שלשה בשאר בגדים מנין". אלא דרשא דרבא היא: גלי רחמנא בנגעים. דרבייה מן "והבגד", וה"ה לשרצים. דכיון דכתיב בהן "בגד" כי התם, מיניה ילפינן בבנין אב: שרצים אין שתי וערב מטמא בהן. דבגד כתיב בהו, ולא שתי ולא ערב: ואידך אי ס"ד. ורבא אמר לך: על כרחיך לשלשה על שלשה בשאר בגדים אתא, דאילו ג' על ג' בצמר ופשתים בשרצים – מנגעים יליף. דאי נגעים חמירי – לכתוב רחמנא האי ריבויא בשרצים ולשתוק מריבויא ד"הבגד" בנגעים, אלא לדרשא אחריתי אתא: בכעדשה. ונגעים בעינן כגרים: מפיק מאידך. כלומר: מוצא הוא מסברת אידך תנא דפליג עליה, דאשכחן דמרבי שאר בגדים לטומאת שרצים: של עזים. קרי נוצה, על שם שאין גוזזין אותם אלא מורטין: רבא אמר כי לית ליה. לתנא דרישא בשאר בגדים בשרצים ג' על ג' דילמד סתום מן המפורש. אבל שלשה על שלשה בשרצים אית ליה בהו, דאיתרבו מ"או בגד": הדר ביה רבא מההיא. ואמר דתנא דבי רבי ישמעאל ורשב"א אמרו דבר אחד. ולאו כאביי, אלא דלתרוייהו בשאר בגדים טומאת ג' על ג' – ליכא, שלשה על שלשה – איכא: ואיבעית אימא הא. שמעתא דסיפא – לאו רבא אמרה, אלא רב פפא אמרה, לאוקמי תרוייהו תרי תנאי דרבי ישמעאל כהדדי, ולמימר דמודה תנא דרישא דיש טומאת שרצים בשאר בגדים: ה"ג: דרב פפא אמר אף כל לאתויי כלאים. "אף כל" דתנא דרישא דקאמר "אף כל בגדים סתם צמר ופשתים" – לאו לפרושי בגדים סתומים דטומאה קא אתי, דבשאר טומאה ודאי מטמאו שאר בגדים, דאיתרבו מ"או בגד". אלא לפרושי בגד האמור בכלאים סתם "ובגד כלאים שעטנז" וגו'. הלכך, לרב פפא *לא מפיק האי תנא מילתיה דהאי תנא. והך פירוקא דסיפא איהו אמרה, ולא איתמר כדאמרת ליה אליבא דרבא דמפליג בין ג' על ג' לשלשה על שלשה, אלא הכי איתמר, רב פפא אמר: לא מפיק האי תנא מאידך תנא, דאף כל לאתויי כלאים. דכי הוה מוקמינן ליה כרבא הוה צריך לפלוגי, דכיון דאף כל לטומאת שרצים נמי אתא – על כרחיך אף כל למעוטינהו משלש על שלש כדין נגעים, ו"או בגד" לרבויי שלשה על שלשה, ואף על גב דלא מטמאו שאר בגדים בנגעים, דהא נתמעטו בתרי מיעוטי – איתרבו בשרצים. אבל לרב פפא לא מיבעי לן לפלוגי, דכיון דאתרבו שאר בגדים לשרצים – איתרבו לכל תורת צמר ופשתים, בין לשלש בין לשלשה: בהדיא כתיבי ביה. צמר ופשתים, "לא תלבש שעטנז" וגו':

תוספות

נפקא ליה מאו בגד דתניא בגד כו'. פירש בקונטרס: דלא גרסינן "דתניא" דאי ברייתא היא – היכי פליג אביי? ולאו פירכא היא, דהא אביי מודה ד"או" אתא לרבות שאר בגדים לאידך תנא דבי רבי ישמעאל, כדאמר אביי גופיה בסמוך. והיינו ההיא ברייתא גופיה דלקמן, אלא שקיצרה רבא. והא דקאמר לאביי: האי "או" מאי עביד ליה – היינו אליבא דרשב"א, והיך תנא דבי רבי ישמעאל. אבל לאידך תנא דבי ר' ישמעאל אתא "או" לרבות שאר בגדים אפי' לשלש על שלש כדפריש' לעיל. *ולרבא דאמר דאידך תנא דבי רבי ישמעאל לא מרבה שאר בגדים אלא לשלשה על שלשה – לא מפיק האי תנא דבי רבי ישמעאל מאידך. וה"נ דהוה מצי למיבעיא הכא: ורבא האי "או" להך תנא דבי ר' ישמעאל מאי עביד ליה? דלא פליגי אביי ורבא אלא אליבא דרשב"א. וכמו שדורש אביי – כן צריך למדרש רבא אליבא תנא דבי ר' ישמעאל דהכא:

תלמוד לומר או בגד. תימה: דלקמן בפרק "במה אשה יוצאה" (דף סג:) דרשינן מ"או בגד" דאריג כל שהוא טמא. וכי תימא שקולים הם ויבואו שניהם, מ"מ כי פריך "ואביי האי או בגד מאי עביד ליה" לימא דאיצטריך לאריג כל שהוא! ואפי' אם נמחק שם ספרים דכתוב בהן "או בגד" וניגרוס דיליף מ"או בבגד פשתים" דכתיב גבי נגעים, הניחא לרבא – דיליף שרצים מנגעים על ידי דגלי רחמנא, וה"ה לענין אריג כל שהוא. אלא לאביי מאי איכא למימר? מה לנגעים שכן שתי וערב טמא בהן. אבל בשרצים לא, כדאמר בפרק "במה אשה" (לקמן דף סד.): יכול שאני מרבה את החבלים ואת המשיחות – ת"ל: "שק", מה שק טווי ואריג – אף כל טווי ואריג: אי ס"ד נגעים חמירי. הא ודאי דנגעים חמירי אלא מפר' הר"ס דה"ק: אי ס"ד כדקאמרת ד"או בגד" לרבות ג' על ג' בצמר ופשתים דהא נגעים חמירי:

שכן מטמא בכעדשה. ורבא, אע"ג דפירכא גמורה היא – לא חשיב ליה, דלא הוי אלא גילוי מילתא בעלמא דגלי רחמנא בנגעים דג' על ג' קרוי בגד בצמר ופשתים, והוא הדין בשרצים. והקשה ה"ר יעקב מקורביי"ל הקדוש, ונימא ק"ו *[הכי]: מה שתי וערב דטהור בשרצים – טמא בנגעים, ג' על ג' שטמא בשרצים – אינו דין שטמא בנגעים! ויש לומר: דכלים יוכיחו, שמטמא בשרצים ולא בנגעים, אף אני אביא ג' על ג'. וכי תימא: מה לכלים – שכן אין מטמאין ואין נעשין אהל המת במחובר דג' על ג' נמי אין נעשה אהל, כיון דלית ביה פותח טפח. אי נמי: שק יוכיח. אי נמי: בגד לבוע ובגד גוי יוכיח, שטמא בשרצים °ולא בנגעים, כדאמר בת"כ. וא"ת: דהכא משמע דעדשה הוי פחות מכגרים. ותימה לר"י: בפסחים בריש "אלו דברים" (ד' סו:) קאמר: מצורע חמור מבעל קרי שכן טעון פריעה ופרימה אדרבה, בעל קרי חמור שכן מטמא במשהו. סבר ליה כרבי נתן, דאמר כחתימת פי האמה. משמע דחתימת פי האמה לא הוי פחות מכגרים. והתם לעיל מיניה קאמר: זב חמור משרץ, שכן טומאה יוצאה עליו מגופו. ואי כעדשה הוי פחות מגרים, ומחתימת פי האמה, ליפרוך: *מה לשרץ שכן מטמא בכעדשה! ומיהו, אי לא משמעתיה מסברא אין להקשות, דאיכא למימר דכעדשה שהיא עבה, כדמרדד לה הוי רחבה טפי מגרים:

מניין לרבות צמר גמלים. וא"ת: צמר גמלים אמאי לא הוי בכלל צמר, ומה צריך ריבוי? וי"ל: דסתם צמר הוא של כבשים, אבל של גמלים לא איקרי צמר סתם אלא צמר גמלים. וכן שאר צמר, והואיל דיש להם שם לווי – איצטריך ריבוי. כדאמר ב"אלו טרפות" (חולין דף סג:): "אזוב" ולא אזוב כוחלית: ונוצה של עזים. תימה: מאי איצטריך ריבוי לנוצה של עזים, הא כתיב שק בהדיא בקרא, ושק הוי מדבר הבא מן העזים, כדמוכח בפרק "במה אשה" (לקמן דף סד:)! ותירץ ר"י: דשק הוי מן השער של עזים, וההיא מיקרי שער ולא נוצה. ומן הדק דאיקרי נוצה עושים בגדים, ולא שק. ועל שם שמורטין אותה כמו נוצת התרנגולין קרי ליה נוצה. ואור"י: דכן משמע בפרק "ראשית הגז" (חולין דף קלז.) דקאמר דראשית הגז אינו נוהג אלא ברחלים. דאמר קרא: "ראשית גז צאנך" ואתיא גיזה גיזה "מגז כבשי יתחמם". (איוב לא) ופריך התם: ונילף גיזה גיזה מבכור, ויהא נוהג אף בשוורים! אמר קרא: "תתן לו" ולא לשקו. ופריך: נוצה של עזים ליחייב! אלמא: נוצה לא הויא בכלל שק:

הדר ביה רבא מההיא. ומשום שלא יחלוק ההוא תנא דבי רבי ישמעאל אהך הדר ביה מההיא דלעיל, ולא מהך דהכא. ואית ליה לרבא: "אף כל" – לאתויי שרצים. וא"ת: בריש יבמות (דף ד: ושם) היכי פריך התלמוד והא תנא דבי רבי ישמעאל לית ליה דרבא! ההיא ד"הכנף" מין כנף מנא ליה דלית ליה? הא רבא אית ליה דאף כל קאי אשרצים. דאי לאו אף כל – ה"א דמיירי גבי שרצים בכל בגדים ו"או" לג' על ג'. אבל השתא דאמר אף כל צמר ופשתים, אצטריך "או" לרבות שלשה על שלשה בשאר בגדים. אבל שלש על שלש בשאר בגדים – לא. וי"ל: דהתם קאמר אליבא דרב נחמן בר יצחק, דאמר: אף כל לאתויי ציצית, דהשתא ודאי לית ליה דרבא, דאיהו מחייב שאר מינים בציצית: אלא הא דרב פפא בדותא היא. תימה לר"י: דבריש יבמות (גם זה שם) משמע דלתנא דבי רבי ישמעאל אף כל לאתויי כלאים, כי היכי דליהוי צמר ופשתים מופנה למדרש

רבינו חננאל

ואסיקנא הדר ביה רבא מההיא. ואיתוקמה דאביי ואמר רב נחמן בר יצחק אהא דתנא דבי רבי ישמעאל הואיל ונאמרו בתורה בגדים סתם ופרט לך הכתוב בא' מהן צמר ופשתים אף כל צמר ופשתים לאיתויי ציצית שאינו חייב בציצית אלא צמר ופשתים ואקשינן ציצית בהדיא כתיב לא תלבש שעטנז צמר ופשתים גדילים תעשה לך. כלומר אינו חייב לעשות גדילים אלא צמר ופשתים. ושנינן איצטריך סד"א כדרבא דרבא רמי כתיב על ציצית הכנף מן כנף. כלומר האי קרא משמע תו ציצית מכנף עצמו של זה הבגד וכתוב אחרינא צמר ופשתים גדילים תעשה לך הא כיצד שאר מינין במינן פוטרין שלא במינן אין פוטרין. אבל אם תעשה ציצית מן צמר ופשתים פוטרין בין במינן בין שלא במינן קמ"ל דליתיה לדרבא ואתינן לרבויי שאר בגדים לציצית מאשר תכסה. ודחינן האי אשר תכסה לרבות כסות סומא שחייב בציצית: האי תנא דתנא אין מטמא בגדים אלא בגד צמר ופשתים מפיק מהאי תנא דבי רבי ישמעאל דתני [דבי] רבי ישמעאל בגד צמר אין לי אלא בגד צמר מנין לרבות צמר גמלים צמר ארנבים נוצה של עזים והשיראין והכלך והסיריקין מניין ת"ל או בגד. ואמרינן

עין משפט נר מצוה

עא א מיי' פכ"ב מהל' כלים הל' א ופכ"ג הלכה ב:
עב ב מיי' פ"א מהל' כלים הלכה יא:
עג ג מיי' פ"י מהלכות כלאים הלכה א סמג לאוין רפג טוש"ע י"ד סימן רצח סעיף א:

מסורת הש"ס

ויקרא יא | דברים כב | מנחות לט: | [כ"ק סז: שבועות כו. בכורות נד:]

[ועי' מעל"ד תוספות ד"ה ר"פ] | [עי' מ"ש על הגליון פסחים יא.]

כ' ת"י וכ"כ הרש"ל דהך ולרבא וכו' עד מאידך הוי גליון:

גליון הש"ס

תוס' ד"ה שכן מטמא וכו' ולא בנגעים כדאית' בת"כ. ומפורש כן במתני' רפי"א דנגעים:

וק"ק דהא רב פפא אמרה משמע ממש מילתא דרבא דאמר כי לית ליה ג' על ג' ונראה דלרב פפא נמי לא מרבינן שאר בגדים אלא דוקא שלשה על שלשה והא דקאמר לאתויי כלאים ניחא ליה למינקט כלאים דמילתא דפסיקא דצמר ופשתים דוקא [ת"י]:

וי"ל דכשילות מתות נפקא לן טמא שרץ מוכל טמא לנפש ולהכי ליכא למיפרך מה לשרץ שכן מטמא בכעדש' דאיכא למימר טמא מת יוכיח אבל צמר ופשתים אמאי לא נימא הכי טמא מת יוכיח דילפינן משרצים מג"ש דבגד ועור ומיהו איכא למיפרך מה להצד השוה שבהן שכן מטמא שק ואהל כלים [ת"י]

רב נסים גאון

מה לשרצים שכן מטמאין בכעדשה. עיקר דילה בתורת כהנים (ויקרא יא) כל הנוגע בהם יכול בכולם כבולו שיעורו חכמים בכעדשה שכן החומט תחילת ברייתו כעדשה ותמצא בגמרא דחגיגה (דף יא) תלמוד לומר מהן אי מהן יכול במקצתן תלמוד לומר בהם הא כיצד עד שיגע במקצתו שהוא בסוף פרק הכל חייבים בראיה ובנזירות (דף נג) בפרק כהן גדול:

לאתויי ציצית. ציצית, בהדיא כתיב: "לא תלבש שעטנז צמר ופשתים" וכתיב: "גדילים תעשה לך"! סד"א כדרבא, *דרבא רמי: כתיב "הכנף" - מין כנף, וכתיב "צמר ופשתים יחדיו" הא כיצד? צמר ופשתים פוטרין בין במינן בין שלא במינן; שאר מינין, במינן - פוטרין, שלא במינן - אין פוטרין. ס"ד כדרבא - קמ"ל. אמר רב אחא בריה דרבא לרב אשי: לתנא דבי רבי ישמעאל מאי שנא לענין טומאה דמרבי שאר בגדים - דכתיב 'או בגד' הכא נמי לימא: לרבות שאר בגדים מ"אשר תכסה בה" - ההוא לאתויי כסות סומא הוא דאתא, דתניא: *"וראיתם אותו" - פרט לכסות לילה. אתה אומר פרט לכסות לילה, או אינו אלא פרט לכסות סומא? כשהוא אומר: "אשר תכסה בה" - הרי כסות סומא אמור, הא מה אני מקיים "וראיתם אותו" - פרט לכסות לילה. ומה ראית לרבות כסות סומא ולהוציא כסות לילה? מרבה אני כסות סומא - שישנה בראייה אצל אחרים, ומוציא אני כסות לילה - שאינה בראייה אצל אחרים. ואימא לרבות שאר בגדים! מסתברא: קאי בצמר ופשתים - מרבה צמר ופשתים, קאי בצמר ופשתים - מרבה שאר בגדים?!§ אמר אביי: רבי שמעון בן אלעזר וסומכוס אמרו דבר אחד. רשב"א - הא דאמרן, סומכוס, דתניא, סומכוס אומר: סיככה בטווי - פסולה, מפני שמטמאה בנגעים. כמאן - כי האי תנא, דתנן: *שתי וערב מטמא בנגעים מיד, *דברי רבי מאיר. ורבי יהודה אומר: השתי משישלה, והערב מיד, והאוני של פשתן משיתלבנו.§

מתני' כל היוצא מן העץ - אין מדליקין בו, אלא פשתן. וכל היוצא מן העץ אינו מטמא טומאת אהלים אלא פשתן.§

גמ' מנלן דפשתן איקרי עץ? אמר מר זוטרא, דאמר קרא: "והיא העלתם הגגה ותטמנם בפשתי העץ".§ "והיוצא מן העץ אינו מטמא טומאת אהלים אלא פשתן".§ מנלן? אמר רבי אלעזר: *גמר 'אהל' 'אהל' ממשכן

תורה אור: דברים כב | שם | במדבר טו | יהושע ב

לאתויי ציצית. דלא מחייבי בציצית אלא בגדי צמר ופשתים: גדילים תעשה לך. לאלו: סד"א כדרבא. כלומר: סד"א דלא דרשינן הני סמוכין לענין טלית, למימר דטלית צמר ופשתים תעשה ציצית, ולא לשאר טלית, אלא לענין ציצית תדרשיה: "גדילים תעשה לך" מצמר ופשתים, ולא משאר מינין, כדדריש ליה רבא: כתיב הכנף מין כנף. דהאי "כנף" קרא יתירא הוא, דהא כתיב: "על כנפי בגדיהם" והוה ליה למכתב: "ונתנו על הציצית פתיל תכלת": מין כנף. מין הטלית יהא הציצית, דהכי משמע: ציצית של כנף תהא. ואם של משי הוא - ציצית של משי פוטר בה: וכתיב צמר ופשתים. "גדילים תעשה לך" דמשמע נמי מהן תעשה: סד"א כדרבא. דאחר ד"הכנף" אתא לאשמועינן דלא תדרוש סמוכין למיפטר שאר בגדים. דודאי מיחייב מיהא בציצית דמינן, קמ"ל "אף כל" דלא תדרוש "הכנף" הכי, אלא אורחיה דקרא הוא, ולאשמעינן דמצות ציצית בשני מיני צבע, שני חוטין של תכלת ושני חוטין של לבן, דהיינו מין כנף - דסתמיה לבן: מאי שנא כו'. אליבא דרב נחמן קבעי לה, דאמר: "אף כל" - לאתויי ציצית: אשר תכסה. ריבויא דקרא הוא: לכסות לילה. כסות המיוחד ללילות, דלא ניחייב: שישנה בראייה אצל אחרים. וקרינן ביה "וראיתם" לאחרים ביום, ולא אתי "אשר תכסה" ומפיק "וראיתם": שאינה בראייה. ואי מרבינן לה מ"אשר תכסה" קא עקרת ליה "וראיתם": ואימא לרבות שאר בגדים. ולא כסות סומא: קאי בצמר ופשתים. כדאמר, דסמך צמר ופשתים לגדילים - מרבה כסות סומא דצמר ופשתים: מרבה שאר בגדים. בתמיה: אמרו דבר אחד. דדבר המיטמא בנגעים אין מסככין, ואע"ג דאינו מטמא בטומאת מגע: הא דאמרן. חוץ מפשתן, ולא קאמר חוץ מבגד פשתן - משמע אע"ג דלאו בגד, שלא נטוה, כגון אונין, או נטוה ולא נארג - אין מסככין, הואיל ומטמו בנגעים, ואע"ג דלא מטמא בשרצים: סיככה בטווי. הואיל ומטמו בנגעים, דכתיב: "או בשתי או בערב", וה"ה נמי לאונין משיתלבנו. והאי דנקט טווי - לאשמעינן דטווי מטמא מיד, דטוויתו הוא גמר מלאכתו, ולא בעי שישלה: כמאן. אמריה סומכוס להא - כר' מאיר, דאמר: מטמא מיד שנטווה. ל"א: כמאן אמריה אביי להאי מילתא, דהאיך חוץ מפשתן - פשתן דווקא קאמר, אע"ג דלאו בגד. ועל כרחיך אפי' אונין במשמע, אלמא: אונין מיטמא בנגעים: כי האי תנא. כר' יהודה: משישלה. שיהיו שולין אותו מן היורה, ששולקין אותו בה ללבנו: משיתלבנו. בתנור: **מתני'** אין מדליקין בו. לעשות פתילה מקנבוס, ובגד קנבוס מצמר גפן: אינו מטמא טומאת אוהלים. אם עשה מהן אהל והמת תחתיו - הוי כשאר בית, וא"ל להטביל האהל עצמו, דלא קבל טומאה אלא כלים שתחתיו: אלא פשתן. שאף אהל טמא, כדכתיב: "והזה על האהל". ובגמ' יליף דבפשתן משתעי קרא: **גמ'** ממשכן

למדרש סמוכין להתיר כלאים בציצית. וי"ל: דהיינו עד דלא ידע דשעטנז לאפנויי, אבל במסקנא דאמר לרבנן שעטנז לאפנויי - הכי נמי לתנא דבי ר' ישמעאל. וצמר ופשתים לגופייהו אתו, הלכך לא צריך אף כל לאתויי כלאים. וא"ת: לתנא דבי ר' ישמעאל "צמר ופשתים" גבי לבישה מ"מ ל"ל דמדכתיב "ובגד כלאים שעטנז לא יעלה עליך" שמעינן דכל בגדים צמר ופשתים הן! וי"ל: דה"א דווקא העלאה, אבל בלבישה כל תרי מיני אסירי. והשתא ליכא למימר לתנא דבי ר' ישמעאל דתיתי "שעטנז שעטנז" מהעלאה, כדאמר בריש סוגיא ביבמות (דף ד: ושם). דהא השתא איצטריך שעטנז לאפנויי למדרש סמוכין, ולא תוענה למדרש מיניה גזירה שוה: *רב פפא אמרה. לא בעי למימר רב נחמן בר יצחק אמרה, דאמר "אף כל" לאתויי ציצית. דאין לטעות ולהחליף דברי רבא לרב נחמן, אלא ברב פפא שהיה תלמידו, ומלך אחריו. וכשהיה אומר דבר לא היו יודעים אם מדעתו אמרה, או למדה לפני רבו*: סד"א כי דוקיא דרבא. ל"ג "כי דוקיא" דהא מגוף מילתא דרבא הוא דמפיק. ובריש יבמות (ג"ז שם) הוא דגרס לה. ונראה, אע"ג דבפרק "התכלת" (מנחות ד' לט: ושם) אמר רב נחמן: השיראין פטורין מן הציצית, קיי"ל כרבא דבתראה הוא, וחייב בציצית מדאורייתא: מסתברא קאי בצמר ופשתים כו'. לא שייך למיפרך: אדרבה \ קאי ברואין - מרבה רואין, קאי ברואין - מרבה סומין?! דהא עיקר המצוה היא בטלית, ולא באדם. שאם אין לו טלית בת ד' כנפות - פטור מן הציצית: רבי שמעון בן אלעזר וסומכוס אמרו דבר אחד. וא"ת: דר"ש בן אלעזר קאמר מסככין בו חוץ מן הפשתן. משמע: אפי' לא נטוה, וכדאמרינן נמי בפ"ק דסוכה (דף יב: ושם): סיככה באניצי פשתן - פסולה. ומשמע התם דהיינו דייק ונפיץ, אע"ג דלא נטוה. וסומכוס קאמר דדוקא בטווי פסולה! וי"ל: דלרשב"א קאסר מדרבנן, *וסבר בדדייק ונפיץ לפי שהוא קרוב לטווי, וטווי הוא דאסור מן התורה, הואיל דמטמא בנגעים. והיינו "אמרו דבר אחד" דהא דקאמר סומכוס "סיככה בטווי פסולה" - היינו דבר תורה, מדאמר "מפני שמטמא בנגעים" דמדרבנן אין סברא לאוסרו אי מדאורייתא שרי לסכך בטומאת נגעים גזירה משום טומאת מת. וכיון דבטווי אסור מדאוריית' - א"כ באניצי פשתן יאסור מדרבנן, מפני שהוא קרוב לטווי, כדפרישית: אונין של פשתן. פי' בקונטרס: שלא נטוה. ודחק לפרש כן מפני דכבר תנא שתי וערב. וקשה לריב"א: דמנלן לטמאותו בנגעים? הא שתי וערב כתיב! ונראה לר"י: דאונין היינו מטוה. וכן פי' בערוך*. ושתי וערב דקאמר - היינו צמר, לפי שבצמר ניכר בין שתי לערב. דהשתי הוא מן הלשונות של צמר הגדול, וטווי כלאחר יד, ולא כמו שטווים הערב. ודרך היה לשולקו, אע"פ שעכשיו אין רגילין. ואונין של פשתן שהוא הטווי - לא הוזכר לא שתי ולא ערב, לפי שלא ניכר איזה של שתי ואיזה של ערב. כדאמר בפ"ק דמס' ע"ז (ד' יז:): אייתו ליה תרי קיבורי, אמרו ליה: הי דשתיא והי דערבא? איתרחיש ליה ניסא אתא זיבורא *(למיתב) על דערבא כו', אלמא: לא מינכר בפשתן*: כל היוצא מן העץ אין מדליקין. פי' בקונטרס לעיל: כגון בקנבוס וצמר גפן. ואין נראה לר"ת: דא"כ יהא אסור להדליק בו. ומעשים בכל יום שמדליקין בצמר גפן, וגם טוב מאד לפתילה! ואור"י: ודאי מותר להדליק בקנבוס וצמר גפן, דאינם יוצאים מן העץ. אלא זרע הוא, כדאמרי' במנחות: קנבוס ולוף אסרה תורה, שאר זרעים כו'. ופשתן נמי מין זרע, כמו קנבוס. אלא דאיצטריך במתני' למשרי פשתן משום דאיקרי עץ, כדכתיב: "ותטמנם בפשתי העץ", וכמו עץ הדעת *למ"ד חטה היתה וקרי לה עץ, אע"פ שאינה עץ. ועוד, דאמר ב"כילד מברכין" (ברכות דף מ: ושם): כל היכא דאי שקלת לפירא ולא הדר אילנא ומפיק - לא מברכינן עליה "בורא פרי העץ", ופשתן וקנבוס וצמר גפן אי שקלת לפירא, היינו הזרע - לא הדר אילנא ומפיק, הלכך: לאו יוצא מן העץ נינהו: ואין מטמא טומאת אהלים אלא פשתן. והא דאמר לעיל בפ"ק (דף יז.): ועל עצמן בכל שהן. משמע דכל הכלים נעשה אהל לקבל טומאה מחמת אהל - הכא איירי בדבר הקבוע, שחיברו לקרקע, אע"ג שמתחילה היה בגד. כיון שחיברו לאהל - בטלו מתורת בגד, ואין מיטמא אלא פשתן, אע"פ שהוא מחובר. כדכתיב: "והזה על האהל" כו'. וקשה לר"י: דתנן באהלות (פ"ח, מ"א) אלו מביאין וחוצצין: השידה והתיבה כו' והסדינים שהם עשוים אהלים. ואיך חוצצין סדינין של פשתן בפני הטומאה? והא כל דבר המקבל טומאה אינו חוצץ בפני הטומאה! וי"ל: דמיירי בסדינין של משי וקנבוס, שאינן מטמאים. ורשב"א פירש במשניות בע"א:

עד א מיי' פ"ג מהל' ציצית הלכה א סמג עשין כו טוש"ע א"ח סי' ט סעיף א:
עה ב מיי' שם הלכה ה טוש"ע שם סעי' ב:
עו ג מיי' שם טוש"ע שם סעיף ג:
עז ד ה מיי' שם הל' ז סמג שם טוש"ע א"ח סי' יז סעיף א וסי' יח סעיף א:
עח ו מיי' פ"ה מהלכות סוכה הלכה ד סמג עשין מג טוש"ע א"ח סי' תרכט סעיף ד:
עט ז מיי' פי"ג מהל' טומאת לרעת ה"ח:
פ ח מיי' פ"ה מהל' שבת הל' ה סמג לאוין סה טוש"ע א"ח סימן רסד סעיף א:
פא ט מיי' פ"ה מהל' טומאת מת הל' יב:

שייך לעיל ע"א
[וע"ע תוס' שבועות כו. ותוס' בכורות נד: ד"ה תלה ותוס' ב"ק סז: ד"ה רבא]
נ"א מסברא
[סוכה כח.]
[ערך אניצי ע"ש]
[נ"ל ויתיב]
[וע"ע תוספות סוכה יב: ד"ה באניצי]
[ברכות מ:]

מנחות לט: יבמות ד: נזיר נח. ע"ש
זבחים יח: מנחות מג.
נגעי' פי"א מ"ח ת"כ פ' תזריע [במשנה דנגעים לא נזכר דברי ר' מאיר ומטעם זה כתבו תוס' בסוכה י"ב: ד"ה באניצי וכו' דניחא דלא קאמר הכא דרשב"א וסומכוס ורבי מאיר אמרו דבר אחד וגם דלא אמר כמאן כר' מאיר ע"ש ודע דגם בת"כ ליתא דברי רבי מאיר]

גליון הש"ס
גמ' אמר מר זוטרא דאמר קרא. ברכות מ"ג ע"ב:

רבינו חננאל
ואמרינן אינן מטמא בג' על ג' אלא צמר ופשתים והאי דתני דמיטמאין בנגעים שאר בגדי' בשלשה על שלשה. אמרנו בתחלת הפרק השיראין והכלך והסיריקין חייבין בציצית. ואמרינן בתחלת יבמות אמר רחמנא עביד ציצית פתיל תכלת ותכלת עמרא הוא. וממאי דתכלת עמרא הוא ואמרינן מדשש כיתנא דכתיב שש ברקמה ממצרים כו'. כמו שנתפרש ביומא. מדשש כיתנא תכלת עמרא הוא שמעינן מינא דעמרא הוא דמיקריא פתיל תכלת הלכך ליכא ציצית אלא עמרא. תנינא שתי וערב מטמאין בנגעים מיד דברי ר' מאיר ר' יהודה אומר השתי משישלה והערב מיד. והאונין של פשתן משיתלבנו: מתני' כל היוצא מן העץ אין מדליקין בו אלא פשתן [כו']: גמרא מנלן דפשתן איקרי עץ שנאמר ותטמנם בפשתי העץ: כל היוצא מן העץ אינו מטמא טומאת אוהלים אלא פשתן מנהני מילי אמר רבי אלעזר יליף אהל אהל ממשכן

ממשכן; אכְּתִיב הָכָא: °"זֹאת הַתּוֹרָה אָדָם כִּי יָמוּת בְּאֹהֶל" (במדבר יט) וּכְתִיב הָתָם: °"וַיִּפְרֹשׂ אֶת הָאֹהֶל עַל הַמִּשְׁכָּן" (שמות מ). מַה לְּהַלָּן – שֶׁל פִּשְׁתָּן קָרוּי אֹהֶל, אַף כָּאן – שֶׁל פִּשְׁתָּן קָרוּי אֹהֶל. אִי מַה לְּהַלָּן – שְׁזוּרִין וְחוּטָן כָּפוּל ו', אַף כָּאן שְׁזוּרִין וְחוּטָן כָּפוּל ו'? ת"ל: *'אֹהֶל', 'אֹהֶל' רִיבָּה. אִי אֹהֶל אֹהֶל רִיבָּה, אֲפִילּוּ כָּל מִילֵּי נַמִּי! אִם כֵּן, גְּזֵירָה שָׁוָה מַאי אַהֲנֵי לֵיהּ? וְאֵימָא: מַה לְּהַלָּן קְרָשִׁים, אַף כָּאן קְרָשִׁים! אָמַר קְרָא: °"וְעָשִׂיתָ קְרָשִׁים לַמִּשְׁכָּן" (שם כו), במִשְׁכָּן – קָרוּי מִשְׁכָּן, וְאֵין קְרָשִׁים קְרוּיִין מִשְׁכָּן. אֶלָּא מֵעַתָּה "וְעָשִׂיתָ מִכְסֶה לָאֹהֶל" הָכִי נַמִּי, מִכְסֶה לָא אִיקְרִי אֹהֶל! אֶלָּא הָא דְּבָעֵי רַבִּי אֶלְעָזָר: עוֹר בְּהֵמָה טְמֵאָה מַהוּ שֶׁיִּטַּמֵּא בְּאֹהֶל הַמֵּת? הַשְׁתָּא עוֹר בְּהֵמָה טְהוֹרָה לָא מְטַמֵּא, עוֹר בְּהֵמָה טְמֵאָה מִיבַּעְיָא?! שָׁאנֵי הָתָם דַּהֲדַר אַהַדְרֵיהּ קְרָא, (נ"ל אלעזר) דִּכְתִיב: °"וְנָשְׂאוּ אֶת יְרִיעֹת הַמִּשְׁכָּן וְאֶת אֹהֶל מוֹעֵד מִכְסֵהוּ וּמִכְסֵה הַתַּחַשׁ אֲשֶׁר עָלָיו" (במדבר ד) – מַקִּישׁ עֶלְיוֹן לַתַּחְתּוֹן, מַה תַּחְתּוֹן קָרוּי אֹהֶל – אַף עֶלְיוֹן קָרוּי אֹהֶל. § גּוּפָא, בָּעֵי רַבִּי אֶלְעָזָר: געוֹר בְּהֵמָה טְמֵאָה, מַהוּ שֶׁיִּטַּמֵּא טוּמְאַת אֹהָלִין? מַאי קָמִיבַּעְיָא לֵיהּ? – אָמַר רַב אַדָּא בַּר אַהֲבָה: תַּחַשׁ שֶׁהָיָה בִּימֵי מֹשֶׁה קָמִיבַּעְיָא לֵיהּ, טָמֵא הָיָה אוֹ טָהוֹר הָיָה? אָמַר רַב יוֹסֵף: מַאי תִּיבְּעֵי לֵיהּ? תְּנֵינָא: לֹא הוּכְשְׁרוּ לִמְלֶאכֶת שָׁמַיִם אֶלָּא עוֹר בְּהֵמָה טְהוֹרָה בִּלְבַד! מְתִיב רַבִּי אַבָּא, רַבִּי יְהוּדָה אוֹמֵר: שְׁנֵי מִכְסָאוֹת הָיוּ, אֶחָד שֶׁל עוֹרוֹת אֵילִים מְאָדָּמִים וְאֶחָד שֶׁל עוֹרוֹת תְּחָשִׁים. רַבִּי נְחֶמְיָה אוֹמֵר: מִכְסֶה אֶחָד הָיָה, וְדוֹמֶה כְּמִין תְּלָא אִילָן. וְהָא תְּלָא אִילָן טָמֵא הוּא! ה"ק: כְּמִין תְּלָא אִילָן הוּא, שֶׁיֵּשׁ בּוֹ גְּוָונִין הַרְבֵּה, וְלֹא תְּלָא אִילָן, דְּאִילּוּ הָתָם – טָמֵא, וְהָכָא – טָהוֹר. *א"ר יוֹסֵף: א"ה הַיְינוּ דְּמְתַרְגְּמִינַן "סַסְגּוֹנָא" – שֶׁשָּׁשׂ בִּגְוָונִין הַרְבֵּה. רָבָא אָמַר: עוֹר בְּהֵמָה טְמֵאָה דְּמִטַּמֵּא בְּאֹהֶל הַמֵּת מִהָכָא, דְּתַנְיָא: 'עוֹר' 'אוֹ בָעוֹר' – רִיבָּה *עוֹר בְּהֵמָה טְמֵאָה, דוְשֶׁלָּקָה בְּיַד כֹּהֵן. *) קָצִיץ מִכּוּלָּן וְעָשָׂה אַחַת מֵהֶן מִנַּיִן? תַּלְמוּד לוֹמַר: °'אוֹ בְּכָל מְלֶאכֶת עוֹר' (ויקרא יג). וְאִיכָּא לְמִיפְרַךְ: מַה לִּנְגָעִים – שֶׁכֵּן שְׁתִי וָעֵרֶב טָמֵא בָּהֶן! אֶלָּא: גָּמַר מִשְּׁרָצִים, דְּתַנְיָא: 'עוֹר' אֵין לִי אֶלָּא עוֹר בְּהֵמָה טְהוֹרָה, עוֹר בְּהֵמָה טְמֵאָה מִנַּיִן – תַּלְמוּד לוֹמַר: 'אוֹ עוֹר'. וְאִיכָּא לְמִיפְרַךְ: מַה לִּשְׁרָצִים – שֶׁכֵּן מְטַמְּאִין בְּכַעֲדָשָׁה, – נְגָעִים יוֹכִיחוּ. וְחָזַר הַדִּין, לֹא רְאִי זֶה כִּרְאִי זֶה, וְלֹא רְאִי זֶה כִּרְאִי זֶה, הַצַּד הַשָּׁוֶה שֶׁבָּהֶן – שֶׁעוֹר טָמֵא בָּהֶן, וְעָשָׂה עוֹר בְּהֵמָה טְמֵאָה כְּעוֹר בְּהֵמָה טְהוֹרָה, אַף אֲנִי אָבִיא אֹהֶל הַמֵּת, שֶׁעוֹר טָמֵא בּוֹ, וְנַעֲשֶׂה בּוֹ עוֹר בְּהֵמָה טְמֵאָה כְּעוֹר בְּהֵמָה טְהוֹרָה. אֲמַר לֵיהּ רָבָא מִבַּרְנִישׁ לְרַב אַשִׁי: אִיכָּא לְמִיפְרַךְ, מַה לְּהַצַּד הַשָּׁוֶה שֶׁבָּהֶן – שֶׁכֵּן טְמֵאִין בִּפְחוֹת מִכְּזַיִת, תֹּאמַר בְּמֵת שֶׁאֵינוֹ מְטַמֵּא אֶלָּא בִּכְזַיִת! אֶלָּא אָמַר רָבָא מִבַּרְנִישׁ: אָתְיָא

*) מגילה יח. ע"ש.

רש"י

ממשכן. דלא הוה ביה שום יוצא מן העץ אלא פשתן, כדכתיב: "עשר יריעות שש משזר": שזורין. דטור"ש בלע"ז, דכתיב: "משזר": וחוטן כפול ששה. כדאמרינן בפ' "בא לו" דסדר יומא (דף עא:): דברים שנאמר בהן שש – חוטן כפול ששה. ואי קשיא, כיון דיליף ממשכן, כלים ואדם שמאהיל גג הבית וכל שאר אהלים דלא דמו למשכן – מנלן דמטמאו? בספרי תניא: מנין לעשות שאר המאהילים כאהל, מה מצורע הקל עשה בו כל המאהיל כו': אף כאן קרשים. ואימא דעד נמי איקרי אהל: משכן קרוי משכן. כגון עשר יריעות שש משזר, ומשכן איקרי אהל, דכתיב (שמות לט) "את משכן אהל מועד": הכי נמי. דמכסה עורות לאו אהל, ולענין טומאה נמי לא מקבל: השתא עור בהמה טהורה. כגון אילים מאדמים: מה תחתון. עשתי עשרה יריעות עזים לאהל על המשכן, דמשכן היינו עשר יריעות המחוברות בקרסי זהב. ולמעלה מהן אהל יריעות עזים, ולמעלה מהן מכסה העורות: מאי קמבעיא ליה. הא ממשכן גמר לה ר' (*אליעזר) לעיל ברישא שמעתין, והתם טהורה היא דהוי למלאכת משכן: מכסה אחד היה. חציו של אילים וחציו של תחשים. ו"למעלה" דקרא – אתרוייהו כתיב, דבין אילים בין תחשים היה מכסה אחד מלמעלה לאהל יריעות העזים: תלא אילן. חיה טמאה היא, ומנומרת בגוונין: אי הכי. סייעתא היא: ששש. ששמח ביופיו בגוונין: עור או בעור. גבי נגעים כתיב: "או בעור", והוה מצי למכתב: "או עור": ושלקה ביד כהן. משהראהו ביד כהן נעשה נגע, ומתחלה לא היה נגע: קציץ מכולן. מכל האמורים בפסוק, וחיברן יחד: שרצים מטמאין בכעדשה ומת בכזית, ונגעים בכגריס, והוא פחות מכזית: אף אני אביא אהל המת שעור טמא בו. כדאמר לעיל: מקיש עליון לתחתון דקרוי אהל: *שאינה מטמאה בנגעים. דהא צמר ופשתים כתיב: מטמא

תוספות

ויפרוש את האהל וגו'. תימה לר"י: מנא ליה דהאי אהל היינו שש משזר? אימא היינו יריעות עזים דאשכחנא בהדיא דאיקרי אהל, כדכתיב: "ועשית יריעות עזים לאהל על המשכן" וכן משמע פשטיה דקרא: "ויפרוש את האהל" – דהיינו יריעות עזים, "על המשכן" – *דהיינו שש משזר. כדכתיב: "ואת המשכן תעשה עשר יריעות שש משזר". ויש לומר: דדייק משום דקרא כתיב בהקמת המשכן, וחשיב לעיל בסדר הקמתן דמתחלה נתן אדנים (ואח"כ עמודים)(א) ואחר כך הקרשים, וכתיב אחר הקרשים: "ויפרוש את האהל" משמע היינו יריעות התחתונות שהם שש משזר דהם תחלת הפרשה. ותימה דאמאי לא יליף מהא דמשכן היינו יריעות שש משזר, כדכתיב: "ואת המשכן תעשה וגו'" ומשכן איקרי אהל, דכתיב: "את משכן אהל מועד"? ושמא אהאי קרא סמיך: אם כן ג"ש מאי אהני ליה. והא דאמר: "כל פותח טפח מביא את הטומאה" – היינו מק"ו ממצורע, כדיליף בספרי וכדפיר' בקונטרס. וא"ת: והיכי יליף, נימא: דיו כמצורע שלא יטמא אלא טומאת ערב, ודווקא בעומד או יושב ולא עובר, כדתניא במסכת נגעים ומייתי לה, *ובפ"ק דקדושין (ד' לג:) (נגעים פי"ג): טמא יושב תחת האילן, וטהור עובר טמא כו'! וי"ל: דאינו אלא גילוי מילתא בעלמא מק"ו דמצורע, דלית לן למילף אהל אהל ממשכן לענין למעט הבאת טומאה בשאר אהלים דלאו פשתן. ולא ילפינן ממשכן אלא לטומאת עלמו, אפילו מחובר, דדוקא פשתן ולא שאר יוצא מן העץ. ולענין אהל שאינו עשוי בידי אדם, לרבי יהודה בפ"ב דסוכה (דף כא. ושם) (ע"ל כא: תוס' ד"ה אהל) דלא מלינן למילף ממצורע, ולא אשכחן ביה קרא לא למעט ולא לרבות(ג) *אהל שאינו עשוי בידי אדם: אי מה להלן קרשים כו'. פירש בקונטרס: דאף עץ יהא קרוי אהל. וקשה לריב"א: דהא דפנות אין קרויות אהל אלא המכס' שמלמעלה הוא קרוי אהל. ומפ' דה"ק: אי מה להלן קרשים בהדי פשתן – אף כאן בטומאת אהל קרשים בהדי פשתן, ואע"ג דאהל אהל ריבה – לענין דלא בעינן שזורים ולכפול ששה, וכן לענין דלא בעינן צמר ופשתים יחד כי התם, אלא אפילו פשתים ולא צמר. מ"מ פריך דליהוי קרשים בהדי פשתים, דסתם אהל קרוי עם הכיסוי ועם הדפנות: ואין קרשים קרוים משכן. וקשה לר"י: הא כתיב: "יהיה פרוח על לדי המשכן מזה ומזה לכסותו", ואמר לקמן ב"הזורק" (דף לח:): לכסות אמה של קרשים, ואיכא למ"ד: אמה של אדנים. אלמא: דקרשים איקרי משכן! ויש לומר: דלדי המשכן איקרי, ולא משכן: ריבה עור בהמה טמאה. פירש רבינו שמואל: דלהכי איצטריך לרבויי עור בהמה טמאה, כדקתני בת"כ (פ' תזריע): "לצמר" אין לי אלא מין בהמה דקה ונאכל כו', דומיא דלצמר שהוא דוקא של כבשים. מנין לרבות עור בהמה דקה ואין נאכלת, בהמה גסה נאכלת ואין נאכלת, עד שתהא מרבה עורות שרצים – תלמוד לומר: *"בעור" "בעור". ונראה דהא דנקט בהמה גסה נאכלת – אגב אחריני נקט, דאיהי לא בעיא קרא, דהא בשמעתין ילפינן לענין טומאת אהל כל מין טהורה מאילים: ושלקה ביד כהן. מפרש נמי רבינו שמואל דאיצטריך לרבויי משום דכתיב: "והבגד כי יהיה בו נגע לרעת וגו' והראה אל הכהן" דמשמע דאם לא היתה בו נגע קודם שהראהו לכהן – טהור: שכן שתי וערב טמא בהן. מה שאין כן במת, כדנפקא לן בפרק "במה אשה" (לקמן דף סד.): אלא גמר משרצים דתניא עור אין לי אלא עור של בהמה טהורה. וא"ת: מנלן דאיירי קרא בעור בהמה טהורה? ויש לומר: כמו בנגעים, דהכא כתיב שק וה"א מה שק מין בהמה דקה ונאכל, כדמוכח בת"כ ולקמן דשק הוי דבר הבא מן העזים, אף עור – מין בהמה דקה ונאכל. אע"ג דבת"כ מרבה אף שק הבא מחזיר שהוא דבר טמא – אפ"ה הוה אמינא דלא הוקשה עור אלא למשמעות דשק, דהיינו של עזים, ולא הוקש למאי דמרבי בשק – לכך איצטריך ריבוי. הרב פורת: מה לשרצים. וליכא למיפרך: שיטמא מת בכעדשה מק"ו. דהא כל שיעורים הם הלכה למשה מסיני. וקשה לר"י: ונילף מת משרצים בגזירה שוה דבגד ועור, כדאמר לקמן בפרק "במה אשה"! (ג"ז שם) ואומר ר"י: משום דג"ש דאהל אהל ממשכן סתרה לה, לכך איצטריך ריבוי. ועוד י"ל: דג"ש לא איירי בטומאת אהל [המת] עלמו המחובר: אתיא

עין משפט נר מצוה

פב א ב ג מיי' פ"ה מהלכות טומאת מת הלכה יב:

פג ד מיי' פ"ו מהלכות טומאת צרעת הל' ו:

לאו על האהל הוי יריעות שש משזר ועל המשכן היינו על הקרשים הא אין הקרשים קרויים משכן [תוס' ישנים]

פד ה מיי' שם פי"ג הלכה יב:

רבינו חננאל

ממשכן כתיב הכא זאת התורה אדם כי ימות באהל וכתיב ויפרוש את האהל על המשכן מה להלן שש ותכלת והן צמר ופשתים. אף הכא צמר ופשתים. כיון דיליף אהל הטומאה מאהל המשכן. בעי ר' אלעזר עור בהמה טמאה מהו שיטמא באהל המת. ומיבעיא ליה תחש שהיה בימי משה טהור היה או טמא היה. ומפרש רב יוסף תנינא לא הוכשרו למלאכת שמים אלא עור בהמה טהורה בלבד. איני והא"ר נחמיה דומה כמין תלא אילן ותלא אילן טמא הוא. ושנינן דומה לו שיש לו גוונין הרבה כמותו. אבל טהור הוא. רבה אמר עור בהמה טמאה דמטמאה באהל המת. אתי בק"ו מנגעים. דתניא היה לו לומר עור למה כתב בעור לרבו' עור בהמה טמאה. ושלקה ביד כהן שמטמאה בנגעים קיצץ מכולן. פי' כגון שנטל מזה העור רצועה ומזה רצועה והדביקן ועשאן אחד. מנין שמטמאה בנגעים ת"ל או בכל מלאכת עור. פי' שלקה ביד כהן כגון שהחזיק הכהן בעור לבודקו ועודנו בידו לקה בצרעת לאלתר. איכא למיפרך מה לנגעים שכן מטמאין שתי וערב כו' מה להצד השוה שבהן שכן מטמאין בכעדשה וכו' הבגד טומאתן בגרעין. והשרץ בעדשה אלא

רב נסים גאון

אי מה להלן שזורין וחוטן כפול ו' אף כאן שזורין וחוטן כפול ו'. ותמצא עיקר במס' דיומא בפרק בא לו כהן גדול (דף עא ע"ב) בגדים שנאמר בהן שש חוטן כפול ו' וכו' ואמרו קרא' במה הוא שהוא אמר חד לגופיה דכתיב נהו וחד שיהו שזורין וחד לחוטן שיהא כפול ו' ומהנה יודע לנו כי בכל עור שכתב בהן שש העשויים במשכן היו שזורים וחוטן כפול ו': תאמר במת שאינו מטמא אלא בכזית עיקר דילה בספרי הנגע במת יכול כל שהוא וכו' אחר שרבה הכתוב מיעט אמרו בזית מן המת טמא שכן היא תחלת ברייתו ובמשנה בנוס' אהלות בפרק ב' אלו מטמאין באהל המת וכזית מן המת ולא היה ברייתו הפרש והוא כבר פירושו בפרק ג' כזית מן המת פתחו בטפח והמת פתחו בד' טפחים ובתוספ' בראש סדר טהרות חומר בכזית (מזה) [מן] המת שכזית פתחו בטפח ומת פתחו בד' טפחים ובתוספתא דמגילה בפרק א' אין בין כזית מן המת למת אלא שכזית מן המת פתחו בטפח והמת פתחו בד'

מסורת הש"ס

הקשה מהרש"מ מה לריך אהל אהל ריבה לילף מק"ו מטלה של עזים דלא מטמאה בנגעים מטמאה באהל המת שאין חוטן כפול ששה דמטמאה בנגעי' לא כ"ש ותי' דהכלל קיימינן אליבא דר"א דלית ליה ק"ו מדכתי' בסמוך עור בהמה טמאה מהו והכי לאית לכו ק"ו דכתי אהל אהל לדרשה אחריתא [מ"ו]

הגהות הב"ח

(א) תוס' ד"ה ויפרוש וכו' דמתחלה נתן אדנים ואח"כ קרשים ואח"כ עמודים וכו' נמחק: (ב) ד"ה ... לא למעט ולא לרבות הס"ד והשאר נמחק:

[שייך לע"ב]

נראה קצת דכל כלי עור דכתיב במת ושכבת זרע לאתי לדרשה אחריתא ולא לעור בהמה טמאה דא"כ תקשי אמאי איצטריך למיכתביניהו דליתי בג"ש דבגד ועור משרצים [מ"ו]

ס"א או בעור

גליון הש"ס

גמ' אמר רב יוסף א"ה היינו דמתרגמינן. עי' קדושין דף מו ע"א תוס' ד"ה אר"י.

אתיא בק"ו מנוצה של עזים שאין מטמא בנגעים – מטמא באהל המת, עור בהמה טמאה שמטמאה בנגעים – אינו דין שמטמאה באהל המת. ואלא הא דתני רב יוסף: לא הוכשרו במלאכת שמים אלא עור בהמה טהורה בלבד, למאי הלכתא? לתפילין. תפילין?! בהדיא כתיב בהו: "למען תהיה תורת ה' בפיך" – *מן המותר בפיך. אלא לעורן. והאמר אביי: שי"ן של תפילין *הל"מ! אלא לכורכן בשערן ולתופרן בגידן. הא נמי הל"מ הוא, *דתניא: תפילין מרובעות הל"מ, *נכרכו' בשערן ונתפרות בגידן. אלא לרצועו'. והא"ר יצחק: רצועות שחורות הל"מ. נהי דגמירי שחורות – טהורות מי גמירי? מאי הוי עלה דתחש שהיה בימי משה? א"ר אלעא אמר רשב"ל, אומר היה ר"מ: תחש שהיה בימי משה בריה בפני עצמה היה, ולא הכריעו בה חכמים אם מין חיה הוא אם מין בהמה הוא, וקרן אחת היתה לו במצחו, ולפי שעה נזדמן לו למשה, ועשה ממנו משכן ונגנז. *מדקאמר קרן אחת היתה לו במצחו – ש"מ טהור היה, *דא"ר יהודה: שור שהקריב אדם הראשון קרן אחת היתה לו במצחו, שנאמר: "ותיטב לה' משור פר מקרין מפריס". 'מקרין' תרתי משמע! אמר ר"נ בר יצחק: 'מקרן' כתיב. וליפשוט מיניה דמין בהמה הוא! כיון דאיכא קרש דמין חיה הוא, ולית ליה אלא חדא קרן – איכא למימר מין חיה הוא.§

מתני' פתילת הבגד שקיפלה ולא הבהבה, ר"א אומר: טמאה היא ואין מדליקין בה, רע"א: טהורה היא ומדליקין בה.§

גמ' בשלמא לענין טומאה – בהא פליגי, דר"א סבר: קיפול אינו מועיל, ובמילתיה קמייתא קיימא. ור"ע סבר: קיפול מועיל ובטולי בטיל. אלא לענין הדלק' במאי פליגי? א"ר אלעזר א"ר אושעיא, וכן א"ר אדא בר אהבה: הכא בג' על ג' מצומצמות עסקינן, ובי"ט שחל להיות ע"ש עסקינן, דכ"ע אית להו דר' יהודה, *דאמר: מסיקין בכלים ואין מסיקין בשברי כלים, ודכ"ע אית להו דעולא, דאמר עולא: *המדליק צריך שידליק ברוב היוצא. ר"א סבר: קיפול אינו מועיל, וכיון דאדליק ביה פורתא – הויא ליה שבר כלי, וכי קא מדליק – בשבר כלי קמדליק. ור"ע סבר: קיפול מועיל, ואין תורת כלי עליו, וכי קמדליק – בעץ בעלמא קמדליק. אמר רב יוסף, היינו דתנינא: "ג' על ג' מצומצמות" ולא ידענא למאי הלכתא. ומדקא מתרץ רב אדא בר אהבה אליבא דר' יהודה – ש"מ כר"י ס"ל; ומי א"ר אדא בר אהבה הכי? והא"ר אדא בר אהבה: גו'

רש"י

מטמא באהל המת. אם עשאו אהל, דהא ממשכן גמר ליה, ועיקר אהל דכתיב במשכן – ביריעות עזים כתיב. הא דכתיב בספרים: "כל מעשה עזים" – ל"ג ליה, דמהכא לא נפקא לן אהל, דבכלים הוא דכתיב, וכדאמר בעלמא: להביא דבר הבא מן העזים מן הקרניים ומן הטלפים: אלא הא דתני רב יוסף כו'. כיון דרבינן עור בהמה טמאה לאהל המת, הא דתני רב יוסף למאי הלכתא? מאי דהוה הוה, אי לאו למילף מיניה לטומאה: לתפילין. איתמר, דהיא נמי מלאכת שמים: לעורן. עור דפוס שלהן, שהכתבים של פרשיות מונחים בו. דהאי לא מ"למען תהיה" נפקא, דהא לאו תורה כתיבא ביה: שי"ן של תפילין. שיהא העור נקמט מבחוץ ג' קמטין ודומה לשי"ן, והרצועה נקשרת כמין דלית. *ויש רצועה כפופה כמין י', דהיינו שדי. וכיון דאות השם נכתב בקמטין שלו, "מותר בפיך" בעינן, ומקרא נפיק: אלא לנברכות בשערן. תניא להיא דרב יוסף, שצריך לקשור איגרות הפרשיות בשער עור בהמה טהורה, ולתופרן בגיד בהמה טהורה: בשערן. בשער *מן הקלף, כלומר בשל טהורה: לרצועותיהן. שיהיו מעור בהמה טהורה: הל"מ. וכיון דהלכתא רצועות מסיני, טהורות נמי הל"מ, ומתניתא דרב יוסף לאו הל"מ קאמר: מאי הוי עלה דתחש. הואיל ולרב יוסף לאו לענין מלאכה דמשכן איתמר, לא איפשיט בעיין: מקרין תרתי משמע. דמשמע מקרין – כל קרניו: **מתני'** שקיפלה. כמו שגודלין פתילות: הבהבה. על השלהבת כדי שתהא מחורכת ותדליק יפה: טמאה היא. דבגד כלי הוא ומקבל טומאה אם היה שלש על שלש, דקיפול אין מבטלה מתורת בגד, הואיל ולא הבהבה: ואין מדליקין בה. כדמפרש טעמא בגמ': **גמ'** קפול מועיל. לבטולה מתורת בגד: מצומצמות. דאי הוה טפי פורתא, לכולי עלמא מדליקין: ובי"ט שחל להיות בע"ש. דשייך ביה איסור מוקצה, עסקינן: ואין מסיקין בשברי כלים. שנשברו בו ביום, דהוו להו נולד. אבל בכלים – מסיקין, דהא חזו לטלטלן: ודכולי עלמא אית להו. צריך המדליק להדליק בידים קודם סילוק ידיו רוב היוצא מן הפתילה חוץ לנר, הלכך על כרחך צריך לעסוק בו לאחר שנפחת משלש, הלכך טעמא דר"א דאסר – קסבר: קיפול אינו מועיל, והוה ליה כלי שנשבר בי"ט, וכי קמדליק ביה פורתא, כיון דמצומצמות הוו – הוו שברי כלי, דפחות משלש לאו כלי הוא, והוה ליה כלי שנשבר בי"ט. וכי קמדליק בידים להשלים רוב היוצא – בשבר כלי קמדליק. והא דאמרינן מסיקין בכלים – דווקא שלא יגע בו אחר שנפחת, אלא אם כן ריבה עליו עצים מוכנים, כדלקמן (דף כט.): קיפול מועיל. ועל כרחך מעי"ט קיפלה. דאין גודלין פתילה בי"ט, כדתניא ב"המביא" (ביצה לב:), וכבר נתבטל הכלי מבע"י, ואין כאן שבר כלי: היינו דתנינא. שהייתי שונה מרבותי משנה "ג' על ג' מצומצמות", ולא הוה ידענא למאי הלכתא איתמר, דאי לענין טמויי – כל שכן דאי איכא טפי דמטמא: ומדקא מתרץ כו'. מילתא באפי נפשיה היא, בתמיה למירמי דרב אדא אדרב אדא. מדקא מתרץ למתניתין ואוקי דכולי עלמא אית להו אין מסיקין בשברים, דהיינו אליבא דר"י דאית ליה נולד, ש"מ כו': שחקק

תוספות

אתיא בק"ו מנוצה של עזים. וא"ת: נימא שתי וערב יוכיח, שמטמא בנגעים ואינו מטמא במת – אף אני אביא עור בהמה טמאה כו'. ועוד קשה: אמאי איצטריך קרא בשרצים לעור בהמה טמאה? ליתי בק"ו מנוצה של עזים שאין מיטמא בנגעים מיטמא בשרצים! וי"ל: דאי לא הוה כתיב קרא בשרצים ליכא למילף עור בהמה טמאה בק"ו מנגעים, לא בשרצים ולא באהל המת. דאיכא למימר: שתי וערב יוכיח. אבל השתא דכתיב טומאה בשרצים ילפינן שפיר בק"ו מנגעים שיטמא באהל המת. וליכא למימר שתי וערב יוכיח, דמה לשתי וערב – שכן אינו מטמא בשרצי', תאמר בעור בהמה טמאה שמטמא בשרצים – הכי נמי יטמא באהל המת:

ור"י אומר דליכא למימר שתי וערב יוכיח. דהכי עביד ק"ו: ומה נוצה של עזים שאין מטמא בנגעים מטמא באהל המת ככלי העשוי מנוצה של עזים, עור בהמה טמאה שטמא בנגעים – אינו דין שיטמא באהל המת ככליו. דהשתא לא שייך למימר שתי וערב יוכיח שמטמא בנגעים ולא באהל המת – דשתי וערב אין שייך בו כלי, ואין לומר דכל היוצא מן העץ ועצם יוכיח שמטמא בנגעים ואינו מטמא במת – דמה שמטמא בנגעים אינו מחמת עצמו, אלא מחמת הבית. דהא בית שסיככו בזרעים אמר ב"העור והרוטב" דמטמא בנגעים. אבל נוצה והעור – מטמא מחמת עצמו. ומהר"ס כתב: דליכא למימר שתי וערב יוכיח – דמה לשתי וערב שכן אין מטמאין לא במת ולא בש"ז תאמר בעור בהמה טמאה דמטמא, דהא כתיב במת ובש"ז "כל בגד וכל כלי עור". ולעיל כי פריך מה לשרצים – ליכא למימר נגיעת מת וש"ז יוכיח, דמה לכולהו שכן פחות מכזית. דנגיעת מת בכשעורה, וש"ז במשהו, או בחתימת פי האמה, (והוא תי': דאיצטריך קרא בשרצים לאפוקי מהיקש דשק) וזה אין נראה, דע"כ דגם לענין אהל הוי שיעורו בכזית להביא טומאה על כל הכלים ועל עצמן, אפי' יוצא מן העץ דזהו תלוש, קיי"ל דמביא. וי"ל דלא שייך כלל למימר אהל תלוש יוכיח – כיון דלא אתינא למילף אלא לענין אהל המחובר דלא מטמא אלא מאי דילפי' ממשכן, וכי האי גוונא איכא בפ"ק דמנחות גבי טריפה שהיתה לה שעת הכושר, דלא ילפינן מטריפה שלא היתה לה שעת הכושר, אפי' במה הצד [ת"י]:

והקשה השר מקוצי: מאי בעי בסמוך "מאי הוי עלה דתחש"? תיפוק ליה דטהור היה – מדאיצטריך קרא בשרצי' לטמא עור בהמה טמאה. דאי טמא היה – לשתוק קרא בשרצים, ותיתי בק"ו מנגעים. דהשתא ליכא למימר שתי וערב יוכיח – דמה לשתי וערב שכן אין מטמאין באהל המת – תאמר בעור בהמה טמאה דמיטמא באהל המת, כיון דתחש טמא היה! וי"ל: דמהכא ליכא למיפשט דטהור היה, דאפילו טמא היה כתיב בשרצים, דמילתא דאתיא בק"ו טרח וכתב לה קרא. ועוד אומר רש"י: דשרצים לא אתו מק"ו מנגעים, דאיכא למיפרך פשוטי כלי עור יוכיח, דמטמא בנגעים ולא בשרצים: **למאי** הלכתא. לא בעי למימר לאשמעינן דתחש טהור היה דמשמע דאתא לאשמעינן שום צורך הוראה: **תפילין** בהדיא כתיב בהו למען תהיה וגו'. תימה לר"י: וכי אין לברייתא לשנות מה שדורש מן הפסוק וכל הנך דמייתי בסמוך, וכי לית ליה לרב יוסף לשנות הברייתא לפי שזה אמרו אמורא אחד או ברייתא! ואומר רבינו יצחק דהכי פריך: תפילין בהדיא כתיב בהו, ואי הא הוה אתי לאשמעי' הוה ליה לאתויי קרא, אע"כ מילתא אחריתי אתא לאשמעי', ודרשה ד"מן המותר בפיך" היתה פשוטה, ולא איצטריך לאשמעי'. וקאמר: אלא לעורן, והאמר אביי; שין של תפילין כו'. ובזה הלשון הוה ליה לרב יוסף למימר, והוה ידעינן שפיר דבעי עור בהמה טהורה, דדרשה ד"מן המותר בפיך" היא פשוטה. אלא לכורכן בשערן צריך בהמה טהורה – הא נמי הל"מ, דתניא כו'. מדלא קתני רב יוסף בהאי לישנא "ונכרכות בשערן" – ש"מ דמילתא אחריתא אתא לאשמעינן, אלא לרצועותיהן – והא"ר יצחק רצועות שחורות הל"מ, וכיון דמצריך שיהו הרצועות שחורות כמו הקציצה – כל שכן דבעינן שיהו טהורות כמו הקציצה, דסברא הוא להקפיד על הטהרה מעל השחרות. ואי הא אתא רב יוסף לאשמעי' לישמעינן – שיהיו שחורות, דהוה שמעינן מינה תרתי, שחורות וטהורות. ומשני: נהי דגמירי שחורות, טהורות מי גמירי – דמשחורות ליכא למיגמר טהורות: **לא צריכא אלא לכורכן בשערן.** קשה לרשב"א: אי הא אתא לאשמעי', אמאי נקט עור במילתיה? רבא

עין משפט נר מצוה

פה א מיי' פ"א מהלכות תפילין הלכה י ופ"ג מהלכות ס"ת הלכה א סמג עשין כב כה טוש"ע או"ח סימן לב סעיף יב וטור וש"ע יו"ד סימן רעא סעיף א:

פו ב מיי' פ"ג מהלכות תפילין הלכה טו סמג עשין כב טור ש"ע או"ח סי' לב סעיף לז:

פז ג מיי' שם הלכה א טוש"ע שם סעיף מב:

פח ד מיי' שם הלכ' ד טוש"ע שם סעיף מט:

פט ה מיי' שם טוש"ע שם סעיף מד:

צ ו מיי' שם הל' יד וש"ע שם סעיף מט. לקמן קח. מנחות לה.

מנחות שם מגילה כד:

צא ז ח מיי' שם הלכה יד טו סמג שם טור ש"ע או"ח סימן לג סעיף ג:

צב ט מיי' פ"א מהל' מאכלות אסורות הלכה יב טור ש"ע יו"ד סימן פ סעיף ד:

צג י טוש"ע או"ח סימן רסד סעיף ט:

צד כ מיי' פ"ה מהלכות שבת הלכה ה סמג לאוין סה טור ש"ע או"ח סימן רסד סעיף ח:

[עי' תוספות חולין נט: ד"ה קרש] ע"ז ח. ע"ש חולין ס.

רבינו חננאל

אתיא בק"ו מנוצה של עזים. ומה נוצה של עזים שאינה מטמאה בנגעים (בג' על ג') מטמא באהלים דילפינן אהל אהל ממשכן. עור בהמה טמאה שמטמא בנגעים אינו דין שיטמא באהלים ואלא הא דתני רב יוסף לא הוכשרו למלאכת שמים אלא עור בהמה טהורה למאי הלכתא ואסיקנא לרצועות של תפילין. שיהו מבהמה טהורה. אבל תפילין עצמן בהדיא כתיב בהו למען תהיה תורת ה' בפיך. ודרשינן מן המותר בפיך. וגם שי"ן של תפילין. וכי נכרכות בשערן ונתפרות בגידן ורצועותיהן שחורות הלכה למשה מסיני הן. ואסיק' נמי תחש בריה בפ"ע היא ולא הכריעו חכמים אי מין חיה הוא [או מין בהמה] וקרן היה לו וטהור היה: **פיסקא** פתילת הבגד שקפלה ולא הבהבה כו'. א"ר אלעזר מתניתין בג' על ג' מצומצמות הוא. וביו"ט שחל להיות בע"ש. וכולי עלמא אית להו דר' יהודה דאמר מסיקין בכלים ואין מסיקין בשברי כלים. וכולי עלמא אית להו דעולא דאמר צריך להדליק ברוב היוצא. ר' אלעזר סבר קיפול אינו מועיל וכיון דאדליק בה פורתא הוה ליה שבר כלי. וכי קא מדליק בשבר כלי קא מדליק. ולפיכך אסור. ור"ע סבר קיפול מועיל וכיון דקפליה בטליה וכי קא מדליק בעץ בעלמא

רב נסים גאון

בר' טפחים: **אתיא** בק"ו מנוצה של עזים שאין מטמא טומאת נגעים. תמצא עיקר דילי' בתורת כהנים והבגד יכול השיראין והסיריקון והכלך וצמר גפן וצמר גמלים וצמר ארנבאין ונוצה של עזים ת"ל בבגד צמר או בבגד פשתים אין לי אלא צמר ופשתים המיוחדין: **כיון** דאיכא קרש דמין חיה הוא ולית ליה אלא קרן אחד. במס' שחיטת חולין בפרק אלו טריפות (דף ס) אמרו וקרש אע"פ שאין

מסורת הש"ס

שמות יג

[לקמן קח.]

תהלים סט

לקמן קח.

[מכות יא.]

[עי' פרש"י מנחות לה: ובתוס' שם ד"ה אלו תפילין שבראש וכו' שהשיגו על פירש"י מסוגי' דהכא דמסיק אלא לרצועות וכו' ועי' רש"י ותוס' לקמן סב. ד"ה שי"ן של תפילין ועי' תוס' מגילה כד: ד"ה תשמישי קדושה וכו' ובכ"ש ותוס' עירובין צז. ד"ה קשר ותוס' ברכות ו. ד"ה אלו]

לקמן קכג: ביצה לב.

לעיל כ:

גליון הש"ס

גמ' והאמר אביי שי"ן של תפילין. ק"ל הא י"ל לשור של תפלה של יד וכו': גמ' אמר רב יוסף היינו דתנינא שלש על שלש. עיין זה יבמות דף עז ע"ב ודף פ ע"א:

שֶׁחָקַק קַב. בְּי"ט, דַּהֲוָה לֵיהּ נוֹלָד: לְדִבְרֵיהֶם דְּר' אֱלִיעֶזֶר וְר' עֲקִיבָא קָאָמַר. הַאי דְּאוֹקִים לְהוּ רַב אַדָּא אַלִּיבָּא דְּר' יְהוּדָה – דַּחֲזָא פְּלוּגְתַּיְיהוּ דְּלָא מִיתוֹקְמָא אֶלָּא אַלִּיבָּא דְּר' יְהוּדָה. וּמִיהוּ, אִיהוּ לָא סְבִירָא לֵיהּ אֶלָּא כְּר' שִׁמְעוֹן: טַעֲמָא דְּר' אֱלִיעֶזֶר. בְּהַדְלָקָה מִשּׁוּם דְּאֵין מַדְלִיקִין בּוֹ, שֶׁאֵין דּוֹלְקִין יָפֶה, וּבְכָל שַׁבְּתוֹת הַשָּׁנָה אָסוּר, וְלָאו מִשּׁוּם נוֹלָד: חוּץ מִן הַמְּלָל. (נ"א בה) דֶּרֶךְ אוֹמְרֵי בְּגָדִים לְמוֹל מִן הַבְּגָדִים לְכוֹפְלָן מְעַט סָבִיב הַתְּפִירָה, וְאַח"כ תּוֹפֵר, וְג' עַל ג' סוֹפוֹ לִתְפּוֹר לִטְלַאי בְּבֶגֶד עָנִי, לָכֵן אַחְשְׁבוּהּ לִהְיוֹת כְּלִי, הִלְכָּךְ צָרִיךְ לִהְיוֹת בּוֹ יוֹתֵר מִשִּׁיעוּר הַמְּלָל, כְּדֵי שֶׁיְּהֵא הַטְּלַאי שָׁלֹשׁ עַל שָׁלֹשׁ: מְכוּוָּנוֹת. מְצוּמְצָמוֹת. וּדְהָכִי אַחְשְׁבוּהּ, (כלים פכ"ח מ"ז) וְאַע"ג דִּכְשֶׁיִּתָּפֵר לֹא הָוֵי שָׁלֹשׁ, וְהַיְינוּ הָךְ דְּרַב יוֹסֵף. וְלָאו מִשּׁוּם דְּאִי הָוֵי טְפֵי לָא מִיטַּמֵּא, (ס"א ל"ג) *(דְּכָל שֶׁכֵּן), אֶלָּא לְאַפּוּקֵי מִדְּתַנָּא קַמָּא: מַסִּיקִין בִּתְמָרִים. דְּאַגַּב דְּמִטַּלְטֵל לְהוּ לַאֲכִילָה חֲזוּ נַמִּי לְהַסָּקָה: אֲכָלָן. בְּיו"ט אֵין מַסִּיקִין בַּגַּרְעִינִין בְּיו"ט, דַּהֲוָה לְהוּ נוֹלָד: וְהַשְׁתָּא מִגַּלְיָין. הִלְכָּךְ נוֹלָד הָוֵי: וְהָא דְּרַב. דַּאֲמַר: לְר' יְהוּדָה אֵין מַסִּיקִין בַּגַּרְעִינִין, לָאו בְּפֵירוּשׁ אִיתְּמַר: אֲבַל תַּמְרֵי. בְּחוֹל: לְבוּכְיָא. כִּירָה שֶׁל רְעָפִים שֶׁקּוֹרִין טיול"ש, וְהִיא חֲלוּלָה. וּסְפָרִים שֶׁכָּתוּב בָּהֶן: לְבֵי תָפֵי – הַיְינוּ נַמִּי כִּירָה, וְהוּא תַּרְגּוּם שֶׁל בֵּית שְׁפִיתַת שְׁתֵּי קְדֵרוֹת: קַשְׁיָיתָא. גַּרְעִינִין: בַּר פַּחְתֵי. בֶּן גְּדוֹלִים: אֲבַל תַּמְרֵי. בְּיוֹם טוֹב: פַּרְסָיָיתָא. (ברכות ע. וש"נ) תְּמָרִים טוֹבִים וּמִתְבַּשְּׁלִים יָפֶה, וְכָל אוֹכֶל שֶׁלָּהֶם נִפְרָשׁ מֵעַל גַּרְעִינֵיהֶן, וְאֵין הַגַּרְעִינִין רְאוּיִן לְטַלְטֵל – וְאַפ"ה שָׁרֵי (גי' הערוך לבוביא) לְטַלְטְלָן לְמִישְׁדִינְהוּ לְחֵיוָתָא. אַלְמָא, לָא קִיבְּלָהּ מִינֵּיהּ: בְּאַרְמָיָתָא. דְּאֵין מִתְבַּשְּׁלוֹת יָפֶה, וְאֵין הָאוֹכֶל נִפְרָשׁ מֵהֶן, וּמִשְׁתַּיֵּיר בְּגַרְעִינֵיהֶן, וַחֲזוּ לְאָדָם: אַגַּב אִימַּיְיהוּ. (פי' תמרי ארמיתא גרעינייהו רכין ונאכלין גרעיניהן עם התמרים ערוך ערך ארם) שֶׁיֵּשׁ עוֹד מֵאוֹכֶל עֲלֵיהֶן: מַרְבֶּה. עֲלֵיהֶן, וּמְבַטְּלָן בָּרוֹב: רַב הַמְנוּנָא אָמַר. מַתְנִיתִין בִּפְחוֹת מִשְּׁלֹשָׁה טְפָחִים עַל שְׁלֹשָׁה טְפָחִים פְּלִיגֵי לְעִנְיַן טוּמְאָה: וּמְקוּלֵּי מַטְלָנִיּוֹת. מַטְלָנִיּוֹת הַקַּלּוֹת בְּעֵינָיו, דּוּמְיָא דְּמִתּוּקָּנוֹת לְפַקּוּק מֶרְחָץ, דְּמִידֵי דְּלָא (ביצה ד.) חָשִׁיב הוּא. וְקִיפּוּל דְּנָקַט בְּמַתְנִיתִין – מִשּׁוּם הָכִי נָקַט דְּנָקַט דַּוְקָא, וְלִפְלוּגְתָּא דְּהַדְלָקָה תְּנָא קִיפּוּל: פָּחוֹת מִשְּׁלֹשָׁה כו'. (לקמן לט:) דְּאִילּוּ שְׁלֹשָׁה עַל שְׁלֹשָׁה חֲשִׁיבֵי, וְלָא בָּטְלֵי. וְאַע"ג דְּקִילֵּי, כְּגוֹן סְמַרְטוּטִין: שֶׁהִתְקִינוֹ לְכָךְ. שֶׁהִקְצוּ לְכָךְ: לְפַקּוּק הַמֶּרְחָץ. (כלים פכ"ח מ"ב) נְקָבִים שֶׁהַמַּיִם בָּאִים דֶּרֶךְ שָׁם לַמֶּרְחָץ: וּלְנַעֵר בּוֹ אֶת הַקְּדֵרָה. לֶאֱחוֹז בָּהֶן שׁוּלֵי הַקְּדֵרָה, וּלְנַעֲרָהּ לְתוֹךְ הַתַּמְחוּי: בֵּין מִן הַמּוּכָן. לְקַמֵּיהּ מְפָרֵשׁ: הִנִּיחוֹ

גּוֹי שֶׁחָקַק קַב בְּבִקַעַת, יִשְׂרָאֵל מַסִּיקָהּ *בְּיו"ט. וְאַמַּאי? נוֹלָד הוּא! לְדִבְרֵיהֶם דְּר"א וְר"ע קָאָמַר לֵיהּ, וְלֵיהּ לָא סְבִירָא לֵיהּ. רָבָא אָמַר: הַיְינוּ טַעְמָא דְּרַבִּי אֱלִיעֶזֶר – לְפִי שֶׁאֵין מַדְלִיקִין בִּפְתִילָה שֶׁאֵינָהּ מְחוֹרֶכֶת, וְלֹא בִּסְמַרְטוּטִין שֶׁאֵינָן מְחוֹרָכִין. אֶלָּא הָא דְּתָנֵי רַב יוֹסֵף: "ג' עַל ג' מְצוּמְצָמוֹת" לְמַאי הִלְכְתָא? לְעִנְיַן טוּמְאָה, *דִּתְנַן: ג' עַל ג' שֶׁאָמְרוּ – חוּץ מִן הַמְּלָל, דִּבְרֵי ר"ש. וַחֲכ"א: [א]ג' עַל ג' מְכוּוָּנוֹת.§ אָמַר רַב יְהוּדָה אָמַר רַב: *[ב]מַסִּיקִין בְּכֵלִים וְאֵין מַסִּיקִין בְּשִׁבְרֵי כֵלִים, דִּבְרֵי רַבִּי יְהוּדָה, וְר"ש מַתִּיר. מַסִּיקִין בִּתְמָרִין, [ג]אֲכָלָן – אֵין מַסִּיקִין בְּגַרְעִינֵיהֶן, דִּבְרֵי רַבִּי יְהוּדָה, וְר"ש מַתִּיר. מַסִּיקִין בֶּאֱגוֹזִים, אֲכָלָן – אֵין מַסִּיקִין בִּקְלִיפּוֹתֵיהֶן, דִּבְרֵי רַבִּי יְהוּדָה, וְרַבִּי שִׁמְעוֹן מַתִּיר. וּצְרִיכָא, דְּאִי אַשְׁמְעִינַן קַמַּיְיתָא – בְּהַהִיא קָאָמַר רַבִּי יְהוּדָה – מִשּׁוּם דִּמְעִיקָּרָא כְּלִי וְהַשְׁתָּא שֶׁבֶר כְּלִי, וַהֲוָה לֵיהּ נוֹלָד – וְאָסוּר. אֲבָל תְּמָרִים, דִּמְעִיקָּרָא גַּרְעִינִין וְהַשְׁתָּא גַּרְעִינִין – אֵימָא שַׁפִּיר דָּמֵי. וְאִי אַשְׁמְעִינַן גַּרְעִינִין – הֲוָה אָמִינָא: דִּמְעִיקָּרָא מִכַּסְיָין, וְהַשְׁתָּא מִיגַּלְיָין. אֲבָל קְלִיפֵּי אֱגוֹזִין, דִּמְעִיקָּרָא מִיגַּלּוּ וְהַשְׁתָּא מִיגַּלּוּ – אֵימָא שַׁפִּיר דָּמֵי, צְרִיכָא. וְהָא דְּרַב – *לָאו בְּפֵירוּשׁ אִיתְּמַר, אֶלָּא מִכְּלָלָא אִיתְּמַר. דְּרַב אֲכַל תַּמְרֵי וּשְׁדָא קַשְׁיָיתָא *לְבוּכְיָא, אֲמַר לֵיהּ רַבִּי חִיָּיא: *בַּר פַּחְתֵי, כְּנֶגְדּוֹ בְּיו"ט – אָסוּר. קִיבְּלָהּ מִינֵּיהּ אוֹ לֹא קִיבְּלָהּ מִינֵּיהּ? ת"ש, דְּכִי אֲתָא רַב לְבָבֶל אֲכַל תַּמְרֵי וּשְׁדָא קַשְׁיָיתָא לְחֵיוָתָא. מַאי לָאו בְּפַרְסָיְיאָתָא וְלָא קִיבְּלָהּ! לָא, *בְּאַרְמָיָיאתָא – הוֹאִיל וַחֲזֵי אַגַּב אִימַּיְיהוּ. א"ל ר' שְׁמוּאֵל בַּר בַּר חָנָה לְרַב יוֹסֵף: לְרַבִּי יְהוּדָה דְּאָמַר "מַסִּיקִין בְּכֵלִים וְאֵין מַסִּיקִין בְּשִׁבְרֵי כֵלִים" [ד]כֵּיוָן דְּאַדְלִיק בְּהוּ פּוּרְתָּא – הֲוָה לֵיהּ שִׁבְרֵי כֵלִים, וְכִי קָא מְהַפֵּךְ – בְּאִיסּוּרָא קָא מְהַפֵּךְ! דַּעֲבַד כִּדְרַב מַתָּנָה, *דְּאָמַר רַב מַתָּנָה אָמַר רַב: [ה]עֵצִים שֶׁנָּשְׁרוּ מִן הַדֶּקֶל לַתַּנּוּר בְּיו"ט מַרְבֶּה עֵצִים מוּכָנִין, וּמַסִּיקָן. רַב הַמְנוּנָא אָמַר: הָכָא בִּפְחוֹת מִשְּׁלֹשָׁה עַל שְׁלֹשָׁה עָסְקִינַן, *וּמְקוּלֵּי מַטְלָנִיּוֹת שָׁנוּ כָּאן. וְאָזְדָא ר' אֱלִיעֶזֶר לְטַעְמֵיהּ וְר"ע לְטַעְמֵיהּ, *דִּתְנַן: פָּחוֹת מִשְּׁלֹשָׁה עַל שְׁלֹשָׁה שֶׁהִתְקִינוֹ לְפַקֵּק בּוֹ אֶת הַמֶּרְחָץ, וּלְנַעֵר בּוֹ אֶת הַקְּדֵירָה, וּלְקַנֵּחַ בּוֹ אֶת הָרֵחַיִם – בֵּין מִן הַמּוּכָן וּבֵין שֶׁאֵין מִן הַמּוּכָן – טָמֵא, דִּבְרֵי רַבִּי אֱלִיעֶזֶר. וְרַבִּי יְהוֹשֻׁעַ אוֹמֵר: בֵּין מִן הַמּוּכָן וּבֵין שֶׁלֹּא מִן הַמּוּכָן – טָהוֹר. ר"ע אוֹמֵר: מִן הַמּוּכָן – טָמֵא וְשֶׁלֹּא מִן הַמּוּכָן – טָהוֹר. וְאָמַר עוּלָּא, וְאִיתֵּימָא רַבָּה בַּר בַּר חָנָה א"ר יוֹחָנָן, הַכֹּל מוֹדִים: זְרָקוֹ בְּאַשְׁפָּה – דִּבְרֵי הַכֹּל טָהוֹר, הִנִּיחוֹ

רבא אמר היינו טעמא דר' אליעזר. משמע דרבא לענין טומאה אית ליה שיעורא דרב אדא בר אהבה, ולקמן משמע דאית ליה שיעורא דרב המנונא, דאמר "מקולי מטלניות שנו כאן", דקאמר: והדר ביה ר' עקיבא לגבי ר' יהושע. על כן נראה דהכא גרס רבה, ולקמן רבא. ונ"ל דבחנם נהגו אנשים להדליק הפתילה ולכבותה כדי שתהא מהובהבת, דהא אין הלכה כרבי אליעזר – דשמותי הוא, ועוד, אמרינן לקמן: הכא בפתילה שצריך להבהבה עסקינן, משמע דיכול להדליק אע"פ שאינה מהובהבת:

ולא בסמרטוטין שאינן מחורכין. קשה: כיון דתנא דאפילו בפתילה שאינה מחורכת אין מדליקין, כ"ש בסמרטוטין שאינם מחורכין! ומיהו, בתוספתא גרס: ולא בסמרטוטין, אפי' מחורכין:

אבלן אין מסיקין בגרעיניהן. (ביצה לב. וש"נ ע"ש) תימה לר"י: דבפרק "נוטל" (לקמן דף קמג:) אמר: למימרא דרבא כרבי יהודה סבירא ליה. פירוש: דאסר נבלה שנתנבלה בשבת, והא"ל לשמעי': טווי לי בר אווזא ושדי מיעיה לשונרא. ומשני: התם כיון דמסרח – דעתיה עילויה מאתמול. אלמא: כיון דדעתו מאתמול לתת לשונרא כשיסריח למחר – שרי, אע"ג דכל זמן שלא הסריח חזי לאדם. *משום דחשיב כאילו הכינו מבעוד יום לשונרא. ה"נ, מאתמול דעתיה עילויה להסיר הגרעינין כשיאכל התמרים למחר, ואמאי חשיב ליה טפי נולד ממיעיה דבר אווזא? וי"ל: דהתם בר אווזא נשחט מעי"ט ואין המעיים צריכים לאווז, וכיון דמבעוד יום דעתיה למיתביה לשונרא אם יסריחו – חשיבה הכנה מעלייתא. אבל הכא הגרעינין צריכין לאוכל, וחשיבי כאוכל עצמו עד שיאכל התמרים, לכך חשיב להו נולד, ולא מהני מה שדעתו עליהם מאתמול:

(ורש"י פי' לקמן משום דאין דרך לאכול מעיים ביו"ט ולא נהירא דמשום זה לא הוי אסור לטלטלו כמו בשר מלוח דמותר לטלטלו [ת"י])

והא דרב לאו בפירוש איתמר כו'. הא פשיטא דרב אסר נולד כרבי יהודה מכרכי דזוזי (לעיל דף יט:), אלא מייתי ראיה דאף בגרעינין, דאיכא למימר מעיקרא גרעינין והשתא גרעינין – אסר רבי יהודה. וא"ת: ובאגוזים דמעיקרא מגלו והשתא מגלו מנלן דאסר? וי"ל: דאע"ג דמטעם זה עושה צריכותא, מ"מ מטעם זה לפי האמת אין נראה לו לחלק ביניהם: (לעיל ג: וש"נ)

בין מן המוכן כו'. פירש בקונטרס: מוכן דרבי אליעזר – קופסא, שאינו מוכן – תלאו במגוד והניחו אחורי הדלת. ומוכן דר' יהושע – תלאו במגוד והניחו אחורי הדלת, *ושאינו מוכן – זרקו לאשפה. ורבי עקיבא: מוכן – תלאו במגוד, ושאינו מוכן – הניחו אחורי הדלת. וקשה לר"י: דהשתא מוכן ושאינו מוכן דהאי תנא לא הוי כאידך. ועוד: מה להם להזכיר בדבריהם קופסא ואשפה דלא פליגי בה? ועוד, דבפרק "כירה" (לקמן דף לט: ושם) קרי לרבי עקיבא מכריע. ואמאי? והלא לא גילו בדבריהם רבי אליעזר ורבי יהושע שיש לחלק בין תלאו במגוד להניחו אחורי הדלת! ונראה לר"י: דמוכן דכולהו – היינו תלאו במגוד, ושאינו מוכן – היינו הניחו אחורי הדלת. והאי דקאמר: "אמאי קרי ליה שלא מן המוכן", פירש רבי אליעזר: אמאי קרי להניחו אחורי הדלת שלא מן המוכן – הואיל והוא טמא – ומשני: משום דלגבי קופסא לאו מוכן הוא. ולא בעי למימר: משום דלגבי מגוד לאו מוכן הוא, דלא חשיב כולי האי תלאו במגוד מאחורי הדלת, דהוה קרי ליה לגביה שלא מן המוכן. וכן לר' יהושע קא בעי: אמאי חשיב לתלאו במגוד מן המוכן, הואיל והוא טהור – ומשני: דלגבי אשפה מוכן הוא. והא דלא קאמר דלגבי אחורי הדלת מוכן הוא – משום דלא גריע כולי האי טפי ממגוד, דליהוי אינו מוכן לגביה: גזירה

(גם בירושלמי פירש כן)

עין משפט נר מצוה

צה א מיי' פכ"ב מהל' כלים הלכה א:

צו ב מיי' פ"ב מהל' יו"ט הלכה יב סמג לאוין סה טוש"ע א"ח סי' תקא סעיף ו:

צז ג מיי' שם טוש"ע שם סעיף ז:

צח ד שם סעיף ו בהג"ה:

צט ה מיי' שם הלכה יא סמג שם טוש"ע א"ח סי' תקז סעיף ב:

רבינו חננאל

מדליק רבא אמר טעמא דר' אליעזר לפי שאין מדליקין לא בסמרטוטין ולא בפתילה שאינה מחורכת. ורבי עקיבא מתיר: ירושלמי מהו מכורכין מפספסן דכת' (דניאל ג') ושער ראשיהון לא התחרך. ג' על ג' מצומצמות שאמרו חוץ מן המלל דברי ר' שמעון וחכ"א ג' על ג' מכוונות:

אמר רב יהודה אמר רב מסיקין בכלים ואין מסיקין בשברי כלים. מסיקין בתמרים. אכלן אין מסיקין בגרעיניהן. מסיקין באגוזים. אכלן אין מסיקין בקליפיהן דברי רבי יהודה. ורבי שמעון מתיר בכולן. וצריכא דאי אשמעינן וכו' ופשוטה היא. עד אבל קליפי אגוזים דמעיקרא מיגלו אימא קא שרי ר' יהודה צריכא. והא דרב מכללן איתמר דרב אכל תמרי ושדא קשייתא לבוביא א"ל ר' חייא בר פחתי כנגדו ביו"ט אסור ואסיקנא קיבלה מיניה והא כי אתא רב לבבל אכל תמרי ושדא קשייתא לחייתא. ואוקימנא בתמרי ארמייתא שגרעיניהן רכים. והואיל וראוין להיאכל בכלל התמרים כאוכל הן ולפיכך טלטלם. אבל שדו גרעינין דלא חזי אגב אימייהו אסור כר' חייא אליבא דרבי יהודה קסבר הלכה כר' יהודה ביו"ט הואיל וסתם לן כוותיה ביו"ט. ומדמתרץ להו דר' יהודה כרב מתנה שמע מינה הלכתא כוותיה. דאמר רב מתנה עצים שנשרו מן הדקל לתנור ביו"ט מרבה עליהם עצים מוכנים ומסיקן. ואוקמה רב המנונא למתני' במטלניות פחות מג' אצבעות והא דמייתי ראיה ממטלת פחותה מג' על ג' מקולי מטלניות שנו כו'. דתנן בכלים בפ' כ"ח פחות מג' על ג' שהתקינו לפקק את המרחץ ולנער בו הקדירה ולקנח בו הריחיים בין מוכן בין שאינו מוכן טמא דברי ר' אליעזר. ר' יהושע אומר בין מוכן בין שאינו מוכן טהור. רע"א

רב נסים גאון

מאי לאו בפריסאתא ולא קבלה לא בארמיאתא הואיל וחזיאן אגב אימיהו. תמצא פירושה בסוף פ' נוטל אדם את בנו (דף קמג) הני גרעיני דתמרי ארמיאתא שרי לטלטולינהו בשבתא הואיל וחזיאן אגב אימן כי התמרים יבשים תאכל אותם הבהמה ודפריסאתא אסור לפי שהרוטב של תמרים לא תאכל הבהמה אלא גרעינא בלבד לא חזיין אגב אימן: מותיב

ק א מיי' פכ"ב מהל' כלים הלכה כב:
קא ב מיי' פ"ה מהל' שבת הל' יב טוש"ע א"ח סי' רסה סעיף א:
קב ג מיי' שם טוש"ע שם סעיף ב:
קג ד מיי' שם טוש"ע שם סעיף א:
קד ה מיי' פ"י מהל' כלאים הל' טז סמג לאוין רפג טוש"ע י"ד סי' שא סעיף ו:
קה ו מיי' פ"א מהל' שבת הלכה ה סמג לאוין סה טוש"ע א"ח סי' של"ז סעיף א:
קו ז ח מיי' פ"א שם הלכה ז ופי"ב הלכה ב סמג שם טוש"ע א"ח סימן רעח:

גזירה עיליתא דשישא אטו עיליתא דעלמא. והא דקאמר בסוף "המצניע" (לקמן דף צה. ושם): אמימר שרא זילחא במחוזא. ומפרש: דטעמא מאי אסור רבנן – דילמא אתי לאשויי גומות, הכא ליכא גומות. ומפרש בקונטרס: דכולה מחוזא רצפה היתה, התם אין לגזור מחוזא אטו שאר עיירות, אבל בעיר אחת גזרינן עלייה זו אטו עלייה אחרת: ה"ג מחלוקת בקטנים אבל בגדולים ד"ה מותר. ול"ג ד"ה אסור. דבפרק "כל שעה" (פסחים דף כה: ושם) משמע דטפי שרי היכא דלא אפשר מהיכא דאפשר:

ובלבד שלא יתכוין בחמה מפני החמה וכו'. ובענין דלא הוי פסיק רישיה, כגון שהוא לבוש מלבושים אחרים להגין עליו מפני החמה ומפני הצינה:

שהמרו

הִנִּיחוֹ בְּקוּפְסָא – דִּבְרֵי הַכֹּל טָמֵא, לֹא נֶחְלְקוּ אֶלָּא שֶׁתְּלָאוֹ בְּמָגוֹד אוֹ שֶׁהִנִּיחוֹ לַאֲחוֹרֵי הַדֶּלֶת. ר' אֱלִיעֶזֶר סָבַר: אמִדְּלָא זְרָקוֹ בְּאַשְׁפָּה – דַּעְתֵּיהּ עִילָּוֵיהּ, וּמַאי(א) קָרֵי לֵיהּ 'שֶׁלֹּא מִן הַמּוּכָן' – דִּלְגַבֵּי קוּפְסָא לָאו מוּכָן הוּא. וְר' יְהוֹשֻׁעַ סָבַר: מִדְּלָא הִנִּיחוֹ בְּקוּפְסָא – בַּטּוֹלֵי בַּטְלֵיהּ, וּמַאי קָרֵי לֵיהּ 'מוּכָן' – דִּלְגַבֵּי אַשְׁפָּה מוּכָן הוּא. וְר' עֲקִיבָא, בִּתְלָאוֹ בְּמָגוֹד – סָבַר כְּרַבִּי אֱלִיעֶזֶר, בְּהִנִּיחוֹ אֲחוֹרֵי הַדֶּלֶת – סָבַר לָהּ כְּרַבִּי יְהוֹשֻׁעַ. *וַהֲדַר בֵּיהּ ר"ע לְגַבֵּיהּ דְּר' יְהוֹשֻׁעַ. מִמַּאי? אָמַר רָבָא: מִדְּקָתָנֵי 'פְּתִילַת הַבֶּגֶד', מַאי אִירְיָא דְּתָנֵי 'פְּתִילַת הַבֶּגֶד', לִיתְנֵי "פְּתִילָה שֶׁל בֶּגֶד"! מַאי 'פְּתִילַת הַבֶּגֶד' – דַּעֲדַיִין בֶּגֶד הוּא.§ **מתני'** בלֹא *יִקּוֹב אָדָם שְׁפוֹפֶרֶת שֶׁל בֵּיצָה וִימַלְּאֶנָּה שֶׁמֶן וְיִתְּנֶנָּה עַל פִּי הַנֵּר בִּשְׁבִיל שֶׁתְּהֵא מְנַטֶּפֶת, וַאֲפִילּוּ הִיא שֶׁל חֶרֶס, וְרַבִּי יְהוּדָה מַתִּיר. אֲבָל אִם חִבְּרָהּ הַיּוֹצֵר מִתְּחִלָּה – מוּתָּר, מִפְּנֵי שֶׁהוּא כְּלִי אֶחָד. גלֹא יְמַלֵּא אָדָם קְעָרָה שֶׁל שֶׁמֶן וְיִתְּנֶנָּה בְּצַד הַנֵּר וְיִתֵּן רֹאשׁ הַפְּתִילָה בְּתוֹכָהּ בִּשְׁבִיל שֶׁתְּהֵא שׁוֹאֶבֶת, וְרַבִּי יְהוּדָה מַתִּיר.§ **גמ'** וּצְרִיכָא, דְּאִי אַשְׁמְעִינַן שְׁפוֹפֶרֶת שֶׁל בֵּיצָה – בְּהָא קָאָמְרִי רַבָּנַן דְּכֵיוָן דְּלָא מְאִיסָא – אָתֵי לְאִסְתַּפּוֹקֵי מִינַּהּ, אֲבָל שֶׁל חֶרֶס דְּמְאִיסָא – אֵימָא מוֹדוּ לֵיהּ לְרַבִּי יְהוּדָה, וְאִי אַשְׁמְעִינַן שֶׁל חֶרֶס – בְּהָא קָאָמַר רַבִּי יְהוּדָה, אֲבָל בְּהַהִיא – אֵימָא מוֹדֵי לְהוּ לְרַבָּנַן, וְאִי אַשְׁמְעִינַן הָנָךְ תַּרְתֵּי – בְּהָנֵי קָאָמַר רַבִּי יְהוּדָה מִשּׁוּם דְּלָא מִיפְסַק, אֲבָל קְעָרָה דְּמִיפְסְקָא – אֵימָא מוֹדֵי לְהוּ לְרַבָּנַן, וְאִי אַשְׁמְעִינַן בְּהַהִיא – בְּהַהִיא קָאָמְרִי רַבָּנַן, אֲבָל בְּהָנֵי תַּרְתֵּי – אֵימָא מוֹדוּ לְרַבִּי יְהוּדָה, צְרִיכָא.§ "וְאִם חִבְּרָהּ הַיּוֹצֵר מִתְּחִלָּה מוּתָּר וכו'".§ תָּנָא: אִם דחִבְּרָהּ בְּסִיד וּבְחַרְסִית – מוּתָּר, וְהָאֲנַן 'יוֹצֵר' תְּנַן! מַאי יוֹצֵר – כְּעֵין יוֹצֵר.§ *תַּנְיָא, א"ר יְהוּדָה: פַּעַם אַחַת שָׁבַתְנוּ בַּעֲלִיַּית בֵּית נִתְזָה בְּלוֹד וְהֵבִיאוּ לָנוּ שְׁפוֹפֶרֶת שֶׁל בֵּיצָה וּמִלֵּאנוּהָ שֶׁמֶן וּנְקַבְנוּהָ וְהִנַּחְנוּהָ עַל פִּי הַנֵּר וְהָיָה שָׁם ר"ט וּזְקֵנִים וְלֹא אָמְרוּ לָנוּ דָּבָר. אָמְרוּ לוֹ: *מִשָּׁם רְאָיָה?! שָׁאנֵי בֵּית נִתְזָה דִּזְרִיזִין הֵן. אָבִין צִיפּוֹרָאָה גְּרַר סַפְסָלָא בְּעִילִּיתָא דְּשִׁישָׁא לְעֵילָּא מֵרַבִּי יִצְחָק בֶּן אֶלְעָזָר, א"ל: אִי שְׁתוֹקִי לָךְ כִּדְשַׁתִּיקוּ לֵיהּ חַבְרַיָּא לְר' יְהוּדָה נָפֵיק מִינֵּיהּ חוּרְבָּא: הגְּזֵירָה עִלִּיתָא דְּשִׁישָׁא אַטּוּ עִלִּיתָא דְּעָלְמָא. רֵישׁ כְּנִישְׁתָּא דְּבָצְרָה גְּרַר סַפְסָלָא לְעֵילָּא מֵר' יִרְמְיָה רַבָּה, א"ל: כְּמַאן – *כר"ש? אֵימַר דַּאֲמַר ר"ש בִּגְדוֹלִים, דְּלָא אֶפְשָׁר, בִּקְטַנִּים מִי אֲמַר?! וּפְלִיגָא דְּעוּלָּא, דְּאָמַר עוּלָּא: מַחֲלוֹקֶת – בִּקְטַנִּים, אֲבָל בִּגְדוֹלִים – ד"ה מוּתָּר. מְתִיב רַב יוֹסֵף, *ר"ש אוֹמֵר: גּוֹרֵר אָדָם מִטָּה כִּסֵּא וְסַפְסָל וּבִלְבַד שֶׁלֹּא יִתְכַּוֵּין לַעֲשׂוֹת חָרִיץ. קָתָנֵי גְּדוֹלִים וְקָתָנֵי קְטַנִּים, קַשְׁיָא לְתַרְוַיְיהוּ! עוּלָּא מְתָרֵץ לְטַעֲמֵיהּ, וְר' יִרְמְיָה רַבָּה מְתָרֵץ לְטַעֲמֵיהּ. עוּלָּא מְתָרֵץ לְטַעֲמֵיהּ: מִטָּה דּוּמְיָא דְּכִסֵּא. וְר' יִרְמְיָה רַבָּה מְתָרֵץ לְטַעֲמֵי': כִּסֵּא דּוּמְיָא דְּמִטָּה. מְתִיב רַבָּה: *מוֹכְרֵי וכְּסוּת מוֹכְרִין כְּדַרְכָּן, וּבִלְבַד שֶׁלֹּא יִתְכַּוֵּין בַּחַמָּה מִפְּנֵי הַחַמָּה וּבַגְּשָׁמִים מִפְּנֵי הַגְּשָׁמִים, וְהַצְּנוּעִין מַפְשִׁילִין בְּמַקֵּל לַאֲחוֹרֵיהֶן. וְהָא הָכָא, דְּאֶפְשָׁר לְמֶיעְבַּד כִּצְנוּעִין, דְּכִי קְטַנִּים דָּמֵי, וְכִי זלֹא מִתְכַּוֵּין – שָׁרֵי ר"ש לְכַתְּחִלָּה! תְּיוּבְתָּא דְּר"י רַבָּה! *תְּיוּבְתָּא.§ **מתני'** חהַמְכַבֶּה אֶת הַנֵּר מִפְּנֵי שֶׁהוּא מִתְיָרֵא מִפְּנֵי גּוֹיִם וּמִפְּנֵי לִיסְטִי', מִפְּנֵי רוּחַ רָעָה, מִפְּנֵי הַחוֹלֶה שֶׁיִּישַׁן – פָּטוּר. כְּחָס עַל הַנֵּר, כְּחָס עַל הַשֶּׁמֶן, כְּחָס עַל הַפְּתִילָה – חַיָּיב. טרַבִּי יוֹסֵי *פּוֹטֵר בְּכוּלָּן, חוּץ מִן הַפְּתִילָה, מִפְּנֵי שֶׁהוּא עוֹשֶׂה פֶּחָם.§

גמ'

הִנִּיחוֹ בְּקוּפְסָא. גַּלֵּי דַּעְתֵּיהּ דַּחֲשִׁיב לֵיהּ: בְּמָגוֹד. קדיל"א, דְּגָרַע מִקּוּפְסָא וְעָדִיף מֵאֲחוֹרֵי הַדֶּלֶת. וַאֲחוֹרֵי הַדֶּלֶת עָדִיף מִזּוֹרְקוֹ לָאַשְׁפָּה. וּמוּכָן דְּר' אֱלִיעֶזֶר הַיְינוּ קוּפְסָא, וְשֶׁלֹּא מִן הַמּוּכָן – מָגוֹד וַאֲחוֹרֵי הַדֶּלֶת: וּמַאי(ב) קָרֵי לֵיהּ שֶׁלֹּא מִן הַמּוּכָן. הוֹאִיל וּלְרַבִּי אֱלִיעֶזֶר חָשִׁיב לְקַבּוּלֵי טוּמְאָה, דִּלְגַבֵּי קוּפְסָא לָאו מוּכָן הוּא: וְרַבִּי יְהוֹשֻׁעַ סָבַר כו'. וּמוּכָן דְּרַבִּי יְהוֹשֻׁעַ – מָגוֹד וַאֲחוֹרֵי הַדֶּלֶת, וְשֶׁלֹּא מִן הַמּוּכָן – זְרָקוֹ לָאַשְׁפָּה: וּמַאי(ג) קָרֵי לֵיהּ. לְמָגוֹד מוּכָן – הוֹאִיל וְלר' יְהוֹשֻׁעַ בָּטֵל, דִּלְגַבֵּי אַשְׁפָּה דְּאַיְירֵי בָּהּ רַבִּי יְהוֹשֻׁעַ – מוּכָן הוּא. וְרַבִּי עֲקִיבָא, תְּלָאוֹ בְּמָגוֹד – קָרֵי "מוּכָן", וַאֲחוֹרֵי הַדֶּלֶת – "שֶׁלֹּא מִן הַמּוּכָן": וַהֲדַר בֵּיהּ ר' עֲקִיבָא לְגַבֵּי רַבִּי יְהוֹשֻׁעַ. וּמְטַהֵר אַף בְּמוּכָן: מִדְּקָתָנֵי. בְּמַתְנִיתִין: "פְּתִילַת הַבֶּגֶד", דְּמַשְׁמַע שֶׁעֲדַיִין בֶּגֶד הוּא קָלָא, וַחֲשָׁבוֹ בְּעֵינָיו. וְאַפ"ה קָאָמַר רַבִּי עֲקִיבָא בְּמַתְנִי' "טְהוֹרָה הִיא", אַלְמָא: הֲדַר בֵּיהּ: שֶׁל בֶּגֶד. מַשְׁמַע שֶׁקִּפְּלָהּ מִבֶּגֶד. "הַבֶּגֶד" – מַשְׁמַע שֶׁקִּפֵּל הַבֶּגֶד עַצְמוֹ שָׁלֵם. וּלְעִנְיַן הַדְלָקָה כִּדְאוֹקִימְנָא לְעֵיל, טַעְמָא דְּרַבִּי אֱלִיעֶזֶר דְּבָעֵי פְּתִילָה מְחוּרֶכֶת שֶׁתִּדְלַק יָפֶה: **מתני'** שֶׁתְּהֵא מְנַטֶּפֶת. וְיִתְקַיֵּים הַנֵּר, שֶׁתְּהֵא הַשֶּׁמֶן מְטַפְטֵף כָּל שָׁעָה לְתוֹךְ הַנֵּר. וְטַעְמָא מִשּׁוּם גְּזֵרָה, שֶׁמָּא יִסְתַּפֵּק הֵימֶנּוּ, וְכֵיוָן שֶׁהִקְנָהוּ לַנֵּר – חַיָּיב מִשּׁוּם מְכַבֶּה, וַאֲפִי' אוֹתָהּ שְׁפוֹפֶרֶת שֶׁל חֶרֶס דִּמְאִיסָא לֵיהּ גָּזְרִינַן: אֲבָל אִם חִיבְּרָהּ. לֵיכָּא לְמֵיחַשׁ, דְּמִשּׁוּם אִיסּוּר שַׁבָּת בָּדֵיל מִינֵּיהּ: וְיִתֵּן רֹאשׁ הַפְּתִילָה. הַשֵּׁנִי שֶׁהוּא יוֹצֵא דֶּרֶךְ הַנֶּקֶב הָאַחֵר שֶׁבַּנֵּר לִשְׁאוֹב, וְשֶׁמֶן נִמְשָׁךְ דֶּרֶךְ הַפְּתִילָה לָרֹאשׁ הַדּוֹלֵק: וְרַבִּי יְהוּדָה מַתִּיר. דְּלָא גָּזַר: **גמ'** דְּלָא מִיפְסַק. מִידֵי, שֶׁהוּא מוּנָּח בְּתוֹךְ חֲלַל הַנֵּר לְמַעְלָה מִכִּיסּוּי: דְּמִפְסְקָא. שֶׁהֲרֵי אֵצֶל הַנֵּר מוּנַּחַת, וְיֵשׁ כָּאן הֶפְסֵק, וְלֵיכָּא לְמֵימַר גּוּפֵיהּ הוּא, אֵימָא מוֹדֶה דְּנִגְזוֹר: תָּנָא אִם חִיבְּרָהּ. בעה"ב עַצְמוֹ מִבְּעוֹד יוֹם בְּסִיד אוֹ בַּחַרְסִית – מוּתָּר: כְּעֵין יוֹצֵר. שֶׁחִבְּרָהּ שַׁפִּיר: דְּשִׁישָׁא. רִצְפָּה שֶׁל שַׁיִשׁ, דְּלָא עָבֵיד בָּהּ חָרִיץ: לְעֵילָּא מֵרַבִּי יִצְחָק. לְפָנָיו: כִּדְשַׁתִּיקוּ לֵיהּ חַבְרַיָּא. רַבִּי טַרְפוֹן וּזְקֵנִים, שֶׁמִּפְּנֵי שֶׁלֹּא אָמְרוּ לוֹ דָּבָר, דִּימָּה וְהֵעִיד דְּמוּתָּר: נָפֵק מִינֵּיהּ חוּרְבָה. וְיִנְהֲגוּ הֶיתֵּר בַּדָּבָר, וְר' יִצְחָק סְבִירָא לֵיהּ כְּרַבִּי יְהוּדָה דְּדָבָר שֶׁאֵין מִתְכַּוֵּין אָסוּר, וְאַע"ג דִּבְשַׁיִשׁ לָא עָבֵיד חָרִיץ – גָּזַר אַטּוּ עִלִּיתָא דְּעָלְמָא: רֵישׁ כְּנִישְׁתָּא. מַפְטִיר כְּנֵסִיּוֹת, הַמַּכְנִיס וּמוֹצִיא וּמְיַישֵּׁב תַּלְמִידִים וְתִינוֹקוֹת: דְּבָצְרָה. שֵׁם מָקוֹם, "כִּי זֶבַח לַה' בְּבָצְרָה" (ישעיה לד): כְּר' שִׁמְעוֹן. דְּאָמַר: "גּוֹרֵר אָדָם": דְּלָא אֶפְשָׁר. אֶלָּא בִּגְרִירָה, שֶׁאֵין יָכוֹל לִיטְּלָן בְּיָדוֹ: מַחֲלוֹקֶת בִּקְטַנִּים. וְאַע"ג דְּאֶפְשָׁר בְּטִלְטוּל – שָׁרֵי רַבִּי שִׁמְעוֹן, הוֹאִיל וְאֵין מִתְכַּוֵּין לְחָרִיץ. וְרַבִּי יְהוּדָה סָבַר: כֵּיוָן דְּאֶפְשָׁר – אָסוּר: קָתָנֵי גְּדוֹלִים. מִטָּה: וְקָתָנֵי קְטַנִּים. כִּסֵּא, וְרַבִּי יְהוּדָה פָּלֵיג עֲלֵיהּ. דִּתְנַן בְּמַסֶּכֶת בֵּיצָה, רַבִּי יְהוּדָה אוֹמֵר: כָּל הַכֵּלִים אֵין נִגְרָרִים. דְּאִי לָאו מִשּׁוּם פְּלוּגְתַּיְיהוּ – לָמָּה לִי לְמִיתְנֵי גְּדוֹלִים? הַשְׁתָּא קְטַנִּים שָׁרֵי רַבִּי שִׁמְעוֹן, גְּדוֹלִים מִיבַּעְיָא?! אֶלָּא תָּנָא קְטַנִּים מִשּׁוּם ר' שִׁמְעוֹן, וְתָנָא גְּדוֹלִים מִשּׁוּם רַבִּי יְהוּדָה: דּוּמְיָא דְּכִסֵּא. קְטַנִּים, וּבְהָא הוּא דְּאָסַר רַבִּי יְהוּדָה, אֲבָל בִּגְדוֹלִים – שָׁרֵי: כִּסֵּא דּוּמְיָא דְּמִטָּה. גְּדוֹלִים, וּבְהָא הוּא דְּשָׁרֵי רַבִּי שִׁמְעוֹן, אֲבָל בִּקְטַנִּים – אָסַר: מוֹכְרִין כְּדַרְכָּן. כְּסוּת שֶׁל כִּלְאַיִם לוֹבְשׁוֹ בַּשּׁוּק כְּדֵי לְהַרְאוֹתוֹ לִמְוֹכְרוֹ, דְּלָא אָסְרָה תּוֹרָה אֶלָּא לְבִישָׁה שֶׁהִיא לְהִתְחַמֵּם, כְּדֶרֶךְ כָּל הַלּוֹבְשִׁים. וְהַעֲלָאָה דּוּמְיָא דִּלְבִישָׁה נַמִי דְּמִיתְהַנֵּי בָּהּ: וּבִלְבַד שֶׁלֹּא יִתְכַּוֵּין כו'. וְר' שִׁמְעוֹן הוּא דְּאָזֵיל בָּתַר כַּוָּונָה: וְהַצְּנוּעִים. כְּשֵׁרִים, שֶׁמַּרְחִיקִין עַצְמָן מִכָּל לָזוּת שְׂפָתַיִם: וְהָא הָכָא דְּאֶפְשָׁר. לְכָל אָדָם לְמֶיעְבַּד שֶׁלֹּא עַל יְדֵי אִיסּוּר, וַאֲפִילּוּ הָכִי שָׁרֵי: **מתני'** מִפְּנֵי נָכְרִים. כְּגוֹן פַּרְסִיִּים שֶׁהָיָה לָהֶם יוֹם חַג שֶׁאֵין מַנִּיחִין אוֹר אֶלָּא בְּבֵית עֲבוֹדָה זָרָה שֶׁלָּהֶם: וּמִפְּנֵי הַלִּסְטִין. שֶׁלֹּא יִרְאוּ שֶׁיֵּשׁ שָׁם אָדָם וְיָבֹאוּ עָלָיו: וּמִפְּנֵי רוּחַ רָעָה. *) הַבָּאָה עָלָיו, וּכְשֶׁאֵינוֹ רוֹאֶה נוֹחַ לוֹ: פָּטוּר. וּבַגְּמָרָא מְפָרֵשׁ לְכוּלַּהּ: כְּחָס עַל הַנֵּר. שֶׁרְאוּהוּ שֶׁמִּתְקַלְקֵל, וְחָס עָלָיו וְכִבָּה אֶת הַפְּתִילָה: הַנֵּר. קרויזי"ל: חַיָּיב. וּבַגְּמָרָא מְפָרֵשׁ לָהּ: פּוֹטֵר בְּכוּלָּן. מְפָרֵשׁ בַּגְּמָרָא (דף לא:): שֶׁהוּא עוֹשֶׂה פֶּחָם. בְּכִיבּוּי זֶה, וַהֲוֵי מְלָאכָה הַצְּרִיכָה לְגוּפָהּ כִּדְאָמַר בַּגְּמָרָא:

*) ס"א מרה שחורה.

גליון הש"ס

גמ' גזירה עיליתא דשישא. עיין לקמן דף קנא ע"ב: תוס' ד"ה גזרה וכו' אטו עלייה אחרת. ועיי' לקמן דף קנא ע"ב ברש"י ד"ה קרקע:

תוספתא פ"ב ע"ש

[לקמן מא: וש"נ]

לעיל כב. לקמן מו: ביצה כג: [תוספ' ביצה פ"ב] פסחים קא. מנחות מא:

כלאים פ"ט מ"ה לקמן מו: פסחים כו:

[לקמן מ.]

פסחים יח.

הגהות הב"ח

(א) גמ' ואמאי קרי ליה שלא וכו' ואמאי קרי ליה מוכן: (ב) רש"י ד"ה ואמאי קרי ליה שלא: (ג) ד"ה ואמאי קרי ליה למגוד:

[לקמן פב. ברכות יח. עירובין יג: מה. פז. ר"ה כד: סוכה ב: יד: כח. לא: לו: לז. מגילה כז: יבמות כה: קד: ב"מ סג. ב"ב קטו: ע"ז כד. מא: מג. מד. סנהדרין יב. מנחות כח: בכורות מה: חולין נז: ערכין לא. נדה נ: סא.]

[עיין תוספות פסחים כה: סד"ה לא אפשר]

אע"ג דר' יוסי אית ליה דהבערה ללאו יצאת בכיבוי מודה לחייב אף בפני עצמו כדתנן בפרק כלל גדול. ושוב אמר מהר"מ למהר"א אמר דבפ' ספק אכל בהדיא פוטר רבי יוסי בהבערה ומחייב בכיבוי [ת"י]

רבינו חננאל

[רע"א מן המוכן טמא שלא מן המוכן טהור] ואוקימנא בשורקו לאשפה דברי הכל טהור הניחו בקופסא דברי הכל טמא. כי פליגי בשתחבו בבגדו או בשהניחו אחורי הדלת. רבי אליעזר סבר מדלא זרקו לאשפה דעתיה עילויה לפיכך הוא טמא ואמאי קרי ליה אינו מוכן דלגבי קופסא לאו מוכן הוא. ורבי יהושע סבר כיון שלא הניחו בקופסא בטליה הלכך טהור הוא. ואמאי קרי ליה מוכן דאחורי הדלת או תחוב בבגדו לגבי אשפה מוכן הוא. ור' עקיבא (סבר מספקא ליה) בתחבו בבגדו סבר לה כר' אליעזר שהוא טמא בהניחו אחורי הדלת סבר לה כר' יהושע והדר ביה ר' עקיבא לגבי ר' יהושע ואמר אפי' התחובה בבגדו טהור ממאי מדקתני במתני' פתילת הבגד ולא קתני פתילה של בגד ש"מ דעדיין בגד הוא ותני ר' עקיבא אומר טהורה ומדליקין בה. ומאן דחזא רב המנונא דאייתי ראיה מג' על ג' מוקים לה לפתילה דקתני במתני' פתילה שיש בה פחות מג' [טפחים] והא דהויה היא דהכי קתני ר' עקיבא אומר טהורה ומשנה שלימה שנינו מפני שאמרו ג' על ג' שנתמעטה טהורה אבל שלשה על שלשה שנתמעטה אע"פ שטהר מן המדרס טמא בכל הטומאות אלא פחות משלש הוא (וכן) [וכיון] דאוקימנא רב אדא בג' אוקימנא רב המנונא בפחות משלש והאי (דקתני) [דקאמר] שלשה דהכנת מטליות בהדיא [בפחות] משלשה קתני לה והוא הדין לפחות מג'*) והלכה כר"ע דקאי ר' יהושע כוותיה דהא הדר ביה ר' עקיבא לגבי דר' יהושע וכן מפורש בבירה: **מתני'** לא יקוב אדם שפופרת של ביצה כו'. ופשוטה היא זו השפופרת של חרס. תנא אם חיברה זו השפופרת של חרס בסיד ובגפסים כעין היוצר מותר. ומלאנוה שמן ונקבנוה והנחנוה ע"פ הנר. והיה שם ר' טרפון והזקנים ולא אמרו לנו דבר אמרו לו משם ראיה מפני כי [בית] נתזה (זהיר) [זריז] הוה: **תנא** (תוספתא פ"ג) נותנין טיט או חרסית תחת [הנר] או גרגיר מלח או גרים של פול ע"ש מבעוד יום ע"פ הנר להיות שוהה. אבין ציפוראה גרר ספסלא בעיליתא דשישא לעילא מר' יצחק בן אלעזר אמר ליה [אי] שתוקי לך כי האי דשתקו ליה חבריא לר' יהודה בשפופרת של ביצה ונפיק מינה חורבה דהוראה להיתר לאו שפיר עבדת בגרירת ספסילא גזירה עיליתא דשישא דלית בה חריץ אטו עיליתא דעלמא. ריש כנישתא דבצרה גרר ספסילא לעילא מר' ירמיה רבה א"ל כמאן כר' שמעון אימור דשרי ר' שמעון בגדולים דלא אפשר להגביהן בקטנים דאפשר להגביהן מי אמר. עולא אמר מחלוקת בקטנים אבל בגדולים דברי הכל מותר ומותבינן לתרווייהו מהאי ר' שמעון אומר גורר אדם מטה כסא וספסל ובלבד שלא יתכוין לעשות חריץ הנה קתני מטה דהיא גדולה וקתני כסא וספסל שהן קטנים מכלל דפליגי בקטנים ובגדולים קשיא לתרווייהו ופרק' ר' ירמיה רבה כסא וספסל גדולים הן דומיא דמטה. עולא מפרק לטעמיה מטה קטנה שיכול להגביהה דומיא דכסא וספסל. מתיב רבא מוכרי כסות של כלאים מוכרין כדרכן ובלבד שלא יתכוין בחמה מפני החמה ובגשמים מפני הגשמים. שאם יתכוין נמצא נהנה מן הכלאים ואסור והצנועין מפשילין במקל לאחוריהן כדי שלא יהא כלאים עולה על גופן כלל. והא הכא דאפשר למעבד כצנועים כי היכי דאפשר להגביה כלים. וכי לא מכוין קא שרי רבי שמעון בהעלאה עליהן. תיובתא דרבי ירמיה רבה תיובתא: **מתני'** המכבה את הנר מפני שהוא מתירא כו'.

*) עי' כרי"ף שסתרו.

אוקימנא

רב נסים גאון

מותיב רבא מוכרי כסות מוכרין כדרכן ובלבד שלא יתכוין בחמה מפני החמה ובגשמים מפני הגשמים. הוצרכו להתיר לאלו דברים שהם רגילים בהם ובלבד שלא יתכוונו בהם להרחיק הזק החמה בעת החום והזק הגשמים בעתם וכמוהו התירו לתופרים כמו ששנינו תופרי כסות תופרין כדרכן כו' זו המשנה שנויה בפרק ט' דמסכת כלאים בסוף המסכת לפי שאמרו קודם לכן אין עראי לכלאים כו' כלומר

גמ' מִדְקָתָנֵי סֵיפָא. כְּחָס עַל הַנֵּר כו' חַיָּיב חַטָּאת אִס שָׁגַג בְּשַׁבָּת, שֶׁשָּׁכַח שֶׁהוּא שַׁבָּת, אוֹ סָבַר שֶׁכִּיבּוּי מוּתָּר בְּשַׁבָּת: ש"מ ר' יְהוּדָה הִיא. דְּאָמַר: *מְלָאכָה שֶׁאֵינָהּ צְרִיכָה לְגוּפָהּ חַיָּיב עָלֶיהָ. דְּכִיבּוּי זֶה אֵין צָרִיךְ לְגוּפוֹ, אֶלָּא לְצוֹרֶךְ דָּבָר אַחֵר, שֶׁלֹּא תִּדָּלֵק הַפְּתִילָה, אוֹ שֶׁלֹּא יִפָּקַע הַנֵּר. וְאֵין לְךָ כִּיבּוּי הַצָּרִיךְ לְגוּפוֹ אֶלָּא כִּיבּוּי שֶׁל פֶּחָמִין כְּשֶׁעוֹשִׂין אוֹתוֹ, וְכִיבּוּי שֶׁל הַבְהוּב פְּתִילָה, שֶׁהַכִּיבּוּי נַעֲשֶׂה לְהַאֲחִיז בּוֹ הָאוּר מַהֵר כְּשֶׁיִּרְצֶה לְהַדְלִיקוֹ. וְכֵיוָן דְּרַבִּי יְהוּדָה הִיא, רֵישָׁא דְּפָטַר – מִשּׁוּם חוֹלֶה, וְה"ה לִשְׁאָר פְּטוּרֵי דְּמַתְנִיתִין: אִי. דְּאִית בְּהוּ סַכָּנַת נְפָשׁוֹת, וּמִשּׁוּם פִּקּוּחַ נֶפֶשׁ שָׁרֵי לְהוּ – לִיתְנֵי "מוּתָּר" לְכַתְּחִלָּה: חַיָּיב מִיבָּעֵי לֵיהּ. הוֹאִיל וְרַבִּי יְהוּדָה הִיא, דְּלָא פָּטַר לֵיהּ מִשּׁוּם דְּאֵינָהּ צְרִיכָה לְגוּפָהּ: וְהָא דְּתָנֵי רַבִּי אוֹשַׁעְיָא. בַּהֲדַיָּא: "אֲבָל אָסוּר": וְר' שִׁמְעוֹן הִיא*. דְּפָטַר לֵיהּ מִשּׁוּם "אֵינָהּ צְרִיכָה לְגוּפָהּ": שָׁאוּל שְׁאֵילְתָא. שָׁאֲלוּ שְׁאֵלָה: לְעֵילָא מַר' תַּנְחוּם. לְפָנָיו. וְכֵן לְשׁוֹן הַתַּלְמוּד (א) וְהַמִּקְרָא: "שְׂרָפִים עוֹמְדִים מִמַּעַל לוֹ" (ישעיה ו'). וְעַל שֵׁם שֶׁיְּרֵאִים לְהִתְקָרֵב לְפָנָיו – עוֹמְדִין מֵרָחוֹק: דְּמִן נֵוֵי. מָקוֹם: בְּאִישָׁא. חוֹלֶה. תַּרְגּוּם שֶׁל רָעָה – בִּישְׁתָּא: פְּתַח וַאֲמַר. כָּךְ הָיוּ רְגִילִין לִפְתּוֹחַ בְּאַגָּדָה תְּחִילָּה, וְהוּא דּוֹמֶה לִשְׁאֵלָה וּדְרָשׁ: כִּי לְכֶלֶב חַי. כְּלוֹמַר: גְּדוֹלִים הַחַיִּים וּפִקּוּחַ נֶפֶשׁ: אָן הִיא. אָנָה הָלְכָה? וְחָזַרְתְּ וְאָמַרְתְּ. לִסְתּוֹר דִּבְרֵי עַצְמְךָ: לָא קַשְׁיָא. אִיהוּ גּוּפֵיהּ הֲוָה מְפָרֵשׁ לְהוּ: דְּאָמַר ר' יוֹחָנָן. קְרָא קָא דָּרֵישׁ "בַּמֵּתִים חָפְשִׁי": וְשַׁבֵּחַ אֲנִי אֶת הַמֵּתִים. שֶׁעָסְקוּ בְּחַיֵּיהֶם בַּתּוֹרָה וּמִצְוֹת וּמֵתוּ, רְאוּיִים לְשַׁבְּחָם אֲפִילּוּ מִצַּדִּיקִים חַיִּים, שֶׁגְּדוֹלִים הֵן בְּמִיתָתָן מִבְּחַיֵּיהֶן: עָמַד מֹשֶׁה. וְאֵין לְךָ צַדִּיק מִמֶּנּוּ, וְלֹא נַעֲנָה בִּזְכוּתוֹ: ד"א וְשַׁבֵּחַ אֲנִי אֶת הַמֵּתִים. הָרִאשׁוֹנִים, מִן הַחַיִּים שֶׁל עַכְשָׁיו, שֶׁהָרִאשׁוֹנִים טוֹבִים מֵאֵלֶּה. תֵּדַע, שֶׁמִּתְקַיְּימוֹת גְּזֵרוֹתָיו שֶׁל מֹשֶׁה, וְאֵין מִתְקַיְּימוֹת גְּזֵירוֹת שָׂרִים שֶׁל עַכְשָׁיו: וְתִקֵּן כַּמָּה תַּקָּנוֹת. כִּי הַהִיא דְּתָנֵי בִּמְגִילָּה (דף ד'. ולב.): מֹשֶׁה תִּיקֵּן לָהֶם לְיִשְׂרָאֵל שֶׁיְּהוּ שׁוֹאֲלִין וְדוֹרְשִׁין בְּעִנְיָנוֹ שֶׁל יוֹם: עַל אוֹתוֹ עָוֹן. דְּבַת שֶׁבַע: דָּבְקוּ שְׁעָרִים. שֶׁל בֵּית קָדְשֵׁי הַקֳּדָשִׁים: כ"ד רְנָנוֹת. "רִנָּה" "תְּפִלָּה" "תְּחִינָּה" כְּתוּבִים בִּתְפִלַּת שְׁלֹמֹה עַד כ"ד. וְיֵשׁ אוֹמְרִים: כ"ד בְּרָכוֹת דְּתַעֲנִית, וְלָא נְהִירָא*): רְהַטוּ שְׁעָרִים בַּתְרֵיהּ לְמִבְלְעֵיהּ. סָבְרֵי דְּעַל עַצְמוֹ אָמַר "מֶלֶךְ הַכָּבוֹד". א"ל שְׁעָרִים: מִי הוּא זֶה מֶלֶךְ הַכָּבוֹד? אָמַר אִיהוּ: ה' עִזּוּז וְגִבּוֹר (תהלים כד): שׂוֹנְאֵי דָּוִד. מִשְׁפַּחַת שָׁאוּל, שִׁמְעִי, וְכַיּוֹצֵא בּוֹ: דְּיוֹם הַכִּפּוּרִים. שֶׁאָכְלוּ וְשָׁתוּ בַּחֲנוּכַּת הַבַּיִת, כִּדְכְתִיב: "אֶת הֶחָג שִׁבְעַת יָמִים וְשִׁבְעַת יָמִים", כִּדְאָמְרִינַן בְּמוֹעֵד קָטָן (דף ט.): וּדְקָאָמַר שְׁלֹמֹה כִּי לְכֶלֶב חַי הוּא טוֹב מֵאַרְיֵה הַמֵּת. לָאו לְעִנְיַן חֲשִׁיבוּתָא אֲמָרוֹ, אֶלָּא לְעִנְיַן הִלְכוֹת שַׁבָּת וְי"ט: קִיצִּי. הָעֲתִידוֹת לָבוֹא עָלַי: *מִדַּת יָמַי. כַּמָּה יְמֵי חַיַּי: מֶה חָדֵל אָנִי. בְּאֵיזֶה יוֹם אֲנִי חָדֵל וּבָטֵל מִן הָעוֹלָם: אָמוּת בְּאֶחָד בְּשַׁבָּת. שֶׁיּוּכְלוּ לְהִתְעַסֵּק בִּי וּבְהֶסְפֵּדִי: כִּי טוֹב יוֹם בַּחֲצֵרֶיךָ. כְּלוֹמַר: כְּבָר אָמַרְתָּ לְפָנַי: טוֹב יוֹם שֶׁאַתָּה עוֹמֵד בַּחֲצֵרַי וְעוֹסֵק בַּתּוֹרָה, מֵאֶלֶף עוֹלוֹת שֶׁעָתִיד בִּנְךָ שְׁלֹמֹה לְהַעֲלוֹת, כִּדְכְתִיב (מלכים א ג): "אֶלֶף עוֹלוֹת יַעֲלֶה שְׁלֹמֹה" וגו':

כָּל

תורה אור

גמ' מִדְקָתָנֵי סֵיפָא 'חַיָּיב' – ש"מ ר' יְהוּדָה הִיא. רֵישָׁא בְּמַאי עָסְקִינַן? אִי בְּחוֹלֶה שֶׁיֵּשׁ בּוֹ סַכָּנָה – 'מוּתָּר' מִיבָּעֵי לֵיהּ! וְאִי בְּחוֹלֶה שֶׁאֵין בּוֹ סַכָּנָה – 'חַיָּיב חַטָּאת' מִיבָּעֵי לֵיהּ! לְעוֹלָם בְּחוֹלֶה שֶׁיֵּשׁ בּוֹ סַכָּנָה, [א]וּבְדִין הוּא דְּלִיתְנֵי 'מוּתָּר', וְאַיְּידֵי *דְּבָעֵי לְמִתְנֵי סֵיפָא 'חַיָּיב' – תְּנָא נַמִי רֵישָׁא 'פָּטוּר'. וְהָדְתָנֵי רַבִּי אוֹשַׁעְיָא: "אִם בִּשְׁבִיל הַחוֹלֶה שֶׁיִּישַׁן – לֹא יְכַבֶּה, וְאִם כִּבָּה – פָּטוּר אֲבָל אָסוּר" – הַהִיא בְּחוֹלֶה שֶׁאֵין בּוֹ סַכָּנָה, וְרַבִּי שִׁמְעוֹן הִיא.§ שָׁאוּל [ב]שְׁאֵילָה זוֹ לְעֵילָּא מַר' תַּנְחוּם דְּמִן נֵוֵי: מַהוּ לְכַבּוֹת בּוּצִינָא דְּנוּרָא מִקַּמֵּי בְּאִישָׁא בְּשַׁבְּתָא? פְּתַח וַאֲמַר: אַנְתְּ שְׁלֹמֹה, אָן חָכְמְתָךְ אָן *סוּכְלְתָנוּתָךְ! לָא דַּיֵּיךְ שֶׁדְּבָרֶיךָ סוֹתְרִין דִּבְרֵי דָּוִד אָבִיךָ אֶלָּא שֶׁדְּבָרֶיךָ סוֹתְרִין זֶה אֶת זֶה! דָּוִד אָבִיךָ אָמַר: °"לֹא הַמֵּתִים יְהַלְלוּ יָהּ" וְאַתְּ אָמַרְתְּ: °"וְשַׁבֵּחַ אֲנִי אֶת הַמֵּתִים שֶׁכְּבָר מֵתוּ", וְחָזַרְתְּ וְאָמַרְתְּ: °"כִּי לְכֶלֶב חַי הוּא טוֹב מִן הָאַרְיֵה הַמֵּת"! לָא קַשְׁיָא, הָא דְּקָאָמַר דָּוִד: "לֹא הַמֵּתִים יְהַלְלוּ יָהּ" הָכִי קָאָמַר: לְעוֹלָם יַעֲסוֹק אָדָם בַּתּוֹרָה וּבְמִצְוֹת קוֹדֶם שֶׁיָּמוּת, שֶׁכֵּיוָן שֶׁמֵּת – בָּטֵל מִן הַתּוֹרָה וּמִן הַמִּצְוֹת, וְאֵין לְהקב"ה שֶׁבַח בּוֹ, וְהַיְינוּ דְּאָמַר ר' יוֹחָנָן, *מַאי דִּכְתִיב: °"בַּמֵּתִים חָפְשִׁי" – כֵּיוָן שֶׁמֵּת אָדָם נַעֲשָׂה חָפְשִׁי מִן הַתּוֹרָה וּמִן הַמִּצְוֹת. וּדְקָאָמַר שְׁלֹמֹה "וְשַׁבֵּחַ אֲנִי אֶת הַמֵּתִים שֶׁכְּבָר מֵתוּ" – שֶׁכְּשֶׁחָטְאוּ יִשְׂרָאֵל בַּמִּדְבָּר עָמַד מֹשֶׁה לִפְנֵי הקב"ה, וְאָמַר כַּמָּה תְּפִלּוֹת וְתַחֲנוּנִים לְפָנָיו וְלֹא נַעֲנָה, וּכְשֶׁאָמַר °"זְכוֹר לְאַבְרָהָם לְיִצְחָק וּלְיִשְׂרָאֵל עֲבָדֶיךָ" – מִיָּד נַעֲנָה, וְלֹא יָפֶה אָמַר שְׁלֹמֹה "וְשַׁבֵּחַ אֲנִי אֶת הַמֵּתִים שֶׁכְּבָר מֵתוּ"? דָּבָר אַחֵר: מִנְהָגוֹ שֶׁל עוֹלָם, שַׂר ב"ו גּוֹזֵר גְּזֵרָה סָפֵק מְקַיְּימִין אוֹתָהּ סָפֵק אֵין מְקַיְּימִין אוֹתָהּ, וְאִם תִּמְצֵי לוֹמַר מְקַיְּימִין אוֹתָהּ – בְּחַיָּיו מְקַיְּימִין אוֹתָהּ, בְּמוֹתוֹ – אֵין מְקַיְּימִין אוֹתָהּ. וְאִילּוּ מֹשֶׁה רַבֵּינוּ, גָּזַר כַּמָּה גְּזֵירוֹת וְתִיקֵּן כַּמָּה תַּקָּנוֹת, וְקַיָּימוֹת הֵם לְעוֹלָם וּלְעוֹלְמֵי עוֹלָמִים. וְלֹא יָפֶה אָמַר שְׁלֹמֹה "וְשַׁבֵּחַ אֲנִי אֶת הַמֵּתִים וגו'"? ד"א: "וְשַׁבֵּחַ אֲנִי וגו'" – כִּדְרַב יְהוּדָה אָמַר רַב, דְּאָמַר רַב יְהוּדָה אָמַר רַב: מַאי דִּכְתִיב °"עֲשֵׂה עִמִּי אוֹת לְטוֹבָה וְיִרְאוּ שׂוֹנְאַי וְיֵבוֹשׁוּ" – אָמַר דָּוִד לִפְנֵי הקב"ה: *רִבּוֹנוֹ שֶׁל עוֹלָם, מְחוֹל לִי עַל אוֹתוֹ עָוֹן! אָמַר לוֹ: מָחוּל לָךְ. אָמַר לוֹ: עֲשֵׂה עִמִּי אוֹת בְּחַיַּי! אָמַר לוֹ: בְּחַיֶּיךָ אֵינִי מוֹדִיעַ, בְּחַיֵּי שְׁלֹמֹה בִּנְךָ אֲנִי מוֹדִיעַ. *כְּשֶׁבָּנָה שְׁלֹמֹה אֶת בֵּית הַמִּקְדָּשׁ בִּיקֵּשׁ לְהַכְנִיס אָרוֹן לְבֵית קָדְשֵׁי הַקֳּדָשִׁים, דָּבְקוּ שְׁעָרִים זֶה בָּזֶה. אָמַר שְׁלֹמֹה עֶשְׂרִים וְאַרְבָּעָה רְנָנוֹת וְלֹא נַעֲנָה. פָּתַח וְאָמַר: °"שְׂאוּ שְׁעָרִים רָאשֵׁיכֶם וְהִנָּשְׂאוּ פִּתְחֵי עוֹלָם וְיָבֹא מֶלֶךְ הַכָּבוֹד" רְהַטוּ בַּתְרֵיהּ לְמִיבְלְעֵיהּ, אָמְרוּ: "מִי הוּא זֶה מֶלֶךְ הַכָּבוֹד?" אָמַר לְהוּ: "ה' עִזּוּז וְגִבּוֹר". חָזַר וְאָמַר: °"שְׂאוּ שְׁעָרִים רָאשֵׁיכֶם וּשְׂאוּ פִּתְחֵי עוֹלָם וְיָבֹא מֶלֶךְ הַכָּבוֹד. מִי הוּא זֶה מֶלֶךְ הַכָּבוֹד ה' צְבָאוֹת הוּא מֶלֶךְ הַכָּבוֹד סֶלָה" וְלֹא נַעֲנָה. כֵּיוָן שֶׁאָמַר: °"ה' אֱלֹהִים אַל תָּשֵׁב פְּנֵי מְשִׁיחֶךָ זָכְרָה לְחַסְדֵי דָּוִד עַבְדֶּךָ" – מִיָּד נַעֲנָה. בְּאוֹתָהּ שָׁעָה נֶהֶפְכוּ פְּנֵי כָּל שׂוֹנְאֵי דָּוִד כְּשׁוּלֵי קְדֵירָה, וְיָדְעוּ כָּל הָעָם וְכָל יִשְׂרָאֵל שֶׁמָּחַל לוֹ הקב"ה עַל אוֹתוֹ עָוֹן. וְלֹא יָפֶה אָמַר שְׁלֹמֹה: "וְשַׁבֵּחַ אֲנִי אֶת הַמֵּתִים שֶׁכְּבָר מֵתוּ"? *וְהַיְינוּ דִּכְתִי': °"בַּיּוֹם הַשְּׁמִינִי שִׁלַּח אֶת הָעָם וַיְבָרְכוּ אֶת הַמֶּלֶךְ וַיֵּלְכוּ לְאָהֳלֵיהֶם שְׂמֵחִים וְטוֹבֵי לֵב עַל כָּל הַטּוֹבָה אֲשֶׁר עָשָׂה ה' לְדָוִד עַבְדּוֹ וּלְיִשְׂרָאֵל עַמּוֹ": 'וַיֵּלְכוּ לְאָהֳלֵיהֶם' – שֶׁמָּצְאוּ נְשׁוֹתֵיהֶן בְּטׇהֳרָה. 'שְׂמֵחִים' – שֶׁנֶּהֱנוּ מִזִּיו הַשְּׁכִינָה. 'וְטוֹבֵי לֵב' – שֶׁנִּתְעַבְּרוּ נְשׁוֹתֵיהֶן שֶׁל כׇּל אֶחָד וְאֶחָד וְיָלְדָה זָכָר. "עַל כָּל הַטּוֹבָה אֲשֶׁר עָשָׂה ה' לְדָוִד עַבְדּוֹ (וּלְיִשְׂרָאֵל עַמּוֹ)". 'לְדָוִד עַבְדּוֹ') – שֶׁמָּחַל לוֹ עַל אוֹתוֹ עָוֹן, 'וּלְיִשְׂרָאֵל עַמּוֹ' – דְּאַחֵיל לְהוּ עֲוֹן דְּיוֹם הַכִּפּוּרִים. וּדְקָאָמַר שְׁלֹמֹה: "כִּי לְכֶלֶב חַי הוּא טוֹב מִן הָאַרְיֵה הַמֵּת" – כִּדְרַב יְהוּדָה אָמַר רַב, דְּאָמַר רַב יְהוּדָה אָמַר רַב: מַאי דִּכְתִיב: °"הוֹדִיעֵנִי ה' קִצִּי וּמִדַּת יָמַי מַה הִיא אֵדְעָה מֶה חָדֵל אָנִי", אָמַר דָּוִד לִפְנֵי הַקָּדוֹשׁ בָּרוּךְ הוּא: רִבּוֹנוֹ שֶׁל עוֹלָם, "הוֹדִיעֵנִי ה' קִצִּי"! אָמַר לוֹ: גְּזֵרָה הִיא מִלְּפָנַי שֶׁאֵין מוֹדִיעִין קִצּוֹ שֶׁל בָּשָׂר וָדָם. "וּמִדַּת יָמַי מַה הִיא"? גְּזֵרָה הִיא מִלְּפָנַי שֶׁאֵין מוֹדִיעִין מִדַּת יָמָיו שֶׁל אָדָם. "וְאֵדְעָה מֶה חָדֵל אָנִי", אָמַר לוֹ: *בְּשַׁבָּת תָּמוּת. אָמוּת בְּאֶחָד בְּשַׁבָּת! אָמַר לוֹ: כְּבָר הִגִּיעַ מַלְכוּת שְׁלֹמֹה בִּנְךָ, *וְאֵין מַלְכוּת נוֹגַעַת בַּחֲבֶרְתָּהּ אֲפִי' כִּמְלֹא נִימָא. אָמוּת בְּעֶרֶב שַׁבָּת! *אָמַר לוֹ: °"כִּי טוֹב יוֹם בַּחֲצֵרֶיךָ מֵאָלֶף" [ג]טוֹב לִי יוֹם אֶחָד שֶׁאַתָּה יוֹשֵׁב וְעוֹסֵק בַּתּוֹרָה מֵאֶלֶף עוֹלוֹת שֶׁעָתִיד שְׁלֹמֹה בִּנְךָ לְהַקְרִיב לְפָנַי עַל גַּבֵּי הַמִּזְבֵּחַ.

כָּל

רב נסים גאון

[ש"מ ר' יהודה היא]. כלומר הדבר שנא' לדעת ר' יהודה שהיה סובר מלאכה שאינה צריכה לגופה חייב עליה וכבר הקדמנו פירושו בפרק הראשון [רישא] במאי עסקי' אי בחולה שיש בו סכנה מותר מיבעי ליה והעיקר דיליה הוא דאמר הכתוב (ויקרא יח) אשר יעשה אותם האדם וחי בהם ובפרק יום הכפורים (יומא דף פה) אמרו וכבר היה רבי ישמעאל ורבי עקיבא ורבי אלעזר בן עזריה מהלכין בדרך ולוי הסדר וישמעאל בנו של רבי אלעזר בן עזריה מהלכין אחריהם נשאלה שאילה זו לפניהם מנין לפיקוח נפש שדוחה את השבת נענה רבי ישמעאל ואמר (שמות כב) אם במחתרת ימצא הגנב ולאחר דבריו אמר רב יהודה אמר שמואל אי הואי התם הוה אמינא מילתא דעדיפא מכולהו וחי בהם ולא שימות בהם אמר רבא לכולהו אית להו פירכא לבר מדשמואל דלית ליה פירכא וכו' וכבר אמרו קודם (שם דף פב) שאין לך דבר שעומד בפני פיקוח נפש חוץ מע"ז וגילוי עריות ושפיכות דמים ובפרק מפנין (דף קכט) אמרו מר זוטרא מתני לקולא טעמא דאמרה אין צריכה הא סתמא מחללין עליה את השבת אמר ליה רבינא [למרימר] הילכתא כמאן אמר ליה כמר זוטרא שספק נפשות להקל ואמרו (שם) אמר רב יהודה אמר שמואל עושין מדורה לחיה בשבת סבור מינה לחיה אין לחולה לא בימות הגשמים אין בימות החמה לא איתמר אמר ר' חייא בר אבין אמר שמואל הקיז דם ונצטנן עושין לו מדורה אפילו בתקופת תמוז ושנו במשנה (פרק ר"א דמילה דף קלד) רבי אלעזר בן עזריה אומר מרחיצין את הקטן ביום השלישי שחל להיות בשבת שנאמר ויהי ביום השלישי בהיותם כואבים ואמרו בתלמוד כי אתא רב דימא אמר רבי אלעזר הלכה כרבי אלעזר בן עזריה הוו בה במערבא הרחצת כל גופו או הרחצת מילה עצמה אמר להו ההוא מרבנן ורבי (עקיבא) [יעקב] שמיה מסתברא דהרחצת כל גופו דאי סלקא דעתך הרחצת מילה עצמה מי גרע מחמין שעל גבי מכה בשבת דאמר רב אין מונעין חמין ושמן מעל גבי מכה בשבת מתקיף לה רב יוסף ולא שני לך בין חמין שהוחמו בשבת לחמין שהוחמו מערב שבת מתקיף לה רב דימי וממאי דהכא בחמין שהוחמו בשבת פליגי דילמא בחמין שהוחמו מערב שבת פליגי אמר אביי אנא בעאי דאישני ליה וקדים ושני ליה רב יוסף מפני שסכנה היא לו כי אתא רבין אמר ר' אבא אמר רבי אלעזר ואמרי לה אמר רבי אבהו אמר רבי יוחנן הלכה כרבי אלעזר בן עזריה בין בחמין שהוחמו בשבת ובין בחמין שהוחמו מערב שבת בין בהרחצת כל גופו ובין בהרחצת מילה מפני שסכנה היא לו ואלו העיקרים אמרו ובחולה שיש בו סכנה מותר מיבעיא ליה ובמסכת ע"ז תמצא כמו אלו העיקרים רבים: **ואילו** משה רבינו גזר כמה גזירות ותיקן כמה תקנות מעצמו לישראל והריני מזכירין מהן מה שיזדמן לנו במסכת דיבמות אמרינן בפרק הערל (דף עט) אמרו ונתינים דוד גזר עליהם משה גזר עליהם מחוטב עציך עד שואב מימיך ובמסכת ברכות בפרק שלשה שאכלו כאחת (דף מח) אמר רב נחמן משה תיקן להם לישראל ברכת הזן בשעה שירד להן המן ובמסכת מגילה בפרק בני העיר (דף לב) תנו רבנן משה תיקן להן לישראל שיהו קורין ודורשין בעניינו של יום ובפ' יוה"כ (יומא דף עה) אמרו עד שבא משה ותיקן להם זמן סעודה (ובפ') [ובמסכת] תעניות (דף כז) [בפרק] בג' פרקים בשנה משה תיקן להם לישראל שמונה משמרות ארבעה מאלעזר וארבעה מאיתמר: **בשלמא** לדור עבדו שמחל לו הקב"ה על אותו עון אלא לישראל עמו מאי היא שמחל להם עון יום הכפורים תמצא פירו' בפרק משקין בית השלחין (מו"ק דף ט) אמר

מסורת הש"ס: [עי' תוספות לקמן לד. ד"ה את המת] · [לקמן נג:] · תהלים קטו · קהלת ד · שם ט · תהלים פח · [שמות לב] · תהלים פו · סנהד' קז: ע"ש מ"ק ט. · תהלים כד · שם · דה"ב ו · מלכים א ח · תהלים לט · [ברכות מח: מ"ק כח. יומא לח: תענית כ:] · *[מכות י.]

הגהות הב"ח

(א) רש"י ד"ה לעילא מר' תנחום וכו' הש"ס והמקרא. נ"ב ע"ל בפ' ר"ע דף פ"ח ע"א פי' בדרך אחר:

גליון הש"ס

גמ' טוב לי יום אחד שאתה יושב ועוסק בתורה. ובירו' פ"ז דברכות איתא חביבי עלי משפט ולדקה שאתה עושה יותר מקרבנות:

ל"א קלי מנין שנותי מדת ימי באיזה יום בשנה לדעת מנין ימי שאני מתקיים בשנה אחרונה כנ"ל

עין משפט נר מצוה: קז א ב מיי' פ"ב מהל' שבת הלכה ב טוש"ע א"ח סימן רעח:

[עירובין טז. פסחים ז: יבמות לח. קב. כתובות ל. נדרים כח: עב. נזיר כח: ב"ק מט: לד. ב"מ סב: סנהדרין נז. זבחים לח: חולין סח. קטו: בכורות מו:]

[תרגום אונקלוס של בחכמה ובתבונה בחוכמתא ובסוכלתנו כפ' תשא]

[לקמן קנא: ע"ש ואז תשכיל ותבין פרש"י דהכא ד"ה לאמר רבי יוחנן וכו' נדה סא:]

רבינו חננאל

אוקימנא למתני' כרבי יהודה ובחולה שיש בו סכנה שאם יראה אור הנר ימות והוא הדין לכל הזכורין במשנתנו ובדין הוא דליתני מותר ואיידי דתני סיפא בפחם חייב תני רישא פטור דמשמע פטור אבל אסור ואינו אלא פטור ומותר והא דתני רבי אושעיא אם בשביל שיישן חולה לא יכבה ואם כבה פטור אבל אסור ההוא בחולה שאין בו סכנה ואליבא דרבי שמעון דאמר דבר שאין מתכוין פטור*) **נשאלה** שאלה זו לפני ר' תנחום דמן נוי שם מקום מן

*) עי' בכריתות כ' ב' ובתוספות שם:

[מ"ק ט.]

[עי' תוספות חגיגה יז. ד"ה אף עלרת כו'] תהלים פד

כָּל יוֹמָא דְשַׁבְּתָא. שֶׁל כָּל שַׁבְּתוֹת הַשָּׁנִים: הֲוָה יָתֵיב וְגָרֵיס. שֶׁלֹּא יִקְרַב מַלְאַךְ הַמָּוֶת אֵלָיו, שֶׁהַתּוֹרָה מְגִינָּה מִמָּוֶת כִּדְאָמְרִינַן בְּסוֹטָה (דף כא.): סָלֵיק וּבָחֵישׁ בְּאִילָנֵי. מְנַעְנֵעַ הַמַּלְאָךְ בָּאִילָנוֹת לְהַשְׁמִיעַ קוֹל אֵימָה: וּכְלָבִים שֶׁל בֵּית אַבָּא רְעֵבִים. לִשְׁתֵּי שְׁאֵלוֹת הַלָּלוּ הוֹלְכָךְ: וְלֹא יָפֶה אָמַר כו'. שֶׁלְּתַקָּנַת הַכְּלָבִים לֹא הִצְרִיכוּהוּ לַעֲשׂוֹת טִלְטוּל נְבֵלָה, וְאֶת הָאַרְיֵה הַמֵּת אָסְרוּ לְטַלְטֵל אֶלָּא עַל יְדֵי כִּכָּר אוֹ תִּינוֹק. ל"א: שֶׁהִקְדִּימוּהוּ תְּשׁוּבַת הַכֶּלֶב לִתְשׁוּבַת הָאַרְיֵה – לְשׁוֹן רַבּוֹתַי: וּלְעִנְיַן שְׁאֵילְתָא. דְּמַהוּ לְכַבּוֹת: דִּשְׁאִילְנָא קֳדָמֵיכוֹן. דֶּרֶךְ עֲנָוָה אָמַר, דַּהֲוָה לֵיהּ לְמֵימַר: דְּשָׁאִילְתּוּן קֳדָמַי: קְרוּיָה נֵר. "נֵר *אֱלֹהִים נִשְׁמַת אָדָם" (משלי כ): מוּטָב תִּכְבֶּה נֵרוֹ כו'. לָאו מֵהָכָא יָלֵיף חִלּוּל שַׁבָּת. דְּפִיקּוּחַ נֶפֶשׁ נָפְקָא לָן* מִ"וָחַי בָּהֶם" וְלֹא שֶׁיָּמוּת בָּהֶם. אֶלָּא לְהַטְעִימָן הַדָּבָר בְּאַגָּדָה הַמּוֹשֶׁכֶת אֶת הַלֵּב, לְפִי שֶׁהָיוּ בָּאִים לִשְׁמוֹעַ הַדְּרָשָׁה נָשִׁים וְעַמֵּי הָאָרֶץ, וְהָיוּ צְרִיכִין הַדַּרְשָׁנִין לִמְשׁוֹךְ אֶת לִבָּם: תְּחִלָּתוֹ וְסוֹפוֹ. וְכ"ש שֶׁיֵּשׁ עוֹד בֵּינְתַיִים: קוֹדֶם הַשֶּׁמֶשׁ. אִם יַעֲמוֹל בַּתּוֹרָה שֶׁקָּדְמָה לַשֶּׁמֶשׁ – *יֵשׁ יִתְרוֹן: לִצְוָות. לַוְותָא = סוֹלַא"ס: מְהוּלָּל. מְשׁוּבָּח: מִשְׂחוֹק שֶׁמְּשַׂחֵק עִם הָרְשָׁעִים. שֶׁנּוֹתֵן לָהֶם שָׁעָה מְשַׂחֶקֶת – כְּדֵי לְהַאֲכִילָן חֶלְקָן, וּלְטוֹרְדָן מִן הָעוֹלָם הַבָּא: שִׂמְחָה שֶׁל מִצְוָה. כְּגוֹן הַכְנָסַת כַּלָּה: שְׂחוֹק. שְׂחוֹק מַמָּשׁ, שֶׁאֵין דַּעַת שׂוֹחֵק מְיוּשֶּׁבֶת עָלָיו. וַאֲפִילּוּ אֵינוֹ שֶׁל לָצוֹן – מ"מ אֵין בּוֹ יִישּׁוּב: קַלּוּת רֹאשׁ. לָצוֹן: קְחוּ לִי מְנַגֵּן. מִלְוָה הִיא לְהַשְׁרוֹת עָלָיו שְׁכִינָה: לִדְבַר הֲלָכָה. צָרִיךְ לִפְתּוֹחַ בְּמִילֵּי דִּבְדִיחוּתָא בְּרֵישָׁא: לַחֲלוֹם טוֹב. אִם בָּא לִישַׁן מִתּוֹךְ שִׂמְחָה – מַרְאִין לוֹ חֲלוֹם טוֹב: נוֹטְפוֹת מַר. מְרִירוּת, מֵחֲמַת אֵימָה: וּבָדְחִי רַבָּנַן. נִפְתָּח לִבָּם מֵחֲמַת הַשִּׂמְחָה: מֵעַזֵּי פָנִים. שֶׁלֹּא יַזִּיקוּנִי: וּמֵעַזּוּת פָּנִים. שֶׁלֹּא יֵצֵא עָלַי שֵׁם מַמְזֵרוּת, דְּהוּא עַז פָּנִים: בְּדִבְרֵי תוֹרָה. מוּתָּר לַעֲנוֹת כְּאִוַּלְתּוֹ: הָרָה וְיוֹלֶדֶת יַחְדָּיו. בְּיוֹם שֶׁהָרָה זֶה – יוֹלֶדֶת וָלָד אַחֵר, כְּמוֹ תַּרְנְגוֹלֶת. וְכֵיוָן שֶׁמְּשַׁמֶּשֶׁת בְּכָל יוֹם – נִמְצֵאת יוֹלֶדֶת בְּכָל יוֹם, דְּהָכִי מַשְׁמַע קְרָא: בְּכָל עֵת שֶׁהִיא מִתְעַבֶּרֶת – יוֹלֶדֶת, שֶׁמְּמַהֶרֶת לִגְמוֹר לוּרַת הַוָּלָד לִזְמַן מוּעָט: בֹּא וְאַרְאֲךָ. טָרַח לַעֲנוֹתוֹ כְּאִוַּלְתּוֹ, כְּדֵי לְהַעֲמִיד דִּבְרֵי תוֹרָה עַל מְכוֹנוֹ: לִיגְלֵג. "זוֹ אִוֶּלֶת": צְלָף. מִין אִילָן הַטּוֹעֵן ג' מִינֵי פֵּירוֹת: אֲבִיּוֹנוֹת, וְקַפְרִיסִין, וְלוּלָבִין. וְכִי אִיתֵיהּ לְהַאי לֵיתֵיהּ לְהַאי, כִּדְאָמַר בְּרֵישׁ "חֶזְקַת הַבָּתִּים"*: פִּסַּת בַּר. מַשְׁמַע גְּלוּסְקָאוֹת שֶׁרְחָבוֹת כְּמִין פַּס יָד, וּמַשְׁמַע כְּלֵי מֵילָת כְּמוֹ "כְּתוֹנֶת פַּסִּים": בַּר. כְּמוֹ "לִשְׁבּוֹר בָּר" (בראשית מב). וּלְעִנְיַן כְּלֵי מֵילָת – "בַּר" – נָקִי, כְּמוֹ "בָּרָה כַּחַמָּה" (שיר ו): כְּמֵהִין וּפִטְרִיּוֹת. שֶׁיּוֹצְאִין כְּמוֹת שֶׁהֵן בְּלַיְלָה אֶחָד, וּרְחָבִין וַעֲגוּלִין כִּגְלוּסְקָאוֹת: נַבְרָא בַּר קוּרָא. סִיב כְּמִין לְבוּשׁ מְלוּפָּף גָּדֵל סְבִיבוֹת הַקּוֹר שֶׁל דֶּקֶל כְּשֶׁהוּא רַךְ. קוֹר – עֲנַף הָאִילָן כְּשֶׁהוּא רַךְ יוֹצֵא בְּכָל שָׁנָה, קוֹדֶם שֶׁיִּתְקַשֶּׁה קָרוּי קוֹר:

תורה אור

כָּל יוֹמָא דְשַׁבְּתָא הֲוָה יָתֵיב וְגָרֵיס כּוּלֵּי יוֹמָא, הַהוּא יוֹמָא דְּבָעֵי לְמֵינָח נַפְשֵׁיהּ קָם מַלְאַךְ הַמָּוֶת קַמֵּיהּ וְלָא יָכֵיל לֵיהּ, דְּלָא הֲוָה פָּסַק פּוּמֵיהּ מִגִּירְסָא. אֲמַר: מַאי אַעֲבֵיד לֵיהּ? הֲוָה לֵיהּ בּוּסְתָּנָא אֲחוֹרֵי בֵיתֵיהּ, אֲתָא מַלְאַךְ הַמָּוֶת סָלֵיק וּבָחֵישׁ בְּאִילָנֵי, נְפַק לְמֶיחֱזֵי. הֲוָה סָלֵיק בְּדַרְגָּא. אִיפְּחִית דַּרְגָּא מִתּוּתֵיהּ, אִישְׁתִּיק וְנָח נַפְשֵׁיהּ. שָׁלַח שְׁלֹמֹה לְבֵי מִדְרָשָׁא: אַבָּא מֵת וּמוּטָּל בַּחַמָּה, וּכְלָבִים שֶׁל בֵּית אַבָּא רְעֵבִים, מָה אֶעֱשֶׂה? שָׁלְחוּ לֵיהּ: *חֲתוֹךְ אנְבֵלָה וְהַנַּח לִפְנֵי הַכְּלָבִים, וְאָבִיךָ – *הַנַּח בעָלָיו כִּכָּר אוֹ תִּינוֹק וְטַלְטְלוֹ. וְלֹא יָפֶה אָמַר שְׁלֹמֹה: °"כִּי לְכֶלֶב חַי הוּא טוֹב מִן הָאַרְיֵה הַמֵּת"? וּלְעִנְיַן שְׁאֵילָה דִּשְׁאִילְנָא קֳדָמֵיכוֹן: נֵר קְרוּיָה נֵר, וְנִשְׁמָתוֹ שֶׁל אָדָם קְרוּיָה נֵר, מוּטָב תִּכְבֶּה נֵר שֶׁל בָּשָׂר וָדָם מִפְּנֵי נֵרוֹ שֶׁל הקב"ה.§ אָמַר רַב יְהוּדָה בְּרֵיהּ דְּרַב שְׁמוּאֵל בַּר שֵׁילַת מִשְּׁמֵיהּ דְּרַב: בִּקְשׁוּ חֲכָמִים לִגְנוֹז סֵפֶר קֹהֶלֶת מִפְּנֵי שֶׁדְּבָרָיו סוֹתְרִין זֶה אֶת זֶה, וּמִפְּנֵי מָה לֹא גְּנָזוּהוּ – מִפְּנֵי שֶׁתְּחִילָּתוֹ דִּבְרֵי תוֹרָה וְסוֹפוֹ דִּבְרֵי תוֹרָה, תְּחִילָּתוֹ דִּבְרֵי תוֹרָה – דִּכְתִיב: °"מַה יִּתְרוֹן לָאָדָם בְּכָל עֲמָלוֹ שֶׁיַּעֲמוֹל תַּחַת הַשָּׁמֶשׁ" וְאָמְרִי דְּבֵי ר' יַנַּאי: תַּחַת הַשֶּׁמֶשׁ הוּא דְּאֵין לוֹ, קוֹדֶם שֶׁמֶשׁ – יֵשׁ לוֹ. סוֹפוֹ דִּבְרֵי תוֹרָה – דִּכְתִיב: °"סוֹף דָּבָר הַכֹּל נִשְׁמָע אֶת הָאֱלֹהִים יְרָא וְאֶת מִצְוֹתָיו שְׁמוֹר כִּי זֶה כָּל הָאָדָם". *מַאי "כִּי זֶה כָּל הָאָדָם"? אָמַר רַבִּי *(אֱלִיעֶזֶר): כָּל הָעוֹלָם כּוּלּוֹ לֹא נִבְרָא אֶלָּא בִּשְׁבִיל זֶה. ר' אַבָּא בַּר כָּהֲנָא אָמַר: שָׁקוּל זֶה כְּנֶגֶד כָּל הָעוֹלָם כּוּלּוֹ. שִׁמְעוֹן בֶּן עַזַּאי אוֹמֵר, וְאָמְרִי לַהּ שִׁמְעוֹן בֶּן זוֹמָא אוֹמֵר: לֹא נִבְרָא כָּל הָעוֹלָם כּוּלּוֹ אֶלָּא לְצַוּוֹת לָזֶה. וּמַאי דְּבָרָיו סוֹתְרִין זֶה אֶת זֶה? כְּתִיב: °"טוֹב כַּעַס מִשְּׂחוֹק" וּכְתִיב: °"לִשְׂחוֹק אָמַרְתִּי מְהוֹלָל". כְּתִיב: °"וְשִׁבַּחְתִּי אֲנִי אֶת הַשִּׂמְחָה" וּכְתִיב: °"וּלְשִׂמְחָה מַה זֹּה עוֹשָׂה". לָא קַשְׁיָא "טוֹב כַּעַס מִשְּׂחוֹק" – טוֹב כַּעַס שֶׁכּוֹעֵס הקב"ה עַל הַצַּדִּיקִים בָּעוה"ז, מִשְּׂחוֹק שֶׁמְּשַׂחֵק הקב"ה עַל הָרְשָׁעִים בָּעוֹלָם הַזֶּה. "וְלִשְׂחוֹק אָמַרְתִּי מְהוֹלָל" – זֶה שְׂחוֹק שֶׁמְּשַׂחֵק הקב"ה עִם הַצַּדִּיקִים בָּעוֹלָם הַבָּא. "וְשִׁבַּחְתִּי אֲנִי אֶת הַשִּׂמְחָה" גשִׂמְחָה שֶׁל מִצְוָה, "וּלְשִׂמְחָה מַה זֹּה עוֹשָׂה" – זוֹ שִׂמְחָה שֶׁאֵינָהּ שֶׁל מִצְוָה. *לְלַמֶּדְךָ דשֶׁאֵין שְׁכִינָה שׁוֹרָה לֹא מִתּוֹךְ עַצְבוּת וְלֹא מִתּוֹךְ עַצְלוּת וְלֹא מִתּוֹךְ שְׂחוֹק וְלֹא מִתּוֹךְ קַלּוּת רֹאשׁ וְלֹא מִתּוֹךְ *שִׂיחָה וְלֹא מִתּוֹךְ דְּבָרִים בְּטֵלִים, אֶלָּא מִתּוֹךְ דְּבַר שִׂמְחָה שֶׁל מִצְוָה, שֶׁנֶּאֱמַר: °"וְעַתָּה קְחוּ לִי מְנַגֵּן וְהָיָה כְּנַגֵּן הַמְנַגֵּן וַתְּהִי עָלָיו יַד ה'". אָמַר רַב יְהוּדָה: וְכֵן לִדְבַר הֲלָכָה. אָמַר רָבָא: וְכֵן לַחֲלוֹם טוֹב. אִינִי?! וְהָאָמַר רַב גִּידֵּל אָמַר רַב: *כָּל תַּלְמִיד חָכָם שֶׁיּוֹשֵׁב לִפְנֵי רַבּוֹ וְאֵין שִׂפְתוֹתָיו נוֹטְפוֹת מֹר – תִּכְוֶינָה, שֶׁנֶּאֱמַר: °"שִׂפְתוֹתָיו שׁוֹשַׁנִּים נוֹטְפוֹת מוֹר עוֹבֵר", אַל תִּקְרֵי 'מוֹר עוֹבֵר', אֶלָּא 'מַר עוֹבֵר', *אַל תִּקְרֵי 'שׁוֹשַׁנִּים' אֶלָּא 'שֶׁשּׁוֹנִים'! לָא קַשְׁיָא, הָא – בְּרַבָּה וְהָא – בְּתַלְמִיד. וְאִיבָּעֵית אֵימָא: הָא וְהָא בְּרַבָּה, וְלָא קַשְׁיָא, הָא – מִקַּמֵּי דְּלִפְתַּח, הָא – לְבָתַר דְּפָתַח. כִּי הָא דְּרַבָּה, מִקַּמֵּי דְּפָתַח לְהוּ לְרַבָּנַן אָמַר מִילְּתָא דִּבְדִיחוּתָא, וּבָדְחִי רַבָּנַן. לְסוֹף יָתֵיב בְּאֵימְתָא וּפָתַח בִּשְׁמַעְתָּא. וְאַף סֵפֶר מִשְׁלֵי בִּקְשׁוּ לִגְנוֹז, שֶׁהָיוּ דְּבָרָיו סוֹתְרִין זֶה אֶת זֶה. וּמִפְּנֵי מָה לֹא גְּנָזוּהוּ – אָמְרִי: סֵפֶר קֹהֶלֶת לָאו עִיַּינִינַן וְאַשְׁכְּחִינַן טַעְמָא? הָכָא נַמִּי לִיעַיְּינַן. וּמַאי דְּבָרָיו סוֹתְרִים זֶה אֶת זֶה – כְּתִיב: °"אַל תַּעַן כְּסִיל כְּאִוַּלְתּוֹ" וּכְתִיב: °"עֲנֵה כְסִיל כְּאִוַּלְתּוֹ" לָא קַשְׁיָא, הָא – בְּדִבְרֵי תוֹרָה, הָא – בְּמִילֵּי דְּעָלְמָא. כִּי הָא דְּהַהוּא דַּאֲתָא לְקַמֵּיהּ דְּרַבִּי, אֲמַר לֵיהּ: אִשְׁתְּךָ אִשְׁתִּי וּבָנֶיךָ בָּנַי. אֲמַר לֵיהּ: רְצוֹנְךָ שֶׁתִּשְׁתֶּה כּוֹס שֶׁל יַיִן? שָׁתָה וּפָקַע. הַהוּא דַּאֲתָא לְקַמֵּיהּ דְּרַבִּי חִיָּיא, אֲמַר לֵיהּ: אִמְּךָ אִשְׁתִּי וְאַתָּה בְּנִי. אֲמַר לֵיהּ: רְצוֹנְךָ שֶׁתִּשְׁתֶּה כּוֹס שֶׁל יַיִן? שָׁתָה וּפָקַע. אָמַר רַבִּי חִיָּיא: אַהֲנְיָא לֵיהּ צְלוֹתֵיהּ לְרַבִּי דְּלָא לְשַׁוְּויֵיהּ בְּנֵי מַמְזֵירֵי. דְּרַבִּי כִּי הֲוָה מְצַלֵּי, אֲמַר: *"יְהִי רָצוֹן מִלְּפָנֶיךָ ה' אֱלֹהֵינוּ שֶׁתַּצִּילֵנִי הַיּוֹם מֵעַזֵּי פָנִים וּמֵעַזּוּת פָּנִים". בְּדִבְרֵי תוֹרָה מַאי הִיא? כִּי הָא דְּיָתֵיב רַבָּן גַּמְלִיאֵל וְקָא דָּרֵישׁ: עֲתִידָה אִשָּׁה *שֶׁתֵּלֵד בְּכָל יוֹם, שֶׁנֶּאֱמַר: °"הָרָה וְיוֹלֶדֶת יַחְדָּיו". לִיגְלֵג עָלָיו אוֹתוֹ תַּלְמִיד, אָמַר: "אֵין כָּל חָדָשׁ תַּחַת הַשָּׁמֶשׁ"! א"ל: בֹּא וְאַרְאֲךָ דּוּגְמָתָן בָּעוה"ז, נְפַק אַחְוֵי לֵיהּ תַּרְנְגוֹלֶת. וְתוּ יָתֵיב רַבָּן גַּמְלִיאֵל וְקָא דָּרֵישׁ: עֲתִידִים אִילָנוֹת שֶׁמּוֹצִיאִין פֵּירוֹת בְּכָל יוֹם, שֶׁנֶּאֱמַר: °"וְנָשָׂא עָנָף וְעָשָׂה פֶרִי", מָה עָנָף בְּכָל יוֹם – אַף פְּרִי בְּכָל יוֹם. לִיגְלֵג עָלָיו אוֹתוֹ תַּלְמִיד, אָמַר: וְהָכְתִיב "אֵין כָּל חָדָשׁ תַּחַת הַשָּׁמֶשׁ"! א"ל: בֹּא וְאַרְאֲךָ דּוּגְמָתָם בָּעוֹלָם הַזֶּה, נְפַק אַחְוֵי לֵיהּ צְלָף. וְתוּ יָתֵיב רַבָּן גַּמְלִיאֵל וְקָא דָּרֵישׁ: *עֲתִידָה אֶרֶץ יִשְׂרָאֵל שֶׁתּוֹצִיא גְּלוּסְקָאוֹת וּכְלֵי מֵילָת, שֶׁנֶּאֱמַר °"יְהִי פִסַּת בַּר בָּאָרֶץ". לִיגְלֵג עָלָיו אוֹתוֹ תַּלְמִיד, וְאָמַר: "אֵין כָּל חָדָשׁ תַּחַת הַשָּׁמֶשׁ"! אֲמַר לֵיהּ: בֹּא וְאַרְאֲךָ דּוּגְמָתָן בָּעוֹלָם הַזֶּה, נְפַק אַחְוֵי לֵיהּ כְּמֵיהִין וּפִטְרִיּוֹת, וְאַכְּלֵי מֵילָת – נַבְרָא בַּר קוּרָא.§ *ת"ר: יה"לְעוֹלָם יְהֵא אָדָם עַנְוְותָן כְּהִלֵּל וְאַל יְהֵא קַפְּדָן כְּשַׁמַּאי. מַעֲשֶׂה בִּשְׁנֵי בְּנֵי אָדָם שֶׁהִמְרוּ

קהלת ט | שם א | שם יב

קח א מיי' פכ"א מהל' שבת הלכה יח סמג לאוין סה טוש"ע א"ח סימן שכד סעיף ז:
קט ב מיי' פכ"ו מהל' שבת הלכה כא סמג שם טוש"ע א"ח סי' שיא סעיף א:
קי ג מיי' פ"ח מהלכות לולב הלכה טו:
קיא ד מיי' פ"ז מהל' יסודי התורה הלכה ד [ברא"ש פ"ה דברכות סימן ב]:
קיב ה מיי' פ"ב מהל' דעות הלכה ג:

לקמן קנו: | ברכות ו: | [נ"ל אלעזר] | שם ב | ס"א שמחה | עיין בערוך ערך טף | [ברכות טז: ושם איתא שתצילנו וכו' וכן כאוי לכיות] | [עי' תוספות ע"ז ה. ד"ה אין בן דוד] | כתובות קיא:

[נ"ל ה'] | [יומא פה:] | [וכלאי' פסחים נד. נדרים לט:] | לקמן מ"ג: קמב: | [דף כח:] | שם ז | שם ח | שם ב | פסחים קיז. ע"ש | מלכים ב ג | שיר השירים ה | [לקמן פח: פסחים קיז.] | משלי כו | ירמיהו לא | יחזקאל יז | תהלים עב | [אבות דר"נ פט"ו ע"ש שינויים רבים]

רב נסים גאון

אמר רבי פרנך אמר רבי יוחנן אותה שנה לא עשו ישראל צום הכפורים כו': **ואביך** הנח עליו ככר או תינוק וטלטלו. תמצא עיקר המעשה בפרק כירה (דף מג) איתמר מת המוטל בחמה רב יהודה אמר שמואל הופכו ממטה למטה ורבי חיננא משמיה דרב אמר מניח עליו ככר או תינוק ומטלטלו ובפרק נוטל (דף קמג) אמרו לא אמרו ככר או תינוק אלא למת בלבד מיכן נלמוד כי אותם שמניחין פת על המנורה שהדליקו את הנר עליה כדי שיסירו המנורה ממקומה עוברין הם על המצות ואסור לעשות כן שלא התירו חכמים להניח ככר אלא למת בלבד ולא לדבר אחר:

פליגו

רבינו חננאל

העיירות: **מהו** לכבות בוצינא דנהורא מקמי באישא בשבתא. פי' באישא שכיב מרע: **פתח** ואמר אנת שלמה אן הוא חכמתנותך וסוכלתנותך לא דייך שדבריך סותרין דברי אביך כו'. ולענין שאילתא דשאילנא ת"ש נשמתו של אדם היא נרו של הקב"ה שנאמר נר ה' נשמת אדם. מוטב תכבה נרו של ב"ו מפני נרו של הקב"ה. כלומר אם הוא חולה שיש בו סכנה שרי: **אין** השכינה שורה אלא מתוך שמחה שנאמר והיה כנגן המנגן ותהי עליו רוח אלהים. וכן לדבר הלכה והני מילי ברבה אבל בתלמיד לא שכל תלמיד שאין שפתותיו נוטפות מר תכוינה: **תנו** רבנן לעולם יהא אדם ענותן כהלל ואל יהא קפדן כשמאי מעשה בב'

שֶׁהִמְרוּ זֶה אֶת זֶה, אָמְרוּ: כָּל מִי שֶׁיֵּלֵךְ וְיַקְנִיט אֶת הִלֵּל – יִטּוֹל ד' מֵאוֹת זוּז. אָמַר אֶחָד מֵהֶם: אֲנִי אַקְנִיטֶנּוּ. אוֹתוֹ הַיּוֹם ע"ש הָיָה, וְהִלֵּל חָפַף אֶת רֹאשׁוֹ. הָלַךְ וְעָבַר עַל פֶּתַח בֵּיתוֹ, אָמַר: מִי כָּאן הִלֵּל? מִי כָּאן הִלֵּל? נִתְעַטֵּף וְיָצָא לִקְרָאתוֹ. אָמַר לוֹ: בְּנִי, מָה אַתָּה מְבַקֵּשׁ? א"ל: שְׁאֵלָה יֵשׁ לִי לִשְׁאוֹל. א"ל: שְׁאַל בְּנִי, שְׁאַל! מִפְּנֵי מָה רָאשֵׁיהֶן שֶׁל בַּבְלִיִּים סְגַלְגַּלּוֹת? א"ל: בְּנִי, שְׁאֵלָה גְּדוֹלָה שָׁאַלְתָּ – מִפְּנֵי שֶׁאֵין לָהֶם חַיּוֹת פִּקְחוֹת. הָלַךְ וְהִמְתִּין שָׁעָה אַחַת, חָזַר וְאָמַר: מִי כָּאן הִלֵּל? מִי כָּאן הִלֵּל? נִתְעַטֵּף וְיָצָא לִקְרָאתוֹ. אָמַר לוֹ: בְּנִי, מָה אַתָּה מְבַקֵּשׁ? א"ל: שְׁאֵלָה יֵשׁ לִי לִשְׁאוֹל. א"ל: שְׁאַל בְּנִי, שְׁאַל! מִפְּנֵי מָה עֵינֵיהֶן שֶׁל תַּרְמוֹדִיִּין תְּרוּטוֹת? אָמַר לוֹ: בְּנִי, שְׁאֵלָה גְּדוֹלָה שָׁאַלְתָּ – מִפְּנֵי שֶׁדָּרִין בֵּין הַחוֹלוֹת. הָלַךְ וְהִמְתִּין שָׁעָה אַחַת, חָזַר וְאָמַר: מִי כָּאן הִלֵּל? מִי כָּאן הִלֵּל? נִתְעַטֵּף וְיָצָא לִקְרָאתוֹ. א"ל: בְּנִי, מָה אַתָּה מְבַקֵּשׁ? א"ל: שְׁאֵלָה יֵשׁ לִי לִשְׁאוֹל. א"ל: שְׁאַל בְּנִי, שְׁאַל! מִפְּנֵי מָה רַגְלֵיהֶם שֶׁל אַפְרִקִיִּים רְחָבוֹת? א"ל: בְּנִי, שְׁאֵלָה גְּדוֹלָה שָׁאַלְתָּ – מִפְּנֵי שֶׁדָּרִין בֵּין בִּצְעֵי הַמַּיִם. אָמַר לוֹ: שְׁאֵלוֹת הַרְבֵּה יֵשׁ לִי לִשְׁאוֹל, וּמִתְיָרֵא אֲנִי שֶׁמָּא תִּכְעוֹס. נִתְעַטֵּף וְיָשַׁב לְפָנָיו, א"ל: כָּל שְׁאֵלוֹת שֶׁיֵּשׁ לְךָ לִשְׁאוֹל – שְׁאַל. א"ל: אַתָּה הוּא הִלֵּל שֶׁקּוֹרִין אוֹתְךָ נְשִׂיא יִשְׂרָאֵל? א"ל: הֵן. א"ל: אִם אַתָּה הוּא – לֹא יִרְבּוּ כְּמוֹתְךָ בְּיִשְׂרָאֵל. א"ל: בְּנִי, מִפְּנֵי מָה? א"ל: מִפְּנֵי שֶׁאִבַּדְתִּי עַל יָדְךָ ד' מֵאוֹת זוּז. א"ל: הֱוֵי זָהִיר בְּרוּחֲךָ, כְּדֵי הוּא הִלֵּל שֶׁתְּאַבֵּד עַל יָדוֹ ד' מֵאוֹת זוּז וְד' מֵאוֹת זוּז – וְהִלֵּל לֹא יַקְפִּיד.§ ת"ר: מַעֲשֶׂה בְּגוֹי אֶחָד שֶׁבָּא לִפְנֵי שַׁמַּאי, אָמַר לוֹ: כַּמָּה תּוֹרוֹת יֵשׁ לָכֶם? אָמַר לוֹ: שְׁתַּיִם, תּוֹרָה שֶׁבִּכְתָב וְתוֹרָה שֶׁבְּעַל פֶּה. א"ל: שֶׁבִּכְתָב – אֲנִי מַאֲמִינְךָ, וְשֶׁבְּעַל פֶּה – אֵינִי מַאֲמִינְךָ. גַּיְּירֵנִי ע"מ שֶׁתְּלַמְּדֵנִי תּוֹרָה שֶׁבִּכְתָב. גָּעַר בּוֹ וְהוֹצִיאוֹ בִּנְזִיפָה. בָּא לִפְנֵי הִלֵּל – גַּיְּירֵיהּ, יוֹמָא קַמָּא א"ל: א"ב ג"ד, לְמָחָר אַפֵּיךְ לֵיהּ. א"ל: וְהָא אֶתְמוֹל לָא אֲמַרְתְּ לִי הָכִי?! א"ל: לָאו עֲלַי דִּידִי קָא סָמְכַתְּ? דְּעַל פֶּה נַמִּי סְמוֹךְ עֲלַי.§ שׁוּב מַעֲשֶׂה בְּגוֹי אֶחָד שֶׁבָּא לִפְנֵי שַׁמַּאי, א"ל: גַּיְּירֵנִי ע"מ שֶׁתְּלַמְּדֵנִי כָּל הַתּוֹרָה כּוּלָּהּ כְּשֶׁאֲנִי עוֹמֵד עַל רֶגֶל אַחַת. דְּחָפוֹ בְּאַמַּת הַבִּנְיָן שֶׁבְּיָדוֹ. בָּא לִפְנֵי הִלֵּל, *גַּיְּירֵיהּ. אָמַר לוֹ: דַּעֲלָךְ סְנֵי לְחַבְרָךְ לָא תַּעֲבֵיד – זוֹ הִיא כָּל הַתּוֹרָה כּוּלָּהּ, וְאִידָךְ – פֵּירוּשָׁהּ הוּא, זִיל גְּמוֹר.§ שׁוּב מַעֲשֶׂה בְּגוֹי אֶחָד שֶׁהָיָה עוֹבֵר אֲחוֹרֵי בֵּית הַמִּדְרָשׁ, וְשָׁמַע קוֹל סוֹפֵר שֶׁהָיָה אוֹמֵר: °"וְאֵלֶּה הַבְּגָדִים אֲשֶׁר יַעֲשׂוּ חוֹשֶׁן וְאֵפוֹד". אָמַר: הַלָּלוּ לְמִי? אָמְרוּ לוֹ: לְכֹהֵן גָּדוֹל, אָמַר אוֹתוֹ גּוֹי בְּעַצְמוֹ: אֵלֵךְ וְאֶתְגַּיֵּיר, בִּשְׁבִיל שֶׁיְּשִׂימוּנִי כֹּהֵן גָּדוֹל. בָּא לִפְנֵי שַׁמַּאי, אָמַר לֵיהּ: גַּיְּירֵנִי עַל מְנָת שֶׁתְּשִׂימֵנִי כֹּהֵן גָּדוֹל. דְּחָפוֹ בְּאַמַּת הַבִּנְיָן שֶׁבְּיָדוֹ. בָּא לִפְנֵי הִלֵּל – גַּיְּירֵיהּ. א"ל: כְּלוּם מַעֲמִידִין מֶלֶךְ אֶלָּא מִי שֶׁיּוֹדֵעַ טַכְסִיסֵי מַלְכוּת? לֵךְ לְמוֹד טַכְסִיסֵי מַלְכוּת. הָלַךְ וְקָרָא, כֵּיוָן שֶׁהִגִּיעַ °"וְהַזָּר הַקָּרֵב יוּמָת" אָמַר לֵיהּ: מִקְרָא זֶה עַל מִי נֶאֱמַר? א"ל: אֲפִי' עַל דָּוִד מֶלֶךְ יִשְׂרָאֵל. נָשָׂא אוֹתוֹ גֵּר קַל וָחוֹמֶר בְּעַצְמוֹ: וּמָה יִשְׂרָאֵל שֶׁנִּקְרְאוּ בָּנִים לַמָּקוֹם, וּמִתּוֹךְ אַהֲבָה שֶׁאֲהֵבָם קָרָא לָהֶם: °"בְּנִי בְכֹרִי יִשְׂרָאֵל" – כְּתִיב עֲלֵיהֶם: "וְהַזָּר הַקָּרֵב יוּמָת", גֵּר הַקַּל שֶׁבָּא בְּמַקְלוֹ וּבְתַרְמִילוֹ – עַל אַחַת כַּמָּה וְכַמָּה! בָּא לִפְנֵי שַׁמַּאי, א"ל: כְּלוּם רָאוּי אֲנִי לִהְיוֹת כֹּהֵן גָּדוֹל? וַהֲלֹא כְּתִיב בַּתּוֹרָה: "וְהַזָּר הַקָּרֵב יוּמָת"! בָּא לִפְנֵי הִלֵּל, א"ל: עַנְוְותָן הִלֵּל, *יָנוּחוּ לְךָ בְּרָכוֹת עַל רֹאשְׁךָ שֶׁהִקְרַבְתַּנִי תַּחַת כַּנְפֵי הַשְּׁכִינָה. לְיָמִים נִזְדַּוְּוגוּ שְׁלָשְׁתָּן לְמָקוֹם אֶחָד, אָמְרוּ: קַפְּדָנוּתוֹ שֶׁל שַׁמַּאי בִּקְּשָׁה לְטוֹרְדֵנוּ מִן הָעוֹלָם, עַנְוְותָנוּתוֹ שֶׁל הִלֵּל קֵרְבָנוּ תַּחַת כַּנְפֵי הַשְּׁכִינָה.§ אָמַר ר"ל, מַאי דִּכְתִיב: °"וְהָיָה אֱמוּנַת עִתֶּיךָ חֹסֶן יְשׁוּעֹת חָכְמַת וָדָעַת וגו'" – 'אֱמוּנַת' זֶה סֵדֶר זְרָעִים, 'עִתֶּיךָ' – זֶה סֵדֶר מוֹעֵד, 'חוֹסֶן' – זֶה סֵדֶר נָשִׁים, 'יְשׁוּעוֹת' – זֶה סֵדֶר נְזִיקִין, 'חָכְמַת' – זֶה סֵדֶר קָדָשִׁים, 'וָדַעַת' – זֶה סֵדֶר טָהֳרוֹת. וַאפ"ה °"יִרְאַת ה' הִיא אוֹצָרוֹ". אָמַר רָבָא: בְּשָׁעָה שֶׁמַּכְנִיסִין אָדָם לַדִּין אוֹמְרִים לוֹ: [א]נָשָׂאתָ *וְנָתַתָּ בֶּאֱמוּנָה, [ב]קָבַעְתָּ עִתִּים לַתּוֹרָה, עָסַקְתָּ בִּפְרִיָּה וּרְבִיָּה, צִפִּיתָ לִישׁוּעָה, פִּלְפַּלְתָּ בְּחָכְמָה, הֵבַנְתָּ דָּבָר מִתּוֹךְ דָּבָר? וַאפ"ה: אִי יִרְאַת ה' הִיא אוֹצָרוֹ – אִין, אִי לָא – לָא. מָשָׁל לְאָדָם שֶׁאָמַר לִשְׁלוּחוֹ: הַעֲלֵה לִי כּוֹר חִטִּין לָעֲלִיָּיה. הָלַךְ וְהֶעֱלָה לוֹ. א"ל: עֵירַבְתָּ לִי בָּהֶן קַב חוֹמְטוֹן? א"ל: לָאו. א"ל: מוּטָב אִם לֹא הֶעֱלִיתָהּ.§ תָּנָא דְּבֵי ר"י: *מְעָרֵב אָדָם קַב חוֹמְטוֹן בְּכוֹר שֶׁל תְּבוּאָה, וְאֵינוֹ חוֹשֵׁשׁ.§ אָמַר רַבָּה בַּר רַב הוּנָא: כָּל אָדָם שֶׁיֵּשׁ בּוֹ תּוֹרָה וְאֵין בּוֹ יִרְאַת

Marginal references beside the Gemara: שמות כח (beside "ואלה הבגדים"); במדבר ח (beside "והזר הקרב יומת"); שמות ד (beside "בני בכורי ישראל"); ישעיהו לג (beside "והיה אמונת עתיך"); שם (beside "יראת ה' היא אוצרו").

רש"י

שֶׁהִמְרוּ. נִתְעָרְבוּ. כְּמוֹ שֶׁ"מַּמְרִין אֶת הַיּוֹנִים" דְּסַנְהֶדְרִין (דף כה:): מִי כָּאן הִלֵּל. כְּלוֹמַר כָּאן הִלֵּל? וּלְשׁוֹן גְּנַאי לִנְשִׂיא יִשְׂרָאֵל: מִפְּנֵי מָה רָאשָׁן שֶׁל בַּבְלִיִּים סְגַלְגַּלּוֹת. בילונ"ה בְּלַע"ז, שֶׁאֵינוֹ עָגוֹל. לִישָּׁנָא אַחֲרִינָא: רֹאשָׁן שֶׁל בַּבְלִיִּים סְגַלְגַּל – עָגוֹל: תְּרוּטוֹת. רַכּוֹת: שֶׁדָּרִים בֵּין הַחוֹלוֹת. וְהָרוּחַ נוֹשֶׁבֶת וְנִכְנָס בְּתוֹךְ עֵינֵיהֶם. וּבְמָקוֹם אַחֵר *מְפָרֵשׁ תְּרוּטוֹת לָשׁוֹן: עֲגוּלוֹת בֵּית מוֹשַׁב שֶׁלָּהֶן. וְאַף כָּאן אֲנִי אוֹמֵר כֵּן. וּמִפְּנֵי שֶׁדָּרִים בֵּין הַחוֹלוֹת שֶׁיָּפֶה אוֹתָם הַמָּקוֹם, שֶׁלֹּא יְהֵא סֶדֶק שֶׁל עֵינֵיהֶם אָרוֹךְ כְּשֶׁלָּנוּ וְיִכָּנֵס בּוֹ הַחוֹל. וְכֵן רַגְלֵיהֶם שֶׁל אַפְרִקִיִּים רְחָבוֹת – שֶׁלֹּא יִטְבְּעוּ בְּבִצְעֵי הַמַּיִם. וְרַבּוֹתֵינוּ מְפָרְשִׁים: שֶׁדָּרִים בֵּין בִּצְעֵי הַמַּיִם וְהוֹלְכִין יְחֵפִין, וּמִתְפַּשְּׁטִין רַגְלֵיהֶן. לְפִי שֶׁהַמִּנְעָל דּוֹחֵק הָרֶגֶל וּמַעֲמִידוֹ עַל דְּפוּס שֶׁלּוֹ: כְּדַי הוּא הִלֵּל. רָאוּי לְכָךְ: הוֹצִיאוֹ בִּנְזִיפָה. דְּתַנְיָא: הַבָּא לְקַבֵּל דִּבְרֵי חֲבֵרוּת חוּץ מִדָּבָר אֶחָד, וְכֵן גֵּר הַבָּא לְהִתְגַּיֵּיר וְקִבֵּל עָלָיו דִּבְרֵי תוֹרָה חוּץ מִדָּבָר אֶחָד – אֵין מְקַבְּלִין אוֹתוֹ. בְּמַסֶּכֶת בְּכוֹרוֹת (דף ל:): גַּיְּירֵיהּ. וְסָמַךְ עַל חָכְמָתוֹ שֶׁסּוֹפוֹ שֶׁיַּרְגִּילֶנּוּ לְקַבֵּל עָלָיו. דְּלָא דָּמְיָא הָא לְ"חוּץ מִדָּבָר אֶחָד" – שֶׁלֹּא הָיָה כּוֹפֵר בַּתּוֹרָה שֶׁבְּעַל פֶּה, אֶלָּא שֶׁלֹּא הָיָה מַאֲמִין שֶׁהִיא מִפִּי הַגְּבוּרָה. וְהִלֵּל הוּבְטַח שֶׁאַחַר שֶׁיְּלַמְּדֶנּוּ יִסְמוֹךְ עָלָיו: אַפֵּיךְ לֵיהּ. כְּגוֹן תשר"ק: לָאו עֲלַי קָא סָמְכַתְּ. מִנַּיִן אַתָּה יוֹדֵעַ שֶׁזּוּ אָלֶף וְזוּ בֵּית – אֶלָּא שֶׁלִּמַּדְתִּיךְ וְסָמַכְתָּ עָלַי, דְּעַל פֶּה נַמִּי סְמוֹךְ עַל דְּבָרַי: אַמַּת הַבִּנְיָן. מַקֵּל שֶׁהוּא אַמַּת אוֹרֶךְ, וּמוֹדְדִים בּוֹ אוֹרֶךְ הַבִּנְיָן. שֶׁהָיוּ קוֹלְנִין עִם הָאוּמָּנִין כָּךְ וְכָךְ אַמּוֹת בְּכָךְ וְכָךְ דָּמִים: דַּעֲלָךְ סְנֵי לְחַבְרָךְ לָא תַּעֲבֵיד. "רֵיעֲךָ וְרֵיעַ אָבִיךָ אַל תַּעֲזוֹב" (משלי כז) – זֶה הקב"ה. אַל תַּעֲבוֹר עַל דְּבָרָיו, שֶׁהֲרֵי עָלֶיךָ סָנְאוּי שֶׁיַּעֲבוֹר חֲבֵירְךָ עַל דְּבָרֶיךָ. ל"א: חֲבֵירְךָ מַמָּשׁ, כְּגוֹן גְּזֵלָה גְּנֵבָה נִיאוּף וְרוֹב הַמִּצְוֹת: אִידָךְ. שְׁאָר דִּבְרֵי תוֹרָה: פֵּירוּשָׁהּ. דְּהָא מִילְּתָא הוּא, לָדַעַת אֵיזֶה דָּבָר סָנְאוּי זִיל גְּמוֹר וְתֵדַע: סוֹפֵר. מְלַמֵּד תִּינוֹקוֹת: טַכְסִיסֵי. תִּיקּוּנֵי דַּרְכֵי הַמֶּלֶךְ לְפִי הַכָּבוֹד: שְׁלָשְׁתָּן. הַגֵּרִים הַלָּלוּ: סֵדֶר זְרָעִים. שֶׁעַל אֱמוּנַת הָאָדָם סוֹמֵךְ לְהַפְרִישׁ מַעַשְׂרוֹתָיו כָּרָאוּי: חוֹסֶן. לְשׁוֹן יוֹרְשִׁין, וְעַל יְדֵי אִשָּׁה נוֹלְדוּ יוֹרְשִׁין: סֵדֶר נְזִיקִין. מוֹשִׁיעַן, מַזְהִיר לִפְרוֹשׁ מֵהֶיזֵּק וּמֵהִתְחַיֵּיב מָמוֹן: דַּעַת. עָדִיף מֵחָכְמָה: הִיא אוֹצָרוֹ. הוּא עִיקָּר הֶחָשׁוּב בְּעֵינָיו לֶאֱצוֹר וְלַעֲשׂוֹת סְגוּלָּה לְזִכָּרוֹן: קָבַעְתָּ עִתִּים. לְפִי שֶׁאָדָם צָרִיךְ לְהִתְעַסֵּק בְּדֶרֶךְ אֶרֶץ, שֶׁאִם אֵין דֶּרֶךְ אֶרֶץ אֵין תּוֹרָה, הוּצְרַךְ לִקְבּוֹעַ עִתִּים לַתּוֹרָה דָּבָר קָצוּב, שֶׁלֹּא יִמָּשֵׁךְ כָּל הַיּוֹם לְדֶרֶךְ אֶרֶץ: בִּפְרִיָּה וּרְבִיָּה. הַיְינוּ חוֹסֶן: צִפִּיתָ לִישׁוּעָה. לְדִבְרֵי הַנְּבִיאִים: הֵבַנְתָּ דָּבָר מִתּוֹךְ דָּבָר. הַיְינוּ דַּעַת: קַב חוֹמְטִין. אֶרֶץ מְלֵחָה, וּמְשַׁמֶּרֶת אֶת הַפֵּירוֹת מֵהִתְלִיעַ: וְאֵינוֹ חוֹשֵׁשׁ. לְמוֹכְרָהּ בִּדְמֵי חִטִּין, דְּלָאו אוֹנָאָה הִיא – שֶׁהֲרֵי שֶׁמִּירְתָּן בְּכָךְ: יִרְאַת

תוספות

שהמרו זה את זה. דיני אסמכתא מפורש במקום אחר. (בבא מציעא דף עד. וסס): אמונת זה סדר זרעים. מפרש בירושלמי: שמאמין בחי העולמים וזורע: וסותר

רבינו חננאל

בג' בני אדם שהמרו זה את זה. כל מי שיקניט הלל יטול [ד' מאות] זוז כו': **אמר** ר"ל והיה אמונת עתיך וגו' אמונת זה סדר זרעים. עתיך זה סדר מועד. חוסן זה סדר נשים. ישועות זה סדר נזיקין. חכמת זה סדר קדשים. ודעת זה סדר טהרות. ואף על פי [כן] יראת ה' היא אוצרו. אי איכא יראת ה' אין ואי לא לא: **רבא** אמר בשעה שמכניסין את האדם לדין אומרים לו נשאת ונתת באמונה. קבעת עתים לתורה. עסקת בפריה ורביה. צפית לישועה. פלפלת בחכמה. הבנת דבר מתוך דבר. אע"פ שיש בידך כל אלו אי איכא יראת שמים אין ואם לא לא. פי' חומטון חול מערבין בתבואה. ואינו בא בה סלמנטון. והיא רצינתא. ומפורש בסוף המוכר את הספינה: **כל** ת"ח שיש בו תורה ואין בו

עין משפט נר מצוה

קיג א טור וש"ע א"ח סי' קנו:

קיד ב מיי' פ"א מהל' ת"ת הלכה ח טור וש"ע א"ח סימן קנה סעיף א:

מסורת הש"ס

[סוטה מז. סנהדרין קז: בכורות מל.]

[ועי' תוס' יבמות קט: ד"ה רעה וכו']

[ברכות נג. וש"נ]

[ועי' תוס' סנהדרין ז. ד"ה אלא ותוס' קדושין מ: ד"ה אין]

זה שייך לדיני מכירה

גליון הש"ס

גמרא הלל גייריה. עי' יבמות דף כד ע"ב תוס' ד"ה לא בימי ודף קט ע"ב תוס' ד"ה רעה:

קטו א מיי' פ"א מהל' שבת הל' ז ופי"ב הל' ב סמג לאוין סה טור או"ח סימן רסח:
קטז ב מיי' פ"ה מהל' שבת הלכה טו:
קיז ג מיי' פ"ה מהל' שבת הל' ג טוש"ע או"ח סי' רסג סעיף ג:

[ילקוט פרשת עקב רמז תתנה איתא רבי ור' אלעזר בר' שמעון הוו יתבי וכו' וע"ע ילקוט קהלת רמז תתקסט]

[מ"ק כח. סנהדרין עו: ע"ש]

יִרְאַת שָׁמַיִם, דּוֹמֶה לְגִזְבָּר שֶׁמָּסְרוּ לוֹ מַפְתְּחוֹת הַפְּנִימִיּוֹת וּמַפְתְּחוֹת הַחִיצוֹנוֹת לֹא מָסְרוּ לוֹ. בְּהֵי עָיֵיל? *מַכְרִיז רַבִּי יַנַּאי: חֲבָל עַל דְּלֵית לֵיהּ דַּרְתָּא, וְתַרְעָא לְדַרְתָּא עָבֵיד. אָמַר רַב יְהוּדָה: לֹא בָּרָא הקב"ה אֶת עוֹלָמוֹ אֶלָּא כְּדֵי שֶׁיִּירְאוּ מִלְּפָנָיו, שֶׁנֶּאֱמַר: °"וְהָאֱלֹהִים עָשָׂה שֶׁיִּירְאוּ מִלְּפָנָיו". *ר' סִימוֹן וְר' אֶלְעָזָר הֲווּ יָתְבִי, חָלֵיף וְאָזֵיל ר' יַעֲקֹב בַּר אַחָא. א"ל חַד לְחַבְרֵיהּ: נֵיקוּ מִקַּמֵּיהּ, דִּגְבַר דָּחֵיל חֲטָאִין הוּא, א"ל אִידָךְ: נֵיקוּ מִקַּמֵּיהּ; דִּגְבַר *בַּר אוֹרְיָין הוּא. א"ל: אָמִינָא לָךְ אֲנָא דִּגְבַר דָּחֵיל חֲטָאִין הוּא – וְאָמְרַתְּ לִי אַתְּ "בַּר אוֹרְיָין הוּא"?! תִּסְתַּיֵּים דְּרַבִּי אֶלְעָזָר הוּא דְּאָמַר "דִּגְבַר דָּחֵיל חֲטָאִין הוּא", דְּא"ר יוֹחָנָן מִשּׁוּם ר' *אֶלְעָזָר: אֵין לוֹ לְהקב"ה בְּעוֹלָמוֹ אֶלָּא יִרְאַת שָׁמַיִם בִּלְבַד, שֶׁנֶּאֱמַר: °"וְעַתָּה יִשְׂרָאֵל מָה ה' אֱלֹהֶיךָ שׁוֹאֵל מֵעִמָּךְ כִּי אִם לְיִרְאָה וגו'" וּכְתִיב: °"וַיֹּאמֶר לָאָדָם הֵן יִרְאַת ה' הִיא חָכְמָה וגו'", *שֶׁכֵּן בִּלְשׁוֹן יְוָנִי קוֹרִין לְאַחַת הֵן. – *תִּסְתַּיֵּים.§ דָּרַשׁ רַב עוּלָּא, מַאי דִּכְתִיב: °"אַל תִּרְשַׁע הַרְבֵּה וגו'", הַרְבֵּה הוּא דְּלָא לִירְשַׁע, הָא מְעַט לִירְשַׁע? אֶלָּא: מִי שֶׁאָכַל שׁוּם וְרֵיחוֹ נוֹדֵף, יַחֲזוֹר וְיֹאכַל שׁוּם אַחֵר וִיהֵא רֵיחוֹ נוֹדֵף?! דָּרַשׁ רָבָא בַּר רַב עוּלָּא, מַאי דִּכְתִיב: °"כִּי אֵין חַרְצֻבּוֹת לְמוֹתָם וּבָרִיא אוּלָם" – אָמַר הקב"ה: לֹא דַּיָּין לָרְשָׁעִים שֶׁאֵינָן חֲרֵדִין וַעֲצֵבִין מִיּוֹם הַמִּיתָה, אֶלָּא שֶׁלִּבָּם בָּרִיא לָהֶן כְּאוּלָם. וְהַיְינוּ דְּאָמַר רַבָּה, מַאי דִּכְתִיב: °"זֶה דַּרְכָּם כֶּסֶל לָמוֹ" – יוֹדְעִין רְשָׁעִים שֶׁדַּרְכָּם לְמִיתָה, וְיֵשׁ לָהֶם חֵלֶב עַל כִּסְלָם. שֶׁמָּא תֹּאמַר: שִׁכְחָה הִיא מֵהֶן – ת"ל: "וְאַחֲרֵיהֶם בְּפִיהֶם יִרְצוּ סֶלָה".§ "כּוֹחֵס עַל הַנֵּר כו'".§ ר' יוֹסֵי כְּמַאן ס"ל? *אִי כְּר' יְהוּדָה ס"ל – אֲפִילּוּ בְּהָנָךְ נַמִי לִיחַיֵּיב, וְאִי כְּרַ"שׁ ס"ל – פְּתִילָה נַמִי לִיפְטַר! אָמַר עוּלָּא: [א]לְעוֹלָם כְּר' יְהוּדָה ס"ל. וְקָסָבַר ר' יוֹסֵי: [ב]סוֹתֵר עַל מְנָת לִבְנוֹת בִּמְקוֹמוֹ – הָוֵי סוֹתֵר, עַל מְנָת לִבְנוֹת שֶׁלֹּא בִּמְקוֹמוֹ – לָא הָוֵי סוֹתֵר. א"ל רַבָּה: מִכְּדִי, *כָּל מְלָאכוֹת יָלְפִינַן לְהוּ מִמִּשְׁכָּן וְהָתָם סוֹתֵר ע"מ לִבְנוֹת שֶׁלֹּא בִּמְקוֹמוֹ הוּא! א"ל: שָׁאנֵי הָתָם, כֵּיוָן דִּכְתִיב: °"עַל פִּי ה' יַחֲנוּ" – כְּסוֹתֵר ע"מ לִבְנוֹת בִּמְקוֹמוֹ דָּמֵי, וְר' יוֹחָנָן אָמַר: לְעוֹלָם כְּרַ"שׁ ס"ל, וּמַאי שְׁנָא פְּתִילָה – כִּדְאָמַר רַב הַמְנוּנָא וְאִיתֵּימָא רַב אַדָּא בַּר אַהֲבָה: הָכָא בִּפְתִילָה שֶׁצָּרִיךְ לְהַבְהֲבָהּ עָסְקִינַן, דִּבְהַהִיא אֲפִילּוּ ר"ש מוֹדֵי דְּקָא מְתַקֵּן מָנָא. אָמַר רָבָא: דַּיְקָא נַמִי דְּקָתָנֵי "שֶׁהוּא עוֹשֶׂה פֶּחָם" וְלָא קָתָנֵי "מִפְּנֵי שֶׁנַּעֲשֵׂית פֶּחָם" – ש"מ.§ **מתני'** עַל שָׁלֹשׁ עֲבֵירוֹת נָשִׁים מֵתוֹת בִּשְׁעַת לֵידָתָן: עַל שֶׁאֵינָן זְהִירוֹת בְּנִדָּה, בְּחַלָּה, [ג]וּבְהַדְלָקַת הַנֵּר.§ **גמ'** נִדָּה מ"ט? א"ר יִצְחָק: הִיא קִלְקְלָה בְּחַדְרֵי בִטְנָהּ – לְפִיכָךְ תִּלְקֶה בְּחַדְרֵי בִטְנָהּ. תֵּינַח נִדָּה, חַלָּה וְהַדְלָקַת הַנֵּר מַאי אִיכָּא לְמֵימַר? כִּדְדָרַשׁ הַהוּא גָּלִילָאָה עֲלֵיהּ דְּרַב חִסְדָּא, אָמַר הקב"ה: *רְבִיעִית דָּם נָתַתִּי בָּכֶם – עַל עִסְקֵי דָם הִזְהַרְתִּי אֶתְכֶם, רֵאשִׁית

(קהלת ג; דברים י; איוב כח; קהלת ז; תהלים עג; תהלים מט; במדבר ט)

רש"י

יִרְאַת שָׁמַיִם דּוֹמֶה. לְפָתְחִים חִיצוֹנִים, שֶׁדֶּרֶךְ לָהֶם נִכְנָסִים לַפְּנִימִיִּים. כָּךְ, אִם יְרֵא שָׁמַיִם הוּא – נַעֲשֶׂה חָרֵד לִשְׁמוֹר וְלַעֲשׂוֹת, וְאִם לָאו – אֵינוֹ חָשׁ לְתוֹרָתוֹ: בְּהֵי עָיֵיל. בְּאֵיזֶה פֶּתַח נִכְנָס, לִפְתּוֹחַ אֶת הַפְּנִימִיִּים:(א) (*וַאֲנָא אָמִינָא לָךְ. כְּלוֹמַר: אַתָּה מִיעַטְתָּ בְּשִׁבְחוֹ: הֵן יִרְאַת ה'. יְחִידָה הִיא הַיִּרְאָה בָּעוֹלָם: מִי שֶׁאָכַל שׁוּם וְרֵיחוֹ נוֹדֵף כו'. פֵּירוּקָא הוּא. כְּלוֹמַר, הָכִי קָאָמַר קְרָא: אִם רָשַׁעְתָּ מְעַט – אַל תּוֹסֵף עַל רִשְׁעֲךָ, דְּמִי שֶׁאָכַל שׁוּם וְרֵיחוֹ נוֹדֵף כְּבָר לַחֲבֵרָיו, כְּלוּם יַחֲזוֹר וְיֹאכַל עוֹד אַחֵר, וְיִהְיֶה נוֹדֵף יוֹתֵר לִזְמַן אָרוֹךְ? חַרְדִּין וַעֲצֵבִין. נוֹטְרִיקוֹן דְּחַרְצוּבּוֹת: כְּאוּלָם. שֶׁפִּתְחוֹ פָּתוּחַ וְרָחָב: זֶה דַּרְכָּם. לְעֵיל מִינֵּיהּ כְּתִיב: "קִרְבָּם בָּתֵּימוֹ לְעוֹלָם", דְּהַיְינוּ קְבוּרָה, וַהֲדַר כְּתִיב: "זֶה דַרְכָּם כֶּסֶל לָמוֹ", כְּלוֹמַר: יוֹדְעִין הֵם שֶׁזּוֹ דַרְכָּם – אֲבָל כֶּסֶל לָמוֹ, כִּלְיוֹתֵיהֶם מְחוּפִּין בְּחֶלְבָּם מֵהָשִׁיב (ב)כִּלְיוֹתֵיהֶם מַחֲשֶׁבֶת סוֹפָם. וְשֶׁמָּא תֹּאמַר מֵחֲמַת הַחֵלֶב שָׁכְחוּ וַהֲרֵי הֵם שׁוֹגְגִין – ת"ל: "וְאַחֲרֵיהֶם" – אֶת הֶעָתִיד לָבֹא לְנַפְשָׁם אַחֲרֵי אוֹבְדָם "בְּפִיהֶם יִרְצוּ" וִיסַפְּרוּ תָּמִיד, וְאעפ"כ – אֵינָן חוֹזְרִין: אֲפִי' בִּפְתִילָה נַמִי לִיפְטַר. דְּחָס עַל הַפְּתִילָה נַמִי אֵינָהּ צְרִיכָה הַמְּלָאכָה לְגוּפָהּ. דִּמְלָאכָה הַיְינוּ כִּיבּוּי, וְכִיבּוּי עַצְמוֹ אֵינוֹ צָרִיךְ לוֹ. דְּאִם לֹא הוּבְעֲרָה מֵעוֹלָם הֲוָה נִיחָא לֵיהּ אִם מִתְּחִלָּה הוּבְהֲבָה, הוֹאִיל וְחָס עָלֶיהָ, כִּי אִית בָּהּ טְפֵי הֲוָה נִיחָא לֵיהּ בָּהּ: לְעוֹלָם כְּר' יְהוּדָה סְבִירָא לֵיהּ. דְּמִשּׁוּם אֵין צְרִיכָה לְגוּפָהּ לָא מִיפְּטַר, הוֹאִיל וּצְרִיכָה לְדָבָר אַחֵר – מְלֶאכֶת מַחֲשֶׁבֶת הוּא. וְכִי מְכַבֶּה לָהּ מִשּׁוּם חַיְיסָא דְּשֶׁמֶן וְנֵר, הַיְינוּ טַעְמָא דְּפָטוּר – קָסָבַר דְּסוֹתֵר ע"מ לִבְנוֹת בִּמְקוֹמוֹ – הָוֵי סוֹתֵר. כָּל מְקַלְקֵל דְּשַׁבָּת – הָוֵי פָּטוּר, דְּלָאו הַיְינוּ מְלֶאכֶת מַחֲשֶׁבֶת. וְסוֹתֵר דִּתְנַן *בַּאֲבוֹת מְלָאכוֹת דְּמִיחַיֵּיב – סוֹתֵר ע"מ לִבְנוֹת הוּא, וְאֵינוֹ יָכוֹל לִבְנוֹת אֶלָּא אִם כֵּן סוֹתְרוֹ, וְהַשְׁתָּא לָאו קִלְקוּל הוּא. וְר"י סָבַר, דְּאִם בִּמְקוֹמוֹ חוֹזֵר וּבוֹנֶה, הוּא דְּמִחַיֵּיב אַסְּתִירָה. וְאִי לָא – לָא. וּמְכַבֶּה דּוּמְיָא דְּסוֹתֵר הוּא, וְכֵן קוֹרֵעַ דּוּמְיָא דְּסוֹתֵר. וּלְהָכִי תְּנַן: "הַקּוֹרֵעַ ע"מ לִתְפּוֹר" וְכֵן מוֹחֵק תְּנַן: "ע"מ לִכְתּוֹב", דְּכוּלְּהוּ סוֹתֵר נִינְהוּ. הִלְכָּךְ, עַל הַפְּתִילָה חַיְיסָא דִּידֵיהּ אֵינָהּ אֶלָּא לְהַדְלִיק. הִלְכָּךְ: מְכַבֶּה עַל מְנָת לְהַדְלִיק – הַיְינוּ בִּמְקוֹמוֹ. אֲבָל כִּי חָס עַל הַנֵּר אוֹ עַל הַשֶּׁמֶן, וְעַל הַפְּתִילָה אֵינוֹ חָס וְאֵינוֹ חוֹשֵׁשׁ אִם מַשְׁלִיכָהּ, אֲפִי' צָרִיךְ לַשֶּׁמֶן לְהַדְלִיק בּוֹ פְּתִילָה אַחֶרֶת לְאַחַר זְמַן בְּתוֹךְ נֵר זֶה – אֵין זֶה סוֹתֵר ע"מ לִבְנוֹת בִּמְקוֹמוֹ, שֶׁאֵין הַכִּיבּוּי וְהַהַבְעָרָה לֹא בַּשֶּׁמֶן וְלֹא בַּנֵּר אֶלָּא בַּפְּתִילָה. הִלְכָּךְ, לָא שַׁיְיכָא סְתִירָה וּבִנְיָן אֶלָּא בַּפְּתִילָה, וְכֵיוָן דְּאֵין מַחֲשֶׁבֶת סוֹפוֹ לַחֲזוֹר וּלְהַדְלִיק פְּתִילָה זוֹ – אֵין כָּאן עוֹד בִּנְיָן בִּמְקוֹם סְתִירָה. וּדְקָתָנֵי: "שֶׁהוּא עוֹשֶׂה פֶּחָם" – כְּלוֹמַר: מִפְּנֵי שֶׁהֵם עוֹשִׂין פֶּחָם מִתְּחִלָּתָהּ, וְעוֹמֶדֶת לַחֲזוֹר וּלְהַאֲחִיז בָּהּ אוּר, וְאִיכָּא בִּנְיָן בִּמְקוֹם סְתִירָה. וְרַבּוֹתֵינוּ מְפָרְשִׁין: נֵר וְשֶׁמֶן – אִיכָּא לְמֵימַר מִיבָּעֵי לֵיהּ לְמִידֵי אַחֲרִינֵי וְלֹא לְהַדְלִיק. וְלִי נִרְאֶה שֶׁאֵין צְרִיכִין אָנוּ לְדוֹחַק זֶה, דְּמִשּׁוּם דְּאִיכָּא לְמֵימַר לֵית לָן לְמִיפְטְרֵיהּ, שֶׁהֲרֵי הוּא יוֹדֵעַ לָמָּה חָס עֲלֵיהֶן, וּסְתָם נֵר אֵינוֹ אֶלָּא לְהַדְלִיק בּוֹ פְּתִילָה: וּמִשְׁכָּן סוֹתֵר עַל מְנָת לִבְנוֹת שֶׁלֹּא בִּמְקוֹמוֹ הוּא. שֶׁהָיוּ סוֹתְרִין אוֹתוֹ בַּחֲנִיָּיה זוֹ, וְנוֹסְעִים לְמָקוֹם אַחֵר וְחוֹנִים, וְחוֹזְרִים וּמְקִימִין אוֹתוֹ: כְּר' שִׁמְעוֹן. דְּפָטַר לֵיהּ מִשּׁוּם דְּאֵין צְרִיכִין לְגוּפָהּ. וְכָחָס עַל הַפְּתִילָה הַיְינוּ טַעְמָא דְּמִחַיֵּיב – כְּגוֹן שֶׁצָּרִיךְ לְהַבְהֲבָהּ, שֶׁלֹּא הוּבְהֲבָה מִבְּעוֹד יוֹם. דְּכִיבּוּי זֶה צָרִיךְ לְגוּפוֹ, שֶׁיְּהֵא הַלַּהַב נוֹחַ לֶאֱחוֹז בָּהּ כְּשֶׁיָּבֹא לְהַדְלִיקָהּ: שֶׁהוּא עוֹשֶׂה פֶּחָם. שֶׁהוּא מִתְכַּוֵּין מַמָּשׁ לַעֲשׂוֹתָהּ כְּמִין פֶּחָם עַכְשָׁיו. אַלְמָא: בְּכִבּוּי הַצָּרִיךְ לְגוּפוֹ מַיְירֵי, וְלֹא קָתָנֵי שֶׁנַּעֲשֵׂית פֶּחָם מִתְּחִלָּתוֹ שֶׁהוּבְהֲבָה, דִּנְהִי לְמֵימַר טַעְמָא מִשּׁוּם דְּבַת בִּנְיָן הִיא דְּאִיכָּא בִּנְיָן בִּמְקוֹם סְתִירָה, מַה שֶּׁאֵין כֵּן בַּשֶּׁמֶן וְנֵר דְּלָא שַׁיָּיךְ בְּהוּ בִּנְיָן וּסְתִירָה: **מתני'** בִּשְׁעַת לֵידָתָן. בַּגְּמָרָא מְפָרֵשׁ מַאי שְׁנָא שְׁעַת לֵידָתָן: **גמ'** הָכִי גָּרְסִינַן. בְּנִדָּה מַאי טַעְמָא: בְּחַדְרֵי בִטְנָהּ. מְקוֹר דָּמָהּ: קִלְקְלָה. מָרְדָה: רְבִיעִית דָּם. חַיֵּי אָדָם תְּלוּיִין בָּהּ: רֵאשִׁית

תוספות

וסותר על מנת לבנות במקומו. ור"ש פוטר אפי' בסותר על מנת לבנות במקומו אלא במקום שע"י סתירה יש תיקון (בבנין אחרון) יותר משלא היה בנין ראשון מעולם שם. כגון בפתילה שצריך להבהבה, דמחייב ר' שמעון כדאמר בסמוך. ואם תאמר: לר' שמעון, הא דתנן בפרק "כלל גדול": (לקמן דף עג.) "המכבה והסותר", בשלמא מכבה – משכחת לה דמתקן כדפירש, כגון לעשות פחמין. אלא סותר – לא משכחת שיהא מתקן בסתירה זו יותר משלא היה בנוי שם מעולם, ואמאי חייב לר' שמעון? וי"ל: דכולהו ממשכן ילפינן לה, ולא היה כיבוי במשכן כ"א לעשות פחמין – ולהכי לא מחייב ר"ש אלא בכה"ג. אבל סותר אשכחן במשכן שאין מתקן בסתירה זו יותר משלא היה בנוי שם מעולם, ולהכי מחייב שם אפי' ר"ש. וא"ת: כיון דסותר ומכבה בעינן ע"מ לבנות ולהבעיר, א"כ בפרק "כלל גדול" (שם) דתנן: "המכבה והסותר" – הוי ליה למיתני "המכבה ע"מ להבעיר" ו"הסותר ע"מ לבנות" כי היכי דקתני "המוחק ע"מ לכתוב שתי אותיות, והקורע ע"מ לתפור שתי תפירות"! וי"ל: דהתם נמי לא קתני ליה אלא משום דבעי למיתני שיעורא דשתי אותיות ושתי תפירות, אבל במכבה וסותר על מנת להבעיר ולבנות כל שהוא – מיחייב, לא איצטריך למיתנייה:

רבינו חננאל

יראת שמים דומה לגזבר שמסרו לו מפתחות הפנימיות והחיצוניות לא מסרו לו בהי עייל מכריז ר' יוחנן חבל על דלית [ליה] דירתא ותרעא לדירתה עביד. אמר להו [רבא] לרבנן במטו מינייכו רבנן לא תירתון תרתי גיהנם*): **א"ר** יוחנן אין להקב"ה אלא יראת שמים בלבד שנא' ויאמר לאדם הן יראת ה' היא חכמה וסור מרע בינה: **פיס' כחס** על הנר כחס על השמן וכו'. אוקימנא למתני' כולה המכבה את הנר כחס על הנר כחס על השמן כחס על הפתילה כו' לר' יהודה דסבר דבר שאין מתכוין אסור וחלק עליו רבי יוסי בכולהו והודה לו בפתילה. ואוקמה עולא דרבי יוסי נמי כרבי יהודה סבירא ליה דדבר שאין מתכוין אסור. מיהו אמר לך לא מחייב אלא היכא דקא מתעבדא מלאכה וסותר ע"מ לבנות במקומו כגון פתילה שכבה ע"מ להדליק במקום שכבה בראש הפתילה הוי סותר ונגמרה מלאכה לפיכך חייב. אבל מכבה הפתילה ליטול השמן או הנר נמצא סותר בפתילה ובונה בנר או בשמן כי האי גוונא לא הוי סותר ואין שם מלאכה כלל לפיכך פטור. ואקשינן מכדי מלאכות דשבת ילפינן להו [ממשכן] ובמשכן סותר מזה המקום שנוסעין ממנו לבנות במקום אחר הוא והנה סותר שלא לבנות במקומו הוי סותר ושנינן כיון דכתיב על פי ה' יחנו ועל פי ה' יסעו. ויתכן שיאמר להם שובו חנו במקום שסרתם כסותר ע"מ לבנות [במקומו] דמי רבי יוחנן אמר לעולם רבי יוסי כרבי שמעון סבירא ליה ומתני' בפתילה שצריך להבהבה עסקי'. דבהא אפילו רבי שמעון מודה דקא מתקן מנא דחירובי משויא ליה מנא ודייקא נמי מתני' הכי דקתני מפני שהוא עושה פחם כלומר מתכוין לעשותה פחם הוא ולא קתני שנעשה פחם בלא כוונתו ש"מ. נתברר כי ההבהוב הוא חירוך (דניאל ג) ושער ראשיהון לא התחרך והחירוך הוא עשויה כמין פחם: **מתני'** על שלש עבירות נשים וכו'. אסיקנא כי הא דדריש ההוא גלילאה

*) לפנינו ליתא כאן מימרא דרבא אלא ביומא ד' עב ע"ב:

נ"ל אנא

יומא עב:

[בגיטין סב. פרש"י בן תורה]

[בילקוט פרשת עקב הג"ל איתא ר' אלעזר בר' שמעון]

[במגילה כז. פרש"י ד"ה תסתיים יש סימון]

[לעיל יב. לקמן עג: וש"נ]

[לקמן מט:]

[סוטה ה. ע"ש רש"י ותוספות ד"ה אדם]

הגהות הב"ח

(א) רש"י ד"ה בהי וכו' הפנימיים הס"ד ואח"כ מ"ה אמינא לך אנא כלומר: (ב) ד"ה זה דרכם וכו' מהשיב אל כליותיהם וכו' ירצו סלה ויספרו:

גליון הש"ס גמרא אין לו להקב"ה בעולמו. עיין ברכות דף לג ע"ב: רש"י ד"ה מפני שהוא עושה פחם. שהוא מתכוין ממש. וק"ל הא בפשוטו י"ל דחוץ מן הפתילה היינו דחוץ כחס על הפתילה חייב דמיירי בלא הובהבה מבעו"י וכיון דרצונו לחזור ולהדליק הפתילה וניחא ליה בפחם מיקרי צריכה לגופה דאפילו באינו מתכוין אלא דהוי פ"ר היכא דניחא ליה מקרי צריכה לגופה כדלקמן קג ע"א בתולש עולשין בארעא דידיה. ומכוונת יותר דבפתילה שצריך להבהבה עסקינן היינו דהוא אינו מתכוין לכך אלא דממילא ניחא ליה:

ראשית קראתי אתכם. "ראשית תבואתה" (ירמיה ב): עסקי ראשית. "ראשית עריסותיכם" (במדבר טו): הריני נוטל נשמתכם. ואחד רביעית דמכם, ויכבה נרכם, ויבטל שם ראשיתכם. ונשים נלקו על כך, כדאמרינן בבראשית רבה: היא איבדה חלתו של עולם – שעל ידה נטרד אדה"ר שנתרם כחלה, וכבתה נרו של עולם, ושפכה דמו. ועוד, שצרכי הבית תלוין בה: נפל תורא. לארץ, שהוא עומד לשחיטה, הכל אומרים: חדדו לסכינא עד שלא יקום, ויהא טורח להשליכו. כך, הואיל ואיתרע מזלה – מזומנת פורענותה לבא: תפיש תירוס אמתא. תרבה פשעים השפחה, וכולן תלקה בחבטה אחת: תפיש. תרבה: תירוס. פשע והתרסה: מחטרא. בטלו"ר בלע"ז. כלומר: אשה עומדת ליסורי לידה על עונשה של חוה, ומצרפין לה עונשין הרבה לאותו מלקות: שבקיה לרוויא. לשיכור, אינך צריך להפילו, שהוא יפול מאליו. כך האשה עומדת לילד משנתעברה, והיא צריכה לבקש להקב"ה לפתוח רחמה, והוא נמנע – והיא מתה מאליה. כל הני – משל הדיוט נינהו: רעיא חגרא ועיזי רהיטין. קשים לרוץ, ואינו יכול להגיען ולהלקותן על סרחונן: אבב חוטרא מילי. כשהיא באה לפני גדרות צאן – שם הוא מדבר עמה להלקותה על פשעה. ואבי דרי – לבית הדיר של צאן באין לחשבון. "גדרות צאן" מתרגמינן "חוטרין דען" (במדבר לב), כלומר: האשה כשהיא בבריאות, פעמים שזכויותיה תולין, ואין כח במקטרג להזכיר עונה. אבל משהגיעה לפתח הסכנה וצריכה לנסים – שם מזכירין עונותיה ומעשיה, אם ראויה היא לנס אם לאו: אבב חנואתא נפישי אחי ומרחמי. לפתח החנות, שמחלקים בו מזונות ויש שם עושר, הרבה אחים והרבה אוהבים יש, הכל נעשים אוהבים: מרחמי. אוהבים: אבב בזיוני. במקום שיש הפסד ועוני – לא אחי ולא מרחמי. כך, בשעת הסכנה הורע מזלה וחשיבותה, וחדלו פרקליטין שלה: וגברי היאך מיבדקי. מעשים שלהם, להזכיר עונם וזכותם: כעין גשר. כל מקום סכנה, כגון קיר נטוי, ויוצא לדרך: דילמא מיפקיד. נכרי דינא על חטאיו, ומתפיסנא בהדיה: מברא. ספינה שעוברין בה את הנהר: בדיק. הספינה, שלא יהא בה נקב: מנכין. פוחתין: קטנתי מכל החסדים. הוקטנו ונתמעטו זכיותי בשביל "החסדים אשר עשית" וגו': יומא דשותא. שמנשבת בו הרוח דרומית חזקה, המפלת חומות ועוקרת אילנות: לביני דקלי. שלא יפיל הרוח דקל עליו: ממנו להביא ראיה. מאחר שהוא נופל – צריך למצוא ממנו וממעשיו ראיה לזכות: מששת ימי בראשית. דכתיב: "קורא הדורות מראש" (ישעיה מא) – שנגלו לפניו הדורות, ומעשיהם, *וקנס פורענותם: שהרי. כשניתנה תורה עדיין לא נפל זה, והכתוב קראו "נופל": על ידי חייב. בע"ה זה, שלא קיים מצות מעקה: אומרים. העומדין שם: שכן דרך כל המומתים מתודין. כדתנן בסנהדרין: "שכל המתודה יש לו חלק" כו', שכן מצינו בעכן שאמר לו יהושע כו'. בפ' "נגמר הדין" (סנהדרין דף מג:): לשוק. מצויים שם מריבות ובעלי דינים נכרים וישראלים: דומה כמו שנמסר לסרדיוט. להוליכו לפני השופט: חש בראשו. חששא בעלמא, מיחוש קל: נתנוהו בקולר. הוי טפי משנמסר לסרדיוט, וגרוע מעולה לגרדום, שאין דנין שם אלא להריגה, ועל סרחון חמור, וצריך פרקליטין גדולים: עלה למטה. שחלה הרבה, שצריך לעלות וליפול למשכב: ואלו הן פרקליטין. (א) שעושה למטה(ב) רצוי לב"ד של מעלה – תשובה ומעשים טובים: באותו מלאך. שמליץ עליו זכות, והוא אחד מני אלף. ואפילו הוא עצמו מעיד עליו חובה – ניצול בפחת של זכות, שנאמר: "מליץ אחד מני אלף" במליצתו של מלאך אין אלא אחת מאלף להגיד ישרו. ומשמע נמי שהמלאך המליץ הוי אחד מני אלף, דהא "מלאך" כתיב, מכלל דהשאר מגידים עליו חובה. אלא מדלא כתיב "אם יש עליו מליץ מלאך אחד מני אלף" איכא למידרשיה אמלאך ואמליצה: יולדות. בשעת לידתן: שלש עבירות. הנך דמתניתין: ילדות. בחורות, ואפילו שלא בשעת לידה: רבי אחא אומר. הילדות מתות על עון שמכבסות: ארנא. כך היו קורין מגדלות שלהם – פריט"י, ובלשונינו משטי"ר: בית עם. לשון בזוי, שמתקבצין בו הכל: ולארון הקודש ארנא. אין קורין אותו ארון הקדש: בדקי(ג). עונות שבודקין אותן בהן בשעת סכנה, כרבנן דאמרי "יולדות": דבקי. שמדבקין ומקרבין מיתה לפני זמנה, כר' אלעזר דתני "ילדות":

ונמסרו

ראשית קראתי אתכם – על עסקי ראשית הזהרתי אתכם, נשמה שנתתי בכם קרויה נר – *על עסקי נר הזהרתי אתכם. אם אתם מקיימים אותם – מוטב, ואם לאו – הריני נוטל נשמתכם. ומ"ש בשעת לידתן? אמר *רבא: נפל תורא – חדד לסכינא. אביי אמר: תפיש תירוס אמתא – בחד מחטרא ליהוי. רב חסדא אמר: שבקיה לרוויא, דמנפשיה נפיל. מר עוקבא אמר: רעיא חגרא ועיזי רהיטן, אבב חוטרא – מילי, ואבי דרי – חושבנא. רב פפא אמר: אבב חנואתא נפישי אחי ומרחמי, אבב בזיוני – לא אחי ולא מרחמי. וגברי היכא מיבדקי? אמר ריש לקיש: בשעה שעוברים על הגשר. גשר ותו לא?! אימא: כעין גשר. רב לא עבר במברא דיתיב ביה גוי, אמר: דילמא מיפקיד ליה דינא עליה, ומתפיסנא בהדיה. שמואל לא עבר אלא במברא דאית ביה גוי, אמר: שטנא בתרי אומי לא שליט. ר' ינאי בדיק ועבר. ר' ינאי לטעמיה, *דאמר: [א]לעולם אל יעמוד אדם במקום סכנה לומר שעושין לו נס – שמא אין עושין לו נס. ואם עושין לו נס – מנכין לו מזכיותיו. אמר רבי חנין: מאי קראה – "קטנתי מכל החסדים ומכל האמת". רבי זירא ביומא דשותא לא נפיק לביני דיקלא. אמר ר' יצחק בריה דרב יהודה: לעולם יבקש אדם רחמים שלא יחלה, שאם יחלה – אומרים לו: הבא זכות והפטר. אמר מר עוקבא: מאי קראה – "כי יפול הנופל ממנו" ממנו להביא ראיה. תנא דבי רבי ישמעאל: "כי יפול הנופל ממנו" (ממנו) ראוי זה ליפול מששת ימי בראשית, שהרי לא נפל, והכתוב קראו נופל. אלא *שמגלגלין זכות על ידי זכאי וחובה על ידי חייב.§ ת"ר: [ב]מי שחלה ונטה למות, אומרים לו: התודה, שכן כל המומתין מתודין. אדם יוצא לשוק - יהי דומה בעיניו כמי שנמסר לסרדיוט, חש בראשו - יהי דומה בעיניו כמי שנתנוהו בקולר, עלה למטה ונפל - יהי דומה בעיניו כמו שהעלוהו לגרדום לידון; שכל העולה לגרדום לידון אם יש לו פרקליטין גדולים - ניצול, ואם לאו - אינו ניצול. ואלו הן פרקליטין של אדם - תשובה ומעשים טובים. ואפי' תשע מאות ותשעים ותשעה מלמדים עליו חובה, ואחד מלמד עליו זכות – ניצול, שנאמר: "אם יש עליו מלאך מליץ אחד מני אלף להגיד לאדם ישרו ויחננו ויאמר פדעהו מרדת שחת וגו'".§ ר' אליעזר בנו של ר' יוסי הגלילי אומר: אפילו תשע מאות ותשעים ותשעה באותו מלאך לחובה ואחד לזכות – ניצול, שנאמר: "מליץ אחד מני אלף".§ תנו רבנן: על שלש עבירות נשים מתות יולדות, רבי אלעזר אומר: נשים מתות ילדות. ר' אחא אומר: בעון שמכבסות צואת בניהם בשבת, וי"א: על שקורין לארון הקודש "ארנא".§ תניא, ר' ישמעאל בן אלעזר אומר: בעון שני דברים עמי הארצות מתים – על שקורין לארון הקודש "ארנא", ועל שקורין לבית הכנסת "בית עם". תניא, ר' יוסי אומר: *שלשה בדקי מיתה נבראו באשה, ואמרי לה: שלשה דבקי מיתה, נדה וחלה והדלקת הנר. חדא כר' אלעזר, וחדא כרבנן. *תניא, רשב"ג אומר: הלכות הקדש תרומות ומעשרות הן הן גופי תורה, ונמסרו

על שקורין לארון הקדש ארנא. לא ארון שעשה בצלאל קאמר, דמסתמא לא היו מזכירים ארון שהיה לפני כמה שנים שנגנז בבית הראשון, אלא לארון שבבית הכנסת. אע"ג דבכל דוכתי קרי ליה "תיבה" כדתנן: העובר לפני התיבה, היורד לפני התיבה. (ברכות פ"ה דף לד.). אור"י: אשכחן נמי דקרי ליה ארון, כדאמר: תשעה וארון מצטרפין (שם פ"ז דף מז:):

מקרא

קיח א מיי' פי"ב מהל' רוצח ושמירת נפש הל' ו סמג עשין עט ש"ע י"ד סי' קיו סעיף ה בהג"ה:

קיט ב מיי' פ"א מהל' תשובה הל' א סמג עשין יג טוש"ע קטז סי' שלח סעיף א:

רבינו חננאל

גלילאה רביעית דם נתתי בכם על עסקי דם הזהרתי אתכם ראשית קראתי אתכם על עסקי ראשית הזהרתי [אתכם] כגון החלה והתרומה נשמה שקרויה נר נתתי בכם על עסקי נר הזהרתי אתכם אם אתם מקיימין אותן מוטב ואם לאו הריני נוטל נשמתכם. ולמה בשעת לידה אמר רבה נפל תורא חדד סכינא תיפוש תירום אמתא חד מחבטא ניהוי פי' תרבה להתרומם השפחה על אדונתה אחת הכאה תהיה עליה. כלומר פעמים רבות מכעסת אדונתה ומקבעת אדונתה את הכל בלבה והיא משלמת לה בהכאה אחת הכל. וכן רעיא מחגרא ועיזא רהיטתא אבב חוטרא ואבי [דרי] חושבנא. *) פי' רועה פסח שאין יכול לרוץ. ועז בורחת ורצה בשדות כשמגיע בשער גדרות הצאן כדמתרגמינן חוטרין דען ובבית הדיר (בו) כדתנן הכונס צאן לדיר שם מעלה חשבון הבריחות שברחה ושם מכה אותה. בחנות של יין הכל (אי הכין) [אוהביו] באין שם ושואלין בשלום בעל החנות כדי שישתו עמו אבל אם רואין שנתפס אדם בבית המכס או בבית המושל להיענש כל אוהביו בורחין אין אחד מהן פונה אליו: **לא** יעמוד אדם במקום סכנה ויאמר עושין לי נס [שמא] אין עושין לו נס. ואם עושין לו מנכין לו מזכיותיו שנא' קטנתי מכל החסדים וגו': **לעולם** יבקש אדם רחמים שלא יחלה שאם יחלה אומרים לו הבא זכיות והפטר: **ת"ר** חלה ונטה למות אומרים לו התודה שכן דרך כל המומתים מתודים אדם יוצא לשוק יהיה דומה כמי [שנמסר] לסרדיוט חש בראשו דומה כמי שנתנוהו בקולר עלה למטה דומה כמי שהעלוהו לגרדום לידון אם יש לו פרקליטין המלמדין עליו זכות נצול אם לאו לא נצול תשובה ומעשים טובים הן פרקליטין של אדם. אפי' תתקצ"ט מלמדין עליו חובה ואחד מלמד עליו זכות נצול שנאמר אם יש עליו מלאך מליץ אחד מני אלף להגיד לאדם ישרו ויחננו ויאמר פדעהו מרדת שחת מצאתי כופר: **שלשה** בדקי מיתה. כרבנן דאמרי מתות יולדות [ואמרי לה ג' דבקי מיתה כר"א דאמר מתות ילדות] כלומר דבקה בהו מיתה שלא בעתה:

פי'

*) ע' ערוך ערך כב.

תורה אור: בראשית לב; דברים כב; איוב לג

[כדכתיב נר ה' נשמת אדם תנחומא ריש פ' נח]

[נ"ל רבה]

תענית כ:

[סנהדרין ח. ב"ב קיט: תוספתא יומא פ"ד]

תוספתא פ"ב ברכות לח:

תוספתא פ"ב

נ"א וזמן

הגהות הב"ח

(א) רש"י ד"ה ואלו הן פרקליטין (שעושה למטה) תא"מ ונ"ב ס"א אין זה: (ב) בא"ד שבכן רצוי לב"ד: (ג) ד"ה בדקי מיתה עונות:

עין משפט נר מצוה

קב א מיי' פ"ג מהל' ציצית הל' יב סמג עשין כו טור א"ח סימן כד:

ונמסרו לעמי הארץ. תניא, רבי נתן אומר: בעון נדרים מתה אשה של אדם, שנאמר: °"אם אין לך לשלם למה יקח משכבך מתחתיך". רבי אומר: *בעון נדרים בנים מתים כשהן קטנים, שנאמר: °"אל תתן את פיך לחטיא את בשרך ואל תאמר לפני המלאך כי שגגה היא למה יקצוף האלהים על קולך וחבל את מעשה ידיך". איזה הן מעשה ידיו של אדם – הוי אומר: בניו ובנותיו של אדם. ת"ר, בעון נדרים בנים מתים – דברי ר"א בר"ש, ר' יהודה הנשיא אומר: בעון ביטול תורה. בשלמא למאן דאמר בעון נדרים – כדאמרן, אלא למ"ד בעון ביטול תורה – מאי קראה? דכתיב: °"לשוא הכיתי את בניכם מוסר לא לקחו". ר"נ בר יצחק אמר: למ"ד בעון נדרים נמי מהכא – "לשוא הכיתי את בניכם" – על עסקי שוא. מכדי, *ר' יהודה הנשיא היינו רבי, ורבי בעון נדרים קאמר! בתר דשמעה מר"א בר' שמעון. פליגי בה ר' חייא בר אבא ור' יוסי, חד אמר: בעון מזוזה, וחד אמר: בעון ביטול תורה. למ"ד "בעון מזוזה" – מקרא נדרש לפניו ולא לפני פניו. ולמ"ד "בעון ביטול תורה" – *מקרא נדרש לפניו ולפני פניו.§ פליגי בה ר"מ ור' יהודה; חד אמר: בעון מזוזה, וחד אמר: בעון ציצית. בשלמא למ"ד בעון מזוזה – דכתיב: °"וכתבתם על מזוזות ביתך" וכתיב בתריה: "למען ירבו ימיכם וימי בניכם". אלא למ"ד בעון ציצית, מ"ט? א"ר כהנא ואיתימא שילא מרי, דכתיב: °"גם בכנפיך נמצאו דם נפשות אביונים נקיים". ר"נ בר יצחק אמר: למ"ד בעון מזוזה נמי מהכא, דכתיב: °"לא במחתרת מצאתים" – שעשו פתחים כמחתרת. אמר ר"ל: *כל הזהיר בציצית זוכה ומשמשין לו ב' אלפים וח' מאות עבדים, שנא': °"כה אמר ה' [צבאות] בימים ההמה אשר יחזיקו עשרה אנשים מכל לשונות הגוים [והחזיקו] בכנף איש יהודי לאמר נלכה עמכם וגו'". סימן: שנא חלה תרומה נגזלת דינא שבועה שיפוכתא גילויא ונבלותא.§ תניא, ר' נחמיה אומר: בעון שנאת חנם – מריבה רבה בתוך ביתו של אדם, ואשתו מפלת נפלים, ובניו ובנותיו של אדם מתים כשהן קטנים.§ ר' אלעזר בר' יהודה אומר: בעון חלה אין ברכה במכונס, ומארה משתלחת בשערים, וזורעין זרעים ואחרים אוכלין, שנאמר: °"אף אני אעשה זאת לכם והפקדתי עליכם בהלה את השחפת ואת הקדחת מכלות עינים ומדיבות נפש וזרעתם לריק זרעכם ואכלהו אויביכם", אל תקרי "בהלה" אלא "בחלה". ואם נותנין – מתברכין, שנאמר: °"[ו]ראשית עריסותיכם תתנו לכהן להניח ברכה אל ביתך".§ בעון ביטול תרומות ומעשרות שמים נעצרין מלהוריד טל ומטר, והיוקר הוה, והשכר אבד, ובני אדם רצין אחר פרנסתן ואין מגיעין, שנאמר: °"ציה גם חום יגזלו מימי שלג שאול חטאו". מאי משמע? *תנא דבי רבי ישמעאל: בשביל דברים שצויתי אתכם בימות החמה ולא עשיתם – יגזלו מכם מימי שלג בימות הגשמים. ואם נותנין – מתברכין, שנאמר: °"הביאו את כל המעשר אל בית האוצר ויהי טרף בביתי ובחנוני נא בזאת אמר ה' צבאות אם לא אפתח לכם את ארובות השמים והריקותי לכם ברכה עד בלי די", *מאי "עד בלי די"? אמר רמי בר (*רב) א"ר: עד שיבלו שפתותיכם מלומר די.§ בעון גזל הגובאי עולה, והרעב הווה, ובני אדם אוכלים בשר בניהן ובנותיהן, שנאמר: °"שמעו הדבר הזה פרות הבשן אשר בהר שומרון העושקות דלים הרוצצות אביונים" אמר רבא: כגון* הני נשי דמחוזא, דאכלן

משלי כב | קהלת ה | ירמיהו ב | דברים יא | ירמיהו ב | שם | זכריה ח | ויקרא כו | יחזקאל מד | איוב כד | מלאכי ג | עמוס ד

רש"י

ונמסרו לעמי הארץ. שלא מסרו לב"ד למצות שומרין לדבר, והאמינה תורה את כל אדם עליהן. והן הן גופי תורה, שחברים אוכלין פתן וסומכין שניטל ממנו חלה ותרומה ומעשרות. והקדש נמי מסור לכל אדם להקדיש, וחל הקדש ע"פ כל אדם, והן גופי תורה, שהיינו צריכים לחוש במטלטלין שמא הקדישו וחזר בו. ואע"ג דתקון רבנן דמאי – מ"מ תורה האמינתו. ורבותי מפרשים: הלכות הקדש – כגון יין לנסכים, כדמפרש ב"חומר בקדש" (חגיגה דף כו:) שעמי הארץ נאמנים עליו. וקשיא לי: אי מדרבנן קאמר, דחשיב מאי דהימנוהו רבנן – לא הוה ליה למיתני תרומות ומעשרות, דרבנן לא הימנוהו: אם אין לך לשלם. עולות והקדשות שתדור: משכבך. אשתך: אל תתן את פיך(א). בנדר, לחטיא את בשרך – לחייב את בניך: לפני המלאך. גזבר של הקדש: כי שגגה. בשוגג קבלתי לנדור, ולא אשלם: על קולך. בשביל קול נדריך: לשוא הכיתי. בתמיה: וכי בחנם הכיתים? אינו אלא בשביל המוסר, דהיינו תורה. לא לקחו – לא למדו, לשון לקח: על עסקי שוא. שמשקרו בנדריהם, דדמי לשבועה: והא "בעון נדרים" אמר בברייתא קמייתא. ומשני: ההיא קמייתא בתר הך איתמר. דמעיקרא אמר "בעון ביטול תורה", ובתר דשמע מר' אלעזר דשמע מר' שמעון אבוה דהוה רביה, דרבי "בעון נדרים" – אמר איהו נמי הכי: מקרא נדרש. "למען ירבו ימיכם וימי בניכם" נדרש לפניו, קאי אקרא דלקמיה דמשתעי במזוזה, ולא לפני פניו "ולמדתם אותם את בניכם": ולפני פניו. ואף בעון בטול תורה קאמר: גם בכנפיך. בשביל כנפיך שבטלת מצותם – נמצאו עליך חובת דם נפשות אביונים נקיים – בנים קטנים שלא חטאו: במחתרת. שאין לה פצימין. הכי אמר קרא: לא במחתרת *פתחיהן מצאתים שלמים במצותי, כי על כל אלה הכיתי. דהאי קרא בתר "לשוא הכיתי את בניכם" כתיב: בכנף איש יהודי. בשכר הכנף יחזיקו בכנף עשרה אנשים מכל לשון, הרי שבע מאות לשבעים לשון, וארבע כנפות יש לו – הרי אלפים ושמונה מאות: שנאת חנם. שלא ראה בו דבר עבירה שיהא מותר לשנאותו – ושונאו: מריבה רבה. מדה כנגד מדה: ובניו קטנים מתים. אהבתו ניטלת ממנו, היינו נמי במדה: במכונס. באוצרות יין ושמן, ומתוך כך באה מארה בשערים – שמוכרים ביוקר: בחלה. בעון חלה: והפקדתי. כמו "לא נפקד ממנו איש" (במדבר לא) – אמעט את מה שעליכם, שכנסתם כבר: השמים נעצרים. ומתוך שאין גשמים – היוקר הוה: והשכר אבד. שכר ריוח: ציה גם חום. ציה כמו 'לווי'. דברים שצויתי אתכם בשעת החום, היינו תרומות ומעשרות: דאכלן

תוספות

מקרא נדרש לפניו ולפני פניו. תימה לר"י: דבפ"ק דקדושין (דף לד. ושם) דאמר: כל מצות עשה כו', ופריך: ונקיש מזוזה לתלמוד תורה. פי': וליפטרי נשים ממזוזה, כי היכי דפטירי מתלמוד תורה! ומשני: לא ס"ד, דכתיב "למען ירבו ימיכם" וגו' אטו גברי בעו חיי, נשי לא בעו חיי? והשתא הא קאי נמי אתלמוד תורה, כדמשמע הכא, אע"פ שאין הנשים חייבות. וי"ל: דבת"ת הוה מחייבינן נמי מהאי טעמא – אי לא מיעט קרא בהדיא, *דכתיב: "ולמדתם אותם את בניכם" ולא את בנותיכם. אבל במזוזה דליכא מיעוט אלא היקשא מהאי טעמא אית לן למימר דאין להקיש: רבי יהודה הנשיא היינו רבי, ורבי בעון נדרים קאמר. והכא לא משני דאף בעון ביטול תורה קאמר, כדמשני לקמן (דף לג:) גבי אף על לשון הרע. דהתם שייך למימר דאף קאמר, דבברייתא שניה שמביא אחריה קאי נמי אתנא קמא דקאמר על לשון הרע, וקאמר איהו אף שאוכלים דברים שאינם מתוקנים. אבל הכא, אי אף קאמר – א"כ ברייתא דלעיל דלא קאי את"ק, הוה ליה למינקט נמי "בעון ביטול תורה":

בעון ציצית כו'. דוקא בימיהם שהיו מלבושיהם כך בארבע כנפות, היו נענשים מי שלא היה להם ציצית. כדמוכח (מנחות מא.) גבי א"ל מלאכא לרב קטינא: כו'. אבל השתא, שאין העולם רגילים במלבושים כאלו אין צריך לקנות. אך טוב לקנות טלית ולברך עליו בכל יום, כדאמר בסוף פרק קמא דסוטה (דף יד.): וכי לאכול מפריה היה רוצה משה? אלא אמר משה: מצוה שאוכל לקיים יתקיים על ידי. [ת"י]:

ה"ג

תורה אור

רבינו חננאל

פי' מקרא נדרש לפניו שנאמר למען ירבו ימיכם וימי בניכם וגו' ולפני זה הפסוק כתיב וכתבתם על מזוזות ביתך וגו'. ונדרש בזכות שתעשה מזוזות ירבו ימי בניכם רבי יהודה הנשיא אמר לפני פניו כתיב ולמדתם אותם את בניכם לדבר והן התורה ומקרא זה למען ירבו ימיכם וימי בניכם נדרש לפניו שהוא המזוזה ולפני פניו בטול תורה: **תניא** רשבג"א הלכות קודש ותרומה ומעשרות הן הן גופי תורה. וכולן נמסרו לעמי הארץ: **ירושלמי** תני רשב"ג הלכות קודש חטאת והבכורות הן הן גופי הלכות ושלשתן נמסרו לעמי הארץ (הלכך הקודש) [וכמו דתנינן בחגיגה כד] אם אמר הפרשתי לתוכה רביעית קודש (שמו) [נאמן] וכו'. ושאר כל השמועה כולה ופשוטה היא:

מסורת הש"ס

[כדאיתא בקדושין כט:]

כתובות עב. ע"ש

[יבמות מח. קדושין סג.]

[ר"ה טז: קדושין טו: ב"מ לה. זבחים כב: מנחות יט: חולין קיח:]

ס"א פלימין

[תענית ז:]

[נ"ל חמא]

מכות כג: תענית ט. [כב: ע"ש]

[פסחים נ:]

הגהות הב"ח

(א) רש"י ד"ה אל תתן את פיך. נ"ב עי' בתוספות ר"פ הדיינין בד"ה ואין בשרך:

גליון הש"ס גמ' שנאמר אל תתן. עי' שבועות דף לט ע"א תוס' ד"ה ואין בשרך: שם בעון ביטול תורה מאי קראה. במסכת כלה איתא רבי יהושע אומר בעון ביטול תורה בנים קטנים מתים דכתיב ותשכח תורת אלהיך אשכח בניך גם אני: שם רבי חייא בר אבא ורבי יוסי. נ"ל ור' אסי או ר' אמי. סדר הדורות בהקדמה אות ד':

רב נסים גאון

פליגי בה ר' אבא (חייה) [חייא] בר אבא ור' יוסי חד אמר בעון מזוזה וחד אמר בעון ביטול תורה. פי' הוא שאמר הקב"ה לישראל (דברים יא) ולמדתם אותם את בניכם לדבר בם וכתיב וכתבתם על מזוזות ביתך ובשעריך ואמר שכרה כנגדה למען ירבו ימיכם וימי בניכם והך דאמר בעון מזוזה הבנים מתים קסבר מקרא נדרש לפניו ולא לפני פניו כלומר כי תתן שכרו של מי שקיים מצות מזוזה שיאריכו חיי בניו וחילופה שאם יעזוב עשייתה ויהיו דברי הכתוב למען ירבו חוזרין על הפסוק שלפניו שהוא וכתבתם על מזוזות ביתך והך דאמר בעון ביטול תורה הבנים מתים קסבר מקרא נדרש לפניו ולפני פניו וכי זו ההבטחה ומתן השכר הכתוב בפסוק שהוא למען ירבו ימיכם שלא הבטיח הקב"ה אלא למי שמלמד את בנו תורה כמו שאמר בפסוק שהוא לפני פניו ולמדתם אותם יהיה עכשיו זה שכתוב למען ירבו ימיכם וימי בניכם חוזר על הפסוק שכתב ולמדתם אותם הלכך כל מי שמלמד תורה לבניו זוכין לאריכות ימים וחילופה כי אם אינו מלמדם תורה לא תהיה להם ארוכות ימים כי הם מתים בעון ביטול תורה: **כל** הזהיר במצות ציצית זוכה ומשמשין אותו שני אלפים ושמונה מאות עבדים שנא' (זכריה ח) כה אמר ה' [צבאות] בימים ההמה אשר יחזיקו עשרה אנשים מכל לשונות הגוים והחזיקו בכנף איש יהודי כבר ידעת כל לשונות הגוים הם שבעים לשון ואם יהיו י' אנשים מכל לשון לע' לשון יהיו הכל שבע מאות הרי אלו יחזיקו בכנף אחד והטלית שעל ישראל יש לה ד' כנפים שנאמר (דברים כב) על ארבע כנפות כסותך הרי אם יהיו שבע מאות מחזיקים בכנף אחד יהיו כל המחזיקים בד' כנפים אלפים ושמונה מאות: אמר

דְּאָכְלָן וְלָא עָבְדָן. וְנִמְלָא שֶׁגּוֹזְלוֹת אֶת בַּעֲלֵיהֶן. וְעוֹד, מִתּוֹךְ שֶׁמְּלוּמָּדוֹת בְּמַאֲכָל וּבְמִשְׁתֶּה גּוֹרְמוֹת לַבְּעָלִים לִגְזוֹל: וּכְתִיב. בְּהַהִיא פָּרָשָׁה בִּנְבוּאַת עָמוֹס: "הִכֵּיתִי אֶתְכֶם בַּשִּׁדָּפוֹן", וְסֵיפֵיהּ דִּקְרָא: "כַּרְמֵיכֶם[ג] וְזֵיתֵיכֶם יֹאכַל הַגָּזָם". וּכְתִיב בְּיוֹאֵל: "יֶתֶר הַגָּזָם", דְּמַשְׁמַע שֶׁהַגָּזָם אֵינוֹ אֶלָּא תְּחִלַּת מַכָּה, וְאַחֲרֶיךָ בָּאִים אַרְבֶּה וְחָסִיל. אַלְמָא: גּוֹבַאי עוֹלֶה בַּעֲוֹן גָּזֵל. וְכֵיוָן דְּמִינֵי גּוֹבַאי עוֹלִין – רָעָב הֹוֶה, וְכֵיוָן דְּהָרָעָב הֹוֶה – כְּתִיב בִּישַׁעְיָה: "וַיִּגְזוֹר עַל יָמִין וְרָעֵב" וגו', וְסֵיפֵיהּ דִּקְרָא: "אִישׁ בְּשַׂר זְרוֹעוֹ יֹאכֵלוּ": עִינּוּי הַדִּין. שֶׁמְּאַחֲרִין הַדַּיָּינִין לְדוּנוֹ, וְלֹא לְשֵׁם שָׁמַיִם, אֶלָּא לְאַחַר שֶׁהוּבְרַר לָהֶן הַדִּין מַשְׁהִין אוֹתוֹ: עִוּוּת הַדִּין. שֶׁמְּעַוְּותִין אוֹתוֹ מְזִידִין: קִלְקוּל

תורה אור

עמוס ד דְּאָכְלָן וְלָא עָבְדָן. וּכְתִיב: "הִכֵּיתִי אֶתְכֶם בַּשִּׁדָּפוֹן וּבַיֵּרָקוֹן הַרְבּוֹת גַּנּוֹתֵיכֶם
יואל א וְכַרְמֵיכֶם וּתְאֵנֵיכֶם וְזֵיתֵיכֶם יֹאכַל הַגָּזָם". וּכְתִיב: "יֶתֶר הַגָּזָם אָכַל הָאַרְבֶּה וְיֶתֶר
ישעיהו ט הָאַרְבֶּה אָכַל הַיֶּלֶק וְיֶתֶר הַיֶּלֶק אָכַל הֶחָסִיל". וּכְתִי': "וַיִּגְזוֹר עַל יָמִין וְרָעֵב וַיֹּאכַל עַל
שְׂמֹאל וְלֹא שָׂבֵעוּ אִישׁ בְּשַׂר זְרוֹעוֹ יֹאכֵלוּ", אַל תִּקְרֵי 'בְּשַׂר זְרוֹעוֹ' אֶלָּא 'בְּשַׂר זַרְעוֹ'.§
בַּעֲוֹן עִינּוּי הַדִּין וְעִיוּוּת הַדִּין וְקִלְקוּל הַדִּין וּבִיטּוּל תּוֹרָה חֶרֶב וּבִיזָּה רַבָּה, וְדֶבֶר
וּבַצּוֹרֶת בָּא, וּבְנֵי אָדָם אוֹכְלִין וְאֵינָן שְׂבֵעִין, וְאוֹכְלִין לַחְמָם בְּמִשְׁקָל, דִּכְתִיב:
ויקרא כו "וְהֵבֵאתִי עֲלֵיכֶם חֶרֶב נוֹקֶמֶת נְקַם בְּרִית וגו'". וְאֵין בְּרִית אֶלָּא תּוֹרָה, *שֶׁנֶּאֱמַר:
ירמיהו לג "אִם לֹא בְרִיתִי יוֹמָם וָלָיְלָה וגו'". וּכְתִיב: "בְּשִׁבְרִי לָכֶם מַטֵּה לֶחֶם וְאָפוּ עֶשֶׂר נָשִׁים ויקרא כו
וגו'". וּכְתִיב: "יַעַן וּבְיַעַן בְּמִשְׁפָּטַי מָאָסוּ".§ בַּעֲוֹן שְׁבוּעַת שָׁוְא וּשְׁבוּעַת שֶׁקֶר וְחִילּוּל שם
הַשֵּׁם וְחִילּוּל שַׁבָּת – חַיָּה רָעָה רַבָּה, וּבְהֵמָה כָּלָה, וּבְנֵי אָדָם מִתְמַעֲטִין, וְהַדְּרָכִים
מִשְׁתּוֹמְמִין, שֶׁנֶּאֱ': "וְאִם בְּאֵלֶּה לֹא תִוָּסְרוּ לִי" אַל תִּקְרֵי בְּאֵלֶּה אֶלָּא בְּאָלָה, וּכְתִיב: שם
שם יט "וְהִשְׁלַחְתִּי בָכֶם אֶת חַיַּת הַשָּׂדֶה וגו'". וּכְתִיב בִּשְׁבוּעַת שֶׁקֶר: "וְלֹא תִשָּׁבְעוּ בִשְׁמִי
שם כב לַשָּׁקֶר וְחִלַּלְתָּ אֶת שֵׁם אֱלֹהֶיךָ" וּבְחִילּוּל הַשֵּׁם כְּתִיב: "וְלֹא תְחַלְּלוּ אֶת שֵׁם קָדְשִׁי"
שמות לא וּבְחִילּוּל שַׁבָּת כְּתִיב: "מְחַלְלֶיהָ מוֹת יוּמָת", וְיָלֵיף חִילּוּל חִילּוּל מִשְּׁבוּעַת שֶׁקֶר.§
בַּעֲוֹן *שְׁפִיכוּת דָּמִים בֵּית הַמִּקְדָּשׁ חָרֵב, וּשְׁכִינָה מִסְתַּלֶּקֶת מִיִּשְׂרָאֵל, שֶׁנֶּאֱמַר:
במדבר לה "וְלֹא תַחֲנִיפוּ וגו' וְלֹא תְטַמֵּא אֶת הָאָרֶץ אֲשֶׁר אַתֶּם יוֹשְׁבִים בָּהּ אֲשֶׁר אֲנִי שׁוֹכֵן
בְּתוֹכָהּ", הָא אַתֶּם מְטַמְּאִים אוֹתָהּ – אֵינְכֶם יוֹשְׁבִים בָּהּ, וְאֵינִי שׁוֹכֵן בְּתוֹכָהּ.§ בַּעֲוֹן
גִּלּוּי עֲרָיוֹת וַעֲבוֹדָה זָרָה וְהַשְׁמָטַת שְׁמִיטִּין וְיוֹבְלוֹת – גָּלוּת בָּא לָעוֹלָם,
ויקרא יח וּמַגְלִין אוֹתָן, וּבָאִין אֲחֵרִים וְיוֹשְׁבִין בִּמְקוֹמָן, שֶׁנֶּאֱמַר: "כִּי אֶת כָּל הַתּוֹעֵבוֹת הָאֵל
עָשׂוּ אַנְשֵׁי הָאָרֶץ וגו'" וּכְתִיב: "וַתִּטְמָא הָאָרֶץ וָאֶפְקוֹד עֲוֹנָהּ עָלֶיהָ וגו'" וּכְתִיב:
שם "וְלֹא תָקִיא הָאָרֶץ אֶתְכֶם בְּטַמַּאֲכֶם אוֹתָהּ" וּבַעֲבוֹדָה זָרָה כְּתִיב: "וְנָתַתִּי אֶת שם כו
פִּגְרֵיכֶם וגו'" וּכְתִיב: "וַהֲשִׁמּוֹתִי אֶת מִקְדְּשֵׁיכֶם וגו' וְאֶתְכֶם אֱזָרֶה בַגּוֹיִם". בִּשְׁמִיטִּין
שם וּבְיוֹבְלוֹת כְּתִיב: "אָז תִּרְצֶה הָאָרֶץ אֶת שַׁבְּתֹתֶיהָ כֹּל יְמֵי הֳשַׁמָּה וְאַתֶּם בְּאֶרֶץ
שם אוֹיְבֵיכֶם וגו'" וּכְתִיב: "כָּל יְמֵי הָשַּׁמָּה תִּשְׁבּוֹת".§ בַּעֲוֹן נַבְלוּת פֶּה צָרוֹת רַבּוֹת,
וּגְזֵירוֹת קָשׁוֹת מִתְחַדְּשׁוֹת, וּבַחוּרֵי שׂוֹנְאֵי יִשְׂרָאֵל מֵתִים, יְתוֹמִים וְאַלְמָנוֹת צוֹעֲקִין
ישעיהו ט וְאֵינָן נַעֲנִין, שֶׁנֶּאֱ': "עַל כֵּן עַל בַּחוּרָיו לֹא יִשְׂמַח ה' וְאֶת יְתוֹמָיו [וְאֶת] (וְ)אַלְמְנוֹתָיו
לֹא יְרַחֵם כִּי כֻלּוֹ חָנֵף וּמֵרַע וְכָל פֶּה דּוֹבֵר נְבָלָה בְּכָל זֹאת לֹא שָׁב אַפּוֹ וְעוֹד יָדוֹ
נְטוּיָה". מַאי *וְעוֹד יָדוֹ נְטוּיָה? א"ר חָנָן בַּר רָבָא: הַכֹּל יוֹדְעִין כַּלָּה לָמָּה נִכְנְסָה
לַחוּפָּה, אֶלָּא כׇּל הַמְנַבֵּל פִּיו אֲפִי' חוֹתְמִין עָלָיו גְּזַר דִּין שֶׁל שִׁבְעִים שָׁנָה לְטוֹבָה
– הוֹפְכִין עָלָיו לְרָעָה. אָמַר רַבָּה בַּר שֵׁילָא אָמַר רַב חִסְדָּא: כׇּל הַמְנַבֵּל אֶת פִּיו
משלי כב – מַעֲמִיקִין לוֹ גֵּיהִנָּם, שֶׁנֶּאֱמַר: "שׁוּחָה עֲמוּקָּה פִּי זָרוֹת". רַב נַחְמָן בַּר יִצְחָק אָמַר: אַף
שם שׁוֹמֵעַ וְשׁוֹתֵק, שֶׁנֶּאֱמַר: "זְעוּם ה' יִפּוֹל שָׁם". אָמַר רַב אוֹשַׁעְיָא: כׇּל הַמְמָרֵק עַצְמוֹ
שם כ לַעֲבֵירָה – חַבּוּרוֹת וּפְצָעִין יוֹצְאִין בּוֹ, שֶׁנֶּאֱמַר: "חַבּוּרוֹת פֶּצַע תַּמְרוּק בְּרָע" וְלֹא
שם עוֹד אֶלָּא שֶׁנִּדּוֹן בְּהִדְרוֹקָן,[א] שֶׁנֶּאֱמַר: "וּמַכּוֹת חַדְרֵי בָטֶן". אָמַר רַב נַחְמָן בַּר יִצְחָק:
*סִימָן לַעֲבֵירָה הִדְרוֹקָן. ת"ר, ג' מִינֵי הִדְרוֹקָן הֵן: שֶׁל עֲבֵירָה – עָבֶה, וְשֶׁל רָעָב – תָּפוּחַ,
וְשֶׁל כְּשָׁפִים – דַּק. שְׁמוּאֵל הַקָּטָן חָשׁ בֵּיהּ אָמַר: רבש"ע, מִי מֵפִים? אִיתַּסֵי. אַבַּיֵי חָשׁ
בֵּיהּ, אָמַר רָבָא: יָדַעְנָא בֵּיהּ *בְּנַחְמָנִי דְּמַכַּפֵּין נַפְשֵׁיהּ. רָבָא חָשׁ בֵּיהּ. וְהָא
רָבָא הוּא דַּאֲמַר: נְפִישֵׁי קְטִילֵי קֵדָר מִנְּפִיחֵי כָפָן! שָׁאנֵי רָבָא, דְּאַנְסִי לֵיהּ רַבָּנַן
בְּעִידָּנֵיהּ בְּעַל כּוֹרְחֵיהּ. ת"ר, ד' סִימָנִין הֵן: סִימָן לַעֲבֵירָה – הִדְרוֹקָן, סִימָן לְשִׂנְאַת
חִנָּם – יֵרָקוֹן, סִימָן *לְגַסּוּת הָרוּחַ – עֲנִיּוּת, סִימָן לְלה"ר – אַסְכָּרָה. ת"ר: אַסְכָּרָה בָּאָה לָעוֹלָם
עַל

[עי' רש"י גטין לד: ד"ה והלכתא והר"ן נדרים נד: ד"ה איתמר טעם דנקרא נחמני]

הַדִּין. שֶׁלֹּא הָיוּ מִתְכַּוְּונִין בּוֹ לְעַיֵּין כׇּל צׇרְכָּן, וְנִתְקַלְקֵל מֵאֵלָיו: חֶרֶב וּבִיזָּה רַבָּה כו'. דִּכְתִיב: "נְקַם בְּרִית", וְאֵין בְּרִית אֶלָּא תּוֹרָה, דִּכְתִיב: "אִם לֹא בְרִיתִי יוֹמָם וָלָיְלָה" וְהָגִיתָ בּוֹ יוֹמָם וָלַיְלָה. וּכְתִיב: "חֶרֶב", וְעַל יְדֵי חֶרֶב – דְּהַיְינוּ מִשְׁלַחַת גְּיָיסֵי מִלְחָמָה, הַבִּיזָּה בָּאָה. וּכְתִיב: "וְשִׁלַּחְתִּי דֶבֶר" – הֲרֵי דֶּבֶר, וּכְתִיב: "בְּשִׁבְרִי לָכֶם מַטֵּה לֶחֶם" – הֲרֵי בַּצּוֹרֶת. וּכְתִיב בְּסוֹף כׇּל הַקְּלָלוֹת: "יַעַן וּבְיַעַן בְּמִשְׁפָּטַי מָאָסוּ" – הֲרֵי עִינּוּי וְעִיוּוּת וְקִלְקוּל בִּכְלָל: שְׁבוּעוֹת שָׁוְא. כׇּל הַמְשַׁנֶּה אֶת הַיָּדוּעַ, כְּגוֹן: עַל הָאִישׁ שֶׁהוּא אִשָּׁה. שְׁבוּעַת שֶׁקֶר – שֶׁאֵין בַּדָּאוּתוֹ נִיכֶּרֶת, וּמַאֲמִין שֶׁקֶר לַבְּרִיּוֹת: וְהַדְּרָכִים מִשְׁתּוֹמְמִין. מֵאֵין עוֹבֵר: אֶלָּא בְּאָלָה. וְיֵשׁ בְּמַשְׁמַע בֵּין שָׁוְא בֵּין שֶׁקֶר. וּכְתִיב בִּשְׁבוּעַת שֶׁקֶר: "וְחִלַּלְתָּ", וּבְשַׁבָּת וּבְחִילּוּל הַשֵּׁם כְּתִיב חִילּוּל, וְגָמְרִינַן מִשְּׁבוּעָה: חִילּוּל הַשֵּׁם. אָדָם גָּדוֹל שֶׁבְּנֵי אָדָם לְמֵדִים הֵימֶנּוּ וְאֵינוֹ נִזְהָר בְּמַעֲשָׂיו, נִמְלְאוּ הַקְּטַנִּים מְזַלְזְלִין בַּתּוֹרָה עַל יָדוֹ, וְאוֹמְרִים: זֶהוּ מֵבִין שֶׁאֵין מַמָּשׁ בַּתּוֹרָה וּבַמִּצְוֹת, וְנִמְצָא הַשֵּׁם מִתְחַלֵּל, נַעֲשָׂה דְּבָרָיו חוּלִּין: אֵין אֲנִי שׁוֹכֵן. אוֹרְבָּן הַבַּיִת בְּמַשְׁמַע, שֶׁאֵין מִשְׁכָּנִי[ג] בְּתוֹכָם: כִּי אֶת כׇּל הַתּוֹעֵבוֹת. בְּפָרָשַׁת עֲרָיוֹת כְּתִיב: וְנָתַתִּי אֶת פִּגְרֵיכֶם עַל פִּגְרֵי גִּלּוּלֵיכֶם. דְּהַיְינוּ ע"ז. וּכְתִיב בַּתְרֵיהּ: "וְאֶתְכֶם אֱזָרֶה בַגּוֹיִם", וּכְתִיב: "וְשָׁמְמוּ עָלֶיהָ אוֹיְבֵיכֶם הַיּוֹשְׁבִים בָּהּ", הֲרֵי שֶׁהֵם גּוֹלִין, וְאוֹיְבֵיהֶם יוֹשְׁבִין בִּמְקוֹמָן: שַׁבְּתוֹתֶיהָ. שְׁמִיטִּין: וְאַתֶּם בְּאֶרֶץ אוֹיְבֵיכֶם. וּלְעֵיל מִינֵּיהּ כְּתִיב: "וְשָׁמְמוּ עָלֶיהָ אוֹיְבֵיכֶם": לֹא יִשְׂמַח. הֲרֵי צָרוֹת וּגְזֵירוֹת. "וְאֶת יְתוֹמָיו וְאֶת אַלְמְנוֹתָיו לֹא יְרַחֵם" – הֲרֵי צוֹעֲקִין וְאֵינָם נַעֲנִין. בַּעֲוֹן מָה – "כִּי כֻלּוֹ חָנֵף וּמֵרַע וְכָל פֶּה דּוֹבֵר נְבָלָה, וְעוֹד יָדוֹ נְטוּיָה". לָשׁוֹן "וָעֶד" כׇּל שְׁנוֹתָיו שֶׁל אָדָם שֶׁהֵן ע' שָׁנָה, יַד הַדִּין נְטוּיָה עָלָיו לְבַטֵּל זְכִיּוֹתָיו בַּעֲוֹן זֶה: הַכֹּל יוֹדְעִין כו'. וְלֹא הוּצְרַךְ לְאָדָם לְפָרֵשׁ לָמָּה נִכְנְסָה. וְהַמְנַבֵּל פִּיו בְּכָךְ – אֲפִילּוּ כו': שׁוּחָה עֲמוּקָּה. מוּכֶנֶת לְפִי זָרוֹת, לְמִי שֶׁפִּיו זָרָה: זְעוּם ה' יִפּוֹל שָׁם. זַעַם שֶׁל הקב"ה הוּא שׁוֹרֶה שָׁם אֵצֶל פִּי זָרוֹת. הַיּוֹשֵׁב אֶצְלוֹ וְשׁוֹמֵעַ קָרוּי זְעוּמוֹ שֶׁל הקב"ה: הַמְמָרֵק עַצְמוֹ. מְפַנֶּה לִבּוֹ לְכָךְ, מְמָרֵק עַצְמוֹ מִשְּׁאָר עֲסָקִים לְהִתְעַסֵּק בַּעֲבֵירוֹת: תַּמְרוּק בְּרָע. הַמְמָרֵק בְּרָע: הִדְרוֹקָן. חוֹלִי הוּא: שֶׁל עֲבֵירָה עָבֶה. הַבָּאָה בִּשְׁבִיל עֲבֵירָה – עָבֶה, בְּשָׂרוֹ מִתְקַשֶּׁה וְעָב וְנָפוּחַ בְּעוֹבִי: תָּפוּחַ. שיינ"ש. נָפוּחַ עוֹרוֹ עַל בְּשָׂרוֹ וּמַיִם בֵּינְתַיִים, וְנִרְאֶה כִּזְכוּכִית, וְרַךְ מִתּוֹכוֹ: דַּק. בְּשָׂרוֹ דַּק וְכָחוּשׁ: מִי מֵפִים. מִי מֵטִיל גּוֹרָל לְהַבְחִין וּלְהוֹדִיעַ שֶׁאֵינוֹ שֶׁל עֲבֵירָה? עַכְשָׁיו יֹאמְרוּ עָלַי שֶׁעָבַרְתִּי עַל דָּת, וְאֵין הַכֹּל יוֹדְעִין בְּג' סִימָנִים שֶׁאָמַרְנוּ, וּפְעָמִים שֶׁמִּשְׁתַּנִּין: יָדַעְנָא בֵּיהּ. שֶׁמִּתְחַמֵּת רָעָב בָּא לוֹ, וְאֵין צָרִיךְ לְחָשְׁדוֹ: וְהָא רָבָא דַּאֲמַר. כְּלוֹמַר: לָמָּה חָשׁ בּוֹ? וְהָא לֹא הִרְעִיב אֶת עַצְמוֹ, מִדְּקָאָמַר "יָדַעְנָא בֵּיהּ בְּנַחְמָנִי" – מִכְּלָל דְּהַמַּרְעִיב עַצְמוֹ רַע בְּעֵינָיו. וְאִי מִשּׁוּם שֶׁהָיָה מַשְׁהֶה נְקָבָיו, וְאָמְרִינַן בִּבְכוֹרוֹת (דף מד:): "לוֹקֶה רַבָּה – הִדְרוֹקָן רַבָּה", שֶׁעַל שֶׁהַיַּית נְקָבִים הוּא בָּא: הָא אִיהוּ אֲמַר נְפִישֵׁי קְטִילֵי קֵדָר. רַבִּים הֲרוּגֵי נְקָבִים מִמּוּתֵי הִדְרוֹקָן שֶׁל רָעָב. קֵדָר – לְשׁוֹן קְדֵרָה, עַל שֵׁם שֶׁשּׁוֹפֵךְ כִּקְדֵרָה: דְּאַנְסִי לֵיהּ רַבָּנַן בְּעִידָּנֵיהּ. הַתַּלְמִידִים הַקְּבוּעִים לָהֶם עֵת לְפָנָיו אוֹנְסִין אוֹתוֹ לְהַשְׁהוֹת נְקָבָיו: סִימָן לְגַסּוּת הָרוּחַ עֲנִיּוּת. בְּפֶרֶק "הָאִישׁ מְקַדֵּשׁ" (קדושין דף מט:) מְפָרֵשׁ: מַאי עֲנִיּוּת – עֲנִיּוּת דְּתוֹרָה: אַסְכָּרָה. חוֹלִי הַמַּתְחִיל בַּמֵּעַיִים וְגוֹמֵר בַּגָּרוֹן, הַנִּקְרָא בונמלא"ן:

עַל

[נדרים לב.]

[יומא פה. ע"ש]

[כתובות ח:]

יבמות ס: ע"ש

[קדושין מט:]

הגהות הב"ח

(א) גמ' שנידון בהדרוקן נ"ב עי' בעירובין דף מא ע"ב: (ב) רש"י ד"ה וכתיב וכו' כרמיכם ותאניכם וזיתיכם: (ג) ד"ה אין אני וכו' משכני (בתוכם) תז"מ ונ"ב ס"א בתוכה:

עין משפט נר מצוה

קכא א מיי׳ פ״ז מהל׳ דעות הלכה ה:

עַל הַמַּעֲשֵׂר, ר׳ אֶלְעָזָר בְּרַ׳ יוֹסֵי אוֹמֵר: עַל לָשׁוֹן הָרַע. אָמַר רָבָא, וְאִיתֵּימָא רִיב״ל: מַאי קְרָאָה – °״וְהַמֶּלֶךְ יִשְׂמַח בֵּאלֹהִים יִתְהַלֵּל כָּל הַנִּשְׁבָּע בּוֹ כִּי יִסָּכֵר פִּי דוֹבְרֵי שָׁקֶר״. אִיבַּעְיָא לְהוּ: רַבִּי אֶלְעָזָר בְּרַבִּי יוֹסֵי ״עַל לָשׁוֹן הָרַע קָאָמַר״ אוֹ דִילְמָא ״אַף עַל לָשׁוֹן הָרַע״ נַמִי קָאָמַר? ת״ש, כְּשֶׁנִּכְנְסוּ רַבּוֹתֵינוּ לַכֶּרֶם בְּיַבְנֶה הָיָה שָׁם רַבִּי יְהוּדָה וְר׳ אֶלְעָזָר בְּר׳ יוֹסֵי וְר״ש. נִשְׁאֲלָה שְׁאֵלָה זוֹ בִּפְנֵיהֶם: מַכָּה זוֹ מִפְּנֵי מָה מַתְחֶלֶת בִּבְנֵי מֵעַיִם וְגוֹמֶרֶת בַּפֶּה? נַעֲנָה רַבִּי יְהוּדָה בְּרַבִּי אִלְעָאִי *רֹאשׁ הַמְדַבְּרִים בְּכָל מָקוֹם וְאָמַר: אע״פ *שֶׁכְּלָיוֹת יוֹעֲצוֹת, וְלֵב מֵבִין, וְלָשׁוֹן מְחַתֵּךְ – פֶּה גּוֹמֵר. נַעֲנָה רַבִּי אֶלְעָזָר בְּרַבִּי יוֹסֵי וְאָמַר: מִפְּנֵי שֶׁאוֹכְלִין בָּהּ דְּבָרִים טְמֵאִין. דְּבָרִים טְמֵאִים סָלְקָא דַּעְתָּךְ? אֶלָּא: שֶׁאוֹכְלִין בָּהּ דְּבָרִים שֶׁאֵינָן מְתוּקָּנִים. נַעֲנָה ר׳ שִׁמְעוֹן וְאָמַר: בַּעֲוֹן בִּיטּוּל תּוֹרָה. אָמְרוּ לוֹ: נָשִׁים יוֹכִיחוּ! שֶׁמְּבַטְּלוֹת אֶת בַּעֲלֵיהֶן. גּוֹיִם יוֹכִיחוּ! שֶׁמְּבַטְּלִין אֶת יִשְׂרָאֵל. תִּינוֹקוֹת יוֹכִיחוּ! שֶׁמְּבַטְּלִין אֶת אֲבִיהֶן. תִּינוֹקוֹת שֶׁל בֵּית רַבָּן יוֹכִיחוּ! הָתָם כִּדְרַבִּי גּוּרְיוֹן, דְּאָמַר רַבִּי גּוּרְיוֹן, וְאִיתֵּימָא רַב יוֹסֵף בְּרַבִּי שְׁמַעְיָה: בִּזְמַן שֶׁהַצַּדִּיקִים בַּדּוֹר – צַדִּיקִים נִתְפָּסִים עַל הַדּוֹר, *אֵין צַדִּיקִים בַּדּוֹר – תִּינוֹקוֹת שֶׁל בֵּית רַבָּן נִתְפָּסִים עַל הַדּוֹר. א״ר יִצְחָק בַּר זְעִירִי וְאָמְרִי לַהּ א״ר שִׁמְעוֹן בֶּן נְזִירָא: מַאי קְרָאָה – °״אִם לֹא תֵדְעִי לָךְ הַיָּפָה בַּנָּשִׁים צְאִי לָךְ בְּעִקְבֵי הַצֹּאן וגו׳״ וְאָמְרִינַן: גְּדָיִים הַמְמוּשְׁכָּנִין עַל הָרוֹעִים. ש״מ: אַף עַל לָשׁוֹן הָרַע נַמִי קָאָמַר, ש״מ. וְאַמַּאי קָרוּ לֵיהּ ״רֹאשׁ הַמְדַבְּרִים בְּכָל מָקוֹם״? דְּיָתְבִי רַבִּי יְהוּדָה וְרַבִּי יוֹסֵי וְרַבִּי שִׁמְעוֹן, וְיָתֵיב יְהוּדָה בֶּן גֵּרִים גַּבַּיְיהוּ. פָּתַח ר׳ יְהוּדָה וְאָמַר: כַּמָּה נָאִים מַעֲשֵׂיהֶן שֶׁל אוּמָּה זוֹ: תִּקְּנוּ שְׁוָוקִים, תִּקְּנוּ גְּשָׁרִים, תִּקְּנוּ מֶרְחֲצָאוֹת. ר׳ יוֹסֵי שָׁתַק. נַעֲנָה רשב״י וְאָמַר: כָּל מַה שֶּׁתִּקְּנוּ – לֹא *תִּקְּנוּ אֶלָּא לְצוֹרֶךְ עַצְמָן, תִּקְּנוּ שְׁוָוקִין – לְהוֹשִׁיב בָּהֶן זוֹנוֹת, מֶרְחֲצָאוֹת – לְעַדֵּן בָּהֶן עַצְמָן, גְּשָׁרִים – לִיטּוֹל מֵהֶן מֶכֶס. הָלַךְ יְהוּדָה בֶּן גֵּרִים ^א^וְסִיפֵּר דִּבְרֵיהֶם, וְנִשְׁמְעוּ לַמַּלְכוּת. אָמְרוּ: יְהוּדָה שֶׁעִילָּה – יִתְעַלֶּה, יוֹסֵי שֶׁשָּׁתַק – יִגְלֶה לְצִיפּוֹרִי, שִׁמְעוֹן שֶׁגִּינָּה – יֵהָרֵג. אֲזַל הוּא וּבְרֵיהּ טְשׁוּ בֵּי מִדְרְשָׁא. כָּל יוֹמָא הֲוָה מַיְיתִי לְהוּ דְּבֵיתְהוּ רִיפְתָּא וְכוּזָא דְּמַיָּא וְכָרְכִי. כִּי תְּקִיף גְּזֵירְתָא, א״ל לִבְרֵיהּ: *נָשִׁים דַּעְתָּן קַלָּה עֲלֵיהֶן דִּילְמָא מְצַעֲרִי לַהּ וּמְגַלְּיָא לָן. אֲזַלוּ טְשׁוּ בִּמְעָרְתָא. אִיתְרְחִישׁ נִיסָּא אִיבְרִי לְהוּ חָרוּבָא וְעֵינָא דְּמַיָּא. וַהֲווּ *מַשְׁלְחִי מָנַיְיהוּ, וַהֲווּ יָתְבִי עַד צַוְּארַיְיהוּ בְּחָלָא, כּוּלֵּי יוֹמָא גָּרְסִי, בְּעִידַּן צַלּוֹיֵי לָבְשׁוּ מִיכְסוּ *וּמְצַלּוּ, וַהֲדַר מַשְׁלְחִי מָנַיְיהוּ כִּי הֵיכִי דְּלָא לִיבְלוּ. אִיתִּבוּ תְּרֵיסַר שְׁנֵי בִּמְעָרְתָא. אֲתָא אֵלִיָּהוּ וְקָם אַפִּיתְחָא דִּמְעָרְתָא, אֲמַר: מַאן לוֹדְעֵיהּ לְבַר יוֹחַי דְּמִית קֵיסָר וּבְטֵיל גְּזֵירְתֵיהּ? נְפַקוּ. חֲזוּ אֱינָשֵׁי דְּקָא כָּרְבִי וְזָרְעִי, אֲמַר: *מַנִּיחִין חַיֵּי עוֹלָם וְעוֹסְקִין בְּחַיֵּי שָׁעָה! כָּל מָקוֹם שֶׁנּוֹתְנִין עֵינֵיהֶן – מִיָּד נִשְׂרָף. יָצְתָה בַּת קוֹל וְאָמְרָה לָהֶם: לְהַחֲרִיב עוֹלָמִי יְצָאתֶם? חִיזְרוּ לִמְעַרַתְכֶם! הֲדוּר אֲזוּל. אִיתִּיבוּ תְּרֵיסַר יַרְחֵי שַׁתָּא. אָמְרִי: *מִשְׁפַּט רְשָׁעִים בְּגֵיהִנָּם – י״ב חֹדֶשׁ. יָצְתָה בַּת קוֹל וְאָמְרָה: צְאוּ מִמְּעָרַתְכֶם! נְפַקוּ, כָּל הֵיכָא דַּהֲוָה מָחֵי ר׳ אֶלְעָזָר – הֲוָה מָסֵי ר״ש. אָמַר לוֹ: בְּנִי, דַּי לָעוֹלָם אֲנִי וְאַתָּה. בַּהֲדֵי פַּנְיָא דְּמַעֲלֵי שַׁבְּתָא חֲזוּ הַהוּא סָבָא דַּהֲוָה נָקֵיט תְּרֵי *מְדָאנֵי אָסָא, וְרָהֵיט בֵּין הַשְּׁמָשׁוֹת. אָמְרוּ לֵיהּ: הָנֵי לָמָּה לָךְ? אָמַר לְהוּ: לִכְבוֹד שַׁבָּת. וְתִיסְגֵּי לָךְ בְּחַד? חַד כְּנֶגֶד °״זָכוֹר״, וְחַד כְּנֶגֶד °״שָׁמוֹר״. א״ל לִבְרֵיהּ: חֲזִי כַּמָּה חֲבִיבִין מִצְוֹת עַל יִשְׂרָאֵל! יְתֵיב דַּעְתַּיְיהוּ. שָׁמַע ר׳ פִּנְחָס בֶּן יָאִיר חַתְנֵיהּ וּנְפַק לְאַפֵּיהּ, עַיְילֵיהּ לְבֵי בָּנֵי הֲוָה קָא *אָרֵיךְ לֵיהּ לְבִישְׂרֵיהּ, חֲזֵי דַּהֲוָה בֵּיהּ פִּילֵי בְּגוּפֵיהּ, הֲוָה קָא בָּכֵי, וְקָא נָתְרוּ דִּמְעַת עֵינֵיהּ וְקָמְצַוְּחָא לֵיהּ. א״ל: אוֹי לִי שֶׁרְאִיתִיךְ בְּכָךְ! א״ל: אַשְׁרֶיךָ שֶׁרְאִיתַנִי בְּכָךְ, שֶׁאִילְמָלֵא לֹא רְאִיתַנִי בְּכָךְ – לֹא מָצָאתָ בִּי כָּךְ. דְּמֵעִיקָּרָא כִּי הֲוָה מַקְשֵׁי ר״ש בֶּן יוֹחַי קוּשְׁיָא – הֲוָה מְפָרֵק לֵיהּ ר׳ פִּנְחָס בֶּן יָאִיר תְּרֵיסַר פֵּירוּקֵי, לְסוֹף כִּי הֲוָה מַקְשֵׁי ר״פ בֶּן יָאִיר קוּשְׁיָא – הֲוָה מְפָרֵק לֵיהּ רשב״י עֶשְׂרִין וְאַרְבָּעָה פֵּירוּקֵי. אָמַר: הוֹאִיל וְאִיתְרְחִישׁ נִיסָּא – אֵיזִיל אַתְקִין מִילְּתָא, דִּכְתִיב: °״וַיָּבֹא יַעֲקֹב שָׁלֵם״ וְאָמַר רַב: שָׁלֵם בְּגוּפוֹ, שָׁלֵם בְּמָמוֹנוֹ, שָׁלֵם בְּתוֹרָתוֹ. °״וַיִּחַן אֶת פְּנֵי הָעִיר״ אָמַר רַב: מַטְבֵּעַ תִּיקֵּן לָהֶם, וּשְׁמוּאֵל אָמַר: שְׁוָוקִים תִּיקֵּן לָהֶם, וְר׳ יוֹחָנָן אָמַר: מֶרְחֲצָאוֹת תִּיקֵּן לָהֶם. אֲמַר: אִיכָּא מִילְּתָא דְּבָעֵי לְתַקּוּנֵי? אֲמַרוּ לֵיהּ: אִיכָּא דּוּכְתָּא דְּאִית בֵּיהּ סְפֵק טוּמְאָה, וְאִית

תהלים סג · שיר א · שמות כ · בראשית לג · שם

ה״ג ר״ת הלך רבי יהודה בן גרים וסיפר דבריס ונשמעו למלכות, ויש ספרים שכתב בהן יהודה, ואין נראה לרבינו תם. דאמרינן בפרק קמא דמועד קטן (דף ט.): כי הוו מיפטרי ר׳ יהודה בן גריס ור״ש בן חלפתא מר׳ שמעון בן יוחי אמר ליה לבריה: אנשים הללו אנשי צורה הם, זיל גבייהו דליברכוך. מכלל דגברא רבה היה. ובסוף שמעתא ל״ג ״גל של עצמות״ בלשון גנאי, אלא ״נח נפשיה״:

עבד

עַל הַמַּעֲשֵׂר. הָאוֹכֵל פֵּירוֹתָיו טְבָלִים, וְהוּא בְּמִיתָה בִּידֵי שָׁמַיִם. וְזוֹהִי מִיתָתוֹ מִדָּה כְּנֶגֶד מִדָּה, דְּדֶרֶךְ גְּרוֹנוֹ נִכְנָס בְּמֵעָיו: יִסָּכֵר. אַסְכָּרָה: לַכֶּרֶם. זֶה בֵּית הַמִּדְרָשׁ שֶׁיּוֹשְׁבִין שׁוּרוֹת שׁוּרוֹת כְּכֶרֶם, כָּךְ מְפוֹרָשׁ בִּירוּשַׁלְמִי בִּבְרָכוֹת: מַכָּה זוֹ. אַסְכָּרָה: רֹאשׁ הַמְדַבְּרִים. בְּמִצְוַת הַמֶּלֶךְ, שֶׁצִּוָּה עָלָיו לְדַבֵּר תְּחִלָּה בְּכָל מָקוֹם, כִּדְלְקַמָּן: פֶּה גּוֹמֵר. לָשׁוֹן הָרַע, וְהוּא בָּא עַל כָּךְ, לְפִיכָךְ מַתְחִיל בַּמֵּעַיִם וּמְסַיֵּים בַּפֶּה. שֶׁהַלֵּב מֵבִין לְסַפֵּר לָשׁוֹן הָרַע, וּבוֹדֶה הַדְּבָרִים מִלִּבּוֹ: פֶּה גּוֹמֵר. הַכֹּל יוֹצֵא מִן הַגָּרוֹן: דְּבָרִים טְמֵאִים סָלְקָא דַעְתָּךְ. וְכִי עוֹנְשָׁהּ מִיתָה? דְּבִשְׁלָמָא לָשׁוֹן הָרַע עוֹנְשָׁהּ מִיתָה, דִּכְתִיב (תהלים קא): ״מְלָשְׁנִי בַסֵּתֶר רֵעֵהוּ אוֹתוֹ אַצְמִית״: מְתוּקָּנִין. מְעוּשָּׂרִים, שֶׁהַטֶּבֶל בְּמִיתָה בִּידֵי שָׁמַיִם, כִּדְיָלֵיף בְּ״אֵלּוּ הֵן הַנִּשְׂרָפִים״ (סנהדרין דף פג.): בַּעֲוֹן בִּטּוּל תּוֹרָה. דְּעָנוּשׁ נַמִי מִיתָה, כְּדַאֲמַרַן: מִקְרָא נִדְרָשׁ לִפְנֵי פָנָיו ״לְמַעַן יִרְבּוּ יְמֵיכֶם״, הָא אִם לֹא תִּלְמְדוּ – יִתְמַעֲטוּ: נָשִׁים יוֹכִיחוּ. שֶׁאֵינָן מְצֻוּוֹת עַל דִּבְרֵי תוֹרָה, דִּכְתִיב: ״וְלִמַּדְתֶּם אוֹתָם אֶת בְּנֵיכֶם״ וְלֹא בְּנוֹתֵיכֶם, וּמֵתוֹת בְּאַסְכָּרָה. אָמַר לָהֶן: אַף הֵן מְבַטְּלוֹת אֶת בַּעֲלֵיהֶן: תִּינוֹקוֹת יוֹכִיחוּ. שֶׁאֵינָן בְּנֵי לִימּוּד. אָמַר לָהֶן: אַף הֵן בַּעֲוֹן שֶׁמְּבַטְּלִים אֶת אֲבִיהֶם לְהוֹלִיכָן לַחַמָּה וְלַצּוֹנֵן, וּלְפַיְּיסָן בֶּאֱגוֹזִים: שֶׁל בֵּית רַבָּן. לֹא בָּטְלִין וְלֹא מְבַטְּלִין: אִם לֹא תֵדְעִי לָךְ. לִשְׁמוֹר מִצְוֹתַי – צְאִי לָךְ וּבַקְּשִׁי רַחֲמִים בִּזְכוּת עִקְבֵי הַצֹּאן – אָבוֹת הָרִאשׁוֹנִים שֶׁהָיוּ רַגְלֵי הַצֹּאן וְחִזּוּקָם, וּרְעִי בִּזְכוּתָן אֶת גְּדִיּוֹתַיִךְ – תִּינוֹקוֹת שֶׁלָּךְ, שֶׁלֹּא יִתָּפְשׂוּ עַל מִשְׁכְּנוֹת הָרוֹעִים – רוֹעֵי הַדּוֹר וּפַרְנָסָיו: ש״מ אַף עַל לָשׁוֹן הָרַע. וְלָא פָּלֵיג אַמַּעֲשֵׂר, דְּהָא קָאָמַר הָכָא שֶׁהֵם אוֹכְלִין דְּבָרִים שֶׁאֵינָן מְתוּקָּנִין: בֶּן גֵּרִים. בֶּן גֵּר וְגִיּוֹרֶת הָיָה: שֶׁל אוּמָּה זוֹ. רוֹמִיִּים: שְׁוָוקִין. סֵדֶר מוֹשַׁב חֲנוּיוֹת עֲיָירוֹת וְחוּצוֹתֵיהֶן: וְסִיפֵּר דִּבְרֵיהֶם. לְתַלְמִידָיו אוֹ לְאָבִיו וְאִמּוֹ, וְלֹא לְהַשְׁמִיעָן לַמַּלְכוּת, וְנִשְׁמְעוּ עַל יָדוֹ לַמַּלְכוּת: יִתְעַלֶּה. לִהְיוֹת רֹאשׁ הַמְדַבְּרִים: אִיבְרִי לְהוּ חָרוּבָא. לֶאֱכוֹל פֵּירוֹתָיו, וְעֵינָא דְּמַיָּא לִשְׁתּוֹת: בְּחָלָא. בְּחוֹל. שֶׁהָיוּ פּוֹשְׁטִין בִּגְדֵיהֶם שֶׁלֹּא יִבְלוּ, וּמְכַסִּין עֶרְוָתָן בְּחוֹל: כָּרְבִי. חוֹרְשִׁים: וְעוֹסְקִין בְּחַיֵּי שָׁעָה. דְּאֶפְשָׁר עַל יְדֵי נָכְרִים, וְהקב״ה מְחַלֵּק מָזוֹן וְרֶיוַח לְעוֹשֵׂי רְצוֹנוֹ: מִשְׁפַּט רְשָׁעִים בְּגֵיהִנָּם י״ב חוֹדֶשׁ. שֶׁנֶּאֱמַר (ישעיה סו): ״וְאִשָּׁם לֹא תִכְבֶּה וְהָיָה מִדֵּי חֹדֶשׁ בְּחָדְשׁוֹ וּמִדֵּי שַׁבָּת בְּשַׁבַּתּוֹ יָבֹא כָל בָּשָׂר״, אַף הַנִּדּוֹנִים בּוֹ בְּמַשְׁמַע. מָה שַׁבָּתוֹת לְמִינּוּי שֶׁלָּהֶם, אַף חֳדָשִׁים לְמִינּוּי שֶׁלָּהֶן. וְהַאי וַדַּאי בְּפוֹשְׁעֵי גֵיהִנָּם מִשְׁתָּעֵי, דִּכְתִיב לְעֵיל מִינֵּיהּ: ״וְיָצְאוּ וְרָאוּ בְּפִגְרֵי הָאֲנָשִׁים הַפּוֹשְׁעִים בִּי״ – הָכִי תָּנֵי לַהּ בְּסֵדֶר עוֹלָם (פ״ו): דַּי לָעוֹלָם. בְּעוֹסְקֵי תוֹרָה אֲנִי וְאַתָּה: תְּרֵי מְדָאנֵי. חֲבִילוֹת שֶׁל הֲדַס לְהָרִיחַ בְּשַׁבָּת: מְדָאנֵי. כְּמוֹ ״מַעֲדַנּוֹת כִּימָה״ (איוב לח): אָרֵיךְ. מְתַקֵּן וּמַחֲלִיק: פִּילֵי. בְּקָעִים סְדָקִים, מֵחֲמַת הַחוֹל: וְקָמְצַוְּוחוּ לֵיהּ. לְר׳ שִׁמְעוֹן, שֶׁהַדְּמָעוֹת מְלוּחִין וּמַכְאִיבִין אֶת הַמַּכָּה בְּתַחִלָּתָן: אַתְקִין מִילְּתָא. כְּדֶרֶךְ שֶׁעָשָׂה יַעֲקֹב כְּשֶׁנִּיצּוֹל מִיַּד עֵשָׂו: שָׁלֵם בְּגוּפוֹ. שֶׁנִּתְרַפֵּא מִצַּלַּעְתּוֹ: שָׁלֵם בְּתוֹרָתוֹ. שֶׁלֹּא שָׁכַח תַּלְמוּדוֹ מִפְּנֵי טוֹרַח הַדֶּרֶךְ: תִּיקֵּן לָהֶם. דִּבְרֵי חֵן וַחֲנִיָּיה. וְלִי נִרְאֶה: מִ״וַּיִּקֶן אֶת חֶלְקַת הַשָּׂדֶה״ – לְשׁוֹן תִּיקּוּן:

תורה אור

גליון הש״ס

שם א״ל לבריה נשים דעתן קלה עליהן. עי׳ מג״א סס״י קנ״ו: שם בעידן צלויי לבשו. עיין לעיל דף יא ע״א תוס׳ ד״ה כגון רשב״י: גמ׳ במערתא אתא אליהו. בירושלמי פ״ט דשביעית הוא בענין אחר ועוד שם ענינים נפלאים מרשב״י:

מסורת הש״ס

[ברכות סא.]

[ברכות סג: מנחות קג:]

[שנאמר וממקדשי תחלו (יחזקאל ט) כך כתב רש״י כתובות ח: ד״ה חשיב את]

ע״ז ב:

[קידושין פ:]

[עי׳ תוספות לעיל יא. ד״ה כגון ר״ש]

[לעיל י. ביצה טו: תעני׳ כא.]

[עדיות פ״ב מ״י ר״ה יז.]

דברים ה

[כלומר עורך בשר גופו ומתקנו ערוך] ע״ש בערך א

[תרגום של ויפשיטו וישלחו ועי׳ רש״י כתובות סה: ד״ה האי תנא וכו׳ ורש״י סוטה ח: ד״ה בהני אית לה]

[גיר׳ הערוך מדני פי׳ מדן עיי״ן מובלע והוא מעדן כדכתיב מעדנות כימה איוב ל״ח ע״כ וע׳ סוכה יג: וברש״י שם ד״ה ראשי מעדנים וכו׳ ולכאורה טוב לגרוס הכא בגמרא וברש״י מעדני אסא]

ואית להו צערא לכהנים לאקופי. אמר: איכא איניש דידע דאיתחזק הכא טהרה? א"ל ההוא סבא: כאן קיצץ *בן זכאי תורמסי תרומה. עבד איהו נמי הכי, כל היכא דהוה קשי – טהריה, וכל היכא דהוה רפי – צייניה. אמר ההוא סבא: טיהר בן יוחי בית הקברות! א"ל: אילמלי *(לא) היית עמנו, ואפי' היית עמנו ולא נמנית עמנו – יפה אתה אומר. עכשיו שהיית עמנו ונמנית עמנו, יאמרו: זונות מפרכסות זו את זו, תלמידי חכמים לא כל שכן? יהב ביה עיניה, ונח נפשיה. נפק לשוקא, חזייה ליהודה בן גרים, אמר: עדיין יש לזה בעולם? *נתן בו עיניו, ועשהו גל של עצמות.§

מתני' [א] ג' דברים צריך אדם לומר בתוך ביתו ערב שבת עם חשכה: עשרתם? ערבתם? הדליקו את הנר. [ב] ספק חשכה ספק אינו חשכה – אין מעשרין את הודאי, ואין מטבילין את הכלים, ואין מדליקין את הנרות. אבל *מעשרין את הדמאי, ומערבין וטומנין את החמין.§

גמ' מנא הני מילי? א"ר יהושע בן לוי, אמר קרא: "וידעת כי שלום אהלך ופקדת נוך ולא *תחטא". אמר רבה בר רב הונא: *אע"ג דאמור רבנן שלשה דברים צריך אדם לומר וכו', [ג] צריך למימרינהו בניחותא, כי היכי דליקבלינהו מיניה. אמר רב אשי: אנא לא שמיע לי הא דרבה בר רב הונא, וקיימתי מסברא. הא גופא קשיא; אמרת: שלשה דברים צריך אדם לומר בתוך ביתו ערב שבת עם חשכה, עם חשכה – אין, ספק חשכה ספק אינו חשכה – לא. והדר תני: ספק חשכה ספק אינו חשכה מערב!§ *סימן: *בגופיא *זימרא *ציפרא *בחבלא *דמילתא.§ א"ר אבא אמר רב חייא בר אשי אמר רב: לא קשיא, [ד] כאן – בעירובי תחומין, כאן – בעירובי חצרות. *ואמר *רבא: [ה] אמרו לו שנים "צא וערב עלינו". לאחד עירב עליו מבעוד יום, ולאחד עירב עליו בין השמשות. זה שעירב עליו מבעוד יום – נאכל עירובו בין השמשות, וזה שעירב עליו בין השמשות – נאכל עירובו משחשכה, שניהם קנה עירוב. מה נפשך, אי בין השמשות יממא הוא – בתרא ליקני, קמא לא ליקני! ואי בין השמשות ליליא הוא, קמא ליקני, בתרא לא ליקני! בין השמשות ספקא הוא, *וספקא דרבנן לקולא.§ *(ואמר) רבא: מפני מה אמרו: *[ו] אין טומנין בדבר שאינו מוסיף הבל משחשכה – גזרה שמא ירתיח. אמר ליה אביי: אי הכי, בין השמשות נמי ניגזר! א"ל: סתם קדירות רותחות הן. ואמר רבא: מפני

* [נ"ל אמר]

רש"י

ואית להו צערא לאקופי. שהיה אותו שוק שהספק בו מקום מעבר העיר לרבים, והכהנים לא היו יכולין ליכנס שם מפני טומאה, וצריך להקיף דרך אחר ארוך: איכא דידע דאיתחזק טהרה. בהאי שוק מימיו, שלא היה בית הקברות גמור ולא ניתן לפנותו: כאן קיצץ בן זכאי. שתלן ועקרן לאחר גידולן: תורה אור תורמסי תרומה. הצריכות לשמרן בטהרה. וגם הוא היה כהן, כדאמרינן [*בתוספתא דפרה] (פ"ג): "אם מה שעשו ידי שכחתי": עבד איהו נמי הכי. היה מקלץ תורמסין ומשליכן שם, ונעשה נס וצף המת במקום שהוא שם, וציינו למקום הקבר – הכי מפרש בפסיקתא דפרשת העומר, ובסדר זרעים ירושלמי*): היית. במעמד: ונמנית. הסכמת לדעתנו להיות מן המנין: מפרכסות זו את זו. את שער חברתה להיות נאה: גל מעצמות. כמת שנרקב בשרו ונפל מזמן הרבה: **מתני'** עם חשכה. שאם ימהר להזכירם מבעוד יום יפשעו, ויאמרו: עדיין יש שהות: עשרתם. פירות האילן לסעודת שבת, שאף אכילת עראי של שבת קובעת למעשר, כדאמרינן במסכת ביצה (דף לד:) דשבת עונג איקרי, מכל שהוא הוי עונג: ערבתם. ערובי *תחומין וחצירות. והני תרי שייכי למימרינהו בלשון שאלה, דשמא כבר עשו, אבל בנר לא שייך "הדלקתם", דדבר הנראה לעין הוא: ספק חשכה. כגון בין השמשות, אין מעשרין את הודאי – דתיקון מעליא הוא, אע"ג דשבות בעלמא היא, קסבר: גזרו על השבות אף על בהש"מ: ואין מטבילין את הכלים. דהוי נמי שבות, כדאמרינן במסכת ביצה (דף יח.) דנראה כמתקן כלי: ואין מדליקין את הנרות. כ"ש דספיקא דאורייתא היא. וזו ואין צריך לומר זו קתני: אבל מעשרין את הדמאי. דלא דמי למתקן, דרוב ע"ה מעשרין הן: ומערבין. עירוב, ובגמרא פריך: הא תנן לעיל עם חשכה ערבתם, מקמי דליהוי ספק: וטומנין את החמין. נותנן בקופה של מוכין להיות חומם משתמר בהן. אבל משחשכה – ודאי אין טומנין בהן, כדמפרש בגמ': **גמ'** עם חשכה. מבעוד יום הוא ויש שהות לעשר ולערב(א): בעירובי תחומין. תיקון מעליא, דאסמכוה רבנן תחומין אקראי. ואפי' למאן דאמר תחומין דרבנן, כדאמרינן בעירובין (דף נא.): ילפינן מקום ממקום ומקום מניסה כו'. אבל עירובי חצרות – חומרא בעלמא הוא, ולא מיקרי שביתה מעלייתא, וספקא דבין השמשות שפיר דמי: בין השמשות קונה עירוב. שהוא תחילת קדושת היום: נאכל. שאכלו כלב או אדם: שעירב עליו מבעוד יום. הפיח עירוב לסוף התחום מבעוד יום, ולא הספיק להחשיך ממש, עד שנאכל בין השמשות: שניהם קנו עירוב. דלגבי האי שנאכל בין השמשות משוינן ליה ליליא, ואמרינן: כבר קדש היום בעוד העירוב קיים, וקנה עירוב, דהלכה כר' יוסי דאמר בעירובין (דף לה.): "ספק עירוב כשר". ולגבי דהאי שהונח עליו בין השמשות ונתקיים עד שחשכה – משוינן לבין השמשות יממא, ועדיין לא קדש היום כשהונח, ונמצא שהיה שם כבר בשעת קניית עירוב: בתרא ליקני. זה שהונח עליו בין השמשות: קמא לא ליקני. שהרי נאכל מבעוד יום: ה"ג: ספקא דרבנן היא. כלומר: הא מילתא דמספקא לן אי בין השמשות יממא או ליליא – במילתא דרבנן איתרע לן, בעירובי תחומין דרבנן. וכל ספקא דרבנן – לקולא: ה"ג: אמר רבא מפני מה אמרו אין טומנין בדבר שאינו מוסיף הבל. כגון למר ומוכין: משחשכה. כדתנן במתניתין: וטומנין את החמין, טעמא – דספק חשכה, הא ודאי חשכה – אין טומנין. וסתם הטמנה בדבר שאינו מוסיף הבל, דאילו בדבר המוסיף הבל – אפי' מבעוד יום אסור, כדתנן בפ"ד (דף מז:): "אין טומנין לא בגפת" כו' גזירה שמא ימלא קדרתו שנצטננה כשירצה להטמינה, ויתיחנה תחילה, ונמצא מבשל בשבת: אי הכי בין השמשות נמי ניגזר. דהא שבות מעלייתא היא, דהא איכא גזירת איסור דאורייתא. ותנא דמתניתין אית ליה דגזרו על השבות ביה"ש, דקתני: "אין מעשרין את הודאי": רותחות הן. שסמוך לביה"ש הוא מעבירם מעל האור, וליכא למיחש לשמא נצטננה וירתיחנה:

תוספות

עבד איהו נמי הכי. מפר"ת: כמו יעקב אבינו ותיקן מילתא: כל היכא דהוה קשי טהריה. כדאיתא בנדה בפרק "האשה" (דף סח. ושם) דתניא, אמר רבי יוסי בן שאול: מעשה בסלע שהיו מחזיקין בה טומאה כו', אמר להו: הביאו לי סדינין – הביאו לו, ושראן במים ופרסו עליו, מקום טומאה – לח, מקום טהרה – נגוב: **לא** קשיא כאן בעירובי תחומין כו'. נראה לר"ת כפירוש הקונטרס, דבעירובי תחומין מחמרינן, משום דאית להו סמך מן המקרא. וכן פר"ת, וכן יש בירושלמי, וכן משמע בפרק "מי שהוציאוהו" (עירובין דף מו: ושם) גבי הא דקאמר: הלכה כדברי המיקל בעירוב. רב פפא אמר, אילטריך, סד"א ה"מ עירובי חצרות, אבל בעירובי תחומין – אימא לא. ומעיקרא היה מפרש ר"ת דעירובי חצרות חמירי טפי, דאין מערבין אלא בפת, כדמשמע בפרק "הדר" (שם דף עא:) וב"חלון" (שם דף פא. ושם). אבל בעירובי תחומין – מערבין בכל דבר חוץ ממים ומלח. *ואין נראה, דהא ר"מ ס"ל דתחומין דאורייתא, בפרק "בכל מערבין" (שם לה.) – ואפ"ה אית ליה ב"הדר"* דעירובי חצרות בפת, ובעירובי תחומין מערבין בכל דבר, דלא אשכחן דפליג ר"מ אסתם משנה ד"בכל מערבין". וטעמא דמקילי בתחומים דלא בעי פת – משום *דאין מערבין אלא לדבר מצוה:

נאכל עירובו משחשכה. לאו דווקא, וה"ה לא נאכל:

שניהם קנו עירוב. פירש בקונטרס: דרבא איירי בעירובי תחומין, וכן משמע לשון "לא וערב". ואע"פ דספק חשכה אין מערבין עירובי תחומין – ה"מ לכתחילה, אבל בדיעבד – כשר, כר' יוסי דאמר (עירובין פ"ג דף לה.): ספק עירוב כשר. וקשה לרשב"א: דר' יוסי לית ליה התם גבי נפל עליו גל או נשרף או תרומה ונטמאה ספק עירוב [כשר] – אלא משום חזקה, כדתניא התם בהדיא (דף לו.): כיצד אמר רבי יוסי ספק עירוב כשר – כו'. אבל בספק כי הכא, שהניחו בין השמשות או נאכל בין השמשות – לא מכשר. ומפר"ת: דהכא מיירי בעירובי חצרות. וכן פר"ח, וכן מוכח בסוף "הדר" (שם דף עו.) ולא – אשכחן נמי דלאו חוץ לעיר קאמר, כמו: "לא ושכור לנו פועלים" (ב"מ דף פג.)*: רבי

עין משפט נר מצוה

קכב א מיי' פ"ה מהל' שבת הל' ג סמג עשין יא טוש"ע א"ח סי' רס סעיף ב:

קכג ב מיי' פ"ד מהל' שבת הל' ד ופ"ה הל' ג ופכ"ג הלכה טו סמג שם טוש"ע א"ח סי' רסא סעיף א:

[עי' בערוך ערך עבד נוסחאות שונות וגרס בן עזאי]

קכד ג טוש"ע א"ח סי' רס סעיף ב:

קכה ד מיי' פ"א מהל' עירובין הלכה כא סמג עשין דרבנן א טוש"ע א"ח סימן רסא סעיף א וסי' שצג סעיף ב וסי' תטו סעיף ב:

קכו ה מיי' פ"ו מהל' עירובין הלכה יג טוש"ע א"ח סימן שצג סעיף ג:

[ועי' תוספות גיטין ו: ד"ה ערבתם]

קכז ו מיי' פ"ד מהל' שבת הלכה ג סמג לאוין סה טוש"ע א"ח סי' רנז סעיף א:

[עירובין לה. פב.]

קכח ז טוש"ע א"ח סי' שיח סעיף ד:

גיטין ו: ע"ש

סימן להלכות שאמר בעל המאמר זה במסכת זו [רש"א]

[נ"ל ר' אבא וכ"כ הש"ל"ה דף מז. ד"ה סימנין] דוק היטב בשל"ה שם ותמלא שענין הגהתו באופן אחר ובמקום ואמר רבא צ"ל אמר רבא וא"כ ואמר רבא הכא בסמוך אין להגיה

[וע"ע תוס' עירובין עו. ד"ה שניהם]

[לקמן נא.]

רבינו חננאל

מתניתין ג' דברים צריך אדם לומר בתוך כו'. ואסיקנא צריך למימרינהו בניחותא כי היכי דנקבלו אינשי ביתיה מיניה מנא לן דצריך הדלקת נר בשבת שנאמר וידעת כי שלום אהלך וגו' ואין שלום אלא באור שנא' וירא אלהים את האור כי טוב ואוקמינן הא דתנן הכא ערבתם עם חשכה הן עירובי תחומין והא דתני בסיפא בספק חשיכה ומערבין וטומנין את החמין ערובי חצרות אמר רבא אמר (לשנים צאו ועירבו עלי) [אמרו לו שנים צא וערב עלינו] פי' ערובי חצרות (אחד) [לאחד] עירב עליו מבע"י (ואחד) [ולאחד] עירב עליו בין השמשות זה שעירב עליו מבע"י נאכל ערובו בין השמשות זה שעירב עליו בין השמשות נאכל עירובו משחשיכה שניהם קנו עירוב. מה נפשך וכו' ואסיקנא בין השמשות ספק מן היום הוא ספק מן הלילה הוא ועירובי חצירות דרבנן וספק דבריהם להקל: **ירושלמי** חדא דתימר בעירובי חצרות אבל בעירובי תחומין דבר תורה הן: **וטומנין** החמין אמר רבא מפני מה אמרו אין טומנין בדבר המוסיף ואפילו מבע"י גזרה שמא ירתיח*) בין השמשות ומפני מה אמרו אין טומנין אפילו בדבר שאינו מוסיף משחשיכה גזרה שמא יטמין

*) נראה דחסר כאן בדברי רבינו וצ"ל ובבין השמשות לא גזרינן דבביה"ש סתם קדרות רותחות הן:

מסורת הש"ס

[עי' תוספות מנחות כה: ד"ה שהכהנים] ופי' לאלו' ועיין בספרי ר"פ חקת

[עיין תוספות מגילה כח. ד"ה אילמלא]

ברכות נח. [ב"ב עה. סנהדרין ק.]

[ועיין פרש"י בגיטין ו:]

[בהלכות סי' סג ובפרשה בהעלותך עוד סימן קכב ... כיון דלא ... מאניה ליכא ... וחי לא ... ולא מעשרי ... ביתיה עכ"ל ... ש שפירש ... עוד כר"ן]

עירובין עו. [שם אי' רבה] ... רבא וכן ... מ ברמב"ס ... נימרא דרבא

הגהות הב"ח

(א) רש"י ד"ה עם חשכה וכו' ולערב הס"ד ואח"כ מ"ה כאן בעירובי תחומין דעירובי תחומין תיקון מעליא הוא דאסמכוה:

גליון הש"ס

גמ' אמר ההוא סבא. עי' חולין קד ו ע"א תוס' ד"ה ...: שם טיהר בן יוחי. עי' תוס' יבמות יומא ... מתני' ספק חשיכה. עי' ר"ה דף ט ע"א תוס' ד"ה ור"ע: שם אבל מעשרין. עי' חולין דף ז ע"א תוס' ד"ה ודילמא וגיטין דף לא ע"א תוס' ד"ה במתשבה: גמ' סימן בגופיא. מבואר במהרש"א. וה"מ למתחשב עוד ההיא לקמן דף נ ע"ב:

רב נסים גאון

אמר רבא מפני מה אין טומנין אפילו בדבר שאינו מוסיף הבל משחשכה (מה שחשבה) דבר המוסיף הוא הנזכר בבמה טומנין (לקמן מז) גפת וזבל ומלח וסיד וחול ודבר שאינו מוסיף תבן זוגין ומוכין ועשבין בזמן שהן יבשים ומה שהתירה המשנה מהטמנה מבעוד יום אבל בשבת לא כמו שאמרה ספק חשיכה ספק אינה חשיכה טומנין את החמין אבל ודאי חשיכה אין טומנין כלל ואפילו בדבר שאינו מוסיף ופירוש דילה בתוספתא (פרק רביעי) אין טומנין את החמין בתחילה ובסוף פרק במה טומנין (דף נא) תנו רבנן אע"פ שאמרו אין טומנין בדבר שאינו מוסיף כו' ולפי שהיתה הטמנת החמין בשבת אסורה מכל צד למדנו ראיה מזה על דבר המשנה שאמרה אבל טומנין בהן יבשין אינן אלא מבעוד יום ערב שבת ואפילו הכי הרי אמרו אין טומנין כו' לא בגפת ולא בזבל כולה ובפ' כירה אמרו (דף לט) אמר רב חסדא ממעשה שעשו אנשי טבריא ואסרו להן רבנן בטלה הטמנה בדבר המוסיף ואפילו מבעוד יום ועמד לנו מדבר זה כי הגפת והזבל וכל דבר שהוא מוסיף הבל לא נכשר ההטמנה בהם ואפילו מבעוד יום ואן

מִפְּנֵי מָה אָמְרוּ [א] אֵין טוֹמְנִין בְּדָבָר הַמּוֹסִיף הֶבֶל וַאֲפִילּוּ מִבְּעוֹד יוֹם – גְּזֵירָה שֶׁמָּא יַטְמִין בְּרֶמֶץ שֶׁיֵּשׁ בָּהּ גַּחֶלֶת. אָמַר לֵיהּ אַבַּיֵי: וְיַטְמִין! גְּזֵירָה שֶׁמָּא יַחְתֶּה בְּגֶחָלִים.§ ת"ר: ביה"ש סָפֵק מִן הַיּוֹם וּמִן הַלַּיְלָה, סָפֵק כּוּלּוֹ מִן הַיּוֹם, סָפֵק כּוּלּוֹ מִן הַלַּיְלָה – מַטִּילִין אוֹתוֹ לְחוֹמֶר שְׁנֵי יָמִים. וְאֵיזֶהוּ בֵּין הַשְּׁמָשׁוֹת – מִשֶּׁתִּשְׁקַע הַחַמָּה כ"ז שֶׁפְּנֵי מִזְרָח מַאֲדִימִין, הִכְסִיף הַתַּחְתּוֹן וְלֹא הִכְסִיף הָעֶלְיוֹן – בֵּין הַשְּׁמָשׁוֹת, הִכְסִיף הָעֶלְיוֹן וְהִשְׁוָה לַתַּחְתּוֹן – זֶהוּ לַיְלָה, דִּבְרֵי רַבִּי יְהוּדָה. ר' נְחֶמְיָה אוֹמֵר: כְּדֵי שֶׁיְּהַלֵּךְ אָדָם מִשֶּׁתִּשְׁקַע הַחַמָּה חֲצִי מִיל. *רַבִּי יוֹסֵי אוֹמֵר: בֵּין הַשְּׁמָשׁוֹת כְּהֶרֶף עַיִן, *זֶה נִכְנָס וְזֶה יוֹצֵא, (א) וְאִי אֶפְשָׁר לַעֲמוֹד עָלָיו. אָמַר מָר: "מַטִּילִין אוֹתוֹ לְחוֹמֶר שְׁנֵי יָמִים", לְמַאי הִלְכְתָא? אָמַר רַב הוּנָא בְּרֵיהּ דְּרַב יְהוֹשֻׁעַ: לְעִנְיַן טוּמְאָה, *כִּדְתְנַן: [ב] רָאָה שְׁנֵי יָמִים בֵּין הַשְּׁמָשׁוֹת – סָפֵק לְטוּמְאָה וּלְקָרְבָּן, רָאָה יוֹם אֶחָד בֵּין הַשְּׁמָשׁוֹת סָפֵק לְטוּמְאָה. הָא גּוּפָהּ קַשְׁיָא; אָמְרַתְּ: אֵיזֶהוּ ביה"ש – מִשֶּׁתִּשְׁקַע הַחַמָּה, כ"ז שֶׁפְּנֵי מִזְרָח מַאֲדִימִין. הָא הִכְסִיף הַתַּחְתּוֹן וְלֹא הִכְסִיף הָעֶלְיוֹן – לַיְלָה הוּא. וַהֲדַר תְּנָא: הִכְסִיף הַתַּחְתּוֹן וְלֹא הִכְסִיף הָעֶלְיוֹן – בֵּין הַשְּׁמָשׁוֹת! אָמַר רַבָּה אָמַר רַב יְהוּדָה אָמַר שְׁמוּאֵל: כְּרוֹךְ וּתְנִי, [ג] אֵיזֶהוּ ביה"ש – מִשֶּׁתִּשְׁקַע הַחַמָּה כָּל זְמַן שֶׁפְּנֵי מִזְרָח מַאֲדִימִין, וְהִכְסִיף הַתַּחְתּוֹן וְלֹא הִכְסִיף הָעֶלְיוֹן – נַמִי בֵּין הַשְּׁמָשׁוֹת, הִכְסִיף הָעֶלְיוֹן וְהִשְׁוָה לַתַּחְתּוֹן – לַיְלָה. וְרַב יוֹסֵף אָמַר רַב יְהוּדָה אָמַר שְׁמוּאֵל: הָכִי קָתָנֵי: מִשֶּׁתִּשְׁקַע הַחַמָּה כ"ז שֶׁפְּנֵי מִזְרָח מַאֲדִימִין – יוֹם, הִכְסִיף הַתַּחְתּוֹן וְלֹא הִכְסִיף הָעֶלְיוֹן – ביה"ש, הִכְסִיף הָעֶלְיוֹן וְהִשְׁוָה לַתַּחְתּוֹן – לַיְלָה. וְאַזְדוּ לְטַעֲמַיְיהוּ, דְּאִיתְּמַר: שִׁיעוּר ביה"ש בְּכַמָּה? אָמַר רַבָּה אָמַר רַב יְהוּדָה אָמַר שְׁמוּאֵל: שְׁלֹשָׁה חֶלְקֵי מִיל. מַאי ג' חֶלְקֵי מִיל? אִילֵימָא תִּלְתָּא פַּלְגֵי מִילָא – נֵימָא מִיל וּמֶחֱצָה! אֶלָּא תִּלְתָּא תִּילְתֵי מִילָא – נֵימָא מִיל! °אֶלָּא: [ד] תִּלְתָּא רִיבְעֵי מִילָא. וְרַב יוֹסֵף אָמַר רַב יְהוּדָה אָמַר שְׁמוּאֵל: שְׁנֵי חֶלְקֵי מִיל. מַאי שְׁנֵי חֶלְקֵי מִיל? אִילֵימָא תְּרֵי פַּלְגֵי מִילָא – לֵימָא מִיל! וְאֶלָּא תְּרֵי רִבְעֵי מִילָא – לֵימָא חֲצִי מִיל! אֶלָּא: תְּרֵי

רש"י

מִפְּנֵי מָה אָמְרוּ אֵין טוֹמְנִין בְּדָבָר הַמּוֹסִיף הֶבֶל וַאֲפִילּוּ מִבְּעוֹד יוֹם. כִּדְתְנַן לְקַמָּן: *לֹא בְּגֶפֶת וְלֹא בְּזֶבֶל, וְאַף עַל גַּב דִּסְתָם הַטְמָנָה מִבְּעוֹד יוֹם הוּא, דְּהָא אָסְרִינַן מִשֶּׁחֲשֵׁכָה: בְּרֶמֶץ. אֵפֶר הַמְעוֹרָב בְּגֶחָלִים: וְיַטְמִין. דְּהָא מִבְּעוֹד יוֹם הוּא: גְּזֵירָה שֶׁמָּא יַחְתֶּה בְּגֶחָלִים. מִשֶּׁחֲשֵׁכָה. שֶׁבָּא לְבַשֵּׁל הַקְּדֵרָה שֶׁלֹּא בִּשְּׁלָה כָּל צָרְכָּהּ, וְגָזְרוּ אַף בְּבִישּׁוּלָהּ כָּל צָרְכָּהּ עַד שֶׁיִּגְרוֹף אוֹ שֶׁיִּקְטוֹם, וְהָכִי מַסְקִינַן בְּפֶרֶק "כִּירָה" (דף לז:) דְּאָמַר *רַבִּי: קְטָמָהּ וְהוּבְעֲרָה – מַשְׁהִין עָלֶיהָ חַמִּין שֶׁהוּחַמּוּ מִבְּעוֹד יוֹם כָּל צָרְכָּן, וְתַבְשִׁיל שֶׁבִּישֵּׁל כָּל צָרְכּוֹ. וְכֵן אָמַר ר' יוֹחָנָן*: מִן הַיּוֹם וּמִן הַלַּיְלָה. כְּלוֹמַר: סָפֵק (ב) יֵשׁ בּוֹ מִשְּׁנֵיהֶם: סָפֵק כּוּלּוֹ מִן הַיּוֹם סָפֵק כּוּלּוֹ מִן הַלַּיְלָה. הֲרֵי ג' סְפֵיקוֹת. לְפִיכָךְ מַטִּילִין עָלָיו חוֹמֶר שְׁנֵי הַיָּמִים. וּלְקַמָּן מְפָרֵשׁ לְמַאי הִילְכְתָא שַׁיָּיךְ לוֹמַר שֶׁמָּא יֵשׁ בּוֹ מִשְּׁנֵיהֶם: מַאֲדִימִין. שֶׁנִּרְאֶה אֲדַמְדְּמוּת חַמָּה בֶּעָבִים: הִכְסִיף. הִשְׁחִיר: הַתַּחְתּוֹן. תַּחְתּוֹן שֶׁל כִּיפַּת הָרָקִיעַ הַסְּמוּכָה לָאָרֶץ: עֶלְיוֹן. גּוֹבְהָהּ שֶׁל כִּפָּה אֵינָהּ מְמַהֶרֶת לְהַכְסִיף. וּלְקַמָּן פָּרֵיךְ: מַאי קָאָמַר, דְּקַשְׁיָא סֵיפָא אַרֵישָׁא: חֲצִי מִיל. זֶהוּ שִׁיעוּר אוֹרֶךְ בֵּין הַשְּׁמָשׁוֹת, וּלְאַחַר חֲצִי מִיל הָוֵי לַיְלָה: כְּהֶרֶף עַיִן. כְּשִׁיעוּר קְרִיצַת עַיִן, בְּרִפְיוֹן וְלֹא בְּחָזְקָה: זֶה נִכְנָס. הַלַּיְלָה נִכְנָס וְהַיּוֹם יוֹצֵא, יְצִיאַת זֶה עִם כְּנִיסַת זֶה. כְּשֶׁהֵם מִתְפָּרְשִׁין קָרֵי בֵּין הַשְּׁמָשׁוֹת. וְכָל דְּמִקַּמֵּי הָכִי – הָוֵי יוֹם מְעַלְּיָא: לְמַאי הִילְכְתָא. יַטִּילוּ עָלָיו סָפֵק שֶׁמָּא מִשְּׁנֵיהֶם יֵשׁ בּוֹ. בִּשְׁלָמָא סָפֵק כּוּלּוֹ מִן הַיּוֹם – אִיכָּא לְמֵימַר לְעִנְיַן מוֹצָאֵי שַׁבָּת לְהָבִיא אָשָׁם תָּלוּי. סָפֵק כּוּלּוֹ מִן הַלַּיְלָה – לְעִנְיַן לֵילֵי שַׁבָּת. אֶלָּא חוֹמֶר שְׁנֵיהֶם לְמַאי הִילְכְתָא? רָאָה שְׁנֵי ביה"ש. זִיבָה דְּזָב מְטַמְּאָה בְּיָמִים וּבִרְאִיּוֹת: בֵּין שֶׁרָאָה שְׁתַּיִם בְּיוֹם אֶחָד, בֵּין שֶׁרָאָה שְׁתַּיִם בִּשְׁנֵי יָמִים רְצוּפִים; בֵּין שֶׁרָאָה אַחַת בִּשְׁנֵי יָמִים, כְּגוֹן בֵּין הַשְּׁמָשׁוֹת – חֲשִׁיב לֵיהּ כִּשְׁתֵּי רְאִיּוֹת מִשּׁוּם יָמִים. דְּיָלְפִינַן מִ"לַּזָּכָר וְלַנְּקֵבָה". מַה נְּקֵבָה בְּיָמִים – אַף זָכָר בְּיָמִים, וּרְאִיּוֹת בְּגוּפֵיהּ מִיפַּרְשָׁא, כִּדְתַנְיָא בִּמְגִילָּה (דף ח.): מָנָה הַכָּתוּב שְׁתַּיִם וּקְרָאוֹ טָמֵא כו': סָפֵק לְטוּמְאָה וּלְקָרְבָּן. סָפֵק טָמֵא סָפֵק טָהוֹר, סָפֵק חַיָּיב קָרְבָּן עִם הַטּוּמְאָה סָפֵק אֵינוֹ חַיָּיב קָרְבָּן. אֲבָל טָמֵא שִׁבְעָה דְּזָב בַּעַל שְׁתֵּי רְאִיּוֹת אוֹ שְׁנֵי יָמִים – כָּל תּוֹרַת טוּמְאַת זָבִין עָלָיו, וּשְׁלִישִׁי מְבִיאָתוֹ לִידֵי קָרְבָּן. וְזֶה שֶׁרָאָה שְׁנֵי בֵּין הַשְּׁמָשׁוֹת, סָפֵק יוֹם אֶחָד הוּא – וְטָמֵא כִּשְׁנֵי רְאִיּוֹת, אוֹ שְׁנֵי יָמִים רְצוּפִין הֵן – וְטָמֵא נַמִי בְּתוֹרַת יָמִים. סָפֵק ב' יָמִים שֶׁאֵין רְצוּפִין הֵן – וְטָהוֹר מִטּוּמְאַת שִׁבְעָה, אֶלָּא כְּבַעַל קֶרִי בְּעָלְמָא, דְּלָאו שְׁתֵּי רְאִיּוֹת בְּיוֹם אֶחָד אִיכָּא וְלֹא שְׁנֵי יָמִים רְצוּפִין אִיכָּא, סָפֵק שֶׁהֵן ג' יָמִים רְצוּפִין – דְּזָב גָּמוּר הוּא אַף לְקָרְבָּן. כֵּיצַד: שֶׁמָּא בֵּין הַשְּׁמָשׁוֹת הָרִאשׁוֹן כּוּלּוֹ מִן הַיּוֹם, וּבֵיה"ש הַשֵּׁנִי כּוּלּוֹ מִן הַלַּיְלָה – וְנִמְצָא יוֹם אֶחָד הֶפְסֵק בֵּינְתַיִים, וְטָהוֹר. אוֹ שְׁנֵיהֶם מִן הַיּוֹם – דְּהָווּ לְהוּ שְׁנֵי יָמִים רְצוּפִין. וְכֵן אִם שְׁנֵיהֶם מִן הַלַּיְלָה – הָווּ לְהוּ נַמִי שְׁנֵי יָמִים רְצוּפִין. אוֹ שֶׁמָּא אִם הָרִאשׁוֹן מִן הַלַּיְלָה וְהַשֵּׁנִי מִן הַיּוֹם – הָווּ לְהוּ נַמִי שְׁתֵּי רְאִיּוֹת בְּיוֹם אֶחָד, וְטָמֵא שִׁבְעָה בְּכָל אֵלּוּ, וְאֵין כָּאן קָרְבָּן. אוֹ שֶׁמָּא שְׁתֵּיהֶן הָרְאִיּוֹת הָיוּ מִקְצָתָן בַּיּוֹם וּמִקְצָתָן בַּלַּיְלָה, וְיֵשׁ כָּאן שְׁלֹשָׁה רְצוּפִים, וְכֵן אִם הָרִאשׁוֹנָה מִקְצָתָהּ בַּיּוֹם וּמִקְצָתָהּ בַּלַּיְלָה וְהַשְּׁנִיָּה כּוּלָּהּ מִן הַלַּיְלָה, אוֹ הָרִאשׁוֹנָה כּוּלָּהּ מִן הַיּוֹם וְהַשְּׁנִיָּה מִקְצָתָהּ בַּיּוֹם וּמִקְצָתָהּ בַּלַּיְלָה – הָווּ לְהוּ ג' יָמִים רְצוּפִין, וְטָעוּן קָרְבָּן. הִלְכָּךְ: סָפֵק אַף לְקָרְבָּן וּמֵבִיא חַטַּאת הָעוֹף הַבָּאָה עַל הַסָּפֵק וְאֵין נֶאֱכֶלֶת. דְּשֶׁמָּא לָאו בַּר קָרְבָּן הוּא, וּמְלִיקַת חוּלִּין נְבֵלָה: רָאָה אַחַת ביה"ש סָפֵק לְטוּמְאָה. שֶׁמָּא מִקְצָתָהּ בַּיּוֹם וּמִקְצָתָהּ בַּלַּיְלָה, וְהַיְינוּ חוֹמֶר ב' יָמִים – וְטָמֵא ז'. אוֹ שֶׁמָּא כּוּלָּהּ אוֹ מִן הַיּוֹם אוֹ מִן הַלַּיְלָה – וְאֵין כָּאן אֶלָּא אַחַת: פְּנֵי מִזְרָח מַאֲדִימִים. עֲדַיִין לֹא הִכְסִיף אֲפִי' תַּחְתּוֹן: כָּרוּךְ וּתְנִי. שְׁנֵי הַדְּבָרִים בְּכֶרֶךְ אֶחָד, בְּתוֹרָה אַחַת: וְאַזְדוּ לְטַעֲמַיְיהוּ. דְּרַבָּה סָבַר שִׁיעוּר ביה"ש נָפִישׁ, וְרַב יוֹסֵף סָבַר זוּטַר: פַּלְגָּא

תוספות

רבי יוסי אומר בין השמשות כהרף עין. פירש רשב"א: דאין להסתפק בו אלא כשהוא כהרף עין, ולא בזמן גדול כמו שמסתפק בו תנא קמא, אבל אין לפרש: רבי יוסי אין מסתפק בבין השמשות כלל, והכי קאמר: כהרף עין אני מכיר ובקי בו מתי זה נכנס וזה יוצא, ויודע אני מתי הוא יום מתי הוא לילה, דהא בתוספתא דמסכת זבים, בפ"ק קתני, וכן היה ר' יוסי אומר: ראה אחד בין השמשות ואחד ודאי – ספק לטומאה ולקרבן. פירוש: שראה במוצאי שבת ביה"ש, וביום שני ראה ביום, ספק לטומאה – דשמא בין השמשות כולו מן היום, והוי יום מפסיק וטהור. או שמא כולו מן הלילה – והוו שני ימים רצופין, וטמא. ושמא מן היום ומן הלילה, ואיכא שלשה ימים רצופין – וחייב קרבן, אלמא דר' יוסי נמי מספקא ליה בההוא כהרף עין: **ספק** לטומאה ולקרבן. פירש בקונטרס: דשמא בין השמשות ראשון כולו מן היום, ושני כולו מן הלילה. ול"נ: דאי ראשון כולו מן היום – שני נמי כולו מן היום. ועוד: דאמר לקמן בשמעתין (דף לה:) "העושה מלאכה בשני בין השמשות – חייב חטאת ממה נפשך. ולפירוש הקונטרס הא איכא למימר: שמא בין השמשות דע"ש כולו יום, ומוצאי שבת כולו לילה, ולא יתחייב חטאת אלא אשם. ומפרש רשב"ם: ספק לטומאה ולקרבן – שראה בין השמשות במוצאי שבת, וביה"ש דמוצאי יום שני, דשמא בין השמשות שניהם כולו מן היום, או כולו מן הלילה מפסיק יום אחד בינתים ואין כאן טומאה, או שמא חציו מן היום וחציו מן הלילה – והוו רצופין וטמא טומאת שבעה ומתחייב קרבן. וקשה לפירושו, חדא: דשני ימים בין השמשות משמע רצופין. ועוד: דלפי זה לא משכחת טומאת ז' בלא קרבן, ולישנא משמע ספק טומאה לחוד ולקרבן לחוד. ועוד קשה לר"י: דאם מיירי כשראה כל בין השמשות, כמו "העושה מלאכה שני בין השמשות" כדמפרש רשב"ם – א"כ בראיה אחת חייב קרבן, דהא ביה"ש הוי לכל הפחות חצי מיל דהוו אלף אמה, דשיעור מיל הוי אלפים אמה כדפי' רש"י בפרק "שני שעירים" (יומא דף סו. ושם). ואמר בפרק "ד' מיתות" (סנהדרין דף סג.): ראה אחת מרובה כג' שהיא כמגדיון לשילה, שהם שתי טבילות ושני סיפוגין – הרי זה זב גמור. ובתוספתא בריש מסכת זבין משמע היינו שיעור ק' אמה, לכך מפרש ר"ת: דמיירי שלא ראה כל בין השמשות אלא שעה אחת מועטת דבין השמשות זה, ושעה אחרת בין השמשות אחר. ובכל שהוא שבין השמשות יש להסתפק שמא כולו מן היום או כולו מן הלילה, או חציו יום וחציו לילה, והשתא אתי שפיר; דספק לטומאה – דשמא הראשון כולו מן היום והשני כולו מן הלילה, ומפסיק יום בינתים, או שמא תרוייהו יום או תרוייהו לילה – ואיכא ב' ימים רצופין – וספק לקרבן. שמא הראשון מן היום ומן הלילה, והשני לילה, או הא' יום והב' חציו יום וחציו לילה, ואיכא ג' רצופין והויא דהעושה

עין משפט נר מצוה

קכט א מיי' פ"ד מהל' שבת הלכה ב סמג לאוין סה טוש"ע א"ח סימן רנז סעיף א:
קל ב מיי' פ"ב מהל' מחוסרי כפרה הל' יב יג יד:
קלא ג ד מיי' פ"ה מהל' שבת הל' ד סמג עשין לב טוש"ע א"ח סימן רסא סעיף ב:

רבינו חננאל

יטמין ברמץ ויבא לחתוי בגחלים: **ת"ר** בין השמשות [ספק] מן היום ומן הלילה ספק כולו מן היום ספק כולו מן הלילה מטילין אותו לחומר ב' ימים ואמרינן למאי הלכתא לטומאה כדתנן במסכת זבין פרק א' ראה ב' ימים בין השמשות ספק לטומאה ולקרבן פי' האיש מטמא בראיות והאשה בג' ימים. עכשיו איש שראה ביום שבת בין השמשות אם תאמר בין השמשות כולו (א') יום הוא הנה [ראה] ראיה אחת בשבת עוד ראה ביום ראשון בין השמשות הנה ראיה שניה ביום ראשון. וא"ת בין השמשות של יום ראשון חציו מליל יום ב' הוא נמצא שראה ג' ימים (בג') [בב'] ראיות בשבת וביום א' ויום שני וקיי"ל ב' לטומאה וג' לקרבן ראה אחד ביה"ש ספק לטומאה יש לומר כולו מן היום ובעל קרי הוא ואינו טמא אלא יומו ויש לומר בין השמשות חציו יום (ותצפרה) [לכ'] [וג'] ימים או (לכ') [וג'] לילות הרי זה זב גמור ותניא בתוספתא (פ"א דזבים) ומודה ר' יוסי שאם ראה אחת בין השמשות אף על פי שאין כאן כדי טבילה וספוג הוא זב ב' ראיות שב' ימים חולקין אותה ובן היה ר' יוסי אומר ראה אחת בין השמשות ספק לטומאה ופטור מן הקרבן ראה שתים בין השמשות ספק לטומאה ולקרבן אחת בין השמשות ואחת בין השמשות (ושתים ודאי) ודאי לטומאה וספק לקרבן שתים ודאי ואחת בין השמשות [או שתים בין השמשות ואחת ודאי] ודאי לטומאה ולקרבן סוף הברייתא ואיזהו בין השמשות משתשקע החמה וכ"ז שפני מזרח מאדים הכסיף התחתון ולא הכסיף העליון [ביה"ש] (והוה יום) הכסיף העליון והשוה לתחתון והו לילה דברי רבי יהודה ור' נחמיה אומר בה"ש משתשקע החמה עד כדי הילוך חצי מיל רבי יוסי אומר ביה"ש כהרף עין הלילה נכנס והיום יוצא ואי אפשר לעמוד עליו ואמרי על הא דר' יהודה הא גופה קשיא ומתרץ רבה כרוך ותני איזהו בה"ש משתשקע החמה וכ"ז שפני מערב מאדימין את המזרח וסימנך כוותא. פי' אם יהיה נר דולק בבית ובו חלון פתוח למערב מתראה אור הנר כנגד פתח החלון במזרח וגם הכסיף התחתון ולא הכסיף העליון עדיין ביה"ש הוא. הכסיף העליון והשוה לתחתון זהו לילה. ורב יוסף תני לה הכי איזהו ביה"ש משתשקע החמה וכ"ז שפני מערב מאדימין למזרח עדיין הוא יום הכסיף התחתון ולא הכסיף העליון ביה"ש הכסיף העליון והשוה לתחתון לילה ואזדו לטעמייהו דאתמר שיעור בין השמשות בכמה רבה אמר כדי הילוך ג' רבעי מיל [ור"י אמר ב' שלישי מיל] נתננו סימן זה לדבר שיהא *(נום) לתלמיד בהין של תורה שהוא י"ב לוגין רביעית ג' לוגין ושליש ד' לוגין נמצאו ג' רביעית ט' לוגין ונמצאו שני שלישי הין ח' לוגין הרי יש בין ג' רביעיות ובין ב' שלישים לוג א' שהוא חצי שתות כמוהו חשבון המיל ששיערו בו רבה ורב יוסף נמצא שיעור רבה יתר על השיעור דרב יוסף כדי הילוך חצי שתות מיל ש"מ שלא נתנו סימן לשיעור אלא לדבר שנחלקו בו שהוא משתשקע החמה וכ"ז שפני מזרח מאדימין והיינו חצי שתות מיל (משיכסיף עליון עד שישוה לתחתון) [משתשקע החמה עד שיכסיף התחתון

*) אולי צ"ל נוח.

מסורת הש"ס

[דף מז:]
שם איתא ר' יונתן בר נחמני א"ר אושעיא
[לקמן לז:]
ברכות ב:
[נדה נג.] [וע' תוספות פסחים ב. ב"ק ס: ד"ה לעולם יכנס]
זבים פ"א מ"ו

הגהות הב"ח

(א) גמ' וזה יוצא (ואי אפשר לעמוד עליו) תא"מ ונ"ב בתוספות משמע דלא גרסי' וא"א לעמוד עליו גם בא"ש כ"ג ליה אבל בתוספתא גרס ליה: (ב) רש"י ד"ה מן היום וכו' ספק כולו מן היום וכו' ספק בו יש בו:

גליון הש"ס

גמ' אלא תלתא רבעי. עיין פירש"י ברכות דף ב ע"ב ד"ה והא כהנים ובנדה דף נג ע"א ברש"י ד"ה ביה"ש וצ"ע:

רב נסים גאון

ואן אל חבן אל יאבם וכל דבר (שמוסיף) [שאינו מוסיף] הבל פי' אלחרארה אנמא אבאה אל הטמנה בהם מבעוד יום אבל משחשיכה אסור*) הרי מכאן אמר רבא מפני מה אמרו אין טומנין בדבר המוסיף ואפי' מבעוד יום ואין טומנין בדבר שאינו מוסיף משחשיכה כי העת שאסרו בו ההטמנה בגפת ובזבל בו בעת עצמו אמרו אבל טומנין בהם יבשים ואי אפשר להיות משחשיכה מפני שאמרו אין טומנין בתחלה בשבת ולא יתכן להיות אלא מבעוד יום ואעפ"כ אסרו דבר שהוא מוסיף ולא התירו אלא דבר שאינו מוסיף ואם היה דבר שאינו מוסיף מבעוד יום הוא שמותר מכלל שמחשיכה אסור: **ראה** ב' ימים בין השמשות ספק לקרבן ראה יום אחד בין השמשות ספק לטומאה. כבר ידענו כי הזב אפילו ראה ג' ראיות מופסקין ביום אחד הרי הוא זב גמור כדתניא (ב"ק פרק כילד הרגל דף כד) תלה הכתוב את הזב בראיות ואת הזבה בימים וכן אם לא יהיו מופסקין אלא מחוברין ויש בהן שיעור שיטבול אדם ב' טבילות ויסתפג ב' סיפוגין הרי (זה) [זב] גמור כדתנן (מס' זבים פ"א משנה ה) ראה אחת מרובה כשלש שהיא (כמי גריון) [כמגן גד יון] לשילות שהן כדי שתי [טבילות] וכשני סיפוגין הרי זה זב גמור וכן נמי אם יראה בסוף היום ראיה אחת מחוברת שלא פסקה עד שנכנס הלילה הרי דינה כדין ב' ראיות כי יציאת היום וכניסת הלילה מחלקין הראיה ומפסקין אותה שאמרה המשנה ראה אחת ביום ואחת בין השמשות אחת בין השמשות ואחת למחר אם ידוע שמקצת הראיה מהיום ומקצתה למחר ודאי לטומאה ולקרבן ואם ספק שמקצתה היום ומקצתה למחר ודאי לטומאה וספק לקרבן אבל אם ראה בין השמשות הואיל ובין השמשות הוא סוף היום שעבר ותחילת יום שאחריו ואנו מסתפקים בו יהיה דין זה האיש ספק לטומאה כי

פַּלְגָּא דְּדַנְקָא. אֶחָד מִי"ב בְּמִיל. דְּשִׁיעוּרָא דְּרַבָּה תְּלָת רִיבְעֵי מִילָא הַיְינוּ תִּשְׁעָה פַּלְגֵי דַּנְקָא. וְשִׁיעוּרָא דְּרַב יוֹסֵף שְׁמוֹנָה פַּלְגֵי דַּנְקָא, דַּנְקָא שְׁתוּת: וְחִילּוּפָה. אִיפְלִיגוּ רַבָּה וְרַב יוֹסֵף בְּחַלְתָּא, דְּהָתָם שִׁיעוּרָא דְּרַב יוֹסֵף נָפִישׁ מִדְּרַבָּה. רַבָּה דְּאָמַר הָכָא תְּלָתָא אָמַר הָתָם תְּרֵי, וְרַב יוֹסֵף דְּאָמַר הָכָא תְּרֵי אָמַר הָתָם תְּלָתָא: חַלְתָּא. כַּוֶּורֶת: שָׁרֵי לְטַלְטוּלָהּ. דְּתוֹרַת כְּלִי עָלֶיהָ: בַּת תְּלָתָא. גְּדוֹלָה יוֹתֵר מִדַּאי, וְאֵין תּוֹרַת כְּלִי עָלֶיהָ: בְּעֵי מִינֵּיהּ דְּמָר. רַבָּה: בִּשְׁעַת מַעֲשֶׂה. שֶׁהָיִיתִי צָרִיךְ לַדָּבָר: כְּמַאן. הָא דַּאֲפִי' בְּתַרְתֵּי כּוֹרֵי לָא שְׁרָא: קַשׁ. זְנָבוֹת שִׁבּוֹלִין, אשטריי"ם: וּבוֹר סְפִינָה אֲלֶכְּסַנְדְּרִית. סְפִינָה גְּדוֹלָה שֶׁפּוֹרְשִׁים בָּהּ לַיָּם הַגָּדוֹל, וּמֵי הַיָּם מְלוּחִין, וְעוֹשִׂין כְּלִי גָּדוֹל כְּמִין בּוֹר, וְנוֹתְנִין לְתוֹכוֹ מַיִם יָפִים: לַח. אֵין בּוֹ גּוֹדֶשׁ: שֶׁהֵן כּוֹרַיִים. שִׁשִּׁים סְאָה, בְּיָבֵשׁ. שֶׁהַגּוֹדֶשׁ מַחֲזִיק שְׁלִישׁ בַּכֵּלִים שֶׁלָּהֶם, שֶׁהָיוּ עֲשׂוּיִין כְּיָם שֶׁעָשָׂה שְׁלֹמֹה, גּוֹבְהָן כַּחֲצִי רָחְבָּן וְהֵם עֲגוּלִּים: טְהוֹרִין. דְּאִיתְקַשׁ כְּלִי עֵץ לְשַׂק דְּמִיטַּלְטֵל מָלֵא וְרֵיקָן, וְזֶה אֵינוֹ מִיטַּלְטֵל מָלֵא – דְּגָדוֹל יוֹתֵר מִדַּאי, וְאִם יְטַלְטְלוּהוּ – יִשָּׁבֵר בִּידֵיהֶם: דָּאוֵי. מַבִּיט עֶרֶב שַׁבָּת לִרְאוֹת אִם יֵשׁ שָׁם אַדְמוּמִית חַמָּה: פָּנִים הַמַּאֲדִימִים אֶת הַמִּזְרָח. לָעֶרֶב חַמָּה שׁוֹקַעַת בַּמַּעֲרָב, וְזַהֲרוּרֵי הַחַמָּה מַאֲדִימִין אֶת הַמִּזְרָח כַּחַלּוֹן, דִּכְשֶׁהַחַמָּה נִכְנֶסֶת בָּהּ מַאֲדֶמֶת כּוֹתֶל שֶׁכְּנֶגְדָּהּ: וְסִימָנָךְ כַּוְּותָא. חַלּוֹן, כְּמוֹ שֶׁפֵּירַשְׁתִּי: כַּרְמֶל. הַר שֶׁעַל שְׂפַת הַיָּם, וְחַמָּה סָמוּךְ לִשְׁקִיעָתָהּ נִרְאֵית עַל רָאשֵׁי הֶהָרִים, וּכְדֵי שֶׁיֵּרֵד וְיִטְבּוֹל וְיַעֲלֶה הָוֵי לַיְלָה: כְּמִין כְּבָרָה. סֶלַע עָגוֹל וְעָשׂוּי כִּכְבָרָה: זֶהוּ בְּאֵרָהּ שֶׁל מִרְיָם. שֶׁהָיָה מִתְגַּלְגֵּל עִם יִשְׂרָאֵל בַּמִּדְבָּר בִּזְכוּתָהּ שֶׁל מִרְיָם, דִּכְתִיב (במדבר כ): "וַתָּמָת שָׁם מִרְיָם", וּסְמִיךְ לֵיהּ "וְלֹא הָיָה מַיִם לָעֵדָה": טָהוֹר. מִלְּקַבֵּל טוּמְאָה, וְטוֹבְלִין בּוֹ – דְּלָאו כִּכְלִי דָּמֵי לִהְיוֹת הַמַּיִם הַנּוֹבְעִין מִמֶּנּוּ כִּשְׁאוּבִין, וְאֵין לָךְ מַעְיָן מִיטַּלְטֵל אֶלָּא בְּאֵרָהּ שֶׁל מִרְיָם: כֹּהֲנִים טוֹבְלִין בּוֹ. וְאַע"פ שֶׁצְּרִיכִין הֶעֱרֵב שֶׁמֶשׁ אַחַר טְבִילָה לֶאֱכוֹל בִּתְרוּמָתָן, קָסָבַר יְמָמָא הוּא וְיֵשׁ שָׁהוּת אַחֲרָיו לִשְׁקִיעַת הַחַמָּה: סָפֵק הוּא. לְדִידֵיהּ, הוֹאִיל וְקָרֵי לֵיהּ "בֵּין הַשְּׁמָשׁוֹת" כּוּלֵּיהּ סְפֵקָא הוּא, וְשֶׁמָּא טָבְלוּ בַּלַּיְלָה וְאֵין כָּאן הֶעֱרֵב שֶׁמֶשׁ: אֶלָּא בֵּין הַשְּׁמָשׁוֹת דְּרַבִּי יוֹסֵי לְרַבִּי יְהוּדָה לָא גָּרְסִינַן, דְּהָא בְּהֶדְיָא אָמַר שְׁמוּאֵל בֵּין הַשְּׁמָשׁוֹת דְּר' יְהוּדָה כֹּהֲנִים טוֹבְלִין בּוֹ. וּמַאן דְּגָרֵים לֵיהּ מְפָרֵשׁ הָכִי: אֶלָּא בֵּין הַשְּׁמָשׁוֹת דְּר' יוֹסֵי לְר' יְהוּדָה. וְהָכִי אִתְּמַר: בֵּין הַשְּׁמָשׁוֹת דְּר' יוֹסֵי לְר' יְהוּדָה – כֹּהֲנִים טוֹבְלִין בּוֹ. וְאַשְׁמְעִינַן שְׁמוּאֵל דְּבֵין הַשְּׁמָשׁוֹת דְּר' יוֹסֵי קָדֵים לְדְר' יְהוּדָה, וּתְחִילַּת בֵּין הַשְּׁמָשׁוֹת דְּר' יְהוּדָה לְר' יוֹסֵי לֵילְיָא הוּא, וּדְר' יוֹסֵי לְר' יְהוּדָה יְמָמָא הוּא. וְהָא בָּעֵי הֶעֱרֵב שֶׁמֶשׁ, נְהִי דִּלְר' יְהוּדָה יְמָמָא הוּא – מִיהוּ הֵיכִי טָבֵיל? הָא בֵּין הַשְּׁמָשׁוֹת דְּר' יְהוּדָה סָפֵק לַיְלָה הוּא, וְכֵיוָן דְּבֵין הַשְּׁמָשׁוֹת דְּר' יוֹסֵי כְּהֶרֶף עַיִן – מִקַּמֵּי דְּסָלֵיק מִטְּבִילָה שָׁלֵים וְעָיֵיל בֵּין הַשְּׁמָשׁוֹת דְּר' יְהוּדָה, וְסָפֵק לַיְלָה הוּא וְאֵין כָּאן הֶעֱרֵב שֶׁמֶשׁ. וְלָאו מִילְּתָא הִיא, דְּלֵיכָּא לְמֵימַר דְּר' יוֹסֵי קָדֵים, מִדְּקָאָמַר בְּסֵיפָא: אֶלָּא דְּר' יְהוּדָה לְר' יוֹסֵי. וּפָרְכִינַן: פְּשִׁיטָא. וְאִי הֲוָה לָן לְסַפּוּקֵי דְּדִילְמָא דְּר' יוֹסֵי קָדֵים, מַאי פְּשִׁיטוּתָא? טוּבָא אַשְׁמְעִינַן שְׁמוּאֵל, דְּאַשְׁמְעִינַן דְּבֵין הַשְּׁמָשׁוֹת דְּר' יְהוּדָה קָדֵים: פְּשִׁיטָא. דִּלְר' יוֹסֵי כֹּהֲנִים טוֹבְלִים בּוֹ כִּדְר' יְהוּדָה, דְּהָא סְפֵקָא דְּר' יוֹסֵי כְּהֶרֶף עַיִן, וְכָל לְמַעְלָה הֵימֶנּוּ יְמָמָא הוּא, וְשִׁיעוּרֵיהּ דְּר' יְהוּדָה נָפִישׁ טוּבָא וּמַעֲרִיב שִׁמְשֵׁיהּ: *בֵּין הַשְּׁמָשׁוֹת דְּר' יוֹסֵי מֵישַׁךְ שַׁיֵּיךְ בִּדְר' יְהוּדָה. בְּסוֹפוֹ הוּא נִכְלָל, וְכִי שָׁלֵים דְּר' יְהוּדָה – לֵילְיָא הוּא אֲפִי' לְר' יוֹסֵי, וְכִי טָבֵיל בְּסוֹף בֵּין הַשְּׁמָשׁוֹת דְּר' יְהוּדָה – תּוּ לֵיכָּא הֶעֱרֵב שֶׁמֶשׁ. קָא מַשְׁמַע לָן שְׁמוּאֵל דְּכָל בֵּין הַשְּׁמָשׁוֹת דְּר' יְהוּדָה לְר' יוֹסֵי יְמָמָא הוּא וְכָשֵׁר לִטְבִילָה, וְהָדַר מַתְחִיל דְּר' יוֹסֵי וְהוּא הֶעֱרֵב שֶׁמֶשׁ: בִּשְׁלָמָא הֲלָכָה כְּר' יְהוּדָה לְעִנְיַן שַׁבָּת לְחוּמְרָא. כְּלוֹמַר: מִדְּקָאָמַר ר' יוֹחָנָן הֲלָכָה כְּר' יְהוּדָה לְהָכִי, וַהֲלָכָה כְּר' יוֹסֵי לְהָכִי, ש"מ מְסַפְּקָא לֵיהּ. הִלְכָּךְ: עַל כָּרְחָךְ לְחוּמְרָא בָּעֵי לְמֵיזַל. וּבִשְׁלָמָא כִּי אָמַר הֲלָכָה כְּר' יְהוּדָה לְעִנְיַן שַׁבָּת – אִיכָּא לְמֵימַר דִּלְחוּמְרָא אֲמָרָהּ, וּבְע"ש אָמַר, שֶׁאִם עָשָׂה בּוֹ מְלָאכָה – מֵבִיא אָשָׁם תָּלוּי. אֲבָל בְּמוֹצ"ש לָא עָבְדִינַן כְּוָותֵיהּ, לְמֵימְרָא דְּבִיה"ש דִּידֵיהּ לֵילְיָא הוּא: אִילֵימָא לִטְבִילָה. דְּס"ל דְּכֹהֲנִים טוֹבְלִין כִּדְר' יְהוּדָה, כִּדְקָאָמַר ר' יוֹסֵי. וְהָא לְר' יוֹחָנָן דְּר' יְהוּדָה סְפֵיקָא הוּא, מִדִּלְעִנְיַן שַׁבָּת קָאֵי כְּוָותֵיהּ לְחוּמְרָא: אֶלָּא

תְּרֵי תִּילְתֵי מִיל. מַאי בֵּינַיְיהוּ? אִיכָּא בֵּינַיְיהוּ פַּלְגָּא דְּדַנְקָא. וְחִילּוּפָה בְּחַלְתָּא, דְּאָמַר רַבָּה: [א]חַלְתָּא בַּת תְּרֵי כּוֹרֵי שָׁרֵי לְטַלְטוּלָהּ, וּבַת תְּלָתָא כּוֹרֵי אָסוּר לְטַלְטוּלָהּ. וְרַב יוֹסֵף אָמַר: בַּת תְּלָתָא כּוֹרֵי נַמִי שָׁרֵי, בַּת אַרְבָּעָה כּוֹרֵי אָסוּר. אָמַר אַבַּיֵי: בְּעֵי מִינֵּיהּ דְּמָר בִּשְׁעַת מַעֲשֶׂה, וַאֲפִילּוּ בַּת תְּרֵי כּוֹרֵי לָא שְׁרָא לִי, כְּמַאן – כְּהַאי תַּנָּא, דִּתְנַן: *[ב]כַּוֶּורֶת הַקַּשׁ וְכַוֶּורֶת הַקָּנִים וּבוֹר סְפִינָה אֲלֶכְּסַנְדְּרִית, אע"פ[א] שֶׁיֵּשׁ לָהֶם שׁוּלַיִם וְהֵן מַחֲזִיקוֹת מ' סְאָה בְּלַח שֶׁהֵן כּוֹרַיִים בְּיָבֵשׁ – טְהוֹרִים. *אָמַר אַבַּיֵי: שְׁמַע מִינָּהּ – *הַאי גּוּדְשָׁא תִּילְתָּא הָוֵי. אַבַּיֵי חַזְיֵיהּ לְרַבָּה דְּקָא דָּאוֵי לְמַעֲרָב, א"ל: וְהָתַנְיָא כָּל זְמַן שֶׁפְּנֵי מִזְרָח מַאֲדִימִין! א"ל: מִי סָבְרַתְּ פְּנֵי מִזְרָח מַמָּשׁ? לֹא, פָּנִים הַמַּאֲדִימִין אֶת הַמִּזְרָח. א"ד, רָבָא חַזְיֵיהּ לְאַבַּיֵי דְּקָא דָּאוֵי לְמִזְרָח, א"ל: מִי סָבְרַתְּ פְּנֵי מִזְרָח מַמָּשׁ? פָּנִים הַמַּאֲדִימִין אֶת הַמִּזְרָח! וְסִימָנָיךְ כַּוְּותָא.§ ר' נְחֶמְיָה אוֹמֵר: כְּדֵי שֶׁיַּהֲלֵךְ אָדָם מִשֶּׁתִּשְׁקַע הַחַמָּה חֲצִי מִיל.§ א"ר חֲנִינָא: הָרוֹצֶה לֵידַע שִׁיעוּרוֹ שֶׁל ר' נְחֶמְיָה יַנִּיחַ חַמָּה בְּרֹאשׁ הַכַּרְמֶל, וְיֵרֵד וְיִטְבּוֹל בַּיָּם וְיַעֲלֶה, וְזֶהוּ שִׁיעוּרוֹ שֶׁל ר' נְחֶמְיָה. א"ר חִיָּיא: הָרוֹצֶה לִרְאוֹת בְּאֵרָהּ שֶׁל מִרְיָם, יַעֲלֶה לְרֹאשׁ הַכַּרְמֶל וְיִצְפֶּה וְיִרְאֶה כְּמִין כְּבָרָה בַּיָּם, וְזוֹ הִיא בְּאֵרָהּ שֶׁל מִרְיָם. אָמַר רַב: מַעְיָן הַמִּיטַּלְטֵל – טָהוֹר, וְזֶהוּ בְּאֵרָהּ שֶׁל מִרְיָם.§ אָמַר רַב יְהוּדָה אָמַר שְׁמוּאֵל: ביה"ש דְּר' יְהוּדָה כֹּהֲנִים טוֹבְלִין בּוֹ. לְמַאן? אִילֵימָא לְר' יְהוּדָה – סְפֵקָא הוּא! אֶלָּא ביה"ש דְּר' יְהוּדָה לְר' יוֹסֵי כֹּהֲנִים טוֹבְלִין בּוֹ. פְּשִׁיטָא! מַהוּ דְּתֵימָא: בֵּין הַשְּׁמָשׁוֹת דְּר' יוֹסֵי – מֵישַׁךְ שַׁיֵּיךְ בִּדְר' יְהוּדָה, קָא מַשְׁמַע לָן: דְּשָׁלֵים בֵּין הַשְּׁמָשׁוֹת דְּר' יְהוּדָה, וַהֲדַר מַתְחִיל בֵּין הַשְּׁמָשׁוֹת דְּר' יוֹסֵי. אָמַר רַבָּה בַּר בַּר חָנָה א"ר יוֹחָנָן: הֲלָכָה כְּר' יְהוּדָה לְעִנְיַן שַׁבָּת, וַהֲלָכָה כְּר' יוֹסֵי לְעִנְיַן תְּרוּמָה. בִּשְׁלָמָא הֲלָכָה כְּר' יְהוּדָה לְעִנְיַן שַׁבָּת – לְחוּמְרָא, אֲבָל לְעִנְיַן תְּרוּמָה מַאי הִיא? אִילֵימָא לִטְבִילָה – סְפֵקָא הִיא!
אֶלָּא

דהעושה מלאכה בשני בין השמשות – היינו שעשה כל בין השמשות, או שעשה בשניהם בתחילת בין השמשות. וכן הא דתניא בתוספתא דמסכת זבים בפ"ק: דשני בין השמשות ודאי לטומאה וספק לקרבן – איירי נמי דידעינן כגון שראה בשניהם בתחילת בין השמשות. ועוד י"ל: דמיירי כשראה כל בין השמשות, דר' יוסי תני לה דאמר בין השמשות כהרף עין, וליכא ביה שיעור שלשה ראיות: **תרי** תילתי מיל. קשה: דהכא משמע דמשקיעת החמה עד הלילה ליכא אלא תלתא ריבעי מיל, ור' יהודה גופיה בפסחים בפרק "מי שהיה טמא (דף צד. ושם) סבר דמשקיעת החמה עד צאת הכוכבים – ארבע מילין, וצאת הכוכבים לילה הוא, כדאמרינן בריש פ"ק דפסחים (דף ב. ושם), וכדמוכח קרא (נחמיה ד): "ואנחנו עושים במלאכה וגו'", דמיניה מפיק בפ"ב דמגילה (דף כ:) דמעלות השחר יממא הוא. ואומר ר"ת: דהתם מיירי בתחילת שקיעה, והכא משתשקע – מסוף שקיעה, אחר שנכנסה חמה בעובי הרקיע. אבל תימה לר"י: דמאי פליגי? דהא ודאי משעת צאת הכוכבים הוי לילה כדפי'! וי"ל: דאמרינן לקמן "לא גדולים הנראים ביום ולא קטנים כו' אלא בינונים". והשתא פליגי, דלר' יהודה מספקא ליה בכל כוכבים הנראים משקיעת החמה עד שהכסיף העליון – אם הם בינונים אם לאו. וע"ק: דניחזי אנן באדם בינוני שילך מתחילת שקיעת החמה ד' מילין, כדאמר בפסחים! י"ל: דמספקא להו מהו אדם בינוני: **ואפילו** בת תרי כורי לא שרא לי. לית הילכתא הכי שיתבטל ממנו תורת כלי משום כובדו, דאמר בפ"ב דעירובין (דף קב. *ושם): ההיא שריתא דהוה בי רבי פדת דהוי שקלי לה עשרה ושדי לה אדשא, אמר: תורת כלי עליה. אפילו אביי גופיה לא קיבלה, כדאמרינן בפרק "כירה" (לקמן דף מה:): מנרתא שאני, שאדם קובע לה מקום. א"ל אביי: והרי כילת חתנים דאדם קובע לה מקום, ומותר לנטותה ולפורקה בשבת. אלא אמר אביי: כו', והא דאמרינן בשילהי "כל כתבי" (לקמן קכא:): פמוטות של בית רבי מותר לטלטלן בשבת. א"ל ר' זירא: בניטלין בידו אחת או בשתי ידים: אמר ליה: כאותן של בית אביך. פירוש: שהן גדולות. ולא כר"ח ורש"י שפירשו כאותן של בית אביך שהם קטנות. דהא מוכח בהדיא בפ' "כירה" (לקמן מו.) דמנורות דלית להו חדקי – דכולי עלמא שרי, דהיינו פמוטות גדולות: **וירד** ויטבול ויעלה. פי' בקונטרס: ובתוך כדי שירד ויעלה הוי לילה, וקשה: דלא ה"ל למינקט סימנא דטבילה אי לאו דאתא לאשמעינן דטבילה מעליא היא. ובירוש' משמע בפ' (ב') [א'] דברכות דמשיעלה מתחיל בין השמשות. והשתא קמ"ל דשפיר טבל, ועלה לו הערב שמש. *וה"ה דלפי זה הוה ליה למינקט: "הרוצה לידע בין השמשות דרבי יהודה", אלא שמא סבר כרב יוסף, דבין השמשות דרבי יהודה אינו מתחיל משתשקע החמה, אלא משהכסיף התחתון:
אלא

רבינו חננאל

והתחתון] כדי הילוך חצי שתות מיל (וכיון שפירשנו רבה) [ועו"ז שפירשנו דרבה] אמר ג' רביעי מיל ורב יוסף אמר ב' שלישי מיל. אמרו וחלופה בחלתא רבה נותן בה מדה ב' כור ורב יוסף נותן בה מדה ג' כור (ביותר) [יותר] אסור נמצא רב יוסף מוסיף על שיעורו של רבה ותרווייהו סבירא להו דכהאי שיעורא מטלטלא מליאה וריקנית ומנא היא והלכך שריא לטלטולה. אמר אביי בעי מיניה דמר הלכה למעשה ואפילו חלתא בת ארבעים סאה שהוא כור ושליש כור לא התיר לי כי האי דתנן בכלים פרק (י"ד) [ט"ו] כוורת הקש וכוורת הקנים ובור ספינה אלכסנדרית אף על פי שיש להם שולים ומחזיקות מ' סאה בלח שהן כוריים ביבש טהורים כלומר אינה כלי לפיכך אינה מקבלת טומאה והלכתא כרבה: **רבי** נחמיא אומר משתשקע החמה עד שיעור כדי הילוך חצי מיל זהו בין השמשות אמר רבי (נחמי') [חנינא] הרוצה לידע שיעורו של ר' נחמיה יניח חמה בראש הכרמל וירד וטבול בימא דטבריא ויעלה וזהו שיעור של ר' נחמיה א"ר

רב נסים גאון

כי בחליפת זה היום וכניסת יום אחר נתחלף הראיה ויהיה על זה האיש דין הטומאה כאילו ראה ב' ראיות ותמצא ברור זה הדבר בפרק ראשון מתוספתא ובין ומודה רבי יוסי שאם ראה אחת בין השמשות אע"פ שאין בה כדי טבילה וסיפוג ויש בידו ב' ראיות מפני שב' ימים חולקין אותו ומטילין אותו לחומרי ב' ימים וספק לטומאה ולדאלך*) אמרו מטילין לחומרי ב' ימים: **אמר** אביי ש"מ מי' גדאשא תילתא הוי דייק לה אביי מדברי המשנה והן מחזיקות ארבעים סאה בלח שהן כורים ביבש כי הכור ל' סאין כמו שתמצא בפרק המוכר את הספינה (ב"ב דף פו) כור בל' סאה בסלע אני מוכר לך והואיל והכלי שיכיל מן היבש כורים שהן ס' סאה לא יכיל מן הלח יותר ממ' סאה והם ב' שלישי הס' מכלל שהשליש הנשאר לא יכילנו הכלי עצמו שלא יהיה גדוש על פי המדה והואיל ובזמן

*) ולדאלך פירושו בלשון ערבי ולזה.

קלב א מיי' פכ"ה מהל' שבת הל' ו [ועי' בכ"מ] סמג לאוין סה טוש"ע א"ח סימן רח סעיף ב:
קלג ב מיי' פ"ג מהל' כלים הלכה ב:

עירובין יד: כלים פט"ו מ"א אהלות פ"ח מ"א

[עי' תוספות עירובין יד: ד"ה ש"מ וכו' הנ"מ לענין מקוה וממכר]

[עירובין יד: קאמר אביי הך מלתא אקרא דש"מ האי גודשא וכו' ונע"ק]

הגהות הגר"א
[א] גמרא (אע"פ) תז"מ:

גיר' רש"ל וקשה לרשב"א דלפי זה לא היה לו להזכיר עלייה אלא כשירד ויטבול ותו לא

הר"י לא גרס הגה תיבות בין השמשות אך גרס ומעריב שמשיה דר"י סוף דיבור ואח"כ מתחיל דיבור מישך שייך והוא נכון

אֶלָּא לַאֲכִילַת תְּרוּמָה, דְּלָא אָכְלִי כֹּהֲנִים תְּרוּמָה עַד דְּשָׁלֵים בֵּין הַשְּׁמָשׁוֹת דְּר' יוֹסֵי. א"ר יְהוּדָה אָמַר שְׁמוּאֵל: [א]כּוֹכָב אֶחָד – יוֹם, שְׁנַיִם – בֵּין הַשְּׁמָשׁוֹת, שְׁלֹשָׁה – לַיְלָה. תנ"ה: כּוֹכָב אֶחָד – יוֹם, שְׁנַיִם – בֵּין הַשְּׁמָשׁוֹת, שְׁלֹשָׁה – לַיְלָה. א"ר יוֹסֵי(א): לֹא כּוֹכָבִים גְּדוֹלִים הַנִּרְאִין בַּיּוֹם, וְלֹא כּוֹכָבִים קְטַנִּים שֶׁאֵין נִרְאִין אֶלָּא בַּלַּיְלָה, [ב]אֶלָּא בֵּינוֹנִים. א"ר יוֹסֵי בַּר' זְבִידָא: [ג]הָעוֹשֶׂה מְלָאכָה בִּשְׁנֵי בֵּין הַשְּׁמָשׁוֹת – חַיָּיב חַטָּאת מִמַּה נַּפְשָׁךְ. א"ל רָבָא לְשַׁמְעֵיהּ: [ד]אַתּוּן דְּלָא קִים לְכוּ בְּשִׁיעוּרָא דְּרַבָּנַן, אַדְּשִׁימְשָׁא אַרֵישׁ דִּיקְלֵי – אַתְלוּ שְׁרָגָא. בְּיוֹם הַמְּעוּנָּן מַאי? בְּמָתָא חֲזִי תַּרְנְגוֹלָא, בְּדַבְרָא – עוֹרְבֵי, אִי נָמֵי אַדְאָנֵי.§ ת"ר, שֵׁשׁ תְּקִיעוֹת תּוֹקְעִין עֶרֶב שַׁבָּת: רִאשׁוֹנָה לְהַבְטִיל אֶת הָעָם מִמְּלָאכָה שֶׁבַּשָּׂדוֹת, שְׁנִיָּה – לְהַבְטִיל עִיר וַחֲנוּיוֹת, שְׁלִישִׁית – לְהַדְלִיק אֶת הַנֵּר, דִּבְרֵי ר' נָתָן. ר' יְהוּדָה הַנָּשִׂיא אוֹמֵר: שְׁלִישִׁית לַחֲלוֹץ תְּפִילִּין. וְשׁוֹהֶה כְּדֵי צְלִיַּית דָּג קָטָן, אוֹ כְּדֵי לְהַדְבִּיק פַּת בַּתַּנּוּר, וְתוֹקֵעַ וּמֵרִיעַ וְתוֹקֵעַ וְשׁוֹבֵת. אָמַר רשב"ג: מַה נַּעֲשֶׂה לָהֶם לַבַּבְלִיִּים, שֶׁתּוֹקְעִין וּמְרִיעִין וְשׁוֹבְתִין – מִתּוֹךְ מְרִיעִין. "תּוֹקְעִין וּמְרִיעִין"?! הָווּ לְהוּ חֲמִשָּׁה! אֶלָּא: שֶׁתּוֹקְעִין, וְחוֹזְרִין וְתוֹקְעִין, וּמְרִיעִין וְשׁוֹבְתִין מִתּוֹךְ מְרִיעִין – מִנְהַג אֲבוֹתֵיהֶן בִּידֵיהֶן. מַתְנֵי לֵיהּ רַב יְהוּדָה לְרַב יִצְחָק בְּרֵיהּ: שְׁנִיָּה – לְהַדְלִיק אֶת הַנֵּר. כְּמַאן? לָא כְּר' נָתָן וְלָא כְּר' יְהוּדָה הַנָּשִׂיא! אֶלָּא: שְׁלִישִׁית לְהַדְלִיק אֶת הַנֵּר, כְּמַאן? כְּרַבִּי נָתָן. תָּנָא דְּבֵי רַבִּי יִשְׁמָעֵאל, [ה]שֵׁשׁ תְּקִיעוֹת תּוֹקְעִין ע"ש: הִתְחִיל לִתְקוֹעַ תְּקִיעָה רִאשׁוֹנָה – נִמְנְעוּ הָעוֹמְדִים בַּשָּׂדֶה מִלַּעֲדוֹר וּמִלַּחֲרוֹשׁ וּמִלַּעֲשׂוֹת כָּל מְלָאכָה שֶׁבַּשָּׂדוֹת, וְאֵין הַקְּרוֹבִין רַשָּׁאִין לִיכָּנֵס עַד שֶׁיָּבוֹאוּ רְחוֹקִין וְיִכָּנְסוּ כּוּלָּם כְּאֶחָד. וַעֲדַיִין חֲנוּיוֹת פְּתוּחוֹת וּתְרִיסִין מוּנָּחִין, הִתְחִיל לִתְקוֹעַ תְּקִיעָה שְׁנִיָּה – נִסְתַּלְּקוּ הַתְּרִיסִין וְנִנְעֲלוּ הַחֲנוּיוֹת, וַעֲדַיִין חַמִּין מוּנָּחִין עַל גַּבֵּי כִּירָה. וּקְדֵירוֹת מוּנָּחוֹת עַל גַּבֵּי כִּירָה הִתְחִיל לִתְקוֹעַ תְּקִיעָה שְׁלִישִׁית – סִילֵּק הַמְסַלֵּק, וְהִטְמִין הַמַּטְמִין, וְהִדְלִיק הַמַּדְלִיק. וְשׁוֹהֶה כְּדֵי צְלִיַּית דָּג קָטָן, אוֹ כְּדֵי לְהַדְבִּיק פַּת בַּתַּנּוּר, וְתוֹקֵעַ וּמֵרִיעַ וְתוֹקֵעַ וְשׁוֹבֵת. א"ר יוֹסֵי *(בַּר) חֲנִינָא: שָׁמַעְתִּי שֶׁאִם בָּא לְהַדְלִיק אַחַר שֵׁשׁ תְּקִיעוֹת – מַדְלִיק, שֶׁהֲרֵי נָתְנוּ חֲכָמִים שִׁיעוּר לַחַזַּן הַכְּנֶסֶת לְהוֹלִיךְ שׁוֹפָרוֹ לְבֵיתוֹ. אָמַר לוֹ: *אִם כֵּן, נָתַתָּ דְּבָרֶיךָ לְשִׁיעוּרִין! אֶלָּא: מָקוֹם צָנוּעַ יֵשׁ לוֹ לַחַזַּן הַכְּנֶסֶת בְּרֹאשׁ גַּגּוֹ, שֶׁשָּׁם מַנִּיחַ שׁוֹפָרוֹ, לְפִי שֶׁאֵין מְטַלְטְלִין לֹא אֶת הַשּׁוֹפָר וְלֹא אֶת הַחֲצוֹצְרוֹת. וְהָתַנְיָא: שׁוֹפָר מִיטַּלְטֵל וַחֲצוֹצְרוֹת אֵינָם מִיטַּלְטְלִין! אָמַר רַב (*יוֹסֵי): לָא קַשְׁיָא, כָּאן – בְּיָחִיד, כָּאן – בְּצִבּוּר. א"ל אַבַּיֵי: וּבְיָחִיד לְמַאי חֲזֵי – הוֹאִיל וְרָאוּי לְגַמַּע בּוֹ מַיִם לְתִינוֹק

רש"י

אֶלָּא לַאֲכִילָה. וְכוּלַּהּ מִילְּתָא דְּר' יוֹחָנָן לְחוּמְרָא. דְּלָא תֵּימָא כִּי שָׁלֵים בֵּין הַשְּׁמָשׁוֹת דְּר' יְהוּדָה לֵילְיָא הוּא, וְנֵיכוּל, וּמִמֵּילָא נַמִי לְעִנְיַן מוֹצָאֵי שַׁבָּת לָא אָמְרִינַן כְּר' יְהוּדָה, דְּנֵימָא דְּר' יוֹסֵי לֵילְיָא הוּא וְשָׁרֵי: בִּשְׁנֵי בֵּין הַשְּׁמָשׁוֹת. עֶרֶב שַׁבָּת וּמוֹצָאֵי שַׁבָּת דְּהֶעְלֵם אֶחָד – אֵין כָּאן עוֹד אָשָׁם תָּלוּי, אֶלָּא חַטָּאת: מִמַּה נַּפְשָׁךְ. אִי לֵילְיָא הוּא – חַיָּיב עַל עֶרֶב שַׁבָּת, וְשֶׁל מוֹצָאֵי שַׁבָּת אֵינוֹ כְּלוּם, וְאִי יְמָמָא הוּא – חַיָּיב עַל מוֹצָאֵי שַׁבָּת, וְאֵין שֶׁל עֶרֶב שַׁבָּת כְּלוּם. וּכְגוֹן דַּעֲבַד לֵיהּ כָּל בֵּין הַשְּׁמָשׁוֹת, דְּלֵיכָּא לְסַפּוּקֵי לְהַאי בִּתְחִילָּתוֹ וּלְהַאי בְּסוֹפוֹ: בְּשִׁיעוּרֵי דְּרַבָּנַן. בֵּין הַשְּׁמָשׁוֹת: אַתְלוּ. הַדְלִיקוּ אֶת הַנֵּר מִבְּעוֹד יוֹם: חֲזוּ תַּרְנְגוֹלִין. הַיּוֹשְׁבִים עַל הַקּוֹרוֹת מִבְּעוֹד יוֹם, וְכֵן הָעוֹרְבִים בַּשָּׂדֶה: אַדְאָנֵי. עֵשֶׂב הַקָּרוּי מלווי"א וְעָלִין שֶׁלּוֹ נוֹטִין לְצַד הַחַמָּה, שַׁחֲרִית כְּפוּפִין לַמִּזְרָח, וּבַחֲצִי הַיּוֹם זְקוּפִין, וְלָעֶרֶב כְּפוּפִים אֵצֶל לַמַּעֲרָב: שֵׁשׁ תְּקִיעוֹת. אַף הַתְּרוּעוֹת בַּמִּנְיָן, דְּסֵדֶר שֶׁלָּהֶן תְּקִיעָה תְּרוּעָה וּתְקִיעָה: לְהַבְטִיל מִמְּלָאכָה שֶׁבַּשָּׂדוֹת. וִיהֵא לָהֶן שָׁהוּת לִיכָּנֵס לָעִיר: לְהַבְטִיל הָעִיר. מִמְּלָאכָה: וְהַחֲנוּיוֹת. מִמִּקָּח וּמִמְכָּר: לַחֲלוֹץ תְּפִילִּין. וְהַדְלָקַת נֵר בָּרְבִיעִית: לְהַדְבִּיק פַּת בַּתַּנּוּר. וַעֲדַיִין יֵשׁ שָׁהוּת כְּדֵי שֶׁיִּקְרְמוּ פָּנֶיהָ, שֶׁהָיוּ מְמַהֲרִים הַתְּקִיעוֹת כְּדֵי לְהוֹסִיף מֵחוֹל עַל הַקֹּדֶשׁ: וְתוֹקֵעַ וּמֵרִיעַ וְתוֹקֵעַ. הֲרֵי שֵׁשׁ: וְשׁוֹבֵת. חָל שַׁבָּת עָלָיו: מִלַּעֲדוֹר. מִלַּחְפּוֹר: וְיִכָּנְסוּ כּוּלָּם כְּאֶחָד. שֶׁלֹּא יַחְשְׁדוּ הַנִּכְנָסִים בָּאַחֲרוֹנָה לוֹמַר שֶׁעָסְקוּ בִּמְלַאכְתָּן אַחַר שֶׁשָּׁמְעוּ קוֹל הַשּׁוֹפָר, שֶׁאֵין הַכֹּל מַכִּירִין מִי קְרוֹבִים וּמִי רְחוֹקִים: תְּרִיסִין. הֵן דַּלְתוֹת *הַחֲנוּיוֹת, וּמְסַלְּקִין אוֹתָן וּמַנִּיחָן ע"ג יְתֵדוֹת וּמוֹכְרִין עֲלֵיהֶן תַּבְלִין וּשְׁאָר דְּבָרִים, וְלָעֶרֶב מַחֲזִירִין אוֹתָן לַפְּתָחִים: חַמִּין. מַיִם חַמִּין לִמְזוֹג בָּהֶן יַיִן לִשְׁתּוֹת: סִילֵּק הַמְסַלֵּק. קְדֵרוֹת הָעֲשׂוּיוֹת לְהִסְתַּלֵּק לְמַאֲכַל הַלַּיְלָה: וְהִטְמִין הַמַּטְמִין. אֶת הָרְאוּיוֹת לְמָחָר: חַזַּן הַכְּנֶסֶת. שַׁמָּשׁ הַצִּיבּוּר: לְהוֹלִיךְ שׁוֹפָרוֹ לְבֵיתוֹ. שֶׁהָיָה גַּג מְיוּחָד בְּגוֹבַהּ הָעִיר וְאֶמְצָעִיתָהּ לִתְקוֹעַ שָׁם, וּמִשָּׁם מוֹלִיכוֹ לְבֵיתוֹ, אַלְמָא אַכַּתִּי לָא נְקִיט קְדוּשַּׁת שַׁבָּת עֲלַיְיהוּ: לְשִׁיעוּרִין. פְּעָמִים שֶׁבֵּיתוֹ קָרוֹב, פְּעָמִים שֶׁבֵּיתוֹ רָחוֹק: בְּרֹאשׁ גַּגּוֹ. שֶׁתָּקַע שָׁם: שֶׁאֵין מְטַלְטְלִין. אֲפִילּוּ בִּרְשׁוּת הַיָּחִיד: וְהָתַנְיָא שׁוֹפָר מִיטַּלְטֵל. לְפִי שֶׁכָּפוּף רֹאשׁוֹ, וְרָאוּי לִשְׁאוֹב בּוֹ מַיִם וְלִשְׁתּוֹת הַתִּינוֹק: חֲצוֹצְרוֹת. פְּשׁוּטָה, וְאֵינָהּ רְאוּיָה אֶלָּא לִתְקוֹעַ, וַהֲוֵי דָּבָר שֶׁמְּלַאכְתּוֹ לְאִיסּוּר, וְאָסוּר מִשּׁוּם מוּקְצֶה:

תוספות

אלא לענין אבילה. קשה: דמשום שיעורא פורתא דהוי כהרף עין לא הוי ליה למיפסק כר' יוסי! וליכא למימר דכהרף עין דר' יוסי אינו מיד אחר בין השמשות דר' יהודה ומתאחר הרבה אחריו. א"כ(ג), הא דאמר רב יהודה כו' בין השמשות דר' יהודה לרבי יוסי כהנים טובלים בו, מאי איריא "בין השמשות"? אחר בין השמשות דר' יהודה נמי כהנים טובלים לר' יוסי! וי"ל: דאינו מתאחר כל כך שיהא שיעור טבילה בינתיים. א"נ: ספק היה להם אם היה מתחיל מיד אחר דר' יהודה או מתאחר הרבה, ולהכי איצטריך למיפסק דלא אכלי כהנים תרומה עד דודאי שלים בין השמשות דרבי יוסי:

הקשה ה"ר פורת דבשבת גופיה הוה מצי למינקט הלכה כר' יהודה בע"ש, וכר' יוסי במוצאי שבת. וכן לענין תרומה הוה מצי למימר: הלכה כר' יהודה לענין טבילה, וכר' יוסי לענין אכילה. ונראה לר"י: דניחא ליה לאשמועינן רבותא, דאפי' בשבת דחמיר – מיקל ר' יוסי, ושרי לעשות מלאכה בבין השמשות דר' יהודה. ואפי' בתרומה דקיל משבת, או בתרומה דרבנן – מחמיר ר' יוסי, דלא אכלי כהנים עד דשלים בין השמשות דידיה:

רבי יהודה הנשיא **אומר** שלישית לחלוץ כו'. פירש"י: ורביעית להדליק את הנר, וכן משמע, דלא פליג אתרתי קמייתא. ועוד: דאמר בסמוך "שניה להדליק את הנר כמאן לא כר' נתן ולא כר' יהודה הנשיא". וליכא למימר נמי דאף לחלוץ תפילין קאמר, ומדליק נמי בשלישית, מדקאמר: אלא ג' להדליק את הנר כמאן – כר' נתן, משמע: ולא כר' יהודה הנשיא. וקשה: דבס"פ "ד' מיתות" (סנהדרין דף סח. ושם) גבי שחלה ר"א, ואותו היום ע"ש היה, ונכנס הורקנוס בנו לחלוץ תפילין, גער בו אביו ויצא בנזיפה. א"ל: היאך מניחין איסור סקילה ועוסקין באיסור שבות. אלמא: הדלקת נר קודם לחליצת תפילין, וי"ל: דשאני התם, דמשום חוליו איחרו מלהדליק את הנר לפי שהיו טרודין בו עד שהיה סמוך לחשכה. ולכך אמר יעסוק באיסור סקילה קודם. ואדרבה, משם יש ראיה דחליצת תפילין קודמת, מדרצה הורקנוס לחלוץ תפילין קודם הדלקה, ומסתמא היה יודע שכך היו רגילין לעשות:

שש תקיעות. כמו שפירש בקונטרס, שהיו תוקעין תקיעה תרועה תקיעה. אע"ג דקצת משמע לקמן דשלש ראשונות תקיעות הן, דקתני: התחיל לתקוע תקיעה שניה – לאו דווקא נקט תקיעה, וכן מוכיח בפרק "החליל" (סוכה דף נג: ושם) דתנן: אין פוחתין מכ"א תקיעות במקדש, ואין מוסיפין על מ"ח תקיעות. וחשיב באותן מ"ח שלש להבטיל את העם ממלאכה, ואמר בגמרא: מתניתין דלא כר' יהודה, דתניא, רבי יהודה אומר: הפוחת אל יפחות משבע, והמוסיף אל יוסיף על ט"ז. ומפרש: במאי פליגי, ר' יהודה סבר: תקיעה תרועה תקיעה אחת היא. ואם ג' להבטיל את העם ממלאכה כולן תקיעות, למה היה ר' יהודה מחשיבם כאחת:

והתניא שופר מטלטלין כו'. תימה לר"י: הא ע"כ האי דשרי לטלטל שופר – היינו לצורך גופו או לצורך מקומו, דמחמה לצל – אפי' ר' שמעון אסר, כמו שאפרש בסמוך, דשופר מלאכתו לאיסור הוא, וברייתא דלעיל דאסר להצניעו – היינו מחמה לצל, והוי כמו מרא שלא יגנב בפרק "כל הכלים" (לקמן דף קכד:) דהיינו טלטול שלא לצורך. ואומר ר"י: דמשמע ליה דאסר בברייתא דלעיל אפי' לצורך גופו ומקומו, מדקתני "לפי שאין מטלטלין" ולא קתני "לפי שאין מצניעין". וא"ת: וכיון דאיירי הכא הא דמטלטל שופר – היינו לצורך גופו, א"כ חצוצרות אמאי אין מטלטלין? וי"ל: דחצוצרות מוקצה יותר משופר, כמו שאפרש בסמוך. ומיהו, מתוך פירוש הקונטרס משמע דשופר הוי מלאכתו להיתר:

הא

רבינו חננאל

חייא הרוצה לראות בארה של מרים יעלה בראש הכרמל ויצפה ויראה כמין כברה בים וזהו בארה של מרים אמר רב יהודה אמר רב מעין המטלטל מטהר זה היא בארה של מרים: ואסיק' בתר דשלים ביה"ש דרבי יהודה מתחיל ביה"ש דר' יוסי הלכך לר' יוסי בבין השמשות דרבי יהודה טובלין הכהנים בו דהא עדיין לא העריב השמש ולכשיעריב השמש לר' יוסי נטהרו. א"ר יוחנן הלכתא כרבי יהודה לענין שבת דאמר משתשקע החמה קידש היום והלכתא כר' יוסי דאין כהנים טבולי יום אוכלין בתרומה עד שלים ביה"ש דר' יוסי אמר רב יהודה אמר שמואל תניא נמי הכי ר' יוסי אומר כוכב א' יום ב' ביה"ש ג' לילה ולא כוכבים גדולים הנראים ביום ולא כוכבים קטנים שאין נראין אלא בלילה אלא בינונים: **ירושלמי** בתחלת ברכות כמה כוכבים יצאו ויהיה לילה ר' פינחס בשם ר' אבא בר אבא כוכב א' ודאי יום שנים ספק ג' לילה. ואסיק' הדא דתימר באילין דלית אורחיהן למיחמי בימּמא ברם באילין דאורחיהן למיתחמי בימּמא לא משערינן בהו א"ר יוסי בר אבין ובלחוד דתיחמון תלתא כוכבים בר מן*) חד כוכבתא. אמר להו רבא לבני מחוזא**) אתון דלא קים לכו בשיעורא דרבנן אדאיכא שמשא בריש דיקלא אתלו [שרגא]. פירוש אדליקו שרגא. ביום המעונן במתא חזי תרנגולא אימתי עיילי בקינייהו בדברא חזי עורבי אימתי עיילו בקינייהו א"נ אדוני פי' ירקות השדה הן ידועין העלין שלהן בבוקר מתפתחין ומתפשטין ומבין השמשות מתכווצין ונראין כסתומין: **העושה** מלאכה בשני בין השמשות בע"ש ובשבת חייב חטאת. ממה נפשך אי ביה"ש יום הוא הנה נתחייב במלאכה שעשה בשבת אם לילה הוא נתחייב במלאכה שעשה בע"ש: **ת"ר** ו' תקיעות תוקעין בע"ש תקיעה אחת להבטיל המלאכה שבשדות שניה להבטיל מלאכה שבעיר ושבחנויות שלישית להדליק נר דברי ר' נתן ר' יהודה הנשיא אומר שלישית לחלוץ את התפילין כו' תנא דבי שמואל ו' תקיעות תוקעין ע"ש התחילו לתקוע ראשונה נמנעו הכל מלחרוש ומלעדור ומלזרוע ואין הקרובים נכנסין עד שיגיעו רחוקים הגיעו רחוקים נכנסו הכל ועדיין חנויות פתוחות ותריסין מונחים. תקע שניה נסתלקו התריסין וננעלו החנויות ועדיין החמין והקדירות מונחין ע"ג הכירה תקע שלישית סילק המסלק

*) לפנינו הגי' שם בירושלמי מן הלא כוכביא וכ"ה בחוסי הרשב"א כתי' ועי' בהגהות מיי' פ"ה מהל' שבת עוד גי' אחרת בירושלמי. **) וכן בספר דברי יוסף מביא ג"כ נוסחא זו בשם ש"ס כ"י.

עין משפט נר מצוה

קלד א ב מיי' פ"ה מהל' שבת הלכה ד ופ"ז מהל' תרומות הל' ב טוש"ע א"ח סי' רלה סעיף א:

קלה ג מיי' פ"ה מהל' שבת הלכה ד:

קלו ד טוש"ע א"ח סי' רסא סעיף ג:

קלז ה מיי' פ"ה מהל' שבת הלכה יח יט סמג עשין ל טוש"ע א"ח סימן רנו:

מסורת הש"ס

(חלונות) עי' ביצה לא: רש"י ד"ה תריסין

(נ"ל ברבי)

(מגילה יח: גיטין יז. ב"ב כט. חולין ט. לב.)

(נ"ל יוסף)

הגהות הב"ח

(א) גמ' אמר רבי יוסי בר אבין לא כוכבים: (ב) תוס' ד"ה אלא וכו' דא"כ הא דאמר:

גליון הש"ס

גמרא ושוהה כדי צליית דג. עי' בר"ן בפירקין בכלל חנוכה דף י ע"ב:

רב נסים גאון

ובזמן שהוא גדול יכיל ס' אע"פ שמן הלח לא יכיל אלא ארבעים נפקא לן מינה הא דאביי שהגדוש על פי המדה הוא שליש מה שתבילנו כלל המדה: **במאי** קמיפלגי **) בפלוגתא דר' אליעזר והורקנוס בנו. תמצא פירוש דבריהם במסכת סנהדרין בסוף פרק ד' מיתות (דף סח) תניא כשחלה ר' אליעזר נכנסו חכמי ישראל אצלו והוא יושב בקינוף שלו והן יושבין בטריקלין שלו אותו היום ערב שבת היה ונכנס הורקנוס בנו לחלוץ תפליו גער בו אביו ויצא בנזיפה אמר להן חבריו של אבא כמדומה שדעתו של אבא נטרפה אמר לו דעתך ודעת אמך נטרפה היאך מניחין איסור סקילה ועוסקים באיסור שבות סבר ר' אליעזר הדלקת הנר שהוא איסור סקילה קודמת לחליצת תפילין שהוא איסור שבות וצריך להקדים הדלקת הנר ואחר כן יחלוץ והורקנוס בנו סבר חליצת תפילין קודמת להדלקת הנר ותמצא בפרק במה מדליקין דבני מערבא מעשה בר' אליעזר שהיה גוסס בערב שבת עם חשיכה ונכנס הורקנוס בנו לחלוץ תפליו אמר לו בני הנחת מצות הנר שהיא שבות וחייבין עליה כרת

**) נראה דחסר כאן בדעת הגאון וצריך לציין על הברייתא דשלישית להדליק את הנר ר"י הנשיא אומר שלישית לחלוץ תפילין וע"ז אמר דקמפלגי בפלוגתא דר"א והורקנוס בנו וכו' ועי' תוס' ד"ה ר"י.

לְתִינוֹק, בְּצִיבּוּר נַמִּי חֲזִי – לְגַמַּע לְתִינוֹק עָנִי! וְתוּ, הָא דְּתַנְיָא: כְּשֵׁם שֶׁמְּטַלְטְלִין אֶת הַשּׁוֹפָר – כָּךְ מְטַלְטְלִין אֶת חֲצוֹצְרוֹת, מַנִּי? אֶלָּא, לָא קַשְׁיָא, הָא – ר' יְהוּדָה, הָא – א"ר שִׁמְעוֹן, הָא – *ר' נְחֶמְיָה. וּמַאי שׁוֹפָר – נַמִּי חֲצוֹצְרוֹת, כִּדְרַב חִסְדָּא. דְּא"ר חִסְדָּא: *הָנֵי תְּלָת מִילֵּי אִשְׁתַּנִּי שְׁמַיְיהוּ מִכִּי חָרַב בֵּית הַמִּקְדָּשׁ: חֲצוֹצְרָתָא שׁוֹפָרָא, שׁוֹפָרָא חֲצוֹצְרָתָא. לְמַאי נָפְקָא מִינָּהּ – לְשׁוֹפָר שֶׁל רֹאשׁ הַשָּׁנָה. עֲרָבָה צַפְצָפָה, צַפְצָפָה עֲרָבָה. לְמַאי נ"מ – לְלוּלָב. פְּתוֹרָה פְּתוֹרְתָּא, פְּתוֹרְתָּא פְּתוֹרָה, לְמַאי נ"מ – לְמִקָּח וּמִמְכָּר. אָמַר אַבַּיֵי: אַף אָנוּ נֹאמַר, הוּבְלִילָא בֵּי כָּסֵי, בֵּי כָּסֵי הוּבְלִילָא. לְמַאי נָפְקָא מִינָּהּ – *לְמַחַט שֶׁנִּמְצֵאת בְּעוֹבִי בֵּית הַכּוֹסוֹת, דְּמִצַּד אֶחָד כְּשֵׁרָה וּמִשְּׁנֵי צְדָדִים טְרֵיפָה. אָמַר רַב אַשִׁי: *אַף אָנוּ נֹאמַר, בָּבֶל *בּוֹרְסִיף, בּוֹרְסִיף בָּבֶל. לְמַאי

רש"י

לְתִינוֹק עָנִי. שֶׁעַל הַצִּיבּוּר לְפַרְנְסוֹ: **הָא ר' יְהוּדָה.** שׁוֹפָר מִיטַּלְטֵל וַחֲצוֹצְרוֹת אֵינָן מִיטַּלְטְלִין, דְּמוּקְצֶה הוּא. אֲבָל שׁוֹפָר – תּוֹרַת כְּלִי עָלָיו, כִּדְאָמְרַן לְעֵיל: **הָא.** דְּקָתָנֵי תַּרְוַיְיהוּ מִטַּלְטְלִין – ר' שִׁמְעוֹן הִיא, דְּלֵית לֵיהּ מוּקְצֶה: **הָא.** דְּקָתָנֵי: אַף שׁוֹפָר אֵין מְטַלְטְלִין – ר' נְחֶמְיָה, דְּאָמַר: *אֲפִי' תַּרְווֹד אֲפִי' טַלִּית אֵין נִיטָּלִין אֶלָּא לְצוֹרֶךְ תַּשְׁמִישׁוֹ הַמְיוּחָד, וְעִיקַּר שׁוֹפָר לָאו לִגְמוֹעַ מַיִם קָאֵי: **וּמַאי שׁוֹפָר.** דְּקָתָנֵי בְּהַהִיא דְּר' נְחֶמְיָה דְּאַקְדְּמֵית בָּהּ לַחֲצוֹצְרוֹת לְאִיסּוּרָא. וְכֵיוָן דְּתָנֵי: אֵין מְטַלְטְלִין אֶת הַשּׁוֹפָר, תּוּ לָא צָרִיךְ לְמִתְנֵי חֲצוֹצְרוֹת, דְּכ"ש הִיא, הוֹאִיל וְאֵינוֹ רָאוּי לְגַמַּע בּוֹ תִּינוֹק. אֶלָּא שׁוֹפָר דְּתָנָא רֵישָׁא הוּא חֲצוֹצְרוֹת, וַחֲצוֹצְרוֹת דְּתָנָא בְּסֵיפָא הוּא שׁוֹפָר. דְּאִישְׁתַּנּוּ שְׁמַיְיהוּ כִּדְרַב חִסְדָּא: **לְשׁוֹפָר שֶׁל רֹאשׁ הַשָּׁנָה.** אֵין תּוֹקְעִין אֶלָּא בְּאוֹתוֹ שֶׁעַם הָאָרֶץ קוֹרִין חֲצוֹצְרוֹת, וְהוּא שׁוֹפָר. אוֹ אִם בָּא עַם הָאָרֶץ לִשְׁאוֹל בַּמֶּה יִתְקַע – אוֹמְרִים לוֹ: בַּחֲצוֹצְרוֹת: **צַפְצָפָה.** פְּסוּלָה לְלוּלָב, וְעָלֶה שֶׁלָּהּ עָגוֹל וְקָנֶה שֶׁלָּהּ לָבָן, כִּדְאָמְרַן בְּסוּכָּה: **פְּתוֹרָה.** מִתְּחִילָּה הָיוּ קוֹרִין לְגָדוֹל פְּתוֹרָה וְלִקְטַנָּה פְּתוֹרְתָּא, וְעַכְשָׁיו נִשְׁתַּנּוּ: **אַף אָנוּ נֹאמַר.** אַף אָנוּ יְכוֹלִים לְהוֹסִיף אַדְּרַב חִסְדָּא לוֹמַר שֶׁגַּם זֶה נִשְׁתַּנָּה: **הוּבְלִילָא.** מִתְּחִילָּה הָיוּ קוֹרִין לְהֶמְסֵס הוּבְלִילָא, וּלְבֵית הַכּוֹסוֹת בֵּי כָּסֵי, וְעַכְשָׁיו נִשְׁתַּנּוּ: **הֶמְסֵס.** הוּא הַסָּמוּךְ לְבֵית הַכּוֹסוֹת, עָשׂוּי סְגַלְגַּל כְּמִין כַּדּוּר, וּבְתוֹכוֹ קְלִיפוֹת קְלִיפוֹת הַרְבֵּה כְּגַלְגַּל שֶׁל רֵיחַיִם, וְקוֹרִין לינפי"ל, וְדוֹפְנוֹ דַּק מְאֹד: **בֵּית הַכּוֹסוֹת.** סוֹף הַכֶּרֶס, שֶׁקּוֹרִין פאנצ"א, וְיֵשׁ בּוֹ עוֹבִי שֶׁקּוֹרִין דובלו"ן, וְתוֹכוֹ עָשׂוּי כְּמִין כּוֹס. עוֹבִי בֵּית הַכּוֹסוֹת – דּוֹפֶן כְּפוּלָה, וּדְבוּקִין הַכְּפָלִים זֶה בָּזֶה בְּשׁוּמָּן: **מִצַּד א'.** שֶׁלֹּא נִיקַּב אֶלָּא א' מִן הַכְּפָלִים – כְּשֵׁרָה, שֶׁחֲבֵירוֹ סוֹתְמוֹ: **מִב' צְדָדִין.** שֶׁנִּיקְּבוּ שְׁנֵיהֶם טְרֵיפָה. וּבְבֵית הַכּוֹסוֹת הוּא דְּאִיכָּא לְפָלוּגֵי בֵּין צַד א' לִשְׁנֵי צְדָדִין, אֲבָל בְּהֶמְסֵס, אֲפִי' מִצַּד א' שֶׁלֹּא נִרְאֶה הַנֶּקֶב לַחוּץ – אֵין זוֹ סְתִימָה, לְפִי שֶׁהַדּוֹפֶן דַּק מְאֹד: לְגִיטֵּי

תוספות

הא ר' יהודה. לר' יהודה מטלטלין שופר. אע"ג דמלאכתו לאיסור – שרי לטלטלו לצורך גופו ומקומו, כדמוכח בפרק "כל הכלים" (לקמן קכד:), דאמר רב: מכבדות של מילתא מותר לטלטל בשבת, ושל תמרה אסור. פירוש: לפי שמלאכתו לאיסור. ור' אלעזר אמר: אף של תמרה. במאי עסקינן? אילימא לצורך גופו ומקומו – בהא לימא רב של תמרה לא? והא רב כרבא ס"ל דשרי דבר שמלאכתו לאיסור לצורך גופו ומקומו. ואי ר' יהודה אסר – והא רב סבר כר' יהודה דאית ליה מוקצה. ובפרק "תולין" (לקמן דף קמא: ושם) גבי הא דפריך לאביי [ורבא] ממנעל שעל גב האימום משמע בהדיא דשרי ר"י בדבר שמלאכתו לאיסור לצורך גופו ומקומו. ותניא נמי בפרק "כירה" (לקמן דף מד.) ר' יהודה אומר: כל הנרות של מתכת מטלטלין חוץ מן הנר שהדליקו בו בשבת אבל בחצוצרות אסר משום דכיון דלא חזי למלאכת היתר אלא מעט מקצה ליה לגמרי ממלאכת היתר והוי כמטה שיחדה למעות והניח עליה מעות דאמר רב יהודה א"ר (לקמן דף מד:) דאסור לטלטלה °ומוקי לה כר' יהודה וכמו קינה של תרנגולים דמשמע לקמן (דף מה:) °דאסור לר' יהודה אפי' לצורך גופו ומקומו: **הא** ר' שמעון. דלית ליה מוקצה אלא מוקצה מחמת חסרון כיס. ודוקא לצורך גופו או מקומו הוא דשרי, אבל מחמה לצל – מודה ר"ש דאסור, דתנן בפרק "כל הכלים" (לקמן דף קכג:): נוטל אדם את הקורנס לפצע בו את האגוזים, קורדום לחתוך בו דבילה – אבל מחמה לצל אסור. וכר' שמעון היא, מדקתני סיפא: מחט של יד ליטול בו את הקוץ. וב"הנחנקין" (סנהדרין דף פד:) מוקי לה כר' שמעון. ובשילהי "האורג" (לקמן קז.) נמי מוכח מינה דמפיס מורסא מותר לכתחילה, וההיא דמפיס מורסא מוקמא כר"ש בריש פ' "ח' שרצים" (לקמן דף קז:). ובפ' בתרא (לקמן קנז.) נמי פשיטא לן דמתניתין דכל הכלים אתיא כר"ש, דקאמר: דמוקצה מחמת חסרון כיס מודה ר"ש, דתנן: כל הכלים ניטלין בשבת חוץ ממסר הגדול ויתד של מחרישה. וגבי מכבדות של תמרה (דף קכד:) דפריך: אלא מחמה לצל בהא לימא ר' אלעזר אף של תמרה?! ואי שרי ר"ש אף מחמה לצל – מאי קושיא? דילמא ר' אלעזר כר"ש ס"ל:

הא ר' נחמיה. ההיא דאסרה שופר וחצוצרות. דתניא בפרק "חבית" (לקמן דף קמו.): אפי' תרווד אפילו טלית אפי' סכין – אין נוטלין אלא לצורך תשמישן. ופי' בקונטרס: תשמישן המיוחד להם. ומשמע לפי' דכלי שמלאכתו לאיסור – אסור לטלטלו לשום צורך, דהא מיוחד למלאכת איסור, ואנן בעינן שיהא מיוחד לצורך אותו דבר שנוטלו בשבת, וקשה לר"ת: דאמר בפרק "חבית" (ג"ז שם): חותלות של תמרים ושל גרוגרות – מתיר, אבל לא מפקיע ולא חותך, ומוקי לה כר' נחמיה. וכן בפרק "בכל מערבין" (עירובין דף לה. ושם): הכא במנעול דקטיר במיתנא ובעי סכינא למיפסקיה, ומוקי כר' נחמיה. ואמאי אסר בסכין כיון שהוא עומד ומיוחד לחתיכה? והר"ר שמעון הזקן הקשה לפירוש הקונטרס: דהיכי קאמר רבה בפרק "כל הכלים" (לקמן דף קכד.) ואתא ר' נחמיה למימר דאפי' כלי שמלאכתו להיתר לצורך גופו או לצורך מקומו – אין, מחמה לצל – לא. היכי שרי לצורך מקומו? והלא אין זה תשמיש המיוחד לו! *ודוחק ר"ת לומר לפי' הקונטרס: דקערות אחר שאכלו בהן, דדרך להסירן כל שעה – חשיב צורך מקומו תשמיש המיוחד לו. ונראה לר"ת: דלא שרי ר' נחמיה אלא תשמיש הרגיל לעשות בו בחול, אפי' אינו תשמיש המיוחד לו, ואפי' דבר שמלאכתו לאיסור שרי, כיון שדרך אותו תשמיש לעשות ממנו בחול – כגון קורנס לפצע בו את האגוזים, וקורדום לחתוך בו את הדבילה – והיינו לצורך תשמישו דקאמר, כלומר: מה שרגיל לעשות בו בחול, ולא אתא לאפוקי אלא מחמה לצל, וכגון תשמיש שאינו רגיל לחתוך, כגון חותלות של תמרים בסכין או מנעול דקטיר במיתנא. ושופר נמי, אין דרך בחול לגמע בו מים לתינוק. והסקה בכלים דתניא בפרק "כל הכלים" (לקמן דף קכד:*): אין מסיקין בכלים כו', ומוקי לה כר' נחמיה. ומביא ר"ת ראיה מפרק "כל הכלים" (ג"ז שם) דתנן: כל הכלים ניטלין לצורך ושלא לצורך, ר' נחמיה אומר: אין ניטלין אלא לצורך. ומפרש רבה בגמרא: דבר שמלאכתו להיתר – לצורך גופו ולצורך מקומו, דבר שמלאכתו לאיסור – לצורך גופו – אין, לצורך מקומו – לא. והשתא מה לו להזכיר דבר שמלאכתו לאיסור, כיון דמתניתין לא איירי אלא במלאכתו להיתר? אלא ודאי משום ר' נחמיה נקטיה, דבעי למימר: ואתא ר' נחמיה למימר דאפי' דבר שמלאכתו להיתר כו'. ומשום דמשוה ר' נחמיה מלאכתו להיתר למלאכתו לאיסור – נקט מלאכתו לאיסור, דלר' נחמיה תרוייהו: לצורך גופו – שרי, ולצורך מקומו – לא. ולרבא – תרוייהו לצורך גופו ומקומו שרי, מחמה לצל – לא. ולשון אפי' משמע נמי הכי:

למחט שנמצאת. דתניא ב"אלו טרפות" (חולין דף נ. ושם) וב"המדיר" (כתובות דף עו:): מצד אחד – כשירה, מב' צדדין – טרפה. ופי' בקונטרס: בעובי בית הכוסות הוא דאיכא לפלוגי הכי, אבל בהמסס – אפי' מצד אחד, שלא נראה הנקב לחוץ – טרפה, דאין זו סתימה. והקשה ה"ר אליעזר ממי"ץ, דהא תנן: *"המסס ובית הכוסות שניקבו לחוץ" משמע דבהמסס נמי לא מיטרפה אלא בנקב מפולש! ואור"י: דהאי "לחוץ" – לא לגמרי "לחוץ", אלא כלומר: לצד חוץ, לאפוקי ניקבו זה לתוך זה דכשירה. כדקתני בתר הכי, וקמ"ל דמצד אחד כשירה אע"ג דניקב עור אחד שלם. אבל הא דקתני: מב' צדדין טרפה – אין חידוש. אי נמי: מב' צדדין טרפה – נמי חידוש הוא, דקמ"ל: אע"פ שסוכך על המסס, וס"ד שמגין כמו חלחולת שנקבה ויריכים מעמידין אותה דכשירה – קמ"ל דהכא טרפה. ור"ת אומר: דבהמסס נמי מצד אחד כשירה, ופשיטא דלא הויא טרפה אא"כ ניקב נקב מפולש לחוץ, דאין סברא שיהיה טרפה בשום מקום אלא בנקב מפולש. והא דנקט בברייתא: "בית הכוסות" – לאשמועינן מצד אחד כשירה, אע"ג דניקב עור שלם. ונפקא מינה הא דשמעינן דאישתני שמייהו אע"ג דדינם שוה, דאי לא אשמעינן – ה"א דהאי דקתני "מחט שנמצאת בעובי בית הכוסות" – היינו דקרו השתא בי כסי, שאין לו אלא עור אחד, והוה אתי למימר דדוקא בההוא מצד אחד כשירה. אבל במאי דקרו הובלילא – אפי' מצד אחד טרפה, כיון שניקב עור אחד שלם. לכך אשמעינן דאישתני שמייהו, דאפי' בהובלילא מצד אחד כשירה. ועוד אור"י: דמלינו למימר כפי' רש"י, דבהמסס – אפי' מצד אחד טרפה, דחיישינן שמא ניקב לחוץ וחזר והבריא. כמו ישב לו קוץ בוושט*, דהכי הלכתא התם: דחיישינן שמא הבריא, וחוששין לספק דרוסה. ואפי' למאן דלא חייש התם בקוץ – שמא במחט שהוא דק חיים. והא דבעי ב"אלו טרפות" ניקבו לחוץ, היינו כגון דידעינן דשוב לא הבריא – כגון שאכלה מחט בפנינו ושחטוה מיד: נפקא

עין משפט נר מצוה

קלח א מיי' פכ"ה מהל' שבת הל' ג סמג לאוין סה טוש"ע א"ח סי' שח סעיף ג ד:

סוכה לד. ע"ש

[עי' בערוך ערך אנגרא ובסנהדרין קט. מאי בורסיף וכו']

רבינו חננאל

והטמין המטמין והדליק המדליק ושוהה כדי לצלות דג קטן או כדי להדביק פת בתנור ותוקע ומריע ותוקע ושובת וכו' ואסיק' מקום צנוע יש בראש גגו ששם מניח את השופר שאין מטלטלין לא את השופר ולא את חצוצרות ותניא מטלטלין שופר וחצוצרות ותניא מטלטלין שופר ולא חצוצרות ואוקימנא להו הא ר' יהודה הא ר' שמעון והא ר' נחמיה:

הדרן עלך במה מדליקין

ועוד קשה הא דא"ל אביי (שם) לרבה אליבא דר"נ קערות היכי מטלטלים להו ולרבה דידיה מי ניחא הא לא מטלטלי אלא לתשמיש המיוחד לו ודוחק ר"ת כו' [ת"י]

רב נסים גאון

ובאת לחלוץ תפילין שהן רשות ואינן אלא מצוה: **למאי** נפקא מינה למחט שנמצאת בעובי בית הכוסות תגד אצל דלך *) בפרק אלו טריפות (דף נ) ובכתובות בפ' המדיר (דף עו)

*) עירושו בערבי תמצא עיקר זה:

מסורת הש"ס

[לקמן קמו.]

[לקמן קכג. קכד. קמו. עירובין לה. ביצה לב.]

[כתובות עו: חולין מח: נ:]

[סוכה לד. ע"ש]

[ושם]

[חולין מב.]

חולין מג:

גליון הש"ס

תוס' ד"ה הא ר' יהודה וכו' ומוקי לה כר' יהודה. וע"ש ע"ב תוס' ד"ה הא אין עליה: בא"ד דאסור לר' יהודה. עי' פירש"י שם ד"ה אלא לתרנגולין:

[דף עח:]

א א ב ג מיי' פ"ג מהל' שבת הלכה ד ה סמג לאוין סה טוש"ע א"ח סי' רנג סעיף א:

לְמַאי נָפְקָא מִינָּהּ – לְגִיטֵּי נָשִׁים.§

הדרן עלך במה מדליקין

כִּירָה אשֶׁהִסִּיקוּהָ בְּקַשׁ וּבִגְבָבָא – נוֹתְנִים עָלֶיהָ תַּבְשִׁיל. בַּגֶּפֶת וּבָעֵצִים – לֹא יִתֵּן עַד שֶׁיִּגְרוֹף, אוֹ עַד שֶׁיִּתֵּן אֶת הָאֵפֶר. בֵּית שַׁמַּאי אוֹמְרִים, חַמִּין אֲבָל לֹא תַּבְשִׁיל וּבֵית הִלֵּל אוֹמְרִים, חַמִּין וְתַבְשִׁיל. בֵּית שַׁמַּאי אוֹמְרִים, נוֹטְלִין אֲבָל לֹא מַחֲזִירִין וּבֵית הִלֵּל אוֹמְרִים, אַף מַחֲזִירִין.§ **גמ'** אִיבַּעְיָא לְהוּ: הַאי 'לֹא יִתֵּן' – לֹא יַחֲזִיר הוּא, אֲבָל לַשְׁהוֹת – מַשְׁהִין אַף עַל פִּי שֶׁאֵינוֹ גָּרוּף וְאֵינוֹ קָטוּם, וּמַנִּי – חֲנַנְיָה הִיא. דְּתַנְיָא, *חֲנַנְיָה אוֹמֵר: בכָּל שֶׁהוּא כְּמַאֲכַל בֶּן דְּרוּסַאי – מוּתָּר לְשַׁהוֹתוֹ עַל גַּבֵּי כִּירָה, אע"פ שֶׁאֵינוֹ גָּרוּף וְאֵינוֹ קָטוּם; אוֹ דִילְמָא: גלַשְׁהוֹת תְּנַן, וְאִי גָּרוּף וְקָטוּם – אִין, אִי לָא – לָא, וְכָל שֶׁכֵּן לְהַחֲזִיר. ת"ש, מִדְּקָתָנֵי תְּרֵי בָּבֵי בְּמַתְנִי': ב"ש אוֹמְרִים: חַמִּין אֲבָל לֹא תַּבְשִׁיל, וּבֵית הִלֵּל אוֹמְרִים: חַמִּין וְתַבְשִׁיל. ב"ש אוֹמְרִים: נוֹטְלִין אֲבָל לֹא מַחֲזִירִין, וּב"ה אוֹמְרִים: אַף מַחֲזִירִין. אִי אָמְרַתְּ בִּשְׁלָמָא לַשְׁהוֹת תְּנַן – הָכִי קָתָנֵי: כִּירָה שֶׁהִסִּיקוּהָ בְּקַשׁ וּבִגְבָבָא – מַשְׁהִין עָלֶיהָ תַּבְשִׁיל, בַּגֶּפֶת וּבָעֵצִים – לֹא יַשְׁהֶא עַד שֶׁיִּגְרוֹף אוֹ עַד שֶׁיִּתֵּן אֵפֶר, וּמָה הֵן מַשְׁהִין? בֵּית שַׁמַּאי אוֹמְרִים: חַמִּין אֲבָל לֹא תַּבְשִׁיל, וּב"ה אוֹמְרִים: חַמִּין וְתַבְשִׁיל. וְכִי הֵיכִי דִּפְלִיגִי בְּלַשְׁהוֹת – פְּלִיגִי נַמִי בְּלְהַחֲזִיר, שֶׁבֵּית שַׁמַּאי אוֹמְרִים: נוֹטְלִין אֲבָל לֹא מַחֲזִירִין, וּבֵית הִלֵּל אוֹמְרִים: אַף מַחֲזִירִין. אֶלָּא אִי אָמְרַתְּ לְהַחֲזִיר תְּנַן, הָכִי קָתָנֵי: כִּירָה שֶׁהִסִּיקוּהָ בְּקַשׁ וּבִגְבָבָא – מַחֲזִירִין עָלֶיהָ תַּבְשִׁיל, בַּגֶּפֶת וּבָעֵצִים – לֹא יַחֲזִיר עַד שֶׁיִּגְרוֹף אוֹ עַד שֶׁיִּתֵּן אֵפֶר. וּמָה הֵן מַחֲזִירִין? בֵּית שַׁמַּאי אוֹמְרִים: חַמִּין אֲבָל לֹא תַּבְשִׁיל, וּבֵית הִלֵּל אוֹמְרִים: חַמִּין וְתַבְשִׁיל. בֵּית שַׁמַּאי אוֹמְרִים: נוֹטְלִין אֲבָל לֹא מַחֲזִירִין, וּבֵית הִלֵּל אוֹמְרִים: אַף מַחֲזִירִין. הָא *תּוּ לָמָּה לִי?! לְעוֹלָם

רש"י

לְגִיטֵּי נָשִׁים. דְּקַיְימָא לָן: בְּנֵי בָּבֶל בְּקִיאִין שֶׁצָּרִיךְ לִכְתּוֹב גֵּט לִשְׁמָהּ וְהַמֵּבִיא גֵּט מִשָּׁם אֵין צָרִיךְ לוֹמַר בְּפָנַי נִכְתַּב וּבְפָנַי נֶחְתַּם, וּבְנֵי שְׁאָר אֲרָצוֹת אֵין בְּקִיאִין וְצָרִיךְ. וְעַכְשָׁיו בְּנֵי בּוֹרְסִיף הִיא בָּבֶל וּבָבֶל שֶׁל עַכְשָׁיו הִיא בּוֹרְסִיף וְהֵן עַמֵּי הָאָרֶץ כִּדְאָמְרִינַן בְּעָלְמָא (סנהדרין דף קט.): בּוֹר שָׁאוּבִי שֶׁנִּטְּלוּ מֵימָיו. וַאֲנִי אוֹמֵר: "נָפְקָא מִינָּהּ לְגִיטֵּי נָשִׁים" – לְעִנְיַן שִׁינָּה שְׁמוֹ וּשְׁמָהּ וְשֵׁם עִירוֹ וְעִירָהּ פָּסוּל וְצָרִיךְ לִכְתּוֹב שֵׁם שֶׁל עַכְשָׁיו:

הדרן עלך במה מדליקין

כִּירָה. עֲשׂוּיָה כְּעֵין קְדֵירָה, וְנוֹתְנִין קְדֵירָה לְתוֹכָהּ: **קַשׁ.** זַנְבוֹת הַשִּׁבּוֹלִין: **גְּבָבָא.** הַנִּגְבָּב מִן הַשָּׂדֶה, אִישְׁטוּבְל"א: **גֶּפֶת.** פְּסוֹלֶת שֶׁל שׁוּמְשְׁמִין שֶׁהוֹצִיא שַׁמְנָן: **עַד שֶׁיִּגְרוֹף.** הַגֶּחָלִים, מִשּׁוּם דְּמוֹסִיף הֶבֶל. וְטַעְמָא פָּרֵישְׁנָא בַּפֶּרֶק דִּלְעֵיל*, שֶׁמָּא יַחְתֶּה בַּגֶּחָלִים: **אוֹ עַד שֶׁיִּתֵּן אֵפֶר.** עַל גַּבֵּי גֶּחָלִים לְכַסּוֹתָם וּלְכַנְּסָם: **בֵּית שַׁמַּאי אוֹמְרִים.** נוֹתְנִין עָלֶיהָ חַמִּין אַחַר שֶׁגְּרָפָהּ, דְּלָא צְרִיכִי לְבִשּׁוּלֵי, דְּלֵיכָּא לְמִגְזַר שֶׁמָּא יַחְתֶּה: **אֲבָל לֹא תַּבְשִׁיל.** דְּנִיחָא לֵיהּ בְּבִשּׁוּלֵיהּ, וְאָתֵי לְאַחְתּוּיֵי. א"נ, נִתְקַיְּימָה מַחֲשַׁבְתּוֹ וּמֶיחֱזֵי כִּמְבַשֵּׁל(א): **לֹא מַחֲזִירִין.** בְּשַׁבָּת, דְּמֶיחֱזֵי כִּמְבַשֵּׁל: **אַף מַחֲזִירִין.** הוֹאִיל וְגָרוּף:

גמ' קָטוּם. הַיְינוּ נָתַן אֵפֶר עַל הַגֶּחָלִים. דְּאֵפֶר מְתַרְגְּמִינַן קִיטְמָא: **תְּרֵי בָּבֵי.** בֵּית שַׁמַּאי אוֹמְרִים חַמִּין וכו', וְתוּ תָּנָא בָּבָא אַחֲרִיתִי: נוֹטְלִין וְלֹא מַחֲזִירִין: **וּמָה הֵן מַשְׁהִין.** בְּגָרוּף וְקָטוּם: **פְּלִיגִי נַמִי בְּלְהַחֲזִיר.** אֶת הַמּוּתָּר לְשַׁהוֹת, כְּגוֹן חַמִּין לְבֵית שַׁמַּאי וְחַמִּין וְתַבְשִׁיל לְב"ה: **אֶלָּא אִי אָמְרַתְּ לְהַחֲזִיר תְּנַן הָכִי קָתָנֵי.** כְּלוֹמַר ע"כ הָכִי מְפָרְשָׁא: **ב"ש אוֹמְרִים נוֹטְלִין וְלֹא מַחֲזִירִין.** ע"כ אַתַּבְשִׁיל קָיְימִי, דְּהָא שָׁרוּ בְּחַמִּין: **הָא תּוּ לָמָּה לִי.** הָא תָּנָא לֵיהּ רֵישָׁא: **אֲבָל לֹא תַּבְשִׁיל:** לְעוֹלָם

תוספות

נפקא מינה לגיטי נשים. מה שפי' בקונטרס: לענין שינה שם עירו ושם עירה – אין נראה לרשב"א, דבבל הוא שם מדינה ולא שם העיר, כדאמר בפרק "עשרה יוחסין" (קדושין דף עא.): כל הארצות עיסה לארץ ישראל, וארץ ישראל עיסה לבבל. וקאמר נמי התם: *עד היכן היא בבל. ולא אשכחן שום דוכתא עיר ששמה בבל, אלא מדינה היא, ואין כותבין שם מדינה בגט:

הדרן עלך במה מדליקין

כירה שהסיקוה בקש ובגבבא. נראה לר"י: דקש היינו זנבות השבולים שנשאר בשדה, הנקרא אשטובל"א בלעז. ותבן הוא הנקצר עם השבולת. דהכי משמע לקמן בפרק "שואל" (לקמן דף קנ:) דקאמר: בשלמא קש – משכחת לה במחובר, אלא תבן היכי משכחת לה? ומסיק: בתבנא סריא. והא דאמר בריש "המקבל" (בבא מציעא דף קג.) גבי מקום שנהגו לקצור אינו רשאי לעקור, משום דאמר ניחא לי דתיתבן ארעאי, הוה ליה למימר דתיתקש, דהנשאר בקרקע נקרא קש, כדפירש רש"י. אלא משום דתיתבן משמע טפי לשון זיבול, נקט ליה*: **לא** יתן עד שיגרוף. פירש בקונטרס: משום תוספת הבל. ואין נראה לר"י, דאפילו גרופה וקטומה היא מוספת הבל יותר מכמה דברים השנויין ב"במה טומנין". ועוד, דחנניה שרי להשהות אף כשאינה גרופה, ולא אסרו מוסיף הבל אלא דוקא בהטמנה, אבל להשהות – שרי. וכשאינה גרופה אסרי רבנן דחנניה, משום דילמא אתי לאחתויי:

חמין ותבשיל. נראה לר"י: דסתם חמין ותבשיל היינו אפי' לא בשיל כל צרכו אלא כמאכל בן דרוסאי. דהא כי מוקי מתניתין להחזיר תנן – הוי מתניתין כחנניה, דשרי חמין ותבשיל להשהות על גבי כירה אפילו בשאינה גרופה, אפילו לא בשיל כל צרכו, ולא כרבנן. ואמאי? ודילמא מתניתין אפילו כרבנן, ומתני' בחמין ותבשיל שנתבשלו כל צרכן, דמודו רבנן דמשהין ע"ג כירה שאינה גרופה וקטומה! אלא ודאי משום דסתם חמין ותבשיל כמאכל בן דרוסאי נמי משמע. ומיהו, סתם חמין ותבשיל – הוי נמי בשיל כל צרכו, כדמוכח בסוף שמעתין (דף לח.) גבי קשיא דרבי מאיר אדרבי מאיר, אע"פ שיש לדחות. ושם אפרש בע"ה. ואפילו אי סתם חמין ותבשיל לא הוה בשיל כל צרכו, צריך לומר: הא דאסרי בית שמאי להחזיר – היינו אפילו חמין שהוחמו כל צרכן, וכן לבית הלל בשאינה גרופה. מדקאמר בגמרא (דף לח:): ואף רבי אושעיא סבר מחזירין אפילו בשבת, דאמר רבי אושעיא: פעם אחת כו' והעלנו לו קומקומוס של חמין ומזגנו לו את הכוס והחזרנוהו למקומו. ואי לא אסיר בהוחמו כל צרכן – מנא ליה דמחזירין אפילו בשבת? דילמא הוחם כל צורכו הוה! ואם תאמר: ואם סתם חמין ותבשיל הוי בין בשיל כל צרכו בין לא בשיל, אם כן סברי בית שמאי מצטמק ויפה לו – אסור, כיון דאסיר תבשיל שבישל כל צרכו. ואם כן, היכי שרי חמין שלא הוחמו כל צרכן, והא יפה לו הוא! ואור"י: דודאי תבשיל אסרי בית שמאי, משום דלעולם יפה לו אע"ג דנתבשל כל צרכו. אבל חמין שאין יפה להם אלא עד כדי צרכן, אבל מכאן ואילך רע להן, כדמוכח לקמן – לא אסרי בית שמאי, דליכא למיגזר שמא יחתה, דבלא חיתוי יוחמו כל צרכן: **וב"ה** אומרים אף מחזירין. אפילו בשבת מחזירין, *כדאמר בגמרא. ולשון "נוטלין" נמי משמע דבשבת מיירי, דבחול לא הוה צריך למיתני נוטלין. ולמאן דאסר להחזיר – אסר אפילו בחול, לבית הלל – כשאינה גרופה, ולבית שמאי – אפי' בגרופה. מדקאמר בגמרא: לדברי האומר "מחזירין" – מחזירין אפילו בשבת, משמע דעיקר פלוגתא הוי בחול. ועוד מדקדק ר"ת: מדקאמר "לא יתן עד שיגרוף", ואי לא יתן לא יחזיר בשבת הוא – איך יגרוף או יקטום בשבת? והוה ליה למימר "אלא אם כן גרף וקטם". אלא בחול נמי אסור להחזיר. וא"ת: מה שיעור הוא נותן לאסור בע"ש? דהיכא דסלקו בהשכמה – פשיטא דשרי להחזיר! ואומר ר"י: דמשעה שלא יוכלו להרתיחו מבעוד יום – אסור להחזיר. ומיהו, בשבת אפילו רותח אסור להחזיר למאן דאסר. דאי לאו הכי – מנא ליה דרבי אושעיא סבר מחזירין אפילו בשבת? דילמא קומקום של חמין רותח הוה. ועוד אומר ר"י: דמצינו למימר דבערב שבת נמי אסור להחזיר אפילו רותח, משעה שאם היה קר לא היה יכול להרתיח מבע"י. וקשה לרשב"א: היכי שרי להחזיר קדרה על גבי כירה בשבת? והא אמר בפרק "המביא כדי יין" (ביצה דף לג: ושם) דיליס וקדרה וחביתא ופוריא – מלמטה למעלה אסור משום אהל! ואור"י: דכי אסרו חכמים אהל עראי – ה"מ כשעושה הדפנות תחלה ואח"כ הכיסוי, אבל הכא שדופני הכירה כבר עשויות מאיליהן לא אחמור רבנן לאסור ליתן קדרה על גבה. ומיהו, הא דאמר ב"המוצא תפילין" (עירובין דף קב.) גבי דיכרי דרב הונא, דאמר ליה: כרוך בודיא ושייר בה טפח, למחר מוסיף על אוהל עראי הוא. משמע: דבלא שיור – אסור, אע"ג דהדפנות כבר עשויות! אור"י: התם – משום דדמי אהל טפי, אסור אפילו בלא עשיית דפנות. אבל קדרה דלא דמי אהל כולי האי – לא אסרו חכמים בלא עשיית דפנות: לעולם

[ועי' תוס' ב"מ קג. ד"ה המקבל]

לעיל כ.

[דף לד:]

רבינו חננאל

פ"ג כירה שהסיקוה בקש ובגבבא וכו'. כירה זו היא מקום שפיתת ב' קדרות. איבעיא להו הא דתנינן לא יתן עד שיגרוף. או עד שיתן האפר על גבי גחלים נתינה זו בע"ש וקמ"ל דאסור לשהות ע"ג כירה אא"כ גרופה וקטומה או דילמא נתינה זו החזרת הקדירה היא בשבת וקמ"ל דאסור להחזיר אלא ע"ג כירה קטומה או גרופה אבל לשהות מותר. ומתני' מני חנניה היא דתניא כל שהוא כמאכל בן דרוסאי מותר לשהותו על גבי כירה אע"פ שאינה גרופה ולא קטומה.

ומיהו רש"י פי' בגמרא מחזירין אפילו בשבת למחרת דנראה דאין דעתו להחזיר ובטלה הטמנה אבל בלילה אין נראה כן [ת"י]

רב נסים גאון

נפקא מינה לגיטי נשים. כלומר בדאלך *) המביא גט מבבל או מבורסיף אין צריך לומר בפני נכתב ובפני נחתם לדבריהם שאמרו במסכת גיטין בפר' א' (דף ו) בבל רב אמר כארץ ישראל לגיטין מכי אתא רב לבבל ובפרק עשרה יוחסין (דף עב) היכא חביל ימא אמר רב פפא סבא משמיה דרב זו פרת בורסיף ובבראשית דר' אושעיא (פרשה לח) חד תלמיד ר' יוחנן הוה יתיב קדמוי הוה מסבר ליה ולא סבר אמר ליה מה דין לית את סבר אמר ליה דאנא גלי מן אתראי אמר ליה מן הדין אתר את אמר ליה מן בורסיף אמר ליה לא תאמר כן אלא בולסיף שנאמר (בראשית יא) כי שם בלל ה' שפת כל הארץ ובגמרא דכל ישראל יש להן חלק (סנהדרין דף קט) אמרו אמר רב יוסף בבל בורסיף סימן רע לתורה מאי בורסיף אמר רב אסי בור שפת ואדוננו האיי ז"ל אמר בבל בורסיף ובורסיף בבל כוונת דבר זה לאותה ששנינו במשנה שינה שמו ושמה שם עירו ושם עירה פסול הרי נודע כי בבל ובורסיף עיר אחת הן והגט כשר: **סליק פרק במה מדליקין**

*) פירושו בזה.

הגהות הב"ח

(א) רש"י ד"ה אבל לא תבשיל וכו' כמבשל הס"ד ואח"כ מ"ה אבל לא:

גליון הש"ס

תוס' ד"ה וב"ה אומרים וכו' והל"ל אא"כ גרף. לענ"ד הא מצינו כזה במ"ק דף ד ע"ב עד שיעמיק כו' כגון שהעמיק:

ולא רצה לומר דתנא רישא דאפילו בחול אין מחזירין לב"ש כדמשמע עד שיגרוף וסיפא קתני דאפילו בשבת מחזירין לב"ה כדמשמע נוטלין דבלאו תרי בבא סברא הוא דבתרווייהו פליגי דהא אי להשהות תנן ליכא אלא חד בבא בהחזרה ומהר"מ אומר דאי משום ב"ה תני סיפא לא ה"ל למיתני דברי בית שמאי [ת"י]

לעולם אימא לך להחזיר תנן, וחסורי מיחסרא והכי קתני: כירה שהסיקוה בקש ובגבבא – מחזירין עליה תבשיל, בגפת ובעצים – לא יחזיר עד שיגרוף או עד שיתן את האפר. אבל לשהות – משהין, אע"פ שאינו גרוף ואינו קטום. ומה הן משהין? בית שמאי אומרים: חמין אבל לא תבשיל, ובית הלל אומרים: חמין ותבשיל. והך חזרה דאמרי לך – לאו דברי הכל היא אלא מחלוקת בית שמאי ובית הלל; שבית שמאי אומרים: נוטלין ולא מחזירין, ובית הלל אומרים: אף מחזירין. ת"ש, דאמר ר' חלבו א"ר חמא בר גוריא אמר רב: לא שנו אלא על גבה, אבל לתוכה – אסור. אי אמרת בשלמא להחזיר תנן – היינו דשני בין תוכה לעל גבה, אלא אי אמרת לשהות תנן – מה לי תוכה מה לי על גבה! מי סברת ר' חלבו ארישא קאי? אסיפא [א]קאי: "ובית הלל אומרים אף מחזירין". ואמר ר' חלבו אמר רב חמא בר גוריא אמר רב: לא שנו אלא על גבה, אבל תוכה – אסור. *תא שמע: [ב]ב' כירות המתאימות, אחת גרופה וקטומה ואחת שאינה גרופה ואינה קטומה – משהין על גבי גרופה וקטומה, ואין משהין על שאינה גרופה ואינה קטומה. ומה הן משהין? בית שמאי אומרים: ולא כלום, ובית הלל אומרים: חמין אבל לא תבשיל. עקר – דברי הכל לא יחזיר, דברי רבי מאיר. רבי יהודה אומר, בית שמאי אומרים: חמין אבל לא תבשיל, ובית הלל אומרים: חמין ותבשיל. בית שמאי אומרים: נוטלין אבל לא מחזירין, ובית הלל אומרים: אף מחזירין". אי אמרת בשלמא לשהות תנן; מתני' מני – רבי יהודה היא, אלא אי אמרת להחזיר תנן, מתניתין מני? לא רבי יהודה ולא ר' מאיר. אי רבי מאיר – קשיא לב"ש בחדא, ולבית הלל בתרתי. אי רבי יהודה – קשיא גרופה וקטומה! לעולם אימא לך: להחזיר תנן, ותנא דידן סבר לה כרבי יהודה בחדא, ופליג עליה בחדא. סבר לה כרבי יהודה בחדא – בחמין ותבשיל, ונוטלין ומחזירין. ופליג עליה בחדא – דאילו תנא דידן סבר: לשהות, ואף על פי שאינו גרוף וקטום, ורבי יהודה סבר: בלשהות נמי, גרוף וקטום – אין, אי לא – לא. איבעיא להו: מהו לסמוך בה? תוכה וגבה – אסור, אבל לסמוך בה – שפיר דמי, או דילמא לא שנא? תא שמע: שתי כירות המתאימות, אחת גרופה וקטומה ואחת שאינה גרופה וקטומה – משהין על גבי גרופה וקטומה, ואף על גב דקא סליק ליה הבלא מאידך. דילמא שאני התם – דכיון דמידליא שליט בה אוירא. תא שמע, דאמר רב ספרא אמר רב חייא: קטמה ונתלבתה – סומכין לה, ומקיימין עליה, ונוטלין ממנה, ומחזירין לה. שמע מינה: לסמוך נמי, קטמה – אין, לא קטמה – לא. ולטעמיך 'נוטלין ממנה' דקתני, קטמה – לא?! אלא: תנא, 'נוטלין' משום 'מחזירין' הכא נמי: תנא סומכין משום מקיימין. הכי השתא! התם – נוטלין ומחזירין בחד מקום הוא, תנא נוטלין משום מחזירין. אלא הכא, סומכין – בחד מקום הוא, ומקיימין – בחד מקום הוא. מאי הוי עלה? ת"ש: *[ג]כירה שהסיקוה בגפת ובעצים – סומכין לה, ואין מקיימין אא"כ גרופה וקטומה. [ד]גחלים שעממו, או שנתן עליה נעורת של פשתן דקה – הרי היא כקטומה. אמר ר' יצחק בר נחמני א"ר אושעיא: קטמה והובערה – משהין עליה חמין שהוחמו כל צורכן, ותבשיל שבישל כל צורכו.

שמע

רש"י

לעולם אימא לך להחזיר תנן. ואילו לשהות, אע"פ שאינו גרוף – שרי: והך חזרה דאמרי לך. "לא יחזיר עד שיגרוף", דכי גרוף מיהא שרי: לאו דברי הכל היא. ולבית שמאי לא סבירא להו: לא שנו. שריותא דמתני' אלא על גבה, דלא נפיש הבלא כולי האי. אבל תוכה – אסור: אי אמרת בשלמא להחזיר תנן. אבל לשהות משהין, אפילו בשאין גרופה, כדמתרצינן ליה הסוגיי. ורבי חלבו אשריותא דלשהות על שאינה גרופה קאי: היינו דשני בין תוכה לעל גבה. דכי משהי לתוכה דשאינה גרופה – מטמין ממש ברמץ: אלא אי אמרת לשהות תנן. דאפילו לשהות בעי גרופה, כיון דגרופה ומבעוד יום הוא נותנו לתוכה, מה לי תוכה מה לי על גבה? ארישא. "עד שיגרוף": אסיפא קאי. דאיירי בחזרה. אבל רישא לשהות הוא, ובין תוכה ובין גבה – שרי: שתי כירות המתאימות. מחוברות יחד, וקיר של חרס מפסקת ביניהם: משהין על גבי גרופה וקטומה. דלא חיישינן משום דסליק לה הבלא מאידך: ומה הן משהין. על הגרופה: לא יחזיר. בשבת: אא"ב. רישא דמתניתין לשהות קאמר, דבעי גרופה, ובלשהות פליגי בחמין ובתבשיל ובגרוף. וסיפא פליגי בחזרה – מתני' ר' יהודה היא. אלא אי אמרת להחזיר תנן, דבעי גרופה, אבל לשהות – לא בעי גרופה, ופלוגתא דחמין ותבשיל – כשאינו גרוף, כדקמחסרת ומתרצת לה: קשיא לב"ש בחדא. דקאמרי ב"ש במתני': משהין חמין אף בשאינו גרוף. והכא קאמר רבי מאיר לב"ש דאפילו גרוף, ולא כלום, וכ"ש כשאינו גרוף. והא כולה חדא פירקא היא, דבית שמאי לא שני להו בין גרוף לשאינו גרוף: ולב"ה בתרתי. דבמתניתין שרי בית הלל להשהות חמין ותבשיל אף בשאינו גרוף, והכא קתני דבגרוף חמין – אין, תבשיל – לא. ובשאינה גרוף אין משהין כלל. הכל לא יחזיר": ואי ר' יהודה. דקאמר נמי כי מתניתין, מ"מ גרופה וקטומה קשיא. דמתניתין שרית פלוגתא קמייתא בשאינו גרוף, ושרו ב"ש חמין ובית הלל חמין ותבשיל. והכא קתני: "אין משהין על גבי שאינה גרופה ואינה קטומה" כלל, ופלוגתא דלשהות – בגרופה וקטומה: בחמין ותבשיל ונוטלים ומחזירין. דמוקי פלוגתא דב"ש וב"ה בשהיית חמין ותבשיל. דבית שמאי שרו חמין, ותבשיל – לא. וב"ה – חמין ותבשיל. ולא כר' מאיר דקאמר: לב"ש לא כלום: מהו לסמוך. קדרה אצל דופן הכירה בלא גרופה, שהכירה מטלטלת היא, ומושיבים אותה על גבי קרקע: גבה. עובי שפתה, או כסוי שעל חללה: דמדלי. הקדרה על גבי הכירה: ונתלבתה. חזרה והובערה: התם נוטלין ומחזירין בחד מקום. ולא שייך למתני "מחזירין" עד דתני "נוטלין": נעורת. אריסט"ש: שהוחמו כל צרכן. דליכא למיחש לחיתויי:

מצטמק

תוספות

לעולם אימא לך להחזיר תנן וחסורי מיחסרא כו'. משום דקיי"ל כחנניה, כמו שאפרש בע"ה, דחיק לאוקמא מתני' כוותיה:

אא"ב להחזיר תנן היינו דשני בין תוכה לעל גבה. פי' בקונטרס: משום דאי להחזיר תנן(א) – א"כ לשהות משהין אפילו באינה גרופה, להכי שני בין תוכה – דהוי מטמין ממש ברמץ – לעל גבה. וקשה להר"ת: דלחנניה אפילו תוכה משהין, אפי' באינה גרופה, דהא תנן (לעיל דף יט:): ולא חררה על גבי גחלים אלא עד שיקרמו פניה. הא קרמו פניה – שרי, אע"ג דחררה בתוכה היא. ונראה הכי אור"י: דבחנם דחק רש"י לפרש כן, דאיכא למימר שפיר: היינו דשני לן בין תוכה לעל גבה, מהא דשרי להחזיר בגרופה. ובהשהאה דוקא לא ניחא ליה לחלק – אבל בהחזרה ניחא ליה שפיר לחלק, כדמוכח במאי דמשני: "מי סברת ארישא קאי אסיפא קאי" כו'. קשה לר"י: *היכי בעי למימר אליבא דרב דמתניתין להחזיר תנן, אם כן אתיא מתניתין כחנניה, ורב דלא כחנניה. דהא חנניה שרי במצטמק ויפה לו, דהא דתנן: (שם) אין צולין בשר ובילה אלא כדי שיצולו מבעוד יום. אתיא כחנניה. ובילה, אמרינן לקמן דמצטמק ויפה לו הוא, ורב אסר לקמן, *דמצטמק ויפה לו. וי"ל: דבלאו הכי לא סבר לה רב כשום תנא, דהא ר"מ ור' יהודה אסרי באינה גרופה אפילו במצטמק ורע לו, ורב שרי במצטמק ורע לו אפילו באינה גרופה. דבגרופה לא אשכחן שום אמורא דאסר, אפילו יפה לו. ועוד: דרב קאי אמילתיה דרבי יוחנן, דאיירי באינה גרופה. וכן רבי יוחנן דשרי לקמן חמין ותבשיל שבישל כל צרכו – באינה גרופה, אבל לא בישל כל צרכו אסור – לא אשכחן תנא דסבר הכי:

מהו לסמוך. באינה גרופה קבעי. ואי מתניתין להשהות תנן – קא בעי להשהות ולהחזיר, ואי להחזיר תנן ושרי להשהות אפי' תוכה וגבה – בעי להחזיר ולהשהות היכא שאינו מבושל כמאכל בן דרוסאי:

תא שמע כירה שהסיקוה כו'. ומסיק דשרי לסמוך. ומכל מקום אין ללמוד מכאן לסמוך אצל האש, דשאני הכא דדופני כירה מפסיקין בינו ולאש:

עין משפט נר מצוה

ב א מיי' פ"ג מהל' שבת הלכה י' סמג לאוין סה טוש"ע א"ח סי' רנג סעיף ב:
ג ב שם סעיף א בהג"ה:
ד ג מיי' שם הלכה ז טוש"ע שם סעיף א:
ה ד מיי' שם הלכה ל:

ואפשר דרב מוקי מתני' בלהחזיר אבל להשהות אפילו אינה גרופה שרי מצטמק ורע לו ולרבי יוחנן אפי' מצטמק ויפה לו [ת"י]

רבינו חננאל

ושקלינן וטרינן ותריצנן כירה שהסיקוה בגפת או בעצים אסור להחזיר אבל לשהות משהין בה אע"פ שאינה גרופה ולא קטומה בין תבשיל בין חמין כחנניה: ואע"ג דעמדה אמרינן תוב תא שמע ב' כירות המתאימות אחת גרופה וקטומה ואחת שאינה גרופה ולא קטומה כו' לר' מאיר אליבא דבית הלל משהין ע"ג גרופה וקטומה חמין אבל לא תבשיל ולב"ש לא כלום לר' יהודה אליבא דב"ש משהין חמין אבל לא תבשיל. וב"ה חמין ותבשיל ב"ש אומרים נוטלין חמין אבל לא (תבשיל) מחזירין. וב"ה [אומרים] נוטלין אף מחזירין בשלמא אי אמרת מתני' לשהות [נמי בעינן] ע"ג גרופה וקטומה מתני' ר' יהודה היא. אלא אי אמרת להחזיר היא אבל לשהות בש"א משהין חמין ובה"א חמין ותבשיל אף על פי שאינה גרופה ולא קטומה. מני מתני' אי ר' מאיר קשיא לב"ש (בהו) [בחדא] במתני' דקתני בש"א חמין אבל לא תבשיל. ורבי מאיר קתני לבית שמאי ולא כלום. ולבית הלל בתרתי דר' מאיר קתני לב"ה משהין חמין אבל לא תבשיל. ומתני' קתני לב"ה חמין ותבשיל. ותוב דרבי מאיר קתני דברי הכל לא יחזיר ומתני' קתני לב"ה אף מחזירין. אי לרבי יהודה קשיא גרופה וקטומה דכי קתני משהין לב"ש חמין לב"ה חמין ותבשיל בגרופה וקטומה קתני ומתני' אע"פ שאינה גרופה וקטומה. ושנינן לעולם אימא לך להחזיר תנן. ותנא דידן סבר לה כרבי יהודה בחדא ופליג עליה בחדא ופשוטה היא ועמדה [הסוגיא] דמתני' להחזיר תנן. עכשיו יש מי שאומר כיון דלא איפשיטא בהדיא להחזיר אשנויי לא סמכינן [ומוקמי] מתני' לשהות. ויש מי שאומר הלכה להחזיר תנן ומסייעא ליה הא דא"ר יוחנן כירה שהסיקוה בגפת ובעצים משהין עליה חמין שלא הוחמו כל צרכן ותבשיל שלא בישל כל צרכו עקר לא יחזיר וקסבר מתני' להחזיר תנן כו'. ועוד מדאמר רבא תרוייהו תנינהי ואמרינן מכדי תרוייהו תנינהי ר' יוחנן מאי אתא לאשמעינן ואמר דיוקא דמתני' קמ"ל ש"מ דרבי יוחנן סבר דוקא דמתני' להחזיר הוא*) ושיהוי זה אינה הטמנה אלא כגון כסא של ברזל והקדירה יושבת עליה והיא תלויה (או) באבנים [או] כיוצא בה. אבל הטמנה ע"ג גחלים דברי הכל אסור. דקי"ל הטמנה בדבר המוסיף אסור ואפילו מבעוד יום: איבעיא להו מהו לסמוך לה. תוכה וגבה אסור. אבל לסמוך שרי או דילמא לא

*) עי' בבעל המאור:

מסורת הש"ס

תוספתא פ"ג

תוספתא [פ"ג]

הגהות הב"ח

(א) תוס' ד"ה אא"ב וכו' דאי להחזיר תנן אבל לשהות:

גליון הש"ס

תוס' ד"ה לעולם וכו' משום דקיי"ל כחנניה. כעין זה בתוספות מגילה דף יט ע"ב ד"ה ודילמא:

ו א ב (מיי' פ"ג מהל' שבת הל' ד') סמג לאוין סה טוש"ע א"ח סימן רנג סעיף א:

שְׁמַע מִינַּהּ: מִצְטַמֵּק וְיָפֶה לוֹ מוּתָּר – שָׁאנֵי הָכָא, דִּקְטָמָהּ. אִי הָכִי, מַאי לְמֵימְרָא? הוּבְעֲרָה אִיצְטְרִיכָא לֵיהּ, מַהוּ דְּתֵימָא: כֵּיוָן דְּהוּבְעֲרָה – הֲדָרָא לַהּ לְמִילְּתָא קַמַּיְיתָא, קָמַשְׁמַע לָן. אָמַר רַבָּה בַּר בַּר חָנָה אָמַר רַבִּי יוֹחָנָן: קְטָמָהּ וְהוּבְעֲרָה – מַשְׁהִין עָלֶיהָ חַמִּין שֶׁהוּחַמּוּ כָּל צוֹרְכָּן וְתַבְשִׁיל שֶׁבִּישֵּׁל כָּל צוֹרְכּוֹ, וַאֲפִי' גֶּחָלִים שֶׁל רוֹתֶם. ש"מ: מִצְטַמֵּק וְיָפֶה לוֹ מוּתָּר. שָׁאנֵי הָכָא דִּקְטָמָהּ. אִי הָכִי, מַאי לְמֵימְרָא? הוּבְעֲרָה אִצְטְרִיכָא לֵיהּ. הַיְינוּ הַךְ! גֶּחָלִים שֶׁל רוֹתֶם אִצְטְרִיכָא לֵיהּ. אָמַר רַב שֵׁשֶׁת אָמַר ר' יוֹחָנָן: כִּירָה שֶׁהִסִּיקוּהָ בְּגֶפֶת וּבְעֵצִים מַשְׁהִין עָלֶיהָ חַמִּין שֶׁלֹּא הוּחַמּוּ כָּל צוֹרְכָּן וְתַבְשִׁיל שֶׁלֹּא בִּישֵּׁל כָּל צוֹרְכּוֹ, עָקַר – לֹא יַחֲזִיר עַד שֶׁיִּגְרוֹף אוֹ עַד שֶׁיִּתֵּן אֵפֶר. קָסָבַר: מַתְנִיתִין לְהַחֲזִיר תְּנַן, אֲבָל לְשְׁהוֹת מַשְׁהִין אע"פ שֶׁאֵינוֹ גָּרוּף וְאֵינוֹ קָטוּם. אֲמַר רָבָא: תַּרְוַויְיהוּ תְּנָנְהִי, לְשְׁהוֹת תָּנֵינָא: *אֵין נוֹתְנִין אֶת הַפַּת בְּתוֹךְ הַתַּנּוּר עִם חֲשֵׁיכָה, וְלֹא חֲרָרָה עַל גַּבֵּי גֶּחָלִים, אֶלָּא כְּדֵי שֶׁיִּקְרְמוּ פָּנֶיהָ. הָא קָרְמוּ פָּנֶיהָ – שָׁרֵי. לְהַחֲזִיר נַמִּי תָּנֵינָא: בֵּית הִלֵּל אוֹמְרִים: אַף מַחֲזִירִין. וְעַד כָּאן לָא קָשָׁרוּ בֵּית הִלֵּל אֶלָּא בִּגְרוּפָה וּקְטוּמָה, אֲבָל בְּשֶׁאֵינָהּ גְּרוּפָה וּקְטוּמָה – לֹא. וְרַב שֵׁשֶׁת נַמִּי – דִּיוּקָא דְּמַתְנִי' קמ"ל. אָמַר רַב שְׁמוּאֵל בַּר יְהוּדָה אָמַר רַבִּי יוֹחָנָן: [א]כִּירָה שֶׁהִסִּיקוּהָ בְּגֶפֶת וּבְעֵצִים מַשְׁהִין(א) עָלֶיהָ תַּבְשִׁיל שֶׁבִּישֵּׁל כָּל צוֹרְכּוֹ וְחַמִּין שֶׁהוּחַמּוּ כָּל צוֹרְכָּן וַאֲפִי' מִצְטַמֵּק וְיָפֶה לוֹ. אֲמַר לֵיהּ הַהוּא מִדְּרַבָּנַן לְרַב שְׁמוּאֵל בַּר יְהוּדָה: הָא רַב וּשְׁמוּאֵל דְּאָמְרִי תַּרְוַויְיהוּ: מִצְטַמֵּק וְיָפֶה לוֹ אָסוּר! אֲמַר לֵיהּ: אַטּוּ לֵית אֲנָא יָדַע דְּאָמַר רַב יוֹסֵף אָמַר רַב יְהוּדָה אָמַר שְׁמוּאֵל: מִצְטַמֵּק וְיָפֶה לוֹ אָסוּר! כִּי קָאָמִינָא לָךְ – לְרַבִּי יוֹחָנָן קָאָמִינָא. אֲמַר לֵיהּ רַב עוּקְבָא מִמֵּישָׁן לְרַב אַשִׁי: אַתּוּן דְּמִקָּרְבִיתוּ לְרַב וּשְׁמוּאֵל – עֲבִידוּ כְּרַב וּשְׁמוּאֵל, אֲנַן – נַעֲבֵיד כְּרַבִּי יוֹחָנָן. אֲמַר לֵיהּ אַבַּיֵי לְרַב יוֹסֵף: מַהוּ לְשְׁהוֹת? אֲמַר לֵיהּ: הָא רַב יְהוּדָה מַשְׁהוּ לֵיהּ וְאָכֵיל. א"ל: בַּר מִינֵּיהּ דְּרַב יְהוּדָה, דְּכֵיוָן דִּמְסוּכָּן הוּא – אֲפִילוּ בְּשַׁבָּת נַמִּי שָׁרֵי לְמֶעֱבַד לֵיהּ, לִי וְלָךְ מַאי? אֲמַר לֵיהּ: בְּסוּרָא מַשְׁהוּ, דְּהָא רַב נַחְמָן בַּר יִצְחָק *מָרֵי דְּעוּבְדָא הֲוָה וּמַשְׁהוּ לֵיהּ וְאָכֵיל. אָמַר רַב אַשִׁי: קָאֵימְנָא קַמֵּיהּ דְּרַב הוּנָא וְשָׁהִין לֵיהּ כָּסָא דְּהַרְסְנָא וַאֲכַל וְלָא יָדַעְנָא אִי מִשּׁוּם דְּקָסָבַר מִצְטַמֵּק וְיָפֶה לוֹ מוּתָּר, אִי מִשּׁוּם דְּכֵיוָן דְּאִית בֵּיהּ מִיחָא מִצְטַמֵּק וְרַע לוֹ הוּא. אָמַר רַב *נַחְמָן: [ב]מִצְטַמֵּק וְיָפֶה לוֹ – אָסוּר, מִצְטַמֵּק וְרַע לוֹ – מוּתָּר. כְּלָלָא דְּמִלְּתָא: כֹּל דְּאִית בֵּיהּ מִיחָא – מִצְטַמֵּק וְרַע לוֹ, לְבַר מִתַּבְשִׁיל דְּלִיפְתָּא, דְּאַף עַל גַּב דְּאִית בֵּיהּ מִיחָא מִצְטַמֵּק וְיָפֶה לוֹ הוּא. וְהָנֵי מִילֵּי – דְּאִית בֵּיהּ בִּשְׂרָא, אֲבָל לֵית בֵּיהּ בִּשְׂרָא – מִצְטַמֵּק וְרַע לוֹ הוּא. וְכִי אִית בֵּיהּ בִּשְׂרָא נַמִּי לָא אֲמַרַן אֶלָּא דְּלָא קָבָעֵי לָהּ לְאוֹרְחִין, אֲבָל קָבָעֵי לָהּ לְאוֹרְחִין – מִצְטַמֵּק וְרַע לוֹ. לְפָדָא דַּיְיסָא וְתַמְרֵי – מִצְטַמֵּק וְרַע לְהֶן. בָּעוּ מִינֵּיהּ מֵרַבִּי חִיָּיא בַּר אַבָּא:

שָׁכַח

רש"י

מִצְטַמֵּק. מִתְמַעֵט וְכָוֵיץ, רטיי"ט. לָשׁוֹן "שָׁדַיִם צוֹמְקִין" (הושע ט). כְּמוֹ שֶׁאַתָּה אוֹמֵר בִּלְשׁוֹן צִוּוּי "נִצְטַוָּה", וּבִלְשׁוֹן צֶדֶק "נִצְטַדֵּק". וְכֵן כָּל תֵּיבָה שֶׁרֹאשׁ יְסוֹדָהּ צד"י, כְּשֶׁהִיא מִתְפַּעֶלֶת – נוֹתֵן ט' אַחַר צד"י: מוּתָּר. לְהַשְׁהוֹתָן בְּכִירָה. דְּאִי לָאו בְּמִצְטַמֵּק וְיָפֶה לוֹ קָאָמַר, מַאי אָתָא לְאַשְׁמְעִינַן? אֶלָּא ע"כ בְּמִצְטַמֵּק וְיָפֶה לוֹ קָאָמַר, וַאֲפִילּוּ הָכִי לֹא גָּזְרוּ מִשּׁוּם חִיתּוּי, הוֹאִיל וְנִתְבַּשֵּׁל כָּל צָרְכּוֹ. וְתָנָא חַמִּין – לְאַשְׁמְעִינַן דְּבָעֵינַן שֶׁהוּחַמּוּ כָּל צָרְכָּן מִבְּעוֹד יוֹם: שָׁאנֵי הָכָא דִּקְטָמָהּ. וְגַלֵּי דַּעְתֵּיהּ דְּלָא נִיחָא לֵיהּ בְּצִמּוּקֵי: גֶּחָלִים שֶׁל רוֹתֶם. חַמִּין יוֹתֵר מִשְּׁאָר גֶּחָלִים, וְאֵינָם מְמַהֲרִין לִכְבּוֹת. כִּדְאָמְרִינַן בְּ"הַמּוֹכֵר אֶת הַסְּפִינָה" (ב"ב דף עד:): מַשְׁהִין עָלֶיהָ. וְאע"פ שֶׁלֹּא קְטָמָהּ. וְאָמוֹרָאֵי נִינְהוּ אַלִּיבָּא דְּר' יוֹחָנָן: מַתְנִיתִין. דְּקָתָנֵי "עַד שֶׁיִּגְרוֹף": לְהַחֲזִיר תְּנַן. דְּלָא שָׁרוּ בֵּית הִלֵּל לְהַחֲזִיר עַד שֶׁיִּגְרוֹף. וּפֵירוּקָא דְּמַתְנִיתִין כִּדְאָמְרִינַן לְעֵיל: חַסּוּרֵי מִיחַסְּרָא, הִלְכָּךְ עָקַר לֹא יַחֲזִיר, הוֹאִיל וְאֵינָהּ גְּרוּפָה: תַּרְוַויְיהוּ תְּנָנְהִי. בֵּין לְשְׁהוֹת בְּשֶׁאֵינָהּ גְּרוּפָה תָּנֵינָא בְּהֶדְיָא סְתָם מִשְׁנָה דְּמוּתָּר. וְעָקַר לֹא יַחֲזִיר נַמִּי תָּנֵינָא, וְלָמָּה לֵיהּ לְר' יוֹחָנָן לְאַשְׁמְעִינַן? הָא קָרְמוּ פָּנֶיהָ שָׁרֵי. וְהַיְינוּ "לֹא בִּישֵּׁל כָּל צָרְכּוֹ". וְתַנּוּר לָאו גָּרוּף וְקָטוּם הוּא. וְאִי נַמִּי גָּרוּף – בְּתַנּוּר לָא מְהַנְּיָא גְּרִיפָה, כִּדְתְנַן בְּמַתְנִיתִין, וְכ"ש פַּת דְּאַדַּעְתָּא לְבַשּׁוּלֵי יְהָבֵיהּ בְּגַוֵּויהּ: וְעַד כָּאן לָא שָׁרוּ כו'. דְּמַתְנִיתִין אַ"לְאַחַר שֶׁיִּגְרוֹף" קָאֵי, דְּקָתָנֵי: "לֹא יִתֵּן עַד שֶׁיִּגְרוֹף". וּבֵין לְמַאן דְּאָמַר לֹא יַשְׁהֶה, וּבֵין לְמ"ד לֹא יַחֲזִיר – מ"מ חֲזָרָה דְּסֵיפָא אַגָּרוּף וְקָטוּם מְהַדַּר: וְרַב שֵׁשֶׁת נַמִּי דִּיוּקָא דְּמַתְנִי' קמ"ל. מִשּׁוּם דְּלָא מַתְנֵי לַהּ בְּהֶדְיָא: הָא קָרְמוּ שָׁרֵי. וַאֲנַן דְּמַשְׁהִינַן קְדֵירָה עַל גַּבֵּי כִּירָה שֶׁאֵינָהּ גְּרוּפָה – אַדַּחֲנַנְיָה סָמְכִינַן, הוֹאִיל וּתְנַן סְתָם מַתְנִיתִין כְּוָותֵיהּ, כִּדְאָמַר הָא קָרְמוּ שָׁרֵי. וְאע"ג דְּלָא בִּישֵּׁל כָּל צָרְכּוֹ. וְאָמַר רַב שֵׁשֶׁת מִשְּׁמֵיהּ דְּר' יוֹחָנָן כְּוָותֵיהּ, דְּמַתְנִיתִין דְּפִרְקִין מִשּׁוּם חֲזָרָה הוּא דְּבָעֵי גְּרוּפָה, אֲבָל לְשְׁהוֹת לֹא. וְכָל הָנֵי אָמוֹרָאֵי דְּאָסְרִי סָבְרִי: מַתְנִיתִין לְשְׁהוֹת תְּנַן: מַהוּ לְשְׁהוֹת. בְּשֶׁאֵינָהּ גְּרוּפָה: מְסוּכָּן הוּא. רָגִיל לְאוֹחֲזוֹ בּוּלְמוּס, וְצָרִיךְ לֶאֱכוֹל מַאֲכָל מָתוֹק וְטוֹב: מָרֵי דְּעוּבְדָא. מְדַקְדֵּק בְּמַעֲשָׂיו: מִיחָא. קֶמַח: כָּסָא דְּהַרְסְנָא. דָּגִים הַמְבוּשָּׁלִים בְּשַׁמְנָן בְּקֶמַח: דְּאִית בֵּיהּ בִּשְׂרָא. מִצְטַמֵּק וְיָפֶה לוֹ, שֶׁשּׁוּמַּן הַבָּשָׂר מְשַׁבֵּר כֹּחַ הַלֶּפֶת, כִּדְאָמַר בִּבְרָכוֹת (דף מד:): לְאוֹרְחִין. צָרִיךְ חֲתִיכוֹת חֲשׁוּבוֹת לָשׂוּם לִפְנֵיהֶם, וְאֵין דֶּרֶךְ כָּבוֹד בְּתַבְשִׁיל הַמִּצְטַמֵּק, שֶׁאֵין הַבָּשָׂר נִיכָּר בּוֹ: לְפָדָא. מַאֲכָל שֶׁעוֹשֶׂה מִתְּאֵנִים: תַּמְרֵי. מַאֲכָל תְּמָרִים:

שָׁכַח

תוספות

שמע מינה מצטמק ויפה לו מותר. פירש בקונטרס: דאי האי תבשיל במצטמק ורע לו – מאי אתא לאשמעינן. וקשה לר"י: הא איצטריך לאפוקי מדרבי מאיר ורבי יהודה דאסרי בשאינה גרופה, אפילו חמין דמצטמק ורע להם! ועוד קשה: כיון דהשתא ס"ד דמשום דהובערה הדרא למילתא קמייתא, כי משני: שאני הכא דקטמה, מאי פריך: "מאי למימרא" הא איצטריך טובא לאפוקי ממאי דס"ד מעיקרא! ונראה לר"י: דהשתא ס"ד דלא חשיבא קטומה כלל, משום דהובערה. ואשמעינן דהדרא למילתא קמייתא, דאי חשיבא קטומה – אמאי נקט "בישל כל צרכו"? אפי' לא בישל כל צרכו שרי. דאפילו רבי מאיר דמחמיר מכולהו תנאי שרי בחמין שלא הוחמו כל צרכן, כדפירשנו לעיל דסתם חמין ותבשיל הוי שלא הוחמו כל צורכן. ופריך: שמע מינה מצטמק ויפה לו – מותר. דהא סתם תבשיל אמר לקמן דמצטמק ויפה לו הוא, ומשני: שאני הכא דקטמה. פירוש: וחשיבא לגמרי קטומה. וה"ה אפילו לא בישל כל צרכו שרי. והא דנקט: "בישל כל צרכו" – לאשמעינן דאי לאו קטומה – אפילו בישל כל צרכו אסור, משום דמצטמק ויפה לו הוא, ופריך: אי הכי מאי למימרא, אף על גב דאשמעינן דאי לא קטמה אסור – מ"מ מדנקט למילתיה בלשון היתר, משמע דהתירא אתי לאורויי לן. ואף על גב דאשמעינן דלא הדרא למילתא קמייתא, נראה לו דהא לא איצטריך לאשמעינן, דסברא הוא דלא הדרא למילתא קמייתא. ואף על גב דמעיקרא הוה בעי למימר דהדרא למילתא קמייתא – לאו משום דסברא הוא לומר כן, אלא משום דנקט במלתיה "בישל כל צרכו" היה ר"ל כן, כדפרישית. ומשני: דמכל מקום אצטריך, דמהו דתימא כו'. ועוד יש לומר: שאני הכא דקטמה – דלאו לגמרי מהניא קטימה, אלא דוקא משום דבישל כל צרכו. אבל לא בישל כל צרכו – אסור, משום דהובערה. והשתא אתי שפיר הא דנקט הכא "קטמה והובערה", ולעיל נקט "ונתלבתה". דנתלבתה הוי פחות מהובערה. והויא לגמרי כקטומה. ופריך: א"ה מאי למימרא? דהא בלאו מילתיה מסברא ה"א דלא הדרא למלתא קמייתא, כמו בנתלבתה – ושרי, ואפי' לא בישל כל צרכו, ובלשון איסור ה"ל לאשמעינן ולא בלשון היתר. ומשני: הובערה איצטריך ליה. ואי לאו מילתיה לא היה פשוט היתר, אלא הוה ס"ד למימרא דהדרא למילתא קמייתא:

אמר רב ששת אמר ר' יוחנן כירה שהסיקוה בגפת ובעצים משהין עליה תבשיל שלא בישל כל צרכו כו'. פסק ר"ח: דהלכה כרב ששת אמר ר' יוחנן. דרבא דאמר: "תרווייהו תננהי" סבירא ליה כוותיה. וכן פסק רש"י, דסתם מתניתין דפרק קמא (דף יט:) כחנניה, ומותר להשהות אפילו באינה גרופה. אבל להחזיר – ודאי אסור, אא"כ גרוף וקטום, ואפילו *בישל כל צרכו. כדפי' לעיל: **דיוקא** דמתני' קמ"ל. פי' רש"י: דקמ"ל דקרמו פניה – שפיר דמי. ואין נראה, דדיוק פשוט הוא, דהא כיון דתנא עד שיקרמו פניה – ממילא שמעינן דקרמו פניה שרי. ונראה לפרש: דדיוקא דמתניתין דכירה אתא לאשמעי', דלהחזיר תנן, וחסורי מחסרא והכי קתני: **מהו** להשהות. באינה גרופה ולא בישל כל צרכו קבעי, או במצטמק ויפה לו:

שכח

רבינו חננאל

לא שנא ופשטנא מהא דתניא כירה שהסיקוה בגפת ובעצים סומכין ואין מקיימין עליה אלא אם כן גרופה וקטומה עממו הגחלים או שנתן לתוכה נעורת של פשתן דקה הרי כקטומה (דבי) [אמר רב] (שמעון) [שמואל] בר יהודה א"ר יוחנן כירה שהסיקוה בגפת ובעצים משהין עליה חמין שהוחמו כל צרכן ותבשיל שבישל כל צרכו ודוקא כירה שהיא שפיתת ב' קדרות אבל אם אין בה אלא שפיתת קדרה אחת אסור ואפי' מצטמק ויפה לו מותר ואע"ג דרב ושמואל פליגי הא קי"ל דרבי יוחנן לגבי רב ושמואל הלכתא כר' יוחנן ומה שאמר רב (עקיבא) [עוקבא] ממישן לרב אשי אתון דמקרביתון לרב ושמואל עבידו כרב ושמואל לאו משום דהלכתא כוותייהו אלא לעולם הלכתא כר' יוחנן דשרי אבל אתון דנהיגתון איסורא כרב ושמואל הוו להו דברים המותרין ואחרים נהגו בהן איסור אי אתה רשאי להתירן בפניהם והא דאמר רב יהודה מסוכן בשבת שרי למיעבד ליה פשוטה הוא: הא דאמר רב נחמן בר יצחק מצטמק ויפה לו אסור מצטמק ורע לו מותר. כללא דמילתא כל דאית ליה מיחא מצטמק ורע לו הוא בר מתבשילא דליפתא דאע"ג דאית ליה מיחא מצטמק ויפה לו הוא כו'. האי כללא (לגברי) [לגבי] רב ושמואל אמרה ולית הלכתא אלא כר' יוחנן דהא סייעיה ר' עקיבא ממישן לרב אשי. **לפדא** דייסא ותמרי מצטמק ורע לו מותר

הגהות הב"ח

(א) גמ' אמר רב שמואל בר יהודה א"ר יוחנן כירה וכו' משהין עליה חמין שהוחמו כל צורכן ותבשיל שבישל כל צורכו ואפי' מצטמק:

לעיל יט:

[ביצה כט: חולין קי.]

לספרי' דגרסי הכא רב"י נ"ל דאליבא דרב ושמואל קאמר דהא איהו גופיה משהי ליה ואכיל [ת"י]

תימה אמאי אסור להחזיר מ"ש מדאמר לקמן [דף מ:] נותן אדם קיתון של מים כנגד המדורה שתפיג צינתן ושמן איכא מאן דשרי אפילו יד סולדת בו ואם כן אמאי אסור תבשיל שבישל כל צרכו להחזיר הא לא שייך ביה בישול ולעיל [דף לז.] נמי לאסור להטמין משחשיכה אפילו באין מוסיף הבל גזרה שמא ירתיח הא לא שייך ביה בישול וי"ל דודאי בשמן לא שייך ביה בישול אבל בתבשיל אפילו במבושל מבעוד יום שייך בישול והא דשרינן קיתון של מים היינו ליתן במקום שאפי' תהיה שם כל היום לא תהיה יד סולדת בו [ת"י]

שָׁכַח קְדֵרָה עַל גַּבֵּי כִּירָה וּבִשְּׁלָה בַּשַּׁבָּת, מַהוּ? אִישְׁתֵּיק וְלָא א"ל וְלָא מִידֵי. לְמָחָר נְפַק דְּרַשׁ לְהוּ: *הַמְבַשֵּׁל [א]בַּשַּׁבָּת, *בְּשׁוֹגֵג – יֹאכַל, בְּמֵזִיד – לֹא יֹאכַל, וְלָא שְׁנָא. מַאי 'וְל"ש'? רַבָּה וְרַב יוֹסֵף דְּאָמְרִי תַּרְוַויְיהוּ לְהֶיתֵּירָא: מְבַשֵּׁל הוּא דְּקָא עָבֵיד מַעֲשֶׂה, בְּמֵזִיד – לֹא יֹאכַל, אֲבָל הַאי דְּלָא קָא עָבֵיד מַעֲשֶׂה – בְּמֵזִיד נַמִי יֹאכַל. רַב נַחְמָן בַּר יִצְחָק אָמַר [ב]לְאִיסּוּרָא: מְבַשֵּׁל הוּא דְּלָא אָתֵי לְאִיעֲרוּמֵי – בְּשׁוֹגֵג יֹאכַל, אֲבָל הַאי דְּאָתֵי לְאִיעֲרוּמֵי – בְּשׁוֹגֵג נַמִי לֹא יֹאכַל. מֵיתִיבִי: *שָׁכַח קְדֵירָה עַל גַּבֵּי כִּירָה וּבִישְּׁלָה בַּשַּׁבָּת, בְּשׁוֹגֵג – יֹאכַל, בְּמֵזִיד – לֹא יֹאכַל. בד"א – בְּחַמִּין שֶׁלֹּא הוּחַמּוּ כָּל צוֹרְכָּן, וְתַבְשִׁיל שֶׁלֹּא בִּישֵּׁל כָּל צוֹרְכּוֹ. אֲבָל חַמִּין שֶׁהוּחַמּוּ כָּל צוֹרְכָּן וְתַבְשִׁיל שֶׁבִּישֵּׁל כָּל צוֹרְכּוֹ, בֵּין בְּשׁוֹגֵג בֵּין בְּמֵזִיד – יֹאכַל, דִּבְרֵי ר"מ. ר' יְהוּדָה אוֹמֵר: חַמִּין שֶׁהוּחַמּוּ כָּל צוֹרְכָּן – מוּתָּרִין, מִפְּנֵי שֶׁמִּצְטַמֵּק וְרַע לוֹ. וְתַבְשִׁיל שֶׁבִּישֵּׁל כָּל צוֹרְכּוֹ – אָסוּר, מִפְּנֵי שֶׁמִּצְטַמֵּק וְיָפֶה לוֹ, וְכֹל הַמִּצְטַמֵּק וְיָפֶה לוֹ, כְּגוֹן כְּרוּב וּפוֹלִים וּבָשָׂר *טָרוּף – אָסוּר, וְכָל הַמִּצְטַמֵּק וְרַע לוֹ – מוּתָּר. קָתָנֵי מִיהָא: תַּבְשִׁיל שֶׁלֹּא בִּישֵּׁל כָּל צוֹרְכּוֹ, בִּשְׁלָמָא לְרַב נַחְמָן בַּר יִצְחָק לָא קַשְׁיָא: כָּאן – קוֹדֶם גְּזֵרָה, כָּאן – לְאַחַר גְּזֵרָה. אֶלָּא רַבָּה וְרַב יוֹסֵף דְּאָמְרִי לְהֶיתֵּירָא, אִי קוֹדֶם גְּזֵרָה – קַשְׁיָא מֵזִיד, אִי לְאַחַר גְּזֵרָה – קַשְׁיָא נַמִי שׁוֹגֵג! קַשְׁיָא. מַאי גְּזֵירְתָא? דְּאָמַר רַב יְהוּדָה בַּר שְׁמוּאֵל א"ר אַבָּא אָמַר רַב כֹּהֲנָא אָמַר רַב: בַּתְּחִילָּה הָיוּ אוֹמְרִים הַמְבַשֵּׁל בַּשַּׁבָּת, בְּשׁוֹגֵג – יֹאכַל, בְּמֵזִיד – לֹא יֹאכַל, וְה"ה לְשׁוֹכֵחַ. מִשֶּׁרַבּוּ מַשְׁהִין בְּמֵזִיד וְאוֹמְרִים 'שְׁכֵחִים אָנוּ' – חָזְרוּ וְקָנְסוּ עַל הַשּׁוֹכֵחַ. קַשְׁיָא דְּר' מֵאִיר אַדְּר' מֵאִיר, קַשְׁיָא דְּר' יְהוּדָה אַדְּר' יְהוּדָה! דְּר' מֵאִיר אַדְּר"מ לָא קַשְׁיָא; הָא – לְכַתְּחִילָּה, הָא – דִּיעֲבַד. דְּר' יְהוּדָה אַדְּר' יְהוּדָה נַמִי לָא קַשְׁיָא: כָּאן – בִּגְרוּפָה וּקְטוּמָה, כָּאן – בְּשֶׁאֵינָהּ גְּרוּפָה וּקְטוּמָה. אִיבַּעְיָא לְהוּ: עָבַר וְשִׁהָה מַאי, מִי קַנְסוּהוּ רַבָּנַן אוֹ לָא? ת"ש, דְּאָמַר שְׁמוּאֵל בַּר נָתָן א"ר חֲנִינָא: כְּשֶׁהָלַךְ רַבִּי יוֹסֵי לְצִיפּוֹרִי מָצָא חַמִּין שֶׁנִּשְׁתַּהוּ עַל גַּבֵּי כִּירָה – וְלֹא אָסַר לָהֶן, בֵּיצִים מְצוּמָּקוֹת שֶׁנִּשְׁתַּהוּ עַל גַּבֵּי כִּירָה – וְאָסַר לָהֶן. מַאי לָאו – לְאוֹתוֹ שַׁבָּת? לֹא, [ג]לַשַּׁבָּת הַבָּאָה. מִכְּלָל דְּבֵיצִים מְצוּמָּקוֹת מִצְטַמְּקוֹת וְיָפֶה לָהֶן נִינְהוּ?! אִין, דְּאָמַר רַב חָמָא בַּר חֲנִינָא: פַּעַם אַחַת נִתְאָרַחְתִּי אֲנִי וְרַבִּי לְמָקוֹם אֶחָד, וְהֵבִיאוּ לְפָנֵינוּ בֵּיצִים מְצוּמָּקוֹת כְּעוּזְרָדִין, וְאָכַלְנוּ מֵהֶן הַרְבֵּה.§ "ב"ה אוֹמְרִים: אַף מַחֲזִירִין".§ אָמַר רַב שֵׁשֶׁת: לְדִבְרֵי הָאוֹמֵר מַחֲזִירִין

רש"י

שָׁכַח קְדֵרָה. אֲלִיבָּא מַאן דְּאָסַר: הַמְבַשֵּׁל בְּשַׁבָּת. מִשְׁנָה הִיא: וְלָא שְׁנָא. אֲבָל הַאי דְּשָׁכַח קְדֵרָה – לָא שְׁנָא בֵּין שׁוֹגֵג לְמֵזִיד. וְהָכִי דָּרֵשׁ לְהוּ סְתָמָא, וְלָא פֵּירֵשׁ אִי אַשּׁוֹגֵג מְדַמֵּה לָהּ – וּמוּתָּר לְאוֹכְלָהּ, אִי אַמֵּזִיד מְדַמֵּה לָהּ – וְאָסוּר: בְּמֵזִיד נַמִי. אִם הִשְׁהָה עַל גַּבֵּי כִּירָה מִבְּעוֹד יוֹם – יֹאכַל: דְּלָא אָתֵי לְאִיעֲרוּמֵי. וְלַעֲשׂוֹת מֵזִיד, וְלוֹמַר: "שׁוֹגֵג הָיִיתִי" – דְּלָא נֶחְשְׁדוּ יִשְׂרָאֵל עַל הַשַּׁבָּתוֹת: דְּאָתֵי לְאִיעֲרוּמֵי. דְּאִיסּוּר דְּרַבָּנַן הוּא, וְקִילָא לֵיהּ, וְאָתֵי לַשְׁהוּיֵי מֵזִיד וְיֹאמַר "שָׁכַחְתִּי": מֵיתִיבֵי שָׁכַח קְדֵרָה כו' בְּשׁוֹגֵג. כְּגוֹן הַאי דְּשָׁכַח יֹאכַל בְּשַׁבָּת: בְּמֵזִיד. דְּלָא שָׁכַח אֶלָּא הִנִּיחַ – לֹא יֹאכַל: וּבָשָׂר טָרוּף. דְּגַלֵּי דַּעְתֵּיהּ דְּלָא לְאוֹרְחִים קָבָעֵי לָהּ: וְכָל הַמִּצְטַמֵּק וְיָפֶה לוֹ. כְּלוֹמַר: וְכֵן כָּל אוֹכֶל הַמִּצְטַמֵּק וְיָפֶה לָהֶם – אָסוּר לְאוֹכְלָן אִם הִשְׁהָן מֵזִיד: קָתָנֵי מִיהַת. בְּשֶׁלֹּא בִּישֵּׁל כָּל צָרְכּוֹ דְּיֵשׁ חִילּוּק בֵּין שׁוֹגֵג לְמֵזִיד בְּמַשְׁהֶה, קַשְׁיָא בֵּין לְרַבָּה וְרַב יוֹסֵף דְּשָׁרוּ מֵזִיד, בֵּין לְרַב נַחְמָן דְּאָסַר שׁוֹגֵג: בִּשְׁלָמָא לְרַב נַחְמָן. מָצֵי לְתָרוּצֵי, כִּי תַּנְיָא הַהִיא דְּשׁוֹגֵג יֹאכַל – לִפְנֵי גְּזֵירָה, דְּאָמְרִינַן לְקַמָּן דְּגָזְרוּ עַל הַשּׁוֹכְחִין. וְכִי אִיתְּמַר דְּרַבִּי חִיָּיא בַּר אַבָּא דְּתָרֵיגְנָא אַלִּיבֵּיהּ דְּשׁוֹגֵג אָסוּר – לְאַחַר גְּזֵירָה: אֶלָּא דְּרַבָּה וְרַב יוֹסֵף. דְּאָמְרֵי אַלִּיבָּא דְּר' חִיָּיא בַּר אַבָּא לְהֶתֵּירָא, אַף בְּמֵזִיד: אִי קוֹדֶם גְּזֵירָה. אִתְּמַר דְּר' חִיָּיא: קַשְׁיָא מִיהָא מֵזִיד. דְּהָכָא תַּנְיָא "בְּמֵזִיד לֹא יֹאכַל": וְאִי לְאַחַר גְּזֵירָה קַשְׁיָא נַמִי שׁוֹגֵג. דַּאֲפִילּוּ שׁוֹגֵג ה"ל לְמֵיסַר, דְּאִילּוּ מַתְנִי' קוֹדֶם גְּזֵירָה נִשְׁנֵית: הַמְבַשֵּׁל בְּשַׁבָּת. בְּיָדַיִם, דְּאִיכָּא חִיּוּבָא דְּאוֹרַיְיתָא: וְה"ה לְשׁוֹכֵחַ. דְּהַמַּשְׁהֶה נַמִי מִבְּעוֹד יוֹם, אִם שָׁכַח בְּשׁוֹגֵג – יֹאכַל, וְאִם בְּמֵזִיד הִשְׁהָה – לֹא יֹאכַל, כְּאִילּוּ בִּשְּׁלָהּ בְּיָדַיִם בְּשַׁבָּת: קַשְׁיָא דְּר' מֵאִיר אַדְּר' מֵאִיר. דִּתְנַן לְעֵיל בְּרֵישׁ פִּירְקִין לְר' מֵאִיר אַלִּיבָּא דְּב"ה: "חַמִּין אֲבָל לֹא תַּבְשִׁיל", וְהָכָא שָׁרֵי חַמִּין וְתַבְשִׁיל שֶׁבִּישֵּׁל כָּל צָרְכּוֹ: וְקַשְׁיָא דְּר' יְהוּדָה אַדְּר' יְהוּדָה. דְּהָתָם א"ר יְהוּדָה: "חַמִּין וְתַבְשִׁיל", וְהָכָא אָסַר תַּבְשִׁיל שֶׁבִּישֵּׁל כָּל צָרְכּוֹ: הָא לְכַתְּחִלָּה. מִשְׁנָה קַמַּיְיתָא לַשְׁהוֹת לְכַתְּחִלָּה קָמַיְירֵי, וְהָךְ – בְּהִשְׁהָה כְּבָר קָאָמַר, דְּמוּתָּר לְאוֹכְלָהּ: כָּאן בִּגְרוּפָה וּקְטוּמָה. הַהִיא דִּלְעֵיל אַיְירֵי בִּגְרוּפָה וּקְטוּמָה כִּדְקָתָנֵי בָּהּ: "מַשְׁהִין עַל גַּבֵּי גְּרוּפָה וּקְטוּמָה וְאֵין מַשְׁהִין עַל שֶׁאֵינָהּ גְּרוּפָה", וּמָה הֵן מַשְׁהִין עַל הַגְּרוּפָה שֶׁהִתַּרְנוּ לַשְׁהוֹת, ר"מ אוֹמֵר כו'. הִלְכָּךְ: אֲפִי' לְכַתְּחִלָּה שָׁרֵי ר' יְהוּדָה. וְהָכָא כְּשֶׁאֵינָהּ גְּרוּפָה – הִלְכָּךְ דִּיעֲבַד אָסַר: עָבַר וְשִׁהָה בְּמֵזִיד מַאי. מוּתָּר לְאוֹכְלָהּ אוֹ לָא? חַמִּין לֹא אָסַר. דְּמִצְטַמֵּק וְרַע לוֹ: בֵּיצִים אָסַר. דְּמִצְטַמֵּק וְיָפֶה לוֹ: מַאי לָאו לְאוֹתוֹ שַׁבָּת. אֲסָרָן עֲלֵיהֶן בַּאֲכִילָה: לֹא לַשַּׁבָּת הַבָּאָה. אָסַר לָהֶן עַכְשָׁיו שֶׁלֹּא לַעֲשׂוֹת כֵּן לַשַּׁבָּת הַבָּאָה, אֲבָל בַּאֲכִילָה שָׁרוּ: מִכְּלָל דְּבֵיצִים מְצוּמָּקוֹת כו'. בָּעֲיָא הִיא: וְהֵבִיאוּ לְפָנָיו. בְּחוֹל: כְּעוּזְרָדִין. שֶׁנִּצְטַמְּקוּ עַד שֶׁנַּעֲשׂוּ דַּקּוֹת כְּעוּזְרָדִין, קורמ"ש בְּלַעַ"ז, וּמִדְּקָאָמַר: "וְאָכַלְנוּ הַרְבֵּה" – מִכְּלָל דְּיָפֶה לָהֶן:

מַחֲזִירִין

תוספות

שכח קדרה על גבי כירה ובישלה בשבת מהו. אע"ג דקיי"ל כחנניא, הכא בעי בדלא בשיל כמאכל בן דרוסאי דמודה ביה חנניא. אי נמי: בעי אפי' בקידרא חייתא. והא דשרינן בפ"ק (דף יח: ושם) קידרא חייתא – היינו דוקא בתנור שחומו רב, דבלא חיתוי יתבשל עד למחר. אבל כירה דשליט בה אוירא – אסור, דאיכא למיחש שמא יחתה:

אבל האי דלא קעביד מעשה במזיד נמי יאכל. תימה: דהא אמר בפ"ק (שם): "לא תמלא אשה קדרה עססיות כו' ואם נתנה למוצאי שבת אסורין בכדי שיעשו"! וי"ל: דבלאו הכי פריך שפיר מברייתא דמייתי:

בשלמא לרב נחמן בר יצחק כאן קודם גזירה כו'. תימה לר"י: *לימא תרווייהו קודם גזירה, והא דשרי בברייתא שוגג – היינו בבשיל כמאכל בן דרוסאי. ורב נחמן איירי בדלא בשיל כמאכל בן דרוסאי כדפי'. ותירץ ר"ת: ד"בישלה בשבת" משמע שלא היתה קודם לכן כלל מבושלת. ולא בעי למימר נמי דרב נחמן סבר כר' יהודה דאסר תבשיל אפי' בישל כל צרכו, וכ"ש לא בישל – משום דדילמא ר' יהודה לא איירי אלא במזיד, אבל בשוגג מודה לר"מ דשרי אפי' לא בישל כל צרכו:

קשיא דר' מאיר אדר' מאיר. כאן משמע דסתם חמין ותבשיל הוי נמי מבושל כל צרכו, דאי לאו הכי – לא הוה פריך מידי. ורשב"א אומר: דאפי' אי סתם חמין ותבשיל הוי בלא בשיל כל צרכו פריך שפיר. דהא בשאינה גרופה משמע בברייתא דלעיל דאין משהין כלל אפי' בישל כל צרכו, דאי הוה שרי בישל כל צרכו – ה"ל לפרש מה הן משהין בשאינה גרופה, כדמפרש אגרופה, והכא שרי ר"מ בישל כל צרכו אפי' בשאינה גרופה. מ"מ נראה דסתם חמין ותבשיל הוי נמי בבשיל כל צרכו, מדפשיטא ליה לתלמודא דמאן דאסר להחזיר אסר אפי' בישל כל צרכו, כדמוכח גבי "ואף ר' אושעיא סבר כו'":

הא לכתחלה הא דיעבד. לא סגי בהאי שינויא. דהא לעיל שרי ר' מאיר סתם חמין, דהויא אפי' לא הוחמו כל צורכן אפי' לכתחלה, והכא אסר חמין שלא הוחמו כל צורכן אפי' דיעבד. אלא צריך לשנויי כדמשני אקשיא דר' יהודה אדר' יהודה: הא בגרופה וקטומה, הא בשאינה גרופה. ואדרבי יהודה נמי צריך לשנויא (דהכא), דהא לכתחלה הא דיעבד. דהא בשאינה גרופה אסר לעיל אפי' חמין שנתבשל כל צרכו, והכא שרי. אלא דאיכא לשנויי: הא לכתחלה הא דיעבד:

עבר ושהה מאי. בדלא בשיל כמאכל בן דרוסאי ליכא לאוקמי, דהא כבר פשט לעיל לאיסורא כרב נחמן בר יצחק. ונראה לר"י דמבעיא ליה בבשיל ובשוגג, ואליבא דר' יהודה אע"ג דאין הלכה כר' יהודה, אי אסר מצטמק ויפה לו דוקא במזיד, או דילמא אפי' בשוגג. ומייתי ראיה ממעשה דר' יוסי דאסר, ומשמע ליה דאפי' בשוגג היה, מדקאמר "ונשתהו" ולא קאמר "ושיהו". ומיהו לשון "עבר ושהה" משמע במזיד, כמו "עברה ולשה" דפסחים (דף מב.) ואומר רשב"א: דקודם גזירה בעו, דאחר גזירה – פשיטא דאסור בשוגג כמו מזיד:

לא לשבת הבאה. כולה סוגיא בשאינה גרופה, דבגרופה ליכא שום אמורא דאסר, כדפרישית לעיל. והיינו כרב דאסר מצטמק ויפה לו: אפי'

עין משפט נר מצוה

ז א מיי' פ"ג מהל' שבת הלכה ד ופ"ו הל' כג סמג לאוין סה טור וש"ע א"ח סימן שיח סעיף א:

ח ב ג מיי' פ"ג מהל' שבת הלכה ט סמג לאוין סה טוש"ע א"ח סימן רנג סעיף א:

[עי' תוספות ע"ז סו: ד"ה אמר רבא]

וסמא לתלמודא לא נראה לחלק כיון דר"מ אוסר אפילו תבשיל

מסורת הש"ס

תוספתא פ"ג ב"ק עא. חולין טו. גיטין נג: ביצה יז: [תרומות פ"ב מ"ג] כתובות לד.

תוספתא פ"ג

[פי' שמחתכין אותו חתיכות קטנות ומרסקין אותו עד שנטרף במקפה או בטיסני שכל זמן שמצטמק יוצא שמנו ומתערב עם הבישול ערוך ערך טרף ג]

רבינו חננאל

הא דבעו מר' חייא בר אבא שכח קדירה ע"ג כירה ובישלה בשבת ודרש להו המבשל בשבת בשוגג יאכל במזיד לא יאכל ולא שנא כלומר במבשל יש להפריש בין שוגג למזיד אבל בשוכח השוגג והמזיד שוין: **רבה** ורב יוסף אמרי שוכח בין שוגג ובין מזיד מותר לא קנסו רבנן אפילו במזיד רב נחמן בר יצחק אמר שניהן אסורין וקי"ל כוותיה ואותבינא עליה שכח קדירה על גבי כירה ובישלה בשבת בשוגג יאכל במזיד לא יאכל כו'. ועלתה לרבה ורב יוסף בקושיא ואקשינן הכא א"ר מאיר חמין שהוחמו כל צרכן ותבשיל שבישל כל צרכו בין בשוגג בין במזיד מותר ובתחלת הפרק אמר ומה הן משהין בש"א ולא כלום ובה"א חמין אבל לא תבשיל [ושנינן התם] לכתחילה דרבי יהודה אדרבי יהודה לא קשיא הא דקתני רבי יהודה הכא תבשיל שבישל כל צרכו אסור כירה שאינה גרופה ולא קטומה ולפיכך אסור והאי דקתני התם משהין ע"ג כירה לב"ה חמין ותבשיל בגרופה וקטומה וכיון שנתקשה רבה ורב יוסף נתקיימו דברי רב נחמן בר יצחק וקי"ל כוותיה כל השוכח קדירה ובישלה קודם גזירה הוה שרי ובתר גזירה קנסו רבנן אפילו שוגג ומאי גזירה דבתחלה היו אומרים המבשל בשבת בשוגג יאכל במזיד לא יאכל וה"ה לשוכח ומשרבו משהי קדירה במזיד ואומרים שוכחים אנן גזרו אף על השוכח. וכיון דסלקי דמצטמק ויפה לו אסור איבעיא לן עבר ושהה מאי ואתינן למפשטא מהא דתניא דאסיר רבי יוסי בצפורי ביצים מצומקים שנשתהו על גבי כירה (שמא) [ש"מ] עבר ושהה קנסו רבנן ודחינן לא אסר להו לעשות

רב נסים גאון

פרק כירה

אמר רבי חנינא כשהלך רבי יוסי לציפורי. הדבר שגרם לו לילך לציפורי הוא שמפורש בבמה מדליקין (דף לג) יוסי ששתק יגלה לציפורי:

ט א ב ג ד ה ו ז מיי' פ"ג מהל' שבת הלכה ה ז י סמג לאוין סה טוש"ע א"ח סימן רנג סעיף ב:
י ח מיי' פט"ז מהל' כלים הלכה יג:
יא ט י מיי' פ"ט מהל' שבת הל' ב ג טוש"ע א"ח סי' שיח סעיף ג:
יב כ מיי' פכ"ב מהל' שבת הלכה ג סמג שם טוש"ע א"ח סימן שכו סעיף ג וסימן רנז סעיף ה ו וסעיף א:
[יב] כ [מיי' פ"ט מהל' שבת הלכה ב]:

[א]מַחֲזִירִין – אֲפִילּוּ בְּשַׁבָּת. וְאַף ר' אוֹשַׁעְיָא סָבַר: אַף מַחֲזִירִין – אֲפִי' בְּשַׁבָּת; דְּא"ר אוֹשַׁעְיָא: פַּעַם אַחַת הָיִינוּ עוֹמְדִים לְעֵילָּא מֵר' חִיָּיא רַבָּה, וְהֶעֱלֵנוּ לוֹ קוּמְקְמוֹס שֶׁל חַמִּין מִדְּיוֹטָא הַתַּחְתּוֹנָה לְדְיוֹטָא הָעֶלְיוֹנָה, וּמָזַגְנוּ לוֹ אֶת הַכּוֹס וְהֶחֱזַרְנוּהוּ לִמְקוֹמוֹ, וְלֹא אָמַר לָנוּ דָּבָר. א"ר זְרִיקָא א"ר אַבָּא א"ר תַּדַּאי: לֹא שָׁנוּ אֶלָּא שֶׁעוֹדָן בְּיָדוֹ, אֲבָל הִנִּיחָן ע"ג קַרְקַע – אָסוּר. א"ר אַמִי: ר' תַּדַּאי *דַּעֲבַד – לְגַרְמֵיהּ הוּא דַּעֲבַד, אֶלָּא הָכִי א"ר חִיָּיא א"ר יוֹחָנָן: אֲפִילּוּ הִנִּיחָהּ עַל גַּבֵּי קַרְקַע – מוּתָּר. פְּלִיגִי בָּהּ רַב דִּימִי וְרַב שְׁמוּאֵל בַּר יְהוּדָה, וְתַרְוַיְיהוּ מִשְּׁמֵיהּ דְּרַבִּי אֶלְעָזָר אָמְרִי. חַד אָמַר: [ב]עוֹדָן בְּיָדוֹ – מוּתָּר, ע"ג קַרְקַע – אָסוּר. וְחַד אָמַר: הִנִּיחָן עַל גַּבֵּי קַרְקַע – נַמִי מוּתָּר. אָמַר חִזְקִיָּה מִשְּׁמֵיהּ דְּאַבַּיֵי: הָא דְּאָמְרַתְּ עוֹדָן בְּיָדוֹ מוּתָּר – לֹא אֲמַרַן אֶלָּא [ג]שֶׁדַּעְתּוֹ לְהַחֲזִיר, אֲבָל אֵין דַּעְתּוֹ לְהַחֲזִיר – אָסוּר. מִכְּלָל דְּעַל גַּבֵּי קַרְקַע, אע"פ שֶׁדַּעְתּוֹ לְהַחֲזִיר – אָסוּר. אִיכָּא דְּאָמְרִי, אָמַר חִזְקִיָּה מִשְּׁמֵיהּ דְּאַבַּיֵי: הָא דְּאָמְרַתְּ עַל גַּבֵּי קַרְקַע אָסוּר – לֹא אֲמַרַן אֶלָּא שֶׁאֵין דַּעְתּוֹ לְהַחֲזִיר, אֲבָל דַּעְתּוֹ לְהַחֲזִיר – מוּתָּר. מִכְּלָל שֶׁבְּעוֹדָן בְּיָדוֹ, אע"פ שֶׁאֵין דַּעְתּוֹ לְהַחֲזִיר – מוּתָּר. בָּעֵי ר' יִרְמְיָה: תְּלָאָן בְּמַקֵּל מַהוּ? הִנִּיחָן עַל גַּבֵּי מִטָּה מַהוּ? בָּעֵי רַב אַשִׁי: פִּינָּן מִמֵּיחַם לְמֵיחַם מַהוּ? תֵּיקוּ.§ **מתני'** [ד]תַּנּוּר שֶׁהִסִּיקוּהוּ בְּקַשׁ וּבִגְבָבָא לֹא יִתֵּן בֵּין מִתּוֹכוֹ בֵּין מֵעַל גַּבָּיו. כּוּפָּח שֶׁהִסִּיקוּהוּ בְּקַשׁ וּבִגְבָבָא – ה"ז כְּכִירַיִים, בְּגֶפֶת וּבְעֵצִים – הֲרֵי הוּא כְּתַנּוּר.§ **גמ'** 'תַּנּוּר שֶׁהִסִּיקוּהוּ' סָבַר רַב יוֹסֵף לְמֵימַר: 'תּוֹכוֹ' – תּוֹכוֹ מַמָּשׁ, 'עַל גַּבָּיו' – עַל גַּבָּיו מַמָּשׁ, אֲבָל לִסְמוֹךְ – שַׁפִּיר דָּמֵי. אֵיתִיבֵיהּ אַבַּיֵי: כּוּפָּח שֶׁהִסִּיקוּהוּ בְּקַשׁ וּבִגְבָבָא – הֲרֵי הוּא כְּכִירַיִים, בְּגֶפֶת וּבְעֵצִים – הֲרֵי הוּא כְּתַנּוּר, וְאָסוּר. הָא כְּכִירָה שָׁרֵי! בְּמַאי עָסְקִינַן? אִילֵימָא עַל גַּבָּיו, וּבְמַאי? אִילֵימָא כְּשֶׁאֵינוֹ גָּרוּף וְקָטוּם, אֶלָּא כִּירָה כִּי אֵינָהּ גְּרוּפָה וּקְטוּמָה עַל גַּבָּיו מִי שָׁרֵי?! אֶלָּא לָאו – לִסְמוֹךְ, וְקָתָנֵי: הֲרֵי הוּא כְּתַנּוּר, וַאֲסִיר? אָמַר רַב אַדָּא בַּר אַהֲבָה: הָכָא בְּכוּפָּח גָּרוּף וְקָטוּם, וְתַנּוּר גְּרוּפָה וּקְטוּמָה עָסְקִינַן. הֲרֵי הוּא כְּתַנּוּר – [ה]דְּאע"ג דְּגָרוּף וְקָטוּם, עַל גַּבָּיו אָסוּר. דְּאִי כְּכִירָה – כִּי גְּרוּפָה וּקְטוּמָה, שַׁפִּיר דָּמֵי.§ תַּנְיָא כְּוָותֵיהּ דְּאַבַּיֵי: [ו]תַּנּוּר שֶׁהִסִּיקוּהוּ בְּקַשׁ וּבִגְבָבָא – אֵין סוֹמְכִין לוֹ, וְאֵין צָרִיךְ לוֹמַר עַל גַּבָּיו, וְאֵין צָרִיךְ לוֹמַר לְתוֹכוֹ, וְאֵין צָרִיךְ לוֹמַר בְּגֶפֶת וּבְעֵצִים. כּוּפָּח שֶׁהִסִּיקוּהוּ בְּקַשׁ וּבִגְבָבָא – סוֹמְכִין לוֹ[א], וְאֵין נוֹתְנִין עַל גַּבָּיו. בְּגֶפֶת וּבְעֵצִים – אֵין סוֹמְכִין לוֹ. אֲמַר לֵיהּ רַב אַחָא בְּרֵיהּ דְּרָבָא לְרַב אַשִׁי: הַאי כּוּפָּח הֵיכִי דָּמֵי? אִי כְּכִירָה דָּמֵי – אֲפִילּוּ בְּגֶפֶת וּבְעֵצִים נַמִי, אִי כְּתַנּוּר דָּמֵי – אֲפִילּוּ בְּקַשׁ וּבִגְבָבָא נַמִי לָא! אֲמַר לֵיהּ: נָפֵישׁ הַבְלֵיהּ מִדְּכִירָה, וְזוּטַר הַבְלֵיהּ מִדְּתַנּוּר. הֵיכִי דָּמֵי כּוּפָּח, הֵיכִי דָּמֵי כִּירָה? א"ר יוֹסֵי בַּר חֲנִינָא: [ז]כּוּפָּח – מְקוֹם שְׁפִיתַת קְדֵרָה אַחַת, כִּירָה מְקוֹם שְׁפִיתַת שְׁתֵּי קְדֵרוֹת. אָמַר אַבַּיֵי, וְאִיתֵימָא רַבִּי יִרְמְיָה: אַף אֲנַן נַמִי תְּנֵינָא: *כִּירָה [ח]שֶׁנֶּחְלְקָה – לְאוֹרְכָּהּ טְהוֹרָה, לְרָחְבָּהּ – טְמֵאָה. כּוּפָּח בֵּין לְאוֹרְכּוֹ בֵּין לְרוֹחְבּוֹ – טָהוֹר.§ **מתני'** [ט]אֵין נוֹתְנִין בֵּיצָה בְּצַד הַמֵּיחַם בִּשְׁבִיל שֶׁתִּתְגַּלְגֵּל, וְלֹא יַפְקִיעֶנָּה בְּסוּדָרִין, וְר' יוֹסֵי מַתִּיר. [י]וְלֹא יַטְמִינֶנָּה בַּחוֹל וּבַאֲבַק דְּרָכִים בִּשְׁבִיל שֶׁתִּצָּלֶה. מַעֲשֶׂה שֶׁעָשׂוּ אַנְשֵׁי טְבֶרְיָא [כ]וְהֵבִיאוּ סִילּוֹן שֶׁל צוֹנֵן לְתוֹךְ אַמָּה שֶׁל חַמִּין, אָמְרוּ לָהֶם חֲכָמִים: אִם בְּשַׁבָּת – כְּחַמִּין שֶׁהוּחַמּוּ בְּשַׁבָּת, וַאֲסוּרִין בִּרְחִיצָה וּבִשְׁתִיָּה. אִם בְּיוֹם טוֹב – כְּחַמִּין שֶׁהוּחַמּוּ בְּיוֹם טוֹב, וַאֲסוּרִין בִּרְחִיצָה וּמוּתָּרִין בִּשְׁתִיָּה.§ **גמ'** אִיבַּעְיָא לְהוּ: גִּלְגֵּל מַאי? אָמַר רַב יוֹסֵף[ב]: גִּלְגֵּל – חַיָּיב חַטָּאת. אָמַר מָר בְּרֵיהּ דְּרַבִּינָא: אַף אֲנַן נַמִי תְּנֵינָא: כָּל

מַחֲזִירִין אֲפִילּוּ בְּשַׁבָּת. בְּיוֹם הַמָּחֳרָת, וְלָא תֵּימָא פְּלוּגְתַּיְיהוּ מִשֶּׁחֲשֵׁכָה, וְהָכָא הוּא דְּשָׁרוּ – מִשּׁוּם דְּמוֹכְחָא מִילְּתָא דְּאַדַּעְתָּא דְּאַהֲדוּרֵי לְאוֹרֶךְ מָחָר שָׁקֵיל לֵיהּ, אֲבָל בַּיּוֹם לָא מוֹכַח דְּשָׁקֵיל לֵיהּ אַדַּעְתָּא דְּאַהֲדוּרֵי, וּבָטְלָה לָהּ הַטְמָנָה, וְה"ל כְּמַטְמִין לְכַתְּחִלָּה: **קוּמְקְמוֹס.** יוֹרָה קְטַנָּה: **דְּיוֹטָא.** עֲלִיָּיה: **לִמְקוֹמוֹ.** לַכִּירָה: **אֲבָל הִנִּיחַ עַל גַּבֵּי קַרְקַע אָסוּר.** לְהַחֲזִיר, דְּבָטְלָה לָהּ הַטְמָנָה דְּאֶתְמוֹל, וְהָוֵי כְּמַטְמִין לְכַתְּחִלָּה: **לְגַרְמֵיהּ.** יָחִיד הוּא בַּדָּבָר, וְאֵין הֲלָכָה כְּמוֹתוֹ: **תְּלָאָן בְּמַקֵּל מַהוּ.** כְּעוֹדָן בְּיָדוֹ דָּמֵי, אוֹ כְּהִנִּיחָן ע"ג קַרְקַע דָּמֵי: **פִּינָּן מִמֵּיחַם לְמֵיחַם מַהוּ.** מִי הָוֵי כְּמַטְמִין לְכַתְּחִלָּה וְאָסוּר לְהַחֲזִירָן לַכִּירָה, אוֹ לָא: **מֵיחַם.** קוּמְקְמוֹס שֶׁמְּחַמֵּם בּוֹ חַמִּין: **מתני' תַּנּוּר.** מִתּוֹךְ שֶׁקָּצָר לְמַעְלָה וְרָחָב לְמַטָּה, נִקְלָט חוּמּוֹ לְתוֹכוֹ טְפֵי מִכִּירָה: **כּוּפָּח.** בַּגְּמָרָא מְפָרֵשׁ לָהּ: עָשׂוּי חָלָל כְּכִירָה, אֲבָל אָרְכּוֹ כְּרָחְבּוֹ, וְאֵין בּוֹ אֶלָּא שִׁיעוּר שְׁפִיתַת קְדֵירָה אַחַת, וְכִירָה יֵשׁ בָּהּ שְׁפִיתַת שְׁתֵּי קְדֵירוֹת: **גמ' עַל גַּבָּיו.** עַל שְׂפָתוֹ: **אֲבָל לִסְמוֹךְ.** אֵצֶל דּוֹפְנוֹ: **הָא כְּבִירָה שָׁרֵי.** כְּלוֹמַר: מִדְּקָתָנֵי "הֲרֵי הוּא כְּתַנּוּר", מִכְּלָל דְּאִי הֲוָה מְדַמֵּי לֵיהּ לְכִירָה – הֲוָה שָׁרֵי, וְשָׁמְעִינַן מִינָּהּ דְּכִירָה שֶׁהוּסַּק בְּגֶפֶת וּבְעֵצִים שָׁרֵי: **וּבְמַאי קָאֵי.** קס"ד בְּשֶׁאֵינָהּ גְּרוּפָה, וְאִי עַל גַּבָּהּ מִי שָׁרֵי?! **תַּנְיָא כְּוָותֵיהּ דְּאַבַּיֵי.** דְּאָסוּר לִסְמוֹךְ לַתַּנּוּר: **אֲפִי' בְּגֶפֶת וְעֵצִים.** לִשְׁתְּרֵי בִּגְרוּפָה וּקְטוּמָה: **שֶׁנֶּחְלְקָה לְאוֹרְכָּהּ.** הֲרֵי בָּטְלוּ שְׁתֵּי שְׁפִיתוֹתֶיהָ, שֶׁנֶּחְלֶקֶת רָחְבָּהּ לִשְׁתַּיִם – הִלְכָּךְ טָהֲרָה מִטּוּמְאָתָהּ, שֶׁהֲרֵי נִיתְּצָה: **נֶחְלְקָה לְרָחְבָּהּ.** נִמְצְאוּ שְׁתֵּי הַשְּׁפִיתוֹת קַיָּימוֹת, זוֹ לְבַדָּהּ וְזוֹ לְבַדָּהּ: **כּוּפָּח בֵּין לְאוֹרְכָּהּ בֵּין לְרָחְבָּהּ טְהוֹרָה.** שֶׁהֲרֵי אָרְכָּהּ כְּרָחְבָּהּ, וְכוּלָּהּ מְקוֹם שְׁפִיתָה אַחַת: **מתני' אֵין נוֹתְנִין בֵּיצָה בְּצַד הַמֵּיחַם.** קוּמְקְמוֹס שֶׁל נְחֹשֶׁת: **בִּשְׁבִיל שֶׁתִּתְגַּלְגֵּל.** שֶׁתִּצָּלֶה קְלָת עַד שֶׁתְּהֵא מְגֻלְגֶּלֶת: **וְלֹא יַפְקִיעֶנָּה בְּסוּדָרִין.** לֹא יְשַׁבְּרֶנָּה עַל סוּדָר שֶׁהוּחַם בַּחַמָּה כְּדֵי שֶׁתִּצָּלֶה מֵחוּמּוֹ שֶׁל סוּדָר: **בַּחוֹל וּבַאֲבַק דְּרָכִים.** שֶׁהוּחַמּוּ מִכֹּחַ חַמָּה. וּבַגְּמָרָא מְפָרֵשׁ אַמַּאי לָא פָּלֵיג ר' יוֹסֵי בְּהָא: **וְהֵבִיאוּ סִילּוֹן.** מִבְּעוֹד יוֹם: **שֶׁל צוֹנֵן.** כְּדֵי לְחַמְמָן, דְּהַמַּיִם נִמְשָׁכִין וּבָאִין כָּל הַשַּׁבָּת: **לְתוֹךְ אַמָּה.** שֶׁל חַמֵּי טְבֶרְיָא: **אִם בְּשַׁבָּת.** אוֹתָן שֶׁבָּאוּ בַּשַּׁבָּת: ה"ג: כְּחַמִּין שֶׁהוּחַמּוּ:

אפילו בשבת. פירש בקונטרס: בשבת ביום המחרת. ולפ"ז ה"ל למינקט אפי' ביום השבת. ולמאי דפרישית דעיקר פלוגתייהו בחול – אתי שפיר: **פינה** ממיחם למיחם מהו. וא"ת: דבפרק "במה טומנין" (לקמן דף נא.) תניא: וכן היה רשב"ג אומר לא אסרו אלא באותו מיחם, אבל פינה ממיחם למיחם – מותר, אלמא במיחם אחר שרי טפי. והכי משמע איפכא! ואור"ת: דהכא גבי השהה ע"ג כירה, כשהוא באותו מיחם שהוא חם – לא אתי לחתויי, אבל במיחם אחר שהוא קר – אתי לחתויי. אבל גבי הטמנה שרי טפי כשהוא קר, דחיתוי מועט לא יועיל: **ורשב"א** מפרש בשם ר"י: דהתם בהטמנה דהוי לצורך מחר – ליכא למיחש לחיתויי, דבלא חיתוי יתחמם הרבה. אבל הכא דבעי לה בלילה – איכא למיחש לחיתויי. ומיהו קצת משמע התם דמיירי במטמין בלילה. (ת"י):

תנור שהסיקוהו בקש ובגבבא לא יתן כו'. אי להחזיר תנן – הכא נמי האי "לא יתן" – לא יחזיר, אבל להשהות משהה אפילו בתנור שאינו גרוף וקטום. כדמשמע בפ"ק (דף יח:) *דשרינן קידרא חייתא ובשיל כמאכל בן דרוסאי אפילו באינו גרוף וקטום. ומשמע התם דבתנור איירי, דקאי אהא דקתני התם לעיל: "לא תמלא אשה קדרה *עססיות כו'":

אילימא בשאינה גרופה. האי לישנא לאו דוקא. דאביי סבר דלא מיתוקמה בגרופה, דבגרופה לא מסתבר ליה שיהא חילוק בין גפת ועצים לקש וגבבא. דאי הוה מצי אביי לאוקמה בגרופה כדמוקי לה רב אדא – לא הוה מצי למפשט מידי. ורב אדא דמוקי לה בגרופה סבר דיש לעולם יותר חום כשהסיקוה בגפת ובעצים אע"ג דגרופה מבקש וגבבא:

תניא כוותיה דאביי כו'. יש דגרסי בסיפא: כופח שהסיקוהו בגפת ובעצים *אין סומכין לה, דאי גרס "סומכין לה" לא אתא כוותיה דאביי, דאית ליה דבכופח נמי אין סומכין, כדאמרינן לעיל. וי"ל: דאי גרסינן "סומכין" איכא לאוקמה בגרופה, ונקט גפת ועצים לרבותא – דאפילו הכי סומכין לה:

לא יטמיננה בחול. אע"ג דאמר ב"לא יחפור" (ב"ב דף יט. ושם) דחול דקריר – מקרר, דחמים – מחים. והכא בילה היא קרה, הכא מיירי בחול שהוחם בחמה, דומיא דאבק דרכים:

מעשה והביאו סילון של צונן לתוך אמה של חמין כו'. מבעוד יום הביאוהו, כדפירש בקונטרס. ואין שום איסור כלל בהבאה, כדתניא בפרק קמא (דף יח.): "פותקין מים לגינה ומתמלאת והולכת כל השבת כולה". ואסרו ברחיצה גזירה שמא יערבם בשבת. ולערבם בשבת אסור משום תולדות האור, ושיבא כתדא גזירה. *ואם היינו מפרשים דבסילון היו בו נקבים, וכשהיו רוחצים בשבת היו פותחים הנקבים ומתערבין הצוננין בחמין – הוה אתי שפיר טפי, דהשתא ליכא אלא חדא גזירה אטו חמי האור. אך בגמרא מדמי לה להטמנה מבעוד יום, ויליף מינה לאסור להטמין

וברכות מת. וש"נ

כלים פ"ז מ"ג

הגהות הגר"א

[א] גמ' סומכין לו ואין נותנין. נ"ב צ"ל סומכין לו ונותנין כו':

גליון הש"ס

תוס' ד"ה תנור כו' דשרינן קידרא חייתא ובשיל כמאכל בן דרוסאי. ק"ל הא שם לא נזכר מן מאכב"ד אלא חמם ובשיל שפיר דמי אלא הא [illegible] כתבו שם דהיינו כמאכב"ד דהא קיימא בן כחנניא וא"כ איך עשו כאן הוכחה מזה דלמא באמת תנור חמיר דכמאכב"ד אסור ולאמרי ובשיל ע"ד היינו כפשוטו ובשיל לגמרי גם אמאי לא הוכיחו כפשוטו דהא קתני ולא תחרה על גבי גחלים אלא כדי שיקרמו פניה תחררה היינו בתנור כמ"ש תוס' לעיל דף לו ע"א ד"ה אלא וכו' אף על גב דתחררה בתוכה הוא. והיינו ע"כ משום דתחררה אופין בתנור. עכ"פ ראייתם מפ"ק תמוה מאד:

ולר מתני' להשהות תנן בתנור נמי אסור להשהות אע"ג דקידרא חייתא לעיל שרי הוא כחנניא ומתני' אי להשהות תנן אתיא דלא כחנניא [ת"י]

ולפ"ז צריך למגרס בתר הכי ואע"ג [illegible] סומכין ע"ג [illegible] ואפילו בתוכה [ת"י]

והא דחשיב לה כחמין שהוחמו בשבת משמע טפי כפי' ראשון [ת"י]

רבינו חננאל

כן אלא לשבת הבאה וכן סוגיא דשמעתא: פיס' בה"א אף מחזירין אוקימנא הא דקתני מחזירין בשבת הוא ואפי' כמה פעמים ודוקא בכירה גרופה וקטומה והני מילי שלא הניחם ע"ג קרקע כלל אלא מחזיקם בידו ודעתו עליהם להחזירם הוא ששנינו אף מחזירין אבל אם הניחם ע"ג קרקע אע"פ שהיה בדעתו להחזירם לכירה אסור ואסיקנא לשמעתא בתרי לשני. וקי"ל כל כי האי גוונא בדאורייתא עבדינן לחומרא. ושבת איסורא דאורייתא היא: תלאם במקל או הניחם ע"ג המטה או הניחם בכרעי המטה או פינם ממיחם למיחם הני כולהו איבעא ולא אפשיטו ועלו בתיקו. וקי"ל כל תיקו דאיסורא לחומרא: **מתני'** תנור שהסיקו בקש ובגבבא כו' אוקמא אביי לא יסמוך. תניא כוותיה תנור שהסיקו בקש ובגבבא אין סומכין לו ואין צ"ל על גביו. ואין צ"ל שהסיקו בגפת או בעצים. כופח שהסיקוה בקש ובגבבא הרי הוא ככירה. בגפת ובעצים הרי הוא כתנור ואסור. ואע"פ שהוא גרוף וקטום. ואסיק' כופח מקום שפיתת קדירה אחת. כירה מקום שפיתת שתי קדירות. [illegible] הבליה מכירה וזוטר הבליה מדתנור וק"ל מתני' בתנור של נחתומין. מפורש בלא יחפור (ב"ב כ:) אבל תנור [דידן] ככירה דמי. פיס' אין נותנין ביצה בצד המיחם בשביל שתתגלגל גלגל

כָּל *שֶׁבָּא בְּחַמִּין מִלִּפְנֵי הַשַּׁבָּת – שׁוֹרִין אוֹתוֹ בְּחַמִּין בַּשַּׁבָּת, וְכָל שֶׁלֹּא בָּא בְּחַמִּין מִלִּפְנֵי הַשַּׁבָּת – מְדִיחִין אוֹתוֹ בְּחַמִּין בַּשַּׁבָּת, חוּץ מִן הַמָּלִיחַ יָשָׁן וְקוֹלְיָּיס הָאִיסְפַּנִין שֶׁהֲדָחָתָן זוֹ הִיא גְּמַר מְלַאכְתָּן. ש"מ.§ "וְלֹא יַפְקִיעֶנָּה בַּסּוּדָרִין"§ וְהָא דִּתְנַן: *"נוֹתְנִין תַּבְשִׁיל לְתוֹךְ הַבּוֹר בִּשְׁבִיל שֶׁיְּהֵא שָׁמוּר, וְאֶת הַמַּיִם הַיָּפִים בָּרָעִים בִּשְׁבִיל שֶׁיִּצַּנְּנוּ, וְאֶת הַצּוֹנֵן בַּחַמָּה בִּשְׁבִיל שֶׁיֵּחַמּוּ" לֵימָא רַבִּי יוֹסֵי הִיא וְלָא רַבָּנַן! אָמַר רַב נַחְמָן: [א]בַּחַמָּה – דְּכ"ע לָא פְּלִיגִי דְּשָׁרֵי, בְּתוֹלְדוֹת הָאוּר – כ"ע לָא פְּלִיגִי דַּאֲסִיר, כִּי פְּלִיגִי – בְּתוֹלְדוֹת הַחַמָּה; מָר סָבַר: גָּזְרִינַן [ב]תּוֹלְדוֹת הַחַמָּה אַטּוּ תּוֹלְדוֹת הָאוּר, וּמָר סָבַר: לָא גָּזְרִינַן.§ "וְלֹא יַטְמִינֶנָּה בַּחוֹל".§ וְלִיפְלוֹג נַמִי ר' יוֹסֵי בְּהָא! רַבָּה אָמַר: גְּזֵרָה שֶׁמָּא יַטְמִין בָּרֶמֶץ. רַב יוֹסֵף אָמַר: מִפְּנֵי שֶׁמֵּזִיז עָפָר מִמְּקוֹמוֹ. מַאי בֵּינַיְיהוּ? אִיכָּא בֵּינַיְיהוּ: עָפָר תִּיחוֹחַ. מֵיתִיבִי, רשב"ג אוֹמֵר: מְגַלְגְּלִין בֵּיצָה עַל גַּבֵּי גַּג רוֹתֵחַ, וְאֵין מְגַלְגְּלִין בֵּיצָה עַל גַּבֵּי סִיד רוֹתֵחַ. בִּשְׁלָמָא לְמַאן דְּאָמַר "גְּזֵרָה שֶׁמָּא יַטְמִין בָּרֶמֶץ" – לֵיכָּא לְמִגְזַר. אֶלָּא לְמַאן דְּאָמַר "מִפְּנֵי שֶׁמֵּזִיז עָפָר מִמְּקוֹמוֹ" – לִיגְזַר! סְתָם גַּג לֵית בֵּיהּ עָפָר. ת"ש: מַעֲשֶׂה שֶׁעָשׂוּ אַנְשֵׁי טְבֶרְיָא וְהֵבִיאוּ סִילוֹן שֶׁל צוֹנֵן לְתוֹךְ אַמָּה שֶׁל חַמִּין וכו'. בִּשְׁלָמָא לְמַאן דְּאָמַר "גְּזֵרָה שֶׁמָּא יַטְמִין בָּרֶמֶץ" – הַיְינוּ דְּדָמְיָא לְהַטְמָנָה, אֶלָּא לְמַאן דְּאָמַר "מִפְּנֵי שֶׁמֵּזִיז עָפָר מִמְּקוֹמוֹ" – מַאי אִיכָּא לְמֵימַר? מִי סָבְרַתְּ מַעֲשֵׂה טְבֶרְיָא אַסֵּיפָא קָאֵי? אַרֵישָׁא קָאֵי: לֹא יַפְקִיעֶנָּה בַּסּוּדָרִין, וְר' יוֹסֵי מַתִּיר. וְהָכִי קָאָמְרִי לֵיהּ רַבָּנַן לְר' יוֹסֵי: הָא מַעֲשֶׂה דְּאַנְשֵׁי טְבֶרְיָא דְּתוֹלְדוֹת חַמָּה הוּא, וְאָסְרִי לְהוּ רַבָּנַן! אֲמַר לְהוּ: הַהוּא – תּוֹלְדוֹת אוּר הוּא, דְּחָלְפִי אַפִּיתְחָא דְּגֵיהִנָּם. אָמַר רַב חִסְדָּא מִמַּעֲשֶׂה

רש"י

גמ' כל שבא בחמין. כָּל מָלוּחַ שֶׁבָּא בְּחַמִּין מֵע"ש מוּדָחִין וְשׁוֹרִין אוֹתוֹ בְּחַמִּין בַּשַּׁבָּת, וְאֵין בּוֹ מִשּׁוּם תִּיקּוּן – שֶׁהֲרֵי נִתְקַן כְּבָר: מדיחין. שֶׁאֵין זֶה גְּמַר מְלַאכְתּוֹ, אֲבָל לֹא שׁוֹרִין: חוץ מדג מלוח ישן או קוליים האיספנין. דָּג שֶׁקּוֹרִין טוניי"א: שֶׁהֲדָחָתוֹ זֶהוּ גְּמַר מְלַאכְתּוֹ. מִדְּקָרֵי לֵיהּ גְּמַר מְלַאכְתּוֹ – ש"מ זֶהוּ בִּישּׁוּלוֹ, וְחַיָּיב: והא דתנן. בְּפֶרֶק "חָבִית": נותנין כו' הַמַּיִם צוֹנֵן: בחמה. בַּשֶּׁמֶשׁ: דשרי. דְּאֵין דֶּרֶךְ בִּישּׁוּלוֹ בְּכָךְ, וְחַמָּה בָּאוּר לָא מִיחַלְּפָא דְּלִיגְזַר הָא אַטּוּ הָא: בתולדות האור. כְּגוֹן אִם הוּחַם הַסּוּדָר הַזֶּה בָּאוּר מִתְּחִילָּה: דאסיר. דְּהָוֵי בִּישּׁוּל: תולדות חמה. שֶׁהוּחַם הַסּוּדָר בַּחַמָּה: אטו תולדות האור. דְּמַאן דְּחָזֵי סָבַר דְּתוֹלְדוֹת הָאוּר נִינְהוּ: שמא יטמין ברמץ. דְּמַאן דְּחָזֵי סָבַר: מִכְּדֵי הַאי לְבַשּׁוּלֵי וְהַאי לְבַשּׁוּלֵי, וְתַרְוַיְיהוּ דֶּרֶךְ הַטְמָנָה – מַה לִּי רֶמֶץ מַה לִּי חוֹל, וּמִשּׁוּם הָכִי מוֹדֶה ר' יוֹסֵי: שמא יזיז עפר. שֶׁמָּא לֹא יְהֵא שָׁם חוֹל עָקוּר לְכָל הַצּוֹרֶךְ, וְאָתֵי לַאֲזוּזֵי עָפָר הַדָּבוּק, וְהָוֵי חוֹפֵר גּוּמָּא: עפר תיחוח. כְּלוֹמַר: תִּיחוֹחַ בְּעוֹמֶק, דְּלֵיכָּא לְמֵיחַשׁ לְמֵזִיז: גג רותח. שֶׁרְתָחוֹ חַמָּה: ואין מגלגלין בסיד רותח. דְּהוּא תּוֹלְדוֹת הָאוּר: ליכא למיגזר. בְּגַג רוֹתֵחַ, דְּהָא לֹא מַטְמִין לֵיהּ: אלא. לְשֶׁמָּא יָזִיז עָפָר וִיכַסֶּנּוּ בּוֹ לִיגְזַר: לתוך אמה של חמין. וְחַמֵּי טְבֶרְיָא לָאו תּוֹלְדוֹת הָאוּר נִינְהוּ, וְאַפ"ה אָסְרוּ לְהוּ, וּמוֹדֶה בְּהָא ר' יוֹסֵי: דדמיא להטמנה. שֶׁמַּטְמִין מַיִם בְּמַיִם: מי סברת מעשה (א)אסיפא קאי. לְסַיְּיעְתָּא דְּחוֹל וְאָבָק, וּלְאוֹרוּיֵי דְּתוֹלְדוֹת חַמָּה כִּי הַאי גַּוְונָא אֲסִירֵי לְדִבְרֵי הַכֹּל: ארישא קאי. אַפְּלוּגְתָּא, וְרַבָּנַן הוּא דְּאָמְרֵי לָהּ. אֲבָל לְר' יוֹסֵי – כה"ג לָא מִיתְסַר אֶלָּא מִשּׁוּם דְּהָנֵי תּוֹלְדוֹת הָאוּר נִינְהוּ: והא מעשה. דְּחַמֵּי טְבֶרְיָא דְּתוֹלְדוֹת חַמָּה נִינְהוּ, וְדָמֵי לְאַפְקַעְתָּא דְּסוּדָרִין דְּלֵיכָּא לְמִגְזַר לְשֶׁמָּא יָזִיז, וְאָסְרֵי לְהוּ:

בָּטְלָה

תוספות

להטמין מבעוד יום בדבר המוסיף הבל, גזירה שמא יטמין ברמץ *ושמא יחתה. ולר"י נראה: דמה שהיו מתערבין צונן בחמין – לא הוה דמי להטמנה, וליכא למילף מינה. דאיכא למימר דאסרי להו מפני שמבשל המים צוננין. ונראה לו דסילון לא היה מתערב בחמין, כי היה מוקף מחילות מכל צד, והיו מתחממין המים צוננים שבסילון מחמת חמי טבריא. ולא היו רוחצות בחמי טבריא עצמן לפי שריחן רע. והשתא דמיא להטמנה, שמים צוננין היו נטמנין בתוך החמין להתחמם:

כל שבא בחמין מלפני השבת. פירוש: שנתבשל לגמרי, כדמפרש לקמן בפרק "חבית" (דף קמה:): כגון תרנגולת דרבי אבא, שורין אותו בחמין אפילו בכלי ראשון וכל שלא בא כו' מדיחין אותו. לפירוש רשב"א דמפרש דעירוי ככלי שני – אתי שפיר הכא דאין שורין אותו בכלי ראשון, אבל מדיחין אותו מכלי ראשון דרך עירוי. אבל לפר"ת, דמפרש דעירוי הוי ככלי ראשון – ע"כ מדיחין אותו מכלי שני קאמר, וא"כ מאי איריא "מדיחין" אפילו שורין נמי! ואומר ר"י: דאפילו בכלי שני אין שורין, דהואיל דהמים חמין – מיחזי כמבשל. ואע"ג דתנן לקמן (דף מב:): "אבל נותן לתוך הקערה או לתוך התמחוי" – היינו דוקא תבלין שהן עשויין למתק את הקדירה, ולא מיחזי כמבשל. א"נ ה"ה שורין אותו, כיון דאיירי בכלי שני. והא דנקט מדיחין – לאשמעינן דאפילו הדחה הויא גמר מלאכה במליח הישן וקוליים האיספנין:

שמא יטמין ברמץ. אבל הפקעת סודרין לא גזרו אטו שמא יטמין ברמץ, דסודרין לא דמו לרמץ. ואטו סודרין שנתחממו באור לא בעי ר' יוסי למיגזר, דאין דרך לחממן כל כך שלא יהיו נשרפין:

מפני שמזיז עפר ממקומו. פי' בקונטרס: מתוך שלא יהיה לו חול עקור כל הצורך לכסות, אתי לאזוזי עפר הדבוק, והוי חופר גומא. וקשה לריב"א: דהא ליכא איסורא דאורייתא בחופר גומא ואינו צריך אלא לעפרה לרבי שמעון דאמר: "מלאכה שאינה צריכה לגופה פטור עליה"! וצריך לומר לפי פירוש הקונטרס: גזירה שמא יחפור הגומא לטמון הבילה בתוכה. ור"ת *הקשה לפירוש הקונטרס: דמאי דמשני בסמוך סתם גג לית ביה עפר, אדרבה: הא סתם גג יש בו מעזיבה, וכיון דגזרינן שמא יחפור לגזור שמא יחפור במעזיבה ויכסה! ועוד, שמצא בספרים ישנים: מפני שמזיז עפר ממקומו. ולפירוש הקונטרס צריך לגרוס "שמא יזיז". ומפרש ר"ת: שמזיז עפר, שהוא מוקצה, ממקומו כשתוחב הבילה בתוך העפר. וסבר רב יוסף דטלטול מן הצד שמיה טלטול, ואיכא בינייהו עפר תיחוח – היינו שהוא תיחוח כל כך כשמניח הבילה מידו ליפול נטמנת מעצמה בתוך העפר, ואינו מזיז עפר ממקומו בידים. והשתא אתי שפיר, דסתם גג לית ביה עפר כל כך שיוכל להטמין בתוכו, ולחפירת מעזיבה לא חיישינן. ולפירוש זה הוה מצי למימר: "איכא בינייהו עפר מוכן". ובלאו הכי איכא בינייהו טובא, כגון גג דאית ביה עפר. שמא יטמין – ליכא למימר, ושמא יזיז – איכא. וכגון מעשה דאנשי טבריא, דשייך "יטמין" ולא שייך "יזיז". אבל קשה לרשב"א: דקאמר בסמוך "אלא למ"ד שמא יזיז עפר לגזור", ולהאי פירוש לא שייך למימר "לגזור", אלא הוה ליה למימר "ליתסר"! ויש ליישב: דמשום דכל איסורי דרבנן הם גזירה אטו דאורייתא – נקט האי לישנא. ועוד פירש רבינו תם בספר הישר: שמזיז עפר ממקומו, והוי חופר שהוא תולדה דחורש, אפילו בעפר תיחוח כגון חול ואבק דרכים, כדמוכח בביצה (דף ח. ושם) דקאמר: והא קעביד כתישה בעפר תיחוח, והא קעביד גומא. אלמא: בעפר תיחוח שייך נמי גומא, והא דקאמר הכא: "איכא בינייהו עפר תיחוח" היינו כל כך תיחוח כשמניח ביצה עליו נשקעת מאליה, דבההוא ודאי לא שייך חורש. וקשה לפי': דאמאי פליג רבה אדרב יוסף, ולא חייש למה שמזיז עפר? מדקאמר: אלא למאן דאמר שמזיז כו', משמע דלרבה ניחא! ויש לומר: דרבה סבר דלא שייך גומא אלא כשנוטל בידו מן העפר, ונשאר מקום מן הגומא, אבל בנעיצת ביצה – לא שייכא גומא, לפי שאינה ניכרת:

איכא בינייהו עפר תיחוח. פירש בקונטרס: דבעפר תיחוח לא שייכא גומא. והא דמשמע בביצה (שם) דבעפר תיחוח נמי שייך גומא – צריך לומר לפי' דהתם איירי שיש מעט עפר תיחוח, וסביבו קרקע קשה, דכשמסיר עפר תיחוח תשאר הגומא קיימת. אבל הכא, כשיש עפר תיחוח הרבה – כשיעשה גומא אינה מתקיימת, כי דופני הגומא יפלו ולא יוכלו להתקיים, לפי שאין הקרקע קשה:

ואין מגלגלין ביצה על גבי סיד רותח. קשה: אדמפליג בין תולדות חמה לתולדות האור – נפלוג בתולדות חמה גופייהו, בין גג רותח לחול ואבק דרכים וגג דאית ביה עפר! ולמ"ד דשמא יטמין ברמץ – אתי שפיר דמפליג בין גג רותח לסיד רותח שלא כדרך הטמנה. אבל בתולדות חמה גופייהו לא מצי למיפלג אלא בין דרך הטמנה לשלא כדרך הטמנה, דבחול נמי אם אינו מטמינו בו אלא מגלגלו על גביו – שרי:

אלא למ"ד שמא יזיז וכו'. וא"ת: לרב יוסף, אטו מי לית ליה גזירה "שמא יטמין ברמץ"? והא מהאי טעמא אסרינן להטמין בדבר המוסיף הבל! ויש לומר: דמבעוד יום איכא למיגזר שמא יטמין ברמץ ושמא יחתה, אבל הכא – לא שייך למיגזר, דאטו אי שרינן לבשל בחמי חמה ניחוש דילמא אתי לבשל בחמי אור בשבת?! וא"ת: הא אסרינן משחשיכה להטמין אף כשאין מוסיף הבל – גזירה שמא ירתיח! ויש לומר: דהני מילי – בדבר המבושל, איכא למיחש שמא ירתיח, אבל בישול גמור כי הכא – לא טעו אינשי אטו תולדות חמה:

ממעשה

עין משפט נר מצוה

ובי"ט נמי אסרי שמא יחתה דאף בי"ט אסור לחתות לצורך רחיצה [ת"י]

יג א ב מיי' פ"ט מהל' שבת הלכה ג ופכ"ב הלכה ט סמג לאוין סה טוש"ע א"ח סימן שיח סעיף ג:

רבינו חננאל

גלגל מאי אמר רב יוסף גלגל חייב חטאת כענין מליח ישן וקולים האיספנין שהדחתן היא גמר מלאכתן: **ולא** יפקיענה בסודרין. ור' יוסי מתיר. ואוקמה רב נחמן [בחמה כ"ע לא פליגי דשרי] בתולדות האור כולי עלמא לא פליגי [דאסור] כי פליגי בתולדות חמה ת"ק סבר גזרינן תולדות חמה אטו תולדות אור. ור' יוסי סבר לא גזרינן ואמרו ליה רבנן לרבי יוסי והא מעשה שעשו אנשי טבריא תולדות חמה הוא ואסרי להו רבנן לאנשי טבריא [אע"ג דדחי ר' יוסי ואמר תולדות אור הן

מסורת הש"ס

לקמן קמה:

שם קמו:

הגהות הב"ח

(א) רש"י ד"ה מי סברת מעשה טבריא אסיפא:

גליון הש"ס

גמרא דחלפי אפיתחא דגיהנם. עיין חולין דף ח ע"א תוס' ד"ה בחמי טבריא:

ואין נראה כ"כ קושיא דלא חיישינן שמא יחפור במעזיב' אלא בחול דוקא חיישינן ובשאין לו כל הצורך וחסר לו מעט [ת"י]

יד א ב מיי׳ פ״ח מהל׳ יו״ט הלכה טז סמג לאוין עה טוש״ע או״ח סימן תקיא סעיף ב:
טו ג מיי׳ פכ״ב מהל׳ שבת הלכה ג סמג לאוין סה טוש״ע או״ח סימן שכו סעיף א:

מִמַּעֲשֶׂה שֶׁעָשׂוּ אַנְשֵׁי טִבֶּרְיָא וְאָסְרִי לְהוּ רַבָּנַן – בָּטְלָה *הַטְמָנָה בְּדָבָר הַמּוֹסִיף הֶבֶל, וַאֲפִילוּ מִבְּעוֹד יוֹם. אָמַר עוּלָּא: הֲלָכָה כְּאַנְשֵׁי טִבֶּרְיָא. א״ל רַב נַחְמָן: כְּבָר תַּבְרִינְהוּ אַנְשֵׁי טִבֶּרְיָא לְסִילוֹנַיְיהוּ.§ ״מַעֲשֶׂה שֶׁעָשׂוּ אַנְשֵׁי טִבֶּרְיָא״.§ מַאי רְחִיצָה? אִילֵימָא רְחִיצַת כָּל גּוּפוֹ, אֶלָּא חַמִּין שֶׁהוּחַמּוּ בְּשַׁבָּת – הוּא דַּאֲסוּרִין, הָא חַמִּין שֶׁהוּחַמּוּ מֵעֶ״שׁ – מוּתָּרִין?! וְהָתַנְיָא: *חַמִּין שֶׁהוּחַמּוּ מֵעֶ״שׁ, לְמָחָר רוֹחֵץ בָּהֶן פָּנָיו יָדָיו וְרַגְלָיו, אֲבָל לֹא כָּל גּוּפוֹ?! אֶלָּא – פָּנָיו יָדָיו וְרַגְלָיו. אֵימָא סֵיפָא: אבְּיוֹ״ט – כְּחַמִּין שֶׁהוּחַמּוּ בְּיוֹ״ט, וַאֲסוּרִין בִּרְחִיצָה וּמוּתָּרִין בִּשְׁתִיָּה. לֵימָא תְּנַן סְתָמָא כְּבֵית שַׁמַּאי; דִּתְנַן, *בֵּית שַׁמַּאי אוֹמְרִים: לֹא יָחֵם אָדָם חַמִּין לְרַגְלָיו אא״כ רְאוּיִין לִשְׁתִיָּה, וּב״ה במַתִּירִין! א״ר אִיקָא בַּר חֲנַנְיָא: לְהִשְׁתַּטֵּף בָּהֶן כָּל גּוּפוֹ עָסְקִינַן; וְהַאי תַּנָּא הוּא, דְּתַנְיָא: *לֹא גיִשְׁתַּטֵּף אָדָם כָּל גּוּפוֹ, בֵּין בְּחַמִּין וּבֵין בְּצוֹנֵן – דִּבְרֵי ר״מ, ר״ש מַתִּיר, ר׳ יְהוּדָה אוֹמֵר: בְּחַמִּין – אָסוּר, בְּצוֹנֵן – מוּתָּר. אָמַר רַב חִסְדָּא: מַחֲלוֹקֶת בִּכְלִי, אֲבָל בְּקַרְקַע – דִּבְרֵי הַכֹּל מוּתָּר. וְהָא מַעֲשֶׂה דְּאַנְשֵׁי טִבֶּרְיָא בְּקַרְקַע הֲוָה, וְאָסְרִי לְהוּ רַבָּנַן! אֶלָּא, אִי אִיתְּמַר הָכִי אִיתְּמַר: דמַחֲלוֹקֶת – בְּקַרְקַע, אֲבָל בִּכְלִי – דִּבְרֵי הַכֹּל אָסוּר. אָמַר רַבָּה בַּר בַּר חָנָה אָמַר רַבִּי יוֹחָנָן: הֲלָכָה כְּרַבִּי יְהוּדָה. א״ל רַב יוֹסֵף: *בְּפֵירוּשׁ שְׁמִיעַ לָךְ, אוֹ מִכְּלָלָא שְׁמִיעַ לָךְ? מַאי כְּלָלָא? דְּאָמַר רַב תַּנְחוּם א״ר יוֹחָנָן א״ר יַנַּאי אָמַר *(רַב): כָּל מָקוֹם שֶׁאַתָּה מוֹצֵא שְׁנַיִם חֲלוּקִין וְאֶחָד מַכְרִיעַ – הֲלָכָה כְּדִבְרֵי הַמַּכְרִיעַ, חוּץ *מִקּוּלֵּי מַטְלָנִיּוֹת, שֶׁאַף עַל פִּי שֶׁרַבִּי אֱלִיעֶזֶר מַחְמִיר וְרַבִּי יְהוֹשֻׁעַ מֵיקֵל, וְר׳ עֲקִיבָא מַכְרִיעַ – אֵין הֲלָכָה כְּדִבְרֵי הַמַּכְרִיעַ. חֲדָא: דְּרַבִּי עֲקִיבָא תַּלְמִיד הוּא, וְעוֹד: הָא הָדַר

רש״י

בָּטְלָה הַטְמָנָה. נֶאֶסְרָה הַטְמָנָה בְּדָבָר הַמּוֹסִיף הֶבֶל, דְּהָא מִבְּעוֹ״י נָתְנוּ שָׁם הַסִּילוֹן, וּמִפְּנֵי שֶׁהַצּוֹנֵן מִתְחַמְּמִין בְּגָוֶן, וְאַע״ג דְּמִמֵּילָא – אָסוּר: לְסִילוֹנַיְיהוּ. לְסִילוֹנִין שֶׁלָּהֶן, שֶׁחָזְרוּ בָּהֶן: רְאוּיִין לִשְׁתִיָּה. דְּמֵחֵיס לְהוּ לִשְׁתִיָּה, וְאִי בָּעֵי רוֹחֵץ בָּהֶן פָּנָיו: לְהִשְׁתַּטֵּף. שֶׁנּוֹתֵן עַל גּוּפוֹ וּמִשְׁתַּטֵּף: וְהַאי תַּנָּא. ר׳ שִׁמְעוֹן הִיא, דְּמַתִּיר לְהִשְׁתַּטֵּף כָּל גּוּפוֹ בְּשַׁבָּת בְּחַמִּין שֶׁהוּחַמּוּ מֵעֶ״שׁ. וְהַיְינוּ דְּקָאָמַר: כְּחַמִּין שֶׁהוּחַמּוּ בְּשַׁבָּת אָסוּר(א), הָא שֶׁהוּחַמּוּ מֵאֶתְמוֹל – שָׁרֵי. וְאִי בְּיוֹ״ט – כְּחַמִּין שֶׁהוּחַמּוּ בְּיוֹ״ט וְאָסוּר בִּרְחִיצָה דַּאֲפִילּוּ בֵּית הִלֵּל לָא שָׁרֵי לְהָחֵם בְּיוֹ״ט אֶלָּא לְפָנָיו יָדָיו וְרַגְלָיו, אֲבָל לְשִׁיטּוּף כָּל גּוּפוֹ – לָא: לֹא יִשְׁתַּטֵּף. בְּשַׁבָּת: בֵּין בְּחַמִּין. וַאֲפִי׳ הוּחַמּוּ בְּחוֹל: בִּכְלִי. דְּהָרוֹאֶה אוֹמֵר: ״הַיּוֹם הוּחַמּוּ״ וּמוּכְחָא מִילְּתָא דְּתוֹלָדוֹת הָאוּר נִינְהוּ, וְאָתֵי לְהָחֵם בְּשַׁבָּת – כְּגוֹן נוֹתֵן צוֹנֵן בְּחַמִּין: אֲבָל בְּקַרְקַע. כְּגוֹן אַמְבָּטָאוֹת שֶׁל מֶרְחֲצָאוֹת וְהֵן חַמֵּי הָאוּר: מוּתָּר. דְּבָטְלֵי לְהוּ מִתּוֹרַת חַמִּין: וְהָא מַעֲשֶׂה דְּאַנְשֵׁי טִבֶּרְיָא כו׳. אַלְמָא בְּמִילְּתַיְיהוּ קָיְימִי:

תוספות

ממעשה שעשו אנשי טבריא ואסרו להם בטלה הטמנה מבע״י בדבר המוסיף הבל. וא״ת: מה לריך למילף ממעשה דאנשי טבריא, הא מתני׳ היא דאין טומנין בדבר המוסיף הבל בפרק ״במה טומנין״ (לקמן ד׳ מז: ושם) ומבע״י איירי, דמשחשיכה – אפי׳ בדבר שאינו מוסיף הבל אסור, כדאמרינן בפ״ב (לעיל דף לד.). ואור״י: דמתניתין דלקמן איכא לאוקמא בבין השמשות, אבל מבעוד יום – ה״א דשרי. וא״ת, והא קתני: ״טומנין בגיזי למר ואין מטלטלין אותן״ ואי בין השמשות – איך טומנין בהן? והא אסור לטלטלן! וי״ל: דהוה מוקמינן כר׳, דאמר (לעיל ד׳ ח:): כל דבר שהוא משום שבות – לא גזרו עליו בין השמשות. וא״ת: אי כר׳ אתיא, אי מבעוד יום שרי להטמין – ביה״ש נמי שרי, דכל דבר שהוא משום שבות כו׳. וי״ל: דה״א – בהטמנה החמירו. וה״ר שמואל מוורדין מפרש: ממעשה אנשי טבריא בטלה הטמנה – דאסור אפי׳ לאכול, כדקתני ״ואסורין בשתיה״. וה״ר יונה מפרש: בטלה אפי׳ בקדירה חייתא, והיינו דקאמר ״בטלה״ – משמע לגמרי מכל דבר: **אלא** פניו ידיו ורגליו כו׳. הכל היה יכול לדקדק מסיפא, דקתני: ״בי״ט כחמין שהוחמו בי״ט״. אילימא רחילת כל גופו – הא הוחמו מעי״ט שרי, והא לקמן אסר רחילה בי״ט, דקאמר: ״למחר נכנס ומזיע אבל רוחץ לא״ ודוקא שטיפה שרי בבית החילון. אלא דרך התלמוד, *מה שיכול לדקדק מרישא – מדקדק. ומיהו, קשה לרשב״א: דמגופה דמתניתין הוי מצי למידק, בלא הך ברייתא דמייתי, מדקתני ״ואסורין בשתיה״ – כ״ש פניו ידיו ורגליו דאסירי: **אלא** אם כן ראויין לשתיה. נראה לר״י: דדוקא שמחמם אותם לצורך שתיה, אבל לצורך רחילה. אע״ג דראויין לשתיה – אסרי ב״ש, דהא לית להו ״מתוך״ (בילה ד׳ יב. ושם). ובפ״ב דבילה (ד׳ כא: ושם) אסרי ב״ש מדורה להתחמם כנגדה, ואע״ג דראויה היא לבשל ולאפות. ועוד אומר ר״י: דמהכא נמי יש לדקדק, דאי שרו ב״ש לצורך רחילה משום דראויין לשתיה – א״כ לא אתיא מתני׳ אפי׳ כב״ש, דקתני ״ואסורין ברחילה ומותרין בשתיה״. ומדקתני ״ומותרין בשתיה״ מכלל דראויין לשתיה, ואפ״ה קתני דאסורין ברחילה. אלא ודאי לא שרו ב״ש אלא כשעושה לצורך שתיה. ונראה לר״י: דיכול לחמם אפי׳ ביותר מכדי שתיה, כדאמר בפרק ״הדר״ (עירובין ד׳ סח.): נשיילי׳ לאימיה, אי לריכה – נחיימו אגב אימיה. ודוקא בכדי שיעור לרגליו, אבל לצורך כל גופו – לא. והיינו טעמא שהבלנים חשודים, דפעמים שיחממו עיקרן לרחילה:

וב״ה מתירין. משמע דוקא לרגליו, אבל לצורך כל גופו – לא. וכן משמע בכולה שמעתין, דמחמירין בחמין שהוחמו בי״ט כחמין שהוחמו בשבת, וגזרו על הזיעה ביו״ט כמו בשבת, כדאמר בבילה ב״המביא״ ולקמן (דף מ. ושם). א״כ משמע שאסור לעשות הבערה משום רחילה, שאם לא כן – לא היו גוזרים על הזיעה. ותימה: דמ״ש הבערה דרחילה מהבערה דזיעה, דשרי מדאורייתא כדמוכח התם? ואומר ר״י בשם ריב״א: דרחילה אינה אלא לתענוג, ואסורה כמו מוגמר, דאסור בפ״ק דכתובות (ד׳ ז. ושם) משום דאין שוה לכל נפש. וכן משמע בירושלמי דהיינו טעמא דרחילה, אבל זיעה – שוה היא לכל נפש, דאינה תענוג אלא לבריאות. והא דתניא לקמן (ד׳ מ.): ״מרחץ שפקקו נקביו מעי״ט למחר נכנס ומזיע״ – ה״ה אפי׳ הוחם בו ביום, אלא נקט מעי״ט, דאפ״ה: דוקא מזיע, אבל רוחץ – לא:

בין בחמין בין בצונן. נראה לר״י: דהיינו אפי׳ חמין שהוחמו מע״ש, דהא אוסר אפי׳ לונן – ומסתמא בהנך חמין אסיר ר׳ יהודה. ועוד: דמסתמא לא מיירי בדעבדי איסורא. והאי תנא הוא דקאמר – היינו ר״ש. ועוד אומר ר״י: דיש להוכיח דבחמין שהוחמו מע״ש פליגי, דאמר בפרק ״חבית״ (לקמן ד׳ קמז. ושם): מה חמי טבריא חמין, אף מי מערה חמין. הרוחץ, דיעבד – אין, לכתחילה – לא. מכלל דלהשתטף אפי׳ לכתחילה. מני – ר״ש היא, דתניא לא ישתטף כו׳. ואי בשהוחמו בשבת פליגי, אבל מערב שבת שרי ר׳ יהודה – אמאי לריך לאוקמה כר״ש? לוקמה כר׳ יהודה, ובהוחמו מע״ש דהא דומיא דחמי טבריא קתני! **והא** מעשה דאנשי טבריא בקרקע הוה ואסרי להו. הקשה ה״ר אליעזר ממי״ן: מאי פריך התם הוחמו בשבת, כדקתני ״כחמין שהוחמו בשבת״, משמע: דבהוחמו מע״ש – שרי. והכא *בהוחמו מע״ש פליגי, כדפרישית. ומפרש הר״ר יוסף: דס״ל להתלמוד מדמחמיר ר״מ כ״כ, דאוסר אפי׳ לונן – מחמיר נמי לאסור ע״ש אטו שבת. ולהכי פריך: והא מעשה דאנשי טבריא בקרקע הוה, ואסרי להו בהוחמו בשבת. ורב חסדא קאמר, אבל בקרקע – ד״ה מותר. אפילו בהוחמו בשבת. דהא לר״מ, אי הוה אוסר להו בהוחמו בשבת – בהוחמו מע״ש נמי הוה אוסר. וקשה: דר״מ אוסר להשתטף בלונן אפי׳ בקרקע, כדמסיק דבקרקע פליגי, ובפרק ״שמונה שרלים״ (לקמן דף קט. ושם) משמע דשרי, דקאמר התם: ״רוחלין במי גרר ובמי חמתן ובמי עסיא ובמי טבריא אבל לא בים הגדול״. ורמינהו: רוחלין במי טבריא ובים הגדול כו׳. ומוקים בתרייתא כר׳ מאיר! וי״ל: דבקרקע דהכא דאסר – היינו דומיא דכלי, דדמי לרוחץ בחמין. והתם בנהר – התירו, שנראה כמיקר בנהר, ואפי׳ בחמי טבריא לא דמי לאדם רוחץ בחמין:

אמר רבה בר בר חנה *)הלכה כר׳ יהודה. אע״ג דר׳ יוחנן אית ליה ״הלכה כסתם משנה״, הכא משום דר׳ יהודה מכריע הוא – אין הלכה כסתם. וקשה: דבפרק קמא דפסחים (דף יג. ודף כא. ושם) פריך: ונימא מר הלכה כר׳ מאיר דסתם לן תנא כוותיה, אע״ג דסבר דרבן גמליאל מכריע הוא. דפריך בתר הכי: ונימא מר הלכה כרבן גמליאל, דהוה ליה מכריע! וי״ל: דסתם דהכא גריע מההוא סתם, דהכא סתם במתני׳ ומחלוקת בברייתא, והלכה כמכריע. ומיהו, אי לאו הכרעה – הוה הלכה כסתם מתני׳, אע״ג דמחלוקת בברייתא: (לעיל) **הא** חמין שהוחמו מבעוד יום מותרים והתניא חמין שהוחמו כו׳. תימה: לוקי ההיא ברייתא דאסרה בכלי משום דהרואה אומר ״היום הוחמו״. ומתניתין – בקרקע, כמשמעה. כדמפליג בסמוך בין כלי לקרקע! וי״ל: דדוקא בשיטוף דקיל איכא לפלוגי, אבל ברחילה דחמירא – לא מסתברא לפלוגי בהכי:

*) [אמר ר׳ יוחנן הלכה כו׳].

דילמא

הא דלא מייתי בעבור וסיפה מהכלה דאסור דקתני הטמנה ד״ה להתמיד [ת״י]

ביצה כח:

[לקמן מ.] ולא תאמר וליגזר דשמא קודם גזירה וי״ל דמסתמא היתה גזירה קדמוני היתה [ת״י]

[לקמן קמז: ע״ש תוספתא פ״ד]

[ברכות ט. וש״נ]

[נ״ל רבי]

[לעיל כט.]

[וכ״ה תוספות עירובין טז. ד״ה אימא וכתובות נא. ד״ה מני וזקף פט. ד״ה ש״מ וב״ב כו. ד״ה הא ועי׳ תוס׳ לקמן מו: ד״ה כבתה ותוס׳ ברכות מב. ד״ה הסבו ותוספות ב״מ יג: ד״ה הא מכני ועי״ע תוספות כ״מ כב: ד״ה הא של ב״ב]

ומהר״מ מפרש דחמין שהוחמו מע״ש היינו שנסתלקו מעל האור מבע״י ושהוחמו בשבת היינו נמי שהוחמו מבע״י כל צורכן אך מתחממים והולכין גם בשבת דומיא דאנשי טבריא ובהנהו פליגי ר״מ ור״י ור״ש וצוננין קרי שהיו חמין כבר ונצטננו אבל בנסתלקו מבע״י אפילו ר״מ מודה דשרי להשתטף ולא לרחוץ והאי תנא הוא ר״מ ור״י דאסרי חמין שמתחממין והולכין גם בשבת והשתא פריך שפיר והא מעשה דאנשי טבריא בקרקע הוי ויתיישב נמי ההיא דפ׳ שמנה שרצים דשרי ר״מ לרחוץ בקרקע וכן בפרק חבית דמוקי כר״ש [ת״י]

רבינו חננאל

קי״ל כת״ק אמר רב חסדא מדאסרו להו רבנן] שמע מיניה דבטלה הטמנה בדבר המוסיף ואפילו מבעוד יום. אסיקנא דכופח מקום שפיתת קדירה אחת הוא. ואם הוסק בגפת או בעצים הרי הוא כתנור ואסור לסמוך בו. וכ״ש בתוכו או על גבו. וכן לשהות בו אע״פ שהוא גרוף וקטום אסור. נמצא האסור שני פנים. צונן שלא הוחמו כל עיקר. ותבשיל שהתחיל להתבשל ולא הגיע למאכל בן דרוסאי. ומותר שני פנים. חמין שהוחמו ולא בשלו כל עיקר ושבשלו כמאכל בן דרוסאי. ואפילו [לא] בשלו כל צרכן מותר. ומאי דקשי ליה [זיקא] מסקנא כלישנא בתראה דרב אשי דבין דגריא ובין [דברחא] בין שריק ובין שלא שריק שרי. ולא יטמיננה בחול ובאבק דרכים בשביל שתצלה דברי הכל אסור: **מעשה** שעשו אנשי טבריא הביאו סילון של צונן כו׳ אין הלכה כאנשי טבריא דהא תברינהו לסילונייהו אוקימנא הא דתנן אסור ברחיצה להשתטף בהן כל גופו ור׳ שמעון הוא דשרי בחמין שהוחמו מע״ש להשתטף דתניא אסור להשתטף בין בחמין בין בצונן דברי רבי מאיר ורבי שמעון מתיר רבי יהודה אומר בחמין אסור בצונן מותר. אמר רבה בר בר חנה אמר רבי יוחנן הלכה כר׳ יהודה: **הא** דקאמר שמואל חמין שהוחמו מע״ש אינו רוחץ בהן בשבת אלא פניו ידיו ורגליו תניא כוותיה וקי״ל כוותיה דשמואל בהא: **א״ל** לרבה בר בר חנה בפירוש שמיע לך מיניה דר׳ יוחנן דהלכתא כר׳ יהודה דבצונן מותר להשתטף אבל בחמין אסור. או מכללא. מאי כללא דא״ר יוחנן א״ר ינאי כל מקום ששנים חולקין ואחד מכריע הלכה כדברי המכריע חוץ מקולי מטליות שפירשנום בפרק של מעלה. והוא זה ששנינו בכלים בפרק כ״ח פחות משלשה על שלשה שהתקינה לפקק בה את המרחץ כו׳. אף על פי שרבי אליעזר מחמיר ורבי יהושע מיקל ורבי עקיבא מכריע שאין הלכה כרבי עקיבא. חדא דתלמיד הוא ואין תלמיד מכריע על רבו.

הגהות הב״ח

(א) רש״י ד״ה והאי תנא וכו׳ שהוחמו בשבת אסור כצ״ל והא שהוחמו:

רב נסים גאון

חדא דר׳ עקיבא לגבי רבי אליעזר ורבי יהושע תלמיד הוא. פירוש שלו תמצאנו בנדרים בפרק הנודר מן המבושל (דף נ) ר׳ עקיבא אקדשא ליה ברתיה דבר כלבא שבוע כו׳ אמרה ליה זיל הוי בבי רב אזל הוה י״ב שנין קמיה רבי אליעזר ורבי יהושע ובהרבה מקומות תמצאנו כשהוא מדבר עם אחד מהן אומר ר׳ תרשני לומר לפניך דבר אחד ממה שלימדתני תגד דאלך (פירושו, תמלא זה) בר״ה (כס) בשעה ששיגר רבן גמליאל לר׳ יהושע גוזר אני עליך שתבוא אצלי במקלך כו׳ דתניא הלך ר״ע לר׳ יהושע מיצר א״ל ר״ע ר׳ תרשני לומר לפניך דבר אחד שלימדתני ובסנהדרין (פ׳ ד׳ מיתות דף סז) ר״ע אומר משום ר׳ יהושע שנים מלקטין קישואין כו׳ ובתלמוד אמרו גמרה מר׳ אליעזר ולא סברה הדר גמרה מר׳ יהושע ואסברה ניהליה. ועוד הא הדר ביה רבי עקיבא לגבי ר׳ יהושע מפורש זה בפרק במה מדליקין (דף כט):

גליון הש״ס גמ׳ הכי איתמר מחלוקת בקרקע. עי׳ מ״ק דף יט ע״ב תוס׳ ד״ה שאסור וצ״ע: תוס׳ ד״ה ממעשה וכו׳ בטלה אפילו בקדירה חייתא. עי׳ לקמן דף מז ע״ב תוס׳ ד״ה במה טומנין: ד״ה אא״כ וכו׳ נראה לר״י דוקא שמחמם. עי׳ לקמן דף עו ע״א תוס׳ ד״ה הואיל ואיון: בא״ד דהא לית להו מתוך. דבריהם צ״ע דלענין מתוך מה הפרש בין ראויים או אינן ראויים. ולאותי ברשב״א שהוסיף ומאן דלית ליה מתוך לית ליה הואיל ויסוד זה נסתר מפירכת הגמ׳ פסחים דף מז ע״ב וכמ״ש תוס׳ שם ד״ה אהבערה לא ליחייב ועע״ג ובתשובה וגם בדרשות הארכתי בזה בעהש״י: בא״ד כדאמרינן פרק הדר נשיילה ק״ל למאי הוצרכו לראיה זו דאפשר לצורך מילה עדיף. הא להדיא איתא ברייתא ערוכה בבילה ממלא נחתום חבית מים אע״פ שא״צ אלא לקיתון אחד:

*הָדַר בֵּיהּ ר"ע לְגַבֵּיהּ דְּרַבִּי יְהוֹשֻׁעַ. *וְאִי מִכְּלָלָא מַאי? דִּילְמָא, ה"מ – בְּמַתְנִיתִין, אֲבָל בְּבָרַיְיתָא – לָא. א"ל: אֲנָא בְּפֵירוּשׁ שְׁמִיעַ לִי. [ברכות יב. וש"נ] אִתְּמַר: חַמִּין שֶׁהוּחַמּוּ מֵעֶ"שׁ; רַב אָמַר: לְמָחָר רוֹחֵץ בָּהֶן כָּל גּוּפוֹ אֵבֶר אֵבֶר, וּשְׁמוּאֵל אָמַר: לֹא הִתִּירוּ לִרְחוֹץ אֶלָּא פָּנָיו יָדָיו וְרַגְלָיו. מֵיתִיבִי: חַמִּין שֶׁהוּחַמּוּ מֵעֶ"שׁ – לְמָחָר רוֹחֵץ בָּהֶן פָּנָיו יָדָיו וְרַגְלָיו, אֲבָל לֹא כָּל גּוּפוֹ, תְּיוּבְתָּא דְּרַב! אָמַר לָךְ רַב: לֹא כָּל גּוּפוֹ – בְּבַת אַחַת, אֶלָּא אֵבֶר אֵבֶר. וְהָא "פָּנָיו יָדָיו וְרַגְלָיו" קָתָנֵי! כְּעֵין פָּנָיו יָדָיו וְרַגְלָיו. תָּא שְׁמַע: לֹא הִתִּירוּ לִרְחוֹץ בְּחַמִּין שֶׁהוּחַמּוּ מֵעֶ"שׁ, אֶלָּא פָּנָיו יָדָיו וְרַגְלָיו! ה"נ: כְּעֵין פָּנָיו יָדָיו וְרַגְלָיו. תַּנְיָא כְּוָותֵיהּ דִּשְׁמוּאֵל*: [א]חַמִּין שֶׁהוּחַמּוּ מֵעֶ"שׁ, לְמָחָר רוֹחֵץ בָּהֶן פָּנָיו יָדָיו וְרַגְלָיו, אֲבָל לֹא כָּל גּוּפוֹ אֵבֶר אֵבֶר, וְאצ"ל חַמִּין שֶׁהוּחַמּוּ בְּיו"ט. רַבָּה מַתְנֵי לָהּ לְהָא שְׁמַעְתָּא דְּרַב בְּהַאי לִישָּׁנָא: חַמִּין שֶׁהוּחַמּוּ מֵעֶ"שׁ, לְמָחָר, אָמַר רַב: רוֹחֵץ בָּהֶן כָּל גּוּפוֹ, וּמְשַׁיֵּיר אֵבֶר אֶחָד. אֵיתִיבֵיהּ כָּל הָנֵי תְּיוּבְתָּא – תְּיוּבְתָּא. א"ל רַב יוֹסֵף לְאַבַּיֵי: רַבָּה מִי קָא עָבֵיד כִּשְׁמַעְתֵּיהּ דְּרַב? א"ל: לָא יָדַעְנָא. מַאי תִּיבָּעֵי לֵיהּ: פְּשִׁיטָא דְּלָא עָבֵיד, דְּהָא אִיתּוֹתַב! (*דִּילְמָא) לָא שְׁמִיעָא לֵיהּ. וְאִי לָא שְׁמִיעָא לֵיהּ – וַדַּאי עָבֵיד, *דַּאֲמַר אַבַּיֵי: כָּל מִילֵּי דְּמָר עָבֵיד כְּרַב, בַּר מֵהָנֵי תְּלָת דְּעָבֵיד כִּשְׁמוּאֵל: (*) מַטִּילִין מִבֶּגֶד לְבֶגֶד, וּמַדְלִיקִין מִנֵּר לְנֵר, וַהֲלָכָה כְּר"ש בִּגְרִירָה. כְּחוּמְרֵי דְּרַב – עָבֵיד, כְּקוּלֵּי דְּרַב – לָא עָבֵיד. *ת"ר: [ב]מֶרְחָץ שֶׁפָּקְקוּ נְקָבָיו מֵעֶ"שׁ, לְמוֹצ"שׁ – רוֹחֵץ בּוֹ מִיָּד. פָּקְקוּ נְקָבָיו [ג]מֵעיו"ט – לְמָחָר נִכְנָס וּמֵזִיעַ, וְיוֹצֵא וּמִשְׁתַּטֵּף בְּבַיִת הַחִיצוֹן. אָמַר רַב יְהוּדָה: מַעֲשֶׂה בְּמֶרְחָץ שֶׁל בְּנֵי בְרַק שֶׁפָּקְקוּ נְקָבָיו מֵעיו"ט, לְמָחָר נִכְנַס ראב"ע וְר"ע, וְהֵזִיעוּ בּוֹ וְיָצְאוּ וְנִשְׁתַּטְּפוּ בְּבַיִת הַחִיצוֹן. אֶלָּא שֶׁחַמִּין שֶׁלּוֹ מְחוּפִּין בִּנְסָרִים. כְּשֶׁבָּא הַדָּבָר לִפְנֵי חֲכָמִים, אָמְרוּ: אַף עַל פִּי שֶׁאֵין חַמִּין שֶׁלּוֹ מְחוּפִּין בִּנְסָרִין. וּמִשֶּׁרַבּוּ עוֹבְרֵי עֲבֵירָה הִתְחִילוּ לֶאֱסוֹר. אַמְבַּטְיָאוֹת שֶׁל כְּרַכִּין – מְטַיֵּיל בָּהֶן וְאֵינוֹ חוֹשֵׁשׁ. מַאי "עוֹבְרֵי עֲבֵירָה"? דְּא"ר שִׁמְעוֹן בֶּן פָּזִי אָמַר ריב"ל מִשּׁוּם בַּר קַפָּרָא: בַּתְּחִילָּה הָיוּ רוֹחֲצִין בְּחַמִּין שֶׁהוּחַמּוּ מֵעֶ"שׁ, הִתְחִילוּ הַבַּלָּנִים לְהָחֵם בַּשַּׁבָּת וְאוֹמְרִים: מֵעֶרֶב שַׁבָּת הוּחַמּוּ, אָסְרוּ אֶת הַחַמִּין וְהִתִּירוּ אֶת הַזֵּיעָה. וַעֲדַיִין הָיוּ רוֹחֲצִין בְּחַמִּין, וְאוֹמְרִים "מְזִיעִין אֲנַחְנוּ" – אָסְרוּ לָהֶן אֶת הַזֵּיעָה, וְהִתִּירוּ חַמֵּי טְבֶרְיָה. וַעֲדַיִין הָיוּ רוֹחֲצִין בְּחַמֵּי הָאוּר, וְאוֹמְרִים "בְּחַמֵּי טְבֶרְיָה רָחַצְנוּ" – אָסְרוּ לָהֶן חַמֵּי טְבֶרְיָה וְהִתִּירוּ לָהֶן אֶת הַצּוֹנֵן. רָאוּ שֶׁאֵין הַדָּבָר עוֹמֵד לָהֶן – [ד]הִתִּירוּ לָהֶן חַמֵּי טְבֶרְיָה, [ה]וְזֵיעָה בִּמְקוֹמָהּ עוֹמֶדֶת. אֲמַר רָבָא: הַאי מַאן דְּעָבַר אַדְּרַבָּנָן – שָׁרֵי לְמִיקְרֵי לֵיהּ עֲבַרְיָינָא, כְּמַאן – כִּי

(*) בכל המקומות איתא מתירין.

רש"י

הָדַר בֵּיהּ ר' עֲקִיבָא. כִּדְאָמְרִינַן בְּפִירְקִין דִּלְעֵיל (דף כט:). לְשׁוֹן "מַכְרִיעַ" – מַכְבִּיד, מַטֶּה כַּף מֹאזְנַיִם וּמַכְרִיעַ אֶת שֶׁכְּנֶגְדּוֹ. כְּגוֹן הָכָא בְּחַמִּין אָסוּר, הָשְׁתָּא הֲוָה לֵיהּ ר' שִׁמְעוֹן דְּמַתִּיר בְּחַמִּין יָחִיד בִּמְקוֹם שְׁנַיִם, נִמְצָא ר' יְהוּדָה מַכְבִּיד אֶת כַּף הַמִּשְׁקוֹלֶת. שֶׁהֲרֵי ר' יְהוּדָה עִם ר' מֵאִיר שָׁוִים לְאִיסּוּר. וּבְצוֹנֵן מוּתָּר – הֲוֵי לֵיהּ ר' מֵאִיר בְּצוֹנֵן יָחִיד בִּמְקוֹם שְׁנַיִם, נִמְצָא ר' יְהוּדָה מַכְבִּיד אֶת כַּף הַמִּשְׁקוֹלֶת: ה"מ. דְּא"ר יוֹחָנָן: "הֲלָכָה כְּדִבְרֵי הַמַּכְרִיעַ" – בְּמַכְרִיעַ בְּמִשְׁנָה, כִּי הַהִיא דְּמַטְלָנִיּוֹת: כְּעֵין פָּנָיו. כְּלוֹמַר: כָּל אֵבֶר בִּפְנֵי עַצְמוֹ: רוֹחֵץ בָּהֶן כָּל גּוּפוֹ. כְּיַחַד, אֶלָּא שֶׁמְּשַׁיֵּיר אֵבֶר אֶחָד: אֵיתִיבֵיהּ כָּל הָנֵי. וְלֵיכָּא לְשַׁנּוּיֵי: "כְּעֵין פָּנָיו יָדָיו וְרַגְלָיו" – דְּהָא כָּל גּוּפוֹ יַחַד קָאָמַר, חוּץ מֵאֵבֶר אֶחָד: א"ל רַב יוֹסֵף לְאַבַּיֵי. מִשּׁוּם דְּגָדַל אַבַּיֵי בְּבֵית רַבָּה בַּר נַחְמָנִי שֶׁהָיָה רֹאשׁ קוֹדֶם לְרַב יוֹסֵף וּמֵת, הָיָה שׁוֹאֲלוֹ רַב יוֹסֵף אֵיךְ הָיָה רוֹאֵהוּ נוֹהֵג: מִי עָבֵיד כִּשְׁמַעְתֵּי' דְּרַב. בְּהָא מִילְּתָא דִּרְחִילָה: מַאי תִּבָּעֵי לֵיהּ. שִׁיטָּה דְּתַלְמוּדָא פָּרְכָא לֵיהּ: לָא שְׁמִיעַ לֵיהּ. *לְרַבָּה הָא תְּיוּבְתָּא, מִשּׁוּם הָכִי מְסַפְּקָא לֵיהּ לְרַב יוֹסֵף בְּרַבָּה, דְּדִילְמָא עָבֵיד כְּרַב: וְאִי לָא שְׁמִיעָא לֵיהּ. אַמַּאי מְסַפְּקָא לֵיהּ לְרַב יוֹסֵף: הָא וַדַּאי עָבֵיד. רַבָּה בְּכָל מִילֵּי כְּרַב: כְּחוּמְרֵי דְּרַב הֲוָה עָבֵיד. בַּר מֵהָנֵי תְּלָת חוּמְרֵי, אֲבָל כְּקוּלֵּי דְּרַב – אִיכָּא דְּלָא עָבֵיד, וְהָא קוּלָּא הִיא, וְדִילְמָא לָא עָבֵיד: שֶׁפָּקְקוּ נְקָבָיו. שֶׁלֹּא יֵצֵא חֲמִימוּתוֹ: רוֹחֵץ בּוֹ מִיָּד. וְאֵין צָרִיךְ לְהַמְתִּין בִּכְדֵי שֶׁיֵּעָשֶׂה. ל"א: שֶׁפָּקְקוּ נְקָבָיו – אוֹתָן נְקָבִים שֶׁמֶּרְחָץ מִתְחַמֵּם עַל יְדֵיהֶן, שֶׁאוּר נִיסֶּקֶת מִבַּחוּץ מִתַּחְתָּיו. *לוי"ה וְעִיקָּר. רוֹחֵץ בּוֹ מִיָּד – שֶׁהֲרֵי לֹא נִתְחַמֵּם בַּשַּׁבָּת, אֲבָל בַּשַּׁבָּת – לֹא, שֶׁהֲרֵי גָּזְרוּ עַל הָרְחִילָה: וּמִשְׁתַּטֵּף בְּבַיִת הַחִיצוֹן. שֶׁלִּפְנֵי הַמֶּרְחָץ, וְלֹא בְּתוֹךְ הַמֶּרְחָץ, שֶׁלֹּא יֹאמְרוּ "רוֹחֵץ הוּא". כִּדַאֲמַרַן, דְּאָסְרוּ אֶת הָרְחִילָה. אֲבָל הַזֵּיעָה הִתִּירוּ. וְהֵיאַךְ הִיא זֵיעָה – עוֹמֵד אוֹ יוֹשֵׁב בְּבֵית הַמֶּרְחָץ, וְאֵינוֹ נוֹתֵן מַיִם עָלָיו, וְהוּא מִתְחַמֵּם וּמֵזִיעַ: מְחוּפִּין בִּנְסָרִים. וְלֹא הָיוּ צְרִיכִין לָחוּשׁ שֶׁמָּא נִתְחַמְּמוּ בַּשַּׁבָּת מֵחוּמּוֹ שֶׁל מֶרְחָץ: הִתְחִילוּ לֶאֱסוֹר. אֶת הַזֵּיעָה: אַמְבַּטְיָאוֹת. בָּתֵּי מֶרְחָץ גְּדוֹלִים: מְטַיֵּיל בָּהֶן. מְהַלֵּךְ בְּתוֹכָן לְפִי דַּרְכּוֹ, וְלֹא לְהָזִיעַ: וְאֵינוֹ חוֹשֵׁשׁ. שֶׁמָּא יֹאמְרוּ מֵזִיעַ הוּא, וְאַע"ג דְּאָסְרוּ אֶת הַזֵּיעָה: מַאי עוֹבְרֵי עֲבֵירָה. דְּקָאָמַר לְעֵיל שֶׁאָסְרוּ זֵיעָה עַל יְדֵיהֶן: אָסְרוּ לָהֶן אֶת הַחַמִּין. לְגַמְרֵי: וַעֲדַיִין הָיוּ רוֹחֲצִין בְּחַמִּין. שֶׁהוּחַמּוּ מִבְּעוֹד יוֹם: שֶׁאֵין הַדָּבָר עוֹמֵד. שֶׁלֹּא הָיוּ צִיבּוּר יְכוֹלִין לְקַבֵּל מִתּוֹךְ שֶׁאָסְרוּ לָהֶם אֶת הַכֹּל: בִּמְקוֹמָהּ עוֹמֶדֶת. לְאִיסּוּר: כִּי

תוספות

דילמא ה"מ במתני' אבל בברייתא לא. °אע"ג דלא קאמר "במשנתינו" *הכא משמע דאין הלכה כמותו, משום דסתם מתני' דלא כוותיה*: **הלכה** כדברי המכריע. הכרעה כגון קולי מטלניות שר"א ור"י הזכירו בפירוש בדבריהם מוכן ושאינו מוכן, דהיינו תלאו במגוד והניחו אחורי הדלת, שגילו בדבריהם שיש סברא לחלק ביניהם, אלא שנראה להם דסוף סוף אין לחלק ביניהם – לכך הוי ר' עקיבא שמחלק ביניהם מכריע. וכן ר' יהודה הוי מכריע, דר' שמעון ור"מ הזכירו בדבריהם חמין וצונן. והכרעה שלישית דלא הויא הכרעה הוי כי ההיא דפ"ק דפסחים (דף כא.): חבית של יין של תרומה שנטמאה, ב"ש אומרים: תשפך *הכל, וב"ה אומר: תיעשה זילוף. אמר ר' ישמעאל בר' יוסי: אני אכריע, בשדה – תשפך *הכל, ובבית – תעשה זילוף. אמרו לו: אין הכרעה שלישית מכרעת. משום דלא הזכירו ב"ש וב"ה בדבריהם בית ושדה, ולא גילו שיש סברא לחלק בין בית לשדה – חשיב לה הכרעה שלישית. ולא כפירוש הקונטרס דפירש התם דטעמייהו דב"ש לא משום תקלה, אלא מטעם אחר, כמו משום ריחא. אלא משום דלא הזכירו בדבריהם בית ושדה כדפי'. וה"ה דהוה מצי למימר ליה דאין הכרעת תלמיד הכרעה, כדאמר הכא אלא רבותא אמרו: דאפי' לא היה תלמיד – אינה הכרעה. והא דתנן בברכות (דף מג:): "ב"ש אומרים: מברך על השמן ואח"כ מברך על ההדס, וב"ה אומרים: מברך על ההדס ואח"כ על השמן" א"ר גמליאל: אני אכריע, שמן זכינו לריחו וזכינו לסיכתו, הדס לריחו זכינו לסיכתו לא זכינו. וא"ר יוחנן: הלכה כדברי המכריע. פר"ת התם: דהויא כהכרעה שבכל התלמוד. ולא נהירא, דלא הויא הכרעה, אלא כדפי'. והתם אינו אלא מפרש טעמא דבית שמאי. ור"ח פי': אין הכרע' שלישית מכרעת – היינו הכרע' דור שלישי, כמו ר' ישמעאל בר' יוסי שהיה דור שלישי לב"ש וב"ה. ולאו דוקא דור שלישי אלא ה"ה שני. ובכל מקום נקט הכרעה שלישית – משום ברייתא דפסחים*:

למוצאי שבת רוחץ מיד. דוקא לרחוץ, אבל להזיע – נכנס אפילו בשבת ומזיע כמו בי"ט, כדאמר בסמוך דאפי' בשבת הוי זיעה שריא עד הגזירה. ולאחר גזירה – אפילו בי"ט אסרו דאיום טוב קתני: "משרבו עוברי עבירה התחילו לאסור". והוה מצי לערובינהו וליתנינהו: מרחץ שפקקו נקביו מערב שבת או מערב יום טוב, למחר נכנס ומזיע, ולמוצאי שבת ויום טוב רוחץ מיד. אלא, אי עריב ותני להו – הוה אמינא דדוקא בשבת אסרו הזיעה, ולא ביום טוב, דעובדא דמייתי – בשבת הוה, להכי מפליג להו. השתא "משרבו עוברי עבירה" קאי איום טוב, אבל לא אשבת, דזיעה לא הוזכרה גבי שבת: **אלא** שחמין שלו מחופין בנסרים: פי' בקונטרס: שלא היו צריכין לחוש שהוחמו בשבת מחום המרחץ. משמע שסובר שנשתטפו בחמין שהוחמו מע"ש, ולעיל אסר רבי יהודה גופיה. ושמא יחלק בין שבת ליום טוב. ומיהו, בתוספתא גרסינן: ונשתטפו בצונן, אלא שחמין שלו מחופים, ולא יסברו העולם שרחצו בחמין: מפני

רבינו חננאל

הדר ביה ר"ע לגבי דר' יהושע. ואסיקנא דאי מכללא מאי הוי ר' יהודה מכריע הוא והלכתא כדברי המכריע ובין [בפי' ובין] מכללא חדא הוא. ואמרינן דילמא הני מילי אם תהיה מחלוקתם במשנה אבל חלוקתם בברייתא לא. אמר ליה בפירוש שמיעא לי. והא דאמר אביי כל מילי דמר עביד כרב בר מהני תלת. אסיקנ' רבה כחומרי דרב הוה עביד. בקולי דרב לא הוה עביד: **ת"ר** מרחץ שפקקו. פי' פקקו סתמו נקביו מע"ש למוצאי שבת רוחץ בה מיד. פקקו נקביו מערב יום טוב למחר נכנס ומזיע ויוצא ומשתטף בבית החיצון. וכן עשו ר' אלעזר בן עזריה ור"ע במרחץ של בני ברק. משרבו עוברי עבירה התחילו לאסור שהיו מחמין בשבת ואומרים מע"ש החמנו. אסרו להן חמין והתירו הזיעה כו'. ואסיקנא אסרו להן אפילו חמין שהוחמו מע"ש ואפילו חמי טבריא וכ"ש חמי האור. ואפילו זיעה אסרו להן

עין משפט נר מצוה

טז א מיי' פכ"ב מהלכות שבת הלכה ב סמג לאוין סה טוש"ע או"ח סימן שכו סעיף א:
יז ב שם סעיף יא:
יח ג מיי' פ"א מהלכות י"ט הלכה טז סמג לאוין עה טור שו"ע או"ח סימן תקיא סעיף ב:
יט ד מיי' פכ"ב מהלכות שבת הלכה ב סמג לאוין סה טוש"ע או"ח סימן שכו סעיף א:
כ ה מיי' שם טוש"ע שם סעיף יב:

[עי' ברכות יט. במשנתינו קאמרינן והא בריי' היא]
[ועי' תוס' מנחות לא: ד"ה מי קאמר וכו' תירצו באופן אחר]
שם איתא חבל
חבל
לעיל כב. פסחים קא. מנחות מח:
תוספתא שבת פי"ד
[ועי' יתר אריכות בתוס' ב"ק קטז. ד"ה הכרעה]

מסורת הש"ס

[לעיל כט:]
[לעיל לט:]
מאן דגרס בגמ' דילמא גרס הכא לא שמיע ליה לרב יוסף
[רש"ל מ"ז]
תיבת לוי"ה רמז לרבינו יהודה הלוי

גליון הש"ס

תוס' ד"ה דילמא ה"מ במתניתין וכו' אע"ג דלא קאמר במשנתנו. עי' משנה למלך ריש הלכות בית הבחירה:

כא א מיי' פכ"ב מהל' שבת הלכה ג סמג לאוין סה טוש"ע או"ח סימן שכו סעיף ד:
כב ב מיי' שם הלכה ד טוש"ע שם סעיף ו:
כג ג ד מיי' וסמג שם טוש"ע או"ח סימן שיח סעיף יד:
כד ה ו מיי' פכ"ב שם הלכה ה ו טור שו"ע שם סעיף יג וטוש"ע יו"ד סימן קה סעיף ב:
כה ז ח ט מיי' פ"ג מהלכות ק"ש הלכה ד ה טוש"ע או"ח סימן פה סעיף ב:
כו י מיי' פכ"א מהלכות שבת הלכה ג טוש"ע או"ח סימן שלז סעיף ג:
כז כ מיי' פ"ט מהלכות שבת הלכה ג:
והכא באמבטי במקום שרגלה להניח הפך היתה יד סולדת בו והא דלא א"ל תן במקום שאין היד סולדת דהיינו במקום שרחץ ולאי לא היה היד סולדת ושמא שם לא הי' יכול להפשיר א"נ פעמים התמירו בכלי ראשון אף אם אין היד סולדת בו וכן התמירו חכמים אפי' בכלי שני לקמן (מב.) גבי ספל ד"ה כאמבטי [תו"י]
כח ל מ מיי' פכ"ג מהל' שבת הלכה ה טור שו"ע או"ח סימן שלט סעיף ב:

כִּי הַאי תַּנָּא. "אַמְבַּטְיָאוֹת שֶׁל כְּרַכִּים מְטַיֵּיל בָּהֶן וְאֵינוֹ חוֹשֵׁשׁ". אָמַר רָבָא: דַּוְקָא כְּרַכִּין, אֲבָל דִּכְפָרִים – לֹא. מ"ט? כֵּיוָן דְּזוּטְרִין, נָפֵישׁ הַבְלַיְיהוּ. ת"ר: [א]מִתְחַמֵּם אָדָם כְּנֶגֶד הַמְּדוּרָה וְיוֹצֵא וּמִשְׁתַּטֵּף בְּצוֹנֵן, וּבִלְבַד שֶׁלֹּא יִשְׁתַּטֵּף בְּצוֹנֵן וְיִתְחַמֵּם כְּנֶגֶד הַמְּדוּרָה, מִפְּנֵי שֶׁמַּפְשִׁיר מַיִם שֶׁעָלָיו. *ת"ר: [ב]מֵיחֵם אָדָם אֲלוּנְטִית וּמַנִּיחָהּ עַל בְּנֵי מֵעַיִם בַּשַּׁבָּת, וּבִלְבַד שֶׁלֹּא יָבִיא קוּמְקוּמוֹס שֶׁל מַיִם חַמִּין וְיַנִּיחֶנּוּ עַל בְּנֵי מֵעַיִם בַּשַּׁבָּת, וְדָבָר זֶה אֲפִי' בַּחוֹל אָסוּר מִפְּנֵי הַסַּכָּנָה. *ת"ר: [ג]מֵבִיא אָדָם קִיתוֹן מַיִם וּמַנִּיחוֹ כְּנֶגֶד הַמְּדוּרָה, לֹא בִּשְׁבִיל שֶׁיֵּחַמּוּ, אֶלָּא בִּשְׁבִיל שֶׁתָּפִיג צִינָּתָן. ר' יְהוּדָה אוֹמֵר: מְבִיאָה אִשָּׁה פַּךְ שֶׁל שֶׁמֶן וּמַנִּיחָתוֹ כְּנֶגֶד הַמְּדוּרָה, לֹא בִּשְׁבִיל שֶׁיִּבְשַׁל אֶלָּא בִּשְׁבִיל שֶׁיִּפְשַׁר. רשב"ג אוֹמֵר: אִשָּׁה סָכָה יָדָהּ שֶׁמֶן וּמְחַמַּמְתָּהּ כְּנֶגֶד הַמְּדוּרָה, וְסָכָה לִבְנָהּ קָטָן, וְאֵינָהּ חוֹשֶׁשֶׁת. אִיבַּעְיָא לְהוּ: שֶׁמֶן מַה הוּא לְתַנָּא קַמָּא? רַבָּה וְרַב יוֹסֵף דְּאָמְרִי תַּרְוַיְיהוּ לְהֶתֵּירָא, רַב נַחְמָן בַּר יִצְחָק אָמַר לְאִיסּוּרָא. רַבָּה וְרַב יוֹסֵף דְּאָמְרִי תַּרְוַיְיהוּ לְהֶתֵּירָא: שֶׁמֶן אע"פ שֶׁהַיָּד סוֹלֶדֶת בּוֹ – מוּתָּר, קָסָבַר ת"ק: שֶׁמֶן אֵין בּוֹ מִשּׁוּם בִּשּׁוּל. וַאֲתָא רַבִּי יְהוּדָה לְמֵימַר: שֶׁמֶן יֵשׁ בּוֹ מִשּׁוּם בִּשּׁוּל, וְהֶפְשֵׁרוֹ לֹא זֶה הוּא בִּשּׁוּלוֹ. וַאֲתָא ר' שִׁמְעוֹן בֶּן גַּמְלִיאֵל לְמֵימַר: שֶׁמֶן – יֵשׁ בּוֹ מִשּׁוּם בִּשּׁוּל, וְהֶפְשֵׁרוֹ זֶהוּ בִּשּׁוּלוֹ. רַב נַחְמָן בַּר יִצְחָק אָמַר לְאִיסּוּרָא: שֶׁמֶן אע"פ שֶׁאֵין הַיָּד סוֹלֶדֶת בּוֹ – אָסוּר, קָסָבַר: שֶׁמֶן יֵשׁ בּוֹ מִשּׁוּם בִּשּׁוּל, וְהֶפְשֵׁרוֹ זֶהוּ בִּשּׁוּלוֹ. וַאֲתָא ר' יְהוּדָה לְמֵימַר: הֶפְשֵׁרוֹ לֹא זֶהוּ בִּשּׁוּלוֹ. וַאֲתָא רשב"ג לְמֵימַר: שֶׁמֶן יֵשׁ בּוֹ מִשּׁוּם בִּשּׁוּל, וְהֶפְשֵׁרוֹ זֶהוּ בִּשּׁוּלוֹ. רשב"ג הַיְינוּ ת"ק! אִיכָּא בֵּינַיְיהוּ כִּלְאַחַר יָד. א"ר יְהוּדָה אָמַר שְׁמוּאֵל: [ד]אֶחָד שֶׁמֶן וְאֶחָד מַיִם, יָד סוֹלֶדֶת בּוֹ – אָסוּר, אֵין יָד סוֹלֶדֶת בּוֹ – מוּתָּר. וְהֵיכִי דָּמֵי יָד סוֹלֶדֶת בּוֹ? אָמַר רַחֲבָא: כֹּל שֶׁכְּרֵיסוֹ שֶׁל תִּינוֹק נִכְוֵית. א"ר יִצְחָק בַּר אַבְדִּימִי: פַּעַם אַחַת נִכְנַסְתִּי אַחַר רַבִּי לְבֵית הַמֶּרְחָץ וּבִקַּשְׁתִּי לְהַנִּיחַ לוֹ פַּךְ שֶׁל שֶׁמֶן בָּאַמְבַּטִי, [ה]וְאָמַר לִי: טוֹל בִּכְלִי שֵׁנִי וְתֵן. שְׁמַע מִינַּהּ תְּלָת, שְׁמַע מִינָּהּ: שֶׁמֶן יֵשׁ בּוֹ מִשּׁוּם בִּשּׁוּל, וש"מ: [ו]כְּלִי שֵׁנִי אֵינוֹ מְבַשֵּׁל, וש"מ: הֶפְשֵׁרוֹ זֶהוּ בִּשּׁוּלוֹ. הֵיכִי עָבֵיד הָכִי? וְהָאָמַר רַבָּה בַּר בַּר חָנָה א"ר יוֹחָנָן: *[ז]בְּכָל מָקוֹם מוּתָּר לְהַרְהֵר – חוּץ מִבֵּית הַמֶּרְחָץ וּבֵית הַכִּסֵּא! וְכ"ת בִּלְשׁוֹן חוֹל א"ל, וְהָאָמַר אַבַּיֵי: [ח]דְּבָרִים שֶׁל חוֹל – מוּתָּר לְאוֹמְרָן בִּלְשׁוֹן קוֹדֶשׁ, שֶׁל קוֹדֶשׁ – אָסוּר לְאוֹמְרָן בִּלְשׁוֹן חוֹל! [ט]אַפְרוּשֵׁי מֵאִיסּוּרָא שָׁאנֵי. תֵּדַע, דְּאָמַר *רַב יְהוּדָה אָמַר שְׁמוּאֵל: מַעֲשֶׂה *בְּתַלְמִידוֹ שֶׁל ר' מֵאִיר שֶׁנִּכְנַס אַחֲרָיו לְבֵית הַמֶּרְחָץ, [י]וּבִקֵּשׁ לְהָדִיחַ קַרְקַע. וְאָמַר לוֹ: אֵין מְדִיחִין. לָסוּךְ לוֹ קַרְקַע, אָמַר לוֹ: אֵין סָכִין. אַלְמָא: אַפְרוּשֵׁי מֵאִיסּוּרָא – שָׁאנֵי, הָכָא נַמִי: לְאַפְרוּשֵׁי מֵאִיסּוּרָא שָׁאנֵי. אָמַר רָבִינָא: שְׁמַע מִינָּהּ, הַמְבַשֵּׁל בְּחַמֵּי טְבֶרְיָא בַּשַּׁבָּת – חַיָּיב. דְּהָא מַעֲשֶׂה דְּר' לְאַחַר גְּזֵירָה הֲוָה, וְאָמַר לֵיהּ: טוֹל בִּכְלִי שֵׁנִי וְתֵן. אִינִי?! *וְהָאָמַר רַב חִסְדָּא: [כ]הַמְבַשֵּׁל בְּחַמֵּי טְבֶרְיָא בַּשַּׁבָּת – פָּטוּר! מַאי 'חַיָּיב' נַמִי דְּקָאָמַר – *מַכַּת מַרְדּוּת. א"ר זֵירָא: אֲנָא חֲזִיתֵיהּ לְר' אַבָּהוּ דְּשָׁט בָּאַמְבַּטִי, וְלָא יָדַעְנָא אִי עֲקַר אִי לָא עֲקַר. פְּשִׁיטָא דְּלָא עֲקַר. דְּתַנְיָא: [ל]לֹא יָשׁוּט אָדָם בִּבְרֵיכָה מְלֵאָה מַיִם, וַאֲפִי' עוֹמֶדֶת בֶּחָצֵר! [מ]לָא קַשְׁיָא, הָא דְּלֵית

תוספות

מפני שמפשיר מים שעליו. בכולה שמעתא ובמתניתין גבי מיחם שפינהו משמע דלהפשיר מים לצורך שתייה – מותר, דהפשירן לא זהו בישולן. והכא דאסורין מפרש ריב"א: דדומה כרוחץ במים חמין, ויבא להחם חמין לרחוץ גופו:

ובלבד שלא יביא קומקומוס כו'. פירוש: כל זמן שהאלונטית שם, שמא יפלו המים על האלונטית ואתי לידי סחיטה. אי נמי: לא יביא – משום רפואה, וגזרו אטו שחיקת סממנים טפי מבאלונטית, דלא מיחזי כרפואה כ"כ:

ושמע מינה כלי שני אינו מבשל. תימה: מאי שנא כלי שני מכלי ראשון? דאי יד סולדת – אפי' כלי שני נמי, ואי אין יד סולדת – אפילו כלי ראשון נמי אינו מבשל! ויש לומר: לפי שכלי ראשון, מתוך שעמד על האור – דופנותיו חמין, ומחזיק חומו זמן מרובה. ולכך נתנו בו שיעור, דכל זמן *שהיד סולדת בו – אסור. אבל כלי שני, אף על גב דיד סולדת בו – מותר, שאין דופנותיו חמין, והולך ומתקרר: **וכי** תימא בלשון חול קאמר ליה. ואע"ג דאסור להרהר, נימא דאין אסור להרהר אלא בלשון קדש, והוא הרהר בלשון חול:
פשיטא

רש"י

כִּי הַאי תַּנָּא. דְּקָאמַר לְעֵיל: מִשֶּׁהִתְחִילוּ עוֹבְרֵי עֲבֵירָה – הִתְחִילוּ לֶאֱסוֹר הַזֵּיעָה. וַהֲרֵי לֹא נֶאֶסְרָה אֶלָּא ע"י הָרוֹחֲצִין בְּחַמִּין מֵאֶתְמוֹל, וְאוֹנְרִים "מְזִיעִין אֲנַחְנוּ", וְאֵין כָּאן אֶלָּא עֲבֵירַת דִּבְרֵיהֶם, שֶׁאָסְרוּ אֶת הַחַמִּין: נָפֵישׁ הַבְלַיְיהוּ. וּמֵזִיעַ: מַפְשִׁיר. מְחַמֵּם, לְשׁוֹן פּוֹשְׁרִין: מֵיחֵם אָדָם. מְחַמֵּם: אֲלוּנְטִית. טיול"א. וְנִרְאֶה לִי: בֶּגֶד שֶׁמִּסְתַּפְּגִין בּוֹ, דְּבְכָל דּוּכְתָּא קָרֵי לָהּ אֲלוּנְטִית: עַל גַּבֵּי מֵעַיִם. כְּשֶׁהוּא חָשׁ בְּמֵעָיו מְחַמְּמִין לוֹ כְּלִי אוֹ בֶּגֶד, וּמַנִּיחוֹ שָׁם, וּמוֹעִיל: וּבִלְבַד שֶׁלֹּא יָבִיא קוּמְקוּמוֹס כו'. שֶׁמָּא יִשָּׁפְכוּ עָלָיו, וְנִמְצָא רוֹחֵץ בַּשַּׁבָּת בְּחַמִּין: מִפְּנֵי סַכָּנָה. פְּעָמִים שֶׁהֵן רוֹתְחִין: לֹא שֶׁיֵּחַמּוּ. לֹא שֶׁיַּנִּיחֵם שָׁם עַד שֶׁיֵּחַמּוּ: אֶלָּא שֶׁתָּפִיג צִינָּתָן. בְּמִקְצָתָן. שֶׁתָּפִיג – שֶׁתִּתְחַלֵּף, כְּמוֹ "וְרֵיחוֹ לֹא נָמָר" (ירמיה מח) מְתַרְגְּמִינַן: "וְרֵיחֵיהּ לָא פָג": לֹא בִּשְׁבִיל שֶׁיִּבְשַׁל. שֶׁלֹּא תַּנִּיחֶנּוּ שָׁם כְּדֵי בִּישּׁוּל, שֶׁתְּהֵא הַיָּד סוֹלֶדֶת בּוֹ: סָכָה יָדָהּ. אֲבָל לְהַפְשִׁירוֹ בְּפַךְ כְּדֶרֶךְ שֶׁעוֹשָׂה בְּחוֹל – לֹא, וּפָלֵיג אַדְּרַב יְהוּדָה: לְהֶתֵּירָא. מַאי דְּאָסַר רַבִּי יְהוּדָה בְּשֶׁמֶן בִּישּׁוּל, שָׁרֵי ת"ק. וּמַיִם דַּוְקָא נָקַט: וְלֹא שֶׁיֵּחַמּוּ, דְּיֵשׁ בָּהֶן בִּישּׁוּל. אֲבָל שֶׁמֶן, אע"פ שֶׁהַיָּד סוֹלֶדֶת, דְּהַיְינוּ בִּישּׁוּלוֹ דְּר' יְהוּדָה – שָׁרֵי לְת"ק: סוֹלֶדֶת. נִמְשֶׁכֶת לַאֲחוֹרֶיהָ מִדְּאָגָה שֶׁלֹּא תִּכָּוֶה. וְזֶהוּ לְשׁוֹן "וַאֲסַלְּדָה בְחִילָה" (איוב ו) – וְאֶדְאַג בִּרְעָדָה, וְאֶמָּשֵׁךְ מִתְּלוּנּוֹתַי מִדַּאֲגַת יוֹם הַדִּין, אִם הָיִיתִי יוֹדֵעַ שֶׁמִּיתָתִי קְרוֹבָה וְלֹא יַחְמוֹל: שֶׁמֶן יֵשׁ בּוֹ מִשּׁוּם בִּישּׁוּל. הִלְכָּךְ לֹא כְּדֵי שֶׁיִּבְשַׁל אֶלָּא כְּדֵי שֶׁיִּפְשַׁר שָׁרֵי, דְּהֶפְשֵׁרוֹ אֵין זֶה בִּישּׁוּלוֹ: וַאֲתָא רַבִּי שִׁמְעוֹן לְמֵימַר דְּהֶפְשֵׁירוֹ זֶהוּ בִּישּׁוּלוֹ. הִלְכָּךְ: כִּדְעָבְדִין בְּחוֹל לָא לֶיעֱבִיד, אֶלָּא כִּלְאַחַר יָד עַל יְדֵי שִׁינּוּי: לְאִיסּוּרָא. אֲמָרָהּ תַּנָּא קַמָּא לְשֶׁמֶן. דְּמַיָּא הוּא דְּשָׁרֵי לְהַפְשִׁיר, אֲבָל שֶׁמֶן – הֶפְשֵׁרוֹ זֶהוּ בִּישּׁוּלוֹ: אִיכָּא בֵּינַיְיהוּ כִּלְאַחַר יָד. דִּלְתַנָּא קַמָּא, אֲפִילּוּ ע"י שִׁינּוּי – אָסוּר: וְהֵיכִי דָּמֵי. סוֹלֵד, יֵשׁ שֶׁסּוֹלֵד מֵרְתִיחָה מוּעֶטֶת, וְיֵשׁ שֶׁאֵינוֹ סוֹלֵד: נִכְנַסְתִּי. בַּשַּׁבָּת, וּבְחַמֵּי טְבֶרְיָא הֲוָה שֶׁלֹּא נֶאֶסְרוּ, כְּדַאֲמַר לְעֵיל: "הִתִּירוּ לָהֶם חַמֵּי טְבֶרְיָא": בָּאַמְבַּטִי. כְּגוֹן בְּרֵיכָה עֲשׂוּיָה בַּקַּרְקַע, שֶׁהַמַּיִם נִכְנָסִים שָׁם וְנֶאֱסָפִין: וּבִקַּשְׁתִּי לְהַנִּיחַ שָׁם פַּךְ שֶׁמֶן. לְהַפְשִׁיר, לָסוּךְ הֵימֶנּוּ קוֹדֶם הָרְחִיצָה: טוֹל. מִן הַמַּיִם: בִּכְלִי שֵׁנִי. שֶׁיִּצְטַנְּנוּ מְעַט, דִּכְלִי שֵׁנִי אֵינוֹ מְבַשֵּׁל, וְאַחַ"כ תֵּן הַפַּךְ לְתוֹךְ אוֹתוֹ כְּלִי שֵׁנִי. דְּהָךְ אַמְבַּטִי שֶׁהַחַמִּין נִמְשָׁכִין לָהּ מִן הַמַּעְיָין חָשֵׁיב לָהּ כִּכְלִי רִאשׁוֹן שֶׁנִּרְתְּחוּ בּוֹ, שֶׁאע"פ שֶׁהֶעֱבִירוֹ מֵעַל הָאוּר – מְבַשֵּׁל, כִּדְתְנַן לְקַמָּן (ד' מב.): "הָאִילְפָּס וְהַקְּדֵירָה שֶׁהֶעֱבִירָן מְרוּתָּחִין – לֹא יִתֵּן לְתוֹכָן תַּבְלִין": וש"מ הֶפְשֵׁרוֹ. בְּמָקוֹם הָרָאוּי לְבִישּׁוּל: זֶהוּ בִּישּׁוּלוֹ. דְּהָא לְהַפְשִׁיר בְּעָלְמָא הוּא דְּקָבָעֵי, וַאֲסַר לֵיהּ: וְהֵיכִי עָבֵיד הָכִי. לְהוֹרוֹת הוֹרָאָה, שֶׁהוּא דְּבַר תּוֹרָה, בְּבֵית הַמֶּרְחָץ? לְהַרְהֵר. בְּדִבְרֵי תוֹרָה: דְּבָרִים שֶׁל קֹדֶשׁ. דִּבְרֵי תוֹרָה: אָסוּר לְאוֹמְרָן. בְּמָקוֹם הַטִּנּוֹפֶת, וַאֲפִילּוּ בִּלְשׁוֹן חוֹל: אֵין מְדִיחִין. דִּלְמָא אָתֵי לְאַשְׁוּוֹיֵי גּוּמּוֹת: דְּהָא מַעֲשֶׂה דְּרַבִּי אַחַר גְּזֵירָה הֲוָה. שֶׁגָּזְרוּ עַל הַזֵּיעָה, וְעַל כָּרְחִין בְּחַמֵּי טְבֶרְיָא הוּא דַּהֲוֵי. וְרַבִּי יְהוֹשֻׁעַ[א] דְּקָאמַר לְעֵיל: בִּימֵי רַבִּי הֲוָה, אַלְמָא: בִּימֵי רַבִּי כְּבָר נִגְזְרָה: וְקָאָמַר לֵיהּ טוֹל בִּכְלִי שֵׁנִי. אֲבָל רִאשׁוֹן – לֹא, אַלְמָא: יֵשׁ בָּהֶן מִשּׁוּם בִּישּׁוּל: מַרְדּוּת. רְדוּי: שָׁט. לָף: דְּשָׁט בָּאַמְבַּטִי. בַּשַּׁבָּת: וְלָא יָדַעְנָא אִי עֲקַר. רַגְלָיו מִן הָאָרֶץ, דְּקָסָבַר: כִּי תְּנַן "אֵין שָׁטִין עַל פְּנֵי הַמַּיִם" בְּ"מַשִּׁילִין פֵּירוֹת" – *בְּנָהָר גָּדוֹל תְּנַן, דְּאִיכָּא לְמִגְזַר שֶׁמָּא יַעֲשֶׂה חָבִית שֶׁל שַׁיָּיטִין, כִּדְאָמְרִינַן הָתָם. אֲבָל בְּאַמְבַּטִי – לֹא: אִי לֹא עֲקַר. רַגְלָיו: לֹא יָשׁוּט. דְּאע"ג דְּלֵיכָּא לְמִיגְזַר – אָסוּר: וַאֲפִילּוּ עוֹמֶדֶת בֶּחָצֵר. דְּלֵיכָּא לְמִיגְזַר שֶׁמָּא יַתִּיז מַיִם בְּרַגְלָיו חוּץ לְאַרְבַּע אַמּוֹת: הָא. דַּאֲסִיר דְּלֵית

רבינו חננאל

להן אלא צונן בלבד. ראו שאין הדבר עומד חזרו והתירו להן חמי טבריא בלבד. וזיעה במקומה עומדת באיסור אמר רבא מאן דעבר על דברי חכמי' שרי למיקרי' עבריינא. כי האי תנא דתנא משרבו עוברי עבירה: **תנא** אמבטאות של כרכין מטייל בהן ואינו חושש. והני מילי דכרכין אבל דכפרין כיון דזוטרן נפיש הבליהון: **ת"ר** מתחמם אדם כנגד המדורה ויוצא (ומשתטף בצונן) [ובלבד שלא ישתטף בצונן] ויתחמם כנגד המדורה מפני שנפשרו המים שעליו: **ת"ר** מיחם אדם אלונטית ומניחה ע"ג מעיו בשבת ובלבד (ישתטף בצונן ויתחמם כנגד המדורה מפני שתפשר המים) שלא יביא קומקומוס של חמין ויניחנו על גבי מעיו בשבת. ודבר זה אפילו בחול [אסור] מפני הסכנה שלא יכוה: **ת"ר** מניח אדם קיתון של מים כנגד המדורה לא שיחמו אלא כדי שתפוג צינתן. ר' יהודה אמר מנחת אשה פך שמן כנגד המדורה לא שיתבשל אלא כדי שתפשר. רשב"א אשה סכה ידה שמן כנגד המדורה. וסכה לבנה קטן ואינה חוששת: **איבעיא** להו שמן מה לי בו אמר ת"ק. ואסיק' אמר רב אמר שמואל אחד שמן ואחד מים אם נתחמם כשעור שהיד סולדת בו אסור אין היד סולדת בו מותר. ושיעור שהיד סולדת בו. פי' (פירוש') [בירושל'] שהיד*) שולטת בו סולדת היא שולטת והוא כל שכריסו של תינוק נכוית הימנו. הא מעשה דר' שבקשו לו פך של שמן באמבטי ואמר להן טלו בכלי שני ותנו. שמעינן מינה תלת. ש"מ שמן יש בו משום בישול. ולפיכך בכלי ראשון אסור. שנמצא מבשל שמן בשבת. וש"מ מדשרי בכלי שני דכלי שני אינו מבשל. וש"מ הפשרו לא זהו בישולו: **אמר** רבינא ש"מ המבשל בחמי טבריא הואיל וגזרו רבנן עלייהו חייבין מכת מרדות מדרבנן. ואקשינן דר' היאך מורה הוראה במרחץ ואמר טלו בכלי שני כלומר זהו מותר וזהו אסור. והא"ר יוחנן כל מקום מותר להרהר חוץ מבית המרחץ ובית הכסא. ולא דאקשינן מדברי ר' יוחנן לר' דר' יוחנן לגבי דר' תלמיד קטן הוא. (ולא) [אלא] הא דר' יוחנן דברי הכל קבלה הוא

*) ע"ש יש כאן ולשון הירושלמי הובא ברא"ש.

תוספתא שבת פ"ד
[תוספתא שם]

הגהות הב"ח
(א) רש"י ד"ה דהא מעשה וכו' ור' יהושע בן לוי דאמר:

ברכות כד: [לעיל י.] לקמן קנ. זבחים קב: ע"ז מד: קדושין לג.
פסחים מח.
[יבמות נב. כתובות מה: נזיר כג. נח: חולין קמא:]
[דף לו:]
[לקמן קנא:]
[עי' תוס' לקמן קמז: ד"ה דתניא]

דלית ליה גידודי, הא – דאית ליה גידודי. וא"ר זירא: אנא חזיתיה לר' אבהו שהניח ידיו כנגד פניו של מטה, ולא ידענא אי נגע אי לא נגע. פשיטא דלא נגע! דתניא, *ר' אליעזר אומר: "כל האוחז באמה ומשתין כאילו מביא מבול לעולם! אמר אביי: עשאוה כבולשת. דתנן: *בולשת שנכנסה לעיר, בשעת שלום, חביות פתוחות – אסורות, סתומות – מותרות. בשעת מלחמה – אלו ואלו מותרות, לפי שאין פנאי לנסך. אלמא: כיון דבעיתי – לא מנסכי, ה"נ כיון דבעית – לא אתי להרהורי. והכא מאי ביעתותא? ביעתותא דנהרא. איני?! והאמר ר' אבא אמר רב הונא אמר רב: כל המניח ידיו כנגד פניו של מטה כאילו כופר בבריתו של אברהם אבינו! לא קשיא, הא – כי נחית, הא – כי סליק. כי הא דרבא שחי, ר' זירא זקיף. רבנן דבי רב אשי, כי קא נחתי – זקפי, כי קא סלקי – שחי. *ר' זירא הוה קא משתמיט מדרב יהודה, דבעי למיסק לארעא דישראל. דאמר רב יהודה: "כל העולה מבבל לא"י עובר בעשה, שנאמר: °"בבלה יובאו ושמה יהיו". אמר: איזיל ואשמע מיניה מילתא, ואיתי ואיסק. אזל אשכחיה דקאי בי באני, וקאמר ליה לשמעיה: הביאו לי נתר, הביאו לי מסרק, פתחו פומייכו ואפיקו הבלא ואשתו ממיא דבי באני. אמר: אילמלא *(לא) באתי אלא לשמוע דבר זה – דיי. בשלמא הביאו נתר הביאו מסרק, קמ"ל: דברים של חול מותר לאומרם בלשון קדש. פתחו פומייכו ואפיקו הבלא – נמי כדשמואל, דאמר שמואל: הבלא מפיק הבלא. אלא, אשתו מיא דבי באני, מאי מעלייותא? דתניא: "אכל ולא שתה – אכילתו דם וזהו תחילת חולי מעיים. *אכל ולא הלך ד' אמות – אכילתו מרקבת, וזהו תחילת ריח רע. הנצרך *לנקביו ואכל – דומה לתנור שהסיקוהו ע"ג אפרו, וזהו תחילת ריח זוהמא. רחץ בחמין ולא שתה מהן – דומה לתנור שהסיקוהו מבחוץ ולא הסיקוהו מבפנים, רחץ בחמין ולא נשתטף בצונן – דומה לברזל שהכניסוהו לאור ולא הכניסוהו לצונן. רחץ ולא סך – דומה למים ע"ג חבית.

מתני' מוליאר הגרוף שותין הימנו בשבת. אנטיכי, אע"פ שגרופה – אין שותין הימנה.

גמ' היכי דמי מוליאר הגרוף? תנא: מים מבפנים וגחלים מבחוץ. אנטיכי, רבה אמר: בי כירי. רב נחמן בר יצחק אמר: בי דודי. מאן דאמר בי דודי – כ"ש בי כירי. ומאן דאמר בי כירי, אבל בי דודי – לא. תניא כוותיה דרב נחמן: אנטיכי אע"פ שגרופה וקטומה – אין שותין הימנה, מפני שנחושתה מחממתה.

מתני' המיחם שפינהו – לא יתן לתוכו צונן בשביל שיחמו, אבל נותן הוא לתוכו, או לתוך הכוס כדי להפשירן.

גמ' מאי קאמר? אמר רב אדא בר מתנא, הכי קאמר: "המיחם שפינה ממנו מים חמין – לא יתן לתוכן מים מועטים כדי שיחמו, אבל נותן לתוכו מים מרובים – כדי להפשירן. והלא

רש"י

דלית ליה גידודי. שאין שפתה גבוהה שיהיו המים עמוקים אצל שפתה כמו באמצע. דכיון שאין עמוקים שם, כי מטי סמוך לשפתה – נועץ רגליו בקרקע וחופר, וממחה העפר לתוך המים ודמי למגבל. ולי נראה: דאית ליה גידודי שרי, דלא דמי לנהר, אלא לכלי. דלית ליה גידודי – דמיא לנהר, ואסור: שהניח ידיו. כשהיה רוחץ, משום צניעות: אי נגע. באמה: כאילו מביא מבול לעולם. שמתחמם ובא לידי קרי, וזה קלקולו של דור המבול, מוציאים שכבת זרע לבטלה, דכתיב: "כי השחית כל בשר" וגו' (בראשית ו): כבולשת. עשאוה להא דר' אבהו. בולשת – חיילות, גייס הבא לעיר. על שם שמחפשין ובולשים את העיר קרי לה בולשת: בשעת שלום. כגון שהוא של אותה מלכות: כאילו כופר. דנראה שהוא בוש בדבר: כי נחית. לנהר, פניו כלפי הנהר, ואין כאן משום צניעות – אסור לכסותו: כי סליק. ופניו כלפי העם – מותר משום צניעות: ר' זירא זקיף. דחייש לדרב שלא יראה ככופר: משתמיט. היה ירא ליראות לו, משום דהוה בעי רבי זירא למיסק לארעא דישראל, ורב יהודה לא סבירא ליה, וירא פן יגזור עליו מליליך: בבלה יובאו ושמה יהיו עד יום פקדי וגו'. ור' זירא אמר לך: האי קרא בכלי שרת כתיב, כדאמרינן ב"שני דייני גזירות" (כתובות קי.): הביאו לי נתר. לחוף את ראשי, וקאמר להו בלשון הקודש: פתחו פומייכו. ויכנס הבל בית המרחץ לתוך הגוף, ויוציא הבל של זיעה: ואשתו. מן מים חמין, ואפילו לא הוחמו אלא לרחיצה: מותר לאומרן. בבית המרחץ, ואפילו בלשון קודש: הבלא. דמרחץ הנכנס דרך הפה: מפיק הבלא. דזיעה: ולא הלך ד' אמות. קודם שישן: מרקבת. אינה מתעכלת לעשות זבל: ריח רע. ריח הפה: ריח זוהמא. כל גופו מזוהם בזיעה תמיד: ולא הסיקוהו מבפנים. שאינו מטיב לכלום: ולא הכניסוהו לצונן. שהן מחזקין את הברזל: למים ע"ג חבית. על שוליו ולדדיו, שאינם נכנסים לתוכו: **מתני'** מוליאר הגרוף. מן הגחלים מבע"י: שותין. ממימיו בשבת, ואע"פ שהוחמו קצת מחמת הכלי; לפי שאינו מוסיף הבל, אלא משמר ומקיים חום שלהם שלא יצטננו. בגמרא מפרש: מוליאר – מים מבפנים וגחלים מבחוץ, כלי שיש בו בית קיבול קטן אצל דופנו מבחוץ מחובר לו, ונותן שם גחלים, והמים בקיבולו הגדול. ורבותינו מפרשים: מוליאר – שני שולים, ואנטיכי בי דודי – מחילה בינתיים. ולי נראה להפך, דאם כן ה"ל למיתני: מים מלמעלה וגחלים מלמטה. ועוד, ד"נחשתה" דתני באנטיכי – לשון שולים הן. והן אומרים: לשון נחושת, ושאני נחשת מחרס: אנטיכי. מפרש בגמרא: **גמ'** בי כירי. חלל יש בכירה אצל חלליה שהגחלים בו, ומים נתונים בחללה השני. ואע"ג דדמי למוליאר, מיהו – כירה דופנה עב, והאור תדיר בתוכה כל ימות החול ודופנה חם מאד, ומוסיף הבל במים אע"פ שגרופה מן הגחלים: בי דודי. יורה גדולה, עושין לה שתי שוליים ונותנין גחלים בין שניהם, והמים על העליונים: וכל שכן. דבי כירי אסור, כדפרישית, שמתוך שהאור תדיר בו ודופנו עב – מרתיח: אבל בי דודי לא. שהרי הוא כמוליאר: שנחושתה. נחושת שלה. אלמא: בירה של נחשת קאי, ונחשת משמר רתיחתו. ואני אומר: "נחושתה" – לשון שולים, כדכתיב (יחזקאל טז): "יען השפך נחשתך". ולשון של המשנה: "נחשתו של תנור" במסכת כלים (פ"ח מ"ג). ושאני אנטיכי ממוליאר, דמתוך שהשולים מכוסים – חומם משתמר, ואע"ג שגרפו גחליהם: **מתני'** המיחם. קומקמוס של חמין: שפינהו. כולה מתניתין מפרש בגמרא: **גמ'** מאי קאמר. מאי "פינהו" ומאי "לא יתן", והדר אמר "אבל נותן": והלא

תוספות

פשיטא דלא נגע דתניא ר' אליעזר אומר כו'. ואע"ג דרבנן פליגי עליה וסברו בפרק "כל היד" (נדה יג. ושם) – לא שרי אלא משום ממזרות, שלא יראה ככרות שפכה, ויוציאו לעז על בניו שהן ממזרים*: **רחץ** ולא סך. ול"ג "מעיקרא", דהא בכולי התלמוד רחילה קודם סיכה כדאמר בפ"ק דקידושין (דף כב:): "רחצו סכו", וקרא כתיב: "ורחצת וסכת" (רות ג). מיהו, קרא איכא לאוקמי בסיכה שהיתה מתקשטת עצמה לריח טוב לכן לא היתה סכה בתחלה, שעל ידי רחיצה היתה מעברת הסיכה מעליה:

מוליאר הגרוף שותין ממנו בשבת. פי' בקונטרס: לפי שאין מוסיף הבל, אלא משמר ומקיים חום שלהן. ואנטיכי אפי' גרופה אין שותין הימנה, לפי שמוספת הבל. ואין נראה, דלא שייך למיגזר במוסיף הבל אלא בהטמנה, גזירה שמא יטמין ברמץ. ועוד: דדוחק לומר דמתני' איירי כשעשה האיסור. ועוד: דאנטיכי אוסר בכל ענין לשתות הימנו, אפילו בהשהאה. ואי להחזיר תנן, "משהין" אפילו באינו גרוף. ועוד: אי משום תוספת הבל אסרה ליה מתני' בשתיה – תקשה לרבה ורב יוסף דשרו לעיל (דף לח.) בשכח קדרה ע"ג כירה ובשלה בשבת אע"ג דלא נתבשלה כמאכל בן דרוסאי, ואפי' במזיד. ונראה כפי' ה"ר פורת: מוליאר הגרוף שותין הימנו בשבת – שמוזגין המים חמין ביין, לפי שהמים אינן כ"כ חמין במוליאר שיתבשל היין מן המים שמוזגין לתוכו. אבל אנטיכי, אע"פ שגרופה – אין שותין הימנה, לפי שאנטיכי יש בה הבל יותר, ומתבשל היין מן המים בשעת מזיגה. וכ"מ בירושלמי: והלא

רבינו חננאל

הוא ומשום דשמעיה מר' יוחנן הוכיח בעל השמועה. ושנינן לאפרושי מאיסורי שרי במעשה דתלמידו של ר' מאיר: **תניא** לא ישוט אדם בבריכה מליאה מים ואפילו עומדת בחצר א"ר זירא חזיתיה לר' אבהו שהניח ידיו כנגד פניו של מטה וכו' פי' ר' אבהו היה יורד בנהר לטבול ואפילו (לא) נגע לא חיישנן (לה) [והא] דתניא ר' אליעזר אומר כל האוחז באמה ומשתין מביא מבול לעולם כלומ' מתחמם ומוציא ש"ז ונמצא משחית זרעו על הארץ. הני מילי היכא דלא מיבעית אבל היכא דמיבעית כגון ר' אבהו דהוה מבעית מעליית הנהר אין לו פנאי להתחמם כמו שאין פנאי לבלשת לנסך. הלכך אפילו נגע לא חיישינן ליה והני מילי דשרי להניח ידיו כנגד פניו של מטה כשעולה מן הנהר אבל כשיורד בנהר לא כרב דאמר כל המניח ידיו כנגד פניו של מטה כאילו כופר בבריתו של אברהם אבינו וכרבנן דבי רב אשי דכי נחתי זקפו כי סלקי שחו: **אמר** רב יהודה כל העולה מבבל לא"י עובר בעשה שנאמר בבלה יובאו ושמה [יהיו] עד יום פקדי אותם נאם ה'. הלך ר' אבא ומצא לר' יהודה במרחץ והי' אומר לשמשיו בלה"ק הביאו לי נתר הביאו לי מסרק פתחו פומייכו והסיקו הבלא ואשתו מיא דבי באני למדנו ממנו כי דברים של חול מותר לאומרן במרחץ בלה"ק. אמר אילו לא [באתי] אלא לשמוע דבר זה דיי: **מתני'** מוליר תנא מים מבחוץ וגחלים מבפנים והוא של חרס ואם גרף גחלים שרי: **אנטיכי** א"ר נחמן בי דודי ושל נחושת היא ותניא כרב נחמן אנטיכי אע"פ שגרופה אין שותין הימנה בשבת מפני שנחושתה מחממתה: **ירושלמי** מולייר שאינו גרוף אסור מפני שהגחלים נוגעות בגופו ר' חנניא בר הלל אמר מפני שהרוח נכנסת לתוכו והגחלים בוערות. ר' יוסי בר אבין א' מפני שעשו פרקין פרקין ומתיירא שמא נתאכל דיבוקו ומוסיף מים. אנטיכי בשם ר' יוחנן אמרי מפני שמתחממת מכתליה: **פיסקא** מיחם שפינהו לא יתן לתוכו צונן

עין משפט נר מצוה

[וע"ע תוספות יומא ל. ד"ה מלוה]

כט א מיי' פכ"א מהל' איסורי ביאה הלכה כג טוש"ע או"ח סימן ג סעיף יד וטשו"ע או"ח סימן כג סעיף ד:

ל ב מיי' פ"ה מהלכות מלכים הלכה יב:

לא ג מיי' פ"ד מהלכות דעות הלכה ב:

לב ד מיי' פי"ב מהל' שבת הלכה א ופכ"ב הלכה ו סמג לאוין סה טוש"ע או"ח סימן שיח סעיף יב:

מסורת הש"ס

נדה יג. מג.

ע"ז ע: כתובות כז. [נדה יג.]

כתובות קי. ברכות כד:

ירמיהו כז

[עי' תוספות מגילה כח. ד"ה אלמלא]

[עי' ב"מ קיג:]

[לקמן פב. ע"ש]

וַהֲלֹא מְצָרֵף! ר' שִׁמְעוֹן הִיא, דְּאָמַר: *דָּבָר שֶׁאֵין מִתְכַּוֵּין – מוּתָּר. מַתְקִיף לָהּ אַבַּיֵי: מִידֵי "מֵיחַם שֶׁפִּינָּה מִמֶּנּוּ מַיִם" קָתָנֵי? "מֵיחַם שֶׁפִּינָּהוּ" קָתָנֵי! אֶלָּא אָמַר אַבַּיֵי, הָכִי קָאָמַר: הַמֵּיחַם שֶׁפִּינָּהוּ וְיֵשׁ בּוֹ מַיִם חַמִּין – לֹא יִתֵּן לְתוֹכוֹ מַיִם מוּעָטִין בִּשְׁבִיל שֶׁיָּחוֹמּוּ, אֲבָל נוֹתֵן לְתוֹכוֹ מַיִם מְרוּבִּים כְּדֵי לְהַפְשִׁירָן. וּמֵיחַם שֶׁפִּינָּה מִמֶּנּוּ מַיִם – לֹא יִתֵּן לְתוֹכוֹ מַיִם *כׇּל עִיקָּר, מִפְּנֵי שֶׁמְּצָרֵף. וְר' יְהוּדָה הִיא, דְּאָמַר: דָּבָר שֶׁאֵין מִתְכַּוֵּין – אָסוּר. אָמַר רַב: ל"ש אֶלָּא לְהַפְשִׁיר, אֲבָל לְצָרֵף – אָסוּר. וּשְׁמוּאֵל אָמַר: אֲפִי' לְצָרֵף נַמִי מוּתָּר. לְצָרֵף לְכַתְּחִילָּה מִי שָׁרֵי? אֶלָּא, אִי אִיתְּמַר הָכִי אִיתְּמַר, אָמַר רַב: לֹא שָׁנוּ אֶלָּא שִׁיעוּר לְהַפְשִׁיר, אֲבָל שִׁיעוּר לְצָרֵף – אָסוּר. וּשְׁמוּאֵל אָמַר: אֲפִי' שִׁיעוּר לְצָרֵף מוּתָּר

וַהֲלֹא מְצָרֵף. כְּשֶׁכְּלִי מַתָּכוֹת חַם וְנוֹתֵן לְתוֹכוֹ צוֹנֵן – מְחַזְּקִים אֶת הַכְּלִי, וְזוֹ הִיא גְּמַר מְלֶאכֶת הַצּוֹרְפִין. שֶׁרְתִיחַת הָאוּר מְפַעְפַּעְתּוֹ וְקָרוֹב לְהִשָּׁבֵר, וְהַמַּיִם מְצָרְפִין פִּעְפּוּעָיו, שולדי"ר בְּלַע"ז: שֶׁפִּינָּהוּ. מַשְׁמַע שֶׁפִּינָּהוּ לְעַצְמוֹ מֵעַל הָאוּר: אֲבָל לְצָרֵף. שֶׁפִּינָּהוּ מִמֶּנּוּ הַחַמִּין: הָכִי אִיתְּמַר לֹא שָׁנוּ. דְּפִינָּהוּ שָׁרֵי לָתֵת לְתוֹכוֹ צוֹנֵן: אֶלָּא שִׁיעוּר לְהַפְשִׁיר. וְלֹא לְצָרֵף, כְּגוֹן שֶׁלֹּא מִלְּאָהוּ כּוּלּוֹ. וְרַב מַשְׁמַע לֵיהּ "פִּינָּהוּ" כְּרַב אַדָּא, שֶׁפִּינָּה מִמֶּנּוּ חַמִּין: אֲפִילוּ שִׁיעוּר לְצָרֵף. שֶׁמִּלְּאָהוּ כּוּלּוֹ: מוּתָּר

והלא מצרף. וליכא לשנויי בשלא הגיע לצירוף, כדתנן בפרק "אמר להם הממונה" (יומא דף לד: ושם) – דהתם מיחם הגיע לצירוף הוא: **מידי** מיחם שפינה הימנו מים קתני המיחם שפינהו קתני. תימה, והכתיב: "ופנו את הבית" (ויקרא יד) "ואנכי פניתי הבית" (בראשית כד) "סולו פנו דרך" (ישעיה נז), וכן בתלמוד: *"פנו מקום לבר לואי" שאינו מפנה אלא מה שבתוכם! וי"ל: כיון דבכמה מקומות הוזכר פינוי על הדבר המפנין, כגון: *"המפנה תפליו מזוית לזוית" *)"מפנין ד' וה' קופות" (*) "פנו כליס (מבית) הטומאה" *"(תבן) ועתיד לפנותו" – לא הוה ליה למנקט פינהו, אלא: פנה ממנו מים, כיון דאיכא למיטעי: **מיחם** שפינה ממנו מים לא יתן לתוכו מים כל עיקר מפני שמצרף ורבי יהודה היא. אבל לר"ש – שרי, אע"פ שמצרף, כיון דאינו מבשל. כגון שיש בו מים הרבה, שאין המיחם מספיק לבשל רוב המים שבתוכו, כדאשכחן בפרק "אמר להם הממונה" (יומא דף לד: ושם) שאין מבשל ומצרף. דקאמר רבי יהודה: מביאין עששיות של ברזל ומטילין לתוך המים שתפיג צינתן. ואם היה מבשל – היה אסור. ואפ"ה פריך: והלא מצרף! ואע"ג דאביי סבר כר"ש, דהא אמר לעיל: *כל מילי דמר עביד כרב, לבר מהני תלת דעביד כשמואל, וחד מינייהו הלכה כר"ש בגרירה. ומסתמא, אביי כרבה רביה סבירא ליה. מ"מ: מוקי מתניתין כרבי יהודה, משום דקשיא ליה: מידי מיחם שפינה ממנו מים קתני. ורב אדא לא חייש לקושיית אביי, ומוקי לה כהלכתא כר"ש. ול"ג לעיל: "אמר רב אדא בר מתנא אמר רב" – דרב סבר *כר' יהודה בגרירה, ועוד: דבהדיא מוקי בסמוך מתני' כר' יהודה. ול"ל דלא הוי פסיק רישיה, שיכול להיות שלא יצרף. דבפסיק רישיה מודה ר"ש. והא דפריך: "והלא מצרף", ה"ק: והלא שמא מצרף. קשה: דהכא משמע דבצירוף אסר ר' יהודה נמי דבר שאין מתכוין, ובפרק "אמר להם הממונה" גריס רש"י: ה"מ – דאורייתא, אבל הכא – צירוף דרבנן, ול"ג: "אין שבות במקדש". ומפרש דדוקא בדבר שהוא מן התורה אית ליה לר' יהודה דבר שאין מתכוין – אסור, אבל בצירוף שהוא דרבנן – לא. ומיהו, בלאו הכי קשה לפי' דהא ר' יהודה אסר בגרירה במתניתין דבילה דפרק "י"ט" (דף כג.) דתנן: ואינה נגררת אלא ע"ג כלים, דמשמע: אבל ע"ג קרקע – לא, ומוקמינא כר' יהודה דאסר באין מתכוין. אע"ג דבגרירה ליכא איסורא דאורייתא אפי' במתכוין, כדמשמע בסוף פירקין דהוי חורש כלאחר יד. ועוד: דשמעתא דהתם קשה, דמשני אביי: אפי' תימא כשהגיע לצירוף, דבר שאינו מתכוין – מותר. ופריך: ומי אמר אביי הכי, והתניא: "ימול בשר ערלתו" אפי' במקום בהרת יקוץ, דברי רבי אושעיא, והוינן בה: קרא ל"ל? ואמר אביי: לא נצרכה אלא לר' יהודה, דאמר "דבר שאין מתכוין אסור". והשתא, אמאי לא מייתי ההיא דבילה דהיא משנה שלמה דאסר ר' יהודה דבר שאין מתכוין, ומייתי מילתיה דאביי! ועוד: מוחק הספר דגרס "ואין שבות במקדש". לכך נראה לפרש התם: אביי אמר אפילו כו' דבר שאין מתכוין מותר. פי': מותר לר' יהודה. ולא אסר ליה ר' יהודה דבר שאין מתכוין – אלא מדרבנן. ופריך מ"ימול בשר ערלתו" דמוקי אביי דאיצטריך לר' יהודה קרא, א"כ ש"מ דאסר ר' יהודה אין מתכוין מן התורה. ומשני, וה"ג: ה"מ – בכל התורה כולה, פי': בכל התורה כולה חוץ משבת – אסור מן התורה. אבל צירוף דגבי שבת לא אסור אין מתכוין אלא מדרבנן, דכיון דאין מתכוין – לא הויא מלאכת מחשבת, ושרי. דאין שבות במקדש. והשתא א"ש הכא, וסוגיא דהתם. וקשה: דבפרק "ספק אכל" (כריתות דף כ: *ושם) א"ר אשי: כגון שנתכוין לכבות העליונות והובערו התחתונות מאליהן, ת"ק סבר לה כר"י דאמר: דבר שאין מתכוין אסור, ולכך קאמר דחייב חטאת. ומאן דפטר – כר"ש, דאמר: "דבר שאין מתכוין מותר". אלמא משמע דדבר שאין מתכוין – אסור לר"י אפי' בשבת מן התורה. וי"ל: דהתם הוי פסיק רישיה. שאי אפשר כלל לכבות העליונות אם לא יובערו התחתונות, וחשיב מלאכת מחשבת, ואע"ג דהוי פסיק רישיה – פטר ר"ש. משום דהויא מלאכה שאינה צריכה לגופה, דאינו צריך להבערת התחתונות. והא דנקט לישנא "מתכוין ושאין מתכוין" ולא נקט ת"ק כר"י דאמר "מלאכה שאינה צריכה כו'" – משום רבותא דר"י נקט, דלא תימא דלא מחייב ר"י מלאכה שאינה צריכה לגופה אלא במקום שמתכוין לעשות המלאכה, כגון מכבה גחלת של עץ שלא יזוקו רבים – שמתכוין לכיבוי, אבל התם שאינו מתכוין להבעיר התחתונות – לא, קמ"ל: כיון דהוי פסיק רישיה – חייב. ובההיא דהחותה גחלים להתחמם והובערו מאליהן, נקט: הא ר"י דאמר "מלאכה שאינה צריכה לגופה – חייב", הא ר"ש כו'. אע"ג דאין כוונתו להבעיר, מדפטר ר"ש. דאי כוונתו להבעיר – הויא צריכה לגופה. מ"מ, כיון דניחא ליה בהך הבערה – לא קרינן ביה שאינו מתכוין, ולהכי לא נקט לישנא דאין מתכוין. אבל בנתכוין לכבות העליונות – לא ניחא ליה בהבערת התחתונות כלל, שהרי בא לכבות – שייך לישנא דאין מתכוין, אע"ג דהוי פסיק רישיה. ור"ש שרי בחותה גחלים להתחמם. אע"ג דבפרק "הבונה" (לקמן קג. ושם) משמע דהתולש לאכילה או לבהמה בארעא דידיה חייב חטאת בכל שהוא, אע"ג דאין מתכוין ליפות הקרקע – לא דמי לכל מלאכה שאינה צריכה לגופה, כגון חותה להתחמם. דהתם, אע"פ שאין מתכוין ליפות – אנן סהדי דניחא ליה, אבל בחותה – אינו נהנה בהבערה זו, דבלא הבערה זו יתחמם. וכיון שאינו נהנה(א) בברור – לא נתכוון להבעיר, והויא מלאכה שאינה צריכה לו*: **לא** שנו אלא להפשיר. מתוך פי' הקונט' משמע דמפרש הסוגיא כן: לא שנו אלא בדבר שאין שייך צירוף אלא פישור, כגון מיחם שפינהו, אבל לצרף, פי' בדבר ששייך צירוף, כגון מיחם שפינו ממנו מים – אסור. ושמואל אמר "אף לצרף", כלומר: אף בדבר ששייך צירוף – מותר. ומשמע: אפי' במתכוין. ולהכי פריך: ולצרף לכתחילה מי שרי?! אלא אי איתמר הכי איתמר: לא שנו דפינה ממנו מים שרי לתת לתוכו צונן אלא שיעור להפשיר ולא לצרף – כגון שלא מלאהו כולו, דליכא צירוף עד שימלאנו על כל גדותיו. ורב מפרש "פינהו" כרב אדא. והא דפריך לעיל: "והא מצרף" – משום דמשמע ליה הא דקאמר: אבל נותן לתוכו מים מרובין, שיש שיעור לצרף, מדקאמר "מרובים", אבל כשפינהו והמים בתוכו – א"א להיות צירוף; ודוחק. ור"י מפרש בענין אחר: דפינהו נמי איכא צירוף כשמילאהו, ובפינה ממנו מים כל שהוא – יש בו שיעור לצרף, מדפריך לעיל "והלא מצרף" ולא משני שאין בו שיעור לצרף. ועוד, מדקאמר אביי: "אבל מיחם שפינה ממנו מים – אסור, מפני שמצרף" משמע דהתם פשיטא ליה שמצרף. ולא שייך לפלוגי ביה דבכל שהוא הוא מצרף. וה"פ: לא שנו אלא להפשיר, פי': שמתכוין להפשיר. השתא סבירא ליה דמיירי רב אפי' בשיעור לצרף. אבל לצרף, שמתכוין לצרף – אסור, כר"ש. ומפרש "פינהו" – שפינה ממנו מים, כרב אדא. אי נמי פינהו עם המים כאביי, ומיירי כשיש בו שיעור לצרף, כגון שממלאו כולו מים צוננין. דאע"ג דהמים חמין שבתוכו לא נסתלקו – יש שיעור לצרף. ומחלק בין אין מתכוין למתכוין כר"ש, ולא כאביי דמוקי לה באין בו שיעור לצרף, וכר' יהודה. וכי פריך אליבא דשמואל: "ולצרף לכתחילה מי שרי" – ה"ה דהוה מצי למיפרך אליבא דרב: כיון דסבר דהלכה כרבי יהודה בגרירה, דהיינו בדבר שאינו מתכוין – מאי דוחקיה לאוקמי מתני' כשיש בו שיעור לצרף וכר"ש? לוקמה כשאין בו שיעור לצרף כאביי, וכרבי יהודה דסבירא ליה כוותיה! אלא אדשמואל קפריך, דעדיפא ליה. "אלא אי איתמר הכי איתמר" – השתא מפרש מתניתין כאביי לגמרי, שפינהו עם המים. וה"פ: לא שנו אלא שיעור להפשיר – שאינו ממלא המיחם על כל גדותיו, אבל שיעור לצרף אע"פ שאינו מתכוין אלא להפשיר – אסור, כרבי יהודה דסבר כוותיה. אבל פינה ממנו מים – לעולם אסור, דבכל ענין יש שיעור לצרף, כדפי'. וכי קאמר אביי: "אבל מיחם שפינה ממנו מים כו'" – ה"ה דמצי למימר: בד"א – בשיעור להפשיר, אבל שיעור לצרף – אסור. אלא ניחא ליה למינקט האי לישנא, משום דמלשון "פינהו" דייק, דאתיא כר' יהודה. שמואל אומר: אף שיעור לצרף מותר כר"ש. וא"ת, מדקאמר שמואל: "אף שיעור לצרף" אם כן מוקי מתני' כאביי דדייק שפינהו. דלרב אדא דמפרש שפינה ממנו מים – לעולם יש שיעור לצרף, ומאי "אף שיעור לצרף" דקאמר שמואל? וכיון דמפרש כאביי – אם כן נידוק דווקא פינהו, הא פינהו ממנו – אסור, כר"י. וי"ל: דשמואל קאי אמילתיה דרב, וקאמר: אף שיעור לצרף שרי, דהנא סבירא לי כר"ש – מוקמי' מתני' כוותיה דרב אדא כשפינה ממנו מים, ויש לעולם שיעור לצרף:

לא שנו אלא להפשיר. פ"ה דרב משמע ליה מתני' פינהו כרב אדא שפינה ממנו המים ושיעור להפשיר כשלא מלאהו ושיעור לצרף כשמילאהו. וקשה, כי פריך לעיל: והלא מצרף, לימא כשלא מילאהו! ועוד, מדקאמר אביי: אבל מיחם שפינה ממנו מים לא יתן לתוכו כל עיקר מפני שהוא מצרף, משמע בכל ענין הוא מצרף אפי' לא מילאהו! וי"ל: דמשמע ליה פינהו כאביי, וקאמר: לא שנו אלא שיעור להפשיר שלא נתן בו מים כ"כ שיצטנני החמין אבל נתן בו מים כ"כ שיצטננו החמין אסור ואע"פ שאינו מתכוין לצרף מיתסר (תו"י בשם מהר"ש ממיזבורג):

*[ערוב' כ:] *) [לק' קטו:] (*) [פנו כלים מפני הטומאה ברכות כח:] [לעיל כט: ביצה כג: כתובות ה: פסחים כה: נזיר מב. לקמן נ. כריתות כ:]

[כתובות עז.]

[עפר ועתיד לפנותו עירובין עט.]

[לסברת התוס' אליבא דר"ש דאינו מצרף אלא כשהוא מלא ממש צריך למחוק תיבות כל עיקר תו"י]

[לעיל כב.]

[ע"ש]

רבינו חננאל

אוקמא מיחם שפינהו מע"ג הכירה ויש בו מים חמין לא יתן לתוכו מים מועטין בשביל שיחמו אבל נותן לתוכו מים מרובין כדי לפשר. פינה ממנה החמין לא יתן לתוכו מים כל עיקר מפני (הוא) שמצרף. ור' יהודה הוא דאמר דבר שאין מתכוון אסור אמר רב לא שנו אלא מים מועטין שיעור להפשיר אבל מים מרובין שיעור לצרף אסור. פי' צירוף הכלי בעת שיתחמם נעשה כנחלת וכשמביאו בשעת גמר מלאכתו בצונן מחוקתו ולוטש פניו ונמצא לו כמו צירוף רב אמר שיעור לצרף אסור ושמואל אמר אפילו שיעור לצרף נמי מותר *) ואוקמה שמואל כר"ש ורב אדא בר מתנה כר' שמעון ודאביי נמי בבא דרישא (נמי) קאי כשמואל וסוגינא כשמואל אליבא דר"ש [ור' אדא] ואקשינן

*) מן ואוקמה עד קאי כשמואל הובא גם ברמב"ן במלחמת בשם ר"ח:

הגהות הב"ח

(א) תוס' סוף ד"ה מיחס וכו' וכיון שאינו נהנה. נ"ב ע"ל פ' כלל גדול דף עח בד"ה טפי ניחא:

רב נסים גאון

ר"ש היא דאמר דבר שאינו מתכוין מותר וזה העיקר בפרק במה מדליקין (דף כט) דתניא ר"ש אומר גורר אדם מטה כסא וספסל ובלבד שלא יתכוין לעשות חריץ. ור' יהודה דאמר דבר שאין מתכוין אסור עיקר דברי ר' יהודה במשנה במס' יו"ט בפ' יום טוב שחל להיות ערב שבת (דף כג) דתנן ר' יהודה אומר אין מקרדין ביו"ט מפני שהוא עושה חבורה ובגמ' גרסי ר' יהודה סבר דבר שאין מתכוין אסור ובמס' בכורות בפ' כל פסולי המוקדשין (דף לג) שנינו בכור שאחזו דם אפילו מת אין מקיזין לו את הדם דברי ר' יהודה כו' ר' שמעון אומר יקיז אע"פ שהוא עושה מום הרי מיכן תדע שר' יהודה סבר דבר שאין מתכוין אסור ור"ש [סבר] דבר שאין מתכוין מותר:

[וע"ע תוספות בסמוך ד"ה ל"ש ותוס' לקמן מב. ד"ה אפי' ותוס' לקמן קג. ד"ה לא צריכא ותוס' לקמן קיא. ד"ה האי ותוספות יומא לד: ד"ה ה"מ ותוספות סוכה לג: ד"ה מודה ותוספות כתובות ה: ד"ה את"ל ועוד שם ו. ד"ה האי ותוס' כריתות כ: ד"ה סבירא]

גליון הש"ס

תוס' ד"ה מיחם שפינה וכו' ליה ר"י דבר שאינו מתכוין אלא מדרבנן. וכ"כ רש"י לקמן קכא ע"ב ד"ה לפי תומו. ועיין לקמן דף לה ע"א תוס' ד"ה המכבד:

אפילו

מסורת הש"ס

מותר. למימרא דשמואל כרבי שמעון סבירא ליה? *והאמר שמואל: [א]מכבין גחלת של מתכת ברה"ר בשביל שלא יזוקו בה רבים, [ב]אבל לא גחלת של עץ. ואי ס"ד סבר לה כרבי שמעון — אפילו של עץ נמי! *בדבר שאין מתכוין — סבר לה כרבי שמעון, במלאכה שאינה צריכה לגופה — סבר לה כרבי יהודה. אמר רבינא: [ג]הלכך *קוץ ברשות הרבים — מוליכו פחות פחות מד' אמות, ובכרמלית אפילו טובא. § "אבל נותן כו'". § ת"ר: נותן אדם חמין לתוך הצונן, ולא הצונן לתוך החמין, דברי בית שמאי. ובית הלל אומרים: [ד]בין חמין לתוך הצונן, ובין צונן לתוך החמין מותר. בד"א — בכוס, אבל באמבטי — חמין לתוך הצונן, ולא צונן לתוך החמין. ורבי שמעון בן מנסיא אוסר. אמר רב נחמן: הלכה כר"ש בן מנסיא. סבר רב יוסף למימר: ספל הרי הוא כאמבטי. א"ל אביי: תני ר' חייא: ספל אינו כאמבטי. ולמאי דסליק אדעתא מעיקרא דספל הרי הוא כאמבטי, ואמר רב נחמן: הלכה כרבי שמעון בן מנסיא, אלא בשבת רחיצה בחמין ליכא?! מי סברת רבי שמעון אסיפא קאי? ארישא קאי: ובית הלל מתירין בין חמין לתוך צונן, ובין צונן לתוך החמין, ורבי שמעון בן מנסיא אוסר צונן לתוך חמין. לימא רבי שמעון בן מנסיא דאמר כב"ש! הכי קאמר: *לא נחלקו ב"ש וב"ה בדבר זה. אמר רב הונא בריה דרב יהושע: חזינא ליה לרבא דלא קפיד *אמנא, מדתני רבי חייא: נותן אדם קיתון של מים לתוך ספל של מים, בין חמין לתוך צונן ובין צונן לתוך חמין. אמר ליה רב הונא לרב אשי: דילמא שאני התם דמיפסק כלי? אמר ליה: 'מערה' איתמר, [ה]מערה אדם קיתון של מים לתוך ספל של מים, בין חמין לתוך צונן, בין צונן לתוך חמין. § **מתני'** *[ו]האילפס והקדרה שהעבירן מרותחין — לא יתן לתוכן תבלין, אבל

זבחים נא: | [שם לב.] | [בילה כח:] | [לקמן קלט. יבמות כח: ב"ק לג. סוכה טו.] | [בהרא"ש ליתא ועי' ברב אלפס] | פסחים מ:

רש"י

מותר. שאין מתכוין לכך: גחלת של מתכת. שמשליכין לחוץ פסולת של ברזל, דלא שייך כבוי בהכי מדאורייתא, ומדרבנן אסורה. והיכא דאיכא נזקא לרבים — לא גזרו על השבות: אבל לא של עץ. דאיסורא דאורייתא היא, וחייב סקילה: אפילו של עץ נמי. דהא לרבי שמעון מלאכה שאינה צריכה לגופה — פטור עליה, וכל כיבוי אינו צריך לגופו, חוץ מעושי פחמין או מהבהבי פתילה: הלכך. כיון דאמרת לא גזרו שבות דכיבוי מתכת במקום נזקא דרבים: קוץ ברשות הרבים מוליכו פחות מד' אמות. עד שיסלקנו לצידי רשות הרבים, דאיסורא דרבנן הוא: ובכרמלית. דטלטול דידיה דרבנן: אפילו טובא. יעבירנו בעקירה אחת: חמין לתוך צונן. דקסבר "תתאה גבר", ואין החמין מרתיחין את הצונן אלא מפשירין: ולא צונן לתוך חמין. שהתחתונים מרתיחים את העליונים, דתתאה גבר: בכוס. דלשתיה קבעי להו, ולא ניחא ליה שיחומו הרבה. ועוד: דכלי שני הוא: אוסר. אפילו חמין לתוך צונן: ספל הרי הוא כאמבטי. ואף על גב דכלי שני הוא, הואיל ולאו לשתיה אלא לרחיצה — אסירי, דניחא ליה שיחמו הרבה, וגזרינן: אלא בשבת רחיצה בחמין ליכא. בתמיה. דהא לרבי שמעון אפילו חמין לתוך צונן אסור, לא משכחת חמין שהוחמו ואפילו מע"ש שלא יהיו צריכין להפיג רתיחתן, ואם כן לא ירחוץ אפילו פניו ידיו ורגליו בחמין: מי סברת ר' שמעון אסיפא קאי. דלא שרי ת"ק אלא חמין לתוך צונן, ואתא איהו ואסר אף חמין לתוך צונן: ארישא קאי. לשתיה, וצונן לתוך חמין דקשרו ב"ה קאסר: **מתני'** שהעבירן. מן האור: מרותחין. בין השמשות: לא יתן לתוכן תבלין. משתחשך, דכלי ראשון כל זמן שרותח מבשל:
אבל

תוספות

אפילו של עץ נמי. ואם תאמר: ומאי ס"ד דמקשה? וכי משום דסבר שמואל כרבי שמעון באין מתכוין, יסבור כמותו במלאכה שאינו צריך לגופה? וי"ל: דס"ד דמקשה דודאי הא בהא תליא, משום דסבר רבי יהודה דמלאכה שאינו צריך לגופה חייב עליה היכא דמתכוין — בשאין מתכוין נמי החמירו חכמים, אבל לרבי שמעון דפטור עליה מן התורה אף במתכוין — לא חש לאסור מדרבנן כשאין מתכוין, כיון דמתכוין עצמו ליכא אלא איסורא דרבנן. ומיהו, לפי האמת לאו הא בהא תליא. דשמואל, אע"ג דבמלאכה שאינה צריכה לגופה סבר כרבי יהודה דחייב [מתיר] באין מתכוין. ולרבי יהודה נמי אסור אין מתכוין אפילו בגרירה, דמתכוין עצמו לא אסיר אלא מדרבנן, כדאמרי' לקמן. ובשילהי "כל התדיר" (זבחים דף נא: ושם*) דאמר שמואל: המתנדב יין מביאו ומזלפו ע"ג האשים. ופריך: והא קא מכבה! ומשני: דסבר דבר שאין מתכוין — מותר. ופריך כי הכא דאמר שמואל מכבין גחלת של מתכת, אבל לא של עץ! והשתא אומר רשב"א: דפריך מכ"ש, דכיון דסבר שמואל דמלאכה שאינה צריכה לגופה חייב — א"כ סבירא ליה נמי בשבת דבר שאין מתכוין — אסור. דסבר המקשה דהתם דהא בהא תליא, כמו מקשה דהכא, וכיון דבשבת אסור אין מתכוין — כ"ש בעלמא. אך הקשה: דמשמע דאי הוי סבר שמואל מלאכה שאינה צריכה לו פטור עליה — הוה אתי שפיר, ואמאי? והא מלאכה שאינה צריכה לגופה בשאר איסורים, דלאו שבת — חייב עליה, וכיון דסבירא ליה דהא בהא תליא — א"כ אמאי קאמר התם "דבר שאין מתכוין מותר"!

נותן אדם חמין לתוך צונן. *אפי' בכלי ראשון, דחמין לתוך צונן אינו מבשל, כמו שאפרש. ולא צונן לתוך חמין אפילו בכלי שני, דגזרי ב"ש כלי שני אטו כלי ראשון. וב"ה דפליגי ושרו צונן לתוך חמין, היינו דוקא בכלי שני, כדקתני: בד"א — בכוס. משמע דבכלי ראשון מודו ב"ה, ולא משום דסברה הך ברייתא ד"תתאה גבר" כדפירש בקונטרס — דאם כן יקשה מהכא למ"ד *"עילאה גבר". ולמאן דאמר "תתאה גבר" נמי, הא מבשל כדי קליפה, כמו שאפרש לקמן בע"ה, אלא נראה כמו שאומר ר"ת: דחמין לתוך צונן — משמע שהצוננין של מטה מרובים, שדרך ליתן המועט במרובה ולכך אין מבשלים החמין המועטין כלל, לפי שמתערבין בצוננין המרובין, ומתבטל חמימותן. ולא צונן לתוך חמין — שהחמין של מטה מרובין, ומתערבין בהן הצוננין המועטין ומתבשלין: **אבל** באמבטי כו'. נראה דהאי אמבטי איירי כגון שהוא כלי שני, ולא הוי כההוא אמבטי דלעיל, *דקאמר: "בקשתי להניח פך באמבטי" מדקאמר ספל אינו כאמבטי, והאי ספל ע"כ כלי שני. דאי כלי ראשון — אמאי אינו כאמבטי? ודכוותיה אמבטי הוי כלי שני. ועוד: דאי באמבטי שהוא כלי ראשון איירי — לא הוה ליה למינקט אמבטי אלא מיחם שהוא לשתיה, דומיא דכוס. ומדנקט אמבטי — משמע דבכלי שני איירי, ואתא לפלוגי בכלי שני בין כוס שהוא לשתיה, לאמבטי לפי שחמין הרבה, ואיכא למיגזר, דהרואה אותן חמין כל כך סבור דכלי ראשון הוא. ובמתני' דנקט במיחם שהוא ראשון: "לא יתן לתוכו מים" — הוה מצי למימר: באמבטי שהוא שני לא יתן לתוכו מים, אלא דמתני' מיירי בשתיה, ומפליג בין מיחם לכוס: **מי** סברת ר"ש בן מנסיא **אסיפא** קאי **ארישא** קאי. היינו דוקא למאי דס"ד לרב יוסף מעיקרא. אבל למאי דמסקי' דספל אינו כאמבטי — קאי אסיפא בכוס, וסבר שפיר ר"ש בן מנסיא כב"ה, דאפילו צונן לתוך חמין מותר, ואתיא מתני' דשריא לתוך הכוס אליבא דהלכתא, כר"ש בן מנסיא. וא"ת: למאי דסלקא דעתך דארישא קאי, ואסר בכוס צונן לתוך חמין, מאי קמ"ל רב יוסף דספל הרי הוא כאמבטי? כוס נמי הרי הוא כאמבטי לר"ש בן מנסיא, דהלכתא כוותיה! וי"ל: דרב יוסף לב"ה אתא לאשמעינן, דשרו בכוס: **נותן** אדם קיתון של מים. וא"ת: ואמאי לא מייתי ברייתא דלעיל, דספל אינו כאמבטי, ואמאי איצטריך נמי רבי חייא למיתני תרוייהו? וי"ל: דהשתא קמ"ל בין חמין לתוך צונן בין צונן לתוך חמין. דההיא דספל אינו כאמבטי — ה"א דקאי אר"ש בן מנסיא, דאסר באמבטי אפי' חמין לתוך צונן. ועליה קאמר דספל אינו כאמבטי, ושרי חמין לתוך צונן. אבל צונן לתוך חמין — ה"א דאסור. ואפשר ההיא דלעיל היינו הך דהכא, אלא שקיצרה, ונקט לישנא דרב יוסף דמייתי עלה: **שאני** התם דמפסיק כלי. וא"ת, דאמר לעיל (דף מ:): "טול בכלי שני ותן" אבל בכלי ראשון לא, אע"ג דמפסיק מנא! וי"ל: דהתם בכלי ראשון, והכא דבכלי שני שאני:
אבל

[זבחים דף נא: ושם לב.] | [דף מ:] | [פסחים עו:]

עוד נוכל לומר דחמין לתוך צונן דוקא בכ"ש שרי ב"ש אבל בכלי ראשון אסור אטו צונן לתוך חמין [תו"י]

עין משפט נר מצוה

לג א ב מיי' פ"א מהל' שבת הלכה ז ופי"ב הלכה ב טוש"ע או"ח סי' שלד סעיף כז:
לד ג מיי' שם פ"א הל' ז טוש"ע או"ח סי' שח סעיף יח:
לה ד ה מיי' פכ"ב מהל' שבת הלכה ו טוש"ע או"ח סימן שיח סעיף יב:
לו ו מיי' שם טור שו"ע שם סעיף ט:

רבינו חננאל

למימרא דשמואל כר' שמעון (ורב אדא) והאמר שמואל מכבין גחלת של מתכת ברה"ר בשביל שלא יזוקו בה רבים אבל גחלת של עץ לא ואילו ר"ש סבר אפילו של עץ מותר לפי שאין מתכוון לכבות אלא כדי שלא יוזק וכי האי גוונא פטר ר' שמעון ואסיק' לעולם כר' יהוד' סבירא לי' דאמר מלאכה שאינה צריכה לגופה חייב עליה*) מיהו דבר שיש בו היזק לרבים כגון צידת נחש וכבוי גחלת של מתכת בזמן שהיא חמה והיא שחורה והרואה אותה דומה שהיא צוננת לפי שאין בה אדמומית כגחלת לוחשת ונמצאו בני אדם ניזוקין בו לפיכך מותר אבל הגחלת של עץ אם תסיר אדמומיתה נכבת כבר ואינה מזקת ואם אדמומיתה בה כל הרואה אותה מתרחק ממנה ומכל פנים אין אדם ניזוק שהשחורה כבר כבתה והאדומה מתרחקין ממנה לפיכך המכבה אותה חייב ולפיכך היה שמואל אוסר בגחלת של עץ. (ומדוקיה) אמר רבינא קוץ ברה"ר מוליכו פחות פחות מד' אמות ואע"ג דרב ושמואל הלכה כרב באיסורי בהא קיי"ל כשמואל דאמר במלאכה שאינה צריכה לגופה סבר לה כר' יהודה בדבר שאין מתכוין סבר לה כר"ש ומדרב אחא ורבינא שמע מינייהו דהלכתא כר' שמעון: **פיסקא** אבל נותן הוא לתוכו או לתוך הכוס כדי להפשירן. ת"ר לא יתן אדם חמין לתוך צונן [ולא צונן] לתוך חמין וב"ה מתירין כו'. ואוקימנא להא דר"ש בן מנסיא שאוסר כלומר לא נחלקו ב"ש וב"ה אלא אפילו ב"ה אוסרין ואע"ג דאמר רב נחמן הלכתא כר' שמעון בן מנסיא כיון דאמר רב הונא חזינא לרבא דלא קפיד זימנין עביד כמר וזמנין עביד כמר מדתני ר' חייא דתני ר' חייא נותן אדם קיתון של מים לתוך ספל כו' ורב אשי מתרץ לה לרב הונא ואמר ליה מערה תניא כלומר מערה אדם קיתון של מים לתוך ספל של מים בין חמין לתוך צונן בין צונן לתוך חמין קיי"ל כוותיהו דאינון בתראי ומעשה רב ולא דמו ספל לאמבטי וכום למיחם דאוקימנא ליה שאסור לתת בתוכו צונן מועטין בהיות חמין בו כדי שיחמו אלא מרובין כדי להפשיר כי המיחם הוא עצמו מייחם אבל ספל ואמבטי וכום מתחממין בכלי אחד ומערין
בתוך

*) עי' ביאור דברי רבינו ז"ל בחידושי הרשב"א ז"ל ד"ה גחלת של מתכות ע"ש היטב.

אבל נותן הוא לתוך הקערה או לתוך התמחוי. רבי יהודה אומר: *לכל הוא נותן, חוץ מדבר שיש בו חומץ וציר.§ **גמ'** איבעיא להו: רבי יהודה ארישא קאי, ולקולא, או דילמא, אסיפא קאי ולחומרא? ת"ש: דתניא, רבי יהודה אומר: לכל אילפסין הוא נותן, לכל הקדירות רותחות הוא נותן, חוץ מדבר שיש בו חומץ וציר. סבר רב יוסף למימר: מלח הרי הוא כתבלין, דבכלי ראשון – בשלה, ובכלי שני לא בשלה. א"ל אביי, תני רבי חייא: מלח אינה כתבלין, דבכלי שני נמי בשלה. ופליגא דרב נחמן, דאמר רב נחמן: צריכא מילחא בישולא כבישרא דתורא. ואיכא דאמרי, סבר רב יוסף למימר: מלח הרי הוא כתבלין, דבכלי ראשון – בשלה, בכלי שני לא בשלה. א"ל אביי, תני ר' חייא: [א]מלח אינה כתבלין, דבכלי ראשון נמי לא בשלה. והיינו דאמר רב נחמן: צריכא מילחא בישולא כבישרא דתורא.§ **מתני'** [ב]אין נותנין כלי תחת הנר לקבל בו את השמן, ואם נתנוה מבעוד יום – מותר. ואין ניאותין ממנו, לפי שאינו מן המוכן.§ **גמ'** אמר רב חסדא: [ג]אע"פ שאמרו אין נותנין כלי תחת תרנגולת לקבל ביצתה – אבל כופה עליה כלי שלא תשבר. אמר רבה: מ"ט דרב חסדא – קסבר: תרנגולת עשויה להטיל ביצתה באשפה, ואינה עשויה להטיל ביצתה במקום מדרון, והצלה מצויה – התירו, והצלה שאינה מצויה – לא התירו. איתיבי' אביי: והצלה שאינה מצויה – לא התירו?! והתניא: *נשברה לו חבית של טבל בראש גגו – מביא כלי ומניח תחתיה! בגולפי חדתי, דשכיחי דפקעי. איתיביה: *נותנין כלי תחת הנר לקבל ניצוצות! ניצוצות נמי שכיחי.

איתיביה

רש"י

אבל נותן הוא לתוך הקערה. דכלי שני אינו מבשל: תמחוי. כעין קערה גדולה שמערה כל האילפס לתוכה, ומשם מערה לקערות: ר' יהודה אומר לכל וכו'. בגמרא מפרש אהי קאי, אכלי ראשון או אכלי שני: חוץ מדבר שיש בו חומץ או ציר. שהן מבשלין את התבלין כשהן רותחין: ציר. הנוטף מן הדגים כשכובשים אותן במכבש: **גמ'** ארישא קאי. אאילפס, דקא אסר ת"ק, וקאמר ר' יהודה לכל אילפסין הוא נותן, דכלי ראשון לא מבשל: או דילמא אסיפא קאי. אקערה ותמחוי, דקא שרי ת"ק. וקא אמר ליה רבי יהודה: בכל קערות ותמחויין מודינא לך, חוץ מדבר שיש בו חומץ, ואפילו כלי שני נמי לא: דבכלי ראשון נמי לא בשלה. ומותר ליתן, ואפילו בכלי ראשון משהעבירו מן האור: **מתני'** אין נותנין. בשבת: כלי תחת הנר. לקבל בו שמן המטפטף, משום דשמן מוקצה הוא, וקסבר "אין כלי ניטל בשבת אלא לצורך דבר הניטל". אי נמי קסבר: אסור לבטל כלי מהיכנו, להושיב כלי במקום שלא יוכל עוד ליטלו, *(משום) דהוי כקובע לו מקום ומחברו בטיט ודמי למלאכה. וכלי זה משיפול בו השמן המוקצה – יהא אסור לטלטלו: מותר. להניחה שם: ואין נאותין. נהנין: **גמ'** אע"פ שאמרו אין נותנין כלי תחת תרנגולת לקבל ביצתה. כשהיא מטילתה במקום מדרון, שמא תתגלגל ותשבר. ומדיוקא דמתניתין שמעינן לה, דדמי לנותן כלי תחת הנר לקבל בו שמן: אבל כופה עליה כלי. ולא תימא: "אין כלי ניטל אלא לצורך דבר הניטל": באשפה. ויש לחוש שמא תשבר ברגלי אדם, וכופה עליה כלי: והצלה מצויה התירו. לטלטל כלי לצרכה, ואף על פי שהביצה דבר שאינו ניטל בשבת: שאינה מצויה. כגון מדרון, וטיפטוף דשמן דמתני': "נשברה לו חבית של טבל" גרסינן: מביא כלי. ואף על גב דטבל דבר שאינו ניטל הוא, וחבית לא שכיחא דפקעה: גולפי. חביות: נותנין כלי. מתניתין היא, ומותיב ליה מינה: ניצוצות. שלהבת הנוטפת מן הנר, כדי שלא ידלק מה שתחתיה, ואע"ג דניצוצות לא מיטלטלי ולא שכיחי:

איתיביה

תוספות

אבל נותן הוא לתוך הקערה כו'. מהכא ליכא למידק דעירוי ככלי שני, מדקתני "לא יתן לתוכה תבלין" ולא אשמעינן רבותא אפילו שלא יערה על הקערה שתבלין בתוכה, דאדרבה דוק מסיפא, דקתני: "אבל נותן הוא לתוך הקערה", ולא קתני: מערה על הקערה שתבלין בתוכה. ורבינו שמואל מביא ראיה דעירוי ככלי שני מהא דקי"ל "תתאה גבר". ולר"י נראה: דעירוי ככלי ראשון, ומביא ראיה דזבחים בפרק "דם חטאת" (דף צה: ושם), ת"ר: "אשר תבושל בו" אין לי אלא שבישל בו, עירה לתוכו רותח מניין? תלמוד לומר "[אשר תבושל] בו ישבר". אלמא: דעירוי חשיב מבשל. ובירושלמי בפרק "כירה" בעי: מהו ליתן תבלין מלמטה ולערות עליהן מלמעלה? ר' יונה אמר: אסור, דעירוי ככלי ראשון. חיליה דר' יונה מן הדא: אחד שבישל בו ואחד שעירה לתוכו רותח. ודחי ר' יוסי: תמן כלי חרס בולע, תבלין אינו מתבשל. השיב רבי יוסי בר בון, והתניא: מניין שבכלי נחשת כן – תלמוד לומר: "ואם בכלי נחשת בשלה" אית לן למימר כלי נחשת בלע? בתמיה. פי': ע"י עירוי, אם אינו מבשל לא בלע. אלמא: דמסיק דעירוי ככלי ראשון. ונראה דעירוי לא הוי ככלי ראשון ולא ככלי שני, אלא מבשל כדי קליפה. דהא קי"ל כשמואל דאמר "תתאה גבר" דתניא כוותיה ב"כילד צולין" (פסחים עו.) – ומ"מ מבשל כדי קליפה, דאמר התם: תניא כוותיה דשמואל "חם לתוך צונן או צונן לתוך צונן – מדיח". ופריך: חם לתוך צונן – אדמיקר ליה בלע! אלא אימא: חם לתוך צונן – קולף, צונן לתוך צונן – מדיח. וכן משמע בשילהי מסכת ע"ז (דף עו.) דאמר: מר *עוקבא זבן יורה מגויס – אהדר ליה גדנפא. ומסיק: כבולעו כך פולטו, מה בולעו בניצוצות – אף פולטו בניצוצות. ואי עירוי ככלי ראשון – °מאי איריא משום דבלע בניצוצות, אפילו בלע בליעה גמורה פלט בניצוצות שהוא עירוי! אלא ודאי לא מבשל אלא כדי קליפה, ואם עירו רותחים על התרנגולת – צריכה קליפה. וכלי שתשמישו ע"י עירוי כגון קערות – יכול להגעילן ע"י עירוי, דכבולעו כך פולטו. אבל כלי שנתבשל בו איסור – לא סגי להגעילו על ידי עירוי. והא דאמר בפרק בתרא דע"ז (דף עד:), דרש רבא: נעוה ארתחיה – דהתם מסתמא ע"י עירוי! שאני התם דאותה נעוה לא בלעה ע"י רותח**: **לכל** קדרות רותחות הוא נותן. נראה דדוקא בתבלין פליג, אבל בשאר דברים – מודה דכלי ראשון מבשל, אף כשהעבירו מעל האור: **והיינו** דר"נ. נראה דאף לפי' הקונטרס, שפי' *)דבכל מקום דאיכא לישני דפליגי, בשל תורה – הלך אחר המחמיר, ובשל סופרים – הלך אחר המיקל; וכן לריב"א שפירש שבכל מקום "איכא דאמרי" טפל לגבי לשון ראשון שהוא עיקר – הכא הלכה כלישנא בתרא. דללישנא קמא פליג ברייתא דרבי חייא אדרב נחמן, וללישנא בתרא היינו דרב נחמן. ומתוך כך פסק רבינו שמואל שמותר לתת מלח בתבשיל בשבת, אפילו בכלי ראשון שהעבירו מן האור. והמחמיר כלישנא קמא שלא ליתן מלח בקערה כל זמן שהיד סולדת בו – תבא עליו ברכה: **ואם** נתנוהו מבעוד יום מותר. הלשון דחוק, דהוה ליה למימר "אבל מבעוד יום נותנין": **ואין** נאותין ממנו לפי שאינו מן המוכן. איכא לאוקמא כר"ש *דמתיר מותר השמן שבנר, "ואין ניאותין" דקתני הכא – היינו כל זמן שדולק, °דבמוקצה מחמת מצוה מודה ר"ש. כדאמר בגמ' לקמן (דף מה.): אין מוקצה לר"ש אלא שמן שבנר בשעה שהוא דולק, הואיל והוקצה למצותו – הוקצה לאיסורו. ולא שבנר ממש קאמר, דההיא אסור בלאו הכי משום מכבה, כדאמר בביצה פ"ב (דף כב. ושם): המסתפק ממנו – חייב משום מכבה. אלא, כלומר: שמן המטפטף מן הנר: והטלטול דנר עצמו אין לאסור מטעם דהוקצה למצותו, ולא אסור לטלטלו אלא משום דנעשה בסיס לדבר האסור, כדאמרינן בסוף פירקין: (דף מז.) הנח לנר שמן ופתילה הואיל ונעשה בסיס לדבר האסור. אבל מטעם דהוקצה למצותו – לא היה אסור לטלטלו, שאין ביטול מצוה במה שמטלטלו: **אע"פ** שאמרו חכמים אין נותנין כו'. אין נותנין כלי תחת הנר לקבל בו את השמן ה"ל למימר דתנן במתניתין וכלי לקבל ביצה לא שמעינן אלא מדיוקא דמתני' אלא משום דבעי למימר אבל כופה עליה כלי נקט ביצה: **הצלה** שאינה מצויה לא התירו. פי' בקונטרס: לדבר שאינו ניטל. וגרס בההוא דפריך אביי מינה בסמוך "נשברה לו חבית של טבל בראש גגו" דטבל אינו ניטל. וקשה לריב"א: דאי גרס בה "טבל" אמאי פריך לרב יוסף מברייתא אחרת? מהך דהכא הוה ליה לאקשויי! ועוד: דבפרק "כל כתבי" (לקמן דף קיז: ושם) משמע בהדיא דלא גרסי' בברייתא דהכא טבל, דלא בשל טבל מיירי, דקתני סיפא: נזדמנו לו אורחין מביא כלי אחר כו'. ונראה לו לפרש: דהצלה שאינה מצויה לא התירו לטרוח בכל דבר, אפילו בדבר הניטל – משום טירחא: **שאינה** מצויה לא התירו. והא דאין נותנין כלי תחת הנר לקבל שמן – חשיב הצלה שאינה מצויה, לפי שרגילים לעולם לתת כלי תחת הנר מבעוד יום. וניצוצות, אע"ג דקאמר בסמוך דשכיחי – לא שכיחי כולי האי שיחושו לתת שם כלי מבעוד יום, ולהכי חשיב לה הצלה מצויה:

דמבטל

מסורת הש"ס

[כהאי גוונא במעשרות פ"א מ"ז]

[נ"ל משם]

לקמן קיז: ע"ש

לקמן מג. מז:

[וע' תוספות זבחים לה: ד"ה עירה כו'] *) [עי' תוס' ע"ז ז. ד"ה בשל תורה]

[לקמן מד.]

עין משפט נר מצוה

לז א מיי' פכ"ב מהל' שבת הלכה ו טוש"ע או"ח סימן שיח סעיף ט:

לח ב מיי' פכ"ה מהלכות שבת הלכה כג ופ"ה הלכה יג סמג לאוין סה טור שו"ע או"ח סימן רסה סעיף ג:

לט ג מיי' פכ"ה שם סמג שם טור ושו"ע או"ח סימן שי סעיף ו וסימן שכב סעיף א וסי' תקיג סעיף ד:

יש ספרים שגורסין כאן בתוס' רב עקביא כמו שהביא הגאון מהרי"ף בע"ז שם בהגהותיו. ואולי ילאה גירסת מר עוקבא מסוגיא דכ"מ ע. ההוא דולא דבני מר עוקבא כמו שהעיר בסה"ד

א"נ ארתחי' שיעשה האש למטה והיא של חרס דבפ' כל שעה איכא למ"ד זה וזה לפטור המעסה והחלוטה ומוגלשין ואיירי בשיש למנוס כשיעור חלה ולהכי בין תתאה גבר בין עילאה גבר מבשל כדי קליפה ובצר ליה משיעור חלה [תו"י]

רבינו חננאל

בתוך חללו לפיכך מותר שנמצאו כלי שני וקיי"ל כלי שני מותר: ר' יהודה אומר לכל הוא נותן כו' אסיק' ר' יהודה ארישא דקתני האלפס והקדירה שהעבירן מרותחין לא יתן בתוכן תבלין התם פליג ומקיל הוא דתניא ר"י אומר לכל אלפסין רותחין [הוא נותן] לכל קדרות רותחין הוא נותן חוץ מדבר שיש בו חומץ וציר. מלח כתבלין הוא אי לא ואסיק' כדתני ר' חייא מלח אינו כתבלין דכלי ראשון נמי לא בשלה והיינו דרב נחמן דאמר צריכה מילחא בשולי כבשרא דתורא ש"מ כי נותן מלח בתבשיל בשבת ואפילו בכלי ראשון אינו בישול: **מתניתין** אין נותנין כלי תחת הנר לקבל בו את השמן כו' אמר רב חסדא אע"פ שאמרו אין נותנין נר תחת התרנגולת כו' כלומר אפילו אם עומדת במקום מדרון ורואין כיון שתלד תפול הביצה במקום מדרון ותשבר לא התירו לו להטיל תחתיה כלי לקבלה לביצה כדי שלא תשבר שזה לילד התרנגולת במקום מדרון דבר שאינו מצוי הוא ומשום אחת שנזדמנה לה כך לא חיישינן לה. אבל כיון שדרך רוב התרנגולת להטיל ביציהן לאשפה התירו לכפות על אותה ביצה כלי בשביל שלא תשבר וזהו פירוש הצלה מצויה התירו הצלה שאינה מצויה לא התירו והא חבית שנשברה בראש גגו כו' ושנינן בגולפי חדתי פי' קנקנים חדשים

גליון הש"ם

תוס' ד"ה אבל. מאי איריא משום דבלע בנילוטות. ק"ל דלטעמיך אף אם עירוי לא הוי ככ"ר היינו בעירוי על צונן אבל הכא דהעירוי על גוף הכלי שהוא חם. אף אם היה העירוי מצונן לחם היה חם לתתאי גבר מכ"ש בעירוי מכ"ר על כ"ר וה' יאיר עיני: שם ד"ה ואין נאותין דמוקצה מחמת מצוה מודה ר"ש. וכיון דאינו ראוי לאכלו ממש באותה שעה הוי מוקצה בעצמותו כדין כל מאכל שאינו חזי לכלום. עי' מג"א ריש סימן תקט"ו ורק בטלטול הנר בשעה שהוא דולק להאיר זהו מדינא מותר אטו"ל טעמא דבסיס ולק"מ קושית המהרש"א:

איתיביה: *כופין קערה על הנר שלא יאחז בקורה! בבתי גחיני, דשכיח בהו דליקה. *וכן קורה שנשברה סומכין אותה בספסל ובארוכות המטה! בכשורי חדתי, דעבידי דפקעי. *נותנין כלי תחת הדלף בשבת! בבתי חדתי דשכיחי דדלפי. רב יוסף אמר: היינו טעמא דרב חסדא – משום *דקא מבטל כלי מהיכנו. איתיביה אביי: *חבית של טבל שנשברה מביא כלי אחר ומניח תחתיה! א"ל: *טבל מוכן הוא אצל שבת, שאם עבר ותקנו – מתוקן. *נותנין כלי תחת הנר לקבל ניצוצות! א"ר הונא בריה דרב יהושע: ניצוצות אין בהן ממש. *וכן קורה שנשברה סומכין אותה בספסל או בארוכות המטה! דרפי, דאי בעי – שקיל ליה. *נותנין כלי תחת הדלף בשבת! בדלף הראוי. *כופין את הסל לפני האפרוחין שיעלו וירדו! קסבר: מותר לטלטלו. והתניא: *אסור לטלטלו! בעודן עליו. והתניא: אע"פ שאין עודן עליו אסור! א"ר אבהו: בעודן עליו כל בין השמשות, מיגו דאיתקצאי לבין השמשות – איתקצאי לכולי יומא. א"ר יצחק: כשם שאין נותנין כלי תחת תרנגולת לקבל ביצתה – כך אין כופין עליה כלי בשביל שלא תשבר. *קסבר: אין כלי ניטל אלא לדבר הניטל בשבת. מיתיבי כל הני תיובתא, ושני: בצריך למקומו. תא שמע: *אחת ביצה שנולדה בשבת, ואחת ביצה שנולדה ביום טוב – אין מטלטלין לא לכסות בה את הכלי, ולסמוך בה כרעי המטה, אבל כופה עליה כלי בשביל שלא תשבר! הכא נמי – בצריך למקומו. *ת"ש: פורסין מחצלות על גבי אבנים בשבת! באבנים מקורזלות, דחזיין לבית הכסא. ת"ש: *פורסין מחצלות על גבי לבנים בשבת! דאישתיור מבנינא, דחזיין למיזגא עלייהו. ת"ש: פורסין מחצלת על גבי כוורת דבורים בשבת, בחמה מפני החמה, ובגשמים מפני הגשמים, ובלבד שלא יתכוין לצוד! הכא במאי עסקינן – דאיכא דבש. א"ל רב עוקבא ממישן לרב אשי: תינח בימות החמה – דאיכא

רש"י

איתיביה כופין קערה. של חרס על גבי הנר כו': גחיני. נמוכין: וכן קורה שנשברה כו'. משנה היא לקמן: שנשברה. בשבת: ארוכות המטה. לימונ"ש: בספסל. דכלי הוא, ומותר לטלטלו: בכשורי חדתי. שלא נבדקו עדיין, וכשמכביד משא הבית עליהן, שהיו טחין על גגותיהן בטיט – שכיחי דפקעי: תחת הדלף. לקבלו: טעמא דרב חסדא. דאין נותנין כלי תחת התרנגולת: מפני שמבטל כלי מהיכנו. שהיה מוכן מתחלה לטלטלו, ועכשיו עושהו מוקצה: מוכן הוא. שאין בו מוקצה, אלא איסורו. ואם בא אחד ועבר על דברי חכמים שאסרו לתרום בשבת, ותיקנו – מתוקן, ומותר לטלטלו ולאוכלו. הלכך לאו מבטל כלי מהיכנו חשיב ליה: אין בהן ממש. ומותר ליטלן אחר שנפלו לתוכו: וכן קורה כו'. קס"ד שמהדקו שם, ואינו יכול שוב ליטלו: הראוי. לשתיה כל אלו משניות הן: כל בין השמשות. אבל נתנו שם משחשיכה – מותר ליטלו אם אין האפרוחים עליו: בצריך למקומו. להשתמש במקום הכלי. ומתוך שיכול ליטלו לצורך מקומו – מוליכו למקום שירצה: לכסות בה את הכלי. לסתום פי צלוחית: על גבי אבנים. מפני הגשמים, שלא ימחו, או לא יקבלו טיט מאחר ששרויות במים: מקורזלות. ראשן חד וראויות לקינוח, דהוי דבר הניטל: למיזגא. להשען. שכל הסבתן כך היתה, יושב קצת ונשען קצת על שמאלו:

דאיכא

לקמן קז. קכח. / לקמן קנח: / ביצה לה: / [לקמן מז: קכח: קנד:] / [תוספתא פ"ד] / [ביצה לד: לה.] לעיל מב: / לקמן מז: / לקמן קכח: / [תוספ' פט"ז] / [תוספתא שם] / [ביצה לו.] / ביצה ג: / [שם לו. כל הסוגיא ע"ש כמה שינויים] / שם לו. / [דף מז:]

תוספות

דמבטל כלי מהיכנו. בפרק בתרא *פירש בקונטרס דאסור משום דמתחזי כסותר. וכאן פירש דחשיב כאלו מחברו בטיט: טבל מוכן הוא אצל שבת. אף על פי שאסור לטלטלו, כדתנן בפרק "מפנין" (לקמן קכו:) מ"מ לא חשיב מבטל כלי מהיכנו, כיון דאם עבר ותיקנו – מתוקן. ק' לרשב"א: דתנן במסכת תרומות בפ"ב (משנה ג), ומייתי לה ב"הניזקין" (גיטין נד.): המעשר בשבת, בשוגג – יאכל, במזיד – לא יאכל. ולישנא דקאמר הכא "אם עבר ותיקנו" משמע במזיד, מדלא קאמר "שאם שגג ותיקנו". ונראה דנקט עבר – כגון דלית ליה פירי אחריני, דאמר בביצה בפרק "י"ט" (דף יז:) דאפילו במזיד יאכל. עוד הקשה: דבפרק בתרא (דף קנד:) תניא: היתה בהמתו טעונה טבל ועששית – מתיר את החבלים והשקים נופלים, ואע"פ שמשתברין. משמע דאסור להניח תחתיהן כרים וכסתות, אלמא טבל לאו מוכן הוא! ואור"י: "דאף על פי שמשתברין" – לא קאי אטבל אלא אעששית. ועוד הקשה: כי היכי דאמר דאם עבר ותיקנו מתוקן – ה"נ כשמניח כלי תחת תרנגולת לקבל ביצתה, נימא שאם עבר והסיר הביצה – מותר הכלי לטלטל, ואם כן ביטלת תורת ביטול כלי מהיכנו! ולאו פירכא היא, דהא כמו שהכלי עם הביצה אין לה היתר – אבל טבל יש לו היתר על ידי תיקון. ועוד הקשה: היכא דאית ליה פירי אחריני, בשוגג אמאי יאכל? נימא: מגו דאיתקצאי לבין השמשות איתקצאי לכולי יומא! ועוד, מ"ש דהכא אמר דאם עבר ותיקנו מתוקן, ובביצה בפ' "אין צדין" (דף כו: ושם) גבי בכור לר"ש דאמר "אין רואין מומין בי"ט". אמר: שאם עבר וביקרו – אינו מבוקר. ואדא בר אוכמי דאמר בשוגג מבוקר אמרינן התם דליתא דמשבש ותני!*: כופין את הסל. לעיל לא מצי פריך מינה, דהצלה מצויה היא: בעודן עליו. אבל אחר שירדו מותר לטלטלו. נראה לר"י דקסבר דאין מוקצה לחצי שבת, דלמ"ד בפ' "אין צדין" (ביצה כו: ושם) דיש מוקצה – אסור לטלטלו אף אחר שירדו. וקשה לרשב"א: למ"ד "יש מוקצה לחצי שבת" אמאי כופין את הסל לפני האפרוחים? והא מבטל כלי מהיכנו! וקי"ל דאסור לבטלו, דבסוף פירקין *פריך סתמא דהתלמוד: "והא קא מבטל כלי מהיכנו", וכן בפ' "מפנין" (לקמן קכח:) ובפ' בתרא (דף קנד:) פריך אליבא דרב הונא, אע"ג דלא מצינו שהיה סובר כן, משמע דלכ"ע אסור לבטל כלי מהיכנו. וכן אפרש בסמוך. וי"ל: דלמ"ד "יש מוקצה לחצי שבת" – הך דכופין את הסל מוקי כר"ש, דלדידיה ודאי שרי לטלטל הסל כשירדו. דאפי' "מיגו דאיתקצאי לבין השמשות איתקצאי לכולי יומא" לית ליה, דהא מתיר להסתפק מן הנר שכבה. א"נ: הא ד"יש מוקצה לחצי שבת" – היינו לאכילה ולא לטלטול. וא"ת: רב יוסף דמפרש מתני' משום דאסור לבטל כלי מהיכנו, לא אתיא מתני' כר"ש, דלדידיה לא מבטל כלי מהיכנו, כיון דשרי לאחר שכבה כי היכי דלא חשבינן הכא כפיית הסל ביטול כלי משום דשרי אחר שירדו! וי"ל: דלא דמי, דהכא – ודאי לא חשיב ביטול כלי, כי מיד כשבאו על הסל בידו להפריחם ולהבריחם משם: בעודן עליו כל בין השמשות. תימה: הא כיון דבידו להפריחם למטה הוי גמרו בידי אדם, ולית לן למימר: "מיגו דאיתקצאי לבין השמשות" כדמוכח בפ' "אין צדין" (ביצה כו:) דפריך ר' זירא: למ"ד "יש מוקצה לחצי שבת" והא פולין ועדשים, דמבשלים בי"ט דמעיקרא חזו לכוס, כי שדינהו בקדרה חייתא(א) – אידחו להו, גמר בישולייהו – אישתרו להו! א"ל אביי: ולטעמיך, תקשי לך קדירות דעלמא דהא קדירות דשבתא בין השמשות רותחות הן, ולאורתא קא אכלינן מינייהו. אלא: גמרו בידי אדם לא קמבעיא ליה, כי קא מיבעיא ליה – גמרו בידי שמים. וי"ל: דשאני קדירות, אם הוה צריך להו בין השמשות – היה מקררן. וכן פולין ועדשים רצונו שיתבשלו בלא שום דיחוי, אבל הכא – רצונו היה שיעלו האפרוחין על הסל, שלכך כפאו והרי שעה אחת הקצה אותו לצרכן. ומיגו דאיתקצאי לבין השמשות – איתקצאי לכולי יומא: ושני ליה בצריך למקומו. ההיא דנותנין כלי תחת הדלף איכא נמי לשנויי בדלף הראוי, כדשני לעיל, ובפרק "משילין" (ביצה לו. ושם) משני ליה הכי לרבי יצחק. תימה לר"י: מ"ש דגבי שמן תנא "אין נותנין" וגבי ניצוצות "נותנין"? בתרוייהו הוה מצי למתני "נותנין" – בצריך למקומו, או בתרוייהו "אין נותנין" – באין צריך למקומו! ונראה לר"י: דמעיקרא אשמעינן דאין כלי ניטל אלא לדבר הניטל בשבת, וגבי ניצוצות דבתר הכי אשמעינן דבצריך למקומו שרי. אי נמי: ר' יצחק אית ליה נמי דאסור לבטל כלי מהיכנו, ולהכי גבי שמן אין נותנין – אפילו בצריך למקומו. ולרב הונא נפרש בסמוך דאית ליה נמי תרוייהו: "אין כלי ניטל אלא לדבר הניטל" ו"אסור לבטל כלי מהיכנו". ואם נאמר דלרב יוסף לא אתיא מתניתין כר"ש, דכיון דלדידיה מותר לאחר שכבה – לא חשיב ביטול כלי, אם כן מצינן למימר דאפילו רבה אית ליה דאסור לבטל כלי מהיכנו, ואיצטריך למימר דהצלה שאינה מצויה לא התירו – כדי לאוקמה מתניתין כר"ש. וא"ת: מאי צריך בכל הני משניות לאשמעינן דבצריך למקומו שרי? ויש לומר: דלגבי ניצוצות איצטריך לאשמעינן, דלא תימא אפילו בצריך למקומו אסור משום דילמא אתי לכבויי. וכן ההיא ד"כופין קערה שלא תאחוז כו'" וההיא דקורה שנשברה – נראה לרשב"א דאיצטריך לאשמעינן דלא חיישינן שמא יעלה את הקורה, דאסור להעלות כדתנן בפ' "שואל" (לקמן קנא:): וכן קורה שנשברה – סומכין אותה כו', לא שתעלה אלא שלא תוסיף: כופה עליה כלי שלא תשבר כו'. כל הנהו דמייתי ידע המקשה דמצי לשנויי בצריך למקומו, אלא שרוצה לידע אם יש לתרץ בענין אחר: דאיתור מבניינא. כדאמר לקמן בפ' "כל הכלים" (דף קכד:): הני לבני דאייתרי מבניינא – שרי לטלטולינהו:

דחשיב

[ודף קנד: וכ"כ רש"י לקמן קכח: ד"ה והא]

[וזה אין אמאי חשיב במתניתין ביטול כלי מהיכנו הא עבר וכיבה מותר השמן כמו גבי טבל שאם עבר כו' וי"ל שא"ה דכיבוי איסורא דאורייתא ולא אמר ביה שאם עבר כו' [תוספות ישנים]]

עין משפט נר מצוה

מ א מיי' פכ"ה מהלכות שבת הלכה כג סמג לאוין סה טור שו"ע או"ח סימן שי סעיף ו:
מא ב מיי' שם הל' כה:
מב ג מיי' שם טוש"ע או"ח סימן שיג סעיף ז:
מג ד מיי' שם הלכה כד טוש"ע או"ח סימן שלח סעיף ח וסימן תקכא סעיף ג:
מד ה ו מיי' שם הלכה כה סמג שם טוש"ע או"ח סימן שח סעיף לט:
מה ז מיי' וסמג שם טוש"ע או"ח סימן שט"ז סעיף ד:

רבינו חננאל

חדשים שהן מצוין להפקיע. וניצוצות תחת הנר נמי מילתא דשכיחא היא ובבתי גחיני כלומר בתים נמוכים להיאחז בהן דליקה מילתא דשכיחא היא וכן כולם. פירק רבא לדבריו דהצלה מצויה התירו הצלה שאינה מצויה לא התירו אליבא דרב חסדא. רב יוסף אמר מ"ט דרב חסדא משום דאי שרית ליה לקבל הביצה בכלי במקום מדרון כבר ביטל אותו הכלי היום שאסור לטלטלו והביצה בתוכו. כשם שאסור לטלטל הביצה. אבל כפיית הכלי על הביצה אינו ביטול שאם הוצרך הכלי מותר לו לטלטלו שהרי אין בכלי כלום ולא מבטל כלי מהיכנו. איתיביה אביי (טלטל) [חבית של טבל] כו' והא טבל אסור לטלטלו ושני ליה טבל מוכן הוא שאם עבר ותיקנו מתוקן הוא. ושני בניצוצות. ניצוצות אין בהם ממש והכלי שמקבל בו הניצוצות לא מיבטיל ומותר להשתמש בה. וספסל שסמוך בה הקורה רפויה היא שיכול ליטלה ולהשתמש בה. והכלי שמקבל בו הדלף בדלף הראוי לשתיה שהמים מותרים וכ"ש הכלי. וכן הסל שכופין שיעלו וירדו בו האפרוחים אוקמה בעודן האפרוחים עומדין על הסל [או שהיו עומדין על הסל] בין השמשות אסור לטלטל אותו הסל שנעשה מוקצה ואם לאו מותר. ור' יצחק חולק על רב חסדא ואומר אפי' כלי לכוף עליה בשביל שלא תישבר ביצה בשבת אסור. קסבר אין כלי ניטל [אלא] לדבר הניטל בשבת. ואותיבנא עליה כל הני תיובתא. ומשני בצריך למקומו. ת"ש אחת ביצה [שנולדה] בשבת ואחת ביצה שנולדה ביו"ט אין מטלטלין אותה לא לכסות בה את הכלי ולא לסמוך בה כרעי המטה. אבל כופה עליה כלי כו' ומשני הכא נמי בצריך לאותו מקום. פי' לאותו מקום של כלי ולא למקום הביצה.

הגהות הב"ח

(א) תוס' ד"ה בעודן וכו' כי שדינהו בקדר' אידחו כצ"ל ותיבת חייתא נמחק:

גליון הש"ס

תוס' ד"ה טבל מוכן. שאם שגג. עי' לעיל לח ע"א תוס' ד"ה עבר ובפסחים דף מב ע"א ברש"י ד"ה היכא דאתמר וברא"ש שם: תוס' ד"ה בעודן עליו. א"נ הא דיש מוקצה. עיין לקמן דף מד ע"ב תוס' ד"ה יש עליה מעות:

רב נסים גאון

באבנים מקורזלות של בית הכסא. תמצא פירושו בפרק המוציא יין (דף פא) זונין על לבי מדרשא אמר להו רבותיי שיעור אבנים מקורזלות בכמה אמרו לו כזית וכאגוז וכביצה תנו רבנן בשבת ג' אבנים מקורזלות מותר להכניסן לבית הכסא כו': בליבני דאיתור מבניינא דחזיין למיזגא עלייהו עיקרם בפרק כל הכלים ניטלין בשבת (דף קכד) אמר רב נחמן הני ליבני דאשתיור מבניינא שרי לטלטולינהו בשבתא משום דחזו למיזגא עלייהו ובמס' יום טוב (דף לג) בפרק המביא כדי יין ממקום למקום. אמר ליה לא נצרכה אלא לאותן ב' חלות מנהג הוא בעת חתיכת הדבש מן הכוורת להניח ב' חלות לעסק הדבורים ותישתכח עיקר דיליה בבבא [בתרא] בפרק המוכר את הספינה (דף פ) חלות דבש מניח שתי חלות חיצונות:

מו א מיי' פכ"ה מהלכו' שבת הלכה ו ופכ"ו הלכה כב סמג לאוין סה טוש"ע או"ח סימן שיא סעיף ו:
מז ב ג מיי' שם פכ"ו הלכה כא טור שו"ע או"ח שם סעיף א:

גמרא

דְּאִיכָּא דְּבַשׁ, בִּימוֹת הַגְּשָׁמִים דְּלֵיכָּא דְּבַשׁ – מַאי אִיכָּא לְמֵימַר? לֹא נִצְרְכָא אֶלָּא לְאוֹתָן שְׁתֵּי חַלּוֹת. וְהָא מוּקְצוֹת נִינְהוּ! דְּחָשֵׁיב עֲלַיְיהוּ. הָא לָא חָשֵׁיב עֲלַיְיהוּ מַאי – אָסוּר? אִי הָכִי, הָא דְּתָנֵי: "וּבִלְבַד שֶׁלֹּא יִתְכַּוֵּין לָצוּד" לִפְלוֹג וְלִתְנֵי בְּדִידָהּ, בד"א – כְּשֶׁחִישֵּׁב עֲלֵיהֶן, אֲבָל לֹא חִישֵּׁב עֲלֵיהֶן – אָסוּר! הָא קמ"ל: אע"פ שֶׁחִישֵּׁב עֲלֵיהֶן – וּבִלְבַד שֶׁלֹּא יִתְכַּוֵּין לָצוּד. מַנִּי? אִי ר"ש – *לֵית לֵיהּ מוּקְצֶה, אִי ר' יְהוּדָה – כִּי לֹא מִתְכַּוֵּין מַאי הָוֵי? הָא דָּבָר שֶׁאֵין מִתְכַּוֵּין אָסוּר! לְעוֹלָם ר' יְהוּדָה, מַאי "וּבִלְבַד שֶׁלֹּא יִתְכַּוֵּין לָצוּד" – שֶׁלֹּא יַעֲשֶׂנָּה כִּמְצוּדָה, דְּלִישְׁבּוֹק לְהוּ רַוְוחָא כִּי הֵיכִי דְּלָא לִיתְצַדוּ מִמֵּילָא. רַב אַשִׁי אָמַר: מִי קָתָנֵי 'בִּימוֹת הַחַמָּה' וּ'בִימוֹת הַגְּשָׁמִים'? 'בַּחַמָּה מִפְּנֵי הַחַמָּה וּבַגְּשָׁמִים מִפְּנֵי הַגְּשָׁמִים' קָתָנֵי – בְּיוֹמֵי נִיסָן וּבְיוֹמֵי תִּשְׁרִי, דְּאִיכָּא חַמָּה (וְאִיכָּא צִינָּה) וְאִיכָּא גְּשָׁמִים, וְאִיכָּא דְּבַשׁ. אֲמַר לְהוּ רַב שֵׁשֶׁת: פּוּקוּ וְאִמְרוּ לֵיהּ לְר' יִצְחָק: כְּבָר תַּרְגְּמָא רַב הוּנָא לִשְׁמַעְתֵּיךְ בְּבָבֶל. דְּא"ר הוּנָא: עוֹשִׂין מְחִיצָּה לְמֵת בִּשְׁבִיל חַי, וְאֵין עוֹשִׂין מְחִיצָּה לְמֵת בִּשְׁבִיל מֵת. מַאי הִיא? דְּא"ר שְׁמוּאֵל בַּר יְהוּדָה, וְכֵן תָּנָא שֵׁילָא מָרִי: [א]מֵת הַמּוּטָּל בַּחַמָּה בָּאִים שְׁנֵי בְּנֵי אָדָם וְיוֹשְׁבִין בְּצִדּוֹ, חַם לָהֶם מִלְּמַטָּה – זֶה מֵבִיא מִטָּה וְיוֹשֵׁב עָלֶיהָ, וְזֶה מֵבִיא מִטָּה וְיוֹשֵׁב עָלֶיהָ. חַם לָהֶם מִלְמַעְלָה – מְבִיאִים מַחֲצֶלֶת וּפוֹרְסִין עֲלֵיהֶן. זֶה זוֹקֵף מִטָּתוֹ וְנִשְׁמָט וְהוֹלֵךְ לוֹ, וְזֶה זוֹקֵף מִטָּתוֹ וְנִשְׁמָט וְהוֹלֵךְ לוֹ, וְנִמְצֵאת מְחִיצָּה עֲשׂוּיָה מֵאֵלֶיהָ. אִיתְּמַר, מֵת הַמּוּטָּל בַּחַמָּה, רַב יְהוּדָה אָמַר שְׁמוּאֵל: [ב]הוֹפְכוֹ מִמִּטָּה לְמִטָּה. רַב חֲנִינָא בַּר שְׁלָמְיָא מִשְּׁמֵיהּ דְּרַב אָמַר: *מַנִּיחַ עָלָיו כִּכָּר אוֹ תִּינוֹק וּמְטַלְטְלוֹ. הֵיכָא דְּאִיכָּא כִּכָּר אוֹ תִּינוֹק – כּוּלֵּי עָלְמָא לָא פְּלִיגִי דְּשָׁרֵי, כִּי פְּלִיגִי – דְּלֵית לֵיהּ. מ"ס: *טִלְטוּל מִן הַצַּד – שְׁמֵיהּ טִלְטוּל, ומ"ס: לָא שְׁמֵיהּ טִלְטוּל. לֵימָא כְּתַנָּאֵי: *אֵין מַצִּילִין אֶת הַמֵּת מִפְּנֵי הַדְּלֵיקָה. אָמַר ר' יְהוּדָה בֶּן לָקִישׁ: שָׁמַעְתִּי שֶׁמַּצִּילִין אֶת הַמֵּת מִפְּנֵי הַדְּלֵיקָה. הֵיכִי דָּמֵי? אִי דְּאִיכָּא כִּכָּר אוֹ תִּינוֹק – מ"ט דְּתַנָּא קַמָּא? אִי דְּלֵיכָּא – מ"ט דְּר' יְהוּדָה בֶּן לָקִישׁ? אֶלָּא לָאו בְּטִלְטוּל מִן הַצַּד פְּלִיגִי: דְּמָר סָבַר: טִלְטוּל מִן הַצַּד – שְׁמֵיהּ טִלְטוּל. ומ"ס לָא שְׁמֵיהּ טִלְטוּל. לָא, [ג]דְּכ"ע – טִלְטוּל מִן הַצַּד שְׁמֵיהּ טִלְטוּל, וְהַיְינוּ טַעְמָא דְּר' יְהוּדָה בֶּן לָקִישׁ: *דְּמִתּוֹךְ שֶׁאָדָם בָּהוּל עַל מֵתוֹ,
אִי

רש"י

דְּאִיכָּא דְּבַשׁ. דָּבָר הַנִּיטָּל: שְׁתֵּי חַלּוֹת. כָּל הַכַּוֶּורֶת עוֹשִׂין אוֹתָהּ הַדְּבוֹרִים חַלּוֹת חַלּוֹת שֶׁל לַפִּיחִית דְּבַשׁ וְשַׁעֲוָה, וּכְשֶׁרוֹדִים אוֹתָן מַנִּיחִין בָּהּ שְׁתַּיִם שֶׁיִּתְפַּרְנְסוּ מֵהֶן הַדְּבוֹרִים כָּל יְמוֹת הַגְּשָׁמִים, כִּדְתְנַן בְּ"הַמּוֹכֵר אֶת הַסְּפִינָה" (ב"ב פ.): הַלּוֹקֵחַ חַלּוֹת כַּוַּורְתּוֹ שֶׁל חֲבֵירוֹ – מַנִּיחַ שְׁתֵּי חַלּוֹת, דִּסְתָמָא לֹא מְכָרָן: מוּקְצוֹת נִינְהוּ. לַדְּבוֹרִים, הָדַר הָוֵה לֵיהּ דָּבָר שֶׁאֵינוֹ נִיטָּל, וְאַפ"ה מְטַלְטְלִין מַחְצֶלֶת לְהַצָּלָתָן: דְּחָשֵׁיב עֲלַיְיהוּ. מֵאֶתְמוֹל לַאֲכִילָה: וּמַנִּי. הִיא שֶׁהִצְרַכְתָּ לְתָרוּצָהּ כְּשֶׁחִישֵּׁב, וְקָתָנֵי דְ"דָבָר שֶׁאֵין מִתְכַּוֵּין מוּתָּר" כְּר"ש: אִי ר"ש. אֲמַר, לָמָּה לִי לְאוֹקְמֵיהּ כְּשֶׁחִישֵּׁב? שֶׁלֹּא יַעֲשֶׂנּוּ כִּמְצוּדָה. שֶׁלֹּא יְכַסֶּנָּה כּוּלָּהּ, אֶלָּא דְּנִשְׁבּוֹק רַוְוחָא שֶׁיּוּכְלוּ לָצֵאת, כִּי הֵיכִי דְּלָא לִיתְיַלְּדוּ בְּהַאי כִּיסּוּי מִמֵּילָא. וְאַע"ג דְּלָא מִיכַּוֵּין לְמֵילַד – אָסוּר: רַב אַשִׁי אָמַר. לְעוֹלָם דְּאִיכָּא דְּבַשׁ טוּבָא. וּדְקַשְׁיָא לָךְ "יְמוֹת הַגְּשָׁמִים" – מִי קָתָנֵי בָּהּ יְמוֹת הַגְּשָׁמִים? לִשְׁמַעְתֵּיהּ. דְּאֵין כְּלִי נִיטָּל אֶלָּא לְדָבָר הַנִּיטָּל: מֵת הַמּוּטָּל בַּחַמָּה. וְיֵשׁ לָחוּשׁ שֶׁמָּא יְמַהֵר לְהַסְרִיחַ: וְיוֹשְׁבִין בְּצִדּוֹ. ע"ג הַקַּרְקַע, כְּדֵי שֶׁיִּצְטַעֲרוּ מֵחוֹם הַקַּרְקַע וְיִצְטָרְכוּ לְהָבִיא מִטּוֹת לֵישֵׁב עֲלֵיהֶן, וְהַמִּטּוֹת יִהְיוּ לִמְחִיצָה, כִּדְמְסַיֵּים וְאָזֵיל: חַם לָהֶם לְמַטָּה. מִן הַקַּרְקַע שֶׁרְתָחוֹ חַמָּה: וּפוֹרְסִין. עַל רָאשָׁן לְצֵל: זֶה זוֹקֵף מִטָּתוֹ. שֶׁתְּהֵא הַמַּחְצֶלֶת מוּנַּחַת עָלֶיהָ, וְכֵן זֶה. נִמְצֵאת מְחִיצָה עֲשׂוּיָה מֵאֵלֶיהָ. וְלִכְשֶׁיִּרְצוּ נִשְׁמָטִין וְהוֹלְכִין לָהֶם. וְדַוְקָא נָקַט חַם לָהֶם מִלְּמַטָּה בְּרֵישָׁא, שֶׁיָּבִיאוּ הַמִּטּוֹת לִישִׁיבָה בְּרֵישָׁא, וַהֲדַר מַחְצֶלֶת לִפְרוֹשׂ עֲלֵיהֶן לְצֵל, וְאוֹחֲזִין אוֹתָהּ בִּידֵיהֶן עַד לְאַחַר שָׁעָה שֶׁיִּזְקְפוּ וְיִשָּׁמְטוּ. דְּהָוֵה לֵיהּ כִּי הַהוּא דְּאָמְרִינַן (עירובין דף קב.): הַאי מְדוּרְתָּא, מִלְמַעְלָה לְמַטָּה – שָׁרֵי. אֲבָל לְאַתּוּיֵי מֵעִיקָּרָא מִטּוֹת לְאוֹרֶךְ הָאֹהֶל – לָא, דַּהֲוָה לֵיהּ מִלְּמַטָּה לְמַעְלָה כְּדֶרֶךְ בִּנְיָן, וְקיי"ל: אֵין עוֹשִׂין אֹהֶל עֲרַאי בַּתְּחִלָּה בְּשַׁבָּת: הוֹפְכוֹ מִמִּטָּה לְמִטָּה. עַד שֶׁמַּגִּיעַ לְצֵל: מִן הַצַּד. כִּלְאַחַר יָד: אִי דְּלֵיכָּא. וְהַאי "מַצִּילִין" דְּקָאָמַר ר' יְהוּדָה בֶּן לָקִישׁ – דִּמְטַלְטֵל לֵיהּ לְהֶדְיָא הוּא: מַאי טַעְמָא דְּר' יְהוּדָה. אֶלָּא לָאו מִן הַצַּד הוּא דְּקָשָׁרֵי:
אִי

תוספות

דחשיב עלייהו. וא"ת: והא אסור לרדותם, כדתניא בסוף פרק "המצניע" (לקמן צה. ושם): הרודה חלות דבש, בשוגג – חייב חטאת דברי ר"א, ולרבנן שבות מיהא איכא, והוי דבר שאינו ניטל! וי"ל: דמיירי ברדויות ומונחות שם בכוורת, אי נמי: רגילות שיש דבש צף ע"ג חלות, ואותו אינו צריך רדייה:

שלא יעשנו כעין מצודה. וא"ת: מאי קמ"ל? פשיטא – דאי עביד כעין מצודה דאסור, *והא לא משמע מברייתא דאע"ג דאינו מתכוין אסור! וי"ל: דאמר בפ' "משילין" (ביצה לו: ושם) דקמ"ל דס"ד: במינו ניצוד – אסור, שאין במינו ניצוד – מותר: רב אשי אמר כו'. מסתמא רב אשי השיב מיד כן לרב עוקבא כששאלו, אלא שסידר התלמוד תירוץ שלו תחילה. ורשב"א אומר: דשניהם השיב רב אשי, דבמסכת ביצה גרס: "א"ל: לא נצרכה אלא לאותן שתי חלות". ובשינויא דהכא גרס: "ואב"א מי קתני בימות החמה כו'":

כבר תירגמ' רב הונא לשמעתיך. בפרק בתרא (דף קנד:) משמע דאית ליה נמי לרב הונא דאסור לבטל כלי מהיכנו, דפריך אמילתיה, דקאמר התם רב הונא: היתה בהמתו טעונה כלי זכוכית – מביא כרים וכסתות ומניח תחתיהן. והא קמבטל כלי מהיכנו! ומשני: בשליפי זוטרי. וא"ת: אכתי תקשה ליה התם, דהא רב הונא סבר הכא דאין כלי ניטל אלא לדבר הניטל! וי"ל: דמיירי בצריך למקומו. וא"ת: וכי פריך ליה התם מההיא דהיתה בהמתו טעונה טבל ועששית, לימא דמיירי באין צריך למקומו? וי"ל: דהוה מצי לשנויי הכי, דה"נ הוה מצי לשנויי בשליפי רברבי. ור"י מתרץ: דאיסור דאין כלי ניטל אלא לדבר הניטל – שרי *היכא דאיכא הפסד מרובה. וכן משמע דקאמר התם: מהו דתימא כי היכי דלהפסד מרובה חששו כו' משמע: חששו והתירו לטלטל אף לדבר שאינו ניטל, דמה חששו *להתיר אם לא זה האיסור:

חם להם מלמטה. תימה: בלא שום חום, מאי איסור איכא שיביאו כל אחד מטה לישב עליה? ותו: אמאי מייתי ברישא מטה והדר מחצלת? ימתינו עד שיחם להם גם מלמעלה, ויביאו מטות ומחצלות יחד! ונראה דאחמור רבנן למיעבד היכרא שהוא לצורך חי, כל כמה דאיפשר למיעבד: ופורסין עליהן זה זוקף כו'. דוקא בכה"ג, כמו שפי' רש"י. אבל ממטה למעלה – אסור משום אהל. כדאמרי' ב"המביא כדי יין" (ביצה לג: ושם), אמר רב יהודה: מדורתא מלמעלה למטה – שרי, מלמטה למעלה – אסור. וכן ביעתא, וכן קידרא, וכן חביתא ופוריא. דהא דאמרי' ב"המוצא תפילין" (עירובין קב.) גבי דיכרי, דרב הונא אתא לקמיה דרב, א"ל: זיל כרוך בודיא ושייר בה טפח, למחר פשטוה – מוסיף על אהל עראי הוא, ושפיר דמי. אבל בלא שיור – אסור. היינו משום שהמחילות התחתונות היו כבר עשויות, ואם היה פורש עליהן – היה עושה אהל כדרך לעשות אהל, ואע"ג דרב הונא אית ליה הכא דאין כלי ניטל אלא לדבר הניטל, מה שהיה מוסיף למחר – לא חשיב טלטול. או שמא היו מושיבין שם אדם. א"נ: משום הפסד מרובה שרי, כדפירש לעיל: זה זוקף מטתו. תימה לר"י: (*) דרבא לא שרי אלא בשביל חי, ובפ' "מי שהוציאוהו" (שם מד. ושם) תניא: זוקף את המטה, פורס עליה סדין שלא תפול החמה על המת ועל האוכלין. והתם מוקי לה במחילה רביעית, שסוכה כשירה בלאו הכי, ולא הוי אלא תוספת אהל. אבל מ"מ – (אין) ניטל הכלי בשביל מת! ויש לומר: דהתם נמי לא שרי אלא בענין שאומר כאן שעושה בשביל חי, אי נמי: שיש אוכלין עם המת: ונשמט והולך לו. ואין צריך לישאר שם תחת האהל, כדי שיהא נראה שנעשה בשביל חי, כיון דבשעת עשייה היה נראה שעושה בשביל חי: דכ"ע טלטול מן הצד שמיה טלטול. נראה לר"י דכן הלכה, מדלא קאמר דכ"ע לא שמיה טלטול, וכגון דליכא ככר ותינוק, ואין לו אלא מטה אחת. וטעם דרבי יהודה בן לקיש מתוך שאדם בהול כו'. אלא משום דהלכתא דשמיה טלטול – נקט הכי. וקשה לר"י: דבריש "כל הכלים" (לקמן קכג.) פסיק רב נחמן כר' אלעזר בן תדאי, דקסבר לא שמיה טלטול! וע"ק דרב אדרב: דהכא סבר "שמיה טלטול", ובסוף פ' "תולין" (שם קמא.), אמרי בי רב: טלטול מן הצד לא שמיה טלטול! ובדוכתא אחריתי פריך מדרב אאמרי בי רב ובפרק "השואל" (ב"מ קב:) ובפרק "בית כור" (ב"ב קה:) מצריך מילתיה דרב ודאמרי בי רב. ועוד, אמאי אסר
רב

(*) נ"ל דהכא.

[ומשמע ליה שיש שם חלות הרבה דלא הוי מוקצה מחמת חסרון כיס [תוס' ישנים]]

[לעיל ל: לקמן קמב:]

[לקמן קכג. קמא.]

[תוספ' פי"ד] יומא פה.

יומא שם

מה"ר שכנא הגיה והלא משמע דאע"ג דאינו כו'

ולעיל מיניה ה"מ לשנויי דשרי משום הפסד אלא דמשני שינויא חדא לכולהו בצריך למקומו [תו"י]

ומיהו דוחק הרשב"א דחששו להתיר טורח (דהמלאכה) [דהא רבה] דמפרש טעמא משום הגלה שאינה מגויה ולית ליה דביטול כלי ולא טעמא דאין כלי ניטל (אלא) [הלא] תיקשי ליה ברייתא דאסר' בפ' בתרא דף קנד: להביא תחתיו כרים וכסתות אלא ולאי משום טורח [תו"י]

רבינו חננאל

וכיון שמותר לפנותו מאותו מקום ולטלטלו מטלטלו למקום הביצה (כו') וכופהו על הביצה וכן כולם*) ולא יתכן לישב ע"ג הביצה כדי שלא יטנפו בגדיו. לפיכך כופה עליה [כלי] וישב עליו. וכל התיובתות פשוטות הן. ושנינו על הכוורת באותן ב' חלות ששנינו בפ' המוכר את הספינה בענין המוכר חלת דבש כוורתו לחבירו שחייב הקונה להניח לו שתי חלות דבש כדי שיהו מזון לדבורים שלא יברחו. ולפיכך אמרנו אותן ב' חלות מוקצות ממאכל אדם הן (לא השאילו) דשאולין לדבורים. ושנינן כגון (שחייב) [שחשב] עליהן בפירוש למאכל אדם. ואקשינן אי הכי אדתני ומזהיר בפריסת ע"ג הכוורת ובלבד שלא יתכוין לצוד. ליפלוג עליה כו'. ואסיקנא לעולם ר' יהודה [היא] והאי דקתני ובלבד שלא יתכוין לצוד. שלא ישלשל המחצלת וידחקנה בבותלי הכוורת שנמצא הדבורין כסתומין בכוורת אלא ירויח כמעט המחצלת מן הנקב של כוורת שהוא פתח לצאת ולכנוס בו הדבורים כו'. אמר רב ששת כבר תירגם רב הונא לשמעתיה דר' יצחק בבבל דאמר עושין מחיצה למת בשביל החי ואין עושין מחיצה למת בשביל המת כיצד מת מוטל בחמה באין ב' בני אדם ויושבין בצידו. חם להם מלמטה [זה] מביא מטה ויושב עליה וזה מביא מטה ויושב עליה כו'. איתמר מת המוטל בחמה רב יהודה אמר שמואל הופכו ממטה למטה. ומשמיה דרב אמרו מניח עליו ככר או תינוק ומטלטלו. ואסקינן בשיש ככר או תינוק כ"ע לא פליגי שמניח עליו ככר או תינוק ומטלטלו (וכ"ע) [כי פליגי היכא דל"ל מ"ס] טלטול מן הצד שמיה טלטול. [ומ"ס לא שמיה טלטול]. ואתינן ואוקמינן בתנאי. אין מצילין [את המת] מפני הדליקה. אמר ר' יהודה בן לקיש שמעתי שמצילין את המת מפני הדליקה. ואמרינן כ"ע טלטול מן הצד שמיה טלטול. היינו טעמא דר' יהודה בן לקיש מתוך שאדם בהול על מת
אי

*) ע"ס כאן ופי' אחר הוא בצריך למקום הכילה לישב.

גליון הש"ס

רש"י ד"ה אי ר"ש למה לי בשחישב. משמע דמכ"מ צריכים לשינויא דאיכא ב' חלות דס"ל לרש"י שם דלר"ש ליכא לדינא דרי"ף היינו אפילו לר"ש דמיקל במוקצה ואולם רש"י בכילה כ' באמת דלפירכת הש"ס דלר"ש ל"ל כלל לתרך דאיכא ב' חלות מבואר דס"ל לרש"י שם (דלר"ש ליכא לדינא דרי"ף). ולדברי רש"י אלו כוונת הרז"ה פ' מי שהחשיך שכתב דרי"ף הוא רק לר"י וכתב עלה שכ"כ רש"י: גמ' כי פליגי דלית ליה. ק"ל אמאי לא הוי המטה עצמה במקום ככר או תינוק ועי' מג"א סי' ש"ח ס"ק כ"א ובתוספת שבת. ומזה לא הערו כלום ולע"ג: תוס' ד"ה ופורסין וכו' מה שהיה מוסיף למחר. עי' לקמן דף נג ע"א תוס' ד"ה מהו ליתן: שם ד"ה דכו"ע וכו' ובדוכתא אחריתי. עי' בכורות דף כז ע"ב:

אי לא שרית ליה – אתי לכבויי. א"ר יהודה בן שילא א"ר אסי א"ר יוחנן: [א]הלכה כר' יהודה בן לקיש במת.§ "אין נאותין הימנו לפי שאינו מן המוכן".§ תנו רבנן: *[ב]מותר השמן שבנר ושבקערה – אסור, ורבי שמעון מתיר.§

מתני' *מטלטלין נר חדש אבל לא ישן. רבי שמעון אומר: כל הנרות מטלטלין, חוץ מן הנר הדולק בשבת.§

גמ' *ת"ר: מטלטלין נר חדש אבל לא ישן, דברי רבי יהודה. ר"מ אומר: [ג]כל הנרות מטלטלין, חוץ מן הנר שהדליקו בו *בשבת. ר' שמעון אומר: חוץ מן הנר הדולק בשבת. כבתה – מותר לטלטלה, אבל כוס וקערה ועששית לא יזיזם ממקומם. ור' אליעזר בר' שמעון אומר: מסתפק מן הנר הכבה, ומן השמן המטפטף, ואפי' בשעה שהנר דולק. אמר אביי: רבי אליעזר ברבי שמעון סבר לה כאבוה בחדא, ופליג עליה בחדא. סבר לה כאבוה בחדא – דלית ליה מוקצה, ופליג עליה בחדא, דאילו אבוה סבר: כבה – אין, לא כבה – לא, ואיהו סבר: אע"ג דלא כבה. "אבל כוס וקערה ועששית לא יזיזם ממקומם" מאי שנא הני? אמר עולא: סיפא אתאן לר' יהודה. מתקיף לה מר זוטרא: אי הכי מאי 'אבל'? אלא אמר מר זוטרא: לעולם רבי שמעון, וכי קשרי רבי שמעון – בנר זוטא דדעתיה עלויה, אבל הני דנפישי – לא. והתניא: מותר השמן שבנר ושבקערה – אסור, ורבי שמעון מתיר. התם – קערה דומיא דנר, הכא – קערה דומיא דכוס. א"ר זירא: פמוט שהדליקו בו בשבת, לדברי המתיר – אסור, לדברי האוסר – מותר. למימרא דרבי יהודה מוקצה מחמת מיאוס – אית ליה, מוקצה מחמת איסור – לית ליה? והתניא, *ר' יהודה אומר: כל הנרות של מתכת מטלטלין, חוץ מן הנר שהדליקו בו *בשבת! אלא, אי איתמר – הכי איתמר: א"ר זירא: פמוט שהדליקו עליו בשבת – ד"ה אסור, לא הדליקו עליו – ד"ה מותר.§ אמר *רב יהודה א"ר: מטה שיחדה למעות – אסור לטלטלה. מיתיבי' רב נחמן בר יצחק: מטלטלין נר חדש, אבל לא ישן. ומה

אי לא שרית ליה וכו'. אבל במוטל לחמה – לא שרי: **מתני'** מטלטלין נר חדש. שאינו מאוס, וחזי לאישתמושי(א) להדיא, שלא דלק בו נר מעולם: אבל לא ישן. דמוקצה מחמת מיאוס הוא: **גמ'** חוץ מן הנר שהדליקו. ואף על גב שכבה – אסור, דאית ליה לרבי מאיר מוקצה מחמת איסור, ולית ליה מוקצה מחמת מיאוס: *חוץ מן הנר הדולק בשבת. בעוד שהוא דולק אסור, שמא יכבה הנר: עששית. כוס גדול של זכוכית, שקורין לנפ"א: לא יזיזם ממקומן. ואפי' כבה הנר, ולקמן מפרש טעמא: מן הנר הכבה. דכיון דכבה והולך – לא מחייב תו משום מכבה: כבה אין לא כבה לא. דלא שמעינן ליה לרבי שמעון דשרי במתני' אלא מותר שמן שבנר ושבקערה, דמשמע לאחר שכבה: מאי אבל. מדקאמר "אבל" – מכלל דבנר מותר: בזוטא. דדעתי' עליה מבע"י, סבר שיכלה השמן מהר, ואשתמש בנר לכשיכבה: אבל הני. לא אסיק אדעתיה שיכבו כל היום: ור' שמעון מתיר. וקערה נפישא, קשיא קערה אקערה: דומיא דנר. קתני לה, דזוטרא: פמוט. מנורה של מתכת – ואינה מאוסה: לדברי המתיר. ר' מאיר, המתיר בנר ישן: אוסר. בהאי, דמוקצה מחמת איסור, כדקתני לעיל: "חוץ מן הנר שהדליקו בו בשבת": לדברי האוסר. ר' יהודה האוסר בנר ישן של חרס – התם הוא דמאיס, אבל הכא – שרי, ולית ליה מוקצה מחמת איסור: נר של מתכת. לא מאיס, כגון של נחשת דלא בלע: שיחדה למעות. מיתסרא בהזמנה בעלמא, ואע"פ שלא הניח עליה מעולם: מטלטלין נר חדש. והא רבי יהודה קאמר לה דאית ליה מוקצה. אלמא לא מיתסר בהזמנה, מדקאמר "אבל לא ישן", ולא קתני "אבל לא המיוחד לכך":

הניח

רב הכא טלטול מן הצד, הא תנן בפ' "נוטל" (לקמן קמב:): מעות שע"ג הכר – מנער את הכר והן נופלות, ואבן שעל פי החבית – מטה על לדה וכו'. ומוקי לה רב התם בשוכח, אבל במניח – נעשה בסיס לדבר האסור. והכא(ב) (חשיב) בשוכח, מדשרי שמואל. וכל דבר שדעתו ליטלו בשבת ולא להניחו כל השבת – אפילו מניח חשיב כשוכח. כי ההיא דמנער את הכיסוי והם נופלות, אע"פ שבמתכוין כיסה בדבר שאינו ניטל. ואפי' רבנן דרבי אלעזר בן תדאי שרו בכי האי גוונא דהכא. דהא שרו פגה שהטמינה בתבן, וחררה שהטמינה בגחלים אם מגולה מקצתה, ובמכוסה כולה פליגי, דרבי אלעזר – שרי אפי' מכוסה כולה, דתוחב בכוש או בכרכר. ואומר ר"י: דיש לחלק, דהכא – עיקר הטלטול לצורך מת, ולא דמי לכל הנהו שעושה עיקר הטלטול לצורך כר וחבית ולא לצורך מעות ואבן, *ולהכי לא מייתי הכא פלוגתא דר' אלעזר בן תדאי ורבנן. וע"ק לר"י: דאפי' בטלטול דמת שיש לאסור יותר משאר טלטול מן הצד, כדפי' – שרי שמואל. ובסוף "במה טומנין" (לקמן דף נ:) אמר שמואל: האי סכינא דביני אורבי, דלה ושלפה והדר דלה – שרי, ואי לא – אסיר, ופירש בקונט' לקמן דאסור משום טלטול מן הצד. וכן קשה, דרב הונא אמר התם: האי סליקוסתא, דלה ושלפה והדר דלה שרי, ואי לאו אסור. א"כ, אסר טלטול מן הצד. ובסוף "חולין" אמרי בי רב: טלטול מן הצד – לא שמיה טלטול. ו"אמרי בי רב" היינו רב הונא, כמו שמפרש ר"ת בספ"ק דסנהדרין* (דף יז: ושם)! ונראה לר"י דרב הונא ושמואל לא אסרי התם משום טלטול מן הצד, אלא משום שמסיר עפר ומרחיב הגומא. ואיידי דאיירי לעיל מיניה בגומא – נקטה. ומותיב מהטומן לפת וצנונות, דהתם לפת וצנונות לאו דלה ושלפה. ולהכי חשיב התלמוד תיובתא. ור"ה ושמואל הוו ידעי לה, דמתני' היא בסדר זרעים, אלא דדחקי לאוקמה בדלה ושלפה. והתלמוד לא ניחא ליה לאוקמה הכי, ועומדת בתיובתא:

*מתוך שאדם בהול על מתו אי לא שרית לי' אתי לכבויי. ואע"ג דגבי ממון אמרינן *איפכא: אי שרית ליה – אתי לכבויי. היינו משום שאין מצטער על ממונו כמו על מתו, ואי שרית ליה, מתוך שיהא טרוד להציל – ישכח שהיום שבת, ויבא לכבות בשוגג. אבל על מתו מצטער ביותר, ואי לא שרית ליה – אתי לכבויי במזיד:

שבנר ושבקערה אסור ור' שמעון מתיר. ואחר הסבת מותר אפי' לר' יהודה. וה"נ תניא לקמן גבי נויי סוכה: אסור להסתפק מהן עד מוצאי י"ט האחרון, אבל בתר הכי – שרי. וקשה לר"י: דמ"ש מנר חנוכה, דתניא: *כבה ליל ראשון – מוסיף עליו בליל ב' ומדליק בו, כבה ליל ח' – עושה לו מדורה בפני עצמו, מפני שהוקצה למצותו! ואומר ר"י: דנר חנוכה עיקרו לא להנאתו בא אלא לפרסומי ניסא, ומשום חביבותא דנס אינו מצפה שיכבה, אלא מקצה לגמרי למצוה. אבל נר שבת – להנאתו בא, יושב ומצפה שיכבה, ולכך מותר. וא"ת: ומ"ש נר שכבה דאסור לטלטל לר' יהודה, מסוכה רעועה דעלמא דמהני בה תנאי? כדאמר לקמן בשמעתין; ואם התנה עליה – הכל לפי תנאו, ומוקי לה במסכת ביצה (דף ל:) בסוכה דעלמא ורעועה, דאתמול דעתיה עילויה שתפול. ונר נמי דעתיה עילויה שיכבה, ואמאי אין מועיל תנאי להסתפק ממותר השמן? ולר"ש נמי יועיל תנאי להסתפק מן השמן המטפטף בשעה שהנר דולק! וי"ל: דהתם סוכה דעלמא היתה עשויה מזמן גדול, ועתה ביה"ש אינו בודל ממנה ויושב ומצפה מתי תפול. אבל נר עיקר הקצאתו הוא ביה"ש, ודחייה בידי' לצורך שבת, וחמיר טפי – ולא מהני ביה תנאי*:

לדברי המתיר אסור. פי' בקונטרס: לדברי ר' מאיר. וא"ת: מאי קמ"ל? הא בהדיא קאסר ר' מאיר נר שהדליקו בה באותו שבת! וי"ל: דה"א ה"מ בנר של חרס, דאית ביה תרתי: מוקצה מחמת מיאוס ומחמת איסור, קמ"ל דאפי' בשל מתכת דלא מאיס, ולית ביה אלא מוקצה מחמת איסור – אסר ר' מאיר. ואין נראה לר"ת: דלפי זה, הא דמסיק דברי הכל אסור – לא הוי אלא ר' מאיר ור' יהודה דקאי עלייהו, ולא ר"ש. ומפרש, וכן פר"ת: לדברי המתיר – היינו ר' שמעון – אסר כאן, בפמוט. דהא פמוט גדול הוא ככוס וקערה ועששית, כמו פמוטות של בית ר' דשילהי "כל כתבי" (לקמן קכא:). לדברי האוסר – היינו ר' מאיר ור' יהודה, דאסרי בנר חרס שהדליקו בו באותו שבת. וה"מ – בנר של חרס דאיכא תרתי, מוקצה מחמת מיאוס ומחמת איסור. אבל בנר מתכת – שרו. ומסיק דאפי' בשל מתכת אסר ר' מאיר, וה"נ אמרי' בפ"ק דחולין (דף טו.): ע"כ לא שרי רבי מאיר אלא במבשל דראוי לכוס, אבל בשוחט – לא*:

מטה שיחדה למעות אסור לטלטלה. נראה דאפי' לצורך גופה או לצורך מקומה אסור, דכיון שיחדה למעות – שוב אין עושין ממנה שום תשמיש. והויא כאבנורות דאסור לטלטלה לרבי יהודה אפילו לצורך גופה ומקומה. ולרבי שמעון לא אסור שום מוקצה לצורך גופו ומקומו, אלא מוקצה מחמת חסרון כיס:

רבינו חננאל

[אי לא] שרית ליה לטלטולי אתי לכבויי ולמעבד איסורא דאוריי' א"ר יהודה בר שילא א"ר אסי א"ר יוחנן הלכה כר' יהודה בן לקיש במת: ואין נאותין ממנו לפי שאינו מן המוכן: **ת"ר** מותר השמן שבנר ושבקערה אסור להסתפק ממנו. ור"ש מתיר (מטלטלין נר חדש אבל לא ישן) אע"ג דקיי"ל דהלכתא כר' שמעון בכולה שבת בהא לית הלכתא כוותיה. דתנא דידן קתני דברי ר' יהודה סתמא במתניתין [מטלטלין נר חדש אבל לא ישן]. ובברייתא מפרש דברי ר' יהודה מטלטלין נר חדש אבל לא ישן. ר' מאיר [אומר] כל הנרות מטלטלין חוץ מן הנר שהדליקו בה באותה שבת. נמצא ר' מאיר ור' יהודה שניהן אוסרין בנר שהדליקו בו באותה שבת. ור"ש מתיר ואין הלכתא כוותיה. דהוא יחיד במקום רבים ואע"פ דא"ר יוחנן אנו אין לנו אלא בנר כר' שמעון [לר' שמעון] אמרו וליה [לר'] יוחנן לא סבירא ליה טעמא דר"ש. ואפילו ר"ש לא שרי לטלטולי בשבת בנר שכבה אלא בנר קטן דכיון דהוא נר קטן ושמנו מעט דעתו עליו מאתמול לכשיכבה יטלטלנו ואינו מוקצה. אבל נר גדול כגון כוס וקערה ועששית שיתכן שידליקו היום כולו לא אמרינן דחשיב עלייהו מאתמול לכשיכבו יטלטלם. אלא אמרינן ודאי כיון דגדולים הן נתייאשו מלטלטלן ומוקצין הן. לפיכך קתני סיפא אבל כוס וקערה ועששית לא יזיזם ממקומן וכן כיוצא בהן. פעמים שיש קערה ועששית קטנה דומיא דנר קטן ודינם כדין נר קטן ופעמים שיש נר גדול דומיא דקערה ועששית ודינו כדינם. והא דא"ר אלעזר [בר"ש] מסתפק אדם מנר הכבה ומשמן המטפטף אע"פ שהנר דולק*) א"ר זירא פמוט שהדליקו עליו לדברי המתיר בנר אסר בפמוט. כלומר לר' שמעון דמתיר בנר קטן בפמוט שהוא גדול אוסר. ולדברי ר' מאיר ור' יהודה שאוסרין בנר של חרש מפני שהוא מטונף. והוא צאו כלי. ולפיכך הוקצהו מאתמול בפמוט שהוא של מתכת ואינו מטונף מתיר: **ירושל'** נר מאוס. פמוט אינו מאוס. תני נר המונח על הדלת פותח ונועל בשבת ובלבד שלא יתכון לכבות. רב ושמואל פותרין לה בשוכח ומקללין למאן דעבד כן [יכרת] ה' לאיש אשר יעשנה וגו'. ואקשי' ולר' יהודה מוקצה מחמת מיאוס אית ליה מוקצה מחמת איסור שהדליקו בה באותה שבת לא. והתניא ר' יהודה אומר כל הנרות של מתכת מטלטלין חוץ מן הנר שהדליקו בה באותה שבת. ואסיקנ' הכי לדברי

*) עי' ברשב"א וברמב"ן.

רב נסים גאון

אמר ר' זירא פמוט שהדליקו עליו באותה שבת לדברי המתיר אוסר לדברי האוסר מתיר פמוט מין מנורה ויש לה קנה אחד ובמנחות בפרק הקומץ את המנחה (דף כח) כשאמרו על דרך קושיא ואימא נמי באה

מח א מיי' פכ"ו מהל' שבת הלכה כא סמג לאוין סה טוש"ע או"ח סימן שיא סעיף א:

מט ב מיי' פ"ה מהל' שבת הלכה יב ופרק כו הלכה יד סמג לאוין סה טוש"ע או"ח סימן רסה סעיף ג וסימן רעט סעיף א:

נ ג מיי' פכ"ה מהלכות שבת הלכה י יא טוש"ע או"ח סימן רעט סעיף א:

וא"ש דהכא שרי טפי ככר או תינוק מטלטול מן הצד ובפ' נוטל (דף קמב:) אמר לא אמרו ככר או תינוק אלא למת בלבד ואסרינן לכ"ע ע"י ככר או תינוק שאר דברים שלא במת אע"ג דשרי טלטול מן הצד למת [ת"י]

בתוד"ה אלא

שייך לעמוד הקודם

[לקמן קיז:]

[ובש"ס לא נמצא מקומו אלא בשאלתות פ' וישלח הביאו הרא"ש פרק במה מדליקין רס"ט ובטור וב"י סימן תרעז]

[דבור זה שייך לעיל במשנה]

[לקמן מו: ביצה ל:]

חולין יד:

תוספתא שבת פ"ד

י"ג באותה שבת

הגהות הב"ח

(א) רש"י ד"ה מטלטלין וכו' לאישתמושי ביה להדיא: (ב) תוס' ד"ה דכ"ע טלטול וכו' אבל במניח נעשה בסיס לדבר האסור והכא חשיב כשכח מדברי שמואל דאפילו מניח דבר שדעתו ליטלו בשבת ולא להניחו כל השבת חשוב כשכח כי ההיא דמנער:

חולין טו.

בכ"י באותה שבת

[לקמ"ש תוס' יבמות קח: ד"ה אמר וכו' גרסת' הכא רב הונא ע"ש]

ורשב"א מפ' דהכא חמיר טפי לפי שהוא בסיס לדבר האסור [ת"י]

ורשב"א מפרש דאפילו למאי דס"ד אתי ההיא דחולין שפיר דבמוקצה מחמת איסור דהתם אפי' ר"ש מוד' אף על גב דשרי בנתנבלה בשבת התם אינו מעלה על לבו שישחטנה שום אדם בשבת והוי כמו דיש במינו במחובר דפרש"י דבילה [דף כח:] דאפילו ר"ש אסור כגרוגרות וצימוקין מדלא לקטן מאתמול אקצינהו [תוספות ישנים]

גליון הש"ס תוס' ד"ה דכ"ע כו' אפילו מניח חשיב כשוכח כי ההיא דמנער. עי' לקמן דף נא ע"א תוס' ד"ה או שטמן: בא"ד דהכא עיקר. עי' לעיל דף לט ע"א תוס' ד"ה מפני שמזיז: בא"ד הוו ידעי לה דמתני' היא. עי' מנחות דף ט ע"א תוס' ד"ה חסר הלוג. ומו"ק דף ה ע"א תוס' ד"ה לאתויי: תוס' ד"ה מטה שיחדה כו' והויא שיחדה כו' והויא כאנגלרות. לעיל דף לו ע"א:

נא א מיי' פכ"ה מהל' שבת הלכה י טוש"ע או"ח סימן שי סעיף ז:

וּמָה נֵר דִּלְהָכִי עֲבִידָא, כִּי לֹא הִדְלִיק בָּהּ – שָׁרֵי לְטַלְטוּלָהּ, מִטָּה דְּלָאו לְהָכִי עֲבִידָא – לֹא כ"ש! אֶלָּא, אִי אִיתְּמַר – הָכִי אִיתְּמַר: אָמַר רַב יְהוּדָה אָמַר רַב: מִטָּה שֶׁיִּחֲדָהּ לְמָעוֹת, הִנִּיחַ עָלֶיהָ מָעוֹת – אָסוּר לְטַלְטְלָהּ, לֹא הִנִּיחַ עָלֶיהָ מָעוֹת – מוּתָּר לְטַלְטְלָהּ. לֹא יִחֲדָהּ לְמָעוֹת, יֵשׁ עָלֶיהָ מָעוֹת – אָסוּר לְטַלְטְלָהּ, אֵין עָלֶיהָ מָעוֹת – מוּתָּר לְטַלְטְלָהּ, וְהוּא שֶׁלֹּא הָיוּ עָלֶיהָ בֵּין הַשְּׁמָשׁוֹת. אָמַר עוּלָּא, מֵתִיב ר' אֱלִיעֶזֶר: "מוּכְנִי שֶׁלָּהּ, בִּזְמַן שֶׁהִיא נִשְׁמֶטֶת – אֵין חִבּוּר לָהּ, וְאֵין נִמְדֶּדֶת עִמָּהּ, וְאֵין מַצֶּלֶת עִמָּהּ בְּאֹהֶל הַמֵּת, וְאֵין גּוֹרְרִין אוֹתָהּ בַּשַּׁבָּת בִּזְמַן שֶׁיֵּשׁ עָלֶיהָ מָעוֹת". הָא אֵין עָלֶיהָ מָעוֹת – שַׁרְיָא, אַף עַל גַּב דְּהָווּ עָלֶיהָ ביה"ש! הַהִיא ר' שִׁמְעוֹן הִיא, דְּלֵית לֵיהּ מוּקְצֶה, וְרַב כְּרַבִּי יְהוּדָה סְבִירָא לֵיהּ. הָכִי

רש"י

הִנִּיחַ עָלֶיהָ מָעוֹת. אֲפִילּוּ בְּחוֹל, הֲרֵי הוּקְצָה לְאִיסּוּר וְאָסוּר לְטַלְטְלָהּ, וַאֲפִילּוּ נִסְתַּלְּקוּ הַמָּעוֹת מִבְּעוֹד יוֹם. וְלָא דָּמֵי לְנֵר שֶׁל מַתֶּכֶת דְּשָׁרֵי רַבִּי יְהוּדָה – דְּהָתָם בְּלֹא יִחֲדוֹ: לֹא יִחֲדָהּ לְמָעוֹת. אֵין עָלֶיהָ מָעוֹת בַּשַּׁבָּת: מוּתָּר לְטַלְטְלָהּ. וְאע"ג דְּהִנִּיחַ עָלֶיהָ מָעוֹת בְּחוֹל: וְהוּא. שֶׁנִּסְתַּלְּקוּ מִבְּעוֹד יוֹם – שֶׁלֹּא הָיוּ עָלֶיהָ כָּל בֵּין הַשְּׁמָשׁוֹת, אֲבָל הָיוּ עָלֶיהָ כָּל בֵּין הַשְּׁמָשׁוֹת – אִיתְקְצַאי לְכוּלֵּי יוֹמָא: מוּכְנִי שֶׁלָּהּ. גַּבֵּי שִׁידָּה תְּנַן, בְּמַסֶּכֶת כֵּלִים, וְהִיא עֲגָלָה שֶׁל עֵץ מוּקֶּפֶת מְחִיצוֹת לְמֶרְכַּב אֲנָשִׁים וְנָשִׁים. מוּכְנִי – אוֹפָן: בִּזְמַן שֶׁהִיא נִשְׁמֶטֶת. כְּעֵין אוֹפַנֵּי עֲגָלָה שֶׁלָּנוּ, שֶׁאָדָם יָכוֹל לְסַלְּקוֹ מִן הָעֲגָלָה: אֵינוֹ חִיבּוּר לָהּ. דַּחֲשׁוּבָה הִיא כְּלִי לְעַצְמָהּ. דְּאִי שִׁידָּה בַּת קַבּוּלֵי טוּמְאָה הִיא, כְּגוֹן שֶׁאֵינָהּ מַחֲזֶקֶת מ' סְאָה בְּלַח, וְנִטְמְאָה הַשִּׁידָּה – לֹא נִטְמָא הַמּוּכְנִי. וְאִי לָאו בַּת קַבּוּלֵי טוּמְאָה הִיא, וְנָגְעָה טוּמְאָה בַּמּוּכְנִי – הַמּוּכְנִי טְמֵאָה לְעַצְמָהּ, דְּלָא חֲשִׁיבָה מִשִּׁידָּה. וְהִיא מִטַּלְטְלָה מְלֵאָה וְרֵיקָנִית, דְּיֵשׁ לָהּ בֵּית קִיבּוּל: וְאֵינָהּ נִמְדֶּדֶת עִמָּהּ. לְעִנְיַן טוּמְאָה, כְּדְפָרִישִׁית. דִּכְלִי עֵץ הַמַּחֲזִיק מ' סְאָה בְּלַח, שֶׁהֵן כּוֹרַיִים בְּיָבֵשׁ – טָהוֹר, כִּדְאָמְרִי' בְּ"בַמֶּה מַדְלִיקִין" (דף לה.) דִּכְלִי עֵץ אִיתְקַשׁ לְשַׂק, שֶׁיְּהֵא מִיטַּלְטֵל מָלֵא וְרֵיקָן, וְזוֹ אֵינוֹ מִיטַּלְטֵל מָלֵא. וּתְנַן בְּמַסֶּכֶת כֵּלִים*, וּמַיְיתִינַן בַּגְּמָ' דִּמְנָחוֹת: *הַשִּׁידָּה, ב"ה אוֹמְרִים נִמְדֶּדֶת מִבַּחוּץ – דְּרוֹאִין אוֹתָהּ כְּאִילּוּ הִיא עוֹמֶדֶת בְּתוֹךְ כְּלִי גָּדוֹל, וְאִם מַחֲזִיק אוֹתוֹ כְּלִי מ' סְאָה – טְהוֹרָה הַשִּׁידָּה, וְאע"פ שֶׁהִיא אֵינָהּ מַחֲזֶקֶת מ' סְאָה, דְּקָסָבַר: אַף עוֹבְיָהּ נִמְדָּד עִמָּהּ. וְהַמּוּכְנִי אֵינוֹ נִמְדָּד עִמָּהּ לְהַשְׁלִים, דְּרוֹאִין כְּאִילּוּ נִיטַּל הַמּוּכְנִי, וְאח"כ תִּנָּתֵן הַשִּׁידָּה לְתוֹךְ הַכְּלִי: וְאֵינָהּ מַצֶּלֶת עִמָּהּ בְּאֹהֶל הַמֵּת. דְּאִם הַשִּׁידָּה מַחֲזֶקֶת מ' [סְאָה], דְּאֵינָהּ מְקַבֶּלֶת טוּמְאָה – מַצֶּלֶת בְּאֹהֶל הַמֵּת, וַהֲוֵי אֹהֶל לְעַצְמָהּ. וְלֹא שֶׁנִּכְנְסָה לַבַּיִת שֶׁהַמֵּת בּוֹ – דְּא"כ אֵין כָּאן הַצָּלָה, שֶׁהֲרֵי הַגַּג מַאֲהִיל עַל הַטְּהָרוֹת מִלְמַעְלָה. אֶלָּא כְּגוֹן שֶׁנִּכְנְסָה לְבֵית הַקְּבָרוֹת, כִּדְאָמְרִינַן בְּעֵירוּבִין*: ר' יְהוּדָה אוֹמֵר אַף בְּבֵה"ק, מִפְּנֵי שֶׁיָּכוֹל לָחוֹץ בְּשִׁידָּה תֵּיבָה וּמִגְדָּל, בְּפֶ' "בַּכֹּל מְעָרְבִין"*, דְּקָסָבַר: אֹהֶל זָרוּק, כְּלוֹמַר אֹהֶל הַמִּיטַּלְטֵל – שְׁמֵיהּ אֹהֶל, וּמַפְסִיק[א] כְּלַפֵּי הַטּוּמְאָה. וְהַמּוּכְנִי, אִם הוּא גָּבוֹהַּ מִדּוֹפְנֵי הַשִּׁידָּה, וְכֵלִים [בּוֹלְטִים] מִלְמַעְלָה מִדּוֹפְנֵי הַשִּׁידָּה, וְגוֹבַהּ הַמּוּכְנִי מֵגֵין עֲלֵיהֶם – אֵינוֹ מַצִּילָן, דְּמוּכְנִי כְּלִי הוּא לְעַצְמוֹ וּמְקַבֵּל טוּמְאָה, וְאֵינוֹ חוֹצֵץ בִּפְנֵי הַטּוּמְאָה. וְרַבּוֹתַי דּוֹחֲקִין וּמְפָרְשִׁין אוֹתָהּ בְּאֹהֶל הַמֵּת מַמָּשׁ, וּבְשֶׁל חֶרֶס הַמּוּקֶּפֶת צָמִיד פָּתִיל. וְהַרְבֵּה תְּשׁוּבוֹת יֵשׁ: חֲדָא, דְּנִמְדֶּדֶת לֹא שַׁיָּיךְ בְּשֶׁל חֶרֶס, דְּלָא אִיתְקַשׁ לְשַׂק, וּבֵין מִיטַּלְטֵל וּבֵין אֵינוֹ מִיטַּלְטֵל – טָמֵא. וְעוֹד: אִם הַמּוּכְנִי מוּקָּף צָמִיד פָּתִיל – יַצִּיל בִּפְנֵי עַצְמוֹ כֵּלִים שֶׁבְּתוֹכוֹ. וְעוֹד: בְּפֵירוּשׁ נִשְׁנֵית בְּמַסֶּכֶת כֵּלִים בְּהִלְכוֹת כְּלֵי עֵץ, וְהִלְכוֹת כְּלֵי חֶרֶס נִשְׁנוּ לְבַדָּן, וְהִלְכוֹת כְּלֵי עֵץ נִשְׁנוּ לְבַדָּן: הַהִיא ר' שִׁמְעוֹן הִיא. וּמִיהוּ, מָעוֹת לָא חֲזוּ מִידֵּי. וּמוֹדֶה רַבִּי שִׁמְעוֹן דְּעוֹדָן עָלָיו – אָסוּר: מַנִּיחִין

תוספות

ומה נר דלהכי עבידא כו'. פי' בקונטרס: דדייק מדקתני "אבל לא ישן". משמע: דוקא ישן, אבל חדש – אפילו יחדו. וקשה לר"י: דלמאי דמסיק נמי מטה שיחדה והניח עליה מעות כו' תקשה ליה מנר של מתכת, דשרי ר' יהודה אפילו יחדו לעיל, מדקתני "חוץ מן הנר שהדליקו בה באותה שבת", אבל לא הדליקו בה באותה שבת – אע"פ שיחדה והדליקו בה בחול – שרי! ונראה לר"י: דלא דייק כלל מדקתני "אבל לא ישן" אלא דוקא בנר של חרס הוא דקאמ', דלהכי עבידא שתחלת עשייתה היא להדלקה, והוי כמו יחוד – שמיד שמדליקין בה פעם אחת נמאסת, ואין ראויה לתשמיש אחר, ולכך, תחלת עשייתה אינה אלא להדלקה, אע"פ שראויה לתשמיש אחר בין עשייה להדלקה – מ"מ אין עושין אותה לכך, שאין זה אלא זמן מועט. אבל בנר מתכת אין עשייתה להדלקה לבד, דראויה כל שעה לתשמיש אחר:

לא הניח עליה מעות מותר לטלטלה. ואגוזרות דאסר ר' יהודה לעיל (דף לו.) – נראה לר"י דאסר אפי' לא תקע בה, דאגוזרות לא חזיא אלא לתקיעה, ואין לחלק בין תקע ללא תקע. אבל מטה ונר חזי לתשמיש אחרינא: יש עליה מעות אסור לטלטלה. ע"כ במניח איירי, *דבשכח תנן פרק "נוטל" (לקמן קמב:): מנער הכר והן נופלות. ובמניח בשבת איירי, דבהניח מבעוד יום והיו עליה בין השמשות אפילו אין עליה מעות – אסור לטלטלה, כדקאמר בסיפא דמילתיה. וקשה: דאיך יכול להיות שמניח לדעת בשבת? וי"ל: כגון שהניח גוי או תינוק לדעת ישראל. וא"ת: אמאי לא מוכח מהכא בפ' "אין לדין" (ביצה כו:) דאין מוקצה לחצי שבת? וי"ל: דאיכא לאוקמא כגון שהניחם לדעת ישראל כדי להסירם אחר שעה, והוו כגמרו בידי אדם. ולמאי דפרישית לעיל דהא דיש מוקצה לחצי שבת היינו באיסור אכילה ולא בטלטול – א"ש: מוכני שלה. פי' בקונטרס: דגבי שידה תנן לה במסכת כלים (פי"ח מ"א) והיא עשויה למרכבת אנשים ונשים. *ואין נראה לר"י, דאי חזיא למדרס – לא שייך בה מדידה, דלא איתקש לשק ולא בעינן מיטלטל מלא וריקן, כדמוכח בפרק "אלו מומין" (בכורות לח. ושם) דפריך: ושאין לו תוך בכלי שטף מקבל טומאה הוא, והא דומיא דשק בעינן? ומשני: בהנך דחזו למדרסות. לכך נראה דאינה עשויה אלא לכלים. והא דאמר לקמן בפרק "רבי עקיבא" (דף פד. ושם), שלש תיבות הן: תיבה שפתחה מלדה – טמאה מדרס, מלמעלה – טמא מת. פי': אבל מדרס לא, לפי שאומרים עמוד ונעשה מלאכתנו. והבאה במדה – טהורה מכלום, פי': שיש לה מ' סאה, אור"י: דצריך לומר דלא קאי אפתחה מלדה דכיון דחזיא למדרס – אפילו באה במדה טמאה, כדפי'*): ואין מצלת עמה באהל המת. פי' בקונט': בבית הקברות[ג], שהכלים על דופני השידה. וקשה: דמי יביא טומא' על הכלים? ומפרש ריב"א: דמיירי שפיר דקיימא השידה באהל המת, ומוקפת צמיד פתיל. ואע"ג דכלי עץ אינו מציל בצמיד פתיל – היכא דמקבל ארבעים סאה מציל, כיון דלא מקבל טומאה. כדתנן במסכת כלים: ואלו מצילין בצמיד פתיל, כלי גללים כו' וכלי עץ הטהורים. ואין צ"ל דמוכני יש לו בית קיבול, אלא פשוטי כלי עץ הוא – ויש נקב בשידה בלדה והכלים בתוך השידה, והמוכני חופפת שם וממעטת אותו נקב עד שאין נשאר פותח טפח. וקאמר: כיון דנשמטת – אינו ממעט, דדוקא כי מבטלו שם ממעט בחלון, כדמוכח ב"לא יחפור" (ב"ב כ: ושם) דפריך אהא דקתני דכלי חרס ממעט בחלון: הא קחזי ליה! פי': ולא מבטל התם, והיכי ממעט? ומשני: דמטונף, ומיירי שאינו סותם כל הנקב. דאם סותם כל הנקב, אפי' אינו מבטלו שם – סותם, כדאמר בפ' בתרא (דף קנז.): בימי אבא שאול בן בטנית פקקו את המאור בטפיח. והתם לא בטלוהו, שאם ביטלוהו בשבת – היה חייב משום בונה, דהא מוסיפים על הבנין. אלא ודאי בלא ביטול איירי, ואפ"ה סותם. ובכלי עץ אמרינן נמי בפ' בתרא דמגילה (דף כו:): ההיא בי כנישתא דרומאי דהות פתיחה להההוא אנדרונא דהוו מחתי בה מיתי, בעו כהני למיזל לצלויי התם, אמרו ליה לרבא. אמר להו: זילו דלו תיבותא ואותבוהו אבבא, דה"ל כלי עץ העשוי לנחת. ומסתמא לא היו מבטלין אותו שם, שהרי ס"ת מניחין בתוכו? ומיהו, תבן וגרוגרות אין להם דין כלים, דאפי' סותמין כל החלון – צריכין ביטול, כדמוכח בפרק "לא יחפור" (ב"ב יט:). ולר"ת אין נראה לפרש דמוכני הוי אופן, דאין דרך להניח מעות על האופן, דקתני: "ואין גוררין אותה בשבת בזמן שיש עליה מעות". ומפרש: דמוכני היינו כן של שידה, כמו "את הכיור ואת כנו" (שמות ל) וכמו "מכונות" במלכים (א ז) פי': בסיס שהשידה מונחת עליו ויש בשידה נקב מתחתיה כנגד המוכני, והיא בבה"ק והטומאה נכנסת דרך נקב בשידה, ואין המוכני מגלת – כיון שהיא נשמטת, ואין מבטלין אותה שם. ומיירי נמי שאין סותמת כל הנקב אלא ממעטת אותו מפותח טפח, כדפי' לעיל. וצ"ל דמיירי שאין הטומאה כנגד הנקב, דכשהטומאה נגד הנקב – אפילו אין בו פותח טפח בוקעת ועולה, כדאמר בפ"ק דסוכה (דף יח. ושם): ארובה בבית ואין בה פותח טפח, טומאה כנגד ארובה – כל הבית טהור, לפי שבוקעת ועולה. וכן במסכת אהלות*, ומייתי לה ב"העור והרוטב" (חולין קכה:): חבילי המטה וסריגי חלונות כו', פירסן על המת באויר הנוגע כנגד הנקב – טמא, שלא כנגד הנקב – טהור. והתם אין בנקבים פותח טפח, דקתני רישא דמפסיק בין בית לעלייה: אין גוררין אותה בשבת בזמן שיש עליה מעות. מפרש ר"י: דכשהיא נשמטת היא כלי בפני עצמה, אבל כשאינה נשמטת – מותר לגוררה, אע"פ שיש עליה מעות דכיון שאינס ע"ג השידה שהיא עיקר הכלי – שרי: הא אין עליה מעות שריא אע"ג דהוו עליה כל בין השמשות. קשה לרשב"א: דמאי פריך? לוקמא בשכח, ולהכי, אין עליה מעות, אע"ג דהוו עליה כל בין השמשות – שריא, כדאמר בפרק "נוטל" (לקמן קמב:). ובזמן שיש עליה מעות – אסור לגוררה, אפי' בשכח שהוא טלטול גמור. וקמ"ל דבאינה נשמטת שרי לגוררה טלטול גמור! ומתרץ: דע"כ במניח איירי, דהא "אין גוררין אותה" משמע אפי' לצורך מקומה, ואי בשכח – הא אמרי' בפרק "נוטל" (ג"ז שם): לא שנו אלא לצורך גופו, אבל לצורך מקומו – מטלטלו ועודן עליו. (*ומיהו, מטה שיחדה והניח עליה מעות איכא למימר דמודה ר"ש דמקפיד עליה מיחד לה מקום, כדאמרי' בריש "כל הכלים" (שם קכג. ושם): הכל מודים, כיון דקפיד עליה – מיחד לה מקום ופר"ת: דהכל מודים – אפי' ר"ש. והא דפריך לעיל מנר – היינו משום שאין לחלק בין מטה לשאר דברים אלא כשהניח עליה מעות, ולפ"ז לא קשה לעיל אפי' הקונטרס שפי' דדייק מדקתני "אבל לא ישן"):

*) [ועי' תוס' מנחות לא. ד"ה שידה].

וכסוכה [מג:] דקאמר גבי מורביות וכו' ע"ש משמע דדוקא ע"י ע"ה אבל ת"ח לא היו עושין אף על גב דבייתוסין לא הניחו לדעתם לא תקיב כשבת א"נ לא היו יכולין לנערס בלא טלטול קצת אע"ג דקאמר ושמטוס [תו"י]

ורשב"א פירש במשניות דכיון דאין נכנסין לה אלא באקראי בעלמא לא הוי בכך מיוחד למדרס שהרי ספינה עשויה ליסב בה בני אדם ואפ"ה כשמחזקת מ' סאה טהורה [תוספות ישנים]

רבינו חננאל

הכל פמוט שהוא מנורה שאין לה אלא קנה אחד ואין על ראשה אלא כף אחת הדליקו עליו באותה שבת דברי הכל (אחד) [אסור]. לא הדליקו עליו דברי הכל מותר. הא דאמר רב מטה שייחדה למעות והניח עליה מעות*) והיו עליה המעות כל בין השמשות. אע"פ שנטלו המעות עכשיו ואינם במטה אסור לטלטלה. אסיקנא דרב כר' יהודה אמרה לשמעתיה. מתיב ר' אליעזר הא דתנן בכלים פ' י"ח מוכני שלה בזמן שהיא נשמטת אינה חבור ואינה נמדדת עמה ואינה נצלת באהל המת. פי' (כאן) [כן] של שידה בזמן שהיא נשמטת אינה כמו השידה ואינה נשלפת עמה ולא נצלת עמה מפני שהשידה כלי וזו אינה כלי**) מכללא לפיכך אמרו אין גוררין

*) ע"ס כאן. **) ע"ס כאן ועי' ברמב"ן וברשב"א.

שהכיר ר' זירא בשמועה זו נחשת היא וחדש ואינו נמאס ואם הדליקו עליו נר באותו שבת הרי הוא מוקצה מחמת איסור ולפי שהוא מנוקה מלכלוך לא הוי מוקצה מחמת מיאום ועל דעת ר' מאיר שהיה אוסר טלטול הפמוט אם לא הדליקו עליו באותה שבת זה הפמוט אע"פ שהוא כחדש שאינו נמאס אסור לטלטלו לפי שנהיה מוקצה מחמת איסורו מפני הנר שהדליקו עליו באותו יום ועל דעת ר' יהודה אוסר טלטול [נר ישן] (חדש) [של חרש] הרי הפמוט מותר לטלטלו לפי שנראה נר חדש ואינו מאום ולפיכך באה הקושיא מידי למימרא דר' יהודה מוקצה מחמת מיאום אית ליה מוקצה מחמת איסורו לית ליה והתניא ובגמ' דבני מערב גרסי מעשה היה וטילטלו פמוט מתחת הנר בשבת מה אנן קיימין אי כר' מאיר אפילו פמוט יהא אסור כמו שאמר כל הנרות מטלטלין חוץ מן הנר שהדליקו בה באותה שבת וזה הפמוט בו באותה שבת והרי הוא לר' מאיר אסור ואי כר"ש אפילו נר עצמו יהא מותר וכל שכן הפמוט שיהא מותר ואין אנו צריכים להודיענו זה ההיתר בפמוט על דעת ר' שמעון שהיה מותר לטלטלו וכ"ש פמוט מתחתיו אלא כן אנן כר' יהודה דר' יהודה אומר נר מאום פמוט אינו מאום וזה סיוע הפירוש שפירשנו אבל בארתי זה הטעם כי ראיתי מי שפירש אותו בטעם אחר וסבר שר' שמעון שהוא

רב נסים גאון

זהב באה קנים אינה באה וזהב אינה באה קנים השיבו ההוא פמוט מיתקרי והפמוט

מסורת הש"ס

[לקמן מו.] כלים פי"ח מ"ב

פי"ח מ"א

[דף לח.]

[דף ל.]

[שם]

[הוא בתוספתא דאהלות פ"טו]

רש"ל מ"ז ומהרש"א כתב שזהו שייך לסוף דיבור שאח"ז ועי' מהר"מ

הגהות הב"ח

(א) רש"י ד"ה ואינה מצלת וכו' ומפסיק בפני הטומאה: (ב) תוס' ד"ה ואין מצלת וכו' בבית הקברות והכלים מעל דופני השידה:

גליון הש"ס

גמ' בזמן שהיא נשמטת. עי' לקמן דף מח ע"ב תוס' ד"ה דבר תורה. תוס' ד"ה הא אין וכו'. והא למימר דמודה ר"ש. עי' לעיל ר' מו ע"א תוס' ד"ה הא ר' יהודה.

הָכִי נַמִי מִיסְתַּבְּרָא דְּרַב כְּרַבִּי יְהוּדָה סְבִירָא לֵיהּ, דְּאָמַר רַב: [א]מַנִּיחִין נֵר עַל גַּבֵּי דֶּקֶל בְּשַׁבָּת, וְאֵין מַנִּיחִין נֵר ע"ג דֶּקֶל בְּיוֹ"ט. אִי אָמְרַתְּ בִּשְׁלָמָא דְּרַב כְּרַבִּי יְהוּדָה סְבִירָא לֵיהּ – הַיְינוּ דְּשַׁנֵּי בֵּין שַׁבָּת לְיוֹ"ט, אֶלָּא אִי אָמְרַתְּ כְּרַבִּי שִׁמְעוֹן סְבִירָא לֵיהּ – מָה לִי שַׁבָּת וּמָה לִי יוֹ"ט! וְרַב כְּרַבִּי יְהוּדָה ס"ל?! וְהָא בְּעוּ מִינֵּיהּ דְּרַב: מַהוּ לְטַלְטוּלֵי שְׁרָגָא דַּחֲנוּכְּתָא מִקַּמֵּי חַבָּרֵי בְּשַׁבַּתָּא? וַאֲמַר לְהוּ: שַׁפִּיר דָּמֵי. – שְׁעַת הַדְּחָק שָׁאנֵי. דְּהָא א"ל רַב כָּהֲנָא וְרַב אַשִׁי לְרַב: הָכִי הִלְכְתָא? אֲמַר לְהוּ: *כְּדַי הוּא ר' שִׁמְעוֹן לִסְמוֹךְ עָלָיו בִּשְׁעַת הַדְּחָק. בְּעָא מִינֵּיהּ רֵישׁ לָקִישׁ מֵר' יוֹחָנָן: חִטִּים שֶׁזְּרָעָן בַּקַּרְקַע, וּבֵיצִים שֶׁתַּחַת תַּרְנְגוֹלֶת מַהוּ? כִּי לֵית לֵיהּ לְר' שִׁמְעוֹן מוּקְצֶה – הֵיכָא דְּלָא דַּחְיֵיהּ בְּיָדַיִם, הֵיכָא דְּדַחְיֵיהּ בְּיָדַיִם – אִית לֵיהּ מוּקְצֶה, אוֹ דִּילְמָא [ב]לָא שְׁנָא? א"ל: אֵין מוּקְצֶה לְרַבִּי שִׁמְעוֹן אֶלָּא שֶׁמֶן שֶׁבַּנֵּר בְּשָׁעָה שֶׁהוּא דּוֹלֵק, הוֹאִיל וְהוּקְצָה לְמִצְוָתוֹ *הוּקְצָה לְאִיסּוּרוֹ. וְלֵית לֵיהּ הוּקְצָה לְמִצְוָתוֹ?! *וְהָתַנְיָא: סִיכְּכָהּ כְּהִלְכָתָהּ, וְעִיטְּרָהּ בְּקְרָמִים וּבִסְדִינִין הַמְצוּיָּירִין, וְתָלָה בָּהּ אֱגוֹזִין, אֲפַרְסְקִין, שְׁקֵדִים וְרִמּוֹנִין, וְאַפַּרְכְּלֵי שֶׁל עֲנָבִים, וַעֲטָרוֹת שֶׁל שִׁבּוֹלִין, יֵינוֹת, שְׁמָנִים וּסְלָתוֹת – אָסוּר לְהִסְתַּפֵּק מֵהֶן עַד מוֹצָאֵי יוֹ"ט הָאַחֲרוֹן, וְאִם הִתְנָה עֲלֵיהֶן הַכֹּל לְפִי תְּנָאוֹ. וּמִמַּאי דְּר' שִׁמְעוֹן הִיא – דְּתָנֵי *ר' חִיָּיא בַּר יוֹסֵף קַמֵּיהּ דְּר' יוֹחָנָן: אֵין נוֹטְלִין עֵצִים מִן הַסּוּכָּה בְּיוֹ"ט אֶלָּא מִן הַסָּמוּךְ לָהּ, וְר' שִׁמְעוֹן מַתִּיר. וְשָׁוִין בְּסוּכַּת הֶחָג בֶּחָג שֶׁהִיא אֲסוּרָה. וְאִם הִתְנָה עָלֶיהָ – הַכֹּל לְפִי תְּנָאוֹ. – כְּעֵין שֶׁמֶן שֶׁבַּנֵּר קָאָמְרִינַן, הוֹאִיל וְהוּקְצָה לְמִצְוָתוֹ הוּקְצָה לְאִיסּוּרוֹ. אִיתְּמַר נַמִי, א"ר חִיָּיא בַּר אַבָּא א"ר יוֹחָנָן: אֵין מוּקְצֶה לְרַבִּי שִׁמְעוֹן אֶלָּא כְּעֵין שֶׁמֶן שֶׁבַּנֵּר בְּשָׁעָה שֶׁהוּא דּוֹלֵק, הוֹאִיל וְהוּקְצָה לְמִצְוָתוֹ – הוּקְצָה לְאִיסּוּרוֹ. אָמַר רַב יְהוּדָה אָמַר שְׁמוּאֵל: אֵין מוּקְצֶה לְר' שִׁמְעוֹן אֶלָּא גְּרוֹגָרוֹת וְצִימּוּקִים בִּלְבַד. וּמִידֵּי אַחֲרִינָא לָא?! וְהָתַנְיָא: *הָיָה אוֹכֵל בִּתְאֵנִים וְהוֹתִיר וְהֶעֱלָן לַגַּג לַעֲשׂוֹת מֵהֶן גְּרוֹגָרוֹת. בַּעֲנָבִים וְהוֹתִיר וְהֶעֱלָן לַגַּג לַעֲשׂוֹת מֵהֶן צִימּוּקִין – לֹא יֹאכַל עַד שֶׁיַּזְמִין. וְכֵן אַתָּה אוֹמֵר בַּאֲפַרְסְקִין וַחֲבוּשִׁין, וּבִשְׁאָר כָּל מִינֵי פֵּירוֹת. מַנִּי? אִילֵימָא רַבִּי יְהוּדָה – וּמָה הֵיכָא דְּלָא דַּחְיֵיהּ בְּיָדַיִם – אִית לֵיהּ מוּקְצֶה, הֵיכָא דְּדַחְיֵיהּ בְּיָדַיִם לֹא כָּל שֶׁכֵּן? אֶלָּא לָאו – ר' שִׁמְעוֹן הִיא! לְעוֹלָם – רַבִּי יְהוּדָה, וְ"אוֹכֵל" אִצְטְרִיכָא לֵיהּ, סד"א: כֵּיוָן דְּקָאָכֵיל וְאָזֵיל – לָא לִיבָּעֵי הַזְמָנָה, קמ"ל: כֵּיוָן דְּהֶעֱלָן לַגַּג – אַסּוּחֵי אַסְּחֵי לְדַעְתֵּיהּ מִינַּיְיהוּ. *בְּעָא מִינֵּיהּ רַבִּי שִׁמְעוֹן בַּר רַבִּי מֵרַבִּי: פַּצְעִילֵי

רש"י

מַנִּיחִין נֵר. מִבְּעוֹד יוֹם: ע"ג דֶּקֶל. וְיִדְלַק שָׁם בְּשַׁבָּת, דְּלֵיכָּא לְמֵיחַשׁ לִכְשֶׁיִּכְבֶּה לִישְׁקְלֵיהּ מִינֵּיהּ וְנִמְצָא מִשְׁתַּמֵּשׁ בִּמְחוּבָּר. דְּכֵיוָן דְּאַקְלְיֵיהּ לְדָבָר הָאָסוּר בֵּין הַשְּׁמָשׁוֹת – אִיתְקְלַי לְכוּלֵּי יוֹמָא: וְאֵין מַנִּיחִין כו' בְּיוֹם טוֹב. דְּשָׁקֵיל וּמַנַּח לֵיהּ, וּמִשְׁתַּמֵּשׁ בְּאִילָן: מַה לִי שַׁבָּת כו'. בְּשַׁבָּת נַמִי שָׁקֵיל לֵיהּ לִכְשֶׁיִּכְבֶּה: שְׁרָגָא דַּחֲנוּכְּתָא. אַחַר שֶׁכָּבָה: מִקַּמֵּי חַבָּרֵי. שֶׁלֹּא יִרְאוּהוּ בֶּחָצֵר, כִּדְאָמְרִינַן בְּפִרְקִין דִּלְעֵיל (דף כא:) דְּנוֹתְנוֹ בַּטֶּפַח הַסָּמוּךְ לִרְשׁוּת הָרַבִּים. וְיֵדְעוּ שֶׁהִדְלִיקוּ בּוֹ נֵר, וְהֵם גָּזְרוּ שֶׁלֹּא לְהַדְלִיק. אִי נַמִי: בְּיוֹם חַגָּם אֵין מַנִּיחִין לִדְלוֹק אוֹר אֶלָּא בְּבֵית ע"ז: חַבָּרֵי. שֵׁם אוּמָּה שֶׁהָיְתָה עִם פַּרְסִיִּים: הָכִי הִילְכְתָא. בִּתְמִיָּה: בִּשְׁעַת הַדְּחָק. סַכָּנָה. אַלְמָא: שֶׁלֹּא בִּשְׁעַת הַדְּחָק – אָסוּר: שֶׁזְּרָעָן בַּקַּרְקַע. וַעֲדַיִין לֹא הִשְׁרִישׁוּ, מַהוּ לִלְקוֹט וְלֶאֱכוֹל? אֵין מוּקְצֶה לְר' שִׁמְעוֹן בְּדָבָר הָרָאוּי. אֶלָּא בְּשֶׁמֶן שֶׁבַּנֵּר, בְּשָׁעָה שֶׁהוּא דּוֹלֵק כִּדְתַנְיָא לְעֵיל: הוֹאִיל וְהוּקְצָה לְמִצְוָתוֹ. לַשַּׁבָּת: הוּקְצָה לְאִיסּוּרוֹ. אִיסּוּר כִּיבּוּי: וְהוּקְצָה לְמִצְוָתוֹ לֵית לֵיהּ. בִּתְמִיָּה. דְּקס"ד: שֶׁמֶן שֶׁבַּנֵּר דַּוְקָא קָאָמַר, דְּאִיכָּא תַּרְתֵּי: מוּקְצֶה לְמִצְוָה, וּמוּקְצֶה שֶׁל שְׁעַת דְּלֵיקָתוֹ מִשּׁוּם אִיסּוּר כִּיבּוּי. אֲבָל מוּקְצֶה לְמִצְוָה גְּרֵידָא – לֹא אָסַר, וַאֲפִילּוּ בִּשְׁעַת הַמִּצְוָה: וְהָתַנְיָא סִיכְּכָהּ. לַסּוּכָּה כו': קְרָמִים. בִּגְדֵי לִבְעוֹנִים, שֶׁקּוֹרִין אוברייכ"א: אֲפַרְסְקִין. פירסיק"ש בְּלַעַ"ז: יֵינוֹת שְׁמָנִים. בִּכְלֵי זְכוּכִית: עַד מוֹצָאֵי יוֹ"ט הָאַחֲרוֹן. וְהָכָא מוּקְצֶה לְמִצְוָה – אִיכָּא, מוּקְצֶה דְּאִיסּוּר – לֵיכָּא. דְּאִי מִשּׁוּם סְתִירַת אֹהֶל – כִּי מָטָא חוּלּוֹ שֶׁל מוֹעֵד לִשְׁתְּרֵי, דּוּמְיָא דְּנֵר שֶׁכָּבָה: וְהָא מִמַּאי דְּר' שִׁמְעוֹן הִיא. דְּמוֹתִיבְנָא לָךְ מִינֵּיהּ: דְּתָנֵי ר' חִיָּיא כו' אֵין נוֹטְלִין עֵצִים. בְּפֶסַח וַעֲצֶרֶת מִסּוּכָּה הָעֲשׂוּיָה לְצֵל, וַאֲפִילּוּ נָפְלוּ – מִשּׁוּם מוּקְצֶה, דְּאִיתְקְצַאי מֵחֲמַת סְתִירַת אֹהֶל בְּיוֹ"ט: אֶלָּא מִן הַסָּמוּךְ לָהּ. אִם סָמַךְ חֲבִילוֹת עֵצִים אֵצֶל דּוֹפְנָהּ – לֵיכָּא אִיסּוּר מוּקְצֶה, דְּדַעְתֵּיהּ עִילָּוֵיהּ מֵאֶתְמוֹל לְמִישְׁקְלִינְהוּ לְמָחָר, דְּלָא סָתַר בְּהוּ אֹהֶלָא. וּמֵהָךְ דְּתָנֵי ר' חִיָּיא בַּר יוֹסֵף הֲוֵי מָצֵי לְאוֹתְבֵי בְּרֵישָׁא, אֶלָּא נִיחָא לֵיהּ לְאוֹתְבֵי מִמַּתְנִיתָא דְּר' חִיָּיא וְר' אוֹשַׁעְיָא, כִּדְאָמְרִינַן בְּעָלְמָא (חולין דף קמא.): כָּל מַתְנִיתָא דְּלָא מִיתַּנְיָא בֵּי ר' חִיָּיא כו': וְר' שִׁמְעוֹן מַתִּיר. אִם נָפְלָה, דְּלֵית לֵיהּ מוּקְצֶה. וְהָכִי מוֹקְמִינַן לֵיהּ בְּמַסֶּכֶת בֵּיצָה: וְשָׁוִין בְּסוּכַּת הֶחָג בֶּחָג. שֶׁהוּקְצָה לְמִצְוָתָהּ. דְּמִצְוָתָהּ כָּל שִׁבְעָה, אַלְמָא: כָּל שְׁעַת מִצְוָתָהּ נוֹהֵג מוּקְצֶה שֶׁלָּהּ, וְאַע"ג דְּלֵיכָּא אִיסּוּר סְתִירָה: כְּעֵין שֶׁמֶן קָאָמִינָא. וְלֹא מִשּׁוּם אִיסּוּר, אֶלָּא מִשּׁוּם מִצְוָה. דְּהוֹאִיל דְּהוּקְצָה לְמִצְוָתוֹ דְּשַׁבָּת – הוּקְצָה לְכָל זְמַן אִיסּוּר דְּלֵיקָתוֹ, וְלֹא יוֹתֵר. דְּאֵין מִצְוָתוֹ אֶלָּא בִּשְׁעַת דְּלֵיקָתוֹ, וּמִשֶּׁכָּבָה – אֵין בּוֹ מִצְוָה. אֲבָל בְּסוּכַּת הֶחָג – מִצְוָתָהּ כָּל שִׁבְעָה, וְהִקְצָאָתָהּ כָּל זְמַן מִצְוָתָהּ: אֶלָּא גְּרוֹגָרוֹת וְצִמּוּקִין. גְּרוֹגָרוֹת תְּאֵנִים שֶׁמַּעֲלֶה לַגַּג לְיַבְּשָׁן, וּמִשֶּׁנִּשְׁתַּהוּ שָׁם מְעַט אֵין רְאוּיִם לַאֲכִילָה עַד שֶׁיִּתְיַיבְּשׁוּ. וְכֵן לִימּוּקִים דַּעֲנָבִים: הָיָה אוֹכֵל בִּתְאֵנִים. רְבוּתָא אַשְׁמְעֵי'[(א)], דַּהֲוָה אָכֵיל וְאָזֵיל, מִכֵּיוָן דְּאַסְּקִינְהוּ – אַסַּח דַּעְתֵּיהּ וְאַקְצְיָן: חֲבוּשִׁין. קויי"ן: וְכֵן אַתָּה אוֹמֵר כו'. וְאַע"ג דְּהָנֵי חֲזֵי כָּל שַׁעְתָּא, וַאֲפִי' נִשְׁתַּהוּ לֹא נִתְקַלְקְלוּ, מִיהוּ, הוֹאִיל וְאַקְצִינְהוּ – אֲסִירִי: אִי נֵימָא ר"י. לָמָּה לִי הָנָךְ דְּנָקַט דְּדַחְיִנְהוּ בְּיָדַיִם? אֲפִי' הִכְנִיסָן נַמִי לָאוֹצָר – בָּעוּ הַזְמָנָה: פַּצְעִילֵי

תוספות

הכי נמי מסתברא דרב כר' יהודה ס"ל. בכמה מקומות אשכחן דרב סבר כר' יהודה דאסר מטה שייחדה למעות והניח עליה מעות ואילו לר' שמעון שרי, דהא שרי אנוגרות אפי' תקע בה כמה זימני. ודכרכי דזוזי (לעיל דף יט:). אלא דבעי לאוכוחי דסבר כר' יהודה ב"מיגו דאיתקצאי בין השמשות" כו': **מקמי** חברי בשבתא. שביום חג שלהם לא היו מניחין נר אלא בבית ע"ז, ומאי דקמבעיא ליה בנר חנוכה טפי מבנר שבת – משום דלצורך אכילה היו מניחים להם, ואע"ג דבשעת הסכנה אמרינן ב"במה מדליקין" (לעיל דף כא:) דמניחה על שולחנו ודיו – הכא מיירי אם יארע שלא הניחה על שולחנו. א"נ אומר ר"י: דשעת הסכנה דלעיל לאו סכנת חברים קאמר, אלא סכנת גזירה, שגזרו שלא להדליק נר חנוכה: **היכא** דדחייה בידים אית ליה. ואף על גב דנר שכבה שרי ר' שמעון, אף על גב דדחייה בידים – דהתם שאני, כיון שכבר פסק דיחוי שלה. אבל הכא – לעולם הן דחויין, כל זמן שמונחין שם: **אלא** שמן שבנר. לאו דווקא שבנר, דההוא אסור משום מכבה, כדאמר בפ"ב דביצה (דף כב.): המסתפק ממנו – חייב משום מכבה, אלא המטפטף מנר. ומשום דמוקצה למצותו לא אסור [א]נר הדולק לטלטל כדפרישית לעיל, אלא כדאמר בסוף פירקין: משום דהוי בסיס לדבר האסור, תימה לר"י: דאמאי נקט שמן שבנר? טפי ה"ל למינקט: אין מוקצה לר' שמעון אלא גרוגרות וצימוקין, דדמו טפי לחיטין שזרען – דלא איתקצאי לא מחמת מצוה, ולא מחמת איסור. וליכא למימר דסבר ר' יוחנן דלר' שמעון אין מוקצה בגרוגרות וצימוקין – דהא רבי קאמר בסמוך דאית ליה לרבי שמעון מוקצה בגרוגרות וצימוקין, ומסתמא לא פליג: **עד** מוצאי י"ט האחרון של חג. הקשה ר"ת: ביום טוב האחרון, דלא אסר אלא מטעם "מיגו דאיתקצאי בין השמשות" מחמת יום שעבר, והא רבי שמעון שרי מותר השמן שבנר, אף על גב דהוקצה בין השמשות למצותו משום יום הבא! ונראה לר"י: דבמה שאוסרת הברייתא יום טוב האחרון – לא אתיא כר' שמעון: **ולא** מן הסמוך לה. בפרק "המביא כדי יין" (ביצה ל: ושם) גרס במשנה: אלא מן הסמוך לה, ופריך בגמ': והא קסתר אוהלא! ומשני: מאי "מן הסמוך לה" – סמוך לדפנות. והשתא, אי גרס בברייתא דהכא "אלא מן הסמוך לה" – הוי בסמוך לדפנות. ואי גרס "ולא מן הסמוך לה" – מיירי במה שעל הסכך. וטעמא משום דסתר אוהלא, כדאמר התם: **ואם** התנה הכל לפי תנאו. בריש "המביא" (ג"ז שם) פריך עלה: והא קא סתר אוהלא! ומוקי לה בסוכה נפולה וברעועה, דמאתמול דעתיה עלה: **אלא** בגרוגרות וצימוקין. בירושלמי מפ': שמסריחין בינתיים, כיון שמתקלקלין כל כך – אין דעתו לקחתם עד שיתקנו היטב: **וכן** אתה אומר באפרסקין. אף על פי שאין מתקלקלין כל כך – מקצה אותם מדעתו: **היכא** דלא דחייה בידים אית ליה מוקצה. כגון הא דתנן בפרק "מפנין" (לקמן קכו:): ולא את האוצר, ותנן נמי בפרק בתרא (דף קנו:), רבי יהודה אומר: אם לא היתה נבלה מע"ש – אסורה כו': **ואוכל** איצטריכא ליה. מדנקט אוכל במוקצה דדחייה בידים, נראה דאזיל ואכיל – שרי ליה לר"י במוקצה דלא דחייה בידים, כגון גבי אוצר: לדבריו

עין משפט נר מצוה

נב א מיי' פ"ה מהלכות שבת הלכה יז ופ"ד מהלכות י"ט הלכה ה סמג לאוין סה טור שו"ע או"ח סימן רעז סעיף ד וסימן תקי"ד סעיף ו:

נג ב מיי' פכ"ו מהלכות שבת הלכה יד סמג לאוין סה טוש"ע או"ח סימן שי סעיף ב:

רבינו חננאל

אותה בשבת. בזמן שיש עליה מעות. פי' מוכני כן. מלשון את הכיור ואת כנו. נמדלת מלשון שילוף. כדתנן המידל בגפנים. וגרסינן במשקין (מ"ק ג) מאי מדלי שלופי. נמצלת מלשון צל. קתני מיהת אין גוררין אותה בשבת בזמן שיש עליה מעות הא אין עליה מעות שרי. ואע"ג דהוו עליה בין השמשות. ושנינן משנה זו לר' שמעון היא. ורב דאמר כרבי יהודה. דהא רב הוא דאמר מניחין נר ע"ג דקל בשבת [ואין מניחין נר ע"ג דקל ביום טוב]. מכלל דרב כר' יהודה סבר ליה דאמר הנר שהדליקו בו בשבת אין מטלטלין אותו. אבל ביו"ט שמטלטלין אותו ונמצא משתמש במחובר לקרקע אסור. (ואין מניחין נר ע"ג דקל ביו"ט) ואוקימנא אליבא דר' יהודה דשני ליה בין שבת ליו"ט. אבל ר' שמעון לא שני ליה בטלטול הנר בין שבת ליו"ט. איני דרב כר' יהודה עביד ליה. והא רב התיר לטלטל נר מפני חבארי בשבת. ושנינן הא אמר רב בהא כדאי הוא ר"ש לסמוך עליו בשעת הדחק מכלל דרב סבר לית הלכתא כר' שמעון. והא דא"ר יוחנן אין מוקצה לר"ש אלא מידי דאיתקצאי לאיסורא כגון שמן שבנר בשעה שדולק או כגון עיטורי סוכה וכיוצא בהן הואיל והוקצו למצוה פשוטה היא

רב נסים גאון

שהוא מתיר בנר אוסר בפמוט ולדבריהם בתלמוד ארץ ישראל או כר' שמעון אפילו נר עצמו יהא מותר נתבאר כבר שר' שמעון מתיר הנר עצמו וכ"ש הפמוט: **מהו** לטלטולי שרגא דחנוכה מיקמי חבארא בשבתא. שמענו כי בימי החברים פרסיי' היו חברים מחזרין בכל בתי ישראל ומכבין את הנרות ולוקחין מכל בית נר והיה צער גדול לישר' מזה המעשה מפני שהיו מוליכין את נרותיהם לע"ז ואשכחנן בפרק ב' (דגיטין דף טז) רבה בר בר חנה חלש על ר' יהודה ורבנן לשיולי ביה בעו מיניה שנים שהביאו גט ממדינת הים צריכים שיאמרו בפנינו נכתב בפנינו נחתם או אין צריכין אמר להו אין צריכין ומה אילו אמרו בפנינו גירשה מי לא מהימני אדהכי אתא ההוא חברא שקלא לשרגא מיקמייהו אמרי רחמנא או בטולך או בטולא דבר עשו למימרא דרומאי מעלו מפרסאי והא תני ר' חייא מאי דכתיב (איוב כח) אלהים הבין דרכה והוא ידע את מקומה ידע הקב"ה בישראל שאין יכולים לקבל גזירות של עשו הרשע לפיכך הגלה אותם לבבל ובמס' יבמות בפרק הבא על יבמתו (דף סג) אמרו מאי דכתיב בגוי נבל אכעיסם ר' יוחנן אמר אלו חברים אמרו ליה לר' יוחנן אתו חבארי לבבל (שאג) [שנא] ונפל [א"ל] מקבלי שוחדא תריץ ויתיב גזרו על שלש מפני שלש על בשר מפני המתנות על מרחצאות מפני טבילה קא מחטטי שכבי מפני ששמחים ביום אידם ובשאלתות דרב אחא מן שבחא כך פי' בפרשת וארא אל אברהם ובמלכות פרסיים היו חברים שבהן מחזרין על בתי ישראל ומכבין את הנרות וחותין את הגחלים ומוליכין אותן לבית האור שלהן שהיא ע"ז ולא היו עוזבים לא אש ולא גחלים שילינו בלילה חוץ מע"ז שלהן שהיא בית נורא: **כדי** הוא ר' שמעון בן יוחי לסמוך עליו בשעת הדחק. הוא ר' שמעון שאמר הנר שכבתה מותר לטלטלה דלית ליה מוקצה וכל ר' שמעון סתם במשנה ובברייתא הוא ר"ש בן יוחאי וכל ר' יהודה סתם הוא ר' יהודה בר' אלעאי ובמס' מנחות בפרק הקומץ (דף יח) אמרו מפני שר' יהודה בנו של ר' אלעאי ור' אילעאי תלמידו של ר' אליעזר שנה לך משנת ר' אליעזר:

מסורת הש"ס

[כריתות ע. עירובין מו. גיטין יט. נדה ו. ט:]

נ"ל והוקצה [תוס' ישנים]

לעיל כב. ביצה ל: סוכה י. [תוספתא סוכה פ"א]

ביצה ל:

ביצה כו:

[ביצה מ.]

הגהות הב"ח

(א) רש"י ד"ה היה אוכל וכו' רבותא אשמעי' אע"פ דהוה:

גליון הש"ס

תוס' ד"ה אלא שמן וכו' נר הדולק לטלטל כדפי' לעיל דף מב ע"ב תוס' ד"ה ואין נאותין:

נד א מיי' פכ"ו מהל' שבת הלכה יד סמג לאוין סה טוש"ע או"ח סימן שי סעיף ב:

[דף כו.]

נה ב ג מיי' פ"ב מהל' יו"ט הלכה ב סמג לאוין עה טור שו"ע או"ח סימן תצז סעיף ב וסימן תצח סעיף ג:

[ועי' תוספות ביצה ט. ד"ה ת"ר]

והא דלא בעי באפרוח חי אם מותר לטלטל הקינה משום דאפשר לאפריחו [תוספות ישנים]

[ביצה ג.]

א"נ הוי מוקצה מחמת חסרון כיס [תו"י]

[ועי' תוספות חולין יט. ד"ה אמר רב הונא]

פצעילי *תמרה לרבי שמעון מהו? א"ל: *אאין מוקצה לר"ש אלא גרוגרות וצימוקין בלבד. ורבי לית ליה מוקצה?! והתנן: *באין משקין ושוחטין את המדבריות, אבל משקין ושוחטין את הבייתות. ותניא: *גאלו הן מדבריות – כל' שיוצאות בפסח ונכנסות ברביעה. בייתות – כל שיוצאות ורועות חוץ לתחום, ובאות ולנות בתוך התחום. ר' אומר: אלו ואלו בייתות הן, ואלו הן מדבריות – כל שרועות באפר ואין נכנסות לישוב לא בימות החמה ולא בימות הגשמים. איבעית אימא: הני נמי כגרוגרות וצימוקין דמיין. ואי בעית אימא: לדבריו דר"ש קאמר ליה, וליה לא סבירא ליה. ואיבעית אימא: לדבריהם דרבנן קאמר להו: לדידי – לית לי מוקצה כלל, לדידכו – אודו לי מיהת, דהיכא דיוצאות בפסח ונכנסות ברביעה, דבייתות נינהו. ורבנן אמרו ליה: לא, מדבריות נינהו. אמר רבה בר בר חנה אמר ר' יוחנן: אמרו "הלכה כרבי שמעון". ומי אמר ר' יוחנן הכי? והא בעא מיניה ההוא סבא קרויא, ואמרי לה סרויא, מר' יוחנן: קינה של תרנגולת מהו לטלטולי בשבת? אמר ליה: כלום עשוי אלא לתרנגולין? הכא במאי עסקינן – דאית ביה אפרוח מת. הניחא למר בר אמימר משמיה *(דרב) *דאמר: מודה היה ר' שמעון בבעלי חיים שמתו שאסורין, אלא למר בריה דרב יוסף משמיה דרבא דאמר: חלוק היה רבי שמעון [אפי'] בבעלי חיים שמתו, שהן מותרין, מאי איכא למימר? הכא במאי עסקינן – בדאית ביה ביצה. והאמר *רב נחמן: מאן דאית ליה מוקצה – אית ליה נולד, דלית ליה מוקצה – לית ליה נולד! דאית ביה ביצת אפרוח. כי אתא רב יצחק בר' יוסף א"ר יוחנן: הלכה כר' יהודה, ור' יהושע בן לוי אמר: הלכה כרבי שמעון. אמר רב יוסף: היינו דאמר רבה בר בר חנה א"ר יוחנן: אמרו "הלכה כרבי שמעון". 'אמרו' – וליה לא סבירא ליה. א"ל אביי לרב יוסף: ואת לא תסברא דר' יוחנן כר' יהודה? הא ר' אבא ורבי אסי איקלעו לבי ר' אבא דמן חיפא, ונפל מנרתא על גלימיה דר' אסי ולא טילטלה. מאי טעמא? לאו משום דרבי אסי תלמידיה דר' יוחנן הוה, ור' יוחנן כר' יהודה ס"ל דאית ליה מוקצה? א"ל: מנרתא קאמרת? מנרתא שאני. דא"ר אחא בר חנינא א"ר אסי: הורה ריש לקיש בצידן: מנורה הניטלת בידו אחת – מותר לטלטלה, בשתי ידיו – אסור לטלטלה. ור' יוחנן אמר: אנו אין לנו אלא בנר כרבי שמעון. אבל מנורה, בין ניטלה בידו אחת בין ניטלה בשתי ידיו – אסור לטלטלה. וטעמא מאי? רבה ורב יוסף דאמרי תרווייהו: הואיל ואדם קובע לה מקום. אמר ליה אביי לרב יוסף: והרי כילת חתנים, דאדם קובע לו מקום, ואמר שמואל משום רבי חייא: *כילת חתנים מותר

מותר

רש"י

פצעילי תמרה.א) תמרים הנלקטים קודם בישולן, וכונסין אותם בסלים שעושין מלולבין, והן מתבשלות מאליהן. מהו לאכול מהן קודם בישולן? מי מודה בהן דמוקצות הן כגרוגרות וצימוקין, או לא: אלא בגרוגרות וצימוקין. דאיכא תרתי: דדחינהו בידים, ולא חזו: ור' לית ליה מוקצה. דקס"ד: מדבעי מיניה אליבא דרבי שמעון, אלמא הוה שמיע ליה מאבוה דכרבי שמעון סבירא ליה: משקין. דרך להשקות בהמה לפני שחיטה, שתהא נוחה להפשיט: המדבריות. הבייתות: ברביעה. במרחשון: ואלו מדבריות כל שרועות באפר. והני מיסא אסירי, אלמא אית ליה מוקצה: איבעית אימא הני. מדבריות נמי כגרוגרות דמי, דדחינהו בידים ויש טורח לילך ולהביאם: ואיבעית אימא. ההיא דפצעילי תמרה – לדבריו דרבי שמעון קאמר, ולר' לא ס"ל: ה"ג: אמר רבה בר בר חנה א"ר יוחנן אמרו הלכה כר' שמעון: אמרו. בני הישיבה: סרוייא קרוייא. על שם מקומו: כלום עשוי. לשום תשמיש: אלא לתרנגולין. הלכך ה"ל מלאכתו לאיסור – ואסור. אלמא: אית ליה מוקצה: דאית ביה אפרוח מת. דלא חזי למיכל, ולכלבים נמי לא חזי. ואף על גב דא"ר שמעון: מחתכין את הנבלה לפני הכלבים – הני מילי במסוכנת, אבל בריאה – לא, דלא הוה דעתיה מאתמול לכלבים. והאי אפרוח שמת בשבת נמי לא הוה דעתיה מאתמול לכלבים: הניחא למר כו' דאמר מודה היה ר"ש. דאע"ג דאמר: מחתכין הנבלה לפני הכלבים – ה"מ במסוכנת, דדעתיה עליה מאתמול לכלבים. אבל מודה הוא בבעלי חיים, כלומר בבריאים שמתו, שאסורין – שפיר קתרצת, דלרבי שמעון גופיה לא חזי לכלבים: מאי איכא למימר. הא חזי לכלבים: דאית בה ביצה. שנולדה היום, ומודה ר' שמעון בנולד: והא אמר רב נחמן כו'. בשמעתא קמייתא דביצה: דאית בה ביצת אפרוח. וכלב לא אכיל לה משום *קליפה: וליה לא סבירא ליה. לר' יוחנן לא סבירא דתיהוי הלכה כר' שמעון, והיינו דרב יצחק: ואת לא תסברא. ומקמי דשמעת ליה לדרב יצחק לא הוה ידעת דר' יוחנן כר' יהודה? בשתי ידים אסור לטלטלה. כדמפרש טעמא לקמיה, דלאו לטלטולי עבידא, דאדם קובע לה מקום: ור' יוחנן אמר אנו אין לנו. שום היתר בהלכות טלטול נרות: אלא בנר. ישן כרבי שמעון דמתיר, אבל מנורה כו'. הלכך, אי לאו מדרב יצחק – לא הוה ידענא ליה, אבל השתא ידענא דכר' יהודה סבירא ליה בכולהו, בר ממוקצה מחמת מיאוס דנר ישן:

תוספות

לדבריו דר' שמעון קאמר ליה וליה לא סבירא ליה. משמע דמספקא ליה אי ר' סבר לה כר' שמעון. ותימה: אמאי לא מוכח מההיא דלקמן, דסבר כר"ש דאמר: פעם אחת הלך ר' כו' והורה במנורה כר"ש בנר. וכן מברייתא, דמייתי ב"אין צדין":* בכור תם שנפל לבור, ר' יהודה הנשיא אומר: ירד מי שבקי במומין ויראה אם יש בו מום יעלה וישחוט כו'. ומיהו, במאי דמתיר לראות במומין לא אתי כר"ש, אלא במאי דלית ליה מוקצה. ומיהו, רש"י לא גריס "בכור תם" אלא "בכור שנפל לבור" והשתא [illegible] אתי כר' יהודה, ויראה אם היה בו מום זה מעי"ט*: הכא במאי עסקינן דאית ביה אפרוח מת. פירש הר"ר יוסף: דלא נקט אפרוח חי – משום דחי חזי לשחק בו תינוק כשבוכה. ואין נראה, דהא בההיא דכופין את הסל לפני האפרוחין (לעיל דף מג.) משמע דאסור לטלטל. ועוד: אי מחיים שרי – אמאי קאמר בסמוך דמודה ר"ש בבעלי חיים שמתו שאסורין? אלא ודאי בעלי חיים *מוקצין הם כגרוגרות וצימוקין, ומקצה אותם גם מכלבים, ולא דמי לבשר תפל שמותר לר"ש, מדפריך בפרק "מפנין" (לקמן קכח.) על רב הונא דשרי: והא תלמיד דרב הוה ורב כר' יהודה סבירא ליה. אבל לר' שמעון – משמע דשרי, משום דאינו מקצהו מכלבים כמו בעלי חיים:

דאית ביה ביצה. דאסור משום נולד. ל"ע: דר' יוחנן גופיה *מפרש טעמא דביצה משום משקין שזבו! ואפשר דמשום הכי לא הוה אסר ר"ש לטלטלה אלא לאכילה:

דאית ביה ביצת אפרוח. נראה לר"י דאסור לר' שמעון משום דכיון דאית ביה אפרוח הוי *כמו גרוגרות וצימוקין, וקא מיבעיא ליה לסבא קירויא אי שרי לטלטולי על ידי שינער משם הביצה, אי חשיב כמו מניח או כשכח. והשיב לו רבי יוחנן: כלום עשוי אלא לתרנגולין, ואין זה כשכח, אלא כמניח – ואסור:

אמר ליה מנרתא שאני. וא"ת: אמאי לא מוכח מהא דא"ר יוחנן בפ' "לולב וערבה" (סוכה מו:) דסוכה אפילו בשמיני אסורה, אלמא אית ליה "מיגו דאיתקצאי כו'" כר' יהודה! ותירץ ר"י: דנר אינו מוקצה למצותו מטלטול, שאין ביטול מצוה בטלטול. ולא דמי לסוכה דאיתקצאי ביה"ש מחמת מצוה, ולהכי אינו יכול להוכיח מסוכה אנר: לעיל לאו משום דר' אסי תלמידו דר' יוחנן כו'. וא"ת: דילמא ר' אסי כרב רביה סבירא ליה, כדאמר לעיל גבי שרגא דחנוכתא אמרו ליה רב כהנא ורב אסי לרב: הילכתא הכי? ונראה דרב אסי דלעיל לאו היינו ר' אסי דהכא, דההוא דלעיל חבירו של רב כהנא, והכא ר' אסי חבירו של ר' אמי*:

אין לנו אלא בנר כר' שמעון. פי': במוקצה מחמת מיאוס, דהיינו נר ישן שלא הדליקו בה באותה שבת. ולעיל דפסיק כרבי יהודה – היינו בהדליקו בה באותה שבת, דהוי מוקצה מחמת איסור. והא דפסיק בפרק בתרא* כר"ש בנבלה לפני הכלבים, אף על גב דנבלה מוקצה מחמת איסור היא, כדפר"ת (לעיל יט: ד"ה ושמואל) – התם *לא דחייה בידים, אבל הכא דדחייה בידים – סבר כר' יהודה. ולפי זה לא קיימי ר' יוחנן וריב"ל דפסקי כר' שמעון אהדא ברייתא, דר' יוחנן קאי אברייתא ד"כל הנרות של מתכת מטלטלין" כו'. אבל במאי דקאמר ר' יהודה בברייתא דלעיל: "מטלטלין נר חדש אבל לא ישן" – לא סבר רבי יוחנן כוותיה. וריב"ל אברייתא ד"מטלטלין נר חדש" קאי, דבההיא ברייתא שרי

רבי

א) אין נראה לר"י פירוש זה דל"ד לגרוגרות ולימוקין דלא דחיה בידים ונ"ל כפירוש הערוך שפירש פצעילי תמרה לשון מפלע שמפלעין תמרים כדי להתבשל ולהתייבש ובשעת הפליעה מתקלקלת מראיתה ואחר זמן משתבחות ודמי לגרוגרות ולימוקין אך שגרוגרות ולימוקין מתקלקלות יותר מהם. [תוספות ישנים]:

מסורת הש"ס

ביצה מ.

שם. [לקמן קנז.]

[ביצה שם]

[נ"ל דרבא]

ביצה כז:

שם ב.

קשה להפשר להסיר הקליפה ויוכלנה הכלב [תוס' ישנים]

עירובין קב. לקמן קלח:

[דף קנו:]

התו"י המתחיל ולפ"ז וכו' הנרשם בס"א נמצא בדף מו ע"א כי שם מקומו

רבינו חננאל

וכן הא דאמר ליה [ר'] לר' שמעון בריה אין מוקצה לר' שמעון אלא גרוגרות וצמוקין בלבד פשוטה היא: **אמר** רבה בר בר חנה א"ר יוחנן אמרו הלכה כר"ש איני והא בעא מיניה ההוא סבא קרוייה קינה של תרנגולין מהו לטלטלה בשבת ואמר ליה אסור כלום עשוי אלא לתרנגולים מכלל דר' יוחנן כר' יהודה סבירא ליה דאית ליה מוקצה. ושנינן בדאית ליה בהאי קינה אפרוח מת ומשום הכי אסורה לטלטלה. הניחא למ"ד בעלי חיים שמתו בשבת דברי הכל אסור לטלטלן בשבת הא אפילו לר' שמעון ואלא למ"ד ר"ש מתיר בבעלי חיים שמתו שמותר לטלטלן אע"ג דאית בהאי קינה אפרוח שמת בשבת ר"ש מתיר אמאי קא אסר ר' יוחנן והא איהו הלכתא כר' שמעון סבירא ליה. ואסיקנא בדאית בהאי קינה ביצה שיש בה אפרוח דלדברי הכל אסורה. ואעפ"כ לא נתברר כי ר' יוחנן כר' שמעון סבירא ליה. וכי אתא רב יצחק בר' יוסף א"ר יוחנן הלכתא כר' יהודה וריב"ל אמר הלכה כר"ש. אמר רב יוסף היינו דאמר רבה בר בר חנה א"ר יוחנן אמרו הלכה כר"ש וליה לא סבירא ליה. ודייק נמי אביי מדר' אסי נפלה מנרתא על גלימיה [בבי] ר' אבא ולא טלטלה. ואמר (משמיה) [משום] דר' אסי תלמיד דר' יוחנן הוא. ור' יוחנן במוקצה סבר לה כר' יהודה. ודחינן להא דאביי. ואמרינן לא אפילו תימא ר' יוחנן כר' שמעון מנרתא

שני

נו א ב מיי' פכ"ו מהל' שבת הלכה יא טוש"ע או"ח סי' רעט סעיף ז:

מוּתָּר לִנְטוֹתָהּ וּמוּתָּר לְפָרְקָהּ בַּשַּׁבָּת! אֶלָּא אָמַר אַבַּיֵי: בְּשֶׁל חוּלְיוֹת. אִי הָכִי, מ"ט דְּר"ש בֶּן לָקִישׁ דְּשָׁרֵי? מַאי "חוּלְיוֹת" – כְּעֵין חוּלְיוֹת, דְּאִית בָּהּ חִידְקֵי. הִלְכָּךְ: [א]חוּלְיוֹת – בֵּין גְּדוֹלָה בֵּין קְטַנָּה אֲסוּרָה לְטַלְטְלָהּ. גְּדוֹלָה נַמִי דְּאִית בָּהּ חִידְקֵי – גְּזֵירָה אַטּוּ גְּדוֹלָה דְּחוּלְיוֹת. כִּי פְּלִיגִי – בִּקְטַנָּה דְּאִית בָּהּ חִידְקֵי. [ב]מָר סָבַר: גָּזְרִינַן, וּמָר סָבַר: לָא גָּזְרִינַן. וּמִי א"ר יוֹחָנָן הָכִי? וְהָאָמַר ר' יוֹחָנָן: *הֲלָכָה כִּסְתָם מִשְׁנָה, וּתְנַן: *"מוּכְנִי שֶׁלָּהּ בִּזְמַן שֶׁהִיא נִשְׁמֶטֶת – אֵין חִיבּוּר לָהּ, וְאֵין נִמְדֶּדֶת עִמָּהּ, וְאֵין מַצֶּלֶת עִמָּהּ בְּאֹהֶל הַמֵּת, וְאֵין גּוֹרְרִין אוֹתָהּ בַּשַּׁבָּת בִּזְמַן שֶׁיֵּשׁ עָלֶיהָ מָעוֹת". הָא אֵין עָלֶיהָ מָעוֹת – שַׁרְיָא, וְאע"ג דַּהֲווּ עָלֶיהָ ביה"ש! א"ר זֵירָא: תְּהֵא מִשְׁנָתֵינוּ שֶׁלֹּא הָיוּ עָלֶיהָ מָעוֹת כָּל ביה"ש, שֶׁלֹּא לִשְׁבּוֹר דְּבָרָיו שֶׁל ר' יוֹחָנָן. א"ר יְהוֹשֻׁעַ בֶּן לֵוִי: פַּעַם אַחַת הָלַךְ רַבִּי לְדְיוֹסְפְּרָא, וְהוֹרָה בַּמְּנוֹרָה כְּר' שִׁמְעוֹן בְּנֵר. אִיבַּעְיָא לְהוּ: הוֹרָה בַּמְּנוֹרָה כְּר' שִׁמְעוֹן בְּנֵר – לְהֶיתֵּרָא, אוֹ דִילְמָא: הוֹרָה בַּמְּנוֹרָה – לְאִיסּוּרָא וּכְר' שִׁמְעוֹן בְּנֵר – לְהֶיתֵּרָא? תֵּיקוּ. רַב מַלְכִּיָּא אִיקְלַע לְבֵי רַבִּי שִׂמְלַאי וְטִילְטֵל שְׁרָגָא וְאִיקְפַּד ר' שִׂמְלַאי. ר' יוֹסֵי גְּלִילָאָה אִיקְלַע לְאַתְרֵיהּ דְּר' יוֹסֵי בְּרַבִּי חֲנִינָא, טִילְטֵל שְׁרָגָא וְאִיקְפַּד ר' יוֹסֵי בְּר' חֲנִינָא. *ר' אַבָּהוּ, כִּי אִיקְלַע לְאַתְרֵיהּ דְּר' יְהוֹשֻׁעַ בֶּן לֵוִי – הֲוָה מְטַלְטֵל שְׁרָגָא, כִּי אִיקְלַע לְאַתְרֵיהּ דְּר' יוֹחָנָן – *לָא הֲוָה מְטַלְטֵל שְׁרָגָא. מַה נַּפְשָׁךְ, אִי כְּרַבִּי יְהוּדָה סְבִירָא לֵיהּ – לֶיעְבַּד כְּרַבִּי יְהוּדָה, אִי כְּר' שִׁמְעוֹן סְבִירָא לֵיהּ – לֶיעְבַּד כְּר' שִׁמְעוֹן! לְעוֹלָם כְּר' שִׁמְעוֹן ס"ל, וּמִשּׁוּם כְּבוֹדוֹ דְּר' יוֹחָנָן הוּא דְּלָא הֲוָה עָבֵיד. [ג]א"ר יְהוּדָה: שְׁרָגָא דְּמִשְׁחָא – שָׁרֵי לְטַלְטוּלָהּ, דְּנַפְטָא – אָסוּר לְטַלְטוּלָהּ. רַבָּה וְרַב יוֹסֵף דְּאָמְרִי תַּרְוַיְיהוּ: דְּנַפְטָא נַמִי שָׁרֵי לְטַלְטוּלָהּ. (דְּהוֹאִיל וַחֲזֵי לְכַסּוֹת בֵּיהּ מָנָא). רַב אָוְיָא אִיקְלַע לְבֵי רָבָא, הֲוָה מְאִיסָן בֵּי כַּרְעֵיהּ בְּטִינָא, אַתִּיבֵי אַפּוּרְיָא קַמֵּיהּ דְּרָבָא. אִיקְפַּד רָבָא, בְּעָא לְצַעוּרֵיהּ. א"ל: מ"ט רַבָּה וְרַב יוֹסֵף דְּאָמְרִי תַּרְוַיְיהוּ שְׁרָגָא דְּנַפְטָא נַמִי שָׁרֵי לְטַלְטוּלֵיהּ? א"ל: הוֹאִיל וְחַזְיָא לְכַסּוֹיֵי בָּהּ מָנָא. אֶלָּא מֵעַתָּה כָּל צְרוֹרוֹת שֶׁבֶּחָצֵר מְטַלְטְלִין, הוֹאִיל וְחַזְיָא לְכַסּוֹיֵי בְּהוּ מָנָא! א"ל: הָא – אִיכָּא תּוֹרַת כְּלִי עָלֶיהָ, הָנֵי – לֵיכָּא תּוֹרַת כְּלִי עָלֶיהָ. מִי לָא תַּנְיָא

הַשֵּׁירִים

רש"י

מוּתָּר לִנְטוֹתָהּ. דְּקָתָנֵי כִּילַּת חֲתָנִים אֵין לָהּ גַּג טֶפַח, שֶׁנַּקְלִיטִין יוֹצְאִין לִשְׁנֵי רָאשֵׁי הַמִּטָּה בְּאֶמְצָעָהּ אֶחָד לְכָאן וְאֶחָד לְכָאן, וְנוֹתֵן כְּלוּנָס מִזֶּה לָזֶה, וּמַשְׁלִיךְ הָאֹהֶל עָלֶיהָ וְהוּא שׁוֹפֵעַ לְכָאן וּלְכָאן. וְכֵיוָן שֶׁאֵינוֹ רֹחַב טֶפַח – אֵינוֹ אֹהֶל, וְאֵין בּוֹ לֹא בִּנְיָן וְלֹא סְתִירָה: בְּשֶׁל חוּלְיוֹת. בִּמְנוֹרָה שֶׁל פְּרָקִים, שֶׁמָּא תִּפּוֹל וְתִתְפָּרֵק וִיַחֲזִירֶנָּה, וְנִמְצָא עוֹשֶׂה כְּלִי: חִידְקֵי. חִיתּוּכִין סָבִיב לָהּ, קרונ"ש, וְדוֹמֶה לִפְרָקִים. וּמַאן דְּחָזֵי, סָבַר: שֶׁל פְּרָקִים הוּא: גְּדוֹלָה. הוֹאִיל וְדַרְכָּהּ לַעֲשׂוֹתָהּ שֶׁל חוּלְיוֹת, כִּי אִית בֵּיהּ חִידְקֵי – סָבְרֵי דְּחוּלְיוֹת הֵן, וְאָסוּר אֲפִילּוּ לְרֵישׁ לָקִישׁ, כְּדַאֲמַר לְעֵיל: נִיטֶּלֶת בִּשְׁתֵּי יָדַיִם – אָסוּר לְטַלְטְלָהּ: כִּי פְּלִיגִי בִּקְטַנָּה דְּאִית בָּהּ חִידְקֵי. דְּכוּלֵּי עָלְמָא יָדְעֵי דְּלָאו חוּלְיוֹת נִינְהוּ: גָּזְרִינַן. אַטּוּ חוּלְיוֹת: וּמִי אָמַר ר' יוֹחָנָן הָכִי. הֲלָכָה כְּר' יְהוּדָה: תְּהֵא מִשְׁנָתֵינוּ. דְּמוּכְנִי, דְּקָתָנֵי: הָא אֵין עָלֶיהָ מָעוֹת שַׁרְיָא – כְּגוֹן שֶׁלֹּא הָיוּ עָלֶיהָ בֵּין הַשְּׁמָשׁוֹת. וְהָכִי תִּידוֹק מִינָּהּ: טַעְמָא דְּיֵשׁ עָלֶיהָ מָעוֹת כְּשֶׁקָּדַשׁ הַיּוֹם, הָא אֵין עָלֶיהָ כְּשֶׁקָּדַשׁ הַיּוֹם – שַׁרְיָא: לְדְיוֹסְפְּרָא. מָקוֹם: אִיבַּעְיָא לְהוּ. חֲדָא הוֹרָאָה הֲוַאי, וְהָכִי קָאָמַר: הוֹרָה בִּמְנוֹרָה לְהֶיתֵּרָא, כְּדֶרֶךְ שֶׁהָיָה ר' שִׁמְעוֹן מַתִּיר בְּנֵר יָשָׁן, אוֹ דִּילְמָא שְׁתֵּי הוֹרָאוֹת הֲווּ: הוֹרָה בִּמְנוֹרָה לְאִיסּוּר, כְּדַאֲמַרַן בְּדְחִידְקֵי, וְגָזְרִינַן אַטּוּ חוּלְיוֹת. וּכְר"ש הוֹרָה בְּנֵר לְהֶיתֵּר: וְטִלְטֵל שְׁרָגָא. נֵר שֶׁכָּבָה: לְעוֹלָם כְּר' שִׁמְעוֹן סְבִירָא לֵיהּ. דְּאִי סְבִירָא לֵיהּ דְּאָסוּר לָא הֲוָה מְטַלְטֵל לֵיהּ לִכְבוֹד ר' יְהוֹשֻׁעַ בֶּן לֵוִי דְּלֶיעְבַּד אִיסּוּרָא: שְׁרָגָא דְּמִשְׁחָא. שֶׁדָּלַק נֵר שֶׁל שֶׁמֶן: שָׁרֵי לְטַלְטוּלָהּ. אַחַר שֶׁכָּבָה כְּר' שִׁמְעוֹן דְּלָא מְאִיס: אֲבָל בְּנַפְטָא. דְּמַסְרַח אֲפִילּוּ רַבִּי שִׁמְעוֹן מוֹדֶה דְּלָא חֲזֵי אֶלָּא לִמְלַאכְתּוֹ: אִיקְפַּד רָבָא. מִשּׁוּם טִינּוּף הַמִּטָּה: וּבְעָא לְצַעוּרֵיהּ. בִּשְׁאֵלוֹת:

תוספות

רבי שמעון נר שהדליקו באותה שבת. והא דלא פסיק רבי יוחנן כרבי מאיר, דהא סבר לגמרי כוותיה – דשרי מוקצה מחמת מיאוס, ואסר מוקצה מחמת איסור – נקט רבי יהודה, משום דבכל מקום הוזכר גבי מוקצה. ועוד דלא מצינו דאית ליה לרבי מאיר מוקצה מחמת איסור גרידא אלא בנר ישן, דאיכא תרתי: מחמת מיאוס ומחמת איסור. אך לפי זה קשה לרשב"א: דמשמע דנקט במנורה אין לנו כרבי שמעון, אבל רבי שמעון מיהא שרי במנורה. ולמאי דמפרש טעמא דמנורה משום דאדם קובע לו מקום – היכי שרי רבי שמעון? הא אמרי' בריש "כל הכלים" (לקמן דף קכג.): הכל מודים בסיכי וזירי ומזורי, כיון דקפיד עלייהו – מיחד להו מקום. ונראה לפרש: דרבי יוחנן פסק כרבי יהודה במוקצה מחמת מיאוס, וכ"ש במוקצה מחמת איסור. *כדמוכח בפרק בתרא (דף קנז.) דקאמר: בכולי שבת הלכה כרבי שמעון, בר ממוקצה מחמת מיאוס. וחד אמר: במוקצה מחמת מיאוס נמי הלכה כרבי שמעון, בר ממוקצה מחמת איסור. דהיינו שהדליקו בה באותה שבת. והא דקאמר: אנו אין לנו אלא בנר כרבי שמעון – לאו משום דסבר כוותיה בנר, אלא כלומר: אין לנו שיתיר אפי' רבי שמעון דמיקל אלא בנר, אבל במנורה – אסר. והשתא קיימי תרווייהו אחד ברייתא, ולא מצי נמי למינקט רבי מאיר:

והא כילת חתנים דאדם קובע לה מקום. פי' רשב"א: דאדם קובע לה מקום כמו למנורה, ואפ"ה שרי שמואל. אלא ודאי לא חשיב קביעות שלה ושל מנורה קביעות אלא היכא דקבע מקום לגמרי, כדאמר בפ' "כל הכלים" (לקמן קכג. ושם):

דחוליות בין גדולה בין קטנה אסורה. קשה לר"י: דבפ"ב דביצה (דף כא:) תנן: ג' דברים ר"ג מחמיר כב"ש, ותשיב אין זוקפין את המנורה, ומשמע דב"ה שרי. ומפרש התם בגמרא: *הכא במנורה של חוליות עסקינן, משום דמיחזי כבונה. דב"ש סברי: יש בנין בכלים ויש סתירה בכלים, וב"ה סברי: אין בנין כו'. אלמא שרי ב"ה מנורה של חוליות להחזיר. ומאן דשרי בסוף פירקא להחזיר מטה של חוליות ברפוי איכא לאוקמא – ה"נ ברפוי. אבל למאן דאסר קשה! ותירץ ר"י: דהתם מיירי כגון שהחוליות מחוברין יחד ואינם מתפרקין, ופעמים מטין אותן ופעמים זוקפין אותן*:

הורה במנורה להיתרא, וכר"ש בנר נמי להיתרא. **או דילמא: במנורה הורה לאיסורא, וכר"ש בנר להיתרא.** וא"ת: אמאי לא קאמר נמי: או דילמא הורה במנורה להיתרא כרבי שמעון בנר, וכרבי שמעון בנר לא סבירא ליה? דכה"ג איתא ב"אלו טריפות" (חולין דף נו: ושם), הורו בטרפחת כרבי בזפק, איבעיא להו: הורו בטרפחת לאיסורא, וכרבי בזפק להיתרא. או דילמא: הורו בטרפחת להיתרא, כרבי בזפק, וכרבי בזפק לא סבירא להו. וי"ל: דהכא לא שייך למיתלי מנורה בנר, כדתלי טרפחת בזפק. דהכא אין טעם אחד לשניהם, דנר – משום מוקצה, ומנורה – משום בנין. ועוד: דלא בעי למימר דר' לא סבר בנר כר"ש, משום דריב"ל פסיק לעיל כר"ש. ואם תאמר: ובההיא ד"אלו טריפות" אמאי לא קאמר נמי תרווייהו להיתרא כדאמר הכא: או דילמא הורו בטרפחת להיתרא, וכר' בזפק נמי להיתרא? ומיהו, בלאו הכי מגיהין שם הספרים ול"ג הורו בטרפחת לאיסורא – דהא כ"ע שרו לה, דתניא התם: *היא האם היא טרפחת היא שלחופית. ובניטל האם *הוה עובדא והאכילה רבי טרפון לכלבים, ואמר: הלכה חמורך טרפון, ואמר ליה רבי עקיבא: טועה בדבר משנה אתה. וגרס התם: הורו בטרפחת להיתרא וכרבי בזפק להיתרא כו'. ורש"י פי': הורה במנורה להיתרא כר"ש בנר, וחדא הוראה הוי. ואין נראה, דאין לתלות מנורה בנר, ועוד: דאכתי הוי ליה למיבעיא: או דילמא תרווייהו להיתרא: **דנפטא** אסור לטלטלה. פי' בקונט': אפילו לר"ש, וכן משמע, דהא שרגא דמשחא דשרי לטלטלה – היינו לר' שמעון. ועוד: מדפריך רבא בסמוך לרבה ורב יוסף מ"ש מצרורות שבחצר. ואי שרי ר' שמעון דנפטא – תיקש' ליה לכ"ע אליבא דרבי שמעון. לכך פי' בקונט' דהכא אליבא דר' שמעון קאי. ואע"ג דרב אית ליה מוקצה *גבי מטה שיחדה למעות, ורבה נמי אית ליה, כדאמר אביי: *כל מילי דמר עביד כרב, ורב יוסף נמי משמע דאית ליה מוקצה, בפ' "נוטל" (לקמן קמג:) דקאמר: כמה חריפא שמעתא דדרדקי, אימור דאמור בשכח – לכתחילה מי אמור? הכא אליבא דר"ש קאמר, וליה לא ס"ל. ומיהו, נראה לפרש דהכא מיירי נמי אליבא דרבי יהודה, ולא מיירי בהדליקו בו באותה שבת, וה"ק: שרגא דמשחא של מתכת שרי לטלטולה ואפילו לרבי יהודה, כדתניא לעיל (ד' מד.): כל הנרות של מתכת מטלטלין, דנפטא אסור אפי' לרבי שמעון, דמאיס טפי מנר ישן. ורבה ורב יוסף שרו אפי' לרבי יהודה, דלא מאיס אלא שריחו רע. וחזי לכסויי ביה מנא. אבל נר ישן מקלה ליה לגמרי משום דמאיס, ואפילו מכיסוי מנא: [ועי' תוס' מנחות מא: ד"ה כל מילי]:

ואמר

הגהות וציונים בגיליון

[לקמן פא: קיב: קמז: קמח: קנו: עירובין נב: ביצה לז: תענית יח. יבמות טז: מב: גיטין פא: ב"ק כט: לב. סט. לד: ב"מ לג: סנהדרין לד: שבועות ג: מנחות כב: חולין לח: מג: נדה נ: נו:]

יבמות יד. ע"ש

[עי' תוספות יבמות יד. ד"ה לא הוה]

רש"ל מוחק זה

[ועי' תוספות ביצה כב. ד"ה וכר"ה]

[לעיל מד: כלים פי"ח מ"ב]

ולפי זה חמור מוקצה מחמת מיאוס ממוקצה מחמת איסור לר' יוחנן דלא דחייה בידים כמו נבילה דפסק כר"ש ורב סבר איפכא דקאמר בפ"ק דחולין [דף טו.] ע"כ לא קרי ר"מ כו' אבל קוטע דאין ראוי לכוס לא ור"מ לית ליה בפרקין [לעיל מד.] מוקצה מחמת מיאוס להכי אמר בפרק בתרא דרב סבר כר"י מדכרכי דזוזי אסור דהוי מוקצה מחמת מיאוס כדפי' ר"ת בפ"ק מוכח מכ"ש דלדידיה מחמת איסור חמיר טפי. [תוס' ישנים]:

[דף כב.]

[חולין נה:]

[סנהדרין לג.]

[לעיל מד:]

[לעיל כב.]

רבינו חננאל

שני דא"ר יוחנן אנו אין לנו כר"ש אלא בנר. אבל מנורה בין ניטלת בידו אחת בין ניטלת בב' ידים אסור לטלטלה וטעמא מאי ואוקמה רחבה במנורה דאית בה חידקי חידקי שהן כעין חוליו' שנראה המעמידה או המטלטלה כבונה. הילכך דחוליות בין גדולה בין קטנה אסורה. לית בה חוליות ואית בה חידקי חידקי גדולה אסורה דמיחלפא בגדול' של חוליות. כי פליגי במנורה קטנה דאית בה חידקי חידקי. ר' יוחנן סבר גזרינן קטנה דאית בה חידקי אטו גדולה דאית בה חידקי. וריש לקיש סבר לא גזרינן. איני דגזר ר' יוחנן והא איהו דאמר הלכה כסתם משנה. ותנן סתמא בכלים פ' י"ח במוכני של שידה ואין גוררין אותה בשבת בזמן שיש עליה מעות. ודייקינן מינה. הא אין עליה מעות שריא. ואע"ג דהוו עליה כל בין השמשות ולא גזרינן כשאין עליה מעות אטו כשיש עליה מעות. וא"ר זירא תהא משנתנו בשלא היו עליה מעות כל בין השמשות (גזרי') שלא לשבור דברי ר' יוחנן. כלומר לא תקשי לך דר' יוחנן אדר' יוחנן. והא דהורה ר' (זירא ספרא) [בדיוספרא] עלתה בתיקו. ועבדינן בה לחומרא ומוקמינן לה הורה ר' במנורה לאיסורא וכר' שמעון בנר להיתרא: ר' אבהו מטלטל שרגא כר"ש. ובאתריה דר' יוחנן לא הוה מטלטל ליה משום כבודו דר' יוחנן (רב) [אמר רב יהודה] שרגא דמשחא שרי לטלטלה. אבל שרגא דנפטא (הוה) אסיר ורבה ורב יוסף שרו אפילו שרגא דנפטא. ואסיקנ' משום דחזו לכסויי בהו מני דנפטא. ואם תאמר אי הכי כל צרורות שבחצר יטלטלו הואיל וחזו לכסויי בהו מנא דנפטא. שני

גליון הש"ס

גמ' אמר ר' יהודה שרגא דמשחא. עי' לקמן דף קכב ע"ב תוס' ד"ה ליתא: תוס' ד"ה דנפטא וכו' ורבה נמי אית ליה. עי' מנחות דף מא ע"ב תוס' ד"ה כל מילי. ובעירובין דף לג ע"ב תוס' ד"ה לא תימא:

א) *השירים והנזמים והטבעות הרי הן ככל
הכלים הניטלים בחצר, ואמר עולא: מה טעם
– הואיל ואיכא תורת כלי עליה. הכא נמי
– הואיל ואיכא תורת כלי עליה. א"ר נחמן בר
יצחק: בריך רחמנא דלא כסיפיה רבא לרב
אויא. רמי ליה אביי לרבה: תניא, *מותר
השמן שבנר ושבקערה – אסור, ורבי שמעון
מתיר. אלמא: לר' שמעון לית ליה מוקצה.
ורמינהו, *רבי שמעון אומר: כל שאין מומו
ניכר מעי"ט – אין זה מן המוכן! הכי השתא!
התם – אדם יושב ומצפה אימתי תכבה נרו,
הכא – אדם יושב ומצפה מתי יפול בו מום?!
מימר אמר: מי יימר דנפיל ביה מומא, ואת"ל
דנפיל ביה מומא – מי יימר דנפיל ביה מום
קבוע, ואם תמצי לומר דנפל ביה מום קבוע –
מי יימר דמזדקק ליה חכם? מתיב רמי בר
חמא: *מפירין נדרים בשבת, [ונשאלין
לנדרים שהן] לצורך השבת. ואמאי? לימא:
מי יימר דמיזדקק לה בעל? התם כדרב פנחס
משמיה דרבא, *דאמר רב פנחס משמיה
דרבא: כל הנודרת – על דעת בעלה היא נודרת. ת"ש: *)נשאלין לנדרים
של צורך השבת בשבת. ואמאי? לימא: מי יימר דמיזדקק ליה חכם? התם
אי לא מיזדקק ליה חכם – סגיא ליה בג' הדיוטות, הכא – מי יימר דמיזדקק ליה
חכם. רמי ליה אביי לרב יוסף: מי אמר ר' שמעון "כבתה מותר לטלטלה", כבתה – אין,
לא כבתה – לא. מאי טעמא – דילמא בהדי דנקיט לה כבתה, הא שמעינן ליה לר'
שמעון דאמר: דבר שאין מתכוין מותר; דתניא, *ר' שמעון אומר: גורר אדם כסא
מטה וספסל, ובלבד שלא יתכוין לעשות חריץ! כל היכא דכי מיכוין איכא
איסורא דאורייתא – כי לא מיכוין גזר ר"ש מדרבנן, כל היכא דכי מיכוין איכא
איסורא דרבנן – כי לא מיכוין שרי ר"ש לכתחילה. מתיב רבא: *מוכרי כסות
מוכרין כדרכן, ובלבד שלא יתכוין בחמה מפני החמה, ובגשמים מפני
הגשמים, והצנועין מפשילין במקל לאחוריהן. והא הכא, דכי מיכוין – איסורא
דאורייתא איכא, כי לא מיכוין – שרי רבי שמעון לכתחילה! אלא אמר רבא:
הנח

*) לקמן קנז. נדרים עז:

רש"י

השירים. אצעדות: הרי הן ככל הכלים. אע"פ שאסור לצאת בהן לרה"ר, כדאמרינן בפרק "במה אשה יוצאה" (לקמן נט:) גזירה דילמא שלפא ומחויא, מיהו תורת כלי עליהן, ומותר לטלטלן שלא כדרך מלבוש: מומו ניכר. גבי בכור קאי: מי יימר דמזדקק ליה חכם. שימלא חכם שיזקק לו ביו"ט לראות אם מום קבוע הוא או לא: מפירין נדרים. בעל לאשתו: ונשאלין לנדרים. לחכם, להתירן: שהן לצורך שבת. כגון: נדר שלא יאכל היום: ואמאי. מותרת לאכול? ואפילו שרי לה בעל – ליתסר לה משום מוקצה, דהא אסחה לדעתה ואמרה: מי יימר דמזדקק לה בעל? על דעת בעלה. ע"מ אם ירצה הבעל, וסמכה עליה דמזדקק לה ביום שמעו: הכא מי יימר כו'. והדיוטות לא מצו למישרייה לבכור אלא במום הידוע לכל, כגון מחוסר אבר: איסורא דאורייתא. כיבוי אב מלאכה הוא, חריץ – ליכא איסור דאורייתא, דחופר כלאחר יד הוא. דחופר דאמר לקמן תולדה דחורש וחייב – ה"מ חופר כדרכו במרא וקרדום: מוכרין כדרכן. ואפי' של כלאים לובשו להראותו בשוק: ובלבד שלא יתכוין. להנאת חימום, והא ר"ש היא, מדקאזיל בתר כוונה: לדבר

תוספות

ואמר עולא מה טעם. להכי איצטריך לפרושי האי טעמא – משום דמשמע ליה דסבר האי תנא כמאן דאסר לקמן להתקשט בהן בחצר, מדקתני: "הרי הן ככל הכלים הניטלין בחצר". פירוש: ככל הכלים שמלאכתן לאיסור, דשרי לצורך גופן ומקומן, ולהכי מפרש עולא דאיכא תורת כלי עליה. וקשה לר"י: דאמר בפ' "מי שהפך" (מ"ק יב: ושם): ר' יהודה נשיאה נפק בחותמתא דמדושא, [עי' פי' רש"י שם] שמע ר' אמי ואיקפיד. אמר רב יוסף: מ"ט איקפיד? והתניא השירים והנזמים כו'. ומאי פריך מינה? אדרבה, מינה משמע דאסור לצאת בהן כדפי'! והתם קאמר נפק – דמשמע דרך מלבוש! ונראה לר"י דחותמתא דמדושא היינו טבעת של עץ, כמו שמפרשים רבותיו של רש"י. ולא של אלמוג כמו שהוא מפרש. דאלמוגין מפרש בראש השנה (דף כג.) "כסיתא", והכא קאמר דמדושא. אלא של עץ אחר הוא ששמו מדושא, ואין שם תכשיט עליו. וכשיוצאים בו דרך מלבוש לא הוי קישוט אלא טלטול בעלמא, ולהכי ידע רב יוסף דר' אמי לא איקפד אלא משום טלטול. והשתא מייתי שפיר מהך ברייתא דשרי לטלטל לצורך גופו או לצורך מקומו, כשאר כלי' שמלאכתן לאיסור, דניטלין לצורך גופו או לצורך מקומו. ונפק לחצר קאמר, אבל לרה"ר – אסור. כדאמרי' בפ' "הדר" (עירובין סט. ושם): ההוא גברא דנפיק בחותמתא דמדושא, חזייה לר' יהודה נשיאה כסייה, אמר: כגון זה מבטל רשות לר' יהודה: **והתנן** ר"ש אומר כל שאין מומו ניכר מעי"ט אין זה מן המוכן. קשה לר"י: מאי קא פריך? הא ע"כ טעמא דר"ש לאו משום מוקצה, אלא משום דסבר דאין רואין מומין ביו"ט. דהא ר' יהודה דאית ליה טפי מוקצה שרי התם, בריש "אין צדין" (ביצה כה: ושם) בכור שנפל לבור – ירד מומחה ויראה, אם יש בו מום – יעלה וישחוט. ואם לאו – לא ישחוט! וי"ל: דדייק מדלא קתני "ר"ש אוסר לפי שאין רואין מומין בי"ט" דהוה משמע לכתחילה אסור, אבל בדיעבד – מבוקר. ומדקתני "אין זה מן המוכן" – משמע דהוי מוקצה, ואפי' בקרו אינו מבוקר. ובהכי פליגי: דר' יהודה סבר: רואין מומין בי"ט, הלכך לא הוי מוקצה, דמיירי בנפל בו מום מעי"ט, כדמוקי לה התם, ור"ש סבר: אין רואין. ולכך, אפי' ביקרו – אינו מבוקר, משום מוקצה. וא"ת: דבביצה משמע דאביי סבר כאדא בר אוכמי, דאמר: לר"ש, היכא דנפל בו מום מעי"ט – אם בקרו מבוקר, דאמר אביי התם: כוותיה דרבה בר רב הונא מסתברא, מדקתני תלת בבי בברייתא, *(ומוקמא הכיא ברייתא כאדא בר אוכמי). וע"כ הא דשני ליה בין נפל בו מום קבוע מעי"ט לנפל בו מום בי"ט משום דבנפל בו בי"ט[ב] איכא תלתא מי יימר כדקאמר בסמוך, ובנפל בו מעי"ט ליכא אלא חד מי יימר דמיזדקיק ליה חכם. מאי קשיא מנר שכבה דליכא כל הני מי יימר. וי"ל דחזר בו אביי ולית ליה *(דאדא בר אוכמי) משמע מתני' דרב אושעיא דאבא בר אוכמי משבש ותני דמתני' דהתם נמי דיקא כרב אושעיא, כדמפרש התם: **מי** יימר דנפל ביה מומא. נראה דכל הני מי יימר דקאמר רבה – לאו דווקא, דהא ר"ש אסר אפי' בנפל בו מום קבוע מעי"ט, דהשתא ליכא אלא חד מי יימר דמיזדקיק ליה חכם דהא קאי אר' יהודה, דלא שרי אלא כשהיה בו מום קבוע מעי"ט. דהא פריך אהא דקאמר ר' יהודה: "ואם לאו לא ישחוט" – פשיטא! ומשני: לא צריכא, דנפל ביה מאתמול מום עובר, והשתא הוה ליה מום קבוע. מהו דתימא: כיון דדעתיה עילויה – נשחטיה, קמ"ל. א"כ, הא דקאמר: אם יש בו מום יעלה וישחוט – היינו ע"כ מום קבוע מעי"ט. ואפי' לאדא בר אוכמי דשרי ר"ש בדיעבד בחד מי יימר – מ"מ בנפל בו מום עובר מעי"ט דאיכא תרתי מי יימר, לכאורה משמע התם דאסר. לכך נראה דלאו דוקא הן דאפי' בחד מי יימר סגי, וכן מוכחא מאתקפתא דרמי בר חמא, דפריך מחד מי יימר: **מי** יימר דמיזדקיק לה בעל. ואע"ג דפירות שנדרה מהם אינם מוקצין לענין טלטול – דהא חזו לשאר בני אדם, מ"מ אית לן למימר: מיגו דאיתקצאי בין השמשות מאכילתם – איתקצאי לכולי יומא. אי נמי: מיירי בפירות שלה, ואסרתן לכל אדם: **מי** יימר דמיזדקיק לה בעל. תימה: מי דמי? התם – ודאי לא מיזדקיק ליה חכם, דאין רואין מומין בי"ט, אבל הכא, דאין לך איסור בדבר – מיזדקק לה בעל! ולית לן למימר מי יימר, דהא לר' יהודה דקסבר רואין מומין בי"ט לא אמרי' מי יימר! *וי"ל: דבעל נמי לא ניחא להזדקק, דזימנין דשרי נדרים שנדרה לדבר מצוה: **התם** אי לא מיזדקיק ליה חכם סגי ליה בג' הדיוטות אבל הכא כו'. ואע"ג דבפ"ק דחולין (דף יח:) אמר רב יהודה אמר ר' ירמיה, ספק משמיה דרב ספק משמיה דשמואל: ג' מתירין את הבכור במקום שאין מומחה – היינו דוקא במומין מובהקין, כגון ניסמת עינו, נקטעה ידו, נשברה רגלו, כדאמרינן בשילהי "כל פסולי המוקדשין" (בכורות לו:) וה"נ דהוה מצי למימר: מי יימר דמזדקקי ליה ג' הדיוטות, דודאי לא מיזדקקי ליה משום דאין רואין מומין בי"ט. והא דנקט דמיזדקק ליה חכם – משום דחכם שרי בכל מומין: ולפ"ז א"ש גבי טבל. דאמר אם עבר ותיקנו מתוקן, דדוקא חכם אמר הכא לא מיזדקיק, אבל בג' הדיוטות לא אמר מי יימר. ומיהו, לפי מ"ש בפנים ה"נ המ"ל כו' לא א"ש טבל כדפי' לעיל, ולהכי נקט חכם משום דמתיר בכל מומין, ועיקר טעמא משום דהכא איכא איסורא והתם ליכא. והא דנקט התם: אם לא מיזדקיק ליה חכם סגיא בג' הדיוטות, אע"ג דשרי חשיב מוקצה, אי לא סגיא ליה בג' הדיוטות. [תו"י]:

כבתה אין לא כבתה לא. כן דרך התלמוד, דאע"ג דהוה מצי לאתויי רישא דקתני בהדיא: "חוץ מן הנר הדולק בשבת" מייתי סיפא, ודייק מינה*:
דכל היכא דקמכוין איכא איסורא דאורייתא. וא"ת: דהכא בכיבוי ליכא איסורא דאורייתא לר"ש, דמלאכה שאינה צריכה לגופה היא! וי"ל דה"ק: דכי מיכוין איכא איסורא דאורייתא, כגון בפתילה וצריך להבהבה. אע"פ שזה התירוץ דחוק הוא – הא בלאו הכי פריך ליה שפיר. הרב פור"ת:
הגה

א) הא דלא מייתי מתניתין דכל הכלים נוטל אדם קורנס לפצוע בו אגוזים משום דהתם נמי מיוחד להיתר לפצוע בו אגוזים אבל השירים כו' אין עושין כ"א ללבוש וכיון דאסור להתקשט בהן ה"ל לאסרן לטלטל אפ"ה כיון דאיכא תורת כלי עליה שרי והכא נמי נ"ש [תו"י]: ב) וליכא למימר דאע"ג דנפל מום מעי"ט איכא ג' מי יימר דהבעלים לא היו יודעים כלל שהיה בו מום לא היה דהתם מפ' כל שאין מומו ניכר לחכם משמע אבל בעלים יודעים ולאדא בר אוכמי נ"ל דאע"ג דר"ש איירי דנפל ביה מום מעי"ט מדקאי על ר"י מ"מ איירי נמי בנפל בו מום בי"ט או מום עובר מעי"ט מדקתני אין זה מן המוכן דמשמע אפילו ביקרו אינו מבוקר [תו"י]:

רבינו חננאל

שני צרורו' הואיל ואינה תורת כלי עליהן כמו (ש"מ עולה) [שא' עולא] בשירים ונזמים וטבעות הואיל [תורת] כלי עליהן: תנא מותר שמן שבנר ושבקערה אסור להסתפק ממנו. ור"ש מתיר. אלמא לר"ש לית ליה מוקצה. איני והא לענין בכור שנפל בו מום ביו"ט אמר ר"ש אין זה מן המוכן. ושנינן שני זה מזה. אדם מצפה מתי תכבה נרו ויסתפק מן השמן ומכין ליה. אבל לגבי מום ליכא למימר הכי. דאמר מי יימר דנפיל ביה מומא. ואי נפל מי יימר דמזדקיק ליה חכם ומותבינן מהא דתנן מפירין נדרים בשבת*) לצורך השבת ושנינן כל הנודרת על דעת בעלה היא נודרת ומבתחלה כך נדרה בחזקת שיפר לה בעלה והא [דתנן] נשאלין נדרים לצורך השבת נימא מי יימר דמיזדקיק ליה חכם. ושנינן שני התם דסגיא בג' הדיוטות: **רמי** אביי ומי אמר ר' שמעון כבה הנר מותר לטלטלו. מכלל דאי לא כבה חייש. דילמא כי מטלטל ליה שמא יכבה והא איהו דאמר גורר אדם מטה כסא וספסל ובלבד שלא יתכוין לעשות חריץ הנה דאע"ג דנעשה חריץ כיון דבלא כוונה נעשה לא חייש ר' שמעון. ושני כל היכא דכי מכוין אתי למגע באיסורא דאורייתא כגון כביית הנר וכיוצא בו חייש ר"ש וגזר מדרבנן. וכל היכא דכי מכוין איסורא [דרבנן] היא. כי לא מכוין שרי ר"ש לכתחלה איני והא מוכרי כסות כו' וכלאים איסורא דאורייתא היא. וכי לא מיכוין שרי ר"ש לכתחלה. ומשני רבא

*) עי' בחלופי גרסאות.

רב נסים גאון

התם אי לא מזדקק ליה חכם סגיא בג' הדיוטות. משתכח עיקר דילה במסכתא דנדרים בפרק נערה מאורסה (דף עח) אהרן ובניו וכל ישראל בפרשת נדרים למאי הילכתא אמר רב אחא בר יעקב להכשיר ג' הדיוטות וכותיה גרסי' בפרק יש נוחלין (בבא בתרא דף קכ):

גליון הש"ס

גמ' ואמר עולא. עי' לקמן דף נט ע"ב תוס' ד"ה מאן דרכה: תוס' ד"ה מי יימר דמזדקק לה בעל ואע"ג וכו' דהא חזי לשאר ב"א. עי' לקמן דף קכז ע"ב תוס' ד"ה כיון דתניא: שם ד"ה דכל היכא וכו' אע"פ שזה התירוץ דחוק. עי' בבכורות דף כה ע"א תוס' ד"ה דהוי ליה:

מסורת הש"ס

מו"ק יב:
[לעיל מד.] ביצה ל:
ביצה כו.
לקמן קנז. נדרים עז.
יבמות כט: גיטין פג: נדרים עג: נדה מו:
[תוספתא ביצה פ"ב] [לעיל כב. כט: ביצה כג: פסחים קח. מנחות מא:]
כלאים פ"ט מ"ה לעיל כט: פסחים כו:
רש"ל מ"ז
רש"ל מ"ז
והר"ם תירץ דהכא בנדרים דלחוא בידים הי' לנו לאסור כי התם דלא דחיא בידים [תוס' ישנים]
[עי' תוס' לעיל ל"ט: ד"ה אלא פניו וע' הר"מ]

הַנַּח לְנֵר שֶׁמֶן וּפְתִילָה – הוֹאִיל(א) דְּנַעֲשָׂה בָּסִים לְדָבָר הָאָסוּר. א"ר זֵירָא א"ר אַסִי א"ר יוֹחָנָן אָמַר ר' חֲנִינָא אָמַר רַבִּי רוֹמָנוּס: לִי הִתִּיר רַבִּי לְטַלְטֵל מַחְתָּה בְּאֶפְרָהּ. א"ל רַבִּי זֵירָא לְרַבִּי אַסִי: מִי אָמַר רַבִּי יוֹחָנָן הָכִי? וְהָתְנַן: *נוֹטֵל אָדָם בְּנוֹ וְהָאֶבֶן בְּיָדוֹ, אוֹ כַּלְכָּלָה וְהָאֶבֶן בְּתוֹכָהּ. וְאָמַר רַבָּה בַּר בַּר חָנָה א"ר יוֹחָנָן: בְּכַלְכָּלָה מְלֵאָה פֵּירוֹת עָסְקִינַן. טַעְמָא – דְּאִית בָּהּ פֵּירֵי, הָא לֵית בָּהּ פֵּירֵי – לָא! *°"אֶשְׁתּוֹמַם כְּשָׁעָה חֲדָא" וַאֲמַר: הָכָא נַמִי – דְּאִית בָּהּ קָרְטִין. אֲמַר אַבַּיֵי: קָרְטִין בֵּי רַבִּי מִי חֲשִׁיבִי? וְכִי תֵּימָא – חֲזוּ לַעֲנִיִּים, וְהָתַנְיָא: *בִּגְדֵי עֲנִיִּים – לַעֲנִיִּים, בִּגְדֵי עֲשִׁירִים – לַעֲשִׁירִים, *אֲבָל דַּעֲנִיִּים לַעֲשִׁירִים – לָא! אֶלָּא אָמַר אַבַּיֵי: מִידֵּי דַּהֲוָה אַגְּרָף שֶׁל רֵיעִי. אָמַר רָבָא: שְׁתֵּי תְּשׁוּבוֹת בַּדָּבָר: חֲדָא: גְּרָף שֶׁל רֵיעִי – מְאִיס, וְהַאי – לָא מְאִיס. וְעוֹד: גְּרָף שֶׁל רֵיעִי – מִיגְלֵי, וְהַאי מִיכְסֵי! אֶלָּא אָמַר רָבָא: כִּי הֲוֵינַן בֵּי רַב נַחְמָן [א]הֲוָה *מְטַלְטְלִינַן כָּנוּנָא אַגַּב קִיטְמָא וְאע"ג דְּאִיכָּא עֲלֵיהּ שִׁבְרֵי עֵצִים. מֵיתִיבִי: וְשָׁוִין שֶׁאִם יֵשׁ בָּהּ שִׁבְרֵי פְתִילָה – שֶׁאָסוּר לְטַלְטֵל! *אָמַר אַבַּיֵי: [ב]בִּגְלִילָא שָׁנוּ. לֵוִי בַּר שְׁמוּאֵל אַשְׁכַּחִינְהוּ לְרַבִּי אַבָּא וּלְרַב הוּנָא בַּר חִיָּיא דַּהֲווּ קָיְימִי אַפִּיתְחָא דְּבֵי רַב הוּנָא, אֲמַר לְהוּ: מַהוּ לְהַחֲזִיר מִטָּה שֶׁל טַרְסִיִּים בְּשַׁבָּת? אֲמַרוּ לֵיהּ: [ג]שַׁפִּיר דָּמֵי. אֲתָא לְקַמֵּיהּ דְּרַב יְהוּדָה, אֲמַר: הָא רַב וּשְׁמוּאֵל דְּאָמְרִי תַּרְוַיְיהוּ: הַמַּחֲזִיר מִטָּה שֶׁל טַרְסִיִּים בְּשַׁבָּת – חַיָּיב חַטָּאת. מֵיתִיבִי: *הַמַּחֲזִיר קְנֵה מְנוֹרָה בְּשַׁבָּת – חַיָּיב חַטָּאת, קְנֵה סַיָּידִין – לֹא יַחֲזִיר, וְאִם הֶחֱזִיר – פָּטוּר אֲבָל אָסוּר. רַבִּי סִימַאי אוֹמֵר: קֶרֶן עֲגוּלָּה – חַיָּיב, קֶרֶן פְּשׁוּטָה – פָּטוּר! אִינְהוּ דַּאֲמוּר כִּי הַאי תַּנָּא – דְּתַנְיָא: מַלְבְּנוֹת הַמִּטָּה, וְכַרְעוֹת הַמִּטָּה, וּלְוָוחִים שֶׁל סְקִיבָס – [ד]לֹא יַחֲזִיר, וְאִם הֶחֱזִיר – פָּטוּר אֲבָל

תורה אור: דניאל ד

רש"י

לְדָבָר הָאָסוּר. לַשַּׁלְהֶבֶת, דִּבְכִי הַאי מוּקְצֶה מוֹדֶה ר"ש שֶׁהַכְּלִי טָפֵל לַשַּׁלְהֶבֶת בְּעוֹדָהּ בּוֹ, וְלָאו מִשּׁוּם דְּקָיֵישׁ לְכָבְיָיה: בָּסִים. מוֹשָׁב. "אֶת כַּנּוֹ" מְתַרְגְּמִינַן "בְּסִיסֵיהּ": א"ר רוֹמָנוּס לִי הִתִּיר רַבִּי לְטַלְטֵל מַחְתָּה. שֶׁל לְבוֹנָה בְּאֶפְרָהּ. קס"ד בְּאֶפְרָהּ – עִם אֶפְרָהּ קָאָמַר, שֶׁהָאֵפֶר מוּקְצֶה וְלֹא הָיוּ צְרִיכִין לוֹ, וְאַשְׁמְעִינַן דְּאַגַּב מַחְתָּה דְּאִיכָּא תּוֹרַת כְּלִי עָלֶיהָ – טִלְטְלָהּ עִם אֶפְרָהּ: נוֹטֵל אָדָם. הַכַּלְכָּלָה בְּשַׁבָּת וְהָאֶבֶן בְּתוֹכָהּ: הָא לֵיכָּא פֵּרִי לָא. דִּכְלִי נַעֲשָׂה בָּסִיס לָאֶבֶן וּטְפֵלָה לוֹ, וּבָטֵל תּוֹרַת כְּלִי דִּידֵיהּ. וְהָכִי נַמִי נַעֲשֵׂית מַחְתָּה בָּסִיס לָאֵפֶר. וְר' יוֹחָנָן שָׁמְעִי' לֵיהּ לְעֵיל, דִּכְר' יְהוּדָה סְבִירָא לֵיהּ: דְּאִית בֵּיהּ קָרְטִין. שֶׁנִּשְׁתַּיְּירוּ מִן הָאוּר, וּלְבוֹנָה דַּחֲזְיָא לְהָרִיחַ. וְאַגַּב לְבוֹנָה מְטַלְטֵל לַמַּחְתָּה עִם אֶפְרָהּ, דּוּמְיָא דְּכַלְכָּלָה מְלֵאָה פֵּירוֹת וְהָאֶבֶן בְּתוֹכָהּ: קָרְטִין. שֶׁל שִׁיּוּר לְבוֹנָה: בֵּי רַבִּי. דְּנָשִׂיא וְעָשִׁיר הֲוָה, מִי חֲשִׁיבִי: בִּגְדֵי עֲנִיִּים. שָׁלֹשׁ עַל שָׁלֹשׁ, אוֹ שֶׁחוּטָן עָבֶה – הָווּ בְּגָדִים לַעֲנִיִּים לְעִנְיַן טוּמְאָה: בִּגְדֵי עֲשִׁירִים. שְׁלֹשָׁה עַל שְׁלֹשָׁה הָווּ בְּגָדִים לַעֲשִׁירִים, וְכָל שֶׁכֵּן לַעֲנִיִּים. אֲבָל בִּגְדֵי עֲנִיִּים לַעֲשִׁירִים – לָא הֲוֵה בֶּגֶד גַּבַּיְיהוּ, וְלָא מְקַבְּלֵי טוּמְאָה. הָכָא נַמִי: בֵּי רַבִּי(ג) בָּטְלֵי קָרְטִין: אֶלָּא אָמַר אַבַּיֵי. הָא דְּשָׁרֵי לֵיהּ לְטַלְטֵל מַחְתָּה בְּאֶפְרָהּ – מִשּׁוּם דְּאֶפְרָהּ מְאִיס עֲלֵיהּ לִרְאוֹתוֹ, וַהֲוֵי כִּגְרָף שֶׁל רְעִי. דְּתַנְיָא בְּמַסֶּכֶת בֵּיצָה (דף לו:): מוּתָּר לְהוֹצִיאוֹ לָאַשְׁפָּה שֶׁבֶּחָצֵר: גְּרָף. כְּלִי חֶרֶס הַמּוּכָן לְכָךְ: מִיכְסֵי. כָּל מַחְתּוֹת מְכוּסוֹת הֵן, וְיֵשׁ בָּהֶן נְקָבִים לְהוֹצִיא הָרֵיחַ: כָּנוּנָא. כְּלִי נְחֹשֶׁת שֶׁמְּבִיאִין בּוֹ הָאוּר לִפְנֵי שָׂרִים לְהִתְחַמֵּם: אַגַּב קִטְמֵיהּ. שֶׁהָיוּ צְרִיכִין לְאֶפְרוֹ לְכַסּוֹת רוֹק אוֹ צוֹאָה. וְא"ת: מַה צַּד אִיסּוּר יֵשׁ כָּאן? הַיְינוּ רְבוּתָא, דְּאע"ג דְּאִיכָּא עֲלֵיהּ שִׁבְרֵי עֵצִים. וְהָא דְּר' רוֹמָנוּס נַמִי, הַאי מַחְתָּה בְּאֶפְרָהּ דְּקָאָמַר, מַחְתָּה בִּשְׁבִיל אֶפְרָהּ שֶׁהָיָה צָרִיךְ לוֹ, וְדַעְתַּיְיהוּ עֲלֵיהּ מֵאֶתְמוֹל. וּרְבוּתָא אַשְׁמְעִינַן, (כֵּיוָן) אע"ג דְּאִיכָּא עֲלֵיהּ שִׁבְרֵי עֵצִים דַּהֲוֵי כְּכַלְכָּלָה שֶׁל פֵּירוֹת וְהָאֶבֶן בְּתוֹכָהּ: וְשָׁוִין. ר' יְהוּדָה וְר"ש שֶׁנֶּחְלְקוּ בְּנֵר יָשָׁן: בִּגְלִילָא שָׁנוּ. שֶׁחֲשׁוּבוֹת לָהֶן שִׁבְרֵי פְתִילָה, שֶׁאֵין בְּגָדִים שֶׁל פִּשְׁתָּן מְצוּיִין לָהֶם – הִלְכָּךְ לָא בָּטְלֵי, וְנַעֲשָׂה נֵר בָּסִיס לָהֶן: טַרְסִיִּים. צוֹרְפֵי נְחֹשֶׁת אוֹ גַּרְדִּיִּים, וְהוֹלְכִין מֵעִיר לְעִיר לִמְלַאכְתָּן, וְנוֹשְׂאִין עִמָּהֶן מִטּוֹת שֶׁל פְּרָקִים: חַיָּיב חַטָּאת. הוּא תְּחִלָּתוֹ וּגְמָרוֹ, וְנִמְצָא עוֹשֶׂה כְּלִי. וְחַיָּיב מִשּׁוּם מַכֶּה בְּפַטִּישׁ – אָב לְכָל גּוֹמְרֵי מְלָאכָה, וְלֹא מִשּׁוּם בּוֹנֶה – דְּאֵין בִּנְיָן בְּכֵלִים: קְנֵה מְנוֹרָה. שֶׁעוֹשִׂין מִמֶּנָּה קָנִים לְנֵרוֹת הַרְבֵּה וְנוֹטְלִין הֵימֶנָּה, וּבִשְׁעַת הַצּוֹרֶךְ מַחֲזִירִין אוֹתוֹ: קָנֶה שֶׁל סַיָּידִין. הַטָּחִין וּמְלַבְּנִין הַבַּיִת בְּסִיד, יֵשׁ לָהֶן קָנִים שֶׁל פְּרָקִים, וְנוֹתֵן מַטְלִית בְּרֹאשָׁהּ וְשׁוֹרִין בְּסִיד הַמָּחוּי, וְטָח אֶת הַבַּיִת. וּכְשֶׁהוּא טָח מִלְּמַטָּה, אִי אֶפְשָׁר לוֹ אֶלָּא בְּקָנֶה קָצָר, וּכְשֶׁהוּא הוֹלֵךְ וּמַגְבִּיהַּ – מוֹסִיף קָנֶה עַל קָנֶה וּמַאֲרִיכוֹ: פָּטוּר. שֶׁאֵין זֶה גְּמָרוֹ, שֶׁהֲרֵי צָרִיךְ לַחֲזוֹר וּלְפָרְקוֹ תָּמִיד: קֶרֶן עֲגוּלָּה וְקֶרֶן פְּשׁוּטָה. שְׁנֵיהֶם מִין כְּלֵי זֶמֶר, וְהוּא עָשׂוּי נְקָבִים נְקָבִים כִּכְבָרָה, וּמַכְנִיס בָּהֶן חֲלִילִים וּמוֹצִיאִין קוֹלוֹת הַרְבֵּה. קֶרֶן עֲגוּלָּה – מַעֲשֵׂה אוּמָּן הוּא, וְצָרִיךְ לִתְקוֹעַ בַּנְּקָבִים בְּחוֹזֶק, וְהָוְיָא מְלָאכָה. וּבְקֶרֶן פָּשׁוּט – מַכְנִיסוֹ בְּרֶוַח, וְדַרְכָּן לְפָרְקָם תָּמִיד, וּפָטוּר. קָתָנֵי מִיהַת בִּקְנֵי מְנוֹרָה דְּחַיָּיב, וְהוּא הַדִּין לְמִטָּה שֶׁל טַרְסִיִּים: אִינְהוּ. רַבִּי אַבָּא וְרַב הוּנָא בַּר חִיָּיא: דַּאֲמוּר כִּי הַאי תַּנָּא. כְּרַבִּי שִׁמְעוֹן, דְּמַתִּיר לְכַתְּחִלָּה: מַלְבְּנוֹת הַמִּטָּה. כְּעֵין רַגְלַיִם קְטַנִּים יֵשׁ לָהֶן בֵּית קִיבּוּל, וּמַכְנִיסִים לְתוֹכָן רָאשֵׁי כַּרְעֵי הַמִּטָּה, שֶׁלֹּא יִרְקְבוּ בָּאָרֶץ: לְוָוחִים שֶׁל סְקִיבָס. עֵץ קָטָן כְּמִין דַּף שֶׁתּוֹקְעִין בְּקֶשֶׁת שֶׁקּוֹרִין אַרְבַּלֶּסְטְרָ"א, שֶׁעָלָיו מוֹשֵׁךְ הַחֵץ: יִתְקַע

תוספות

הנח לנר שמן ופתילה הואיל ונעשה בסים לדבר האסור. אילטריך למימר בשמן דנעשה בסיס לדבר האסור, דאי לאו הכי – לא היה הנר אסור לטלטל, דהוי בסיס לדבר האסור ולדבר המותר ושרי, כדאמר בסמוך: כי הוינן בי רב נחמן הוה מטלטלינן כנונא אגב קיטמא, אע"ג דאיכא עליה שברי עצים. ואם תאמר: פתילה אמאי קאמר דהויא בסיס לדבר האסור? היא עצמה הויא דבר האסור, כדאמר לקמן: "ושוין שאם יש בה שברי פתילות שאסור לטלטלה"! וי"ל דשברי פתילה הוי שברי כלים, ודמי לצרורות. אבל פתילה שלימה שהיא כלי – הוה שרי, אי לאו דנעשה בסיס לדבר האסור:

לי התיר רבי לטלטל מחתה באפרה. השתא ס"ד דאפר מחתה מוקצה הוא: **ואמר** רבה ב"ב חנה א"ר יוחנן כו'. תימה: אמאי לא פריך בלאו מילתיה דרבי יוחנן ממתני' דפ' "נוטל" (לקמן דף קמב:), דתנן: מעות שע"ג הכר – מנער את הכר והן נופלות, וכן אבן שעל פי החבית – מטה על צדה והיא נופלת, אבל טלטול גמור אסור! ואור"י דה"א דשאני מעות דחשיבי ולא בטלי. ואבן שע"פ החבית ה"א דמיירי שהוא מתוקן לסתום פי החבית והחבית צריכה לה, ולכך לא בטלה:

בגדי עניים לעניים. אומר ר"ת: דדוקא בטומאת מדרס, דביחוד תליא מלתא. אבל בשאר טומאות – לא תליא מלתא ביחוד, דאפילו היה מוטל באשפה מרבינן *מ"והבגד" דשלש על שלש מיטמא, בין לעניים בין לעשירים, דבקרא לא מפליג מידי. ומייתי ר"ת ראיה, דתנן במסכת כלים (פרק כ"ז מ"ב): דבגד מטמא משום שלשה על שלשה למדרס, משום שלש על שלש לטמא מת. וע"כ בעשירים מיירי, דבפכ"ח תנן התם: בגדי עניים, אע"פ שאין בהם שלשה על שלשה – טמאין מדרס. וא"ת: הכא דפריך מברייתא, אמאי לא פריך ממתני' דפכ"ח דכלים שהבאתי? ואור"י: דאי ממתני' – ה"א דבגדי עניים היינו כעין שק, שעיקרו עשוי לעניים ואפי' ביד עשירים אינו צריך שלשה על שלשה. אבל שאר בגדים – בעי שלשה על שלשה, שאינו עומד אלא לעשירים להכי מייתי ברייתא דלא שייך לפרשה הכי:

הוה מטלטלין כנונא אגב קיטמא. פי' "כנונא", מחתה. והיינו מחתה באפרה דלעיל, פי': אגב אפרה שהוסק מע"ש, דמוכן הוא, דחזי לכסות בה רוק או צואה. וקשה, דמשמע דוקא אגב קיטמא שרי, הא לאו הכי – נעשה בסיס לדבר האסור. ואילו בפ"ב דבילה (כא: ושם) אמר, גבי אין מזמנין גוי בשבת משום שיורי כוסות, פריך: וניטלטלינהו אגב כסא, מי לא אמר רבא: כי הוינן בי רב נחמן הוה מטלטלינן כנונא אגב קיטמא, אף על גב דאיכא עליה שברי עצים! ומאי פריך? שאני כנונא דאגב קטמא מטלטל לה, אבל בכוס ליכא אלא דבר האסור! ואור"י, דשיורי כוסות לא חשיבי למיהוי כוס בטל לגבייהו, אף על גב שאין היתר עמהן בכוס טפי גרעי משברי עצים שעם הקיטמא בכנונא: **אע"ג** דאיכא עליה שברי עצים. נראה לרבינו תם: דשברי עצים חשיבי טפי מאבן שבכלכלה. דאם לא כן – מאי קמ"ל ואדמקשי ליה מברייתא דשוין כו' ליסייעיה ממתני' דכלכלה והאבן בתוכה. אלא שברי עצים חשיבי טפי ויש לדמות שברי עצים לגבי אפר כשברי פתילה לגבי שמן:

בגלילא שנו. פירש בקונט' שחשובות להן שברי פתילה שאין בגדי פשתן מצויין להם. ואין נראה לר"ת דהא אמרי' בשילהי ב"ק (דף קיט.): לוקחין מן הנשים כלי צמר ביהודה וכלי פשתן בגליל, משמע שמצוי פשתן הרבה שם. ומפרש ר"ת: בגלילא שנו – שהיה להם רוב שמן, ולהכי לא בטלי שברי פתילה אגב שמן. וכן משמע בפ"ק דסנהדרין (דף יא:) גבי טול איגרת וכתוב לאחנא בני גלילאה עילאה ותתאה כו' דזמן ביעורא מטא לאפרושא מעשרא ממעטני זיתא. ואמר בנזיר בפרק "בית שמאי" (דף לא:) בגלילא שנו, דחמרא עדיף ממשחא. ויין היה מצוי להם הרבה, כדאמר ב"המוציא יין" (לקמן עח.) גבי מים כדי לשוף בהן את הקילור וקאמר בגלילא שנו, *דרפואת מים שכיח טפי משתיה, שהיה להן רוב יין והיו שותין הכל יין. ואפילו הכי חמרא עדיף להו ממישחא, כי השמן היה להם בזול יותר. ורש"י פי' נמי ב"המוציא" (שם) שמחמת עניותא היו עושין רפואה מן המים ואין עושין מן היין רק שתייה, ולפיכך היתה רפואת מים שכיחא. ואין נראה, דכיון שלא היה להם יין לשיפות הקילור, א"כ שכיחא שתיית מים טובא! ואמרי' בעלמא: *אף ערב יוה"כ בגליל, שהיו מרבים בסעודה. משמע שעשירים היו. [וע"ע תוספות חגיגה כה: ד"ה בגלילא]:

*[חולין פג.]

ורבינו מאיר פי' כי מרוב שתיית יין הי' להם חכלילי עינים ושכיחי רפואת מים טובא [תו"י]

עין משפט נר מצוה

נז א ב מיי' פכ"ו מהל' שבת הלכה יג טור שו"ע או"ח סימן שי סעיף סעיף ח:

נח ג ד מיי' פכ"ב מהל' שבת הלכה כו כח סמג לאוין סה טור שו"ע או"ח סימן שיג סעיף ו:

רבינו חננאל

הנח לנר ופתילה ושמן דלא גזר ר"ש אלא הואיל ונעשה כל אחד בסים לדבר האסור. ופשוטה היא: **אמר** רבא כי היינו בי רב נחמן היינו מטלטלי כנונא אגב קיטומה אף על גב דאיכא עליה שברי עצים. מיתיבי ושוין שאם יש בה שברי פתילה שאסור לטלטלה. ופריק אביי בגלילא שנו. פירוש בגליל שנו שדרכם להדליק בשברי פתילות. וכיון שדרכם להדליק בשברי פתילות נעשו מוקצות בשבת לפיכך אסור לטלטל אפילו הנרות שיש בהן שברי פתילות. אבל שברי עצים דכנונא לא חשיבי ובטלי: **לוי** בר שמואל בעא מר' אבא ומרב הונא בר חייא מהו להחזי' מטה של (פרסיים) [טרסיים] בשבת אמרו ליה שרי. אמר להו רב יהודה רב ושמואל דאמרי תרווייהו המחזיר מטה של (פרסיים) [טרסיים] בשבת חייב חטאת. מיתיבי המחזיר קנה מנורה בשבת חייב חטאת קנה של ציירין לא יחזיר ואם החזיר פטור אבל אסור. ר' סימאי א' קרן [עגולה חייב קרן] פשוטה פטור. קתני מיהת המחזיר קנה מנורה בשבת חייב חטאת. קשיא לר' אבא ולרב הונא דשרי. ושני' אינהו דאמור כי האי תנא דתניא אם היה רפוי מותר. דתניא מלבנות המטה וכרעי המטה [ולווחין] של סקיבם לא יחזיר. ואם החזיר פטור אבל

רב נסים גאון

אלא אמר אביי מידי דהוה אגרף של רעי. משתכח במס' יום טוב בפרק משילין פירות (דף לו) אמר שמואל גרף של רעי ועביט מימי רגלים מותר להוציאו לאשפה ובפרק נוטל אדם את בנו (דף קמג) אמרו הני גרעיני דתמרי כול' רב הונא בריה דרב יהושע עביד להו גרף של רעי וכן אמימר עביד להו גרף של רעי: **אמר** אביי בגלילא שנו. כבר טרחו בזה השינוי ששינה אביי הרבה מן החכמים ולא שמעתי מהם כלום ולא מצאתי בו לאחד מן הגאונים פירוש אבל טרחתי על שינויו ומצאתי במס' נזירות בפ' בית שמאי אומרים הקדש טעות הקדש (דף לא) והא שמן עדיף מיין אי משום הא לא קשיא בגלילא שנו דחמרא עדיף ממשחא זה מודיע שהשמן היה אצלם מצוי הרבה וכי מה שהושם בנר ויש בו שברי פתילה אין לו חשיבות אצלם ואינן משתמשין בו לצרכם והרי הוא כדין המוקצה שאסור לטלטלו ולכך

רשב"ג

שנו חכמים כי בגליל אסור לטלטל נר שיש בו שברי פתילה לפי שהשמן הנותר בנר לא חשיב להו וכבר זה הפירוש הודענו באלו הימים לתלמידנו ופירשנו להם בזה הענין ואפשר להיאמר בו פירוש אחר שאנשי גליל לפי שלא היו מקפידין על לשונם ולא דייקי לישאנא ולא גמיר מחד רבה ולא גלו מסכתא למסכתא כמו שהוא מפורש במסכת עירובין בפרק כיצד מעברין (דף נג) ולא היה תלמודם מקויים בידם אסרו עליהם החכמים טלטול נר שיש בתוכו שברי פתילה *) עלי דרך האיסורים ואל תחבט ואל תסייג ויקוי דאלך איצא קולהום פי עדה (מוצאע) [מואצע] מן אל תלמוד מתל הדא אל קול עלי טריק אל תנקין להם

*) פירושם בערבי על דרך האיסורים והגדר והסייג ונמצא סיוע לזה במקומות הרבה מהתלמוד משל זה המאמר על דרך הגידרון להם נזכיר מזה מה שנמצא בפ' תומר בקודש.

מסורת הש"ס

לקמן קמא:

[מו"ק ג: קידושין לט: סוכה מב. חולין כח.]

[עירובין כט:]

[עי' תוספות לקמן קכז: ד"ה כיון וכו']

ביצה כא: ע"ש

[לקמן עח.]

[תוספ' פי"ג]

הגהות הב"ח

(א) גמ' ופתיל' הואיל ונעשה בסים: (ב) רש"י ד"ה בגדי עשירים וכו' ה"נ בי ר' לא חשיבי קרטין ובטלי הס"ד:

גליון הש"ס

גמ' קרן עגולה חייב. עי' כלים פי"א מ"ז:

אֲבָל אָסוּר. ^א^וְלֹא יִתְקַע, וְאִם תָּקַע – חַיָּיב חַטָּאת. רשב"ג אוֹמֵר: ^ב^אִם הָיָה רָפוּי – מוּתָּר. בֵּי רַב חָמָא הֲוָה מִטָּה גָּלְלַנִיתָא, הֲוָה מְהַדְרִי לַהּ בְּיוֹמָא טָבָא. א"ל הַהוּא מִדְּרַבָּנָן לְרָבָא: מַאי דַּעְתִּיךְ, בִּנְיָן מִן הַצַּד הוּא, נְהִי דְּאִיסּוּרָא דְּאוֹרַיְיתָא – לֵיכָּא, אִיסּוּרָא דְּרַבָּנַן מִיהָא אִיכָּא! אֲמַר לֵיהּ: אֲנָא כְּרשב"ג סְבִירָא לִי, דְּאָמַר: אִם הָיָה רָפוּי – מוּתָּר.§ **מתני'** *^ג^נוֹתְנִין כְּלִי תַּחַת הַנֵּר לְקַבֵּל נִיצוֹצוֹת. וְלֹא יִתֵּן לְתוֹכוֹ מַיִם – מִפְּנֵי שֶׁהוּא מְכַבֶּה.§ **גמ'** וְהָא *קָמְבַטֵּל כְּלִי מֵהֵיכָנוֹ! אֲמַר רַב הוּנָא בְּרֵיהּ דְּרַב יְהוֹשֻׁעַ: נִיצוֹצוֹת אֵין בָּהֶן מַמָּשׁ.§ "וְלֹא יִתֵּן לְתוֹכוֹ מַיִם מִפְּנֵי שֶׁהוּא מְכַבֶּה".§ לֵימָא תְּנַן סְתָמָא כְּרַבִּי יוֹסֵי, *דְּאָמַר: גּוֹרֵם לְכִיבּוּי – אָסוּר! וְתִסְבְּרָא?! אֵימוּר דְּאָמַר ר' יוֹסֵי – בַּשַּׁבָּת, בְּעֶרֶב שַׁבָּת מִי אֲמַר? וְכִי תֵּימָא הָכָא נַמִי בַּשַּׁבָּת – וְהָתַנְיָא: נוֹתְנִין כְּלִי תַּחַת הַנֵּר לְקַבֵּל נִיצוֹצוֹת בַּשַּׁבָּת – וְאֵין צָרִיךְ לוֹמַר בְּע"ש, וְלֹא יִתֵּן לְתוֹכוֹ מַיִם מִפְּנֵי שֶׁהוּא מְכַבֶּה מֵע"ש, וְאֵין צָרִיךְ לוֹמַר בַּשַּׁבָּת! אֶלָּא אָמַר רַב אַשִׁי: אֲפִילּוּ תֵּימָא רַבָּנַן, שָׁאנֵי הָכָא – מִפְּנֵי שֶׁמְּקָרֵב אֶת כִּיבּוּיוֹ.§

הדרן עלך כירה

בַּמֶּה *^ד^טוֹמְנִין וּבַמָּה אֵין טוֹמְנִין? אֵין טוֹמְנִין לֹא בְּגֶפֶת, וְלֹא בְּזֶבֶל, לֹא בְּמֶלַח, וְלֹא בְּסִיד, וְלֹא בְּחוֹל, בֵּין לַחִין בֵּין יְבֵשִׁין. וְלֹא בְּתֶבֶן וְלֹא בְּזַגִּין וְלֹא בְּמוֹכִין וְלֹא בַּעֲשָׂבִין בִּזְמַן שֶׁהֵן לַחִין, אֲבָל טוֹמְנִין בָּהֶן כְּשֶׁהֵן יְבֵשִׁין.§ **גמ'** אִיבַּעְיָא לְהוּ: גֶּפֶת שֶׁל זֵיתִים תְּנַן, אֲבָל דְּשׁוּמְשְׁמִין – שַׁפִּיר דָּמֵי, אוֹ דִּילְמָא: דְּשׁוּמְשְׁמִין תְּנַן, וְכָל שֶׁכֵּן דְּזֵיתִים? ת"ש, דְּאָמַר ר' זֵירָא מִשּׁוּם חַד דְּבֵי ר' יַנַּאי: קוּפָּה שֶׁטָּמַן בָּהּ אָסוּר לַהֲנִיחָהּ עַל גֶּפֶת שֶׁל זֵיתִים, ש"מ: שֶׁל זֵיתִים תְּנַן. לְעוֹלָם אֵימָא לָךְ: לְעִנְיַן הַטְמָנָה – דְּשׁוּמְשְׁמִין נַמִי אָסוּר, לְעִנְיַן אַסּוּקֵי

רש"י

יִתְקַע. בְּחוֹזֶק, עַל יְדֵי יְתֵדוֹת שֶׁקּוֹרִין קוויי"ש: מִטָּה גָּלְלַנִיתָא. טירנדי"ן, וְהוּא כְּעֵין שֶׁל טַרְסִיִּים*: מִן הַצַּד. מִפְּנֵי שֶׁאֵינָהּ תְּקוּעָה, וּמְהַדְּקָהּ בְּחוֹזֶק קָרֵי לָהּ מִן הַצַּד – כְּלוֹמַר ע"י שִׁינּוּי: **גמ'** וְהָא קָא מְבַטֵּל כְּלִי מֵהֵיכָנוֹ. דְּלֹא יוּכַל לִיטְּלוֹ מִשָּׁם כָּל הַיּוֹם, דְּנַעֲשָׂה בָּסִיס לַנִּיצוֹצוֹת. לֵימָא תֶּהֱוֵי תְּיוּבְתֵּיהּ דְּרַב חִסְדָּא דְּאָסַר בְּפִירְקִין (דף מג.): אֵין בָּהֶן מַמָּשׁ. מִשֶּׁכָּבוּ, וּמוּתָּר לִיטְּלָן: כְּרַבִּי יוֹסֵי. בְּ"כָל כִּתְבֵי הַקֹּדֶשׁ", דְּקָתָנֵי: עוֹשֶׂה מְחִילָּה בְּכָל הַכֵּלִים, בֵּין מְלֵאִין בֵּין רֵיקָנִין, כְּדֵי שֶׁלֹּא תַּעֲבוֹר הַדְּלֵיקָה. ר' יוֹסֵי אוֹסֵר בִּכְלֵי חֶרֶס חֲדָשִׁים מְלֵאִים מַיִם, שֶׁאֵין יְכוֹלִין לְקַבֵּל הָאוּר וְהֵן מִתְבַּקְּעִים וּמְכַבִּין אֶת הַדְּלֵיקָה: בְּעֶרֶב שַׁבָּת. כְּגוֹן זֶה, שֶׁנּוֹתֵן הַמַּיִם מִבְּעוֹד יוֹם בִּכְלִי תַּחַת הַנֵּר: וְכִי תֵּימָא הָכָא נַמִי. אֵין נוֹתְנִין לְתוֹכוֹ מַיִם בְּשַׁבָּת קָאָמַר, וְר' יוֹסֵי הִיא: וְהָתַנְיָא. אֲפִילּוּ בְּע"ש אָסוּר. וְאִי לִגְרַס כִּיבּוּי מְדַמֵּית לָהּ – אֲפִילּוּ כְּרַבִּי יוֹסֵי לָא מִיתּוֹקְמָא, דִּבְע"ש לֹא אָמַר רַבִּי יוֹסֵי: אֶלָּא אָמַר רַב אַשִׁי. מַתְנִיתִין אֲפִילּוּ לְרַבָּנַן, דְּלָא דָּמֵי לִגְרַס כִּיבּוּי. דְּהָתָם כִּי מָטֵי דְּלֵיקָה לַכֵּלִים – דְּלֵיקָה הוּא דְּפָקַע לְהוּ, וּגְרָמָא בְּעָלְמָא הוּא. אֲבָל זֶה שֶׁנָּתַן הַמַּיִם מַמָּשׁ תַּחַת הַנֵּר – מְכַבֶּה מַמָּשׁ הוּא, וּגְזֵירָה מִבְּעוֹד יוֹם אַטּוּ מִשֶּׁחֲשֵׁכָה: שֶׁמְּקָרֵב אֶת כִּיבּוּיוֹ. זְמַן כִּיבּוּי לְהֶדְיָא, וַהֲוָה לֵיהּ מְכַבֶּה מַמָּשׁ אִי הֲוָה יָהֵיב לֵיהּ בְּשַׁבָּת:

הדרן עלך כירה

בַּמֶּה טוֹמְנִין. הַבָּא לְסַלֵּק קְדֵירָה מֵעַל גַּבֵּי כִּירָה וּלְטוֹמְנָהּ בְּדָבָר אַחֵר, וְאָמְרוּ חֲכָמִים:* אֵין טוֹמְנִין בְּדָבָר הַמּוֹסִיף הֶבֶל אֶלָּא בְּדָבָר הַמַּעֲמִיד הֶבֶל, מִי הוּא הַמּוֹסִיף וְאָסוּר. גֶּפֶת. פְּסוֹלֶת שֶׁל בֵּית הַבַּד שֶׁל שֶׁמֶן, שֶׁהוּא כָּנוּס יַחַד וְחַם מְאֹד לִהְיוֹת. יֵשׁ בָּהֶן הֶבֶל הַרְבֵּה יוֹתֵר מִיבֵשִׁין. זַגִּין. פְּסוֹלֶת שֶׁל יֶקֶב יַיִן: מוֹכִין. כָּל דָּבָר רַךְ קָרוּי מוֹכִין, כְּגוֹן צֶמֶר גֶּפֶן, וּתְלִישֵׁי צֶמֶר רַךְ שֶׁל בְּהֵמָה וּגְרִירַת בְּגָדִים בְּלוּיִים: **גמ'** קוּפָּה שֶׁטָּמַן בָּהּ. שֶׁטּוֹמֵן בָּהּ מוֹכִין וְטוֹמֵן בָּהּ קְדֵירָה: לְעִנְיַן הַטְמָנָה. לְטוֹמְנוֹ בְּתוֹכָהּ: אַסּוּקֵי

תוספות

רבן שמעון בן גמליאל אומר אם היה רפוי מותר. ולעיל נמי מיירי ברפוי וקשה קלת: דהיכי פליגי כולי האי? דמר מחייב חטאת ומר שרי אפי' לכתחלה? ועוד: הא אין בנין וסתירה בכלים! ועוד: תקשה לרב יהודה הך ברייתא, דליכא תנא דמחייב חטאת! וי"ל דהכי קאמר לעיל, הא רב ושמואל דאמרי תרווייהו "המחזיר מטה של טרסיים בשבת חייב חטאת" כשאינו רפוי, ואם כן ברפוי – אין סברא להתיר לכתחלה:

לימא תנן סתמא כרבי יוסי דאמר גורם לכיבוי אסור. הוה מצי למימר: וליטעמיך, הא רבי יוסי גופיה לא אמרה אלא בדליקה, משום דאדם בהול על ממונו אי שרינא ליה אתי לכבויי, והכי מפרש ב"כל כתבי" (לקמן קכ:) אבל הכא – ליכא למגזר, דהא יש כלי תחת הנר ואינו בהול! ובכמה מקומות בהתלמוד יכול לומר "וליטעמיך" ואינו אומר:

מפני שמקרב את כבויו. פירוש: דגזרינן ע"ש אטו שבת, ובשבת יכול לבא לידי כיבוי אם יגביה הכלי בשעת נפילת הנילולות. ואם תאמר: מאי שנא שריית דיו וסממנים ופריסת מצודה, דשרינן בפ"ק (דף יח:) עם השמש, והכא אסרינן מע"ש שלא יבא לעשות בשבת? ותירץ הרב פור"ת: דהתם ליכא למיחש שמא יעשה כן בשבת – דהא אב מלאכה הן, אבל הכא איכא למיחש – דלא דמי איסור כל כך במה שמניח כלי תחת הנילולות, ואיכא למיחש שמא יבא לידי כיבוי, שיתחיל ליתן המים קודם נפילת הנילולות, וקודם גמר הנתינה יפלו ומכבה בידים, או שיגביה הכלי עם המים כנגד הנילולות, כדפרישית. ואף על גב דאותו כיבוי אין בו חיוב חטאת לר' שמעון, דמלאכה שאינה צריכה לגופה היא – החמירו אטו כיבוי דחיוב חטאת. ואע"ג דהוי גזירה לגזירה – קים להו לרבנן דהכא שייך למגזר טפי. ורש"י דפי' דהוה מכבה ממש – לאו דוקא, אלא כלומר: שיוכל לבא לידי כיבוי. ור"ת גרים כפירוש ר"ח: מפני שמקרב כיבוי, דהתם הוא דשרי לעשות מחילה מכלים שיש בתוכן מים – שאינו מכבה כלום עד שיתבקעו הכלים, אבל הכא אין הפסק בין מים לנילולות – ומיד נכבות כשנופלות בכלי, והוי כמחילת מים דאסירא, כגון מחילת שלג וברד. וקשה לפירושו, דירושלמי מוקי מתני' כר' יוסי, אבל לרבנן – אפי' מחילות של מים מותר ובפ' "כל כתבי" (לקמן קכ:) נמי שרו רבנן דר' יוסי בטלית שאחז בו האור מצד אחד ליתן עליו מים מצד אחר, ואם כבתה – כבתה, ונראה דלפי התלמוד שלנו יש לחלק: דבמחילה של מים אע"ג דאין דבר מפסיק – מ"מ שרי, שאין האש נופלת לתוך המים להדיא כי הכא, שהמים תחת הנילולות ומקרב כיבוין טפי. ועוד: דאיכא למימר דהתלמוד שלנו אוסר במחילות של מים לרבנן, ומשום הכי מוקי מתניתין כרבנן, ופליג אירושלמי. ולא דמי לטלית שאחז בו האור מצד אחד שאינו אלא שלא תתפשט האור. ומה שרגילים לתת מים בזכוכית שקורין לאמפ"א ונותנין עליה שמן בע"ש – אין זה קרוי קירוב כיבוי, דכיון שאין מתכוין לכיבוי כלל אלא להגביה את השמן – לא שייך למגזר מידי שמא יעשה בשבת, ושרי אפי' לר' יוסי, וכ"ש לרבנן. דאל"כ – אפי' בלא מים אסור, שהנילולות נופלות בשמן: ועוד איכא למימר: דהתלמוד שלנו אסר מחילה של מים לרבנן, ומש"ה מוקי מתני' כר' יוסי, ופליג אירושלמי, ול"ד לטלית שאחז בו האור מצד אחד, שאינו אלא שלא תתפשט האור [ת"י]:

הדרן עלך כירה

במה טומנין וכו' אין טומנין לא בגפת. פירש הר"ר יוסף בשם רבינו שמואל: דמיירי בבשיל ולא בשיל. אבל קדרה חייתא ובשיל – שרינן בפ"ק (דף יח:). ואין נראה לר"ת: דהא אית לן לאוקמא מתניתין בכסס קדרות שהן מבושלים בין השמשות. ועוד: דמסתמא איירי מתני' דומיא דמתני' דכירה, דמיירי בבשיל כמאכל בן דרוסאי. ונראה לר"ת: שיש לחלק בין השהאה להטמנה. דודאי להשהות מותר כשהוא מאכל בן דרוסאי, שאין חיתוי מעט מועיל לו שהרי מגולה הוא, ושליט ביה אוירא. אבל הטמנה, שעושין לצורך מחר והוא מוטמן – יש לחוש שמא יחתה, שמעט חיתוי מועיל לו ליתפס חומו, וגזרו להטמין בכל דבר המוסיף הבל – גזירה שמא יטמין ברמץ ויחתה: דזיתים

רבינו חננאל

אסור. לא יתקע ואם תקע חייב חטאת רבן שמעון בן גמליאל אומר אם היה רפוי מותר המחזיר קני מנורה חייב חטאת כמשמעו מפני שמתקן כלי כבנין. קנה של ציידין הדכם לתת קנה דק דק בתוך ראש קנה עבה כדי שיהא (נכוה) [גבוה] ולא יהא משבר וזהו פטור אבל אסור. קרן עגולה חייב פשוטה פטור. אלו הן כלי שיר. והן של חליות ויש מהן קרן עגולה וקרן פשוטה כדכתיב (דניאל ג) קל קרנא משרוקיתא. וזה שהיא עגולה היא כלי יש בו מלאכה להחזירה לפיכך חייב חטאת אבל פשוטה אין בה עסק כלום כדתנן בכלים פ' י"א. הכוש והאימא והמקל וסומפאניא וחליל של מתכת טמאין והמצופין טהורין וסמפאניא שיש בה בית קיבול כנפים בין כך ובין כך טמאה. קרן עגולה טמאה וכו' טמאין ובשעת חבורן הכל טמאה בי רב חמא הוה ליה מיטה גליתא והוו מהדרי ליה בי"ט א"ל לרב חמא מאי דעתיך בנין מן הצד הוא נהי דאיסורא דאורי' ליכא דרבנן מידא איכא. א"ל רב חמא אנא כרבן שמעון בן גמליאל סבירא לי אם היה רפוי מותר. נמצא רב חמא כר' אבא ורב הונא דשרו. ומסתברא מטה של טורסיים הוא כגון מטה גליתא: **נותנין** כלי תחת הנר לקבל בו ניצוצות. והא קא מבטל כלי מהיכנו. אמר רב הונא בריה דרב יהושע ניצוצות אין בהן ממש ומותר להשתמש באותו כלי ולא יתן בתוכו מים מפני שהוא מכבה. לימא תנן סתמא כר' יוסי דאמר גרם כבוי אסור דתנן ר' יוסי אוסר לעשות מחיצה שלא תעבור הדליקה בבלי חרש חדשים מלאים מים שאין יכולין לקבל את האור והן מתבקעין ומכבין הדליק' ודחי אימור דאסר ר' יוסי בשבת. בע"ש מי אסר. וכי תימא הכא נמי כי תנן אסור בשבת אבל בע"ש שרי. והא תניא נותנין כלי תחת הנר לקבל ניצוצות בשבת ואין צורך לומר בע"ש. ולא יתן לתוכו מים בע"ש מפני שהוא מכבה ואין צריך לומר בשבת. ואוקמה רב אשי אפילו לרבנן דפליגי עליה דר' יוסי הכא אסרי מפני שמקרב כיבויו פי' כיון שנופלין הניצוצות במים מיד נכבין ובכלים עד שיתבקעו. וקי"ל דהלכתא כר"ש דאפי' במוקצה מחמת מיאוס שרי: **ואין** הלכה כר"ש במוקצה מחמת איסור כגון במנורה ופמוט שהדליקו עליהן באותה שבת וכיוצא בהן וכגון מטה שיחדה למעות ונכרי שהביא דורון לישראל דבר המחובר לקרקע וכיוצא בהן דמוקצה מחמת איסור הן. וגרסי' במי שהחשיך בדרך פליגי בה רב אחא ורבינא חד אמר בכולה שבת הלכתא כר"ש בר ממוקצה מחמת מיאוס וחד אמר אפילו במוקצה נמי הלכתא כר"ש בר ממוקצה מחמת איסור בלבד וקי"ל דבכל התורה רב אחא לחומרא ורבינא לקולא והלכתא כרבינא לקולא בר מהני תלת אומצא כו' ואע"ג דעולא ולוי ורב אמרו הלכה כר' יהודא הא שמואל וזעירי ור' יוחנן אמרו הלכתא כר' שמעון. ורבינא דהוא בתראה פסק הלכתא כר' שמעון כדאמרן. לפיכך כל מוקצה מותר לבר ממוקצה מחמת איסור כמו שפירשנו. ומוקצה מחמת חסרון כים מודה ר' שמעון וגרוגרות וצמוקין כדאמרן:

הדרן עלך כירה

פרק רביעי במה טומנין ובמה אין טומנין כו' אין טומנין בגפת. אוקימנא בגפת של שומשין וכל שכן בגפת של זיתים דמסיק נמי הבלא אסיק אמר רבא אנוחי

עין משפט נר מצוה

נח א מיי' פכ"ב מהל' שבת הלכה ו וסמג שם טוש"ע סי' שח סעיף ו וסעיף ט:

נט ב מיי' שם טור שו"ע שם סעיף ו:

ס ג מיי' שם פ"ה הלכה יג סמג שם טוש"ע או"ח סימן רסה סעיף ד:

סא ד ה מיי' פ"ד מהלכות שבת הלכה א טוש"ע או"ח סימן רנז סעיף ג:

מסורת הש"ס

עי' לקמן קלח. רש"י ד"ה וכסא גלין

[לעיל מב: מג.]

[לעיל מג: וש"נ]

לקמן קכ.

כבת בתו"ח ינ. ונדרים כו: מיר ל.

עי' לעיל יח:

גליון הש"ס

תוס' ד"ה רשב"ג וכו' וקשה קלת. עי' לקמן קף קלח ע"א: שם בד"ה במה טומנין וכו' אבל קדירה חייתא. עי' לעיל יח ע"ב תוספות ד"ה ממעטת:

רב נסים גאון

נדבר מן דאלך מא יתצרנא בפרק חומר בקודש (דף כה) אמרו אמר רב יוסף בגלילא שנו מינו דלא מהימני אקודש לא מהימני אתרומה נמי בנדרים בפרק *) ואלו נדרים ובגליל אסורין שאין אנשי גליל מכירין את חרמי כהנים ובפרק המוציא יין (דף עח) ובפרק מקום שנהגו (דף נה) בפסחים עוד ובגמרא (ירושלמי שבת פרק כל כתבי הלכה ח) גרסי אמר עולא י"ח שנין עבד רבן יוחנן בן זכאי יתיב בהדה ערב ולא אתא קומי אלא אילין תרתין עובדיה אמר גליל גליל שנאת את התורה סופך להעשות כמציקן וכל דין סיוע לפירושנו: **לימא** תנן סתמא כר' יוסי דאמר גרם כיבוי אסור. עיקר דיליה במשנה בפרק כל כתבי הקודש (דף קכ) דתנן ר' יוסי אוסר בכלי חרש חדשים מלאים מים שאין יכולין לקבל את האור והם מתבקעין ומכבין את הדליקה ובגמ' גרסי ר' יוסי סבר גרם כיבוי אסור: **סליק פרק כירה**

*) נ"ל ואלו מותרין דף יח במשנה.

Image **Credits**